P9-DFX-581

MACROECONOMICS

SECOND EDITION

MACROECONOMICS

SECOND EDITION

ANDREW B. ABEL

THE WHARTON SCHOOL OF THE
UNIVERSITY OF PENNSYLVANIA

BEN S. BERNANKE

WOODROW WILSON SCHOOL OF
PUBLIC AND INTERNATIONAL AFFAIRS
PRINCETON UNIVERSITY

ADDISON-WESLEY PUBLISHING COMPANY

READING, MASSACHUSETTS ◦ MENLO PARK, CALIFORNIA ◦ NEW YORK
DON MILLS,ONTARIO ◦ WOKINGHAM, ENGLAND ◦ AMSTERDAM ◦ BONN
SYDNEY ◦ SINGAPORE ◦ TOKYO ◦ MADRID ◦ SAN JUAN ◦ MILAN ◦ PARIS

Editor-in-Chief: Barbara Rifkind
Senior Sponsoring Editor: Marjorie Williams
Development Editor: Jane Tufts
Managing Editor: Kazia Navas
Production Supervisor: Kathy Diamond
Senior Production Coordinator: Patricia Oduor
Production Technology Supervisor: Laurie Petrycki
Electronic Production Specialist: John F. Webber
Electronic Production Administrator: Sally L. Simpson
Copyeditor: Jerrold Moore
Art and Design Manager: Karen Rappaport
Text Designer: Carol H. Rose
Cover Designer: Marshall Henrichs
Art Buyer: Joseph Vetere
Technical Art Consultant: Susan London-Payne
Illustrator: Scientific Illustrators
Proofreader: Phyllis Coyne
Permissions Editor: Mary Dyer
Senior Marketing Manager: Dave Theisen
Marketing Manager: Craig Bleyer
Prepress Services Manager: Sarah McCracken
Senior Manufacturing Manager: Roy Logan
Film Output Source: Pre-Press Co., Inc.
Printer: R. R. Donnelley & Sons

LIBRARY OF CONGRESS CATALOGING-IN-PUBLICATION DATA

Abel, Andrew B. 1952–
Macroeconomics / Andrew B. Abel, Ben S. Bernanke. —2nd ed.
p. cm.
Includes index.
ISBN 0-201-54392-3
1. Macroeconomics. 2. United States—Economic conditions.
I. Bernanke, Ben. II. Title.
HB172.5.A24 1994
339—dc20 93-41631
CIP

Reprinted with corrections, April 1995.

ISBN 0-201-54392-3

3 4 5 6 7 8 9 10-DOW-979695

ABOUT THE AUTHORS

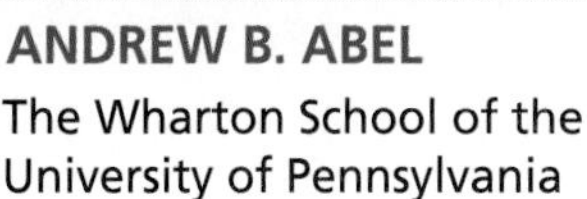

ANDREW B. ABEL

The Wharton School of the University of Pennsylvania

Robert Morris Professor of Finance at The Wharton School and professor of economics at the University of Pennsylvania, Andrew Abel received his A.B. *summa cum laude* from Princeton University and his Ph.D. from the Massachusetts Institute of Technology.

Since his appointment to The Wharton School in 1986, Abel has held the Ronald O. Perelman and the Amoco Foundation Professorships. He began his teaching career at the University of Chicago and Harvard University, and has held visiting appointments at both Tel Aviv University and The Hebrew University of Jerusalem.

A prolific researcher, Abel has published extensively on fiscal policy, capital formation, monetary policy, asset pricing, and social security—as well as serving on the editorial boards of numerous journals. He has been honored as an Alfred P. Sloan Fellow, a National Science Foundation Graduate Fellow, a Fellow of the Econometric Society, and a recipient of the John Kenneth Galbraith Award for teaching excellence. Abel has served as a visiting scholar at the Federal Reserve Bank of Philadelphia and as a member of the Economics Advisory Panel of the National Science Foundation. He is also a Research Associate of the National Bureau of Economic Research and a member of the Advisory Board of the Carnegie-Rochester Conference Series.

BEN S. BERNANKE

Woodrow Wilson School of Public and International Affairs, Princeton University

Class of 1926 Professor of Economics and Public Affairs at Princeton University, Ben Bernanke received his B. A. in economics from Harvard University, *summa cum laude*—capturing both the Allyn Young Prize for best Harvard undergraduate economics thesis and the John H. Williams prize for outstanding senior in the economics department. Like coauthor Abel, he holds a Ph.D. from the Massachusetts Institute of Technology.

Bernanke began his career at the Stanford Graduate School of Business in 1979, moving to Princeton University in 1985. He has twice been visiting professor at M.I.T. and once at New York University, and has taught in undergraduate, M.B.A., M.P.A., and Ph.D. programs. He has authored more than 40 publications in macroeconomics, macroeconomic history, and finance.

Bernanke has served as a visiting scholar for the Federal Reserve System in Philadelphia, Boston, and New York and is currently an advisor to the Federal Reserve Bank of New York. He is co-editor of *Economic Letters* and associate editor of four other journals. He has been variously honored as an Alfred P. Sloan Research Fellow, a Hoover Institution National Fellow, a National Science Foundation Graduate Fellow, and a Research Associate of the National Bureau of Economic Research.

Brief Contents

DETAILED CONTENTS

BUSINESS CYCLES AND MACROECONOMIC POLICY 287

MACROECONOMIC POLICY: ITS ENVIRONMENT AND INSTITUTIONS 443

Summary Tables

Key Diagrams

PREFACE TO THE SECOND EDITION

The first edition of *Macroeconomics* was well received by instructors and students, who welcomed its modern coverage, extensive use of real-world applications, clear writing, and effective learning aids. In the second edition we built on those strengths and, at the same time, significantly shortened and streamlined the book.

As with the First Edition, our goal with the Second is to help students learn to think critically and coherently about today's macroeconomic agenda. Toward that end, we provide lively and up-to-date coverage of a wide range of macroeconomic issues and ideas:

- ***Long-term economic growth.*** Because the rate of economic growth plays a central role in determining living standards, we devote much of Part II to growth and related issues. We first discuss factors contributing to growth, such as productivity (Chapter 3) and rates of saving and investment (Chapter 4), and then in Chapter 6 turn to a full-fledged analysis of the growth process. In Chapter 6 we use tools such as growth accounting and the Solow model to discuss various growth-related topics, including the post-1973 productivity slowdown, the factors that determine long-run living standards, the prospect for the convergence of living standards around the world, government policies to stimulate growth (including some controversial ideas such as industrial policy), and the "new growth theory."
- ***International macroeconomic issues.*** We address the increasing integration of the world economy in two ways; First, throughout the text we make frequent use of cross-country comparisons and applications that draw on the experiences of countries other than the United States; for example, Chapter 15 compares recent monetary policy strategies in Germany, Japan, and the United States. In addition, we devoted two innovative chapters specifically to international issues. Chapter 5 shows how the trade balance is related to a nation's rates of saving and investment and then applies this framework to discuss issues such as the less developed country (LDC) debt crisis, the effect of economic development in Eastern Europe on world interest rates, and the link between the trade deficit and the government budget deficit. Chapter 14 uses a simple supply–demand framework to discuss the determination of exchange rates and then shows how economic openness and the exchange rate system affect the operation of monetary and fiscal policy and the transmission of economic shocks among countries. Chapter 14 features new material on fixed exchange rates, including an explanation of why a currency may face a speculative

run, a discussion of Bretton Woods and the European monetary system (EMS), and a comparison of the relative advantages of fixed- and flexible-rate systems.

- ***Business cycles.*** Our analysis of business cycles begins with facts rather than theories: A unique chapter, Chapter 9, gives a history of U.S. business cycles and then describes the observed cyclical behavior of a variety of important economic variables (the "business cycle facts"). Alternative classical and Keynesian theories of the cycle, presented in Chapters 10-12, are then evaluated by how well they explain the facts.
- ***Monetary and fiscal policy.*** We discuss the effects and potential role of macroeconomic policies in nearly every chapter of the book, both in terms of theory and applications. We present classical (Chapter 11), Keynesian (Chapter 12), and monetarist (Chapter 15) views on the appropriate use of policy. Among the policy-related topics we cover are rational expectations and monetary policy (Chapter 11), the importance of central bank credibility (Chapters 13 and 15), money targeting (Chapter 15), and the intergenerational implications of budget deficits (Chapter 16). We also provide useful background on the institutional framework of policy-making; for example, Chapter 15 explains the operation of the Federal Reserve System and Chapter 16 discusses the Federal budget process.
- ***Labor market issues.*** Because of their relevance to students, we pay close attention to issues relating to employment, unemployment, and real wages. We introduce the basic supply–demand model of the labor market and discuss unemployment briefly in Chapter 3. Chapter 13 covers unemployment more extensively, including the inflation–unemployment tradeoff, the costs of unemployment, and government policies for reducing unemployment. Other labor market topics include: the dynamics of job creation and job destruction in manufacturing (Chapter 11); efficiency wages (Chapter 12); hysteresis in unemployment (Chapter 13); and the effects of marginal and average tax rate changes on labor supply (Chapter 16).

BALANCED PRESENTATION

Macroeconomics is full of controversies, many of which arise from the split between classicals and Keynesians (of the old, new, and neo varieties). Sometimes the controversies overshadow the broad common ground that exists between the two schools. We emphasize that common ground: First, we pay greater attention to long-run issues (over which classicals and Keynesians disagree less). Second, we develop the classical and Keynesian analyses of short-run fluctuations within a single framework, in which we show that the two approaches differ principally in their assumptions about how quickly wages and prices adjust. Where differences in viewpoint remain—for example, in the search versus efficiency–wage interpretations of unemployment—we present and critique both perspectives. This balanced approach gives the student the benefit of hearing all the best ideas in modern macroeconomics. At the same time, an instructor of either classical or Keynesian inclinations can easily base his or her course on this book.

Although we cover a wide range of topics, we avoid the strategy of developing a new model or theory for each issue. Instead we emphasize the wide applicability of a set of core economic ideas (such as the production function, the tradeoff between consuming today and saving for tomorrow, and supply–demand analysis). Using these core ideas, we build a theoretical framework that encompasses all the types of macroeconomic analyses in the book: long-run and short-run, open-economy and closed-economy, and classical and Keynesian.

STREAMLINED ORGANIZATION

One of our major goals for the second edition was to improve the book's organization and make it more accessible to students. Our search for a simpler, more logical organization led to a substantially shorter text and a number of other changes:

- ***New placement of the IS–LM model and an optional algebraic treatment.*** We used a new chapter, Chapter 10, to introduce the *IS–LM* model, devoting Part II entirely to long-run issues in a full-employment framework. The introduction of *IS–LM* in Chapter 10 bridges the long-run analysis of Part II and the short-run analyses (both classical and Keynesian) of Part III. In addition, although we continue to emphasize a graphical approach to the *IS–LM/AD–AS* model, we present a fully developed algebraic treatment in Appendixes to Chapters 10, 11, 12, and 14.
- ***New optional chapter (Chapter 8) combines material on household decisions.*** Detailed analyses of the microeconomics of household decisions (consumption, saving, and labor supply) are brought together in a new, optional chapter. Putting this material together in one chapter serves two purposes: First, it allows for a more coherent and integrated treatment of household decisions (including, in this edition, analyses based on indifference curves). Second, it isolates this relatively more difficult material so that instructors who want to skip it can do so without any loss of continuity. Suggestions on how to use Chapter 8 in your course are given later in the Preface under the heading "Flexibility."
- ***Simplified treatment of exchange rates.*** We now present the determination of exchange rates in Chapter 14 in a simplified, supply–demand framework,[1] which we use to analyze both flexible-exchange-rate and fixed-exchange-rate systems.

THE STRUCTURE OF THE SECOND EDITION

Part I introduces the field of macroeconomics (Chapter 1) and discusses issues of economic measurement, including national income accounting (Chapter 2).

[1]The more detailed first-edition analysis of exchange rates, including interest rate parity, is retained in the Instructor's Manual for those who want to use it.

Part II focuses on long-run issues, for which it is reasonable to assume full employment. Chapter 3 covers the supply side of the economy (the production function and the labor market), and Chapter 4 introduces the demand side (consumption, saving, and investment). Chapter 5 extends the analysis to the open economy and considers the links among saving, investment, output, and the trade balance. Chapter 6 takes up capital formation, productivity change, and long-run economic growth.

Chapters 3–6 focus on real (nonmonetary) variables; Chapter 7 introduces money supply, money demand, and inflation into the full-employment version of the model. Chapter 8, an optional chapter on the microeconomics of household decision-making, concludes Part II.

Part III is devoted to the study of short-run economic fluctuations and stabilization policy. Chapter 9 presents an empirical description of the business cycle. Chapter 10 introduces the *IS–LM* model, bringing together earlier analyses of the labor, goods, and asset markets into a complete model of the economy. We then use the *IS–LM* model (and its *AD–AS* interpretation) as a general framework for macroeconomic analysis. Chapter 11 uses the flexible-price version of the *IS–LM* model to study classical theories of short-run fluctuations, including real business cycle theory and the Lucas supply curve. Chapter 12 uses the sticky-price version of the *IS–LM* model to develop the modern Keynesian approach to cyclical fluctuations and stabilization.

Part IV looks at issues and institutions of policy-making in greater detail. Chapter 13 examines the inflation–unemployment tradeoff and policies to control inflation and unemployment. Our coverage of international issues is rounded out by Chapter 14's analysis of exchange rates and macroeconomic policy in the open economy. Chapter 15 is devoted to monetary policy and the Fed, and Chapter 16 takes a deeper look at a variety of issues relating to fiscal policy.

Appendix A identifies and discusses useful algebraic and graphical tools.

SPECIAL FEATURES

Economists sometimes get caught up in the elegance of formal models and forget that the ultimate test of a model or theory is its practical relevance. In the first edition of *Macroeconomics* we dedicated a significant portion of each chapter to showing how the theory could be applied to real events and issues. Our efforts were well received by instructors and by students. In this edition we go even further to help the student learn how to "think like an economist."

- ***Applications.*** Applications in each chapter show students how they can use theory to understand an important episode or issue, such as the impact of tax reform (Chapter 16) or the causes and effects of the LDC debt crisis (Chapter 5). *New or updated applications* in this edition include the link between technical change and growing wage inequality (Chapter 3); consumer sentiment and the 1990–1991 recession (Chapter 4); the recent problems of the European Monetary System (Chapter 14); and the evolution of monetary policy strategies in the United States, Germany, and Japan (Chapter 15), among others.

- ***Boxes.*** Boxes provide interesting additional information or sidelights, often drawn from current research. Among the topics covered are the relationship between the business cycle and the seasonal cycle (Chapter 9), the treatment of natural resources and the environment in the national income accounts (Chapter 2), and Henry Ford's high-wage policies as an example of efficiency wages (Chapter 12). *New or updated boxes* include evidence on the rationality of price forecasts (Chapter 11), the Lucas critique (Chapter 13), and intergenerational accounts for fiscal policy (Chapter 16).
- ***In Touch with the Macroeconomy.*** One important component of thinking like an economist is being familiar with macroeconomic data—what data are available and their strengths and shortcomings. To put students *in touch with the macroeconomy,* we provide a series of boxes that show where to find important macroeconomic data—such as the index of leading indicators, balance of payments data, and labor market data—and how to interpret them.
- ***The Political Environment.*** In talking about economic policy, students frequently note the discrepancy between the recommendations of economists (assuming they even agree!) and the decisions that politicians or government institutions make. We address this discrepancy in a special series of boxes that highlight the *political environment* of economic issues and policies. These special boxes examine topics such as the link between the state of the economy and presidential elections (Chapter 13) and the relationship between democracy and economic growth (Chapter 6).

LEARNING AIDS

The text contains many features aimed at helping students understand, apply, and retain important concepts.

- ***Detailed, full-color graphs.*** The book is liberally illustrated with *data graphs,* which emphasize the empirical relevance of theory, and *analytical graphs,* which guide students through the development of model and theory in a well-paced, step-by-step manner. Both types of graphs include descriptive captions that summarize the details of events shown in the graph.

  Our use of color in an analytical graph is demonstrated by Figure 11.9 on the next page, which shows the effects of a shifting curve on a set of endogenous variables. Note that the original curve is in black, and its new position is in red, with arrows indicating the direction of the shift. A peach-colored "shock box" indicates the reason for the shift, and a blue "result box" lists the main effects of the shock on endogenous variables. We consistently use these and similar conventions to make it easier for students to gain a clear understanding of the analysis.
- ***Key Diagrams.*** Key diagrams, a unique study feature found at the end of selected chapters, are self-contained descriptions of the most important analytical graphs in the book (see the list on p. xvii for their locations). For each key diagram we present the graph (the production function, p. 100, or the classical *AD–AS* diagram, p. 388, for example) and define and describe

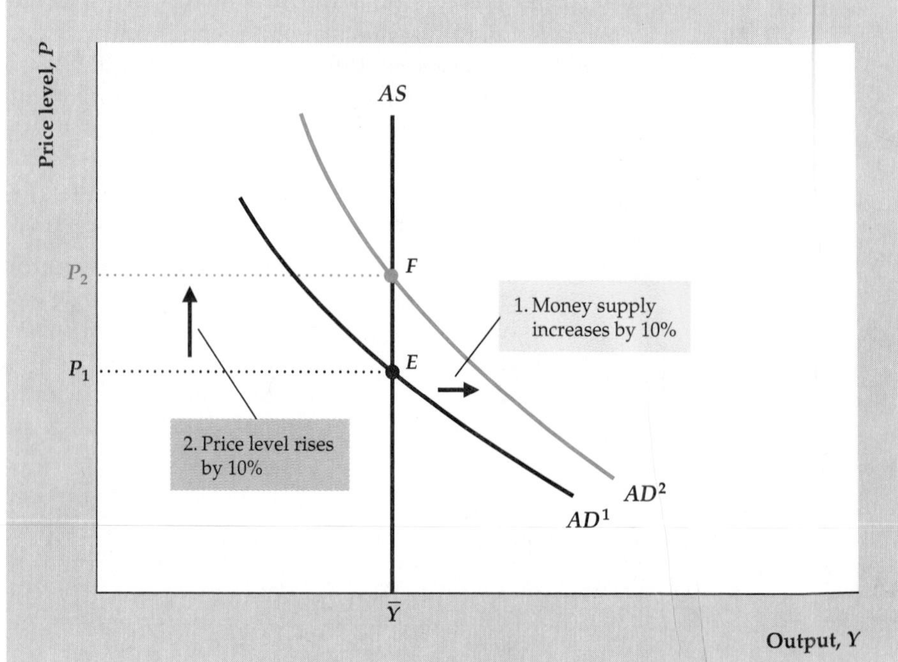

Figure 11.9
Monetary neutrality in the *AD–AS* framework
If we start from general equilibrium at point *E*, a 10% increase in the nominal money supply shifts the *AD* curve up by 10% at each level of output, from AD^1 to AD^2. The *AD* curve shifts up by 10% because at any given level of output, a 10% increase in the price level is needed to keep the real money supply, and thus the aggregate quantity of output demanded, unchanged. In the new equilibrium at point *F*, output is unchanged at $\bar{Y}$, and the price level P_2 is 10% higher than the initial price level P_1. Because the increase in the money supply raises prices but doesn't affect real variables such as output, money is neutral in this framework.

its elements in words and equations. We then present an analysis of what the graph reveals and discuss the factors that shift the curves in the graph.

- ***Summary tables.*** Throughout the book summary tables compile the main results of analyses. These summary tables reduce the time the student must spend learning and writing results, allowing a greater concentration on understanding and applying these results.
- ***End-of-chapter review materials.*** To facilitate review, at the end of each chapter the student will find a *chapter summary*, covering the chapter's main points; a list of *key terms*, with page references; an annotated list of *key equations* (a unique feature!); and *review questions* for self-testing.
- ***End-of-chapter problems.*** An extensive set of problems for practice and review (more than 160 in all) includes *numerical* problems, which have explicit numerical solutions and are especially useful for checking students' understanding of basic relationships and concepts; and *analytical problems*, which ask the student to use or extend theories qualitatively. Answers and additional problems are provided in the *Instructor's Manual*.
- ***Review of useful analytical tools.*** Although we use no mathematics beyond high school algebra, some students will find helpful a review of the main analytical tools used in the book. Appendix A (at the end of the text) succinctly discusses functions of one and several variables, graphs, slopes, exponents, and formulas for finding the growth rates of products and ratios.
- ***Glossary.*** The Glossary at the end of the text includes definitions of all key terms (set in boldface in the chapters and listed at the end of each chapter) and refers the student to the page on which the term is fully defined and discussed. Also included are selected terms that are not key terms.

FLEXIBILITY

We recognize that instructors have different preferences about what to include in their courses and that their choices may be constrained by their students' backgrounds and the length of the term. The text is designed to be flexible in accommodating these different needs. In planning how to use *Macroeconomics* in your course, you might find the following suggestions useful.

- ***Core chapters.*** We recommend that every course include these chapters:

  Chapter 1 Introduction to Macroeconomics
  Chapter 2 The Measurement and Structure of the National Economy
  Chapter 3 Productivity, Output, and Employment
  Chapter 4 Consumption, Saving, and Investment
  Chapter 7 The Asset Market, Money, and Prices
  Chapter 10 The *IS–LM* Model: A General Framework for Macroeconomic Analysis

  Chapters 1 and 2 provide an introduction to macroeconomics, including national income accounting. The next four chapters on the list make up the analytical core of the book: Chapter 3 introduces the labor market, Chapters 3 and 4 together develop the goods market, and Chapter 7 discusses the asset market. Chapter 10 combines the three markets into a general equilibrium model usable for short-run analysis (in either classical or Keynesian terms).

  To a syllabus containing the above six chapters, the instructor can add various combinations of the other chapters according to preference and need.

- ***Short-run versus long-run focus.*** We placed the discussion of long-run issues early in the text because of their intrinsic importance and because we believe that the student should understand the full-employment version of the model before tackling deviations from full employment. However, an instructor who prefers to emphasize short-run issues (business cycle fluctuations and stabilization policy) may omit Chapters 5, 6, and 8 without loss of continuity. Although we don't recommend it, an instructor may also go directly from the introductory materials of Chapters 1 and 2 to Chapter 10 on the *IS–LM* model; in that case the instructor would have to provide background on the various behavioral relationships and equilibrium conditions.

- ***Classical or Keynesian emphasis.*** For instructors who want to teach the course with a modern classical emphasis, all the chapters in Part II (including optional Chapter 8 on household decision-making) are recommended. Chapters 9–11 provide a self-contained presentation of classical business cycle theory. Other material of interest includes the Friedman–Phelps interpretation of the Phillips curve (Chapter 13), the role of credibility in monetary policy (Chapter 15), and Ricardian equivalence with multiple generations (Chapter 16).

  Instructors who prefer a Keynesian emphasis may omit Chapter 8 (household decision-making) and Chapter 11 (classical business cycle analysis), except for the derivation of the aggregate demand curve in Section 11.3. As noted, if a short-run focus is preferred, Chapter 5 (full-employment analysis of the open economy) and Chapter 6 (long-term economic growth) may also be omitted without loss of continuity.

- ***International macroeconomic issues.*** Chapter 5 discusses saving, investment, and the trade balance in an open economy with full employment. Chapter 14 discusses exchange rate determination and macroeconomic policy in an open-economy model in which short-run deviations from full employment are possible. Chapter 5 is a useful but not essential prerequisite for Chapter 14. Both chapters may be omitted without loss of continuity for a course focusing on the domestic economy.
- ***Household decision-making (Chapter 8).*** The basic economics of consumption, saving, and labor supply are discussed in Chapters 3 and 4 as part of the development of our macroeconomic model. However, for instructors who want to emphasize the microeconomic foundations of macroeconomics, Chapter 8 presents a more formal analysis of household decision making. The first part of the chapter uses indifference curves and the consumer's budget line to analyze consumption and saving decisions, and the second part of the chapter discusses the household's labor supply decision in terms of substitution and income effects. *Chapter 8 is strictly optional* and should be skipped by instructors who are short on time and want to focus on other areas. However, if time permits, including Chapter 8 should be considered, particularly for courses in which students have some background in microeconomics.

  As Chapter 8 extends material introduced in Chapters 3 and 4, it may be assigned to follow those chapters directly; or it may be assigned as optional background reading for Chapters 3 and 4. Another possibility is to assign only portions of the chapter: Section 8.3 on the life-cycle model of consumption and saving and Section 8.5 on the labor supply decision may be used on a largely stand-alone basis, with some help from the instructor.

THE SUPPLEMENTS

A full range of supplementary materials for further learning, substantially expanded and improved for the second edition, accompanies the text.

- ***Study Guide.*** The *Study Guide* by Charles Johnston provides a review of each chapter, as well as multiple-choice and short-answer problems (and answers).
- ***Instructor's Manual.*** The *Instructor's Manual* by Dean Croushore with contributions from Joyce Howland provides guidance for instructors on using the text in their courses, solutions to all end-of-chapter problems in the text, an extensive set of additional questions for testing and practice, and suggested topics for additional class discussion.
- ***Software.*** A brand-new software package by Ernie Stokes includes a complete macroeconomic data set with sophisticated data-handling capability; data-based problems that allow students to do their own empirical work; and a model simulation program for studying both textbook-based and user-provided macroeconomic models.

- ***Transparencies.*** Full-color transparencies of all figures in the text are provided for classroom use.
- ***Videos.*** A new set of *MacNeil-Lehrer Business Report* videos provide interesting background for a range of economic issues.

ACKNOWLEDGMENTS

These days a textbook is not the lonely venture of its author or coauthors but is the joint project of dozens of skilled and dedicated people. We extend special thanks to Barbara Rifkind, our first-edition editor, and Marjorie Williams, our second-edition editor, for their outstanding management; Jane Tufts, our superb developmental editor for both editions, who contributed substance as well as style to the manuscript; Kathy Diamond and Patricia Oduor (production), Dave Theisen and Craig Bleyer (marketing), Kim Crowley, Ericka Perry, and Bunny Ames (supplements), and many others at Addison-Wesley for their painstaking effort, care, and craft.

We also thank the reviewers and colleagues who offered valuable comments on succeeding drafts of the book, as well as those who responded to our mail survey:

Ugur Aker, Hiram College
Edward Allen, University of Houston
Richard G. Anderson, Federal Reserve Board, Washington, D.C., Division of Monetary Affairs
David Backus, New York University
Parantap Basu, Fordham University
Valerie R. Bencivenga, Cornell University
Charles A. Bennett, Gannon University
Scott Bloom, North Dakota State University
Bruce R. Bolnick, Northeastern University
David Brasfield, Murray State University
Maureen Burton, California Polytechnic University–Pomona
John Campbell, Princeton University
J. Lon Carlson, Illinois State University
Wayne Carroll, University of Wisconsin–Eau Claire
Stephen Cecchetti, Ohio State University
Anthony Chan, Woodbury University
Jen–Chi Cheng, Wichita State University
Menzie Chinn, University of California
K.A. Chopra, SUNY–Oneonta
Reid Click, Brandeis University
Dean Croushore, Federal Reserve Bank of Philadelphia
Steven R. Cunningham, University of Connecticut
Bruce R. Dalgaard, St. Olaf College
Joe Daniels, Marquette University
A. Edward Day, University of Central Florida
Greg Delemeester, Marietta College
Johan Deprez, Texas Tech University
James Devine, Loyola Marymount University
Patrick Dolenc, Keene State College
Robert Driskill, Vanderbilt University
Donald H. Dutkowsky, Syracuse University
James E. Eaton, Bridgewater College
Janice C. Eberly, University of Pennsylvania
Andrew Economopoulos, Ursinus College
Alejandra Cox Edwards, California State University–Long Beach
Carlos G. Elias, Manhattan College
Sharon J. Erenburg, Eastern Michigan University
Jim Fackler, University of Kentucky
Steven Fazzari, Washington University–St. Louis
J. Peter Ferderer, Clark University
David W. Findlay, Colby College
Thomas J. Finn, Wayne State University
Charles C. Fischer, Pittsburg State University
John A. Flanders, Central Methodist College
Juergen Fleck, Hollins College
R.N. Folsom, San Jose State University
J.E. Fredland, U.S. Naval Academy
William T. Ganley, Buffalo State College
Charles B. Garrison, University of Tennessee–Knoxville
Kathie Gilbert, Mississippi State University
Carlos G. Glias, Manhattan College
Roger Goldberg, Ohio Northern University
A.R. Gutowsky, California State University–Sacramento
Michael Haliassos, University of Maryland
John C. Haltiwanger, University of Maryland
James Hamilton, University of California–San Diego
David Hammes, University of Hawaii
Reza Hamzaee, Missouri Western State College
Robert Stanley Herren, North Dakota University
Fenn Horton, Naval Postgraduate School
E. Philip Howrey, University of Michigan–Ann Arbor

John Huizinga, University of Chicago
Nayyer Hussain, Tougaloo College
Matthew Hyle, Winona State University
Kenneth Inman, Claremont McKenna College
Philip N. Jefferson, Columbia University
Charles W. Johnston, University of Michigan–Flint
Paul Junk, University of Minnesota
George Karras, University of Illinois–Chicago
Roger Kaufman, Smith College
Adrienne Kearney, University of Delaware
Patrick R. Kelso, West Texas State University
Kusum Ketkar, Seton Hall University
F. Khan, University of Wisconsin–Parkside
Robert King, University of Virginia
Nobuhiro Kiyotaki, University of Minnesota
Kenneth Koelln, University of North Texas
Douglas Koritz, Buffalo State College
Eugene Kroch, Villanova University
Kishore Kulkarni, Metro State College of Denver
Maureen Lage, Miami University
John S. Lapp, North Carolina State University
G. Paul Larson, University of North Dakota
James Lee, Fort Hays State University
Keith J. Leggett, Davis and Elkins College
Mary Lorely, Syracuse University
Richard MacDonald, St. Cloud State University
Thampy Mammen, St. Norbert College
Linda M. Manning, University of Missouri
Michael Marlow, Cal Poly State University
Patrick Mason, University of California–Riverside
J. Harold McClure, Jr., Villanova University
Ken McCormick, University of Northern Iowa
John McDermott, University of South Carolina
Michael B. McElroy, North Carolina State University
Randolph McGee, University of Kentucky
Tim Miller, Denison University
B. Moore, Wesleyan University
K.R. Nair, West Virginia Wesleyan College
Stephen A. O'Connell, Swarthmore College
William P. O'Dea, SUNY–Oneonta
Heather O'Neill, Ursinus College
Maurice Obstfeld, University of California–Berkeley
Spencer Pack, Connecticut College
Walter Park, American University
Randall Parker, East Carolina University
Allen Parkman, University of New Mexico
David Parsley, Vanderbilt University
James E. Payne, Eastern Kentucky University
Mark Pernecky, St. Olaf College
Paul Pieper, University of Illinois–Chicago
Andrew J. Policano, SUNY–Stony Brook
Richard Pollock, University of Hawaii–Manoa
Jay B. Prag, Claremont McKenna College
Kojo Quartey, Talladega College
Vaman Rao, Western Illinois University
Charles Revier, Colorado State University
Patricia Reynolds, University of Southern California
Jack Rezelman, SUNY–Potsdam
Robert Rich, Vanderbilt University
Libby Rittenberg, Colorado College
Rosemary Rossiter, Ohio University
Benjamin Russo, University of North Carolina
Plutarchos Sakellaris, University of Maryland
Christine Sauer, University of New Mexico
Edward Schmidt, Randolph–Macon College
Bill Seyfried, University of Central Arkansas
Dorothy Siden, Salem State College
Scott Simkins, University of North Carolina–Greensboro
Abdol Soofi, University of Wisconsin
David E. Spencer, Brigham Young University
Don Stabile, St. Mary's College
Richard Startz, University of Washington
Gabriel Talmain, SUNY–Albany
Bryan Taylor, California State University–Los Angeles
Susan Washburn Taylor, Millsaps College
M. Dekalb Terrell, Kansas State University
Stephen J. Turnosky, University of Washington
Michael Ulan, U.S. Department of State
David D. VanHoose, University of Alabama
Walter A. Verdon, Tiffin University
Doug Waldo, University of Florida
Charles Wallis, Trinity College
Lee J. Weissert, Saint Vincent College
Robert Wofford, University of the Ozarks
Mark Wohar, University of Nebraska–Omaha
Martha Wojtowycz, Syracuse University
Larry Wolfenbarger, Georgia College
Michael Woodford, University of Chicago
Diane Zannoni, Trinity College

We are grateful to Mark Gertler, Rick Mishkin, and Steve Zeldes for valuable assistance with the first edition. We are also grateful to several cohorts of students at the University of Pennsylvania and Princeton University who—not entirely of their own free will but nonetheless very graciously—assisted us in the development of this textbook.

Last and most important, we thank our families for their patience and support. We dedicate this book to them.

Philadelphia A.B.A.
Princeton B.S.B.

MACROECONOMICS

SECOND EDITION

PART I

INTRODUCTION

CHAPTER 1

INTRODUCTION TO MACROECONOMICS

1.1 WHAT MACROECONOMICS IS ABOUT

Macroeconomics is the study of the structure and performance of national economies and of the policies that governments use to try to affect economic performance. The issues that macroeconomists address include the following:

- *What determines a nation's long-run economic growth?* In 1870 income per capita in Norway was smaller than in Argentina. But today, income per capita is more than twice as high in Norway as in Argentina. Why do some nations' economies grow quickly, providing their citizens with rapidly improving living standards, while other nations' economies are relatively stagnant?
- *What causes a nation's economic activity to fluctuate?* After nearly a decade of prosperity during the 1980s, the U.S. economy began to falter in 1990. By the spring of 1991, output in the United States had fallen by more than 1.5% from its level six months earlier. Why do economies sometimes experience sharp short-run fluctuations, lurching between periods of prosperity and periods of hard times?
- *What causes unemployment?* During the 1930s one quarter of the work force in the United States was unemployed. A decade later, during World War II, less than 2% of the work force was unemployed. Why does unemployment sometimes reach very high levels? Why, even during times of relative prosperity, is a significant fraction of the work force unemployed?
- *What causes prices to rise?* The rate of inflation in the United States crept steadily upward during the 1970s, and reached 10% per year in the early 1980s before dropping to less than 4% per year in the mid 1980s. Germany's inflation experience has been much more extreme: Although Germany has earned a reputation for low inflation in recent decades, following its defeat in World War I Germany experienced an eighteen-month period

(July 1922–December 1923) during which prices rose by a factor of several billion! What causes inflation and what can be done about it?

- *How does being part of a global economic system affect nations' economies?* According to many observers, the recovery from the 1990–1991 recession in the United States was hampered by slow economic growth abroad, which restrained the demand for U.S. products. During this period tension between the United States and Japan heightened, as American trade negotiators demanded freer access to Japanese markets so that U.S. producers could sell more of their goods to Japan. How do economic links between nations, such as international trade and borrowing, affect the performance of individual economies and the world economy as a whole?
- *Can government policies be used to improve a nation's economic performance?* The 1992 presidential election campaign that brought President Clinton to office focused on the nation's economic problems and the potential role of the government in helping solve these problems. One of the greatest of the perceived problems—and one of the first to be addressed by the new President—was the large and longstanding Federal budget deficit. How do national economic policies, such as government taxation and spending policies, affect the behavior of the overall economy? How should economic policy be conducted in order to keep the economy as prosperous and stable as possible?

Macroeconomics seeks to offer answers to such questions, which are of great practical importance and are constantly debated by politicians, the press, and the public. In the rest of this section we consider these key macroeconomic issues in more detail.

Long-Run Economic Growth

If you have ever traveled in a developing country, you could not help but observe the difference in living standards relative to those of countries such as the United States. The problems of inadequate food, shelter, and health care experienced by the poorest citizens of rich nations often represent the average situation for the people of a developing country. From a macroeconomic perspective, the difference between rich nations and developing nations may be summarized by saying that rich nations have at some point in their history experienced extended periods of rapid economic growth but that the poorer nations either have never experienced sustained growth or have had periods of growth offset by periods of economic decline.

Figure 1.1 summarizes the growth in output of the U.S. economy since 1869.[1] The record is an impressive one: Over the past century and a quarter, the annual output of U.S. goods and services has increased by more than 56 times. The performance of the U.S. economy is not unique, however; other industrial nations have had similar, and in some cases higher, rates of growth

1. Output is measured in Fig. 1.1 by two very similar concepts, called real gross national product (real GNP) and real gross domestic product (real GDP), both of which attempt to measure the physical volume of production in each year. We discuss the measurement of output in detail in Chapter 2.

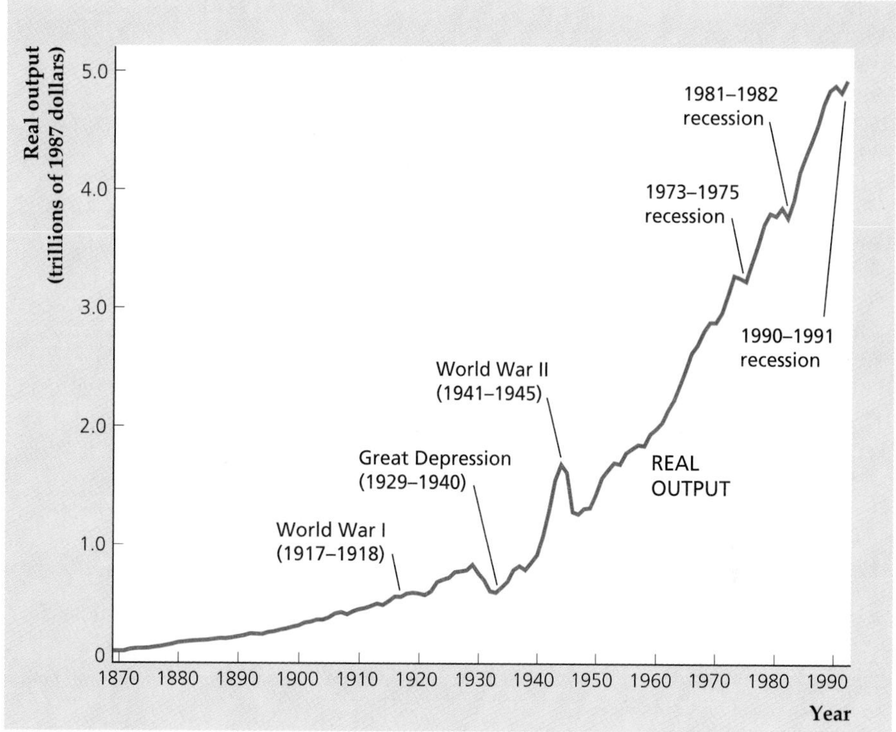

Figure 1.1
Output of the U.S. economy, 1869–1992
In this graph the output of the U.S. economy is measured by real gross domestic product (real GDP) for the period 1919–1992 and by real gross national product (real GNP) for the period prior to 1919, with goods and services valued at their 1987 prices in both cases (see Chapter 2). Note the strong upward trend in output over time, as well as sharp fluctuations during the Great Depression (1929–1940), World War II (1941–1945), and the recessions of 1973–1975, 1981–1982, and 1990–1991.

Sources: 1869–1918: GNP from Christina D. Romer, "The Prewar Business Cycle Reconsidered: New Estimates of Gross National Product, 1869–1908," *Journal of Political Economy*, February 1989, pp. 22–23; 1919–1928: GDP from *Historical Statistics of the United States, 1889–1970*, Series F 125, p. 232; 1929–1992: GDP from *Survey of Current Business*, December 1992, pp. 11, 30. Data from Romer and *Historical Statistics of the United States* were rescaled and merged with data from *Survey of Current Business*.

over this period of time. This massive increase in the output of industrial economies is one of the central facts of modern history and has had enormous political, military, social, and even cultural implications.

In part, the long-term growth of the U.S. economy is the result of a rising population, which has meant a steady increase in the number of available workers. But another significant factor is the increase in the amount of output that can be produced with a given amount of labor. The amount of output produced per unit of labor input—for example, per worker or per hour of work—is called **average labor productivity.** Figure 1.2 shows how average labor productivity, defined in this case as output per employed worker, has changed since 1900. In 1992 the average U.S. worker produced about three and a half times as much output as the average worker at the beginning of the twentieth century, despite working fewer hours over the course of the year. Because today's typical worker is so much more productive, Americans enjoy a significantly higher standard of living than would have been possible earlier in the century.

Although the long-term record of productivity growth in the U.S. economy is excellent, in recent years average labor productivity in the United States has grown slowly. In the twenty-two-year period between 1968 and 1990, output per U.S. worker grew only about 11%, which compares poorly with the more than 50% total improvement that occurred in the eighteen-year period from 1950 to 1968. As a result, living standards rose relatively slowly in the 1970s and 1980s. Labor productivity growth did rise some in the mid 1980s, as you can see from Fig. 1.2. Still, the possibility that the

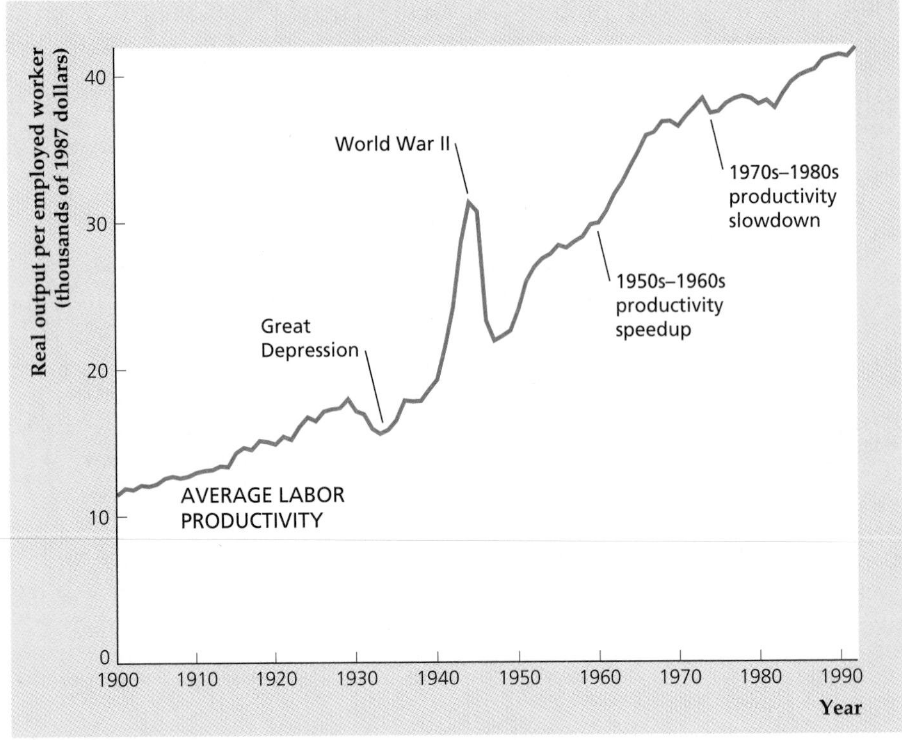

Figure 1.2
Average labor productivity in the United States, 1900–1992
Average labor productivity (output per employed worker) has risen over time, with a peak during World War II reflecting increased wartime production. Productivity growth was particularly strong in the 1950s and 1960s but slowed in the 1970s and 1980s. For the calculation of productivity, output is measured as in Fig. 1.1.

Sources: Employment: 1900–1946: ***Historical Statistics of the United States***, Part I, Series D 1–10, p. 126 (people aged 14 and over); 1947–1992: ***Economic Report of the President***, 1993, Table B-31 (people aged 16 and over). We combined the two series by multiplying the series from the ***Historical Statistics of the United States*** by the ratio of employment of people aged 16 and above to employment of people aged 14 and above in 1947. Average labor productivity is output divided by employment.

productivity growth slowdown will continue underlies many of the concerns that have been expressed about the health and long-term future of the U.S. economy.

Because the rates of growth of output and, particularly, of output per worker ultimately determine whether a nation will be rich or poor, understanding what determines growth is one of the most important goals of macroeconomics. Unfortunately, explaining why economies grow is not easy. Why, for example, did resource-poor Japan and Korea experience growth rates that transformed them in a generation or two from war-torn nations to industrial powers, whereas several resource-rich nations of Latin America have had erratic or even negative growth in recent years? Although macroeconomists have nothing close to a complete answer to the question of what determines rates of economic growth, they do have some ideas to offer. For example, as we discuss in some detail in this book, most macroeconomists believe that rates of saving and investment are important for growth. Another key determinant of growth we discuss is the rate at which technological change and other factors help increase the productivity of machines and workers.

Business Cycles

If you look at the history of U.S. output in Fig. 1.1, you will notice that the growth of output isn't always smooth but has hills and valleys. Most striking is the period between 1929 and 1945, which contains the Great Depression and World War II. During the 1929–1933 economic collapse that marked the first major phase of the Great Depression, the output of the U.S. economy fell by nearly 30%. Over the period 1939–1944, as the United States entered World War II and expanded production of armaments, output nearly doubled. No fluctuations in U.S. output since 1945 have been as severe as those of the 1929–1945 period. However, during the postwar era there have been periods of unusually rapid economic growth, such as during the 1960s, and times during which output actually declined from one year to the next, as in 1973–1975, 1981–1982, and 1990–1991.

Macroeconomists use the term *business cycle* to describe short-run, but sometimes sharp, contractions and expansions in economic activity.[2] The downward phase of a business cycle, during which national output may be falling or perhaps growing only very slowly, is called a recession. Even when they are relatively mild, recessions mean hard economic times for many people. Recessions are also a major political concern, because almost every politician wants to be reelected and the chances of reelection are better if the nation's economy is expanding rather than declining. Macroeconomists put a lot of effort into trying to figure out what causes business cycles and into deciding what can or should be done about them. In this book we describe a variety of features of business cycles, compare alternative explanations for cyclical fluctuations, and evaluate the policy options that are available for affecting the course of the cycle.

Unemployment

One important aspect of recessions is that they usually are accompanied by an increase in **unemployment,** or the number of people who are available for work and are actively seeking work but cannot find jobs. Along with growth and business cycles, the problem of unemployment is a third major issue in macroeconomics.

The best-known measure of unemployment is the unemployment rate, which is the number of unemployed divided by the total labor force (the number of people either working or seeking work). Figure 1.3 shows the unemployment rate in the United States over the past century. The highest and most prolonged period of unemployment occurred during the Great Depression of the 1930s. In 1933 the unemployment rate was 24.9%, indicating that about one of every four potential workers was unable to find a job. In contrast, the tremendous increase in economic activity that occurred during World War II significantly reduced unemployment. In 1944, at the peak of the wartime boom, the unemployment rate was 1.2%.

Recessions have led to significant increases in unemployment in recent years. For example, during the 1981–1982 recession the U.S. unemployment rate reached 10.8%.[3] Even during periods of economic expansion, however, the unemployment rate remains well above zero, as you can see from Fig. 1.3. In early 1990, after eight years of economic growth with no recession, the unemployment rate remained above 5%. Why the unemployment rate can remain

2. A more exact definition is given in Chapter 9. Business cycles do not include fluctuations lasting only a few months, such as the increase in activity that occurs around Christmas.
3. The unemployment rate was 10.8% in November and December 1982. Figure 1.3 shows the unemployment rates for each year. For the entire year of 1982, the unemployment rate was 9.7%.

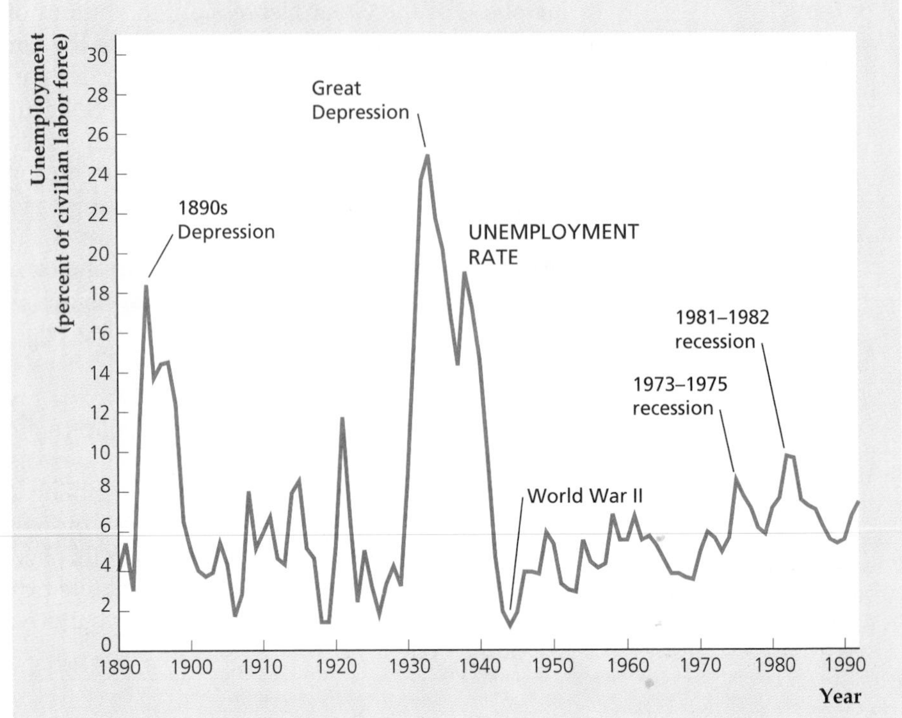

Figure 1.3
The U.S. unemployment rate, 1890–1992
The figure shows the percentage of the civilian labor force (excluding people in the military) that was unemployed in each year since 1890. Unemployment peaked during the depression of the 1890s and the Great Depression of the 1930s, and reached its low point during World War II. Since World War II, the highest unemployment rates occurred during the 1973–1975 and 1981–1982 recessions.

Sources: 1890–1947: *Historical Statistics of the United States*, p. 135 (people aged 14 and above); 1948–1992: *Economic Report of the President*, 1993, Table B-37 (people aged 16 and above).

fairly high even when the economy as a whole is doing well is another important question in macroeconomics.

Inflation

When the prices of most goods and services are rising over time, the economy is said to be experiencing **inflation.** Figure 1.4 shows a measure of the average level of prices faced by consumers in the United States over the past two centuries.[4] Note that prior to World War II inflation usually occurred only during wartime, such as during the War of 1812, the Civil War, and World War I. These wartime periods of inflation were followed by periods of **deflation,** during which the prices of most goods and services fell. The result of these offsetting periods of inflation and deflation was that, over the long run, the level of prices was fairly constant: For example, prices at the end of World War I (1918) stood at about the same level as in 1800, more than a century earlier.

The last significant deflation in the United States occurred during 1929–1933, the initial phase of the Great Depression. Since then inflation, with-

4. This measure is called the consumer price index, or CPI, which is discussed in Chapter 2. Conceptually, the CPI is intended to measure the cost of buying a certain fixed set, or "basket," of consumer goods. However, the construction of a consumer price index over a period as long as two centuries involves many compromises. One is that the basket of goods priced by the CPI is not literally the same over the entire period shown in Fig. 1.4 but is periodically changed to reflect the different mix of consumer goods available at different times.

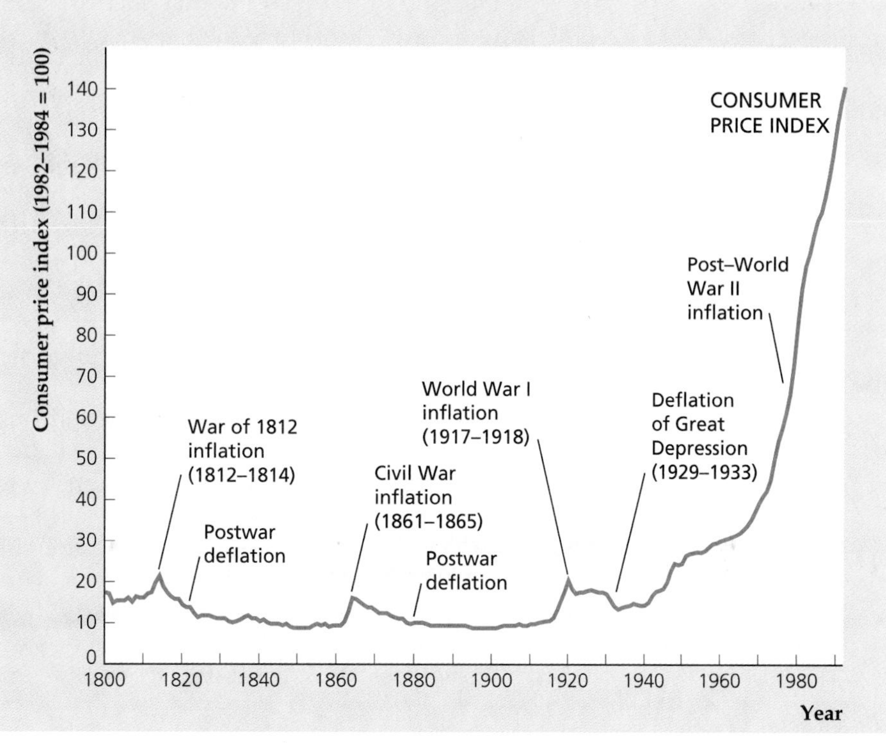

Figure 1.4
Consumer prices in the United States, 1800–1992
Prior to World War II, the average level of prices faced by consumers remained relatively constant, with periods of inflation (rising prices) offset by periods of deflation (falling prices). Since World War II, however, prices have risen more than sevenfold. In the figure the average level of prices is measured by the consumer price index, or CPI (see Chapter 2). The CPI measures the cost of a fixed set, or basket, of consumer goods relative to the cost of the same goods in a base period, in this case 1982–1984. Thus a CPI of 140.3 in 1992 means that a basket of consumer goods that cost $100 in 1982–1984 would cost $140.30 in 1992.

Sources: 1800–1945 (1967 = 100): *Historical Statistics of the United States*, Part I, p. 211; 1946–1989 (1982–1984 = 100) *Economic Report of the President*, 1990, Table C-58; 1990–1991 *Economic Report of the President*, 1993, Table B-56. Data prior to 1946 were adjusted to a base with 1982–1984 = 100.

out offsetting deflation, has become the normal state of affairs. Figure 1.4 shows that consumer prices have risen significantly since World War II, with the measure of prices shown increasing more than sevenfold.

The percentage increase in the average level of prices over a year is called the inflation rate. If the inflation rate in consumer prices is 10%, for example, then on average the prices of items that consumers buy are rising by 10% per year. Rates of inflation may vary dramatically both over time and across countries, from a few percent per year in low-inflation countries (such as Switzerland) to 1000% per year or more in countries (such as Bolivia or Argentina in recent years) that are experiencing hyperinflations, or extreme inflations. When the inflation rate reaches an extremely high level, with prices changing daily or hourly, the economy tends to function poorly. High inflation also means that the purchasing power of money erodes quickly, which forces people to scramble to spend their money almost as soon as they receive it.

The International Economy

Today every major economy is an **open economy,** or one that has extensive trading and financial relationships with other national economies. (A **closed economy** doesn't interact economically with the rest of the world.) Macroeconomists study patterns of international trade and borrowing to understand better the links between national economies. For example, an important topic in macroeconomics is how international trade and borrowing relationships can help transmit business cycles from country to country.

Another issue for which international considerations are central is trade imbalances. Figure 1.5 shows the historical behavior of the imports and exports of goods and services by the United States. U.S. imports are goods and services produced abroad and purchased by Americans; U.S. exports are goods and services produced in the United States and sold to foreigners. To give you a sense of the relative importance of international trade, Fig. 1.5 expresses exports and imports as percentages of total U.S. output. Currently, both exports and imports are larger fractions of U.S. output than they were during the 1950s and 1960s, reflecting both the recovery of trade from the disruptions of the Great Depression and World War II and the trend toward greater economic interdependence among nations. Note, though, that a century ago exports and imports already were important relative to the size of the overall economy.

You can see from Fig. 1.5 that exports and imports need not be equal in each year. For example, following World War I and World War II, U.S. exports outstripped U.S. imports because the country was sending large quantities of supplies to countries whose economies had been damaged by war. When exports exceed imports, a **trade surplus** exists. In the 1980s, however, U.S. exports declined sharply relative to imports, as you can see from Fig. 1.5. This recent excess of imports over exports, or **trade deficit,** has received considerable attention from policymakers and the press even after it declined somewhat in the early 1990s. What causes these trade imbalances? Are they bad for

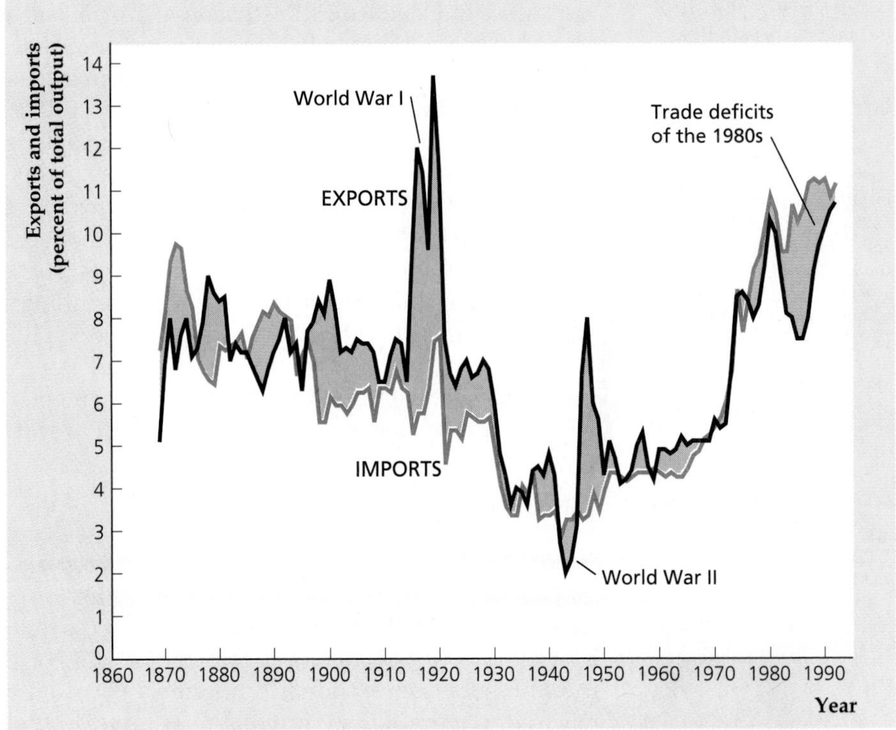

Figure 1.5
U.S. exports and imports, 1869–1992
The figure shows U.S. exports (black) and U.S. imports (red), each expressed as a percentage of total output. Exports and imports need not be equal in each year: U.S. exports exceeded imports (shaded gray) during much of the twentieth century. During the 1980s, however, U.S. exports were smaller than U.S. imports (shaded red).

Sources: Exports and imports in current dollars. 1869–1932: ***Historical Statistics of the United States***, p. 864; 1933–1992: ***Survey of Current Business,*** December 1992, pp. 11, 27. For output (measured by GNP until 1928 and GDP thereafter), the 1869–1928 series is current GNP data from Romer; the 1929–1992 series is GDP data from ***Survey of Current Business***. (See sources for Fig. 1.1.)

the U.S. economy or for the economies of this country's trading partners? These are among the questions that macroeconomists try to answer.

Macroeconomic Policy

A nation's economic performance depends on many factors, including its natural and human resources, its capital stock (buildings and machines), its technology, and the economic choices made by its citizens, both individually and collectively. Another extremely important factor affecting economic performance is the set of macroeconomic policies pursued by the government.

Macroeconomic policies affect the performance of the economy as a whole. The two major types of macroeconomic policies are fiscal policy and monetary policy. **Fiscal policy,** which is determined at the national, state, and local levels, concerns government spending and taxation. **Monetary policy** determines the rate of growth of the nation's money supply and is under the control of a government institution known as the central bank. In the United States the central bank is the Federal Reserve, or the Fed.

One of the main macroeconomic policy issues of recent years in the United States has been in the realm of fiscal policy. This issue concerns the potential effects on the economy of the Federal government's large budget deficit, the annual excess of government spending over tax collections. The recent deficit is put into a long-term perspective in Fig. 1.6, which presents data on Federal

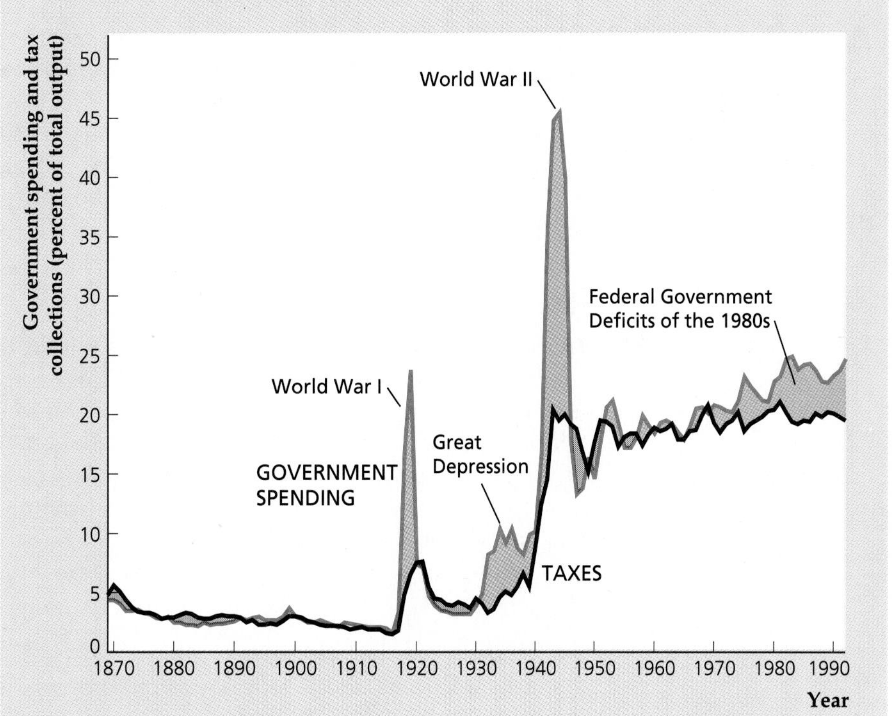

Figure 1.6
U.S. Federal government spending and tax collections, 1869–1992
U.S. Federal government spending (red) and U.S. Federal government tax collections (black) are shown as a percentage of total output. Deficits, or excesses of spending over tax collections, are shaded red, and surpluses (excesses of taxes over spending) are shaded gray. The government sector's share of the economy has grown since World War II. Large deficits occurred during the two world wars, the Great Depression, and in recent years.

Sources: Federal spending and tax collections in billions of current dollars. 1869–1939 (fiscal years): ***Historical Statistics of the United States***, p. 1104; 1940–1958 (calendar years): ***Economic Report of the President***, 1991, Table B-79; 1959–1990 (calendar years): ***Economic Report of the President***, 1993, Table B-77; 1991–1992: ***Survey of Current Business***, December 1992. For output (measured by GNP until 1928 and GDP thereafter), the 1869–1928 series is current GNP data from Romer; the 1929–1992 series is GDP data from ***Survey of Current Business***. (See sources for Fig. 1.1.)

government spending and tax revenues for the past century and a quarter.[5] Again, so that their importance relative to the economy as a whole is indicated, spending, tax collections, and government budget deficits and surpluses are expressed as percentages of total output.

Two obvious features of Fig. 1.6 are the peaks in government spending and deficits that resulted from military buildups in World War I and World War II. At its high point during World War II, Federal government spending exceeded 45% of total output. Significant deficits also occurred during the Great Depression of the 1930s because the government increased its spending on various programs designed to help the economy, such as government-financed jobs programs. Also shown clearly is the increase in the size of the government sector since World War II, an increase reflected in both the major upward shift in government spending and in tax collections relative to national output that occurred in about 1940 and the mild upward trend in both variables that has occurred since then.

The Federal budget deficits of the 1980s and 1990s appear in the right-hand portion of Fig. 1.6. These large and persistent deficits are historically unusual in that they occurred during a period of peace and relative prosperity. Critics of the government's fiscal policies argue that the deficits, which must be financed by borrowing from the public, divert funds that might otherwise be put to more productive uses, such as investment in modern equipment. Some critics also claim a close link between the Federal budget deficits since 1980 and the excess of U.S. imports over exports that occurred during the same period (see Fig. 1.5). Indeed, the Federal budget deficit and the trade imbalance have been called the "twin deficits." Are these claims true? If so, what can be done? These questions too fall under the study of macroeconomics.

The possible link between the government's budget deficit and the trade imbalance illustrates an important aspect of macroeconomics: Macroeconomic issues and problems are frequently interconnected. For this reason studying one macroeconomic question, such as the effects of the government budget deficit, in isolation generally is not sufficient. Instead, macroeconomists usually study the economy as a complete system, recognizing that changes in one sector or market may affect the behavior of the entire economy.

Aggregation

Macroeconomics is one of two broad areas within the field of economics, the other being microeconomics. Macroeconomics and microeconomics have many basic economic ideas and methods in common; the difference between them is the level at which the economy is studied. Microeconomists focus on individual consumers, workers, and firms, each of whom is too small to have an impact on the national economy. Macroeconomists ignore the fine distinctions among the many different kinds of goods, firms, and markets that exist in the economy and instead focus on national totals. For example, in their

5. Government spending includes both government purchases of goods and services, such as purchases of military equipment and the salaries of government officials, and government benefits paid to individuals, such as Social Security payments.

analyses macroeconomists do not care whether consumers are buying VCRs or compact disc players, beef or chicken, Pepsi or Coke. Instead, they add consumer expenditures on all goods and services to get an overall total called aggregate consumption. The process of summing individual economic variables to obtain economywide totals is called **aggregation.** The use of aggregation and the emphasis on aggregate quantities such as aggregate consumption, aggregate investment, and aggregate output are the primary factors that distinguish macroeconomics from microeconomics.

1.2 WHAT MACROECONOMISTS DO

How do macroeconomists use their skills, and what do they do with all the data they gather and the theories they develop? Besides teaching economics, macroeconomists engage in a wide variety of activities, including forecasting, macroeconomic analysis, basic research, and data development.

Macroeconomic Forecasting

Many people believe that economists spend most of their time trying to forecast the performance of the economy. In fact, except for a relatively small number of forecasting specialists, forecasting is a minor part of what macroeconomists do. One reason macroeconomists don't emphasize forecasting is that on the whole they are not terribly good at it! Forecasting is difficult not only because our understanding of how the economy works is imperfect but also because of the impossibility of taking into account *all* the factors—many of them not strictly economic—that might affect future economic trends. Here are some questions that a forecaster, in trying to project the course of the economy, might have to try to answer: How will events abroad affect congressional authorizations for military spending over the next few years? What oil price will the Organization of Petroleum Exporting Countries (OPEC) decide on at its next meeting? Will there be a severe drought in agricultural regions with adverse effects on food quantities and prices? Will new technologies that are being developed ever come to market? Because answers to such questions are highly uncertain, macroeconomic forecasters rarely offer a single prediction. Instead, they usually combine a "most likely" forecast with "optimistic" and "pessimistic" alternative scenarios.

Does the fact that macroeconomics can't be used to make highly accurate forecasts of economic activity mean that it is a pointless field of study? Some people may think so, but that's really an unreasonable standard. Meteorology is an example of a field in which forecasting is difficult (will it *definitely* be nice this weekend?) but in which there is also a lot of useful knowledge (meteorologists helped discover the depletion of the earth's ozone layer and pointed out its dangers). Similarly, cardiologists can't usually predict if or when a patient will have a heart attack—they can only talk about probabilities. Like meteorologists and doctors, economists deal with a system whose complexity makes gaining a thorough understanding difficult and forecasting the system's behavior even more difficult. Rather than predicting what will happen, most macroeconomists are engaged in analyzing and interpreting events as they happen (macroeconomic analysis) or in trying to understand the structure of the economy in general (macroeconomic research).

Macroeconomic Analysis

Macroeconomic analysts monitor the economy and think about the implications of current economic events. Many analysts are employed in the private sector, such as in banks or large corporations. Private-sector analysts try to determine how general economic trends will affect their employers' financial investments, their opportunities for expansion, the demand for their products, and so on. Some private firms specialize in macroeconomic analysis and assist clients on a fee-for-service basis.

The public sector, which includes national and regional governments and international agencies such as the World Bank and the International Monetary Fund, also employs many macroeconomic analysts. The main function of public sector analysts is to assist in policymaking—for example, by writing reports that assess various macroeconomic problems and by identifying and evaluating possible policy options. Among U.S. policymakers, the officials who set monetary policy may call on the aid of several hundred Ph.D. economists employed within the Federal Reserve System, and the President has the advice of the Council of Economic Advisers and the professional staffs of numerous departments and agencies. For members of Congress a frequent source of macroeconomic analysis is the Congressional Budget Office. Economic policymakers also often go outside the government to seek the advice of macroeconomists from business or academia.

If a country has many well-trained macroeconomic analysts, as is true in the United States, does that mean that its macroeconomic policies will always be intelligent and farsighted? The answer, unfortunately, is "no." Because of the complexity of the economy, macroeconomic policy analysis, like macroeconomic forecasting, often is difficult and uncertain. Perhaps even more important, though, *politicians, not economists, usually make economic policy.* Politicians are typically less concerned with the abstract desirability of a policy than with the policy's immediate effects on their constituents. Thus in late 1990 international talks intended to reduce trade barriers failed because European governments found it politically inadvisable to reduce high subsidy payments to their farmers—despite the nearly universal opposition of economists to both trade barriers and farm price support payments. To reflect the importance of politics in economic policymaking, at various points in this book we include a feature called "The Political Environment," in which we discuss political aspects of macroeconomics.

Although the technical advice provided by macroeconomic analysts is not the sole basis on which macroeconomic policy is made, such advice is probably necessary for making good policy decisions, especially if dramatic changes are being considered. In recent years, for example, a number of countries in Eastern Europe, Latin America, and elsewhere have undertaken radical reforms of their economies. In most of these cases the countries' leaders have sought the technical advice of domestic and foreign economists, and this advice has been influential in policymaking. In the former Soviet Union, economists have played an important role in the debate over restructuring and reform, both as technical specialists and as political advocates.

Macroeconomic Research

Macroeconomic research takes an amazing variety of forms, from abstract mathematical analysis to psychological experimentation to massive number-crunching projects in which supercomputers are used to process large amounts of economic data. Nevertheless, the goal of all macroeconomic research is to make general statements about how the economy works. The general insights about the economy gained from successful research form the basis for the analyses of specific economic problems, policies, or situations.

To see why research is important, imagine that you are an economist with the International Monetary Fund whose task is to help a small African country control its high rate of inflation. On what basis can you offer advice? Basically, you should know what inflation-fighting policies other countries had used in the past, what the results had been, how the results had depended on the characteristics of the country employing the policy, and so on. Particularly if the situation you are analyzing is not identical to any of the previous cases, having some theoretical principles would also help identify and understand the main factors contributing to that country's inflation. Analyzing the historical cases and working out the theoretical principles by yourself from scratch might involve many years' effort. The value of ongoing research activities is that many of the results and ideas that you need would already be available in books or professional journals or circulated in unpublished form. Because it forms the basis for activities such as economic analysis and forecasting, in a very real sense macroeconomic research is the engine that pulls the whole enterprise of macroeconomics behind it.

Macroeconomic research takes place primarily in colleges and universities, in nonprofit institutions (such as the National Bureau of Economic Research, the Brookings Institution, and the American Enterprise Institute), and in the public sector (the government and international agencies). Particularly in the public sector, the line between economic analysis and macroeconomic research is much fuzzier than we have drawn it here. The reason is that many economists move back and forth between analysis of specific problems (such as an African country's inflation problem) and more basic macroeconomic research (such as an analysis of inflation in general).

Economic Theory. How is macroeconomic research carried out? As in many other fields, macroeconomic research proceeds primarily through the formulation and testing of theories. An **economic theory** is a set of ideas about the economy that have been organized in a logical framework. Most economic theories are developed in terms of an **economic model,** which is a simplified description of some aspect of the economy, usually expressed in mathematical form. Economists evaluate an economic model or theory by applying four criteria:

1. Are its assumptions reasonable and realistic?
2. Is it understandable and manageable enough to be used in studying real problems?

3. Does it have implications that can be tested by **empirical analysis**? That is, can its implications be evaluated by comparing them with data obtained in the real world?
4. When the implications and the data are compared, are the implications of the theory consistent with the data?

For a theory or model—of any type, not just economic—to be useful, the answer to each of these questions must be "yes." Unfortunately, though, economists may not always agree in their evaluation of a particular model, which means that controversies about the best way to model a given economic situation sometimes persist.

We present a summary of the main steps in developing and testing an economic theory or model in Box 1.1.

BOX 1.1

Developing and Testing an Economic Theory

To illustrate the process of developing and testing an economic theory, suppose that we want to develop a theory that explains the routes that people take when they commute from home to work and back. Such a theory would be useful, for example, to a traffic planner who is concerned about how a proposed housing development will affect traffic patterns. Here are the steps we would take:

Step 1. State the research question.

Example: What determines traffic flows in the city during rush hours?

Step 2. Make *provisional* assumptions that describe the economic setting and the behavior of the economic actors. These assumptions should be simple yet capture the most important aspects of the problem.

Example: The setting is described by the map of the city. The assumption about behavior is that commuters choose routes that minimize driving time.

Step 3. Work out the implications of the theory.

Example: Use the map of the city to plot a route that minimizes driving time between home and place of work.

Step 4. Conduct an *empirical analysis* to compare the implications of the theory with the data.

Example: Conduct a survey of commuters to identify (1) home locations; (2) work locations; and (3) routes taken to work. Then see whether the routes predicted by the model are generally the same as those reported in the commuter survey.

Step 5. Evaluate the results of your comparisons.

If the theory fits the data well: Use the theory to predict what would happen if the economic setting or economic policies change.

Example: Use the minimum-driving time assumption to evaluate the traffic effects of a new housing development by figuring out which routes the residents of the development are likely to take.

If the theory fits the data poorly: Start from scratch with a new model. Repeat steps 2–5.

Example: Change the provisional behavioral assumption to the following: Commuters choose the route that minimizes the *distance* they must drive (not the time they spend driving).

If the theory fits the data moderately well: Either make do with a partially successful theory or modify the model with additional assumptions and then repeat steps 3–5.

Example: A possible modification of the minimum-driving time assumption is that commuters will choose more scenic over less scenic routes, if driving time is not increased by more than a certain number of minutes. To test the model with this modified assumption, you must determine which routes are more scenic (those that pass a lake) and which are less scenic (those that pass a dump).

Data Development

The collection of economic data is a vital part of macroeconomics, and many economists are involved in the data development process. In the United States as well as all other major countries, data on thousands of economic variables are collected and analyzed. We have already presented some important macroeconomic data series, such as measures of output and the price level, and will look at these and others in more detail in Chapter 2. Macroeconomists use economic data to assess the current state of the economy, make forecasts, analyze policy alternatives, and test macroeconomic theories.

Most economic data are collected and published by the government—for example, by agencies such as the Bureau of the Census, the Bureau of Labor Statistics, and the Bureau of Economic Analysis in the United States, and by central banks such as the Federal Reserve. To an increasing degree, however, these activities also take place in the private sector. For example, marketing firms and private economic forecasting companies are important collectors, users, and sellers of economic data. In this book boxes called "In Touch with the Macroeconomy" describe major macroeconomic data series and tell you how they are collected and where to find them.

Much of the data collection and preparation process is routine. However, because providers of data want their numbers to be as useful as possible while keeping costs down, the organization of major data collection projects is typically the joint effort of many skilled professionals. Providers of data must decide what types of data should be collected based on who is expected to use the data and how. They must take care that measures of economic activity correspond to abstract concepts (such as "capital" and "labor") that are suggested by economic theory. In addition, data providers must guarantee the confidentiality of data that may reveal information about individual firms and people in the economy. In a large data-gathering organization, such as the Bureau of the Census, each of these issues is exhaustively analyzed by economists and statisticians before data collection begins.[6]

1.3 WHY MACROECONOMISTS DISAGREE

Over the years, the efforts of thousands of analysts, data collectors, and researchers have greatly enhanced the understanding of macroeconomic phenomena. Yet no matter what the macroeconomic issue, the news media seemingly can find an economist to argue either side of it. Why do macroeconomists appear to disagree so much?[7]

To a certain extent, the amount of disagreement among macroeconomists is exaggerated by the tendency of the public and the media to focus on the

---

6. For a readable discussion of issues that face data collectors, see Janet L. Norwood, "Distinguished Lecture on Economics in Government: Data Quality and Public Policy," *Journal of Economic Perspectives*, Spring 1990, pp. 3–12.

7. Not only do macroeconomists often seem to disagree with each other, but they also sometimes are accused of not being able to agree with themselves. President Harry Truman expressed the frustration of many policymakers when he said he wanted a one-handed economist—one who wouldn't always say, "On the one hand, . . .; on the other hand. . . ."

most difficult and controversial issues. In addition, the very fact that economic policy and performance are of such broad interest and concern contributes to the intensity of debate: More than controversies in many other fields, debates in macroeconomics tend to take place in public, rather than in the seminar room or the laboratory. Although important disagreements among macroeconomists certainly exist, there also are many areas of substantial agreement in macroeconomics.

We can provide an insight into why macroeconomists disagree by drawing the important distinction between positive and normative analyses of economic policy. A **positive analysis** of an economic policy examines the economic consequences of a policy but doesn't address the question of whether those consequences are desirable. A **normative analysis** of policy tries to determine whether a certain policy *should* be used. For example, if an economist is asked to evaluate the effects on the economy of a 5% rise in the income tax, the response involves a positive analysis. But if asked whether the income tax *should* be raised 5%, the economist's response requires a normative analysis. This normative analysis will involve not only the economist's objective, scientific understanding of how the economy works but also personal value judgments—for example, about the appropriate size of the government sector or the amount of income redistribution that is desirable.

Economists may agree on the positive analysis of a question yet disagree on the normative part because of differences in values. Value differences also are common in other fields: Physicists may be in perfect agreement on what would happen *if* a nuclear bomb were detonated (a positive analysis). But physicist "hawks" and physicist "doves" may disagree strongly about whether nuclear weapons *should* be deployed (a normative question).

Disagreement may occur on positive issues, however, and these differences are important in economics. In macroeconomics there always have been many schools of thought, each with a somewhat different perspective on how the economy works. Examples include monetarism and supply-side economics, both of which we discuss in this book. However, the most important—and enduring—disagreements on positive issues in macroeconomics involve the two schools of thought called the classical approach and the Keynesian approach.

Classicals Versus Keynesians

The classical approach and the Keynesian approach are the two major intellectual traditions in macroeconomics. We discuss the differences between the two approaches briefly here and in much greater detail later in the book.

The Classical Approach. The origins of the classical approach go back more than two centuries, at least to the famous Scottish economist Adam Smith. In 1776 Smith published his classic, *The Wealth of Nations,* in which he proposed the concept of the "invisible hand." The idea of the **invisible hand** is that, if there are free markets and individuals conduct their economic affairs in their own best interests, the overall economy will work well. As Smith put it, in a market economy individuals, while pursuing their own self-interests, seem to be led by an invisible hand to maximize the general welfare of everyone in the economy.

However, we must not overstate what Smith claimed: To say that an invisible hand is at work does *not* mean that no one in a market economy will be hungry or dissatisfied; free markets cannot insulate a nation from the effects of drought, war, or political instability. Nor does the invisible hand rule out the existence of great inequalities between the rich and the poor, because in Smith's analysis he took the initial distribution of wealth among people as given. Rather, the invisible-hand idea says that *given* a country's resources (natural, human, and technological) and its initial distribution of wealth, the use of free markets will make people as economically well off as possible.

Validity of the invisible-hand idea depends on a key assumption: The various markets in the economy, including financial markets, labor markets, and markets for goods and services, must function smoothly and without impediments such as minimum wages and interest rate ceilings. In particular, wages and prices must adjust rapidly enough to maintain **equilibrium**—a situation in which the quantities demanded and supplied are equal—in all markets. In markets where quantity demanded exceeds quantity supplied, prices must rise to bring the market into equilibrium. In markets where more of a good is available than people want to buy, prices must fall to bring the market into equilibrium.

Wage and price flexibility is crucial to the invisible-hand idea, because in a free-market system changes in wages and prices are the signals that coordinate the actions of people in the economy. To illustrate, suppose that war abroad disrupts oil imports. This drop in supply will drive up the price of oil. A higher oil price will make it profitable for domestic oil suppliers to pump more oil and to drill more wells. The higher price will also induce domestic consumers to conserve oil and to switch to alternative sources of energy. Increased demand for alternative energy sources will raise their prices and stimulate *their* production, and so on. Thus in the absence of impediments such as government price controls, the adjustment of prices helps the free-market economy respond in a constructive and coordinated way to the initial disruption of supplies.

The classical approach to macroeconomics builds on Smith's basic assumptions that people pursue their own economic self-interests and that prices adjust reasonably quickly to achieve equilibrium in all markets. With these two assumptions as a basis, followers of the classical approach attempt to construct models of the macroeconomy that are consistent with the data and that can be used to answer the questions raised at the beginning of this chapter.

The use of the classical approach carries with it some strong policy implications. Because the classical assumptions imply that the invisible hand works well, classical economists often argue (as a normative proposition) that the government should have, *at most,* a limited role in the economy. As a positive proposition, classical economists also often argue that government policies will be ineffective or counterproductive at achieving their stated goals. Thus, for example, most classicals believe that the government should not try actively to eliminate business cycles.

The Keynesian Approach. Compared with the classical approach, the Keynesian approach is relatively recent. The book that introduced it, *The General Theory of Employment, Interest, and Money,* by British economist John Maynard

Keynes, appeared in 1936—160 years after Adam Smith's *The Wealth of Nations.* In 1936 the world was suffering through the Great Depression: Unprecedentedly high rates of unemployment had afflicted most of the world's economies for years, and the invisible hand of free markets seemed completely ineffective. From the viewpoint of 1936, the classical theory appeared to be seriously inconsistent with the data, creating a need for a new macroeconomic theory. Keynes provided this theory.

In his book Keynes offered an explanation for persistently high unemployment.[8] He based this explanation on an assumption about wage and price adjustment that was fundamentally different from the classical assumption. Instead of assuming that wages and prices adjust rapidly to achieve equilibrium in each market, as in the classical tradition, Keynes assumed that wages and prices adjust slowly. Slow wage and price adjustment meant that markets could be out of equilibrium—with quantities demanded not equal to quantities supplied—for long periods of time. In the Keynesian theory unemployment can persist because wages and prices don't adjust quickly enough to equalize the number of people firms want to employ with the number of people who want to work.

Keynes's proposed solution to high unemployment was to have the government increase its purchases of goods and services, thus raising the demand for output. Keynes argued that this policy would reduce unemployment because, to meet the higher demands for their products, businesses would have to employ more workers. In addition, Keynes suggested, the newly hired workers would have more income to spend, creating another source of demand for output that would raise employment further. More generally, in contrast to classicals, Keynesians tend to be skeptical about the invisible hand and thus are more willing to advocate a role for government in improving macroeconomic performance.

The Evolution of the Classical–Keynesian Debate. Because the Great Depression so strongly shook the faith of many economists in the classical approach, the Keynesian approach dominated macroeconomic theory and policy from World War II until about 1970. At the height of Keynesian influence, economists widely believed that, through the skillful use of macroeconomic policies, the government could promote economic growth while avoiding inflation or recession. The main problems of macroeconomics apparently had been solved, with only some details to be filled in.

However, in the 1970s the United States suffered from both high unemployment and high inflation—called "stagflation," or stagnation plus inflation. This experience weakened economists' and policymakers' confidence in the traditional Keynesian approach, much as the Great Depression had undermined the traditional classical approach. In addition, the Keynesian assumption that prices and wages adjust slowly, so that markets may be out of equilibrium, was criticized as being without sound theoretical foundations. While the Keynesian approach was coming under attack, developments in economic theory made classical macroeconomics look more interesting and at-

8. Actually, Keynes presented a number of explanations of unemployment in his book, and debate continues about "what Keynes really meant." Our interpretation of what Keynes meant is the one adopted by his major followers.

tractive to many economists. Starting in the early 1970s a modernized classical approach enjoyed a major resurgence among macroeconomic researchers, although classical macroeconomics did not achieve the dominance that Keynesianism enjoyed in the early postwar years.

In the past twenty years advocates of both approaches have reworked them extensively to repair their weaknesses. Economists working in the classical tradition have improved their explanations of business cycles and unemployment. Keynesians have worked on the development of sound theoretical foundations for the slow adjustment of wages and prices, and Keynesian models can now accommodate stagflation. Currently, excellent research is being conducted with both approaches, and substantial communication and cross-fertilization is occurring between them.

A Unified Approach to Macroeconomics

In writing this book, we needed a strategy to deal with the fact that there are two major macroeconomic schools of thought. One strategy would have been to emphasize one of the two schools of thought and to treat the other only briefly. The problem with that strategy is that it would not expose you to the full range of ideas and insights that comprise modern macroeconomics. Alternatively, we might have presented the two approaches separately and then compared and contrasted their conclusions; but you would have missed the opportunity to explore the large common ground shared by the two schools of thought.

Our choice was to take an approach to macroeconomics that is as balanced and unified as possible. In keeping with this unified approach, all our analyses in this book—whether of economic growth, business cycles, inflation, or policy, and whether classical or Keynesian in spirit—are based on a *single economic model,* or on components or extensions of the basic model. This economic model, which draws heavily from both the classical and Keynesian traditions, has the following characteristics.

1. *Individuals, firms, and the government interact in goods markets, asset markets, and labor markets.* We have already discussed the need for aggregation in macroeconomics. In the economic model of this book we follow standard macroeconomic practice and aggregate all the markets in the economy into three major markets: the market for goods and services, the asset market (in which assets such as stocks, bonds, and real estate are traded), and the labor market. We show how participants in the economy interact in each of these three markets and how these markets relate to each other and the economy as a whole.

2. *The model's macroeconomic analysis is based on the analysis of individual behavior.* Macroeconomic behavior reflects the behaviors of many individuals and firms interacting in markets. To understand how individuals and firms behave, we take a "bottom-up" approach and focus our analysis at the level of individual decision making (as in Box 1.1 where we discuss a model of individual choices about the route to take to work). The insights gained are then used for studying the economy as a whole.

The guiding principle in analyzing the behavior of individuals and firms is the assumption that they *try to maximize their own economic satisfaction, given their needs, desires, and resources.* Although the founder of classical economics, Adam

Smith, emphasized this assumption, it is generally accepted by Keynesians and classicals alike; and it is used in virtually all modern macroeconomic research.

3. Although Keynesians reject the classical assumption that wages and prices quickly adjust to achieve equilibrium in the short run, *Keynesians and classicals both agree that in the long run prices and wages fully adjust to achieve equilibrium in the markets for goods, assets, and labor.* Because complete flexibility of wages and prices in the long run is not controversial, we examine the long-term behavior of the economy (Chapters 3–8) before discussing short-run issues associated with business cycles (Chapters 9–14).

4. *The basic model that we present may be used with either the classical assumption that wages and prices are flexible or the Keynesian assumption that wages and prices are slow to adjust.* This aspect of the model allows us to compare classical and Keynesian conclusions and policy recommendations within a common theoretical framework.

CHAPTER SUMMARY

1. Macroeconomics is the study of the structure and performance of national economies and the policies that governments use to try to affect economic performance. Important topics in macroeconomics include the determinants of long-run economic growth, business cycles, unemployment, inflation, international trade and lending, and macroeconomic policy.
2. Because macroeconomics covers the economy as a whole, macroeconomists ignore the fine distinctions among different kinds of goods, firms, or markets and focus on national totals such as aggregate consumption. The process of adding individual economic variables to obtain economywide totals is called aggregation.
3. The activities engaged in by macroeconomists include (in addition to teaching) forecasting, macroeconomic analysis, macroeconomic research, and data development.
4. The goal of macroeconomic research is to be able to make general statements about how the economy works. Macroeconomic research makes progress toward this goal by developing economic theories and testing them empirically—that is, by seeing whether they are consistent with data obtained from the real world. A useful economic theory is based on reasonable and realistic assumptions, is easy to use, has implications that can be tested in the real world, and is consistent with the data and the observed behavior of the real-world economy.
5. A positive analysis of an economic policy examines the economic consequences of the policy but does not address the question of whether those consequences are desirable. A normative analysis of a policy tries to determine whether the policy *should* be used. Disagreements among macroeconomists may arise because of differences in normative conclusions, the result of differences in personal values and beliefs, and differences in the positive analysis of a policy proposal.
6. The classical approach to macroeconomics is based on the assumptions that individuals and firms act in their own best interests and that wages and prices adjust quickly to achieve equilibrium in all markets. Under these assumptions the invisible hand of the free-market economy works well, with only a limited scope for government intervention in the economy.
7. The Keynesian approach to macroeconomics assumes that wages and prices do not adjust

rapidly and thus the invisible hand may not work well. Keynesians argue that, because of slow wage and price adjustment, unemployment may remain high for a long time. Keynesians are usually more inclined than classicals to believe that government intervention in the economy may help improve economic performance.

Key Terms

aggregation, p. 13
average labor productivity, p. 5
closed economy, p. 9
deflation, p. 8
economic model, p. 15
economic theory, p. 15
empirical analysis, p. 16
equilibrium, p. 19
fiscal policy, p. 11
inflation, p. 8
invisible hand, p. 18
macroeconomics, p. 3
monetary policy, p. 11
normative analysis, p. 18
open economy, p. 9
positive analysis, p. 18
trade deficit, p. 10
trade surplus, p. 10
unemployment, p. 7

Review Questions

1. How have total output and output per worker changed over time in the United States? How have these changes affected the lives of typical Americans?
2. What is a business cycle? How does the unemployment rate behave over the course of a business cycle? Does the unemployment rate ever reach zero?
3. Define *inflation* and *deflation*. Compare the behavior of consumer prices in the United States in the years before and after World War II.
4. Define *budget deficit*. Historically, when has the Federal government been most likely to run deficits? What has been the recent experience?
5. What is meant by *aggregation*? Why is aggregation important for macroeconomic analysis?
6. List the principal professional activities of macroeconomists. What role does macroeconomic research play in each of these activities?
7. What steps are involved in developing and testing an economic theory or model? What are the criteria for a useful theory or model?
8. Might two economists agree about the effects of a particular economic policy but disagree about the desirability of implementing the policy? Explain your answer.
9. Compare the classical and Keynesian views on the speed of wage and price adjustment. What are the important consequences of the differences in their views?

Numerical Problems

1. Here are some macroeconomic data for the country of Oz for the years 1993 and 1994.

	1993	1994
Output	12,000 tons of potatoes	14,300 tons of potatoes
Employment	1,000 workers	1,100 workers
Unemployed	100 workers	50 workers
Total labor force	1,100 workers	1,150 workers
Prices	2 shekels/ton of potatoes	2.5 shekels/ton of potatoes

As the data suggest, Oz produces only potatoes, and its monetary unit is the shekel. Calculate each of the following macroeconomic variables for Oz, being sure to give units.
a. Average labor productivity in 1993 and 1994.
b. The growth rate of average labor productivity between 1993 and 1994.
c. The unemployment rate in 1993 and 1994.
d. The inflation rate between 1993 and 1994.

2. In a recent issue of the *Survey of Current Business*, find the data section entitled "Selected NIPA Tables." In Table 1.1, "Gross Domestic Product," find data on gross domestic product (a measure of total output), exports, and imports. In Table 3.2, "Federal Government Receipts and Expenditures," find data on the government's total receipts (taxes) and expenditures.
a. Calculate the ratio of exports to GDP, the ratio of imports to GDP, and the ratio of the trade imbalance to GDP in the latest reported quarter. Compare the answers with the values reported for the previous two complete years.
b. Calculate the ratio of Federal government receipts to GDP, the ratio of Federal government expenditures to GDP, and the ratio of the budget deficit to GDP, for the most recent quarter and for the previous two complete years.

Analytical Problems

1. Can average labor productivity fall even though total output is rising? Can the unemployment rate rise even though total output is rising?
2. Prices were much higher in the United States in 1993 than in 1890. Does this fact mean that people were economically better off in 1890? Why or why not?
3. State a theory for why people vote Republican or Democratic that potentially could satisfy the criteria for a useful theory given in the text. How would you go about testing your theory?
4. Which of the following statements are positive in nature and which are normative?

   a. A tax cut will raise interest rates.

   b. A reduction in the payroll tax would primarily benefit poor and middle-class workers.

   c. Payroll taxes are too high.

   d. A cut in the payroll tax would improve the President's popularity ratings.

   e. Payroll taxes should not be cut unless capital gains taxes are cut also.
5. In 1993 the debate heated up in the United States about the North American Free Trade Agreement (NAFTA), which proposed to reduce barriers to trade (such as taxes on or limits to imports) among Canada, the United States, and Mexico. Some people strongly opposed the agreement, arguing that an influx of foreign goods under NAFTA would disrupt the U.S. economy, harm domestic industries, and throw American workers out of work. How might a classical economist respond to these concerns? Would you expect a Keynesian economist to be more or less sympathetic to these concerns than the classical economist? Why?

CHAPTER 2

The Measurement and Structure of the National Economy

Measurement is a crucial part of scientific study. Accurate measurement is essential for making new discoveries, evaluating competing theories, and predicting future events or trends. During the first half of the twentieth century, painstaking research by economists such as Nobel Prize winner Simon Kuznets (the first person to obtain comprehensive measures of national output) and the team of Arthur Burns and Wesley Mitchell (who performed detailed measurements of the stages of the business cycle) showed that careful economic measurement is not only possible but also necessary for any serious understanding of the economy. Their work, and the efforts of many other researchers, transformed economics from a field in which scholars relied on informal observations and broad generalizations to one in which numbers and statistical analysis play an essential role.

In this chapter we present some of the conceptual and practical issues involved in measuring the macroeconomy. We focus on the national income accounts, a framework for measuring economic activity that is widely used by economic researchers and analysts. Learning about the national income accounts will familiarize you with some useful economic data. In addition, because the national income accounts are set up in a logical way that mirrors the structure of the economy, working through these accounts is an important first step toward understanding how the macroeconomy works. When you finish this chapter, you will have a much clearer understanding of the relationships that exist among key macroeconomic variables and among the different sectors of the economy.

2.1 NATIONAL INCOME ACCOUNTING: THE MEASUREMENT OF PRODUCTION, INCOME, AND EXPENDITURE

The **national income accounts** are an accounting framework used in measuring current economic activity. Almost all countries have some form of official national income accounts. (For background information on the U.S. national income accounts, see the box, "In Touch with the Macroeconomy: The National Income and Product Accounts," p. 28.) In this section we discuss the basic idea that underlies national income accounting. We then show how the national income accounts are used in measuring economic activity in the United States and other countries.

The national income accounts are based on the idea that the amount of economic activity that occurs during a period of time can be measured in terms of

1. the amount of output produced, excluding output used up in intermediate stages of production (the product approach);
2. the incomes received by the producers of output (the income approach); and
3. the amount of spending by the ultimate purchasers of output (the expenditure approach).

Each approach gives a different perspective on the economy. However, the fundamental principle underlying national income accounting is that, except for problems such as incomplete or misreported data, *all three approaches give identical measurements of the amount of current economic activity.*

We can illustrate why these three approaches are equivalent by an example. Imagine an economy with only two businesses, called OrangeInc and JuiceInc. OrangeInc owns and operates orange groves. It sells some of its oranges directly to the public. It sells the rest of its oranges to JuiceInc, which produces and sells orange juice. The following table shows the transactions of each business during a year.

OrangeInc Transactions

Wages paid to OrangeInc employees	$15,000
Taxes paid to government	5,000
Revenue received from sale of oranges	35,000
Oranges sold to public	10,000
Oranges sold to JuiceInc	25,000

(*Note:* After-tax profit of OrangeInc = revenue − costs − taxes = $15,000)

JuiceInc Transactions

Wages paid to JuiceInc employees	$10,000
Taxes paid to government	2,000
Oranges purchased from OrangeInc	25,000
Revenue received from sale of orange juice	40,000

(*Note:* After-tax profit of JuiceInc = revenue − costs − taxes = $3000)

OrangeInc pays $15,000 per year in wages to workers to pick oranges, and it sells these oranges for $35,000 ($10,000 worth of oranges to households and $25,000 worth of oranges to JuiceInc). Thus OrangeInc's profit before taxes is

$35,000 – $15,000 = $20,000. Because OrangeInc pays taxes of $5000, its after-tax profit is $15,000.

JuiceInc buys $25,000 of oranges from OrangeInc and pays wages of $10,000 to workers to process the oranges into orange juice. It sells the orange juice for $40,000, so that its profit before taxes is $5000 ($40,000 – $25,000 – $10,000). After paying taxes of $2000, its after-tax profit is $3000.

What is the total value, measured in dollars, of the economic activity generated by these two businesses? The product approach, income approach, and expenditure approach are three different ways of arriving at the answer to this question; all yield the same answer.

1. The **product approach** measures economic activity by adding the market values of goods and services produced, excluding any goods and services used up in intermediate stages of production. This approach makes use of the value-added concept. The **value added** of any producer is the value of its output minus the value of the inputs it purchases from other producers. The product approach computes economic activity by summing the value added of all producers.

In our example, OrangeInc produces output worth $35,000 and JuiceInc produces output worth $40,000. However, measuring overall economic activity by simply adding $35,000 and $40,000 would "double count" the $25,000 of oranges that JuiceInc purchased from OrangeInc and processed into juice. To avoid this double counting, we sum value added rather than output: Because JuiceInc processed oranges worth $25,000 into a product worth $40,000, JuiceInc's value added is $15,000 ($40,000 – $25,000). OrangeInc doesn't use any inputs purchased from other businesses so its value added equals its revenue of $35,000. Thus total value added in the economy is $35,000 + $15,000 = $50,000.

2. The **income approach** measures economic activity by adding all income received, including wages, taxes (the government's income), and after-tax profits (the income of the owners of OrangeInc and JuiceInc). The incomes generated in the example are as follows.

Incomes Received

Wage income ($15,000 at OrangeInc; $10,000 at JuiceInc)	$25,000
Taxes ($5000 from OrangeInc; $2000 from JuiceInc)	7,000
Profits ($15,000 at OrangeInc; $3000 at JuiceInc)	18,000
Total income	$50,000

The income approach concludes that the value of economic activity is $50,000, the same amount determined by the product approach.

3. Finally, the **expenditure approach** measures activity by adding the amount spent by all ultimate users of output. In this example, households are ultimate users of oranges. JuiceInc is not an ultimate user of oranges because it sells the oranges (in processed, liquid form) to households. Thus ultimate users purchase $10,000 of oranges from OrangeInc and $40,000 of orange juice from JuiceInc for a total of $50,000, the same amount computed in both the product and the expenditure approaches.[1]

1. In the example, each business also purchases labor services from employees, but as these services are used in production, they aren't counted as services purchased by ultimate users.

IN TOUCH *WITH THE MACROECONOMY*

THE NATIONAL INCOME AND PRODUCT ACCOUNTS

In the United States the national income accounts are officially called the National Income and Product Accounts, or NIPA. These accounts provide comprehensive measurements of production, income, and expenditure for the U.S. economy. Developed in the 1930s and 1940s by the Department of Commerce, the U.S. national income accounts were used for economic planning during World War II. Official accounts have been constructed as far back as 1929, and some official data are available from as early as 1909.

Currently, the accounts are constructed quarterly by government economists and statisticians in the Bureau of Economic Analysis (BEA), a part of the Department of Commerce. In constructing the accounts, the BEA relies heavily on data provided by other government agencies, such as the Census Bureau and the Bureau of Labor Statistics. The BEA also uses data from tax returns and from private sources, such as industry associations.

Initial estimates of quarterly economic activity are released three or four weeks after the end of each quarter. Revised estimates, which may differ significantly from the initial estimates, are released in each of the next two months. More detailed revisions are done annually.

Historical NIPA data may be obtained from numerous sources, including the *Survey of Current Business* (the BEA's monthly publication), *Business Statistics* (the BEA's biennial publication), and the *Economic Report of the President,* which is issued each February by the President's Council of Economic Advisers. Latest-quarter NIPA data appear in the business press, which gives extensive coverage to the BEA's monthly releases. National income accounts data for other countries are available in *National Accounts,* a publication of the Organization for Economic Cooperation and Development (OECD), in *World Economic Outlook* (published by the International Monetary Fund), and in the United Nations' *National Accounts Statistics.*

Why the Three Approaches Are Equivalent

That the product, income, and expenditure approaches all give the same answer is no accident. The logic of these three approaches is such that they must *always* give the same answer.

To see why, first observe that the market value of goods and services produced in a given period is *by definition* equal to the amount that buyers must spend to purchase them. JuiceInc's orange juice has a market value of $40,000 only because that is what people are willing to spend to buy it. The market value of a good or service and the spending on that good or service are always the same, so the product approach (which measures market values) and the expenditure approach (which measures spending) must give the same measure of economic activity.[2]

2. Our explanation implicitly assumes that everything produced is sold. What if a firm produces some goods that it can't sell? As we demonstrate shortly, the national income accounts treat unsold goods as though they were purchased by the firm from itself; that is, accumulation of unsold goods in inventory is treated as part of expenditure. Thus expenditure and production remain equal even if some goods remain unsold.

Next, observe that what the seller receives must equal what the buyers spend. The seller's receipts in turn equal the total income generated by the economic activity, including the incomes paid to workers and suppliers, taxes paid to the government, and profits (whatever is left over). Thus total expenditure must equal total income generated, implying that the expenditure and income approaches must also produce the same answer. Finally, as both product value and income equal expenditure, they also must be equal.

Because of the equivalence of the three approaches, over any specified time period

$$\text{total production} = \text{total income} = \text{total expenditure}, \tag{2.1}$$

where production, income, and expenditure all are measured in the same units (for example, in dollars). Equation (2.1) is called the **fundamental identity of national income accounting** and forms the basis for national income accounting. (An identity is an equation that is true by definition.) In Section 2.2 we show how this fundamental identity is used in measuring current economic activity for the economy as a whole.

2.2 GROSS DOMESTIC PRODUCT

The broadest measure of aggregate economic activity, as well as the best-known and most often used, is the gross domestic product, or GDP. As in the example in Section 2.1, a country's GDP may be measured by the product approach, the expenditure approach, or the income approach. Although the three approaches arrive at the same value for GDP, each views GDP differently. Using all three approaches gives a more complete picture of an economy's structure than any single approach could.

The Product Approach to Measuring GDP

The product approach defines a nation's **gross domestic product** (GDP) as the market value of final goods and services newly produced within a nation during a fixed period of time. In working through the various parts of this definition, we discuss some practical issues that arise in measuring GDP.

Market Value. Goods and services are counted in GDP at their market values, that is, at the prices at which they are sold. The advantage of using market values is that it allows adding the production of different goods and services. Imagine, for example, that you want to measure the total output of an economy that produces 7 cars and 100 pairs of shoes. Adding the number of cars and the number of pairs of shoes to get a total output of 107 wouldn't make much sense because cars and shoes aren't of equal economic value. But suppose that each car sells for $10,000 and each pair of shoes sells for $60. Taking these market-determined prices as measures of relative economic values, you can calculate the value of cars produced as $70,000 (7 × $10,000) and the value of shoes produced as $6000 (100 × $60). The total market value of production, or GDP, is $70,000 + $6000 = $76,000. Using market values to measure production makes sense because it takes into account differences in the relative economic importance of different goods and services.

A problem with using market values to measure GDP is that some useful goods and services are not sold in formal markets. Ideally, GDP should be adjusted upward to reflect the existence of these goods and services. However, because of the difficulty of obtaining reliable measures, some nonmarket goods and services simply are ignored in the calculation of GDP.[3] Homemaking and child-rearing services performed within the family without pay, for example, are not included in GDP, although homemaking and child care that are provided for pay (for example, by professional housecleaners or by private day-care centers) are included. Similarly, because the benefits of clean air and water aren't bought and sold in markets, actions to reduce pollution or otherwise improve environmental quality usually are not reflected in GDP (see Box 2.1).

Some nonmarket goods and services are partially incorporated in official GDP measures. An example is activities that take place in the so-called underground economy. The **underground economy** includes both legal activities hidden from government record keepers (to avoid payment of taxes or compliance with regulations, for example) and illegal activities such as drug dealing, prostitution, and (in some places) gambling. Some might argue that activities such as drug dealing are "bads" rather than "goods" and shouldn't be included in GDP anyway—although a consistent application of this argument might rule out many goods and services currently included in GDP. Clearly, though, the services of a housepainter who is paid in cash in order to avoid taxes should be included in GDP. Government statisticians regularly adjust GDP figures to include estimates of the underground economy's size. Because cash is the favored means of payment for off-the-books transactions, one clue to the size of the underground economy is the amount of cash in circulation.[4]

A particularly important component of economic activity that does not pass through markets are the services provided by government, such as defense, public education, and the building and maintenance of roads and bridges. The fact that most government services are not sold in markets implies a lack of market values to use when calculating the government's contribution to GDP. In this case the solution that has been adopted is to value government services at their cost of production. Thus the contribution of national defense to GDP equals the government's cost of providing defense: the salaries of service and civilian personnel, the costs of building and maintaining weapons and bases, and so on. Similarly, the contribution of public education to GDP is measured by the cost of teachers' salaries, new schools and equipment, and so on.

---

3. Periodically, attempts have been made by private economists to devise measures that include nonmarket economic activity. See, for example, Robert Eisner, "The Total Incomes System of Accounts," *Survey of Current Business*, January 1985, pp. 24–48.

4. A detailed discussion of NIPA adjustments for the underground economy is given in "The Underground Economy: An Introduction" in the May and July 1984 issues of the *Survey of Current Business*. On the use of cash in circulation to estimate the size of the underground economy, see Vito Tanzi, "The Underground Economy in the United States: Annual Estimates, 1930–1980," IMF Staff Papers, June 1983, pp. 283–305.

BOX 2.1

Natural Resources, the Environment, and the National Income Accounts

Much of any country's economic well-being flows from natural, rather than human-made, assets—land, rivers and oceans, natural resources (such as oil and timber), and indeed the air that everyone breathes. Ideally, for the purposes of economic and environmental planning, the use and misuse of natural resources and the environment should be appropriately measured in the national income accounts. Unfortunately, they are not. There are at least two important conceptual problems with the way the national income accounts currently handle the economic use of natural resources and the environment.

1. *Natural resource depletion.* When an oil driller pumps oil from an underground field, the value of the oil produced is counted as part of the nation's GDP; there is no offsetting deduction to account for the fact that nonrenewable resources are being depleted. In principle, the draining of the oil field can be thought of as a type of negative inventory investment because in a sense it reduces the inventory of oil. If it were included in the national income accounts, this negative inventory investment would reduce the computed value of GDP.

2. *The costs and benefits of pollution control.* Imagine that a company has the following choices: It can produce $100 million worth of output and in the process pollute the local river by dumping its wastes; alternatively, by using 10% of its workers to dispose properly of its wastes, it can avoid polluting but will get only $90 million of output. Under current national income accounting rules, if the firm chooses to pollute rather than not to pollute, its contribution to GDP will be larger ($100 million rather than $90 million) because the national income accounts attach no explicit value to a clean river. In an ideal accounting system the economic costs of environmental degradation would be subtracted in the calculation of a firm's contribution to output, and activities that improve the environment—because they provide real economic benefits—would be added to output.

Discussing the national income accounting implications of resource depletion and pollution may seem to trivialize these important problems. Actually, because GDP and related statistics are used continually in policy analyses, abstract questions of measurement often may turn out to have significant real effects. For example, economic development experts have expressed concern that some poor countries, in attempting to raise measured GDP as quickly as possible, have done so in part by overexploiting their natural resources and harming the environment. Conceivably, explicitly incorporating "hidden" resource and environmental costs into official measures of economic growth might cause these policies to be modified. Similarly, in industrialized countries political debates about the environment at times have emphasized the impact on conventionally measured GDP of proposed pollution control measures, rather than their impact on overall economic welfare. Better accounting for environmental quality might serve to refocus these debates to the more relevant question of whether, for any particular environmental proposal, the benefits (economic and noneconomic) exceed the costs.

Newly Produced Goods and Services. As a measure of current economic activity, GDP includes only goods or services that are newly produced within the current period. GDP excludes purchases or sales of goods that were produced in previous periods. Thus, although the market price paid for a newly constructed house would be included in GDP, the price paid in the sale of a used house is not counted in GDP. (The value of the used house would have been included in GDP for the year it was built.) However, the value of the services of the real estate agent involved in the sale of the used house *is* part of GDP, because those services are provided in the current period.

Final Goods and Services. Goods and services produced during a period of time may be classified as either intermediate goods and services or final goods and services. **Intermediate goods and services** are those used up in the production of other goods and services *in the same period that they themselves were produced.* For example, flour that is produced and then used to make bread in the same year is an intermediate good. The trucking company that delivers the flour to the bakery provides an intermediate service.

Final goods and services are those goods and services that are not intermediate. Final goods and services are the end products of a process. For example, bread produced by the bakery is a final good, and a shopper's bus ride home from the bakery is a final service. Because the purpose of economic activity is the production of final goods and services, with intermediate goods being but a step along the way, only final goods and services are counted in GDP.

Sometimes the distinction between intermediate goods and final goods is subtle. For example, is a new lathe sold to a furniture manufacturer an intermediate good or a final good? Although the lathe is used to produce other goods, it is not used up during the year. Hence it is not an intermediate good; it is a final good. In particular, the lathe is an example of a type of final good called a capital good. Other more general examples of capital goods include factory equipment, office equipment, and factories and office buildings themselves. A **capital good** is a good that is itself produced (this rules out natural resources such as land) and is used to produce other goods; however, unlike an intermediate good, a capital good is not used up in the same period that it is produced. The preparers of the national income accounts decided to classify capital goods as final goods and thus to include their production in GDP. Their reasoning was that the addition to productive capacity that new capital goods represent is an important purpose of economic activity.

Another subtle distinction between intermediate and final goods arises in the treatment of inventory investment. **Inventories** are stocks of unsold finished goods, goods in process, and raw materials held by firms. Inventory investment is the amount by which inventories increase during the year.[5] For example, suppose that a baker began the year with $1000 worth of flour in her storeroom, and at the end of the year she is holding $1100 worth of flour. The difference between her beginning and ending stocks, or $100 worth of flour, equals the baker's inventory investment during the year. Even though the ultimate purpose of the baker's flour is for making bread, her increase in inventory represents production of flour that is not used up during the year. As in the case of capital goods, inventory investment is treated as a final good and thus part of GDP because increased inventories on hand imply greater productive capacity in the future.

In the OrangeInc–JuiceInc example, we showed that total economic activity could be measured by summing the value added (value of output minus value of purchased inputs) for each producer. The advantage of the value added technique is that it automatically includes final goods and excludes intermediate goods from the measure of total output. If you go back to that example, you will see that, by summing the value added of the two companies, we obtained a measure of economic activity that included

5. When inventories decline during the year, inventory investment is negative.

the value of final sales of the two businesses to the public, but that excluded the intermediate goods (unprocessed oranges) sold to JuiceInc by OrangeInc.

GNP Versus GDP. Until fairly recently most economists working with U.S. data focused on a measure of economic activity known as gross national product (GNP) rather than on GDP. However, in 1991, primarily in order to conform with national income accounting practices in other major industrialized countries, the Department of Commerce began to use GDP as its basic measure of economic activity. The difference between GNP and GDP concerns the treatment of output produced by capital and labor working outside its home (domestic) country. Specifically, **gross national product** is the market value of final goods and services newly produced *by domestic factors of production* during the current period (as opposed to production taking place within a country, which is GDP).

When U.S. capital and labor—also called factors of production—are used abroad, they produce output and earn income. This output and income are included in U.S. GNP but not in U.S. GDP because they don't represent production taking place within the United States. So, for example, the value of roads built by a U.S. construction company in Saudi Arabia, as measured by the fees that the construction company receives from the Saudi government, is counted in U.S. GNP but not in U.S. GDP. Similarly, when foreign capital or labor is used in the United States, the output produced and the income earned are part of U.S. GDP (because the production occurs within the United States) but not of U.S. GNP (they are counted in the foreign country's GNP instead). For example, the portion of the value of Japanese cars built in the United States that is attributable to Japanese capital and management counts in Japanese GNP and U.S. GDP, but not in U.S. GNP.

We define **net factor payments from abroad** (*NFP*) to be income paid to domestic factors of production by the rest of the world, minus income paid to foreign factors of production by the domestic economy. Using this concept, we express the relationship between GDP and GNP as

$$\text{GDP} = \text{GNP} - NFP. \tag{2.2}$$

For the United States, GDP and GNP give similar measures of economic activity. For example, in 1992 the U.S. GDP was $5951 billion and the U.S. GNP was $5962 billion, a difference of about 0.2%. The distinction between GNP and GDP is more important for countries such as Egypt and Turkey that have many citizens working abroad. The reason is that remittances sent home by workers abroad are part of a country's GNP but not its GDP.

The Expenditure Approach to Measuring GDP

A different perspective on the components of GDP is obtained by looking at the expenditure side of the national income accounts. The expenditure approach measures GDP as total spending on final goods and services produced within a nation during a specified period of time. Four major categories of spending are added to get GDP: consumption, investment, government purchases of goods and services, and net exports of goods and services. In symbols,

$$\begin{aligned} Y = \text{GDP} &= \text{total production (or output)} \\ &= \text{total income} \\ &= \text{total expenditure;} \\ C &= \text{consumption;} \\ I &= \text{investment;} \\ G &= \text{government purchases of goods and services;} \\ NX &= \text{net exports of goods and services.} \end{aligned}$$

With these symbols, we express the expenditure approach to measuring GDP as

$$Y = C + I + G + NX. \tag{2.3}$$

Equation (2.3), like Eq. (2.1), is one of the basic relationships in macroeconomics. Equation (2.3) is called the **income–expenditure identity** because it states that income Y equals total expenditure $C + I + G + NX$. Recent U.S. data for the four categories of spending, along with some major subcategories, are given in Table 2.1. As you read the rest of this section, you should look at Table 2.1 to get some feel for the relative sizes of different components of spending in the U.S. economy.

Consumption. **Consumption** is spending by domestic households on final goods and services, including those produced abroad.[6] It is the largest component of expenditure, usually accounting for about two thirds of GDP in the United States. Consumption expenditures are grouped into three categories:

1. *consumer durables,* which are long-lived consumer items, such as cars, televisions, furniture, and major appliances (but not houses, which are classified under investment);
2. *nondurable goods,* which are shorter-lived items, such as food, clothing, and fuel; and
3. *services,* such as education, health care, financial services, and transportation.

Investment. **Investment** includes both spending for new capital goods, called *fixed investment,* and increases in firms' inventory holdings, called *inventory investment.* Fixed investment in turn has two major components:

1. *business fixed investment,* which is spending by businesses on structures (factories, warehouses, and office buildings, for example) and equipment (such as machines, vehicles, and furniture); and
2. *residential investment,* which is spending on the construction of new houses and apartment buildings. Houses and apartment buildings are treated as capital goods because they provide a service (shelter) over a long period of time.

Like consumption, investment includes spending on foreign-produced goods. Overall, fixed investment in the United States usually is about one sixth or one seventh of GDP.

As we have mentioned, increases in inventories are included in investment spending, regardless of why inventories rose. In particular, if a firm produces

---

6. Later, we subtract imports to get total spending on the goods and services produced in the domestic economy.

Table 2.1 Expenditure Approach to Measuring GDP in the United States, 1992

	Billions of dollars	Percent of GDP
Personal consumption expenditures	**4096**	**68.8**
Durable goods	480	8.1
Nondurable goods	1291	21.7
Services	2325	39.1
Gross private domestic investment	**770**	**12.9**
Business fixed investment	548	9.2
Nonresidential structures	168	2.8
Producers' durable equipment	380	6.4
Residential investment	218	3.7
Inventory investment	4	0.1
Government purchases of goods and services	**1115**	**18.7**
Federal	449	7.5
National defense	316	5.3
Nondefense	133	2.2
State and local	666	11.2
Net exports	**−30**	**−0.5**
Exports	636	10.7
Imports	667	11.2
Total (equals GDP)	**5951**	**100.0**

Note: Numbers may not add to totals shown owing to rounding.

Source: *Survey of Current Business,* April 1993, Table 1.1.

goods that it can't sell, the resulting rise in inventories counts as investment by the firm. For the purposes of national income accounting, the firm has, in effect, purchased the unsold goods from itself. This accounting rule is useful because it guarantees that production and expenditure will always be equal in the national income accounts. Anything that is produced must by definition either be bought by a customer or "purchased" by the firm itself.

Government Purchases of Goods and Services. **Government purchases** of goods and services, which include any expenditure by the government for a currently produced good or service, foreign or domestic, is the third major component of spending. Government purchases in the United States recently have been about one fifth of GDP. Note in Table 2.1 that in the United States the majority of government purchases are made by state and local governments, not the Federal government.

Not all the checks written by the government are for purchases of goods and services. **Transfers,** a category that includes government payments for Social Security and Medicare benefits, unemployment insurance, welfare payments, and so on, are payments (primarily to individuals) by the government that are not made in exchange for current goods or services. As a result, they are excluded from the government purchases category and are not counted in GDP as calculated by the expenditure approach. Similarly, interest payments on the national debt are not counted as part of government purchases.

Net Exports. **Net exports** are exports minus imports. As discussed in Chapter 1, exports are the goods and services produced within a country that are purchased by foreigners; imports are the goods and services produced abroad that are purchased by a country's residents. Net exports are positive if exports are greater than imports and negative if imports exceed exports.

Exports are added to total spending because they represent spending (by foreigners) on final goods and services produced in a country. Imports are subtracted from total spending because consumption, investment, and government purchases are defined to include imported goods and services. Subtracting imports ensures that total spending, $C + I + G + NX$, reflects spending only on output produced in the country. For example, an increase in imports may mean that Americans are buying Japanese cars instead of American cars. For fixed total spending by domestic residents, therefore, an increase in imports lowers spending on domestic production.

The Income Approach to Measuring GDP

The third and final way to measure GDP is the income approach. It calculates GDP by adding the incomes received by producers, including profits, and taxes paid to the government. A key part of the income approach is a concept known as national income. **National income** is the sum of five types of income (see Table 2.2 for recent U.S. data).

1. *Compensation of employees.* Compensation of employees is the income of workers (excluding the self-employed) and includes wages, salaries, employee benefits (including contributions by employers to pension plans), and employer contributions to Social Security. As you can see from Table 2.2, compensation of employees is the largest component of national income, comprising 59% of GDP in 1992.[7]

2. *Proprietors' income.* Proprietors' income is the income of the nonincorporated self-employed. As many self-employed people own some capital (examples are a farmer's tractor or a dentist's X-ray machine), so proprietors' income includes both labor income and capital income. Proprietors' income was 7% of GDP in 1992.

3. *Rental income of persons.* Rental income of persons, a small item, is the income earned by individuals who own land or structures that they rent to others. Some miscellaneous types of income, such as royalty income paid to

7. Compensation of employees overstates the take-home income of workers. As in each of the other measures of income on this list, part of the income received by employees must be paid to the government as taxes.

Table 2.2 Income Approach to Measuring GDP in the United States, 1992

	Billions of dollars	Percent of GDP
Compensation of employees	3525	59.2
Proprietors' income	405	6.8
Rental income of persons	5	0.1
Corporate profits	394	6.6
Net interest	415	7.0
Total (equals **National Income**)	**4743**	**79.7**
Plus Indirect business taxes (and other small items)	565	9.5
Equals **Net National Product**	**5309**	**89.2**
Plus Consumption of fixed capital	653	11.0
Equals **Gross National Product** (GNP)	**5962**	**100.2**
Less Factor income received from rest of world	129	2.2
Plus Payments of factor income to rest of world	118	2.0
Equals **Gross Domestic Product** (GDP)	**5951**	**100.0**

Note: Numbers may not add to totals shown owing to rounding.

Source: *Survey of Current Business,* April 1993, Tables 1.9 and 1.14.

authors, recording artists and others, also are included in this category. Rental income of persons was about 0.1% of GDP in 1992.[8]

4. *Corporate profits.* Corporate profits are the profits earned by corporations and represent the remainder of corporate revenue after wages, interest, rents, and other costs have been paid. Corporate profits are used to pay taxes levied on corporations, such as the corporate income tax, and to pay dividends to shareholders. The rest of corporate profits after taxes and dividends, called retained earnings, is kept within the corporation. Corporate profits generally are a modest fraction of GDP (7% of GDP in 1992), but the amount of profits earned by corporations may change dramatically from year to year or even from quarter to quarter.

5. *Net interest.* Net interest is interest earned by individuals from businesses and foreign sources minus interest paid by individuals. In 1992 net interest was 7% of GDP, down from 11% in 1990. The recent decline in net interest reflects falling interest rates and some reduction in the use of debt by corporations.

In addition to the five components of national income just described, three other items need to be accounted for to obtain GDP:

8. Rental income of persons is a tiny fraction of GDP because it represents net rental income, or rents received minus the cost of replacing worn-out or depreciated structures. Also, rental income of persons does not include all rents paid in the economy because it excludes rents received by corporations.

- indirect business taxes;
- depreciation; and
- net factor payments.

Indirect business taxes, such as sales and excise taxes, are paid by businesses to Federal, state, and local governments. Indirect business taxes do not appear in any of the five categories of income discussed, but because they are income to the government, they must be added to national income in order to measure all of a country's income. National income plus indirect business taxes equals **net national product** (NNP), as indicated in Table 2.2.[9]

Depreciation (also known as capital consumption allowances) is the value of the capital that wears out during the period over which economic activity is being measured.[10] In the calculation of the components of national income (specifically, proprietors' income, corporate profits, and rental income), depreciation is subtracted from total, or gross, income. Thus, to compute the total or gross amount of income, we must add back in depreciation. The sum of net national product and depreciation is gross national product (GNP). Gross national product and gross domestic product are called *gross* because they measure the nation's total production or output of goods and services without subtracting depreciation.

As we discussed earlier, to go from GNP to GDP we have to subtract net factor payments from abroad, *NFP* (see Eq. 2.2). As we have already mentioned and as you can see from Table 2.2, for the United States net factor payments are relatively small and so GDP and GNP are very close.

Private Sector and Government Sector Income. In this section we have measured economic activity as the sum of all the incomes received in an economy. Sometimes, however, economists need to know how much of total income was received by the private sector (households and businesses) and how much accrues to the government sector, which in the United States consists of Federal, state, and local governments. For example, in trying to predict the demand for consumer goods, focusing on the income available to the private sector might be more useful than focusing on the income of the economy as a whole.

The income of the private sector, known as **private disposable income**, measures the amount of income the private sector has available to spend. In general, as for an individual family, the disposable income of the private sector as a whole equals income received from private-sector activities, plus payments received by the private sector from the government, minus taxes paid to the government. The precise definition is

$$\text{private disposable income} = Y + NFP + TR + INT - T, \qquad (2.4)$$

where

9. A few small additional items are included in NNP, such as net subsidies to government enterprises. We do not discuss these items here.

10. Depreciation (capital consumption allowances) includes both capital that physically wears out and capital that is scrapped because it is no longer economically useful. For instance, still-functioning computers that are scrapped because they have been made obsolete by later models would be included in depreciation.

Y = gross domestic product (GDP);
NFP = net factor payments from abroad;
TR = transfers received from the government;
INT = interest payments on the government's debt;
T = taxes.

As you can see from Eq. (2.4), private disposable income equals private sector income earned at home (GDP) and abroad (net factor payments from abroad, *NFP*);[11] plus payments to the private sector from the government sector (transfers, *TR*, and interest on the government debt, *INT*); minus taxes paid to the government, *T*.

The part of GDP that is not at the disposal of the private sector is the net income of the government sector. The government's net income equals taxes paid by the private sector, *T*, minus payments from the government to the private sector (transfers, *TR*, and interest payments on the government debt, *INT*):

$$\text{net government income} = T - TR - INT. \quad (2.5)$$

Adding Eqs. (2.4) and (2.5) yields the sum of private disposable income and net government income, $Y + NFP$, which is gross national product.

2.3 SAVING AND WEALTH

If you wanted to assess the economic situation of a household, the current income of the household would be an important piece of information. However, someone with a high current income isn't necessarily better off economically than someone with a low current income. For example, a retired tycoon who has no current earnings but owns real estate worth $10 million probably is economically better off than a newly graduated doctor with a high salary but heavy debts left over from medical school. To determine how well off a household is, in addition to knowing current income, you also need to know what the household owns (its assets) and owes (its liabilities). The difference between assets and liabilities is called **wealth.**

As for a household, the economic well-being of a country depends not only on its income but also on its wealth. The wealth of an entire nation is called **national wealth.**

An important determinant of wealth is the rate of saving: A family that puts aside a quarter of its income each month will accumulate wealth much more quickly than a family that spends nearly all its income. Similarly, the rate at which national wealth increases depends on the rate at which individuals, businesses, and governments in the economy save. Thus rates of saving and wealth accumulation are closely related.

In this section we present some concepts of aggregate saving and wealth and examine the relationships among them. Our main interest here is measurement. Questions such as what determines the rate of saving in a country are covered in later chapters.

---

11. Note that the sum of incomes earned at home and abroad, GDP + *NFP*, equals GNP.

Measures of Aggregate Saving

In general, the **saving** of any economic unit is the unit's current income minus its spending on current needs. The saving *rate* of an economic unit is its saving divided by its income. From a macroeconomic perspective, three important measures of saving are private saving, government saving, and national saving. Summary table 1 outlines the definitions of each measure.

Private Saving. The saving of the private sector, known as **private saving,** equals private disposable income minus consumption. Using the definition of private disposable income from Eq. (2.4), we have

$$\begin{aligned} S_{pvt} &= \text{private disposable income} - \text{consumption} \\ &= (Y + NFP - T + TR + INT) - C, \end{aligned} \tag{2.6}$$

where S_{pvt} is private saving. Consumption is subtracted from private disposable income to obtain private saving because consumption represents the private sector's spending to meet current needs. Investment, although part of private sector spending, is not subtracted from private disposable income because capital goods are purchased to enhance future productive capacity rather than to satisfy current needs. The private saving *rate* is private saving divided by private disposable income.[12]

Government Saving. **Government saving** equals net government income minus government purchases of goods and services, *G*. With the definition of net government income from Eq. (2.5), government saving, S_{govt}, is

12. A measure of aggregate saving that you may hear reported and discussed is *personal saving,* which is the saving of the household portion of the private sector. Personal saving differs from private saving by excluding saving done within businesses. The personal saving rate in the United States has been notoriously low. However, because businesses are owned and controlled by households, it makes little economic sense to distinguish between the portion of private saving done within households and the portion done within businesses. Thus we focus on private rather than personal saving.

SUMMARY 1

Measures of Aggregate Saving

Saving Measure	Definition and Formula
Private saving	Private disposable income less consumption $S_{pvt} = (Y + NFP - T + TR + INT) - C$
Government saving	Government receipts less government outlays $S_{govt} = T - (G + TR + INT)$
National saving	Private saving plus government saving; also GNP (Y+NFP) less consumption and government purchases $S = S_{pvt} + S_{govt}$ $= Y + NFP - C - G$

$$S_{govt} = \text{net government income} - \text{government purchases} \qquad (2.7)$$
$$= (T - TR - INT) - G.$$

If you think of government purchases as the government's spending to meet current needs, this definition of government saving fits the general definition of saving. In reality, though, some goods that the government purchases—roads, military aircraft, and government buildings, for example—are not used up during the year and thus are available to satisfy future needs. An ideal measure of government saving would exclude these longer-lived items from current government purchases. However, unlike those of some countries, the national income accounts of the United States do not distinguish these longer-lived government purchases from spending to meet current needs. For simplicity we follow U.S. practice and define government saving to be net government income less *all* government purchases, even though this definition tends to underestimate the true amount of saving that the government does.[13]

Another, probably more familiar, name for government saving is the government budget surplus. The government **budget surplus** equals government receipts minus government outlays. **Government receipts** equal tax revenue, T. **Government outlays** are the sum of government purchases of goods and services, G, transfers, TR, and interest payments on government debt, INT. Thus the government budget surplus equals $T - (G + TR + INT)$, which, as you can see from Eq. (2.7), is the same as government saving.

When government receipts are less than government outlays, the difference between outlays and receipts is known as the government **budget deficit.** Thus, when the government runs a budget deficit, with its outlays greater than its receipts, government saving is negative.

National Saving. **National saving,** or the saving of the economy as a whole, equals private saving plus government saving. Using the definitions of private and government saving, Eqs. (2.6) and (2.7), we obtain national saving, S:

$$S = S_{pvt} + S_{govt}$$
$$= (Y + NFP - T + TR + INT - C) + (T - TR - INT - G) \qquad (2.8)$$
$$= Y + NFP - C - G.$$

Equation (2.8) shows that national saving equals the total income of the economy, $Y + NFP$ (which equals GNP), minus spending to satisfy current needs (consumption, C, and government purchases, G).

The Uses of Private Saving

How is private saving in an economy put to use? Here we show that private saving is used to fund new capital investment, provide the resources the government needs to finance its budget deficits, and acquire assets from or lend to foreigners.

To derive an important identity that illustrates the uses of private saving, we first use the income–expenditure identity (Eq. 2.3) and substitute $C + I + G + NX$ for Y in the expression for national saving (Eq. 2.8):

---

13. A similar argument suggests that expenditures on cars and other long-lived consumer durables should not be subtracted from disposable income in the calculation of private saving, although in practice they are subtracted.

$$S = (C + I + G + NX) + NFP - C - G.$$

Simplifying the above expression, we obtain

$$S = I + (NX + NFP). \qquad (2.9)$$

The expression for national saving in Eq. (2.9) contains the term NX + NFP, which is the sum of net exports and net factor payments, and is called the current account balance, CA.[14] The **current account balance** equals payments received from abroad in exchange for currently produced goods and services (including factor services), minus the analogous payments made to foreigners by the domestic economy. Substituting CA for $NX + NFP$ in Eq. (2.9), we obtain

$$S = I + CA. \qquad (2.10)$$

We now have an expression for national saving, S; our goal is an expression for private saving, S_{pvt}. Equation (2.8) shows that private saving, S_{pvt}, equals national saving, S, minus government saving, S_{govt}. Then, subtracting S_{govt} from both sides of Eq. (2.10), we get

$$S_{pvt} = I + (-S_{govt}) + CA, \qquad (2.11)$$

where $-S_{govt}$ is the government budget deficit.

Equation (2.11) is another important macroeconomic identity, called the **uses-of-saving identity**. It states that an economy's private saving is used in three ways:

1. *Investment* (I). Firms borrow from private savers to finance the construction and purchase of new capital (including residential capital) and inventory investment.

2. *The government budget deficit* ($-S_{govt}$). When the government runs a budget deficit (so that S_{govt} is negative and $-S_{govt}$ is positive), it must borrow from private savers to cover the difference between outlays and receipts.

3. *The current account balance* (CA). When the U.S. current account balance is positive, foreigners' receipts of payments from the United States are not sufficient to cover the payments they make to the United States. To make up the difference, foreigners must either borrow from U.S. private savers or sell to U.S. savers some of their assets, such as land, factories, stocks, and bonds. Thus financing the current account balance is a use of a country's private saving.

In contrast, when the U.S. current account balance is negative, as during most of the 1980s and early 1990s, American receipts of payments from foreigners are not sufficient to cover U.S. payments to foreigners. To offset this excess of payments over receipts, the United States must borrow from foreigners or sell to foreigners some U.S. assets. In this case foreigners use their saving to lend to the United States or to acquire American assets.[15]

---

14. Actually, the current account balance also includes a term called net unilateral transfers, which measures transfers between countries such as private gifts or official foreign aid (see Chapter 5). In our analysis we generally ignore this term.

15. The current account and its relationship to international borrowing and lending are discussed in greater detail in Chapter 5.

APPLICATION

The Uses of Saving and the Government Budget Deficit in the 1980s and 1990s

Understanding the uses-of-saving identity is a helpful first step for analyzing some complicated macroeconomic issues. For example, the effects of government budget deficits on the economy are argued endlessly. Equation (2.11) shows that if the government budget deficit increases, at least one of the following three things, or a combination of them, must happen: (1) private saving must rise, (2) investment must fall, and/or (3) the current account balance must fall.

Figure 2.1 shows the behavior of private saving and its three uses in the United States since 1980, all measured as a percentage of GDP. The increase in the U.S. government budget deficit in 1982 and subsequent years is striking. During the early 1980s the increase in the budget deficit was offset by a drop in investment relative to private saving. However, from about 1984 until near the end of the decade, investment nearly equaled private saving, so the large government budget deficit was mirrored by a negative current account balance. Since the late 1980s a surge in the government budget deficit has been accompanied by a widening gap between national saving and investment and a less negative current account balance.

Relating Saving and Wealth

Saving is a key economic variable because it is closely related to the rate of wealth accumulation. In the rest of this section we discuss the relationship of saving and wealth. To do so, however, we must first introduce the concept of stocks versus flows.

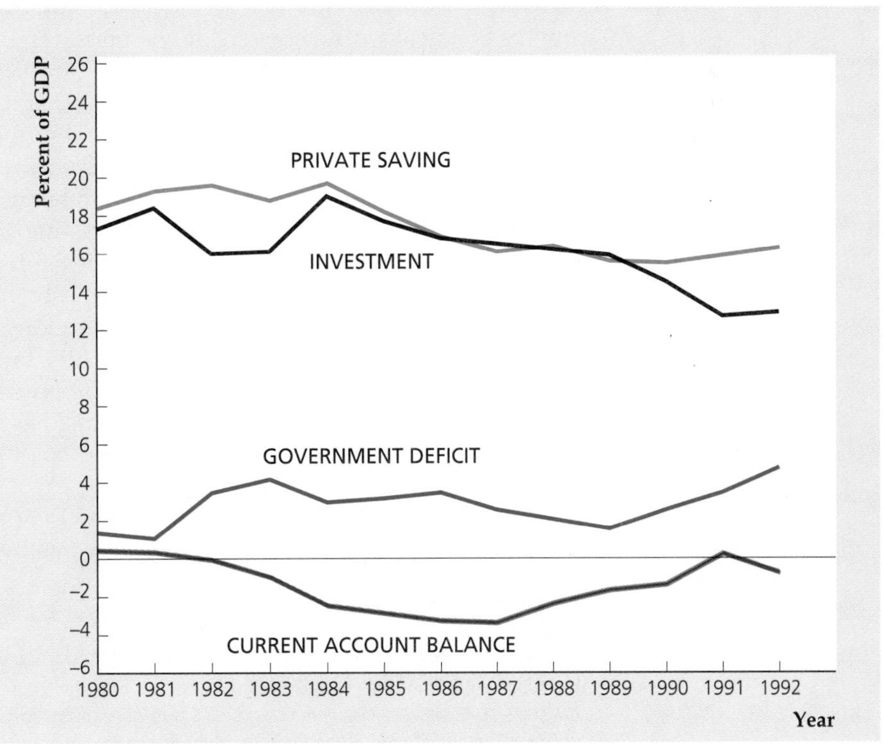

Figure 2.1
The uses-of-saving identity in the United States, 1980–1992
The figure illustrates the uses-of-saving identity—which states that private saving equals the sum of investment, the government budget deficit, and the current account balance—for the United States over the period 1980–1992. All variables are measured as a percentage of GDP, and the government budget deficit is the combined deficit of Federal, state, and local governments.

Source: GDP 1980–1991 from 1993 *Economic Report of the President*, Table B-1; 1992 from *Survey of Current Business*, April 1993, Table 1.1. Gross private saving, government saving, gross investment, and net foreign investment 1980–1991 from 1993 *Economic Report of the President*, Table B-26; 1992 from *Survey of Current Business*, April 1993, Table 5.1.

Stocks and Flows. The economic variables we have discussed so far in this chapter—such as GDP and the various types of expenditure, income, and saving—are measured per unit of time (for example, per quarter or per year). For instance, annual GDP figures measure the economy's production per year. Variables that are measured per unit of time are called **flow variables.**

In contrast, some economic variables, called **stock variables,** are defined at a point in time. Examples of stock variables are the amount of money in your bank account on September 15 of this year and the total value of all houses in the United States on January 1, 1995.

In many applications a flow variable is the rate of change in a stock variable. A classic example is a bathtub with water flowing in from a faucet. The amount of water in the tub at any moment is a stock variable. The units of a stock variable (gallons, in this case) don't have a time dimension. The rate at which water enters the tub is a flow variable; its units (gallons per minute) have a time dimension. In this case the flow is equal to the rate of change of the stock.

Wealth and Saving as Stock and Flow. Saving and wealth are related to each other in much the same way that the flow and stock of water in a bathtub are related. The wealth of any economic unit, also called net worth, is its assets (the things that it owns, including IOUs from other economic units) minus its liabilities (what it owes to other units). Wealth is measured in dollars at a point in time and is a stock variable. Saving is measured in dollars per unit time and is a flow variable. Because saving takes the form of an accumulation of assets or a reduction in liabilities (for example, if saving is used to pay off debts), it adds to wealth just as water flowing into a bathtub adds to the stock of water.

National Wealth. National wealth is the total wealth of the residents of a country. National wealth consists of two parts: (1) the country's domestic physical assets, such as its stock of capital goods and land;[16] and (2) its net foreign assets. The **net foreign assets** of a country equal the country's foreign assets (foreign stocks, bonds, and factories owned by domestic residents) minus its foreign liabilities (domestic physical and financial assets owned by foreigners). Net foreign assets are part of national wealth because they represent claims on foreigners that are not offset by foreigners' claims on the domestic economy.

Domestic financial assets held by domestic residents are not part of national wealth because the value of any domestic financial asset is offset by a domestic financial liability. For example, a checking account held by an American in a U.S. bank is an asset for the depositor but a liability for the bank; it thus does not represent wealth for the economy as a whole. In contrast, an American's checking account in a foreign bank has no corresponding domestic liability (it is a liability of a foreigner) and so is part of American national wealth.

National wealth can change in two ways over time. First, the value of the existing assets or liabilities that make up national wealth may change. Thus an increase in the value of American farmland raises U.S. national wealth, as does an increase in the value of foreign stocks held by Americans. The wearing out

---

16. In principle, national wealth should also include the value of the skills and training of the country's residents—what economists call human capital. In practice, because of measurement problems, human capital is not usually included in measures of national wealth.

or depreciation of physical assets, which corresponds to a fall in the value of those assets, reduces national wealth.

The second way that national wealth can change is through national saving. Over any particular period of time, with the value of existing assets and liabilities held constant, each extra dollar of national saving adds a dollar to national wealth. That is,

$$S = I + CA,$$

which you will recognize as Eq. (2.10). This equation shows that national saving has two uses: (1) to increase the stock of domestic physical capital through investment, I, and (2) to increase the nation's stock of net foreign assets by lending to foreigners or acquiring foreign assets in an amount equal to the current account balance, CA. But each dollar by which domestic physical assets or net foreign assets increase is a dollar by which national wealth increases. Thus, as we claimed, increases in national saving increase national wealth dollar for dollar. As in the example of water flowing into a bathtub, the more rapid the flow of national saving, the more quickly the stock of national wealth will rise.

APPLICATION

An International Comparison of National Saving and Investment Rates

How do national saving and investment in the United States compare with saving and investment in other developed countries? Figure 2.2 shows saving and investment for 1963–1991 for some member countries of the Organization for Economic Cooperation and Development (OECD), a group of 25 industrialized countries. National saving as a percentage of GDP, investment as a percentage of GDP, and current account balances are shown for each of the seven largest OECD countries and for all OECD countries combined. From the relationship $S = I + CA$ (Eq. 2.10), we know that the excess of national saving over investment, $S - I$, for each country equals the country's current account balance, CA.

Figure 2.2 shows that the United States is a low-saving country, with a national saving rate well below that of all OECD countries taken together. As a percentage of GDP, investment in the United States also is fairly low.[17] Japan stands out as the country with the highest saving rate.

Two other conclusions may be drawn from Fig. 2.2. First, national saving rates of many countries have fallen substantially since 1970. Second, within individual OECD countries national saving and investment generally have tended to move in tandem. This point implies that the current account balances of individual OECD countries, which equal the difference between each country's national saving and investment, typically have been small as a percentage of GDP. The exception is the period since the early 1980s, during which the United States, the United Kingdom, and Canada generally have had sharply negative current account balances (investment greater than saving), whereas Japan and Germany have had positive current account balances (saving greater than investment).

17. Some economists have suggested that the low U.S. saving and investment rates reflect various measurement problems as much as fundamental differences in behavior. See, for example, William Dewald and Michael Ulan, "Appreciating U.S. Saving and Investment," *Business Economics*, January 1992, pp. 42–46.

Figure 2.2
Trends in national saving and investment rates
National saving (green) and investment (red) as a percentage of GDP are shown for 1963–1991 for seven OECD countries separately and for all 25 OECD countries taken together. The shaded areas indicate the current account balance, or the excess of national saving over investment. Gray indicates a positive current account balance (national saving greater than investment); red indicates a negative current account balance (investment greater than national saving).

Source: ***National Accounts***, 1970–1991, OECD. (This publication contains data prior to 1970 for national saving and investment.)

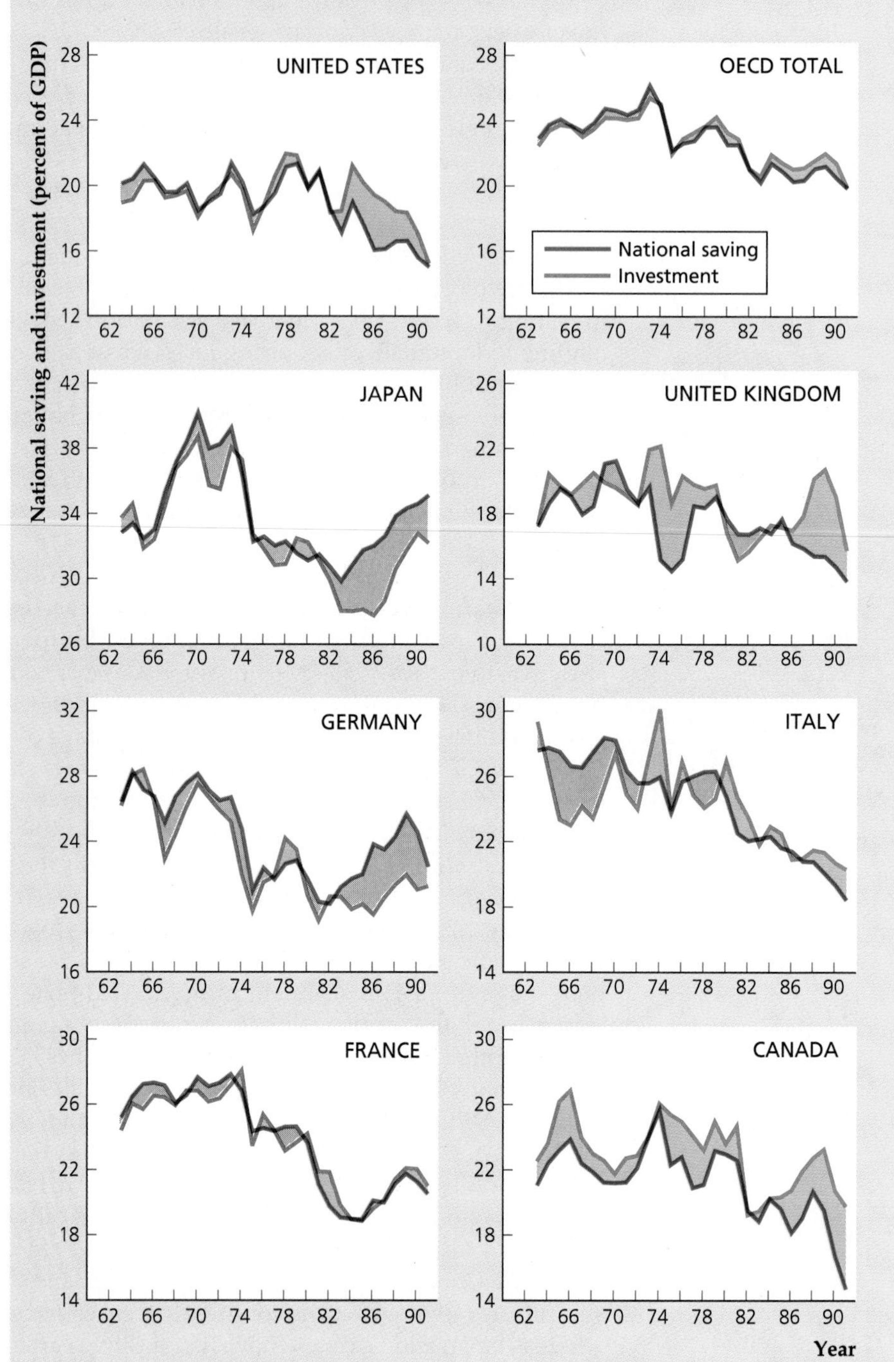

2.4 PRICE INDEXES, INFLATION, AND INTEREST RATES

All the key macroeconomic variables that we have discussed so far in this chapter—GDP, the components of expenditure and income, national wealth, and saving—are measured in terms of current market values. Such variables are called **nominal variables.** The advantage of using market values to measure economic activity is that it allows summing of different types of goods and services.

However, a problem with measuring economic activity in nominal terms arises if you want to compare the values of an economic variable—GDP, for example—at two different points in time. If the current market value of the goods and services included in GDP changes over time, you can't tell whether this change reflects changes in the quantities of goods and services produced, changes in the prices of goods and services, or a combination of these factors. For example, a large increase in the current market value of GDP might mean that a country has greatly expanded its production of goods and services, or it might mean that the country has experienced inflation, which raised the prices of goods and services.

Economists have devised methods for breaking down changes in nominal variables into the part owing to changes in physical quantities and the part owing to changes in prices. Consider the numerical example in Table 2.3, which gives production and price data for the Outasite Golf Ball Company. Five years ago the nominal value of Outasite's production was $200,000 (60,000 golf balls worth $3.00 each and 40,000 tees worth $0.50 each). This year the nominal value of Outasite's production is $480,000 (80,000 balls at $5.00 plus 80,000 tees at $1.00). Although the nominal value of Outasite's production has increased by 140% over the past five years, this increase does not reflect either a 140% increase in output or a 140% increase in prices. Instead, as you can see from Table 2.3, both quantities and prices rose.

Suppose that you were interested primarily in the growth of Outasite's output, perhaps because you wanted to study how the company's work-force productivity has changed over time. How much of the increase in the nominal value of Outasite's production reflects changes in the quantity of balls and tees produced, not changes in price? A standard way to eliminate the influence of price changes is to measure the value of production in each period by using

Table 2.3 Production and Price Data for Outasite Golf Ball Company

	Five Years Ago (Base Year)	This Year (Current Year)	Change from Five Years Ago
Product			
Balls	60,000	80,000	+20,000
Tees	40,000	80,000	+40,000
Price			
Balls	$3.00/ball	$5.00/ball	+$2.00/ball
Tees	$0.50/tee	$1.00/tee	+$0.50/tee
Value			
Balls	$180,000	$400,000	+$220,000
Tees	$20,000	$80,000	+$60,000
Total	**$200,000**	**$480,000**	**+$280,000**

prices from some base year. For this example, let's choose five years ago as the base year. For Outasite's current production of 80,000 balls at \$3.00 per ball (the price of balls five years ago) and its current production of 80,000 tees at \$0.50 per tee (the price of tees five years ago), the value of Outasite's production this year is \$280,000. This calculation is summarized in Table 2.4, step 1.

In general, an economic variable that is measured by the prices of a base year is called a **real variable.** Thus \$280,000 is the real value of Outasite's current production. Real economic variables measure the physical volume of economic activity.

What was Outasite's real production five years ago? To find it, multiply Outasite's production of balls and tees from five years ago by the prices of balls and tees in the base year, or five years ago. This calculation gives (60,000 balls × \$3.00 per ball) + (40,000 tees × \$0.50 per tee) = \$200,000. This value is the same as that for Outasite's nominal production five years ago. This result is a general one: Because current and base-year prices are the same in the base year, real and nominal quantities also are the same in the base year.

Comparing Outasite's current real production of \$280,000 with its real production of \$200,000 five years ago shows that the company's real production rose by 40% over the five years. Note that the estimated increase in real production of 40% lies between the 33% increase in ball production and the 100% increase in tee production. The overall increase in production actually is closer to 33% than 100% because the value of ball production is much greater than the value of tee production. Hence the increase in ball production receives greater weight in the overall growth rate.

Real Versus Nominal GDP

Just as an individual firm's production can be expressed in either nominal or real terms, the output of an entire economy also can be expressed in both nominal and real terms. **Nominal GDP,** also called current-dollar GDP, is the market value of an economy's final output at current market prices. **Real GDP,** also called constant-dollar GDP, measures the market value of an economy's final output at prices that prevailed during a specified base year or period. Use real rather than nominal GDP when looking at how an economy's physical production has evolved over time. (Figure 1.1, p. 5, shows the long-run behavior of real output in the United States.)

Currently, the base year used to calculate real GDP in the United States is 1987. Thus to calculate real GDP for, say, 1992 multiply the quantities of goods and services produced in 1992 by the 1987 prices for those goods and services. In contrast, to calculate nominal GDP for 1992 multiply the quantities of goods and services produced in 1992 by their 1992 prices. Nominal GDP in 1992 of \$5951 billion exceeded real GDP in 1992 of \$4923 billion because prices generally rose between 1987 and 1992. In contrast, real and nominal GDP were equal at \$4540 billion in 1987 because current and base-year prices were the same in 1987.

All macroeconomic variables discussed in this chapter—consumption, investment, saving, wealth, and so on—may be expressed in real terms. Because they measure physical quantities, real variables are better indicators than nominal variables of how a country's living standards and productive capacity are changing over time. In most of this book we focus on the real determinants of

Table 2.4 Calculation of Real Output and Price Level for Outasite Golf Ball Company

1. Calculation of the real value of current output

Real value of current output =

	current quantities	x	base-year prices		
Balls	80,000		$3.00		= $240,000
Tees	80,000		$0.50		= $40,000
				Total	$280,000

2. Calculation of the price level (variable-weight index)

$$\text{Price level} = \frac{\text{value of current output at current prices}}{\text{value of current output at base-year prices}}$$

Value of current output at current prices =

	current quantities	x	current prices		
Balls	80,000		$5.00		= $400,000
Tees	80,000		$1.00		= $80,000
				Total	$480,000

Value of current output at base-year prices =

	current quantities	x	base-year prices		
Balls	80,000		$3.00		= $240,000
Tees	80,000		$0.50		= $40,000
				Total	$280,000

$$\text{Price level (variable-weight)} = \frac{\$480,000}{\$280,000} = 1.71$$

3. Calculation of the price level (fixed-weight index)

$$\text{Price level} = \frac{\text{value of base-year output at current prices}}{\text{value of base-year output at base-year prices}}$$

Value of base-year output at current prices =

	base-year quantities	x	current prices		
Balls	60,000		$5.00		= $300,000
Tees	40,000		$1.00		= $40,000
				Total	$340,000

Value of base-year output at base-year prices =

	base-year quantities	x	base-year prices		
Balls	60,000		$3.00		= $180,000
Tees	40,000		$0.50		= $20,000
				Total	$200,000

$$\text{Price level (fixed-weight)} = \frac{\$340,000}{\$200,000} = 1.70$$

economic well-being. Therefore from now on, unless otherwise stated, when we refer to output, Y, consumption, C, investment, I, and so on, we are referring to these variables measured in real rather than nominal terms.

Price Indexes and Inflation

Measuring GDP in real terms eliminates the effects of price changes from the measure of national output. Sometimes, however, as when studying the determinants of inflation, you may want to determine how much prices have changed over a period of time. A measure of the average level of prices for some specified set of goods and services, relative to the prices in a specified base year, is called a **price index.**

The simplest type of price index is an index for one good, say, hamburgers. Suppose that hamburgers cost \$1.50 each in the base year, say, 1987, and cost \$2.25 each today. The price index for hamburgers, which measures the price of hamburgers today relative to 1987, then is \$2.25/\$1.50 = 1.50, indicating that hamburger prices have risen 50% since 1987.

Usually, however, economists want to know how prices have changed not just for one good but for a larger set of goods and services, perhaps even all the goods and services produced in the economy. So they must somehow combine the prices of many goods into a single index. Two basic types of price indexes, called variable-weight indexes and fixed-weight indexes, are used to measure average price change for a set of goods and services.

A **variable-weight price index** starts with the set of goods and services produced in the current period and compares today's cost of those goods and services with what they would have cost in the base year. More precisely:

$$\text{variable-weight price index} = \frac{\text{value of current output at current prices}}{\text{value of current output at base-year prices}}$$

If the goods and services produced today are much more costly than in the base year, the variable-weight price index will be high. Table 2.4, step 2, shows how to calculate a variable-weight price index for Outasite. Its current output is worth \$480,000 at today's prices and \$280,000 at the prices of five years ago. Thus the price index for Outasite for the current year is \$480,000/\$280,000 = 1.71. Thus, on average, Outasite's prices now are 71% higher than five years earlier.

An often-used variable-weight price index, which is constructed as part of the national income accounts, is the GDP deflator. For any period, the **GDP deflator** is the ratio of current nominal GDP to current real GDP:

$$\text{GDP deflator} = \frac{\text{nominal GDP}}{\text{real GDP}}.$$

The GDP deflator is the variable-weight price index that covers all final goods and services in the economy. The value of current output in current prices is the same as nominal GDP, and the value of current output in base-year prices equals real GDP. Thus the definition of the GDP deflator fits the general form of a variable-weight price index. Published values of the GDP deflator and other price indexes often are multiplied by 100 to get rid of the decimal point. In that case you will see a notation such as 1987 = 100, which means that the index equals 100 (rather than 1.00) in the base year, 1987.

The second type of price index is a fixed-weight index. A **fixed-weight price index** measures how much a fixed basket of goods costs relative to a base period:

$$\text{fixed-weight price index} = \frac{\text{value of fixed basket at current prices}}{\text{value of fixed basket at base-year prices}}.$$

The fixed-weight price index for Outasite is calculated in Table 2.4, step 3, for a fixed basket that equals Outasite's base-year production. The value of Outasite's base-year output in current prices is \$340,000, and the value of its base-year output in base-year prices is \$200,000. Thus the fixed-weight price index is \$340,000/\$200,000 = 1.70, or not much different from the value of 1.71 obtained for the variable-weight index.

The most-used fixed-weight price index is the **consumer price index,** or CPI. (See Fig. 1.4 for historical values of the CPI.) The Bureau of Labor Statistics constructs the CPI by sending people out each month to find the current prices of a fixed list, or basket, of consumer items, including many specific items of food, clothing, housing, and fuel. The CPI for that month is then calculated as the current cost of the basket of consumer items divided by the cost of the basket of items in the base year.[18]

Variable-weight and fixed-weight indexes of the price level have different advantages. The advantage of variable-weight indexes over fixed-weight indexes is that they reflect the prices of the basket of goods that people actually purchased in the current year, rather than the basket they purchased in the base year. The relative disadvantage of variable-weight indexes is that the current basket may contain many goods that did not exist or were of different quality in the base year. For such goods economic statisticians must estimate what a new or improved good would have cost had it existed in the base year, which introduces a source of error.[19]

An important variable that is measured with price indexes is the rate of inflation. The rate of inflation equals the percentage rate of increase in the price index per period. Thus if the CPI rises from 100 in one year to 105 the next, the rate of inflation between the two years is (105 – 100)/100 = 5/100 = 0.05 = 5% per year. If in the third year the CPI is 112, the rate of inflation between the second and third years is (112 – 105)/105 = 7/105 = 0.0667 = 6.67% per year. More generally, if P_t is the price level in period t and P_{t+1} is the price level in period $t + 1$, the rate of inflation between t and $t + 1$, or π_{t+1}, is

$$\pi_{t+1} = \frac{(P_{t+1} - P_t)}{P_t} = \frac{\Delta P_{t+1}}{P_t},$$

where ΔP_{t+1}, or $P_{t+1} - P_t$, represents the change in P_t.

Figure 2.3 (on p. 52) shows the U.S. inflation rate for 1960–1992, based on the GDP deflator as the measure of the price level. Inflation rose during the 1960s and 1970s and fell sharply in the early 1980s.

---

18. Like the GDP deflator, the CPI often is multiplied by 100, so base-year prices equal 100 rather than 1.00.

19. Base years also are periodically changed, so as not to be too far in the past. Updating the base year reduces the problem of having current goods that are very different from the goods that existed in the base year.

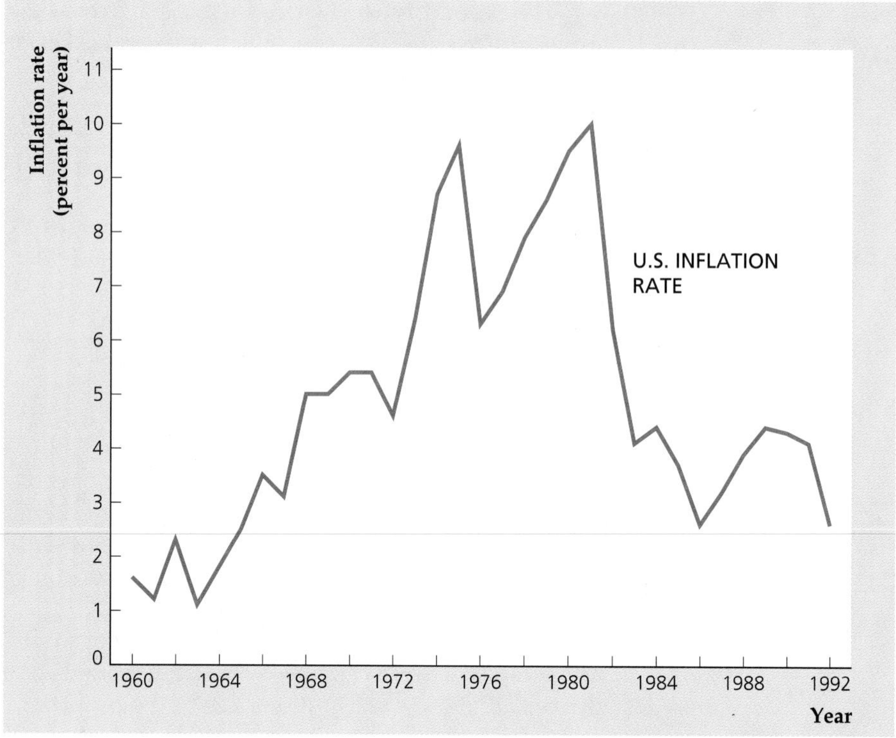

Figure 2.3
The inflation rate in the United States, 1960–1992
Here, inflation is measured as the annual percentage change in the GDP deflator. Inflation rose during the 1960s and 1970s and fell sharply in the early 1980s.

Source: Implicit price deflator for GDP, 1959–1991 from *Economic Report of the President*, Table B-3; 1992 from *Survey of Current Business*, April 1993, Table 7.1.

Interest Rates

Interest rates are another important—and familiar—type of economic variable. An **interest rate** is a rate of return promised by a borrower to a lender. If, for example, the interest rate on a $100, one-year loan is 8%, the borrower has promised to repay the lender $108 one year from now, or $8 interest plus repayment of the $100 borrowed.

As we discuss in more detail in Chapter 4, there are many different interest rates in the economy. Interest rates vary according to who is doing the borrowing, how long the funds are borrowed for, and other factors. There are also many assets in the economy, such as shares of corporate stock, that do not pay a specified interest rate but do pay their holders a return; for shares of stock the return comes in the form of dividends and capital gains (increases in the stock's market price). The existence of so many different assets, each with its own rate of return, has the potential to complicate greatly the study of macroeconomics. Fortunately, however, most interest rates and other rates of return tend to move up and down together. For purposes of macroeconomic analysis we usually speak of "the" interest rate, as if there were only one. If we say that a certain policy causes "the" interest rate to rise, for example, we mean that interest rates and rates of return in general are likely to rise.

Real Versus Nominal Interest Rates. Interest rates and other rates of return share a measurement problem with nominal GDP: An interest rate indicates how quickly the nominal or dollar value of an interest-bearing asset increases over time, but it does not reveal how quickly the value of the asset changes in real, or purchasing-power, terms. Consider, for example, a savings account with an interest rate of 4% per year that has $300 in it at the beginning of the year. At the end of the year the savings account is worth $312, which is a relatively good deal for the depositor if inflation is zero; with no inflation the price level is unchanged over the year, and $312 buys 4% more goods and services in real terms than the initial $300 did a year earlier. If inflation is 4%, however, what cost $300 a year earlier now costs $312, and in real terms the savings account is worth no more today than it was a year ago.

To distinguish changes in the real value of assets from changes in nominal value, economists frequently use the concept of the real interest rate. The **real interest rate** (or real rate of return) on an asset is the rate at which the real value or purchasing power of the asset increases over time. To distinguish them from real interest rates, we refer to conventionally measured interest rates, such as those reported in the newspaper, as nominal interest rates. The **nominal interest rate** (or nominal rate of return) tells us the rate at which the nominal value of an asset increases over time. The symbol for the nominal interest rate is i.

The real interest rate is related to the nominal interest rate and the inflation rate:

$$\begin{aligned}\text{real interest rate} &= \text{nominal interest rate} - \text{inflation rate} \\ &= i - \pi\end{aligned} \tag{2.12}$$

We derive and discuss Eq. (2.12) further at the end of the book in Appendix A, Section A.7.[20] For now, consider again the savings account paying 4% interest. If the inflation rate is zero, the real interest rate on that savings account is the 4% nominal interest rate minus the 0% inflation rate, or 4%. A 4% real interest rate on the account means that the depositor will be able to buy 4% more goods and services at the end of the year than at the beginning. But, if inflation is 4%, the real interest rate on the savings account is the 4% nominal interest rate minus the 4% inflation rate, or 0%. In this case the purchasing power of the account is no greater at the end of the year than at the beginning.

Nominal and real interest rates for the United States for 1960–1992 are shown in Fig. 2.4 on the next page. The real interest rate was unusually low in the mid 1970s; indeed, it was negative, which means that the real values of interest-bearing assets actually were declining over time. Both nominal and real interest rates rose to record highs in the early 1980s before returning to a more normal level in recent years.

The Expected Real Interest Rate. When you borrow, lend, or make a bank deposit, the nominal interest rate is specified in advance. But what about the real interest rate? For any nominal interest rate, Eq. (2.12) states that the real interest rate depends on the rate of inflation over the period of the loan or deposit, say, a year. However, the rate of inflation during the year generally can't be determined until the year is over. Thus at the time that a loan or deposit is made, the real interest rate that will be received is uncertain.

---

20. Equation (2.12) is an approximation, rather than an exact relationship. This approximation holds most closely when interest rates and inflation rates are not too high.

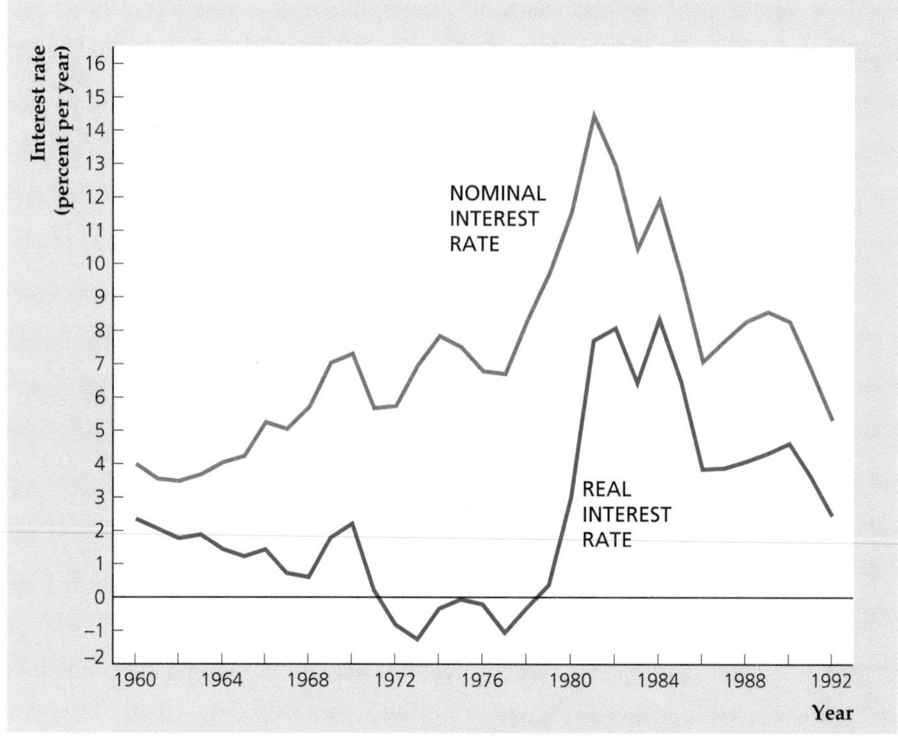

Figure 2.4
Nominal and real interest rates in the United States, 1960–1992
The nominal interest rate shown is the interest rate on three-year Treasury securities. The real interest rate is measured as the nominal interest rate minus the average inflation rate (using the GDP deflator) over the current and subsequent two years. The real interest rate was unusually low (actually negative) in the mid 1970s. In the early 1980s both the nominal and real interest rates were very high. Nominal and real interest rates have returned to more normal levels recently.

Source: The implicit price deflator for GDP is the same as for Fig. 2.3. Inflation rates for 1993 and 1994 are assumed to be 3%. The nominal interest rate on three-year Treasury securities is from the 1993 ***Economic Report of the President***, Table B-69.

Because borrowers, lenders, and depositors don't know what the actual real interest rate will be, they must make their decisions about how much to borrow, lend, or deposit on the basis of the real interest rate they expect to prevail. They know the nominal interest rate in advance, so the real interest rate they expect depends on what they think inflation will be. The **expected real interest rate** is the nominal interest rate minus the expected rate of inflation, or

$$r = i - \pi^e, \tag{2.13}$$

where r is the expected real interest rate and π^e is the expected rate of inflation.

Comparing Eqs. (2.13) and (2.12), you can see that if people are correct in their expectations—so that expected inflation and actual inflation turn out to be the same—the expected real interest rate and the real interest rate actually received will be the same.

The expected real interest rate is the correct interest rate to use for studying most types of economic decisions, such as people's decisions about how much to borrow or lend. However, a problem in measuring the expected real interest rate is that economists generally don't know exactly what the public's expected rate of inflation is. Economists use various means to measure expected inflation. One approach is to survey the public and simply ask what rate of inflation people expect. A second method is to assume that the public's expectations of inflation are the same as publicly announced government or private forecasts. A third possibility is to assume that people's inflation expectations are an extrapolation of recently observed rates of inflation. Unfortunately, none of these methods is perfect, so the measurement of the expected real interest rate always contains some error.

CHAPTER SUMMARY

1. The national income accounts are an accounting framework used in measuring current economic activity. The national income accounts measure activity in three ways: the product approach, the expenditure approach, and the income approach. Although each gives the same value for current economic activity, all three approaches are used because each gives a different perspective on the economy.

2. Gross domestic product (GDP) is the broadest measure of aggregate economic activity occurring during a specified period of time. The product approach measures GDP by adding the market values of final goods and services newly produced in an economy; this approach is implemented by summing the value added by all producers. The expenditure approach measures GDP by adding the four categories of spending: consumption, investment, government purchases, and net exports. The income approach measures GDP by adding all the incomes, including taxes and profits, generated by economic activity.

3. The income of the private sector (domestic households and businesses) is called private disposable income. Private disposable income equals income received from private-sector activities (GDP plus net factor payments from abroad, or GNP) plus payments received from the government (transfers and interest on government debt) minus taxes paid to the government. The net income of the government sector equals taxes collected minus transfer payments and interest paid on government debt. Private disposable income and net government income sum to GNP, which is the income of all domestic factors of production.

4. Saving is the portion of an economic unit's current income that it does not spend to meet current needs. Saving by the private sector, called private saving, equals private disposable income minus consumption. Government saving, which is the same as the government budget surplus, equals the government's net income minus its purchases of goods and services; equivalently, government saving equals government receipts minus government outlays. National saving is the sum of private saving and government saving; it equals GDP plus net factor payments from abroad minus consumption and government purchases.

5. The uses-of-saving identity states that private saving equals the sum of investment, the government budget deficit, and the current account balance. Equivalently, national saving equals the sum of investment and the current account balance.

6. The national wealth of a country equals its physical assets, such as capital, plus its net foreign assets. National wealth increases in two ways: through changes in the value of existing assets and through national saving. National saving adds to national wealth because national saving is used either for investment, thus adding to physical capital, or for lending to foreigners an amount that equals the current account balance, which increases the country's net foreign assets.

7. Nominal GDP is the value of an economy's final output measured at current market prices. Real GDP measures the market value of the economy's final output at prices that prevailed in some base year or period. Because prices are held constant in the calculation of real GDP, changes in real GDP over time capture changes in production volume. More generally, nominal variables measure current market values; real variables are intended to measure physical quantities.

8. A price index is a measure of the current price level relative to a base year. A variable-weight price index, such as the GDP deflator, compares the cost of a set of goods and services produced in the current period with what that set of goods and services would have cost in the base year. A fixed-weight price index, such as the consumer price index, measures how much a fixed basket of goods and services costs in each period, relative to what they cost in the base year. Inflation

is the percentage rate of change of the price level, as measured by a price index such as the GDP deflator or the CPI.

9. An interest rate is a rate of return promised by a borrower to a lender. The nominal interest rate is the rate at which the nominal value of an interest-bearing asset increases over time. The real interest rate, or the nominal interest rate minus the rate of inflation, is the rate at which the value of an asset grows in real, or purchasing-power, terms. Borrowing and lending decisions are based on the expected real interest rate, which is the nominal interest rate less the expected rate of inflation.

Key Terms

budget deficit, p. 41
budget surplus, p. 41
capital good, p. 32
consumer price index, p. 51
consumption, p. 34
current account balance, p. 42
depreciation, p. 38
expected real interest rate, p. 54
expenditure approach, p. 27
final goods and services, p. 32
fixed-weight price index, p. 51
flow variable, p. 44
fundamental identity of national income accounting, p. 29
GDP deflator, p. 50
government outlays, p. 41
government purchases, p. 35
government receipts, p. 41
government saving, p. 40
gross domestic product, p. 29
gross national product, p. 33
income approach, p. 27
income–expenditure identity, p. 34
interest rate, p. 52
intermediate goods and services, p. 32
inventories, p. 32
investment, p. 34
national income, p. 36
national income accounts, p. 26
national saving, p. 41
national wealth, p. 39
net exports, p. 36
net factor payments from abroad, p. 33
net foreign assets, p. 44
net national product, p. 38
nominal GDP, p. 48
nominal interest rate, p. 53
nominal variables, p. 47
price index, p. 50
private disposable income, p. 38
private saving, p. 40
product approach, p. 27
real GDP, p. 48
real interest rate, p. 53
real variable, p. 48
saving, p. 40
stock variable, p. 44
transfers, p. 35
underground economy, p. 30
uses-of-saving identity, p. 42
value added, p. 27
variable-weight price index, p. 50
wealth, p. 39

Key Equations

$$\text{Total production} = \text{total income} = \text{total expenditure} \tag{2.1}$$

The fundamental identity of national income accounting states that the same measure of total economic activity is obtained whether activity is measured by the production of final goods and services, the amount of income generated by the economic activity, or the expenditure on final goods and services.

$$Y = C + I + G + NX \tag{2.3}$$

According to the income–expenditure identity, total income or product or output, Y, equals the sum of the four types of expenditure: consumption, C, investment, I, government purchases, G, and net exports, NX.

$$S_{pvt} = (Y + NFP - T + TR + INT) - C \tag{2.6}$$

Private saving equals private disposable income less consumption, C. Private-sector disposable income equals gross domestic product, Y, plus net factor payments from abroad, NFP, plus transfers, TR, and interest, INT, received from the government, less taxes paid, T.

$$S_{govt} = (T - TR - INT) - G \tag{2.7}$$

Government saving equals government receipts from taxes, T, less outlays for transfers, TR, interest on the national debt, INT, and government purchases, G. Government saving is the same as the government budget surplus and is the negative of the government budget deficit.

$$S = S_{pvt} + S_{govt} = Y + NFP - C - G \quad (2.8)$$

National saving, S, is the sum of private saving and government saving. Equivalently, national saving equals gross domestic product, Y, plus net factor payments from abroad, NFP, less consumption, C, and government purchases, G.

$$S = I + CA \quad (2.10)$$

National saving, S, has two uses: to finance investment, I, and to lend to foreigners (or to acquire foreign assets) an amount that equals the current account balance, CA. The current account balance equals the increase in net foreign assets.

$$S_{pvt} = I + (-S_{govt}) + CA \quad (2.11)$$

According to the uses-of-saving identity, private saving is used to finance investment spending, I, to provide the government with the funds it needs to cover its budget deficit, $-S_{govt}$, and to lend to foreigners (or to acquire foreign assets) an amount that equals the current account balance, CA.

$$r = i - \pi^e \quad (2.13)$$

The expected real interest rate, r, equals the nominal interest rate, i, minus expected inflation π^e.

Review Questions

1. What are the three approaches to measuring economic activity? Why do they give the same answer?
2. Why are goods and services counted in GDP at market value? Are there any disadvantages or problems in using market values to measure production?
3. What is the difference between intermediate and final goods and services? In which of these categories do capital goods, such as factories and machines, fall? Why is the distinction between intermediate and final goods important for measuring GDP?
4. List the four components of total spending. Why are imports subtracted when GDP is calculated in the expenditure approach?
5. Define private saving. How is private saving used in the economy? What is the relationship between private saving and national saving?
6. What is national wealth, and why is it important? How is national wealth linked to national saving?
7. For the purposes of assessing an economy's growth performance, which is the more important statistic: real GDP or nominal GDP? Why?
8. Describe how the GDP deflator and the CPI are calculated. What are the basic differences between these two price indexes?
9. Explain the differences among the nominal interest rate, the real interest rate, and the expected real interest rate. Which interest rate concept is the most important for the decisions made by borrowers and lenders? Why?

Numerical Problems

1. After a boat rescues everyone else from Gilligan's Island, the Professor and Gilligan remain behind, afraid of getting shipwrecked again with the same bunch of people. The Professor grows coconuts and catches fish. Last year he harvested 1000 coconuts and caught 500 fish. He values one fish as worth two coconuts. The Professor gave 200 coconuts to Gilligan in exchange for help in the harvest, and he gave Gilligan 100 fish in exchange for collecting worms for use in fishing. The Professor stored 100 of his coconuts in his hut for consumption at some future time. He also used 100 fish as fertilizer for the coconut trees, as he must every year to keep the trees producing. Gilligan consumed all his coconuts and fish.

   In terms of fish, what is the GDP of Gilligan's Island? What are consumption and investment? What are the incomes of the Professor and Gilligan?
2. ABC Computer Company has a \$20,000,000 factory in Silicon Valley. During the current year ABC builds \$2,000,000 worth of computer components. ABC's costs are labor, \$1,000,000; interest on debt, \$100,000; and taxes, \$200,000.

   ABC sells all its output to XYZ Supercomputer. Using ABC's components, XYZ builds four supercomputers at a cost of \$800,000 each (\$500,000 worth of components, \$200,000 in labor costs, and \$100,000 in taxes per computer). XYZ has a \$30,000,000 factory.

   XYZ sells three of the supercomputers for \$1,000,000 each; but at year's end, it had not sold the fourth. The unsold computer is carried on XYZ's books as an \$800,000 increase in inventory.

   a. Calculate the contributions to GDP of these transactions, showing that all three approaches give the same answer.

b. Repeat part (a), but now assume that in addition to its other costs, ABC also paid $500,000 for imported computer chips.

3. For each of the following transactions, determine the contribution to the current year's GDP. Explain the effects on the product, income, and expenditure accounts.

a. On January 1 you purchase 10 gallons of gasoline at $1.40 per gallon. The gas station purchased the gasoline the previous week at a wholesale price (transportation included) of $1.30 per gallon.
b. Colonel Hogwash purchases a Civil War–era mansion for $1,000,000. The broker's fee is 6%.
c. A homemaker enters the work force, taking a job that will pay $20,000 over the year. The homemaker must pay $8000 over the year for professional child care services.
d. The Japanese build an auto plant in Tennessee for $100,000,000, using only local labor and materials. (*Hint:* The auto plant is a capital good produced by Americans and purchased by the Japanese.)
e. You are informed that you have won $3,000,000 in the New Jersey State Lottery, to be paid to you, in total, immediately.
f. The New Jersey state government pays you an additional $5000 fee to appear in a TV commercial publicizing the state lottery.
g. Hertz Rent-a-Car replaces its rental fleet by buying $100,000,000 worth of new cars from General Motors. It sells its old fleet to a consortium of used-car dealers for $40,000,000. The consortium resells the used cars to the public for a total of $60,000,000.

4. You are given the following data on an economy.

Gross national product	1000
Government purchases of goods and services	200
Government deficit	50
National saving	200
Investment	150
Net factor payments from abroad	25

Find the following:
a. Consumption
b. Private saving
c. Disposable income
d. Gross domestic product
e. Net exports

5. Consider an economy that produces only three types of fruit: apples, oranges, and bananas. In the base year (a few years ago), the production and price data were as follows.

Fruit	Quantity	Price
Apples	3000 bags	$2 per bag
Bananas	6000 bunches	$3 per bunch
Oranges	8000 bags	$4 per bag

In the current year the production and price data are as follows.

Fruit	Quantity	Price
Apples	4000 bags	$3 per bag
Bananas	14,000 bunches	$2 per bunch
Oranges	32,000 bags	$5 per bag

a. What are the values of nominal and real GDP in the base year and the current year?
b. How much did nominal GDP grow between the base year and the current year?
c. How much did real GDP grow between the base year and the current year?
d. What was the percentage change in the price level between the base year and the current year, as measured by the GDP deflator? As measured by a fixed-weight price index that takes actual production in the base year as the fixed basket of goods?

6. For the consumer price index values shown, calculate the rate of inflation in each year from 1930 to 1933. What is unusual about this period, relative to recent experience?

Year	1929	1930	1931	1932	1933
CPI	51.3	50.0	45.6	40.9	38.8

7. Hy Marks buys a one-year government bond on January 1, 1994, for $500. He receives principal plus interest totaling $545 on January 1, 1995. Suppose that the CPI is 200 on January 1, 1994 and 214 on January 1, 1995. This increase in prices is more than Hy had anticipated; his guess was that the CPI would be at 210 by the beginning of 1995.

Find the nominal interest rate, the inflation rate, the real interest rate, Hy's expected inflation rate, and Hy's expected real interest rate.

8. The GDP deflator in Econoland is 200 on January 1, 1993. The deflator rises to 242 by January 1, 1995, and to 266.2 by January 1, 1996.
a. What is the annual rate of inflation over the two-year period between January 1, 1993, and January 1, 1995? In other words, what constant yearly rate of inflation would lead to the price rise observed over those two years?

b. What is the annual rate of inflation over the three-year period from January 1, 1993, to January 1, 1996?
c. In general, if P_0 is the price level at the beginning of an n-year period, and P_n is the price level at the end of that period, show that the annual rate of inflation π over that period satisfies the equation $(1 + \pi)^n = (P_n/P_0)$.

Analytical Problems

1. A reputable study shows that a particular new workplace safety regulation will reduce the growth of real GDP. Is this an argument against implementing the regulation? Explain.
2. Economists have tried to measure the GDPs of virtually all the world's nations. This problem asks you to think about some practical issues that arise in that effort.
a. Before the fall of communism, the economies of the Soviet Union and Eastern Europe were centrally planned. One aspect of central planning is that most prices are set by the government. A government-set price may be too low, in that people want to buy more of the good at the fixed price than there are supplies available; or the price may be too high, so that large stocks of the good sit unsold on store shelves. During the past several years central planning has been largely eliminated in Eastern Europe and the former Soviet Union, but government price-setting has not been completely abandoned. For example, Russia still keeps energy prices well below market-clearing levels.
What problem does government control of prices create for economists attempting to measure a country's GDP? Suggest a strategy for dealing with this problem.
b. In very poor, agricultural countries, many people grow their own food, make their own clothes, and provide services for each other within a family or village group. Official GDP estimates for these countries are often extremely low, perhaps just a few hundred dollars per person. Some economists have argued that the official GDP figures underestimate these nations' actual GDPs. Why might this be so? Again, can you suggest a strategy for dealing with this measurement problem?
3. In the NIPA section of a recent issue of the *Survey of Current Business,* find Table 5.1, "Gross Saving and Investment." Using the table, find private saving and national saving in the United States for the past two years. Show that private saving equals the sum of its three uses in each year. The table refers to private saving as gross private saving, to investment as gross private domestic investment, and to the current account balance as net foreign investment.

PART II

The Macroeconomics of Full Employment

CHAPTER 3

PRODUCTIVITY, OUTPUT, AND EMPLOYMENT

In Chapter 2 we discussed the measurement of several economic variables used to gauge the economy's health. The measurement of economic performance is a prelude to the main objective of macroeconomics: *to understand how the economy works.* Understanding how the economy works requires a shift from economic *measurement* to economic *analysis.*

In Part II of this book, which begins with this chapter, we have two main goals. The first is to analyze the factors that affect the longer-term performance of the economy, including the rate of economic growth, productivity and living standards, the long-run levels of employment and unemployment, saving and capital formation, and the rate of inflation, among others.

The second goal is to develop a theoretical model of the macroeconomy that you can use to analyze the economic issues covered in this book and others that you may encounter in the future. As outlined in Chapter 1, our model is based on the assumption that individuals, firms, and the government interact in three composite markets: the labor market (covered in this chapter), the goods market (Chapter 4), and the asset market (Chapter 7). In developing and using this model in Part II, we generally assume that the economy is at full employment, with quantities supplied and demanded equal in each of the three major markets. As we are focusing on the long-term behavior of the economy, this assumption is a reasonable one. In Part III, in which we explore business cycles, we allow for the possibility that quantities supplied and demanded may not be equal in the short run.

This chapter begins the discussion of how the economy works with what is perhaps the most fundamental determinant of economic well-being in a society: the economy's productive capacity. Everything else being equal, the greater the quantity of goods and services an economy can produce, the more people will be able to consume in the present and the more they will be able to save and invest for the future.

The first section of the chapter shows that the amount of output an economy produces depends on two factors: (1) the quantities of inputs (such as labor, capital, and raw materials) utilized in the production process; and (2) the **productivity** of the inputs, that is, the effectiveness with which they are used. As discussed in Chapter 1, an economy's productivity is basic to determining living standards. In this chapter we show how productivity affects people's incomes by helping to determine how many workers are employed and how much they receive in wages.

Of the various inputs to production, the most important (as measured by share of total cost) is labor. For this reason, we spend most of the chapter analyzing the labor market, using the tools of supply and demand. We first consider the factors that affect how much labor employers demand and workers supply and then look at the forces that tend to bring the labor market into equilibrium. Equilibrium in the labor market determines wages and employment; in turn, the level of employment, together with the quantities of other inputs (such as capital) and the level of productivity determine how much output an economy produces.

Our basic model of the labor market rests on the assumption that the quantities of labor supplied and demanded are equal so that all labor resources are fully utilized. In reality, however, some fraction of workers always is unemployed. The latter part of the chapter introduces unemployment and looks at the relationship between the unemployment rate and the amount of output produced in the economy.

3.1 HOW MUCH DOES THE ECONOMY PRODUCE? THE PRODUCTION FUNCTION

Every day the business news reports many economic variables that influence the economy's performance—the rate of consumer spending, the value of the dollar, the gyrations of the stock market, the growth rate of the money supply, and so on. All of these variables are important. However, no determinant of economic performance and living standards is more basic than the economy's physical capacity to produce goods and services. If an economy's factories, farms, and other businesses all shut down for some reason, other economic factors wouldn't mean much.

What determines the quantity of goods and services that an economy can produce? A key factor is the quantity of inputs—such as capital goods, labor, raw materials, land, and energy—that producers in the economy use. Economists refer to inputs to the production process as **factors of production.** All else being equal, the greater the quantities of factors of production used, the more goods and services are produced.

Of the various factors of production, the two most important are capital (factories and machines, for example) and labor (workers). Hence we focus on these two factors in discussing an economy's capacity to produce goods and services. In modern economies, however, output often responds strongly to changes in the supply of other factors, such as energy or raw materials. Later in this chapter the Application "Output, Employment, and the Real Wage During Oil Price Shocks," p. 86, discusses the effects of a disruption in oil supplies on the economy.

The quantity of capital and labor (and other inputs) used in production doesn't completely determine the amount of output produced. Equally important is how effectively these factors are used. For the same stocks of capital and labor, an economy with superior technologies and management practices, for example, will produce more output than an economy without those strengths.

The effectiveness with which capital and labor are used may be summarized by a relationship called the production function. The **production function** is a mathematical expression relating the amount of output produced to quantities of capital and labor utilized. A convenient way to write the production function is

$$Y = AF(K, N), \tag{3.1}$$

where

Y = real output produced in a given period of time;
A = a number measuring overall productivity;
K = the capital stock, or quantity of capital used in the period;
N = the number of workers employed in the period;
F = a function relating output Y to capital K and labor N.

The production function in Eq. (3.1) applies both to an economy as a whole (where Y, K, and N refer to the economy's output, capital stock, and number of workers) and to an individual firm, in which case Y, K, and N refer to the firm's output, capital, and number of workers.

According to Eq. (3.1), the amount of output Y that an economy (or firm) can produce during any period of time depends on the size of the capital stock K and the number of workers N. The symbol A in Eq. (3.1), which multiplies the function $F(K, N)$, is a measure of the overall effectiveness with which capital and labor are used. We refer to A as total factor productivity, or simply productivity. Note that, for any values of capital and labor, an increase in productivity A of, say, 10% implies a 10% increase in the amount of output that can be produced. Thus increases in productivity A correspond to improvements in production technology or to any other change in the economy that allows capital and labor to be utilized more effectively.

APPLICATION

The Production Function of the U.S. Economy and U.S. Productivity Growth

Empirical studies show that the relationship between output and inputs in the U.S. economy is described reasonably well by the following production function:[1]

$$Y = AK^{0.3}N^{0.7}. \tag{3.2}$$

The production function in Eq. (3.2) is a specific example of the general production function in Eq. (3.1), in which we set the general function $F(K, N)$ equal to $K^{0.3}N^{0.7}$. (Note that this production function contains exponents; if you need to review the properties of exponents, see Appendix A, Section A.6.)

Equation (3.2) shows how output Y relates to the use of factors of production, capital K and labor N, and to productivity A in the United States.

1. This type of production function is called a Cobb–Douglas production function. Cobb–Douglas production functions take the form $Y = AK^aN^{1-a}$, where $0 < a < 1$. Under certain conditions, the parameter a in the Cobb–Douglas production function corresponds to the share of income received by owners of capital, whereas labor receives a share of income equal to $1 - a$. Thus observing the actual shares of income received by capital and labor provides a way of estimating the parameter a.

Table 3.1 presents data on these variables for the U.S. economy for a dozen years beginning in 1980. Columns (1), (2), and (3) show output (real GDP), capital stock, and labor for each year. Real GDP and the capital stock are measured in billions of 1987 dollars, and labor is measured in millions of employed workers. Column (4) shows the U.S. economy's productivity for each year.

Output, capital, and labor in Table 3.1 are measured directly, but there is no way to measure productivity directly. Instead, the productivity index A shown in column (4) is measured indirectly by assigning to A the value necessary to satisfy Eq. (3.2). Specifically, for each year A is determined by the formula $A = Y/(K^{0.3}N^{0.7})$, which is just another way of writing Eq. (3.2). In 1991, for example, Table 3.1 reports that $Y = 4821$, $K = 4824$, and $N = 116.9$; therefore the value of A for 1991 is $4821/[(4824)^{0.3}(116.9)^{0.7}]$, or $A = 13.51$. Calculating productivity in this way ensures that the production function relationship, Eq. (3.2), is satisfied exactly for each year.

The levels of the productivity index A reported in Table 3.1 depend on the units in which output, capital, and labor are measured—for example, the values of A would change if we measured workers in thousands rather than millions—and thus are hard to interpret. In contrast, the year-to-year growth rates of the productivity measure shown in column (5) are units-free and are therefore easier to work with. A close look at the productivity growth rates shown in Table 3.1 emphasizes two points.

Table 3.1 The Production Function of the United States, 1980–1991

Production function: $Y = AK^{0.3}N^{0.7}$

Year	(1) Real GDP, Y (Billions of 1987 dollars)	(2) Capital, K (Billions of 1987 dollars)	(3) Labor, N (Millions of workers)	(4) Total Factor Productivity, A[a]	(5) Growth in Total Factor Productivity (% Change in A)
1980	3776	3677	99.3	12.86	
1981	3843	3811	100.4	12.86	−0.1
1982	3760	3901	99.5	12.57	−2.2
1983	3907	3970	100.8	12.88	2.4
1984	4149	4097	105.0	13.16	2.2
1985	4280	4248	107.2	13.24	0.6
1986	4405	4362	109.6	13.31	0.5
1987	4540	4457	112.4	13.39	0.6
1988	4719	4562	115.0	13.60	1.6
1989	4838	4673	117.3	13.66	0.4
1990	4878	4773	117.9	13.63	−0.2
1991	4821	4824	116.9	13.51	−0.9

[a] Total factor productivity is calculated by the formula $A = Y/(K^{0.3}N^{0.7})$.

Source: Y is GDP in billions of 1987 dollars from Table B-2 in *Economic Report of the President*, February 1993; K is constant-cost net stock of fixed private non-residential capital in billions of 1987 dollars from *Survey of Current Business*, October 1992, p. 30; N is civilian employment (aged 16 and over) in millions of workers from Table B-31 in *Economic Report of the President*, February 1993.

First, productivity growth can vary sharply from year to year. Most strikingly, productivity in the United States fell 2.2% in 1982, a deep recession year, then rose 2.4% in 1983 and 2.2% in 1984, a period of economic recovery. Productivity also fell during the 1990–1991 recession. Productivity normally falls in recessions and rises in recoveries, but explanations for its behavior over the business cycle are controversial. We return to this issue in Part III of this book, which is devoted to business cycles.

Second, since 1980 productivity in the United States has been growing relatively slowly, averaging slightly less than 0.5% per year during the 1980–1991 period. This result is better than the performance of the 1970s, when productivity growth essentially was zero, but notably less than in the 1950–1970 period, when productivity growth exceeded 1.3% a year.[2] This trend is bad news for the economy because the rate of productivity growth is closely related to the rate of improvement of living standards. Chapter 6 discusses the relationship between productivity and living standards in greater detail.

The Shape of the Production Function

The production function in Eq. (3.1) can be shown graphically. The easiest way to graph it is to hold one of the two factors of production, either capital or labor, constant and then graph the relationship between output and the other factor.[3] Suppose that we use the U.S. production function for the year 1991 and hold labor N at its actual 1991 value of 116.9 million workers (see Table 3.1). We also use the actual 1991 value of 13.51 for A. The production function (Eq. 3.2) becomes

$$Y = AK^{0.3}N^{0.7} = (13.51)(K^{0.3})(116.9^{0.7}) = 378.54K^{0.3}.$$

This relationship is graphed in Fig. 3.1 on the next page, with capital stock K on the horizontal axis and output Y on the vertical axis. With labor and productivity held at their 1991 values, the graph shows the amount of output that could have been produced in that year for any value of the capital stock. Point A on the graph shows the situation that actually occurred in 1991: The value of the capital stock ($4824 billion) appears on the horizontal axis, and the value of real GDP ($4821 billion) appears on the vertical axis.

The U.S. production function graphed in Fig. 3.1 shares two properties with most production functions:

1. *The production function slopes upward from left to right.* The slope of the production function tells us that, as the capital stock increases, more output can be produced.
2. *The slope of the production function becomes flatter from left to right.* This property implies that although more capital always leads to more output, it does so at a decreasing rate.

Before discussing the economics behind the second property of the production function, we can illustrate it numerically using Fig. 3.1. Suppose that

2. Other countries also have experienced slower productivity growth since the mid 1970s, as discussed further in Chapter 6.

3. To show the relationship among output and both factors of production simultaneously would require a three-dimensional graph.

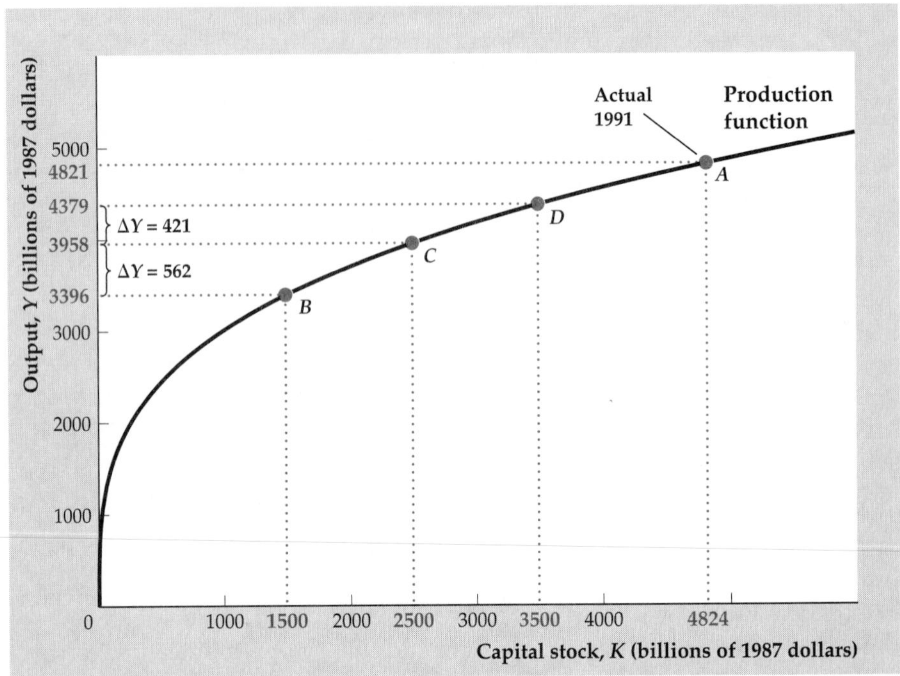

Figure 3.1
The production function relating output and capital
This production function shows how much output the U.S. economy could produce for each level of U.S. capital stock, holding U.S. labor and productivity at 1991 levels. Point *A* corresponds to the actual 1991 output and capital stock. The production function has diminishing marginal productivity of capital: Raising the capital stock by $1000 billion in order to move from point *B* to point *C* raises output by $562 billion, but adding another $1000 billion in capital to go from point *C* to point *D* increases output by only $421 billion.

we are initially at point *B*, where the capital stock is $1500 billion. Adding $1000 billion in capital moves us to point *C*, where the capital stock is $2500 billion. How much extra output has this expansion in capital provided? The difference in output between points *B* and *C* is $562 billion ($3958 billion output at *C* minus $3396 billion output at *B*). This extra $562 billion in output is the benefit from raising the capital stock from $1500 billion to $2500 billion, with productivity and employment held constant.

Now suppose that, starting at *C*, we add another $1000 billion of capital. This new addition of capital takes us to *D*, where the capital stock is $3500 billion. The difference in output between *C* and *D* is only $421 billion ($4379 billion output at *D* minus $3958 billion output at *C*), which is less than the $562 billion increase in output between *B* and *C*. Thus, although the second $1000 billion of extra capital raises total output, it does so by less than did the first $1000 billion of extra capital. This result illustrates that the production function rises less steeply between points *C* and *D* than between points *B* and *C*.

The Marginal Product of Capital. The two properties of the production function are closely related to a concept known as the marginal product of capital. To understand this concept, let's suppose that we start from some given capital stock K and increase the capital stock by some amount ΔK (other factors held constant). This increase in capital would cause output Y to increase by some amount ΔY. The **marginal product of capital,** or ***MPK,*** is the increase in output produced resulting from a one-unit increase in the capital stock. Because ΔK additional units of capital permit the production of ΔY additional units of output, the amount of additional output produced per additional unit of capital is $\Delta Y/\Delta K$. Thus the marginal product of capital is $\Delta Y/\Delta K$.

The marginal product of capital $\Delta Y/\Delta K$ is the change in the variable on the vertical axis of the production function graph (ΔY) divided by the change in the variable on the horizontal axis (ΔK), which you might recognize as a slope.[4] For small increases in the capital stock, the *MPK* can be measured by the slope of a line drawn tangent to the production function. Figure 3.2 illustrates this way of measuring the *MPK*. When the capital stock is 1500, for example, the *MPK* equals the slope of the line tangent to the production function at point *B*.[5] We can use the concept of the marginal product of capital to restate the two properties of production functions listed earlier.

1. *The marginal product of capital is positive.* Whenever the capital stock is increased, more output can be produced. Because the marginal product of capital is positive, the production function slopes upward from left to right.
2. *The marginal product of capital declines as the capital stock is increased.* Because the marginal product of capital is the slope of the production function, the slope of the production function decreases as the capital stock is increased. As Fig. 3.2 shows, the slope of the production function at point *D*, where the capital stock is 3500, is smaller than the slope at point *B*, where the capital stock is 1500. Thus the production function becomes flatter from left to right.

The tendency for the marginal product of capital to decline as the amount of capital in use increases is called the **diminishing marginal productivity** of capital. The economic reason for diminishing marginal productivity of capital

4. For definitions and a discussion of slopes of lines and curves, see Appendix A, Section A.2.
5. We often refer to the slope of the line tangent to the production function at a given point as simply the slope of the production function at that point, for short.

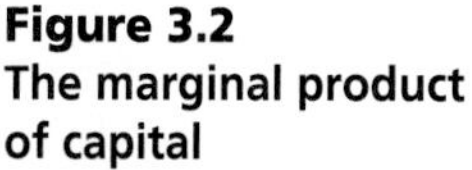

Figure 3.2
The marginal product of capital
The marginal product of capital (*MPK*) at any point can be measured as the slope of the line tangent to the production function at that point. Because the slope of the line tangent to the production function at point *B* is greater than the slope of the line tangent to the production function at point *D*, we know that the *MPK* is greater at *B* than at *D*. At higher levels of capital stock, the *MPK* is lower, reflecting diminishing marginal productivity of capital.

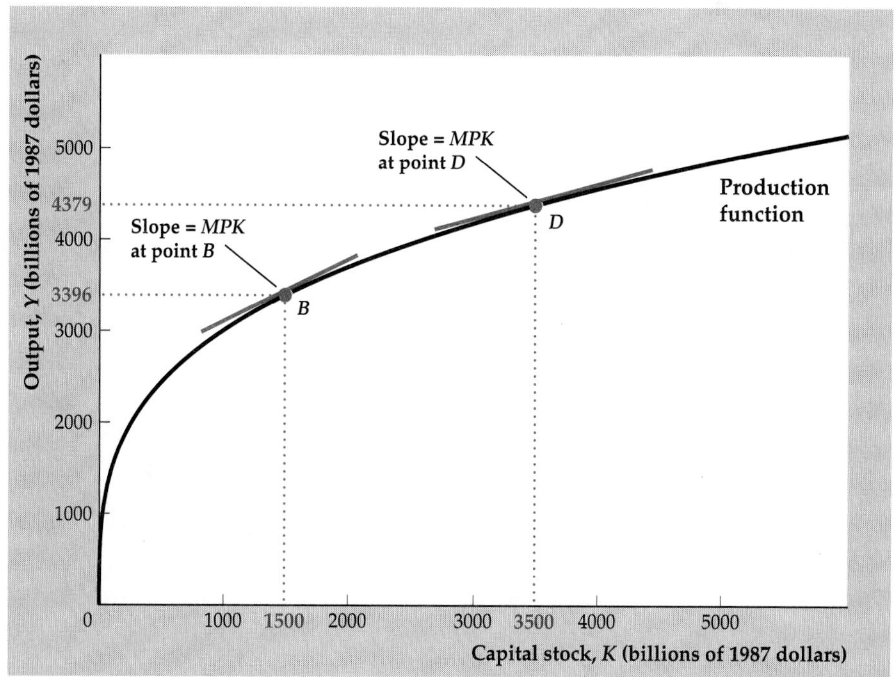

is as follows: When the capital stock is low, there are many workers for each machine, and the benefits of increasing capital further are great; but when the capital stock is high, workers already have plenty of capital to work with, and little benefit is to be gained from expanding capital further. For example, in a secretarial pool in which there are many more secretaries than electric typewriters, each typewriter is constantly being utilized and secretaries must waste time waiting for a free machine. In this situation, the benefits in terms of increased output of adding extra typewriters are high. However, if there are already as many typewriters as secretaries, so that typewriters often are idle and there is no waiting for a machine to become available, little additional output can be obtained by adding yet another typewriter.

The Marginal Product of Labor. In Figs. 3.1 and 3.2 we graphed the relationship between output and capital implied by the 1991 U.S. production function, holding constant the amount of labor. Similarly, we can look at the relationship between output and labor, holding constant the quantity of capital. Suppose that we fix capital K at its actual 1991 value of \$4824 billion and hold productivity A at its actual 1991 value of 13.51 (see Table 3.1). The production function (Eq. 3.2) becomes

$$Y = AK^{0.3}N^{0.7} = (13.51)(4824^{0.3})(N^{0.7}) = 172.05N^{0.7}.$$

This relationship is shown graphically in Fig. 3.3. Point A, where $N = 116.9$ million workers and $Y = \$4821$ billion, corresponds to the actual 1991 values.

The production function relating output and labor looks generally the same as the production function relating output and capital.[6] As in the case of capital, increases in the number of workers raise output but do so at a diminishing rate. Thus the principle of diminishing marginal productivity also applies to labor, and for similar reasons: the greater the number of workers already using a fixed amount of capital and other inputs, the smaller the benefit (in terms of increased output) of adding even more workers.

The **marginal product of labor,** or ***MPN***, is the additional output produced by each additional unit of labor, $\Delta Y/\Delta N$. As with the marginal product of capital, for small increases in employment the *MPN* can be measured by the slope of the line tangent to a production function that relates output and labor. In Fig. 3.3, when employment equals 30 million workers, the *MPN* equals the slope of the line tangent to the production function at point B; and when employment is 90 million workers the *MPN* is the slope of the line that touches the production function at point C. Because of the diminishing marginal productivity of labor, the slope of the production function relating output to labor is greater at B than at C, and the production function flattens from left to right.

Supply Shocks

The production function of an economy doesn't usually remain fixed over time. Economists use the term **supply shock**—or, sometimes, productivity shock—to refer to a change in an economy's production function.[7] A positive, or beneficial,

6. Because N is raised to the power of 0.7 but K is raised to the power of 0.3, the production function relating output and labor is not as sharply bowed as the production function relating output and capital.

7. The term shock is a slight misnomer. Not all changes in the production function are sharp or unpredictable, although many are.

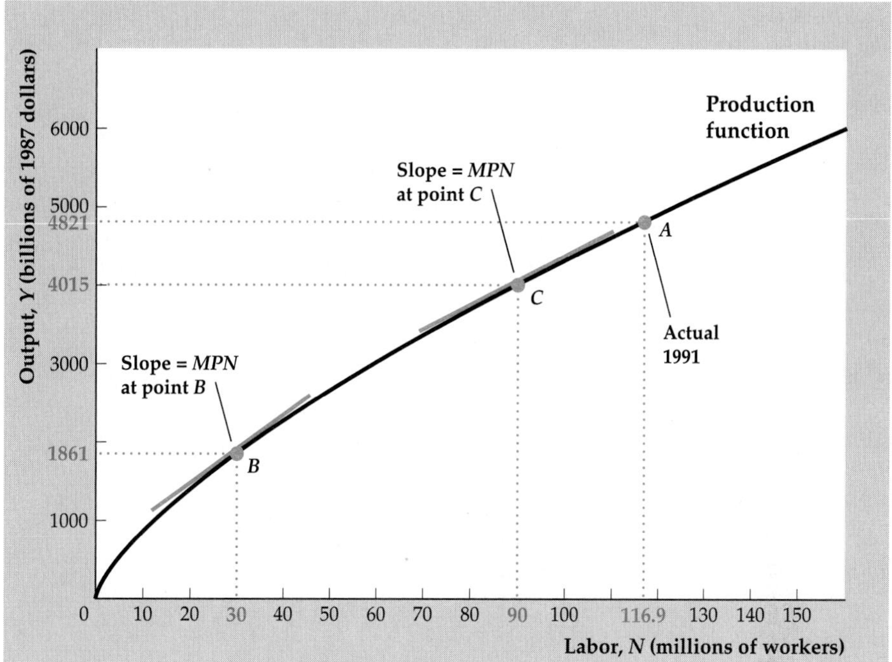

Figure 3.3 The production function relating output and labor This production function shows how much output the U.S. economy could produce at each level of employment (labor input), holding productivity and the capital stock constant at 1991 levels. Point *A* corresponds to actual 1991 output and employment. The marginal product of labor (*MPN*) at any point is measured as the slope of the line tangent to the production function at that point. The *MPN* is lower at higher levels of employment, reflecting diminishing marginal productivity of labor.

supply shock raises the amount of output that can be produced for given quantities of capital and labor. A negative, or adverse, supply shock lowers the amount of output that can be produced for each capital–labor combination.

Real-world examples of supply shocks include changes in the weather, such as a drought or an unusually cold winter; inventions or innovations in management techniques that improve efficiency, such as minicomputers or statistical analysis in quality control; and changes in government regulations, such as antipollution laws, that affect the technologies or production methods used. Also included in the category of supply shocks are changes in the supplies of factors of production *other than capital and labor* that affect the amount that can be produced.

Figure 3.4, on the next page, shows the effects of an adverse supply shock on the production function relating output and labor. The negative supply shock shifts the production function downward so that less output can be produced for specific quantities of labor and capital. In addition, the supply shock shown reduces the slope of the production function so that the output gains from adding a worker (the marginal product of labor) are lower at every level of employment.[8] Similarly, a beneficial supply shock makes possible the production of more output with given quantities of capital and labor and thus shifts the production function upward.[9]

---

8. Logically, an adverse supply shock need not always reduce the marginal products of labor and capital; for example, the production function could make a parallel downward shift. However, thinking of an adverse supply shock reducing marginal products as being the normal case seems reasonable. A shift of the production function like that shown in Fig. 3.4 would occur if there were a decline in total factor productivity *A*, for example.

9. The effects of supply shocks on the production function relating output and capital would be similar.

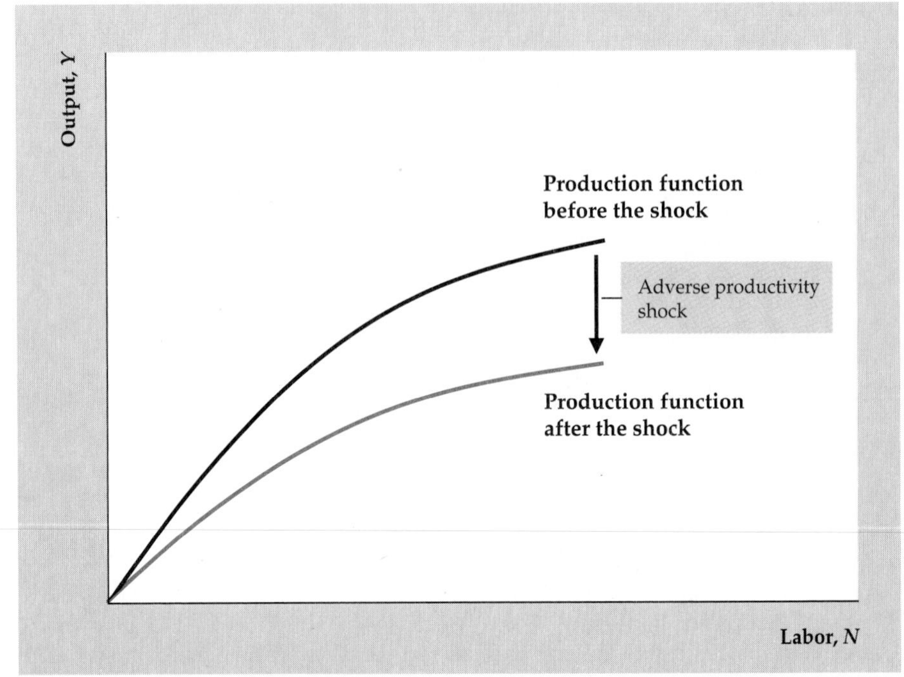

Figure 3.4
An adverse supply shock that lowers the *MPN*
An adverse supply shock is a downward shift of the production function. For any level of labor, the amount of output that can be produced is now less than before. The adverse shock reduces the slope of the production function at every level of employment.

3.2 THE DEMAND FOR LABOR

We have shown that the amount of output produced by a country, or by a firm, depends both on productivity and the quantities of inputs used in the production process. In Section 3.1 our focus was on productivity—its measurement and factors such as supply shocks that cause it to change. In this section we examine what determines the quantities of inputs that producers use. Recall that the two most important inputs are capital and labor. The capital stock in an economy changes over time as a result of investment by firms and the scrapping of worn-out or obsolete capital. However, because the capital stock is long-lived and has been built up over many years, new investment and the scrapping of old capital only slowly have a significant effect on the overall quantity of capital available. Thus, for analyses spanning only a few quarters or years, economists often treat the economy's capital stock as fixed. For now we follow this practice and assume a fixed capital stock. In taking up long-term economic growth in Chapter 6, we drop this assumption and examine how the capital stock evolves over time.

In contrast to the amount of capital, the amount of labor employed in the economy can change fairly quickly. For example, firms may lay off workers or ask them to work overtime without much notice. Workers may quit or decide to enter the work force quickly. Thus year-to-year changes in production often can be traced to changes in employment. To explain why employment changes, for the remainder of this chapter we focus on how the labor market works, using a supply and demand approach. In this section we look at labor demand, and in Section 3.3 we discuss factors affecting labor supply.

As a step toward understanding the overall demand for labor in the economy we consider how an individual firm decides how many workers to employ. To keep things simple for the time being, we make the following assumptions:

1. *Workers are all alike.* We ignore differences in workers' aptitudes, skills, ambition, and so on.
2. *Firms view the wage of the workers they hire as being determined in a competitive labor market and not set by the firms themselves.* For example, a competitive firm in Cleveland that wants to hire machinists knows that it must pay the going local wage for machinists if it wants to attract qualified workers. The firm then decides how many machinists to employ.
3. *In making the decision about how many workers to employ, a firm's goal is to earn the highest possible level of profit* (the value of its output minus its costs of production, including taxes). The firm will demand the amount of labor that maximizes its profit.

To figure out the profit-maximizing amount of labor, the firm must compare the costs and benefits of hiring each additional worker. The cost of an extra worker is the worker's wage, and the benefit of an extra worker is the value of the additional goods or services the worker produces. As long as the benefits of additional labor exceed the costs, hiring more labor will increase the firm's profits. The firm will continue to hire additional labor until the benefit of an extra worker (the value of extra goods or services produced) equals the cost (the wage).

The Marginal Product of Labor and Labor Demand: An Example

Let's make the discussion of labor demand more concrete by looking at The Clip Joint, a small business that grooms dogs. The Clip Joint uses both capital, such as clippers, tubs, and brushes, and labor to produce its output of groomed dogs.

The production function that applies to The Clip Joint appears in Table 3.2, on the next page. For given levels of productivity and the capital stock, it shows how The Clip Joint's daily output of groomed dogs, column (2), depends on the number of workers employed, column (1). The more workers The Clip Joint has, the greater its daily output is.

The *MPN* of each worker at The Clip Joint is shown in column (3). Employing the first worker raises The Clip Joint's output from 0 to 11, so the *MPN* of the first worker is 11. Employing the second worker raises The Clip Joint's output from 11 to 20, an increase of 9, so the *MPN* of the second worker is 9; and so on. Column (3) also shows that, as the number of workers at The Clip Joint increases, the *MPN* falls so that labor at The Clip Joint has diminishing marginal productivity. The more workers there are on the job, the more they must share the fixed amount of capital (tubs, clippers, brushes), and the less benefit there is to adding yet another worker.

The marginal product of labor measures the benefit of employing an additional worker in terms of the extra *output* produced. A related concept, the **marginal revenue product of labor,** or *MRPN,* measures the benefit of employing an additional worker in terms of the extra *revenue* produced. To calculate

Table 3.2 The Clip Joint's Production Function

(1) Number of Workers, N	(2) Number of Dogs Groomed, Y	(3) Marginal Product of Labor, MPN	(4) Marginal Revenue Product of Labor, $MRPN = MPN \times P$ (when P = \$10 per grooming)
0	0		
		11	\$110
1	11		
		9	\$90
2	20		
		7	\$70
3	27		
		5	\$50
4	32		
		3	\$30
5	35		
		1	\$10
6	36		

the *MRPN*, we need to know the price of the firm's output. If The Clip Joint receives \$10 for each dog it grooms, the *MRPN* of the first worker is \$110 per day (11 additional dogs groomed per day at \$10 per grooming). More generally, the marginal revenue product of an additional worker equals the price of the firm's output, *P*, times the extra output gained by adding the worker, *MPN*:

$$MRPN = P \times MPN. \tag{3.3}$$

At The Clip Joint the price of output *P* is \$10 per grooming, so the *MRPN* of each worker, column (4), equals the *MPN* of the worker, column (3), multiplied by \$10.

Now suppose that the wage *W* that The Clip Joint must pay to attract qualified workers is \$80 per day. (We refer to the wage *W*, when measured in the conventional way in terms of today's dollars, as the *nominal* wage.) How many workers should The Clip Joint employ in order to maximize its profits? To answer this question, The Clip Joint compares the benefits and costs of employing each additional worker. The benefit of employing an additional worker, in dollars per day, is the worker's marginal revenue product *MRPN*. The cost of an additional worker, in dollars per day, is the nominal daily wage *W*.

Table 3.2 shows that the *MRPN* of the first worker is \$110 per day, which exceeds the daily wage of \$80, so employing the first worker is profitable for The Clip Joint. Adding a second worker increases The Clip Joint's profit as well because the *MRPN* of the second worker (\$90 per day) also exceeds the daily wage. However, employing a third worker reduces The Clip Joint's profit because the third worker's *MRPN* of \$70 per day is less than the \$80 daily wage. Therefore The Clip Joint's profit-maximizing level of employment at \$80/day—equivalently, the quantity of labor demanded by The Clip Joint—is two workers.

In finding the quantity of labor demanded by The Clip Joint, we measured the benefits and costs of an extra worker in nominal, or dollar, terms. If we measure the benefits and costs of an extra worker in real terms, the results would be the same. In real terms the benefit to The Clip Joint of an extra worker is the number of extra groomings that the extra worker provides, which is the marginal product of labor, *MPN*. The real cost of adding another worker is the **real wage,** which is the wage measured in terms of units of output. Algebraically, the real wage, w, equals the nominal wage, W, divided by the price of output, P.

In this example the nominal wage W is \$80 per day and the price of output P is \$10 per grooming, so the real wage w equals (\$80 per day)/(\$10 per grooming), or 8 groomings per day. To find the profit-maximizing level of employment, The Clip Joint compares this real cost of an additional worker with the real benefit of an additional worker, the *MPN*. The *MPN* of the first worker is 11 groomings per day, which exceeds the real wage of 8 groomings per day, so employing this worker is profitable. The second worker also should be hired, as the second worker's *MPN* of 9 groomings per day also exceeds the real wage of 8 groomings per day. However, a third worker should not be hired, as the third worker's *MPN* of 7 groomings per day is less than the real wage. The quantity of labor demanded by The Clip Joint is therefore two workers, which is the same result we got when we compared costs and benefits in nominal terms.

This example shows that when the benefit of an additional worker exceeds the cost of an additional worker, the firm should increase employment in order to maximize profits. Similarly, if at the firm's current employment level the benefit of the last worker employed is less than the cost of the worker, the firm should reduce employment. Summary table 2 compares benefits and costs of additional labor in both real and nominal terms. In the choice of the profit-maximizing level of employment, comparison of benefits and costs in real or nominal terms is equally valid.

SUMMARY 2

Comparing the Benefits and Costs of Changing the Amount of Labor

To maximize profits, the firm should:	Increase employment if	Decrease employment if
Real terms	$MPN > w$ $(MPN > W/P)$	$MPN < w$ $(MPN < W/P)$
Nominal terms	$P \times MPN > W$ $(MRPN > W)$	$P \times MPN < W$ $(MRPN < W)$

MPN = marginal product of labor
P = price of output
$MRPN$ = marginal revenue product of labor = $P \times MPN$
W = nominal wage
w = real wage = W/P

A Change in the Wage

The Clip Joint's decision to employ two workers was based on a nominal wage of $80 per day. Now suppose that for some reason the nominal wage needed to attract qualified workers drops to $60 per day. How will the reduction in the nominal wage affect the number of workers that The Clip Joint wants to employ?

To find the answer, we can compare costs and benefits in either nominal or real terms. Let's make the comparison in real terms. If the nominal wage drops to $60 per day while the price of groomings remains at $10, the real wage falls to ($60 per day)/($10 per grooming), or 6 groomings per day. Column (3) of Table 3.2 shows that the *MPN* of the third worker is 7 groomings per day, which is now greater than the real wage. Thus, at the lower wage, expanding the quantity of labor demanded from two to three workers is profitable for The Clip Joint. However, the firm will not hire a fourth worker because the *MPN* of the fourth worker (5 groomings per day) is less than the new real wage (6 groomings per day).

This example illustrates a general point about the effect of the real wage on labor demand: All else being equal, *a decrease in the real wage raises the amount of labor demanded.* Similarly, *an increase in the real wage decreases the amount of labor demanded.*

The Marginal Product of Labor and the Labor Demand Curve

Using The Clip Joint as an example, we showed the negative relationship between the real wage and the quantity of labor that a firm demands. Figure 3.5 shows in more general terms how the link between the real wage and the quantity of labor demanded is determined. The amount of labor N is on the horizontal axis. The *MPN* and the real wage, both of which are measured in goods per unit of labor, are on the vertical axis. The downward-sloping curve is the *MPN* curve; it relates the marginal product of labor, *MPN*, to the amount of labor employed by the firm, N. The *MPN* curve slopes downward because of the diminishing marginal productivity of labor. The horizontal line represents the real wage faced by firms in the labor market, which the firms take as given. Here, the real wage is w^*.

For any real wage w^*, the amount of labor that yields the highest profit (and therefore the amount of labor demanded) is determined at point A, the intersection of the real-wage line and the *MPN* curve. At A the quantity of labor demanded is N^*. Why is N^* a firm's profit-maximizing level of labor input? At employment levels of less than N^*, the marginal product of labor exceeds the real wage (the *MPN* curve lies above the real-wage line); thus, if the firm's employment is initially less than N^*, it can increase its profit by expanding the amount of labor it uses. Similarly, if the firm's employment is initially greater than N^*, the marginal product of labor is less than the real wage ($MPN < w^*$) and the firm can raise profits by reducing employment. Only when employment equals N^* will the firm be satisfied with the number of workers it has. More generally, for any real wage, the profit-maximizing amount of labor input—labor demanded—corresponds to the point at which the *MPN* curve and the real-wage line intersect.

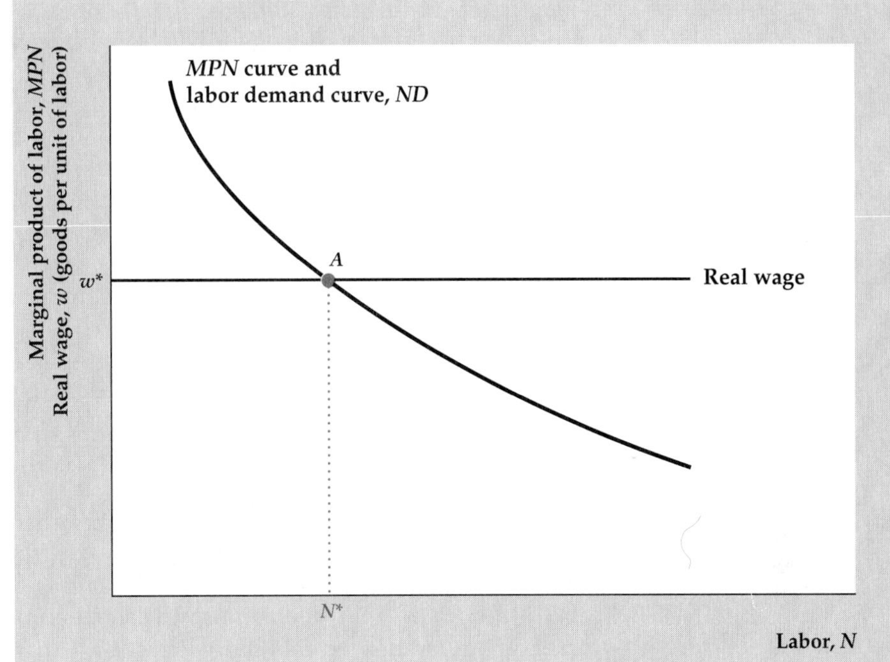

Figure 3.5
The determination of labor demand
The amount of labor demanded is determined by locating the point on the *MPN* curve at which the *MPN* equals the real wage rate; the amount of labor corresponding to that point is the amount of labor demanded. For example, when the real wage is w^*, the *MPN* equals the real wage at point *A* and the quantity of labor demanded is N^*. The labor demand curve, *ND*, shows the amount of labor demanded at each level of the real wage. The labor demand curve is identical to the *MPN* curve.

The graph of the relationship between the amount of labor demanded by a firm and the real wage that the firm faces is called the *labor demand curve.* Because the *MPN* curve also shows the amount of labor demanded at any real wage, *the labor demand curve is the same as the MPN curve,* except that the vertical axis measures the real wage for the labor demand curve and measures the marginal product of labor for the *MPN* curve.[10] Like the *MPN* curve, the labor demand curve slopes downward, indicating that the quantity of labor demanded falls as the real wage rises.

This labor demand curve is more general than that in the example of The Clip Joint in a couple of ways that are worth mentioning. First, we referred to the demand for labor and not specifically to the demand for workers, as in The Clip Joint example. In general, labor *N* can be measured in various ways—for example, as total hours worked, total weeks worked, or the number of employees—depending on the application. Second, although we assumed in the example that The Clip Joint had to hire a whole number of workers, the labor demand curve shown in Fig. 3.5 allows labor *N* to have any positive value, whole or fractional. Allowing *N* to take any value is sensible because people may work fractions of an hour.

Factors That Shift the Labor Demand Curve

Because the labor demand curve shows the relation between the real wage and the amount of labor that firms want to employ, changes in the real wage are represented as movements *along* the labor demand curve. Changes in the

10. Recall that the real wage and the *MPN* are measured in the same units, goods per unit of labor.

real wage do not cause the labor demand curve to shift. The labor demand curve shifts in response to factors that change the amount of labor that firms want to employ *at any given level of the real wage*. For example, we showed earlier in this chapter that beneficial or positive supply shocks are likely to increase the *MPN* at all levels of labor input, and adverse or negative supply shocks are likely to reduce the *MPN* at all levels of labor input. Thus a beneficial supply shock shifts the *MPN* curve upward and to the right and raises the quantity of labor demanded at any given real wage; an adverse supply shock does the reverse.

The effect of a supply shock on The Clip Joint's demand for labor can be illustrated by imagining that the proprietor of The Clip Joint discovers that playing New Age music soothes the dogs. It makes them more cooperative and doubles the number of groomings per day that the same number of workers can produce. This technological improvement gives The Clip Joint a new production function, as described in Table 3.3. Note that doubling total output doubles the *MPN* at each employment level.

The Clip Joint demanded two workers when faced with the original production function (Table 3.2) and a real wage of 8 groomings per day. Table 3.3 shows that the productivity improvement increases The Clip Joint's labor demand at the given real wage to four workers, because the *MPN* of the fourth worker (10 groomings per day) now exceeds the real wage. The Clip Joint will not hire a fifth worker, however, because this worker's *MPN* (6 groomings per day) is less than the real wage.

The effect of a beneficial supply shock on a labor demand curve is shown in Fig. 3.6. The shock causes the *MPN* to increase at any level of labor input, so

Table 3.3 The Clip Joint's Production Function After a Beneficial Productivity Shock

(1) Number of Workers, N	(2) Number of Dogs Groomed, Y	(3) Marginal Product of Labor, MPN	(4) Marginal Revenue Product of Labor, $MRPN = MPN \times P$ (when P = \$10 per grooming)
0	0		
		22	\$220
1	22		
		18	\$180
2	40		
		14	\$140
3	54		
		10	\$100
4	64		
		6	\$60
5	70		
		2	\$20
6	72		

the *MPN* curve shifts upward and to the right. Because the *MPN* and labor demand curves are identical, the labor demand curve also shifts upward and to the right, from ND^1 to ND^2 in Fig. 3.6. When the labor demand curve is ND^2, the firm hires more workers at any real wage level than when the labor demand curve is ND^1. Thus worker productivity and the amount of labor demanded are closely linked.

Another factor that may affect labor demand is the size of the capital stock. Generally, an increase in the capital stock *K*—by giving each worker more machines or equipment to work with—raises workers' productivity and increases the *MPN* at any level of labor. Hence an increase in the capital stock will cause the labor demand curve to shift upward and to the right, raising the amount of labor that a firm demands at any particular real wage.[11]

Aggregate Labor Demand

So far we have focused on the demand for labor by an individual firm, such as The Clip Joint. For macroeconomic analysis, however, we usually work with the concept of the **aggregate demand for labor,** or the sum of the labor demands of all the firms in an economy.

Because the aggregate demand for labor is the sum of firms' labor demands, the factors that determine the aggregate demand for labor are the same as for an individual firm. Thus the aggregate labor demand curve looks the same as the labor demand curve for an individual firm (Fig. 3.5). Like the firm's labor demand curve, the aggregate labor demand curve slopes downward,

11. An increase in the capital stock may reduce the demand for labor if the new capital substitutes for the use of labor. For example, the installation of automatic elevators reduced the marginal product of elevator operators and thus the demand for these workers.

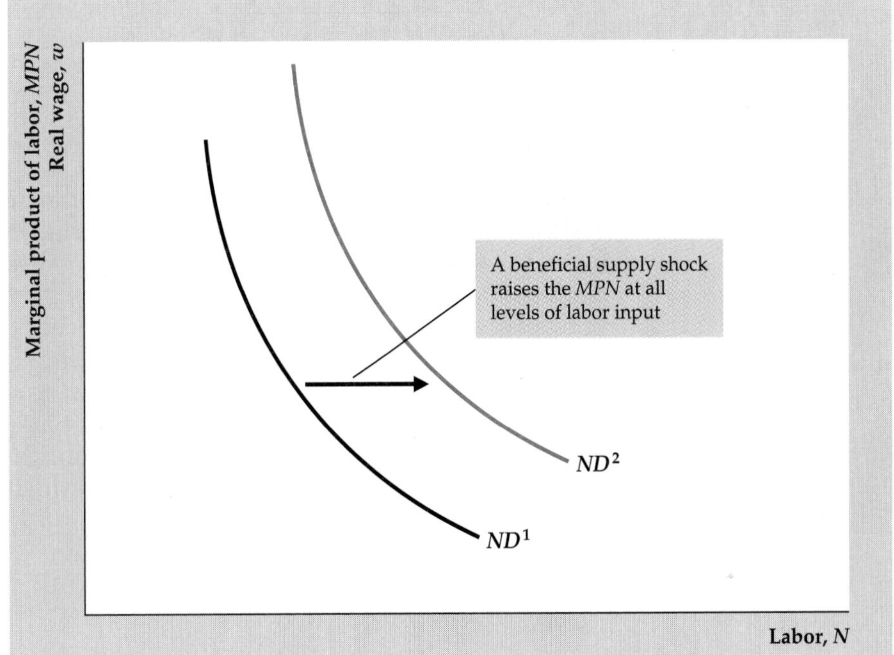

Figure 3.6
The effect of a beneficial supply shock on labor demand
A beneficial supply shock that raises the *MPN* at every level of labor shifts the *MPN* curve upward and to the right. Because the labor demand curve is identical to the *MPN* curve, the labor demand curve shifts upward and to the right from ND^1 to ND^2. For any real wage, firms demand more labor after a beneficial supply shock.

SUMMARY 3

Factors that Shift the Aggregate Labor Demand Curve

An increase in	Causes the labor demand curve to shift	Reason
Productivity	Right	Beneficial supply shock increases *MPN* and shifts *MPN* curve up and to the right.
Capital stock	Right	Higher capital stock increases *MPN* and shifts *MPN* curve up and to the right.

showing that an increase in the economywide real wage reduces the total amount of labor that firms want to use. Similarly, a beneficial supply shock or an increase in the aggregate capital stock shifts the aggregate labor demand curve upward and to the right; an adverse supply shock or a drop in the aggregate capital stock shifts it downward and to the left. The factors affecting aggregate labor demand are listed for convenience in Summary table 3.

3.3 THE SUPPLY OF LABOR

The demand for labor is determined by firms, but the supply of labor is determined by individuals or members of a family making a joint decision. Each person of working age must decide how much (if at all) to work in the wage-paying sector of the economy versus non-wage-paying alternatives, such as taking care of the home and children, going to school, or being retired. The **aggregate supply of labor** is the sum of the labor supplied by everyone in the economy.

Recall that, in determining how much labor to demand, firms compare the costs and benefits of hiring additional workers. Similarly, in deciding how much to work, an individual should weigh the benefits against the costs of working. Beyond any psychological satisfaction gained from having a job, the principal benefit of working is the income earned, which can be used to buy necessities and luxuries. The principal cost of working is that it involves time and effort that are no longer available for other activities. Economists use the term **leisure**[12] for all off-the-job activities, including eating, sleeping, working around the house, spending time with family and friends, and so on. To make themselves as well off as possible, individuals should choose to supply labor

12. The term *leisure* does not imply that all off-the-job activities (housework or schoolwork, for example) are "leisurely"!

up to the point at which the income obtained from working an extra hour just makes up for the extra hour of leisure they have to forego.

We discuss the details of the labor supply decision in Chapter 8. Here we present a general discussion that begins with the relationship between the real wage and labor supply.

The Labor Supply Curve

The economic benefit that people derive from working is the real value of the income that they receive for each unit of time spent at work, which is the same as the real wage. Recall that the real wage w equals the nominal wage W divided by the price level P. Thus, if the nominal wage is \$12/hour and the price level is \$3/good, the real wage is 4 goods/hour. In this case, the worker earns wages with purchasing power equal to 4 goods by working an additional hour.

In discussing labor supply, we distinguish between the *current* real wage (which the worker can earn by working today) and the *expected future* real wage (which the worker expects to earn at some future date). Labor supply reacts differently to changes in the current real wage and the expected future real wage. We consider first the effect of the current real wage.

When the current real wage rises, working (instead of enjoying leisure) becomes more attractive. For example, if hamburger flipping pays very little in real terms—barely enough to cover uniforms and medication for grease burns—a student may prefer hanging out at the beach to taking a summer job at the Burger Barn. But if the Burger Barn pays a high real wage—high enough, say, not only to cover uniforms and medication but also to allow the student to buy a used car by the beginning of the fall term—the student may choose to work. Thus increases in the current real wage should raise the quantity of labor supplied.

The *labor supply curve* of an individual worker relates the amount of labor supplied to the current real wage, with other factors (including the expected future real wage) held constant. Figure 3.7 (on the next page) is a graph of a typical labor supply curve. The current real wage is measured on the vertical axis, and the amount of labor supplied is measured on the horizontal axis. The labor supply curve slopes upward because an increase in the current real wage leads to an increase in the amount of labor supplied.

Factors that Shift the Labor Supply Curve

Any factor that changes the amount of labor supplied at a given level of the current real wage shifts the labor supply curve. Let's look at the effects on labor supply of changes in wealth and in the expected future real wage.

Wealth. The effect of wealth on labor supply is most easily illustrated by an extreme example: A person is working two jobs to make ends meet when she learns that she has won the multimillion-dollar state lottery. Although predicting exactly how the person will use the lottery winnings is impossible, she probably will no longer work two jobs and in fact may choose not to work at all. In any case, she will reduce the amount of labor she supplies. This extreme example illustrates a general point: Because a person who is wealthier can

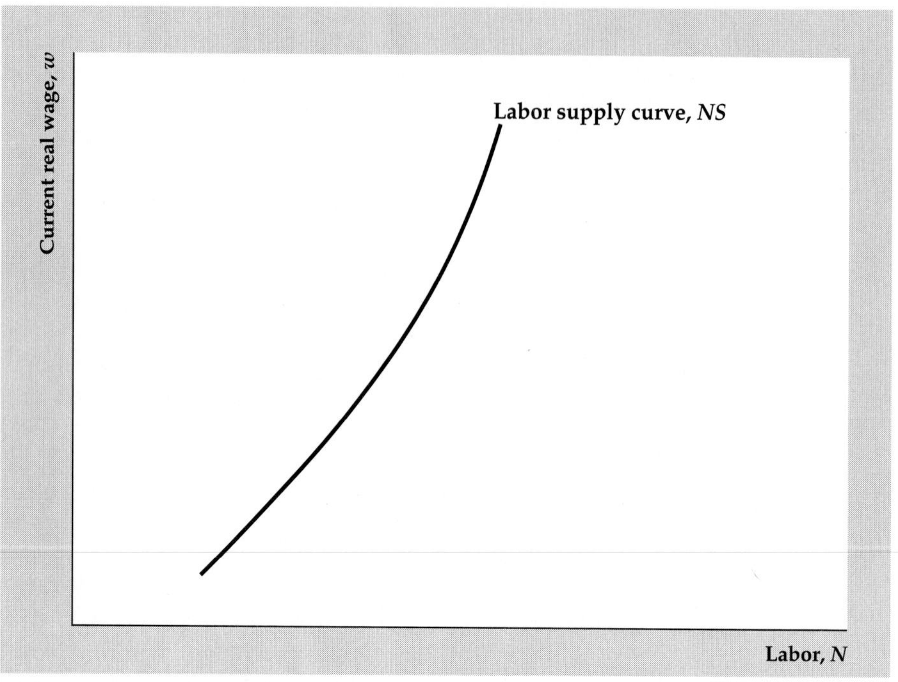

Figure 3.7
The labor supply curve of an individual worker
The horizontal axis shows the amount of labor that a worker will supply for any given current real wage on the vertical axis. The labor supply curve slopes upward, indicating that—with other factors including the expected future real wage held constant—an increase in the current real wage raises the amount of labor supplied.

afford to enjoy more leisure, an increase in wealth tends to reduce the amount of labor supplied at any level of the current real wage. Thus an increase in wealth shifts the labor supply curve to the left, as in Fig. 3.8.

The Expected Future Real Wage. An increase in the real wage that a worker expects to receive in the future makes that person effectively wealthier and thus reduces the amount of labor supplied at any current real wage. For example, a recent college graduate who has been promised a highly paid job starting in the fall is less likely to take a low-paying summer job than is another graduate without such good prospects. Thus an increase in the expected future real wage causes the labor supply curve to shift to the left, as in Fig. 3.8.

Aggregate Labor Supply

As we mentioned earlier, the aggregate supply of labor is the total amount of labor supplied by everyone in the economy. Just as the quantity of labor supplied by an individual rises when the person's current real wage rises, the aggregate quantity of labor supplied increases when the economywide real wage rises. An increase in the current economywide real wage raises the aggregate quantity of labor supplied for two reasons. First, when the real wage rises, people who are already working may supply even more hours—by offering to work overtime, by changing from part-time to full-time work, or by taking a second job. Second, a higher real wage may entice some people who are not currently in the labor force to decide to look for work. Because higher current real wages induce people to want to work more, the aggregate labor supply

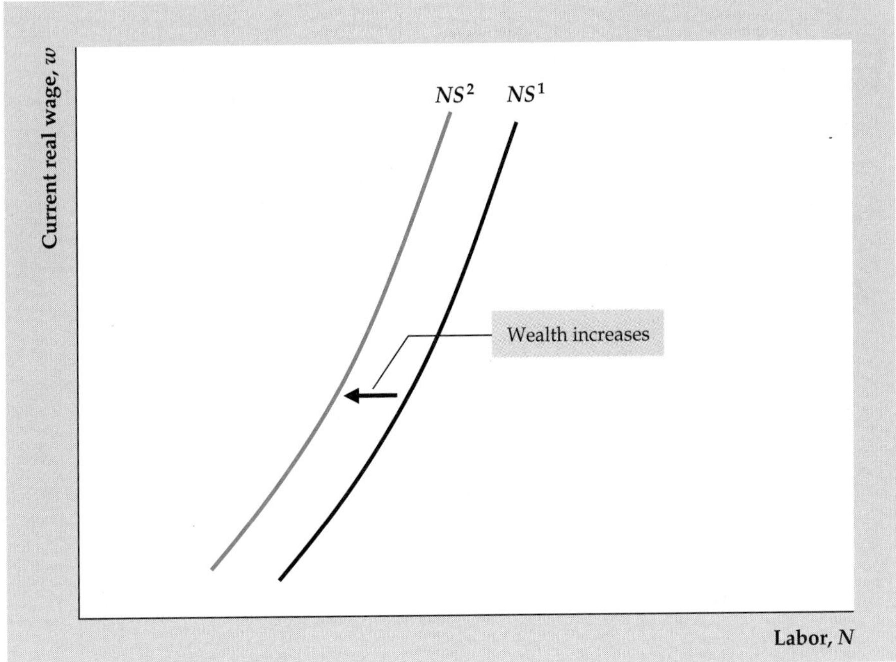

Figure 3.8
The effect on labor supply of an increase in wealth
An increase in wealth reduces the amount of labor supplied at any real wage. Therefore, an increase in wealth causes the labor supply curve to shift to the left. Similarly, an increase in the expected future real wage, which has the effect of making the worker wealthier, reduces the amount of labor supplied at any given current real wage and shifts the labor supply curve to the left.

curve—which shows the relation between the aggregate amount of labor supplied and the current real wage—slopes upward.

Factors other than the current real wage that change the amount of labor that people want to supply cause the aggregate labor supply curve to shift. Summary table 4, p. 84, lists the factors that shift aggregate labor supply. We discussed the first two factors in the table, wealth and the expected future real wage, when we considered the individual's labor supply decision. Aggregate labor supply will also increase if the country's working-age population increases (for example, because of an increased birth rate or immigration), or if changes in the social or legal environment cause a greater proportion of the working-age population to enter the labor force (increased labor force participation). For example, evolving attitudes about the role of women in society contributed to a large increase in the number of women in the U.S. labor market during the 1970s and 1980s; and the elimination of mandatory retirement in many fields may increase the participation rates of older workers.

3.4 LABOR MARKET EQUILIBRIUM

Equilibrium in the labor market requires that the aggregate quantity of labor demanded equal the aggregate quantity of labor supplied. The basic supply–demand model of the labor market introduced here (called the *classical model of the labor market*) is based on the assumption that the real wage adjusts reasonably quickly to equate labor supply and labor demand. Thus, if labor

SUMMARY 4

Factors that Shift the Aggregate Labor Supply Curve

An increase in	Causes the labor supply curve to shift	Reason
Wealth	Left	Increase in wealth increases amount of leisure workers can afford.
Expected future real wage	Left	Increase in expected future real wage increases amount of leisure workers can afford.
Working-age population	Right	Increased number of potential workers increases amount of labor supplied.
Participation rate	Right	Increased number of people wanting to work increases amount of labor supplied.

supply is less than labor demand, firms competing for scarce workers bid up the real wage, whereas if many workers are competing for relatively few jobs, the real wage will tend to fall.

Labor market equilibrium is represented graphically by the intersection of the aggregate labor demand curve and the aggregate labor supply curve at point E in Fig. 3.9. The equilibrium level of employment, achieved after the complete adjustment of wages and prices, is known as the **full-employment level of employment,** $\bar{N}$. The corresponding market-clearing real wage is $\bar{w}$.

Factors that shift either the aggregate labor demand curve or the aggregate labor supply curve affect both the equilibrium real wage and the full-employment level of employment. An example of such a factor is a temporary adverse supply shock. A temporary adverse supply shock—because of, say, a spell of unusually bad weather—decreases the marginal product of labor at every level of employment. As Fig. 3.10 shows, this decrease causes the labor demand curve to shift to the left, from ND^1 to ND^2. Because the supply shock is temporary, however, it is not expected to affect future marginal products or the future real wage, so the labor supply curve doesn't shift. Equilibrium in the labor market moves from point A to point B. Thus the model predicts that a temporary supply shock will lower both the current real wage (from w_1 to w_2) and the full-employment level of employment (from $\bar{N}_1$ to $\bar{N}_2$).

The classical supply–demand model of the labor market has the virtue of simplicity and is quite useful for studying how economic disturbances or changes in economic policy affect employment and the real wage. However, a significant drawback of this basic model is that it cannot be used to study unemployment. Because it assumes that any worker who wants to work at the

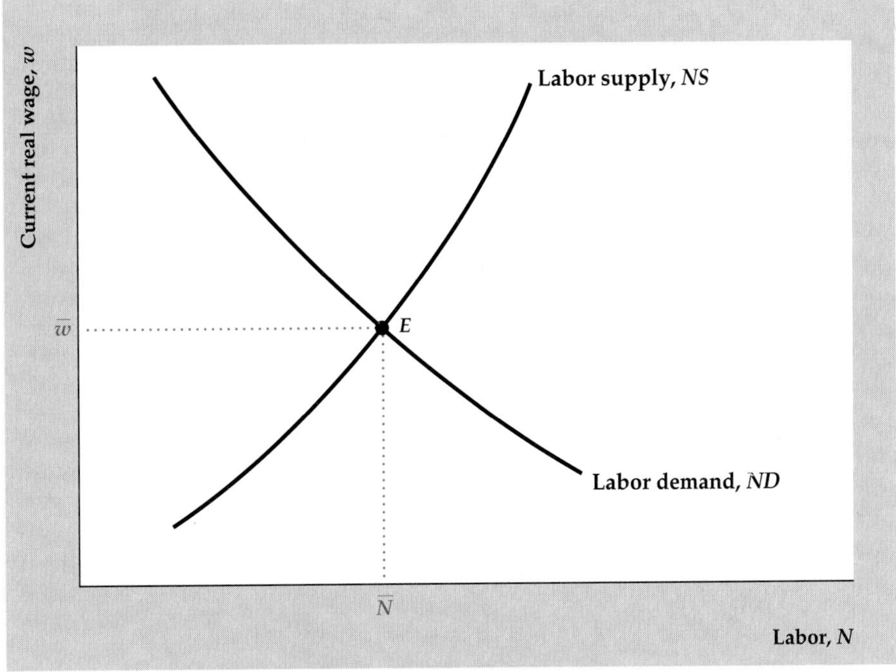

Figure 3.9
Labor market equilibrium
The quantity of labor demanded equals the quantity of labor supplied at point E. The equilibrium real wage is $\bar{w}$, and the corresponding equilibrium level of employment is $\bar{N}$, the full-employment level of employment.

equilibrium real wage can find a job, the model implies zero unemployment, which never occurs.

One way to get unemployment into the model is to drop the assumption that the real wage adjusts rapidly to equate supply and demand. The assumption

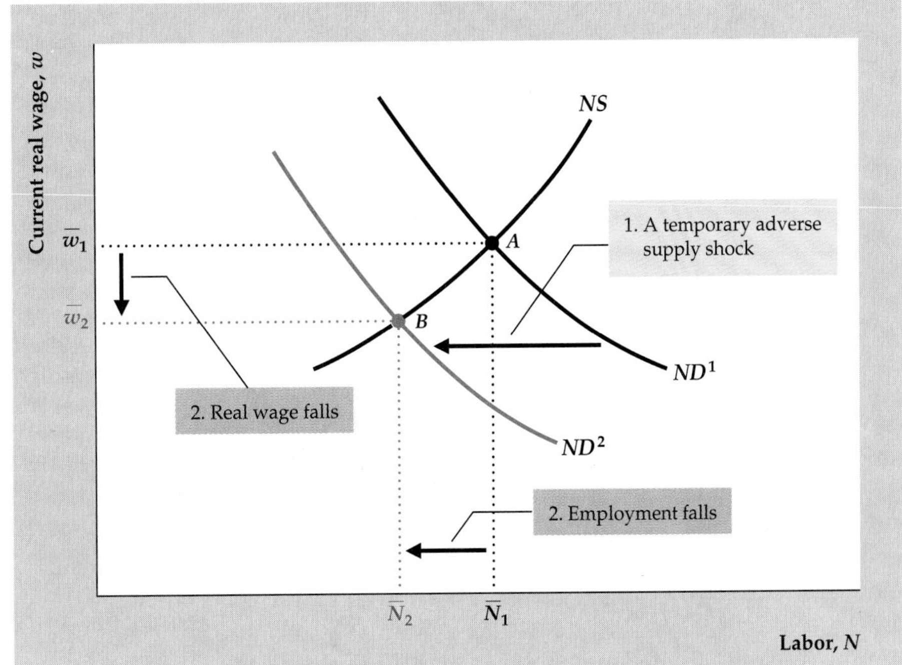

Figure 3.10
Effects of a temporary adverse supply shock on the labor market
An adverse supply shock that lowers the marginal product of labor (see Fig. 3.4) reduces the quantity of labor demanded at any real wage level. Thus the labor demand curve shifts left, from ND^1 to ND^2, and the labor market equilibrium moves from point A to point B. The adverse supply shock causes the real wage to fall from $\bar{w}_1$ to $\bar{w}_2$ and reduces the full-employment level of employment from $\bar{N}_1$ to $\bar{N}_2$.

that the real wage is slow to adjust underlies the Keynesian approach to business cycle analysis (Chapter 12). Another way to extend the model of the labor market to allow for unemployment is to recognize that the process of matching people who would like to work with the appropriate available jobs is not immediate but takes time. Because matching workers with jobs is a time-consuming process, at any particular time some workers will be without jobs. We discuss the matching process and its relationship to unemployment later in this chapter.

Full-Employment Output

By combining labor market equilibrium and the production function, we can determine how much output firms want to supply. **Full-employment output,** $\bar{Y}$, sometimes called *potential output,* is the level of output that firms in the economy supply when wages and prices have fully adjusted. Equivalently, full-employment output is the level of output supplied when aggregate employment equals its full-employment level $\bar{N}$. Algebraically, we can define full-employment output $\bar{Y}$ by using the production function (Eq. 3.1):

$$\bar{Y} = AF(K, \bar{N}). \tag{3.4}$$

Equation (3.4) shows that, for constant capital stock K, full-employment output is determined by two general factors: the full-employment level of employment $\bar{N}$ and the production function relating output to employment.

Anything that changes either the full-employment level of employment $\bar{N}$ or the production function will change full-employment output $\bar{Y}$. For example, an adverse supply shock that reduces the *MPN* (Fig. 3.10) works in two distinct ways to lower full-employment output:

1. The adverse supply shock lowers output directly, by reducing the quantity of output that can be produced with any fixed amounts of capital and labor. This direct effect can be thought of as a reduction in the productivity measure A in Eq. (3.4).
2. The adverse supply shock reduces the demand for labor and thus lowers the full-employment level of employment $\bar{N}$, as Fig. 3.10 shows. A reduction in $\bar{N}$ also reduces full-employment output $\bar{Y}$, as Eq. (3.4) confirms.

APPLICATION

Output, Employment, and the Real Wage During Oil Price Shocks

Among the most severe supply shocks hitting the U.S. and world economies since World War II were sharp increases in the prices of oil and other energy products. Figure 3.11 shows how the price of energy paid by firms, measured relative to the GDP deflator (the general price level of all output), varied during the period 1960–1992. Two adverse oil price shocks stand out: one in 1973–1974, when the Organization of Petroleum Exporting Countries (OPEC) first imposed an oil embargo and then greatly increased crude oil prices; and a second in 1979–1980, after the Iranian revolution disrupted oil supplies. The 1979–1980 oil price shock turned out to be temporary, as energy prices subsequently fell. A third increase in oil prices followed Iraq's invasion of Kuwait in August 1990. However, the 1990 shock had less of an impact on overall energy prices than the previous two oil price shocks and thus doesn't appear as much more than a blip in Fig. 3.11.

When energy prices rise, firms cut back on energy use, implying that less output is produced at any particular levels of capital and labor. Thus an increase in energy prices is an adverse supply shock. How important were these supply shocks? In an empirical study of the 1979–1980 oil price shock, John A. Tatom[13] of the Federal Reserve Bank of St. Louis used post–World War II data to estimate a production function for the United States, in which he allowed for effects of energy price changes. Tatom estimated that the 1979–1980 increase in the relative price of energy reduced the amount of output that could be produced by given quantities of capital and labor by about 5.7%. Tatom's results, if correct, suggest a large impact on the supply of output from oil price shocks, at least in the 1979–1980 case.

Our analysis predicts that an adverse supply shock will lower labor demand, reducing employment and the real wage, as well as reducing the supply of output. In fact, the economy went into a recession following both the 1973–1974 and the 1979–1980 oil shocks, with negative GDP growth each time. In both cases the fraction of the adult population employed and the real wage fell substantially. The real wage declined by about 5% between 1973 and 1975 and by more than 8% between 1978 and 1981. Care must be taken in interpreting these results because macroeconomic policies and other factors were changing at the same time; however, our model appears to account for the response of

13. "Are the Macroeconomic Effects of Oil Price Changes Symmetric?" in K. Brunner and A. Meltzer, eds., *Carnegie-Rochester Conference Series on Public Policy*, Vol. 28, Spring 1988.

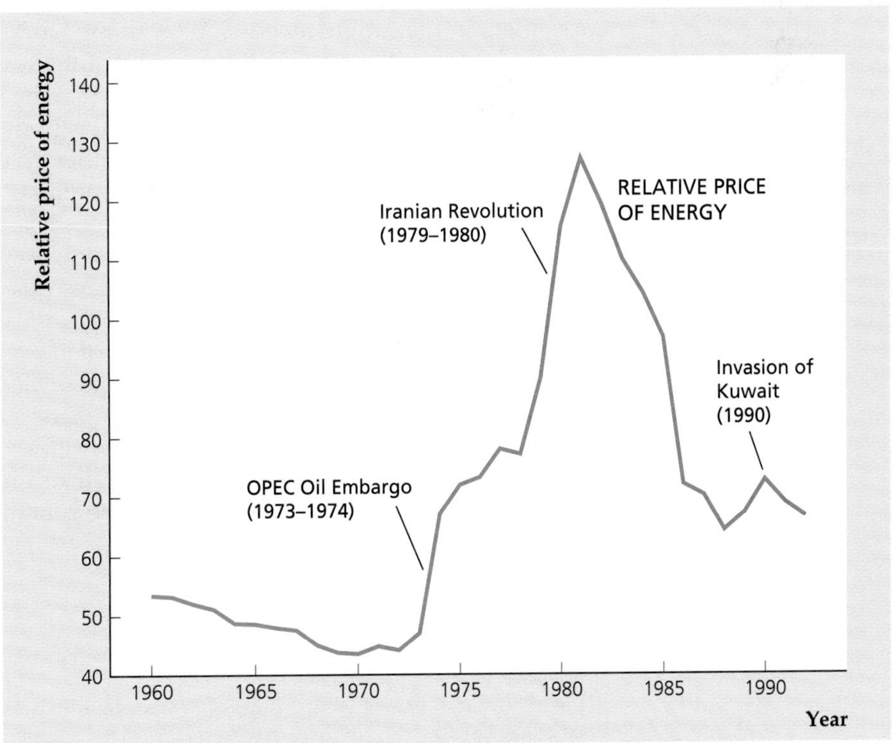

Figure 3.11 Relative price of energy, 1960–1992

The figure shows the producer price index of fuels and related products and power (an index of energy prices paid by producers) relative to the GDP deflator. Note the impact of the 1973–1974 and 1979–1980 oil shocks and the decline in energy prices in the first half of the 1980s. The 1990 Iraqi invasion of Kuwait also increased this price index.

Source: Producer price index (1982 = 100), from Table B-63, *Economic Report of the President,* 1993; GDP deflator (1987 = 100), from *Economic Report of the President,* 1993, Table B.3 (1992 data from *Survey of Current Business,* March 1993, Table 7.13).

the economy to the two oil price shocks of the 1970s. The U.S. economy showed a similar response to the smaller 1990 shock, with a recession beginning at about the same time the shock occurred and continuing into 1991.

APPLICATION

Technical Change and Wage Inequality

Because many families have little income other than wage income, trends in real wages have important implications for the standard of living of a large segment of the society. During the twenty-five years after World War II, real wages in the United States grew strongly. Since about 1970, however, there have been two disturbing trends: (1) overall real wage growth has slowed considerably; and (2) real wages have become more unequal, with wages of the best-paid workers continuing to rise but wages of the worst-paid workers actually falling in real terms.

These two trends are illustrated by Fig. 3.12, which is drawn from a study by Chinhui Juhn of the University of Houston and Kevin M. Murphy and Robert Topel of the University of Chicago.[14] It shows how real hourly wages of different groups of American workers (as reported by the workers to an ongoing government survey) have changed over time. In Fig. 3.12 real wages are measured as percentage differences relative to real wages paid in 1970; positive values indicate that the real wage is above its 1970 level and negative values indicate that the real wage is below its 1970 level. The line marked 1–10 shows the change in the average real wage of workers whose wages are in the bottom 10% of the distribution in any year, the line marked 11–20 shows change in the real wage of workers in the next lowest 10% of the wage distribution, and so on. The top line, marked 61–100, shows the change in the real wage of the best-paid workers, whose wages are in the top 40% of the wage distribution. Figure 3.12 shows both that there has been little overall improvement in real wages since 1970 (even the workers with the highest wage growth—those with wages in the top 40% of the wage distribution—received only modest increases in the real wage) and that the lowest-paid workers have actually had significant declines in their real earnings in the last two decades. Similar trends have been observed in most other industrialized countries.[15]

The explanations offered by most economists for both of these trends focus on the pattern of technological change. The overall slowdown in real wage growth is generally attributed to the slowdown in productivity growth in the U.S. economy over the past two decades (discussed in the Application, "The Production Function of the U.S. Economy and U.S. Productivity Growth," earlier in the chapter). Because of slow productivity growth, the marginal product of labor, *MPN*, and thus labor demand have grown slowly. Coupled with relatively rapid increases in labor supply (the fraction of the adult population in the work force has risen from about 60% to more than 66% during this period), slow growth in labor demand has held down the growth of real wages. Chapter 6 discusses further the general slowdown in productivity growth and its implications.

---

14. "Why Has the Natural Rate of Unemployment Increased Over Time?" *Brookings Papers on Economic Activity,* 1991:2, pp. 75–126.

15. Steven Davis, "Cross-Country Patterns of Change in Relative Wages," in Olivier Blanchard and Stanley Fischer, eds., *NBER Macroeconomics Annual,* Cambridge, Mass.: MIT Press, 1992.

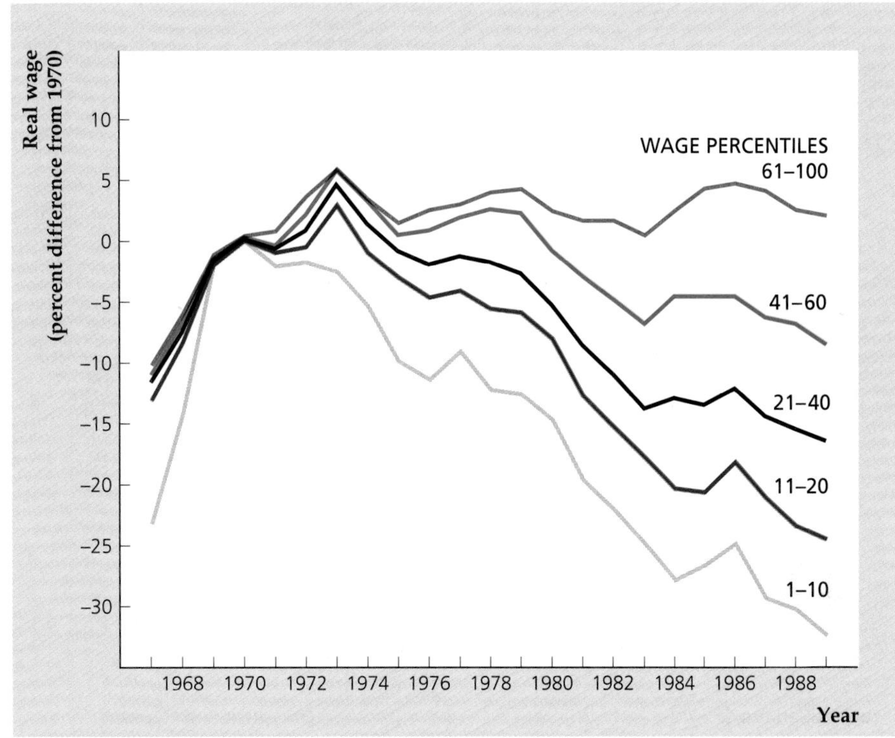

Figure 3.12
The increase in real wage inequality since 1970
The figure shows the real hourly wages of different groups of workers, measured as percentage differences relative to real wages paid in 1970. The line marked 1–10 shows the change in the average real wage of workers whose wages are in the bottom 10% of the distribution, the line marked 11–20 shows the change in the real wage of workers in the next lowest 10% of the wage distribution, and so on. The top line, marked 61–100, shows the change in the real wage of workers whose wages are in the top 40% of the wage distribution. Note both the slow growth of wages since 1970 (even the workers in the top 40% of the wage distribution, who had the highest wage growth, have had only modest increases in the real wage) and the trend toward increased inequality (the distance between the highest and lowest curve has increased since 1970).

From Chinhui Juhn, Kevin M. Murphy and Robert Topel, "Why Has the Natural Rate of Unemployment Increased Over Time?" *Brookings Papers on Economic Activity,* 1991:2, pp. 75–126, Figure 6. Reprinted with the permission of The Brookings Institution.

Some economists link the rising inequality in real wages to the character, not the pace, of technical change. In particular, they argue that technical change during the past two decades has been *skill-biased,* meaning that it has raised the productivity of highly trained or educated workers more than that of the less skilled.[16] For example, some new manufacturing techniques rely considerably more on worker initiative and problem solving than did the traditional assembly-line approach and thus require better-skilled workers. Computerization is another development that has in many cases increased the productivity of more skilled workers while squeezing out those without the education or training to use this new tool effectively. For example, a study by Alan Krueger of Princeton University found that workers who are able to use computers in their jobs enjoy a 10–15% wage premium over similar workers who are not trained to use computers.[17]

Figure 3.13, on the next page, illustrates the labor market effects of a skill-biased technical change. Here we drop the simplifying assumption made earlier that all workers are identical and instead allow for two types of workers,

16. This conclusion is drawn by, among others, John Bound and George Johnson, "Changes in the Structure of Wages in the 1980's: An Evaluation of Alternative Explanations," *American Economic Review,* June 1992, pp. 371–392.

17. "How Computers Have Changed the Wage Structure: Evidence from Microdata, 1984–1989," *Quarterly Journal of Economics,* February 1993, pp. 33–60.

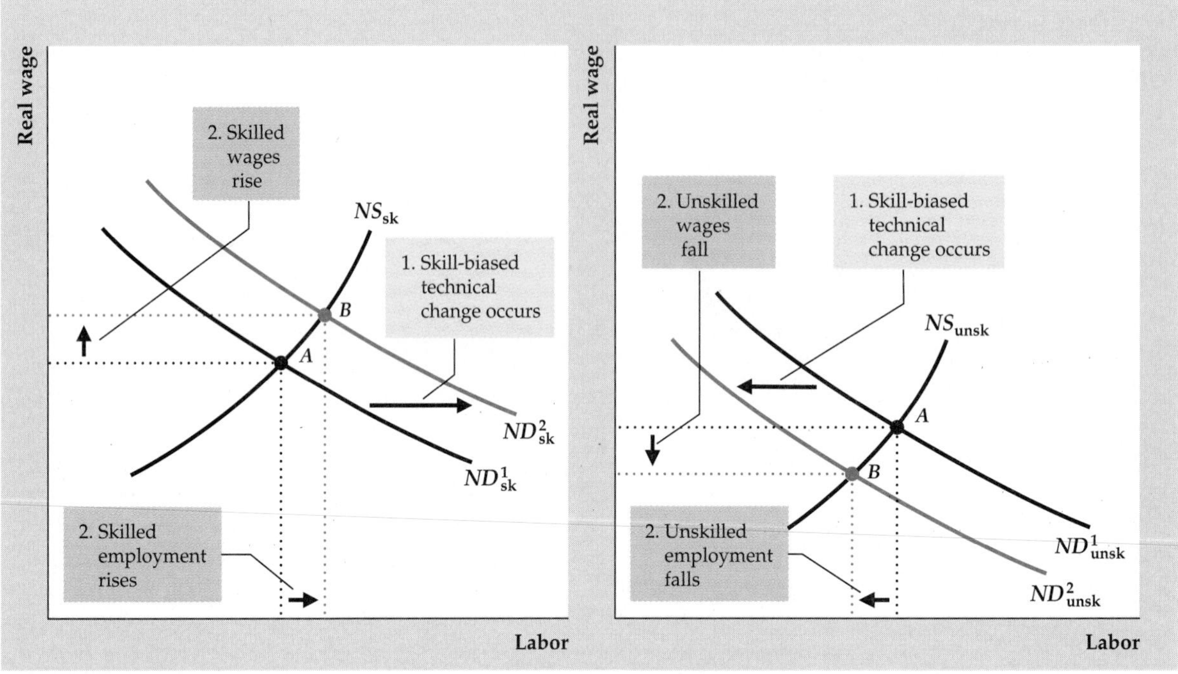

(a) Skilled workers **(b) Unskilled workers**

Figure 3.13
The effects of skill-biased technical change on wage inequality
The supply and demand for skilled labor is shown in (a), and the supply and demand for unskilled labor is shown in (b). The initial equilibrium is shown as point *A* in both parts. Because skilled workers have a higher *MPN* than unskilled workers, their real wage is higher.

A skill-biased technical change increases the *MPN* of skilled workers relative to the *MPN* of unskilled workers. A rise in the *MPN* of skilled workers raises the demand, from ND^1_{sk} to ND^2_{sk} in (a). If the *MPN* of unskilled workers actually falls, demand for unskilled labor falls, from ND^1_{unsk} to ND^2_{unsk} in (b). At the new equilibrium, point *B* in both parts, the wages of skilled workers have risen relative to those of unskilled workers.

skilled and unskilled.[18] Supply and demand for each type of worker are shown separately, with the market for skilled workers shown in Fig. 3.13(a) and the market for unskilled workers shown in Fig. 3.13(b). The supply of each type of worker reflects the number of people in the labor force with each level of skills. For simplicity, and to focus on the effects of a skill-biased technical change, we ignore population growth and changing participation rates and assume that the labor supply curves are fixed. The demand for each type of worker depends on the *MPN* of that type of worker, for constant capital stock and number of employed workers of the other type.

18. With two types of workers, there are three factors of production: capital, skilled labor, and unskilled labor. The production function thus becomes $Y = AF(K, N_{sk}, N_{unsk})$, where N_{sk} is the number of skilled and N_{unsk} the number of unskilled workers employed. A skill-biased technical change changes the function F so that the marginal product of skilled workers rises relative to the marginal product of unskilled workers.

The initial labor demand curves are ND^1_{sk} in Fig. 3.13(a) and ND^1_{unsk} in Fig. 3.13(b), and the initial labor market equilibrium is at point A in both parts. The real wages of skilled workers are higher than those of unskilled workers (i.e., the equilibrium real wage at point A in Fig. 3.13a is higher than the equilibrium real wage at point A in Fig. 3.13b). This difference reflects the higher *MPN* and lower supply of skilled workers, relative to unskilled workers.

A skill-biased technical change, such as the introduction of computers, raises the *MPN* of skilled workers (who can accomplish more with the aid of a computer than they could without one) but reduces the *MPN* of unskilled workers (who do not have the training to be productive in a computerized workplace). Because the *MPN* curve and the demand curve for labor are the same, this technical change raises the demand for skilled workers (from ND^1_{sk} to ND^2_{sk} in Fig. 3.13a) but reduces the demand for unskilled workers (from ND^1_{unsk} to ND^2_{unsk} in Fig. 3.13b). At the new equilibrium, at point B in both parts, skilled workers' real wages and employment have risen, and the wages and employment of the unskilled have fallen. The increased wage inequality predicted by this analysis is consistent with the facts. It also appears to be true that the fraction of employment composed of skilled workers has increased while the fraction composed of unskilled workers has decreased. Juhn, Murphy, and Topel found that, in particular, unskilled workers have responded to the very low wages available to them by significantly reducing the amount of labor they supply.[19]

3.5 UNEMPLOYMENT

Our classical model of the labor market, which relies on supply–demand analysis, is useful for studying the wage rate and the level of employment in an economy and for showing how these variables are linked to output and productivity. However, this model of the labor market is based on the strong assumption that, when the labor market is in equilibrium, all workers who are willing to work at the prevailing wage are able to find jobs. In reality, of course, not everyone who would like to work has a job; there is always some unemployment. The existence of unemployment implies that, at any time, not all of society's labor resources are actively involved in producing goods and services.

We discuss the problem of unemployment several times in this book, notably in Chapter 13. Here we introduce the topic by presenting some basic facts about unemployment and then turning to a preliminary economic analysis of it.

19. A complication not shown in Fig. 3.13 arises if workers expect the skill bias of technical change to be permanent. In that case, skilled workers expect both their current and future wage to rise, which shifts their labor supply curve left; expected declines in the future wage of the unskilled shifts their labor supply curve to the right. This complication may reverse the predictions of the analysis about employment but only reinforces the main conclusion drawn here, that skilled workers' wages rise relative to those of unskilled workers.

Measuring Unemployment

In order to estimate the unemployment rate in the United States, each month the Bureau of Labor Statistics (BLS) surveys about 60,000 households. Each person over sixteen in the surveyed households is assigned to one of three categories:

1. *employed,* if the person worked full-time or part-time during the past week (or was on sick leave or vacation from a job);
2. *unemployed,* if the person didn't work during the past week but looked for work during the past four weeks; or
3. *not in the labor force,* if the person didn't work during the past week and didn't look for work during the past four weeks (examples are full-time students, homemakers, and retirees).

Table 3.4 shows the number of people in each category in May 1993. (A good source for these and other data about the labor market is described in the box, "In Touch with the Macroeconomy: Labor Market Data," p. 93.) In that month there were 119.3 million employed and 8.9 million unemployed workers. The **labor force** consists of all employed and unemployed workers, so in May 1993 it totaled 128.1 million workers (119.3 million employed plus 8.9 million unemployed, which doesn't exactly equal 128.1 because of rounding). The working-age population in May 1993 was 193.3 million, which leaves 65.2 million adults not in the labor force (total population of 193.3 million less 128.1 million in the labor force).

Table 3.4 Employment Status of the U.S. Adult Population, May 1993

Category	Number (Millions)	Share of Labor Force (Percent)	Share of Adult Population (Percent)
Employed workers	119.3	93.1	61.7 (employment ratio)
Unemployed workers	8.9	6.9 (unemployment rate)	4.6
Labor force (employed + unemployed workers)	128.1	100.0	66.3 (participation rate)
Not in labor force	65.2		33.7
Adult population (labor force + not in labor force)	193.3		100.0

Note: Figures may not add up because of rounding.

Source: *The Employment Situation,* May 1993, released by the Bureau of Labor Statistics of the U.S. Department of Labor. Table A-1, seasonally adjusted data.

IN TOUCH *WITH THE MACROECONOMY*

LABOR MARKET DATA

Government agencies collect and distribute a remarkable variety of data pertaining to the labor market. A useful summary of labor market data can be found in *The Employment Situation,* a monthly report issued by the Bureau of Labor Statistics. This report, which is usually released on the first Friday of the month, includes data for the previous month on employment, unemployment, average hours worked each week, and average weekly and hourly earnings. The data are presented for the aggregate U.S. economy and for various categories of workers based on age, gender, race, occupation, and industry. Many of these data are later reprinted in a variety of sources, including *Employment and Earnings, Economic Indicators,* and the *Economic Report of the President.*

The data in *The Employment Situation* are obtained from two different surveys, a household survey and an establishment survey. The household survey is the monthly survey described earlier in this chapter and is used to calculate employment and the unemployment rate. The establishment survey (also known as the payroll survey) is based on the responses of more than 300,000 business establishments about their employment, hours worked, and employee earnings.

Both the household survey and the establishment survey provide information on employment, but they sometimes give conflicting signals about what happened to employment in the previous month. An important difference between the two surveys is that the establishment survey counts *jobs* whereas the household survey counts *people.* Thus a worker with two jobs could be counted twice in the establishment survey but only once in the household survey. The employment data from the establishment survey are more comprehensive and seem to be more closely related to output than are the employment data from the household survey.* However, the household survey provides information about unemployment and the establishment survey doesn't.

* See Roy Webb, ed., *Macroeconomic Data: A User's Guide,* Federal Reserve Bank of Richmond, 1990, pp. 22–23.

Some useful measures of the labor market are the unemployment rate, the participation rate, and the employment ratio. The **unemployment rate** is the fraction of the labor force that is unemployed. In May 1993, the unemployment rate was 6.9% (8.9 million unemployed divided by 128.1 million in the labor force). Figure 1.3 shows the U.S. unemployment rate for the period since 1890.

The fraction of the working-age population in the labor force is the **participation rate.** Of the 193.3 million working-age people in the United States in May 1993, 128.1 million were in the labor force, so the participation rate was 66.3%.

The **employment ratio** is the employed fraction of the working-age population. In May 1993 the employment ratio was 61.7% (119.3 million employed divided by the working-age population of 193.3 million). With an employment ratio of 61.7%, 38.3% of the adult population was not employed in May 1993. Of this 38.3%, 4.6% reflected unemployment and the remaining 33.7% reflected people not in the labor force. Thus a large majority of working-age people who are not employed at any given time are not in the labor force rather than unemployed.

Changes in Employment Status

The labor market is in a constant state of flux. Even when the unemployment rate remains unchanged from one month to the next, during the month hundreds of thousands of U.S. workers become unemployed and hundreds of thousands become employed.

Figure 3.14 shows how workers change their employment status (that is, whether they are employed, unemployed, or not in the labor force) in a typical month. The arrows between each pair of boxes represents a change from one employment status to another, and the number on the arrow shows the fraction of the people in one status that switch to the other status in a typical month.[20] Thus, for example, the arrow from the employed box to the unemployed box has the label 1%, indicating that 1% of employed workers in a typical month will become unemployed by the following month.

What are the employment prospects of an unemployed worker? Figure 3.14 shows that 22% of the unemployed people in a typical month will be employed the following month and that 13% of the unemployed people will be out of the labor force the next month. The remaining 65% of the unemployed people will still be unemployed the following month. Of the 13% of the unemployed who leave the labor force each month, some are **discouraged workers,** or people who have become so discouraged by lack of success at finding a job that they stop searching. Other unemployed workers leave the labor force to engage in some activity outside the labor market, such as homemaking or going to school.

20. Figure 3.14 makes use of data on employed and unemployed people and people not in the labor force from Table 3.4. The flow rates are from John M. Abowd and Arnold Zellner, "Estimating Gross Labor-Force Flows," *Journal of Business and Economic Statistics*, July 1985, pp. 254–283. Abowd and Zellner calculated these figures from monthly data for the period January 1977–December 1982.

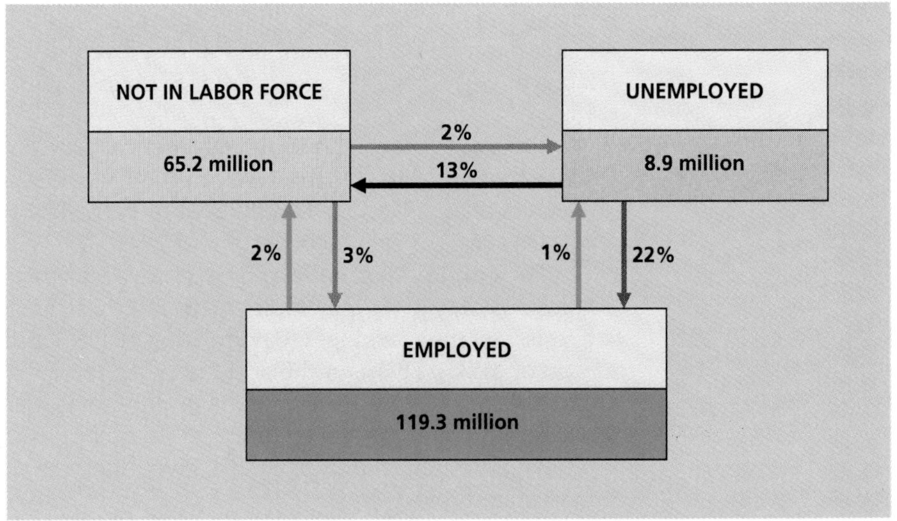

Figure 3.14
Changes in employment status in a typical month
The arrow between two boxes represents a change from one employment status to another; the label on the arrow shows the fraction of the people in one status that switch to the other status in a typical month. For example, the arrow from the unemployed box to the employed box indicates that 22% of unemployed workers become employed the following month; the arrow from the employed box to the unemployed box indicates that 1% of employed workers become unemployed the following month.

How Long Are People Unemployed?

Of the 65% of those unemployed in a typical month who remain unemployed the following month, some may remain unemployed for a considerable period of time. The length of time that an individual is continuously unemployed is called an **unemployment spell.** The length of time that an unemployment spell lasts is called its **duration.** The duration of an unemployment spell determines in large part the degree of hardship suffered by an unemployed worker. At one extreme, a one-week unemployment spell will cost a worker a week's pay but probably will not seriously affect the worker's standard of living. At the other extreme, an unemployment spell that lasts for several months may force an unemployed worker to exhaust his or her life savings or to sell the car or house.

The duration of unemployment spells in the United States is characterized by two seemingly contradictory statements:

1. Most unemployment spells are of short duration, about two months or less.
2. Most people who are unemployed on a given date are experiencing unemployment spells with long duration.

To understand how both of these statements can be true, consider an economy with 100 people in the labor force. Suppose that at the beginning of every month, two workers become unemployed and remain unemployed for one month before finding a new job. In addition, at the beginning of every year four workers become unemployed and remain unemployed for the entire year.

In this example there are twenty-eight spells of unemployment during a year: twenty-four spells that last one month, and four spells that last one year. Thus twenty-four of twenty-eight, or 86%, of the spells last only one month, which is consistent with the first statement: Most spells are short.

How many people are unemployed on a given day, say, on May 15? There are six unemployed workers on May 15: two unemployed workers who began one-month spells of unemployment on May 1, and four unemployed workers who began one-year spells of unemployment on January 1. Thus four of six, or 67%, of the workers unemployed on May 15 are experiencing one-year spells of unemployment, which is consistent with the second statement: Most people who are unemployed on a given date are experiencing long spells of unemployment.

Why There Always Are Unemployed People

Even when the economy is growing vigorously and many new jobs are being created, some people remain unemployed. Why is unemployment apparently a permanent feature of the economy? Here we discuss frictional unemployment and structural unemployment, two types of unemployment that always exist in the labor market and thus prevent the unemployment rate from ever reaching zero.

Frictional Unemployment. The labor market is characterized by a great deal of searching by both workers and firms. Unemployed workers search for suitable jobs, and firms with vacancies search for suitable workers. If all workers were identical and all jobs were identical, these searches would be short and easy: Unemployed workers would simply have to find firms that had vacancies and they would immediately be hired. The problem, of course, is that neither jobs nor workers are identical. Workers vary in their talents, skills, experience, goals, geographic location (and willingness to move), and in the amount of time and energy they are willing to commit to their job. Similarly, jobs vary in the skills and experience required, working conditions, location, hours, and pay. Because of these differences, an unemployed worker may search for several weeks or more before finding a suitable job; similarly, a firm may search for a considerable time before it is able to hire a suitable worker.

The unemployment that arises as workers search for suitable jobs and firms search for suitable workers is called **frictional unemployment.** Because the economy is dynamic, with jobs continually being created and destroyed and workers continually entering and exiting the labor force, there is always some frictional unemployment as workers are matched with appropriate jobs.

Structural Unemployment. In addition to those suffering long spells of unemployment, many people are chronically unemployed. Although their unemployment spells may be broken by brief periods of employment or being out of the labor force, workers who are **chronically unemployed** are unemployed a large part of the time. Long spells of unemployment and chronic unemployment can't be attributed primarily to the matching process. People in these situations don't seem to search for work very intensively and don't generally find stable employment. The long-term and chronic unemployment that exists even when the economy is not in a recession is called **structural unemployment.**

Structural unemployment occurs for two primary reasons. First, unskilled or low-skilled workers often are unable to obtain desirable, long-term jobs. The jobs available to them typically offer relatively low wages and little chance for training or advancement. Most directly related to the issue of structural unemployment is the fact that jobs held by low-skilled workers often don't last long. After a few months the job may end, or the worker may quit or be fired, thus entering another spell of unemployment. Some workers with low skill levels eventually get enough training or experience to obtain more secure, long-term jobs. Because of factors such as inadequate education, discrimination, and language barriers, however, some unskilled workers never make the transition to long-term employment and remain chronically unemployed.

The second source of structural unemployment is the reallocation of labor from industries that are shrinking, or regions that are depressed, to areas that are growing. When industries find that their product is no longer in demand (for example, buggy whip manufacturers) or that they are no longer competitive (for example, U.S. producers of color television sets who lost much of the market to the Japanese), workers in these industries lose their jobs. At the same time, some industries will be growing (for example, health care providers and computer software developers). To prevent unemployment from rising requires that workers who lose jobs in declining industries be matched somehow with jobs in growing industries. This matching may involve a long period of unemployment, especially if workers need to relocate or be trained for a new job.

The Natural Rate of Unemployment. Because of the combination of frictional and structural unemployment, an economy's unemployment rate is never zero, even when the economy is at its full-employment level. The rate of unemployment that prevails when output and employment are at the full-employment level is called the **natural rate of unemployment,** $\bar{u}$. The natural rate of unemployment reflects unemployment owing to frictional and structural causes. Although there is no single official measure of the natural rate of unemployment, many economists believe that the natural rate was in the range of 4–5% during the 1950s and increased gradually to about 6% in the 1980s. Chapter 13 discusses the reasons for the increase in the natural rate.

As output fluctuates around its full-employment level, the unemployment rate fluctuates around the natural rate. The difference between actual unemployment rate and the natural rate of unemployment is called **cyclical unemployment.** Specifically, cyclical unemployment = $u - \bar{u}$, where u is the actual unemployment rate and $\bar{u}$ is the natural rate. Cyclical unemployment is positive whenever the economy's output and employment are below full-employment levels; it is negative when output and employment exceed full-employment levels.

3.6 RELATING OUTPUT AND UNEMPLOYMENT: OKUN'S LAW

Earlier in this chapter we said that many short-run output fluctuations result from changes in employment. When employment falls and unemployment rises, the reduction in the number of people working leads to a decline in the quantity of goods and services produced. We can use the concept of cyclical unemployment to provide a more precise link between the state of the labor market and aggregate output.

The quantitative impact on aggregate output of a change in the unemployment rate is described by Okun's law, a rule of thumb (rather than a "law") first stated by Arthur Okun, chairman of the Council of Economic Advisers in the 1960s during the Johnson administration. According to **Okun's law,** the gap between an economy's full-employment output and its actual level of output increases by 2.5 percentage points for each percentage point the unemployment rate increases.[21, 22] We express Okun's law algebraically as

$$\frac{\bar{Y} - Y}{\bar{Y}} = 2.5(u - \bar{u}). \tag{3.5}$$

The left-hand side of Eq. (3.5) equals the amount by which actual output Y falls short of full-employment output $\bar{Y}$, expressed as a percentage of $\bar{Y}$. Thus Eq. (3.5) says that the percentage gap between potential and actual output equals 2.5 times the cyclical unemployment rate.

Let's apply Okun's law by supposing that the natural rate of unemployment is 6% and the full-employment level of output is \$6000 billion. If the actual unemployment rate is 7%, or 1 percentage point above the natural rate, cyclical unemployment, $u - \bar{u}$, equals 1%. If cyclical unemployment is 1%, Okun's law predicts that actual output Y will be 2.5% (2.5 times 1%) lower

21. When the unemployment rate increases (for example, from 6% to 9%), we say that it increases by 3 percentage points (9% – 6%), or that it increases by 50 percent (3% is 50 percent of 6%).

22. In Okun's original work ("Potential GNP: Its Measurement and Significance," reprinted in Arthur Okun, *The Political Economy of Prosperity*, Washington, D.C.: Brookings Institution, pp. 132–145), the "Okun's law coefficient" was 3.0 rather than 2.5, so each percentage point of cyclical unemployment was associated with a difference between actual output and full-employment output of 3.0 percentage points. Current estimates put the Okun's law coefficient closer to 2.5.

than full-employment output $\bar{Y}$. Because $\bar{Y}$ equals \$6000 billion, Okun's law says that actual output will be \$150 billion below the full-employment level (2.5% times \$6000 billion).

You may wonder why a 1 percentage point increase in the unemployment rate, which reduces employment by about 1% leads (according to Okun's law) to a drop in output that is about two and a half times as large in percentage terms. The reason is that when cyclical unemployment increases, other factors that determine output—the number of people in the labor force, the number of hours each worker works per week, the average productivity of labor—also fall, which magnifies the effect of the increase in unemployment. Numerical Problem 10 at the end of this chapter illustrates this point.

Sometimes we express Okun's law in a slightly different form:

$$\frac{\Delta Y}{Y} = \frac{\Delta \bar{Y}}{\bar{Y}} - 2.5\ \Delta u, \tag{3.6}$$

where $\Delta Y/Y$ is the percentage growth rate of output, $\Delta\bar{Y}/\bar{Y}$ is the percentage growth rate of full-employment output, and Δu is the change in the actual unemployment rate from one year to the next. Equation (3.6) says that when unemployment is rising ($\Delta u > 0$), actual output Y is growing more slowly than full-employment output $\bar{Y}$. Equation (3.6), which requires the assumption that the natural rate of unemployment is constant, is called the growth rate form of Okun's law. See Appendix 3.A at the end of this chapter for a derivation of Eq. (3.6).

Figure 3.15 illustrates the growth rate form of Okun's law. The figure shows the relation between the annual change in the unemployment rate

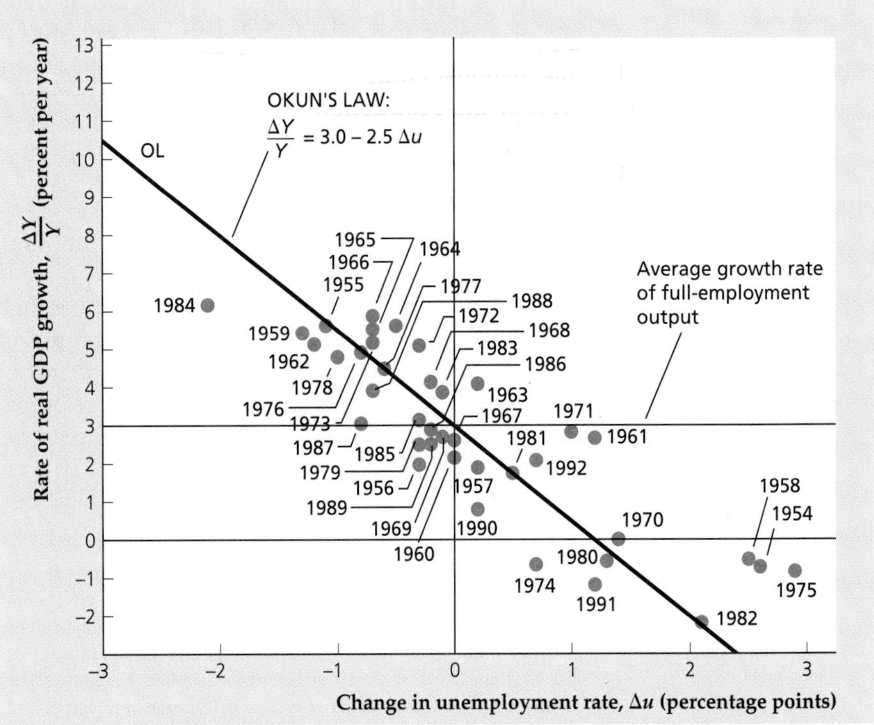

Figure 3.15
Okun's law in the United States: 1954–1992
This figure shows the relation between the growth rate of real GDP (vertical axis) and the change in the unemployment rate (horizontal axis). Line OL is a graph of Okun's law (Eq. 3.6). The slope of this line is −2.5, indicating that a 1 percentage point change in the unemployment rate changes the growth rate of output by 2.5 percentage points in the opposite direction. The horizontal line at 3% shows the approximate average growth rate of full-employment output, equaling the rate at which actual output would grow if there were no change in the unemployment rate ($\Delta u = 0$).

Source: Civilian unemployment rate from *Economic Report of the President*, 1993, Table B-37. GDP 1953–1958 from *National Income and Product Accounts of the United States*, Vol. 1, 1929–1958, U.S. Department of Commerce, February 1993, Table 1.2; GDP 1959–1991 from *Economic Report of the President*, 1993, Table B-2 (1992 GDP from *Survey of Current Business*, July 1993, Table 1.2).

(measured on the horizontal axis) and the annual growth rate of U.S. output (measured on the vertical axis) for the period 1954–1992. Line OL in this figure represents Okun's law. Its slope is –2.5, indicating that a 1 percentage point increase in the unemployment rate is associated with a 2.5% drop in output. The vertical line rising from 0 on the horizontal axis intersects OL at 3%. This intercept indicates that, when there's no change in the unemployment rate, the growth rate of actual output is 3%, or the approximate average growth rate of full-employment output in the United States.

CHAPTER SUMMARY

1. The production function tells us the amount of output that can be produced with any given quantities of capital and labor. The production function can be graphed as a relationship between output and capital, holding labor fixed, or as a relationship between output and labor, holding capital fixed. In either case the production function slopes upward, implying that greater use of capital or labor leads to more output. A shift in the production function, which indicates a change in the amount of output that can be produced with given amounts of capital and labor, is called a supply shock.

2. The extra output that can be produced when the capital stock is increased by one unit, with labor held constant, is called the marginal product of capital (*MPK*). In a graph of the production function relating output to capital, the *MPK* can be measured as the slope of the production function. The *MPK* falls as the capital stock increases, reflecting the diminishing marginal productivity of capital. Similarly, the marginal product of labor (*MPN*) is the extra output that can be produced when labor increases by one unit, with capital held constant. The *MPN*—which can be measured as the slope of the production function relating output to labor—falls as employment rises, indicating that labor also has diminishing marginal productivity.

3. To maximize profits, firms demand labor to the point that the marginal revenue product of labor (*MRPN*) equals the nominal wage, *W*; or, equivalently, to the point that the *MPN* equals the real wage, *w*.

4. The labor demand curve is identical to the *MPN* curve. Because an increase in the real wage causes firms to demand less labor, the labor demand curve slopes downward. Factors that increase the amount of labor demanded at any real wage, such as a beneficial supply shock or an increase in the capital stock, shift the labor demand curve to the right. Aggregate labor demand is the sum of the labor demands of firms in the economy.

5. An individual's decision about how much labor to supply reflects a trade-off between income and leisure. Labor is supplied to the point where the income received for working an extra hour just compensates the worker for giving up an extra hour of leisure.

6. The labor supply curve relates the amount of labor supplied to the current real wage. The labor supply curve slopes upward, indicating that an increase in the current real wage—with other factors, including the expected future real wage, held fixed—raises the amount of labor supplied. Factors that decrease the quantity of labor supplied at the current real wage, and thus shift the labor supply curve to the left, include an increase in wealth and an increase in the expected future real wage. Aggregate labor supply, which is the sum of labor supplies of the individuals in the economy, is also influenced by changes in the working-age population and social or legal factors that affect the number of people participating in the labor market.

7. The classical supply–demand model of the labor market is based on the assumption that the real wage adjusts relatively quickly to equalize the quantities of labor demanded and supplied. The equilibrium level of employment, which arises

when wages and prices in the economy have fully adjusted, is called the full-employment level of employment. Fluctuations in employment and the real wage are the result of factors that shift the labor supply curve and/or the labor demand curve.

8. Full-employment output, or potential output, is the amount of output produced when employment is at its full-employment level. Increases in the full-employment level of employment or beneficial supply shocks increase the full-employment level of output.

9. Working-age people without jobs are classified as unemployed if they looked for work during the preceding four weeks; they are classified as not in the labor force if they haven't been looking for work. The labor force consists of all employed workers plus all unemployed workers. The unemployment rate is the fraction of the labor force that is unemployed.

10. Frictional unemployment reflects the time required for potential workers to find suitable jobs and for firms with vacancies to find suitable workers. Structural unemployment—long-term and chronic unemployment that exists even when the economy isn't in recession—occurs because some workers don't have the skills needed to obtain long-term employment, or because of delays in reallocating workers from economically depressed areas to those that are growing. Frictional and structural unemployment together account for the natural rate of unemployment, which is the unemployment rate that exists when employment is at its full-employment level. Cyclical unemployment is the excess of the actual unemployment rate over the natural rate of unemployment.

11. According to Okun's law, a 1 percentage point increase in the rate of cyclical unemployment reduces output by 2.5 percentage points.

KEY DIAGRAM 1

The Production Function

The production function indicates how much output an economy or a firm can produce with any given quantities of capital and labor.

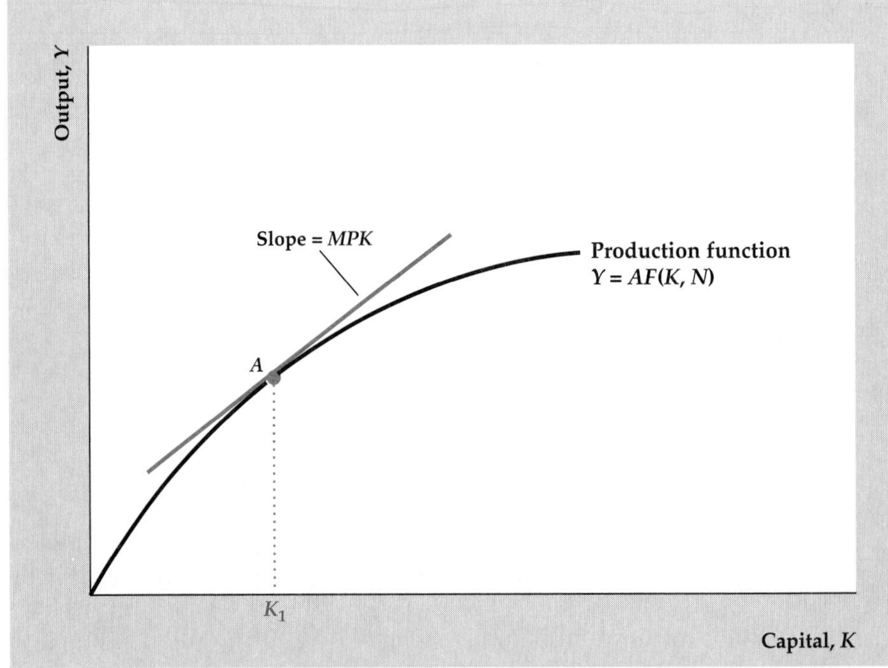

Diagram Elements

■ The production function graphed here has the amount of output produced, Y, on the vertical axis and the quantity of capital used, K, on the horizontal axis, with labor, N, held constant. It can also be drawn as a relationship between output and labor, with capital held constant. The production function relating output to labor looks like the graph shown here.

■ The equation for the production function is $Y = AF(K, N)$, where A (total factor productivity, or simply productivity) measures how effectively the economy uses capital and labor.

Analysis

■ The production function slopes upward, reflecting the fact that an increase in the quantity of capital will allow more output to be produced.

■ The production function becomes flatter from left to right, implying that the larger the capital stock already is, the less extra output is gained by adding another unit of capital. The fact that extra capital becomes less productive as the capital stock grows is called diminishing marginal productivity of capital.

■ With labor held constant, if an increase in capital of ΔK leads to an increase in output of ΔY, then $\Delta Y/\Delta K$ is called the marginal product of capital, or *MPK*. The *MPK* is measured graphically by the slope of the line tangent to the production function. For example, in the diagram the *MPK* when the capital stock is K_1 equals the slope of the line tangent to the production function at point A.

Factors that Shift the Curve

■ Any change that allows more output to be produced for given quantities of capital and labor—a beneficial supply shock—shifts the production function upward. Examples of beneficial supply shocks include new inventions and improved management techniques.

■ Any change that reduces the amount of output that can be produced for given quantities of capital and labor—an adverse supply shock—shifts the production function downward. Examples of adverse supply shocks include bad weather and the depletion of natural resources.

KEY DIAGRAM 2

The Labor Market

An economy's level of employment and the real wage are determined in the labor market.

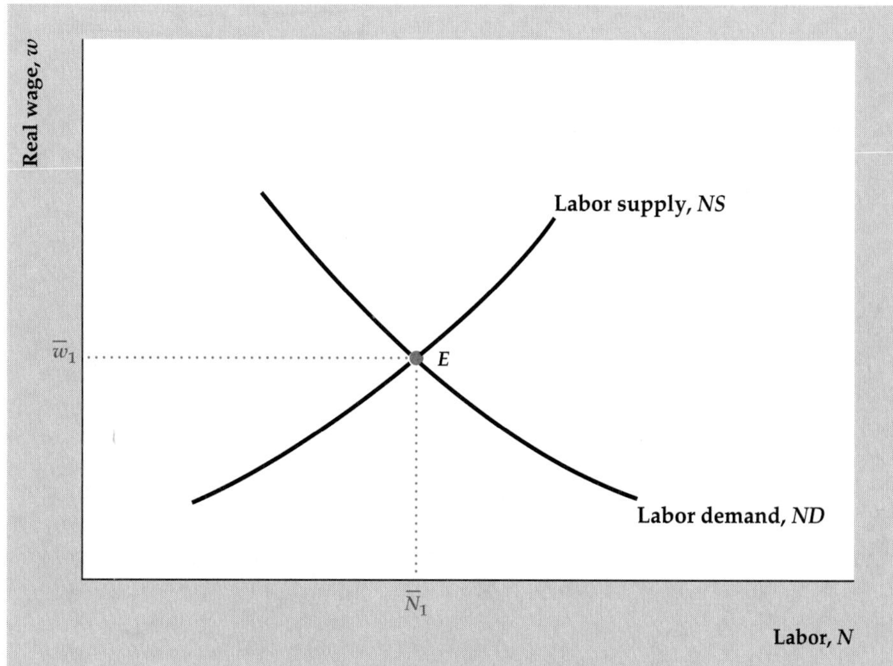

Diagram Elements

■ The current real wage, w, is on the vertical axis, and the level of employment, N, is on the horizontal axis. The variable N may also represent alternative measures of labor, such as total hours worked.

■ The labor demand curve, *ND*, shows the amount of labor that firms want to employ at each current real wage. The labor demand curve slopes downward because firms find hiring more labor profitable when the real wage falls. The labor demand curve for an individual firm is the same as the *MPN* curve, which shows the marginal product of labor at each level of employment.

■ The labor supply curve, *NS*, shows the amount of labor offered by workers at each current real wage. The labor supply curve slopes upward because an increase in the current real wage, with other factors held constant, increases the amount of labor supplied.

Analysis

■ Equilibrium in the labor market occurs when the quantity of labor demanded equals the quantity of labor supplied. In the figure equilibrium employment is N_1, and the equilibrium real wage is w_1. The equilibrium level of employment, which occurs after wages and prices have fully adjusted, is called the full-employment level of employment.

Factors that Shift the Curves

■ Any factor that increases the amount of labor demanded at a given current real wage shifts the labor demand curve to the right. Such factors include an increase in the marginal product of labor at any given level of employment and an increase in the capital stock. See Summary table 3.

■ Any factor that increases the amount of labor supplied at a given current real wage shifts the labor supply curve to the right. Such factors include a decline in wealth, a drop in the expected future real wage, a rise in the working-age population, and an increase in labor force participation. See Summary table 4.

Key Terms

aggregate demand for labor, p. 79
aggregate supply of labor, p. 80
chronically unemployed, p. 96
cyclical unemployment, p. 97
diminishing marginal productivity, p. 69
discouraged workers, p. 94
duration, p. 95
employment ratio, p. 93
factors of production, p. 64
frictional unemployment, p. 96
full-employment level of employment, p. 84
full-employment output, p. 86
labor force, p. 92
leisure, p. 80
marginal product of capital (*MPK*), p. 68
marginal product of labor (*MPN*), p. 70
marginal revenue product of labor (*MRPN*), p. 73
natural rate of unemployment, p. 96
Okun's law, p. 97
participation rate, p. 93
production function, p. 65
productivity, p. 63
real wage, p. 75
structural unemployment, p. 96
supply shock, p. 70
unemployment rate, p. 93
unemployment spell, p. 95

Key Equations

$$Y = AF(K, N) \tag{3.1}$$

The *production function* indicates how much output Y can be produced for given quantities of capital K and labor N and for a given level of total factor productivity A.

$$\bar{Y} = AF(K, \bar{N}) \tag{3.4}$$

Full-employment output $\bar{Y}$ is the quantity of output supplied by firms when wages and prices have fully adjusted, and employment equals its equilibrium value $\bar{N}$.

$$\frac{\bar{Y} - Y}{\bar{Y}} = 2.5(u - \bar{u}) \tag{3.5}$$

Okun's law states that a 1 percentage point increase in the unemployment rate u reduces output Y by 2.5% of the full-employment level of output $\bar{Y}$. When the unemployment rate equals the natural rate of unemployment $\bar{u}$, output equals its full-employment level.

$$\frac{\Delta Y}{Y} = \frac{\Delta \bar{Y}}{\bar{Y}} - 2.5\ \Delta u \qquad (3.6)$$

The growth rate form of Okun's law relates the growth rate of output $\Delta Y/Y$ to the growth rate of full-employment output $\Delta \bar{Y}/\bar{Y}$ and the change in the unemployment rate Δu. According to Eq. (3.6), output grows more slowly than full-employment output when unemployment is rising and more quickly than full-employment output when unemployment is falling. This version of Okun's law is based on the assumption that the natural rate of unemployment is constant.

Review Questions

1. What is a production function? What are some factors that can cause a nation's production function to shift over time? What do you have to know besides an economy's production function to know how much output the economy can produce?
2. The production function slopes upward, but its slope declines from left to right. Give an economic interpretation of each of these properties of the production function.
3. Define *marginal product of capital*, or *MPK*. How can the *MPK* be shown graphically?
4. Explain why the profit-maximizing level of employment for a firm occurs when the marginal revenue product of labor equals the nominal wage. How can this profit-maximizing condition be expressed in real terms?
5. What is the *MPN* curve? How is the *MPN* curve related to the production function? How is it related to labor demand?
6. What two variables are related by the aggregate labor supply curve? What are some factors that cause the aggregate labor supply curve to shift?
7. Define *full-employment output*. How is full-employment output affected by an increase in labor supply? By a beneficial supply shock?
8. Why is the classical model of the labor market discussed in this chapter not very useful for studying unemployment?
9. Define the following: *labor force, unemployment rate, participation rate,* and *employment ratio*.
10. Define *unemployment spell* and *duration*. What are the two seemingly contradictory facts about unemployment spells? Why are the two facts not actually contradictory?
11. What is frictional unemployment? Why is a certain amount of frictional unemployment probably necessary in a well-functioning economy?
12. What is structural unemployment? What are the two principal sources of structural unemployment?
13. Define the *natural rate of unemployment* and *cyclical unemployment*. What does negative cyclical unemployment mean?
14. What is Okun's law? If the unemployment rate increases by 2 percentage points between this year and next year, by how much will output change during the same period? Assume that the natural unemployment rate and full-employment output are constant.

Numerical Problems

1. The following data give real GDP, Y, capital, K, and labor, N, for the U.S. economy in various years.

Year	Y	K	N
1960	1971	1637	65.8
1970	2874	2544	78.7
1980	3776	3677	99.3
1990	4878	4773	117.9

Units and sources are the same as in Table 3.1. Assume that the production function is $Y = AK^{0.3}N^{0.7}$.

a. How much did U.S. total factor productivity grow between 1960 and 1970? Between 1970 and 1980? Between 1980 and 1990?

b. What happened to the marginal product of labor between 1960 and 1990? Calculate the marginal product numerically as the extra output gained by adding 1 million workers in each of the two years. (The data for employment, N, is measured in millions of workers, so an increase of one million workers is an increase of 1.0.)

2. An economy has the production function

$$Y = 0.2(K + \sqrt{N}).$$

In the current period $K = 100$ and $N = 100$.

a. Graph the relationship between output and capital, holding labor constant at its current value. What is the *MPK*? Does the marginal productivity of capital diminish?

b. Graph the relationship between output and labor, holding capital constant at its current value. Find the *MPN* for an increase of labor from 100 to 110. Compare this result with the *MPN* for an increase in labor from 110 to 120. Does the marginal productivity of labor diminish?

3. Acme Widget, Inc., has the following production function.

Number of Workers	Number of Widgets Produced
0	0
1	8
2	15
3	21
4	26
5	30
6	33

a. Find the *MPN* for each level of employment.
b. Acme can get $5 for each widget it produces. How many workers will it hire if the nominal wage is $38? If it is $27? If it is $22?
c. Graph the relationship between Acme's labor demand and the nominal wage. How does this graph differ from a labor demand curve? Graph Acme's labor demand curve.
d. With the nominal wage fixed at $38, the price of widgets doubles from $5 each to $10 each. What happens to Acme's labor demand and production?
e. With the nominal wage fixed at $38 and the price of widgets fixed at $5, the introduction of a new automatic widget maker doubles the number of widgets that the same number of workers can produce. What happens to labor demand and production?
f. What is the relationship between your answers to part (d) and part (e)? Explain.

4. The marginal product of labor (measured in units of output) for a certain firm is

$$MPN = A(100 - N),$$

where A measures productivity and N is the number of labor hours used in production. The price of output is $2.00 per unit.
a. If $A = 1.0$, what will be the demand for labor if the nominal wage is $10? If it is $20? Graph the demand curve for labor. What is the equilibrium real wage if the supply of labor is fixed at 95?
b. Repeat part (a) for $A = 2.0$.

5. For an economy the *MPN* is

$$MPN = 500 - 0.5N,$$

where N is aggregate employment. The aggregate quantity of labor supplied is $400 + 8(1 - t)w$, where w is the real wage and t is the income tax rate. The expression for labor supply reflects the fact that workers care about their after-tax real wage, $(1 - t)w$, rather than their before-tax real wage, w. Employers aren't taxed.
a. Find the before-tax real wage and employment when $t = 0.50$.
b. Find the before-tax real wage and employment when $t = 0.25$. Compare the result with that in part (a). Explain why the cut in the income tax rate has the effect that it does on the labor market.

6. In this problem you are to find the effects of a legal minimum wage on the labor income of unskilled workers. Assume that the marginal product of labor for unskilled labor is

$$MPN = 100 - 0.2N.$$

The supply of unskilled labor is $80 + 2w$, where w is the real wage received by unskilled labor.
a. If there is no minimum wage, find the equilibrium values of the real wage, employment, and labor income for unskilled workers.
b. Now suppose that a minimum wage that sets the real wage at 70 is instituted. What are the new levels of employment and total labor income for unskilled workers?
c. Repeat parts (a) and (b) for $MPN = 100 - 0.9N$. How does the imposition of a minimum real wage of 70 affect labor income now? How does the impact of a minimum wage on labor income depend on the sensitivity of labor demand to the real wage?

7. Consider an economy with 500 people in the labor force. At the beginning of every month 5 people lose their jobs and remain unemployed for exactly one month; one month later, they find new jobs and become employed. In addition, on January 1 of each year 20 people lose their jobs and remain unemployed for six months before finding new jobs. Finally, on July 1 of each year 20 people lose their jobs and remain unemployed for six months before finding new jobs.
a. What is the unemployment rate in this economy in a typical month?
b. What fraction of unemployment spells lasts for one month? What fraction lasts for six months?
c. What is the average duration of an unemployment spell?
d. On any particular date, what fraction of the unemployed are suffering a long spell (six months) of unemployment?

8. Use the data in Fig. 3.14 to calculate how many people become unemployed during a typical month. How many become employed? How many leave the labor force?

9. You are given the following data on the unemployment rate and output.

Year	1	2	3	4
Unemployment rate	8%	6%	7%	5%
Output	950	1030	1033.5	1127.5

a. Assume that the natural rate of unemployment is 6% and that $(\bar{Y} - Y)/\bar{Y} = 2.5(u - \bar{u})$. Find the full-employment level of output in each year.

b. Calculate the growth rate of full-employment output in years 2, 3, and 4 two different ways. First, calculate the growth rates by using the values for full-employment output that you found in part (a). Then calculate the growth rate of full-employment output by using only the change in the unemployment rate, the growth rate of output, and the growth rate version of Okun's law, Eq. (3.6). Compare your answers from the two sets of calculations.

10. Consider an economy that initially has a labor force of 2000 workers. Of these workers, 1900 are employed and each works 40 hours per week. Ten units of output are produced by each hour of labor.

a. What is the total number of hours worked per week in the economy? What is the total output per week in the economy?

b. The economy enters a recession. Employment falls by 4%, and the number of hours per week worked by each employed worker falls by 2.5%. In addition, 0.2% of the labor force becomes discouraged at the prospect of finding a job and leaves the labor force. Finally, suppose that whenever total hours fall by 1%, total output falls by 1.4%.

After the recession begins, what is the size of the labor force? How many workers are unemployed and what is the unemployment rate? What is the total output per week in the economy?

By what percentage has total output fallen relative to the initial situation? What is the value of the Okun's law coefficient relating the loss of output to the increase in the unemployment rate?

Analytical Problems

1. a. A technological breakthrough raises a country's total factor productivity A by 10%. Show how this change affects the graphs of both the production function relating output to capital and the production function relating output to labor.

b. Show that a 10% increase in A also increases the MPK and the MPN by 10% at any level of capital and labor. (*Hint:* What happens to ΔY for any increase in capital ΔK or for any increase in labor ΔN?)

c. Can a beneficial supply shock leave the MPK and MPN unaffected? Show graphically.

2. How would each of the following affect the current level of full-employment output? Explain.

a. A large number of immigrants enter the country.

b. Energy supplies become depleted.

c. New teaching techniques improve the educational performance of high school seniors.

d. A new law mandates the shutdown of some unsafe forms of capital.

3. During the 1980s the average rate of unemployment in Europe was high. Some economists claimed that this rate was in part the result of "real-wage rigidity," a situation in which unions kept real wages above their market-clearing levels.

a. Accepting for the sake of argument that real wages were too high in Europe in the 1980s, show how this would lead to unemployment (a situation where people who would like to work at the going wage cannot find jobs).

b. What is the effect of real-wage rigidity on the output actually supplied by firms, relative to the output they would supply if there were no real-wage rigidity?

4. How would each of the following affect Helena Handbasket's supply of labor?

a. The value of Helena's home triples in an unexpectedly hot real estate market.

b. Originally an unskilled worker, Helena acquires skills that give her access to a higher-paying job. Assume that her preferences about leisure are not affected by the change in jobs.

c. A temporary income tax surcharge raises the percentage of her income that she must pay in taxes, for the current year only. (Taxes are proportional to income in Helena's country.)

5. Suppose that under a new law all businesses must pay a tax equal to 6% of their sales revenue. Assume that this tax is not passed on to consumers. Instead, consumers pay the same prices after the tax is imposed as they did before. What is the effect of this tax on labor demand? If the labor supply curve is unchanged, what will be the effect of the tax on employment and the real wage?

6. Can the unemployment rate and the employment ratio rise during the same month? Can the participation rate fall at the same time that the employment ratio rises? Explain.

APPENDIX 3.A THE GROWTH RATE FORM OF OKUN'S LAW

To derive the growth rate form of Okun's law, Eq. (3.6), we start with the basic form of Okun's law, Eq. (3.5):

$$\frac{\bar{Y} - Y}{\bar{Y}} = 2.5(u - \bar{u}). \tag{3.5}$$

After multiplying by −1, we rewrite Eq. (3.5) as

$$-1 + \frac{Y}{\bar{Y}} = -2.5u + 2.5\bar{u}.$$

We now calculate the change from the previous year to the current year for each side of this equation. Setting the change on the left-hand side equal to the change on the right-hand side, and assuming that $\bar{u}$ is constant (so that $\Delta\bar{u} = 0$), we get

$$\Delta(Y/\bar{Y}) = -2.5\,\Delta u.$$

The left-hand side of this equation, which is the change in $Y/\bar{Y}$, is very close to the growth rate of $Y/\bar{Y}$, which is $\Delta(Y/\bar{Y})/(Y/\bar{Y})$. (To go from the change to the growth rate, we divide by $Y/\bar{Y}$, which is a number close to 1.) Approximating the change in $Y/\bar{Y}$ by the growth rate, and using the formula that states that the growth rate of a ratio is the growth rate of the numerator minus the growth rate of the denominator (Appendix A, Section A.7), we rewrite the equation once more as

$$\frac{\Delta Y}{Y} - \frac{\Delta\bar{Y}}{\bar{Y}} = -2.5\,\Delta u.$$

Rearranging this equation gives the growth rate form of Okun's law, Eq. (3.6).

CHAPTER 4

CONSUMPTION, SAVING, AND INVESTMENT

Chapter 3 focused on some of the factors determining the amount of output produced, or *supplied,* in the economy. This chapter considers the factors that underlie the economywide *demand* for goods and services. In other words, we move from examining how much is produced to examining how that production is used.

Recall from Chapter 2 that aggregate demand (spending) in the economy has four components: the demand for consumer goods and services by households (consumption), the demand for new capital goods by firms (investment), government purchases of goods and services, and the net demand for domestic goods by foreigners (net exports). Because the level of government purchases is determined primarily by the political process, macroeconomic analysis usually treats that component of spending as given. For this chapter we also assume that the economy is closed so that net exports are zero (we drop the closed-economy assumption in Chapter 5). That leaves two major components of spending—consumption and investment—to be discussed in this chapter. Section 4.1 presents the factors that determine how much households choose to consume, and Section 4.2 looks at the decision by firms about how much to invest.

We have said that this chapter is about the aggregate demand for goods and services. However, we could just as easily say that it is about a seemingly very different (but equally important) topic: the determination of saving and capital formation. Studying the aggregate demand for goods and services is the same as studying the factors that determine saving and capital formation for the following reasons: First, saving is simply what is left after an economic unit (say, a household) decides how much of its income to consume. Thus the decision about how much to consume is the same as the decision about how much to save. Second, investment spending is part of the aggregate demand for goods and services, but it also represents the acquisition of new capital goods by firms; and so, in studying investment spending, we are also looking at the factors that lead an economy to acquire new factories, machines, and housing. In effect, we do two things at once in this chapter:

- We explore the determinants of the aggregate demand for goods, which prepares you for future discussions of topics such as the role of spending fluctuations in business cycles.
- While exploring aggregate demand we also examine the factors affecting saving and capital formation, which prepares you for future discussions of the sources of economic growth and other issues.

In making many economic decisions, including those we consider in this chapter, people must trade off the present against the future. In deciding how much to consume and save, for example, a household must weigh the benefits of enjoying more consumption today against the benefits of putting aside some of its income as saving for the future. Similarly, in deciding how much to invest, a firm's manager must determine how much to spend today in order to increase the firm's productive capacity one, five, or even twenty years from now. In making these trade-offs, households and firms must take into account their expectations about the future of the economy, including expectations about government policy.

In Chapter 3 we asked, What forces act to bring the labor market into equilibrium? We close this chapter by asking the same question for the goods market. The goods market is in equilibrium when the quantity of goods and services that producers want to supply (discussed in Chapter 3) equals the quantity of goods and services demanded by households, firms, and the government (discussed in this chapter). Equivalently, the goods market is in equilibrium when desired saving in the economy equals desired investment. We show that the real interest rate plays a key role in bringing the goods market into equilibrium.

4.1 CONSUMPTION AND SAVING

We begin consideration of the demand for goods and services by discussing the factors that affect consumer spending. Because consumption spending by households is by far the largest component of the demand for goods and services—accounting for about two thirds of total spending—changes in consumers' willingness to spend have major implications for the behavior of the economy.

Besides the sheer size of consumption spending, another reason to study consumption is that the individual's or household's decision about how much to consume is closely linked to another important economic decision, the decision about how much to save. Indeed, for given levels of disposable income, the decision about how much to consume and the decision about how much to save are really the same decision. For example, a college student with a part-time job that pays $4000 per year after taxes might decide to spend $3700 per year on clothes, food, entertainment, and other consumption. If she does consume this amount, her saving will automatically be $300 ($4000 minus $3700) per year. Equivalently, she might decide to save $300 per year. If she succeeds in saving $300, her consumption automatically is $3700 ($4000 minus $300) per year. Because the decision about how much to consume and the decision about how much to save actually are two sides of the same coin, we analyze them together.

What determines how much of their current income people choose to consume and how much they choose to save? An important insight is that, in making their economic decisions, most people think about the future as well as the present. They save part of their current income—instead of immediately spending everything they receive—because they care not only about the consumption they get to enjoy today but also about the consumption they hope to enjoy next week, next year, and when they retire. By limiting their current consumption and saving more, people hope to improve their standard of living in the future. Thus consumers face a trade-off between the present and the future: greater current consumption means less saving and (all else being equal) less consumption in the future.

Recognizing that people save now primarily to consume in the future, we can identify the major factors determining current consumption and saving. Here we describe these factors in general terms. We present a more detailed analysis based on a formal model of household decision making in Chapter 8.

Current Income

If you received a one-time bonus at work that raised your current income by \$3000, what would you do with it? Probably you would spend part of the extra income on consumption goods, perhaps a vacation or a new CD player. You might save the rest—for example, by increasing the balance in your bank account or paying off some debts (a form of saving, because it reduces your liabilities and therefore increases your wealth). Thus the increase in your current income would raise both your total consumption and your total saving.

This response to an increase in current income makes good economic sense: When a person's current income rises, that person feels better off and will thus want to consume more today. But one benefit of a rise in current income is that, in addition to enjoying more consumption today, an individual also can plan for greater future consumption by saving part of the current increase in income. Thus *both consumption and saving should rise when current income rises.* Note that the increases in consumption and in saving must sum to the increase in income, so each separately is less than the increase in income.

The same argument works in reverse if current income falls. Because a decline in income makes an individual worse off, that person will respond both by consuming less today and putting less aside for future consumption. In response to a decline in current income, therefore, both consumption and saving will fall (although each separately must fall by less than income does).

To demonstrate what these observations about individual behavior imply about consumption and saving at the macroeconomic level, we first have to define two terms: desired consumption and desired national saving.

- *Desired consumption*, C^d, is the aggregate quantity of goods and services that households want to consume, given income and other factors affecting households' economic opportunities.
- *Desired national saving*, S^d, is the level of national saving that occurs when consumption is at its desired level.

Recall from Chapter 2 that, if net factor payments from abroad (NFP) equal zero (as must be true in a closed economy), national saving S equals $Y - C - G$ (Eq. 2.8), where Y is output, C is consumption, and G is government purchases. Because desired national saving S^d is the level of national saving S that occurs when consumption equals the desired level, we obtain an expression for desired national saving by substituting desired consumption C^d for consumption C in the definition of national saving. This substitution yields

$$S^d = Y - C^d - G. \tag{4.1}$$

We use Eq. (4.1), which defines desired national saving, to look at the effects of an increase in current income at the aggregate level. In macroeconomic terms, a rise in current income corresponds to an increase in total output Y. Our preceding discussion of the effect of current income on an individual's consumption and saving suggests that, when current output Y rises, desired current consumption C^d also rises, but not by as much as the increase in output. Desired consumption rises less than output increases, so desired national saving $Y - C^d - G$ also must rise when output rises.

The relationship between desired consumption C^d and aggregate output Y is sometimes expressed as

$$C^d = c_0 + c_Y Y, \tag{4.2}$$

where c_0 and c_Y are constants. Equation (4.2) simply says that desired consumption depends on current aggregate output. This relationship is called the **Keynesian consumption function** because Keynes wrote about it in his *General Theory.* The parameter c_Y is called the marginal propensity to consume. The **marginal propensity to consume,** or *MPC,* is the amount by which desired consumption rises when current output rises by one unit. Because an increase in current output causes desired consumption to rise, but by less than the increase in output, the *MPC* lies between 0 and 1.

The Keynesian consumption function is useful for building simple models of the economy, but it leaves out some important factors besides current output that affect desired consumption. We look at some of these additional influences on consumption next.

Expected Future Income

Suppose that, instead of receiving the $3000 bonus in your current paycheck, you are told that you will receive the bonus next year. This bonus is legally guaranteed and you have no doubt that you will receive it as promised. What will happen to your current (this year's) consumption and saving? Most likely, *the increase in expected future income will cause your current consumption to rise and your current saving to fall.* Because you know that you will receive the bonus next year, you have less need to save for the future and can enjoy more current consumption instead. Similarly, a drop in expected future income—for example, you learn that your employer is going out of business, which will cost you your job—should make you want to save more and consume less today.

In macroeconomic terms, a rise in expected future income or output raises today's desired consumption C^d. If we assume that today's output Y is unchanged, an increase in C^d will lower desired national saving $Y - C^d - G$.

Economists can't measure expected future income directly, so how do they take this variable into account when predicting consumption and saving behavior? As the following application discusses, one approach is to survey consumers and ask them about their expectations.

Application

Consumer Sentiment and the 1990–1991 Recession

The theory of consumer behavior tells us that consumers' decisions on how much to consume and how much to save should depend on their expectations about the economy's future. When consumers are generally optimistic about the future, they consume more and save less than when they are pessimistic about it. Thus economic forecasters and other analysts may find it useful to know what consumers are thinking about the future at any particular time.

Various surveys regularly try to measure consumers' expectations. Two of the best known are that of the Conference Board, which summarizes its results in a "consumer confidence index," and that of the Survey Research Center at the University of Michigan, which publishes an "index of consumer sentiment." In this application we focus on the index of consumer sentiment.

The Survey Research Center has reported its index of consumer sentiment monthly since 1946. The index is based on the responses of about five hundred households to questions about their own current and future expected financial situation and about what they think the economy will do in the next one to five years. The index is measured relative to a value of 100 for 1966, with higher values corresponding to greater consumer optimism. The Survey Research Center publishes the index in a detailed monthly report called *Surveys of Consumer Attitudes.* It is also available in the press and in the *Survey of Current Business.*

Historically, the index has been a sensitive indicator of recessions and other macroeconomic shocks. Figure 4.1(a), on the next page, shows monthly data for the index of consumer sentiment for the six-year period March 1987–March 1993, and Fig. 4.1(b), also on the next page, shows quarterly real consumption data for the same period. Note that the stock market crash of October 1987 caused a drop in the index of consumer sentiment, but one that quickly reversed. At the same time, real consumption fell slightly.

When Iraq invaded Kuwait in August 1990, the index of consumer sentiment took its sharpest decline ever, reflecting consumers' fears about the long-term implications of the invasion and perhaps broader economic worries as well. As Fig. 4.1(b) shows, consumer spending also dropped sharply in the fourth quarter of 1990 as a recession began.

As Fig. 4.1 indicates, the index of consumer sentiment was volatile during 1991, soaring in March after the Gulf War, then falling later in the year. In 1992 the index of consumer sentiment dropped in each of the four months preceding the presidential election, perhaps reflecting the economic concerns of voters that led them to vote President Bush out of office. The index of consumer sentiment strengthened sharply at about the time of the election but fell again in the spring of 1993. Reflecting this consumer pessimism and uncertainty, growth in real consumption spending was slow and erratic during the uneven economic recovery that began in March 1991.

Wealth

Another factor that affects consumption and saving is the stock of wealth. Recall from Chapter 2 that the wealth of any entity, such as a household or an entire nation, equals its assets minus its liabilities.

To see the effect of wealth on consumption and saving, imagine that you learn that your old baseball card collection (which you had always thought to be of no value) is worth $3000. You sell the collection and deposit the money

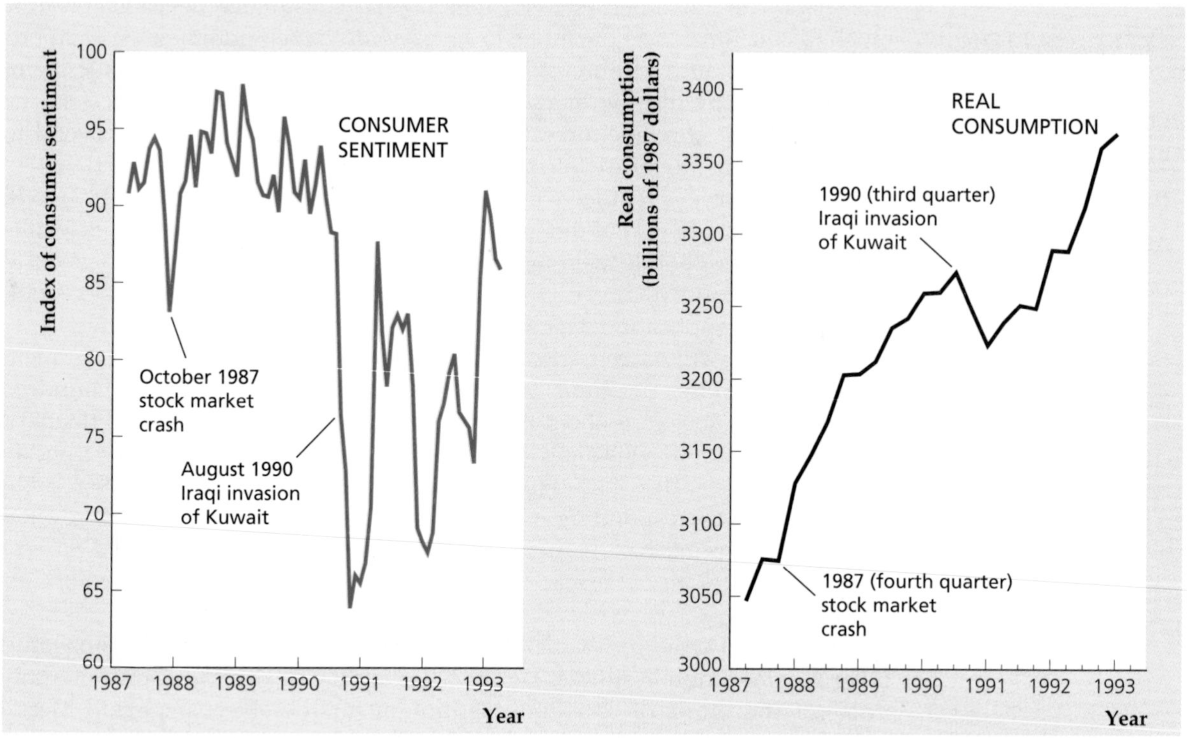

Figure 4.1(a)
The index of consumer sentiment, March 1987–March 1993
The index of consumer sentiment is based on what consumers tell interviewers about their expectations for the future of the economy. The index of consumer sentiment dipped after the October 1987 stock market crash, then fell sharply after the August 1990 Iraqi invasion of Kuwait. The index was volatile during 1991 and 1992.

Source: ***Survey of Current Business and Business Conditions Digest***, various issues. The index of consumer sentiment is a copyrighted series published by the Surveys of Consumers, Survey Research Center, University of Michigan.

Figure 4.1(b)
Consumption, second quarter 1987 to first quarter 1993
The figure shows real consumption expenditures from the second quarter of 1987 through the first quarter of 1993. Consumption declined slightly after the stock market crash of 1987 and then fell sharply along with the index of consumer sentiment after the 1990–1991 recession began in the third quarter of 1990. Consumption growth was erratic during the uneven recovery that began in March 1991.

Source: ***Survey of Current Business***, various issues.

in your bank account. How does this \$3000 increase in wealth affect your economic behavior? In terms of your economic well-being, receiving this unexpected windfall of \$3000 is effectively the same as receiving a \$3000 bonus at work; as when you received the bonus at work, you would probably use some of the \$3000 to increase current consumption. What about saving? Because your current income hasn't changed,[1] the increase in current consumption nec-

1. An increase in the value of assets that you own, such as the baseball card collection, is an increase in wealth but is not counted as an increase in income. Analogously, for the economy as a whole, an increase in stock prices raises national wealth but the increase in stock values is not counted as part of income.

essarily implies that your saving is lower. Generally, when wealth increases there is less need to save for the future out of current income. Hence *an increase in wealth raises current consumption and lowers current saving.*

In macroeconomic terms, the results are analogous: An increase in aggregate wealth increases desired consumption C^d. However, if we assume that current output Y is unchanged by the increase in wealth, the increase in wealth reduces desired national saving $Y - C^d - G$. Similarly, if wealth decreases, desired consumption will fall and desired national saving will rise. The next application illustrates the effects of a change in wealth on consumer behavior.

APPLICATION

The 1987 Stock Market Crash and Consumer Spending

On October 19, 1987, stock prices took their biggest ever one-day plunge. The Standard and Poor's index of 500 stocks fell 20%, coming on top of an overall decline of 16% since the market's peak in August. Although estimates differ, apparently about $1 trillion of financial wealth (equal in value to nearly three months of GDP) was eliminated through declining stock values on October 19 alone.

According to economic theory, how should a stock market crash affect consumers' spending? There are two possible channels.

First, the crash reduced households' wealth, which should have reduced consumption. According to theory, however, the effect on current consumption should have been much smaller than the $1 trillion reduction in wealth; the reason is that consumers would be expected to spread the effects of their losses in wealth over a long period of time, reducing the consumption they had planned for future years as well as current consumption. We can get a quick estimate of the effect of a $1 trillion drop in stock values on current consumption by supposing that consumers spread their reduction in consumption over twenty-five years. Also, for simplicity, let's assume that the real interest rate is zero.[2] Hence, in response to a $1 trillion loss in wealth, consumers would plan to reduce their consumption in each of the next twenty-five years by 1/25 of $1 trillion, or $40 billion per year. This number is consistent with an estimate presented in the 1988 *Economic Report of the President* (p. 42) of the likely effects of the stock market crash on current consumption. To the extent that current income was unaffected by the crash, saving would have to rise by the same amount that consumption falls.

The second way a crash could affect consumption is that it might lead consumers to expect bad economic times ahead and falling future incomes. As discussed previously, a reduction in expected future income tends to reduce current consumption and raise current saving. Surveys of consumer attitudes did find significant declines in consumer confidence about the future in the months following the crash (see the preceding application, "Consumer Sentiment and the 1990–1991 Recession"). This effect appeared to be temporary, however; by early 1988, consumer confidence had recovered completely (see Fig. 4.1a).

What, then, was the actual effect of the October 19 crash on consumption? Consumption behavior is affected by many factors, and isolating the influence

2. If the real interest rate were positive, in calculating the effect on consumption we would have to take into account the interest that the lost $1 trillion would have earned in future years.

of any single factor isn't easy. However, C. Alan Garner[3] of the Kansas City Federal Reserve Bank estimated that the crash led to a \$7.5–10 billion shortfall in consumption between October 1987 and January 1988, or \$30–40 billion at an annual rate. (The weakness of consumption in the fourth quarter of 1987 is apparent in Fig. 4.1b.) Garner's estimates are reasonably close to the direct impact of the change in wealth on consumption that we calculated, but they leave no room for an impact on expected future incomes. David Runkle[4] of the Minneapolis Federal Reserve Bank argued that the overall effect of the crash on the economy was surprisingly small, probably less than the \$40 billion predicted.

The theory was correct, then, in predicting that the loss of financial wealth in the crash should reduce consumption and increase saving, but the effects on consumption and saving appeared to be even smaller than the small effect predicted by the theory. Why? One possible explanation is connected with the unusually erratic behavior of stock prices during 1987. The tremendous decline in stock prices after August mirrored equally impressive gains earlier in the year—39% between December 31, 1986, and August 25, 1987. Because the earlier increase of stock prices was so rapid, it is possible that by August 1987 stockholders had not yet fully adjusted their consumption and saving behavior to their higher level of wealth. Thus when the market fell, consumption did not have to decline by very much in order to fall back into line with wealth.

The Expected Real Interest Rate

An important aspect of saving is that the funds people put aside usually earn interest or some other form of return. We showed in Chapter 2 that the rate at which the real value of a financial investment is expected to grow over time is the expected real interest rate, or the nominal interest rate minus the expected rate of inflation.

Suppose that the real interest rate that people expect to earn on their saving increases. How will this higher real interest rate affect the amount of saving that people do (and hence the amount that they consume)?

Economists have pointed out that a higher real interest rate affects people's incentive to save in two opposite ways. On the one hand, a higher real interest rate means that saving today will have a larger payoff in the future, in terms of the goods and services the accumulated saving will be able to buy. This greater future reward for saving tends to make people more eager to save when the real interest rate rises.

On the other hand, a higher real interest rate means that less saving has to be done today to achieve any future savings target. Consider the doting parents of a young genius who know that they have to accumulate \$100,000 (in 1994 dollars) by the year 2005 to pay college tuition. The higher the real interest rate, the faster their savings will grow and the less they will have to put aside each month to achieve their long-run goal. Thus to the extent that some people are "target savers," a higher real interest rate will depress saving.

3. "Has the Stock Market Crash Reduced Consumer Spending?" *Economic Review,* Federal Reserve Bank of Kansas City, April 1988, pp. 3–16. Some of the other information in this application is also taken from this article.

4. "Why No Crunch from the Crash?" *Quarterly Review,* Federal Reserve Bank of Minneapolis, Winter 1988, pp. 2–7. Interestingly, when the Japanese stock market fell sharply in early 1990, the effect on consumption again appeared to be quite small.

Economic theory doesn't indicate whether the positive or the negative effect on saving of a higher real interest rate is the stronger, so we must rely on empirical studies (studies that examine this relationship by using actual data). Unfortunately, interpretation of the empirical evidence from the many studies done is still disputed. The most widely accepted conclusion seems to be that an increase in the real interest rate reduces consumption and increases saving but that this effect isn't very strong.

Taxes and the Real Return to Saving. In discussing the real return that savers earn, we have not yet mentioned an important practical consideration: Interest earnings (and other returns on savings) are taxed. Because part of interest earnings must be paid as taxes, the real return earned by savers is actually less than the difference between the nominal interest rate and expected inflation.

A useful measure of the returns received by savers that recognizes the effects of taxes is the *expected after-tax real interest rate*. To define this concept, we let i represent the nominal interest rate and t the rate at which interest income is taxed. In the United States, for example, most interest earnings are taxed as ordinary income, so t is the income tax rate. Savers retain a fraction $(1 - t)$ of total interest earned so that the after-tax *nominal* interest rate, received by savers after payment of taxes, is $(1 - t)i$. The **expected after-tax real interest rate,** $r_{a\text{-}t}$, is the after-tax nominal interest rate minus the expected inflation rate π^e, or

$$r_{a\text{-}t} = (1 - t)i - \pi^e. \tag{4.3}$$

The expected after-tax real interest rate is the appropriate interest rate for consumers to use in making consumption and saving decisions because it measures the increase in the purchasing power of their saving after payment of taxes.

Table 4.1 shows how to calculate the after-tax nominal interest rate and the expected after-tax real interest rate. Note that, given the nominal interest rate and expected inflation, a reduction in the tax rate on interest income increases

Table 4.1 Calculating After-Tax Interest Rates

i = nominal interest rate = 5% per year
π^e = expected inflation rate = 2% per year

Example 1
t = tax rate on interest income = 30%
After-tax nominal interest rate = $(1 - t)i = (1 - 0.30)5\% = 3.5\%$
Expected after-tax real interest rate = $(1 - t)i - \pi^e = (1 - 0.30)5\% - 2\% = 1.5\%$

Example 2
t = tax rate on interest income = 20%
After-tax nominal interest rate = $(1 - t)i = (1 - 0.20)5\% = 4\%$
Expected after-tax real interest rate = $(1 - t)i - \pi^e = (1 - 0.20)5\% - 2\% = 2\%$

IN TOUCH *WITH THE MACROECONOMY*

INTEREST RATES

Although in our theoretical discussions we refer to "the" interest rate, as if there were only one, actually there are many different interest rates, each of which depends on the identity of the borrower and the terms of the loan. Shown here are some interest rates that appeared in the daily "Key Rates" box in the business section of the *New York Times* on July 7, 1993.

	CURRENT	YEAR EARLIER
Prime rate	6.00%	6.50%
Federal funds	3.06	3.15
3-month Treasury bills	2.96	3.23
6-month Treasury bills	3.11	3.32
7-year Treasury notes	5.43	6.43
30-year Treasury bonds	6.68	7.61
Municipal bonds	5.72	6.39

The prime rate is the basic rate that banks charge on loans to their best customers. The Federal funds rate is the rate at which banks make overnight loans to each other. Treasury bills, notes, and bonds are debts of the U.S. government, and municipal bonds are obligations of state and local governments. With the exception of the prime rate, these interest rates vary continuously as financial market conditions change. The prime rate is an average of lending rates set by major banks and changes less frequently.

The interest rates charged on these different types of loans need not be the same. One reason for this variation is differences in the risk of nonrepayment, or default. Federal government debt is believed to be free from default risk, but there is always a chance that a business, bank, or municipality may not be able to repay what it borrowed. Lenders charge risky borrowers extra interest to compensate themselves for the risk of default. Thus the prime rate, the Federal funds rate, and the municipal bond rate are higher than they would be if there were no default risk.

A second factor affecting interest rates is the length of time for which the funds are borrowed. Comparing the different Treasury obligations, you can see that generally (although not always) lenders charge a higher interest rate on long-term loans than on short-term loans. Thus the interest rate on Treasury bills repayable in three months or six months was about 3% (annual rate) at that time, the interest rate on seven-year loans to the government was more than 5%, and the interest rate on thirty-year loans to the government was well above 6% per year. The Federal funds rate, the rate on overnight loans between banks, is one of the lowest of the interest rates in the list, even though this rate reflects some default risk.

A final factor affecting interest rates is tax status. Interest on municipal bonds is not taxable, which is the primary reason that lenders are willing to accept relatively low rates on these loans.

Although the levels of the various interest rates are quite different, interest rates tend to go up and down together. For example, all the interest rates in the list had fallen from a year earlier (although by different amounts). Because interest rates tend to move together, it is reasonable to talk about a change in "the" interest rate in our economic analyses.

the nominal and real after-tax rates of return that a saver receives. Thus, by reducing the rate at which it taxes interest, the government can increase the real rate of return earned by savers and (possibly) increase the rate of saving in the economy. The stimulation of saving is the motivation for tax provisions such as Individual Retirement Accounts (IRAs), which allow savers to shelter part of their interest earnings from taxes and thus earn higher after-tax rates of return. Unfortunately, because economists disagree about the effect of higher real interest rates on saving, the effectiveness of IRAs and similar tax breaks for saving also is in dispute.

Fiscal Policy

We've just demonstrated how government tax policies can affect the real return earned by savers and thus, perhaps, the saving rate. However, even when government fiscal policies—its decisions about spending and taxes—aren't intentionally directed at affecting the saving rate, these policies have important implications for the amount of consumption and saving that takes place in the economy. Although understanding the links between fiscal policy and consumer behavior requires some difficult economic reasoning, these links are so important that we introduce them here. We discuss several of these issues further in this book, particularly in Chapters 8 and 16.

To make the discussion of fiscal policy effects as straightforward as possible, we take the economy's aggregate output Y as a given. That is, we ignore the possibility that the changes in fiscal policy that we consider affect the aggregate supply of goods and services. This assumption is valid if the economy is at full employment (as we are assuming throughout Part II of this book) and if the fiscal policy changes don't significantly affect the capital stock or labor supply. Later we relax the fixed-output assumption and discuss both the classical and Keynesian views about how fiscal policy changes can affect output.

In general, fiscal policy affects *desired consumption* C^d primarily by affecting households' current and expected future incomes. More specifically, fiscal changes that increase the tax burden on the private sector, either by raising current taxes or by leading people to expect that taxes will be higher in the future, will cause people to consume less.

For a given level of output Y, government fiscal policies affect *desired national saving* S^d, or $Y - C^d - G$, in two basic ways. First, as we just noted, fiscal policy can influence desired consumption: For any levels of output Y and government purchases G, a fiscal policy change that reduces desired consumption C^d by one dollar will at the same time raise desired national saving S^d by one dollar. Second, for any levels of output and desired consumption, increases in government purchases directly lower desired national saving, as is apparent from the definition of desired national saving, $S^d = Y - C^d - G$.

To illustrate these general points, we consider how desired consumption and desired national saving would be affected by two specific fiscal policy changes: an increase in government purchases and a tax cut.

Government Purchases. Suppose that current government purchases G increase by \$10 billion, say, because the government increases military spending. Assume that this increase in G is temporary so that plans for future government purchases are unchanged. (Analytical Problem 5 at the end of this chapter looks at the case of a permanent increase in government purchases.) For any level of output Y, how will this change in fiscal policy affect desired consumption and desired national saving in the economy?

Let's start by finding the effect of the increased government purchases on consumption. As already mentioned, changes in government purchases affect consumption because they affect private sector tax burdens. Suppose for example that the government pays for the extra \$10 billion in military spending by raising current taxes by \$10 billion. For given total (before-tax) output Y, this tax increase implies a \$10 billion decline in consumers' current (after-tax) incomes. We know that consumers respond to a decline in their current incomes by reducing consumption, although by less than the decline in current income.[5] So, in response to the $10 billion tax increase, consumers might reduce their current consumption by $6 billion.

What happens to consumption if the government doesn't raise current taxes when it increases its purchases? The analysis in this case is more subtle. If the government doesn't raise current taxes, it will have to borrow the $10 billion to pay for the extra spending. The government will have to repay the $10 billion it borrows, plus interest, sometime in the future, implying that future taxes will have to rise.[6] If taxpayers are clever enough to understand that increased government purchases today mean higher taxes in the future, households' expected future (after-tax) incomes will fall, and again they will reduce desired consumption. For the sake of illustration, we can imagine that they again reduce their current consumption by $6 billion, although the reduction in consumption might be less if some consumers don't understand that their future taxes are likely to rise.

What about the effects on desired national saving? The increase in government purchases affects desired national saving, or $Y - C^d - G$, directly by increasing G and indirectly by reducing desired consumption C^d. In our example, the increase in government purchases reduces desired consumption by $6 billion, which by itself would raise national saving by $6 billion. However, this effect is outweighed by the increase in G of $10 billion so that overall desired national saving $Y - C^d - G$ falls by $4 billion, with output Y held constant.[7] More generally, because the decline in desired consumption can be expected to be less than the initial increase in government purchases, a temporary increase in government purchases will lower desired national saving.

To summarize, for the current level of output Y, we conclude that a temporary increase in government purchases reduces both desired consumption and desired national saving.

Taxes. Now suppose that government purchases G remain constant but that the government reduces current taxes T by $10 billion. To keep things as simple as possible, we suppose that the tax cut is a *lump sum,* giving each taxpayer the same amount (think of the country's 100 million taxpayers receiving $100 each). With government purchases G and output Y held constant, desired national saving $Y - C^d - G$ will change only if desired consumption C^d changes. So the question is, how will desired consumption respond to the cut in current taxes?

Again the key issue is, how does the tax cut affect people's current and expected future incomes? The $10 billion current tax cut directly increases current (after-tax) incomes by $10 billion, so the tax cut should increase desired consumption (by somewhat less than $10 billion). However, the $10 billion current tax cut also should lead people to expect *lower* after-tax incomes in the

5. Recall that the marginal propensity to consume out of current income is positive but less than 1.
6. For example, in 1993 President Clinton asked for tax increases to help control the Federal budget deficit, much of which reflects interest on earlier government borrowings.
7. Note that national saving would fall by even more than $4 billion if consumers ignored the prospect of future tax increases and thus didn't reduce their current consumption.

future. The reason is that, because the government hasn't changed its spending, to cut taxes by $10 billion today the government must also increase its current borrowing by $10 billion. Because the extra $10 billion of government debt will have to be repaid with interest in the future, future taxes will have to be higher, which in turn implies lower future disposable incomes for households. All else being equal, the decline in expected future incomes will cause people to consume less today, offsetting the positive effect of increased current income on desired consumption. Thus, in principle, a current tax cut—which raises current incomes but lowers expected future incomes—could either raise or lower current desired consumption.

Interestingly, some economists argue that the positive effect of increased current income and the negative effect of decreased future income on desired consumption should exactly cancel so that the overall effect of a current tax cut on consumption is zero! The idea that tax cuts do not affect desired consumption and (therefore) also do not affect desired national saving,[8] is called the **Ricardian equivalence proposition.**[9]

The Ricardian equivalence idea can be briefly explained as follows (see Chapter 16 for a more detailed discussion). In the long run, all government purchases must be paid for by taxes. Thus if the government's current and planned purchases do not change, a cut in current taxes can affect the *timing* of tax collections but (advocates of Ricardian equivalence emphasize) not the ultimate tax burden borne by consumers. A current tax cut with no change in government purchases doesn't really make consumers any better off (any reduction in taxes today is balanced by tax increases in the future), so they have no reason to respond to the tax cut by changing their desired consumption.

Although the logic of the Ricardian equivalence proposition is sound, many economists question whether it makes sense in practice. Most of these skeptics argue that, even though the proposition predicts that consumers will not increase consumption when taxes are cut, in reality lower current taxes likely will lead to increased desired consumption and thus reduced desired national saving. One reason that consumption may rise after a tax cut is that many, perhaps most, consumers do not understand that increased government borrowing today is likely to lead to higher taxes in the future. Thus consumers may simply respond to the current tax cut, as they would to any other increase in current income, by increasing their desired consumption.

The effects of a tax cut on consumption and saving may be summarized as follows: According to the Ricardian equivalence proposition, with no change in current or planned government purchases, a tax cut doesn't change desired consumption and desired national saving. However, the Ricardian equivalence proposition may not apply if consumers fail to take account of possible future

8. In this example private disposable income rises by $10 billion, so if desired consumption doesn't change, desired private saving rises by $10 billion. However, the government deficit also rises by $10 billion because of the tax cut, so government saving falls by $10 billion. Therefore desired national saving—private saving plus government saving—doesn't change.

9. The argument was first advanced by the nineteenth-century economist David Ricardo, although he expressed some reservations about its applicability to real-world situations. The word "equivalence" refers to the idea that, if Ricardian equivalence is true, taxes and government borrowing have equivalent effects on the economy.

SUMMARY 5

Determinants of Desired National Saving

An increase in	Causes desired national saving to	Reason
Current output, Y	Rise	Part of the extra income is saved to provide for future consumption.
Expected future output	Fall	Anticipation of future income raises current desired consumption, lowering current desired saving.
Wealth	Fall	Some of the extra wealth is consumed, which reduces saving for given income.
Expected real interest rate, r	Probably rise	An increased return makes saving more attractive, probably outweighing the fact that less must be saved to reach a specific savings target.
Government purchases, G	Fall	Higher government purchases directly lower desired national saving.
Taxes, T	Unchanged or rise	Saving doesn't change if consumers take into account an offsetting future tax cut; saving rises if consumers don't take into account a future tax cut and thus reduce current consumption.

tax increases in their planning; in that case, a tax cut will increase desired consumption and reduce desired national saving.

The factors that affect consumption and saving are listed in Summary table 5.

4.2 INVESTMENT

Let's now turn to a second major component of spending: investment spending by firms. Like consumption and saving decisions, the decision about how much to invest depends largely on expectations about the economy's future. Investment also shares in common with saving and consumption the idea of a trade-off between the present and the future. In making a capital investment, a firm commits its current resources (which could otherwise be used, say, to pay increased dividends to shareholders) to increasing its capacity to produce and earn profits in the future.

Recall from Chapter 2 that investment refers to the purchase or construction of capital goods, including residential and nonresidential buildings, machines and equipment used in production, and additions to inventory stocks. From a macroeconomic perspective, there are two main reasons to study investment behavior. First, more so than the other components of aggregate spending, investment spending fluctuates sharply over the business cycle, falling in recessions and rising in booms. Even though investment is only about one sixth of GDP, in the typical recession half or more of the total decline in spending is reduced investment spending. Hence explaining the behavior of investment is important for understanding the business cycle, which we explore further in Part III.

The second reason for studying investment behavior is that investment plays a crucial role in determining the long-run productive capacity of the economy. Because investment creates new capital goods, a high rate of investment means that the capital stock is growing quickly. As discussed in Chapter 3, capital is one of the two most important factors of production (the other is labor). All else being equal, output will be higher in an economy that has invested rapidly and thus built up a large capital stock than in an economy that hasn't acquired much capital.

The Desired Capital Stock

To understand what determines the amount of investment, we must consider how firms decide how much capital they want. If firms attempt to maximize profit, as we assume, a firm's **desired capital stock** is the amount of capital that allows the firm to earn the largest expected profit. Managers can determine the profit-maximizing level of the capital stock by comparing the costs and benefits of using additional capital—a new machine, for example. If the benefits outweigh the costs, expanding the capital stock will raise profits. But if the costs outweigh the benefits, the firm shouldn't increase its planned capital stock and may even want to reduce it. As you might infer from this brief description, the economic logic underlying a firm's decision about how much capital to use is similar to the logic of its decision about how many workers to employ, discussed in Chapter 3.

In real terms, the benefit to a firm of having an additional unit of capital is the marginal product of capital, *MPK*. Recall from Chapter 3 that the *MPK* is the increase in output that a firm can obtain by adding a unit of capital, holding constant the firm's work force and other factors of production. Because lags occur in obtaining and installing new capital, the expected *future* marginal product of capital, MPK^f, is the benefit from increasing investment today by one unit of capital. This expected future benefit must be compared to the expected cost of using that extra unit of capital, or the user cost of capital.

The User Cost of Capital. To make the discussion of the user cost of capital more concrete, let's consider the case of Kyle's Bakery, Inc., a company that produces specialty cookies. Kyle, the bakery's owner-manager, is considering investing in a new solar-powered oven that will allow him to produce more cookies in the future. If he decides to buy such an oven, he must also determine its size. In making this decision, Kyle has the following three items of information:

1. A new oven can be purchased in any size at a price of $100 per cubic foot, measured in real (base-year) dollars.

2. Because the oven is solar powered, using it does not involve energy costs. The oven also does not require maintenance expenditures.[10] However, the oven becomes less efficient as it ages: With each year that passes, the oven produces 10% fewer cookies. Because of this depreciation, the real value of an oven falls 10% per year. For example, after one year of use, the real value of the oven is $90 per cubic foot.
3. Kyle can borrow (from a bank) or lend (to the government, by buying a one-year government bond) at the prevailing expected real interest rate of 8% per year.

In calculating the user cost of capital, we use the following symbols (the numerical values are from the example of Kyle's Bakery):

p_K = real price of capital goods ($100 per cubic foot);
d = rate at which capital depreciates (10% per year);
r = expected real interest rate (8% per year).

The **user cost of capital** is the expected real cost of using a unit of capital for a specified period of time. For Kyle's Bakery, we consider the expected costs of purchasing a new oven, using it for a year, then selling it. The cost of using the oven has two components: a depreciation cost and an interest cost.

In general, the depreciation cost of using capital is the value lost as the capital wears out. Because of depreciation, after one year the oven that Kyle pays $100 per cubic foot for when new will be worth only $90 per cubic foot. The $10-per-cubic-foot loss that Kyle suffers over the year is the depreciation cost of using the oven. Even if Kyle doesn't sell the oven at the end of a year, he suffers this loss because at the end of the year the asset's (the oven's) economic value will be 10% less.

The interest cost of using capital equals the expected real interest rate times the price of the capital. As the expected real interest rate is 8%, Kyle's interest cost of using the oven for a year is 8% of $100 per cubic foot, or $8 per cubic foot. To see why the interest cost is a cost of using capital, imagine first that Kyle must borrow the funds necessary to buy the oven; in this case, the interest cost of $8 per cubic foot is the interest he pays on the loan, which is obviously part of the total cost of using the oven. Alternatively, if Kyle uses profits from the business to buy the oven, he gives up the opportunity to use those funds to buy an interest-bearing asset, such as a government bond. For every $100 that Kyle puts into the oven, he is sacrificing $8 in interest that he would have earned by purchasing a $100 government bond. This foregone interest is a cost to Kyle of using the oven. Thus the interest cost is part of the true economic cost of using capital, whether the capital's purchase is financed with borrowed funds or with the firm's own retained profits.

The user cost of capital is the sum of the depreciation cost and the interest cost. The interest cost is rp_K, the depreciation cost is dp_K, and the user cost of capital, uc, is

$$uc = rp_K + dp_K = (r + d)p_K. \tag{4.4}$$

---

10. These assumptions simplify the example. If there were operating costs, such as fuel and maintenance costs, we would subtract them from the expected future marginal product of capital when calculating the benefit of using the machine.

In the case of Kyle's Bakery,

$$\begin{aligned} uc &= 0.08(\$100 \text{ per cubic foot}) + 0.10(\$100 \text{ per cubic foot}) \\ &= \$18 \text{ per cubic foot.} \end{aligned}$$

Thus Kyle's user cost of capital is \$18 per cubic foot per year.

Determining the Desired Capital Stock. Now we can find a firm's profit-maximizing capital stock, or desired capital stock. A firm's desired capital stock is the capital stock at which the expected future marginal product of capital equals the user cost of capital.

Figure 4.2 shows the determination of the desired capital stock for Kyle's Bakery. The capital stock K, expressed as cubic feet of oven capacity, is measured along the horizontal axis. Both the MPK^f and the user cost of capital are measured along the vertical axis.

The downward-sloping curve shows the value of the MPK^f for different sizes of the capital stock K; at each level of K, the MPK^f equals the expected real value of the extra cookies that could be produced if oven capacity were expanded an additional cubic foot. The MPK^f curve slopes downward because the marginal product of capital falls as the capital stock is increased (we discussed reasons for the diminishing marginal productivity of capital in Chapter 3). The user cost (equal to \$18 per cubic foot in the example) doesn't depend on the amount of capital and is represented by a horizontal line.

The amount of capital that maximizes the expected profit of Kyle's Bakery is 5000 cubic feet, represented by point A in Fig. 4.2. At A, the expected benefit of an additional unit of capital, MPK^f, equals the user cost, uc. For any amount of oven capacity of less than 5000 cubic feet, Kyle's Bakery could increase its

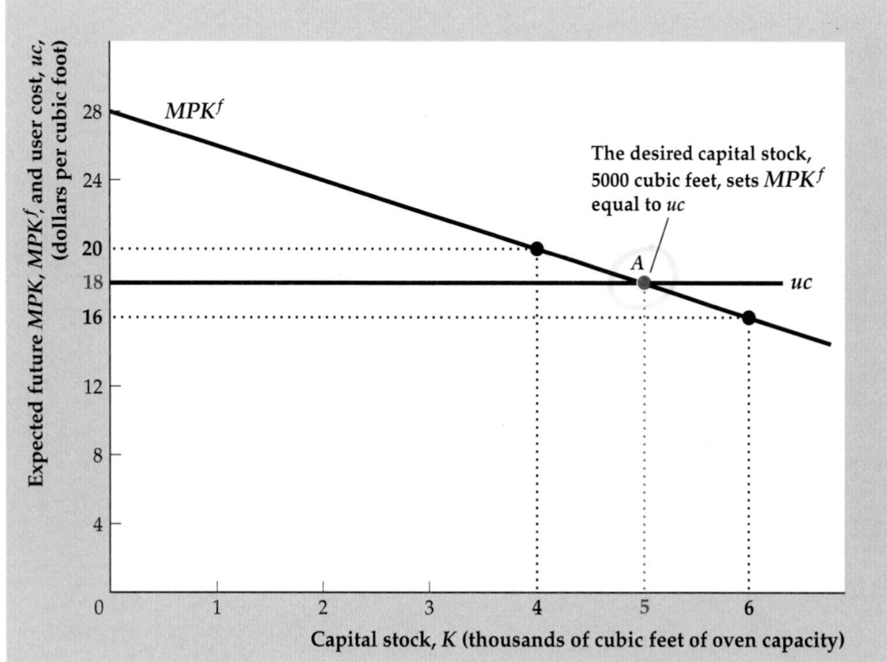

Figure 4.2
Determination of the desired capital stock
The desired capital stock (5000 cubic feet of oven capacity in this example) is the capital stock that maximizes profits. When the capital stock is 5000 cubic feet, the expected future marginal product of capital MPK^f is equal to the user cost of capital uc. If the MPK^f is larger than uc, as it is when the capital stock is 4000 cubic feet, the benefit of extra capital exceeds the cost, and the firm should increase its capital stock. If the MPK^f is smaller than uc, as it is at 6000 cubic feet, the cost of extra capital exceeds the benefit, and the firm should reduce its capital stock.

expected profit by increasing oven capacity. For example, Fig. 4.2 shows that at a planned capacity of 4000 cubic feet the MPK^f of an additional cubic foot is \$20 worth of cookies per year, which exceeds the \$18 expected cost of using the additional cubic foot of capacity. Starting from a planned capacity of 4000 cubic feet, if Kyle adds an extra cubic foot of capacity, he will gain an additional \$20 worth of future output while incurring only \$18 in expected future costs. Thus expanding beyond 4000 cubic feet is profitable for Kyle. Similarly, Fig. 4.2 shows that at an oven capacity of more than 5000 cubic feet, the expected future marginal product of capital, MPK^f, is less than the user cost, uc; in this case Kyle's Bakery could increase expected profit by reducing its capital stock. Only when $MPK^f = uc$ will the capital stock be at the level that maximizes expected profit.

As mentioned earlier, the determination of the desired capital stock is similar to the determination of the firm's labor demand, described in Chapter 3. Recall that the firm's profit-maximizing level of employment is the level at which the marginal product of labor equals the wage. Analogously, the firm's profit-maximizing level of capital is the level at which the expected future marginal product of capital equals the user cost, which can be thought of as the "wage" of capital (the cost of using capital for one period).

Changes in the Desired Capital Stock

Any factor that shifts the MPK^f curve or changes the user cost of capital changes the firm's desired capital stock. For Kyle's Bakery, suppose that the real interest rate falls from 8% to 6%. If the real interest rate r is 0.06 and the depreciation rate d and the price of capital p_K remain at 0.10 and \$100 per cubic

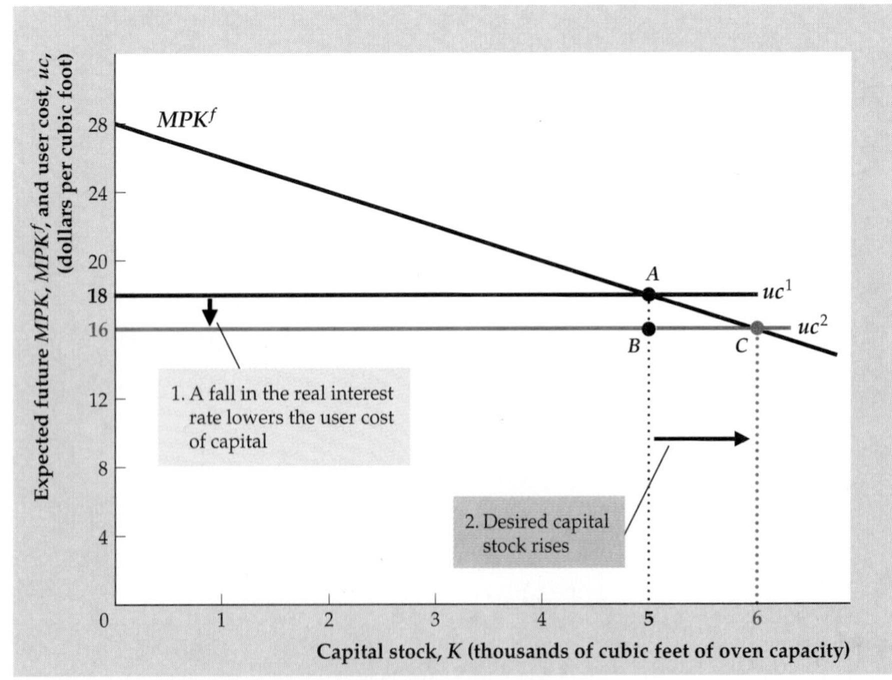

Figure 4.3
A decline in the real interest rate raises the desired capital stock
For the Kyle's Bakery example, a decline in the real interest rate from 8% to 6% reduces the user cost uc of a cubic foot of oven capacity from \$18 to \$16 per cubic foot and shifts the user cost line down from uc^1 to uc^2. The desired capital stock rises from 5000 (point A) to 6000 (point C) cubic feet of oven capacity. At 6000 cubic feet the MPK^f and the user cost of capital again are equal, at \$16 per cubic foot.

foot, respectively, the decline in the real interest rate reduces the user cost of capital $(r + d)p_K$ from \$18 per cubic foot to (0.06 + 0.10)\$100 per cubic foot, or \$16 per cubic foot.

This decline in the user cost is shown as a downward shift of the user cost line, from uc^1 to uc^2 in Fig. 4.3. After that shift, the MPK^f at the original desired capital stock of 5000 cubic feet (point *A*), or \$18 per cubic foot, exceeds the user cost of capital, now \$16 per cubic foot (point *B*). Kyle's Bakery can increase its profit by raising planned oven capacity to 6000 cubic feet, where the MPK^f equals the user cost of \$16 per cubic foot (point C). This example illustrates that a decrease in the expected real interest rate—or any other change that lowers the user cost of capital—increases the desired capital stock.

Technological changes that affect the MPK^f curve also affect the desired stock of capital. Suppose that Kyle invents a new type of cookie dough that requires less baking time, allowing 12.5% more cookies to be baked daily. Such a technological advance would cause the MPK^f curve for ovens to shift upward by 12.5% at each value of the capital stock. Figure 4.4 shows this effect as a shift of the MPK^f curve from MPK^{f1} to MPK^{f2}. If the user cost remains at \$18 per cubic foot, the technological advance causes Kyle's desired capital stock to rise from 5000 to 6000 cubic feet. At 6000 cubic feet (point *D*) the MPK^f again equals the user cost of capital. In general, with the user cost of capital held constant, an increase in the expected future marginal product of capital at any level of capital raises the desired capital stock.

Taxes and the Desired Capital Stock. So far we have ignored the role of taxes in the investment decision. But Kyle is interested in maximizing the profit his firm gets to keep after paying taxes. Thus he must take into account taxes in evaluating the desirability of an additional unit of capital.

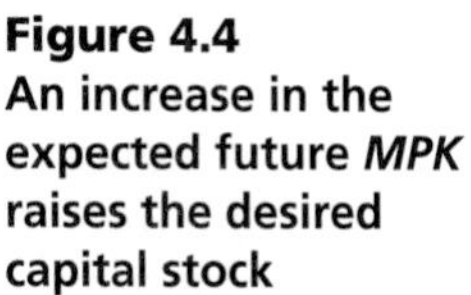

Figure 4.4
An increase in the expected future *MPK* raises the desired capital stock
A technological advance raises the expected future marginal product of capital, MPK^f, shifting the MPK^f curve upward from MPK^{f1} to MPK^{f2}. The desired capital stock increases from 5000 (point *A*) to 6000 (point *D*) cubic feet of oven capacity. At 6000 cubic feet the MPK^f equals the user cost of capital *uc* at \$18 per cubic foot.

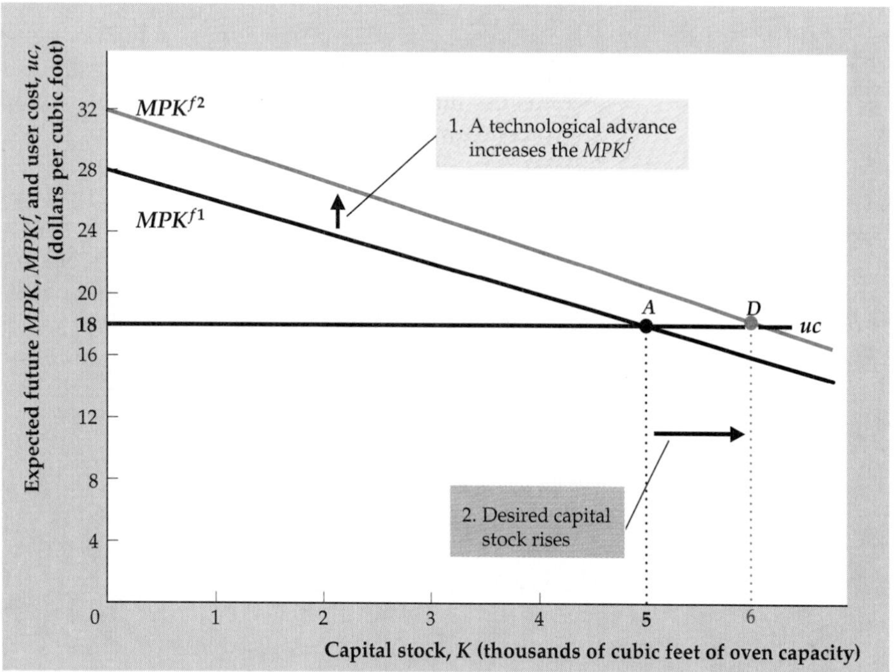

Suppose that Kyle's Bakery pays 20% of its revenues in taxes. In this case extra oven capacity that increases the firm's future revenues by, say, \$20 will raise Kyle's after-tax revenue by only \$16, with \$4 going to the government. To decide whether to add this extra capacity, Kyle should compare the after-tax MPK^f of \$16—not the before-tax MPK^f of \$20—with the user cost. In general, if τ is the tax rate on firm revenues, the after-tax future marginal product of capital is $(1-\tau)MPK^f$. The desired capital stock is the one for which the after-tax future marginal product equals the user cost, or

$$(1-\tau)MPK^f = uc.$$

Dividing both sides of this equation by $1-\tau$, we obtain

$$MPK^f = \frac{uc}{1-\tau} = \frac{(r+d)p_K}{1-\tau}. \qquad (4.5)$$

In Eq. (4.5), the term $uc/(1-\tau)$, is called the tax-adjusted user cost of capital. The **tax-adjusted user cost of capital** shows how large the before-tax future marginal product of capital must be for a firm to willingly add another unit of capital. An increase in the tax rate τ raises the tax-adjusted user cost and thus reduces the desired stock of capital.

To derive the tax-adjusted user cost we assumed that taxes are levied as a proportion of firms' revenues. However, actual corporate taxes in the United States and other countries are much more complicated. Firms generally pay taxes on their profits rather than on their revenues, and the part of profit that is considered taxable may depend on how much the firm invests. For example, when a firm purchases some capital, it is allowed to deduct part of the purchase price of the capital from its taxable profit in both the year of purchase and in subsequent years. By reducing the amount of profit to be taxed, these deductions, known as *depreciation allowances,* allow the firm to reduce its total tax payment.

Another important tax provision, which has been used at various times in the United States and whose revival was proposed by President Clinton in 1993, is the *investment tax credit.* An investment tax credit permits the firm to subtract a percentage of the purchase price of new capital directly from its tax bill. So, for example, if the investment tax credit is 10%, a firm that purchases a \$15,000 piece of equipment can reduce its taxes by \$1500 (10% of \$15,000) in the year the equipment is purchased.

Economists summarize the many provisions of the tax code affecting investment by a single measure of the tax burden on capital called the **effective tax rate.** Essentially, the idea is to ask, What tax rate τ on a firm's revenue would have the same effect on the desired capital stock as do the actual provisions of the tax code? The hypothetical tax rate that answers this question is the effective tax rate. Changes in the tax law that, for example, raise the effective tax rate are equivalent to an increased tax on firm revenue and a rise in the tax-adjusted user cost of capital. Thus, all else being equal, an increase in the effective tax rate lowers the desired capital stock.

Table 4.2 shows effective tax rates on capital for several countries in 1990. The highest effective tax rates were in the United Kingdom (28.0%), Canada (25.9%), and the United States (24.0%). Although other factors besides the effective tax rate affect investment, investment-to-GDP ratios in these countries generally are lower than in the other countries listed (see the Application "An

Table 4.2 Effective Tax Rate on Capital, 1990, Selected Countries

Country	Effective Tax Rate on Capital (Percent)
Australia	14.6
Canada	25.9
France	−33.4†
Germany	4.6
Italy	−72.8†
Japan	6.1
Sweden	1.0
United Kingdom	28.0
United States	24.0

Source: Dale Jorgenson, "Tax Reform and the Cost of Capital: An International Comparison," *Tax Notes International*, April 19, 1993, Table 1.

† A negative effective tax rate indicates that the tax system subsidizes investment.

International Comparison of National Saving and Investment Rates" in Chapter 2, p. 45). In contrast, 1990 effective tax rates on capital in France and Italy actually were negative, reflecting tax systems that subsidize investment in those countries.

APPLICATION

The Effective Tax Rates on Equipment and Structures

Does the effective tax rate on capital significantly affect investment patterns? To help answer this question, let's look at spending on different types of capital that have different effective tax rates.

In the United States, investment in equipment (such as furniture, computers, and automobiles) is treated differently in the tax laws than investment in structures (such as factories, warehouses, and office buildings). Figure 4.5(a), on the next page, shows the effective tax rates on equipment and structures as calculated in a study of the period 1946–1980.[11] From 1946 to 1961, the effective tax rate was greater for equipment than for structures. However, a major revision of the tax code under President Kennedy in 1962 introduced an investment tax credit for equipment. The effective tax rate on equipment fell sharply from 0.428 in 1961 to 0.250 in 1962, while the effective tax rate on structures remained virtually unchanged. After 1962 (except for 1969 and 1970, when the tax credit was temporarily rescinded) equipment was less heavily taxed than structures.

Figure 4.5(b) (on p. 129) shows that over the period 1962–1980 equipment investment grew much more quickly than did investment in structures (a trend that has continued since 1980). The change in the relative taxation of equipment and structures probably was a major reason for this shift in investment toward equipment.

11. Dale W. Jorgenson and Martin A. Sullivan, "Inflation and Capital Recovery," in Charles R. Hulten, ed., *Depreciation, Inflation, and the Taxation of Income from Capital*, Washington, D.C.: The Urban Institute Press, 1981.

Figure 4.5(a)
Effective tax rates, 1946–1980
The effective tax rates on equipment investment and structures investment in the United States are shown for the period 1946–1980. Before 1962 equipment was taxed more heavily than structures, but passage of an investment tax credit for equipment in 1962 reduced the relative tax burden on equipment.

Source: Dale W. Jorgenson and Martin A. Sullivan, "Inflation and Capital Recovery," Table 11, in Charles R. Hulten, ed., ***Depreciation, Inflation, and the Taxation of Income from Capital***, Washington, D.C.: The Urban Institute Press, 1981.

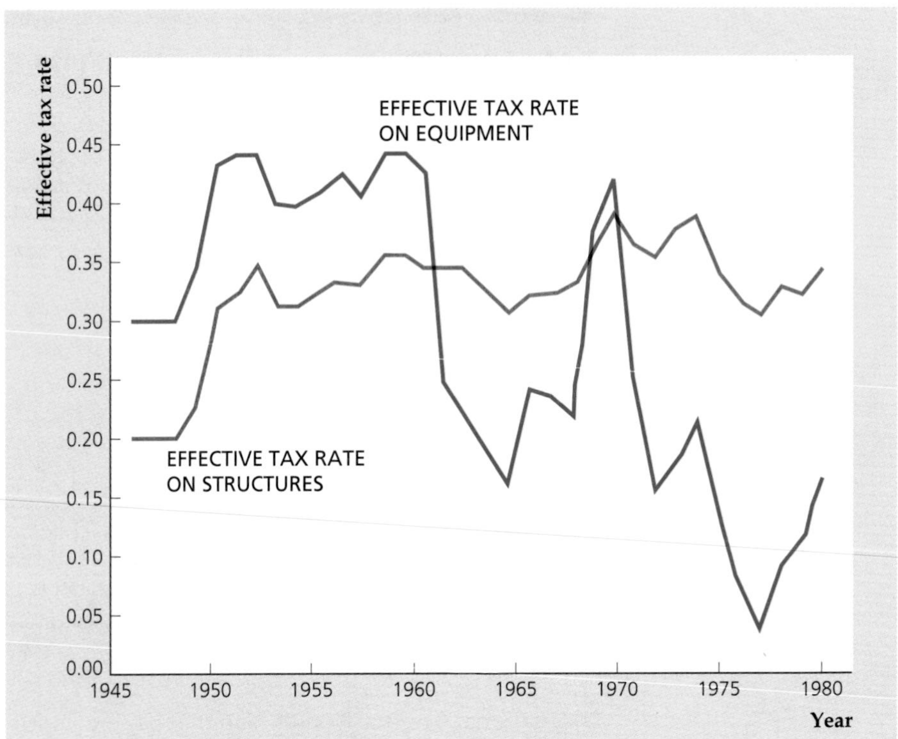

Figure 4.5(b)
Investment in equipment and structures, 1946–1980
Investment in equipment and investment in structures were about the same around 1960, but since then equipment investment has grown noticeably faster. One reason for the expansion of investment in equipment is the more favorable tax treatment since 1962, shown as a lower effective tax rate on equipment investment in (a).

Source: ***Economic Report of the President***, February 1991, Table B-1.

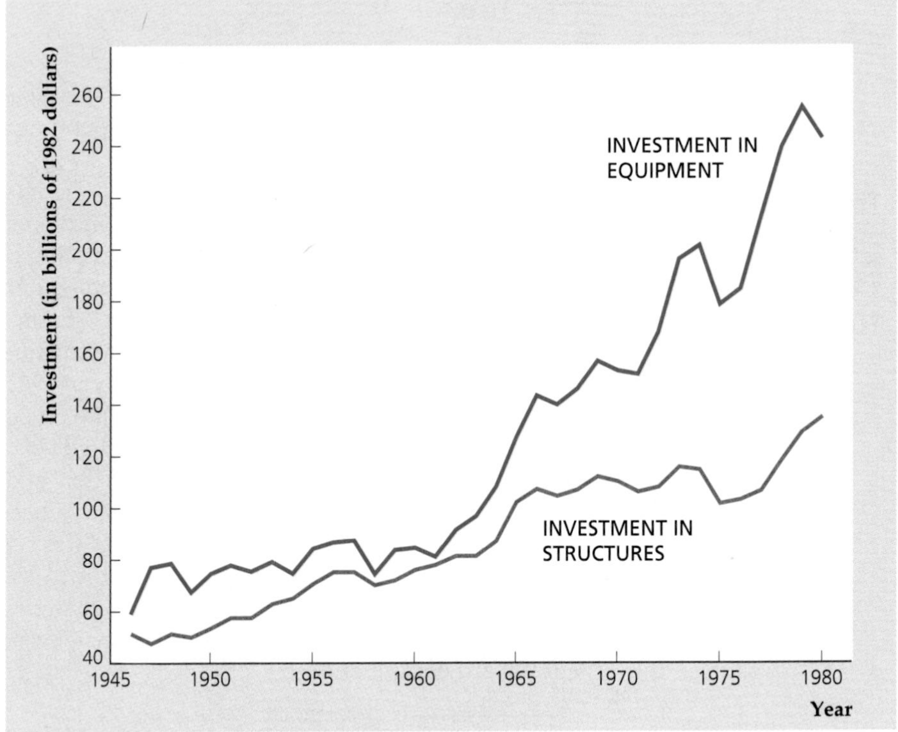

The tax advantage of equipment relative to structures continued into the 1980s; indeed, between 1980 and 1985 the effective tax rate on equipment investment was negative.[12] However, the Tax Reform Act of 1986 eliminated the investment tax credit for equipment and significantly reduced the difference in effective tax rates on equipment and structures. But investment in equipment relative to total investment did *not* decline, suggesting that tax factors alone do not explain the behavior of investment. One reason for continued investment in equipment after the reduction in its tax advantage was the surge in demand by businesses for all types of computer hardware (computer purchases count as equipment investment).

From the Desired Capital Stock to Investment

Now let's look at the link between a firm's desired capital stock and the amount it invests. In general, the capital stock (of a firm or of a country) changes over time through two opposing channels. First, the purchase or construction of new capital goods increases the capital stock. We've been calling the total purchase or construction of new capital goods that takes place each year "investment," but its precise name is **gross investment.** Second, the capital stock depreciates or wears out, which reduces the capital stock.

Whether the capital stock increases or decreases over the course of a year depends on whether gross investment is greater or less than depreciation during the year; when gross investment exceeds depreciation, the capital stock grows. The change in the capital stock over the year—or, equivalently, the difference between gross investment and depreciation—is **net investment.**

We express these concepts algebraically with the symbols:

I_t = gross investment during year t,
K_t = capital stock at the beginning of year t, and
K_{t+1} = capital stock at the beginning of year $t + 1$ (equivalently, at the end of year t).

Net investment, the change in the capital stock during period t, equals $K_{t+1} - K_t$. The amount of depreciation during year t is dK_t, where d is the fraction of capital that depreciates each year. The relationship between net and gross investment is

$$\text{net investment} = \text{gross investment} - \text{depreciation};$$
$$K_{t+1} - K_t = I_t - dK_t. \tag{4.6}$$

In most but not all years, gross investment is larger than depreciation so that net investment is positive and the capital stock increases. Figure 4.6, on the next page, shows the behavior since 1929 of gross and net investment in the United States, expressed as percentages of GDP; the difference between gross and net investment is depreciation. Note the occasional large swings in both gross and net investment and the negative rates of net investment that occurred in several years during the Great Depression of the 1930s and World War II (1941–1945).

12. See Dale Jorgenson, "Tax Reform and the Cost of Capital: An International Comparison," *Tax Notes International,* April 19, 1993, pp. 981–1008, Table 1.

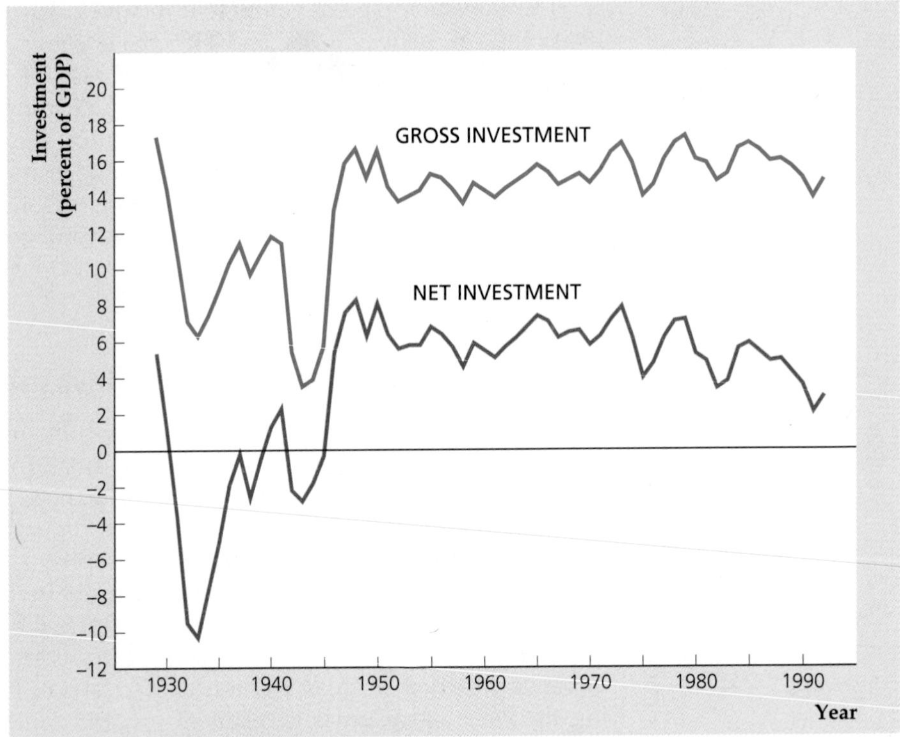

Figure 4.6
Gross and net investment, 1929–1991
Gross and net investment in the United States since 1929 are shown as percentages of GDP. During some years of the Great Depression and World War II net investment was negative, implying that the capital stock was shrinking.

Source: Gross and net investment from Table 5.3 of ***National Income and Product Accounts of the United States***, Volume 1, 1929–58; Volume 2, 1959–88; updates from ***Survey of Current Business***, various issues, Tables 1.1 and 5.3.

We can use Eq. (4.6) to illustrate the relationship between the desired capital stock and investment. First, rewriting Eq. (4.6) gives

$$I_t = K_{t+1} - K_t + dK_t,$$

which states that gross investment equals net investment plus depreciation.

Now suppose that firms use information available at the beginning of year t about the expected future marginal product of capital and the user cost of capital and determine the desired capital stock K^* they want by the end of year t (beginning of year $t+1$). For the moment, suppose also that capital is easily obtainable so that firms can match the actual capital stock at the end of year t, K_{t+1}, with the desired capital stock K^*. Substituting K^* for K_{t+1} in the preceding equation yields

$$I_t = K^* - K_t + dK_t. \tag{4.7}$$

Equation (4.7) shows that firms' gross investment, I_t, during a year has two parts: (1) the desired net increase in the capital stock over the year, $K^* - K_t$; and (2) the investment needed to replace worn-out or depreciated capital, dK_t. The amount of depreciation that occurs during a year is determined by the depreciation rate and the initial capital stock. However, the desired net increase in the capital stock over the year depends on the factors—such as taxes, interest rates, and the expected future marginal product of capital—that affect the desired capital stock. Indeed, Eq. (4.7) shows that any factor that leads to a change in the desired capital stock K^* results in an equal change in gross investment I_t.

Lags and Investment. The assumption just made, that firms can obtain capital quickly enough to match actual capital stocks with desired levels each year, isn't realistic in all cases. Although most types of equipment are readily available, a skyscraper or a nuclear power plant may take years to construct. Thus, in practice, a $1 million increase in a firm's desired capital stock may not translate into a $1 million increase in gross investment within the year; instead, the extra investment may be spread over several years as planning and construction proceed. Despite this qualification, factors that increase firms' desired capital stocks also tend to increase the current rate of investment. Summary table 6 brings together the factors that affect investment.

Investment in Inventories and Housing

Our discussion so far has emphasized what is called business fixed investment, or investment by firms in structures (such as factories and office buildings) and equipment (such as drill presses and jetliners). However, there are two other components of investment spending: inventory investment and residential investment. As discussed in Chapter 2, inventory investment equals the increase in firms' inventories of unsold goods, unfinished goods, or raw materials. Residential investment is the construction of housing, such as single-family homes, condominiums, or apartment buildings.

Fortunately, the concepts of future marginal product and the user cost of capital, which we used to examine business fixed investment, apply equally well to inventory investment and residential investment. Consider, for example, a new-car dealer trying to decide whether to increase the number of cars she normally keeps on her lot from 100 to 150, that is, to make an inventory investment of 50 cars. The benefit of having more cars to show is that potential car buyers will have a greater variety of models to select from and may not have to wait for delivery, enabling the car dealer to sell more cars. The increase in sales commissions the car dealer expects to make, measured in real terms and with the same sales force, is the expected future marginal product of the increased inventory. The cost of holding more cars reflects (1) depreciation of the cars sitting on the lot, and (2) the interest the car dealer must pay on the loan obtained to finance the higher inventory. The car dealer will make the inventory investment if the expected benefits of increasing her inventory, in terms of increased sales, are at least as great as the interest and depreciation

SUMMARY 6

Determinants of Desired Investment

An increase in	Causes desired investment to	Reason
Real interest rate, r	Fall	The user cost increases, which reduces desired capital stock.
Effective tax rate	Fall	The tax-adjusted user cost increases, which reduces desired capital stock.
Expected future *MPK*	Rise	The desired capital stock increases.

costs of adding 50 cars. This principle is the same one that applies to business fixed investment.

We can also use this same approach to analyze residential investment. The expected future marginal product of an apartment building, for example, is the real value of rents that can be collected from the tenants, minus taxes and operating costs. The user cost of capital for an apartment building during a year is its depreciation, or loss of value from wear and tear, plus the interest cost (reflected in mortgage payments, for example). As for other types of capital, constructing an apartment building is profitable only if its expected future marginal product is at least as great as its user cost.

4.3 GOODS MARKET EQUILIBRIUM

In Chapter 3 we showed that the quantity of goods and services supplied in an economy depends on the level of productivity—as determined, for example, by the technology used—and on the quantity of inputs, such as the capital and labor used. In this chapter we have discussed the factors that affect the demand for goods and services, particularly the demand for consumption goods by households and the demand for investment goods by firms. But how do we know that the amount of goods and services that consumers and investors want to buy will be the same as the amount that producers are willing to provide? Putting the question another way, What economic forces bring the goods market into equilibrium, with quantities demanded equal to quantities supplied? In this section, we show that the real interest rate is the key economic variable whose adjustments help bring the quantities of goods supplied and demanded into balance; thus a benefit of our analysis is an explanation of what determines interest rates. Another benefit is that, by adding the analysis of goods market equilibrium to the analysis of labor market equilibrium in Chapter 3, we take another large step toward constructing a complete model of the macroeconomy.

The goods market is in equilibrium when the aggregate quantity of goods supplied equals the aggregate quantity of goods demanded. (For brevity, we refer only to "goods" rather than to "goods and services," but services always are included.) Algebraically, this condition is

$$Y = C^d + I^d + G. \tag{4.8}$$

The left-hand side of Eq. (4.8) is the quantity of goods Y supplied by firms, which is determined by the factors discussed in Chapter 3. The right-hand side of Eq. (4.8) is the aggregate demand for goods. If we continue to assume no foreign sector, so that net exports are zero, the quantity of goods demanded is the sum of desired consumption by households, C^d, desired investment by firms, I^d, and government purchases G.[13] Equation (4.8) is called the goods market equilibrium condition.

The goods market equilibrium condition is different in an important way from the income–expenditure identity for a closed economy, $Y = C + I + G$

13. We assume that G always equals the level desired by the government and so don't distinguish between desired and actual G.

(this identity is Eq. 2.3, with $NX = 0$). The income–expenditure identity is a relationship between actual income (output) and actual spending, which by definition, is always satisfied. In contrast, the goods market equilibrium condition does not always have to be satisfied. For example, firms may produce output faster than consumers want to buy it so that undesired inventories pile up in firms' warehouses. In this situation the income–expenditure identity is still satisfied (because the undesired additions to firms' inventories are counted as part of total spending—see Chapter 2); but the goods market wouldn't be in equilibrium because production exceeds *desired* spending (which does *not* include the undesired increases in inventories). Although in principle the goods market equilibrium condition need not always hold, strong forces act to bring the goods market into equilibrium fairly quickly.

A different, but equivalent, way to write the goods market equilibrium condition emphasizes the relationship between desired saving and desired investment. To obtain this alternative form of the goods market equilibrium condition, we first subtract $C^d + G$ from both sides of Eq. (4.8):

$$Y - C^d - G = I^d.$$

The left-hand side of this equation, $Y - C^d - G$, is desired national saving, S^d (see Eq. 4.1). Thus the goods market equilibrium condition becomes

$$S^d = I^d. \tag{4.9}$$

This alternative way of writing the goods market equilibrium condition says that the goods market is in equilibrium when desired national saving equals desired investment.

Because saving and investment are central to many issues we present in this book, and because the desired-saving-equals-desired-investment form of the goods market equilibrium condition often is easier to work with, we utilize Eq. (4.9) in most of our analyses. However, we emphasize once again that Eq. (4.9) is equivalent to the condition that the supply of goods equals the demand for goods, Eq. (4.8).

The Saving–Investment Diagram

For the goods market to be in equilibrium, then, the aggregate supply of goods must equal the aggregate demand for goods, or equivalently, desired national saving must equal desired investment. We demonstrate in this section that adjustments of the real interest rate allow the goods market to attain equilibrium.[14]

The determination of goods market equilibrium can be shown graphically with a saving–investment diagram (Fig. 4.7 on the next page). The real interest rate is measured along the vertical axis, and national saving and investment are measured along the horizontal axis. The saving curve, S, shows the relationship between desired national saving and the real interest rate. The upward slope of the saving curve reflects the empirical finding (Section 4.1) that a higher real interest rate raises desired national saving. The investment curve, I, shows

14. Strictly speaking, we should refer to the expected real interest rate rather than simply the real interest rate. The two are the same if expected inflation and actual inflation are equal.

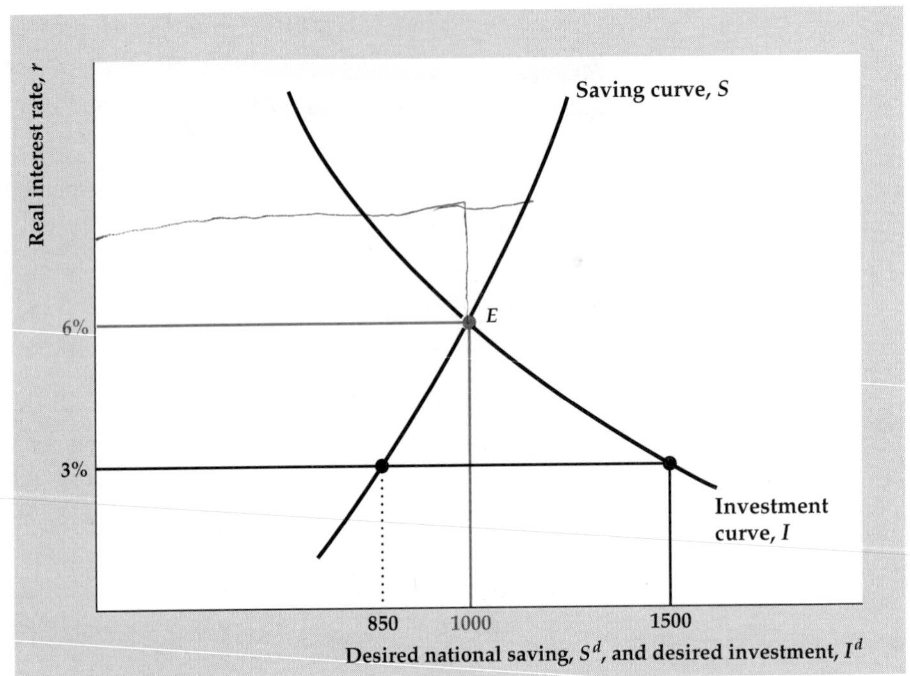

Figure 4.7
Goods market equilibrium
Goods market equilibrium occurs when desired national saving equals desired investment. In the figure equilibrium occurs when the real interest rate is 6% and both desired national saving and desired investment equal 1000. If the real interest rate were, say, 3%, desired investment (1500) would not equal desired national saving (850), and the goods market would not be in equilibrium. Competition among borrowers for funds would then cause the real interest rate to rise until it reaches 6%.

the relationship between desired investment and the real interest rate. The investment curve slopes downward because a higher real interest rate increases the user cost of capital and thus reduces desired investment.

Goods market equilibrium is represented by point E, at which desired national saving equals investment, as required by Eq. (4.9). The real interest rate corresponding to E (6% in this example) is the only real interest rate that clears the goods market. When the real interest rate is 6%, both desired national saving and desired investment equal 1000.

How does the goods market come to equilibrium at E, where the real interest rate is 6%? Suppose instead that the real interest rate is 3%. As Fig. 4.7 shows, when the real interest rate is 3%, the amount of investment that firms want to do (1500) exceeds desired national saving (850). With investors wanting to borrow more than savers want to lend, the "price" of saving—the real interest rate that lenders receive—will be bid up. The return to savers will rise until it reaches 6%, and desired national saving and desired investment are equal. Similarly, if the real interest rate exceeds 6%, the amount that savers want to lend will exceed what investors want to borrow, and the real return paid to savers will be bid down. Thus adjustments of the real interest rate, in response to an excess supply or excess demand for saving, bring the goods market into equilibrium.

Although Fig. 4.7 shows goods market equilibrium in terms of equal saving and investment, keep in mind that an equivalent way to express goods market equilibrium is that the supply of goods, Y, equals the demand for goods, $C^d + I^d + G$ (Eq. 4.8). Table 4.3 illustrates this point with a numerical example consistent with the values shown in Fig. 4.7. Here the assumption is that output Y and government purchases G are fixed at values of 4500 and 1500, respectively. Desired consumption C^d and desired investment I^d depend on the real interest rate. Desired consumption depends on the real interest rate because a higher real interest rate raises desired saving, which necessarily reduces desired consumption. Desired investment depends on the real interest rate because an increase in the real interest rate raises the user cost of capital, which lowers desired investment.

In the example in Table 4.3, when the real interest is 6%, desired consumption $C^d = 2000$. Therefore desired national saving $S^d = Y - C^d - G = 4500 - 2000 - 1500 = 1000$. Also, when the real interest rate is 6%, desired investment $I^d = 1000$. As desired national saving equals desired investment when $r = 6\%$, the equilibrium real interest rate is 6%, as in Fig. 4.7.

Note, moreover, that when the real interest rate is at the equilibrium value of 6%, the aggregate supply of goods, Y, which is 4500, equals the aggregate demand for goods, $C^d + I^d + G = 2000 + 1000 + 1500 = 4500$. Thus both forms of the goods market equilibrium condition, Eqs. (4.8) and (4.9), are satisfied when the real interest rate equals 6%.

Table 4.3 also illustrates how adjustments of the real interest rate bring about equilibrium in the goods market. Suppose that the real interest rate initially is 3%. Both components of private sector demand for goods (C^d and I^d) are higher when the real interest rate is 3% than when it is 6%. The reason is that consumers save less and firms invest more when real interest rates are relatively low. Thus, at a real interest of 3%, the demand for goods ($C^d + I^d + G = 2150 + 1500 + 1500 = 5150$) is greater than the supply of goods ($Y = 4500$). Equivalently, at a real interest rate of 3%, Table 4.3 shows that desired investment ($I^d = 1500$) exceeds desired saving ($S^d = 850$). As Fig. 4.7 shows, an increase in the real interest rate to 6% eliminates the disequilibrium in the goods market by reducing desired investment and increasing desired national saving. An alternative explanation is that the increase in the real interest rate eliminates the excess of the demand for goods over the supply of goods by reducing both consumption demand and investment demand.

Shifts of the Saving Curve. For any real interest rate, a change in the economy that raises desired national saving shifts the saving curve to the right, and a change that reduces desired national saving shifts the saving curve to the left. (Summary table 5 lists the factors affecting desired national saving.)

A shift of the saving curve leads to a new goods market equilibrium with a different real interest rate and different amounts of saving and investment. Figure 4.8, on the next page, illustrates the effects of a decrease in desired national saving—resulting, for example, from a temporary increase in cur-

Table 4.3 Components of Aggregate Demand for Goods (An example)

Real Interest Rate, r	Output, Y	Desired Consumption, C^d	Desired Investment, I^d	Government Purchases, G	Desired National Saving, $S^d = Y - C^d - G$	Aggregate Demand for Goods, $C^d + I^d + G$
3%	4500	2150	1500	1500	850	5150
6%	4500	2000	1000	1500	1000	4500

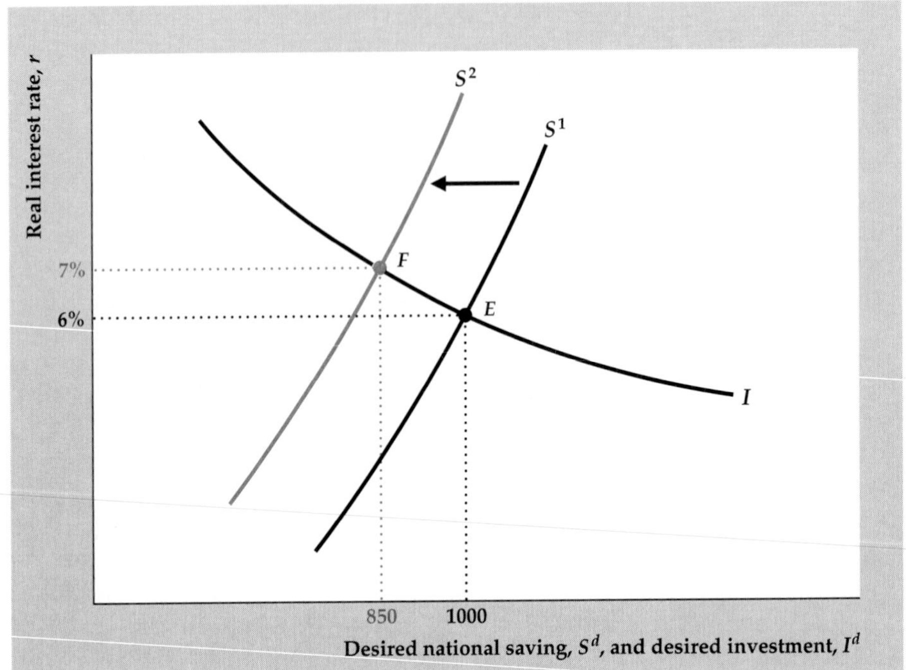

Figure 4.8
A decline in desired saving
A change that reduces desired national saving, such as a temporary increase in current government purchases, shifts the saving curve to the left, from S^1 to S^2. The goods market equilibrium point moves from E to F. The decline in desired saving raises the real interest rate, from 6% to 7%, and lowers saving and investment, from 1000 to 850.

rent government purchases. The initial equilibrium point is at E, where (as in Fig. 4.7) the real interest rate is 6% and desired national saving and desired investment both equal 1000. When current government purchases increase, the resulting decrease in desired national saving causes the saving curve to shift to the left, from S^1 to S^2. At the new goods market equilibrium point, F, the real interest rate is 7%, reflecting the fact that at the initial real interest rate of 6% the demand for funds by investors now exceeds the supply of saving.

Figure 4.8 also shows that, in response to the increase in government purchases, national saving and investment both fall, from 1000 to 850. Saving falls because of the initial decrease in desired saving, which is only partially offset by the increase in the real interest rate. Investment falls because the higher real interest rate raises the user cost of capital that firms face. When increased government purchases cause investment to decline, economists say that investment has been *crowded out*. The crowding out of investment by increased government purchases occurs, in effect, because the government is using more real resources, some of which would otherwise have gone into investment.

APPLICATION

The Effect of Wars on Investment and the Real Interest Rate

Economically, an important aspect of war and military buildups in general is that government purchases rise sharply as expenditures for military pay and equipment increase. Also, to a greater degree than other types of increases in government purchases, increases owing to military buildups are temporary because military expenditures tend to return to lower peacetime levels after a war. Thus thinking of a war as a largely temporary increase in current government purchases is reasonable. Our model predicts that a temporary increase in government purchases associated with a war will increase the real interest rate and reduce investment.

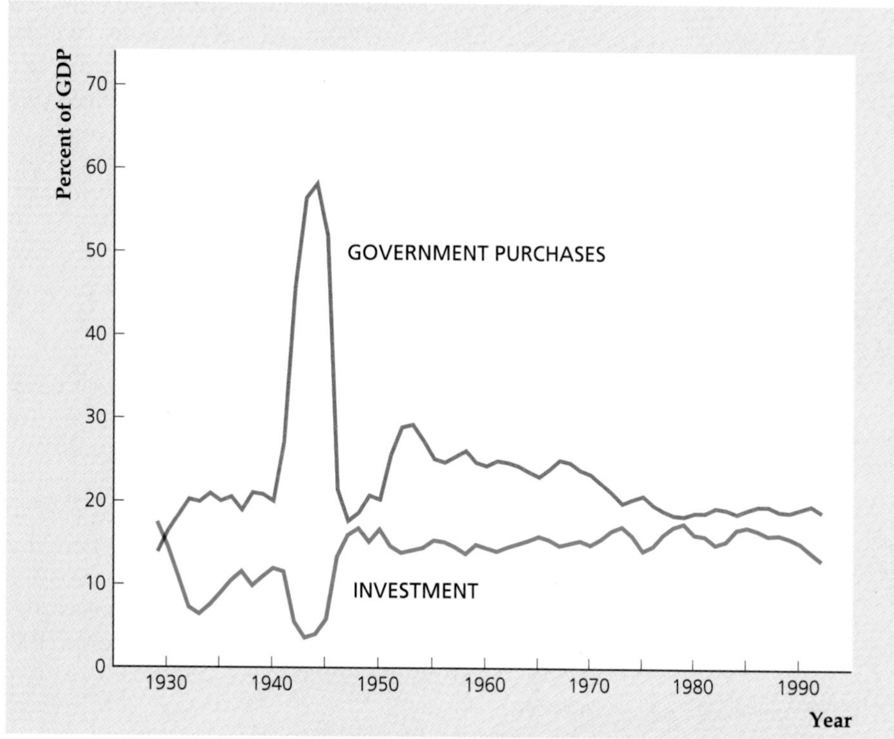

Figure 4.9
Shares of government purchases and investment in U.S. GDP, 1929–1992
The graph shows the percentages of U.S. GDP devoted to government purchases and to investment since 1929. Note the sharp increases in government purchases during World War II and the Korean War, as well as the tendency for investment's share to fall during those military buildups.

Sources: Investment, as in Fig. 4.6. GDP and government purchases, ***Survey of Current Business***, December 1992, Table 2, p. 30, and more recent issues.

How well do these predictions hold up? Historically, wars (especially large ones) often have had negative effects on investment. Figure 4.9 shows U.S. real investment spending and real government purchases, measured relative to real GDP, for the period 1929–1992. During World War II a large decline in private investment spending mirrored the sharp increase in government purchases. A similar pattern developed during the Korean War in the early 1950s. Interestingly, the military buildups of the Vietnam era and the early 1980s didn't change total government purchases enough to show clearly.

Besides predicting that military buildups will crowd out investment, our analysis also implies that real interest rates will be higher during wars. Robert Barro[15] of Harvard University has studied the behavior of real interest rates during wars. He found that this prediction of the model does not fit the data well for the United States: Although real interest rates were slightly above normal during the Korean and Vietnam wars, they were below normal during the Civil War, World War I, and World War II.

For the U.S. case, especially during the two world wars, government price controls, rationing, and control of production decisions may have prevented the private economy from functioning normally. As an alternative test of the theory, Barro used British data for the period 1730–1913. The British fought many wars, both large and small, during that period, and they rarely invoked price or production controls. Thus the British data should provide a good test of the theory.

---

15. "The Neoclassical Approach to Fiscal Policy," in Robert Barro, ed., *Modern Business Cycle Theory*, Cambridge, Mass.: Harvard University Press, 1989.

Barro found evidence in the British data that real interest rates do rise during wars. Long-term nominal interest rates (which, because inflation was essentially zero over this period, were about the same as real rates) were normally about 3.5% in Britain for this time span. During the American Revolution, however, British rates rose to about 5.5%, and they reached 6% during the Napoleonic Wars. This effect is not huge, but it is statistically significant. For the British case, at least, Barro's evidence is consistent with the prediction that wars raise real interest rates.

Shifts of the Investment Curve. Like the saving curve, the investment curve can shift. For any real interest rate, a change in the economy that raises desired investment shifts the investment curve to the right, and a change that lowers desired investment shifts the investment curve to the left. (See Summary table 6 for the factors affecting desired investment.)

The effects on goods market equilibrium of an increase in desired investment—as from an invention that raises the expected future marginal product of capital—are shown in Fig. 4.10. The increase in desired investment shifts the investment curve to the right, from I^1 to I^2, changing the goods market equilibrium point from E to G. The real interest rate rises from 6% to 8% because the increased demand for investment funds causes the real interest rate to be bid up. Saving and investment also increase, from 1000 to 1100, with the higher saving reflecting the willingness of savers to save more when the real interest rate rises.

In these last two chapters we have presented supply–demand analyses of the labor and goods markets and developed tools needed to understand the behavior of various macroeconomic variables, including employment, the real

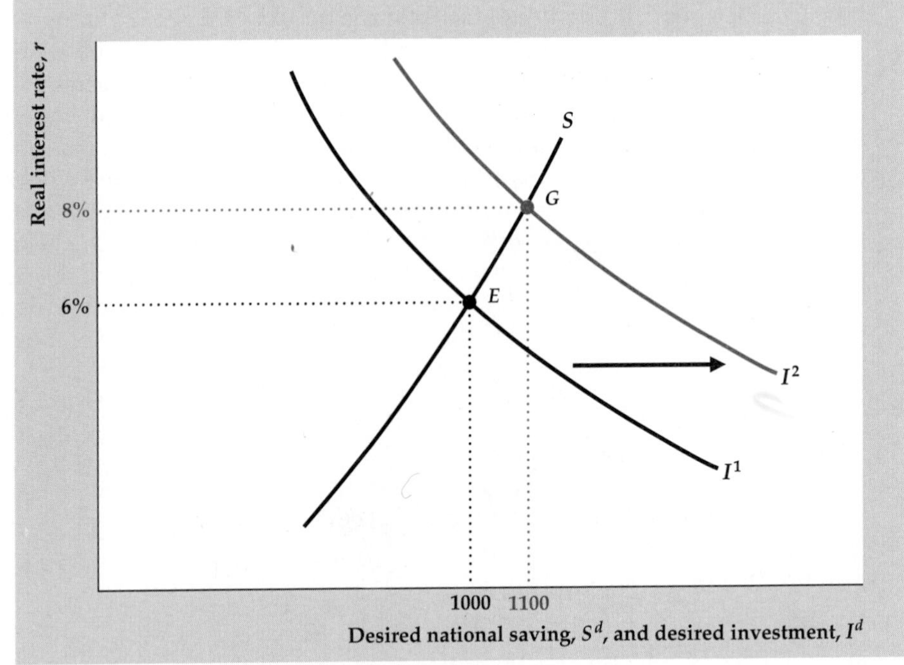

Figure 4.10
An increase in desired investment
A change in the economy that increases desired investment, such as an invention that raises the expected future *MPK*, shifts the investment curve to the right, from I^1 to I^2. The goods market equilibrium point moves from E to G. The real interest rate rises from 6% to 8%, and saving and investment also rise, from 1000 to 1100.

wage, output, saving, investment, and the real interest rate. These concepts—and a few more developed in the study of asset markets in Chapter 7—form the basis for the economic analysis presented in the rest of this book. In Chapter 5 we use the concepts developed so far to examine the determinants of trade flows and international borrowing and lending. In Chapter 6 we use them to tackle the fundamental question of why some countries' economies grow more quickly than others'.

CHAPTER SUMMARY

1. Because saving equals income minus consumption, a household's decisions about how much to consume and how much to save are really the same decision. Individuals and households save because they value both future consumption and current consumption; for the same amount of income, an increase in current saving reduces current consumption but increases the amount that the individual or household will be able to consume in the future.

2. For an individual or household, an increase in current income raises both desired consumption and desired saving. Analogously, at the national level, an increase in current output raises both desired consumption and desired national saving. At both the household and national levels, an increase in expected future income or in wealth raises desired consumption; however, because these changes raise desired consumption without affecting current income or output, they cause desired saving to fall.

3. An increase in the expected real interest rate has two contradictory effects on saving: An increase in the real interest rate increases the reward to saving but also reduces the amount of saving that must be done to reach a specific target. Empirical estimates suggest that an increase in the real interest rate raises desired national saving (and thus reduces desired consumption)—but not by very much. The expected after-tax real interest rate is the real return that savers expect to earn after paying a portion of interest received in taxes.

4. With total output held constant, a temporary increase in government purchases reduces desired consumption. The reason is that higher government purchases imply increases in present or future taxes, which makes consumers feel poorer. However, the decrease in desired consumption is smaller than the increase in government purchases, so that desired national saving, $Y - C^d - G$, falls as a result of a temporary increase in government purchases.

5. According to the Ricardian equivalence proposition, a current lump-sum tax cut should have no effect on desired consumption or desired national saving. The reason is that, if there is no change in current or planned government purchases, a tax cut that increases current income must be offset by future tax increases that lower expected future income. If consumers do not take account of expected future tax changes, however, the Ricardian equivalence proposition will not hold and a tax cut is likely to raise desired consumption and lower desired national saving.

6. The desired capital stock is the level of capital that maximizes expected profits. At the desired capital stock the expected future marginal product of capital equals the user cost of capital. The user cost of capital is the expected real cost of using a unit of capital for a period of time; it is the sum of the depreciation cost (the loss in value because the capital wears out) and the interest cost (the interest rate times the price of the capital good).

7. Any change that reduces the user cost of capital or increases the expected future marginal product of capital increases the desired capital stock. A reduction in the taxation of capital, as measured by the effective tax rate, also increases the desired capital stock.

8. Gross investment is spending on new capital goods. Gross investment minus depreciation (worn-out or scrapped capital) equals net investment, or the change in the capital stock. Firms invest in order to achieve their desired level of capital stock; when the desired capital stock increases, firms invest more.

9. The goods market is in equilibrium when the aggregate quantity of goods supplied equals the aggregate quantity of goods demanded, which (in a closed economy) is the sum of desired consumption, desired investment, and government purchases of goods and services. Equivalently, the goods market is in equilibrium when desired national saving equals desired investment. For any given level of output, the goods market is brought into equilibrium by changes in the real interest rate.

10. The determination of goods market equilibrium, for any supply of output Y, is represented graphically by the saving–investment diagram. The saving curve slopes upward because empirical evidence suggests that a higher real interest rate raises desired saving. The investment curve slopes downward because a higher real interest rate raises the user cost of capital, which lowers firms' desired capital stocks and thus the amount of investment they do. At constant output, changes in variables that affect desired saving or investment shift the saving or investment curves and change the real interest rate that clears the goods market.

KEY DIAGRAM 3

The Saving–Investment Diagram

In an economy with no foreign trade the goods market is in equilibrium when desired national saving equals desired investment. Equivalently, the goods market is in equilibrium when the aggregate quantity of goods supplied equals the aggregate quantity of goods demanded.

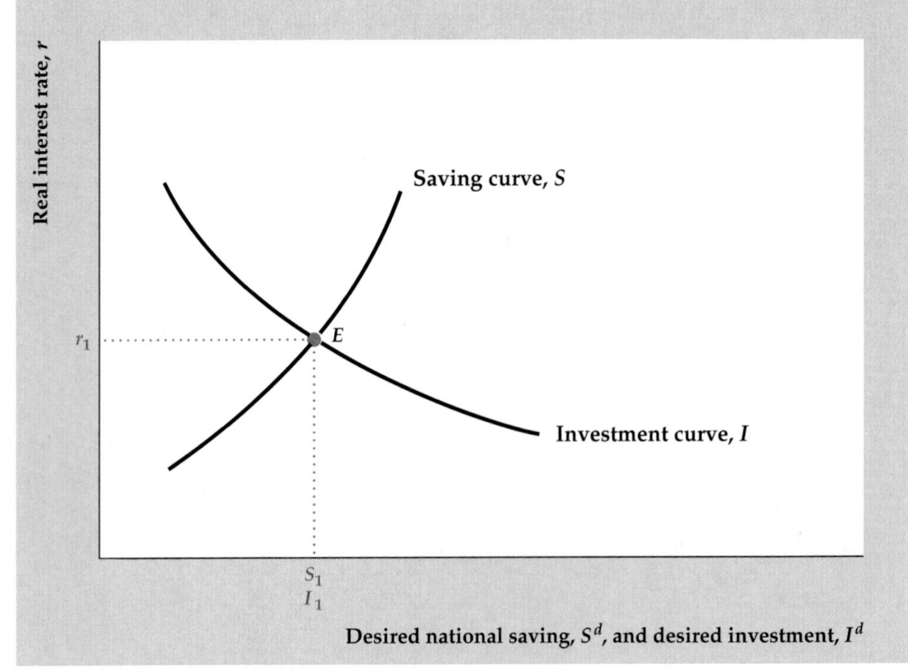

Diagram Elements

■ The real interest rate r is on the vertical axis; desired national saving S^d and desired investment I^d are on the horizontal axis.

■ The saving curve, S, shows the level of desired national saving at each real interest rate. The saving curve slopes upward because a higher real interest rate increases the reward for saving and causes households to save more. (Empirically, this effect outweighs the tendency of a higher real interest rate to lower saving by reducing the amount of saving necessary to reach any specified target.) Desired national saving is defined as $S^d = Y - C^d - G$, where Y is output, C^d is desired consumption, and G is government purchases.

■ The investment curve, I, shows the amount that firms want to invest in new capital goods at each real interest rate. The investment curve slopes downward because a higher real interest rate raises the user cost of capital and thus lowers the amount of capital that firms want to use.

Analysis

■ Goods market equilibrium requires that desired national saving equal desired investment, or $S^d = I^d$.

■ Goods market equilibrium occurs in the diagram at point E, where the saving curve and investment curve intersect. At E desired national saving equals S_1, desired investment equals I_1, and $S_1 = I_1$. The real interest rate at E, r_1, is the real interest rate that clears the goods market.

■ An alternative way to express the goods market equilibrium condition is as follows: The quantity of goods supplied, Y, equals the quantity of goods demanded by households, C^d, firms, I^d, and the government, G, or $Y = C^d + I^d + G$. As $S^d = Y - C^d - G$, this condition is equivalent to $S^d = I^d$.

Factors That Shift the Curves

■ Any factor that raises desired national saving at a given real interest rate shifts the saving curve to the right; similarly, any factor that lowers desired national saving shifts the saving curve to the left. Factors that affect desired national saving are listed in Summary table 5. Similarly, factors that change desired investment for a given real interest rate shift the investment curve; see Summary table 6 for factors that affect desired investment. Shifts of either curve change the goods market equilibrium point and thus change national saving, investment, and the real interest rate.

Key Terms

desired capital stock, p. 121
effective tax rate, p. 126
expected after-tax real interest rate, p. 115
gross investment, p. 128
Keynesian consumption function, p. 110
marginal propensity to consume, p. 110
net investment, p. 129
Ricardian equivalence proposition, p. 119
tax-adjusted user cost of capital, p. 126
user cost of capital, p. 122

Key Equations

$$S^d = Y - C^d - G \tag{4.1}$$

Desired national saving, S^d, is the level of national saving that occurs when consumption is at its desired level. Equation (4.1) is obtained by substituting desired consumption C^d for actual consumption C in the definition of national saving.

$$r_{a\text{-}t} = (1 - t)i - \pi^e \tag{4.3}$$

The expected after-tax real interest rate, $r_{a\text{-}t}$, is the after-tax nominal interest rate, $(1 - t)i$, minus the expected rate of inflation π^e. The expected after-tax real interest rate is the real return earned by a saver when a portion t of interest income must be paid as taxes.

$$uc = rp_K + dp_K = (r + d)p_K \tag{4.4}$$

The user cost of capital, uc, is the sum of the interest cost, rp_K, and the depreciation cost, dp_K, where d is the depreciation rate and p_K is the price of a new capital good.

$$MPK^f = \frac{uc}{1-\tau} = \frac{(r+d)p_K}{1-\tau} \tag{4.5}$$

The desired capital stock, or the capital stock that maximizes the firm's expected profits, is the capital stock for which the expected future marginal product of capital, MPK^f, equals the tax-adjusted user cost of capital, $uc/(1 - \tau)$, where τ is the tax rate on firm revenues (equivalently, the effective tax rate).

$$Y = C^d + I^d + G \tag{4.8}$$

The *goods market equilibrium condition* says that the goods market is in equilibrium when the aggregate quantity of goods supplied, Y, equals the aggregate quantity of goods demanded, $C^d + I^d + G$.

$$S^d = I^d \tag{4.9}$$

Another way of stating the goods market equilibrium condition is that desired national saving, S^d, must equal desired investment, I^d. This equation is equivalent to Eq. (4.8).

Review Questions

1. Given income, how are consumption and saving linked? What is the basic motivation for saving?
2. How are desired consumption and desired saving affected by increases in current income, expected future income, and wealth? Why is the effect on desired saving of an increase in the expected real interest rate potentially ambiguous?
3. What effect does a temporary increase in government purchases—for example, to fight a war—have on desired consumption and desired national saving, for a constant level of output? What is the effect on desired national saving of a lump-sum tax increase? Why is the effect of a lump-sum tax increase controversial?
4. What are the two components of the user cost of capital? Explain why each is a cost of using a capital good.
5. What is the desired capital stock? How does it depend on the expected future marginal product of capital, the user cost of capital, and the effective tax rate?
6. What is the difference between gross investment and net investment? Can gross investment be positive when net investment is negative?
7. Give two equivalent ways of describing equilibrium in the goods market. Use a diagram to show how goods market equilibrium is attained.
8. Explain why the saving curve slopes upward and the investment curve slopes downward in the saving–investment diagram. Give two examples of changes that would shift the saving curve to the right, and two examples of changes that would shift the investment curve to the right.

Numerical Problems

1. A consumer is making saving plans for this year and next. She knows that her real income after taxes will be $50,000 in both years. Any part of her income saved this year will earn a real interest rate of 10% between this year and next year. Currently, the consumer has no wealth (no money in the bank or other financial assets, and no debts). There is no uncertainty about the future.

   The consumer wants to save an amount this year that will allow her to (1) make college tuition payments next year equal to $12,600 in real terms; (2) enjoy exactly the same amount of consumption this year and next year, not counting tuition payments as part of next year's consumption; and (3) have neither assets nor debts at the end of next year.

   a. How much should the consumer save this year? How much should she consume?

   How are the amounts that the consumer should save and consume affected by each of the following changes (taken one at a time, with other variables held at their original values)?

   b. Her current income rises from $50,000 to $54,200.

   c. The income she expects to receive next year rises from $50,000 to $54,200.

   d. During the current year she receives an inheritance of $1050 (an increase in wealth, not income).

   e. The expected tuition payment for next year rises from $12,600 to $14,700.

   f. The real interest rate rises from 10% to 25%.
2. Hula hoop fabricators cost $100 each. The Hi-Ho Hula Hoop Company is trying to decide how many of these machines to buy. HHHHC expects to produce the following number of hoops each year for each level of capital stock shown.

Number of Fabricators	Number of Hoops Produced per Year
0	0
1	100
2	150
3	180
4	195
5	205
6	210

Hula hoops have a real value of $1 each. HHHHC has no other costs besides the cost of fabricators.

a. Find the expected future marginal product of capital (in terms of dollars) for each level of capital. The MPK^f for the third fabricator, for example, is the real value of the extra output obtained when the third fabricator is added.

b. If the real interest rate is 12% per year and the depreciation rate of capital is 20% per year, find the user cost of capital (in dollars per fabricator per year). How many fabricators should HHHHC buy?

c. Repeat part (b) for a real interest rate of 8% per year.

d. Repeat part (b) for a 40% tax on HHHHC's sales revenues.

e. A technical innovation doubles the number of hoops a fabricator can produce. How many fabricators should HHHHC buy when the real interest rate is 12% per year? 8% per year? Assume that there are no taxes and that the depreciation rate is still 20% per year.

3. You have just taken a job that requires you to move to a new city. In relocating, you face the decision of whether to buy or rent a house. A suitable house costs $200,000 and you have saved enough for the down payment. The (nominal) mortgage interest rate is 10% per year, and you can also earn 10% per year on savings. Mortgage interest payments are tax deductible, interest earnings on savings are taxable, and you are in a 30% tax bracket. Interest is paid or received, and taxes are paid, on the last day of the year. The expected inflation rate is 5% per year.

The cost of maintaining the house (replacing worn-out roofing, painting, and so on) is 6% of the value of the house. Assume that these expenses also are paid entirely on the last day of the year. If the maintenance is done, the house retains its full real value. There are no other relevant costs or expenses.

a. What is the expected after-tax real interest rate on the home mortgage?

b. What is the user cost of the house?

c. If all you care about is minimizing your living expenses, at what (annual) rent level would you be just indifferent between buying a house and renting a house of comparable quality? Rent is also paid on the last day of the year.

4. Consider a firm that faces the following expected future marginal product of capital:

$$MPK^f = 1000 - 2K,$$

where MPK^f is the expected future marginal product of capital and K is the capital stock. The price of capital, p_K, is 1000, the real interest rate, r, is 10%, and the depreciation rate, d, is 15%.

a. What is the user cost of capital?

b. What is the value of the firm's desired capital stock?

c. Now suppose that the firm must pay a 50% tax on its revenue. What is the value of the desired capital stock?

d. Now suppose that in addition to the 50% tax rate on revenue, the firm can take advantage of a 20% investment tax credit, which allows it to reduce its taxes paid by 20% of the value of new capital purchased. What is the firm's desired capital stock now? (*Hint:* An investment tax credit effectively reduces the price of capital to the firm.)

5. An economy has full-employment output of 9000, and government purchases are 2000. Desired consumption and desired investment are as follows:

Real interest rate (%)	Desired consumption	Desired investment
2	6100	1500
3	6000	1400
4	5900	1300
5	5800	1200
6	5700	1100

a. Why do desired consumption and desired investment fall as the real interest rate rises?

b. Find desired national saving for each value of the real interest rate.

c. If the goods market is in equilibrium, what are the values of the real interest rate, desired national saving, and desired investment? Show that both forms of the goods market equilibrium condition, Eqs. (4.8) and (4.9), are satisfied at the equilibrium. Assume that output is fixed at its full-employment level.

d. Repeat part (c) for the case in which government purchases fall to 1600. Assume that the amount people desire to consume at each real interest rate is unchanged.

6. An economy has full-employment output of 6000. Government purchases, G, are 1200. Desired consumption and desired investment are

$$C^d = 3600 - 2000r + 0.10Y, \text{ and}$$
$$I^d = 1200 - 4000r,$$

where Y is output and r is the real interest rate.

a. Find an equation relating desired national saving S^d to r and Y.

b. Using both versions of the goods market equilibrium condition, Eqs. (4.8) and (4.9), find the real interest rate that clears the goods market. Assume that output equals full-employment output.
c. Government purchases rise to 1440. How does this increase change the equation describing desired national saving? Show the change graphically. What happens to the market-clearing real interest rate?

Analytical Problems

1. Use the saving–investment diagram to analyze the effects of the following on national saving, investment, and the real interest rate. Explain your reasoning.
   a. Consumers become more future-oriented and thus decide to save more.
   b. The government announces a large, one-time bonus payment to veterans returning from a war. The bonus will be financed by additional taxes levied on the general population over the next five years.
   c. The government introduces an investment tax credit (offset by other types of taxes, so total tax collections remain unchanged).
   d. A large number of accessible oil deposits are discovered, which increases the expected future marginal product of oil rigs and pipelines. It also causes an increase in expected future income.
2. A country loses much of its capital stock to a war.
   a. What effects should this event have on the country's current employment, output, and real wage?
   b. What effect will the loss of capital have on desired investment?
   c. The effects on desired national saving of the wartime losses are ambiguous. Give one reason for desired saving to rise and one reason for it to fall.
   d. Assume that desired saving doesn't change. What effect does the loss of capital have on the country's real interest rate and the quantity of investment?
3. **a.** Analyze the effects of a temporary increase in the price of oil (a temporary adverse supply shock) on current output, employment, the real wage, national saving, investment, and the real interest rate. Because the supply shock is temporary, you should assume that the expected future *MPK* and households' expected future incomes are unchanged. Assume throughout that output and employment remain at full-employment levels (which may change).
   b. Analyze the effects of a permanent increase in the price of oil (a permanent adverse supply shock) on current output, employment, the real wage, national saving, investment, and the real interest rate. Show that in this case, unlike the case of a temporary supply shock, the real interest rate need not change. (*Hint:* A permanent adverse supply shock lowers the current productivity of capital and labor, just as a temporary supply shock does. In addition, a permanent supply shock lowers both the expected future *MPK* and households' expected future incomes.)
4. Economists often argue that a temporary increase in government purchases, say, for military purposes, will crowd out private investment. Use the saving–investment diagram to illustrate this point, explaining why the curve(s) shift. Does it matter whether the temporary increase in military spending is funded by taxes or by borrowing?

   Alternatively, suppose that the temporary increase in government purchases is for infrastructure (roads, sewers, bridges) rather than for military purposes. The government spending on infrastructure makes private investment more productive, increasing the expected future *MPK* at each level of the capital stock. Use the saving–investment diagram to analyze the effects of government infrastructure spending on current consumption, national saving, investment, and the real interest rate. Does investment by private firms get crowded out by this kind of government investment? If not, what kind of spending, if any, does get crowded out? Assume that there is no change in current productivity or current output and assume also (for simplicity) that households do not expect a change in their future incomes.
5. "A permanent increase in government purchases has a larger effect than a temporary increase of the same amount." Use the saving–investment diagram to evaluate this statement, focusing on effects on consumption, investment, and the real interest rate for a fixed level of output. (*Hint:* The permanent increase in government purchases implies larger increases in current and future taxes.)

CHAPTER 5

SAVING AND INVESTMENT IN THE OPEN ECONOMY

With virtually no exceptions, modern economies are open economies, which means that they engage in international trade of goods and services and in international borrowing and lending. Economic openness is of tremendous benefit to the average person. Because the United States is an open economy, U.S. consumers can enjoy products from around the world (Japanese videocassette recorders, Italian shoes, Irish woolens) and U.S. businesses can find new markets abroad for their products (computers, beef, financial services). Similarly, the internationalization of financial markets means that U.S. savers have the opportunity to purchase German government bonds or shares in Taiwanese companies as well as domestic assets, and U.S. firms who want to finance investment projects can borrow in London or Tokyo as well as in New York.

Beyond the economic diversity and opportunity it creates, economic openness carries another important implication: In an open economy, *a country's spending need not equal its production in every period,* as would be required in a closed economy with no foreign trade and no international borrowing and lending. In particular, by importing more than they export and borrowing from abroad to pay for the difference, the residents of an open economy can temporarily spend more than they produce.

The ability of an open economy to spend more than it produces is both an opportunity and a potential problem. For example, by borrowing abroad, the United States was able to finance a large excess of imports over exports during the 1980s and early 1990s. As a result, Americans enjoyed higher levels of consumption, investment, and government purchases than they could have otherwise. At the same time, however, they incurred foreign debts that may be a future burden to the U.S. economy. Similarly, by borrowing heavily from abroad during the 1970s, some less developed countries (LDCs) were able to avoid large reductions in domestic spending even though the two oil price shocks of that decade caused sharp declines in their output. During the 1980s, however, many LDC borrowers were unable to cope with the burden of their foreign debts—a situation that became known as the LDC debt crisis—and perhaps as a result suffered severely reduced economic growth.

Why do countries sometimes borrow abroad to pay for an excess of imports over exports but at other times export more than they import and lend the difference to other countries? Why doesn't each country just balance its books and import as much as it exports each year? As this chapter explains, the fundamental determinants of a country's trade position are the country's saving and investment decisions. Thus, although the issues of trade balances and international lending introduced here may seem at first to be unrelated to the topics covered in Chapter 4, the two sets of questions actually are closely related.

To explore how desired national saving and desired investment help determine patterns of international trade and lending, we extend the idea of goods market equilibrium, described by the saving–investment diagram, to include a foreign sector. We show that, unlike the situation in a closed economy, in an open economy desired national saving and desired investment don't have to be equal. Instead, we show that, when a country's desired national saving exceeds its desired investment, the country will be a lender in the international capital market and will have a current account surplus. Similarly, when a country's desired national saving is less than its desired investment, the country will be an international borrower and will have a current account deficit.

In its emphasis on saving and investment, this chapter develops an important theme of this part of the book. However, in order to focus on the role of saving and investment, we ignore some other factors that also influence international trade and lending. The most important of these factors is the exchange rate, or the rate at which domestic currency can be exchanged for foreign currency. We discuss exchange rates and their role in the open economy fully in Chapter 14.

5.1 BALANCE OF PAYMENTS ACCOUNTING

Examining the factors that affect international trade and lending first requires an understanding of the basics of balance of payments accounting. The **balance of payments accounts,** which are part of the national income accounts discussed in Chapter 2, are the record of a country's international transactions. (The box "In Touch with the Macroeconomy: The Balance of Payments Accounts," p. 148, contains information about how the balance of payments accounts are constructed and where to find these data.) As you read this section, you should refer to Table 5.1, which presents U.S. balance of payments data for 1992; note that some of the numbers are positive and that others are negative. To sort out which international transactions are entered with a plus sign and which are entered with a minus sign, keep the following principle in mind: Any transaction that involves a flow of funds *into* the United States is a *credit* item and is entered with a plus sign; any transaction that involves a flow of funds *out of* the United States is a *debit* item and is entered with a minus sign. We illustrate this principle as we discuss the various components of the balance of payments accounts.

Table 5.1 Balance of Payments Accounts of the United States, 1992 (Billions of Dollars)

CURRENT ACCOUNT				
Net exports			**−41.2**	
Exports		617.8		
Merchandise	439.3			
Services	178.5			
Imports		−658.9		
Merchandise	−535.6			
Services	−123.4			
Net income from assets			**10.1**	
Income receipts on investments		109.2		
Income payments on investments		−99.1		
Net unilateral transfers			**−31.4**	
Current Account Balance (*CA*)				**−62.5**
CAPITAL ACCOUNT				
Increase in U.S.-owned assets abroad (capital outflow)			**−44.9**	
U.S. official reserve assets		3.9		
Other U.S. assets		−48.8		
Increase in foreign-owned assets in U.S. (capital inflow)			**120.4**	
Foreign official assets		40.3		
Other foreign assets		80.1		
Capital Account Balance (*KA*)				**75.5**
Statistical discrepancy				**−13.1**
Addendum				
Official settlements balance = balance of payments = increase in U.S. official reserve assets − increase in foreign official assets = −3.9 − 40.3 =				**−44.2**

Note: Numbers may not add to totals shown owing to rounding.

Source: *Survey of Current Business,* March 1993, p. 66.

The Current Account

The **current account** measures a country's trade in currently produced goods and services, along with unilateral transfers between countries. For convenience we divide the current account into three separate components: (1) net exports of goods and services, (2) investment income from assets abroad, and (3) net unilateral transfers.

Net Exports of Goods and Services. We discussed the concept of net exports, *NX*, or exports minus imports, as part of the expenditure approach to

IN TOUCH *WITH THE MACROECONOMY*

THE BALANCE OF PAYMENTS ACCOUNTS

The data on U.S. international transactions that make up the balance of payments accounts are produced quarterly by the Bureau of Economic Analysis (BEA) in the U.S. Department of Commerce. The BEA's data are released to the public about two and a half months after the end of the quarter to which they refer, and detailed figures appear in the March, June, September, and December issues of the *Survey of Current Business.* Summary data, much like those in Table 5.1, appear in various publications, including the monthly *Federal Reserve Bulletin* and the *Economic Report of the President,* which is published each February. The *Economic Report* also is a good source of historical balance of payments data. Balance of payments data are revised each June to reflect more complete information, with revisions being made to data as much as four years old.

Although full information about the balance of payments accounts is available only quarterly, some components of the accounts are released monthly. The best-known example is the merchandise trade balance, which equals exports of goods minus imports of goods. These data are initially tabulated by the U.S. Bureau of the Census (which then passes them on to the BEA) and are based primarily on information provided by the U.S. Customs Service, the government agency responsible for monitoring flows of goods in and out of the country. In recent years the Census Bureau has also negotiated with the data collection agencies of major U.S. trading partners to swap information about trade flows. The benefit of exchanging trade information is that it allows the Census Bureau to find out, for example, whether Canadian estimates of the imports they receive from the United States are similar to U.S. estimates of exports shipped to Canada. In principle, of course, the two numbers should be the same.

For more information, see Bureau of Economic Analysis, *The Balance of Payments of the United States: Concepts, Data Sources, and Estimating Procedures,* Washington, D.C.: U.S. Government Printing Office, 1990.

measuring GDP in Chapter 2. Here we point out that net exports often are broken into two categories: merchandise (goods) and services.

Merchandise consists of currently produced goods, such as American soybeans, French perfume, Brazilian coffee, and Japanese cars. When an American buys a Japanese car, for example, the transaction is recorded as a merchandise import for the United States (a debit item for the United States, because funds flow out of the United States to pay for the car) and a merchandise export for Japan (a credit item for Japan because funds flow into Japan to pay for the car). The difference between a country's merchandise exports and its merchandise imports is called the **merchandise trade balance,** or simply the trade balance. The merchandise trade balance receives a lot of attention from the public and the press.[1] This attention doesn't seem entirely warranted, however, because merchandise trade is only one component of the current account.

Internationally traded services include transportation, tourism, insurance, education, and financial services, among others. When a U.S. family spends a week's vacation in Mexico, for example, the family's expenditures for accom-

1. This attention may in part reflect the availability of merchandise trade data monthly, whereas most balance of payments data are available only quarterly. See the box "In Touch with the Macroeconomy: The Balance of Payments Accounts."

modations, food, sight-seeing tours, and so on, are counted in the U.S. current account as an import of tourism services (a debit item for the United States because funds are flowing out of the country). The family's expenditures count as an export of tourism services for Mexico (a credit item in the Mexican current account). Similarly, when a foreign student attends college in the United States, her tuition payments are included as an export of services for the United States and an import of services for her home country.

Investment Income from Assets Abroad. Investment income received from assets abroad includes interest payments, dividends, royalties, and other returns that residents of a country receive from assets (such as bonds, stocks, or patents) that they own outside their own country. For example, the interest that a U.S. saver receives from a French government bond he owns, or the profits a U.S. company receives from a foreign subsidiary, are income receipts from assets abroad. These are credit items in the current account because the receipts are payments from foreigners to domestic residents.

Payment of investment income to foreign owners of assets in a country are debit items because they represent funds that flow out of the country. *Net* investment income from assets abroad equals investment income received from assets abroad minus investment income paid to foreign owners of domestic assets.

For the United States, net investment income from assets abroad is quantitatively almost the same as net factor payments from abroad, *NFP*, discussed in Chapter 2. The difference between the two concepts is that net factor payments from abroad also include wages and salaries of Americans working outside the country, less the wages and salaries of foreigners working in the United States. In practice, the wage and salary component of *NFP* is very small, so we ignore it and treat *NFP* and net investment income from abroad as equivalent concepts.

Net Unilateral Transfers. **Unilateral transfers** are payments from one country to another that do not correspond to the purchase of any good, service, or asset. Examples are official foreign aid (a payment from one government to another) or a gift of money from a resident of one country to family members living in another country. When the United States makes a transfer to another country, the amount of the transfer is a debit item because funds flow out of the United States. A country's net unilateral transfers equal unilateral transfers received by the country minus unilateral transfers flowing out of the country. The negative value of net unilateral transfers in Table 5.1 shows that the United States is a net donor to other countries.

Current Account Balance. Adding all the credit items and subtracting all the debit items in the current account yields a number called the **current account balance.** If the current account balance is positive—with the value of credit items exceeding the value of debit items—the country has a current account surplus. If the current account balance is negative—with the value of debit items exceeding the value of credit items—the country has a current account deficit. As Table 5.1 shows, in 1992 the United States had a $62.5 billion current account deficit, equal to the sum of net exports ($NX = -\$41.2$ billion), net investment income from abroad (*NFP* = $10.1 billion), and net unilateral transfers (–$31.4 billion).

The Capital Account

Not all transactions with foreign countries are tallied in the current account. If a Japanese investor purchases a ten-year-old vacation house in Hawaii, for example, the purchase is *not* included in the current account of either the United States or Japan. The reason is that the current account includes only the trade of currently produced goods and services. A ten-year-old house is an existing asset rather than a currently produced good or service, so its sale isn't part of the current account.

Trade between countries in existing assets, either real or financial, is recorded in the **capital account.** When the home country sells an asset to another country, the transaction is recorded as a **capital inflow** for the home country and as a credit item in the capital account. So, for example, if an American hotel is sold to Italian investors, the transaction is counted as a capital inflow to the United States and as a credit item in the U.S. capital account. (Why is a capital inflow a credit item? Because when an American sells an asset to a foreigner, funds flow *into* the United States.) Similarly, when the home country buys an asset from abroad—say, an American obtains a Swiss bank account—the transaction is a **capital outflow** from the home country (the United States in this example) and a debit item in the home country's capital account (funds are flowing *out of* the United States).

The **capital account balance** equals the value of capital inflows (credit items) minus the value of capital outflows (debit items). When residents of a country sell more assets to foreigners than they buy from foreigners, the capital account balance is positive, creating a capital account surplus. When residents of the home country purchase more assets from foreigners than they sell, the capital account balance is negative, creating a capital account deficit. Table 5.1 shows that in 1992 Americans increased their holdings of foreign assets by $44.9 billion while foreigners increased their holdings of U.S. assets by $120.4 billion. Thus the United States had a capital account surplus (a net capital inflow) of $75.5 billion in 1992 ($120.4 billion minus $44.9 billion).

The Official Settlements Balance. In Table 5.1 one set of capital account transactions, transactions in official reserve assets, has been broken out separately. These transactions differ from other capital account transactions in that they are conducted by central banks (such as the Federal Reserve in the United States), which are the official institutions that determine national money supplies. Held by central banks, **official reserve assets** are assets, other than domestic money or securities, that can be used in making international payments. Historically, gold was the primary official reserve asset, but now the official reserves of central banks also include government securities of major industrialized economies, foreign bank deposits, and special assets created by the International Monetary Fund (an international agency that facilitates trade and financial relationships among countries).

Central banks can change the quantity of official reserve assets they hold by buying or selling reserve assets on open markets. For example, the Federal Reserve could increase its reserve assets by using dollars to buy gold. According to Table 5.1 (see the line "U.S. official reserve assets"), in 1992 the U.S. central bank sold \$3.9 billion of its official reserve assets.[2] In the same year foreign central banks accumulated \$40.3 billion in dollar-denominated reserve assets (see the line "Foreign official assets"). The **official settlements balance**—also called the **balance of payments**—is the net increase (domestic less foreign) in a country's official reserve assets. A country that increases its net holdings of reserve assets during a year has a balance of payments surplus, and a country that reduces its net holdings of reserve assets has a balance of payments deficit. For the United States in 1992 the official settlements balance was –\$3.9 billion (the change in U.S. reserve assets) less \$40.3 billion (the change in foreign dollar-denominated reserve assets), or –\$44.2 billion. Thus the United States had a balance of payments deficit of \$44.2 billion in 1992.

For the issues we discuss in this chapter, the balances on current account and capital account play a much larger role than the balance of payments. The macroeconomic significance of the balance of payments is explained in Chapter 14, when we discuss the determination of exchange rates.

The Relationship between the Current Account and the Capital Account

The logic of balance of payments accounting implies a close relationship between the current account and the capital account. Except for errors arising from problems of measurement, *in each period the current account balance and the capital account balance must sum to zero.* That is, if

$$CA = \text{current account balance,}$$
$$KA = \text{capital account balance,}$$

then

$$CA + KA = 0. \qquad (5.1)$$

The reason that Eq. (5.1) holds is that every international transaction involves a swap of goods, services, or assets between countries. The two sides of the swap always have offsetting effects on the sum of the current and capital account balances, $CA + KA$. Thus the sum of the current and capital account balances must equal zero.

Table 5.2, shown on the next page, helps clarify this point. Suppose that an American buys an imported British sweater, paying \$75 for it. This transaction is an import of goods to the United States and thus reduces the U.S. current account balance by \$75. However, the British exporter who sold the sweater now holds \$75. What will he do with it? There are several possibilities, any of which will offset the effect of the purchase of the sweater on the sum of the current and capital account balances.

The Briton may use the \$75 to buy a U.S. product, say, a computer game. This purchase is a \$75 export for the United States. This U.S. export together with the original import of the sweater into the United States results in no net

2. Remember that a positive number in the capital account indicates a capital inflow, or a sale of assets.

Table 5.2 Why the Current Account Balance and the Capital Account Balance Sum to Zero: An Example (Balance of Payments Data Refer to the United States)

***Case I:* United States Imports \$75 Sweater from Britain; Britain Imports \$75 Computer Game from United States**	
Current Account	
Exports	+\$75
Imports	–\$75
Current account balance, CA	0
Capital Account	
No transaction	
Capital account balance, KA	0
Sum of current and capital account balances, $CA + KA$	0
***Case II:* United States Imports \$75 Sweater from Britain; Britain Buys \$75 Bond from United States**	
Current Account	
Imports	–\$75
Current account balance, CA	–\$75
Capital Account	
Capital inflow	+\$75
Capital account balance, KA	+\$75
Sum of current and capital account balances, $CA + KA$	0
***Case III:* United States Imports \$75 Sweater from Britain; Federal Reserve Sells \$75 of British Pounds to British Bank**	
Current Account	
Imports	–\$75
Current account balance, CA	–\$75
Capital Account	
Capital inflow (reduction in U.S. official reserve assets)	+\$75
Capital account balance, KA	+\$75
Sum of current and capital account balances, $CA + KA$	0

change in the U.S. current account balance *CA*. The U.S. capital account balance *KA* hasn't changed, as no assets have been traded. Thus the sum of *CA* and *KA* remains the same.

A second possibility is that the Briton will use the \$75 to buy a U.S. asset, say, a bond issued by a U.S. corporation. The purchase of this bond is a capital inflow to the United States. This \$75 increase in the U.S. capital account offsets the \$75 reduction in the U.S. current account caused by the original import of the sweater. Again, the sum of the current and capital account balances, *CA* + *KA*, is unaffected by the combination of transactions.

Finally, the Briton may decide to go to his bank and trade his dollars for British pounds. If the bank sells these dollars to another Briton for the purpose of buying U.S. exports or assets, or if it buys U.S. assets itself, one of the previous two cases is repeated. Alternatively, the bank may sell the dollars to the Federal Reserve in exchange for pounds. But in giving up $75 worth of British pounds, the Federal Reserve reduces its holdings of official reserve assets by $75, which counts as a capital inflow. As in the previous case, the capital account balance rises by $75, offsetting the decline in the current account balance caused by the import of the sweater.[3]

This example shows why, conceptually, the current account balance and capital account balance must always sum to zero. In practice, problems in measuring international transactions prevent this relationship from holding exactly. The amount that would have to be added to the sum of the current and capital account balances for this sum to reach its theoretical value of zero is called the **statistical discrepancy.** As Table 5.1 shows, in 1992 the statistical discrepancy was about –$13.1 billion. Box 5.1 discusses a puzzle that arises because of statistical discrepancies in the balance of payments accounts.

3. In this case the balance of payments falls by $75, reflecting the Fed's loss of official reserves. We didn't consider the possibility that the Briton would just hold $75 in U.S. currency. As dollars are an obligation of the United States (in particular, of the Fed), the Briton's acquisition of dollars would be a credit item in the U.S. capital account, which would offset the effect of the sweater import on the U.S. current account.

BOX 5.1

Does Mars Have a Current Account Surplus?

The exports and imports of any individual country need not be equal in value. However, as every export is somebody else's import, for the world as a whole exports must equal imports and the current account surplus must be zero.

Or must it? When official current account figures for all nations are added up, the result is a current account deficit for the world. For example, International Monetary Fund (IMF) projections for 1993 were that industrial countries would have a collective $35.6 billion current account deficit, developing countries would have a $52.9 billion deficit, and former centrally planned economies would have a $24.6 billion deficit, all of which adds up to a current account deficit for the world as a whole of $113.1 billion. Is planet Earth a net importer, and does Mars have a current account surplus?

Since extraterrestrial trade seems unlikely, the explanation of the Earth's current account deficit must lie in statistical and measurement problems. A study by the IMF concluded that the main problem is the misreporting of income from assets held abroad. For example, interest earned by an American on a foreign bank account should in principle be counted as a credit item in the U.S. current account and a debit item in the current account of the foreign country. However, if the American fails to report this interest income to the U.S. government, it may show up only as a debit to the foreign current account, leading to a measured Earth-wide current account deficit. The fact that the world's current account deficit is generally larger during periods of high interest rates provides some support for this explanation.

Sources: International Monetary Fund, *Report on the World Current Account Discrepancy,* September 1987; and IMF, *World Economic Outlook,* October 1992, Table A30.

Net Foreign Assets and the Balance of Payments Accounts

In Chapter 2 we defined the net foreign assets of a country as the foreign assets held by the country's residents (including, for example, foreign stocks, bonds, or real estate) minus the country's foreign liabilities (domestic physical and financial assets owned by foreigners). Net foreign assets are part of a country's national wealth, along with the country's domestic physical assets, such as land and the capital stock. The total value of a country's net foreign assets can change in two ways: (1) the value of existing foreign assets and foreign liabilities can change, as when stock held by an American in a foreign corporation increases in value or the value of U.S. farmland owned by a foreigner declines; and (2) the country can acquire new foreign assets or incur new foreign liabilities.

What determines the quantity of new foreign assets that a country can acquire? In any period *the net amount of new foreign assets that a country acquires equals its current account surplus.* For example, suppose a country exports $10 billion more in goods and services than it imports and thus runs a $10 billion current account surplus (assuming that net investment income from abroad and net unilateral transfers both are zero). The country must then use this $10 billion to acquire foreign assets or reduce foreign liabilities. In this case we say that the country has undertaken net foreign lending of $10 billion.

Similarly, if a country has a $10 billion current account deficit, it must cover this deficit either by selling assets to foreigners or borrowing from foreigners. Either action reduces the country's net foreign assets by $10 billion. We describe this situation by saying that the country has engaged in net foreign borrowing of $10 billion.

Equation (5.1) emphasizes the link between the current account and the acquisition of foreign assets. Because $CA + KA = 0$, if a country has a current account surplus, it must have an equal capital account deficit. In turn, a capital account deficit implies that the country is experiencing capital outflows, or a net increase in holdings of foreign assets. Similarly, a current account deficit implies a capital account surplus and a decline in the country's net holdings of foreign assets. Summary table 7 presents some equivalent ways of describing a country's current account position and its acquisition of foreign assets.

SUMMARY 7

Equivalent Measures of a Country's International Trade and Lending

Each Item Describes the Same Situation

A current account surplus of $10 billion
A capital account deficit of $10 billion
Net acquisition of foreign assets of $10 billion
Net foreign lending of $10 billion
Net exports of $10 billion (if net factor payments, *NFP*, and net unilateral transfers equal zero)

Application

Is the United States the World's Largest International Debtor?

From about World War I until the 1980s, the United States was a net creditor internationally, in that it had more foreign assets than liabilities. However, beginning in the early 1980s the United States ran up large annual current account deficits, which had to be financed by net foreign borrowing.[4]

According to official statistics released at the time by the Bureau of Economic Analysis (BEA), U.S. foreign obligations drew even with its foreign assets in 1984; by the end of the decade foreign liabilities exceeded foreign assets by nearly $700 billion. Journalists and others often cited the implication of these numbers: that during the 1980s the United States had become the world's largest international debtor and was in economic decline.

It is certainly true that years of current account deficits have eroded America's net foreign assets. However, the claim that the United States is the world's largest debtor needs to be put into perspective. First, the economic burden created by any debt depends not on the absolute size of the debt but on its size relative to the debtor's economic resources. Even if the $700 billion estimate for U.S. net foreign debt in the late 1980s were correct (and there are reasons to question this number), that debt would have represented about 13% of American annual GDP—a much smaller share of national output than the debt of countries such as Mexico (debt equals 78% of output), Chile (125%), Nigeria (123%), and Jamaica (176%),[5] although larger than the debt-to-GDP ratio of most other industrial countries. Thus the actual burden of foreign debt borne by the United States surely is smaller than that of many nations, particularly developing nations.

Second, the official estimates of America's foreign debt that circulated in the 1980s have not gone unchallenged. The main point raised by critics was that, in calculating American net foreign assets, the BEA valued many assets and liabilities at their original cost, or book value, rather than at their current market value. So, for example, a company purchased for $10,000,000 ten years ago would still have been valued at $10,000,000 in the BEA's calculation, even though inflation and economic growth might mean that the company's dollar value is much greater today. Because many U.S. investments abroad were made years ago, but many foreign investments in the United States were made relatively recently, the BEA's valuing of investments at original cost understated the value of American investments abroad more than it understated the value of foreign investments in the United States.

Studies that have attempted to correct for measurement problems have generally obtained more optimistic results for the U.S. net foreign asset position. For example, Michael Ulan and William G. Dewald,[6] economists at the U.S. Department of State, estimated that as late as 1989, America's foreign assets and liabilities were of approximately equal value. Another piece of evidence in favor of the view that the United States is not a large net debtor is that U.S. receipts from assets abroad remain about the same size as payments

4. Keep in mind that we have defined net foreign borrowing broadly to include the sale of U.S. foreign and domestic assets as well as the incurring of new foreign debts.

5. These data, which are for 1987, are from Kenneth Rogoff, "Symposium on New Institutions for Developing Country Debt," *Journal of Economic Perspectives,* Winter 1990, pp. 3–6, Table 1.

6. "Appreciating America's Foreign Investments," *The American Enterprise,* September/October 1990, pp. 73–75.

made to foreign holders of U.S. assets (see Table 5.1). Recently, the BEA modified its methods to allow for changes in market values, obtaining estimates of America's foreign debt much closer to those calculated by Ulan and Dewald and others.[7]

In evaluating the significance of a nation's foreign debt, you must also remember that net foreign assets are only one component of national wealth, the other being domestic physical assets. If national wealth is growing at a healthy rate overall, there isn't much reason to be concerned if one of its components is falling. For example, if a country were to incur large foreign debts in order to build up its capital stock, and if the new capital were highly productive, the foreign debt would not be an economic burden. Unfortunately, this scenario doesn't apply to the United States: Although our measurements are imprecise, the national wealth of the United States apparently has grown relatively slowly in real terms over the past decade,[8] reflecting low rates of national saving (see Fig. 2.2). This relatively slow growth of total national wealth should be of greater concern to policymakers than the behavior of net foreign assets viewed in isolation.

5.2 GOODS MARKET EQUILIBRIUM IN AN OPEN ECONOMY

We are now ready to investigate the economic forces that determine international trade and borrowing. In the remainder of this chapter we demonstrate that a country's current account balance and foreign lending are closely linked to its domestic spending and production decisions. Understanding these links first requires developing the open-economy version of the goods market equilibrium condition.

In Chapter 4 we derived the goods market equilibrium condition for a closed economy. We showed that this condition can be expressed either as desired national saving equals desired investment or, equivalently, as the aggregate supply of goods equals the aggregate demand for goods. With some modification, we can use these same two conditions to describe goods market equilibrium in an open economy.

Let's begin with the open-economy version of the condition that desired national saving equals desired investment. In Chapter 2 we derived the national income accounting identity (Eq. 2.9):

$$S = I + CA = I + (NX + NFP). \quad (5.2)$$

Equation (5.2) is a version of the uses-of-saving identity. It states that national saving S has two uses: (1) to increase the nation's stock of capital by funding investment I, and (2) to increase the nation's stock of net foreign assets by

7. See Russell B. Scholl, Raymond J. Mataloni, Jr., and Steve D. Bezirganian, "The International Investment Position of the United States in 1991," *Survey of Current Business*, June 1992, pp. 46–59. Scholl et al. find that the U.S. became a net foreign debtor in 1987 or 1988, depending on the method of estimation used.

8. According to Federal Reserve estimates, real U.S. national wealth grew 2.0% per year during the period 1980–1991, compared to 3.5% per year during 1970–1980 and 3.3% per year during 1960–1970. See the *Economic Report of the President*, February 1993, Table B-110.

lending to foreigners (recall that the current account balance CA equals the amount of funds that the country has available for net foreign lending). Equation (5.2) also reminds us that (assuming no net unilateral transfers) the current account CA is the sum of net exports NX and net factor payments from abroad NFP.

Because Eq. (5.2) is an identity, it must always hold (by definition). For the economy to be in goods market equilibrium, actual national saving and investment must also equal their desired levels. If actual and desired levels are equal, Eq. (5.2) becomes

$$S^d = I^d + CA = I^d + (NX + NFP), \tag{5.3}$$

where S^d and I^d represent desired national saving and desired investment, respectively. Equation (5.3) is the goods market equilibrium condition for an open economy, in which the current account balance CA equals net lending to foreigners, or capital outflows. Hence Eq. (5.3) states that *in goods market equilibrium in an open economy, the desired amount of national saving S^d must equal the desired amount of domestic investment I^d plus the amount lent abroad CA.* Note that the closed-economy equilibrium condition is a special case of Eq. (5.3), with $CA = 0$.

In general, net factor payments NFP are determined by past investments and aren't much affected by current macroeconomic developments. If for simplicity we assume that net factor payments NFP are zero, the current account equals net exports and the goods market equilibrium condition, Eq. (5.3), becomes

$$S^d = I^d + NX. \tag{5.4}$$

Equation (5.4) is the form of the goods market equilibrium condition that we will work with. Under the assumption that net factor payments are zero, we can refer to the term NX interchangeably as net exports or as the current account balance.

As for the closed economy, we can also write the goods market equilibrium condition for the open economy in terms of the aggregate supply and aggregate demand for goods. In an open economy, where net exports NX are part of the aggregate demand for goods, this alternative condition for goods market equilibrium is

$$Y = C^d + I^d + G + NX, \tag{5.5}$$

where Y is output, C^d is desired consumption spending, and G is government purchases. This way of writing the goods market equilibrium condition is equivalent to the condition in Eq. (5.4).[9]

We can rewrite Eq. (5.5) as

$$NX = Y - (C^d + I^d + G), \tag{5.6}$$

Equation (5.6) states that in goods market equilibrium the amount of net exports a country sends abroad equals the country's total output (gross domestic product) Y less total desired spending by domestic residents, $C^d + I^d + G$. Total spending by domestic residents is called **absorption.** Thus Eq. (5.6) states that

9. To see that Eq. (5.5) is equivalent to Eq. (5.4), subtract $C^d + G$ from both sides of Eq. (5.5) to obtain $Y - C^d - G = I^d + NX$. The left-hand side of this equation equals desired national saving S^d, so it is the same as Eq. (5.4).

an economy in which output exceeds absorption will send goods abroad ($NX > 0$) and have a current account surplus and that an economy that absorbs more than it produces will be a net importer ($NX < 0$), with a current account deficit.

5.3 SAVING AND INVESTMENT IN A SMALL OPEN ECONOMY

To show how saving and investment are related to international trade and lending, we first present the case of a small open economy. A **small open economy** is an economy that is too small to affect the world real interest rate. The **world real interest rate** is the real interest rate that prevails in the international capital market, the market in which individuals, businesses, and governments borrow and lend across national borders. Because changes in saving and investment in the small open economy aren't large enough to affect the world real interest rate, this interest rate is fixed in our analysis, which is a convenient simplification. Later in this chapter we consider the case of an open economy, such as the U.S. economy, that is large enough to affect the world real interest rate.

As with the closed economy, we can describe the goods market equilibrium in a small open economy by using the saving–investment diagram. The important new assumption that we make is that residents of the economy can borrow or lend in the international capital market at the (expected) world real interest rate r^w, which for now we assume is fixed. If the world real interest rate is r^w, the domestic real interest rate must be r^w as well, as no domestic borrower with access to the international capital market would pay more than r^w to borrow, and no domestic saver with access to the international capital market would accept less than r^w to lend.[10]

Figure 5.1 shows the saving and investment curves for a small open economy. In a closed economy, goods market equilibrium would be represented by point E, the intersection of the curves. The equilibrium real interest rate in the closed economy would be 4% (per year), and national saving and investment would be \$3 billion (per year). In an open economy, however, desired national saving need not equal desired investment. If the small open economy faces a fixed world real interest rate r^w higher than 4%, desired national saving will be greater than desired investment. For example, if r^w is 6%, desired national saving is \$5 billion and desired investment is \$1 billion, so desired national saving exceeds desired investment by \$4 billion.

Can the economy be in equilibrium when desired national saving exceeds desired investment by \$4 billion? In a closed economy it could not. The excess saving would have no place to go, and the real interest rate would have to fall to bring desired saving and desired investment into balance. However, in the open economy the excess \$4 billion of saving can be used to buy foreign assets. This capital outflow uses up the excess national saving, so that there is no disequilibrium. Instead, the goods market is in equilibrium with desired national

10. For simplicity we ignore factors such as differences in risk or taxes that might cause the domestic real interest rate to differ from the world rate. We also assume that there are no legal barriers to international borrowing and lending (when they exist, such barriers are referred to as capital controls).

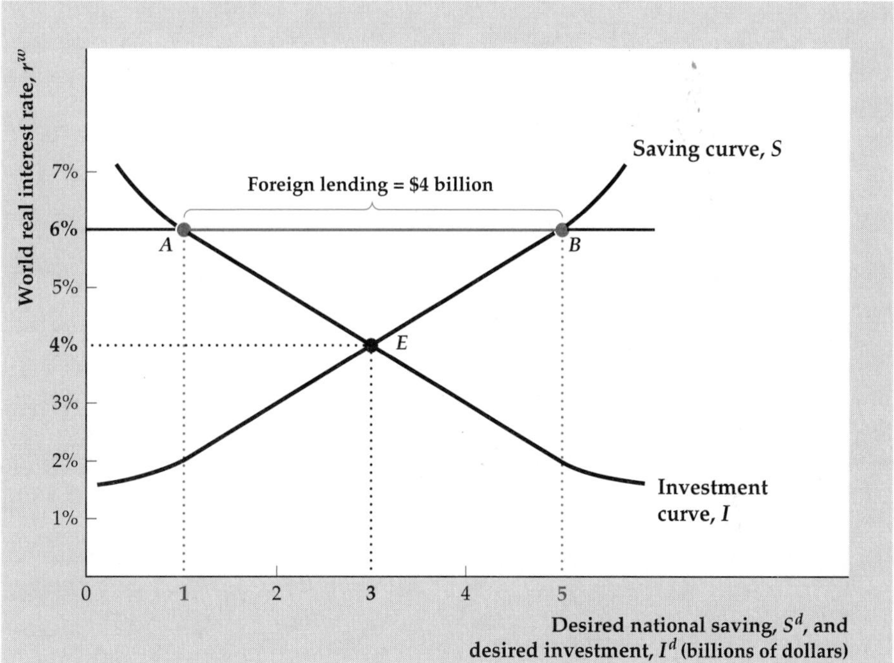

Figure 5.1
A small open economy that lends abroad
The graph shows the saving–investment diagram for a small open economy. The country faces a fixed world real interest rate of 6%. At this real interest rate national saving is \$5 billion (point *B*) and investment is \$1 billion (point *A*). The part of national saving not used for investment is lent abroad, so foreign lending is \$4 billion (distance *AB*).

saving of \$5 billion, desired investment of \$1 billion, and net foreign lending of \$4 billion (see Eq. 5.4 and recall that net exports *NX* and net foreign lending are the same).

Alternatively, suppose that the world real interest rate r^w is 2% instead of 6%. As Fig. 5.2, on the next page, shows, in this case desired national saving is \$1 billion and desired investment is \$5 billion so that desired investment exceeds desired saving by \$4 billion. Now firms desiring to invest will have to borrow \$4 billion in the international capital market. Is this also a goods market equilibrium? Yes it is, because desired national saving (\$1 billion) again equals desired investment (\$5 billion) plus net foreign lending (minus \$4 billion). Indeed, a small open economy can achieve goods market equilibrium for any value of the world real interest rate. All that is required is that net foreign lending equal the difference between the country's desired national saving and its desired investment.

A more detailed version of the example illustrated in Figs. 5.1 and 5.2 is presented in Table 5.3 on page 161. As shown in the top panel, we assume that in this small country gross domestic product *Y* is fixed at its full-employment value of \$20 billion and government purchases *G* are fixed at \$4 billion. The middle panel shows three possible values for the world real interest rate r^w and the assumed levels of desired consumption and desired investment at each of these values of the real interest rate. Note that higher values of the world real interest rate imply lower levels of desired consumption (because people choose to save more) and lower desired investment. The bottom panel shows the values of various economic quantities implied by the assumed values in the top two panels.

The equilibrium in this example depends on the value of the world real interest rate r^w. Suppose that r^w = 6%, as shown in Fig. 5.1. Column (3) of Table

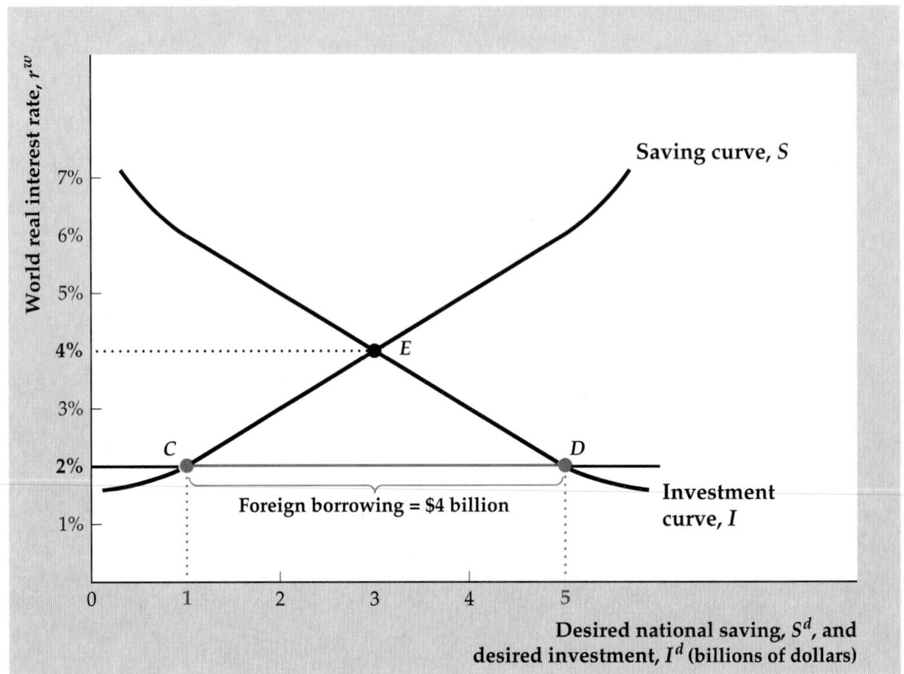

Figure 5.2
A small open economy that borrows abroad
The same small open economy shown in Fig. 5.1 now faces a fixed world real interest rate of 2%. At this real interest rate national saving is $1 billion (point *C*) and investment is $5 billion (point *D*). Foreign borrowing of $4 billion (distance *CD*) makes up the difference between what investors want to borrow and what domestic savers want to lend.

5.3 shows that, if $r^w = 6\%$, desired consumption C^d is $11 billion (row 2) and that desired investment I^d is $1 billion (row 3). With C^d at $11 billion, desired national saving, $Y - C^d - G$, is $5 billion (row 5). Desired net foreign lending, $S^d - I^d$, is $4 billion (row 7)—the same result illustrated in Fig. 5.1.

If $r^w = 2\%$, as in Fig. 5.2, column (1) of Table 5.3 shows that desired national saving is $1 billion (row 5) and that desired investment is $5 billion (row 3). Thus desired foreign lending, $S^d - I^d$, equals –$4 billion (row 7)—that is, foreign borrowing totals $4 billion. Again, the result is the same as illustrated in Fig. 5.2.

An advantage of working through the numerical example in Table 5.3 is that we can also use it to demonstrate how the goods market equilibrium, which we've been interpreting in terms of desired saving and investment, can be interpreted in terms of output and absorption. Suppose again that $r^w = 6\%$, giving a desired consumption C^d of $11 billion and a desired investment I^d of $1 billion. Government purchases G are fixed at $4 billion. Thus when r^w is 6%, desired absorption (the desired spending by domestic residents), $C^d + I^d + G$, totals $16 billion (row 4, column 3).

In goods market equilibrium a country's net exports—the net quantity of goods and services that it sends abroad—equal gross domestic product Y minus desired absorption (Eq. 5.6). When r^w is 6%, Y is $20 billion and desired absorption is $16 billion so that net exports NX are $4 billion. Net exports of $4 billion imply that the country is lending $4 billion abroad, as in Fig. 5.1. If the world real interest rate drops to 2%, desired absorption rises (because people want to consume more and invest more) from $16 billion to $24 billion (row 4, column 1). Because in this case absorption ($24 billion) exceeds domestic

Table 5.3 Goods Market Equilibrium in a Small Open Economy: An Example (Billions of Dollars)

Given			
Gross domestic product, Y	20		
Government purchases, G	4		
Effect of real interest rate on desired consumption and investment			
	(1)	**(2)**	**(3)**
(1) World real interest rate, r^w (%)	2	4	6
(2) Desired consumption, C^d	15	13	11
(3) Desired investment, I^d	5	3	1
Results			
(4) Desired absorption, $C^d + I^d + G$	24	20	16
(5) Desired national saving, $S^d = Y - C^d - G$	1	3	5
(6) Net exports, $NX = Y -$ desired absorption	−4	0	4
(7) Desired foreign lending, $S^d - I^d$	−4	0	4

Note: We assume that net factor payments, *NFP*, equal zero.

production ($20 billion), the country has to import goods and services from abroad ($NX = -\$4$ billion). Note that desired net imports of $4 billion imply net foreign borrowing of $4 billion, as shown in Fig. 5.2.

The Effects of Economic Shocks in a Small Open Economy

The saving–investment diagram can be used to determine the effects of various types of economic disturbances in a small open economy. Briefly, any change that increases desired national saving relative to desired investment at a given world real interest rate will increase net foreign lending, the current account balance, and net exports (which are all equivalent[11]). A decline in desired national saving relative to desired investment reduces those quantities. Let's look at two examples, both of which are useful in the application that follows.

Example 1: A Temporary Adverse Supply Shock. Suppose that a small open economy is hit with a severe drought—an adverse supply shock—that temporarily lowers output. The effects of the drought on the nation's saving, investment, and current account are shown in Fig. 5.3 on the next page. The initial saving and investment curves are S^1 and I^1. For the world real interest rate r^w, initial net foreign lending (equivalently, net exports or the current account balance) is length AB.

11. Remember that we are assuming that net factor payments from abroad and net unilateral transfers are zero so that net exports equal the current account balance.

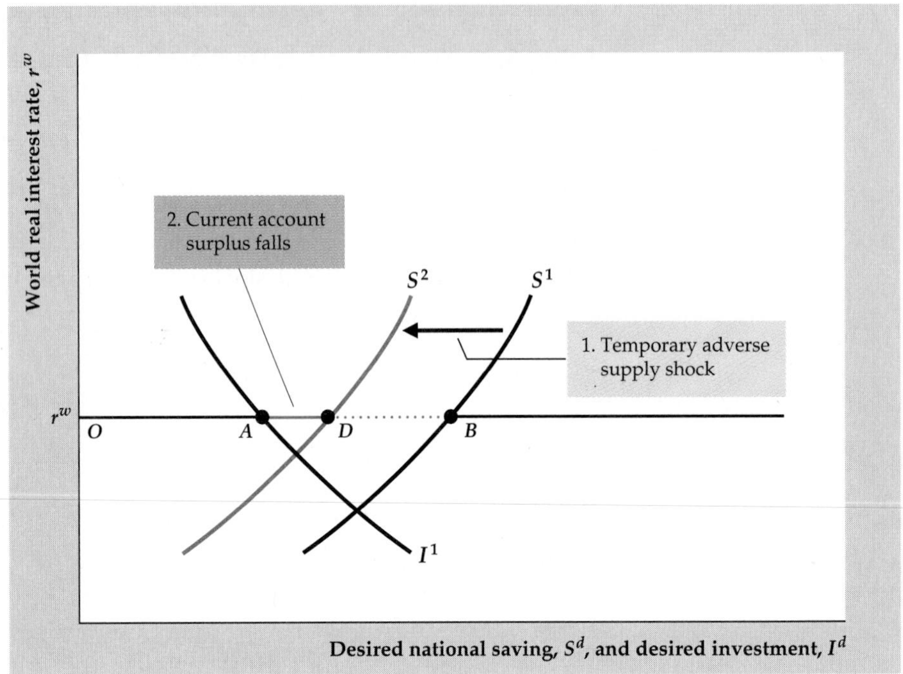

Figure 5.3
A temporary adverse supply shock in a small open economy
Curve S^1 is the initial saving curve, and curve I^1 is the initial investment curve of a small open economy. With a fixed world real interest rate of r^w, national saving equals the distance *OB* and investment equals distance *OA*. The current account surplus (equivalently, net foreign lending) is the difference between national saving and investment, shown as distance *AB*. A temporary adverse supply shock lowers current output and causes consumers to save less at any real interest rate, which shifts the saving curve left, from S^1 to S^2. National saving decreases to distance *OD*, and the current account surplus decreases to distance *AD*.

The drought brings with it a temporary decline in income. A drop in current income causes people to reduce their saving at any prevailing real interest rate, so the saving curve shifts left, from S^1 to S^2. If the supply shock is temporary, as we have assumed, the expected future marginal product of capital is unchanged. As a result, desired investment at any real interest rate is unchanged, and the investment curve does not shift. The world real interest rate is given and does not change.

In the new equilibrium, net foreign lending and the current account have shrunk to length *AD*. The current account shrinks because the country saves less and thus is not able to lend abroad as much as before.

In this example we assumed that the country started with a current account surplus, which is reduced by the drought. If, instead, the country had begun with a current account deficit, the drought would have made the deficit larger. In either case the drought reduces (in the algebraic sense) net foreign lending and the current account balance.

Example 2: An Increase in the Expected Future Marginal Product of Capital. Suppose that technological innovations increase the expected future marginal product MPK^f of current capital investments. The effects on a small open economy are shown in Fig. 5.4. Again, the initial national saving and investment curves are S^1 and I^1 so that the initial current account surplus equals length *AB*.

An increase in the MPK^f raises the capital stock that domestic firms desire to hold so that desired investment rises at every real interest rate. Thus the

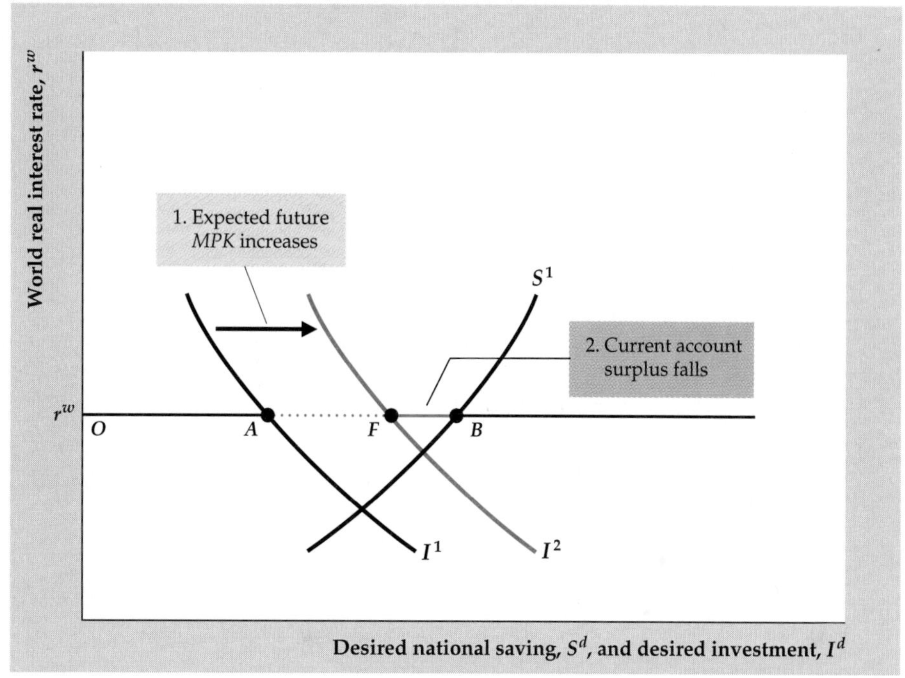

Figure 5.4
An increase in the expected future *MPK* in a small open economy
As in Fig. 5.3, the small open economy's initial national saving and investment curves are S^1 and I^1. At the fixed world real interest rate of r^w, there is an initial current account surplus equal to the distance *AB*. An increase in the expected future marginal product of capital (MPK^f) shifts the investment curve right, from I^1 to I^2, causing investment to increase from distance *OA* to distance *OF*. The current account surplus, which is national saving minus investment, decreases from distance *AB* to distance *FB*.

investment curve shifts right, from I^1 to I^2. The current account and net foreign lending shrink to length *FB*. Why does the current account fall? Because building capital has become more profitable in the home country, more of the country's output is absorbed by domestic investment, leaving less to send abroad.[12]

APPLICATION: The LDC Debt Crisis

During the 1970s less developed countries (LDCs) greatly increased their international borrowing. Table 5.4, shown on the next page, presents data for a group of fifteen developing countries, ten of which are in Latin America, that had become heavily indebted by the early 1980s. Over the 1972–1981 period, these countries ran current account deficits averaging more than 18% of their exports of goods and services (column 1). These current account deficits were financed by borrowing abroad, primarily from private commercial banks in the United States, Japan, and Europe. By 1982—the year in which the LDC debt crisis became generally recognized—foreign debt was 41% of the gross domestic product of the fifteen countries.

12. A possibility that we have neglected so far is that technological innovations also cause savers to expect a higher future income, which would reduce current saving at every level of the world real interest rate. A leftward shift of the saving curve would further reduce the current account balance. This effect would only reinforce the effect on the country's current account of the rightward shift of the investment curve, so for simplicity we continue to ignore this potential change in desired saving.

Table 5.4 Macroeconomic Data for Fifteen Heavily Indebted Countries

Year	(1) Current Account Balance[a]	(2) Interest Payments on Debt[a]	(3) Balance on Merchandise Trade[a]	(4) Per Capita Real GDP Growth
1972–1981	–18.2%	—	—	2.2%
1982	–35.7	32.0%	3.1%	–2.6
1983	–11.3	30.3	21.1	–4.9
1984	–1.5	30.8	28.8	0.2
1985	–0.5	30.1	27.6	1.6
1986	–14.5	30.9	16.2	1.1
1987	–6.2	26.0	18.0	0.7
1988	–5.9	25.5	18.0	–0.8
1989	–3.6	24.4	16.4	–0.9
1990	–2.2	21.8	16.0	–2.2
1991	–11.8	20.7	8.5	–0.5
1992	–12.9	17.4	4.2	–1.7
1993	–12.8	15.0	3.6	1.6

[a] As a percentage of exports of goods and services.

Source: International Monetary Fund, *World Economic Outlook,* October 1992, Tables A6, A35, and A39. The fifteen heavily indebted countries are Argentina, Bolivia, Brazil, Chile, Colombia, Cote d'Ivoire, Ecuador, Mexico, Morocco, Nigeria, Peru, the Philippines, Uruguay, Venezuela, and Yugoslavia. Data for 1993 and part of 1992 are IMF estimates.

During 1982, for reasons that we discuss shortly, banks began to lose confidence that their LDC loans would be repaid as promised and refused to make new loans. Unable to obtain new credit to replace maturing loans or to make planned investments, dozens of countries came under intense financial pressure. Negotiations with the banks and international agencies such as the International Monetary Fund and the World Bank resulted in some modest reductions in outstanding LDC debt, as did some unilateral decisions by debtor countries to reduce or delay payments to the banks. Mainly, though, the debtors did not default on (refuse to repay) their debts and attempted to keep making interest payments.

In the years following, interest payments on international debt were a serious burden on LDC economies. Column (2) of Table 5.4 shows that for the fifteen heavily indebted countries, interest payments during 1982–1989 were between a quarter and a third of the total value of those countries' exports. In the balance of payments accounts, payments of interest on debt (which are part of investment income paid to foreigners) are debit items in the current account. Because the LDC debtors couldn't get new loans (capital inflows) for use in making interest payments, they were forced to expand exports and cut imports of goods and services. In particular, merchandise exports for LDC debtors substantially exceeded merchandise imports throughout the decade (column 3). Lower imports, especially reductions in imports of capital goods and intermediate goods, contributed to poor growth performance during the 1980s (column 4), with living standards in some countries falling sharply.

In March 1989 U.S. Treasury Secretary Nicholas Brady announced what has become known as the Brady plan. It amounted to a three-way deal among the commercial banks holding LDC debt, the international agencies such as the World Bank that make loans to poor countries, and the debtor nations themselves. The Brady plan called on the commercial banks to accept significant reductions in the interest and principal owed to them by developing countries, in exchange for guarantees that the reduced LDC obligations would in fact be met. The role of the international agencies was to help the debtor nations meet their reduced debt payments by providing loans and other assistance. For their part, besides making continued debt payments, the LDC debtors were required to undertake reforms to improve the performance of their economies.

The Brady plan, together with falling world interest rates, contributed to a reduced burden of LDC debt after 1989. Table 5.4, column (2) shows that, between 1986 and 1993, the ratio of interest payments to exports had been approximately halved. Unfortunately, the economic troubles of these countries continued. The worldwide recession of the early 1990s reduced demand for LDC exports, leading both their trade balances and GDP growth rates to deteriorate (columns 3 and 4).

The LDC debt crisis raises several important questions:

1. *Why Did the LDCs Borrow So Much in the First Place, and Why Were Lenders Willing to Lend?* There were two main causes of the increase in LDC debt, both of which can be analyzed with our model of the small open economy. The first cause is that heavy foreign borrowing is a normal part of the process of economic development. The United States and Canada, for example, both piled up large international debts during their early growth. Figure 5.5, shown on the next page, illustrates the reasons. In a developing economy the capital stock is low, whereas other types of resources (labor, land, minerals) may be relatively abundant. As a result, the expected future marginal product of capital investments is potentially high. This high expected future *MPK* is reflected by a desired investment curve that is quite far to the right.

At the same time, at early stages of development a country's income is low, so desired national saving is low. Reflecting this low desired saving, the saving curve is far to the left. The combination of high desired investment and low desired national saving at the given world real interest rate results in large capital inflows, or foreign borrowing, represented by length *AB*. Corresponding to the capital inflows are current account deficits, which arise because the developing country is importing large quantities of capital goods and other supplies without yet producing much for export. In a growing LDC attractive investment opportunities exceed the domestic population's capacity to save, so borrowing abroad is profitable for domestic investors, and lending is profitable for foreign lenders.

The second cause of the increase in LDC debt was specific to the 1970s. The oil shocks of 1973–1974 and 1979–1980 represented severe adverse supply shocks, which sharply depressed income in non-oil-exporting LDCs. Presumably because they thought that these shocks would be temporary, consumers in non-oil-exporting LDCs responded by reducing saving, so they would not have to reduce current consumption by as much as the current drop in output.

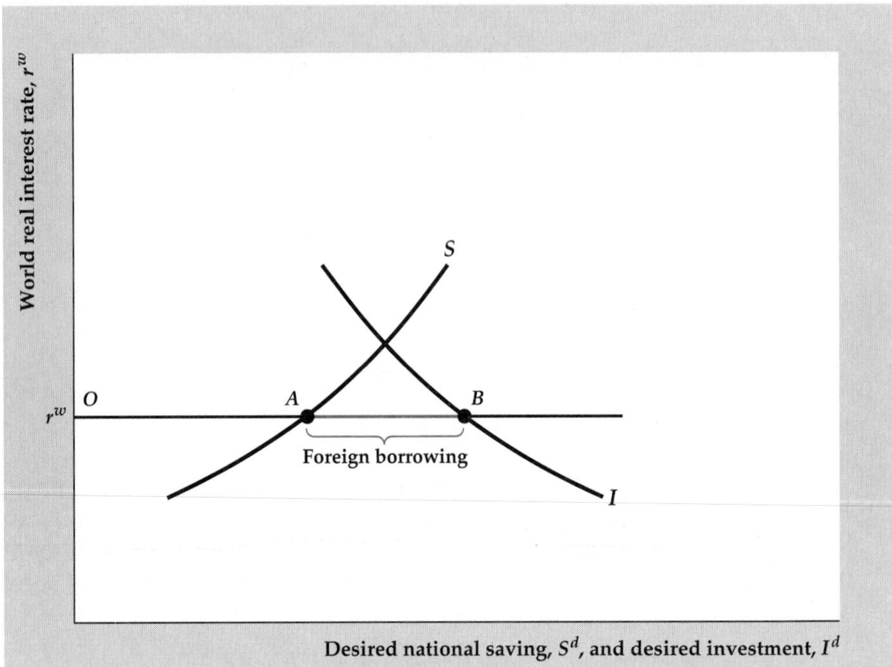

Figure 5.5 International borrowing in a developing economy In a small developing economy income and desired national saving are low, so the saving curve *S* is far to the left. Investment opportunities are good (the expected future *MPK* is high), so the investment curve *I* is far to the right. At the world real interest rate of r^w, investment (distance *OB*) greatly exceeds national saving (distance *OA*). To fund its desired investment, the country must borrow abroad. Distance *AB* is the developing country's foreign borrowing or, equivalently, its current account deficit.

Lower desired saving at given values of the world real interest rate led to increased current account deficits and foreign borrowing. Our analysis of a temporary adverse supply shock in Fig. 5.3 predicts such a result.

Ironically, the ultimate source of a significant portion of the funds borrowed by LDCs was the oil-exporting countries themselves, which needed someplace to invest the huge increase in their oil revenues created by the higher prices. In practice, the oil exporters lent to banks in industrialized countries, who then re-lent the funds to LDCs in a process known as "recycling petro-dollars."

2. *If the LDC Lending Was Justified, Why Did the Loans Go Bad?* Various adverse macroeconomic developments, not foreseen when most of the LDC loans were made, caused problems for the LDC debtors. Among these developments was a worldwide recession in 1979–1982 that lowered the demand for LDC exports. Reduced export sales kept LDC borrowers from achieving the large surpluses on the merchandise and services portion of the current account that they needed to pay interest on their debts.[13] Another adverse macroeconomic development of the early 1980s was sharp increases in interest rates. Because most LDC debt was in the form of floating-rate loans, whose required interest payments rise automatically when current interest rates rise, the interest obligations of the LDC debtors increased greatly.

Although the macroeconomic problems that arose generally were unexpected, it is probably also true that many of the loans made to the LDCs in the 1970s were not adequately researched by lenders, and some borrowing firms

13. The open-economy macroeconomic model used in this chapter is too simplified to explain the effects of a decline in demand for a country's exports. We incorporate this type of effect into the model in Chapter 14.

THE POLITICAL ENVIRONMENT

DEFAULT AND SOVEREIGN DEBT

If an individual consumer defaults on a loan, the creditors have well-established legal means to try to force repayment. For example, they may be able to seize the consumer's assets, or a court may rule that part of the consumer's future wages may be attached in repayment. In contrast, default on sovereign debt, or debt owed by an independent nation, leaves creditors with limited options. There is no international authority to enforce repayment of sovereign debts, and creditors can neither seize the debtors' domestic assets nor "attach" its income.

With this lack of legal enforceability, why do sovereign debtors usually try to repay what they owe, even when doing so imposes economic hardship on their people? Some researchers emphasize that defaulting countries may face significant economic costs. Such costs may include seizure of the country's assets held abroad, disruption of international trade (as creditors interfere with shipments or payments), and denial of future international loans.

Although the economic costs of default are part of the reason that international debtors usually repay, key political considerations are equally important:

1. *Creditors' political power within their own country.* When there were widespread defaults on foreign bonds during the Great Depression, the American holders of the foreign bonds were politically unorganized and received little help from the U.S. government (well-organized British bondholders got much more help from their government in the 1930s).* In the 1980s, in contrast, concern about the health of the domestic banking system (which stood to suffer from LDC defaults) prompted the United States to put diplomatic and political pressures on the debtor countries to repay.
2. *Relations between creditor and debtor countries.* History has shown that debtors are more likely to repay when they value the political, economic, and military relations they have with creditors. A debt-laden Australia did not default during the Great Depression because it wanted good relations with its main creditor, Great Britain. At the opposite extreme, in 1990 Iraq tried to "solve" its foreign debt problems by invading a principal creditor, Kuwait. Similarly, creditors are less likely to be tough when they value their relationships with the debtors. The United States has forgiven many of the war debts owed it by its military allies, for example.
3. *Relations among the debtor countries.* If many LDC debtors defaulted simultaneously, the creditor countries would have much greater difficulty punishing them. Enforcing trade sanctions against one country is easier than enforcing them against thirty countries, for example. For this reason some LDC leaders have called for the formation of a "debtors' cartel," an organization of debtor countries that would negotiate with the creditors as a bloc. The feasibility of such debtor cooperation depends on the ability of the debtors to get along and cooperate politically. So far, differing goals and animosities among debtors, and political pressures from the creditor nations, have prevented the emergence of a debtors' cartel.

* For an interesting discussion of the debt crisis in historical perspective, see Barry Eichengreen, "Historical Research on International Lending and Debt," *Journal of Economic Perspectives*, Spring 1991, pp. 149–169.

and governments wasted or mismanaged the funds they received. The rapidity with which lending was expanded in the 1970s may have been one reason that careless lending and investment decisions were made.

3. *Why Has the LDC Debt Crisis Taken So Long to Be Resolved?* Because the true economic values of LDC loans fell dramatically below their "paper" values, someone had to bear large losses; the long delay in resolving the crisis was (and remains) a result of continuing disagreement over how the losses should be shared. The borrowers, of course, could have escaped their debts by defaulting. However, default itself may impose sufficient economic and political costs on the borrowers to make it unattractive (see the box "The Political Environment: Default and Sovereign Debt," p. 167). The banks that made the LDC loans had little incentive to make concessions, particularly when their own financial health was at serious risk early in the decade. Only over a long period of time, as the costs of an ongoing debt crisis have become clear, have political leaders begun to take steps toward finding a comprehensive resolution of the debt problem.

5.4 SAVING AND INVESTMENT IN LARGE OPEN ECONOMIES

Although the model of a small open economy facing a fixed real interest rate is appropriate for studying many of the countries in the world, it isn't the right model to use for analyzing the world's major developed economies. The problem is that significant changes in the saving and investment patterns of a major economy can and do affect the world real interest rate, which violates the assumption made for the small open economy that the world real interest rate is fixed. Fortunately, we can readily adapt the analysis of the small open economy to the case of a **large open economy,** that is, an economy large enough to affect the world real interest rate.

To begin, let's think of the world as comprising only two large economies: (1) the home or domestic economy, and (2) the foreign economy (representing the economies of the rest of the world combined). Figure 5.6 shows the saving–investment diagram that applies to this case. Figure 5.6(a) shows the saving curve S and the investment curve I of the home economy. Figure 5.6(b) displays the saving curve S_{For} and the investment curve I_{For} of the foreign economy. These saving and investment curves are just like those for the small open economy.

Instead of taking the world real interest rate as given, as we did in the model of a small open economy, we determine the world real interest rate within the model for a large open economy. What determines the value of the world real interest rate? Remember that for the closed economy, the real interest rate was set by the condition that the amount that savers want to lend must equal the amount that investors want to borrow. Analogously, in the case of two large open economies, *the world real interest rate will be such that desired international lending by one country equals desired international borrowing by the other country.*

To illustrate the determination of the equilibrium world real interest rate, we return to Fig. 5.6. Suppose, arbitrarily, that the world real interest rate r^w is 6%. Does this rate result in a goods market equilibrium? Figure 5.6(a) shows that, at a 6% real interest rate, in the home country desired national saving is \$450 billion and desired investment is \$150 billion. Because desired national saving exceeds desired investment by \$300 billion, the amount that the home country would like to lend abroad is \$300 billion.

To find how much the foreign country wants to borrow, we turn to Fig. 5.6(b). When the real interest rate is 6%, desired national saving is \$550 billion and desired investment is \$650 billion in the foreign country. Thus at a 6% real interest rate the foreign country wants to borrow \$100 billion (\$650 billion less \$550 billion) in the international capital market. Because this amount

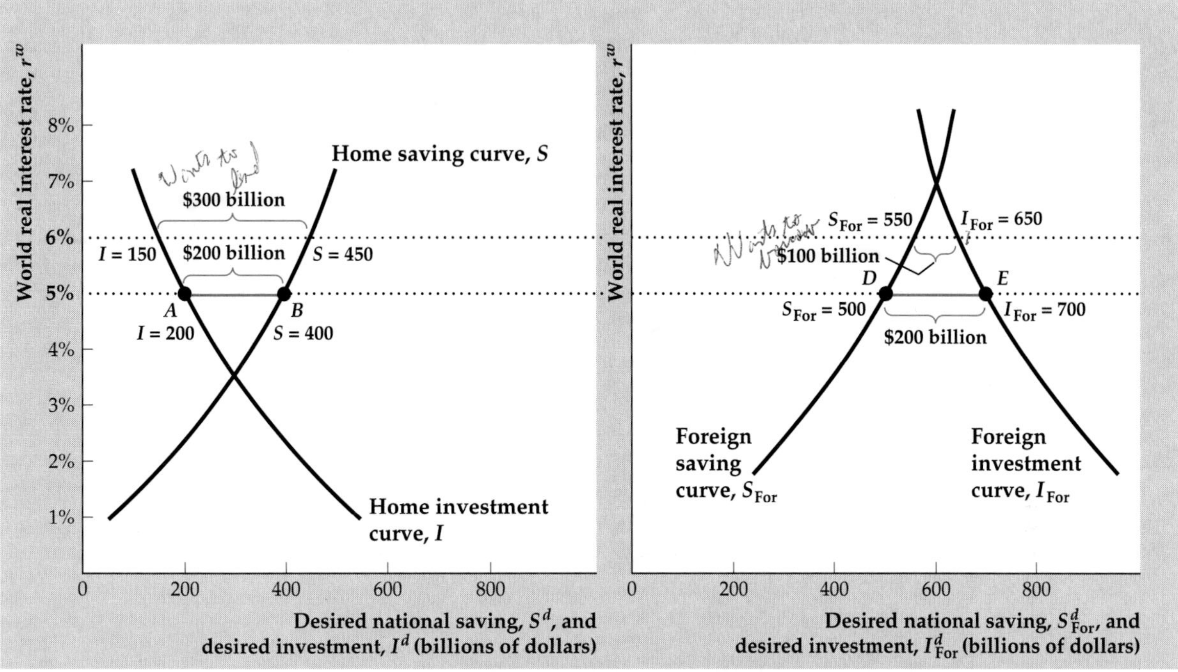

(a) Home country **(b) Foreign country**

Figure 5.6
The determination of the world real interest rate with two large open economies
The equilibrium world real interest rate is the real interest rate at which desired international lending by one country equals desired international borrowing by the other country. In the figure, when the world real interest rate is 5%, desired international lending by the home country is $200 billion ($400 billion desired national saving less $200 billion desired investment, or distance *AB*), which equals the foreign country's desired international borrowing of $200 billion ($700 billion desired investment less $500 billion desired national saving, or distance *DE*). Thus 5% is the equilibrium world real interest rate. Equivalently, when the interest rate is 5%, the current account surplus of the home country equals the current account deficit of the foreign country (both are $200 billion).

is less than the $300 billion the home country wants to lend, 6% is *not* the real interest rate that is consistent with equilibrium in the international capital market.

At a real interest rate of 6%, desired international lending exceeds desired international borrowing, so the equilibrium world real interest rate must be less than 6%. Let's try a real interest rate of 5%. Figure 5.6(a) shows that at that interest rate desired national saving is $400 billion and desired investment is $200 billion in the home country, so the home country wants to lend $200 billion abroad. In Fig. 5.6(b), when the real interest rate is 5%, desired national saving in the foreign country is $500 billion and desired investment is $700 billion, so the foreign country's desired international borrowing is $200 billion. At a 5% real interest rate, desired international borrowing and desired international lending are equal (both are $200 billion), so the equilibrium world real interest rate is 5% in this example.

Graphically, the home country's desired lending when r^w equals 5% is length *AB* in Fig. 5.6(a), and the foreign country's desired borrowing is length *DE* in Fig. 5.6(b). Because length *AB* equals length *DE*, desired international lending and borrowing are equal when the world real interest rate is 5%.

We defined international equilibrium in terms of desired international lending and borrowing. Equivalently, we can define equilibrium in terms of international flows of goods and services. The amount the lending country desires to lend (distance *AB* in Fig. 5.6a) is the same as its current account surplus. The amount the borrowing country wants to borrow (distance *DE* in Fig. 5.6b) equals its current account deficit. Thus saying that desired international lending must equal desired international borrowing is the same as saying that the desired net outflow of goods and services from the lending country (its current account surplus) must equal the desired net inflow of goods and services to the borrowing country (its current account deficit).

In summary, for a large open economy the equilibrium world real interest rate is the rate at which the desired international lending by one country equals the desired international borrowing of the other country. Equivalently, it is the real interest rate at which the lending country's current account surplus equals the borrowing country's current account deficit.

Unlike the situation in a small open economy, for large open economies the world real interest rate is not fixed but will change when desired national saving or desired investment changes in either country. Generally, any factor that increases desired international lending relative to desired international borrowing at the initial world real interest rate causes the world real interest rate to fall. Similarly, a change that reduces desired international lending relative to desired international borrowing at the initial world real interest rate will cause the world real interest rate to rise. We illustrate this principle further in an application.

APPLICATION

German Reunification and the World Real Interest Rate

The collapse of communism in Eastern Europe in 1989 revealed a legacy of economic decay. Factories and equipment were outmoded and in poor repair, infrastructure (roads, utilities, and communications systems) was inadequate, and substantial environmental problems had to be addressed. Clearly, to give market-oriented reforms a chance to work, large infusions of capital were (and are) needed to modernize the Eastern European economies. Among the great uncertainties for those economies are where the funds needed for investment will come from and how fast modernization can take place.

Among the Eastern European economies, the one that seems best situated to receive new investment is the former East Germany's, because of its reunification with West Germany. The new, united Germany has announced plans for major infrastructure spending in the east, and private firms, attracted by the former East Germany's educated labor force and its new attachment to capitalism, have expressed interest in making capital investments there. The question we address here is, Assuming that substantial new investment does occur in eastern Germany and Eastern Europe generally, what will be the effect on international capital markets and trade patterns in the rest of the world? More narrowly, What would be the effect of an investment boom in eastern Germany and Eastern Europe on the world real interest rate?

Figure 5.7 shows an analysis of this issue. The home economy, shown in Fig. 5.7(a), is a united Germany. We label the foreign economy in Fig. 5.7(b) as

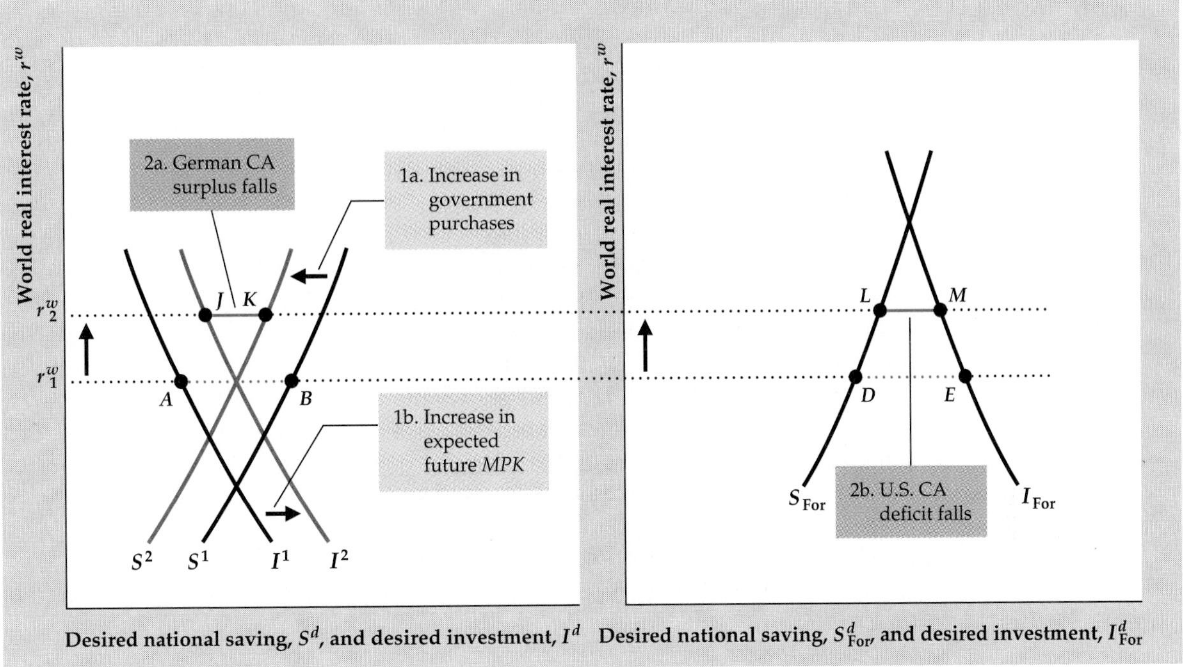

(a) Home country (Germany) **(b) Foreign country (United States)**

Figure 5.7
German reunification and the world real interest rate
The figure represents two large open economies, Germany (the home economy) and the United States (the foreign economy). Before reunification, the German saving and investment curves are S^1 and I^1. The equilibrium world real interest rate, r_1^w, is the real interest rate at which the German current account surplus *AB* just equals the U.S. current account deficit *DE*. Reunification raises government purchases in Germany, which shifts the German saving curve left from S^1 to S^2, and also improves investment opportunities in Germany, which shifts the German investment curve right from I^1 to I^2. The U.S. saving and investment curves do not shift. The new world real interest rate is r_2^w, where the German current account surplus *JK* again equals the U.S. current account deficit *LM*. Reunification raises the world real interest rate, lowers the German current account surplus, and lowers the U.S. current account deficit.

the United States, although the foreign economy might more accurately be taken to represent all of Germany's trading partners as a group.

In Fig. 5.7 the initial (before reunification) equilibrium world real interest rate is r_1^w. At that interest rate Germany has a current account surplus, represented by length *AB*, and the United States has a current account deficit, represented by length *DE*. As required for equilibrium, before reunification the U.S. current account deficit equals the German current account surplus. That is, lengths *AB* and *DE* are equal.

Two likely results of reunification are (1) temporarily increased German government purchases as the infrastructure in eastern Germany is rebuilt; and (2) an increase in the expected future marginal product MPK^f for German investment, resulting from eastern Germany's switch to a capitalist system and the opening up of the economy. To determine the impact of reunification, we consider how these two factors should affect desired national saving and desired investment in a united Germany.

Recall that a temporary increase in government purchases lowers desired national saving at any real interest rate. Thus the German saving curve shifts left, from S^1 to S^2 in Fig. 5.7(a). The effect of the increase in the MPK^f in eastern Germany is to raise desired investment at any real interest rate, leading the German investment curve to shift right, from I^1 to I^2. There is no reason to expect any change in desired national saving or desired investment in the United States at any given world real interest rate.

Because of the reduction in desired national saving and the increase in desired investment in Germany, the international capital market is no longer in equilibrium at the original world real interest rate r_1^w. At that real interest rate the amount the Germans want to lend abroad has fallen, so desired international borrowing exceeds desired international lending. Thus the world real interest rate must rise. Figure 5.7 shows that the new equilibrium interest rate is r_2^w. When the real interest rate is r_2^w, desired international lending by Germany, distance *JK*, equals desired international borrowing by the United States, distance *LM*. Because r_2^w is greater than r_1^w, we conclude that German reunification will tend to raise the world real interest rate.

Other possible effects of reunification shown in Fig. 5.7 include:

- a lower German current account surplus (length *JK* is shorter than length *AB*);
- a lower U.S. current account deficit (length *LM* is shorter than length *DE*); and
- more national saving and less investment in the United States.

The German current account surplus falls in this analysis because new investment opportunities in eastern Germany raise German desired investment at the same time that increased government purchases reduce German desired national saving. The increase in U.S. national saving and the drop in U.S. investment, which imply a smaller U.S. current account deficit, are responses by U.S. savers and investors to the higher world real interest rate.

We can't yet say whether these predictions are on target. As the analysis suggests, since reunification the German current account balance has declined significantly, from a surplus exceeding 4% of German output in 1989 to a deficit greater than 1% of output in 1992. However, because of uncertainties about the outcomes of the ongoing reforms, capital inflows to eastern Germany and to Eastern Europe more generally have not yet been very large, and they probably have not yet had much impact on the world real interest rate.[14] No doubt additional developments will affect the pace of investment in Eastern Europe, and many other types of shocks may affect international capital markets. Nevertheless, this analysis provides a way to think about these questions; and indeed, our results are consistent with projections made by economists in both the private and the public sectors.[15]

---

14. See International Monetary Fund, *World Economic Outlook,* Table A51 for data on international saving and investment flows. Data on the German current account are from Table A31 of the same publication.

15. See, for example, Alessandro Giustiniani, Francesco Papadia, and Daniela Porciani, "Growth and Catch-up in Central and Eastern Europe: Macroeconomic Effects on Western Countries," Princeton Essays in International Finance no. 186, April 1992; see also "Economic Reform in Eastern Europe and the U.S.S.R.," in IMF, *World Economic Outlook,* May 1990, particularly the box on the effects of German reunification.

5.5 FISCAL POLICY AND THE CURRENT ACCOUNT

The 1980s in the United States were characterized by large government budget deficits and large current account deficits. Were these two phenomena related? Many economists and other commentators argue that they were, suggesting that in fact the budget deficit was the primary cause of the current account deficit. Those supporting this view often use the phrase "twin deficits" to convey the idea that the government budget deficit and the current account deficit were closely linked. Not all economists agree with this interpretation, however; some argue that the two deficits were largely unrelated. In this section we briefly discuss what the theory has to say about this issue and then turn to the evidence.

The Critical Factor: The Response of National Saving

In theory, the issue of whether there is a link between the government budget deficit and the current account deficit revolves around the following proposition: *An increase in the government budget deficit will raise the current account deficit only if the increase in the budget deficit reduces desired national saving.*

Let's first look at why the link to national saving is crucial. Figure 5.8 shows the case of the small open economy. The world real interest rate is fixed at r^w. We draw the initial saving and investment curves S^1 and I so that, at the world real interest rate r^w, the country is running a current account surplus, represented by length AB. Now suppose that the government budget deficit rises. For simplicity, we assume throughout this section that the change in fiscal policy does not affect the tax treatment of investment so that the investment

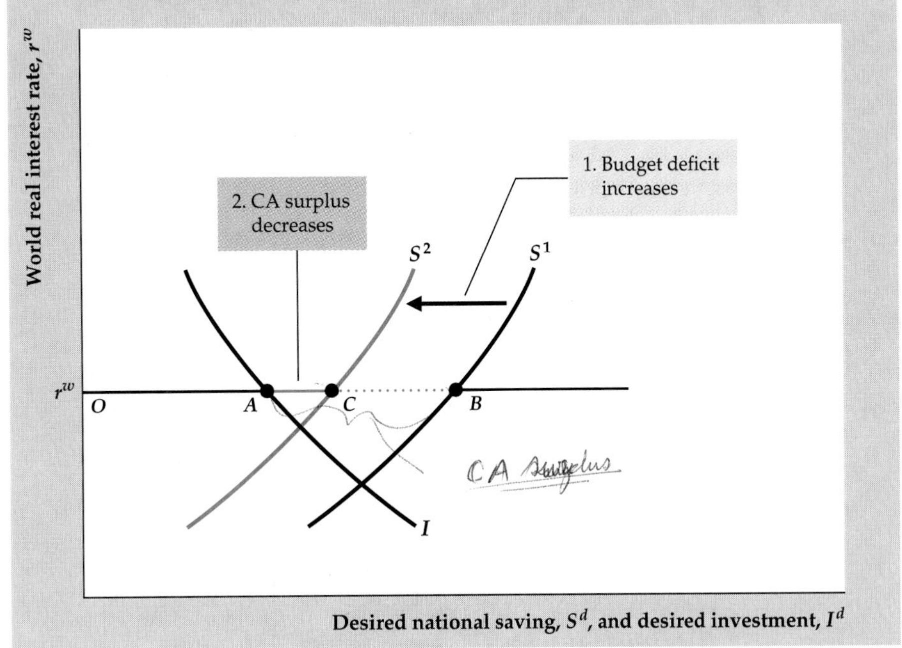

Figure 5.8
The government budget deficit and the current account in a small open economy
An increase in the government budget deficit affects the current account only if the increased budget deficit reduces national saving. Initially, the saving curve is S^1 and the current account surplus is distance AB. If an increase in the government deficit reduces national saving, the saving curve shifts left, from S^1 to S^2. With no change in the effective tax rate on capital, the investment curve I doesn't move. Thus the increase in the budget deficit causes the current account surplus to decrease from distance AB to distance AC. In contrast, if the increase in the budget deficit has no effect on national saving, the current account is also unaffected and remains equal to distance AB.

curve doesn't shift. Hence, as Fig. 5.8 shows, the government deficit increase will change the current account balance only if it affects desired national saving.

The usual claim made by supporters of the twin-deficits idea is that an increase in the government budget deficit reduces desired national saving. If it does, the increase in the government deficit shifts the desired national saving curve left, from S^1 to S^2. The country still has a current account surplus, now equal to distance AC, but it is less than the original surplus AB.

We conclude that in a small open economy an increase in the government budget deficit reduces the current account balance by the same amount that it reduces desired national saving. By reducing saving, the increased budget deficit reduces the amount that domestic residents want to lend abroad at the world real interest rate, thus lowering capital outflows. Equivalently, reduced national saving means that a greater part of domestic output is absorbed at home; with less output to send abroad, the country's current account falls. Similar results hold for the large open economy (you are asked to work out this case in Analytical Problem 4 at the end of the chapter).

The Government Budget Deficit and National Saving

Let's now turn to the link between the budget deficit and saving and consider two cases: a budget deficit arising from an increase in government purchases and a deficit rising from a cut in taxes.

A Deficit Caused by Increased Government Purchases. Suppose that the source of the government budget deficit is a temporary increase in government purchases, perhaps owing to a military buildup. In this case there is no controversy: Recall (Chapter 4) that, with output Y held constant at its full-employment level, an increase in government purchases G directly reduces desired national saving, $S^d = Y - C^d - G$.[16, 17] Because economists agree that a deficit owing to increased government purchases reduces desired national saving, they also agree that a deficit resulting from increased government purchases reduces the nation's current account balance.

A Deficit Resulting from a Tax Cut. Suppose instead that the government budget deficit is the result of a cut in current taxes, with current and planned future government purchases unchanged. With government purchases G unchanged and with output Y held constant at its full-employment level, the tax cut will cause desired national saving, $S^d = Y - C^d - G$, to fall only if it causes desired consumption C^d to rise.

Will a tax cut cause people to consume more? As we discussed in Chapter 4, believers in the Ricardian equivalence proposition argue that a lump-sum tax change (with current and future government purchases held constant)

16. Because the increase in government purchases also means that taxes may be raised in the future, lowering consumers' expected future income, desired consumption C^d may fall. However, because the increase in G is temporary so that the future tax increase need not be too large, this drop in C^d should not offset the effect of increased G on desired national saving.
17. In general, in an open economy, $S^d = Y + NFP - C^d - G$, but we are assuming that $NFP = 0$ so that $S^d = Y - C^d - G$.

won't affect desired consumption or desired national saving. These economists point out that a cut in taxes today forces the government to borrow more to pay for its current purchases; when this extra borrowing plus interest is repaid in the future, future taxes will have to rise. Thus, although a tax cut raises consumers' current after-tax incomes, the tax cut creates the need for higher future taxes and lowers the after-tax incomes that consumers can expect to receive in the future. Overall, according to this argument, a tax cut doesn't benefit consumers and thus won't increase their desired consumption.

If the Ricardian equivalence proposition is true, a budget deficit resulting from a tax cut will have no effect on the current account because it doesn't affect desired national saving. However, as we noted in Chapter 4, many economists argue that—despite the logic of Ricardian equivalence—in practice many consumers do respond to a current tax cut by consuming more. For example, consumers simply may not understand that a higher deficit today makes higher taxes tomorrow more likely. If for any reason consumers do respond to a tax cut by consuming more, the deficit resulting from a tax cut will reduce national saving and thus also will reduce the current account balance.

APPLICATION

The Twin Deficits

The relationship between the U.S. government budget deficit and the U.S. current account deficit—the twin deficits—is shown in Fig. 5.9 (on the next page) for the period 1960–1992. Here, fiscal policy is measured by government purchases and government net receipts (taxes less transfers and interest paid), in both cases relative to GDP and for combined Federal, state, and local governments. The difference between government purchases and net receipts is the government budget deficit, shown in pink. Figure 5.9 also shows the current account balance. Negative values of the current account balance indicate a current account deficit.

The key movements in the data occurred in the early 1980s. Between 1981 and 1983 the government budget deficit increased from 1% of GDP to almost 4% of GDP. This increase mostly reflected a drop in net receipts (particularly important were tax cuts phased in following the Economic Recovery Tax Act of 1981), but military spending also increased. The current account, which was in surplus in 1981, fell between 1982 and 1984 to a deficit of almost 3% of GDP. Both the government budget deficit and the current account deficit remained large throughout the 1980s.[18]

The apparently close relationship of the U.S. government budget deficit and current account deficit during the 1980s is evidence in favor of the twin-deficits idea, that budget deficits cause current account deficits. Because the rise in the budget deficit primarily reflected tax cuts (or increases in transfers and interest, which reduced net government receipts) rather than increased government purchases, this behavior of the two deficits seems also to contradict the Ricardian equivalence proposition, which says that tax cuts should have no effect on saving or the current account.

However, even though the U.S. experience of the 1980s seems to confirm the link between the government budget and the current account, the evidence from other episodes is less supportive of this hypothesis. For example, the

18. During 1991 the current account was in approximate balance. This improvement was largely the result of one-time unilateral transfers to the United States from allies to help defray the costs of the Persian Gulf war.

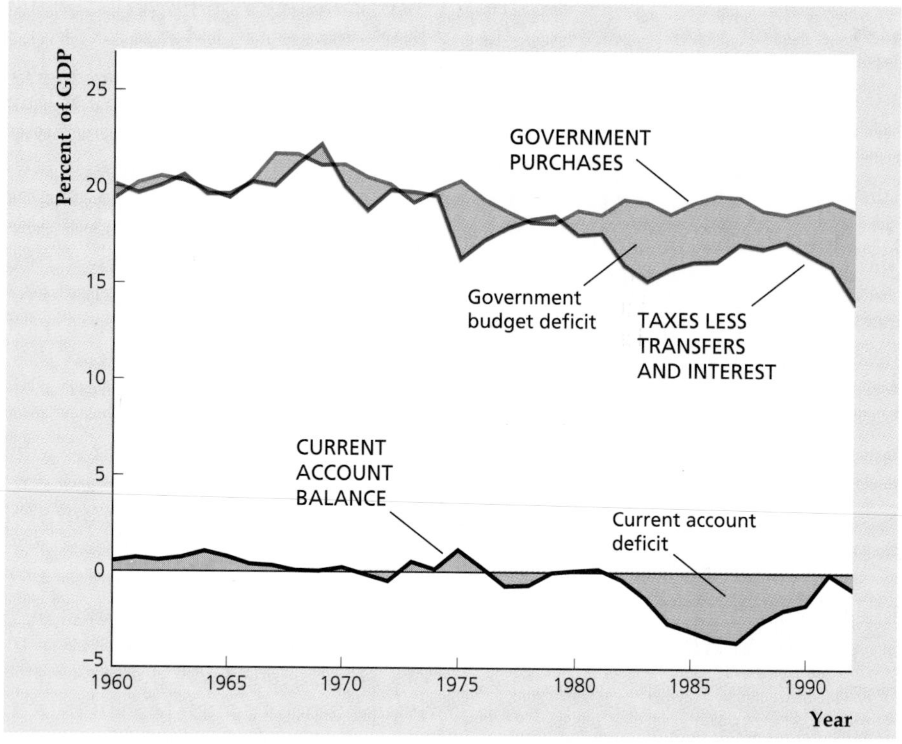

Figure 5.9
The government budget deficit and the current account in the United States, 1960–1992
Shown are government purchases, net government income (taxes less transfers and interest), and the current account balance for the United States for 1960–1992. Government data are for state, local, and Federal governments, and all series are measured as a percentage of GDP. The government deficit (pink) is the difference between government purchases and net receipts. The expansion of both the government deficit and the current account deficit in the early 1980s is the twin-deficits phenomenon.

Source: *Economic Report of the President*, February 1993, Tables B-1, B-78, B-100.

United States simultaneously ran large government budget deficits and large current account *surpluses* during both world wars (compare Figs. 1.6 and 1.5). Another situation in which the twin-deficits idea failed to hold occurred in 1975, when a one-time tax rebate contributed to a large (4% of GDP) government budget deficit; and yet the U.S. current account balance rose noticeably in 1975, as Fig. 5.9 shows.

The evidence from abroad on the relationship between fiscal and current account deficits is equally mixed. For example, Germany's budget deficit and current account deficit both recently increased, as the twin deficits view would predict. But during the mid-1980s Canada and Italy both ran government budget deficits that were considerably larger than those in the United States (as a percentage of GDP), without experiencing severe current account problems. Because of the lack of clear evidence, a good deal of disagreement remains among economists about the relationship between government budget deficits and the current account.[19] What we can say for sure (because it is implied by the uses-of-saving identity, Eq. 2.11) is that, if an increase in the government budget deficit is not offset by an equal increase in private saving, the result must be a decline in domestic investment, a rise in the current account deficit, or both.

19. For a review of this debate, including useful references, see Ellis Tallman and Jeffrey Rosensweig, "Investigating U.S. Government and Trade Deficits," in Federal Reserve Bank of Atlanta, *Economic Review*, May/June 1991, pp. 1–11.

CHAPTER SUMMARY

1. The balance of payments accounts consist of the current account and the capital account. The current account records trade in currently produced goods and services, investment income from assets held abroad, and transfers between countries. The capital account records trade in existing assets, both real and financial.

2. In the current account, exports of goods and services, receipts of investment income from assets held abroad, and unilateral transfers received from abroad count as credit (plus) items. Imports of goods and services, payments of investment income to foreigners holding assets in the home country, and unilateral transfers sent abroad are debit (minus) items in the current account. The current account balance, *CA*, equals the value of credit items less debit items in the current account. Setting net factor payments and net unilateral transfers to zero makes the current account balance the same as net exports, *NX*. The capital account balance, *KA*, is the value of assets sold to foreigners (capital inflows) minus the value of assets purchased from foreigners (capital outflows).

3. In each period, except for measurement errors, the current account balance and the capital account balance must sum to zero. The reason is that any international transaction amounts to a swap of goods, services, or assets between countries; the two sides of the swap always have offsetting effects on the sum of the current account and capital account balances.

4. In an open economy, goods market equilibrium requires that the desired amount of national saving equal the desired amount of domestic investment plus the amount the country lends abroad. Equivalently, net exports must equal the country's output (gross domestic product) less desired total spending by domestic residents (absorption).

5. A small open economy faces a fixed real interest rate in the international capital market. In goods market equilibrium in a small open economy, national saving and investment equal their desired levels at the prevailing world real interest rate; foreign lending, net exports, and the current account all equal the excess of national saving over investment. Any factor that increases desired national saving or reduces desired investment at the world real interest rate will increase the small open economy's foreign lending (equivalently, its current account balance).

6. The levels of saving and investment of a large open economy affect the world real interest rate. In a model of two large open economies, the equilibrium real interest rate in the international capital market is the rate at which desired international lending by one country equals desired international borrowing by the other country. Equivalently, it is the rate at which the lending country's current account surplus equals the borrowing country's current account deficit. Any factor that increases desired national saving or reduces desired investment at the initial interest rate for either large country will increase the supply of international loans relative to the demand and cause the world real interest rate to fall.

7. According to the "twin-deficits" hypothesis, the large U.S. government budget deficits of the 1980s helped cause the sharply increased U.S. current account deficits of that period. Whether budget deficits cause current account deficits is the subject of disagreement. In theory, and if we assume no change in the tax treatment of investment, an increase in the government budget deficit will raise the current account deficit only if it reduces national saving. Economists generally agree that an increase in the budget deficit caused by a temporary increase in government purchases will reduce national saving, but whether an increase in the budget deficit caused by a tax cut reduces national saving is controversial.

KEY DIAGRAM 4

National Saving and Investment in a Small Open Economy

This open-economy version of the saving–investment diagram shows the determination of national saving, investment, and the current account balance in a small open economy that takes the world real interest rate as given.

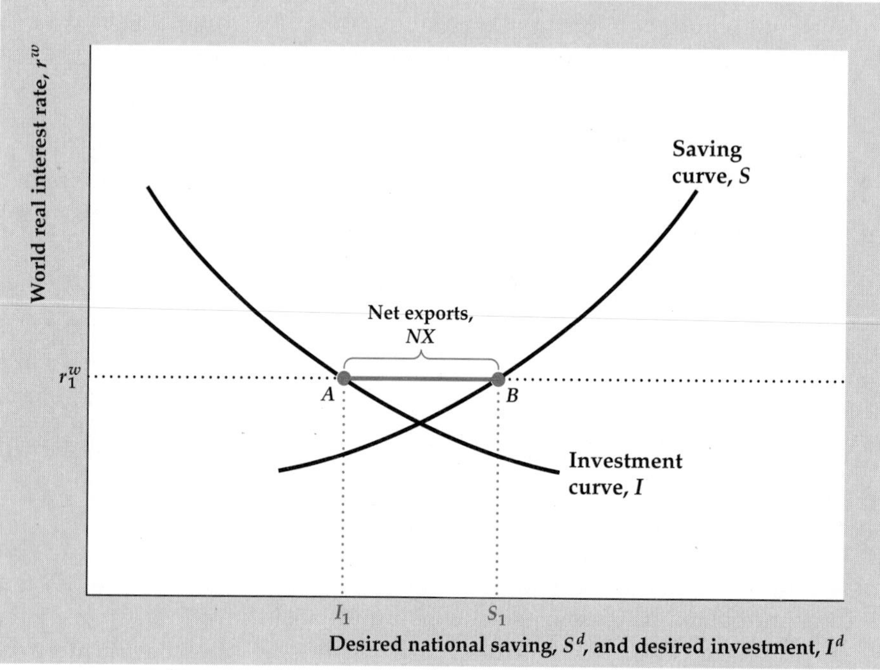

Diagram Elements

■ The world real interest rate is measured on the vertical axis, and the small economy's desired national saving S^d and desired investment I^d are measured on the horizontal axis.

■ The world real interest rate r^w is fixed, as indicated by the horizontal line.

■ The saving curve S and the investment curve I are the same as in the closed-economy saving–investment diagram, Key Diagram 3 (p. 140).

Analysis

■ Goods market equilibrium in a small open economy requires that desired national saving equal desired investment plus net exports (Eq. 5.4). In the diagram when the world real interest rate is r_1^w desired national saving is S_1 and desired investment is I_1. The country's net exports NX and current account balance CA, or $S_1 - I_1$, is distance AB. Equivalently, distance AB, the excess of desired national saving over desired investment, is the amount that the small open economy is lending abroad, or its capital account deficit.

Factors that Shift the Curves

■ Anything that increases desired national saving in the small open economy, for a fixed value of the world real interest rate, shifts the saving curve right. Factors that shift the saving curve right (see Summary table 5, p. 120) include

- an increase in current output, Y,
- a decrease in expected future output,
- a decrease in wealth,
- a decrease in current government purchases, G, and
- an increase in current taxes, T, if Ricardian equivalence doesn't hold and taxes affect saving.

■ Anything that increases desired investment at the prevailing real interest rate shifts the investment curve right. Factors that shift the investment curve right (see Summary table 6, p. 131) include

an increase in the expected future marginal product of capital, MPK^f, and
a decrease in the effective tax rate on capital.

■ An increase in desired national saving shifts the saving curve right and raises net exports and the current account balance. Equivalently, an increase in desired national saving raises the country's net foreign lending, which equals its capital account deficit. Similarly, an increase in desired investment shifts the investment curve right and lowers net exports, the current account balance, net foreign lending, and the capital account deficit.

■ An increase in the world real interest rate r^w raises the horizontal line in the diagram. Because an increase in the world real interest rate increases national saving and reduces investment, it raises net foreign lending, net exports, the current account surplus, and the capital account deficit.

KEY DIAGRAM 5

National Saving and Investment in Large Open Economies

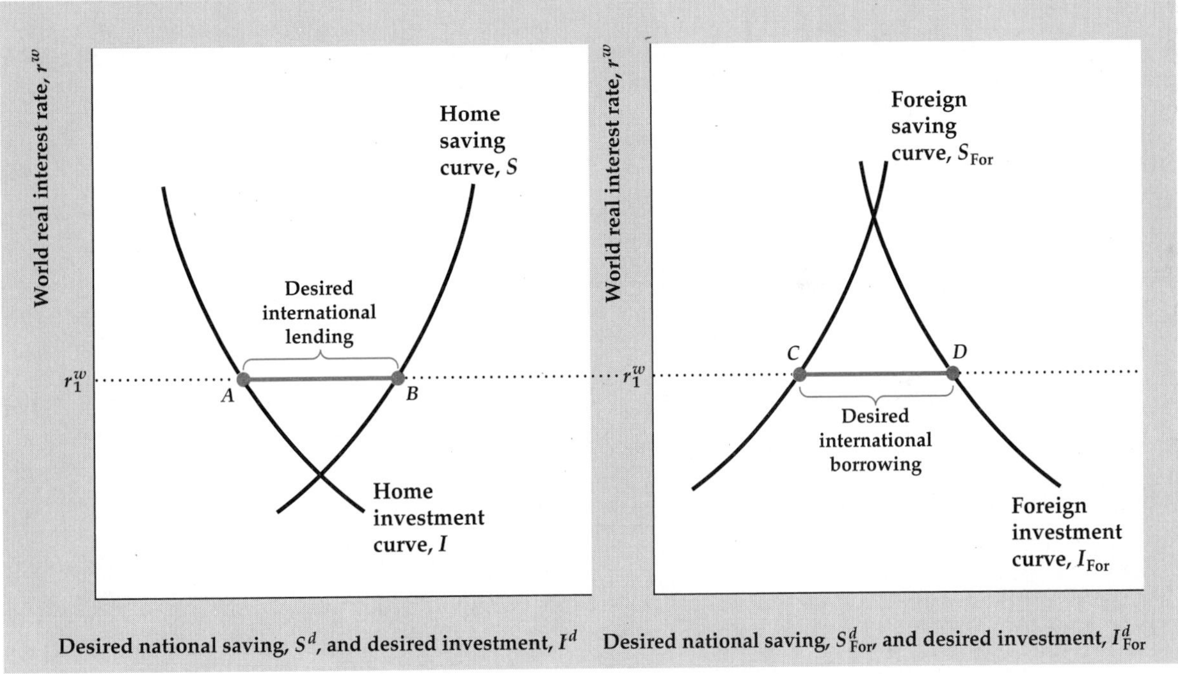

(a) Home country **(b) Foreign country**

This diagram shows the determination of national saving, investment, and the current account balance in large open economies, economies large enough to affect the world real interest rate.

Diagram Elements

■ The figure consists of two saving–investment diagrams, one for the home country and one for the foreign country (representing the rest of the world).

■ The world real interest rate r^w, measured on the vertical axis, is the real interest rate faced by both countries in the international capital market.

■ The saving and investment curves in the home country (S and I) and in the foreign country (S_{For} and

I_{For}) are the same as the saving and investment curves presented before (Key Diagram 3, p. 140, and Key Diagram 4).

Analysis

■ This case differs from the case of the small open economy (Key Diagram 4) in that the world real interest rate r^w is determined within the model, not given.

■ Goods market equilibrium for large open economies requires that the desired international lending of one country equal the desired international borrowing of the other. Equivalently, because a country's international lending equals its current account balance, goods market equilibrium requires that one country's current account surplus equal the other country's current account deficit.

■ The world real interest rate adjusts to achieve goods market equilibrium. In the diagram r_1^w is the equilibrium world real interest rate, because at that interest rate the home country's desired international lending (its desired national saving less desired investment, or distance AB) equals the foreign country's desired international borrowing (its desired investment less desired national saving, or distance CD).

Factors that Shift the Curves

■ The saving and investment curves in the two countries are shifted by the same factors as in Key Diagram 3, p. 140, and Key Diagram 4.

■ The world real interest rate changes when desired national saving or desired investment changes in either country. Any change that increases desired international lending relative to desired international borrowing at the initial world real interest rate will cause the world real interest rate to fall to restore equilibrium in the international capital market. Changes that increase desired international lending relative to desired international borrowing include an increase in desired national saving or a decrease in desired investment in either country. Similarly, a decrease in desired national saving or an increase in desired investment in either country reduces desired international lending relative to desired international borrowing and raises the world real interest rate.

Key Terms

absorption, p. 157
balance of payments, p. 151
balance of payments accounts, p. 146
capital account, p. 150
capital account balance, p. 150
capital inflow, p. 150
capital outflow, p. 150
current account, p. 147
current account balance, p. 149
large open economy, p. 168
merchandise trade balance, p. 148
official reserve assets, p. 150
official settlements balance, p. 151
small open economy, p. 158
statistical discrepancy, p. 153
unilateral transfers, p. 149
world real interest rate, p. 158

Key Equations

$$CA + KA = 0 \tag{5.1}$$

Except for problems of measurement, the current account balance, CA, and the capital account balance, KA, always sum to zero. The reason is that every international transaction involves a swap of goods, services, or assets; and the two sides of the swap always have offsetting effects on $CA + KA$.

$$S^d = I^d + NX \tag{5.4}$$

The goods market equilibrium condition in an open economy holds that desired national saving, S^d, must equal desired investment, I^d, plus the amount lent abroad. The amount lent abroad equals the current account balance, which (if we assume that net factor payments and unilateral transfers are zero) also equals net exports, NX.

$$NX = Y - (C^d + I^d + G) \quad (5.6)$$

An alternative way of writing the goods market equilibrium condition, this equation states that net exports must equal the country's output, Y, less its desired absorption, $C^d + I^d + G$.

Review Questions

1. List the categories of credit items and debit items that appear in a country's current account. What is the current account balance? What is the relationship between the current account balance and net exports?
2. What is the key difference that determines whether an international transaction appears in the current account or the capital account?
3. An American publisher sells $200 worth of books to a resident of Brazil. By itself, this item is a credit item in the U.S. current account. Describe some offsetting transactions that could ensure that the U.S. current and capital account balances would continue to sum to zero.
4. How do a country's current and capital account balances affect its net foreign assets? If country A has greater net foreign assets per citizen than does country B, is country A necessarily better off than country B?
5. Explain why, in a small open economy, (a) national saving does not have to equal investment, and (b) output does not have to equal absorption.
6. Generally, what types of factors will cause a small open economy to run a large current account deficit and thus borrow abroad? More specifically, what two major factors contributed to heavy LDC borrowing in the 1970s?
7. In a world with two large open economies, what determines the world real interest rate? What relationship between the current accounts of the two countries is satisfied when the world real interest rate is at its equilibrium value?
8. How does an increase in desired national saving in a large open economy affect the world real interest rate? How does an increase in desired investment affect it? Why do changes in desired saving or investment in large open economies affect the world real interest rate but changes in desired saving or investment in small open economies do not?
9. Under what circumstances will an increase in the government budget deficit affect the current account balance in a small open economy? In the cases in which the current account balance changes, by how much does it change?
10. What are the twin deficits? What is the connection between them?

Numerical Problems

1. Here are some balance of payments data (without pluses and minuses):

   Merchandise exports, 100
   Merchandise imports, 125
   Service exports, 90
   Service imports, 80
   Investment income receipts from assets, 110
   Investment income payments on assets, 140
   Transfers from home country to other countries, 10
   Increase in home country's ownership of assets abroad, 160
   Increase in foreign ownership of assets in home country, 200
   Increase in home reserve assets, 30
   Increase in foreign reserve assets, 35

   Find the merchandise trade balance, net exports, the current account balance, the capital account balance, the official settlements balance, and the statistical discrepancy.
2. In a small open economy output (gross domestic product) is $25 billion, government purchases are $6 billion, and net factor payments from abroad are zero. Desired consumption and desired investment are related to the world real interest rate in the following manner:

World Real Interest Rate	Desired Consumption	Desired Investment
5%	$12 billion	$3 billion
4%	$13 billion	$4 billion
3%	$14 billion	$5 billion
2%	$15 billion	$6 billion

   For each value of the world real interest rate, find national saving, foreign lending, and absorption. Calculate net exports as the difference between output and absorption. What is the relationship between net exports and foreign lending?
3. In a small open economy,

   desired national saving, $S^d = \$10\text{ billion} + (\$100\text{ billion})r^w$;

   desired investment, $I^d = \$15\text{ billion} - (\$100\text{ billion})r^w$;

output, $Y = \$50$ billion;

government purchases, $G = \$10$ billion;

world real interest rate, $r^w = 0.03$.

a. Find the economy's national saving, investment, current account surplus, net exports, desired consumption, and absorption.
b. Owing to a technological innovation, the country's desired investment rises by \$2 billion at each level of the world real interest rate. Repeat part (a).

4. Consider two large open economies, the home economy and the foreign economy. In the home country the following relationships hold:

desired consumption, $C^d = 320 + 0.4(Y - T) - 200r^w$;

desired investment, $I^d = 150 - 200r^w$;

output, $Y = 1000$;

taxes, $T = 200$;

government purchases, $G = 275$.

In the foreign country the following relationships hold:

desired consumption, $C^d{}_{For} = 480 + 0.4(Y_{For} - T_{For}) - 300r^w$;

desired investment, $I^d{}_{For} = 225 - 300r^w$;

output, $Y_{For} = 1500$;

taxes, $T_{For} = 300$;

government purchases, $G_{For} = 300$.

a. What is the equilibrium interest rate in the international capital market? What are the equilibrium values of consumption, national saving, investment, and the current account balance in each country?
b. Suppose that in the home country government purchases increase by 50 to 325. Taxes also increase by 50 to keep the deficit from growing. What is the new equilibrium interest rate in the international capital market? What are the new equilibrium values of consumption, national saving, investment, and the current account balance in each country?

5. A small island nation is endowed with indestructible coconut trees. These trees live forever and no new trees can be planted. Every year \$1 million worth of coconuts fall off the trees and can be eaten locally or exported to other countries. In past years the island nation ran current account surpluses and capital account deficits, acquiring foreign bonds. It now owns \$500,000 of foreign bonds. The interest rate on these bonds is 5% per year. The residents of the island nation consume \$1,025,000 per year. What are the values of investment, national saving, the current account balance, the capital account balance, net exports, GDP, and GNP in this country?

Analytical Problems

1. Explain how each of the following t ransactions would enter the U.S. balance of payments accounts. Discuss only the transactions described. Do not be concerned with possible offsetting transactions.
a. The U.S. government sells F-16 fighter planes to a foreign government.
b. A London bank sells yen to, and buys dollars from, a Swiss bank.
c. The Federal Reserve sells yen to, and buys dollars from, a Swiss bank.
d. A New York bank receives the interest on its loans to Brazil.
e. A U.S. collector buys some ancient artifacts from a collection in Egypt.
f. A U.S. oil company buys insurance from Lloyds of London to insure its oil rigs in the Gulf of Mexico.
g. A U.S. company borrows from a British bank.

2. For each transaction described in Analytical Problem 1 that by itself changes the sum of the U.S. current account balance, CA, and the U.S. capital account balance, KA, give an example of an offsetting transaction that would leave $CA + KA$ unchanged.

3. A large country imposes capital controls that prohibit foreign borrowing and lending by domestic residents. Analyze the effects on the country's current account balance, national saving, and investment, and on domestic and world real interest rates. Assume that, before the capital controls were imposed, the large country was running a capital account surplus.

4. The text showed, for a small open economy, that an increase in the government budget deficit raises the current account deficit only if it affects desired national saving in the home country. Show that this result is true also for a large open economy. Then assume that an increase in the government budget deficit does affect desired national saving in the home country. What effects will the increased budget deficit have on the foreign country's current account, investment in both countries, and the world real interest rate?

5. How would each of the following affect national saving, investment, the current account balance, and the real interest rate in a large open economy?
   a. An increase in the domestic willingness to save (which raises desired national saving at any given real interest rate).
   b. An increase in the willingness of foreigners to save.
   c. An increase in foreign government purchases.
   d. An increase in foreign taxes (consider both the case in which Ricardian equivalence holds and the case in which it doesn't hold).
6. Analyze the effects on a large open economy of a temporary adverse supply shock that hits only the foreign economy. Discuss the impact on the home country's national saving, investment, and current account balance—and on the world real interest rate. How does your answer differ if the adverse supply shock is worldwide?

Long-Run Economic Growth

A nation's ability to provide improving standards of living for its people depends crucially on its long-run rate of economic growth. Over a long period of time even an apparently small difference in the rate of economic growth can translate into a large difference in the income of the average person.

Compare, for example, the historical experiences of Australia and Japan. In 1870 real GDP per person was about five times greater in Australia than in Japan, as the data on national growth performances in Table 6.1 show. Indeed, of sixteen major economies considered by British economist Angus Maddison in his important research on long-run growth (and from whose work the data in Table 6.1 are taken), Australia was the richest and Japan the poorest in 1870. Australia's economy didn't stand still after 1870. Over the next 119 years, according to Maddison's data, Australian real GDP per person grew by 1.2% per

Table 6.1 Economic Growth in Eight Major Countries, 1870–1989

	Levels of Real GDP per Capita				Annual growth rate (%),
Country	**1870**	**1913**	**1950**	**1989**	**1870–1989**
Australia	3,123	4,523	5,931	13,584	1.2%
Canada	1,347	3,560	6,113	17,576	2.2
France	1,571	2,734	4,149	13,837	1.8
Germany	1,300	2,606	3,339	13,989	2.0
Japan	618	1,114	1,563	15,101	2.7
Sweden	1,316	2,450	5,331	14,912	2.1
United Kingdom	2,610	4,024	5,651	13,468	1.4
United States	2,247	4,854	8,611	18,317	1.8

Note: Figures are in U.S. dollars at 1985 prices, adjusted for differences in the purchasing power of the various national currencies.

Source: Angus Maddison, *Dynamic Forces in Capitalist Development: A Long-run Comparative View*, New York: Oxford University Press, 1991, Table 1.1.

year, so that by 1989 the real income of the average Australian was more than four times higher than it had been in 1870. However, during the same period Japanese real GDP per person grew at a rate of 2.7% per year, reaching a level in 1989 that was more than twenty-four times larger than it had been in 1870.

The Japanese growth rate of 2.7% per year may not seem dramatically greater than the Australian growth rate of 1.2% per year. Yet by 1989 Japan, which had been far poorer than Australia a century earlier, had surpassed its Pacific neighbor in per capita GDP. Other, similar comparisons can be drawn from Table 6.1; compare, for example, the long-term growth performance of the United Kingdom against that of Canada or Sweden. Note, however, that even those countries that grew relatively slowly have dramatically increased their output per person during the past century.

Although the comparisons highlighted by Table 6.1 span a long period of time, a change in the rate of economic growth can have important effects over even a decade or two. For example, since about 1973 the United States and other industrialized countries have experienced a sustained slowdown in their rates of growth. Between 1947 and 1973, total (not per capita) real GDP in the United States grew by more than 3.7% per year, but between 1973 and 1992 America's real GDP grew by only 2.2% per year. To appreciate the significance of this slowdown, imagine that the 1947–1973 growth trend had continued—that is, suppose that real GDP in the United States had continued to grow at 3.7% per year instead of at the 2.2% per year rate actually achieved. Then in 1992 the U.S. real GDP would have been about a third higher than its actual value—a bonus of about $2 trillion, or $8000 per person (in 1992 dollars). Surely, if this growth had occurred, many of America's pressing economic problems would be far less severe. Just to give one (very speculative) example, if Federal government tax collections in 1992 had reflected a tax base that was a third higher, the Federal government budget would have shown a healthy surplus instead of a $200 billion deficit.

No one understands completely why economies grow, and no one has a magic formula for inducing rapid growth. Indeed, if such a formula existed, there would be no poor nations. Nevertheless, economists have gained useful insights about the growth process. In this chapter we identify the forces that determine the growth rate of an economy over long periods of time and examine various policies that governments may use to try to influence the rate of growth. Once again, saving and investment decisions play a central role in the analysis. Along with changes in productivity, the rates at which a nation saves and invests—and thus the rate at which it accumulates capital goods—are important factors in determining the standard of living that the nation's people can attain.

6.1 THE SOURCES OF ECONOMIC GROWTH

An economy's output of goods and services depends on the quantities of available inputs, such as capital and labor, and on the productivity of those inputs. The relationship between output and inputs is described by the production function, introduced in Chapter 3:

$$Y = AF(K, N). \tag{6.1}$$

Equation (6.1) relates total output Y to the economy's use of capital K and labor N and to productivity A.

If inputs and productivity are constant, the production function states that output also will be constant—there will be no economic growth. For the quantity of output to grow, either the quantity of inputs must grow or productivity must improve, or both. The relationship between the rate of output growth and the rates of input growth and productivity growth is

$$\frac{\Delta Y}{Y} = \frac{\Delta A}{A} + a_K \frac{\Delta K}{K} + a_N \frac{\Delta N}{N}, \tag{6.2}$$

where

$\frac{\Delta Y}{Y}$ = rate of output growth;

$\frac{\Delta K}{K}$ = rate of capital growth;

$\frac{\Delta N}{N}$ = rate of labor growth;

$\frac{\Delta A}{A}$ = rate of productivity growth;

a_K = elasticity of output with respect to capital;

a_N = elasticity of output with respect to labor.

In Eq. (6.2) the elasticity of output with respect to capital, a_K, is the percentage increase in output resulting from a 1% increase in the capital stock, and the elasticity of output with respect to labor, a_N, is the percentage increase in output resulting from a 1% increase in the amount of labor used. The elasticities a_K and a_N both are numbers between 0 and 1 that must be estimated from historical data.[1]

Equation (6.2), called the **growth accounting equation,** is the production function (Eq. 6.1) written in growth rate form. Some examples will be helpful for understanding the growth accounting equation.

Suppose that a new invention allows firms to produce 10% more output for the same amount of capital and labor. In terms of the production function, Eq. (6.1), for constant capital and labor inputs, a 10% increase in productivity A raises output Y by 10%. Similarly, from the growth accounting equation, Eq. (6.2), if productivity growth $\Delta A/A$ equals 10% and capital and labor growth are zero, output growth $\Delta Y/Y$ will be 10%. Thus the production function and the growth accounting equation give the same result, as they should.

Now suppose that firms' investments cause the economy's capital stock to rise by 10% ($\Delta K/K$ = 10%) while labor input and productivity remain unchanged. What will happen to output? The production function shows that, if the capital stock grows, output will increase. However, because of the diminishing marginal productivity of capital (see Chapter 3), the extra capital will be

1. Elasticities and growth rate formulas such as Eq. (6.2) are discussed further in Appendix A, Sections A.3 and A.7.

less productive than that used previously, so the increase in output will be less than 10%. Diminishing marginal productivity of capital is the reason that the growth rate of capital, $\Delta K/K$, is multiplied by a factor less than 1 in the growth accounting equation. For the United States this factor, a_K, the elasticity of output with respect to capital, is about 0.3. Thus the growth accounting equation, Eq. (6.2), indicates that a 10% increase in the capital stock, with labor and productivity held constant, will increase U.S. output by about 3%, or (0.3)(10%).

Similarly, the elasticity of output with respect to labor a_N is about 0.7 in the United States. Thus, according to Eq. (6.2), a 10% increase in the amount of labor used ($\Delta N/N = 10\%$), with no change in capital or productivity, will raise U.S. output by about 7%, or (0.7)(10%).[2]

Growth Accounting

According to Eq. (6.2), output growth $\Delta Y/Y$ can be broken into three parts:

1. that resulting from productivity growth, $\Delta A/A$,
2. that resulting from increased capital inputs, $a_K\,\Delta K/K$, and
3. that resulting from increased labor inputs, $a_N\,\Delta N/N$.

Growth accounting measures empirically the relative importance of these three sources of output growth. A typical growth accounting analysis involves the following four steps (see Table 6.2 on the next page for a summary and numerical example).

- *Step 1.* Obtain measures of the growth rates of output, $\Delta Y/Y$, capital, $\Delta K/K$, and labor, $\Delta N/N$, for the economy over any period of time. In the calculation of growth rates for capital and labor, more sophisticated analyses make adjustments for changing quality as well as quantity of inputs. For example, to obtain a quality-adjusted measure of N, an hour of work by a skilled worker is counted as more labor than an hour of work by an unskilled worker. Similarly, to obtain a quality-adjusted measure of K, a machine that can turn fifty bolts a minute is treated as being more capital than a machine that can turn only thirty bolts a minute.
- *Step 2.* Estimate values for the elasticities a_K and a_N from historical data. Keep in mind the estimates for the United States of 0.3 for a_K and 0.7 for a_N.
- *Step 3.* Calculate the contribution of capital to economic growth as $a_K\,\Delta K/K$ and the contribution of labor to economic growth as $a_N\,\Delta N/N$.
- *Step 4.* The part of economic growth assignable to neither capital growth nor labor growth is attributed to improvements in total factor productivity. The rate of productivity change $\Delta A/A$ is calculated from the formula

$$\frac{\Delta A}{A} = \frac{\Delta Y}{Y} - a_K\frac{\Delta K}{K} - a_N\frac{\Delta N}{N},$$

2. Chapter 3 examined the production function for the U.S. economy, $Y = AK^{0.3}N^{0.7}$. In that production function, called a Cobb–Douglas production function, the exponent on the capital stock K, 0.3, equals the elasticity of output with respect to capital, and the exponent on the quantity of labor input N, 0.7, equals the elasticity of output with respect to labor. See Appendix A, Section A.7.

Table 6.2 The Steps of Growth Accounting: A Numerical Example

Step 1. Obtain measures of output growth, capital growth, and labor growth over the period to be studied.

Example:

$$\text{Output growth} = \frac{\Delta Y}{Y} = 40\%;$$
$$\text{Capital growth} = \frac{\Delta K}{K} = 20\%;$$
$$\text{Labor growth} = \frac{\Delta N}{N} = 30\%.$$

Step 2. Using historical data, obtain estimates of the elasticities of output with respect to capital and labor, a_K and a_N.

Example: $a_K = 0.3$ and $a_N = 0.7$.

Step 3. Find the contributions to growth of capital and labor.

Example:

$$\text{Contribution to output growth of growth in capital} = a_K \frac{\Delta K}{K} = (0.3)(20\%) = 6\%;$$
$$\text{Contribution to output growth of growth in labor} = a_N \frac{\Delta N}{N} = (0.7)(30\%) = 21\%.$$

Step 4. Find productivity growth as the residual (the part of output growth not explained by capital or labor).

Example:

$$\text{Productivity growth} = \frac{\Delta A}{A} = \frac{\Delta Y}{Y} - a_K \frac{\Delta K}{K} - a_N \frac{\Delta N}{N}$$
$$= 40\% - 6\% - 21\% = 13\%.$$

which is the growth accounting equation, Eq. (6.2), rewritten with $\Delta A/A$ on the left-hand side. Thus the growth accounting technique treats productivity change as a residual, that is, the portion of growth not otherwise explained.[3]

Growth Accounting and the Productivity Slowdown. What does growth accounting say about the sources of U.S. economic growth? Among the best-known research using the growth accounting framework was done at the

3. The growth accounting method for calculating productivity growth is similar to the method we used to find productivity growth in Section 3.2, where we also determined productivity growth as the part of output growth not explained by increases in capital and labor. The differences are that growth accounting uses the growth accounting equation, which is the production function in growth rate form, instead of using the production function directly, as we did in Chapter 3; and growth accounting analyses usually adjust measures of capital and labor for changes in quality, which we did not do in Chapter 3.

Brookings Institution by Edward Denison. Table 6.3 summarizes Denison's findings for the period 1929–1982.

The last entry in column (4) shows that, over the 1929–1982 period, output grew at an average rate of 2.92% per year. According to Denison's measurements (column 4), the growth of labor accounted for output growth of 1.34% per year. The growth of labor in turn resulted primarily from an increase in population, an increase in the percentage of the population in the labor force, and higher educational levels, which raised workers' skills. (Offsetting these trends to a degree was a decline in the number of hours worked per person.) According to Denison, the growth of the capital stock accounted for output growth of 0.56% per year. So, together, labor and capital growth contributed 1.90% to the annual growth rate of output.

The difference between total growth (2.92%) and the amount of growth attributed to capital and labor growth (1.90%) is 1.02%. By the growth accounting method, this remaining 1.02% per year of growth is attributed to increases in productivity. Thus, according to Denison, increased quantities of factors of production and improvements in the effectiveness with which those factors were used both played an important role in U.S. growth after 1929.

Data for three shorter periods are given in columns (1)–(3) of Table 6.3. This breakdown highlights a striking conclusion: productivity growth during 1973–1982 was negative (fourth entry in column 3). In other words, Denison estimated that any combination of capital and labor would have produced less output in 1982 than it could have in 1973! Comparing columns (2) and (3) reveals that the decline in U.S. productivity growth between the 1948–1973 and 1973–1982 periods of 1.80 percentage points (1.53 minus −0.27) accounts for the bulk of the overall slowdown in output growth between those periods of 2.15 percentage points (3.70 minus 1.55).

The finding of a significant slowdown in productivity growth beginning in the early 1970s has been confirmed by many more-recent studies, both for the United States and for other industrialized countries. Table 6.4, shown on the next page, reports some results from a recent study by Kumiharu Shigehara,

Table 6.3 Sources of Economic Growth in the United States (Denison) (Percent per Year)

	(1) 1929–1948	(2) 1948–1973	(3) 1973–1982	(4) 1929–1982
Source of Growth				
Labor growth	1.42	1.40	1.13	**1.34**
Capital growth	0.11	0.77	0.69	**0.56**
Total input growth	1.53	2.17	1.82	**1.90**
Productivity growth	1.01	1.53	−0.27	**1.02**
Total output growth	**2.54**	**3.70**	**1.55**	**2.92**

Source: Edward F. Denison, *Trends in American Economic Growth, 1929–1982,* Washington, D.C.: The Brookings Institution, 1985, Table 8.1, p. 111.

Table 6.4 Growth Rates of Output and Productivity Before and After 1973 (Percent per Year)

	Output growth		Productivity growth	
	1960–1973	1973–1990	1960–1973	1973–1990
United States	4.0	2.5	1.6	0.0
Japan	10.0	4.0	5.9	1.8
Europe	4.9	2.3	3.2	1.3
OECD	5.3	2.7	2.8	0.7

Notes: Output is business-sector output, and productivity growth refers to total factor productivity. OECD refers to members of the Organization for Economic Cooperation and Development, a group of 25 industrialized countries. "Europe" refers to European members of the OECD.

Source: Kumiharu Shigehara, "Causes of Declining Growth in Industrialized Countries," in Federal Reserve Bank of Kansas City, *Policies for Long-Run Economic Growth,* 1992, Table 1.

head of the Department of Economics and Statistics for the Organization for Economic Cooperation and Development (OECD), an organization of the major industrialized countries. The table updates the measurement of U.S. productivity growth to 1990 and also includes results for Japan, European members of the OECD, and the OECD membership as a whole. Note that the major industrialized countries other than the United States also experienced slower growth after 1973 and that much of the reduction in output growth is attributable to slower rates of productivity improvement.

The widespread slowdown in productivity growth of the past two decades is a major economic concern and has a direct impact on living standards, real wages, and other basic economic issues. Unfortunately, the source of the worldwide slowdown remains something of a puzzle, as the next Application discusses.

APPLICATION: The Post-1973 Slowdown in Productivity Growth

Since about 1973, the rate of economic growth, both in the United States and in other countries, has declined significantly. The consequences of this slowdown have been severe: The United States in particular has been jolted both in terms of its role as a world economic leader and its ability to solve domestic economic and social problems. Explaining this slowdown obviously is important and has been the subject of a great deal of research.

Growth accounting was useful in showing that the slowdown in output growth primarily reflects reduced growth of productivity, rather than slower growth in the amount of capital and labor available. But this finding only pushes the puzzle back one step. The obvious next question is, What caused productivity performance to deteriorate so sharply? In this application we discuss some alternative explanations, including possible measurement problems, deterioration in the legal and human environment, reduced rates of technological innovation, and the effects of high oil prices.

Measurement. Interestingly, several economists have suggested that the productivity slowdown really isn't a genuine economic problem. Instead, they argue, the slowdown is an illusion, the result of measurement problems that have overstated the extent of the decline.

The key issue in productivity measurement is whether the official output statistics adequately capture changes in quality. Consider the case of a firm producing air conditioners that, using unchanged quantities of capital and labor, makes the same number of air conditioners this year as last year. However, this year's air conditioners are of much higher quality than last year's because they are more reliable and energy-efficient. The firm's output this year has a greater real economic value than last year's output, so the true productivity of the firm's capital and labor has risen over the year, even though the firm produces the same *number* of air conditioners as before. However, if statisticians measuring the firm's output counted only the number of air conditioners produced and failed to adjust for quality change, they would miss this improvement in productivity. (Numerical Problem 3 at the end of this chapter illustrates the proper way to measure productivity when the quality of goods is changing.)

In fact, official output measures do try to account for quality improvements —for example, by counting a more energy-efficient air conditioner as contributing more to output than a less efficient model. However, measuring quality change is difficult, and to the extent that improvements are not fully accounted for in the data, productivity growth will be underestimated.

A careful study of the measurement issue was done for the Brookings Institution by Martin N. Baily and Robert J. Gordon.[4] They found that measurement problems may be important for explaining the productivity slowdown in some industries. A striking example is the construction industry: According to the official data, productivity in the construction industry *declined* by 40% between 1967 and 1986! Baily and Gordon argue that this result is implausible and point to various quality improvements in residential construction (such as more frequent installation of central air-conditioning, more custom woodwork, and better insulation and landscaping), which official measures of construction output don't recognize.

However, Baily and Gordon also point out that measurement problems aren't new, that they also existed before 1973. For inadequate measurement to explain the post–1973 productivity decline, we must show not only that current measurement procedures understate productivity growth but also that recent productivity growth is understated by much more than it was before 1973. Overall, Baily and Gordon conclude that measurement problems could explain at most a third of the reported post–1973 slowdown. Thus the productivity slowdown is not, for the most part, simply a measurement problem.

The Legal and Human Environment. In his growth accounting study, Edward Denison didn't stop at reporting the decline in productivity growth but went on to offer some explanations for the decline. One explanation given by Denison for the negative productivity growth during 1973–1982 is the change in what he called *the legal and human environment,* which includes several diverse factors. For example, since 1973 a cleaner environment and worker safety and health have been emphasized. To the extent that capital and labor

4. "The Productivity Slowdown, Measurement Issues, and the Explosion of Computer Power," *Brookings Papers on Economic Activity,* 1988:2, pp. 347–420.

resources are devoted to these goals, measured output and productivity will decline.[5]

In addition to pollution control and improvements in worker health and safety, changes in the legal and human environment include factors that reduce productivity but do not yield any benefit to the society. For example, Denison estimated that increased dishonesty and crime reduced the annual growth rate of output by 0.05% per year, because productive resources were diverted to protection against crime or were lost to theft, arson, or vandalism. A potentially more important problem was an apparent decline in educational quality during the 1970s, which led to slower improvement in workers' skills. A study by John H. Bishop of Cornell University found that some slowdown in productivity growth could be attributed to declines in student achievement, as measured by standardized tests, that took place primarily between 1967 and 1980.[6]

Technological Depletion and Slow Commercial Adaptation. Improvements in technology are a fundamental source of productivity growth and economic growth. The production processes used and the products and services available today are vastly different from those of 50 years ago. One explanation of the productivity slowdown is that the major technological advances of the past have now been largely exploited, but commercially significant new technologies haven't arrived fast enough to maintain earlier rates of productivity growth. The idea that technological innovation has at least temporarily dried up is part of the "depletion hypothesis" suggested by William Nordhaus[7] of Yale University.

Why should the pace of technological innovation have slowed down since 1973? One argument is that the high rate of innovation in the decades following World War II was abnormal, reflecting a backlog of technological opportunities that were not exploited earlier because of the Great Depression and World War II. According to this view, in recent years we have simply returned to a more normal rate of innovation. Some economists also point out that nothing requires economically valuable inventions to arrive at a steady rate. Perhaps the United States has just been unlucky in that the recent scientific and engineering breakthroughs in computerization and gene splicing, for example, haven't yet produced all the expected economic payoffs.

A variation of the technological depletion hypothesis holds that there is no shortage of breakthroughs in basic science. Instead, the problem is that U.S. corporations have been slow or unable to adapt the most recent breakthroughs to commercial uses. In contrast, studies have found that Japanese firms do a much better job than U.S. companies of maintaining communication and

---

5. Of course, the reduction in measured productivity caused by reducing pollution or increasing worker safety is not in any way an argument against pursuing these goals. The proper criterion for evaluating proposed environmental regulations, for example, is whether the benefits to society of the regulations, in terms of cleaner air or water, exceed the costs they will impose. For a discussion of the problems of accounting for environmental quality when measuring output, see Box 2.1, p. 31.

6. "Is the Test Score Decline Responsible for the Productivity Growth Decline?" *American Economic Review,* March 1989, pp. 178–197.

7. "Economic Policy in the Face of Declining Productivity Growth," *European Economic Review,* May/June 1982, pp. 131–158.

cooperation between the laboratory and the shop floor and of bringing new scientific results quickly into the marketplace—even when the original scientific breakthroughs occurred in other countries.[8]

The Oil Price Explanation. A popular explanation for the productivity slowdown is the large increase in energy prices that followed the OPEC oil embargo in 1973. The idea is that, as companies responded to high energy prices by using less energy, the amount of output they could produce with the same amount of capital and labor declined, reducing productivity. What makes this explanation plausible is not only that the timing is right—the productivity decline appears to have begun in earnest in about 1973—but that, unlike several of the other explanations, the oil price story explains why all major industrial countries, not just the United States, experienced a slowdown.

Pinning the blame for the productivity slowdown on oil price increases isn't easy, though. For many industries energy costs are a relatively small part of total costs. Why then should energy price increases have had such dramatic effects? One answer, proposed by Martin N. Baily,[9] is that the rise in oil prices may have made many older, more energy-intensive machines and factories unprofitable to operate, thus effectively reducing the nation's capital stock. Such a decline in the "true" capital stock below the measured capital stock would show up in the data as a drop in productivity. If Baily's explanation were correct, however, the prices of used capital goods should have dropped sharply when oil prices rose, reflecting their diminished economic value. Generally, though, the predicted decline in the prices of used capital goods didn't happen.[10]

In a detailed growth accounting analysis, Dale Jorgenson[11] of Harvard University argued that the impact of oil prices shows up in an analysis of productivity performance industry by industry. Some basic industries rely heavily on energy and were hurt badly by the oil price increases. According to Jorgenson, the effect of oil price increases on productivity is underestimated in economywide data. Despite these points, however, proponents of the oil price explanation face the problem of explaining why productivity growth did not resurge when oil prices fell in real terms in the 1980s.

Conclusion. The problem involved in explaining the post–1973 slowdown in productivity growth may not be a lack of reasonable explanations but too many. We should not dismiss the possibility that there was no single cause of the slowdown but that many factors contributed to it. Unfortunately, if there are multiple explanations for the slowdown, no single policy action by

8. See Edwin Mansfield, "Industrial R&D in Japan and the United States: A Comparative Study," *American Economic Review,* May 1988, pp. 223–228; Nathan Rosenberg and W. Edward Steinmueller, "Why Are Americans Such Poor Imitators?" *American Economic Review,* May 1988, pp. 229–234. The argument that the U.S. problem is slow commercial adaptation of new scientific findings is also made by an influential MIT study; see MIT Commission on Industrial Productivity, *Made in America: Regaining the Productive Edge,* Cambridge, Mass.: MIT Press, 1989.

9. "Productivity and the Services of Capital and Labor," *Brookings Papers on Economic Activity,* 1982:2, pp. 423–454.

10. See Charles R. Hulten, James W. Robertson, and Frank C. Wykoff, "Energy, Obsolescence, and the Productivity Slowdown," NBER working paper no. 2404, October 1987.

11. "Productivity and Economic Growth," Harvard Institute of Economic Research discussion paper no. 1487, June 1990.

itself is likely to rev up the productivity engine. Instead, policies to improve productivity growth will have to address many problems at the same time.

6.2 GROWTH DYNAMICS: THE SOLOW MODEL

Although growth accounting provides useful information about the sources of economic growth, it doesn't completely explain a country's growth performance. Because growth accounting takes the economy's rates of input growth as given, it can't explain why capital and labor grow at the rates that they do. The growth of the capital stock in particular is the result of the myriad saving and investment decisions of households and firms. By taking the growth of the capital stock as given, the growth accounting method leaves out an important part of the story.

In this section we take a closer look at the dynamics of economic growth, or how the growth process evolves over time. In doing so, we drop the assumption made in Chapter 3 that the capital stock is fixed and study the factors that cause the economy's stock of capital to grow. Our analysis is based on a famous model of economic growth developed in the late 1950s by Nobel laureate Robert Solow[12] of MIT, a model that has become the basic framework for most subsequent research on growth. Besides clarifying how capital accumulation and economic growth are interrelated, the Solow model is useful for examining three basic questions about growth:

1. What is the relationship between a nation's long-run standard of living and fundamental factors such as its saving rate, its population growth rate, and its rate of technical progress?
2. How does a nation's rate of economic growth evolve over time? Will economic growth stabilize, accelerate, or stop?
3. Do economic forces exist that will ultimately allow poorer countries to catch up with the richest countries in terms of living standards?

Setup of the Solow Model

The Solow model examines an economy as it evolves over time. In order to analyze the effects of labor force growth as well as changes in capital, we assume that the population is growing and that at any particular time a fixed share of the population is of working age. For any year t,

$$N_t = \text{the number of workers available.}$$

We assume that the population and work force both grow at fixed rate n. So, if $n = 0.05$, the number of workers in any year is 5% greater than in the previous year.

At the beginning of each year t the economy has available a capital stock K_t. (We demonstrate shortly how this capital stock is determined.) During each year t capital, K_t, and labor, N_t, are used to produce the economy's total output,

12. The original article is Robert M. Solow, "A Contribution to the Theory of Economic Growth," *Quarterly Journal of Economics*, February 1956, pp. 65–94.

Y_t. Part of the output produced each year is invested in new capital or in replacing worn-out capital. We further assume that the economy is closed and that there are no government purchases,[13] so the uninvested part of output is consumed by the population. If

$$Y_t = \text{output produced in year } t,$$
$$I_t = \text{gross (total) investment in year } t, \text{ and}$$
$$C_t = \text{consumption in year } t,$$

the relationship among consumption, output, and investment in each year is

$$C_t = Y_t - I_t. \tag{6.3}$$

Equation (6.3) states that the uninvested part of the economy's output is consumed.

Because the population and the labor force are growing in this economy, focusing on output, consumption, and the capital stock *per worker* is convenient. Hence we use the following notation:

$$y_t = \frac{Y_t}{N_t} = \text{output per worker in year } t;$$
$$c_t = \frac{C_t}{N_t} = \text{consumption per worker in year } t;$$
$$k_t = \frac{K_t}{N_t} = \text{capital stock per worker in year } t.$$

The capital stock per worker, k_t, is also called the **capital–labor ratio.** An important goal of the model is to understand how output per worker, consumption per worker, and the capital–labor ratio change over time.[14]

The Per-Worker Production Function. In general, the amount of output that can be produced by specific quantities of inputs is determined by the production function. Until now we have written the production function as a relationship between total output Y and the total quantities of capital and labor inputs K and N. However, we can also write the production function in per-worker terms as

$$y_t = f(k_t). \tag{6.4}$$

Equation (6.4) indicates that, in each year t, output per worker y_t depends on the amount of available capital per worker k_t.[15] Here we use a small f instead of a capital F for the production function to emphasize that the measurement of output and capital is in *per-worker* terms. For the time being we focus

13. Analytical Problem 3 at the end of this chapter adds government purchases to the model.

14. For purposes of analysis, discussing output and consumption per worker is more convenient than discussing output and consumption per member of the population as a whole. Under the assumption that the work force is a fixed fraction of the population, anything we say about the growth rate of output or consumption per worker also will be true of the growth rate of output or consumption per member of the population.

15. To write the production function in the form of Eq. (6.4) requires the assumption of constant returns to scale, which means that an equal percentage increase in both capital and labor inputs results in the same percentage increase in total output. So, for example, with constant returns to scale, a 10% increase in both capital and labor raises output by 10%. In terms of the growth accounting equation, Eq. (6.2), constant returns to scale requires that $a_K + a_N = 1$. See Analytical Problem 6 at the end of this chapter.

on the role of the capital stock in the growth process by assuming no productivity growth and thus leaving the productivity term out of the production function, Eq. (6.4).[16] We bring productivity growth back into the model later.

The per-worker production function is graphed in Fig. 6.1. The capital–labor ratio (the amount of capital per worker) k_t is measured on the horizontal axis, and output per worker y_t is measured on the vertical axis. The production function slopes upward from left to right because an increase in the amount of capital per worker allows each worker to produce more output. As with the standard production function, the bowed shape of the per-worker production function reflects the diminishing marginal productivity of capital. Thus when the capital–labor ratio is already high, an increase in the capital–labor ratio has a relatively small effect on output per worker.

Steady States. One of the most striking conclusions obtained from the Solow model is that in the absence of productivity growth the economy reaches a steady state in the long run. A **steady state** is a situation in which the economy's output per worker, consumption per worker, and capital stock per worker are constant—that is, in the steady state, y_t, c_t, and k_t don't change over time.[17] To explain how the Solow model works, we first examine the characteristics of a steady state and then discuss how the economy might attain it.

Let's begin by looking at investment in a steady state. In general, gross (total) investment in year t, I_t, is devoted to two purposes: (1) replacing worn-out or depreciated capital, and (2) expanding the size of the capital stock. If d is the capital depreciation rate, or the fraction of capital that wears out each

16. More precisely, we set the total factor productivity term A at 1.

17. Note that if output, consumption, and capital per worker are constant, then total output, consumption, and capital all are growing at rate n, the rate of growth of the work force.

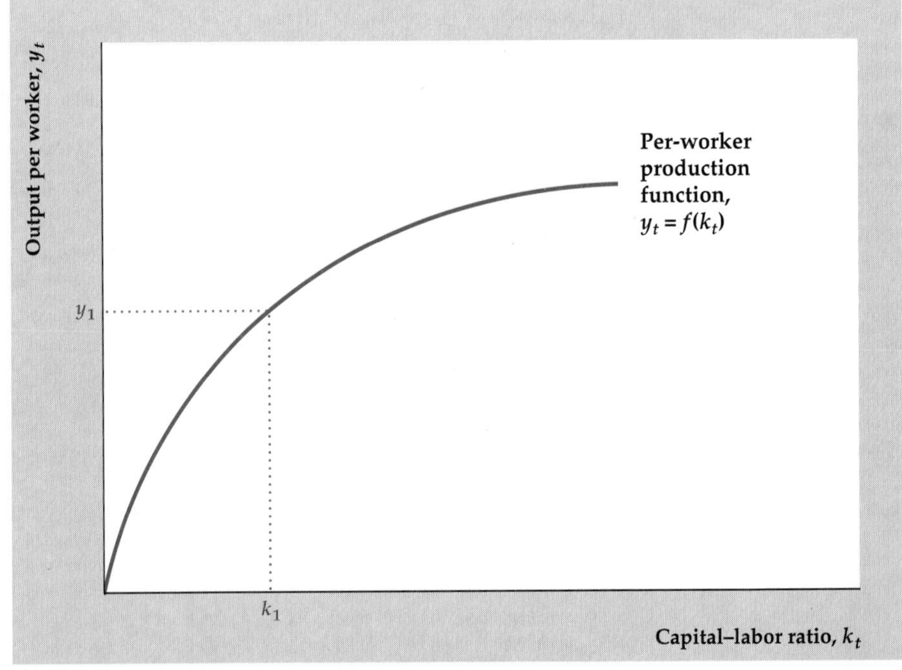

Figure 6.1
The per-worker production function
The per-worker production function, $y_t = f(k_t)$, relates the amount of output produced per worker, y_t, to the capital–labor ratio, k_t. For example, when the capital–labor ratio is k_1, output per worker is y_1. The per-worker production function slopes upward from left to right because an increase in the capital–labor ratio raises the amount of output produced per worker. The bowed shape of the production function reflects the diminishing marginal productivity of capital.

year, the total amount of depreciation in year t is dK_t. The amount by which the capital stock is increased is net investment. What is net investment in a steady state? Because capital per worker, K_t/N_t, is constant in a steady state, the total capital stock grows at the same rate as the labor force, that is, at rate n. Net investment is therefore nK_t in a steady state.[18] To obtain steady-state investment we add net investment nK_t and depreciation dK_t:

$$I_t = (n + d)K_t \quad \text{(in a steady state).} \tag{6.5}$$

To obtain steady-state consumption (output less investment), we substitute Eq. (6.5) into Eq. (6.3):

$$C_t = Y_t - (n + d)K_t \quad \text{(in a steady state).} \tag{6.6}$$

Equation (6.6) measures consumption, output, and capital as economy-wide totals rather than in per-worker terms. To put them in per-worker terms, we divide both sides of Eq. (6.6) by the number of workers N_t, recalling that $c_t = C_t/N_t$, $y_t = Y_t/N_t$, and $k_t = K_t/N_t$. Then we use the per-worker production function, Eq. (6.4), to replace y_t with $f(k_t)$ and obtain

$$c = f(k) - (n + d)k \quad \text{(in a steady state).} \tag{6.7}$$

Equation (6.7) shows the relationship between consumption per worker c and the capital–labor ratio k in the steady state. Because consumption per worker and the capital–labor ratio are constant in the steady state, we dropped the time subscripts, t.

Equation (6.7) shows that an increase in the steady-state capital–labor ratio k has two opposing effects on steady-state consumption per worker c. First, an increase in the steady-state capital–labor ratio raises the amount of output each worker can produce, $f(k)$. Second, an increase in the steady-state capital–labor ratio also increases the amount of output per worker that must be devoted to investment, $(n + d)k$. More goods devoted to investment leaves fewer goods to consume.

Figure 6.2, on the next page, shows the trade-off between these two effects. In Fig. 6.2(a) different possible values of the steady-state capital–labor ratio k are measured on the horizontal axis. The curve is the per-worker production function, $y = f(k)$, as in Fig. 6.1. The straight line shows steady-state investment per worker, $(n + d)k$. Equation (6.7) indicates that steady-state consumption per worker c equals the height of the curve $f(k)$ minus the height of the straight line $(n + d)k$. Thus consumption per worker is the height of the shaded area.

The relationship between consumption per worker and the capital–labor ratio in the steady state is shown more explicitly in Fig. 6.2(b). For each value of the steady-state capital–labor ratio k, steady-state consumption c is the difference between the production function and investment in Fig. 6.2(a). Note that starting from low and medium values of k (values less than k_1 in Fig. 6.2(b), increases in the steady-state capital–labor ratio lead to greater steady-state consumption per worker. However, for high values of k (values greater than k_1), increases in the steady-state capital–labor ratio may actually result in lower steady-state consumption per worker because so much investment is needed to maintain the high level of capital per worker. In the extreme case,

18. Algebraically, net investment in year t is $K_{t+1} - K_t$. If total capital grows at rate n, then $K_{t+1} = (1 + n)K_t$. Substituting for K_{t+1} in the definition of net investment, we find that net investment $= (1 + n)K_t - K_t = nK_t$ in a steady state.

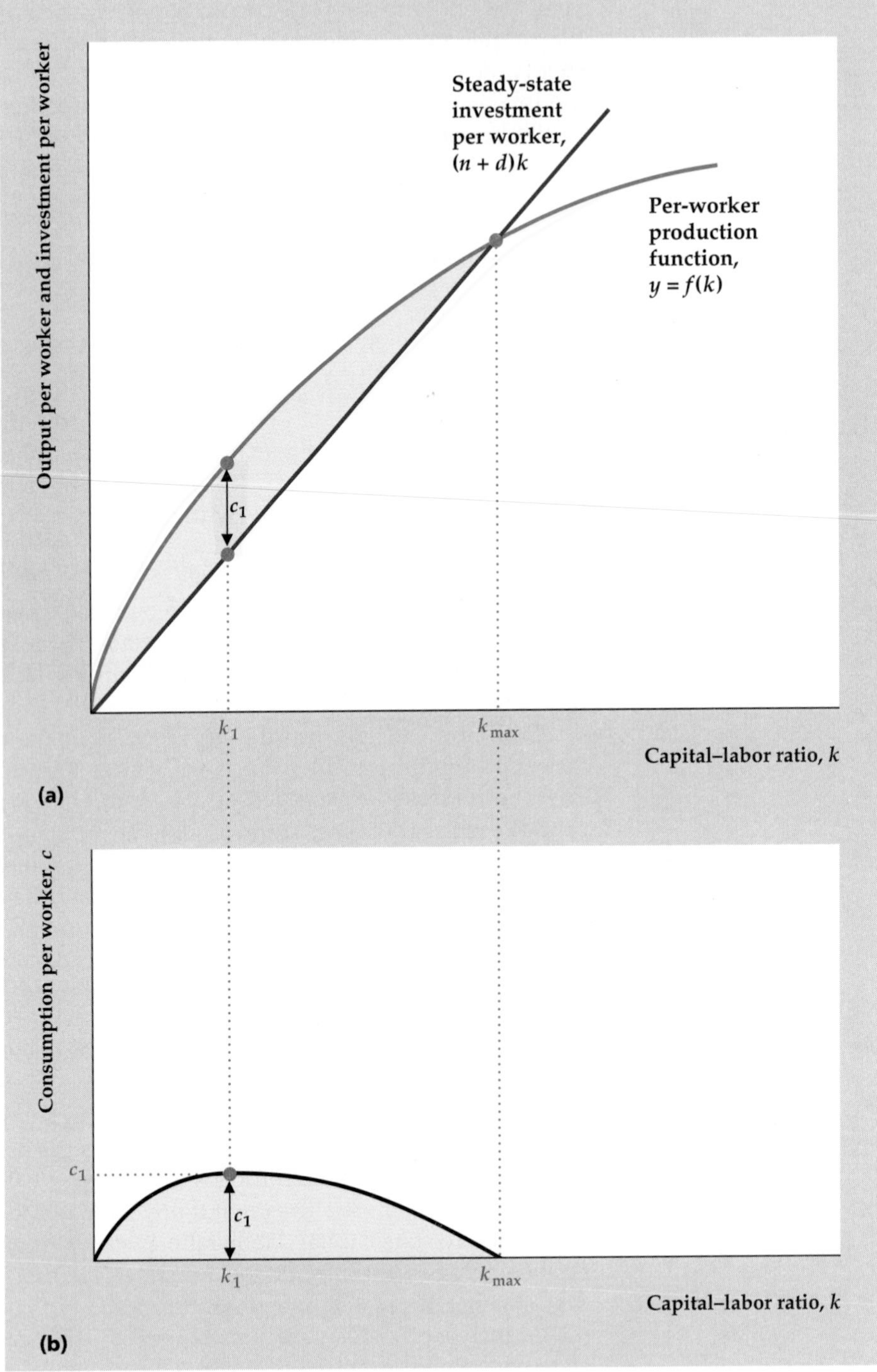

Figure 6.2
The relationship of consumption per worker to the capital–labor ratio in the steady state
(a) For each value of the capital–labor ratio, k, steady-state output per worker, y, is given by the per-worker production function, $f(k)$. Steady-state investment per worker, $(n + d)k$, is a straight line with slope $n + d$. Steady-state consumption per worker, c, is the difference between output per worker and investment per worker (the shaded area). For example, if the capital–labor ratio is k_1, steady-state consumption per worker is c_1.
(b) For each value of the steady-state capital–labor ratio, k, steady-state consumption per worker, c, is derived in (a) as the difference between output per worker and investment per worker. Thus the shaded area (peach) in (b) corresponds to the shaded area in (a). Note that, starting from a low value of the capital–labor ratio, an increase in the capital–labor ratio raises steady-state consumption per worker. However, starting from a capital–labor ratio greater than k_1, an increase in the capital–labor ratio actually lowers consumption per worker. When the capital–labor ratio equals k_{max}, all output is devoted to investment, and steady-state consumption per worker is zero.

where $k = k_{max}$ in Fig. 6.2, all output has to be devoted to replacing and expanding the capital stock, with nothing left to consume!

Policymakers often try to improve long-run living standards with policies aimed at stimulating saving and investment—and thus increasing the rate of capital formation. Figure 6.2 shows the limits to this strategy. A country with a low amount of capital per worker may hope to improve long-run (steady-state) living standards substantially by increasing rates of saving and investment. However, a country that already has a high level of capital per worker may find that further increases in saving and investment fail to raise steady-state consumption much. The fundamental reason for this outcome is the diminishing marginal productivity of capital—that is, the larger the capital stock already is, the smaller the benefit from expanding the capital stock still further. Indeed, Fig. 6.2 shows that, theoretically, capital per worker can be so high that further increases will actually *lower* steady-state consumption per worker.[19]

In any economy in the world today could a higher capital stock lead to less consumption in the long run? A recent study of seven advanced industrial countries concluded that the answer is "no." Even for high-saving Japan, further increases in capital per worker would lead to higher steady-state consumption per worker.[20] Thus in our analysis we will always assume that an increase in the steady-state capital–labor ratio raises steady-state consumption per worker.

Reaching the Steady State. Our discussion of steady states leaves two loose ends. First, we need to say something about why an economy like the one we describe here eventually will reach a steady state, as we claimed earlier. Second, we have not yet shown *which* steady state the economy will reach; that is, we would like to know the steady-state level of consumption per worker and the steady-state capital–labor ratio that the economy will eventually attain.

To tie up these loose ends, we need one more piece of information: the rate at which people save. To keep things as simple as possible, suppose that saving in this economy is proportional to current income:

$$S_t = sY_t, \tag{6.8}$$

where S_t is national saving[21] in year t and s is the saving rate, which we assume to be constant. Because a $1 increase in current income raises saving, but by less than $1 (see Chapter 4), we take s to be a number between 0 and 1. Equation (6.8) ignores some other determinants of saving discussed in earlier chapters, such as the real interest rate. However, including these other factors wouldn't change our basic conclusions, so for simplicity we omit them.

In every year, national saving S_t equals investment I_t. Therefore

$$sY_t = (n + d)K_t \quad \text{(in a steady state)}, \tag{6.9}$$

where the left-hand side of Eq. (6.9) is saving (see Eq. 6.8) and the right-hand side of Eq. (6.9) is steady-state investment (see Eq. 6.5).

Equation (6.9) shows the relation between total output Y_t and the total capital stock K_t that holds in the steady state. To determine steady-state capital

19. The level of the capital stock that maximizes consumption per worker in the steady state, shown as k_1 in Fig. 6.2, is known as the Golden Rule level of the capital stock, so-called because it maximizes the economic welfare of future generations. Readers familiar with calculus might try to use Eq. (6.7) to show that, at the Golden Rule level of the capital stock, the marginal product of capital equals $n + d$.

20. See Andrew B. Abel, N. Gregory Mankiw, Lawrence H. Summers, and Richard J. Zeckhauser, "Assessing Dynamic Efficiency: Theory and Evidence," *Review of Economic Studies,* January 1989, pp. 1–20.

21. With no government in this model, national saving and private saving are the same.

per worker, we divide both sides of Eq. (6.9) by N_t. We then use the production function, Eq. (6.4), to replace y_t with $f(k_t)$:

$$sf(k) = (n + d)k \quad \text{(in the steady state).} \tag{6.10}$$

Equation (6.10) indicates that saving per worker $sf(k)$ equals steady-state investment per worker $(n + d)k$. Because the capital–labor ratio k is constant in the steady state, we again drop the subscripts t from the equation.

With Eq. (6.10) we can now determine the steady-state capital–labor ratio that the economy will attain, as shown in Fig. 6.3. The capital–labor ratio is measured along the horizontal axis. Saving per worker and investment per worker are measured on the vertical axis.

The bowed curve shows how the amount of saving per worker $sf(k)$ is related to the capital–labor ratio. This curve slopes upward because an increase in the capital–labor ratio implies higher output per worker and thus more saving per worker. The saving-per-worker curve has the same general shape as the per-worker production function, because saving per worker equals the per-worker production function $f(k)$ multiplied by the fixed saving rate s.

The line in Fig. 6.3 represents steady-state investment per worker $(n + d)k$. The steady-state investment line slopes upward because, as the capital–labor ratio rises, more investment per worker is required to replace depreciating capital and equip new workers with the same high level of capital.

According to Eq. (6.10), the steady-state capital–labor ratio must ensure that saving per worker and steady-state investment per worker are equal. The one level of the capital–labor ratio for which this condition is satisfied is shown in Fig. 6.3 as k^*, the value of k at which the saving curve and the

Figure 6.3
Determining the capital–labor ratio in the steady state
The steady-state capital–labor ratio, k^*, is determined by the condition that saving per worker, $sf(k)$, equals steady-state investment per worker, $(n + d)k$. The steady-state capital–labor ratio k^* corresponds to point A, where the saving curve and the steady-state investment line cross. From any starting point, eventually the capital–labor ratio reaches k^*. If the capital–labor ratio happens to be below k^*, say, at k_1, saving per worker, $sf(k_1)$, exceeds the investment per worker, $(n + d)k_1$, needed to maintain the capital–labor ratio at k_1. As this extra saving is converted into capital, the capital–labor ratio will rise, as indicated by the arrows. Similarly, if the capital–labor ratio is greater than k^*, say, at k_2, saving is too low to maintain the capital–labor ratio, and it will fall over time.

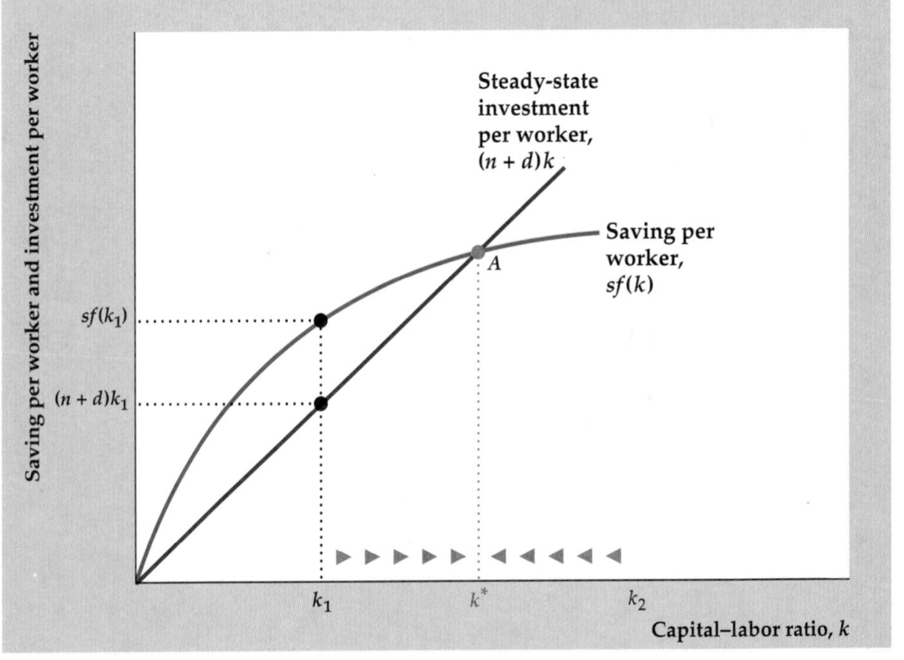

steady-state investment line cross. For any other value of k, saving and investment won't be equal in the steady state. Thus k^* is the only possible steady-state capital–labor ratio for this economy.[22]

With the unique steady-state capital–labor ratio k^*, we can also find steady-state output and consumption per worker. From the per-worker production function, Eq. (6.4), if the steady-state capital–labor ratio is k^*, steady-state output per worker y^* is

$$y^* = f(k^*).$$

From Eq. (6.7) steady-state consumption per worker, c^*, equals steady-state output per worker, $f(k^*)$, minus steady-state investment per worker, $(n + d)k^*$:

$$c^* = f(k^*) - (n + d)k^*.$$

Recall that, in the empirically realistic case, a higher value of the steady-state capital–labor ratio k^* implies greater steady-state consumption per worker c^*.

Using the condition that in a steady state, national saving equals steady-state investment, we found the steady-state capital–labor ratio k^*. When capital per worker is k^*, the amount that people choose to save will just equal the amount of investment necessary to keep capital per worker at k^*. Thus when the economy's capital–labor ratio reaches k^*, it will remain there forever.

But is there any reason to believe that the capital–labor ratio will ever reach k^* if it starts at some other value? Yes, there is. Suppose that the capital–labor ratio happens to be less than k^*; for example, it equals k_1 in Fig. 6.3. When capital per worker is k_1, the amount of saving per worker, $sf(k_1)$, is greater than the amount of investment needed to keep the capital–labor ratio constant, $(n + d)k_1$. When this extra saving is converted into capital, the capital –labor ratio will rise. As indicated by the arrows on the horizontal axis, the capital–labor ratio will increase from k_1 toward k^*.

If capital per worker is initially greater than k^*—for example, if k equals k_2 in Fig. 6.3—the explanation of why the economy converges to a steady state is similar. If the capital–labor ratio exceeds k^*, the amount of saving that is done will be less than the amount of investment that is necessary to keep the capital–labor ratio constant. (In Fig. 6.3 when k equals k_2, the saving curve lies below the steady-state investment line.) Thus the capital–labor ratio over time will fall from k_2 toward k^*, as indicated by the arrows. Output per worker will also fall until it reaches its steady-state value.

To summarize, if we assume no productivity growth, the economy must eventually reach a steady state. In this steady state the capital–labor ratio, output per worker, and consumption per worker remain constant over time. (However, total capital, output, and consumption grow at rate n, the rate of growth of the labor force.) This conclusion might seem gloomy, since it implies that living standards must eventually stop improving. However, we shall see that this conclusion can be avoided if, in fact, productivity continually increases.

---

22. Actually, there is also a steady state at the point $k = 0$, at which the capital stock, output, and consumption are zero forever. However, as long as the economy starts out with a positive amount of capital, it will never reach the zero-capital steady state.

The Fundamental Determinants of Long-Run Living Standards

What determines how well off the average person in an economy will be in the long run? If we measure long-run well-being by the steady-state level of consumption per worker, we can use the Solow model to answer this question. Here, we discuss three factors that affect long-run living standards: the saving rate, population growth, and productivity growth (see Summary table 8).

The Saving Rate. According to the Solow model, a higher saving rate implies higher living standards in the long run, as illustrated in Fig. 6.4. Suppose that the economy's initial saving rate is s_1 so that saving per worker is $s_1 f(k)$. The saving curve when the saving rate is s_1 is labeled "Initial saving per worker." The initial steady-state capital–labor ratio k_1^* is the capital–labor ratio at which the initial saving curve and the investment line cross (point A).

Suppose now that, say, because the government introduces policies that strengthen the incentives for saving, the country's saving rate rises from s_1 to s_2. The increased saving rate raises saving at every level of the capital–labor ratio. Graphically, the saving curve shifts upward from $s_1 f(k)$ to $s_2 f(k)$. The new steady-state capital–labor ratio k_2^* corresponds to the intersection of the new saving curve and the investment line (point B). Because k_2^* is larger than k_1^*, the higher saving rate has increased the steady-state capital–labor ratio. Gradually, this economy will move to the higher steady-state capital–labor ratio, as indicated by the arrows on the horizontal axis. In the new steady state, output per worker and consumption per worker will be higher than in the original steady state.

An increased saving rate leads to higher output, consumption, and capital per worker in the long run, so it seems that a policy goal should be to make the country's saving rate as high as possible. However, this conclusion isn't necessarily correct: Although a higher saving rate raises consumption per worker in the long run, an increase in the saving rate initially causes consumption

SUMMARY 8

The Fundamental Determinants of Long-Run Living Standards

An Increase in	Causes Long-Run Output, Consumption, and Capital per Worker to	Reason
The saving rate, s	Rise	Higher saving allows for more investment and a larger capital stock.
The rate of population growth, n	Fall	With higher population growth more output must be used to equip new workers with capital, leaving less output available to increase consumption or capital per worker.
Productivity	Rise	Higher productivity directly increases output; by raising incomes, it also raises saving and the capital stock.

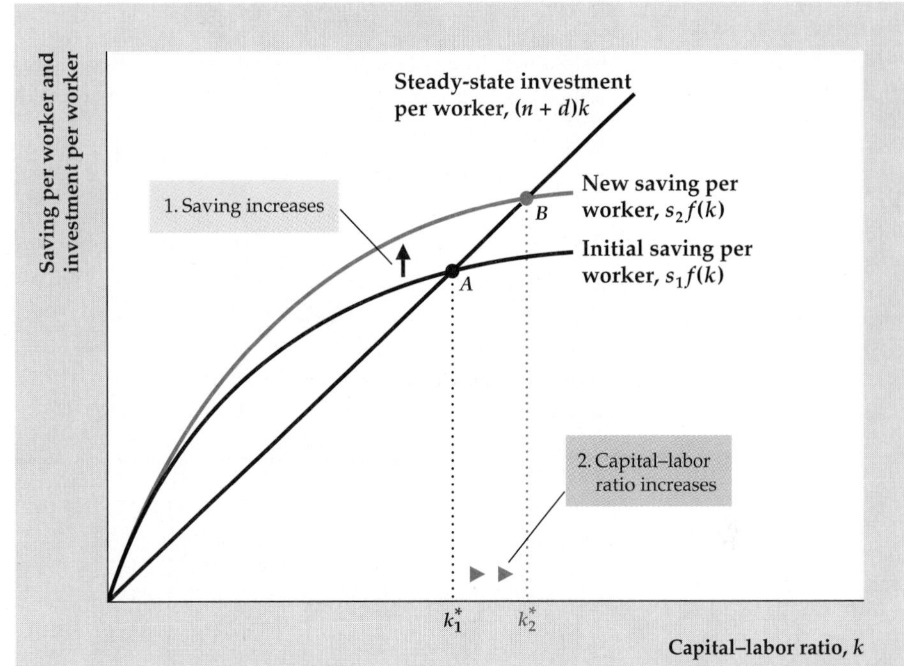

Figure 6.4
The effect of an increased saving rate on the steady-state capital–labor ratio
An increase in the saving rate from s_1 to s_2 raises the saving curve from $s_1 f(k)$ to $s_2 f(k)$. The point where saving per worker equals steady-state investment per worker moves from point A to point B, and the corresponding capital–labor ratio rises from k_1^* to k_2^*. Thus a higher saving rate raises the steady-state capital–labor ratio.

to fall. This decline occurs because, at the initial level of output, increases in saving and investment leave less available for current consumption. Thus higher future consumption has a cost in terms of lower present consumption. Society's choice of a saving rate should take into account this trade-off between current and future consumption. Beyond a certain point the cost of reduced consumption today will outweigh the long-run benefits of a higher saving rate.

Population Growth. In many developing countries a high rate of population growth is considered to be a major problem, and reducing it is a primary policy goal. What is the relationship between population growth and a country's level of development, as measured by output, consumption, and capital per worker?

The Solow model's answer to this question is shown in Fig. 6.5 on the next page. An initial steady-state capital–labor ratio k_1^* corresponds to the intersection of the steady-state investment line and the saving curve at point A. Now suppose that the rate of population growth, which is the same as the rate of labor force growth, rises from an initial level of n_1 to n_2. What happens?

An increase in the population growth rate means that workers are entering the labor force more rapidly than before. These new workers must be equipped with capital. Thus to maintain the same steady-state capital–labor ratio, the amount of investment per current member of the work force must rise. Algebraically, the rise in n increases steady-state investment per worker from $(n_1 + d)k$ to $(n_2 + d)k$. This increase in the population growth rate causes the steady-state investment line to pivot up and to the left, as its slope rises from $(n_1 + d)$ to $(n_2 + d)$.

After the pivot of the steady-state investment line, the new steady state is at point B. The new steady-state capital–labor ratio is k_2^*, which is lower than

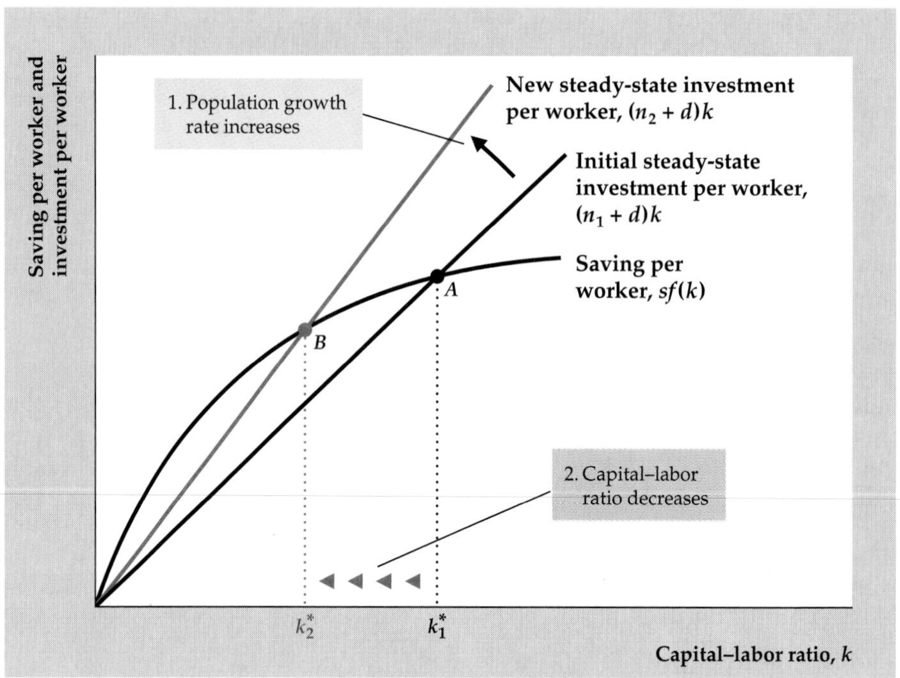

Figure 6.5
The effect of a higher population growth rate on the steady-state capital–labor ratio
An increase in the population growth rate from n_1 to n_2 increases steady-state investment per worker from $(n_1 + d)k$ to $(n_2 + d)k$. The steady-state investment line pivots up and to the left as its slope rises from $n_1 + d$ to $n_2 + d$. The point where saving per worker equals steady-state investment per worker shifts from point A to point B, and the corresponding capital–labor ratio falls from k_1^* to k_2^*. A higher population growth rate therefore causes the steady-state capital-labor ratio to fall.

the original capital–labor ratio k_1^*. Because the new steady-state capital–labor ratio is lower, the new steady-state output per worker and consumption per worker will be lower as well.

Thus the Solow model implies that increased population growth will lower living standards. The basic problem is that when the work force is growing rapidly, a large part of current output must be devoted just to providing capital for the new workers to use. This result suggests that policies to control population growth will indeed improve living standards.

There are some counterarguments to the conclusion that policy should aim to reduce population growth. First, although a reduction in the rate of population growth n raises consumption *per worker,* it also reduces the growth rate of *total* output and consumption, which grow at rate n in the steady state. Having fewer people means more for each person but also less total productive capacity. For some purposes (military, political) a country may care about its total output as well as output per person. Thus, for example, some countries of Western Europe are concerned about projections that their populations will actually shrink in the next century, possibly reducing their ability to defend themselves or influence world events.

Second, an assumption in the Solow model is that the proportion of the total population that is of working age is fixed. When the population growth rate changes dramatically, this assumption may not hold. For example, declining birth rates in the United States imply that the ratio of working-age people to retirees will become unusually low early in the twenty-first century, a development that may cause problems for Social Security funding and other areas such as health care.

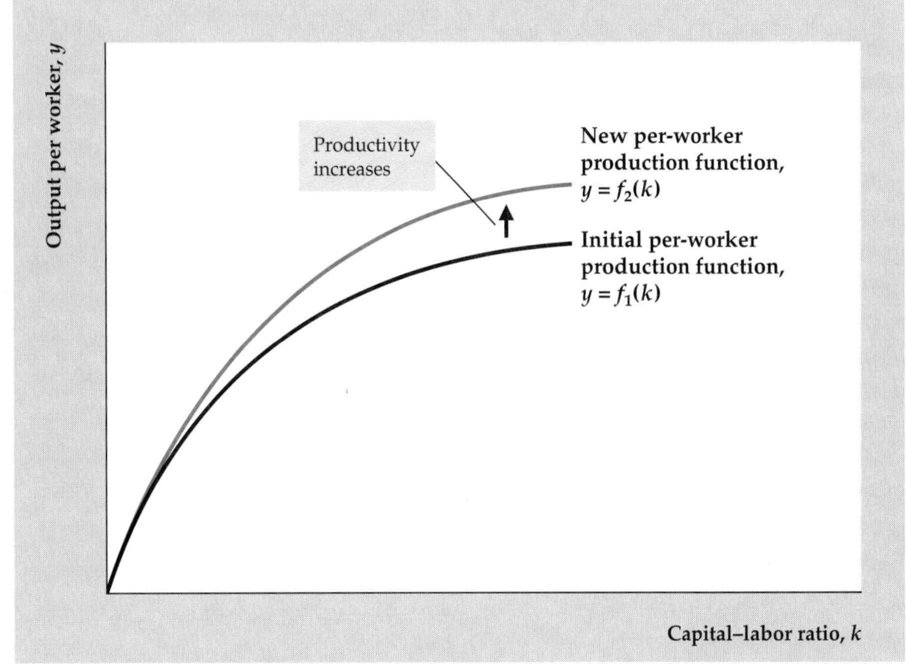

Figure 6.6
An improvement in productivity
An improvement in productivity shifts the per-worker production function upward from the initial production function $y = f_1(k)$ to the new production function $y = f_2(k)$. After the productivity improvement, more output per worker y can be produced at any capital–labor ratio k.

Productivity Growth. A significant aspect of the basic Solow model is that, ultimately, the economy reaches a steady state in which output per capita is constant. But in the introduction to this chapter we described how Japanese output per person has grown by a factor of 24 since 1870! How can the Solow model account for that sustained growth? The key is a factor that we haven't yet made part of the analysis: productivity growth.

The effects of a productivity improvement—the result of, say, a new technology—are shown in Figs. 6.6 and 6.7. An improvement in productivity corresponds to an upward shift in the per-worker production function because, at any prevailing capital–labor ratio, each worker can produce more output. Figure 6.6 shows a shift from the original production function $y = f_1(k)$ to a "new, improved" production function $y = f_2(k)$. The productivity improvement corresponds to a beneficial supply shock, as explained in Chapter 3.

Figure 6.7, on the next page, shows the effects of this productivity improvement in the Solow model. As before, the initial steady state is determined by the intersection of the saving curve and the steady-state investment line at point A; the corresponding steady-state capital–labor ratio is k_1^*. The productivity improvement raises output per worker for any level of the capital –labor ratio. As saving per worker is a constant fraction s of output per worker, saving per worker also rises at any capital–labor ratio. Graphically, the saving curve shifts upward from $sf_1(k)$ to $sf_2(k)$, now intersecting the steady-state investment line at point B. The new steady-state capital–labor ratio is k_2^*, which is higher than the original steady-state capital–labor ratio k_1^*.

Overall, a productivity improvement raises steady-state output and consumption per worker in two ways. First, it directly increases the amount that

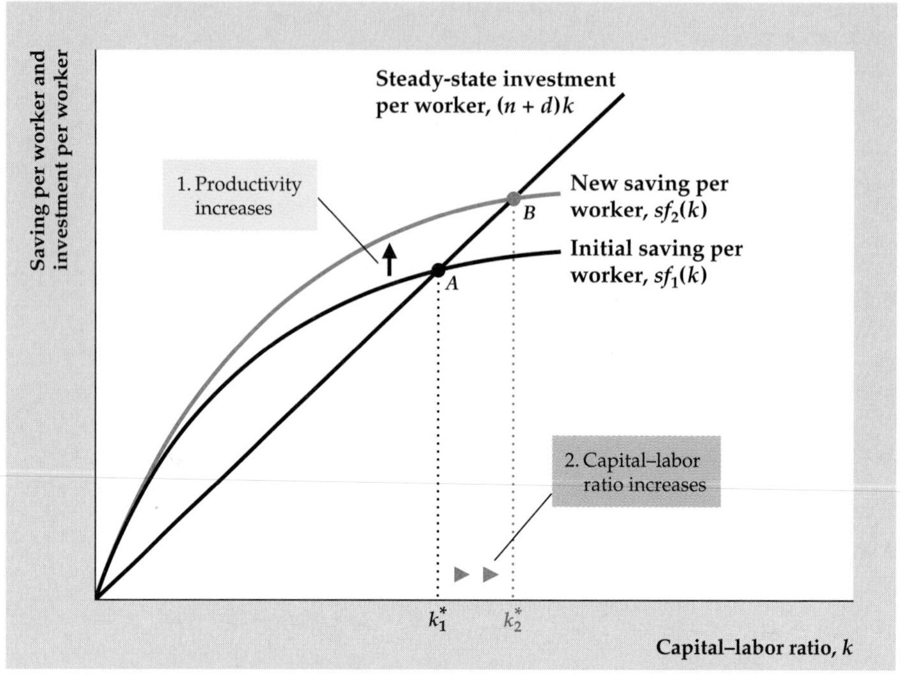

Figure 6.7
The effect of a productivity improvement on the steady-state capital–labor ratio
A productivity improvement shifts the production function upward from $f_1(k)$ to $f_2(k)$, raising output per worker for any capital–labor ratio. Because saving is proportional to output, saving per worker also rises, from $sf_1(k)$ to $sf_2(k)$. The point where saving per worker equals steady-state investment per worker shifts from point A to point B, and the corresponding steady-state capital–labor ratio rises from k_1^* to k_2^*. Thus a productivity improvement raises the steady-state capital–labor ratio.

can be produced at any capital–labor ratio. Second, as Fig. 6.7 shows, by raising the supply of saving, a productivity improvement also causes the long-run capital–labor ratio to rise. Thus a productivity improvement has a doubly beneficial impact on the standard of living.

Like a one-time increase in the saving rate or decrease in the population growth rate, a one-time productivity improvement shifts the economy only from one steady state to a higher one. When the economy reaches the new steady state, consumption per worker once again becomes constant. Is there some way to keep consumption per worker growing indefinitely?

In reality, there are limits to how high the saving rate can rise (it certainly can't exceed 100%!) or how low the population growth rate can fall. Thus higher saving rates or slower population growth aren't likely sources of continually higher living standards. However, since the Industrial Revolution, if not before, people have shown remarkable ingenuity in becoming more and more productive. In the very long run, according to the Solow model, only these continuing increases in productivity hold the promise of perpetually better living standards. Thus we conclude that, in the long run, *the rate of productivity improvement is the dominant factor determining how quickly living standards rise.*

APPLICATION
Do Economies Converge?

A wide gulf separates living standards in the richest and the poorest nations of the world. Will this difference persist forever? Will, indeed, the "rich get richer and the poor get poorer"? Or will national living standards ultimately converge? These questions obviously are of immense importance for humanity's future. In this Application we discuss what the Solow model says about the prospects for convergence and then turn to the empirical evidence.

There are at least three possible scenarios for the evolution of living standards throughout the world: We will refer to them as unconditional convergence, conditional convergence, and no convergence.

By **unconditional convergence** we mean that the poor countries eventually will catch up to the rich countries so that in the long run living standards around the world become more or less the same. The Solow model predicts unconditional convergence under certain special conditions. For example, let's suppose that the world's economies differed principally in terms of their capital–labor ratios, with rich countries having high capital–labor ratios and high levels of output per worker, and poor countries having low capital–labor ratios and low levels of output per worker. Suppose, however, that on other dimensions—specifically in terms of saving rates, population growth rates, and the production functions to which they had access—rich and poor countries were the same. If each of a group of countries has the same saving rate, population growth rate, and production function, the Solow model predicts that—despite any differences in initial capital–labor ratios—these countries all will eventually reach the same steady state. In other words, according to the Solow model, if countries have the same fundamental characteristics, capital–labor ratios and living standards will unconditionally converge, even though some countries may start from way behind.

But if countries differ in characteristics such as their saving rates, population growth rates, and access to technology, according to the Solow model they will converge to different steady states, with different capital–labor ratios and different living standards in the long run. If countries differ in fundamental characteristics, the Solow model predicts **conditional convergence,** by which we mean that living standards will converge only within groups of countries having similar characteristics. For example, if there is conditional convergence, a poor country with a low saving rate may catch up someday to a richer country that also has a low saving rate, but it will never catch up to a rich country that has a high saving rate.

For a variety of reasons (such as different cultures, political systems, and economic policies) countries do differ in characteristics such as saving rates, so conditional convergence seems to be the most likely outcome. However, our discussion so far assumes that these economies are all closed economies. According to the Solow model, if economies are open and international borrowing and lending flow freely, some additional economic forces support unconditional convergence. In particular, as poor countries have less capital per worker and thus higher marginal products of capital than do rich countries, savers in all countries will be able to earn the highest return by investing in poor countries. Thus foreign investment should cause capital stocks in poor countries to grow rapidly, even if domestic saving rates are low. Eventually, borrowing abroad should allow initially poor countries' capital–labor ratios and output per worker to be the same as in initially rich countries.[23]

The third possibility is *no convergence,* by which we mean that poor countries don't catch up over time. Living standards may even diverge (the poor get poorer and the rich get richer). Although reconciling no convergence with

23. Although output per worker in poor countries converges to that of rich countries, consumption per worker will remain at a lower level in poor countries because part of output must be used to repay foreign investors.

the Solow model isn't impossible (for example, permanent differences in productivity growth rates across countries could lead to divergence), this outcome would be inconsistent with the spirit of that model, which tends to favor the general idea of convergence.

What is the evidence? Unfortunately (from the perspective of the world's poor countries), there is little empirical support for unconditional convergence: Most studies have uncovered little tendency for poor countries to catch up with rich ones. For example, in a study of seventy-two countries over the period 1950–1985, William Baumol[24] of Princeton University and New York University found no overall tendency toward convergence. Using data beginning in 1870, Baumol did find some evidence for convergence among a group of sixteen major free-market economies, with the countries in the sample that were relatively poorest in 1870 growing somewhat faster over the period. However, J. Bradford DeLong[25] of Harvard University pointed out that the countries Baumol studied were the richest countries as of 1980. In choosing this set of countries, DeLong argued, Baumol created a bias in favor of finding convergence, because countries that failed to converge to high levels of output per hour would not be included among the sample of currently rich countries. DeLong showed that if Baumol's sample were expanded to include countries that were relatively rich in 1870 but are not among the richest countries today—countries such as Argentina, Chile, the area that until recently was East Germany, Ireland, New Zealand, Portugal, and Spain—Baumol's evidence for convergence disappears.

The evidence for conditional convergence, however, seems much better. For example, an article by N. Gregory Mankiw of Harvard University, David Romer of University of California at Berkeley, and David Weil[26] of Brown University examined a sample of 98 countries for the period 1960–1985. While finding no evidence for unconditional convergence in their data, Mankiw, Romer, and Weil showed that the failure of poor countries to catch up reflected high rates of population growth and low rates of saving (defined broadly to include resources devoted to education along with those devoted to accumulation of physical capital). After correcting for differences in national saving rates and population growth rates, Mankiw, Romer, and Weil found strong tendencies for countries with similar characteristics to converge. Similar results were obtained by Robert Barro of Harvard University and Xavier Sala-i-Martin[27] of Yale University, who also demonstrated a convergence of living standards among the states of the United States. Because the states are similar in fundamental economic characteristics, such as saving rates and access to technology, this result also is consistent with conditional convergence.

The findings in support of conditional convergence are encouraging for the Solow model, and they provide some empirical confirmation that factors such as the saving rate (including the provision of resources for education) are

---

24. "Productivity Growth, Convergence, and Welfare: What the Long-Run Data Show," *American Economic Review,* December 1986, pp. 1072–1085.
25. "Productivity Growth, Convergence and Welfare: Comment," *American Economic Review,* December 1988, pp. 1138–1154.
26. "A Contribution to the Empirics of Economic Growth," *Quarterly Journal of Economics,* May 1992, pp. 407–438.
27. "Convergence," *Journal of Political Economy,* April 1992, pp. 223–251.

important for growth. These results also suggest that international capital markets linking rich and poor countries are not as efficient as we might hope, since evidently foreign investment in poor countries has been insufficient to overcome the problem of low domestic saving rates. Possibly, political barriers such as legal limits or high taxes on foreign investment prevent enough foreign lending from flowing into poor countries. Alternatively, potential lenders in rich nations may not be able to obtain adequate information about investment opportunities in countries that are both physically distant and also have different languages, cultures, and legal systems.

The New Growth Theory

The traditional Solow model of economic growth has proved to be quite useful. However, it does have one serious shortcoming: The Solow model takes the rate of productivity growth as given, providing no explanation for why productivity improvements are sometimes rapid and sometimes slow. We have argued that the rate of productivity growth is the most important determinant of long-run living standards, so treating this important variable as a "black box" isn't very satisfying. Instead, a better understanding of how economic forces affect the evolution of productivity would be desirable.

In recent years researchers have tried to expand the Solow framework to include explanations of productivity change within the model. This so-called **new growth theory** has two principal strands.[28]

First, some new growth theorists have focused on the role of **human capital,** the economist's term for the knowledge, skills, and training of individuals. The links between human capital and growth flow two ways: On the one hand, as economies become richer they become more likely to "invest in people," through improved nutrition, schooling, and on-the-job training. On the other hand, a healthier and more highly skilled labor force is more productive, which leads to improved living standards. New growth theorists have examined the implications of adding human capital formation to the Solow growth model. They found that it better describes the actual process of economic growth. In particular, many empirical studies reveal strong links between educational and literacy levels in the population and the rate at which the economy is able to grow subsequently.[29]

A second strand of the new growth theory emphasizes the importance of *technological innovation by private firms* as a source of productivity growth. Firms improve product design and production efficiency in various ways: Some innovation takes place in formal research and development programs, as when a cosmetics company's lab works on a better shampoo or an underarm deodorant that won't stick to your clothes. Much innovation also takes place informally, as when workers on the shop floor suggest a better production

---

28. Two important early articles in the new growth theory are Paul Romer, "Increasing Returns and Long-Run Growth," *Journal of Political Economy,* October 1986, pp. 1002–1037 and Robert E. Lucas, Jr., "On the Mechanics of Economic Development," *Journal of Monetary Economics,* July 1988, pp. 3–42. For a recent discussion of the "old" and "new" growth theories, see Gene Grossman and Elhanan Helpman, "Endogenous Innovation in the Theory of Growth," *Journal of Economic Perspectives,* Winter 1994, pp. 23–44.

29. One such study is the Mankiw-Romer-Weil article cited earlier.

method or feedback from customers leads to a change in product design. Economists refer to innovations that arise in the process of making and marketing a good or service as *learning by doing*.[30] New growth theorists have studied the economic incentives that lead firms to innovate and have tried to incorporate the process of innovation by firms into the Solow growth model. Clearly, this strand of the new growth theory is closely related to the strand that emphasizes human capital formation, as the development and use of technological innovations often requires a skilled work force.

The new growth theory is promising. Although drawing strong policy lessons from this work may be premature, one implication is worth mentioning: In the traditional Solow model, the ability of government policies to influence long-run living standards is limited. For example, if policy succeeded in raising the saving rate, according to the Solow model the result would be a one-time improvement in living standards, as the economy moves to a new, higher steady state. In some new growth theory models, in contrast, a rise in the saving rate can result in a permanent rise in the *growth rate* of output, leading to ongoing improvements in living standards. The reason for the ongoing effect is that, according to the new growth theory, more output not only raises living standards but also leads to more human capital formation and innovation, which increase productivity and output, which increase human capital and innovation again, and so on in a "virtuous circle." Thus, in the new growth theory models, the impact of an increase in the saving rate in the long run can be much greater than that predicted by the traditional Solow model.

6.3 GOVERNMENT POLICIES TO RAISE LONG-RUN LIVING STANDARDS

Increased growth and a higher standard of living in the long run often are cited by political leaders as primary policy goals. Let's take a closer look at government policies that may be useful in raising a country's long-run standard of living. (The Political Environment: Economic Growth and Democracy, p. 211, discusses whether the *form* of government—democratic or nondemocratic—affects the long-run growth rate of an economy.)

Policies to Affect the Saving Rate

The Solow model suggests that the rate of national saving is a principal determinant of long-run living standards. However, this conclusion doesn't necessarily mean that policymakers should try to force the saving rate upward because more saving means less consumption in the short run. Indeed, if the "invisible hand" of free markets is working well, the saving rate freely chosen by individuals should be the one that optimally balances the benefit of saving

30. The term is originally from Kenneth Arrow, "The Economic Implications of Learning by Doing," *Review of Economic Studies*, June 1962, pp. 155–173.

The Political Environment

ECONOMIC GROWTH AND DEMOCRACY

Economic growth is an important social goal, but it is certainly not the only one. Most people also highly value political freedom and a democratic political process. Are these two goals conflicting or mutually supporting? If the citizens of poor countries succeed in achieving democracy, as many did during the 1980s and early 1990s, can they expect to enjoy faster economic growth as well? Or does increased political freedom involve economic sacrifice?

There are several reasons to believe that democracy may promote growth. Relative to dictatorships, democratic governments that command popular support might be expected to be more stable, to be less likely to start wars, and to have better relations with the advanced industrial nations, most of which are democracies. Constitutional protections of both human and property rights should increase the willingness of both foreigners and residents to invest in the country, and freedoms of speech and expression probably are essential for the full development of a nation's educational and scientific potential. However, the ability of a democratic government to undertake unpopular but necessary economic reforms or make other tough choices may be hampered by pressures of interest groups or fluctuations of public opinion. Similarly, a dictatorial government may be better able than a democratic one to enforce a high national saving rate and keep government spending under control.

What does empirical evidence show about the relationship between democracy and economic growth? A simple fact is that, for the most part, the richest countries of the world are democratic, and the poorest nations are nondemocratic. (There are exceptions: India is poor but is more democratic than wealthy Saudi Arabia or Singapore.) Not too much should be read into this fact, however, because many wealthy nations that are currently democratic initially achieved economic leadership under kings, princes, or emperors.

A more relevant empirical test is to compare the current economic growth rates (rather than the current levels of output) of democratic and nondemocratic countries. Here the findings of recent research have been generally good news for democracy. In a study of 115 market economies over the period 1960–1980, Gerald Scully* of the University of Texas at Dallas found that "politically open" societies grew at an average of 2.7% per year, compared to only 0.9% per year for repressive societies. Other researchers found a somewhat smaller advantage for democracy or even a slight edge for nondemocratic economies. For example, a study of 98 countries over the period 1960–1985 by John Helliwell† of Harvard University found essentially no statistical link between democracy and subsequent economic growth, although he did find that democracy promoted improved education and raised investment rates. There seems to be no support, however, for the view that adopting democratic institutions imposes high costs in terms of lost economic growth.

---

* "The Institutional Framework and Economic Development," *Journal of Political Economy,* June 1988, pp. 652–662.

† "Empirical Linkages Between Democracy and Economic Growth," NBER working paper no. 4066, May 1992.

more (higher future living standards) against the cost of saving more (less present consumption).

Despite the argument that saving decisions are best left to private individuals and the free market, some people claim that Americans save too little and that U.S. policy should aim at raising the saving rate. One possible justification for this claim is that existing tax laws discriminate against saving by taxing away part of the returns to saving; a "pro-saving" policy thus is necessary to offset this bias. Another, stronger view is that Americans are just too shortsighted in their saving decisions and must be encouraged to save more.

What policies can be used to increase saving? If saving were highly responsive to the real interest rate, tax breaks that increase the real return that savers receive would be effective. For example, some economists advocate taxing households on how much they consume rather than on how much they earn, thereby exempting from taxation the income that is saved. But as Chapter 4 noted, although saving appears to increase when the expected real return available to savers rises, most studies find this response to be small.

An alternative and perhaps more direct way to increase the national saving rate is by increasing the amount that the government saves; in other words, the government should try to reduce its deficit or increase its surplus. Our analysis of the "twin deficits" debate (Chapter 5) indicated that reducing the deficit by reducing government purchases will lead to more national saving. Many economists also argue that raising taxes to reduce the deficit will also increase national saving by leading people to consume less. However, believers in Ricardian equivalence contend that tax increases without changes in current or planned government purchases won't affect consumption or national saving.

Policies to Raise the Rate of Productivity Growth

Of the factors affecting long-run living standards, the rate of productivity growth may well be the most important in that—according to the Solow model—only ongoing productivity growth can lead to continuing improvement in output and consumption per worker. Government policy can attempt to increase productivity in several ways.

Improving Infrastructure. Some research findings suggest a significant link between productivity and the quality of a nation's infrastructure—its highways, bridges, utilities, dams, airports, and other publicly owned capital.[31] The construction of the interstate highway system in the United States, for example, significantly reduced the cost of transporting goods and stimulated tourism and other industries. In the past two decades the rate of U.S. government investment in infrastructure has fallen, leading to a decline in the quality and quantity of public capital.[32] Reversing this trend, some economists argue, might help achieve higher productivity. However, not everyone agrees that more infrastructure investment is needed. For example, some critics have pointed out that the links between productivity growth and infrastructure aren't clear. If rich countries are more likely to build roads and hospitals, perhaps higher productivity growth leads to more infrastructure, rather than vice-versa. Others worry that infrastructure investments by the government may involve political considerations (for example, favoring the districts of powerful members of Congress) more than promoting economic efficiency.

---

31. See, for example, David A. Aschauer, "Rx for Productivity: Build Infrastructure," *Chicago Fed Letter,* Federal Reserve Bank of Chicago, September 1988.

32. For data and discussion, see Clifford Winston and Barry Bosworth, "Public Infrastructure," in Henry J. Aaron and Charles L. Schultze, eds., *Setting Domestic Priorities: What Can Government Do?,* Washington: Brookings Institution, 1992.

Building Human Capital. Recent research findings point to a strong connection between productivity growth and human capital. The government affects human capital development through educational policies, worker training or relocation programs, health programs, and in other ways. Specific programs should be examined carefully to see whether benefits exceed costs, but a case may be made for greater commitment to human capital formation as a way to fight productivity slowdown.

One crucial form of human capital, which we haven't yet mentioned, is entrepreneurial skill. People with the ability to build a successful new business or to bring a new product to market play a key role in economic growth. Productivity growth may increase if the government were to remove unnecessary barriers to entrepreneurial activity (such as excessive red tape) and give people with entrepreneurial skills greater incentives to use those skills productively.[33]

Encouraging Research and Development. The government also may be able to stimulate productivity growth by affecting rates of scientific and technical progress. The U.S. government directly supports much basic scientific research (through the National Science Foundation, for example). Most economists agree with this type of policy because the benefits of scientific progress, like those of human capital development, spread throughout the economy. Basic scientific research may thus be a good investment from society's point of view, even if no individual firm finds such research profitable. Some economists would go further and say that even more applied, commercially oriented research deserves government aid.

Industrial Policy

Beyond support for basic science and technology, an aggressive approach that has been proposed for encouraging technological development is industrial policy. Generally, **industrial policy** is a growth strategy in which the government—using taxes, subsidies, or regulation—attempts to influence the nation's pattern of industrial development. More specifically, some advocates of industrial policy argue that the government should subsidize and promote "high-tech" industries, in order to try to achieve or maintain national leadership in technologically dynamic areas.

The idea that the government should try to determine the nation's mix of industries is controversial. Economic theory and practice suggest that under normal circumstances the free market can allocate resources well without government assistance. Thus advocates of industrial policy must explain why the free market fails in the case of high technology. Two possible sources of market failure that have been suggested are borrowing constraints and spillovers.

Borrowing constraints are limits imposed by lenders on the amounts that individuals or small firms can borrow.[34] Because of borrowing constraints, private companies, especially start-up firms, may have difficulty obtaining

33. For a discussion of the importance of entrepreneurial activity and how it is affected by government policy and the social environment, see William J. Baumol, "Entrepreneurship: Productive, Unproductive, and Destructive," *Journal of Political Economy*, October 1990 (part 1), pp. 893–921.
34. Chapter 8 presents further discussion of borrowing constraints.

enough financing for some projects. Development of a new supercomputer, for example, is likely to require heavy investment in research and development and involve a long period during which expenses are high and no revenues are coming in.

Spillovers occur when a given company's innovation—say, the development of an improved computer memory chip—stimulates a flood of related innovations and technical improvements by other companies and industries. The innovative company thus may enjoy only some of the total benefits of its breakthrough while bearing the full development cost. Without a government subsidy (argue advocates of industrial policy), such companies may not have a sufficiently strong incentive to innovate.

A third argument for industrial policy has less to do with market failure and more with nationalism. In some industries (such as aerospace) the efficient scale of operation is so large that the world market has room for only a few firms. For the world, the most desirable outcome is that those few firms be the most efficient, lowest-cost producers. However, in terms of a single country, say, the United States, at least some of the firms in the market should be American so that profits from the industry will accrue to the United States. Moreover, having U.S. firms in the market may enhance U.S. prestige and yield military advantages. These perceived benefits might lead the United States to subsidize its firms in that industry, helping them to compete with the firms of other nations in the race to capture the world market. Of course, other nations may well retaliate by introducing or increasing existing subsidies to their own firms.

These theoretical arguments for government intervention all assume that the government is skilled at picking "winning" technologies and that its decisions about which industries to subsidize would be free from purely political considerations. However, both assumptions are questionable. A danger of industrial policy is that the favored industries would be those with the most powerful congressional supporters, rather than those with the most economic promise.

The available evidence on the arguments for industrial policy has been surveyed by Gene Grossman[35] of Princeton University. Grossman concludes that, in general, industrial policy is not desirable because, in choosing industries to target, governments have frequently "backed the wrong horse"; the costly attempt of European governments to develop the supersonic transport (SST) and other new types of commercial airplanes is a case in point. Grossman also points out that alternative policies—such as a tax break for all research and development spending—promote technology without requiring the government to target specific industries.

However, Grossman also concedes that government intervention may be desirable in some cases, notably in the early development stages of technologically innovative products, such as computers and CAT scanners. Empirically, the potential for beneficial spillovers in these cases appears so large that government intervention may be justified, even though many projects the government may choose to support ultimately will not prove worthwhile.

---

35. "Promoting New Industrial Activities: A Survey of Recent Arguments and Evidence," *OECD Economic Studies,* Spring 1990, pp. 87–125.

CHAPTER SUMMARY

1. Economic growth is the principal source of improving standards of living over time. Over long periods even small differences in growth rates can have a large effect on nations' standards of living.

2. Growth accounting is a method for breaking total output growth into the portions resulting from growth in capital inputs, growth in labor inputs, and growth in productivity. All three factors have contributed to long-run economic growth in the United States. However, the slowdown in U.S. output growth after 1973 (and in other countries) primarily reflects a sharp decline in productivity growth. This decline in productivity growth in turn is the result of various factors, including problems in the legal and human environment, slower technical progress, and increased oil prices.

3. The Solow model of economic growth examines the interaction of growth, saving, and capital accumulation over time. It predicts that in the absence of productivity growth the economy will reach a steady state in which output, consumption, and capital per worker are constant.

4. According to the Solow model, each of the following leads to higher output, consumption, and capital per worker in the long run: an increase in the saving rate, a decline in the population growth rate, and an increase in productivity.

5. The Solow model implies that living standards of countries with similar saving rates, population growth rates, and production functions will tend to converge over time (conditional convergence). Empirical evidence tends to support conditional convergence. Unconditional convergence—the idea that living standards in most poor countries will eventually catch up to those of rich countries—is not supported by the data.

6. The new growth theory incorporates explanations of productivity growth into the Solow model. One strand of the new growth theory emphasizes the formation of human capital, including the acquisition of skills and training by workers. A second strand focuses on the economic incentives for technological innovation by private firms.

7. Government policies to raise long-run living standards include raising the rate of saving and increasing productivity. Possible ways of increasing productivity involve investing in public capital (infrastructure), encouraging the formation of human capital, and increasing research and development. A more aggressive strategy is industrial policy, in which the government uses subsidies and other tools to influence the nation's pattern of industrial development—and, in particular, to stimulate high-tech industries. Theoretical arguments for the use of industrial policy include the possible existence of borrowing constraints and spillovers. Critics of this approach contend that in practice the government cannot successfully pick and subsidize only "winning" technologies.

Key Terms

capital–labor ratio, p. 195
conditional convergence, p. 207
growth accounting, p. 187
growth accounting equation, p. 186
human capital, p. 209
industrial policy, p. 213
new growth theory, p. 209
steady state, p. 196
unconditional convergence, p. 207

Key Equations

$$\frac{\Delta Y}{Y} = \frac{\Delta A}{A} + a_K \frac{\Delta K}{K} + a_N \frac{\Delta N}{N} \qquad (6.2)$$

The growth accounting equation states that output growth, $\Delta Y/Y$, depends on the growth rate of productivity, $\Delta A/A$, the growth rate of capital, $\Delta K/K$, and the growth rate of labor, $\Delta N/N$. The elasticity of output with respect to capital, a_K, gives the percentage increase in output that results when capital increases by 1%. The elasticity of output with respect to labor, a_N, gives the percentage increase in output that results when labor increases by 1%.

$$y_t = f(k_t) \qquad (6.4)$$

For any year t the per-worker production function relates output per worker, y_t, to capital per worker (also called the capital–labor ratio), k_t.

$$c = f(k) - (n + d)k \qquad (6.7)$$

Steady-state consumption per worker c equals steady-state output per worker $f(k)$ minus steady-state investment per worker $(n + d)k$. Steady-state output per worker is determined by per-worker production $f(k)$, where k is the steady-state capital–labor ratio. Steady-state investment per worker has two parts: equipping new workers with the per-worker capital stock, nk, and replacing worn-out or depreciated capital, dk.

$$sf(k) = (n + d)k \qquad (6.10)$$

The steady state is determined by the condition that saving per worker $sf(k)$ equals steady-state investment per worker $(n + d)k$. Saving per worker equals the saving rate s times output per worker $f(k)$.

Review Questions

1. According to the growth accounting approach, what are the three sources of economic growth? From what basic economic relationship is the growth accounting approach derived?
2. Of the three sources of growth identified by growth accounting, which one is primarily responsible for the slowdown in U.S. economic growth after 1973? What explanations have been given for the decline in this source of growth?
3. According to the Solow model of economic growth, if there is no productivity growth, what will happen to output per worker, consumption per worker, and capital per worker in the long run?
4. True or false? The higher the steady-state capital–labor ratio is, the more consumption each worker can enjoy in the long run. Explain your answer.
5. What effect should each of the following have on long-run living standards, according to the Solow model?
   a. An increase in the saving rate.
   b. An increase in the population growth rate.
   c. A one-time improvement in productivity.
6. What is *convergence?* Explain the difference between *unconditional convergence* and *conditional convergence.* What prediction does the Solow model make about convergence? What does the evidence say?
7. What two explanations of productivity growth does the new growth theory offer?
8. What types of policies are available to a government that wants to promote economic growth? For each type of policy you identify, explain briefly how the policy is supposed to work and list its costs or disadvantages.

Numerical Problems

1. Two economies, Hare and Tortoise, each start with a real GDP per person of $5000 in 1950. Real GDP per person grows 3% a year in Hare and 1% a year in Tortoise. In the year 2000, what will be real GDP per person in each economy? Make a guess first; then use a calculator to get the answer.
2. Over the past twenty years an economy's total output has grown from 1000 to 1300, its capital stock has risen from 2500 to 3250, and its labor force has increased from 500 to 575. All measurements are in real terms. Calculate the contributions to economic growth of growth in capital, labor, and productivity
   a. assuming that $a_K = 0.3$ and $a_N = 0.7$.
   b. assuming that $a_K = 0.5$ and $a_N = 0.5$.
3. This problem illustrates how allowing for quality change can affect estimates of labor productivity and other variables.

   An economy with four workers produces only pizzas and six-packs of beer. Quantities of each product and the prices they sold for in two different years were as follows:

Year		Quantity	Price
1987	Pizza	5000	$8.00
1987	Beer	5000	$4.00
1993	Pizza	7000	$12.00
1993	Beer	6000	$5.00

   a. Calculate nominal GDP and real GDP for both years, assuming that 1987 is the base year. What is average labor productivity (real GDP per worker) in each of the two years? What is the total percentage change in the GDP deflator between 1987 and 1993?

b. Pizzas produced in 1993 contain more anchovies than 1987 pizzas did. Indeed, a taste test study concludes that one-and-a-half 1987-style pizzas are needed to produce as much consumer satisfaction as a 1993-style pizza. To adjust for this quality change, restate the number of pizzas produced in 1993 as the number of "1987 pizza equivalents" produced in 1993. Also restate the 1993 pizza price so that it is the cost of the amount of 1993 pizza needed to give the same satisfaction obtained from a 1987 pizza. (*Hint:* These two adjustments should not affect total nominal spending on pizzas for 1993.) Now recalculate real GDP and average labor productivity for 1993 and the percentage change in the GDP deflator from 1987 to 1993. How does the quality adjustment affect these variables?

4. For a particular economy, the following capital input K and labor input N were reported in four different years.

Year	K	N
1	200	1000
2	250	1000
3	250	1250
4	300	1200

The production function in this economy is

$$Y = K^{0.3}N^{0.7},$$

where Y is total output.

a. Find total output, the capital–labor ratio, and output per worker in each year. Compare year 1 with year 3 and year 2 with year 4. Can this production function be written in per-worker form? If so, write algebraically the per-worker form of the production function.

b. Repeat part (a) but assume now that the production function is $Y = K^{0.3}N^{0.8}$.

5. Use the data from Table 6.1 to calculate annual growth rates of GDP per capita for each country listed over the period 1950–1989. (*Note:* The annual growth rate z will satisfy the equation $(1 + z)^{39} = \text{GDP}_{1989}/\text{GDP}_{1950}$. To solve this equation for z using a calculator, take logs of both sides of the equation.) You will find that Germany and Japan, two countries that suffered extensive damage in World War II, had the two highest growth rates after 1950. Give a reason, based on the analysis of the Solow model, for these countries' particularly fast growth during this period.

6. An economy has the per-worker production function

$$y_t = 3k_t^{0.5},$$

where y_t is output per worker and k_t is the capital–labor ratio. The depreciation rate is 0.1, and the population growth rate is 0.05. Saving is

$$S_t = 0.3Y_t,$$

where S_t is total national saving and Y_t is total output.

a. What are the steady-state values of the capital–labor ratio, output per worker, and consumption per worker?

The rest of the problem shows the effects of changes in the three fundamental determinants of long-run living standards.

b. Repeat part (a) for a saving rate of 0.4 instead of 0.3.

c. Repeat part (a) for a population growth rate of 0.08 (with a saving rate of 0.3).

d. Repeat part (a) for a production function of

$$y_t = 4k_t^{0.5}.$$

Assume that the saving rate and population growth rate are at their original values.

Analytical Problems

1. According to the Solow model, how would each of the following affect consumption per worker in the long run (that is, in the steady state)? Explain.

a. The destruction of a portion of the nation's capital stock in a war.

b. A permanent increase in the rate of immigration (which raises the overall population growth rate).

c. A permanent increase in energy prices.

d. A temporary rise in the saving rate.

e. A permanent increase in the fraction of the population in the labor force (the population growth rate is unchanged).

2. An economy is in a steady state with no productivity change. Because of an increase in acid rain, the rate of capital depreciation rises permanently. Determine the effects on steady-state capital per worker, output per worker, and consumption per worker. Is the long-run growth rate of the total capital stock affected? If so, in what way?

3. This problem adds the government to the Solow model. Suppose that a government purchases goods in the amount of g per worker every year; with N_t

workers in year t, total government purchases are gN_t. The government has a balanced budget so that its tax revenue in year t, T_t, equals total government purchases. Total national saving S_t is

$$S_t = s(Y_t - T_t),$$

where Y_t is total output and s is the saving rate.

a. Graphically show the steady state for the initial level of government purchases per worker.

b. Suppose that the government permanently increases its purchases per worker. What are the effects on the steady-state levels of capital per worker, output per worker, and consumption per worker? Does your result imply that the optimal level of government purchases is zero?

4. In a Solow-type economy total national saving S_t is

$$S_t = sY_t - hK_t.$$

The extra term, $-hK_t$, reflects the idea that when wealth (as measured by the capital stock) is higher, saving is lower. (Wealthier people have less need to save for the future.)

Find the steady-state values of per-worker capital, output, and consumption. What is the effect on the steady state of an increase in h?

5. Two countries are identical in every way except that one has a much higher capital–labor ratio than the other. According to the Solow model, which country's total output will grow more quickly? Does your answer depend on whether one country or the other is in a steady state? In general terms, how will your answer be affected if the two countries are allowed to trade with each other?

6. Suppose that total capital and labor both increase by the same percentage amount, so that the amount of capital per worker k doesn't change. Writing the production function in per-worker terms, $y = f(k)$, requires that this increase in capital and labor must not change the amount of output produced per worker y. Use the growth accounting equation to show that equal percentage increases in capital and labor will leave output per worker unaffected only if $a_K + a_N = 1$.

CHAPTER 7

The Asset Market, Money, and Prices

Chapters 3 and 4 discussed the labor market and the goods market, two of the three markets in our model of the macroeconomy. In this chapter we consider the third market, the asset market. By *asset market* we mean the entire set of markets in which people buy and sell real and financial assets, including, for example, gold, houses, stocks, and bonds.

A type of asset that has long been believed to have special macroeconomic significance is money. Money is the economist's term for assets that can be used in making payments, such as cash and checking accounts. One reason that money is important is that most prices are expressed in units of money, such as dollars, yen, or francs. Because prices are measured in money terms, understanding the role of money in the economy is basic to studying issues related to the price level, such as inflation and its causes. In addition, many economists believe that the amount of money in the economy affects real economic variables, such as output and employment. If it does, then it may be possible to use monetary policy to promote stable output growth and fight unemployment, as we discuss in Part III.

Because money is such an important asset, it is the focus of our discussion of the asset market. The first part of the chapter explains what money is and why people choose to hold it. We show that a person's decision about how much money to hold (his or her money demand) is part of a broader decision about how to allocate wealth among the various assets that are available. We then bring together the demand for money and the supply of money (which is determined by the central bank) to analyze equilibrium in the asset market. This analysis demonstrates that the price level in an economy is closely related to the amount of money in the economy. Thus high rates of inflation—that is, rapid increases in prices—are likely when the money supply is growing rapidly.

7.1 WHAT IS MONEY?

In economics the meaning of the term *money* is different from its everyday meaning. People often say *money* when they mean *income* or *wealth*, as in: That job pays good money, or Her family has a lot of money. In economics, however, **money** refers specifically to assets that are widely used and accepted as payment. Historically, the forms of money have ranged from beads and shells to gold and silver—and even to cigarettes (see Box 7.1). In modern economies the most familiar forms of money are coins and paper money, or currency. Another common form of money is checkable deposits, or bank accounts on which checks can be written for making payments.

The Functions of Money

Since the earliest times almost all societies—from the most primitive to the most sophisticated and with many types of political and economic systems—have used money. Money has three useful functions in an economy: It is a medium of exchange, a unit of account, and a store of value.

Medium of Exchange. In an economy with no money, trading takes the form of barter, or the direct exchange of certain goods for other goods. Even today some people belong to barter clubs, in which members swap goods and services among themselves. Generally, though, barter is an inefficient way to trade, because finding someone who has the item you want and is willing to exchange that item for something you have is both difficult and time-consuming. In a barter system, if one of the authors of this book wanted a restaurant meal, he would first have to find a restaurateur willing to trade his blue-plate special for an economics lecture—which might not be easy to do.

Money makes searching for the perfect trading partner unnecessary. In an economy that utilizes money, the economics professor doesn't have to find a restaurant owner who is hungry for knowledge. Instead, he can first exchange his economics lecture to students for money and then use the money to buy a meal. In functioning as a **medium of exchange,** or a device for making transactions, money permits people to trade at less cost in time and effort. Having a medium of exchange also raises productivity by allowing people to specialize in economic activities at which they are most skilled. In an economy with money, specialized producers have no problem trading their goods or services for the things they need. In a barter economy, though, the difficulty of trading would leave people no choice but to produce most of their own food, clothing, and shelter. Thus in a barter economy the opportunity to specialize is greatly reduced.

Unit of Account. As a **unit of account,** money is the basic unit for measuring economic value. In the United States, for example, virtually all prices, wages, asset values, and debts are expressed in dollars. Having a single, uniform measure of value is convenient. For example, pricing all goods in the United States in dollars—instead of some goods being priced in yen, some in gold, and some in General Motors shares—simplifies comparison among different goods.

The medium-of-exchange and unit-of-account functions of money are closely linked. Because goods and services are most often exchanged for

BOX 7.1

Money in a Prisoner-of-War Camp

Among the Allied soldiers liberated from German prisoner-of-war (POW) camps at the end of World War II was a young man named R. A. Radford. Radford had been trained in economics, and shortly after his return home he published an article entitled "The Economic Organisation of a POW Camp."* This article, a minor classic in the economics literature, is a fascinating account of the daily lives of soldiers in several POW camps. It focuses particularly on the primitive "economies" that grew up spontaneously in the camps.

The scope for economic behavior in a POW camp might seem severely limited, and to a degree that's so. There was little production of goods within the camps, although there was some trade in services, such as laundry or tailoring services and even portraiture. However, prisoners were allowed to move around freely within the compound, and they actively traded goods obtained from the Red Cross, the Germans, and other sources. Among the commodities exchanged were tinned milk, jam, butter, biscuits, chocolate, sugar, clothing, and toilet articles. In one particular camp, which at various times had up to fifty thousand prisoners of many nationalities, active trading centers were run entirely by the prisoners.

A key practical issue was how to organize the trading. At first, the camp economies used barter, but it proved to be slow and inefficient. Then the prisoners hit on the idea of using cigarettes as money. Soon prices of all goods were quoted in terms of cigarettes, and cigarettes were accepted as payment for any good or service. Even nonsmoking prisoners would happily accept cigarettes as payment, because they knew that they could easily trade the cigarettes for other things they wanted. The use of cigarette money greatly simplified the problem of making trades and helped the camp economy function much more smoothly.

Why were cigarettes, rather than some other commodity, used as money by the POWs? Cigarettes satisfied a number of criteria for a good money: A cigarette is a fairly standardized commodity whose value was easy for both buyers and sellers to ascertain. An individual cigarette is low enough in value that making "change" wasn't a problem. Cigarettes are portable, are easily passed from hand to hand, and don't spoil quickly.

A drawback was that, as a commodity money (a form of money with an alternative use), cigarette money had a resource cost: Cigarettes that were being used as money could not simultaneously be smoked. In the same way, the traditional use of gold and silver as money was costly, in that it diverted these metals—and the labor and capital used to locate and mine them—from alternative uses.

The use of cigarettes as money isn't restricted to POW camps. Just before the collapse of communism in Eastern Europe, cigarette money reportedly was used in Romania and other countries instead of the nearly worthless official money.

---

* *Economica*, November 1945, pp. 189–201.

money (the medium-of-exchange function), expressing economic values in money terms (the unit-of-account function) is natural. Otherwise, we could just as well express economic values in terms of, say, bushels of wheat. However, the medium of exchange and the unit of account aren't always the same. In countries with high and erratic inflation, for example, fluctuating currency value makes money a poor unit of account because prices must be changed frequently. In such cases economic values are commonly stated in terms of a more stable unit of account, such as dollars or ounces of gold, even though transactions may continue to be carried out in the local currency.

Store of Value. As a **store of value,** money is a way of holding wealth. An extreme example is a miser who keeps his life's savings in cash under the mattress. But even someone who spends his cash wages fifteen minutes after receiving them is using money as a store of value for that short period.

In most cases only money functions as a medium of exchange or a unit of account, but any asset—for example, stocks, bonds, or real estate—can be a store of value. As these other types of assets normally pay the holder a higher return than money does, why do people use money as a store of value? The answer is that money's usefulness as a medium of exchange makes it worthwhile to hold, even though its return is relatively low.

Measuring Money: The Monetary Aggregates

Money is defined as those assets that are widely used and accepted in payment. This definition suggests a hard-and-fast line between assets that should be counted as money and those that should not. Actually, the distinction between monetary assets and nonmonetary assets isn't so clear.

Consider, for example, money market mutual funds (MMMFs), which first became popular in the late 1970s. MMMFs are organizations that sell shares to the public and invest the proceeds in short-term government and corporate debt. MMMFs strive to earn a high return for their shareholders. At the same time, MMMFs typically allow their shareholders to write a small number of checks each month against their accounts, perhaps for a fee. Thus, although MMMF shares can be used to make payments, they are not as convenient as cash or regular checking accounts for this purpose. Should MMMF shares be counted as money or not? There is no definitive answer.

Because assets differ in their "moneyness," no single measure of the amount of money in the economy—or the money stock, as it is often called—is likely to be completely satisfactory. For this reason, in most countries economists and policymakers use several different measures of the money stock. These official measures are known as **monetary aggregates.** The various monetary aggregates differ in how narrowly they define the concept of money. In the United States the two most widely used monetary aggregates are called M1 and M2. Summary definitions and data for these two aggregates are given in Table 7.1. Information about where to find data on the monetary aggregates

Table 7.1 The U.S. Monetary Aggregates (March 1993)

M1	**$1030.4 billion**
Currency	$297.9 billion
Travelers' checks	$7.8 billion
Demand deposits	$336.3 billion
Other checkable deposits	$388.5 billion
M2	**$3478.5 billion**
Components of M1	$1030.4 billion
Savings deposits, including MMDAs	$1184.8 billion
Small-denomination time deposits	$849.2 billion
Money market mutual funds	$342.2 billion
Overnight repurchase agreements and Eurodollars	$71.9 billion

Source: *Federal Reserve Bulletin,* June 1993, Table 1.21. There, M2 is M1 plus lines 33, 34, 36, 37, 39, and 41. Data are not seasonally adjusted.

IN TOUCH *WITH THE MACROECONOMY*

THE MONETARY AGGREGATES

The official monetary aggregates*—currently M1, M2, M3, and L—are compiled and reported by the Board of Governors of the Federal Reserve System in Washington. Only data for M1 were reported until 1971, when the Fed introduced M2 and M3. Since then the definitions of the monetary aggregates have changed several times, reflecting the evolution of the financial system.

The Fed reports estimates of the aggregates both weekly and monthly, using data supplied by banks, the Treasury, money market mutual funds, foreign central banks, and other sources. Each Thursday at 4:30 P.M. the Fed announces figures for M1, M2, and M3 for the week ending the Monday of the previous week. These announcements are regularly reported by the business media; see, for example, the "Federal Reserve Data" column that appears on Fridays in the *Wall Street Journal.* Historical data are available in the *Federal Reserve Bulletin,* the Federal Reserve's *Annual Statistical Digest,* the *Economic Report of the President,* and in numerous other sources. Monetary data are revised frequently, reflecting the receipt of new data by the Federal Reserve or changes in the definitions of monetary aggregates.

Publication of the monetary aggregates helps keep the public and Congress informed about how the Fed is changing the nation's money supply. In addition, twice a year the Federal Reserve must report to Congress its plans for the future growth of the monetary aggregates. These semiannual reports allow public discussion and review of current monetary policy.

---

* For more details on the monetary aggregates, see John R. Walter, "Monetary Aggregates," in Roy H. Webb, ed., *Macroeconomic Data: A User's Guide,* Federal Reserve Bank of Richmond, 1990.

is presented in the box "In Touch with the Macroeconomy: The Monetary Aggregates".

The M1 Monetary Aggregate. The most narrowly defined official money measure, **M1**, consists primarily of currency and balances held in checking accounts. More precisely, M1 is made up of currency and travelers' checks held by the public, demand deposits (non-interest-bearing checking accounts), and other checkable deposits. The category "other checkable deposits" includes interest-bearing checkable deposits, such as NOW (negotiated order of withdrawal) accounts and ATS (automatic transfer service) accounts. M1 is perhaps the closest counterpart of the theoretical definition of money because all its components are actively used and widely accepted for making payments.

The M2 Monetary Aggregate. Everything in M1 plus other assets that are somewhat less "moneylike" comprise **M2**. The main additional assets in M2 include savings deposits, small-denomination (under $100,000) time deposits, noninstitutional[1] holdings of money market mutual funds (MMMFs), and money market deposit accounts (MMDAs). Time deposits are interest-bearing deposits with a fixed term (early withdrawal usually involves a penalty). As mentioned, MMMFs invest their shareholders' funds in short-term securities, pay market-based interest rates, and allow holders to write checks. MMDAs are like MMMFs, except they are offered by banks or thrift institutions such as

---

1. Holdings of MMMFs by institutions, such as pension funds, are included in the broader monetary aggregate M3, which we discuss briefly next.

savings and loan associations. In Table 7.1 we followed the presentation in the *Federal Reserve Bulletin* and included MMDAs as part of savings deposits.

Additional small components of M2 are overnight repurchase (RP) agreements and overnight Eurodollars issued to U.S. residents. In an RP agreement a bank borrows overnight from a nonbank customer by selling a security, such as a government bond, to the customer and promising to buy the security back the next day. Overnight Eurodollars are short-term deposits held in foreign branches of U.S. banks.

Other Monetary Aggregates. Two additional monetary aggregates, generally less well known and used than M1 and M2, are M3 and L. The aggregate M3 contains everything in M2 and other assets, such as large-denomination (over $100,000) time deposits and MMMFs held by institutions. The L aggregate is broader still: It includes everything in M3 and assets such as short-term Treasury debt, commercial paper (short-term debt of large corporations), and U.S. savings bonds.

Many of the assets included in M3 or L (as well as some that are in M2) are not money in the strict sense of being directly acceptable in payment. For example, assets such as Treasury bills or commercial paper, which are part of the broadest monetary aggregate L, cannot be used directly for making purchases. However, because these assets can be quickly and cheaply converted into currency or checkable deposits, economists include them in the broader measures of money.

Weighted Monetary Aggregates. The monetary aggregates are constructed by simply adding the outstanding amounts of various types of assets. Thus a dollar of currency contributes no more to the measured money stock than does a dollar of savings deposits. This standard way of measuring the money stock ignores the fact that some assets, such as currency, are more moneylike than others. Recently, some economists have experimented with weighted monetary aggregates. In this approach a dollar of a very moneylike asset such as currency is given a greater weight in the total than is a dollar of a less moneylike asset such as a savings deposit. Several studies conclude that weighted monetary aggregates are more useful measures of money than are the standard aggregates.[2] Disagreements about the best way to weight the various monetary assets remain, however, and so far this approach hasn't been officially adopted.

The Money Supply

The **money supply** is the amount of money available in an economy.[3] In modern economies the money supply is determined by the central bank—in the United States, the Federal Reserve System.

A detailed explanation of how central banks control the money supply raises issues that would take us too far afield at this point, so we defer that discussion to Chapter 15. To grasp the basic idea, however, let's consider the simple hypothetical situation in which the only form of money is currency. In

2. For a recent technical discussion of weighted aggregates, see William A. Barnett, Douglas Fisher, and Apostolos Serletis, "Consumer Theory and the Demand for Money," *Journal of Economic Literature*, December 1992, pp. 2086–2119.

3. The terms *money supply* and *money stock* are used interchangeably.

this case to increase the money supply the central bank only needs to increase the amount of currency in circulation. How can it do so?

One way—which is close to what happens in practice—is for the central bank to use newly minted currency to buy financial assets, such as government bonds, from the public. In making this swap, the public increases its holdings of money, and the amount of money in circulation rises. When the central bank uses money to purchase government bonds from the public, thus raising the money supply, it is said to have conducted an *open-market purchase*.

To reduce the money supply, the central bank can make this trade in reverse, selling government bonds that it holds to the public in exchange for currency. After the central bank removes this currency from circulation, the money supply is lower. When the central bank sells government bonds to the public to reduce the money supply, the transaction is an *open-market sale*. Open-market purchases and sales together are called **open-market operations.**

In addition to buying government bonds from the public, the central bank can also increase the money supply by buying newly issued government bonds directly from the government itself. For example, if a country's treasury needs \$1 billion to pay for some new fighter planes, it might give an IOU for \$1 billion (government bonds) to the central bank in exchange for \$1 billion in newly minted currency. The treasury then gives the \$1 billion of currency to the manufacturer of the fighter planes. After the treasury has distributed this currency, the amount of money in circulation—the money supply—will be higher by \$1 billion. Effectively, this second way of increasing the money supply amounts to the government financing its expenditures by printing money.[4] This practice is most common in poor countries or in countries wracked by war or natural disaster, in which government spending often greatly exceeds the amount that can be raised through taxes.[5]

For the rest of this chapter we assume that the economy has a money supply of M dollars, which is determined by the central bank. The term M may represent M1, M2, or some other measure of money. For the purpose of developing the theoretical model, which measure of money M refers to doesn't matter.

7.2 PORTFOLIO ALLOCATION AND THE DEMAND FOR ASSETS

Our next goal is to understand how people determine the amount of money they choose to hold. We begin by considering the broader question of how people allocate their wealth among the many different assets that are available, of which money is only one example.

A consumer, a business, a pension fund, a university, or any other holder of wealth must decide how to distribute that wealth among many types of assets.

4. In Chapter 2 we said that the portion of government outlays not covered by taxes had to be borrowed from the private sector. Is this still true when the government has the option of paying for its outlays by printing money? Yes; for national income accounting purposes, the Federal Reserve is treated as part of the private sector. So when the Treasury sells government bonds to the Federal Reserve in exchange for currency, it is still technically borrowing from the private sector.

5. The financing of government spending through money creation is discussed further in Chapter 16.

The set of assets that a holder of wealth chooses to own is called a *portfolio*. The decision about which assets and how much of each asset to hold is called the **portfolio allocation decision.**

The portfolio allocation decision can be complex. Many people make their living by giving financial advice to holders of wealth, and a major branch of economics, called financial economics, is devoted largely to the study of the portfolio allocation decision. But, fundamentally, only three characteristics of assets matter for the portfolio allocation decision: expected return, risk, and liquidity.

Expected Return

The rate of return to an asset is the rate of increase in its value per unit of time. For example, the return on a bank account is the interest rate on the account. The return on a share of stock is the dividend paid by the stock plus any increase in the stock's price. Clearly, a high return is a desirable feature for an asset to have: All else being equal, the higher the return a wealth holder's portfolio provides, the more consumption she can enjoy in the future for any given amount of saving done today.

Of course, the return on an asset is not always known in advance. Stock prices may go up or down, for example. Thus holders of wealth must base their portfolio allocation decisions on **expected returns,** or their best guesses about returns on assets. Everything else being equal, the higher an asset's expected return (after subtracting taxes and fees such as brokers' commissions), the more desirable the asset is and the more of it holders of wealth will want to own.[6]

Risk

The uncertainty about the return an asset will earn relates to the second important characteristic of assets—riskiness. An asset or a portfolio of assets has high **risk** if there is a significant chance that the actual return received will be very different from the expected return. An example of a risky asset is a share in a start-up gene-splicing company that will be worthless if the company fails but will triple in value if the company succeeds. Because most people don't like risk, they hold risky assets only if the expected return is higher than that on relatively safe assets, such as government bonds.

Liquidity

Besides risk and return a third characteristic, liquidity, affects the desirability of assets. The **liquidity** of an asset is the ease and quickness with which it can be exchanged for goods, services, or other assets. Because it is accepted directly in payment, money is a highly liquid asset. An example of an illiquid asset is your automobile: Time and effort are required to exchange a used car for other goods and services; you must find someone interested in buying the

6. For the purpose of comparing expected returns among assets, returns may be expressed in either real or nominal terms. For any expected rate of inflation, if asset A's nominal return is 1% higher than asset B's nominal return, asset A's expected real return (its nominal return minus expected inflation) will also be 1% higher than asset B's expected real return.

car and arrange legal transfer of ownership. Between liquid money and illiquid autos are many assets, such as stocks and bonds, of intermediate liquidity. A share of stock, for example, can't be used directly to pay for groceries as cash can, but stock can be transformed into cash with a short delay and at the cost of a broker's fee.

In addition to making transactions easier and cheaper, liquidity provides flexibility to the holder of wealth. A liquid asset can easily be disposed of if there is an emergency need for funds or if an unexpectedly good financial investment opportunity arises. Thus, everything else being equal, the more liquid an asset is, the more attractive it will be to holders of wealth.

Asset Demands

Typically, there is a trade-off among the three characteristics that make an asset desirable: a high expected return, safety (low risk), and liquidity. For example, a safe and liquid asset, such as a checking account, is likely to have a low expected return. The essence of the portfolio allocation decision is determining which assets, taken together, achieve the wealth holder's preferred combination of expected return, safety, and liquidity.

The amount of each particular asset that a holder of wealth desires to include in her portfolio is called her demand for that asset. Because all wealth must be held as some type of asset, the sum of a wealth holder's asset demands must equal her total wealth. For example, suppose that you have wealth of $10,000 and decide to hold $5000 in stock, $4000 in bonds, and $1000 in cash. The sum of your three asset demands must equal your total wealth of $10,000.

7.3 THE DEMAND FOR MONEY

The **demand for money** is the quantity of monetary assets, such as cash and checking accounts, that people choose to hold in their portfolios. Choosing how much money to demand is thus a part of the broader portfolio allocation decision. In general, the demand for money—like the demand for any other asset—will depend on the expected return, risk, and liquidity of money and of other assets.

In practice, two features of money are particularly important. First, money is the most liquid asset. This liquidity is the primary benefit of holding money.[7] Second, money pays a low return (indeed, currency pays a zero nominal return). The low return earned by money, relative to other assets, is the major cost of holding money. People's demand for money is determined by how they trade off their need for liquidity against the cost of a lower return.

In this section we look at how some key macroeconomic variables affect the demand for money. Although we primarily consider the aggregate, or total, demand for money, the same economic arguments apply to individual money demands. This relation is to be expected, as the aggregate demand for money is the sum of all individual money demands.

---

7. Money also has low risk, but many alternative assets (such as short-term government bonds) are no riskier than money and pay a higher return.

The macroeconomic variables that have the greatest effects on money demand are the price level, real income, and interest rates. Higher prices or incomes increase people's need for liquidity and thus raise the demand for money. Interest rates affect money demand through the expected return channel: The higher the interest rate on money, the more money people will demand; however, the higher the interest rate paid on alternative assets to money, the more people will want to switch from money to those alternative assets.

The Price Level

The higher the general level of prices, the more dollars people need to conduct transactions and thus the more dollars people will want to hold. For example, sixty years ago the price level in the United States was about one tenth of its level today; as your grandfather will tell you, in 1935 a good restaurant meal cost a dollar. Because less money was needed for transactions, the number of dollars your grandfather held in the form of currency or checking accounts—his nominal demand for money—was probably much smaller than the amount of money you hold today. The general conclusion is that a higher price level, by raising the need for liquidity, increases the nominal demand for money. In fact, because prices are ten times higher today than they were in 1935, an identical transaction takes ten times as many dollars today as it did back then. Thus, everything else being equal, the nominal demand for money is *proportional* to the price level.

Real Income

The more transactions that individuals or businesses conduct, the more liquidity they need and the greater is their demand for money. An important factor determining the number of transactions is real income. For example, a large, high-volume supermarket has to deal with a larger number of customers and suppliers and pay more employees than does a corner grocery. Similarly, a high-income individual makes more and larger purchases than a low-income individual. Because higher real income means more transactions and a greater need for liquidity, the amount of money demanded should increase when real income increases.

Unlike the response of money demand to changes in the price level, the increase in money demand need not be proportional to an increase in real income. Actually, a 1% increase in real income usually leads to less than a 1% increase in money demand. One reason that money demand grows more slowly than income is that higher-income individuals and firms typically use their money more efficiently. For example, a high-income individual may open a special cash management account in which money not needed for current transactions is automatically invested in nonmonetary assets paying a higher return. Because of minimum-balance requirements and fees, such an account might not be worthwhile for a lower-income individual.

Another reason that money demand grows more slowly than income is that nations' financial sophistication tends to increase as national income grows. In poor countries people may hold much of their saving in the form of money, for lack of anything better; in richer countries people have many attractive alternatives to money. Money substitutes such as credit cards also become more common as a country becomes richer, again leading to aggregate money demand's growing more slowly than income.

Interest Rates

The theory of portfolio allocation implies that, with risk and liquidity held constant, the demand for money depends on the expected returns of both money and alternative, nonmonetary assets. An increase in the expected return on money increases the demand for money, and an increase in the expected return on alternative assets causes holders of wealth to switch from money to higher-return alternatives, thus lowering the demand for money.

For example, suppose that, of your total wealth of $10,000, you have $8000 in government bonds earning 8% interest and $2000 in a NOW account (an interest-bearing checking account) earning 3%. You are willing to hold the NOW account at a lower return because of the liquidity it provides. But if the interest rate on bonds rises to 10%, and the NOW account interest rate remains unchanged, you may decide to switch $1000 from the NOW account into bonds. In making this switch, you reduce your holding of money (your money demand) from $2000 to $1000. Effectively, you have chosen to trade some liquidity for the higher return offered by bonds.

Similarly, if the interest rate paid on money rises, holders of wealth will choose to hold more money. In the example, if the NOW account begins paying 5% instead of 3%, with bonds still at 8%, you may sell $1000 of your bonds, lowering your holdings of bonds to $7000 and increasing your NOW account to $3000. The sacrifice in return associated with holding money is less than before, so you increase your NOW account balance and enjoy the flexibility and other benefits of extra liquidity. Thus a higher interest rate on money makes the demand for money rise.

In principle, the interest rate on each of the many alternatives to money should affect money demand. However, as previously noted, the many interest rates in the economy generally tend to move up and down together. For the purposes of macroeconomic analysis, therefore, assuming that there is just one nominal interest rate, i, which measures the nominal return on nonmonetary assets, is simpler and not too misleading. The nominal interest rate i minus the expected inflation rate π^e gives the expected real interest rate r that is relevant to saving and investment decisions, as discussed in Chapter 4.

Also, in reality, various interest rates are paid on money. For example, currency pays zero interest, but different types of checkable accounts pay varying rates. Again for simplicity, let's assume that there is just one nominal interest rate for money, i^m. The key conclusions are that an increase in the interest rate on nonmonetary assets, i, reduces the amount of money demanded, and an increase in the interest rate on money, i^m, raises the amount of money demanded.

The Money Demand Function

We express the effects of the price level, real income, and interest rates on money as

$$M^d = PL(Y, i), \tag{7.1}$$

where

M^d = the aggregate demand for money, in nominal terms;
P = the price level;
Y = real income or output;
i = the nominal interest rate earned by alternative, nonmonetary assets;
L = a function relating money demand to real income and the nominal interest rate.

Equation (7.1) holds that nominal money demand M^d is proportional to the price level P. Hence, if the price level P doubles (and real income and interest rates don't change), nominal money demand M^d also will double, reflecting the fact that twice as much money is needed to conduct the same real transactions. Equation (7.1) also indicates that, for any price level P, money demand depends (through the function L) on real income Y and the nominal interest rate on nonmonetary assets i. An increase in real income Y raises the demand for liquidity and thus increases money demand. An increase in the nominal interest rate i makes nonmonetary assets more attractive, which reduces money demand.

We could have included the nominal interest rate on money, i^m, in Eq. (7.1), because an increase in the interest rate on money makes people more willing to hold money and thus increases money demand. Historically, however, the nominal interest rate on money has varied much less than the nominal interest rate on nonmonetary assets (for example, currency and a portion of checking accounts always have paid zero interest) and thus has been ignored by many statistical studies of Eq. (7.1). Thus for simplicity we do not explicitly include i^m in the equation.

An equivalent way of writing the demand for money expresses the nominal interest rate i in terms of the expected real interest rate and the expected rate of inflation. Recall from Eq. (2.13) that the expected real interest rate r equals the nominal interest rate i minus the expected rate of inflation π^e. Therefore the nominal interest rate i equals $r + \pi^e$. Substituting $r + \pi^e$ for i in Eq. (7.1) yields

$$M^d = PL(Y,\ r + \pi^e). \qquad (7.2)$$

Equation (7.2) shows that, for any expected rate of inflation π^e, an increase in the real interest rate increases the nominal interest rate and reduces the demand for money. Similarly, for any real interest rate, an increase in the expected rate of inflation increases the nominal interest and reduces the demand for money.

Nominal money demand M^d measures the demand for money in terms of dollars (or lire, or francs). But, sometimes, measuring money demand in real terms is more convenient. If we divide both sides of Eq. (7.2) by the price level P, we get

$$\frac{M^d}{P} = L(Y,\ r + \pi^e). \qquad (7.3)$$

The expression on the left-hand side of Eq. (7.3), M^d/P, is called real money demand or, sometimes, the demand for real balances. Real money demand is the amount of money demanded in terms of the goods it can buy. Equation (7.3) states that real money demand M^d/P depends on real income (or output)

Y and on the nominal interest rate, which is the sum of the real interest r and expected inflation π^e. The function L that relates real money demand to output and interest rates in Eq. (7.3) is called the **money demand function.**

Other Factors Affecting Money Demand

The money demand function in Eq. (7.3) captures the main macroeconomic determinants of money demand, but some other factors should be mentioned. Besides the nominal interest rate on money, which we have already discussed, additional factors influencing money demand include wealth, risk, liquidity of alternative assets, and payment technologies. Summary table 9 contains a comprehensive list of variables that affect the demand for money.

Wealth. When wealth increases, part of the extra wealth may be held as money, increasing total money demand. However, with income and the level of

SUMMARY 9

Macroeconomic Determinants of the Demand for Money

An Increase in	Causes Money Demand to	Reason
Price level, P	Rise proportionally	A doubling of the price level doubles the number of dollars needed for transactions.
Real income, Y	Rise less than proportionally	Higher real income implies more transactions and thus a greater demand for liquidity.
Real interest rate, r	Fall	Higher real interest rate means a higher return on alternative assets and thus a switch away from money.
Expected inflation, π^e	Fall	Higher expected inflation means a higher return on alternative assets and thus a switch away from money.
Nominal interest rate on money, i^m	Rise	A higher return on money makes people more willing to hold money.
Wealth	Rise	Part of an increase in wealth may be held in the form of money.
Risk	Rise, if risk of alternative asset increases	Higher risk of alternative asset makes money more attractive.
	Fall, if risk of money increases	Higher risk of money makes it less attractive.
Liquidity of alternative assets	Fall	Higher liquidity of alternative assets makes these assets more attractive.
Efficiency of payments technologies	Fall	People can operate with less money.

transactions held constant, a holder of wealth has little incentive to keep extra wealth in money rather than in higher-return alternative assets. Thus the effect of an increase in wealth on money demand is likely to be small.

Risk. Money usually pays a fixed nominal interest rate (zero in the case of cash), so holding money itself usually isn't risky. However, if the risk of alternative assets such as stocks and real estate increases greatly, people may demand safer assets, including money. Thus increased riskiness in the economy may increase money demand.[8]

However, money doesn't always carry a low risk. In a period of erratic inflation, even if the nominal return on money is fixed, the real return on money (the nominal return minus inflation) may become quite uncertain, making money risky. Money demand then will fall as people switch to inflation hedges (assets whose real returns are less likely to be affected by erratic inflation) such as gold, consumer durable goods, and real estate.

Liquidity of Alternative Assets. The more quickly and easily alternative assets can be converted into cash, the less need there is to hold money. In recent years the joint impact of deregulation, competition, and innovation in financial markets has made alternatives to money more liquid. For example, with a home equity line of credit, a family can now write checks that are backed by the value of its home. We have mentioned individual cash management accounts whose introduction allowed individuals to switch wealth easily between high-return assets, such as stocks, and more liquid forms. As alternative assets become more liquid, the demand for money declines.

Payment Technologies. A last factor affecting money demand are the technologies available for making and receiving payments. For example, the introduction of credit cards allowed people to make transactions without money—at least until the end of the month, when a check must be written to pay the credit card bill. Automatic teller machines (ATMs) probably have reduced the demand for cash because people know that they can obtain cash quickly whenever they need it. In the future more innovations in payment technologies undoubtedly will help people operate with less and less money. Some experts even predict that ultimately we will live in a "cashless society," in which almost all payments will be made through immediately accessible computerized accounting systems and that the demand for money will be close to zero.

Elasticities of Money Demand

The theory of portfolio allocation helps economists identify factors that should affect the aggregate demand for money. However, for many purposes—such as forecasting and quantitative analyses of the economy—economists need to

8. For some evidence that this effect occurred in the early 1980s, see James M. McGibany and Farokh Nourzad, "Interest Rate Volatility and the Demand for Money," *Quarterly Review of Economics and Business*, Autumn 1986, pp. 73–83.

know not just which factors affect money demand but also how strong the various effects are. This information can be obtained only through statistical analysis of the data.

Over the past three decades, economists have performed hundreds of statistical studies of the money demand function. The results of these studies often are expressed in terms of elasticities, which measure the change in money demand resulting from changes in factors affecting the demand for money. Specifically, the **income elasticity of money demand** is the percentage change in money demand resulting from a 1% increase in real income. Thus, for example, if the income elasticity of money demand is 2/3, a 3% increase in real income will increase money demand by 2% ($2/3 \times 3\% = 2\%$). Similarly, the **interest elasticity of money demand** is the percentage change in money demand resulting from a 1% increase in the interest rate.

When we work with the interest elasticity of money demand, some care is needed to avoid a potential pitfall. To illustrate, suppose that the interest rate increases from 5% per year to 6% per year. To describe this increase in the interest rate as a 1% increase in the interest rate is tempting (but incorrect). In fact, it is a 20% increase in the interest rate, because 6 is 20% larger than 5.[9] If the interest elasticity of money demand is −0.1, for example, an increase in the interest rate from 5% to 6% reduces money demand by 2% ($-0.1 \times 20\% = -2\%$). Note that, if the interest elasticity of money demand is negative, as in this example, an increase in the interest rate reduces money demand.

What are the actual values of the income elasticity and interest elasticity of money demand? Although the many statistical studies of money demand provide a range of answers, some common results emerge. First, there is widespread agreement that the income elasticity of money demand is positive. For example, in his classic 1973 study of M1 money demand, which established the framework for many later studies, Stephen Goldfeld of Princeton University found this elasticity to be about 2/3.[10] A positive income elasticity of money demand implies that money demand rises when income rises, as predicted by our theory. Goldfeld's finding that the income elasticity of money demand is less than 1.0 is similar to that of many other empirical analyses, although some studies have found values for this elasticity as large as 1.0. An income elasticity of money demand smaller than 1.0 implies that money demand rises less than proportionally with income. Earlier in the chapter we discussed some reasons why, as an individual or nation becomes richer, the demand for money might be expected to grow more slowly than income.

Second, for the interest elasticity of money demand, most studies find a small negative value. For example, Goldfeld found the interest elasticity of money demand to be about −0.1 or −0.2. A negative value for the interest elasticity of money demand implies that when interest rates on nonmonetary assets rise, people reduce their holdings of money, again as predicted by the theory.

---

9. The change from 5% to 6% can be described as "a one *percentage point* increase" or as "a twenty *percent* increase."

10. "The Demand for Money Revisited," *Brookings Papers on Economic Activity*, 1973:4, pp. 577–638. Goldfeld reported elasticities of money demand that applied to the short run and the long run. The figures we present here are long-run elasticities.

Finally, Goldfeld's study and others have confirmed empirically that the nominal demand for money is proportional to the price level. Again, this result is consistent with the theory, as reflected in the money demand equation, Eq. (7.3).

APPLICATION

Financial Innovation and the "Case of the Missing Money"

Goldfeld's 1973 study showed that a money demand function for M1 in a form similar to Eq. (7.3) fit the existing data well. Shortly after Goldfeld's article was published, however, problems arose. Between late 1974 and early 1976 the demand for M1 was much lower than predicted by Goldfeld's equation—a puzzle that Goldfeld referred to in a later article as the "case of the missing money."[11] After getting back on track in the late 1970s, demand for M1 went the other way in the early 1980s, coming in higher than predicted by money demand equations. Thus the relationship between money demand and its principal macroeconomic determinants—the price level, income, and interest rates—seems to have shifted erratically.

Numerous explanations have been offered for the surprising instability of money demand. One factor emphasized by many economists was an increased pace of innovation and change in the financial system during the 1970s and 1980s. Spurred by deregulation and intense international competition during this period, banks and other financial institutions provided the public with many new financial assets to choose from, as well as a variety of new portfolio management techniques. Some of these innovations reduced the demand for narrowly defined money (M1); others increased it.

During the 1970s some of the major innovations tended to reduce the demand for M1. New liquid and interest-bearing assets that provided attractive alternatives to the assets in M1, which paid no interest at the time, were introduced. Examples of these new assets were money market mutual funds (utilized by consumers) and overnight repurchase agreements (utilized by firms), both now included in M2. As interest rates reached new peaks in the 1970s, these alternatives to M1 became widely used, reducing the demand for M1 (and increasing the demand for M2).

But, during the 1980s, financial innovations tended to increase M1 money demand. Holdings of new interest-bearing checking accounts, such as NOW accounts, grew rapidly in the early 1980s. Because these accounts are included in M1, their increased use raised total holdings of M1. Indeed, holdings of interest-bearing checkable accounts increased from 4% of M1 in November 1979 to 21% of M1 by December 1982.[12] Thus financial innovation helps explain why M1 demand was lower than predicted in the 1970s and higher than predicted in the 1980s.

Financial innovation continues to be a powerful force. Regulatory changes are likely to have a large impact on the structure of the banking system in the years ahead, and technological changes will continue to transform the nature of banking services. However, although financial innovation is good for the

---

11. Goldfeld, "The Case of the Missing Money," *Brookings Papers on Economic Activity,* 1976:3, pp. 683–730.

12. This figure is cited in James L. Pierce, "Did Financial Innovation Hurt the Great Monetarist Experiment?" *American Economic Review,* May 1984, pp. 392–396. This article contains additional discussion and references on the topic of the effects of financial innovation.

economy in general, changes in the financial system may continue to make money demand hard to predict.

Velocity and the Quantity Theory of Money

A concept related to money demand, which at times is used in discussions of monetary policy, is velocity. It measures how often the money stock "turns over" each period. Specifically, **velocity** is nominal GDP (the price level P times real output Y) divided by the nominal money stock M. If we let V represent velocity,

$$V = \frac{\text{nominal GDP}}{\text{nominal money stock}} = \frac{PY}{M}. \tag{7.4}$$

If velocity rises, each dollar of the money stock is being used in a greater dollar volume of transactions in each period, if we assume that the volume of transactions is proportional to GDP. Figure 7.1 shows the M1 and M2 velocities for the United States during 1959–1992.

The concept of velocity comes from one of the earliest theories of money demand, the quantity theory of money.[13] The **quantity theory of money** asserts that real money demand is proportional to real income, or

13. The quantity theory of money was developed by several classical economists, notably Irving Fisher, in the late nineteenth and early twentieth centuries. A famous statement of the theory is contained in Fisher's book *The Purchasing Power of Money* (New York: Macmillan, 1911).

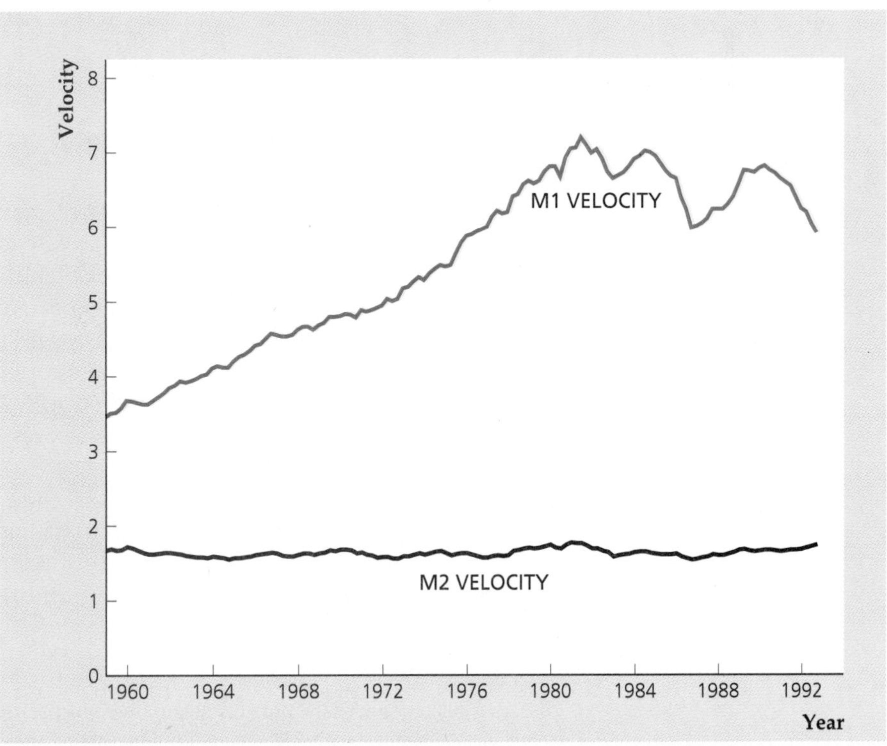

Figure 7.1
Velocity of M1 and M2, 1959–1992
M1 velocity is nominal GDP divided by M1, and M2 velocity is nominal GDP divided by M2. M1 velocity moved steadily upward until about 1981, but in the early 1980s M1 velocity fell and it has behaved erratically since then. M2 velocity has no clear trend and is more stable than M1 velocity, but it has been unpredictable over some short periods, such as 1990–1991.

Source: M1 and M2 money stock revisions from Federal Reserve Board, Release H.6. Nominal GDP from *Survey of Current Business,* various issues.

$$\frac{M^d}{P} = kY, \qquad (7.5)$$

where M^d/P is real money demand, Y is real income, and k is a constant. In Eq. (7.5) the real money demand function $L(Y, r + \pi^e)$ takes the simple form kY. This way of writing money demand is based on the strong assumption that velocity is a constant, $1/k$, and doesn't depend on income or interest rates.[14]

Is velocity actually a constant? As Fig. 7.1 shows, M1 velocity clearly is not a constant: M1 velocity rose steadily until about 1980 but then fell sharply in the early 1980s and behaved erratically since then. Financial innovations played a role in the 1980s' M1 velocity decline. As discussed, the popularity of new interest-bearing checking accounts during this period raised the demand for M1 at any level of GDP and thereby lowered its velocity. But, in addition, the quantity theory's assumption that interest rates don't affect money demand—an assumption contradicted by most empirical studies—probably contributed to that theory's misprediction of M1 demand in the 1980s. Lower interest rates on nonmonetary assets in the 1980s increased people's willingness to hold low-interest or zero-interest money, which raised the demand for M1 at any level of GDP and thus reduced M1 velocity.

M2 velocity, also shown in Fig. 7.1, is closer to being a constant. It shows no upward or downward trend and doesn't exhibit the instability of M1 velocity. However, even M2 velocity has been somewhat unpredictable over short periods. During the 1990–1991 recession, for example, M2 velocity rose significantly more than Federal Reserve economists predicted. Thus, although M2 velocity is more stable than M1 velocity, most economists would be reluctant to treat M2 velocity as a constant.

7.4 ASSET MARKET EQUILIBRIUM

Recall that the asset market actually is a set of markets, in which real and financial assets are traded. The demand for any asset (say, government bonds) is the quantity of the asset that holders of wealth want in their portfolios. The demand for each asset depends on its expected return, risk, and liquidity relative to other assets. The supply of each asset is the quantity of that asset that is available. At any particular time the supplies of individual assets are typically fixed, although over time asset supplies change (the government may issue more bonds, firms may issue new shares, more gold may be mined, and so on).

The asset market is in equilibrium when the quantity of each asset that holders of wealth demand equals the (fixed) available supply of that asset. In this section we examine asset market equilibrium, focusing on the role of money. We then show how asset market equilibrium is linked to the price level.

---

14. To derive velocity under the quantity theory, we must assume that nominal money demand M^d equals the actual money stock M, an assumption that we justify later in the chapter. Under this assumption, you should verify that $V = 1/k$.

Asset Market Equilibrium: An Aggregation Assumption

In analyzing the labor market in Chapter 3 and the goods market in Chapter 4, we relied on aggregation to keep things manageable. That is, instead of looking at the supply and demand for each of the many different types of labor and goods in the economy, we studied the supply and demand for both labor and goods in general. Aggregating in this way allowed us to analyze the behavior of the economy as a whole without getting lost in the details.

Because there are many different types of assets, aggregation is equally necessary for studying the asset market. Thus we adopt an aggregation assumption for the asset market that economists often make for macroeconomic analysis: We assume that all assets may be grouped into two categories, money and nonmonetary assets. Money includes assets that can be used in payment, such as currency and checking accounts. All money is assumed to have the same risk and liquidity and to pay the same nominal interest rate, i^m. The fixed nominal supply of money is M. Nonmonetary assets include all assets other than money, such as stocks, bonds, land, and so on. All nonmonetary assets are assumed to have the same risk and liquidity and to pay a nominal interest rate of $i = r + \pi^e$, where r is the expected real interest rate and π^e is the expected rate of inflation. The fixed nominal supply of nonmonetary assets is NM.

Although the assumption that assets can be aggregated into two types ignores many interesting differences among assets, it greatly simplifies our analysis and has proved to be very useful. One immediate benefit of making this assumption is that, if we allow for only two types of assets, *asset market equilibrium reduces to the condition that the quantity of money supplied equals the quantity of money demanded.*

To demonstrate this point, let's look at the portfolio allocation decision of an individual named Ed. Ed has a fixed amount of wealth that he allocates between money and nonmonetary assets. If m^d is the nominal amount of money and nm^d is the nominal amount of nonmonetary assets that Ed wants to hold, the sum of Ed's desired money holdings and his desired holdings of nonmonetary assets must be his total wealth, or

$$m^d + nm^d = \text{Ed's total nominal wealth.}$$

This equation has to be true for every holder of wealth in the economy.

Suppose that we sum this equation across all holders of wealth in the economy. Then the sum of all individual money demands m^d equals the aggregate demand for money M^d. The sum of all individual demands for nonmonetary assets is the aggregate demand for nonmonetary assets, NM^d. Finally, adding nominal wealth for all holders of wealth gives the aggregate nominal wealth of the economy, or

$$M^d + NM^d = \text{aggregate nominal wealth.} \tag{7.6}$$

Equation (7.6) states that the total demand for money in the economy plus the total demand for nonmonetary assets must equal the economy's total nominal wealth.

Next, we relate the total supplies of money and nonmonetary assets to aggregate wealth. Because money and nonmonetary assets are the only assets in the economy, aggregate nominal wealth equals the supply of money M plus the supply of nonmonetary assets NM, or

$$M + NM = \text{aggregate nominal wealth}. \tag{7.7}$$

Finally, we subtract Eq. (7.7) from Eq. (7.6) to obtain

$$(M^d - M) + (NM^d - NM) = 0. \tag{7.8}$$

The term $M^d - M$ in Eq. (7.8) is the *excess demand for money,* or the amount by which the total amount of money demanded exceeds the money supply. Similarly, the term $NM^d - NM$ in Eq. (7.8) is the *excess demand for nonmonetary assets.*

Now suppose that the demand for money M^d equals the money supply M so that the excess demand for money $M^d - M$ is zero. Equation (7.8) shows that, if $M^d - M$ is zero, $NM^d - NM$ must also be zero; that is, if the amounts of money supplied and demanded are equal, the amounts of nonmonetary assets supplied and demanded also must be equal. By definition, if quantities supplied and demanded are equal for each type of asset, the asset market is in equilibrium.

If we make the simplifying assumption that assets can be lumped into monetary and nonmonetary categories, the asset market is in equilibrium only if the quantity of money supplied equals the quantity of money demanded. This result is convenient, because it means that in studying asset market equilibrium we only have to look at the supply and demand for money and can ignore nonmonetary assets. As long as the amounts of money supplied and demanded are equal, the entire asset market will be in equilibrium.

The Asset Market Equilibrium Condition

Equilibrium in the asset market occurs when the quantity of money supplied equals the quantity of money demanded. This condition is valid whether money supply and demand are expressed in nominal terms or real terms. We work with this condition in real terms, or

$$\frac{M}{P} = L(Y,\ r + \pi^e). \tag{7.9}$$

The left-hand side of Eq. (7.9) is the nominal supply of money M divided by the price level P, which is the supply of money measured in real terms. The right-hand side of the equation is the same as the real demand for money M^d/P, as in Eq. (7.3). Equation (7.9), which states that the real quantity of money supplied equals the real quantity of money demanded, is called the asset market equilibrium condition.

The asset market equilibrium condition involves five variables: the nominal money supply M, the price level P, real income Y, the real interest rate r, and the expected rate of inflation π^e. The nominal money supply M is determined by the central bank through its open-market operations. For now, we treat the expected rate of inflation π^e as fixed (we return to the determination of expected inflation later in the chapter). That leaves three variables in the asset market equilibrium condition whose values we haven't yet specified: output Y, the real interest rate r, and the price level P.

In this part of the book we have made the assumption that the economy is at full employment or, equivalently, that all markets are in equilibrium. Both classical and Keynesian economists agree that the full-employment assumption is reasonable for analyzing the long-term behavior of the economy. If we continue to assume full employment,[15] we can use the analysis from previous chapters to describe how output and the real interest rate are determined. Recall from Chapter 3 that if the labor market is in equilibrium—with employment at its full-employment level—output equals full-employment output $\bar{Y}$. Chapter 4 showed that, for any level of output, the real interest rate must take the value that makes desired national saving and desired investment equal (the goods market equilibrium condition).

With the values of output and the real interest rate established by equilibrium in the labor and goods markets, the only variable left to be determined by the asset market equilibrium condition is the price level P. To emphasize that the price level is the variable determined by asset market equilibrium, we multiply both sides of Eq. (7.9) by P and divide both sides by real money demand, $L(Y, r + \pi^e)$, to obtain

$$P = \frac{M}{L(Y,\ r + \pi^e)}. \tag{7.10}$$

According to Eq. (7.10), the economy's price level P equals the ratio of the nominal money supply M to the real demand for money $L(Y, r + \pi^e)$. For given values of real output Y, the real interest rate r, and the expected rate of inflation π^e, the real demand for money $L(Y, r + \pi^e)$ is fixed. Thus Eq. (7.10) states that the price level is proportional to the nominal money supply. A doubling of the nominal money supply M, for instance, would double the price level P, with other factors held constant. The existence of a close link between the price level and the money supply in an economy is one of the oldest and most reliable conclusions about macroeconomic behavior, having been recognized in some form for hundreds if not thousands of years. We discuss the empirical support for this link in Section 7.5.

What forces lead the price level to its equilibrium value, Eq. (7.10)? A complete description of how the price level adjusts to its equilibrium value involves an analysis of the goods market as well as the asset market; we leave this task until Chapter 10, where we discuss the links among the three main markets of the economy in more detail. Briefly, in Chapter 10 we show that an increase in the money supply leads people to increase their nominal spending on goods and services; this increased nominal demand for output leads prices to rise. Prices continue to rise until people are content to hold the increased nominal quantity of money in their portfolios, satisfying the asset market equilibrium condition (rewritten as Eq. 7.10).

7.5 MONEY GROWTH AND INFLATION

In Section 7.4 we established that, when the markets for labor, goods, and assets are all in equilibrium, the price level P is proportional to the nominal money supply M. However, the price level itself generally is of less concern to policymakers and the public than is the rate of inflation, or the percentage rate of increase of the price level. In this section we extend our analysis of the price level to show how inflation is determined. We conclude that the inflation rate,

15. We relax this assumption in Part III when we discuss short-run economic fluctuations.

which is the growth rate of the price level, is closely related to the growth rate of the nominal money supply.

To obtain an equation for the rate of inflation in a full-employment economy, we set the growth rate of the left-hand side of Eq. (7.10) equal to the growth rate of its right-hand side to obtain

$$\frac{\Delta P}{P} = \frac{\Delta M}{M} - \frac{\Delta L(Y, r + \pi^e)}{L(Y, r + \pi^e)}, \tag{7.11}$$

where the symbol Δ indicates the change in a variable from one year to the next. The left-hand side of Eq. (7.11) is the growth rate of the price level, $\Delta P/P$, which is the same as the inflation rate π. The right-hand side of Eq. (7.11) expresses the growth rate of the ratio on the right-hand side of Eq. (7.10) as the growth rate of the numerator, M, minus the growth rate of the denominator, $L(Y, r + \pi^e)$. (Appendix A, Section A.7 provides some useful formulas for calculating growth rates.) Equation (7.11) shows that, if the asset market is in equilibrium, *the rate of inflation equals the growth rate of the nominal money supply minus the growth rate of real money demand.*

Equation (7.11) highlights the point that the rate of inflation is closely related to the rate of growth of the nominal money supply. However, to use Eq. (7.11) to predict the behavior of inflation we must also know how quickly real money demand is growing. The money demand function, Eq. (7.3), focused on two macroeconomic variables with significant effects on real money demand: income (or output) Y and the nominal interest rate $r + \pi^e$. We show later in this section that, in a long-run equilibrium with a constant growth rate of money, the nominal interest rate will be constant. Therefore here we look only at growth in income as a source of growth in real money demand.

Earlier we defined the income elasticity of money demand to be the percentage change in money demand resulting from a 1% increase in real income. If $\Delta Y/Y$ is the percentage change in real income from one year to the next and η_Y is the income elasticity of money demand, $\eta_Y \Delta Y/Y$ is the resulting increase in the real demand for money, with other factors affecting money demand held constant. Substituting π for $\Delta P/P$ and $\eta_Y \Delta Y/Y$ for the growth rate of real money demand in Eq. (7.11) yields

$$\pi = \frac{\Delta M}{M} - \eta_Y \frac{\Delta Y}{Y}. \tag{7.12}$$

Equation (7.12) is a useful simple expression for the rate of inflation. According to Eq. (7.12), the rate of inflation equals the growth rate of the nominal money supply minus an adjustment for the growth rate of real money demand arising from growth in real output. For example, suppose that nominal money supply growth is 10% per year, real income is growing by 3% per year, and the income elasticity of money demand is 2/3. Then Eq. (7.12) predicts that the inflation rate will be 10% – (2/3)(3%), or 8% per year.

APPLICATION

Inflation in Low-Money-Growth and High-Money-Growth Countries

Both the growth of the nominal money supply and the growth of real money demand (resulting from real income growth, for example) affect the rate of inflation. Generally, however, the growth rate of real money demand doesn't vary significantly among countries. For example, if the income elasticity of money demand in a country is 1/2 and real output growth is 6% per year, according to Eq. (7.12) real money demand will grow at 3% per year (1/2 × 6%) in that country. If a second country also has an income elasticity of money demand of 1/2, but its income is growing by a more modest 2%, the rate of growth of real money demand in the second country is 1% per year. In this example, the difference in the growth of real money demand in the two countries is only 2 percentage points (3% – 1%) per year.

In contrast to growth in real money demand, rates of growth of nominal money supplies may vary dramatically among countries, from rates that are near zero or even negative to rates of thousands of percent per year. Thus huge differences in inflation rates among countries almost always are the result of large differences in rates of money growth.

Evidence on the link between inflation and money supply growth in different countries is provided in Table 7.2. Starting with International Monetary

Table 7.2 Inflation in Low-Money-Growth and High-Money-Growth Countries, 1988–1991

Low-Money-Growth Countries

Country	Money Growth Rate (% per year)	Inflation Rate (% per year)
1. Cote d'Ivoire	−4.1	2.0
2. Senegal	−0.5	−0.7
3. Switzerland	0.7	4.1
4. Rwanda	1.0	6.7
5. Niger	1.4	−3.2
6. France	2.9	3.2
7. United States	3.6	4.6
8. Czechoslovakia	3.8	15.2
9. Canada	3.8	4.8
10. Burkina Faso	5.2	1.4

High-Money-Growth Countries

Country	Money Growth Rate (% per year)	Inflation Rate (% per year)
1. Peru	1052.6	1694.3
2. Zaire	207.7	251.4
3. Poland	144.9	184.7
4. Uruguay	78.3	88.3
5. Mexico	67.0	41.4
6. Turkey	57.4	66.2
7. Zambia	56.6	94.7
8. Ecuador	50.8	57.4
9. Sudan	50.8	78.5
10. Nigeria	36.6	29.6

Source: International Monetary Fund, International Financial Statistics.

Fund data for 1988–1991 for more than 140 countries, we eliminated small countries (population under 5 million) and countries with any missing data. Of the remaining countries, Table 7.2 lists the ten countries with the lowest average rates of money growth over 1988–1991 and the ten countries with the highest average rates of money growth over the same period. Also given is each country's inflation rate (as measured by the rate of change of the consumer price index) for that period.

Note the close relationship between money growth rates and inflation. Countries such as Peru and Zaire, with triple-digit money growth rates, also had triple-digit inflation rates. Countries such as Cote d'Ivoire or Senegal, in contrast, had both low money growth rates and low inflation rates. Figure 7.2 graphs the relationship between money growth and inflation for nineteen of the twenty countries (Peru is omitted from the graph for readability); again, the close relationship between money growth rates and inflation is apparent.

If rapid money growth causes inflation, why do countries allow their money supplies to grow so quickly? As discussed earlier, governments sometimes find that printing money (borrowing from the central bank) is the only way that they can finance their expenditures, which is most likely to occur in poor countries or countries suffering from war or natural disaster. Unfortunately, the almost inevitable result of financing government expenditures in this way is increased inflation.

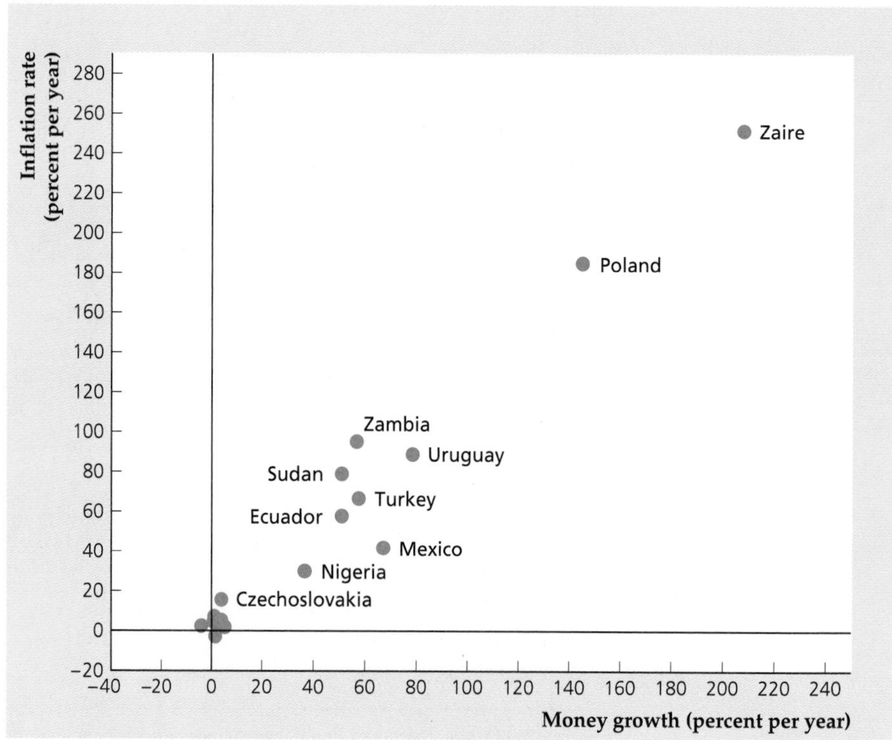

Figure 7.2
The relationship between money growth and inflation
Nominal money growth and inflation for 1988–1991 are plotted for the countries listed in Table 7.2, excluding Peru for readability. There is a strong relationship between money growth rates and inflation rates, with low-money-growth countries having low inflation and high-money-growth experiencing high inflation.

Source: See Table 7.2 and text.

The Expected Inflation Rate and the Nominal Interest Rate

In our earlier discussion of asset market equilibrium, we made the assumption that the expected inflation rate is fixed. For a given real interest rate r (which is determined by the goods market equilibrium condition), if the expected inflation rate π^e is fixed, so is the nominal interest rate, at $r + \pi^e$. We close the chapter with a brief look at the factors that determine the expected inflation rate and the nominal interest rate.

What should holders of wealth and others expect the inflation rate to be in the future? As we demonstrated, Eq. (7.12), which relates inflation to the growth rates of the nominal money supply and real income, is useful for predicting inflation. For expected values of money growth (based, for example, on plans announced by the central bank) and real income growth, as well as an estimate of the income elasticity of money demand, Eq. (7.12) can be used to calculate the expected inflation rate. Suppose that people in a particular country expect their nation's money supply to grow much more rapidly over the next two years because the government is committed to large military expenditures and can pay for these expenditures only by printing money. In this case, Eq. (7.12) shows that people should expect much higher inflation rates in the future.

The inflation prediction equation, Eq. (7.12), is particularly easy to apply when the growth rates of the nominal money supply and real income are constant over time. In this case, the expected growth rates of the nominal money supply and real income equal their current growth rates, and (from Eq. 7.12) the expected inflation rate equals the current inflation rate (assuming no change in the income elasticity of money demand). In practice, the current inflation rate often approximates the expected inflation rate, as long as people don't expect money or income growth to change too much in the near future.

The public's expected inflation rate is not directly observable, except perhaps through surveys and similar methods. However, an observable economic variable that is strongly affected by expected inflation is the nominal interest rate. At any real interest rate r, which is determined by the goods market equilibrium condition that desired national saving equals desired investment, the nominal interest rate $r + \pi^e$ changes one-for-one with changes in the expected inflation rate π^e. Thus policy actions (such as rapid expansion of the money supply) that cause people to fear future increases in inflation should cause nominal interest rates to rise, all else being equal.

But, as already noted, if people don't expect large changes in the growth rates of the money supply or real income, expected inflation won't be much different from current inflation. In this case, nominal interest rates and current inflation rates should move together. If current inflation is high, for example, expected inflation also is likely to be high; but high expected inflation also causes nominal interest rates to be high, all else being equal.

The historical relationship between nominal interest rates and inflation is illustrated by Fig. 7.3, on the next page, which shows the nominal interest rate on six-month Treasury bills and the annual inflation rate measured by the GDP deflator in the United States from 1959 to 1992. The nominal interest rate and the inflation rate have tended to move together, rising during the 1960s and 1970s and then falling sharply after reaching a peak in 1981. However, movements in the inflation rate aren't perfectly matched by movements in the

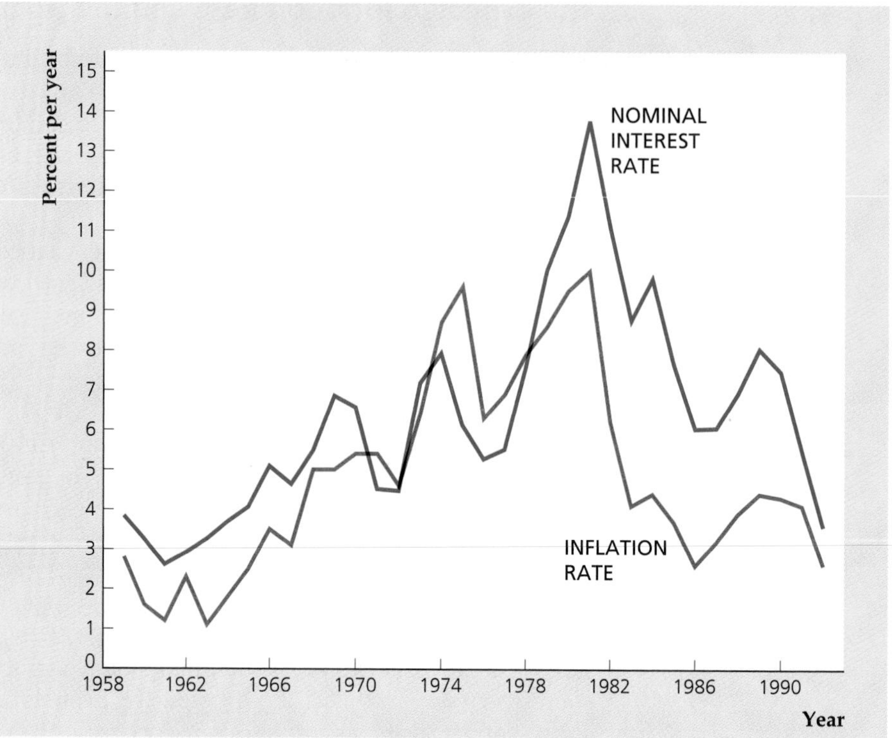

Figure 7.3
Inflation and the nominal interest rate in the United States, 1959–1992
The figure shows the nominal interest rate on six-month Treasury bills and the annual rate of inflation as measured by the GDP deflator. The nominal interest rate tends to move together with inflation, although there are periods such as the early 1980s when the two variables diverge.

Source: Nominal interest rate is the yield on six-month Treasury bills from Table B-69 of the *Economic Report of the President,* February 1993. Inflation is the rate of change of the GDP deflator from Table B-3 of the same source. The inflation rate for 1992 is from *Survey of Current Business.*

nominal interest rate because the real interest rate hasn't been constant over this period. In particular, during the late 1970s and early 1980s, the rise in the nominal interest rate was much greater than the rise in the inflation rate, reflecting an increase in the real interest rate from a negative value in the mid 1970s to much higher, positive values in the 1980s.

CHAPTER SUMMARY

1. Money is the set of assets that are widely used and accepted as payment, such as currency and checking accounts. Money functions as a medium of exchange, a unit of account, and a store of value.

2. The supply of money is set by the central bank—the Federal Reserve System in the United States. The central bank's official measures of money are called the monetary aggregates. M1, which is made up primarily of currency and checking accounts, and M2, which includes a broader set of monetary assets, are the monetary aggregates that are most widely watched.

3. A portfolio allocation decision is made by a holder of wealth when determining which assets and how much of each asset to hold. The three characteristics of assets that most affect their desirability are expected return, risk, and liquidity.

4. Money demand is the total amount of money that people choose to hold in their portfolios.

The principal macroeconomic variables that affect money demand are the price level, real income, and interest rates. Nominal money demand is proportional to the price level. Higher real income increases the number of transactions and thus raises real money demand. A higher interest rate on alternative, nonmonetary assets lowers real money demand by making the alternative assets more attractive than money. The money demand function measures the relationship between real money demand and these macroeconomic variables.

5. Velocity is the ratio of nominal GDP to the nominal money stock. The quantity theory of money is an early theory of money demand that assumes that velocity is constant, so that money demand is proportional to income. Historically, M2 velocity has been more stable than M1 velocity, although even M2 velocity isn't constant.

6. Under the simplifying assumption that assets can be grouped into two categories—money and nonmonetary assets—the asset market is in equilibrium if the quantity of money supplied equals the quantity of money demanded. When all markets are in equilibrium (the economy is at full employment), the level of output is determined by equilibrium in the labor market, the real interest rate is determined by equilibrium in the goods market, and the price level is determined by equilibrium in the asset market. The equilibrium price level is proportional to the nominal money supply.

7. When all markets are in equilibrium, the inflation rate equals the growth rate of the nominal money supply minus the growth rate of real money demand. The growth rate of real money demand in turn depends primarily on the real income growth rate. Expected inflation depends on expected growth rates of the nominal money supply and real income. For a given real interest rate, the nominal interest rate responds one-for-one to changes in expected inflation.

Key Terms

demand for money, p. 227
expected returns, p. 226
income elasticity of money demand, p. 233
interest elasticity of money demand, p. 233
liquidity, p. 226
M1, p. 223
M2, p. 223
medium of exchange, p. 220
monetary aggregates, p. 222
money, p. 220
money demand function, p. 231
money supply, p. 224
open-market operations, p. 225
portfolio allocation decision, p. 226
quantity theory of money, p. 235
risk, p. 226
store of value, p. 221
unit of account, p. 220
velocity, p. 235

Key Equations

$$\frac{M^d}{P} = L(Y,\ r + \pi^e) \qquad (7.3)$$

According to the money demand function, the real quantity of money demanded, M^d/P, depends on output and the nominal interest rate on alternative, nonmonetary assets. An increase in output, Y, raises the number of transactions people make and thus raises the demand for money. An increase in the nominal interest rate on nonmonetary assets, i (which equals the real interest rate, r, plus the expected rate of inflation, π^e) raises the attractiveness of alternative assets and thus reduces the demand for money.

$$V = \frac{\text{nominal GDP}}{\text{nominal money supply}} = \frac{PY}{M} \qquad (7.4)$$

Velocity V is nominal GDP, or P times Y, divided by the nominal money stock, M. Velocity is assumed to be constant by the quantity theory of money.

$$\frac{M}{P} = L(Y,\ r + \pi^e) \qquad (7.9)$$

The asset market equilibrium conditions states that the real supply of money, M/P, and the real demand for money, $L(Y, r + \pi^e)$, are equal.

$$\pi = \frac{\Delta M}{M} - \eta_Y \frac{\Delta Y}{Y} \qquad (7.12)$$

The inflation rate, π, equals the growth rate of the nominal money supply, $\Delta M/M$, minus the growth rate of real money demand. The growth rate of real money demand equals the income elasticity of money demand, η_Y, times the growth rate of real income or output, $\Delta Y/Y$.

Review Questions

1. Define *money*. How does the economist's use of this term differ from its everyday meaning?
2. What are the three functions of money? How does each function contribute to a more smoothly operating economy?
3. Who determines the nation's money supply? Explain how the money supply could be expanded or reduced in an economy in which all money is in the form of currency.
4. What are the three characteristics of assets that are most important to holders of wealth? How does money compare with other assets for each characteristic?
5. List and discuss the macroeconomic variables that affect the aggregate demand for money.
6. Define *velocity*. Discuss the role of velocity in the quantity theory of money.
7. Why is equilibrium in the asset market described by the condition that real money supply equal real money demand? What is the aggregation assumption that is needed to allow ignoring the markets for other assets?
8. What is the relationship between the price level and the nominal money supply when all markets are in equilibrium? What is the relationship between inflation and the nominal money supply?
9. Give an example of a factor that would increase the public's expected rate of inflation. All else being equal, how would this increase in the expected inflation rate affect interest rates?

Numerical Problems

1. Money demand in an economy in which no interest is paid on money is

$$\frac{M^d}{P} = 500 + 0.2Y - 1000i.$$

a. You know that $P = 100$, $Y = 1000$, and $i = 0.10$. Find real money demand, nominal money demand, and velocity.
b. The price level doubles from $P = 100$ to $P = 200$. Find real money demand, nominal money demand, and velocity.
c. Starting from the values of the variables given in part (a) and assuming that the money demand function as written holds, determine how velocity is affected by an increase in real income. By an increase in the nominal interest rate. By an increase in the price level.

2. Mr. Midas has wealth of \$100,000 that he invests entirely in money (a checking account) and government bonds. Mr. Midas instructs his broker to invest \$50,000 in bonds, plus \$5000 more in bonds for every percentage point that the interest rate on bonds exceeds the interest rate on his checking account.
a. Write an algebraic formula that gives Mr. Midas's demand for money as a function of bond and checking account interest rates.
b. Write an algebraic formula that gives Mr. Midas's demand for bonds. What is the sum of his demand for money and his demand for bonds?
c. Suppose that all holders of wealth in the economy are identical to Mr. Midas. Fixed asset supplies per person are \$80,000 of bonds and \$20,000 of checking accounts. Checking accounts pay no interest. What is the interest rate on bonds in asset market equilibrium?
3. Assume that the quantity theory of money holds and that velocity is constant at 5.0. Output is fixed at its full-employment value of 10,000, and the price level is 2.0.
a. Determine the real demand for money and the nominal demand for money.
b. In this same economy the government fixes the nominal money supply at 5000. With output fixed at its full-employment level and with the assumption that prices are flexible, what will be the new price level? What happens to the price level if the nominal money supply rises to 6000?
4. Consider an economy with a constant nominal money supply, a constant level of real output $Y = 100$, and a constant real interest rate $r = 0.10$. Suppose that the income elasticity of money demand is 0.5 and the interest elasticity of money demand is -0.1.
a. By what percentage does the equilibrium price level differ from its initial value if output increases to $Y = 106$ (and r remains at 0.10)? (*Hint:* Use Eq. 7.11.)
b. By what percentage does the equilibrium price level differ from its initial value if the real interest increases to $r = 0.11$ (and Y remains at 100)?

c. Suppose that the real interest rate increases to $r = 0.11$. What would real output have to be in order for the equilibrium price level to remain at its initial value?

5. Suppose that the real money demand function is

$$L(Y,\ r + \pi^e) = \frac{0.01Y}{(r + \pi^e)},$$

where Y is real output, r is the real interest rate, and π^e is the expected rate of inflation. Real output is constant over time at $Y = 150$. The real interest is fixed in the goods market at $r = 0.05$ per year.

a. Suppose that the nominal money supply is growing at the rate of 10% per year and that this growth rate is expected to persist forever. Currently, the nominal money supply is $M = 300$. What are the values of the real money supply and the current price level? (*Hint:* What is the value of the expected inflation rate that enters the money demand function?)

b. Suppose that the nominal money supply is $M = 300$. The central bank announces that from now on the nominal money supply is going to grow at the rate of 5% per year. If everyone believes this announcement, and if all markets are in equilibrium, what are the values of the real money supply and the current price level? Explain the effects on the real money supply and the current price level of a slowdown in the rate of money growth.

Analytical Problems

1. All else being equal, how would each of the following affect the demand for M1? The demand for M2? Explain.

a. The maximum number of checks per month that can be written on money market mutual funds and money market deposit accounts is raised from three to thirty.

b. Home equity lines of credit that allow homeowners to write checks against the value of their homes are introduced.

c. The stock market crashes, and further sharp declines in the market are widely feared.

d. Banks introduce overdraft protection, under which funds are automatically transferred from savings to checking as needed to cover checks.

e. A crackdown reduces the illegal drug trade (which is carried out largely in currency).

2. Figure 7.1 shows that, before the 1980s, M1 velocity generally rose over time. Suggest some explanations for this upward trend.

3. The prisoner-of-war camp described by Radford (Box 7.1) periodically received large shipments of cigarettes from the Red Cross or other sources.

a. How did cigarette shipments affect the price level (the prices of goods in terms of cigarettes) in the POW camp?

b. (More difficult) On some occasions the prisoners knew in advance when the cigarette shipments were to arrive. What happened to the demand for cigarette money and the price level in the camp in the days just before an anticipated shipment?

4. Assume that prices and wages adjust rapidly so that the markets for labor, goods, and assets are always in equilibrium. What are the effects of each of the following on output, the real interest rate, and the current price level?

a. A temporary increase in government purchases.

b. A reduction in expected inflation.

c. A temporary increase in labor supply.

d. An increase in the interest rate paid on money.

CHAPTER 8

Household Decisions to Consume, Save, and Work: A More Formal Treatment[1]

The focus of macroeconomics is on aggregate quantities such as GDP, national saving, investment, and employment. However, you mustn't lose sight of the fact that these aggregate quantities reflect the individual decisions of millions of people, from assembly-line workers to corporate executives to homemakers to government officials. One useful strategy for trying to understand the behavior of aggregate quantities is to think about the forces that affect the economic behavior of individuals and firms.

We have already analyzed the economic behavior of business firms. In Chapter 3 we looked at firms' decisions about how much labor to employ and how much output to produce; in Chapter 4 we examined firms' decisions about how much capital to use. In this chapter we focus on the economic behavior of households (individuals and families). Although we discussed household economic behavior in general terms earlier, here we use some tools from microeconomics to examine certain aspects of household decision making in greater detail. These decisions are the ones having the greatest macroeconomic significance: the household's choices about how much to consume, how much to save, and how much to work.

As you might expect, the main conclusions that we draw in this chapter about household economic behavior are not much different from those reached in our earlier, briefer discussions. The principal benefit of this chapter's more formal approach is not a new set of conclusions but rather a deeper insight into the factors affecting household economic behavior and clarification of some ongoing controversies. The chapter will also give you a sense of

1. This chapter is optional; it can be used alone or to supplement Chapters 3 and 4. See the Preface for additional information and suggestions.

some of the methods that professional economists use in economic analysis and research, and as a basis for policy advice.

8.1 CONSUMPTION AND SAVING: THE PRESENT VERSUS THE FUTURE

Let's begin by taking a closer look at the household's decision about how much of its income to consume and how much to save. (Recall from Chapter 4 that, because saving is the portion of income left after the household decides how much to consume, the decisions about how much to consume and how much to save are really two aspects of the same decision.) We have already stressed the significance of the consumption–saving decision from the macroeconomic perspective. For example, in Chapter 5 we discussed the close link between national saving and the trade balance. In Chapter 6 we demonstrated that the national saving rate is one of the primary factors that determines a country's long-run standard of living.

Why do people save? Recall from Chapter 4 that the benefit of saving is that, by putting some of its income aside today, a household increases its ability to consume in the future. The cost of saving is that the household must reduce the amount of consumption that it presently enjoys. Thus, fundamentally, in choosing how much to consume and save today the household is making a trade-off between the present and the future. In this section we present an economic model of this trade-off. To illustrate how the model works, we follow the fortunes of an individual consumer named Prudence.

To keep the analysis of the model manageable, we make three simplifying assumptions. (At various points in the chapter we discuss the implications for our analysis of dropping each of these assumptions.)

1. We assume that the time horizon over which Prudence makes her plans (her "lifetime") consists of only two periods: the present, or current, period and the future period. You might think of the two periods as corresponding to Prudence's working years and her retirement years, for example. A two-period model is the simplest framework that captures the essential idea of a trade-off between the present and the future.

2. We assume that Prudence takes her current and future income and her wealth as given, ignoring the possibility that, by working overtime or taking on a second job, she might be able to increase her income. In Section 8.4 we discuss what happens when Prudence can vary the amount of labor she supplies.

3. We assume that Prudence can choose how much to borrow or save at a given real interest rate. For now we ignore the facts that consumers typically have to pay a higher real interest rate to borrow than they can earn on their savings and that in practice lenders may restrict the amount that consumers can borrow. Later we discuss how Prudence's behavior might change when limits are placed on how much she can borrow.

How Much Can the Consumer Afford? The Budget Constraint

To analyze Prudence's decision about how much to consume and save, we first examine how her economic resources determine the choices available to her. To have some specific numbers to work with, let's suppose that Prudence receives a fixed after-tax income, measured in real terms[2], of 14,000 in the current period and expects to receive a real income of 11,000 in the future period. In addition, she begins the current period with real wealth of 6000 in a savings account.

Next, we list the symbols used to represent Prudence's situation. We used capital letters as symbols for aggregate variables in earlier chapters, so we use lowercase letters for an individual's variables:

y = Prudence's current real income (14,000);
y^f = Prudence's future real income (11,000);
a = Prudence's real wealth (assets) at the beginning of the current period (6000);
a^f = Prudence's real wealth at the beginning of the future period (not yet determined);
c = Prudence's current real consumption (not yet determined);
c^f = Prudence's future real consumption (not yet determined).

Many different combinations of current and future consumption—that is, of c and c^f—are available to Prudence. Here is one possibility: In the current period she could consume all her initial wealth (6000) plus all her current income (14,000), for a total (real) consumption of 20,000. If she did so, in the future period Prudence would be able to consume 11,000, her future income. Thus one consumption combination available to Prudence is

$$c = 20{,}000 \quad \text{and} \quad c^f = 11{,}000.$$

If Prudence makes this particular consumption choice, how much does she save in the first period? Saving, s, is current income minus current consumption, or

$$\begin{aligned} s &= y - c \\ &= 14{,}000 - 20{,}000 = -6000. \end{aligned} \tag{8.1}$$

Hence Prudence's saving (−6000) is negative; the term for negative saving is *dissaving*. Here, Prudence dissaves by spending her initial wealth *and* all her current income. She could have consumed even more—and dissaved even more—in the current period by borrowing and repaying the loan in the future.

In general, any amount of current consumption c that Prudence chooses will determine the amount of future consumption c^f that she will be able to enjoy. To work out the relationship between Prudence's current consumption and her future consumption, we note first that the funds that Prudence has on hand in the current period are her current income y and her initial wealth a. If her current consumption is c, at the end of the current period she has $y + a - c$ left.

2. The units in which Prudence's income is measured are base-year dollars. Or you can think of a world in which there is only one good, say hamburgers, which provides the unit of measurement.

Prudence can put these leftover current resources in the bank to earn interest. If the real interest rate that Prudence can earn on her deposit is r, the real value of her bank account (principal plus interest) in the future period will be $(y + a - c)(1 + r)$. The amount $(y + a - c)(1 + r)$ corresponds to a^f, Prudence's assets at the beginning of the future period.

In the future period the funds available to Prudence consist of her assets a^f plus the income she receives in the future period y^f, for a total of $(y + a - c)(1 + r) + y^f$. Because the future period is the last period of Prudence's "life" (and there is no one that she wants to leave an inheritance to), she spends all her remaining resources on consumption. Thus Prudence's future consumption c^f is

$$c^f = (y + a - c)(1 + r) + y^f. \tag{8.2}$$

Equation (8.2) is called the consumer's budget constraint. For any level of current consumption c, the **budget constraint** indicates how much future consumption c^f Prudence can afford, based on her current and future income and initial wealth.[3]

Some sample calculations using the budget constraint, under the assumption that the real interest rate r equals 10%, are shown in Table 8.1. Column (1)

3. In our derivation of Eq. (8.2), we assumed that Prudence's current consumption was less than her total current resources so that she had some resources left to deposit in the bank. However, the budget constraint, Eq. (8.2), still works if Prudence's current consumption exceeds her total current resources so that she must borrow from the bank. See Analytical Problem 2 at the end of the chapter.

Table 8.1 Consumption Combinations Available to Prudence

y = current real income = 14,000.
y^f = expected future real income = 11,000.
a = initial real wealth or assets = 6000.
r = real interest rate = 10%.

(1) Current Consumption, c	(2) Saving, $s = y - c$	(3) Leftover Current Resources, $y - c + a$	(4) Future Assets, $a^f = (y - c + a) \times (1 + r)$	(5) Future Consumption, $c^f = a^f + y^f$	
0	14,000	20,000	22,000	33,000	A
5,000	9,000	15,000	16,500	27,500	B
10,000	4,000	10,000	11,000	22,000	C
15,000	−1,000	5,000	5,500	16,500	D
20,000	−6,000	0	0	11,000	E
25,000	−11,000	−5,000	−5,500	5,500	F
30,000	−16,000	−10,000	−11,000	0	G

The letters in the final column correspond to the lettered points in Figure 8.1.

shows different values of current consumption c that Prudence might choose. Column (2) shows the implied level of current saving s, or current income y minus current consumption c. Column (3) gives the total amount of current resources left, $y + a - c$, after Prudence enjoys her current consumption. Prudence's wealth at the beginning of period 2, a^f (column 4), equals leftover current resources times $1 + r$ (negative values of a^f imply that Prudence enters the second period in debt). Finally, future consumption (column 5) equals Prudence's wealth at the beginning of the future period a^f, plus future income y^f.[4] Future consumption can be calculated directly from the budget constraint, Eq. (8.2).

The Budget Line

The **budget line** is the graph of the budget constraint, Eq. (8.2); it shows the combinations of current and future consumption that Prudence can afford, based on her current and future income, her initial level of wealth, and the real interest rate. Figure 8.1 shows Prudence's budget line, with current consumption c on the horizontal axis and future consumption c^f on the vertical axis. The possible consumption combinations calculated in Table 8.1 appear as points A–G on the budget line.

4. We do not include in future income y^f the interest that Prudence earns on her saving. Future income y^f includes only labor income or transfers received, such as Social Security payments.

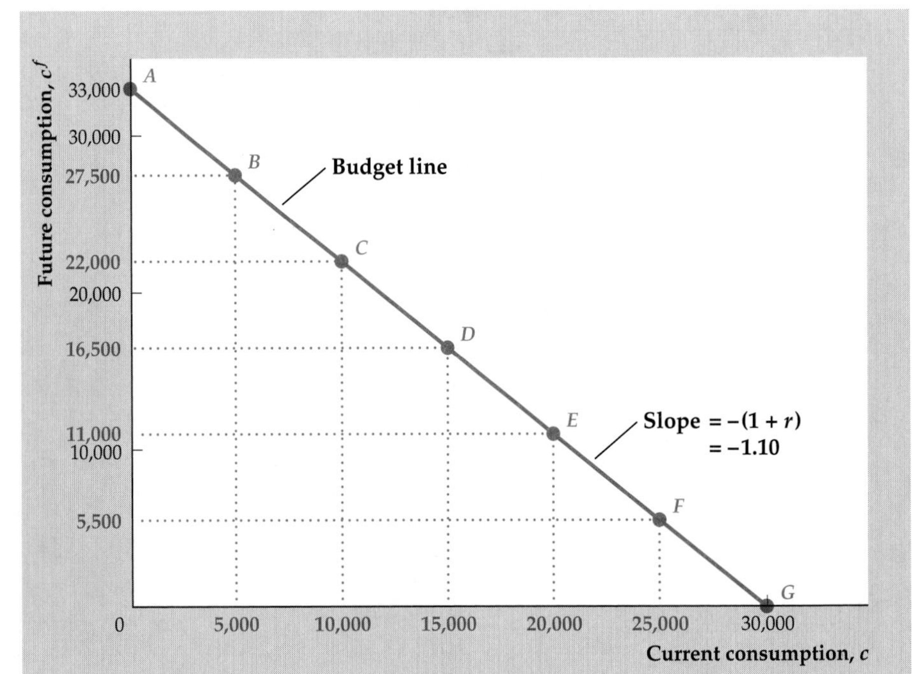

Figure 8.1
The budget line
The budget line shows the combinations of current and future consumption c and c^f available to Prudence, as presented in Table 8.1. Each lettered point corresponds to a consumption combination in Table 8.1. The slope of the budget line is $-(1 + r) = -1.10$. The slope equals $-(1 + r)$ because each extra unit of current consumption implies one less unit of saving; savings earn interest at rate r, so each unit reduction in saving in turn implies a reduction of $1 + r$ units in Prudence's future consumption.

Figure 8.1 shows that the budget line slopes downward, which reflects the trade-off between current and future consumption. If Prudence increases her current consumption by one unit, her saving falls by one unit; and because saving earns interest at rate r, a one-unit decline in saving today implies that Prudence's future wealth—and thus her future consumption—will be lower by $1 + r$ units. Because an increase in current consumption by one unit lowers future consumption by $1 + r$ units, the slope of the budget line is $-(1 + r)$. In our numerical example the real interest rate is 10%, so the slope of the budget line in Fig. 8.1 is –1.10.

Present Values

To describe Prudence's budget constraint seemingly requires four separate quantities: Prudence's current income y, her future income y^f, her initial wealth a, and the real interest rate r. However, by using the present value concept, we can conveniently summarize Prudence's economic resources, both current and future, with a single number.

Present value measures the value of payments to be made in the future in terms of today's dollars or goods. To illustrate, suppose that you know that you must make a payment of $13,200 one year from now. How much money would you have to put aside today so that you could make that future payment? The answer to this question is the present value of $13,200.

The present value of a future payment depends on the interest rate. If the current nominal interest rate i is 10% per year, the present value of $13,200 to be paid one year from now is $12,000. The reason is that $12,000 deposited in the bank today at a 10% interest rate will earn $1200 (10% of $12,000) of interest in one year, which added to the initial $12,000 equals $13,200. Therefore at an interest rate of 10%, having $13,200 one year from now is economically equivalent to having $12,000 today.

More generally, if the nominal interest rate is i per year, each dollar in the bank today is worth $1 + i$ dollars one year from now. To have $13,200 one year from now requires $\$13{,}200/(1 + i)$ in the bank today; thus the present value of $13,200 to be paid one year from now is $\$13{,}200/(1 + i)$. So, as we have already shown, if $i = 10\%$ per year, the present value of $13,200 one year from now is $\$13{,}200/1.10 = \$12{,}000$. If $i = 20\%$ per year, the present value of $13,200 one year in the future is $\$13{,}200/1.20 = \$11{,}000$. Hence an increase in the interest rate reduces the present value of a future payment; the higher the interest rate is, the less must be put aside today to attain that amount in the future.[5]

In this discussion we have measured future payments in nominal, or dollar, terms. When future payments are measured in nominal terms, the appropriate interest rate for calculating present values is the nominal interest rate i. If future payments are measured in real terms, present values are calculated exactly the same way, except that the real interest rate r rather than the nominal interest rate i is used. In analyzing Prudence's consumption–saving decision,

5. Our examples consider only payments due in one year, but present values can be calculated for payments at any time in the future. See Numerical Problem 2 at the end of the chapter.

we're measuring everything in real terms, so we use the real interest rate r to calculate the present values of Prudence's future income and consumption.

Present Value and the Budget Constraint

We now use the concept of present value to restate Prudence's budget constraint in a convenient form. We define the **present value of lifetime resources (*PVLR*)** as the present value of the income the consumer expects to receive in current and future periods plus initial wealth. In the two-period case the present value of lifetime resources is

$$PVLR = y + \frac{y^f}{1+r} + a, \tag{8.3}$$

which is the sum of Prudence's current income, y,[6] the present value of her future income, $y^f/(1 + r)$, and her current wealth, a.

Using the *PVLR* concept, we restate the budget constraint as follows: The present value of lifetime consumption (*PVLC*) must equal the present value of lifetime resources (*PVLR*).

Let's show that this restatement of the budget constraint holds for our example. Recall that Prudence has y = 14,000, y^f = 11,000, and a = 6000. With a real interest rate r of 10%, Prudence's *PVLR* is 14,000 + 11,000/1.10 + 6000, or 30,000 (see Eq. 8.3). According to the budget constraint, therefore, the present value of current and future consumption at any point on her budget line is 30,000. At point *E* in Fig. 8.1, for example, c = 20,000 and c^f = 11,000. The present value of c is 20,000 and the present value of c^f is 11,000/1.10 = 10,000; thus the present value of lifetime consumption at *E* is 20,000 + 10,000 = 30,000, the same as Prudence's *PVLR*. As you may verify, the present value of lifetime consumption equals 30,000 at every point along the budget line in Fig. 8.1.

The restatement of the budget constraint in terms of present values may also be shown algebraically. First, we divide both sides of Eq. (8.2) by $(1 + r)$ and then add c to both sides to get

$$c + \frac{c^f}{1+r} = y + \frac{y^f}{1+r} + a; \tag{8.4}$$

$$PVLC = PVLR.$$

Equation (8.4) states that the present value of lifetime consumption, $c + c^f/(1 + r)$, equals the present value of lifetime resources, $y + y^f/(1 + r) + a$.

In terms of Fig. 8.1, and indeed for any graph of the budget line, the *PVLR* equals the value of current consumption, c, at the horizontal intercept of the budget line. To understand why, note that the horizontal intercept is the point on the budget line at which future consumption c^f equals zero. Setting future consumption c^f at zero in Eq. (8.4) yields current consumption c on the left-hand side, which must equal the *PVLR* on the right-hand side. Thus $c = PVLR$ at the horizontal intercept of the budget line. In our numerical example the

6. Note that the present value of current income is just current income.

budget line's horizontal intercept (point G in Fig. 8.1) occurs at c = 30,000, which is the same as the value of Prudence's *PVLR*.

What Does the Consumer Want? Consumer Preferences

The budget constraint, represented graphically as the budget line, shows the combinations of current and future consumption *available* to Prudence. To determine which of the many possible consumption combinations Prudence will actually choose, we need to know something about Prudence's preferences for current versus future consumption.

Economists use the term **utility** to describe the satisfaction or well-being of an individual. Preferences about current versus future consumption are summarized by how much utility a consumer obtains from each combination of current and future consumption.

We can graphically represent Prudence's preferences for current versus future consumption by using indifference curves. An **indifference curve** shows all consumption combinations that yield the same level of utility. Because Prudence is equally happy with all consumption combinations on an indifference curve, she doesn't care (that is, she is indifferent) about which combination she actually gets. Figure 8.2 shows two of Prudence's indifference curves. Because the consumption combinations corresponding to points X, Y, and Z all are on the same indifference curve (IC^1), Prudence would obtain the same level of utility at X, Y, and Z.

Indifference curves have three important properties, each of which has an economic interpretation, and each of which appears in Fig. 8.2.

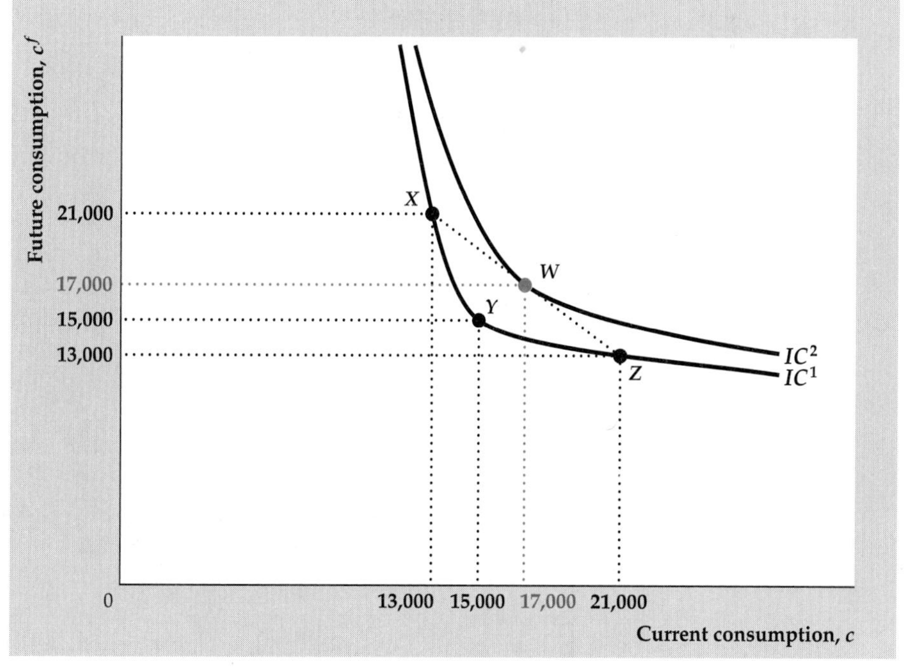

Figure 8.2
Indifference curves
All points on an indifference curve represent consumption combinations that yield the same level of utility. Indifference curves slope downward because a consumer can be compensated for a reduction in current consumption by an appropriate increase in future consumption. All points on IC^2 represent consumption combinations that are preferred to all consumption combinations represented by points on IC^1. Indifference curves are bowed toward the origin to reflect the consumption-smoothing motive. Prudence prefers the consumption combination at point W, which is an average of the combinations at points X and Z because W represents a smoother pattern of consumption. Thus the indifference curve containing W (IC^2) lies above and to the right of the indifference curve containing X, Y, and Z (IC^1).

1. *Indifference curves slope downward from left to right.* To understand why, let's suppose that Prudence has selected the consumption combination at point Y, where $c = 15{,}000$ and $c^f = 15{,}000$.[7] Now suppose that Prudence must reduce her current consumption to $c = 13{,}000$. Clearly, if she reduces current consumption while maintaining future consumption, she will suffer a reduction in utility. However, Prudence can be compensated for this reduction in current consumption by increasing her future consumption. Suppose that, if her future consumption is increased to $c^f = 21{,}000$ while her current consumption is reduced to $c = 13{,}000$ so that she moves to point X, her level of utility remains unchanged. If this is true, she is indifferent between the consumption combinations at X and Y because the higher level of future consumption at X makes up for the lower level of current consumption at X. In general, any change in the level of current consumption must be accompanied by a change in the *opposite* direction in the level of future consumption in order to keep Prudence's level of utility unchanged. Thus indifference curves, which represent consumption combinations with equal levels of utility, must slope downward from left to right.

2. *Indifference curves that are farther up and to the right represent higher levels of utility.* Consider for example point W, which lies above and to the right of point Y in Fig. 8.2. Both current consumption and future consumption are higher at W than at Y. Because Prudence obtains utility from both current and future consumption, W offers a higher level of utility than does Y; that is, Prudence prefers W to Y. In fact, as all points on the indifference curve IC^1 yield the same level of utility as Y, Prudence prefers W to all points on the indifference curve IC^1. Furthermore, as all points on indifference curve IC^2 yield the same level of utility as W, Prudence prefers all points on IC^2 to all points on IC^1. In general, for any two indifference curves, consumers prefer consumption combinations on the indifference curve that is above and to the right of the other indifference curve.

3. *Indifference curves are bowed toward the origin.* This characteristic shape of indifference curves for current and future consumption captures the commonsense idea that most consumers prefer relatively smooth consumption over time to having large amounts of consumption in one period and small amounts in the other. For example, most people would rather have a moderate lunch on both Tuesday and Wednesday to the alternative of stuffing themselves on Tuesday and having only a slice of bread on Wednesday. Similarly, most people would prefer a moderate living standard during both their working lives and their retirement to an alternative of opulence during their working lives and poverty during retirement. This preference for relatively smooth consumption is known as the **consumption-smoothing motive.**

We can illustrate the link between the shape of indifference curves and the consumption-smoothing motive by considering the following three consumption combinations in Fig. 8.2: point X ($c = 13{,}000$; $c^f = 21{,}000$), point W ($c = 17{,}000$; $c^f = 17{,}000$), and point Z ($c = 21{,}000$; $c^f = 13{,}000$). Note that W corresponds to

7. Point Y lies below Prudence's budget line shown in Fig. 8.1, which means that not only could Prudence afford this consumption combination, but she would have resources left over at the end of the future period. Unless she wants to leave a bequest, she would not actually choose such a combination for the resources shown in Fig. 8.1.

complete consumption smoothing, with equal consumption in both periods. In contrast, X and Z represent consumption combinations with large changes in consumption between the first period and the second period. Note also that W represents a consumption combination that is the average of the consumption combinations at X and Z: Current consumption at W, 17,000, is the average of current consumption at X and Z (13,000 and 21,000); similarly, future consumption at W, also 17,000, is the average of future consumption at X and Z (21,000 and 13,000).

Even though point W essentially is an average of points X and Z, and Prudence is indifferent between X and Z, she prefers W to X and Z because W represents much "smoother" (more even) consumption. Graphically, Prudence's preference for W over X and Z is indicated by W's position above and to the right of indifference curve IC^1 (which runs through X and Z). Note that W lies on a straight line drawn between X and Z. The only way that W can lie above and to the right of IC^1 is if IC^1 bows toward the origin, as depicted in Fig. 8.2. Thus the bowed shape of the indifference curve captures the consumption-smoothing motive.

The Optimal Level of Consumption

Combining Prudence's budget line (which describes Prudence's available consumption combinations) and her indifference curves (which describe her preferences for current versus future consumption), we can find the levels of current consumption and saving that make her happiest. This best available, or *optimal,* level of current consumption and saving is represented graphically by the point at which Prudence's budget line is tangent to an indifference curve, shown as point D in Fig. 8.3.

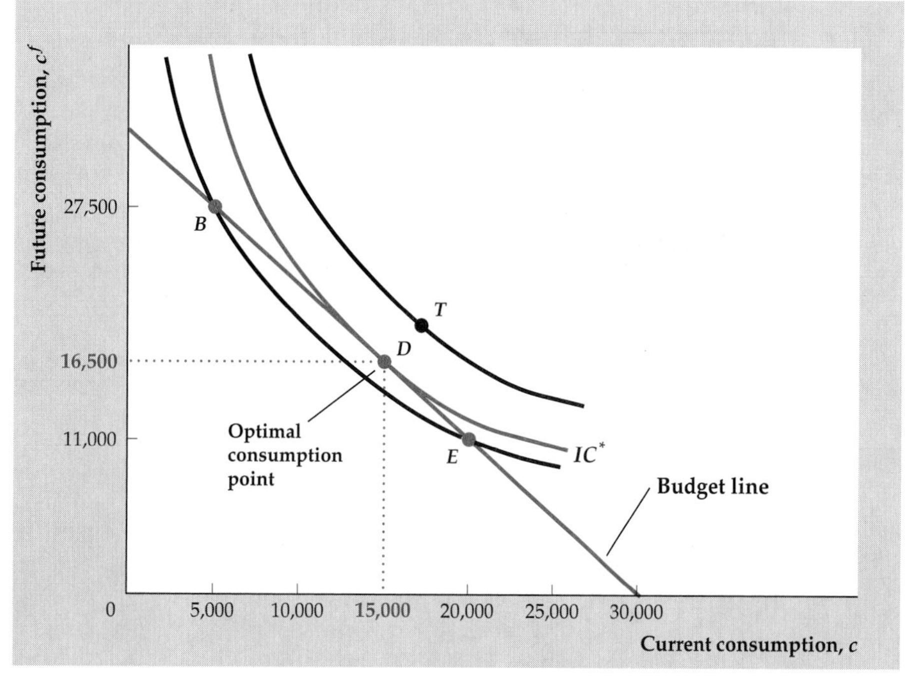

Figure 8.3
The optimal consumption combination
The optimal (highest-utility) combination of current and future consumption is represented by the point of tangency between the budget line and an indifference curve (point *D*). All other points on the budget line, such as *B* and *E*, lie on indifference curves below and to the left of indifference curve IC^* and thus yield lower utility than the consumption combination at *D*, which lies on IC^*. Prudence would prefer the consumption combination at point *T* to the one at *D*, but as *T* lies above the budget line she can't afford the consumption combination that *T* represents.

How do we know that Prudence achieves her highest possible level of satisfaction, or utility, at point *D*? First, note that *D* lies on indifference curve *IC**, which means that all consumption combinations on *IC** yield the same level of utility as *D*. All points on Prudence's budget line other than point *D*—points such as *B* and *E*, for example—lie on indifference curves that are below and to the left of *IC**. Thus the consumption combinations represented by all these other points yield a lower level of utility than the consumption combination at *D*. Prudence would prefer the consumption combination represented by a point such as *T* in Fig. 8.3 to the consumption combination represented by *D*, because *T* lies on an indifference curve above and to the right of *IC**; however, because *T* also lies above the budget line, Prudence can't afford the consumption combination represented by that point. With her budget constraint, Prudence can't do any better than *D*.

We conclude that Prudence's utility-maximizing consumption and saving choice is represented by point *D*, where her budget line is tangent to an indifference curve. Here, her optimal level of current consumption is 15,000, and her optimal level of future consumption is 16,500. Prudence's choice of current consumption automatically determines her current saving. Her optimal saving s equals her current income (14,000) minus her optimal current consumption:

$$s = y - c = 14{,}000 - 15{,}000 = -1000.$$

Thus Prudence chooses to dissave (decrease her initial assets) by 1000. As Table 8.1 shows, if Prudence dissaves 1000 in the current period, she will be able to consume 16,500 in the future period, consistent with her consumption plan, represented by point *D*.

8.2 THE EFFECTS OF CHANGES IN INCOME AND WEALTH ON CONSUMPTION AND SAVING

Two key factors that affect consumption and saving are the levels of income and wealth in an economy. In Chapter 4 we discussed generally the linkage between these variables and household decisions. In this section we use our model of consumer behavior to examine it further. The formal model provides a helpful insight: *The effect on consumption of a change in current income, expected future income, or wealth depends only on how that change affects the consumer's present value of lifetime resources, or PVLR.*

An Increase in Current Income

Let's begin by analyzing the effects on consumption and saving of a change in *current income*. Suppose that Prudence receives a bonus at work of 4000, which raises her current real income from 14,000 to 18,000. Her initial assets (6000), future income (11,000), and the real interest rate (10%) are unchanged; hence the increase of 4000 in current income implies an equal increase in Prudence's present value of lifetime resources, or *PVLR*. If she hasn't yet committed herself to her original consumption–saving plan, how might Prudence revise that plan in light of her increased current income?

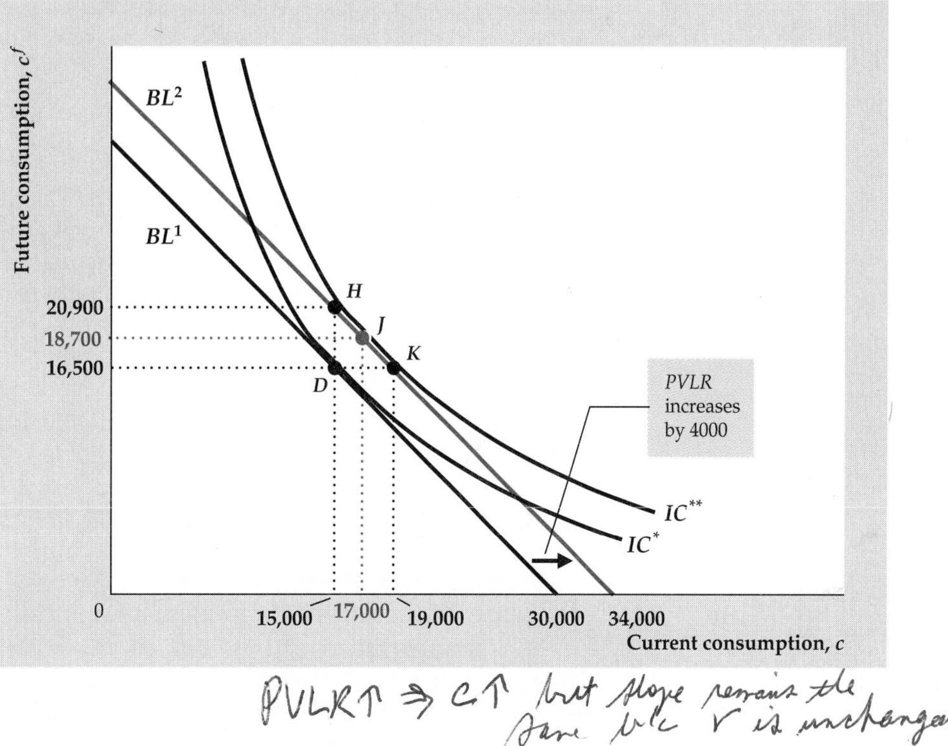

Figure 8.4
An increase in income or wealth
An increase in current income, future income, and/or initial wealth that raises Prudence's *PVLR* by 4000 causes the budget line to make a parallel shift to the right by 4000, from BL^1 to BL^2. If Prudence's original consumption plan was to consume at point *D*, she could move to point *H* by spending all the increase on future consumption and none on current consumption; or she could move to point *K* by spending all the increase on current consumption and none on future consumption. However, if Prudence has a consumption-smoothing motive she will move to point *J*, which has both higher current consumption and higher future consumption than *D*. Point *J* is optimal because it lies where the new budget line BL^2 is tangent to an indifference curve, IC^{**}.

We use the graph in Fig. 8.4 to answer this question. In Fig. 8.4, BL^1 is Prudence's original budget line, and point *D*, where $c = 15{,}000$ and $c^f = 16{,}500$, represents Prudence's original, prebonus consumption plan. Prudence's bonus will allow her to consume more, both currently and in the future, so the increase in her income causes her budget line to shift. To see exactly how the budget line shifts, note that the increase of 4000 in Prudence's current income implies that her *PVLR* also increases by 4000. Because the horizontal intercept of the budget line occurs at $c = PVLR$, the bonus shifts the horizontal intercept to the right by 4000. The slope of the budget line, $-(1 + r)$, remains unchanged because the real interest rate r is unchanged. Thus the increase in current income of 4000 causes a parallel shift of the budget line to the right by 4000, from BL^1 to BL^2.

That shift demonstrates graphically that, after receiving her bonus, Prudence can enjoy greater current and future consumption. Two particular consumption combinations now available are represented by points *H* and *K* on the new budget line BL^2. At *H*, which lies directly above point *D*, Prudence's current consumption is unchanged from what it was at *D*, but her future consumption is higher by 4400. To reach *H*, Prudence must save all of her bonus, then use both the bonus and the interest of 400 earned on the bonus to increase future consumption. An alternative possibility is represented by *K*, where future consumption is unchanged from that at *D* but current consumption has risen by 4000. To reach *K*, Prudence must spend all of her bonus on current consumption, saving none of it for the future.

Both *H* (save all of the bonus) and *K* (save none of the bonus) represent extreme strategies for Prudence. If Prudence has a consumption-smoothing motive, she will use her bonus *both* to increase her current consumption and (by saving part of her bonus) to increase future consumption. If her indifference curves are as shown in Fig. 8.4, she will move to *J*, where her new budget line, BL^2, is tangent to the indifference curve IC^{**}. At *J*, current consumption c = 17,000, future consumption c^f = 18,700, and saving s = 18,000 – 17,000 = 1000. Both current and future consumption are higher at *J* than at *D* (where c = 15,000 and c^f = 16,500). Prudence's current saving of 1000 at *J* is higher than her saving was at *D* (where she dissaved by 1000) because the increase in her current consumption of 2000 is less than the increase in her current income of 4000. This example demonstrates the conclusion of Chapter 4—that an increase in current income raises both current consumption and current saving.

An Increase in Future Income

Suppose that Prudence doesn't get her bonus of 4000 in the current period, so that her current income y remains at its initial level of 14,000. Instead, because of an improved company pension plan, she learns that her future income will increase by 4400, so y^f rises from 11,000 to 15,400. How will this good news affect Prudence's current consumption and saving?

At a real interest rate of 10%, the improvement in the pension plan increases the present value of Prudence's future income by 4400/1.10, or 4000. So, as in the case of the current-period bonus just discussed, the improved pension plan raises Prudence's *PVLR* by 4000 and causes a parallel shift of the budget line to the right by that amount. The effects on current and future consumption are therefore exactly the same as they were for the increase of 4000 in current income (and Fig. 8.4 applies equally well here).

Although increases in current income and expected future income that are equal in present value will have the same effects on current and planned future consumption, the effects of these changes on current saving are different. We showed that an increase in current income raises current saving. In contrast, because the increase in future income raises current consumption (by 2000, in this example) but doesn't affect current income, it causes saving to fall (by 2000, from –1000 to –3000). Prudence knows that she will be receiving more income in the future, so she has less need to save today.

An Increase in Wealth

Changes in wealth also affect consumption and saving. Suppose that, while rummaging through her attic, Prudence unexpectedly finds a passbook for a savings account that her grandmother had opened for her. When Prudence checks with the bank, she learns that the real value of the account is 4000. How will this unexpected increase in wealth affect Prudence's consumption and saving?

Our work so far makes this analysis easy. As in the cases of current and future income, the effect of a change in wealth on consumption depends only on how much the *PVLR* changes. In this example, the increase in wealth of 4000 raises the *PVLR* by 4000; thus its effect on consumption must be the same as that of an increase in current income of 4000 or that of an increase in future income of 4400, each of which also raises the PVLR by 4000. Again, we use Fig. 8.4. Prudence's increase in wealth raises her *PVLR* by 4000 and thus shifts the budget line to the right by 4000, from BL^1 to BL^2. As before, her optimal consumption choice goes from point D (before she finds the passbook) to point J (after her increase in wealth). Because the increase in wealth raises current consumption (from 15,000 at D to 17,000 at J) but leaves current income (14,000) unchanged, it results in a decline in current saving (from −1000 at D to −3000 at J). Being wealthier, Prudence doesn't have to save as much of her current income (actually, she is increasing her dissaving) in order to provide for the future.

The preceding analyses show that changes in current income, future income, and initial wealth all lead to parallel shifts of the budget line by the amount that they change the *PVLR*. Thus the effect of any of these changes on current and future consumption may be summarized by their effect on the *PVLR*. Economists use the term **income effect** to describe the impact of any change that causes a parallel shift of the budget line. Because increases in current income, future income, or wealth raise current and future consumption, the income effect on current and future consumption is positive.

The Permanent Income Theory

Some increases in income—winning money in a contest or getting a one-time bonus at work—are purely one-shot, or temporary, increases. Other increases in income, such as finding a new long-term job at a higher salary, are permanent. Our analysis implies that consumption and saving will react differently to these two types of changes.

In terms of our model, a temporary increase in income represents a rise in current income y, with future income y^f held constant. In contrast, a permanent increase in income raises *both* current income y *and* future income y^f. Therefore a permanent one-unit increase in income leads to a larger increase in the *PVLR* than does a temporary one-unit increase in income.

Because income changes affect consumption only to the extent that they lead to changes in the *PVLR*, our theory predicts that a permanent one-unit increase in income will raise current and future consumption more than a temporary one-unit increase in income will. Equivalently, because current consumption rises more when an income increase is permanent, the amount saved from a permanent increase in income will be less than the amount saved from a temporary increase in income.

This distinction between the effects of permanent and temporary income changes is emphasized in the **permanent income theory** of consumption and saving, developed in the 1950s by Nobel laureate Milton Friedman.[8] He pointed out that income should affect consumption only through the *PVLR* in a many-period version of the model we present here. Thus permanent changes in income, because they last for many periods, may have much larger effects on consumption than temporary changes in income. As a result, temporary income increases would be mostly saved, and permanent income increases would be mostly consumed.

Friedman also provided some of the first empirical evidence for this theory. For example, he found that the consumption of farm families on average

8. Friedman, *A Theory of the Consumption Function,* Princeton, N.J.: Princeton University Press, 1957.

responded less to changes in income than did the consumption of nonfarm families. Friedman's explanation was that, as farm incomes depend heavily on weather and crop prices, both of which are volatile, changes in farm incomes are much more likely to be temporary than are changes in nonfarm incomes. Current changes in farm incomes have a smaller effect on the *PVLR* and therefore have a smaller effect on current consumption.

APPLICATION

Aggregate Consumption During Recessions

Recessions are periods during which real GDP declines (or grows very slowly) so that consumers' real incomes also decline. However, recessions are usually short-lived, and the losses in income suffered by consumers are to some degree temporary.[9] If the declines in GDP during recessions are at least partly temporary, the permanent income theory predicts that aggregate consumption should fall by less than GDP falls when the economy turns down. More generally, if output fluctuations are partly temporary, the theory predicts that aggregate consumption should be "smoother" than real GDP, reflecting the consumption-smoothing motive of consumers.

Figure 8.5 shows the behavior of real GDP and real aggregate consumption, excluding spending on consumer durables, for the period 1970–1992. (We

9. There is some debate about how much of the decline in income in a typical recession is temporary and how much is permanent. Box 9.1 discusses the issue and reports the results of a study that found about 70% of the decline in income during a recession to be temporary.

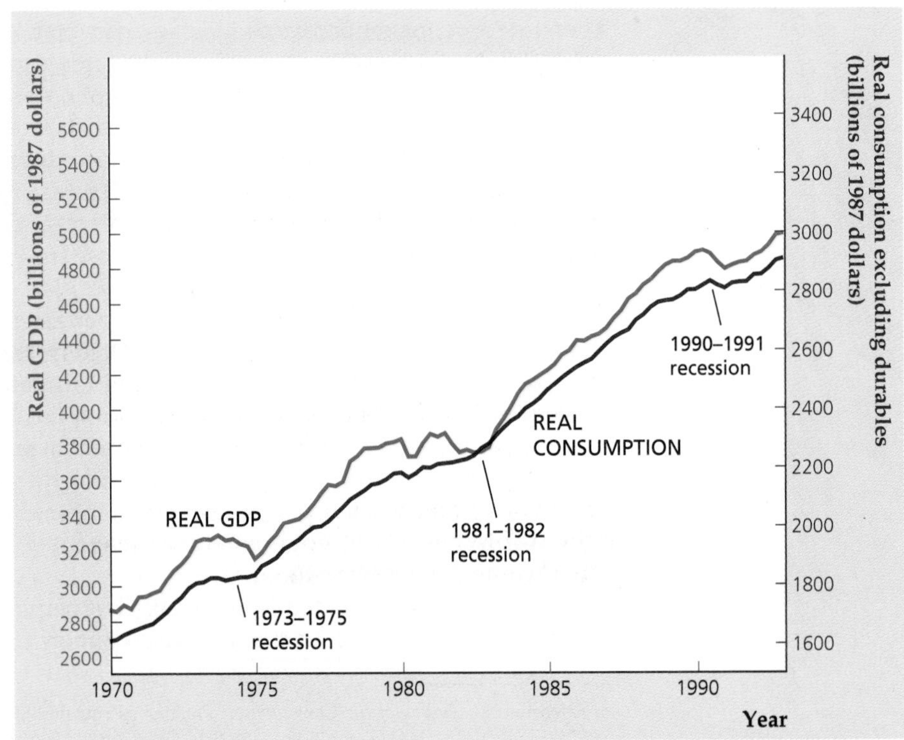

Figure 8.5
Consumption during recessions
The figure shows real GDP (green) and aggregate real consumption (burgandy), excluding expenditures on consumer durables. Because of the consumption-smoothing motive, the path of consumption generally is smoother than that of output, and consumption doesn't fall as sharply as output during recessions.

exclude spending on consumer durables from the consumption measure because items such as cars or furniture aren't completely consumed during the period in which they are purchased, but instead are used over many years.) The period 1970–1992 included three major recessions: 1973–1975, 1981–1982, and 1990–1991. Figure 8.5 generally confirms the predictions of the permanent income theory that consumption is smoother than output and doesn't plunge sharply in recessions. Because consumption drops less in recessions than income does, saving must decline during recessions.

Ricardian Equivalence

Although consumption and saving decisions are made by households, there are times when policymakers would like to influence these decisions. For example, as we pointed out in Chapter 6, some economists argue that U.S. consumption is "too high" and U.S. national saving is "too low" relative to what is needed to provide a high living standard in the long run. Many of those who make this argument go on to suggest that higher taxes are needed to depress desired consumption, C^d, and raise desired national saving, $Y - C^d - G$. At times, such as during recessions, others have proposed that taxes be cut to stimulate consumer spending (we discuss the role of spending in cyclical fluctuations in Part III of this book).

Whether (lump-sum) changes in taxes do in fact affect desired consumption is a controversial issue in macroeconomics. In Chapter 4 we introduced the Ricardian equivalence proposition, which states that, if there is no change in current or planned government purchases, lump-sum changes in taxes will *not* affect desired consumption or desired national saving. Our explanation of this proposition in Chapter 4 was intuitive rather than analytical. A benefit of the analysis of this chapter is that we can now explain Ricardian equivalence both precisely and simply.

The most significant result of this analysis is that changes in income or wealth affect desired consumption only to the extent that they affect the consumer's *PVLR*. The point made by advocates of Ricardian equivalence is that, holding current and future government purchases constant, *a change in current taxes does not affect the consumer's PVLR and thus should not affect desired consumption, C^d, or desired national saving, $Y - C^d - G$.*

Suppose that—in an attempt to raise aggregate consumption—the government cuts Prudence's current taxes by 100. This tax reduction increases Prudence's current income by 100, which (all else being equal) would cause her to consume more. However, because the government's revenue has been reduced by 100 and its expenditures have not changed, the government must increase its current borrowing from the public by 100 (per taxpayer). Further, the government must pay interest on its borrowings. So if the real interest rate that the government must pay on its debt is 10%, as we have been assuming, in the future period the government's outstanding debt will be 110 greater than it would have been without the tax cut.

As a taxpayer, Prudence is ultimately responsible for the government's debts. Suppose that the government decides to repay its borrowings and accumulated interest in the future period (Chapter 16 discusses what happens if the government's debt is left for Prudence's descendants to repay). To repay its debt plus interest the government must raise taxes in the future period by

110, so Prudence's expected future income falls by 110. Overall, then, the government's tax program has raised Prudence's current income by 100 but reduced her future income by 110. At a real interest rate of 10%, the present value of the future income change is –100, which cancels out the increase in current income of 100. Thus Prudence's *PVLR* is unchanged by the tax cut, and (as the Ricardian equivalence proposition implies) she should not change her current consumption.

Ricardian equivalence is closely linked to the consumer model presented in this chapter and, in particular, to the idea that consumption should depend only on the *PVLR*. To assess the practical validity of Ricardian equivalence, we need to know how well our model fits the empirical evidence.

Excess Sensitivity and Borrowing Constraints

Many-period versions of our two-period model of consumer behavior, such as the permanent-income theory, have been extensively tested with empirical data.[10] In general, the model has held up well. A variety of studies confirm that consumption is affected by current income, expected future income, and wealth, and that permanent income changes have larger effects on consumption than do temporary income changes—all of which are implied by the model.

However, not all researchers have accepted a more specific prediction of the model—that the impact of a change in income or wealth on consumption depends only on the change in the *PVLR*. In particular, some studies show that the response of consumption to a change in current income is greater than would be expected based on the effect of the current income change on the *PVLR*. This tendency of consumption to respond to current income more strongly than the model predicts is called the *excess sensitivity* of consumption to current income.[11]

If consumption is in fact "excessively" sensitive to current income, what is the explanation? One possibility is that people are more short-sighted than assumed for the model and don't always think about their future prospects when making current consumption and saving decisions. Another possibility, which is more in the spirit of the model, is that the amount that people can borrow is limited.

In developing our two-period model of consumption and saving, we assumed that consumers can borrow and lend as much as they desire at a single real interest rate. Realistically, though, banks and other lenders typically restrict the amount that a consumer may borrow.[12] Sometimes they deny credit altogether because they believe that a heavily indebted consumer is likely to

10. An extensive survey of the literature is provided by Angus Deaton, *Understanding Consumption*, New York: Oxford University Press, 1992.

11. An important early article that found excess sensitivity was Marjorie Flavin, "The Adjustment of Consumption to Changing Expectations About Future Income," *Journal of Political Economy*, October 1981, pp. 974–1009.

12. Most consumer borrowing is used to finance purchases of housing or consumer durables. In those cases the consumer has an asset—the house or the durable goods—that the bank can seize if payments aren't made on time. In contrast, if the reason for borrowing is to finance a level of current consumption that exceeds current income and assets, the bank may have no assets to take if the payments aren't made.

go bankrupt or fail to repay the loan. A restriction imposed by lenders on the amount that someone can borrow against future income is called a **borrowing constraint.**

The effect of a borrowing constraint on a consumer's consumption–saving decision depends on whether the consumer would want to borrow in the absence of a borrowing constraint. If the consumer wouldn't want to borrow even if borrowing were possible, the borrowing constraint is said to be *nonbinding*. A nonbinding borrowing constraint has no effect on a consumer's consumption or saving behavior because the consumer doesn't want to borrow anyway. In contrast, when a consumer wants to borrow but is prevented from doing so, the borrowing constraint is said to be *binding*. In this case, the consumer will spend all available current income and wealth on current consumption in order to come as close as possible to the consumption combination desired in the absence of borrowing constraints.

Now consider the effect on consumption of an increase in current income. Because a consumer facing a binding borrowing constraint spends all her current income and wealth on current consumption, she consumes all of any increase in current income, whether the increase is temporary or permanent. An unconstrained consumer saves part of an increase in current income. Thus the effect of an increase in current income on current consumption is greater for a constrained consumer than for an unconstrained consumer. In macroeconomic terms this result implies that—if a significant number of consumers face binding borrowing constraints—the response of aggregate consumption to an increase in aggregate income (output) will be greater than implied by the basic theory in the absence of borrowing constraints. In other words, if there are borrowing constraints, consumption may be excessively sensitive to current income.

Empirically, how prevalent are borrowing constraints in the U.S. economy? We have no direct way of counting how many consumers are constrained from borrowing. However, several studies estimate that, to account for the observed relationship between aggregate consumption and current income, during any year some 20% to 50% of U.S. consumers face binding borrowing constraints.[13]

8.3 CONSUMPTION AND SAVING OVER MANY PERIODS: THE LIFE-CYCLE MODEL

The two-period model suggests that a significant part of saving is done to pay for retirement. However, the two-period model doesn't reflect other important aspects of the consumer's lifetime income and consumption patterns. For example, income typically rises over most of a person's working life, and people

13. See, for example, John Y. Campbell and N. Gregory Mankiw, "Consumption, Income, and Interest Rates: Reinterpreting the Time Series Evidence," in O. Blanchard and S. Fischer, eds., NBER *Macroeconomics Annual,* Cambridge, Mass.: MIT Press, 1989; and Robert E. Hall and Frederic S. Mishkin, "The Sensitivity of Consumption to Transitory Income: Estimates from Panel Data on Households," *Econometrica,* March 1982, pp. 461–481.

save for reasons other than retirement. The **life-cycle model** of consumption and saving, originated in the 1950s by Nobel laureate Franco Modigliani[14] and his associates, extends the two-period model to many periods and focuses on the patterns of income, consumption, and saving throughout an individual's life.

The essence of the life-cycle model is shown in Fig. 8.6. In Fig. 8.6(a) the typical consumer's patterns of income and consumption are plotted against the consumer's age, from age twenty (the approximate age of economic independence) to age eighty (the approximate age of death). Two points about Fig. 8.6(a) are significant.

14. A review of the life-cycle theory is provided by Franco Modigliani, "Life Cycle, Individual Thrift, and the Wealth of Nations," *American Economic Review*, June 1986, pp. 297–313.

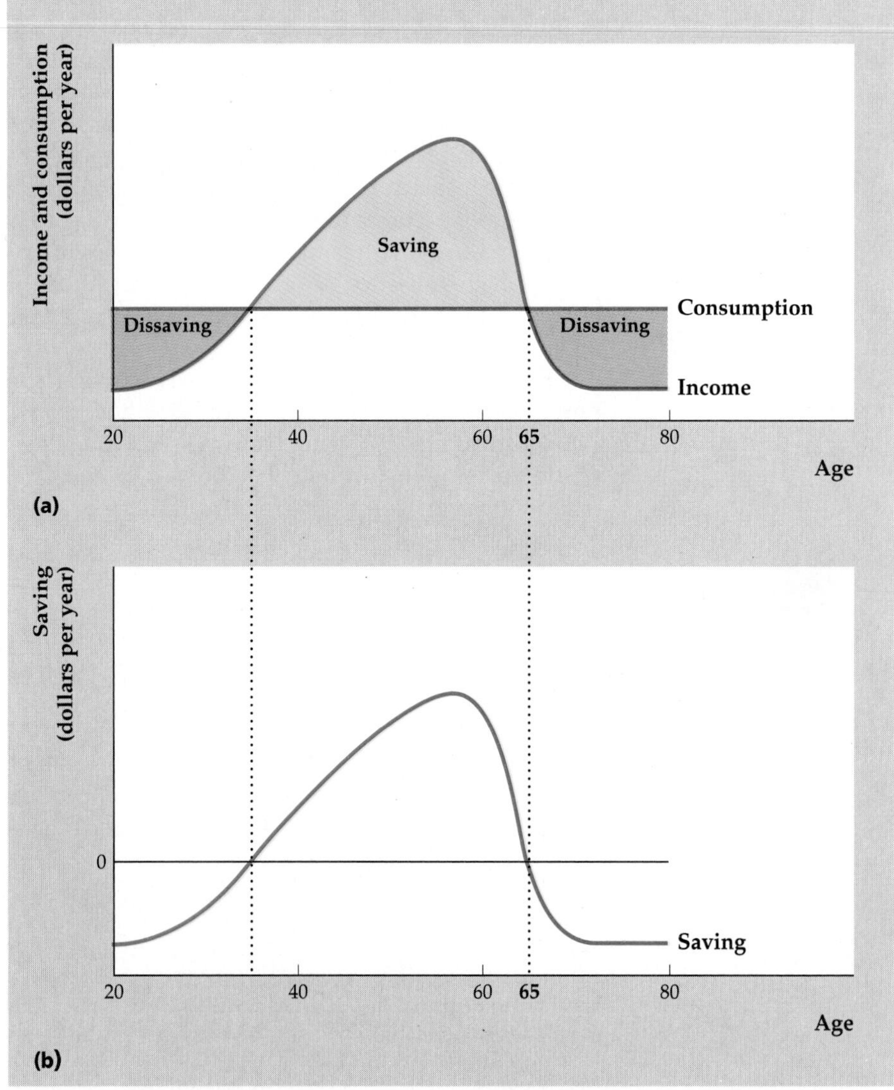

Figure 8.6
Life-cycle consumption, income, and saving
(a) Income and consumption are plotted against age. Income typically rises gradually throughout most of a person's working life and peaks shortly before retirement. The desire for a smooth pattern of consumption means that consumption varies less than income over the life cycle. Consumption here is constant.
(b) Saving is the difference between income and consumption; the saving pattern is hump-shaped. Early in a person's working life consumption is larger than income, so saving is negative. In the middle years saving is positive; the excess of income over consumption is used to repay debts incurred earlier in life and to provide for retirement. During retirement people dissave.

First, the average worker experiences steadily rising real income, with peak earnings typically occurring between the ages of fifty and sixty. After retirement, income (excluding interest earned from previous saving) drops fairly sharply.

Second, the lifetime pattern of consumption is much smoother than the pattern of income over time, which is consistent with the consumption-smoothing motive discussed earlier. Because consumers do not like large changes in their consumption levels, they spread their lifetime resources to maintain a fairly even standard of living over time. Although shown as perfectly flat in Fig. 8.6(a), consumption, in reality, varies somewhat by age; for example, it will be higher during years of high child-rearing expenses. An advantage of using the life-cycle model to study consumption and saving is that it may be easily modified to allow for various patterns of lifetime income and consumption.

The lifetime pattern of saving, shown in Fig. 8.6(b), is the difference between the income and consumption curves in Fig. 8.6(a). This overall hump-shaped pattern has been confirmed empirically. Saving is minimal or even negative during the early working years, when income is low. Maximum saving occurs when the worker is between fifty and sixty, when income is highest. Finally, during retirement there is dissaving, as the consumer draws down accumulated wealth to meet living expenses.

An important implication of the hump-shaped pattern of saving is that national saving rates depend on the age distribution of a country's population. Countries with unusually young or unusually old populations have low saving rates, and countries with relatively more people in their middle years have higher saving rates.

The Life-Cycle Model: An Example

Some additional insight into the implications of the life-cycle model can be gained from a simple example. Imagine a consumer who is "young" for 20 years, "middle-aged" for 20 years, and "retired" for 20 years (after which he dies). He has no initial wealth, earns a salary of \$20,000 per year when young, earns a salary of \$60,000 per year when middle-aged, and receives retirement benefits of \$10,000 per year when retired (all incomes are in real terms).

Suppose that the real interest rate is zero so that the present value of any future income just equals the future income itself. Then the consumer's *PVLR* simply equals total lifetime earnings, or

$$\begin{aligned} PVLR &= \text{total lifetime income} \\ &= (20 \times \$20{,}000) + (20 \times \$60{,}000) + (20 \times \$10{,}000) \\ &= \$1{,}800{,}000. \end{aligned}$$

Suppose also that the consumer is an extreme "consumption-smoother," that is, he tries to keep his annual real consumption c at a constant level for each of his 60 adult years. With a zero real interest rate, the present value of his consumption is $60c$. The budget constraint, which states that the present value of consumption must equal the *PVLR*, is therefore

$$\text{present value of consumption} = 60c = PVLR = \$1{,}800{,}000,$$

or, solving for c,

$$c = \$30,000.$$

If his consumption is $30,000 per year, what will the consumer's pattern of saving be? When the consumer is young, earning $20,000 per year and consuming $30,000 per year, his saving will be –$10,000 per year (he will dissave, borrowing to do so). During middle age, he will save $60,000 – $30,000 = $30,000 per year. Finally, during retirement, the consumer will dissave at the rate of $20,000 per year (his saving will be $10,000 – $30,000 = –$20,000 per year).

Bequests and Saving

In both the two-period model and the life-cycle model, we assumed that the consumer plans to spend all his wealth and income during his lifetime, leaving nothing to heirs. Empirically, however, many people leave bequests, or inheritances, to children, charities, and others. What effect does a **bequest motive,** or a desire to leave inheritances, have on saving behavior?

Let's return to the life-cycle example. Suppose that the consumer doesn't plan to spend all his economic resources but wants to leave $120,000 to his heirs. Because the consumer's adult life spans 60 years, he can achieve this bequest by reducing consumption and increasing saving by $2000 per year. (Remember that the real interest rate is zero.) We conclude that, to the extent that consumers desire to leave bequests, they will consume less and save more than when they simply consume all their resources during their lifetimes.

APPLICATION

Why Do the Japanese Save So Much?

The Japanese are known for their high saving rate, especially in comparison with the saving rate in the United States. To some extent, the perceived difference between Japan and the United States may reflect different accounting practices. For example, the Japanese count government investment projects, such as roads, as part of national saving, but the United States does not. Even with corrections, though, the Japanese saving rate seems to be significantly higher.

Numerous explanations for high Japanese saving were examined by Fumio Hayashi of the University of Pennsylvania.[15] Several of these explanations were related to life-cycle factors, including the following:

1. *Population age structure.* The Japanese have among the world's highest life expectancies and thus long expected retirements. To finance these long retirements, they must save more during their working years. The Japanese also had a postwar baby boom, followed by a population growth slowdown, which means that a relatively large proportion of the population is now middle-aged, the peak saving period.

2. *High income growth.* Because of Japan's rapid economic growth during the past forty years, current Japanese workers earn much higher real incomes

15. "Why Is Japan's Saving Rate So Apparently High?" in Stanley Fischer, ed., *NBER Macroeconomics Annual,* Cambridge, Mass.: MIT Press, 1986.

than their now-retired parents did when they were working in the 1950s or 1960s. Thus current workers can plan to consume more when they retire than their parents did. This rise in incomes implies that current workers will save much more than current retirees are dissaving, leading to a high aggregate saving rate for the country as a whole.[16]

3. *High housing and land prices, including high required down payments.* Despite recent decreases, Japanese housing prices are fantastically high. Potential home buyers not only must face these high prices but also must make down payments that in percentage terms are much higher than in the United States. Thus young people frequently must save for years to buy a home.

4. *High bequests.* Japanese customarily leave large bequests, perhaps because many elderly Japanese live with their children. To be able to leave large bequests, the Japanese must save more during their working lives.

Hayashi's paper discusses these factors in detail. Although all may contribute, his tentative conclusion is that the desire to leave large bequests may be the single most important cause of high Japanese saving.

8.4 THE REAL INTEREST RATE AND THE CONSUMPTION–SAVING DECISION

Until now, we have focused on the effects of changes in income and wealth on consumption and saving, holding constant the real interest rate. Actually, the real interest rate may change sharply, as when it rose from negative values in the late 1970s to about 8% in 1982. Government policies, such as tax breaks designed to encourage saving, also may lead to changes in the after-tax real interest rate faced by households, even when the real interest rate itself doesn't change. Building on our more general discussion in Chapter 4, we now use our model of consumer behavior to analyze the link between the real interest rate and the amounts that households choose to consume and save.

The Real Interest Rate and Saving in the Two-Period Model

To explore the effects of a change in the real interest rate on consumption and saving, let's return to the two-period model and Prudence's situation. Recall that Prudence initially has current real income y of 14,000, future income y^f of 11,000, initial wealth a of 6000, and faces a real interest rate r of 10% (which should be thought of as the after-tax real interest rate; see Section 4.1). At this real interest rate Prudence's present value of lifetime resources, $PVLR$, is

16. Numerical Problem 6 at the end of the chapter further develops the relationship of income growth and saving.

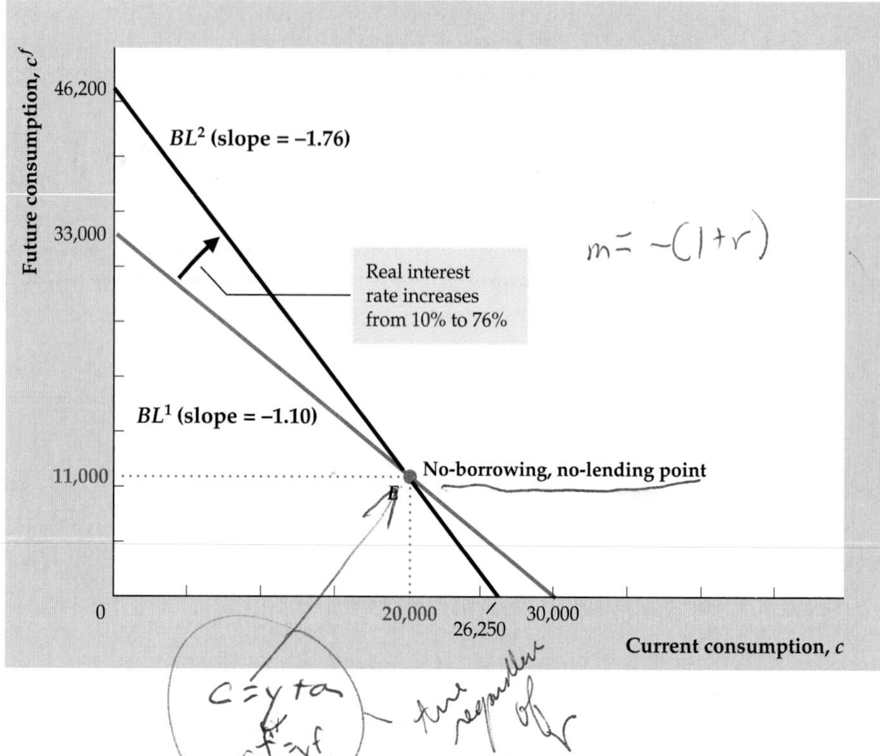

Figure 8.7
The effect of an increase in the real interest rate on the budget line
The figure shows the effect on Prudence's budget line of an increase in the real interest rate r from 10% to 76%. Because the slope of a budget line is $-(1 + r)$ and the initial real interest rate is 10%, the slope of Prudence's initial budget line BL^1 is –1.10. The initial budget line BL^1 also passes through the no-borrowing, no-lending point E, which represents the consumption combination that Prudence obtains by spending all her current income and wealth on current consumption. Because E can still be obtained when the real interest rate rises, it also lies on the new budget line BL^2. However, the slope of BL^2 is –1.76, reflecting the rise in the real interest rate to 76%. Thus the higher real interest rate causes the budget line to pivot clockwise around the no-borrowing, no-lending point.

30,000. Her budget line, which is the same as in Fig. 8.1, is shown in Fig. 8.7 as BL^1. Now let's see what happens when for some reason the real interest rate jumps from 10% to 76%.[17]

The Real Interest Rate and the Budget Line. To see how Prudence's budget line is affected when the real interest rate rises, let's first consider point E on the budget line BL^1. Point E is special in that it is the only point on the budget line at which current consumption equals current income plus initial wealth ($c = y + a = 20{,}000$) and future consumption equals future income ($c^f = y^f = 11{,}000$). If she chooses this consumption combination, Prudence doesn't need to borrow (her current income and initial wealth are just enough to pay for her current consumption) nor does she have any current resources left to deposit in (lend to) the bank. Thus E is the **no-borrowing, no-lending point.** Because E involves neither borrowing nor lending, the consumption combination it represents is available to Prudence regardless of the real interest rate. Thus the no-borrowing, no-lending point remains on the budget line when the real interest rate changes.

Next, recall that the budget line's slope is $-(1 + r)$, reflecting the fact that sacrificing one unit of current consumption allows Prudence to increase her future consumption by $(1 + r)$ units. When the real interest rate r jumps from 10% to 76%, the slope of the budget line changes from –1.10 to –1.76; that is, the new budget line is steeper. Knowing one point on the new budget line (E) and the slope of the new budget line (–1.76) is enough information to draw the

17. A 76% real interest rate isn't realistic, but assuming this large a change makes its effects more obvious.

new budget line, BL^2. Comparing BL^2 to BL^1 shows that an increase in the real interest rate causes the budget line to pivot clockwise around the no-borrowing, no-lending point, E.

The Substitution and Income Effects of a Change in the Real Interest Rate

Because an increase in the real interest rate changes the budget line and thus the combinations of current and future consumption available to Prudence, she may respond by altering the amounts consumed and saved. A change in the real interest rate can affect the consumption–saving decision in two ways, referred to as the substitution effect and the income effect.

The Substitution Effect. If Prudence reduces her consumption by one unit today, thereby increasing her saving by one unit, she will be able to consume $1 + r$ additional units in the future. Thus when the real interest rate r increases, the amount of future consumption that can be obtained in exchange for giving up a unit of current consumption rises. In effect, a higher real interest rate makes future consumption cheaper, relative to current consumption.

In the same way that a drop in the price of coffee relative to the price of tea leads consumers to buy more coffee and less tea, a drop in the price of future consumption relative to current consumption leads consumers to switch from current consumption toward future consumption—that is, they save more. The tendency to save more in response to a higher reward for saving is called the **substitution effect,** because a higher real interest rate causes consumers to substitute future consumption for current consumption. When people argue that a higher real interest rate raises saving by increasing the reward for saving, they are talking about the substitution effect.

The substitution effect is illustrated graphically in Fig. 8.8 shown on the next page. Initially, the real interest rate is 10% and the budget line is BL^1. Suppose for now that Prudence's preferences are such that BL^1 is tangent to an indifference curve, IC^1, at the no-borrowing, no-lending point, E.[18] At a real interest rate of 10%, then, Prudence chooses the consumption combination at E.

When the real interest rate rises from 10% to 76%, the budget line pivots clockwise to BL^2. Because Prudence's original consumption point, the no-borrowing, no-lending point, E, also lies on the new budget line BL^2, she has the option of remaining at E and enjoying the same combination of current and future consumption after the real interest rate rises. But note that points along BL^2 immediately above and to the left of E lie above and to the right of IC^1. These points represent consumption combinations that are available to Prudence and yield a higher level of utility than the consumption combination at E. Prudence can attain the highest level of utility along BL^2 at point V, where indifference curve IC^2 is tangent to BL^2. In response to the increased incentive to save, Prudence reduces her current consumption, from 20,000 to 17,000, and moves from E to V on BL^2. Prudence's reduction of 3000 in current consumption between E and V is equivalent to an increase of 3000 in saving. The

18. Note that Prudence's indifference curves in Fig. 8.8 are different from those in Fig. 8.4.

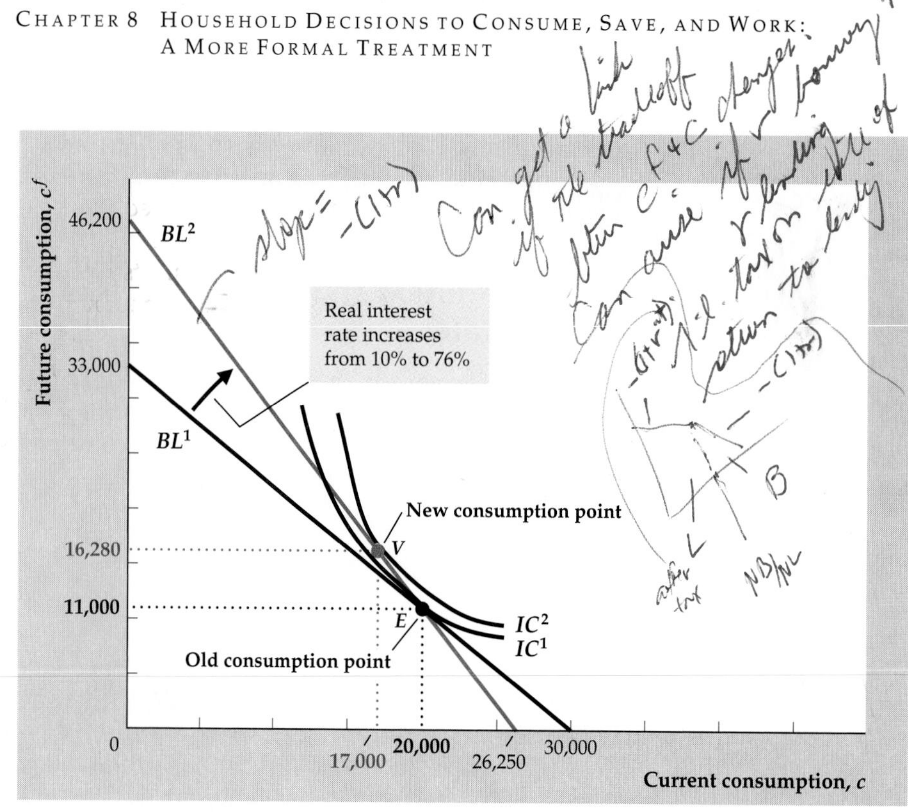

Figure 8.8
The substitution effect of an increase in the real interest rate
We assume that Prudence's preferences are such that when the real interest rate is 10% she chooses the consumption combination at the no-borrowing, no-lending point, point E, on the initial budget line BL^1. Point E lies on the indifference curve IC^1. An increase in the real interest rate to 76% causes the budget line to pivot clockwise from BL^1 to BL^2, as in Fig. 8.7. By substituting future consumption for current consumption along the new budget line BL^2, Prudence can reach points that lie above and to the right of IC^1; these points represent consumption combinations that yield higher utility than the consumption combination at E. Her highest utility is achieved by moving to point V, where the new budget line BL^2 is tangent to indifference curve IC^2. The drop in current consumption (by 3000) and the resulting equal rise in saving that occur in moving from E to V reflect the substitution effect of the increase in the real interest rate.

increase in saving between E and V reflects the substitution effect on saving of a higher real interest rate.

The Income Effect. If Prudence's current consumption initially equals her current resources (current income plus initial wealth) so that she is neither a lender nor a borrower, a change in the real interest rate has only a substitution effect on her saving, as shown in Fig. 8.8. However, if Prudence's current consumption is initially less than her current resources (so that she has resources to lend), or if her current consumption initially exceeds her current resources (so that she must borrow to pay for her current consumption), a change in the real interest rate has an additional effect (the income effect) on her saving decision.

We can illustrate the income effect by supposing that Prudence plans to consume only part of her current income and wealth in the first period, leaving some resources to be deposited in the bank. When the real interest rate rises, as a lender Prudence will be able to earn a higher return, which makes her better off. More precisely, an increase in the real interest rate increases the amount of current and future consumption that a lender can enjoy. Because she is made economically better off by the increase in the real interest rate, Prudence will tend to increase her current consumption and thus save less when the real interest rate rises.

But, if Prudence initially is a borrower, an increase in the real interest rate makes her worse off, because she must pay more interest on any loans that she takes out. Because she is made worse off by the increase in the real interest rate, Prudence will choose to consume less in the first period and thus increase her saving (actually, reduce the amount she dissaves). The tendency of lenders to consume more and save less in response to being economically better off, and of borrowers to consume less and save more in response to being economically worse off, is called the **income effect** of an increase in the real interest rate. For a lender note that the income effect of an increase in the real interest rate works in the opposite direction as the substitution effect, whereas for a borrower the income and substitution effects work in the same direction.

The full impact of an increase in the real interest rate on Prudence's saving, including the substitution and income effects—assuming that Prudence initially is a lender—is shown in Fig. 8.9. As before, Prudence's original budget line is BL^1 when the real interest rate is 10%. However, we now assume that Prudence's preferences are such that BL^1 is tangent to an indifference curve, IC^1, at point D. Thus, at a 10% real interest rate, Prudence plans current consumption of 15,000 and future consumption of 16,500. Prudence's current resources equal 20,000 (current income of 14,000 plus initial assets of 6000), so if she enjoys current consumption of 15,000 she will have resources of 5000 to lend. Her chosen point, D, being to the left of the no-borrowing, no-lending point, E (current consumption is lower at D than at E) shows that Prudence is a lender.

The increase in the real interest rate from 10% to 76% causes Prudence's budget line to pivot clockwise through the no-borrowing, no-lending point, E, ending at BL^2 as before. To separate the substitution and income effects of the increase in the real interest rate, think of the movement of the budget line from BL^1 to BL^2 as taking place in two steps.

First, imagine that the original budget line BL^1 pivots clockwise around Prudence's original consumption combination, point D, until it is parallel with the new budget line BL^2 (that is, its slope is –1.76). The resulting intermediate budget line is the dashed line BL^{int}. Second, imagine that BL^{int} makes a parallel shift to the right to BL^2.

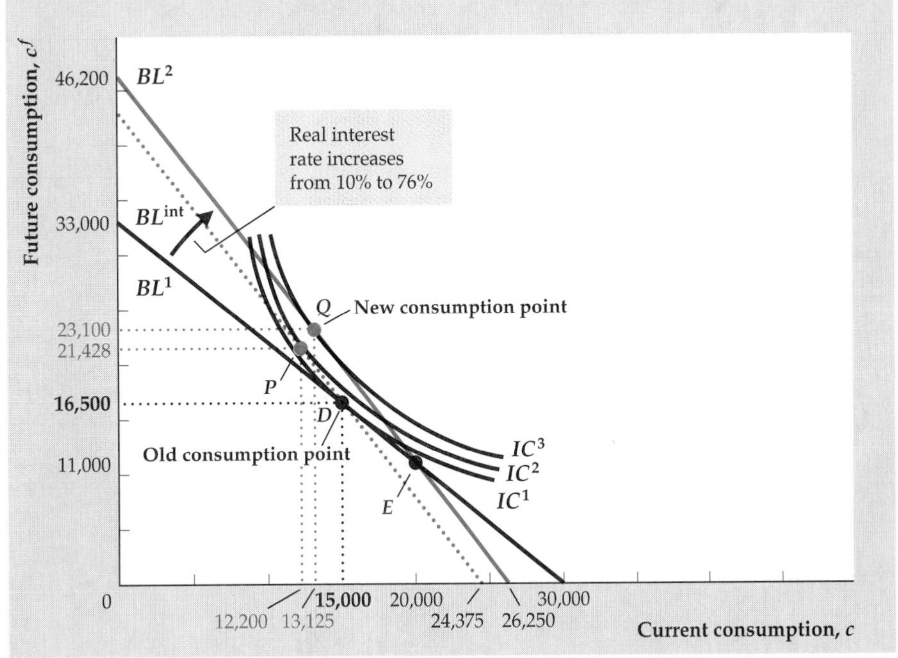

Figure 8.9
An increase in the real interest rate with both an income effect and a substitution effect
We assume that Prudence initially consumes at point D on the original budget line BL^1. An increase in the real interest rate from 10% to 76% causes the budget line to pivot clockwise from BL^1 to the new budget line BL^2. We break the overall shift of the budget line into two parts: (1) a pivot around the original consumption point, D, to yield an intermediate budget line BL^{int}, and (2) a parallel shift from BL^{int} to the final budget line BL^2. The substitution effect is measured by the movement from the original consumption point, D, to point P on BL^{int}, and the income effect is measured by the movement from P to Q on BL^2. As drawn, the substitution effect is larger than the income effect so that the overall effect is for current consumption to fall and saving to rise.

The response of Prudence's saving and current consumption to the increase in the real interest rate can also be broken into two steps. First, consider her response to the pivot of the budget line through point D, from BL^1 to BL^{int}. If this were the only change in Prudence's budget line, she would move from D to P ($c = 12{,}200$ and $c^f = 21{,}428$) on BL^{int}. At P, she would save more and enjoy less current consumption than at D. The increase in saving between D and P, similar to Prudence's shift from E to V in Fig. 8.8, measures the substitution effect on Prudence's saving of the increase in the real interest rate.

Second, consider the effect of the parallel shift from BL^{int} to BL^2. The new budget line BL^2 is tangent to an indifference curve, IC^3, at point Q, so Prudence will choose the consumption combination at Q. Current and future consumption are higher, and saving is lower, at Q than at P. The increase in current consumption and the decrease in saving between P and Q reflect the income effect of the increase in the real interest rate. Thus, as discussed earlier, income effects occur when a change in some variable causes a parallel shift of the budget line. Because it corresponds to a parallel shift of the budget line, the income effect of a change in the real interest rate on consumption and saving is the same as the effect of a change in income or wealth.

The total change in Prudence's consumption and saving resulting from the rise in the real interest rate is shown in Fig. 8.9 as the change in saving between point D and point Q. This change is the sum of the substitution effect, measured by the increase in saving in moving from D to P, and the income effect, measured by the decline in saving in moving from P to Q. As Fig. 8.9 is drawn, current consumption is lower and saving is higher at the final point, Q, than at the original point, D. However, we could just as easily draw it so that saving is less at the final point, Q, than at the initial point, D. Thus the theory fails to predict whether Prudence's saving will rise or fall in response to an increase in the real interest rate.

The reason that we cannot say for sure how Prudence's saving will change is that, for the case of a lender analyzed in Fig. 8.9, the income and substitution effects work in opposite directions; the final result depends on which effect is stronger. In contrast, for a borrower the income and substitution effects work in the same direction (you are asked to show this result in Analytical Problem 5 at the end of the chapter). A higher real interest rate increases a borrower's reward for saving, which tends to make him save more (the substitution effect); and, because a borrower pays rather than receives interest, a higher real interest rate also makes him poorer, leading him to consume less and save more.

To summarize, the two-period model implies that an increase in the real interest rate increases saving by borrowers. However, because of conflicting income and substitution effects, economic theory is not decisive about the effect of the real interest rate on the saving of lenders. In the U.S. economy, which of course includes both borrowers and lenders, empirical studies show that an increase in the real interest rate tends to increase aggregate saving, although often the effect is found to be relatively small.

APPLICATION

Tax Policy and the Divergence of Canadian and U.S. Private Saving

Because Canada and the United States have similar and closely integrated economies, you might expect private saving in the two countries to be similar. However, a study by Chris Carroll of the Federal Reserve Board and Lawrence

Summers of Harvard University[19] found that, although private saving rates in the two countries moved in parallel over much of the post–World War II period, beginning in about 1971 private saving behavior in the United States and Canada began to diverge. During the 1970s and early 1980s Canadian private saving surged, but U.S. private saving declined. By the mid 1980s the Canadian private saving rate was substantially higher than the U.S. rate.[20]

Carroll and Summers concluded that differences in general macroeconomic conditions could not explain the differences in saving behavior between Canada and the United States. Instead, they argued that, relative to U.S. policies, Canadian tax policies have been more favorable toward saving by leading to a higher after-tax real interest rate. They focused on two differences in tax policy.

First, Canada has tax-favored saving plans (including employer-sponsored Registered Pension Plans, or RPPs, and individual Registered Retirement Savings Plans, or RRSPs), which were expanded substantially in the early 1970s. The Canadian plans allow a significant portion of interest income to go untaxed. The United States has had similar "tax-sheltered" saving plans, such as Individual Retirement Accounts (IRAs), but these plans were not made widely available until 1981 and were limited after 1986. Because before-tax real interest rates in the United States and Canada were similar in the 1970s and 1980s, the differences in tax policy implied that Canadian savers were able to obtain higher after-tax real interest rates than U.S. savers were, which may help explain why the Canadians saved more.

Second, compared to the Canadian tax system, the U.S. tax system encourages borrowing and consumption, which, of course, reduces saving. In contrast to Canada, where consumers who borrow are not allowed to deduct their interest payments from their taxable incomes, in the United States prior to 1986 all consumer interest payments were tax-deductible.[21] We can demonstrate the effect of this difference in tax laws by comparing two borrowers (one in the United States and one in Canada) both of whom have borrowed $10,000 at a 10% rate of interest and assuming that the U.S. borrower is in a 30% tax bracket. Both borrowers pay $1000 each year in interest, but the U.S. borrower gets to deduct the $1000 from his taxable income, which saves him $300 (30% of $1000) in taxes. After taxes, the U.S. borrower's interest cost is $700 ($1000 less $300 in reduced taxes), for an after-tax nominal interest rate of 7% ($700 divided by the principal of $10,000). The Canadian borrower gets no tax break, so the after-tax interest rate she pays on her loan equals her before-tax interest rate of 10%—three percentage points higher than that of the U.S. borrower. Further, the benefit of tax deductibility of interest to the borrower is highest when interest rates are high, so that the difference in borrowing costs between

19. "Why Have Private Savings Rates in the United States and Canada Diverged?" *Journal of Monetary Economics*, September 1987, pp. 249–279.

20. The private saving measure used by Carroll and Summers is net private saving, or private saving less depreciation of capital, divided by GNP. Using this measure, they found that the private saving rate in Canada rose from 7.8% in the 1971–1975 period to 11.9% in the 1981–1985 period; between the same two periods the U.S. private saving rate fell from 8.7% to 6.2%.

21. The U.S. Tax Reform Act of 1986 began a phaseout of some types of consumer interest deductions. However, mortgage interest is still deductible, as is interest paid on home equity lines of credit.

Canadians and U.S. citizens was greatest in the high-interest-rate periods of the 1970s and early 1980s, when the saving rates diverged most.

In the case of borrowers, the substitution and income effects work in the same direction, and the theory tells us unambiguously that higher after-tax borrowing rates should reduce borrowing and consumption and increase aggregate saving. Thus it is likely that the different tax treatment of borrowers' interest payments contributed to the difference in aggregate saving between the United States and Canada.

8.5 THE SUPPLY OF LABOR: THE INCOME–LEISURE TRADE-OFF

The decision about how much to consume and save isn't the only decision made by households that has macroeconomic significance. Equally important is the household's decision about whether and how much to work—that is, how much labor to supply. In Chapter 3 we introduced the concept of labor supply and showed that the amount of labor that people choose to supply helps determine the level of real wages, employment, and output in the economy.

Here, we reexamine some of the factors that affect labor supply. Although the labor supply decision can be analyzed in the same formal model as consumption and saving,[22] for simplicity and to conserve space we stay with a less formal discussion here. Nevertheless, concepts from the earlier part of this chapter—in particular, the ideas of income and substitution effects—are quite useful in our analysis of labor supply.

To illustrate the key issues in the determination of labor supply with an example, let's look at how Prudence decides how much to work. Suppose that, having played on the professional golf tour when she was younger, Prudence's best job opportunity is to work as a golf instructor. After paying taxes and job-related expenses, she finds that by giving golf lessons she can earn a real income of 100 per day. Furthermore, by varying the number of students she allows to sign up for lessons, she can work anywhere from 0 to 365 days this year. Prudence is reluctant to work too much, though, because every day she spends on the golf course means one less day available to devote to her real passion, skydiving. The decision Prudence faces is how many days to work this year—or, in other words, how much labor to supply.

Prudence approaches this question by asking herself: Economically speaking, what really makes me happy? After a little reflection, she concludes that her level of satisfaction, or utility, depends on the amount of goods and services she consumes (in the present and in the future) and on the amount of leisure time she has available to jump out of airplanes. Her question can thus be recast as: "How much should I work this year in order to obtain the highest possible level of utility?"

To find the level of labor supply that maximizes her utility, Prudence must compare the costs and benefits of working an extra day. The cost of an extra

22. To do so, the necessary change is to drop the assumption that incomes are given and allow current and future incomes to depend on the amount that Prudence chooses to work.

day of work is the loss of a day of leisure; this cost can be measured as the loss in utility that Prudence experiences when she has to work for a day instead of skydive. The benefit of working an extra day is an increase of 100 in real income, which allows Prudence to enjoy more current and future consumption. Specifically, the benefit of the extra day of work is the increase in utility that results when Prudence optimally distributes her extra real income of 100 between current and future consumption.[23]

If the benefit of working an extra day (utility gained from extra income) exceeds the cost (utility lost by reducing leisure), Prudence should work the extra day. In fact, she should continue to increase her time at work until the utility she receives from extra real income of 100 just equals the loss of utility associated with missing a day of leisure. Prudence's labor supply at that point is the one that maximizes her utility.[24] Using the idea that the labor supply decision results from a trade-off of leisure against income, we can discuss factors that influence the amount of labor Prudence supplies.

Real Wages and Labor Supply

The real wage is the amount of real income that a worker receives in exchange for giving up a unit of leisure (an hour, day, or week for example) for work. It is thus an important determinant of the quantity of labor that is supplied.

Generally, as discussed in Chapter 3, an increase in the real wage affects the labor supply decision in two ways. First, an increase in the real wage raises the benefit (in terms of extra real income) of working an extra day and thus tends to make the worker want to supply more labor. The tendency of workers to supply more labor in response to a higher reward for working is called the **substitution effect** of a higher real wage on the quantity of labor supplied.

Second, an increase in the real wage also makes workers effectively wealthier because for the same amount of work they now earn a higher real income. Someone who is wealthier will be more able to afford extra leisure and, as a result, will supply less labor. The tendency of workers to supply less labor in response to becoming wealthier is called the **income effect** of a higher real wage on the quantity of labor supplied. Note that the substitution and income effects of a higher real wage work in opposite directions, with the substitution effect tending to raise the quantity of labor supplied and the income effect tending to reduce it.

A Pure Substitution Effect: A One-Day Rise in the Real Wage. We can illustrate the substitution effect by supposing that, after some consideration, Prudence decides to work six days per week, leaving every Wednesday free to go skydiving. She could work and earn real income of 100 each Wednesday, but her highest utility is obtained by taking leisure on that day instead.

Now imagine that one Tuesday, an eccentric golfer calls Prudence and requests a lesson on Wednesday to help him prepare for a weekend amateur

---

23. Another benefit of increased income in the present is that it would allow Prudence to work less in the future.

24. Not everyone can choose his or her labor supply as flexibly as Prudence; for example, some jobs are available for forty hours a week or not at all. Still, by choosing to work overtime, part-time, or at a second job, or by varying the number of family members who are working, households do have a significant amount of latitude over how much labor to supply.

tournament. He offers Prudence her regular wage of 100 per day, but Prudence declines, explaining that she is going skydiving on Wednesday. Not willing to take no for an answer, the golfer then offers to pay a fee of 1000 for an all-day lesson on Wednesday. When Prudence hears this offer to work for ten times her usual wage rate, she thinks: "I don't get offers like this every day. I'll go skydiving some other day, but this Wednesday, I'm going to work."

Prudence's decision to work rather than skydive (that is, to substitute labor for leisure) on this one Wednesday is a response to a very high reward, in terms of extra income, that the extra day of work will bring. Thus her decision to work the extra day is the result of the substitution effect. Because receiving a very high wage for only one day doesn't make Prudence substantially wealthier, the income effect of the one-day wage increase is negligible. Thus the effect of a one-day increase in the real wage on the quantity of labor supplied by Prudence is an almost pure example of the substitution effect.

A Pure Income Effect: A Gift. By the next week Prudence has forgotten all about the eccentric golfer. But then she hears that he managed to win his amateur tournament. Furthermore, in gratitude he sends Prudence a check worth 30,000, or nearly a year's pay. Prudence's response is to reduce the amount she works from six to five days a week.

Why did Prudence reduce the quantity of labor she supplied when she received the unexpected gift? Prudence treasures the time she spends skydiving but decided to work six days per week to pay for food, clothes, rent, and skydiving trips. However, when the large check arrives, suddenly she can afford to take more time off from work— and so she does. Because the gift made her wealthier, she reduces her labor supply. This is an example of a pure income effect.

In Chapter 3 we concluded that either an increase in wealth or an increase in the expected future real wage would reduce current labor supply. Both results are examples of pure income effects. An increase in wealth— say, winning a lottery prize—is like the gift that Prudence received from the golfer; a wealthier worker can afford more leisure—and more consumption—and thus will supply less labor. Similarly, an increase in the expected future real wage raises the worker's present value of lifetime resources, *PVLR*, by raising expected future income; so again, the worker is better off and will choose more current leisure. Neither an increase in wealth nor an increase in the expected future real wage has any effect on the current reward for working, so neither change has any substitution effect on labor supply.

The Substitution Effect and the Income Effect Together: A Long-Term Increase in the Real Wage. Now imagine that, some weeks following her windfall, Prudence receives a call from a nearby country club offering her a long-term position as the resident golf pro. She will receive a wage of 200 per day (twice her previous wage) and will continue to be free to set the number of days she works. Prudence accepts the offer immediately.

On her new job, will Prudence work more days or fewer days than she did before? In this case two effects work in opposite directions. On the one hand, because the reward for working is greater, she will be tempted to work more than she did previously. This tendency to increase labor supply in response to a higher real wage is the substitution effect. On the other hand, at double her original wage Prudence can pay for food, rent, and skydiving expenses by working only three or four days a week, tempting her to work less and spend more time skydiving. This tendency to reduce labor supply because she is wealthier is the income effect.

Which effect wins? One factor that will influence Prudence's decision is the length of time she expects her new, higher wage to last. The longer the higher wage is expected to last, the larger its impact is on Prudence's lifetime resources, and the stronger the income effect is. Thus, if Prudence expects to hold the new job until she retires, the income effect is strong (she is much wealthier) and she is more likely to reduce the amount she works. If Prudence believes that the job may not last very long, the income effect is weak (the increase in her lifetime resources is small) and she may choose to work more to take advantage of the higher wage while she can. In general, the longer an increase in the real wage is expected to last, the larger the income effect is and the more likely it is that the quantity of labor supplied will be reduced.

Empirical Evidence on Real Wages and Labor Supply. Because of conflicting income and substitution effects, there is some ambiguity about how a real-wage change will affect labor supply. What is the empirical evidence?

In his book on labor supply Mark Killingsworth[25] of Rutgers University surveyed the results of more than sixty studies of the labor supply decision in the United States, the United Kingdom, Canada, West Germany, Japan, and Taiwan. Although the studies differed in many respects and didn't all yield precisely the same results, generally they showed that the aggregate amount of labor supplied rises in response to a temporary increase in the real wage but falls in response to a permanent increase in the real wage. The finding that a temporary increase in the real wage raises the amount of labor supplied confirms the substitution effect: If the reward for working rises for a short period, people will take advantage of the opportunity to work more. The result that a permanent increase in the real wage lowers the aggregate amount of labor supplied indicates that for long-lived increases in the real wage the income effect outweighs the substitution effect: If permanently higher wages make workers much better off, they will choose to work less. The effect of permanent increases in real wages is further illustrated in the following Application.

APPLICATION

Weekly Hours of Work and the Wealth of Nations

In 1869 the typical worker in the U.S. manufacturing sector worked about 56 hours per week. However, as shown in Fig. 8.10 on the next page, the average workweek in U.S. manufacturing declined steadily into the 1930s. Although various forces contributed to the shortening of the workweek before 1930, the major reason was sharply rising real wages. Increases in real wages over the late nineteenth and early twentieth centuries in the United States were driven by technological innovation and increased productivity and thus were largely permanent. In response to permanent increases in the real wage, workers reduced the amount of labor they supplied.

25. *Labor Supply*, Cambridge, England: Cambridge University Press, 1983. See especially Tables 3.1–3.5 and 4.2–4.4.

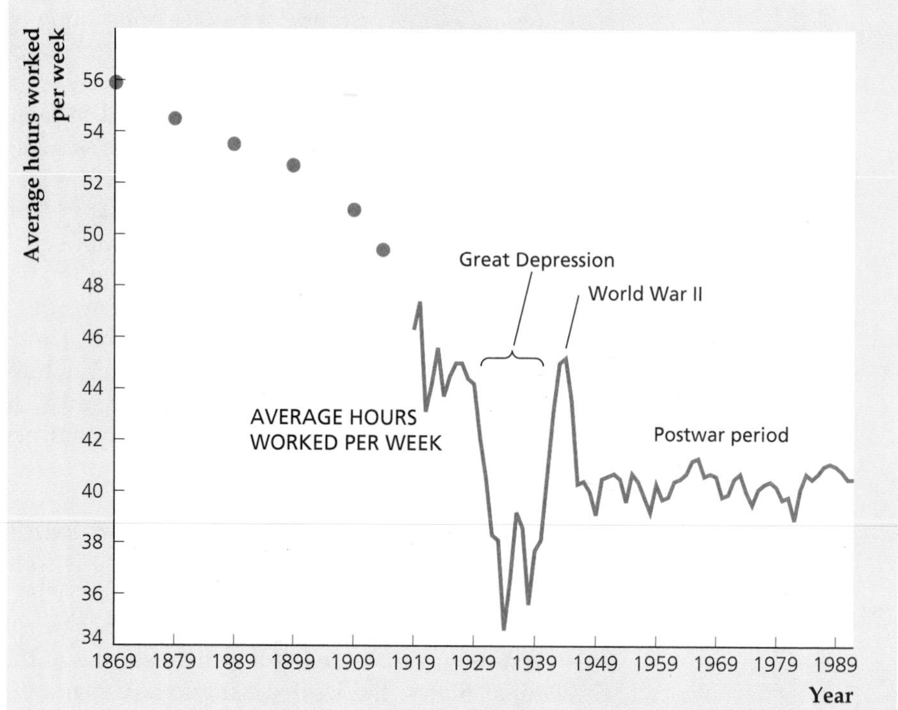

Figure 8.10
Average weekly hours, U.S. manufacturing
Reflecting the income effect of wages on labor supply, the steady increase in the real wage in the United States during the late nineteenth and early twentieth centuries tended to reduce the average weekly hours of manufacturing workers. Weekly hours fluctuated sharply during the Great Depression and World War II but stabilized in the postwar period. *Note:* Data were available only for selected years prior to 1919.

Source: Average weekly hours, production workers in manufacturing establishments: Bureau of Economic Analysis, *Long-Term Economic Growth 1860–1970*, June 1973, pp. 212–213; and *Employment and Earnings*, Table C-1, various issues.

The response of labor supply to increases in real wages doesn't explain all of the changes in weekly hours worked. For example, the relatively low number of hours worked per week during the 1930s reflects primarily the general economic collapse that occurred during the Great Depression; and the sharp increase in weekly hours of work during the 1940s resulted in part from the threat to national survival posed by World War II, which induced workers to work more hours per week. Since World War II the workweek in U.S. manufacturing has stabilized at around forty hours, with little decline despite increases in the real wage in the 1950s and 1960s. However, since World War II workers have reduced the quantities of labor supplied in other ways, notably by retiring earlier and taking more vacation time.

The historical data in Fig. 8.10 provide some evidence that, in response to a permanent increase in the real wage, workers choose to have more leisure and to work fewer hours per week. Figure 8.11 presents additional evidence, drawn from thirty-six nations. Each point in the diagram represents a different country. The horizontal axis measures real gross domestic product (GDP) per person, and the vertical axis measures the average number of hours worked per week by production workers in manufacturing. Workers in richer countries with higher wage rates (United States, Canada) tend to work fewer hours per week than workers in poorer countries with lower wage rates (South Korea, Bolivia). Because the differences in wages among countries reflect long-term differences in productivity, the fact that high-wage countries have shorter workweeks provides further support for the finding that permanent increases in the real wage cause workers to supply less labor.

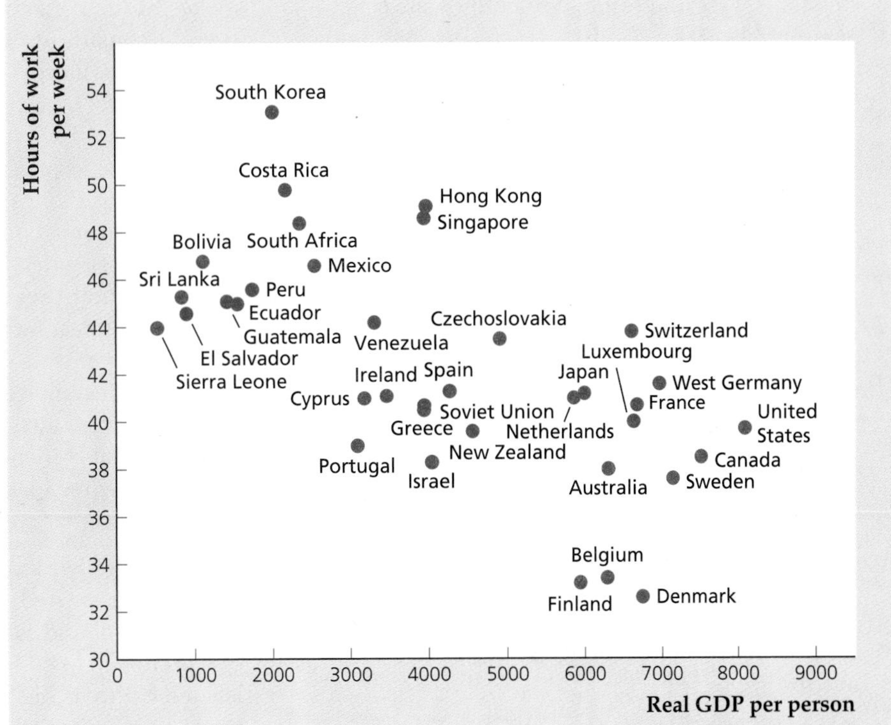

Figure 8.11
The work week and real GDP per person in 36 countries
The point corresponding to each country shows the country's real GDP per person in 1980 on the horizontal axis and the average number of hours worked per week in manufacturing on the vertical axis. Because of the income effect on labor supply, richer countries tend to have short work weeks.

Source: Average hours per week: *United Nations Statistical Yearbook*, 1985–1986, p. 89; real GDP per capita (in 1975 dollars): Robert Summers and Alan Heston, "Improved International Comparisons of Real Product and Its Components: 1950–1980," *Review of Income and Wealth*, June 1984, pp. 259–261.

CHAPTER SUMMARY

1. In deciding how much to consume and to save, households trade off present consumption against future consumption. This tradeoff can be analyzed most simply in a two-period model of consumer behavior.

2. For any possible level of current consumption, the budget constraint shows how much future consumption an individual can afford, based on the individual's economic resources. The graph of the budget constraint, in a diagram with current consumption on the horizontal axis and future consumption on the vertical axis, is called the budget line. The budget line slopes downward [with slope = $-(1 + r)$, where r is the real interest rate] because an increase in current consumption implies less saving and thus less consumption in the future.

3. Present values measure payments to be made in the future in terms of today's dollars. The budget constraint can be expressed in terms of present values: The present value of an individual's lifetime consumption, *PVLC*, equals that person's present value of lifetime resources, *PVLR*. Thus a change in income or wealth affects an individual's consumption opportunities only to the extent that it changes the *PVLR*.

4. Preferences about current and future consumption are represented by indifference curves. All combinations of current and future consumption on an indifference curve yield the same level of utility, or economic satisfaction. Indifference curves slope downward, and indifference curves that are higher and to the right represent higher levels of utility. Indifference curves are

bowed toward the origin, which indicates that households prefer relatively even consumption over time (the consumption-smoothing motive).

5. Consumers choose the available combination of current and future consumption that yields the highest level of utility. Graphically, this consumption combination is represented by the point at which the budget line is tangent to an indifference curve.

6. An increase in current income, expected future income, or initial wealth raises the *PVLR* and shifts the budget line parallel and to the right by an amount equal to the increase in the *PVLR*. This rise in economic resources increases both current and future consumption. An increase in current income raises saving, but increases in future income or initial wealth—because they increase current consumption without raising current income—reduce saving. The effects of any parallel shift in the budget line are called income effects.

7. Friedman's permanent income theory of consumption and saving predicts that permanent increases in income, because they have a larger effect on the individual's *PVLR*, should have a larger effect on current consumption than do temporary increases in income.

8. Empirically, some studies show that current consumption responds more strongly to current income than the theory predicts (the excess sensitivity phenomenon). Borrowing constraints—limits imposed by lenders on the amounts that households can borrow—may help explain why consumption responds so strongly to changes in current income.

9. Modigliani's life-cycle model of consumption and saving focuses on patterns of income, consumption, and saving throughout an individual's life. Because income is highest during an individual's middle years and because people try to keep consumption relatively constant over time, the life-cycle model predicts that middle-aged people will have high saving rates and people in their early working years or in retirement will have low or negative saving rates.

10. An increase in the real interest rate has two effects on saving. First, a higher real interest rate makes future consumption cheaper in terms of current consumption, which causes people to want to save more; this effect is called the substitution effect. Second, an increase in the real interest rate makes lenders better off (inducing them to save less) and makes borrowers worse off (inducing them to save more); this effect is called the income effect. The income and substitution effects work in opposite directions for lenders so that their saving may either rise or fall when the real interest rate rises. For borrowers, the income and substitution effects work in the same direction so that a borrower always increases saving when the real interest rate rises. The empirical evidence isn't conclusive but suggests that aggregate saving rises modestly in response to a higher real interest rate.

11. The benefit of working an extra hour is the extra real income earned, which can be used to increase current and future consumption. The cost of working an extra hour is the loss of an hour's leisure. Utility is highest when labor is supplied to the point where the cost of working an extra hour (utility lost because of reduced leisure) equals the benefit (utility gained because of increased income).

12. An increase in the real wage has competing substitution and income effects on the amount of labor supplied. The substitution effect of a higher real wage increases the amount of labor supplied, as the worker responds to the increased reward for working. The income effect reduces the amount of labor supplied, as the higher real wage makes the worker wealthier and thus able to afford a greater amount of leisure. The longer an increase in the real wage is expected to last, the stronger is the income effect. Thus permanent increases in the real wage typically reduce the quantity of labor supplied.

Key Terms

bequest motive, p. 268
borrowing constraint, p. 265
budget constraint, p. 251
budget line, p. 252
consumption-smoothing motive, p. 256
income effect, p. 261
income effect (of the real interest rate on saving), p. 273

income effect (of the real wage on labor supply), p. 277
indifference curve, p. 255
life-cycle model, p. 266
no-borrowing, no-lending point, p. 270
permanent income theory, p. 261
present value, p. 253
present value of lifetime resources (*PVLR*), p. 254
substitution effect (of the real interest rate on saving), p. 271
substitution effect (of the real wage on labor supply), p. 277
utility, p. 255

Key Equations

$$c^f = (y + a - c)(1 + r) + y^f \tag{8.2}$$

For any possible level of current consumption, c, the budget constraint shows how much future consumption, c^f, the consumer can afford, given current real income, y, expected future real income, y^f, and initial wealth (assets), a.

$$c + \frac{c^f}{1+r} = y + \frac{y^f}{1+r} + a \tag{8.4}$$

$$PVLC = PVLR$$

An alternative way to state the budget constraint is that the present value of lifetime consumption (*PVLC*), $c + c^f/(1 + r)$, equals the present value of lifetime resources (*PVLR*), $y + y^f/(1 + r) + a$.

Review Questions

1. Explain how, in choosing how much to consume and how much to save out of current income, an individual or household is making a tradeoff between the present and the future.
2. Without using numbers or equations, sketch a consumer's budget line, labeling the axes of the graph. What can be said about points that lie on the budget line? Why does the budget line slope the way it does? If the budget line you have drawn were to shift to the left, would the consumer be better off or worse off? Why?
3. How is the present value of a given future payment affected if the interest rate rises? In words, how can the consumer's budget constraint be expressed in terms of present values?
4. Sketch an indifference curve. Why does it have the slope that it does? Why does it have the shape that it does? What is the relationship between one indifference curve and another that lies below it and to the left of the first?
5. What are the effects on current consumption and saving of an increase in current income? An increase in expected future income? An increase in wealth? Explain in words (without using a diagram).
6. Compare the effects of a \$1000 permanent increase in income on current consumption, future consumption, and saving to the effects of a \$1000 temporary increase in income. Explain your answer by using the concept of the *PVLR*.
7. Define *borrowing constraint*, and distinguish between binding and nonbinding borrowing constraints. Does your answer to Review Question 6 change if there is a binding borrowing constraint? If there is a nonbinding borrowing constraint?
8. According to the life-cycle model, when during a consumer's life is saving likely to be high? When is saving likely to be low? Explain.
9. What are the two effects that an increase in the real interest rate has on desired saving? Describe each effect briefly. What is the overall effect of an increase in the real interest rate on saving? How does your answer depend on whether the consumer is a borrower or a lender?
10. What two effects does an increase in the real wage have on the amount of labor supplied? What determines which effect is the stronger?
11. Using the concepts of income and substitution effects, discuss how the amount of labor a household supplies should react to (a) a decline in wealth and (b) an increase in the real wage that household members expect to earn in the future.

Numerical Problems

1. A consumer has initial real wealth of 20, current real income of 90, and future real income of 110. The real interest rate is 10% per period.
   a. Find the consumer's *PVLR*.
   b. Write the equation for the consumer's budget constraint (using the given numerical values) and graph the budget line.

   Suppose that the consumer's goal is to smooth consumption completely. That is, he wants to have the same level of consumption in both the current and future periods.

c. How much will he save and consume in the current period?

d. How will his current saving and consumption be affected by an increase of 11 in current income?

e. How will his current saving and consumption be affected by an increase of 11 in future income?

f. How will his current saving and consumption be affected by an increase of 11 in his initial wealth?

2. a. The present value of a nominal payment P one year from now is $P/(1 + i)$, where i is the (annual) nominal interest rate. If the nominal interest rate i is constant, show that the present value of a payment P to be received in n years is $P/(1 + i)^n$. (*Hint:* If the nominal interest rate is i, how much would you have to put in the bank today in order to have P dollars in n years?)

b. When taking out a $100,000 mortgage you are offered two options: First, you can repay $10,000 at the end of each of the first four years after you get the loan, then repay $110,000 at the end of the fifth year. Or second, you can repay $12,000 at the end of each of the first four years, then repay $100,000 at the end of the fifth year. At a 10% constant annual interest rate, which option is the better deal in present value terms? (To find the present value of a series of payments, add the present values of the individual payments.)

3. Bill Melater has a current real income after taxes of 300, an expected future real income after taxes of 360, and no initial wealth. The real interest rate is fixed at 20% throughout the problem. Bill always consumes an amount equal to half his *PVLR* in the current period.

a. What is Bill's *PVLR*, current-period consumption, and current-period saving?

b. The government raises Bill's current taxes by 30 but does not change its spending. Assuming that future taxes are adjusted to offset the effect of the current tax increase on the government debt, does Ricardian equivalence hold in this example? Explain.

c. Repeat part (b) under the assumption that Bill isn't allowed to borrow against future income.

d. Repeat part (b) under the assumption that the current tax increase is accompanied by an equal increase in the government's current-period foreign aid program.

4. In a particular town each of its 2000 residents makes consumption and saving plans over a current period and a future period. All want to smooth consumption completely (that is, make current and future consumption equal), if possible. For 1000 of the residents current income is 120 and future income is 100. For the remaining 1000 residents current income is 100 and future income is 120. None has any initial wealth. The real interest rate is zero (and is unaffected by decisions made by the residents). The residents can freely borrow from and lend to people in other towns at the fixed real interest rate.

a. What is the town's aggregate consumption in the current period?

b. What is the effect on aggregate consumption if all consumers receive a temporary (current-period-only) increase in income of 10?

c. What is the effect on aggregate consumption if all consumers receive a permanent (both current- and future-period) income increase of 10?

Suppose that consumers aren't allowed to borrow, but they may save if they want.

d. Now what is the town's aggregate consumption in the current period?

e. What is the effect on aggregate consumption if all consumers receive a temporary increase in income of 10?

f. Comparing the change in aggregate consumption in part (e) to the change that occurred in part (b), can you conclude that the presence of borrowing constraints makes consumption "excessively sensitive" to current income? Why or why not?

5. A consumer lives three periods, called the learning period, the working period, and the retirement period. Her income is 200 during the learning period, 800 during the working period, and 200 again during the retirement period. The consumer's initial assets are 300. The real interest rate is zero. The consumer desires perfectly smooth consumption over her lifetime.

a. What are consumption and saving in each period, assuming no borrowing constraints? What happens if the consumer faces a borrowing constraint that prevents her from borrowing?

b. Assume that the consumer's initial wealth is zero instead of 300. Repeat part (a). Does being borrowing-constrained mean that her consumption is lower in all three periods of her life than it would be if there were no borrowing constraints?

6. This problem analyzes the relationship between the rate of income growth in a country and its rate of saving. (See item 2 in the application "Why Do the Japanese Save So Much?" p. 268.)

An economy lasts three periods. One hundred people called "parents" live during the first and second periods. Each parent earns a real income of 10,000 in the first period and earns nothing (is retired) in the second period. Parents desire to have equal consumption during their working lives and retirement. The real interest rate is zero in all periods.

One hundred people called "children" live during the second and third periods. Children each earn a real income of $(1 + g)$ times 10,000 in the second period, where g is the real growth rate of the economy. Children earn no income (are retired) in the third period. Children also desire perfectly even consumption over their lives.

Calculate total saving (adding the saving of parents and children) during the second period, assuming a growth rate of $g = 0$. (*Hint:* Remember that parents dissave during retirement.) What happens if $g = 0.10$? If $g = 0.50$? How is saving in the second period related in general to the growth rate of the economy?

7. Rudy Day has current real income of 12,000, has initial real wealth of 2000, and expects future real income of 12,000. The real interest rate is 20%.
   a. Draw Rudy's budget line, and give numerical values for the budget line's horizontal intercept and its slope.
   b. The real interest rate rises to 50%. Repeat part (a).
   c. Initially, Rudy's current consumption is 12,000. Show diagrammatically the substitution and income effects of the increase in the real interest rate on Rudy's saving. Do you have enough information to know whether his saving will increase or decrease? Explain.
   d. Suppose that initially Rudy's current consumption is 16,000 rather than 12,000. Repeat part (c).

Analytical Problems

1. If you are a utility-maximizing consumer with no borrowing constraints, how would each of the following affect your current consumption and saving?
   a. You are informed that a long-lost relative has left you a large bequest. However, the bequest is to be kept in a trust, and you will not be able to withdraw any of the money for ten years.
   b. Your doctor tells you that you have an amazingly healthy constitution and that you should easily live to age ninety. This prediction doesn't change your plan to retire at age sixty-five in order to perfect your fishing skills.
   c. You are a taxpayer, and you read in the paper that your state government's deficit is much worse than thought. A tax increase next year now seems inevitable.
   d. You work in the auto industry and read in the newspaper that a serious recession and tough foreign competition are predicted to drive down car sales.
   e. Your son's dentist tells you that in three or four years he will need a very expensive set of braces.
   f. After several years of litigation you receive an insurance award compensating you for losses incurred in a fire. Though fairly large, the award is less than what you had been expecting.
2. To derive the budget constraint, Eq. (8.2), we assumed that Prudence's current consumption was less than her current resources so that she had some resources to put in the bank until the future period. Show that Eq. (8.2) still holds if Prudence's current consumption exceeds her current resources. (*Hint:* In this case Prudence must borrow an amount equal to the difference between her consumption and her resources in the current period and then repay this amount with interest in the future period. Her future consumption then equals her future income less her loan repayment.)
3. Many taxpayers have more income withheld from their paychecks than they owe in taxes, with the result that after filing their tax returns, they receive refund checks from the Internal Revenue Service. In early 1985 the installation of a new computer system at the IRS delayed the processing of individual income tax returns. During February and March, a period in which many refund checks are usually mailed out, relatively few were processed. However, as the new computer came on line, the IRS moved to catch up. Refunds were above normal in April and much higher than normal in May. By June nearly all refunds had been mailed out, as is usually the case. Thus the aggregate income of U.S. consumers, including tax refunds, was noticeably below normal in February and March and higher than normal in April, May, and June.

   Some economic forecasters predicted that the IRS's computer problems would lead to a weakening in February and March consumer purchases. Discuss this prediction, using the concept of *PVLR*.

What happens if many consumers have binding borrowing constraints?[26]

4. One of the many innovations in U.S. financial markets during the past fifteen years has been the increased availability of home equity lines of credit (HELs). Home equity lines (technically a form of second mortgage, usually offered by a bank or savings and loan association) allow homeowners to borrow against the value of the equity in their house, often just by writing a check when funds are needed.[27] This contrasts with earlier periods, when borrowing against a home at any time other than the initial purchase date was typically a complex and costly process. What effect should the increased availability of HELs have on household consumption and saving? Discuss.[28]

5. Draw a budget line and indifference curves for a consumer who initially is a borrower. Be sure to indicate the no-borrowing, no-lending point and the optimal consumption point. Then show the effect on the budget line and the consumer's optimal consumption of an increase in the real interest rate. Using an intermediate budget line, show the income effect and the substitution effect. Do they work in the same direction or in opposite directions? Explain.

6. Consumers typically pay a higher real interest rate to borrow than they receive when they lend (by making bank deposits, for example). Draw a consumer's budget line under the assumption that the real rate of return earned on funds lent, r_l, is lower than the real interest rate paid to borrow, r_b. Show how the budget line is affected by an increase in r_l, an increase in r_b, or an increase in the consumer's initial wealth.

   Show that changes in r_l and r_b may leave current and future consumption unchanged. (*Hint:* Draw the consumer's indifference curves so that the consumer initially chooses the no-borrowing, no-lending point.)

7. Repeat Analytical Problem 4 in Chapter 3, p. 105. Discuss each part in terms of income and substitution effects.

8. John Doe learns that the percentage of his wages paid into the Social Security fund has been permanently raised.

   a. Suppose that John's expected Social Security benefits are not changed; instead, the increase in his Social Security tax is used to make up some unexpected shortfalls in the current Social Security program. John also doesn't expect his before-tax real wages in the future to change. John is well below the Social Security "cap"; that is, none of his labor earnings is exempt from the Social Security tax. What will be the effect of the increase in the Social Security tax on the amount of labor that John supplies?

   b. Repeat part (a), but assume that John's extra Social Security taxes all go directly to increase his expected retirement benefits. Assume also that John will get the full increase in retirement benefits whether or not he keeps working at his present rate. What happens to John's labor supply now?

---

26. This problem is based on David W. Wilcox, "Income Tax Refunds and the Timing of Consumption Expenditure," Board of Governors of the Federal Reserve System, revised May 1990. Wilcox found that, empirically, the delay in making refunds did not affect the timing of consumer purchases.

27. A homeowner's equity in her house is the value of the house minus the value of any mortgage she owes against the house. Consumer use of home equity lines was particularly stimulated by tax law changes in 1986, which eliminated the tax deductibility of interest on most types of consumer debt but not on home equity lines and other mortgages. However, growth in this type of borrowing had been strong even before 1986.

28. In a study of individual families ("Second Mortgages and Household Saving," *Regional Science and Urban Economics*, May 1989, pp. 325–346) Joyce Manchester of Dartmouth and James Poterba of the Massachusetts Institute of Technology found that with family characteristics held constant, each extra dollar of second-mortgage borrowing was associated with about 75 cents less total saving by the family.

Business Cycles and Macroeconomic Policy

CHAPTER 9

BUSINESS CYCLES

Since the Industrial Revolution, the economies of the United States and many other countries have grown tremendously. That growth has transformed economies and greatly improved living standards. Yet even in prosperous countries, economic expansion has been periodically interrupted by episodes of declining production, income, and spending and rising unemployment. Sometimes—fortunately, not very often—these episodes have been severe and prolonged. But whether brief or more extended, declines in economic activity have been followed almost invariably by a resumption of economic growth.

This repeated sequence of economic expansion giving way to temporary decline followed by recovery, is known as the *business cycle*. The business cycle is a central concern in macroeconomics because business cycle fluctuations—the ups and downs in overall economic activity—are felt throughout the economy. When the economy is growing strongly, prosperity is shared by most of the nation's industries and their workers and owners of capital. When the economy weakens, many sectors of the economy experience declining sales and production, and the number of unemployed workers increases. Because the effects of business cycles are so widespread, and because economic downturns can cause great hardship, economists have tried to find the causes of these episodes and to determine what, if anything, can be done to counteract them. The two basic questions of (1) what causes business cycles and (2) how policymakers should respond to cyclical fluctuations are the main concern of Part III of this book.

Unfortunately, these two questions remain highly controversial. Much of this controversy involves the proponents of the classical and Keynesian approaches to macroeconomics, introduced in Chapter 1. In brief, classical economists view business cycles as generally representing the economy's best response to disturbances in production or spending. Thus classical economists do not see much, if any, need for government action to counteract these fluctuations. In contrast, Keynesian economists argue that, because wages and prices adjust slowly, disturbances in production or spending may drive the economy away from its most desirable level of output and employment for long periods of time. According to the Keynesian view, government should intervene to smooth business cycle fluctuations.

We explore the debate between classicals and Keynesians, and the implications of that debate for economic analysis and macroeconomic policy, in Chapters

10–12. This chapter provides essential background for that discussion by presenting the basic features of the business cycle. We begin with a definition and a brief history of the business cycle in the United States. We then turn to a more detailed discussion of business cycle characteristics, or "business cycle facts."

9.1 WHAT IS A BUSINESS CYCLE?

Countries have experienced ups and downs in overall economic activity since they began to industrialize. Economists have measured and studied these fluctuations for more than a century. Marx and Engels referred to "commercial crises," an early term for business cycles, in their Communist Manifesto in 1848. In the United States, the National Bureau of Economic Research (NBER), a private nonprofit organization of economists founded in 1920, pioneered business cycle research. The NBER developed and continues to update the **business cycle chronology,** a detailed history of business cycles in the United States and other countries. The NBER has also sponsored many studies of the business cycle: One landmark study was the 1946 book *Measuring Business Cycles,* by Arthur Burns (who served as Federal Reserve chairman from 1970 until 1978) and Wesley Mitchell (a principal founder of the NBER). This work was among the first to document and analyze the empirical facts about business cycles. It begins with the following definition:

> Business cycles are a type of fluctuation found in the aggregate economic activity of nations that organize their work mainly in business enterprises. A cycle consists of expansions occurring at about the same time in many economic activities, followed by similarly general recessions, contractions, and revivals which merge into the expansion phase of the next cycle; this sequence of changes is recurrent but not periodic; in duration business cycles vary from more than one year to ten or twelve years.[1]

Five points in this definition should be clarified and emphasized.

1. *Aggregate economic activity.* Business cycles are defined broadly as fluctuations of "aggregate economic activity" rather than as fluctuations in a single, specific economic variable such as real GDP. Although real GDP may be the single variable that most closely measures aggregate economic activity, Burns and Mitchell also thought it important to look at other indicators of activity, such as employment and financial market variables.

2. *Expansions and contractions.* Figure 9.1—a diagram of a typical business cycle—helps explain what Burns and Mitchell meant by expansions and contractions. The dashed line shows the average, or normal, growth path of aggregate economic activity, and the solid curve shows the rises and falls of actual business activity. The period of time during which aggregate economy

1. Burns and Mitchell, *Measuring Business Cycles,* New York: National Bureau of Economic Research, 1946, p. 1.

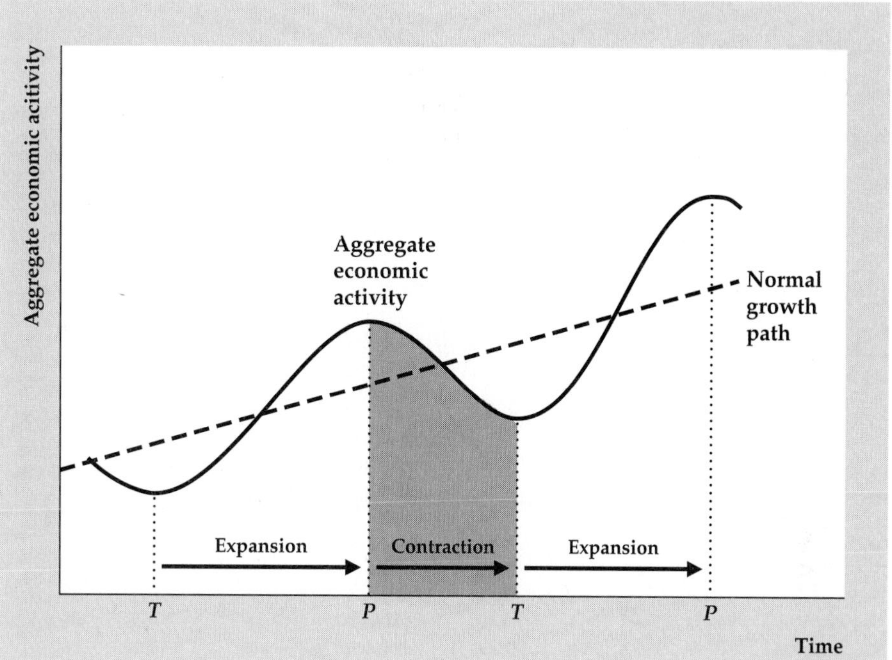

Figure 9.1
A business cycle
The solid curve graphs the behavior of aggregate economic activity over a typical business cycle. The dashed line shows the economy's normal growth path. During a contraction aggregate economic activity falls until it reaches a trough, *T*. The trough is followed by an expansion during which economic activity increases until it reaches a peak, *P*. A complete cycle is measured from peak to peak or trough to trough.

activity is falling is a **contraction** or **recession.** If the recession is particularly severe, it becomes a **depression.** After reaching the low point of the contraction, the **trough** (*T*), economic activity begins to increase. The period of time during which aggregate economic activity grows is an **expansion** or a **boom.** After reaching the high point of the expansion, the **peak** (*P*), aggregate economic activity begins to decline again. The entire sequence of decline followed by recovery, measured from peak to peak or trough to trough, is a **business cycle.**

Figure 9.1 suggests that business cycles are purely temporary deviations from the economy's long-run growth path. However, part of the output losses and gains that occur during a business cycle may become permanent (see Box 9.1 on the next page).

Peaks and troughs in the business cycle are known collectively as **turning points.** One goal of business cycle research is to identify when turning points occur. Aggregate economic activity isn't measured directly by any single variable, so there's no simple formula that tells economists when a peak or trough has been reached.[2] In practice, a small group of economists who form the NBER's Business Cycle Dating Committee determine that date. The committee meets only when its members believe that a turning point may have occurred. By examining a variety of economic data, the committee determines whether a peak or trough has been reached and, if so, the month it happened. However,

2. A conventional definition used by the media—that a recession has occurred when there are two consecutive quarters of negative real GDP growth—isn't widely accepted by economists. The reason that economists tend not to like this definition is that real GDP is only one of many possible indicators of economic activity.

BOX 9.1

Temporary and Permanent Components of Recessions

Until the 1980s, economists generally believed that business cycles are temporary events. According to this view, after the economy recovers from a recession, it returns to the level it would have reached had the recession not occurred. Thus, although a recession creates short-run problems, it has no important long-run effects on a country's standard of living.

However, in a 1982 article* Charles Nelson of the University of Washington and Charles Plosser of the University of Rochester showed that business cycles are not entirely temporary events. Instead, some permanent reduction in output is associated with the typical recession. Nelson and Plosser examined many macroeconomic variables, including measures of output and employment. Using statistical techniques, they found that for every variable except the unemployment rate, part of a typical cyclical fluctuation represents a permanent change. Only in the unemployment rate did they find fluctuations to be completely transitory.

The severe 1973–1975 recession illustrates the potential permanence of cyclical changes in output. The solid curve in the accompanying figure shows actual real GDP in the United States from 1947 to the first quarter of 1993. The dashed curve in the figure shows the trend in real output, based on the period 1947–1973 and extended through 1993.† In the 1980s GDP remained well below the levels it would have reached on the basis of the earlier trend, suggesting that the 1973–1975 recession was associated with a permanent reduction in real GDP. Of course, we can't conclude that the 1973–1975 recession directly caused the subsequent slowdown. External factors, such as OPEC's quadrupling of oil prices, may have caused both the recession and the subsequent slowdown. Alternatively, the slowdown of growth after 1973 may have been purely coincidental and unrelated to the 1973–1975 recession. Whatever the reason, much of the 1973–1975 drop in output became permanent.

In a typical recession, what fraction of the decline in output is permanent? This question is not easily answered. One problem is that the nature of a decline in output—temporary or permanent—can't be determined until several years afterward. Another problem is that all cyclical output changes may not be alike in their degree of permanence. For example, it is perhaps

Permanent components of the business cycle
The figure shows actual U.S. real GDP (measured quarterly) and a trend line based on real GDP growth from 1947 to 1973. The economy didn't return to the earlier trend after the 1973 recession. Hence much of the output loss of the 1973 recession was permanent.

Source: *Survey of Current Business,* real GDP.

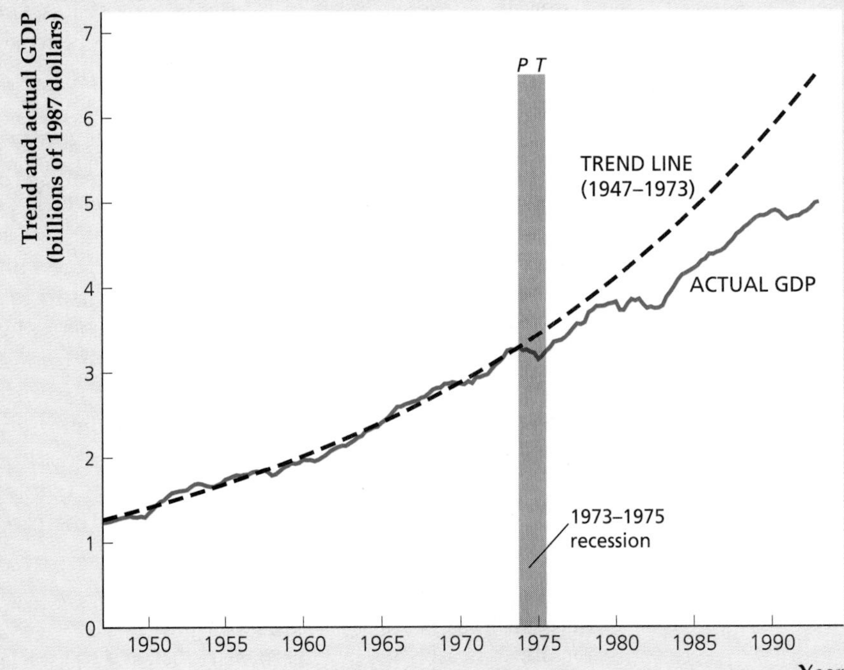

(*Continued*)

not so surprising that a portion of the output decline during the 1973–1975 recession turned out to be permanent, because that recession was associated with a large and long-lasting change in the economy: a fourfold increase in the price of oil. Output declines in recessions not associated with long-lasting supply shocks, in contrast, may well be less permanent than the 1973–1975 decline. Indeed, one recent statistical analysis—by Pierre Perron[‡] of Princeton University—concluded that, of post–World War II U.S. recessions, only the 1973–1975 downturn had a significant permanent effect on the level of output.

Another interesting statistical study of the degree of permanence of cycles was carried out by George Evans[§], now of the London School of Economics. Evans used the unemployment rate, which Nelson and Plosser found has only temporary fluctuations, as a measure of how far output is from its long-run or permanent level at any particular time. He used unusually high unemployment rates, for example, to indicate periods when output is well below its long-run level. Evans estimated that, on average, changes in real output are 30% permanent and 70% temporary in the postwar U.S. economy.

* "Trends and Random Walks in Macroeconomic Time Series: Some Evidence and Implications," *Journal of Monetary Economics*, September 1982, pp. 139–162.

† The trend line in the figure curves upward slightly because it is based on the assumption of a constant growth rate. The graph of a variable that grows by the same percentage every year will curve upward over time, rather than being a straight line.

‡ "The Great Crash, the Oil Price Shock and the Unit Root Hypothesis," *Econometrica*, November 1989, pp. 1361–1401.

§ "Output and Unemployment Dynamics in the United States: 1950–1985," *Journal of Applied Econometrics*, 1989, pp. 213–237.

the committee's announcements usually come well after a peak or trough occurs, so their judgments are more useful for historical analysis of business cycles than as a guide to current policymaking

3. *Comovement.* Business cycles do not occur in just a few sectors or in just a few economic variables. Instead, expansions or contractions "occur at about the same time in many economic activities." Thus, although some industries are more sensitive to the business cycle than others, output and employment in most industries tend to fall in recessions and rise in expansions. Many other economic variables, such as prices, productivity, investment, and government purchases, also have regular and predictable patterns of behavior over the course of the business cycle. This tendency is called **comovement.**

4. *Recurrent but not periodic.* The business cycle isn't periodic, in that it does not occur at regular, predictable intervals and does not last for a fixed or predetermined length of time. (Box 9.2, p. 310, discusses the seasonal cycle—or economic fluctuations over the seasons of the year—which, unlike the business cycle, is periodic.) Although the business cycle isn't periodic, it is recurrent; that is, the standard pattern of contraction–trough–expansion–peak recurs again and again in industrial economies.

5. *Persistence.* The duration of a complete business cycle can vary greatly, from about a year to more than a decade, and predicting it is extremely difficult. However, once a recession begins, the economy tends to keep contracting for a period of time, perhaps for a year or more. Similarly, an expansion once begun usually lasts a while. This tendency for declines in economic activity to be followed by further declines, and for growth in economic activity to be followed by more growth, is called **persistence.** Because movements in economic activity have some persistence, economic forecasters are always on the lookout for turning points, which are likely to indicate a change in the direction of economic activity.

9.2 THE AMERICAN BUSINESS CYCLE: THE HISTORICAL RECORD

An overview of American business cycle history is provided by the NBER's monthly business cycle chronology,[3] as summarized in Table 9.1. It gives the dates of the troughs and peaks of the thirty-one complete business cycles that the U.S. economy has experienced since 1854. Also shown are the number of months that each contraction and expansion lasted.

The Pre–World War I Period

The period between the Civil War (1861–1865) and World War I (1917–1918) was one of rapid economic growth in the United States. Nevertheless, as Table 9.1 shows, recessions were a serious problem during that time. Indeed, the longest contraction on record is the 65-month-long decline between October 1873 and March 1879, a contraction that was worldwide in scope and is referred to by economic historians as the Depression of the 1870s. Overall, during the 1854–1914 period the economy suffered 338 months of contraction, or nearly as many as the 382 months of expansion. In contrast, from the end of World War II in 1945 through July 1993, the number of months of expansion (476) outnumbered months of contraction (96) by about five to one.

The Great Depression and World War II

The worst economic contraction in the history of the United States was the Great Depression of the 1930s. After a prosperous decade in the 1920s, aggregate economic activity reached a peak in August 1929, two months before the stock market crash in October 1929. Between the 1929 peak and the 1933 trough, real GDP fell by nearly 30%. During the same period the unemployment rate rose from about 3% to nearly 25%, with many of those lucky enough to have jobs able to work only part-time. To appreciate how severe the Great Depression was, compare it with the two worst post–World War II recessions of 1973–1975 and 1981–1982. In contrast to the 30% real GDP decline and 25% unemployment rate of the Depression, in the 1973–1975 recession real GDP fell by 4.1% and the unemployment rate rose from about 4% to about 9%; in the 1981–1982 recession real GDP fell by 2.8% and the unemployment rate rose from about 7% to about 11%.

---

3. For a detailed discussion of the NBER chronologies, see Geoffrey H. Moore and Victor Zarnowitz, "The NBER's Business Cycle Chronologies," in Robert J. Gordon, ed., *The American Business Cycle: Continuity and Change*, Chicago: University of Chicago Press, 1986.

Table 9.1 NBER Business Cycle Turning Points and Durations of Post-1854 Business Cycles

Trough	Expansion (Months from Trough to Peak)	Peak	Contraction (Months from Peak to Next Trough)
Dec. 1854	30	June 1857	18
Dec. 1858	22	Oct. 1860	8
June 1861	46	Apr. 1865	32
Dec. 1867	18	June 1869	18
Dec. 1870	34	Oct. 1873	65
Mar. 1879	36	Mar. 1882	38
May 1885	22	Mar. 1887	13
Apr. 1888	27	July 1890	10
May 1891	20	Jan. 1893	17
June 1894	18	Dec. 1895	18
June 1897	24	June 1899	18
Dec. 1900	21	Sep. 1902	23
Aug. 1904	33	May 1907	13
June 1908	19	Jan. 1910	24
Jan. 1912	12	Jan. 1913	23
Dec. 1914	44 (WWI)	Aug. 1918	7
Mar. 1919	10	Jan. 1920	18
July 1921	22	May 1923	14
July 1924	27	Oct. 1926	13
Nov. 1927	21	Aug. 1929	43 (Depression)
Mar. 1933	50	May 1937	13 (Depression)
June 1938	80 (WWII)	Feb. 1945	8
Oct. 1945	37	Nov. 1948	11
Oct. 1949	45 (Korean War)	July 1953	10
May 1954	39	Aug. 1957	8
Apr. 1958	24	Apr. 1960	10
Feb. 1961	106 (Vietnam War)	Dec. 1969	11
Nov. 1970	36	Nov. 1973	16
Mar. 1975	58	Jan. 1980	6
July 1980	12	July 1981	16
Nov. 1982	92	July 1990	8
Mar. 1991			

Source: *Survey of Current Business*, April 1993, page C-25: Business Cycle Expansions and Contractions.

Although no sector escaped the Great Depression, some were particularly hard hit. In the financial sector stock prices continued to collapse after the crash. Depositors withdrew their money from banks, and borrowers, unable to repay their bank loans, were forced to default; as a result, thousands of banks were forced to go out of business or merge with other banks. In agriculture farmers were bankrupted by low crop prices, and a prolonged drought in the

Midwest turned thousands of farm families into homeless migrants. Investment, both business and residential, fell to extremely low levels, and a "trade war"—in which countries competed in erecting barriers to imports—virtually halted international trade.

Although most people think of the Great Depression as a single episode, technically it consisted of two business cycles, as Table 9.1 shows. The contraction phase of the first cycle lasted forty-three months, from August 1929 until March 1933, and was the most precipitous economic decline in U.S. history. After Franklin Roosevelt took office as President in March 1933 and instituted a set of policies known collectively as the New Deal, a strong expansion began and continued for fifty months, from March 1933 to May 1937. By 1937 real GDP was almost back to its 1929 level, although at 14% the unemployment rate remained high. Unemployment remained high in 1937 despite the recovery of real GDP because the number of people of working age had grown since 1929 and because increases in productivity allowed employment to grow more slowly than output.

The second cycle of the Great Depression began in May 1937 with a contraction phase that lasted more than a year. Despite a new recovery that began in June 1938, the unemployment rate was still more than 17% in 1939.

The Great Depression ended dramatically with the advent of World War II. Even before the Japanese attack on Pearl Harbor brought the United States into the war in December 1941, the economy was gearing up for increased armaments production. After the shock of Pearl Harbor the United States prepared for total war. With production supervised by government boards and driven by the insatiable demands of the military for more guns, planes, and ships, real GDP almost doubled between 1939 and 1944. Unemployment dropped sharply, averaging less than 2% of the labor force in 1943–1945 and bottoming out at 1.2% in 1944.

Post–World War II U.S. Business Cycles

As World War II was ending in 1945, economists and policymakers were concerned that the economy would relapse into depression. As an expression of this concern, Congress passed the Employment Act of 1946, which required the government to fight recessions and depressions with any measures at its disposal. But instead of falling into a new depression as feared, the U.S. economy began to grow strongly.

Only a few relatively brief and mild recessions interrupted the economic expansion of the early postwar period. None of the five contractions that occurred between 1945 and 1970 lasted more than a year, whereas eighteen of the twenty-two previous cyclical contractions in the NBER's monthly chronology had lasted a year or more. The largest drop in real GDP between 1945 and 1970 was 3.3% during the 1957–1958 recession, and throughout this period unemployment never exceeded 8.1% of the work force. Again, there was a correlation between economic expansion and war: The 1949–1953 expansion corresponded closely to the Korean War, and the latter part of the strong 1961–1969 expansion occurred during the military buildup to fight the Vietnam War.

Because no serious recession occurred between 1945 and 1970, some economists suggested that the business cycle had been "tamed," or even that it was "dead." This view was especially popular during the record 106-month expansion of 1961–1969, which was widely attributed not only to high rates of military spending during the Vietnam War but also to the macroeconomic policies of Presidents Kennedy and Johnson. Some argued that policymakers should stop worrying about recessions and focus their attention on inflation, which had been gradually increasing over the 1960s.

Unfortunately, reports of the business cycle's death proved premature. Shortly after the Organization of Petroleum Exporting Countries (OPEC) succeeded in quadrupling oil prices in the fall of 1973, the U.S. economy and the economies of many other nations fell into a severe recession. In the 1973–1975 recession American real GDP fell by 4.1% and the unemployment rate reached 9%—not a depression but a serious downturn, nonetheless. Also disturbing was the fact that inflation, which had fallen during most previous recessions, shot up to unprecedented double-digit levels. Inflation continued to be a problem for the rest of the 1970s, even as the economy recovered from the 1973–1975 recession.

More evidence that the business cycle wasn't dead came with the sharp 1981–1982 recession. This contraction lasted sixteen months, the same length as the 1973–1975 decline, and the unemployment rate reached 11%, a postwar high. Many economists claim that the Fed knowingly created this recession to reduce inflation, a claim we discuss in Chapter 12. Inflation did drop dramatically, from about 11% to less than 4% per year. The recovery from this recession was strong, however, and the ensuing expansion continued until the summer of 1990.

In July 1990 the expansion of almost eight years ended, and the economy entered a recession. This recession was relatively short (the trough came in March 1991, only eight months after the peak) and shallow (the unemployment rate peaked in mid 1992 at 7.7%, not particularly high for a recession). However, the recovery from the 1990–1991 recession was slow and erratic, prompting public concern about the state of the economy two years or more after the official trough had been passed.

Have American Business Cycles Become Less Severe?

Until recently, macroeconomists believed that, over the long sweep of history, business cycles generally have become less severe. Obviously, no recession in the United States since World War II can begin to rival the severity of the Great Depression. Even putting aside the Depression, economists generally believed that business downturns before 1929 were longer and deeper than those since 1945. According to the NBER business cycle chronology (Table 9.1), for example, the average contraction before 1929 lasted nearly twenty-one months and the average expansion lasted slightly more than twenty-five months. Since 1945, contractions have shortened to an average of eleven months, and expansions have lengthened to an average of fifty months. Standard measures of economic fluctuations, such as real GDP growth and the unemployment rate, also show considerably less volatility since 1945, relative to data available for the pre–1929 era.

Since World War II a major goal of economic policy has been to reduce the size and frequency of recessions. If researchers found—contrary to the generally accepted view—that business cycles had *not* moderated in the postwar period, serious doubt would be cast on the ability of economic policymakers to achieve this goal. For this reason, although the question of whether the business cycle has moderated over time may seem to be a matter of interest only to economic historians, this issue is of great practical importance.

Thus Christina Romer, now at the University of California at Berkeley, sparked a heated controversy by writing a series of articles denying the claim that the business cycle has moderated over time.[4] Romer's main point concerned the dubious quality of the pre–1929 data. Unlike today, in earlier periods the government didn't collect comprehensive data on economic variables such as GDP. Instead, economic historians, using whatever fragmentary information they could find, have had to estimate historical measures of these variables.

Romer argued that methods used for estimating historical data typically overstated the size of earlier cyclical fluctuations. For example, the widely accepted estimates of pre–1929 GNP[5] compiled by Nobel laureate Simon Kuznets made heavy use of data, originally collected by William Shaw, on the economy's total output of "commodities" during those years. Shaw's commodity output data measured the output of the goods-producing sectors of the economy (agriculture, mining, manufacturing, and to some extent construction) but left out important components of GNP such as wholesale and retail distribution, transportation, and services. Because manufacturing and construction are among the most cyclically volatile components of the modern economy—and distribution, transportation, and services are much less volatile—Romer argued that basing GNP estimates only on commodity output tends to overstate the size of business cycle fluctuations. She used statistical methods to create new estimates of GNP that showed much less volatility in the pre-Depression economy than implied by Kuznets's work. Indeed, she concluded that pre–Depression business cycles, on average, were only about 25% larger than post–1945 cycles, rather than roughly twice as severe, as Kuznets's figures implied.

Since Romer raised the issue, much new research has been done, including work on the historical experience of countries other than the United States. Some of this research has supported Romer's view that cycles haven't moderated. For example, Matthew Shapiro[6] of the University of Michigan showed that the returns earned in the stock market—which are closely related to production and profitability and thus might be used as an indicator of cyclical conditions—were no more variable before the Great Depression than they are today. Steven Sheffrin[7] of the University of California at Davis looked at historical data for six European countries (United Kingdom, Denmark, Sweden,

4. The articles included "Is the Stabilization of the Postwar Economy a Figment of the Data?" *American Economic Review*, June 1986, pp. 314–334; "The Prewar Business Cycle Reconsidered: New Estimates of Gross National Product, 1869–1908," *Journal of Political Economy*, February 1989, pp. 1–37; and "The Cyclical Behavior of Individual Production Series, 1889–1984," *Quarterly Journal of Economics*, February 1991, pp. 1–31.

5. As discussed in Chapter 2, until 1991 the U.S. national income and product accounts focused on GNP rather than GDP. As a result, studies of business cycle behavior have, until very recently, focused on GNP rather than GDP.

6. "The Stabilization of the United States Economy: Evidence from the Stock Market," *American Economic Review*, December 1988, pp. 1067–1079.

7. "Have Economic Fluctuations Been Dampened? A Look at Evidence Outside the United States," *Journal of Monetary Economics*, January 1988, pp. 73–83.

Italy, France, and Norway) and found evidence for postwar moderation of the business cycle only in Sweden.

But the traditional view that the cycle has moderated also has defenders. In a comprehensive study of historical GNP[8] Nathan Balke of Southern Methodist University and Robert Gordon of Northwestern University used previously unutilized data on transportation, communications, and construction for the period 1869–1928. Although these historical data had been available for more than twenty years, they hadn't been used in previous estimates of GNP. When Balke and Gordon combined these data with the Shaw–Kuznets data on commodity output to construct a new series for pre–Depression GNP, they found that the size of pre–1929 business cycle fluctuations was closer to Kuznets's original findings than to Romer's revised estimates.

If Balke and Gordon are right, Romer's challenge will have been answered, and the original belief that the business cycle has moderated over time will be reconfirmed. Even if the traditional view is true, though, the debate served the useful purpose of forcing a careful reexamination of the historical data.

9.3 BUSINESS CYCLE FACTS

Although no two business cycles are identical, all (or most) cycles have features in common. This point has been made strongly by a leading business cycle theorist, Robert E. Lucas, Jr., of the University of Chicago:

> Though there is absolutely no theoretical reason to anticipate it, one is led by the facts to conclude that, with respect to the qualitative behavior of comovements among series [that is, economic variables], *business cycles are all alike.* To theoretically inclined economists, this conclusion should be attractive and challenging, for it suggests the possibility of a unified explanation of business cycles, grounded in the *general* laws governing market economies, rather than in political or institutional characteristics specific to particular countries or periods.[9]

Lucas's statement that business cycles are all alike (or more accurately, that they have many features in common) is based on examinations of comovements among economic variables over the business cycle. In this section, we study these comovements, which we call business cycle facts, for the post–World War II period in the United States. Knowing these business cycle facts is useful for interpreting economic data and evaluating the state of the economy. In addition, they provide guidance and discipline for developing economic theories of the business cycle. When we discuss alternative theories of the business cycle in Chapters 11 and 12, we evaluate the theories principally by determining how well they account for business cycle facts. To be successful,

---

8. "The Estimation of Prewar Gross National Product: Methodology and New Evidence," *Journal of Political Economy,* February 1989, pp. 38–92.

9. Robert E. Lucas, Jr., "Understanding Business Cycles," in K. Brunner and A. H. Meltzer, eds., *Carnegie-Rochester Conference Series on Public Policy,* vol. 5, Autumn, 1977, p. 10.

a theory of the business cycle must explain the cyclical behavior of not just a few variables, such as output and employment, but of a wide range of key economic variables.

The Cyclical Behavior of Economic Variables: Direction and Timing

Two characteristics of the cyclical behavior of macroeconomic variables are important to our discussion of the business cycle facts. The first is the *direction* in which a macroeconomic variable moves, relative to the direction of aggregate economic activity. An economic variable that moves in the same direction as aggregate economic activity (up in expansions, down in contractions) is **procyclical.** A variable that moves oppositely to aggregate economic activity (up in contractions, down in expansions) is **countercyclical.** Variables that do not display a clear pattern over the business cycle are **acyclical.**

The second characteristic is the *timing* of the variable's turning points (peaks and troughs) relative to the turning points of the business cycle. An economic variable is a **leading variable** if it tends to move in advance of aggregate economic activity. In other words, the peaks and troughs in a leading variable occur before the corresponding peaks and troughs in the business cycle. A **coincident variable** is one whose peaks and troughs occur at about the same time as the corresponding business cycle peaks and troughs. Finally, a **lagging variable** is one whose peaks and troughs tend to occur later than the corresponding peaks and troughs in the business cycle.

The fact that some economic variables consistently lead the business cycle suggests that they might be used to forecast the future course of the economy. This idea is behind the **index of leading indicators,** discussed in the box, "In Touch with the Macroeconomy: The Index of Leading Indicators", p. 302.

In some cases the cyclical timing of a variable is obvious from a graph of its behavior over the course of several business cycles; in other cases elaborate statistical techniques are needed to determine timing. Conveniently, the Statistical Indicators Branch of the Bureau of Economic Analysis (BEA) has analyzed the timing of dozens of economic variables. This information is published monthly in the *Survey of Current Business,* along with the most recent data for these variables. For the most part, in this chapter we rely on the BEA's timing classifications.

Let's now examine the cyclical behavior of some key macroeconomic variables. We showed the historical behavior of several of these variables in Figs. 1.1–1.4. Those figures covered a long time period and were based on annual data. To provide a better view of short-run cyclical behavior, we now look at quarterly or monthly data. The direction and timing of the variables considered are presented in Summary table 10.

Production

Because the level of production is a basic indicator of aggregate economic activity, peaks and troughs in production tend to occur at about the same time as peaks and troughs in aggregate economic activity. Thus production is a coincident and procyclical variable. Figure 9.2, on page 304, shows the behavior of the industrial production index in the United States since 1960. This index is a

SUMMARY 10

The Cyclical Behavior of Key Macroeconomic Variables (The Business Cycle Facts)

Variable	Direction	Timing
Production		
Industrial production	Procyclical	Coincident
Durable goods industries are more volatile than nondurable goods and services		
Expenditure		
Consumption	Procyclical	Coincident
Business fixed investment	Procyclical	Coincident
Residential investment	Procyclical	Leading
Inventory investment	Procyclical	Leading
Government purchases	Procyclical	—[a]
Investment is more volatile than consumption		
Labor Market Variables		
Employment	Procyclical	Coincident
Unemployment	Countercyclical	Unclassified[b]
Average labor productivity	Procyclical	Leading[a]
Real wage	Procyclical	—[a]
Money Growth and Inflation		
Money growth	Procyclical	Leading[c]
Inflation	Procyclical	Lagging
Financial Variables		
Stock prices	Procyclical	Leading
Nominal interest rates	Procyclical	Lagging
Real interest rates	Acyclical	—[a]

[a] Timing is not officially designated by Bureau of Economic Analysis.
[b] Officially designated as "unclassified" by the Bureau of Economic Analysis.
[c] M1 money growth is a leading variable; M2 money growth leads the cycle at peaks but is coincident at troughs and is officially "unclassified" overall.

Source: *Survey of Current Business,* May 1993. Industrial production: series 47 (total industrial production); consumption: series 57 (manufacturing and trade sales, 1987 dollars); business fixed investment: series 86 (gross private nonresidential fixed investment); residential investment: series 89 (gross private residential fixed investment); inventory investment: series 30 (change in business inventories); employment: series 41 (employees on nonagricultural payrolls); unemployment: series 43 (civilian unemployment rate); money supply: series 85 (percent change in money supply, M1) and series 102 (percent change in money supply, M2); inflation: series 120 (CPI for services, change from previous month, smoothed); stock prices: series 19 (index of stock prices, 500 common stocks); nominal interest rates: series 119 (Federal funds rate), series 114 (discount rate on new issues of 91-day Treasury bills), series 109 (average prime rate charged by banks)

broad measure of production in manufacturing, mining, and utilities. The vertical lines P and T in Figs. 9.2–9.12 indicate the dates of business cycle peaks and troughs, as determined by the NBER (see Table 9.1). The turning points in industrial production correspond closely to the turning points of the cycle.

Although almost all types of production rise in expansions and fall in recessions, the cyclical sensitivity of production in some sectors of the economy

IN TOUCH *WITH THE MACROECONOMY*

THE INDEX OF LEADING INDICATORS

The index of leading indicators is a weighted average of eleven economic variables that lead the business cycle. Its purpose is to aid in forecasting future aggregate economic activity. The index was originally developed in 1938 at the National Bureau of Economic Research by Wesley Mitchell and Arthur Burns,* whose important early work on business cycles was mentioned earlier in the chapter. The index of leading indicators is currently updated by the Statistical Indicators Branch of the BEA, with results published monthly in the *Survey of Current Business.* (The index of leading indicators previously appeared in *Business Conditions Digest,* until that publication was discontinued in March 1990.)

The eleven variables that make up the index of leading indicators are listed in the accompanying table. They were chosen because each has a tendency to predict (lead) economic activity and because data on them are frequently and promptly reported. This second characteristic is essential because a variable can't be of much help in forecasting if accurate data on the variable arrive only after a long delay.

Components of the index of leading indicators, June 1993

1. Average weekly hours of production or nonsupervisory workers in manufacturing
2. Average weekly initial claims for unemployment insurance
3. Manufacturers' new orders in the consumer goods and materials industries in 1982 dollars
4. Vendor performance (a measure of delays reported by purchasing agents in obtaining goods from suppliers)
5. Contracts and orders for plant and equipment in 1982 dollars
6. Index of new private housing units authorized by local building permits
7. Change in manufacturers' unfilled orders for durable goods industries in 1982 dollars
8. Change in prices of sensitive materials (raw industrial, crude, and intermediate materials)
9. Index of stock prices for 500 common stocks
10. M2 money supply in 1982 dollars
11. Index of consumer expectations

Although the components of the index are varied, there are good economic reasons for why each component helps predict economic activity. For example, new orders for manufactured goods, new orders for plant and equipment, and new building permits all are direct measures of the amount of future production being planned in the economy. The index of stock prices reflects the optimism or pessimism of stock market participants about the economy's future.

The percentage change in the index of leading indicators is reported monthly, with two or three consecutive monthly declines being regarded as the warning sign that a recession is on the way. The behavior of the index of leading indicators since 1948 is shown in the accompanying figure. Note how the index tends to turn down in advance of cyclical peaks. On the whole, the index is a valuable and much-watched forecasting device, correctly predicting a large majority of economic turning points during the post–World War II period. However, the index is not without problems, including the following:

1. Despite the emphasis on the use of data that are promptly available, the data on the eleven components of the index and thus the index of leading indicators itself are usually revised during the first two months after their initial release. As a result, an early signal of recession or recovery may be reversed when the revised data become available.

2. On several occasions the index has given false warnings, predicting a recession when in fact no recession occurred in the several months following the drop in the index.

3. Although it may forecast that a recession is coming, the index doesn't provide much information about how far in the future the recession is or how severe it will be when it arrives.

4. Changes in the structure of the economy over time may cause some variables to become better predictors of the economy and others to become worse. For this reason, the index of leading indicators must be revised periodically, either to change the list of component indicators or to change the weights of the components.

IN TOUCH *WITH THE MACROECONOMY*

(Continued)

The Index of Leading Indicators
Used for forecasting, the index of leading indicators is a weighted average of eleven economic variables that typically lead the business cycle. The index turns down in advance of business cycle peaks, signaling the onset of recession.

Source: *Business Conditions Digest* and *Survey of Current Business*, composite index of leading indicators.

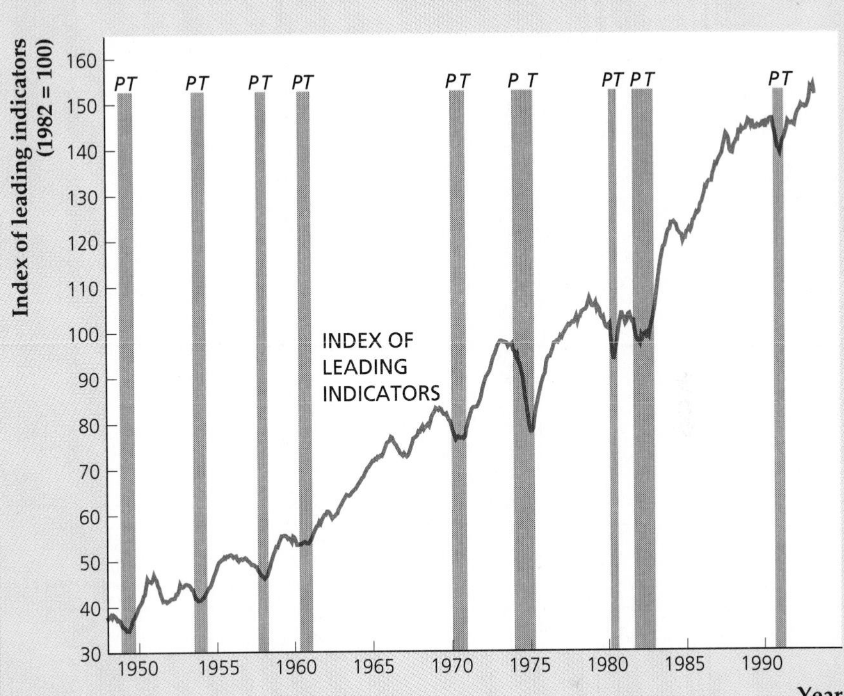

Alternatives to the official index of leading indicators were developed recently by James Stock of Harvard University and Mark Watson of Northwestern University,[†] working under the auspices of the NBER. Stock and Watson proposed a new index of leading indicators, designed specifically to estimate the rate of economic growth six months into the future, that relies more heavily on financial market data than does the official index. An advantage of relying on financial market data is that these data are available very quickly and are rarely revised. A second index proposed by Stock and Watson, called the recession index, is intended to estimate the probability that the economy will be in recession six months in the future.

* Wesley Mitchell and Arthur Burns, *Statistical Indicators of Cyclical Revivals*, New York: NBER, 1938.
† "New Indexes of Coincident and Leading Economic Indicators," in Stanley Fischer and Olivier Blanchard, eds., NBER *Macroeconomics Annual*, Cambridge, Mass.: MIT Press, 1989.

is greater than in others. Industries that produce relatively durable, or long-lasting, goods—houses, consumer durables (refrigerators, cars, washing machines), or capital goods (drill presses, computers, factories)—respond strongly to the business cycle, producing at high rates during expansions and at much lower rates during recessions. In contrast, industries that produce relatively nondurable or short-lived goods (foods, paper products) or services (education, insurance) are less sensitive to the business cycle.

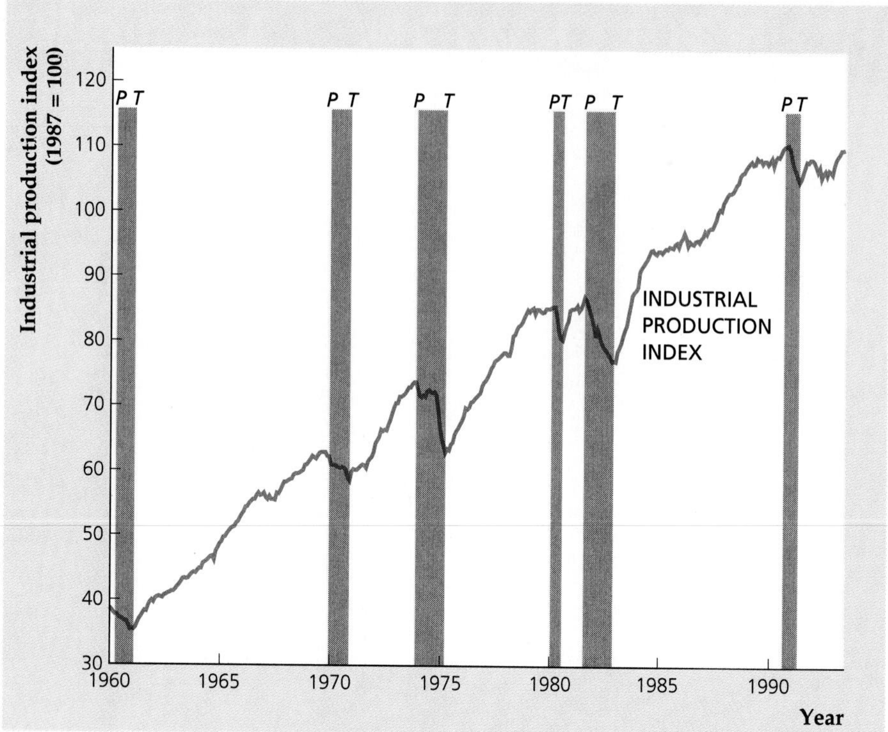

Figure 9.2
Cyclical behavior of the index of industrial production
The index of industrial production, a broad measure of production in manufacturing, mining, and utilities, is procyclical and coincident. The peaks and troughs of the business cycle are shown by the vertical lines *P* and *T*. The shaded areas represent recessions.

Source: *Business Conditions Digest* and *Survey of Current Business,* industrial production index, total.

Expenditure

For components of expenditure, as for types of production, durability is the key to determining sensitivity to the business cycle. Figure 9.3 shows the cyclical behavior of consumption spending and fixed investment (both measured in real terms). Fixed investment, which consists of business fixed investment (structures, equipment) and residential investment, is made up primarily of spending on durable goods and is strongly procyclical. However, consumption expenditures, which include expenditures on nondurable goods and services, in addition to consumer durables, are relatively smoother. A breakdown of consumption into its components would show that spending on consumer durables is strongly procyclical (sales of cars, furniture, and washing machines go up sharply during an economic expansion) but that consumption of nondurable goods and services is much less affected by the business cycle. With respect to timing, consumption and investment are generally coincident with the business cycle, although individual components of fixed investment vary in their cyclical timing.[10]

One component of spending that seems to follow its own rules is inventory investment, or changes in business inventories, shown in Fig. 9.4. Inventory investment is procyclical and leading. Even though goods kept in inventory need not be durable, inventory investment is also very volatile. Although, on

10. Summary table 10 shows that residential investment leads the cycle.

Figure 9.3
Cyclical behavior of consumption and investment
Both consumption and investment are procyclical. However, investment is more sensitive than consumption to the business cycle, reflecting the fact that durable goods are a larger part of investment spending than they are of consumption spending.

Source: *Business Conditions Digest* and *Survey of Current Business,* consumption expenditures and fixed investment.

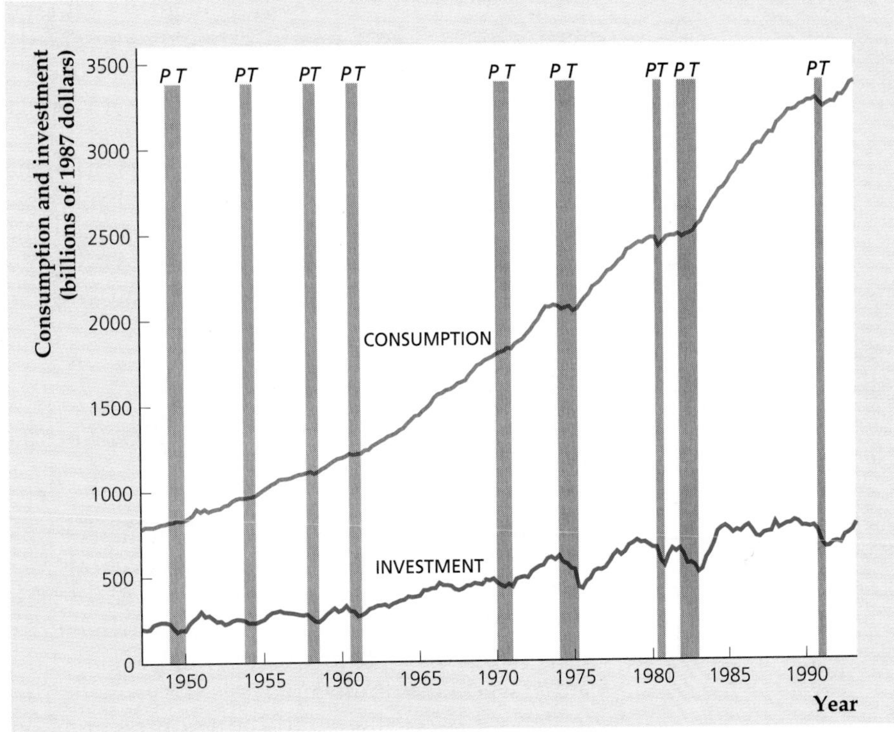

Figure 9.4
Cyclical behavior of changes in business inventories
Inventory investment, or changes in business inventories, is procyclical and leading but also extremely volatile. For example, between 1982 and 1990 inventory investment fluctuated sharply despite the fact that the economy was continuously in expansion.

Source: *Business Conditions Digest* and *Survey of Current Business,* inventory investment.

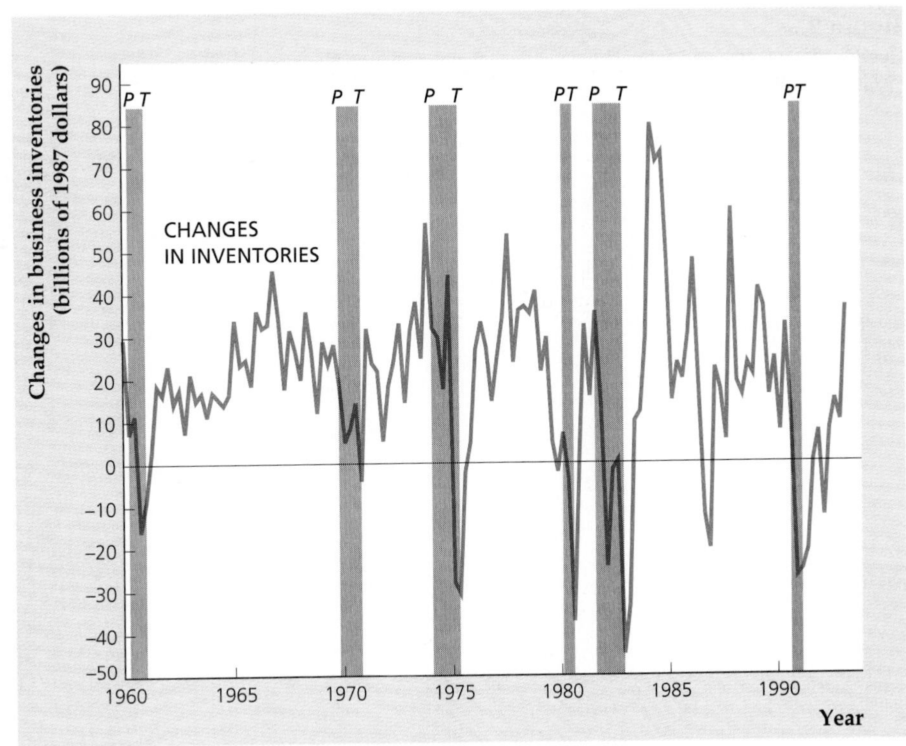

average, inventory investment is a small part (about 1%) of total spending, sharp declines in inventory investment represented a large part of the total decline in spending in some recessions, most notably those of 1973–1975 and 1981–1982. The sense in which inventory investment follows its own rules is that it often displays large fluctuations that aren't associated with business cycle peaks and troughs, as during the expansion that began in 1982.

Government purchases of goods and services generally are procyclical (see Fig. 4.9 for annual data that captures the main movements). Rapid military buildups, as during World War II, the Korean War, and the Vietnam War, are usually associated with economic expansions.

Employment and Unemployment

Business cycles are strongly felt in the labor market. In a recession, employment grows slowly or falls, many workers are laid off, and jobs become more difficult to find.

Figure 9.5 shows the number of civilians employed in the United States since 1960. Employment is clearly procyclical, as more people have jobs in booms than in recessions, and also is coincident with the cycle.

Figure 9.6 shows the civilian unemployment rate, which is the fraction of the civilian labor force (the number of people who are available for work and want to work) that is unemployed. The civilian unemployment rate is strongly countercyclical, rising sharply in contractions but falling more slowly in expansions. Although the BEA has studied the timing of unemployment,

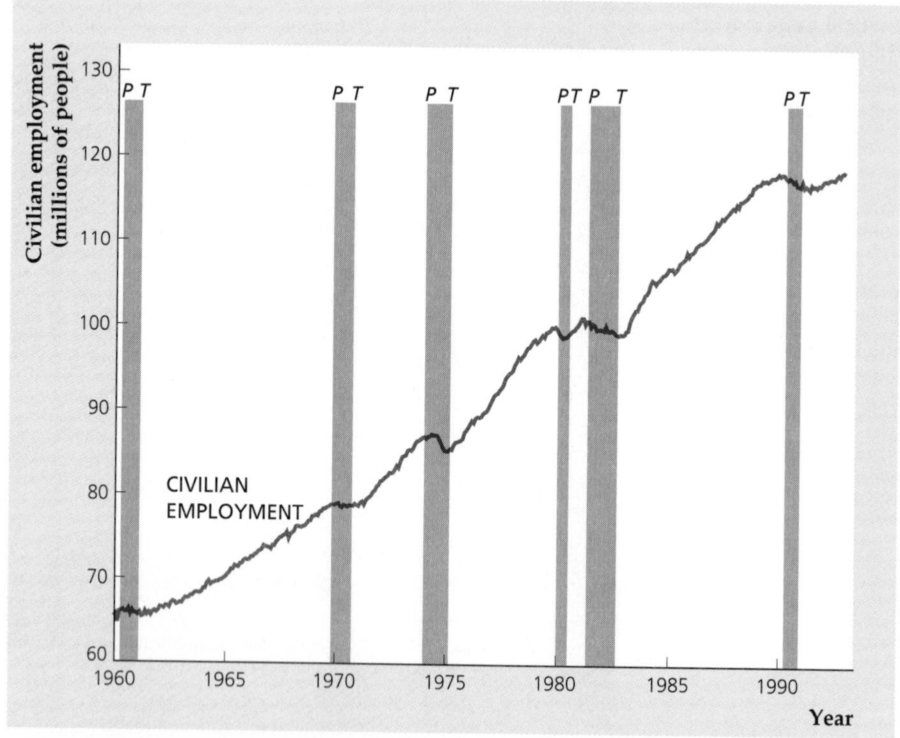

Figure 9.5
Cyclical behavior of civilian employment
Civilian employment is procyclical and coincident with the business cycle.

Source: *Business Conditions Digest* and *Survey of Current Business*, civilian employment.

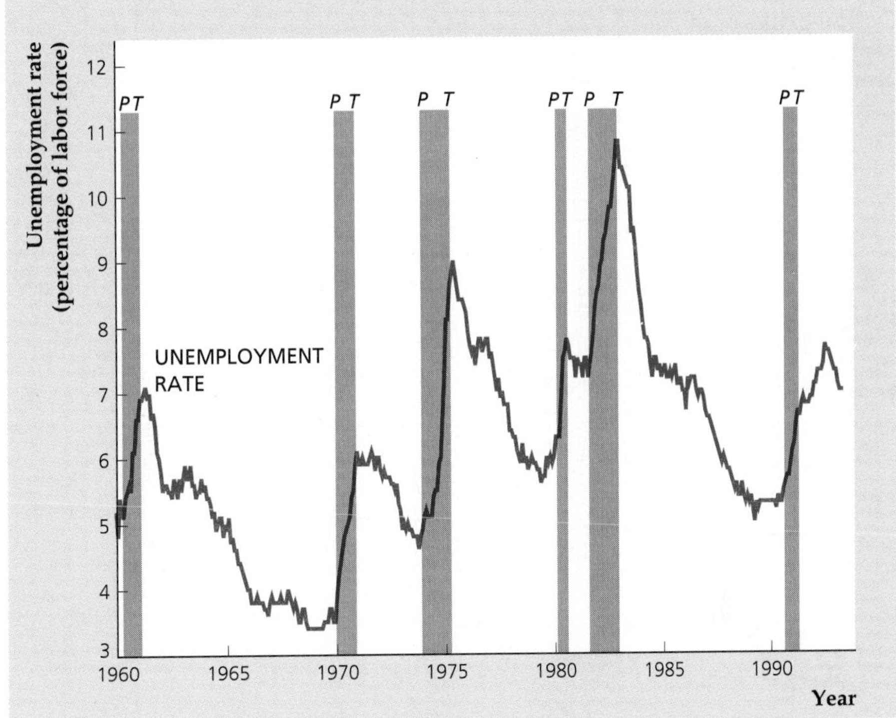

Figure 9.6
Cyclical behavior of the unemployment rate
The unemployment rate is countercyclical and very sensitive to the business cycle. Its timing pattern relative to the cycle is unclassified, meaning that it has no definite tendency to lead, be coincident, or lag.

Source: *Business Conditions Digest* and *Survey of Current Business*, civilian unemployment rate.

Summary table 10 shows that the timing of this variable is officially "unclassified," owing to the absence of a clear pattern in the data. Figure 9.6 illustrates a somewhat unusual aspect of the 1990–1991 recession: The unemployment rate continued to climb for several months after the recession's trough was reached.

Average Labor Productivity and the Real Wage

Two other significant labor market variables are average labor productivity and the real wage. As discussed in Chapter 1, average labor productivity is output per unit of labor input. Figure 9.7, on the next page, shows average labor productivity measured as total real output in the U.S. economy (excluding farms) divided by the total number of hours worked to produce that output. Average labor productivity tends to be procyclical: In booms workers produce more output during each hour of work than they do in recessions.[11] Although the BEA doesn't officially designate the timing of this variable, studies show that average labor productivity tends to lead the business cycle.[12]

Recall from Chapter 3 that the real wage is the compensation received by workers per unit of time (such as an hour or a week) measured in real, or purchasing-power, terms. The real wage is an especially important variable in the

11. The Application in Chapter 3, "The Production Function of the U.S. Economy and U.S. Productivity Growth," p. 65, made the point that total factor productivity A also tends to be procyclical.
12. See Robert J. Gordon, "The 'End of Expansion' Phenomenon in Short-Run Productivity Behavior," *Brookings Papers on Economic Activity*, 1979:2, pp. 447–461.

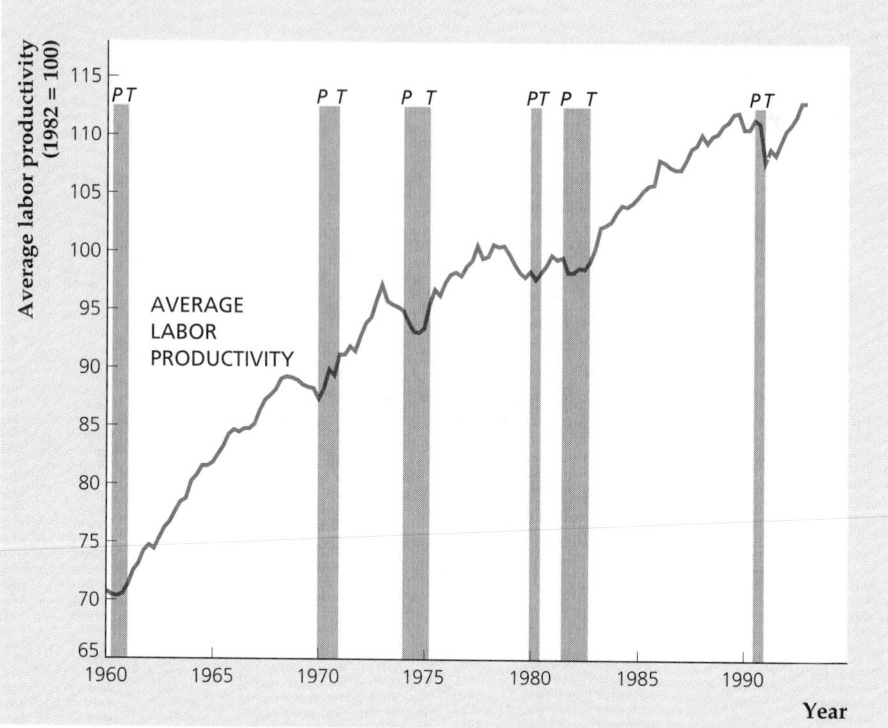

Figure 9.7
Cyclical behavior of average labor productivity
Average labor productivity, measured as real output per employee hour in the nonfarm business sector, is procyclical and leading.

Source: *Business Conditions Digest* and *Survey of Current Business,* index of output per hour, all persons, nonfarm business sector.

study of business cycles because it is one of the main determinants of the amount of labor supplied by workers and demanded by firms.

Generally speaking, two types of studies attempt to characterize the cyclical behavior of real wages. One examines the average real wage for the economy as a whole. In these studies the wage usually is measured as the total real compensation paid to all workers in the economy divided by the total number of hours worked. As Fig. 9.8 suggests, the average real wage measured in this way is mildly procyclical. (The most striking feature of Fig. 9.8 is how much the growth of the average real wage has slowed since about 1973.)

However, some economists point out that the economywide average real wage may not be a good indicator of the real wage received by the typical worker. An example illustrates the potential problem. Imagine that an economy consisted of two employed workers, each earning \$9 per hour, and one unemployed worker. Clearly, the average wage paid to workers in this economy is \$9 per hour. Now suppose that this economy expands, with the result that the two employed workers get raises to \$10 per hour and that the previously unemployed worker finds a job that pays \$7 per hour. If all three workers work the same number of hours, the economywide average wage is the same as before: (\$10 + \$10 + \$7)/3, or \$9 per hour. Thus, although all three workers are earning more in the expansion than they did before, the economywide average wage hasn't changed. The reason is that the increase in the employed individuals' wages has been offset by a change in the composition of the work force, which now includes a relatively low-wage worker who wasn't working before the expansion.

To eliminate effects of changing labor force composition on the measured real wage, the second type of study attempts to measure the cyclical behavior

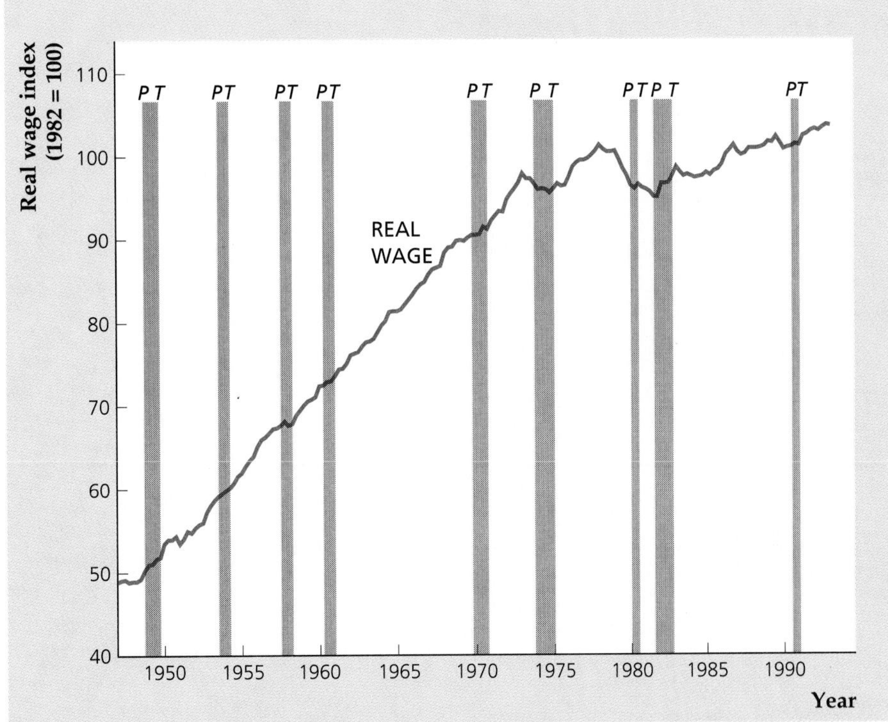

Figure 9.8
Cyclical behavior of the real wage
The economywide average real wage is mildly procyclical. Note how sharply real wage growth has slowed since 1973.

Source: *Business Conditions Digest* and *Survey of Current Business,* average hourly compensation, all employees, nonfarm business sector.

of the real wages of specific individual workers. Unfortunately, this type of study suffers from a lack of good data on individual wages and from a number of technical statistical problems. Because of these problems, results range from the finding that real wages are acyclical to the finding that they are highly procyclical. However, several recent studies of individual wages support the finding of the aggregate studies that the real wage is mildly procyclical.[13]

Overall, most of the evidence points to the conclusion that real wages are mildly procyclical, but the range of results from the studies of individuals' wages suggests that this conclusion isn't definite.

Money Growth and Inflation

Another variable whose cyclical behavior is somewhat controversial is the money supply. Figure 9.9, on page 311, shows the behavior since 1960 of the growth in the M2 measure of the money supply.[14] Note that (nominal) money growth fluctuates a great deal and doesn't always display an obvious cyclical pattern. However, as Fig. 9.9 shows, money growth often falls sharply at or

13. See, for example, Michael Keane, Robert Moffitt, and David Runkle, "Real Wages Over the Business Cycle: Estimating the Impact of Heterogeneity with Micro Data," *Journal of Political Economy,* December 1988, pp. 1232–1266. Stronger procyclicality for the real wage is claimed by Gary Solon, Robert Barsky, and Jonathan Parker, "Measuring the Cyclicality of Real Wages: How Important Is Composition Bias?" NBER working paper no. 4202, October 1992.

14. See Table 7.1 for a definition of M2. To reduce the effect of high month-to-month volatility in money growth, Fig. 9.9 presents a six-month moving average of money growth rates; that is, the reported growth rate in each month is actually the average of the growth rate in the current month and in the previous five months.

BOX 9.2

The Seasonal Cycle and the Business Cycle

Did you know that the United States has a large economic boom, followed by a deep recession, every year? The boom always occurs in the fourth quarter of the year (October through December). During this quarter output is 5% higher than in the third quarter (July–September) and about 8% higher than in the following first quarter (January–March). Fortunately, the first-quarter recession is always a short one, with output rising by almost 4% in the second quarter (April–June). This regular seasonal pattern, known as the seasonal cycle, actually accounts for more than 85% of the total fluctuation in the growth rate of real output!

Why don't large seasonal fluctuations appear in Figs. 9.2–9.12? Normally, macroeconomic data are seasonally adjusted, meaning that regularly recurring seasonal fluctuations are removed from the data. Seasonal adjustment allows users of economic data to ignore seasonal changes and focus on business cycle fluctuations and longer-term movements in the data. However, Robert Barsky of the University of Michigan and Jeffrey Miron of Boston University* argue that the practice of seasonally adjusting macroeconomic data may throw away information that could help economists better understand the business cycle. Using data that hadn't been seasonally adjusted, Barsky and Miron determined that the comovements of variables over the seasonal cycle are similar to their comovements over the business cycle. Specifically, they obtained the following results:

1. Of the types of expenditure, expenditures on durable goods vary most over the seasonal cycle and expenditures on services vary least.
2. Government spending is seasonally procyclical.
3. Employment is seasonally procyclical, and the unemployment rate is seasonally countercyclical.
4. Average labor productivity is seasonally procyclical, and the real wage hardly varies over the seasonal cycle.
5. The nominal money stock is seasonally procyclical.

Each observation appears to be true for both the business cycle and the seasonal cycle (although, as discussed, there is some controversy about the cyclical behavior of the real wage). However, the seasonal fluctuations of inventory investment, the price level, and the nominal interest rate are much smaller than their fluctuations over the business cycle.

The seasonal cycle illustrates three potential sources of aggregate economic fluctuations: (1) changes in consumer demand, as at Christmastime; (2) changes in productivity, as when construction workers become less productive because of winter weather in the first quarter; and (3) changes in labor supply, as when people take summer vacations in the third quarter. Each of these three sources of fluctuation may also contribute to the business cycle.

As we discuss in Chapter 11, classical economists believe that business cycles generally represent the economy's best response to changes in the economic environment, a response that macroeconomic policy need not try to eliminate. Although it doesn't necessarily confirm this view, the seasonal cycle shows that large economic fluctuations may be desirable responses to various factors (Christmas, the weather) and do not need to be offset by government policy.

* "The Seasonal and the Business Cycle," *Journal of Political Economy,* June 1989, pp. 503–534.

just before the onset of a recession. Moreover, many statistical and historical studies—including a classic work by Milton Friedman and Anna J. Schwartz[15] that used data back to 1867—demonstrate that money growth is procyclical and leads the cycle.

The cyclical behavior of inflation presents a somewhat clearer picture (Fig. 9.10 on the next page). Inflation is procyclical but with some lag. Inflation

15. *A Monetary History of the United States, 1867–1960,* Princeton, N.J.: Princeton University Press for NBER, 1963. We discuss this study further in Chapter 11.

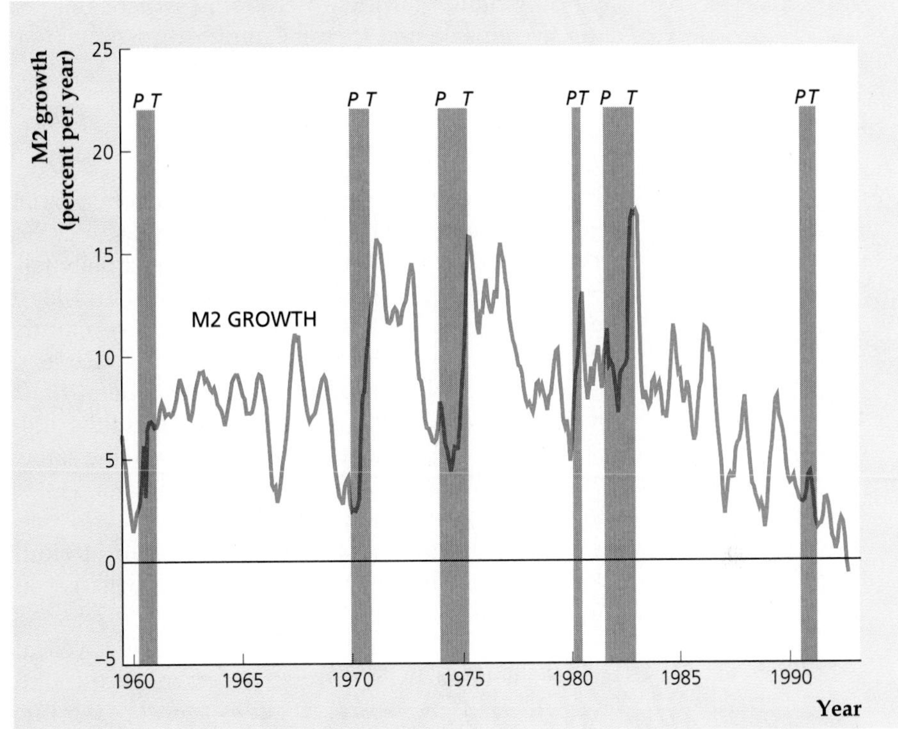

Figure 9.9
Cyclical behavior of nominal money growth
Nominal money growth, here measured as the six-month moving average of monthly growth rates in M2 (expressed in annual rates), is volatile. However, the figure shows that money growth often falls at or just before a cyclical peak. Statistical and historical studies suggest that, generally, money growth is procyclical and leading.

Source: Federal Reserve Board, money stock revisions, release H.6.

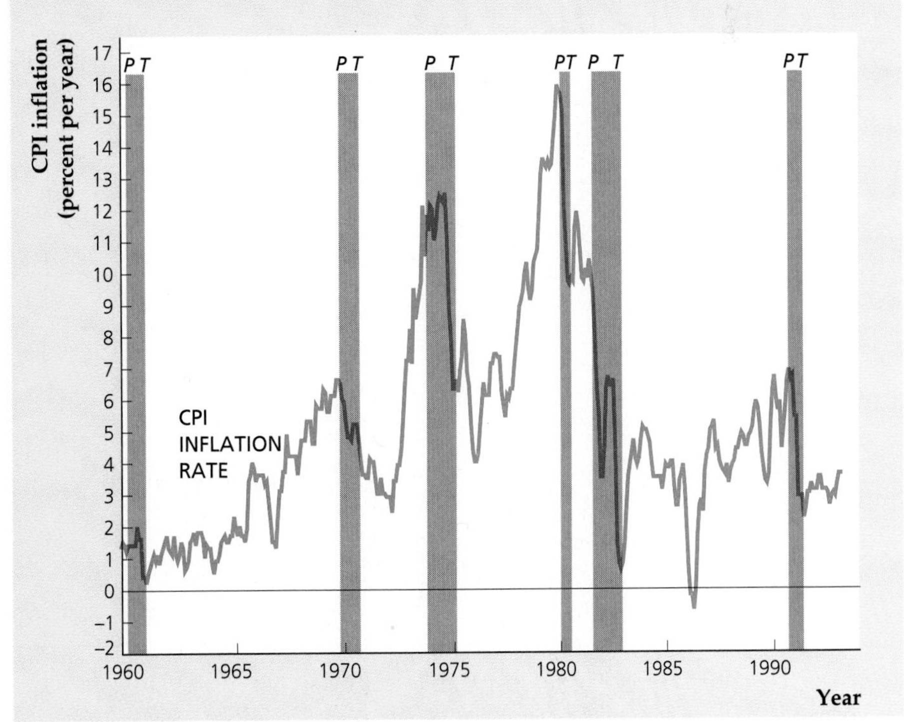

Figure 9.10
Cyclical behavior of inflation
Inflation, here measured as the six-month moving average of monthly growth rates of the CPI (expressed in annual rates), is procyclical and lags the business cycle. A typical pattern is for inflation to build up during the expansion and then to fall after the cyclical peak.

Source: *Business Conditions Digest* and *Survey of Current Business,* consumer price index for all urban consumers.

typically builds during an economic expansion, peaks slightly after the business cycle peak, and then falls until some time after the business cycle trough is reached.

Financial Variables

Financial variables are another class of economic variables that are sensitive to the cycle. For example, stock prices are generally procyclical (stock prices rise in good economic times) and leading (stock prices usually fall in advance of a recession).

Nominal interest rates are procyclical and lagging. The nominal interest rate shown in Fig. 9.11 is the rate on three-month Treasury bills. However, other interest rates examined by the BEA, such as the prime rate (charged by banks to their best customers) and the Federal funds rate (the interest rate on overnight loans made from one bank to another) also are procyclical and lagging. Note that nominal interest rates have the same general cyclical pattern as inflation; Chapter 7 discussed why nominal interest rates tend to move up and down with the inflation rate.

The real interest rate doesn't have an obvious cyclical pattern. For instance, the real interest rate actually was negative during the 1973–1975 recession but was very high during the 1981–1982 recession. (Annual values of the real interest rate are shown in Fig. 2.4.) The acyclicality of the real interest rate doesn't necessarily mean its movements are unimportant over the business cycle. Instead, the lack of a stable cyclical pattern may reflect the facts that individual business cycles have different causes and that these different sources of cycles have different effects on the real interest rate.

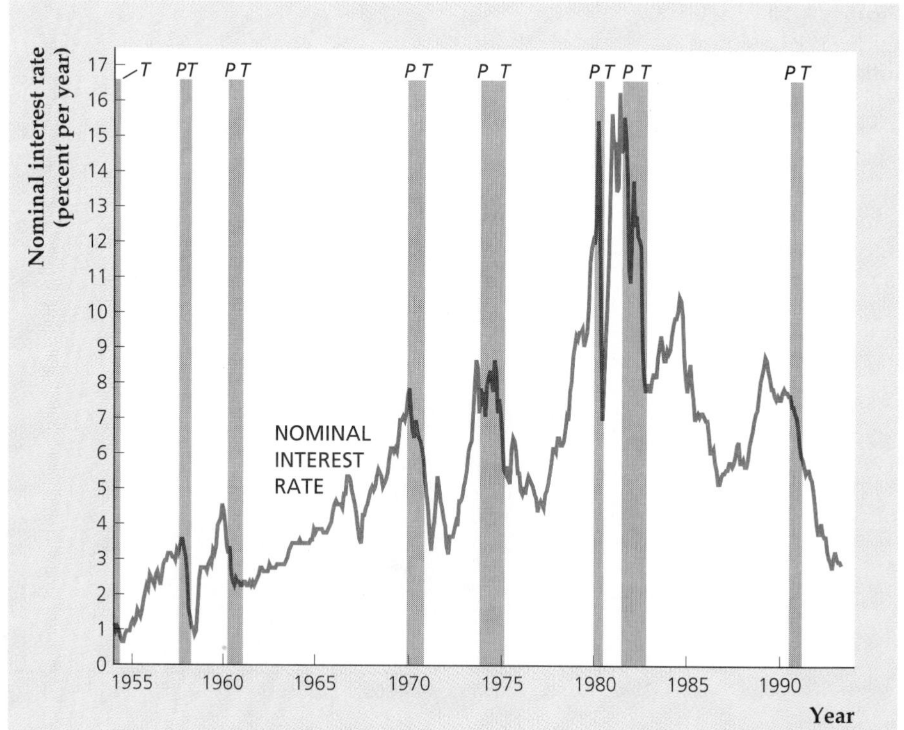

Figure 9.11
Cyclical behavior of the nominal interest rate
The nominal interest rate, measured here as the interest rate on three-month Treasury bills, is procyclical and lagging.

Source: *Business Conditions Digest* and *Survey of Current Business,* discount rate on new issues of 91-day Treasury bills.

International Aspects of the Business Cycle

So far we have concentrated on business cycles in the United States. However, business cycles are by no means unique to the United States, having been regularly observed in all industrialized market economies. In most cases the cyclical behavior of key economic variables in these other economies is similar to that described for the United States.

The business cycle is an international phenomenon in another sense: Frequently, the major industrial economies undergo recessions and expansions at about the same time, suggesting that they share a common cycle. Figure 9.12 illustrates this common cycle by showing the index of industrial production since 1960 for each of six major industrial countries. Note in particular the effects of worldwide recessions in about 1975, 1982, and 1991. Figure 9.12 also shows that each economy experiences many small fluctuations not shared by the others.

Looking Ahead

The business cycle facts presented in this chapter would be useful even if we took them no further: For example, being familiar with the typical cyclical patterns of key macroeconomic variables helps forecasters project the course of the economy, businesspeople make their investment and hiring plans, and holders of wealth choose portfolios that provide the right combinations of risk and return. However, macroeconomists generally are interested not only in *what* happens during business cycles but also *why* it happens. Thus, using

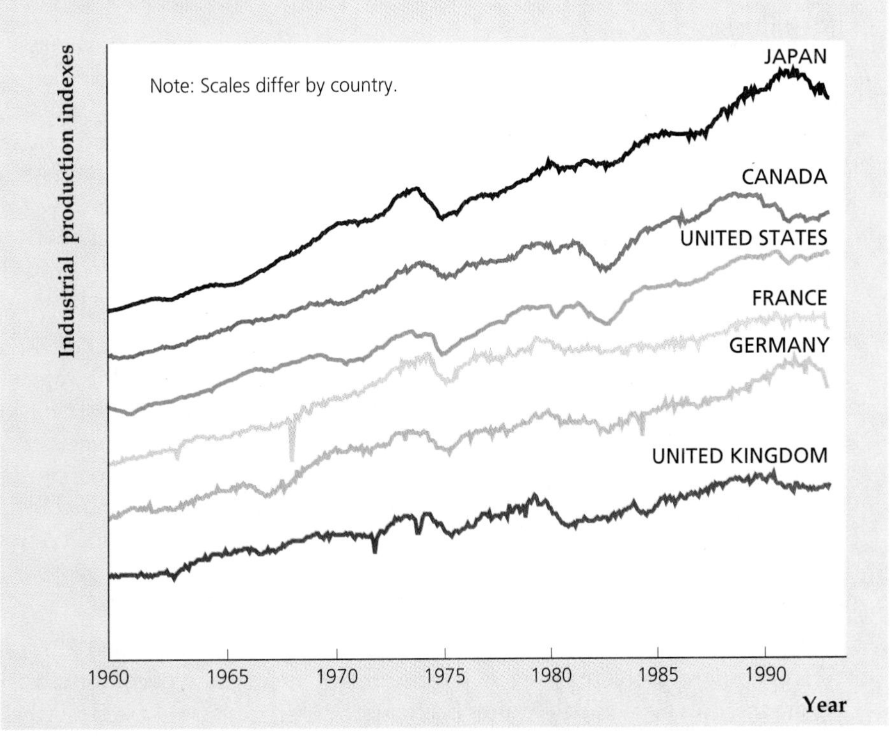

Figure 9.12
Industrial production indexes in six major countries
The worldwide effect of business cycles is reflected in the similarity of the behavior of industrial production in each of the six countries shown. But individual countries also have fluctuations not shared with other countries.
Note: The scales for the industrial production indexes differ by country; for example, the figure does not imply that Japan's total industrial production is the highest of the six countries.

Source: *Business Conditions Digest* and *Survey of Current Business,* industrial production indexes.

these business cycle facts as background, in the rest of Part III we study some alternative explanations of cyclical fluctuations and policy recommendations based on those explanations.

As a general framework for our analysis of the business cycle, in Chapter 10 we present a macroeconomic model called the *IS–LM* model. It combines the labor market (from Chapter 3), the goods market (from Chapter 4) and the asset market (from Chapter 7). Depending on the assumption of how quickly prices and wages adjust to balance quantities supplied and demanded in all markets, we can use the *IS–LM* model to study either classical (Chapter 11) or Keynesian (Chapter 12) theories of the business cycle. Ultimately, these different approaches to macroeconomics should be judged on how well they explain the business cycle facts presented in this chapter.

CHAPTER SUMMARY

1. A business cycle consists of a period of declining aggregate economic activity (a contraction or recession) followed by a period of rising economic activity (an expansion or a boom). The low point of the contraction is called the trough, and the high point of the expansion is called the peak. Business cycles have been observed in market economies since the beginning of industrialization.

2. Many economic variables have regular and predictable patterns of behavior over the course of the cycle. That tendency is called comovement. We refer to the typical cyclical patterns of key macroeconomic variables as the "business cycle facts."

3. The fluctuations in aggregate economic activity that constitute business cycles are recurrent, having been observed again and again in industrialized market economies. However, they aren't periodic, in that they don't occur at regular or predictable intervals. Business cycle fluctuations also are persistent, which means that once a recession or expansion begins, it usually lasts for a while.

4. Economists believe that the U.S. economy before 1929 had longer recessions and more cyclical volatility than the post–World War II economy. However, data problems prevent precise measurements of how much more cyclical the pre–World War I economy was. The Great Depression that began in 1929 and didn't end until the onset of World War II was the most severe cyclical decline in U.S. history. Moderation of the business cycle after World War II led to premature pronouncements that the cycle was "dead." However, the U.S. economy suffered severe recessions in 1973–1975 and 1981–1982.

5. The direction of a variable relative to the business cycle can be procyclical, countercyclical, or acyclical. A procyclical variable moves in the same direction as aggregate economic activity, rising in booms and falling in recessions. A countercyclical variable moves oppositely to aggregate economic activity, falling in booms and rising in recessions. An acyclical variable has no clear cyclical pattern.

6. The timing of a variable relative to the business cycle may be coincident, leading, or lagging. A coincident variable's peaks and troughs occur at about the same time as peaks and troughs in aggregate economic activity. Peaks and troughs in a leading variable come before, and peaks and troughs in a lagging variable come after, the corresponding peaks and troughs in aggregate economic activity.

7. The cyclical direction and timing of major macroeconomic variables—the business cycle facts—are described in Summary table 10. In

brief, production, consumption, and investment are procyclical and coincident. Investment is much more volatile over the business cycle than consumption is. Employment is procyclical, but the unemployment rate is countercyclical. Average labor productivity and the real wage are procyclical, although according to most studies the real wage is only mildly so. Money and stock prices are procyclical and lead the cycle. Inflation and nominal interest rates are procyclical and lagging. The real interest rate is acyclical.

Key Terms

acyclical, p. 300
boom, p. 291
business cycle, p. 291
business cycle chronology, p. 290
coincident variable, p. 300
comovement, p. 293
contraction, p. 291
countercyclical, p. 300
depression, p. 291
expansion, p. 291
index of leading indicators, p. 300
lagging variable, p. 300
leading variable, p. 300
peak, p. 291
persistence, p. 293
procyclical, p. 300
recession, p. 291
trough, p. 291
turning points, p. 291

Review Questions

1. Draw a diagram showing the phases and turning points of a business cycle. Using the diagram, illustrate the concepts of recurrence and persistence.
2. What is *comovement*? How is comovement related to the business cycle facts presented in this chapter?
3. What is the evidence for the view that the U.S. business cycle has become less severe over time? Why is the question of whether the cycle has moderated over time an important one?
4. What terms are used to describe the way a variable moves when economic activity is rising or falling? What terms are used to describe the timing of cyclical changes in economic variables?
5. If you knew that the economy was falling into a recession, what would you expect to happen to production during the next few quarters? To investment? To average labor productivity? To the real wage? To the unemployment rate?
6. How is the fact that some economic variables are known to lead the cycle used in macroeconomic forecasting?

Analytical Problems

1. Consumer expenditures on durable goods such as cars and furniture, as well as purchases of new houses, fall much more than expenditures on nondurable goods and services during recessions. Why do you think that is?
2. Output, total hours worked, and average labor productivity all are procyclical.
   a. Which variable, output or total hours worked, increases by a larger percentage in expansions and falls by a larger percentage in recessions? (*Hint:* Average labor productivity = output ÷ total hours worked so that the percentage change in average labor productivity equals the percentage change in output minus the percentage change in total hours worked.)
   b. How is the procyclical behavior of average labor productivity related to Okun's Law, discussed in Chapter 3?

CHAPTER 10

THE *IS-LM* MODEL: A GENERAL FRAMEWORK FOR MACROECONOMIC ANALYSIS

Chapter 9 *described* business cycles by presenting the business cycle facts. This and the following two chapters *explain* business cycles and how policymakers should respond to them. First, we must develop a macroeconomic model that we can use to analyze cyclical fluctuations and the effects of policy changes on the economy. By examining the labor market in Chapter 3, the goods market in Chapter 4, and the asset market in Chapter 7, we already have identified the three components of a complete macroeconomic model. Now we put these three components together into a single framework that allows us to analyze them simultaneously. This chapter, then, consolidates our previous analyses to provide the theoretical structure for the rest of the book.

The macroeconomic model developed in this chapter is the *IS–LM* model. (As we discuss later, this name originates in two of its basic equilibrium conditions: that investment, *I*, must equal saving, *S*, and that money demanded, *L*, must equal money supplied, *M*.) The *IS–LM* model was developed in 1937 by Nobel laureate Sir John Hicks,[1] who intended it as a graphical representation of the ideas presented by Keynes in his famous 1936 book, *The General Theory of Employment, Interest, and Money.* Reflecting Keynes's belief that wages and prices don't adjust quickly to clear markets (see Section 1.3), in his original *IS–LM* model Hicks assumed that the price level was fixed, at least temporarily. Since Hicks, several generations of economists have worked to refine the *IS–LM* model, and it has been widely applied in analyses of cyclical fluctuations and macroeconomic policy, and in forecasting.

Because of its origins, the *IS–LM* model is commonly identified with the Keynesian approach to business cycle analysis. Classical economists—who

1. Hicks outlined the *IS–LM* framework in an article entitled "Mr. Keynes and the Classics: A Suggested Interpretation," *Econometrica,* April 1937, pp. 137–159.

believe that wages and prices move rapidly to clear markets—would reject Hicks's *IS–LM* model because of his assumption that the price level is fixed. However, the conventional *IS–LM* model may be easily adapted to allow for rapidly adjusting wages and prices. Thus the *IS–LM* framework, although originally developed by Keynesians, also may be used to present and discuss the classical approach to business cycle analysis.

Using the *IS–LM* model as a framework for both classical and Keynesian analyses has several practical benefits: First, using a single model for both classical and Keynesian analyses avoids the need to learn two different models. Second, utilizing a single framework emphasizes the large areas of agreement between the Keynesian and classical approaches while showing clearly how the two approaches differ. Moreover, because versions of the *IS–LM* model (and its concepts and terminology) are so often applied in analyses of the economy and macroeconomic policy, studying this framework will help you understand and participate more fully in current economic debates.

We use a graphical approach to develop the *IS–LM* model. Appendix 10.A, as extended by appendixes at the ends of Chapters 11 and 12, presents the identical analysis in algebraic form. If you have difficulty understanding why the curves used in the graphical analysis have the slopes they do or why they shift, you may find the algebra in the appendix helpful.

To keep things as simple as possible, in this chapter we assume that the economy is closed. In Chapter 14 we show how to extend the *IS–LM* model to allow for a foreign sector.

10.1 THE *FE* LINE: EQUILIBRIUM IN THE LABOR MARKET

Previous chapters discussed the three main markets of the economy: the labor market, the goods market, and the asset market. We also identified some of the links among these markets, but now we want to be more precise about how they fit into a complete macroeconomic system.

Let's turn first to the labor market and recall from Chapter 3 the concepts of the full-employment level of employment and full-employment output. The *full-employment level of employment* $\bar{N}$ is the equilibrium level of employment reached after wages and prices have fully adjusted so that the quantity of labor supplied equals the quantity of labor demanded. *Full-employment output* $\bar{Y}$ is the amount of output produced when employment is at its full-employment level, given the current level of the capital stock and the production function. Algebraically, full-employment output $\bar{Y}$ equals $AF(K, \bar{N})$, where K is the capital stock, A is productivity, and F is the production function (see Eq. 3.4).

Our ultimate goal is a diagram that has the real interest rate on the vertical axis and output on the horizontal axis. In such a diagram equilibrium in the labor market is represented by the **full-employment line,** or *FE*, in Fig. 10.1 on the next page. The *FE* line is vertical at $Y = \bar{Y}$ because, when the labor market is in equilibrium, output equals its full-employment level, regardless of the interest rate.[2]

2. The real interest rate affects investment and thus the amount of capital that firms will have in the future, but it doesn't affect the current capital stock, and hence does not affect current output.

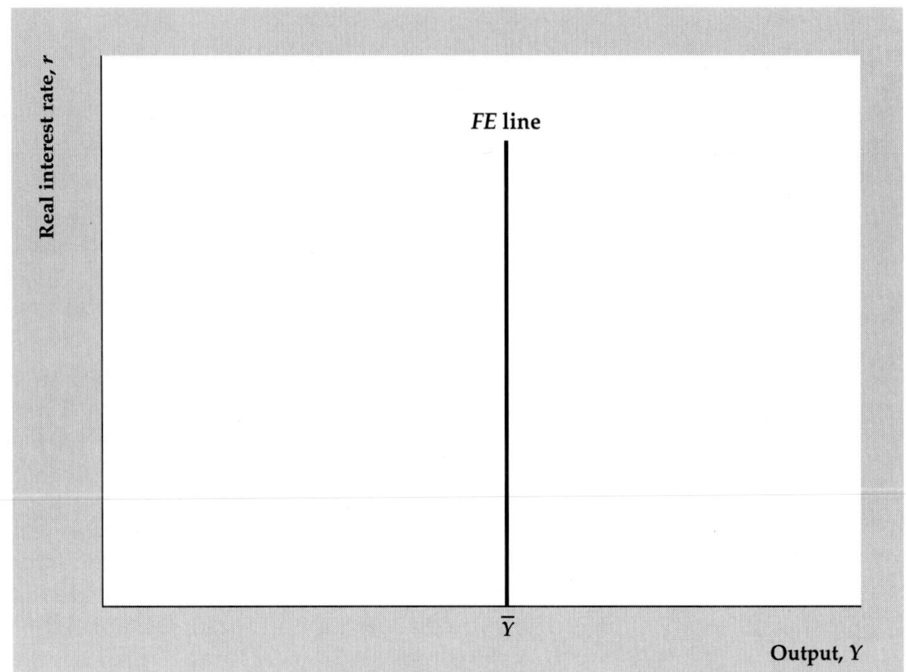

Figure 10.1
The *FE* line
The full-employment (*FE*) line represents labor market equilibrium. When the labor market is in equilibrium, employment equals its full-employment level $\bar{N}$ and output equals its full-employment level $\bar{Y}$, regardless of the value of the real interest rate. Thus the *FE* line is vertical at $Y = \bar{Y}$.

Factors that Shift the *FE* Line

The full-employment level of output is determined by the current levels of labor, capital, and productivity. Any change that affects the full-employment level of output $\bar{Y}$ will cause the *FE* line to shift. Recall that full-employment output $\bar{Y}$ increases—and thus the *FE* line shifts to the right—when the labor supply increases (which raises equilibrium employment $\bar{N}$) or when there is a beneficial supply shock. Similarly, a drop in the labor supply or an adverse supply shock lowers full-employment output $\bar{Y}$ and shifts the *FE* line to the left. Summary table 11 lists the factors that shift the *FE* line.

10.2 THE *IS* CURVE: EQUILIBRIUM IN THE GOODS MARKET

The second of the three markets in our model is the goods market. Recall from Chapter 4 that the goods market is in equilibrium when desired investment and desired national saving are equal or, equivalently, when the aggregate quantity of goods supplied equals the aggregate quantity of goods demanded. In Chapter 4 we demonstrated that adjustments in the real interest rate help bring about equilibrium in the goods market.

In a diagram with the real interest rate on the vertical axis and real output on the horizontal axis, equilibrium in the goods market is described by a curve called the *IS* curve. Specifically, for any level of output (or income) Y, the ***IS* curve** shows the real interest rate r for which the goods market is in equilibrium. The *IS* curve is so named because at all points on the curve desired investment, I, equals desired national saving, S.

SUMMARY 11

Factors that Shift the Full-Employment (*FE*) Line

A(n)	Shifts the *FE* Line	Reason
Beneficial supply shock	Right	1. More output can be produced for the same amount of capital and labor. 2. If the *MPN* rises, labor demand increases and raises employment. Full-employment output increases for both reasons.
Increase in labor supply	Right	Equilibrium employment rises, raising full-employment output.
Increase in the capital stock	Right	More output can be produced with the same amount of labor. In addition, increased capital may increase the *MPN*, which increases labor demand and equilibrium employment.

Figure 10.2, on the next page, shows the derivation of the *IS* curve from the saving–investment diagram introduced in Chapter 4 and used extensively in Chapters 4 and 5 (see Key Diagram 3, p. 140). Figure 10.2(a) shows the saving–investment diagram drawn for two randomly chosen levels of output, 4000 and 5000. Corresponding to each level is a saving curve, with the value of output indicated in parentheses next to it. Each saving curve slopes upward because an increase in the real interest rate causes households to increase their desired level of saving. An increase in current output (income) leads to more desired saving at any real interest rate, so the saving curve S for $Y = 5000$ lies to the right of the saving curve S for $Y = 4000$.

Also shown in Fig. 10.2(a) is an investment curve. Recall from Chapter 4 that the investment curve slopes downward because an increase in the real interest rate increases the user cost of capital, which reduces the desired capital stock and hence desired investment. Desired investment isn't affected by current output, so the investment curve is the same whether $Y = 4000$ or $Y = 5000$.

Each level of output implies a different market-clearing real interest rate. When output is 4000, goods market equilibrium is at point D and the market-clearing real interest rate is 7%. When output is 5000, goods market equilibrium occurs at point F and the market-clearing real interest rate is 5%.

Figure 10.2(b) shows the *IS* curve for this economy, with output on the horizontal axis and the real interest rate on the vertical axis. For any level of output, the *IS* curve shows the real interest rate that clears the goods market. Thus $Y = 4000$ and $r = 7\%$ at point D on the *IS* curve. (Note that point D in Fig. 10.2b corresponds to point D in Fig. 10.2a.) Similarly, when output is 5000, the real interest rate that clears the goods market is 5%. This combination of output and the real interest rate occurs at point F on the *IS* curve in Fig. 10.2(b); it corresponds to point F in Fig. 10.2(a). In general, because a rise in output increases national desired saving, thereby reducing the real interest rate that clears the goods market, the *IS* curve slopes downward.

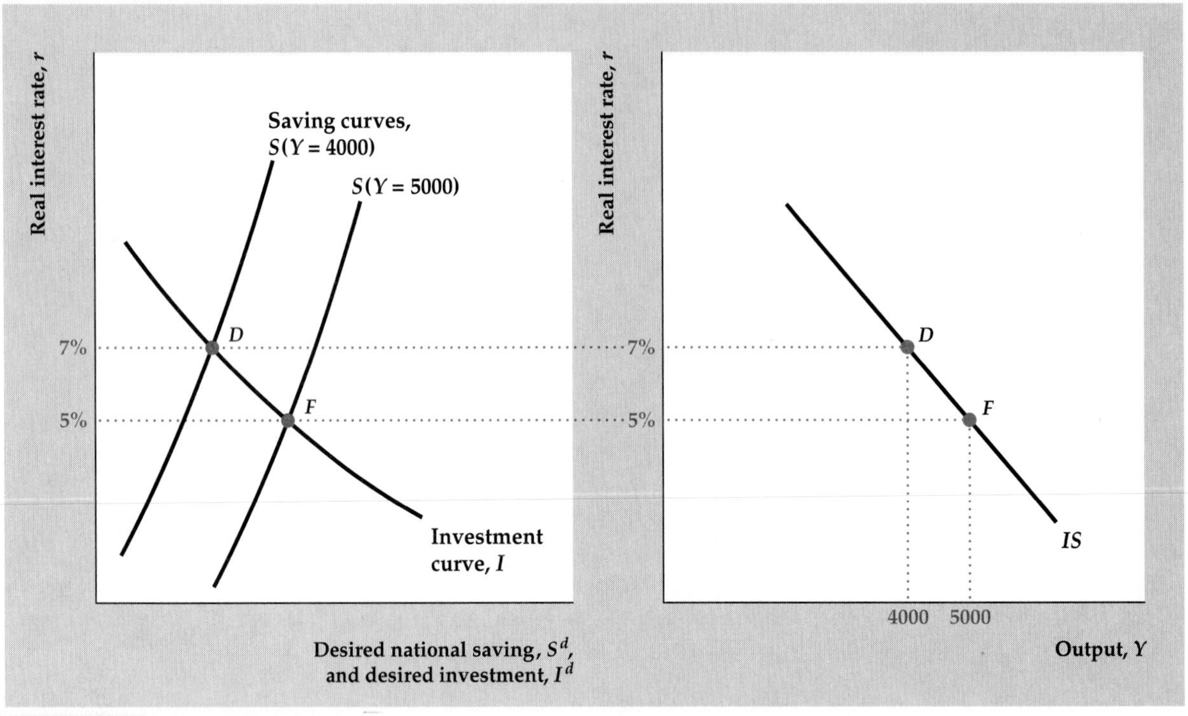

(a)

(b)

Figure 10.2
Deriving the *IS* curve
(a) The graph shows the goods market equilibrium for two different levels of output: 4000 and 5000 (the output corresponding to each saving curve is indicated in parentheses next to the curve). Higher levels of output (income) increase desired national saving and shift the saving curve to the right. When output is 4000, the real interest rate that clears the goods market is 7% (point *D*). When output is 5000, the market-clearing interest rate is 5% (point *F*).

(b) For each level of output the *IS* curve shows the corresponding real interest rate that clears the goods market. Thus each point on the *IS* curve corresponds to an equilibrium point in the goods market. As in (a), when output is 4000, the real interest rate that clears the goods market is 7% (point *D*); when output is 5000, the market-clearing interest rate is 5% (point *F*). Because higher output raises saving and leads to a lower market-clearing interest rate, the *IS* curve slopes downward.

The slope of the *IS* curve may also be interpreted in terms of the alternative (but equivalent) version of the goods market equilibrium condition, which states that in equilibrium the aggregate quantity of goods demanded must equal the aggregate quantity of goods supplied. To illustrate, suppose that the economy is initially at point *F* in Fig. 10.2(b). The aggregate quantities of goods supplied and demanded are equal at point *F*, because *F* lies on the *IS* curve, which means that the goods market is in equilibrium at that point.[3]

Now suppose that for some reason the real interest rate *r* rises from 5% to 7%. Recall from Chapter 4 that an increase in the real interest rate reduces both desired consumption C^d (because people desire to save more when the

3. We have just showed that desired national saving equals desired investment at point *F*, or $S^d = I^d$. Substituting the definition of desired national saving, $Y - C^d - G$, for S^d in the condition that desired national saving equals desired investment shows also that $Y = C^d + I^d + G$ at *F*.

real interest rate rises) and desired investment I^d, thereby reducing the aggregate quantity of goods demanded. If output Y remained at its initial level of 5000, the increase in the real interest rate would imply that more goods were being supplied than demanded. For the goods market to reach equilibrium at the higher real interest rate, the quantity of goods supplied has to fall. At point D in Fig. 10.2(b), output has fallen enough (from 5000 to 4000) that the quantities of goods supplied and demanded are equal, and the goods market has returned to equilibrium.[4] Again, higher real interest rates are associated with less output in goods market equilibrium, so the *IS* curve slopes downward.

Factors that Shift the *IS* Curve

For any level of output, the *IS* curve shows the real interest rate needed to clear the goods market. With output held constant, any economic disturbance or policy change that changes the value of the goods-market-clearing real interest rate will cause the *IS* curve to shift. More specifically, for constant output, *any change in the economy that reduces desired national saving relative to desired investment will increase the real interest rate that clears the goods market and thus shifts the IS curve up.* Similarly, for constant output, changes that increase desired saving relative to desired investment, thereby reducing the market-clearing real interest rate, shift the *IS* curve down. Factors that shift the *IS* curve are described in Summary table 12, on the next page.

We can use a change in current government purchases to illustrate *IS* curve shifts in general. The effects of a temporary increase in government purchases on the *IS* curve are shown in Fig. 10.3 on page 323. Figure 10.3(a) shows the saving–investment diagram, with an initial saving curve S^1 and an initial investment curve I. The S^1 curve represents saving when output (income) is fixed at $Y = 4500$. Figure 10.3(b) shows the initial *IS* curve, IS^1. The initial goods market equilibrium when output Y equals 4500 is represented by point E in both (a) and (b). At E, the initial market-clearing real interest rate is 6%.

Now suppose that the government increases its current purchases of goods, G. Desired investment at any level of the real interest rate isn't affected by the increase in government purchases, so the investment curve doesn't shift. However, as discussed in Chapter 4, a temporary increase in government purchases reduces desired national saving (see Summary table 5, p. 120), so the saving curve shifts to the left from S^1 to S^2 in Fig. 10.3(a). As a result of the reduction in desired national saving, the real interest rate that clears the goods market when output equals 4500 increases from 6% to 7% (point F in Fig. 10.3a).

The effect on the *IS* curve is shown in Fig. 10.3(b). With output constant at 4500, the real interest rate that clears the goods market increases from 6% to 7%, as shown by the shift from point E to point F. The new *IS* curve, IS^2,

---

4. Although a drop in output Y obviously reduces the quantity of goods supplied, it also reduces the quantity of goods demanded. The reason is that a drop in output is also a drop in income, which reduces desired consumption. However, although a drop in output of one dollar reduces the supply of output by one dollar, a drop in income of one dollar reduces desired consumption C^d by *less* than one dollar (that is, the marginal propensity to consume, defined in Chapter 4, is less than 1). Thus a drop in output Y reduces goods supplied more than goods demanded and therefore reduces the excess supply of goods.

SUMMARY 12

Factors that Shift the *IS* Curve

An Increase in	Shifts the *IS* Curve	Reason
Expected future output	Up	Desired saving falls (desired consumption rises), raising the real interest rate that clears the goods market.
Wealth	Up	Desired saving falls (desired consumption rises), raising the real interest rate that clears the goods market.
Government purchases, G	Up	Desired saving falls (demand for goods rises), raising the real interest rate that clears the goods market.
Taxes, T	No change or Down	No change, if consumers take into account an offsetting future tax cut and do not change consumption (Ricardian equivalence); down, if consumers don't take into account a future tax cut and reduce desired consumption, increasing desired national saving and lowering the real interest rate that clears the goods market.
Expected future marginal product of capital, MPK^f	Up	Desired investment increases, raising the real interest rate that clears the goods market.
Effective tax rate on capital	Down	Desired investment falls, lowering the real interest rate that clears the goods market.

passes through F and lies above and to the right of the initial *IS* curve, IS^1. Thus a temporary increase in government purchases shifts the *IS* curve up.

So far our discussion of *IS* curve shifts has focused on the goods market equilibrium condition that desired national saving must equal desired investment. However, factors that shift the *IS* curve may also be described in terms of the alternative (but equivalent) goods market equilibrium condition—that the aggregate quantities of goods demanded and supplied are equal. In particular, for a given level of output, *any change that increases the aggregate demand for goods shifts the IS curve up.*

This rule works because, for the initial level of output, an increase in the aggregate demand for goods causes the quantity of goods demanded to exceed

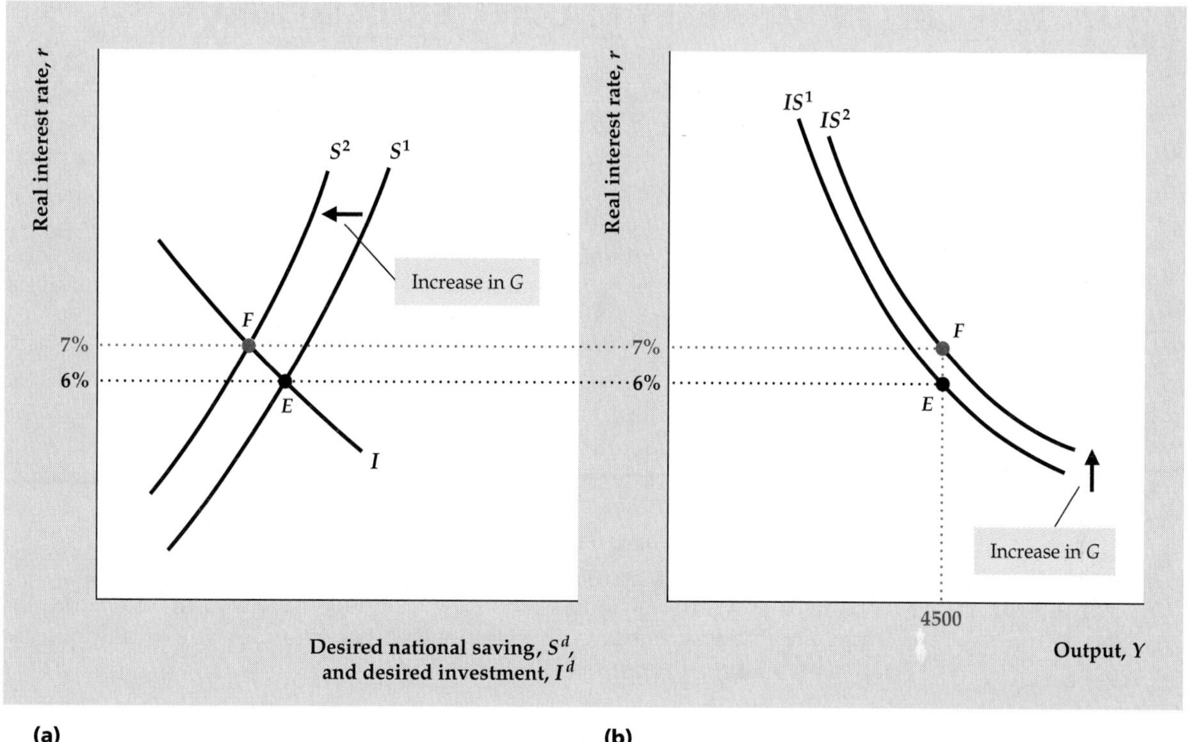

Figure 10.3
Effect on the *IS* curve of a temporary increase in government purchases
(a) The saving–investment diagram shows the effects of a temporary increase in government purchases, G, with output Y constant at 4500. The increase in G reduces desired national saving and shifts the saving curve to the left, from S^1 to S^2. The goods market equilibrium point moves from point E to point F, and the real interest rate rises from 6% to 7%.
(b) The increase in G raises the real interest rate that clears the goods market for any level of output. Thus the *IS* curve shifts upward from IS^1 to IS^2. In this example, with output held constant at 4500, an increase in government purchases raises the real interest rate that clears the goods market from 6% (point E) to 7% (point F).

the quantity supplied. Goods market equilibrium can be restored at the same level of output by an increase in the real interest rate, which reduces desired consumption C^d and desired investment I^d. For any level of output, an increase in aggregate demand for goods raises the real interest rate that clears the goods market, so we conclude that an increase in the aggregate demand for goods shifts the *IS* curve up.

To illustrate this alternative way of thinking about *IS* curve shifts, we again use the example of a temporary increase in government purchases. Note that an increase in government purchases, G, directly raises the demand for goods, $C^d + I^d + G$, leading to an excess demand for goods at the initial level of output. The excess demand for goods can be eliminated and goods market equilibrium at the initial level of output restored by an increase in the real interest rate, which reduces C^d and I^d. Because a higher real interest rate is required for goods market equilibrium when government purchases increase, an increase in G causes the *IS* curve to shift up.

10.3 THE *LM* CURVE: ASSET MARKET EQUILIBRIUM

The third and final market in our macroeconomic model is the asset market, presented in Chapter 7. The asset market is in equilibrium when the quantities of assets demanded by holders of wealth for their portfolios equal the supplies of those assets in the economy. In reality, there are many different assets, both real (houses, consumer durables, office buildings) and financial (checking accounts, government bonds). Recall, however, that we aggregated all assets into two categories—money and nonmonetary assets. We assumed that the nominal supply of money is M and that money pays a fixed nominal interest rate i^m. Similarly, we assumed that the nominal supply of nonmonetary assets is NM and that these assets pay a nominal interest rate i and (given expected inflation π^e) an expected real interest rate r.

With this aggregation assumption, we showed that the asset market equilibrium condition reduces to the requirement that the quantities of money supplied and demanded be equal. In this section we show that asset market equilibrium can be represented by the *LM* curve. However, in order to discuss how the asset market comes into equilibrium—a task that we didn't complete in Chapter 7—we first introduce an important relationship used every day by traders in financial markets: the relationship between the *price* of a nonmonetary asset and the *interest rate* on that asset.

The Interest Rate and the Price of a Nonmonetary Asset

The price of a nonmonetary asset, such as a government bond, is what a buyer has to pay for it. Its price is closely related to the interest rate that it pays (sometimes called its *yield*). To illustrate this relationship with an example, let's consider a bond that matures in one year. At maturity, we assume, the bondholder will redeem it and receive \$10,000; the bond doesn't pay any interest before it matures.[5] Suppose that this bond can now be purchased for \$9615. At this price, over the coming year the bond will increase in value by \$385 (\$10,000 – \$9615), or approximately 4% of its current price of \$9615. Therefore the nominal interest rate on the bond, or its yield, is 4% per year.

Now suppose that for some reason the current price of a \$10,000 bond that matures in one year drops to \$9524. The increase in the bond's value over the next year will be \$476 (\$10,000 – \$9524), or approximately 5% of the purchase price of \$9524. Therefore, when the current price of the bond falls to \$9524, the nominal interest rate on the bond increases to 5% per year. More generally, given the promised schedule of repayments of a bond or other nonmonetary asset, the higher the price of the asset, the lower is the nominal interest rate that the asset pays. Thus a media report that, in yesterday's trading, the bond market "strengthened" (bond prices rose), is equivalent to saying that nominal interest rates fell.

We have just indicated why the price of a nonmonetary asset and its nominal interest rate are negatively related to each other. For a given expected rate of inflation π^e, movements in the nominal interest rate are matched by equal movements in the real interest rate, so the price of a nonmonetary asset and its

5. A bond that doesn't pay any interest before maturity is called a *discount bond*.

real interest rate are also inversely related. This relationship is a key to deriving the *LM* curve and explaining how the asset market comes into equilibrium.

The Equality of Money Demanded and Money Supplied

To derive the *LM* curve, which represents asset market equilibrium, recall again that the asset market is in equilibrium only if the quantity of money demanded equals the currently available money supply. We depict the equality of money supplied and demanded using the *money supply–money demand diagram*, shown in Fig. 10.4(a). The real interest rate is on the vertical axis and money, measured in real terms, is on the horizontal axis.[6] The *MS* line shows

6. Asset market equilibrium may be expressed as either nominal money supplied equals nominal money demanded, or as real money supplied equals real money demanded. As in Chapter 7, we work with the condition expressed in real terms.

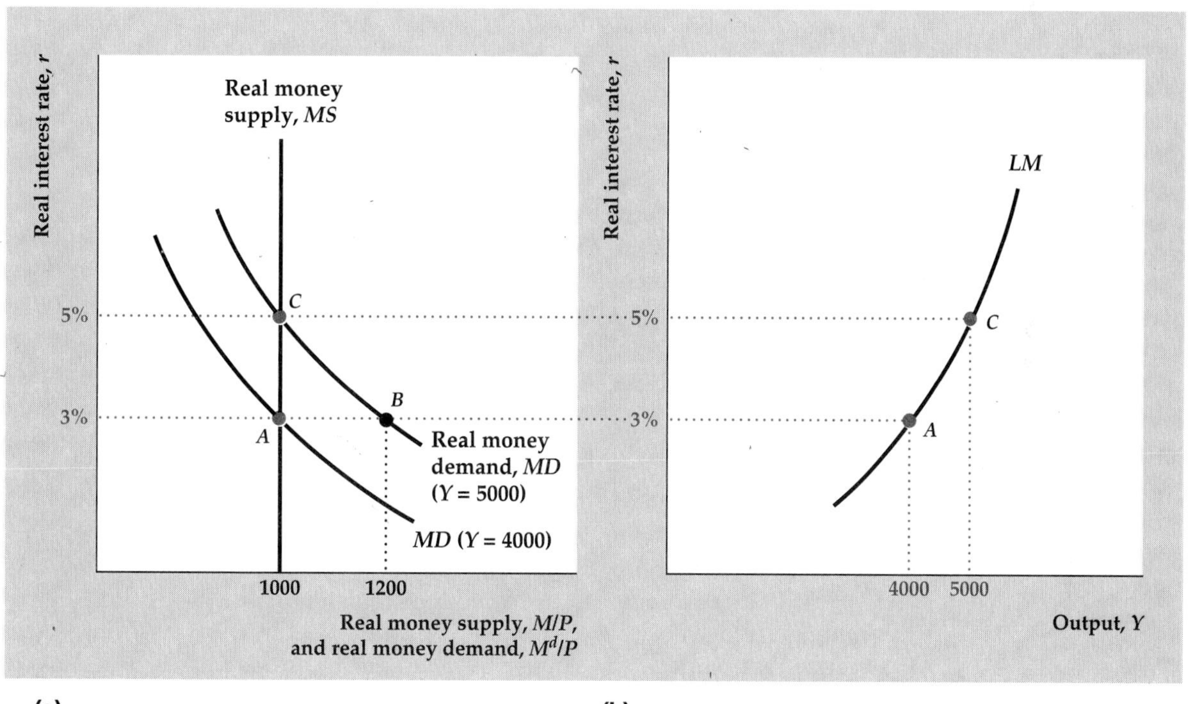

Figure 10.4
Deriving the *LM* curve

(a) The curves show real money demand and real money supply. Real money supply is fixed at 1000. When output is 4000, the real money demand curve is *MD* ($Y = 4000$); the real interest rate that clears the asset market is 3% (point *A*). When output is 5000, more money is demanded at the same real interest rate, so the real money demand curve shifts to the right to *MD* ($Y = 5000$). In this case the real interest rate that clears the asset market is 5% (point *C*).

(b) The graph shows the corresponding *LM* curve. For each level of output the *LM* curve shows the real interest rate that clears the asset market. Thus when output is 4000, the *LM* curve shows that the real interest rate that clears the goods market is 3% (point *A*). When output is 5000, the *LM* curve shows a market-clearing real interest rate of 5% (point *C*). Because higher output raises money demand, and thus raises the real interest rate that clears the asset market, the *LM* curve slopes upward.

the economy's real money supply, M/P. The nominal money supply M is set by the central bank. Thus, for a given price level P, the real money supply M/P is a fixed number and the *MS* line is vertical. For example, if $M = 2000$ and $P = 2$, the *MS* line is vertical at $M/P = 1000$.

Real money demand at two different levels of income Y is shown by the two *MD* curves in Fig. 10.4(a). Recall from Chapter 7 that a higher real interest rate r increases the relative attractiveness of nonmonetary assets and causes holders of wealth to demand less money. Thus the money demand curves slope downward. The money demand curve *MD* for $Y = 4000$ shows the real demand for money when output is 4000; similarly, the *MD* curve for $Y = 5000$ shows the real demand for money when output is 5000. Because an increase in income increases the amount of money demanded at any real interest rate, the money demand curve for $Y = 5000$ is farther to the right than the money demand curve for $Y = 4000$.

Graphically, asset market equilibrium occurs at the intersection of the money supply and money demand curves, where the real quantities of money supplied and demanded are equal. For example, when output is 4000, so that the money demand curve is *MD* ($Y = 4000$), the money demand and money supply curves intersect at point *A* in Fig. 10.4(a). The real interest rate at *A* is 3%. Thus when output is 4000, the real interest rate that clears the asset market (equalizes the quantities of money supplied and demanded) is 3%. At a real interest rate of 3% and an output of 4000, the real quantity of money demanded by holders of wealth is 1000, which equals the real money supply made available by the central bank.

What happens to the asset market equilibrium if output rises from 4000 to 5000? People need to conduct more transactions, so their real money demand increases at any real interest rate. As a result, the money demand curve shifts to the right, to *MD* for $Y = 5000$. If the real interest rate remained at 3%, the real quantity of money demanded would exceed the real money supply. At point *B* in Fig. 10.4(a) the real quantity of money demanded is 1200, which is greater than the real money supply of 1000. To restore equality of money demanded and supplied and thus bring the asset market back into equilibrium, the real interest rate must rise to 5%. When the real interest rate is 5%, the real quantity of money demanded declines to 1000, which is equal to the fixed real money supply (point C in Fig. 10.4a).

How does an increase in the real interest rate eliminate the excess demand for money, and what causes this increase in the real interest rate? Recall that the prices of nonmonetary assets and the interest rates they pay are negatively related. At the initial real interest rate of 3%, the increase in output from 4000 to 5000 causes people to demand more money (the *MD* curve shifts to the right in Fig. 10.4a). To satisfy their desire to hold more money, people will try to sell some of their nonmonetary assets for money. But when people rush to sell a portion of their nonmonetary assets, the prices of these assets will fall, which will cause the real interest rates on these assets to rise. Thus it is the public's attempt to increase its holdings of money by selling nonmonetary assets that causes the real interest rate to rise.

Because the real supply of money in the economy is fixed, the public as a whole cannot increase the amount of money it holds. As long as people attempt to do so by selling nonmonetary assets, the real interest rate will continue to rise. But the increase in the real interest rate paid by nonmonetary assets makes those assets more attractive relative to money, reducing the real quantity of money demanded (here the movement is *along* the *MD* curve for $Y = 5000$, from point B to point C in Fig. 10.4a). The real interest rate will rise until the real quantity of money demanded again equals the fixed supply of money and restores asset market equilibrium. The new asset market equilibrium is at C, where the real interest rate has risen from 3% to 5%.

The preceding example shows that when output rises, increasing real money demand, a higher real interest rate is needed to maintain equilibrium in the asset market. In general, the relationship between output and the real interest rate that clears the asset market is expressed graphically by the *LM* curve. For any level of output, the ***LM* curve** shows the real interest rate for which the asset market is in equilibrium, with equal quantities of money supplied and demanded. The term *LM* comes from the asset market equilibrium condition that the real quantity of money demanded, as determined by the real money demand function L, must equal the real money supply M/P.

The *LM* curve corresponding to our numerical example is shown in Fig. 10.4(b), with the real interest rate r on the vertical axis and output Y on the horizontal axis. Points A and C lie on the *LM* curve. At A, which corresponds to point A in the money supply–money demand diagram of Fig. 10.4(a), output Y is 4000 and the real interest rate r is 3%. Because A lies on the *LM* curve, when output is 4000 the real interest rate that clears the asset market is 3%. Similarly, because C lies on the *LM* curve, when output is 5000 the real interest rate that equalizes money supplied and demanded is 5%; this output–real interest rate combination corresponds to the asset market equilibrium at point C in Fig. 10.4(a).

Figure 10.4(b) illustrates the general point that the *LM* curve always slopes upward from left to right. It does so because increases in output, by raising money demand, also raise the real interest rate on nonmonetary assets needed to clear the asset market.

Factors that Shift the *LM* Curve

In deriving the *LM* curve we varied output but held constant other factors, such as the price level, that affect the real interest rate that clears the asset market. Changes in any of these other factors will cause the *LM* curve to shift. In particular, for constant output, *any change that reduces real money supply relative to real money demand will increase the real interest rate that clears the asset market and cause the LM curve to shift up.* Similarly, for constant output, anything that raises real money supply relative to real money demand will reduce the real interest rate that clears the asset market and shift the *LM* curve down. Here we discuss in general terms how changes in real money supply or demand affect the *LM* curve. Summary table 13, shown on the next page, describes the factors that shift the *LM* curve.

Changes in the Real Money Supply. An increase in the real money supply M/P will reduce the real interest rate that clears the asset market and shift the *LM* curve down. Figure 10.5, on page 329, illustrates this point and extends our previous numerical example.

Figure 10.5(a) contains the money supply–money demand diagram. Initially, suppose that the real money supply M/P is 1000 and output is 4000, so the money demand curve is *MD* ($Y = 4000$). Then equilibrium in the asset market occurs at point A with a market-clearing real interest rate of 3%. The *LM* curve

SUMMARY 13

Factors that Shift the *LM* Curve

An Increase in	Shifts the *LM* Curve	Reason
Nominal money supply, M	Down	Real money supply increases, lowering the real interest rate that clears the asset market (equates money supplied and money demanded).
Price level, P	Up	Real money supply falls, raising the real interest rate that clears the asset market.
Expected inflation, π^e	Down	Demand for money falls, lowering the real interest rate that clears the asset market.
Nominal interest rate on money, i^m	Up	Demand for money increases, raising the real interest rate that clears the asset market.

In addition, for constant output, any factor that increases real money demand raises the real interest rate that clears the asset market and shifts the *LM* curve up. Other factors that increase real money demand (see Summary table 9, p. 231) include

- an increase in wealth;
- an increase in the risk of alternative assets relative to the risk of holding money;
- a decline in the liquidity of alternative assets; and
- a decline in the efficiency of payment technologies.

corresponding to the real money supply of 1000 is shown as *LM* (M/P = 1000) in Fig. 10.5(b). At point *A* on this *LM* curve, as at point *A* in the money supply–money demand diagram in Fig. 10.5(a), output is 4000 and the real interest rate is 3%. Because *A* lies on the initial *LM* curve, when output is 4000 and the money supply is 1000, the real interest rate that clears the asset market is 3%.

Now suppose that, with output constant at 4000, the real money supply rises from 1000 to 1200. This increase in the real money supply causes the vertical money supply curve to shift to the right, from MS^1 to MS^2 in Fig. 10.5(a). The asset market equilibrium point is now point *D*, where, with output remaining at 4000, the market-clearing real interest rate has fallen to 2%.

Why has the real interest rate that clears the asset market fallen? At the initial real interest rate of 3%, there is an excess supply of money—that is, holders of wealth have more money in their portfolios than they want to hold and, consequently, they have a smaller share of their wealth than they would like in nonmonetary assets. To eliminate this imbalance in their portfolios, holders of wealth will want to use some of their money to buy nonmonetary assets. However, when holders of wealth as a group try to purchase nonmonetary assets, the price of nonmonetary assets is bid up and hence the real interest rate paid on these assets declines. As the real interest rate falls, nonmonetary assets become less attractive relative to money. The real interest rate continues

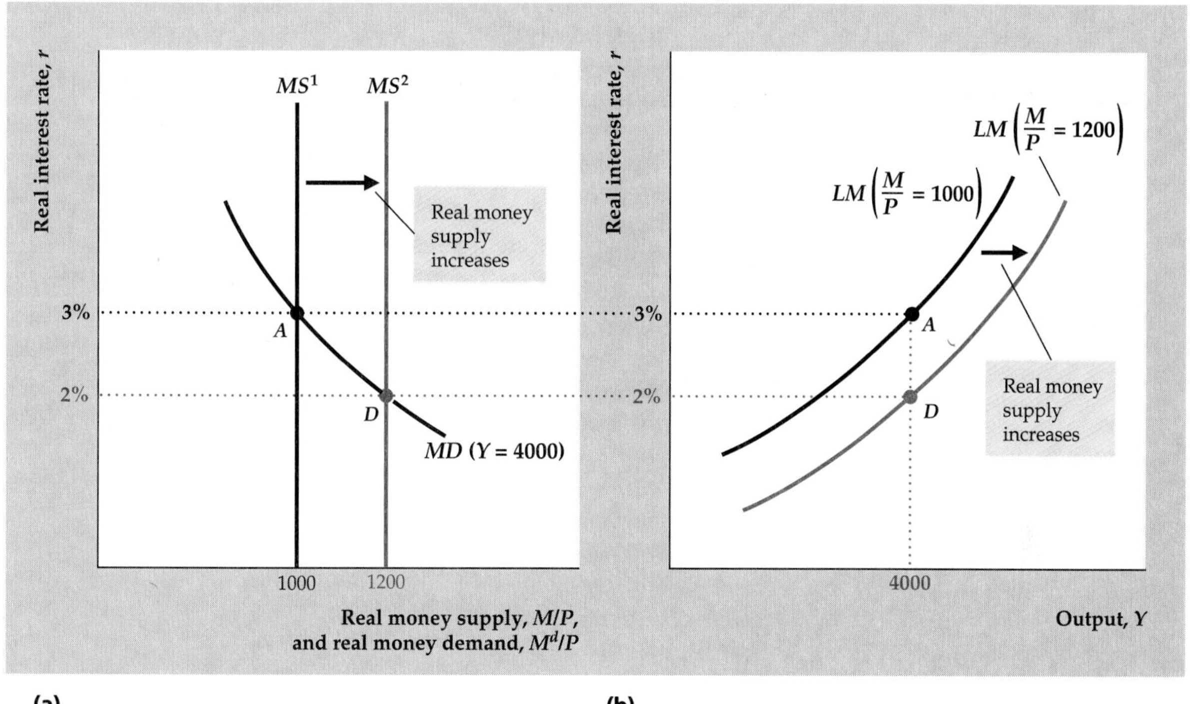

(a)

(b)

Figure 10.5
An increase in the real money supply shifts the *LM* curve down

(a) An increase in the real supply of money shifts the money supply curve to the right, from MS^1 to MS^2. For a constant level of output, the real interest rate that clears the asset market falls. If output is fixed at 4000, for example, the money demand curve is *MD* ($Y = 4000$) and the real interest rate that clears the asset market falls from 3% (point *A*) to 2% (point *D*).

(b) The graph shows the effect of the increase in real money supply on the *LM* curve. For any level of output, the increase in the real money supply causes the real interest rate that clears the asset market to fall. So, for example, when output is 4000, the increase in the real money supply causes the real interest rate that clears the asset market to fall from 3% (point *A*) to 2% (point *D*). Thus the *LM* curve shifts down, from *LM* for $M/P = 1000$ to *LM* for $M/P = 1200$.

to fall until it reaches 2% at point *D* in Fig. 10.5(a), where the excess supply of money and the excess demand for nonmonetary assets are eliminated and the asset market is back in equilibrium.

The effect of the increase in real money supply on the *LM* curve is illustrated in Fig. 10.5(b). With output constant at 4000, the increase in the real money supply lowers the real interest rate that clears the asset market, from 3% to 2%. Thus point *D*, where $Y = 4000$ and $r = 2\%$, is now a point of asset market equilibrium, and point *A* no longer is. More generally, for any given level of output, an increase in the real money supply lowers the real interest rate that clears the asset market. Therefore the entire *LM* curve shifts down. The new *LM* curve, *LM* for $M/P = 1200$, passes through the new equilibrium point *D* and lies below the old *LM* curve, *LM* for $M/P = 1000$.

Thus, with fixed output, an increase in the real money supply lowers the real interest rate that clears the asset market and causes the *LM* curve to shift down. A similar analysis would show that a drop in the real money supply causes the *LM* curve to shift up.

What might cause the real money supply to increase? In general, because the real money supply equals M/P, the real money supply will increase whenever the nominal money supply M, which is controlled by the central bank, grows more quickly than the price level P.

Changes in Real Money Demand. A change in any variable that affects real money demand, other than output or the real interest rate, will also shift the *LM* curve. More specifically, with output constant, an increase in real money demand raises the real interest rate that clears the asset market and thus shifts the *LM* curve up. Analogously, with output constant, a drop in real money demand shifts the *LM* curve down.

Figure 10.6 shows a graphical analysis of an increase in money demand similar to that for a change in money supply shown in Fig. 10.5. As before, the money supply–money demand diagram is shown on the left, Fig. 10.6(a). Output is constant at 4000, and the real money supply again is 1000. The initial money demand curve is MD^1. The initial asset market equilibrium point is at A, where the money demand curve MD^1 and the money supply curve MS

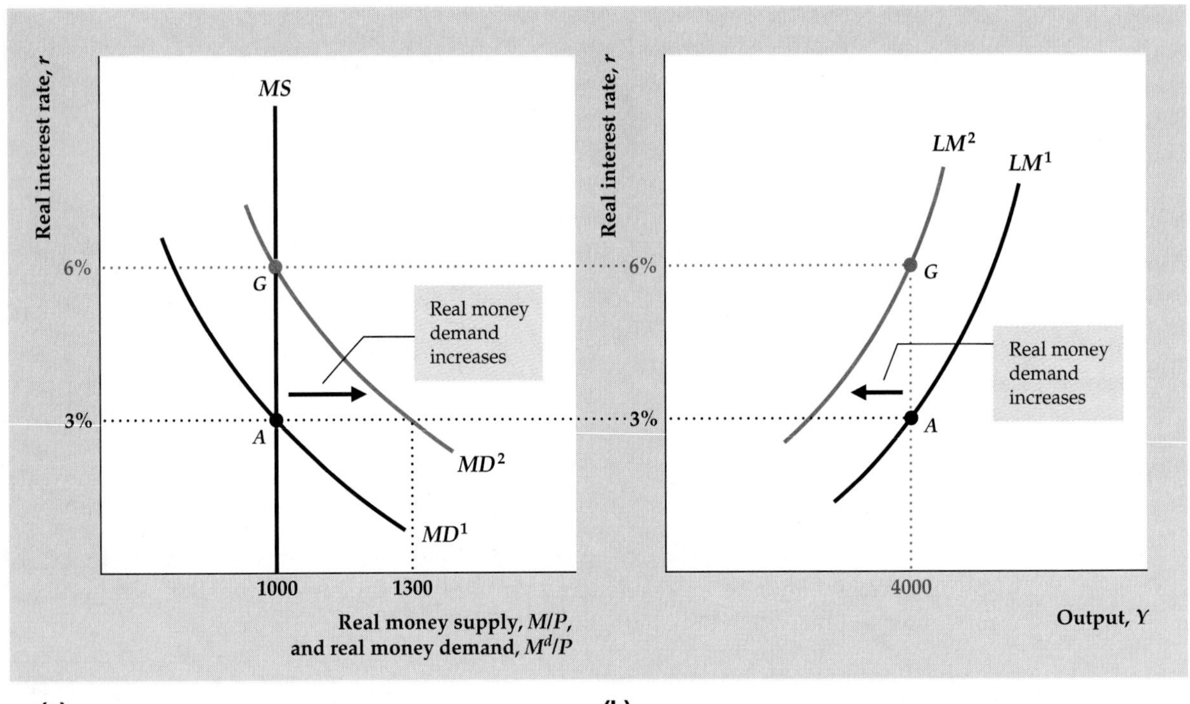

Figure 10.6
An increase in real money demand shifts the *LM* curve up
(a) With output constant at 4000 and the real money supply at 1000, an increase in the interest rate paid on money raises real money demand. The money demand curve shifts to the right, from MD^1 to MD^2, and the real interest rate that clears the asset market rises from 3% (point *A*) to 6% (point *G*).
(b) The graph shows the effect of the increase in real money demand on the *LM* curve. When output is 4000, the increase in real money demand raises the real interest rate that clears the asset market from 3% (point *A*) to 6% (point *G*). More generally, for any level of output, the increase in real money demand raises the real interest rate that clears the asset market. Thus the *LM* curve shifts up, from LM^1 to LM^2.

intersect. At initial equilibrium, point *A*, the real interest rate that clears the asset market is 3%.

Now suppose that, for a fixed level of output, a change occurs in the economy that increases real money demand. For example, if banks decided to increase the interest rate paid on money, i^m, the public would want to hold more money at the same levels of output and the real interest rate. Graphically, the increase in money demand shifts the money demand curve to the right, from MD^1 to MD^2 in Fig. 10.6(a). At the initial real interest rate of 3% the real quantity of money demanded is 1300, which exceeds the available supply of 1000; so 3% is no longer the value of the real interest rate that clears the asset market.

How will the real interest rate that clears the asset market change after the increase in money demand? If holders of wealth want to hold more money, they will exchange nonmonetary assets for money. Increased sales of nonmonetary assets will drive down their price and thus raise the real interest rate that they pay. The real interest rate will rise, reducing the attractiveness of holding money, until the public is satisfied to hold the available real money supply (1000). The real interest rate rises from its initial value of 3% at *A* to 6% at *G*.

Figure 10.6(b) shows the effect of the increase in money demand on the *LM* curve. The initial *LM* curve, LM^1, passes through point *A*, showing that when output is 4000 the real interest rate that clears the asset market is 3%. (Point *A* in Fig. 10.6b corresponds to point *A* in Fig. 10.6a.) Following the increase in money demand, with output fixed at 4000, the market-clearing real interest rate rises to 6%. Thus the new *LM* curve must pass through point *G* (corresponding to point *G* in Fig. 10.6a), where $Y = 4000$ and $r = 6\%$. The new *LM* curve, LM^2, is higher than LM^1 because the real interest rate that clears the asset market is now higher for any level of output.

10.4 GENERAL EQUILIBRIUM IN THE COMPLETE *IS–LM* MODEL

The next step is to put the labor market, the goods market, and the asset market together and examine the equilibrium of the economy as a whole. A situation in which all markets in an economy are simultaneously in equilibrium is called a **general equilibrium.** Figure 10.7, on the next page, shows the complete *IS–LM* model, illustrating how the general equilibrium of the economy is determined. Shown are

- the full-employment, or *FE*, line, along which the labor market is in equilibrium;
- the *IS* curve, along which the goods market is in equilibrium; and
- the *LM* curve, along which the asset market is in equilibrium.

The three curves intersect at point *E*, indicating that all three markets are in equilibrium at that point. Therefore *E* represents a general equilibrium and, because it is the only point that lies on all three curves, it represents the only general equilibrium for this economy.

Although point *E* obviously is a general equilibrium point, not so clear is what forces, if any, act to bring the economy to that point. To put it another way, although the *IS* curve and *FE* line must intersect somewhere, we haven't explained why the *LM* curve must pass through that same point. In

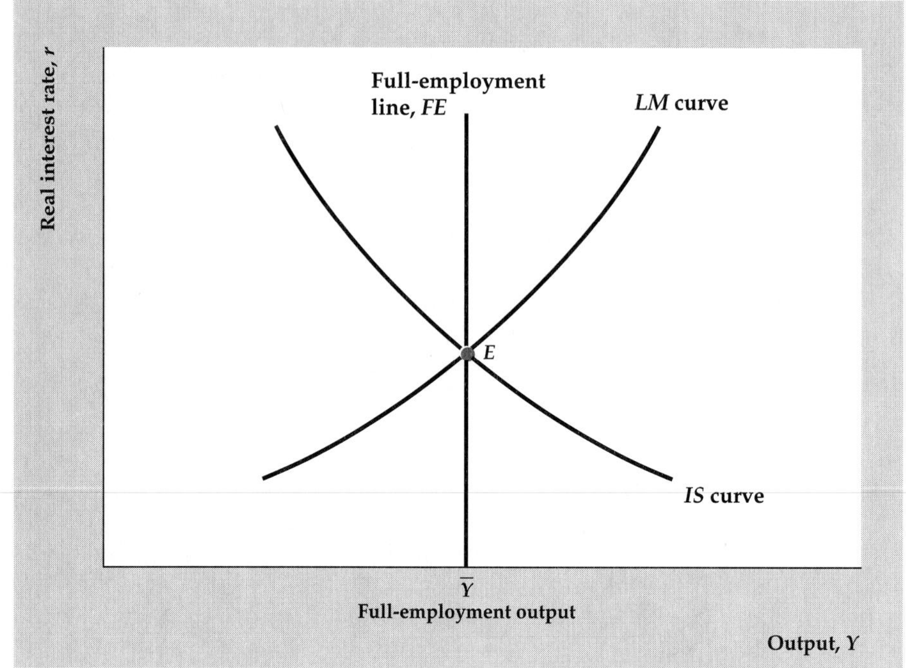

Figure 10.7
General equilibrium in the *IS–LM* model
The economy is in general equilibrium when quantities supplied equal quantities demanded in every market. The general equilibrium point, *E*, lies on the *IS* curve, the *LM* curve, and the *FE* line. Thus at *E*, and only at *E*, the goods market, the asset market, and the labor market are simultaneously in equilibrium.

Section 10.5 we discuss the economic forces that lead the economy to general equilibrium. There we show that (1) the general equilibrium of the economy always occurs at the intersection of the *IS* curve and the *FE* line; and (2) adjustments of the price level cause the *LM* curve to shift until it passes through the general equilibrium point defined by the intersection of the *IS* curve and the *FE* line. Before discussing the details of this adjustment process, however, let's consider an example that illustrates the use of the complete *IS–LM* model.

Applying the *IS–LM* Framework: A Temporary Adverse Supply Shock

An economic shock relevant to business cycle analysis is an adverse supply shock. Specifically, suppose that (because of bad weather or a temporary increase in oil prices) the productivity parameter *A* in the production function drops temporarily.[7] We can use the *IS–LM* model to analyze the effects of this shock on the general equilibrium of the economy and the general equilibrium values of economic variables such as the real wage, employment, output, the real interest rate, the price level, consumption, and investment.

Suppose that the economy is initially in general equilibrium at point *E* in Fig. 10.8(a), where the initial *FE* line, FE^1, *IS* curve, and *LM* curve, LM^1, for this economy intersect. To determine the effects of a temporary supply shock on the general equilibrium of this economy, we must consider how the temporary drop in productivity *A* affects the positions of the *FE* line and the *IS* and *LM* curves.

The *FE* line describes equilibrium in the labor market. Hence to find the effect of the supply shock on the *FE* line we must start by looking at how the

7. Recall that the production function, Eq. (3.1), is $Y = AF(K, N)$, so a drop in *A* reduces the amount of output that can be produced for any quantities of capital *K* and labor *N*.

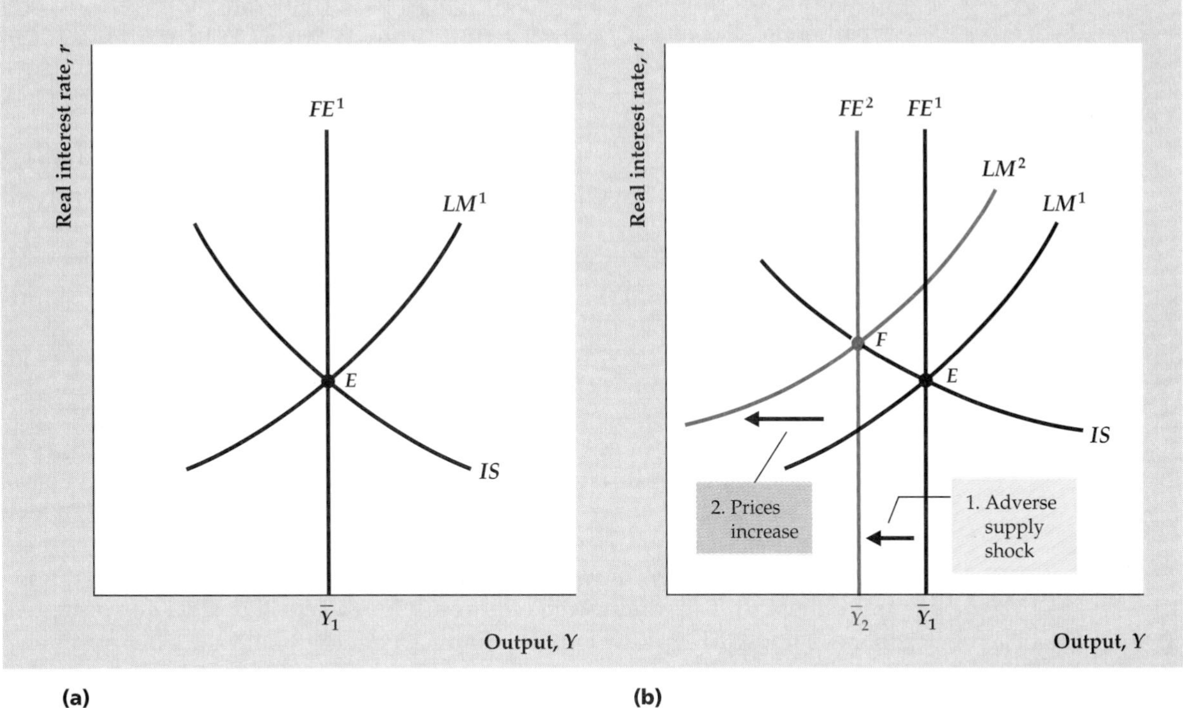

Figure 10.8
Effects of a temporary adverse supply shock
(a) Initially, the economy is in general equilibrium at point E, with output at its full-employment level $\bar{Y}_1$.
(b) A temporary adverse supply shock reduces full-employment output from $\bar{Y}_1$ to $\bar{Y}_2$ and shifts the FE line to the left from FE^1 to FE^2. The new general equilibrium is represented by point F, where FE^2 intersects the unchanged IS curve. The price level increases and shifts the LM curve up and to the left, from LM^1 to LM^2, until it passes through F. At the new general equilibrium point, F, output is lower, the real interest rate is higher, and the price level is higher than at the original general equilibrium point, E.

shock affects labor supply and labor demand. In Chapter 3 we demonstrated that an adverse supply shock reduces the marginal product of labor and thus shifts the labor demand curve down (see Fig. 3.10). Because the supply shock is temporary, we assume that it doesn't affect workers' wealth or expected future wages and so doesn't affect labor supply. As a result of the decline in labor demand, the equilibrium values of the real wage and employment, $\bar{N}$, fall.

The *FE* line shifts only to the degree that full-employment output $\bar{Y}$ changes. Does $\bar{Y}$ change? Yes. Recall from Chapter 3 that an adverse supply shock reduces full-employment output $\bar{Y}$, which equals $AF(K, \bar{N})$, for two reasons: (1) as we just mentioned, the supply shock reduces the equilibrium level of employment $\bar{N}$, which lowers the amount of output that can be produced; and (2) the drop in productivity A directly reduces the amount of output produced by any combination of capital and labor. The reduction in $\bar{Y}$ is represented by a shift to the left of the *FE* line, from FE^1 to FE^2 in Fig. 10.8(b).

Now consider the effects of the temporary adverse supply shock on the *IS* curve. Recall that we derived the *IS* curve by changing the level of current output in the saving–investment diagram (Fig. 10.2) and finding for each level of current output the real interest rate for which desired saving equals desired investment. A *temporary* adverse supply shock reduces current output but doesn't change any other factor affecting desired saving or investment (such as wealth, expected future income, or the future marginal product of capital). Therefore a temporary supply shock is just the sort of change in current output that we used to trace out the *IS* curve. We conclude that a temporary adverse supply shock is a movement *along* the *IS* curve, *not a shift* of the *IS* curve, leaving it unchanged.[8]

Finally, we consider the *LM* curve. A temporary supply shock has no direct effect on the demand or supply of money and thus doesn't shift the *LM* curve.

We now look for the new general equilibrium of the economy. In Fig. 10.8(b), there is no point at which FE^2 (the new *FE* line), *IS*, and LM^1 all intersect. As we mentioned—and demonstrate in Section 10.5—when the *FE* line, the *IS* curve, and the *LM* curve don't intersect at a common point, the *LM* curve shifts until it passes through the intersection of the *FE* line and *IS* curve. This shift in the *LM* curve is caused by changes in the price level *P*, which change the real money supply M/P and thus affect the equilibrium of the asset market. As Fig. 10.8(b) shows, to restore general equilibrium at point *F*, the *LM* curve must shift up and to the left, from LM^1 to LM^2. For it to do so the real money supply M/P must fall (see Summary table 13) and thus the price level *P* must rise. We infer (although we haven't yet given an economic explanation) that an adverse supply shock will cause the price level to rise.

What is the effect of a temporary supply shock on the inflation rate, as distinct from the price level? As the inflation rate is the growth rate of the price level, during the period in which prices are rising to their new, higher level, a burst of inflation will occur. However, after the price level stabilizes at its higher value (and is no longer rising), inflation subsides. Thus a temporary supply shock should cause a temporary rather than a permanent increase in the rate of inflation.

Let's pause and review our results.

1. As we had already shown in Chapter 3, a temporary adverse supply shock lowers the equilibrium values of the real wage and employment.
2. Comparing the new general equilibrium, point *F*, to the old general equilibrium, point *E*, in Fig. 10.8(b), we see that the supply shock lowers output and raises the real interest rate.
3. The supply shock raises the price level and causes a temporary burst in inflation.
4. Because in the new general equilibrium the real interest rate is higher and output is lower, consumption must be lower than before the supply shock. The higher real interest rate also implies that investment must be lower after the shock.

In the following Application we check out how well our model explains the historical behavior of the economy. However, note that economic models, such as the *IS–LM* model, also are used extensively in forecasting economic conditions (Box 10.1).

---

8. Analytical Problem 2 at the end of the chapter examines the effect of a permanent adverse supply shock and identifies factors that shift the *IS* curve in that case.

BOX 10.1

Econometric Models and Macroeconomic Forecasts

The *IS–LM* model developed in this chapter is a relatively simple example of a macroeconomic model. Much more complicated models of the economy, many though not all of them based on the *IS–LM* framework, are used in applied macroeconomic research and analysis.

A common use of macroeconomic models is to help economists forecast the course of the economy. In general, using a macroeconomic model to obtain quantitative economic forecasts involves three steps. First, numerical values for the parameters of the model (such as the income elasticity of money demand) must be obtained. In *econometric* models, these values are estimated through statistical analyses of the data. Second, projections must be made of the likely behavior of relevant *exogenous* variables, or variables whose values are not determined within the model. Examples of exogenous variables include policy variables (such as government spending and the money supply), oil prices, and changes in productivity. Third, based on the expected path of the exogenous variables and the model parameters, the model can be solved (usually on a computer) to give forecasts of variables determined within the model (such as output, employment, and interest rates). Variables determined within the model are *endogenous* variables.

Although a relatively simple model like the *IS–LM* model developed in this chapter could be used to create real forecasts, the results probably would not be very good. Because real-world economies are complex, macroeconomic models actually used in forecasting tend to be much more detailed than the *IS–LM* model presented here. For example, instead of a single aggregate production function, an econometric model used for forecasting might include production functions estimated separately for many individual industries. The complexity of models used in commercial forecasting is illustrated by the accompanying table, based on an article by Stephen McNees and John Ries* of the Federal Reserve Bank of Boston. For the three well-known forecasting firms shown, the number of economic variables forecasted ranged from about 700 to about 1200. Generally, the number of equations in an econometric model exceeds the number of variables forecasted, so these models become quite complex.

Despite the amount of detail in some econometric models, they typically do not capture all information relevant to forecasting the economy. As the accompanying table also illustrates, most forecasters combine the results from their econometric models with other forecasting techniques, including personal judgment, time-series methods (statistical methods that attempt to extrapolate economic trends without the explicit use of an economic model), and detailed analysis of current data (including partial and preliminary data). Studies have shown that combining several different forecasting methods usually provides more accurate forecasts than relying on a single approach.†

* "The Track Record of Macroeconomic Forecasts," *New England Economic Review*, November/December 1983, pp. 5–18.

† See Stephen McNees, "Man vs. Model? The Role of Judgment in Forecasting," *New England Economic Review*, July/August 1990, pp. 41–52, and Victor Zarnowitz, *Business Cycles: Theory, History, Indicators, and Forecasting*, Chicago: University of Chicago Press, 1992, especially Chapter 18.

Forecaster	**Number of variables forecasted**	**Forecasting techniques (approximate weights)**	
Chase Econometrics	About 700	Econometric model	70%
		Judgment	20%
		Time-series methods	5%
		Current data analysis	5%
Data Resources, Inc.	About 1000	Econometric model	55%
		Judgment	30%
		Time-series methods	10%
		Current data analysis	5%
Wharton Econometric Forecasting Associates	About 1200	Econometric model	60%
		Judgment	30%
		Current data analysis	10%

Source: Based on McNees and Ries (1983), Table 1.

APPLICATION

Oil Price Shocks Revisited

In Chapter 3 we pointed out that an increase in the price of oil is an example of an adverse supply shock, and we looked at the effects of the 1973–1974 and 1979–1980 oil price shocks on the U.S. economy (see the Application, "Output, Employment, and the Real Wage During Oil Price Shocks", p. 86). The theory's predictions—that adverse supply shocks reduce output, employment, and the real wage—were confirmed for those two episodes. Our analysis using the complete *IS–LM* model is consistent with that earlier discussion. However, it adds the predictions that, following an oil price shock, consumption and investment decline, inflation increases, and the real interest rate rises.

Figure 9.3 shows that consumption fell slightly and that investment fell sharply immediately after these oil price shocks. From the beginning of the recession in the fourth quarter of 1973 until the fourth quarter of 1974, real consumption fell by 1.3% and real investment fell by 13.2%. Following the onset of the recession in the first quarter of 1980, real consumption fell by 2.0% and real investment fell by 11.2% in just one quarter. Inflation also behaved as predicted by our analysis, surging temporarily in 1973–1974 and again in 1979–1980 (see Fig. 9.10).

Our analysis also predicted that an oil price shock will cause the real interest rate to rise. However, this result depends somewhat on the assumption we made that people expected the oil price shock to be temporary. In Analytical Problem 2 at the end of the chapter, you will find that, if the adverse supply shock is expected to be permanent, the rise in the real interest rate will be less than when the adverse supply shock is expected to be temporary (and the real interest rate may not rise). However, we don't really know what people's expectations were about the duration of the two major oil price shocks. Therefore we can't state with confidence what the effect of such a shock on the real interest rate should have been. Actually, the real interest rate rose during the 1979–1980 shock but not during the 1973–1974 shock (see Fig. 2.4). On the basis of these data only, our model suggests that people expected the 1973–1974 oil shock to be permanent and the 1979–1980 shock to be temporary. Interestingly, those expectations were essentially correct: Figure 3.11 shows that the oil price increase of 1979–1980 was reversed rather quickly but that the price increase of 1973–1974 was not.

10.5 PRICE ADJUSTMENT AND THE ATTAINMENT OF GENERAL EQUILIBRIUM

We now explain the economic forces that lead prices to change and shift the *LM* curve until it passes through the intersection of the *IS* curve and the *FE* line. In discussing the role of price adjustments in bringing the economy back to general equilibrium, we also show the basic difference between the two main approaches to business cycle analysis, classical and Keynesian.

To illustrate the adjustment process, let's use the complete *IS–LM* model to consider what happens to the economy if the nominal money supply increases. This analysis allows us to discuss monetary policy (the control of the money supply) and to introduce some ongoing controversies about the effects of monetary policy on the economy.

The Effects of a Monetary Expansion

Suppose that the central bank decides to raise the nominal money supply M by 10%. For now we hold the price level P constant so that the real money supply M/P also increases by 10%. What effects will this monetary expansion have on the economy? Figure 10.9, on the next page, helps us answer this question with the complete *IS–LM* model.

The three parts of Fig. 10.9 show the sequence of events involved in the analysis. For simplicity, suppose that the economy initially is in general equilibrium so that in Fig. 10.9(a) the *IS* curve, the *FE* line, and the initial *LM* curve, LM^1, all pass through the general equilibrium point, E. At E output equals its full-employment value of 1000, and the real interest rate is 5%. Both the *IS* and *LM* curves pass through E, so we know that 5% is the market-clearing real interest rate in both the goods and asset markets. For the moment the price level, P, is fixed at its initial level of 100.

The 10% increase in the real supply of money M/P doesn't shift the *IS* curve or the *FE* line because, with output and the real interest rate held constant, a change in M/P doesn't affect desired national saving, desired investment, labor demand, labor supply, or productivity. However, Fig. 10.5 showed that an increase in the real money supply does shift the *LM* curve down, which we show here as a shift of the *LM* curve from LM^1 to LM^2, in Fig. 10.9(b). The *LM* curve shifts down because, at any level of output, an increase in the money supply lowers the real interest rate needed to clear the asset market.

Note that, after the *LM* curve has shifted down to LM^2, there is no point in Fig. 10.9(b) at which all three curves intersect. In other words, the goods market, the labor market, and the asset market no longer are simultaneously in equilibrium. We now must make some assumptions about how the economy behaves when it isn't in general equilibrium.

Of the three markets in the *IS–LM* model, the asset market (represented by the *LM* curve) undoubtedly adjusts the most quickly, because financial markets can respond within minutes to changes in economic conditions. The labor market (the *FE* line) is probably the slowest to adjust, because the process of matching workers and jobs takes time and wages may be renegotiated only periodically. The adjustment speed of the goods market (*IS* curve) probably is somewhere in the middle. We assume that, when the economy isn't in general equilibrium, the asset market and the goods market are in equilibrium so that *output and the real interest rate are given by the intersection of the IS and LM curves.* Note that, when the economy isn't in general equilibrium, the *IS–LM* intersection doesn't lie on the *FE* line, so the labor market isn't in equilibrium.

Immediately after the increase in the nominal money supply, therefore, the economy is out of general equilibrium with the level of output and the real interest rate represented by point F in Fig. 10.9(b), where the new *LM* curve, LM^2, intersects the *IS* curve. At F, output (1200) is higher and the real interest rate (3%) is lower than at the original general equilibrium, point E. We refer to F, the point at which the economy comes to rest before any adjustment occurs in the price level, as the *short-run equilibrium* point. (Although we refer to F as a short-run equilibrium point, keep in mind that only the asset and goods markets are in equilibrium there—the labor market isn't.)

In economic terms, why does the increase in the money supply shift the economy to point F? The sequence of events can be described as follows: After

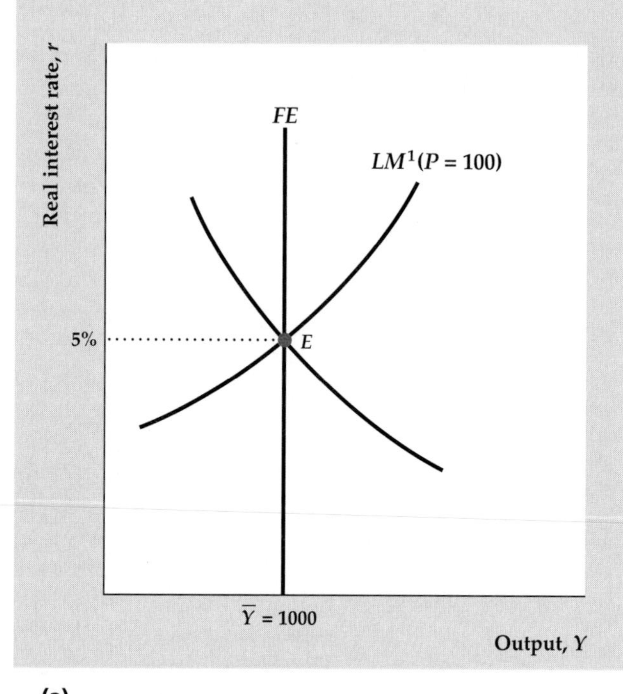

(a)

Figure 10.9
Effects of a monetary expansion
(a) The economy is in general equilibrium at point *E*. Output equals the full-employment level of 1000, the real interest rate is 5%, and the price level is 100.
(b) With the price level fixed, a 10% increase in the nominal money supply *M* raises the real money supply *M*/*P* and shifts the *LM* curve down from LM^1 to LM^2. At point *F*, the intersection of the *IS* curve and the new *LM* curve, LM^2, the real interest rate has fallen to 3%, which raises the aggregate demand for goods. If firms produce extra output to meet the increase in aggregate demand, output rises to 1200 (higher than full-employment output of 1000).
(c) Because aggregate demand exceeds full-employment output at point *F*, firms raise prices. A 10% rise in *P*, from 100 to 110, restores the real money supply to its original level and shifts the *LM* curve back to its original position at LM^1. This returns the economy to point *E*, where output again is at its full-employment level of 1000, but the price level has risen 10% from 100 to 110.

the increase in the money supply, holders of wealth are holding more money in their portfolios than they desire at the initial values of output and the real interest rate. To bring their portfolios back into balance, they will try to use their excess money to buy nonmonetary assets. However, as holders of wealth bid for nonmonetary assets, they put upward pressure on the price of those assets, which reduces their interest rate. Thus, after an increase in the money supply, wealth-holders' attempts to achieve their desired mix of money and nonmonetary assets cause the interest rate to fall.

The drop in the real interest rate isn't the end of the story, however. Because the lower real interest rate increases the demand by households for consumption, C^d, and the demand by firms for investment, I^d, the aggregate demand for goods rises. Here we make a fundamental assumption, to which we return shortly: When demanders increase their spending on goods, firms are willing (at least temporarily) to produce enough to meet the extra demand for their output. After the decline in the real interest rate raises the aggregate demand for goods, therefore, we assume that firms respond by increasing production, leading to higher output at the short-run equilibrium point, *F*.

To summarize, with the price level constant, an increase in the nominal money supply takes the economy to the short-run equilibrium point, *F*, in Fig. 10.9(b), at which the real interest rate is lower and output is higher than at the initial general equilibrium point, *E*. We made two assumptions: (1) when the economy isn't in general equilibrium, the economy's short-run equilibrium occurs at the intersection of the *IS* and *LM* curves; and (2) when the aggregate demand for goods rises, firms are willing (at least temporarily) to produce enough extra output to meet the expanded demand.

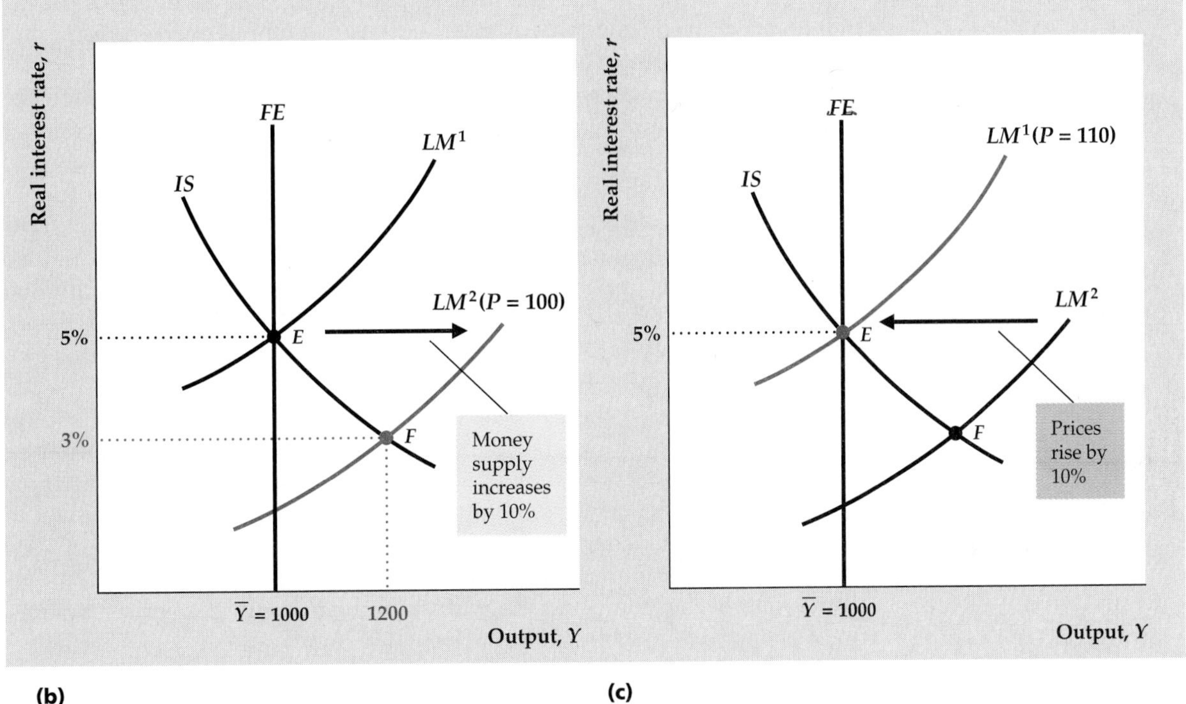

(b)

(c)

The Adjustment of the Price Level. So far we have simply taken the price level P as fixed. In reality, prices respond to conditions of supply and demand in the economy. The price level P refers to the price of output (goods), so to think about how prices are likely to adjust in this example, let's reconsider the effects of the increase in the money supply on the goods market.

In Fig. 10.9(b), the short-run equilibrium point, F, lies on the *IS* curve, implying that the goods market is in equilibrium at that point with equal aggregate quantities of goods supplied and demanded. Recall our assumption that firms are willing to meet any increases in aggregate demand by producing more. In that sense, then, the aggregate quantity of goods supplied equals the aggregate quantity of goods demanded. However, in another sense the goods market is *not* in equilibrium at point F. The problem is that, in order to meet the aggregate demand for goods at F, firms have to produce more output than their full-employment level of output $\bar{Y}$. Full-employment output $\bar{Y}$ is the level of output that maximizes firms' profits because that level of output corresponds to the profit-maximizing level of employment (Chapter 3). Therefore, in meeting the higher level of aggregate demand, firms are producing more output than they want to. In the sense that, at point F, the production of goods by firms is *not* the level of output that maximizes their profits, the goods market isn't truly in equilibrium.

At point F the aggregate demand for goods exceeds firms' desired supply of output $\bar{Y}$, so we can expect firms to begin raising their prices, causing the price level P to rise. With the nominal money supply M set by the central bank, an increase in the price level P lowers the real money supply M/P, which in turn causes the *LM* curve to shift up. Indeed, as long as the aggregate quantity of goods demanded exceeds what firms want to supply, prices will keep rising. Thus the *LM* curve will keep shifting up and to the left until the aggregate quantity of goods demanded equals full-employment output. Aggregate demand equals full-employment output only when the *LM* curve has returned to its initial position, LM^1 in Fig. 10.9(c), where it passes through the original general equilibrium point, *E*. At *E* all three markets of the economy again are in equilibrium, with output at its full-employment level.

Compare Fig. 10.9(c) to the initial situation in Fig. 10.9(a) and note that after the adjustment of the price level the 10% increase in the nominal money supply has had no effect on output or the real interest rate. Employment also is unchanged from its initial value, as the economy has returned to its original level of output. However, as a result of the 10% increase in the nominal money supply, the price level is 10% higher (so that $P = 110$). How do we know that the price level changes by exactly 10%? To return the *LM* curve to its original position, the increase in the price level had to return the real money supply M/P to its original value. Because the nominal money supply *M* was raised by 10%, to return M/P to its original value, the price level *P* had to rise by 10% as well. Thus the change in the nominal money supply causes the price level to change proportionally. This result is the same result obtained in Chapter 7 (see Eq. 7.10), where we assumed that all markets are in equilibrium.

Note that, because in general equilibrium the price level has risen by 10% but real economic variables are unaffected, all nominal economic variables must also rise by 10%. In particular, for the real wage to have the same value after prices have risen by 10% as it did before, the nominal wage must rise by 10%. Thus the return of the economy to general equilibrium requires adjustment of the nominal wage (the price of labor) as well as the price of goods.

Trend Money Growth and Inflation. In Fig 10.9 we analyzed the effects of a one-time 10% increase in the nominal money supply, followed by a one-time 10% adjustment in the price level. In reality, in most countries the money supply and the price level grow continuously. Our framework easily handles this situation. Suppose that in some country both the nominal money supply *M* and the price level *P* are growing steadily at 7% per year, which implies that the real money supply M/P is constant. The *LM* curve depends on the real money supply M/P, so in this situation the *LM* curve will not shift, even though the nominal money supply and prices are rising.

Now suppose that for one year the money supply of this country is increased an additional 3%—for a total of 10%—while prices rise 7%. Then the real money supply M/P grows by 3% (10% minus 7%), and the *LM* curve shifts down and to the right. Similarly, if for one year the nominal money supply increased by only 4%, with inflation still at 7% per year, the *LM* curve would shift up, reflecting the 3% drop ($-3\% = 4\% - 7\%$) in the real money supply.

This example illustrates that changes in *M* or *P* *relative to the expected or trend rate of growth of money and inflation* (7% in this example) shift the *LM* curve. Thus, when we analyze the effects of "an increase in the money supply," we have in mind an increase in the money supply relative to the expected, or trend, rate of money growth (for example, a rise from 7% to 10% growth for one year); by a "decrease in the money supply," we mean a drop relative to a trend rate (such as a decline from 7% to 4% growth in money). Similarly, if we say something like "the price level falls to restore general equilibrium," we don't necessarily mean that the price level literally falls but only that it rises by less than its trend or expected rate of growth would suggest.

Classical versus Keynesian Versions of the *IS–LM* Model

Our diagrammatic analysis of the effects of a change in the money supply highlights two questions that are central to the debate between the classical and Keynesian approaches to macroeconomics: (1) How rapidly does the economy reach general equilibrium? and (2) What are the effects of monetary policy on the economy? We conclude this chapter by briefly discussing these two closely related questions. Because they are important, we return to them in Chapters 11 and 12.

Price Adjustment and the Self-Correcting Economy. In our analysis of the effects of a monetary expansion, we showed that *the economy is brought into general equilibrium by adjustment of the price level.* In graphical terms, if the intersection of the *IS* and *LM* curves lies to the right of the *FE* line—so that the aggregate quantity of goods demanded exceeds full-employment output, as in Fig. 10.9(b)—the price level will rise. The increase in *P* shifts the *LM* curve up, reducing the quantity of goods demanded, until all three curves intersect at the general equilibrium point, as in Fig. 10.9(c). Similarly, if the *IS–LM* intersection lies to the left of the full-employment line—so that desired spending on goods is below firms' profit-maximizing level of output—firms will cut prices. A decrease in the price level raises the real money supply and shifts the *LM* curve down, until all three curves again intersect, returning the economy to general equilibrium.

There is little controversy about the idea that, after some sort of economic disturbance, price level adjustments will eventually restore the economy to general equilibrium. However, the *speed* at which this process takes place is a much-debated issue in macroeconomics. Under the classical assumptions that we used in Chapters 3, 4, and 7, prices are flexible and the adjustment process is rapid. When prices are flexible, the economy is effectively self-correcting, automatically returning to full employment after a shock moves it away from general equilibrium.[9] Indeed, if firms respond to increased demand by raising prices rather than by temporarily producing more (as we earlier assumed), the adjustment process would be almost immediate.

According to the opposing Keynesian view, however, sluggish adjustment of prices (and of wages, the price of labor) might prevent general equilibrium from being attained for a much longer period, perhaps even several years. While the economy is not in general equilibrium, Keynesians argue, output is determined by the level of aggregate demand, represented by the intersection of the *IS* and *LM* curves; the economy is not on the *FE* line, and the labor market is not in equilibrium. This assumption of sluggish price adjustment, and the consequent disequilibrium in the labor market, distinguishes the Keynesian version of the *IS–LM* model from the classical version.

Monetary Neutrality. Closely related to the issue of how fast the economy reaches general equilibrium is the question of how a change in the nominal money supply affects the economy. We showed that, after the economy reaches its general equilibrium, an increase in the nominal money supply has no effect on real variables such as output, employment, or the real interest rate but raises the price level. Economists say that there is **monetary neutrality,** or simply that

9. The proposition that a free-market economy with flexible prices is automatically self-correcting is consistent with Adam Smith's invisible-hand idea, discussed in Chapter 1.

money is neutral, if a change in the nominal money supply changes the price level proportionally but has no effect on real variables. Our analysis shows that, after the complete adjustment of prices, money is neutral in the *IS–LM* model.

The practical relevance of monetary neutrality is much debated by classicals and Keynesians. The basic issue again is the speed of price adjustment. In the classical view a monetary expansion is rapidly transmitted into prices and has, at most, a transitory effect on real variables; that is, the economy moves quickly from the situation shown in Fig. 10.9(a) to the situation shown in Fig. 10.9(c), spending little time in the position shown in Fig. 10.9(b). Keynesians agree that money is neutral after prices fully adjust but believe that, because of slow price adjustment, the economy may spend a long time in disequilibrium. During this period the increased money supply causes output and employment to rise and the real interest rate to fall (compare Fig. 10.9b with Fig. 10.9a).

In brief, Keynesians believe in monetary neutrality in the long run (after prices adjust) but not in the short run. Classicals are more accepting of the view that money is neutral even in the relatively short run. We return to the issue of monetary neutrality when we develop the classical and Keynesian models of the business cycle in more detail in Chapters 11 and 12.

CHAPTER SUMMARY

1. The *IS–LM* model represents the three main markets of the economy—the labor market, the goods market, and the asset market—simultaneously, in a diagram that has the real interest rate on the vertical axis and output on the horizontal axis. Although the *IS–LM* model was originally developed by Keynesians, it may be used to illustrate both classical and Keynesian analyses of the economy.

2. In the *IS–LM* model, equilibrium in the labor market is represented graphically by the full-employment, or *FE*, line, which is vertical at full-employment output. Factors that raise full-employment output shift the *FE* line to the right, and factors that reduce full-employment output shift the *FE* line to the left.

3. For any level of output, the *IS* curve shows the value of the real interest rate that clears the goods market. The *IS* curve slopes downward because higher output leads to more desired saving and thus a lower goods-market-clearing real interest rate. For constant output, any change that reduces desired national saving relative to desired investment increases the real interest rate that clears the goods market and shifts the *IS* curve up. Equivalently, for constant output, any change that increases the aggregate demand for goods increases the real interest rate that clears the goods market and shifts the *IS* curve up.

4. For any level of output, the *LM* curve identifies the real interest rate that equates the quantities of money supplied and demanded and thus clears the asset market. The *LM* curve slopes upward because an increase in output raises money demand, implying that a higher real interest rate is needed to clear the asset market. With output fixed, any change that reduces the money supply relative to money demand increases the real interest rate that clears the asset market and causes the *LM* curve to shift up.

5. General equilibrium in the macroeconomy occurs when all markets are in equilibrium. Graphically, the general equilibrium point is where the *IS* curve, the *FE* line, and the *LM* curve intersect. Price level adjustments push the economy toward general equilibrium.

Specifically, changes in the price level, P, change the real money supply, M/P, which causes the LM curve to shift until it passes through the point at which the FE line and the IS curve intersect.

6. A temporary adverse supply shock causes the general equilibrium levels of the real wage, employment, output, consumption, and investment to fall, and the general equilibrium levels of the real interest rate and price level to increase.

7. A change in the money supply is neutral if it leads to a proportional change in the price level but doesn't affect real variables. In the IS–LM model, money is neutral after prices have adjusted and the economy has returned to general equilibrium.

8. Classical macroeconomists argue that prices and wages adjust rapidly so that following shocks or changes in policy the economy reaches its general equilibrium point quickly. In contrast, Keynesians argue that prices and wages adjust slowly enough that the economy can remain away from its general equilibrium for a prolonged period of time. Keynesians agree with classicals, however, that eventually prices and wages fully adjust and the economy reaches its general equilibrium.

KEY DIAGRAM 6

The *IS–LM* diagram

The *IS–LM* diagram shows general equilibrium in the goods, asset, and labor markets. It can be used to analyze the effects of economic shocks on output, the real interest rate, the price level, and other macroeconomic variables.

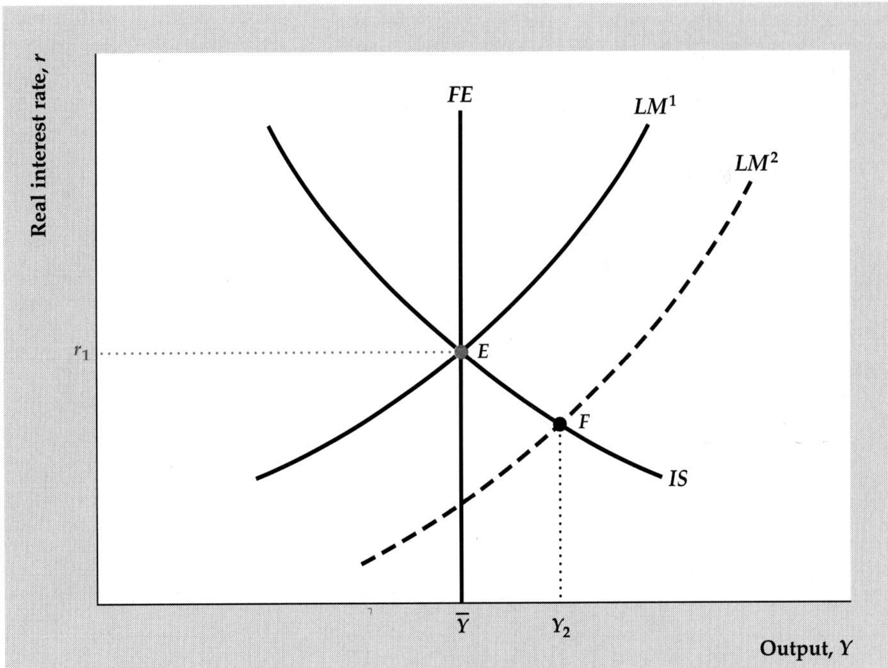

Diagram Elements

- The real interest rate, r, is on the vertical axis, and output, Y, is on the horizontal axis.
- The full-employment line, FE, is vertical at full-employment output. Full-employment output, $\bar{Y}$, is the level of output that firms supply when wages and prices have fully adjusted, so employment is at its full-employment level, $\bar{N}$. Full-employment output is determined by the equation $\bar{Y} = AF(K, \bar{N})$.
- For any level of output Y, the IS curve gives the real interest rate r that clears the goods market—or, in

other words, the rate that equalizes desired national saving, S^d, and desired investment, I^d. Because higher output raises desired saving and lowers the real interest rate that clears the goods market, the *IS* curve slopes downward. Equivalently, the *IS* curve gives combinations of output Y and the real interest rate r that equalize the aggregate quantities of goods supplied and demanded, $Y = C^d + I^d + G$.

- For given values of the price level and output, the *LM* curve gives the real interest rate that clears the asset market, making the real money supply, M/P, and the real quantity of money demanded, $L(Y, r + \pi^e)$, equal. Because an increase in income raises real money demand, which raises the real interest rate that clears the asset market, the *LM* curve slopes upward.

Factors that Shift the Curves

- Any factor that raises full-employment output shifts the *FE* line to the right. See Summary table 11.
- For constant output, any change that reduces desired national saving relative to desired investment increases the real interest rate that clears the goods market and shifts the *IS* curve up. Equivalently, any change that increases the aggregate demand for goods at a specific level of income raises the real interest rate that clears the goods market and shifts the *IS* curve up. See Summary table 12.
- For constant output, any change that reduces real money supply relative to real money demand increases the real interest rate that clears the asset market and shifts the *LM* curve up. See Summary table 13.

Analysis

- If we assume that the *LM* curve is LM^1, the economy is in general equilibrium at point E, which lies on all three curves. At E the labor market (*FE* line), the goods market (*IS* curve), and the asset market (*LM* curve) are all in equilibrium. At E output equals full-employment output $\bar{Y}$; and the real interest rate, r_1, clears both the goods and asset markets.
- If we assume that the *LM* curve is LM^2, the *FE* line and *IS* and *LM* curves don't all intersect, and the economy is out of general equilibrium. We assume that, when the economy is out of general equilibrium, the short-run equilibrium of the economy occurs at the intersection of the *IS* and *LM* curves (point F), where the goods and asset markets are in equilibrium but the labor market isn't. If we further assume that (at least temporarily) firms produce enough output to meet the increased aggregate demand at F, in short-run equilibrium the economy's output is Y_2.
- At the short-run equilibrium point, F, output Y_2 is greater than firms' profit-maximizing level of output $\bar{Y}$. Because aggregate demand at F exceeds what firms want to produce, they raise prices. An increase in the price level P lowers the real money supply M/P and shifts the *LM* curve up to LM^1, and general equilibrium is reached at E. At E output again equals full-employment output $\bar{Y}$. Similarly, if the short-run equilibrium had been to the left of the *FE* line, declines in the price level P would have shifted the *LM* curve to the right and restored general equilibrium at E.
- According to classical economists, the price adjustment process quickly restores the economy to general equilibrium at point E, so the economy spends little or no time away from full employment at point F. Keynesians argue that prices and wages are slow to adjust, so the economy may remain at the short-run equilibrium point, F, with output different from $\bar{Y}$, for an extended period of time.

Key Terms

full-employment line, p. 317
general equilibrium, p. 331
IS curve, p. 318
LM curve, p. 327
monetary neutrality, p. 341

Review Questions

1. What determines the position of the *FE* line? Give two examples of changes in the economy that would shift the *FE* line to the right.
2. What relationship does the *IS* curve capture? Derive the *IS* curve graphically and show why it slopes as

it does. Give two examples of changes in the economy that would cause the *IS* curve to shift down and to the left.

3. What relationship does the *LM* curve capture? Derive the *LM* curve graphically and show why it slopes as it does. Give two examples of changes in the economy that would cause the *LM* curve to shift down and to the right.
4. For constant output, if real money supply exceeds the real quantity of money demanded, what will happen to the real interest rate that clears the asset market? In describing the adjustment of the real interest rate, use the relationship that exists between the price of a nonmonetary asset and the interest rate that it pays.
5. Define *general equilibrium* and show the general equilibrium point in the *IS–LM* diagram. If the economy isn't in general equilibrium, what determines output and the real interest rate? What economic forces act to bring the economy back to general equilibrium?
6. Define *monetary neutrality*. Show that, after prices adjust completely, money is neutral in the *IS–LM* model. What are the classical and Keynesian views about whether money is neutral in the short run? In the long run?

Numerical Problems

1. Desired consumption and investment are

$$C^d = 3600 - 2000r + 0.10Y;$$
$$I^d = 1200 - 4000r.$$

As usual, Y is output and r is the real interest rate. Government purchases G are 1200.

a. Find an equation relating desired national saving S^d to r and Y.

b. What value of the real interest rate clears the goods market when $Y = 6000$? Use both forms of the goods market equilibrium condition. What value of the real interest rate clears the goods market when $Y = 6400$? Graph the *IS* curve.

c. Government purchases rise to 1320. How does this increase change the equation for national saving in part (a)? What value of the real interest rate clears the goods market when $Y = 6000$? Use both forms of the goods market equilibrium condition. How is the *IS* curve affected by the increase in G?

2. In a particular economy the real money demand function is

$$\frac{M^d}{P} = 2000 + 0.2Y - 20,000i.$$

Assume that $M = 3000$, $P = 2.0$, and $\pi^e = 0.05$.

a. What is the real interest rate r that clears the asset market when $Y = 5000$? When $Y = 6000$? Graph the *LM* curve.

b. Repeat part (a) for $M = 3600$. How does the *LM* curve in this case compare with the *LM* curve in part (a)?

c. Use $M = 3000$ again and repeat part (a) for $\pi^e = 0.04$. Compare the *LM* curve in this case with the one in part (a).

3. An economy has full-employment output of 1000. Desired consumption and desired investment are

$$C^d = 200 + 0.8(Y - T) - 500r;$$
$$I^d = 200 - 500r.$$

Government purchases are 196 and taxes are

$$T = 20 + 0.25Y.$$

Money demand is

$$\frac{M^d}{P} = 0.5Y - 250(r + \pi^e),$$

where the expected rate of inflation $\pi^e = 0.10$. The nominal supply of money $M = 9890$.

a. What are the general equilibrium values of the real interest rate, price level, consumption, and investment?

b. Suppose that government purchases are increased to $G = 216$. What are the new general equilibrium values of the real interest rate, the price level, consumption, and investment?

4. The production function in an economy is

$$Y = A(5N - 0.0025N^2),$$

where A is productivity. With this production function, the marginal product of labor is

$$MPN = 5A - 0.005AN.$$

Suppose that $A = 2$. The labor supply curve is

$$NS = 55 + 10(1 - t)w,$$

where NS is the amount of labor supplied, w is the real wage, and t is the tax rate, which is 0.5.

Desired consumption and investment are

$$C^d = 300 + 0.8(Y - T) - 200r;$$
$$I^d = 258.5 - 250r.$$

Taxes and government purchases are

$$T = 20 + 0.5Y;$$
$$G = 50.$$

Money demand is

$$\frac{M^d}{P} = 0.5Y - 250(r + \pi^e).$$

The expected rate of inflation π^e is 0.02, and the nominal money supply M is 9150.

a. What are the general equilibrium levels of the real wage, employment, and output?

b. For any level of output Y, find an equation that gives the real interest rate r that clears the goods market; this equation describes the *IS* curve. (*Hint:* Write the goods market equilibrium condition and solve for r in terms of Y and other variables.) What are the general equilibrium values of the real interest rate, consumption, and investment?

c. For any level of output Y, find an equation that gives the real interest rate that clears the asset market; this equation describes the *LM* curve. (*Hint:* As in part (b), write the appropriate equilibrium condition and solve for r in terms of Y and other variables.) What is the general equilibrium value of the price level?

d. Suppose that government purchases increase to $G = 72.5$. Now what are the general equilibrium values of the real wage, employment, output, the real interest rate, consumption, investment, and the price level?

5. (Appendix). This question asks you to use the formulas in Appendix 10.A to find the general equilibrium values of variables for the economy described in Numerical Problem 4. Assume that $G = 50$.

a. Use the data from Numerical Problem 4 to find the numerical values of the parameters $A, f_1, f_2, n_0, n_w, c_0, c_Y, c_r, t_0, t, i_0, i_r, \ell_0, \ell_Y$, and ℓ_r defined in Appendix 10.A.

b. Substitute the values of these behavioral parameters into the relevant equations in Appendix 10.A to compute the general equilibrium values of the real wage, employment, output, the real interest rate, and the price level.

c. Assume that government purchases G increase to 72.5, and repeat part (b).

Analytical Problems

1. Use the *IS–LM* model to determine the effects of each of the following on the general equilibrium values of the real wage, employment, output, the real interest rate, consumption, investment, and the price level.

a. A reduction in the effective tax rate on capital that increases desired investment.

b. The expected rate of inflation rises.

c. An influx of working-age immigrants increases labor supply (ignore any other possible effects of increased population).

d. The introduction of automatic teller machines reduces the demand for money.

2. Use the *IS–LM* model to analyze the general equilibrium effects of a permanent increase in the price of oil (a permanent adverse supply shock) on current output, employment, the real wage, national saving, consumption, investment, the real interest rate, and the price level. Assume that, besides reducing the current productivity of capital and labor, the permanent supply shock lowers both the expected future *MPK* and households' expected future incomes. Show that, if the real interest rate rises at all, it will rise less than in the case of a temporary supply shock that has an equal effect on current output.

3. Suppose that the price level is fixed in the short run so that the economy doesn't reach general equilibrium immediately after a change in the economy. For each of the following changes, what are the short-run effects on the real interest rate and output? Assume that, when the economy is in disequilibrium, only the labor market is out of equilibrium; assume also that for a short period firms are willing to produce enough output to meet the aggregate demand for output.

a. A decrease in the expected rate of inflation.

b. An increase in consumer optimism that increases desired consumption at each level of income and the real interest rate.

c. An increase in government purchases.

d. An increase in lump-sum taxes, with no change in government purchases (consider both the case in which Ricardian equivalence holds and the case in which it doesn't).

e. A scientific breakthrough increases the expected future *MPK*.

4. (Appendix) In some macroeconomic models, desired investment depends on the current level of output as well as on the real interest rate. One possible reason that desired investment may depend on output is that, when current production and sales are high, firms may expect continued strong demand for their products in the future, which leads them to want to expand capacity.

Algebraically, we can allow for a link between desired investment and current output by replacing Eq. (10.A.10) with

$$I^d = i_0 - i_r r + i_Y Y,$$

where i_Y is a positive number. Use this alternative equation for desired investment to derive the algebraic expressions for the general equilibrium values of employment, the real wage, output, the real interest rate, and the price level.

5. (Appendix) Recall from Chapter 7 that an increase in i^m, the nominal interest rate on money, increases the demand for money. To capture that effect, let's replace Eq. (10.A.17) with

$$\frac{M^d}{P} = \ell_0 + \ell_Y Y - \ell_r (r + \pi^e - i^m).$$

How does this modification change the solutions for the general equilibrium values of the variables discussed in Appendix 10.A, including employment, the real wage, output, the real interest rate, and the price level?

APPENDIX 10.A AN ALGEBRAIC VERSION OF THE *IS-LM* MODEL

This appendix presents an algebraic version of the *IS–LM* model. For each of the three markets—labor, goods, and assets—we first present equations that describe demand and supply in that market, then find the market equilibrium. After considering each market separately, we solve for the general equilibrium of the complete *IS–LM* model. Appendixes 11.A and 12.B extend the algebraic approach to short-run departures of the economy from general equilibrium, with Appendix 11.A illustrating the classical approach and Appendix 12.B illustrating the Keynesian approach.

The Labor Market

The demand for labor is based on the marginal product of labor, as determined by the production function. Recall from Chapter 3 (Eq. 3.1) that the production function can be written as $Y = AF(K, N)$, where Y is output, K is the capital stock, N is labor input, and A is productivity. Holding the capital stock K fixed, we can write the production function with output Y as a function only of labor input N and productivity A. A useful specific production function is

$$Y = A(f_1N - \frac{1}{2}f_2N^2), \qquad (10.A.1)$$

where f_1 and f_2 are positive numbers.

The marginal product of labor, *MPN*, is the slope of the production function. The slope of the production function in Eq. (10.A.1) at any level of employment N equals[10] $A(f_1 - f_2N)$, so the marginal product of labor is

$$MPN = A(f_1 - f_2N) \qquad (10.A.2)$$

Firms hire labor to the point at which the marginal product of labor equals the real wage. Thus, the relation between the real wage w and the amount of labor demanded ND is

$$w = A(f_1 - f_2ND) \qquad (10.A.3)$$

The supply of labor is an increasing function of the current, after-tax real wage. If t is the tax rate on wage income (we assume that $0 < t < 1$) so that $(1 - t)w$ is the after-tax real wage, a simple form of the labor supply curve is

$$NS = n_0 + n_w(1 - t)w, \qquad (10.A.4)$$

10. Students who know calculus can derive the slope of the production function by taking the derivative of Eq. (10.A.1) with respect to N.

where *NS* is the amount of labor supplied, and n_0 and n_w are positive numbers. Factors other than the after-tax real wage that affect labor supply, such as wealth or the working-age population, are captured by the constant term n_0 in Eq. (10.A.4).

Equilibrium in the Labor Market. In equilibrium, the amounts of labor demanded *ND* and supplied *NS* are equal; their common value is the full-employment level of employment $\overline{N}$. If we substitute $\overline{N}$ for *NS* and *ND* in Eqs. (10.A.3) and (10.A.4), we have two linear equations in the two variables $\overline{N}$ and w. Solving these equations for w and $\overline{N}$ yields[11]

$$w = A\left[\frac{f_1 - f_2 n_0}{1 + (1-t)Af_2 n_w}\right] \tag{10.A.5}$$

and

$$\overline{N} = \frac{n_0 + (1-t)Af_1 n_w}{1 + (1-t)Af_2 n_w}. \tag{10.A.6}$$

Using the full-employment level of employment $\overline{N}$ in Eq. (10.A.6), we obtain the full-employment level of output $\overline{Y}$ by substituting $\overline{N}$ into the production function (10.A.1):

$$\overline{Y} = A\left[f_1\overline{N} - \frac{1}{2}f_2\overline{N}^2\right], \text{ } FE \text{ line.} \tag{10.A.7}$$

The value of full-employment output in Eq. (10.A.7) is the horizontal intercept of the *FE* line.

We can use these equations to analyze the effects on the labor market of changes in productivity and in labor supply. First consider an increase in productivity A. Equation (10.A.5) shows that an increase in A leads to an increase in the equilibrium real wage (an increase in A raises the ratio $A/[1 + (1-t)Af_2n_w]$). Although not directly evident from Eq. (10.A.6), an increase in A also increases $\overline{N}$.[12] To see why, note first that an increase in A doesn't affect the labor supply curve, Eq. (10.A.4). Second, an increase in A raises the real wage. Hence the implication is that an increase in A raises the equilibrium amount of labor supplied and thus also the full-employment level of employment $\overline{N}$. Because an increase in A raises $\overline{N}$, it must also raise full-employment output $\overline{Y}$ (see Eq. 10.A.7) and shift the *FE* line to the right.

Now consider an increase in the amount of labor supplied at each level of the after-tax real wage, represented algebraically as an increase in n_0 in Eq. (10.A.4). Equations (10.A.5) and (10.A.6) show that an increase in n_0 reduces the equilibrium real wage and increases employment $\overline{N}$. Because an increase in labor supply raises $\overline{N}$, it also raises full-employment output $\overline{Y}$ and shifts the *FE* line to the right.

11. We assume that the constants f_1, f_2, and n_0 are such that $f_1 - f_2n_0 > 0$. This assumption is needed to guarantee that the marginal product of labor and the equilibrium real wage are positive.

12. Students who know calculus can compute the derivative of $\overline{N}$ with respect to A in Eq. (10.A.6) and will find that the sign of this derivative is positive only if $f_1 - f_2n_0 > 0$. As we have assumed that $f_1 - f_2n_0 > 0$ (see preceding footnote), an increase in A does indeed increase $\overline{N}$.

The Goods Market

To find equilibrium in the goods market, we start with equations describing desired consumption and desired investment. Desired consumption is

$$C^d = c_0 + c_Y(Y - T) - c_r r, \tag{10.A.8}$$

where $Y - T$ is disposable income (income Y minus taxes T), r is the real interest rate, and c_0, c_Y, and c_r are positive numbers. The number c_Y in Eq. (10.A.8) is the marginal propensity to consume, as defined in Chapter 4; because people consume only part of an increase in disposable income, saving the rest, a reasonable assumption is that $0 < c_Y < 1$. According to Eq. (10.A.8), an increase in disposable income causes desired consumption to increase, and an increase in the real interest rate causes desired consumption to fall (and desired saving to rise). Other factors that affect desired consumption, such as wealth or expected future income, are included in the constant term c_0.[13]

Taxes in Eq. (10.A.8) are

$$T = t_0 + tY, \tag{10.A.9}$$

where t is the tax rate on income (the same tax rate that is levied on wages) and t_0 is a lump-sum tax. As mentioned earlier, $0 \le t < 1$, so an increase in income Y increases total taxes T and also increases disposable income $Y - T$, thereby increasing consumption.

Desired investment is

$$I^d = i_0 - i_r r, \tag{10.A.10}$$

where i_0 and i_r are positive numbers. Equation (10.A.10) indicates that desired investment falls when the real interest rate rises. Other factors affecting desired investment, such as the expected future marginal product of capital, are included in the constant term i_0.

Equilibrium in the Goods Market. The goods market equilibrium condition in a closed economy is given by Eq. (4.8), which we repeat here:

$$Y = C^d + I^d + G. \tag{10.A.11}$$

Equation (10.A.11) is equivalent to the goods market equilibrium condition, $S^d = I^d$, which could be used equally well here.

If we substitute the equations for desired consumption (Eq. 10.A.8, with taxes T as given by Eq. 10.A.9) and desired investment (Eq. 10.A.10) into the goods market equilibrium condition (Eq. 10.A.11), we get

$$Y = c_0 + c_Y(Y - t_0 - tY) - c_r r + i_0 - i_r r + G. \tag{10.A.12}$$

---

13. Because an increase in taxes T reduces desired consumption in Eq. (10.A.8), this formulation of desired consumption appears, at first glance, to be inconsistent with the Ricardian equivalence proposition discussed in Chapter 4. However, essential to the idea of Ricardian equivalence is that consumers expect an increase in current taxes T to be accompanied by lower taxes in the future. This decrease in expected future taxes would increase desired consumption, which would be captured in Eq. (10.A.8) as an increase in c_0. According to the Ricardian equivalence proposition, after an increase in T with no change in current or planned government purchases, an increase in c_0 would exactly offset the reduction in $c_Y(Y - T)$ so that desired consumption would be unchanged.

Collecting the terms that multiply Y on the left-hand side yields

$$[1-(1-t)c_Y]Y = c_0 + i_0 + G - c_Y t_0 - (c_r + i_r)r. \qquad (10.A.13)$$

Equation (10.A.13) relates output Y to the real interest rate r that clears the goods market. This relationship between Y and r defines the *IS* curve. Because the *IS* curve is graphed with r on the vertical axis and Y on the horizontal axis, we rewrite Eq. (10.A.13) with r on the left-hand side and Y on the right-hand side. Solving Eq. (10.A.13) for r gives

$$r = \alpha_{IS} - \beta_{IS}Y, \qquad \textit{IS} \text{ curve.} \qquad (10.A.14)$$

In Eq. (10.A.14), α_{IS} and β_{IS} are positive numbers defined as

$$\alpha_{IS} = \frac{c_0 + i_0 + G - c_Y t_0}{c_r + i_r} \qquad (10.A.15)$$

and

$$\beta_{IS} = \frac{1-(1-t)c_Y}{c_r + i_r}. \qquad (10.A.16)$$

Equation (10.A.14) yields the graph of the *IS* curve. In Eq. (10.A.14), the coefficient of Y, or $-\beta_{IS}$, is the slope of the *IS* curve; because this slope is negative, the *IS* curve slopes downward. Changes in the constant term α_{IS} in Eq. (10.A.14), which is defined in Eq. (10.A.15), shift the *IS* curve. Anything that increases α_{IS}—such as (1) an increase in consumer optimism that increases desired consumption by increasing c_0; (2) an increase in the expected future marginal product of capital MPK^f that raises desired investment by raising i_0; or (3) an increase in government purchases G—shifts the *IS* curve up. Similarly, anything that decreases α_{IS} shifts the *IS* curve down.

The Asset Market

In general, the real demand for money depends on real income Y and on the nominal interest rate on nonmonetary assets i, which in turn equals the expected real interest rate r plus the expected rate of inflation π^e. We assume that the money demand function takes the form

$$\frac{M^d}{P} = \ell_0 + \ell_Y Y - \ell_r(r + \pi^e), \qquad (10.A.17)$$

where M^d is the nominal demand for money, P is the price level, and ℓ_0, ℓ_Y, and ℓ_r are positive numbers. The constant term ℓ_0 includes factors other than output and the interest rate that affect money demand, such as the liquidity of alternative assets. The real supply of money equals the nominal supply of money M, which is determined by the central bank, divided by the price level P.

Equilibrium in the Asset Market. As we showed in Chapter 7, if we assume that there are only two types of assets (money and nonmonetary assets), the asset market is in equilibrium when the real quantity of money demanded equals the real money supply M/P. Using the money demand function in Eq. (10.A.17), we write the asset market equilibrium condition as

$$\frac{M}{P} = \ell_0 + \ell_Y Y - \ell_r (r + \pi^e). \qquad (10.A.18)$$

For fixed levels of the nominal money supply M, price level P, and expected rate of inflation π^e, Eq. (10.A.18) relates output Y and the real interest rate r that clears the asset market. Thus Eq. (10.A.18) defines the *LM* curve. To get Eq. (10.A.18) into a form that is easier to interpret graphically, we rewrite the equation with r alone of the left-hand side:

$$r = \alpha_{LM} - \left(\frac{1}{\ell_r}\right)\left(\frac{M}{P}\right) + \beta_{LM} Y, \qquad LM \text{ curve}, \qquad (10.A.19)$$

where

$$\alpha_{LM} = \left(\frac{\ell_0}{\ell_r}\right) - \pi^e \qquad (10.A.20)$$

and

$$\beta_{LM} = \left(\frac{\ell_Y}{\ell_r}\right). \qquad (10.A.21)$$

The graph of Eq. (10.A.19) is the *LM* curve. In Eq. (10.A.19), the coefficient of Y, or β_{LM}, is the slope of the *LM* curve; because this coefficient is positive, the *LM* curve slopes upward. Variables that change the intercept of the equation in Eq. (10.A.19), $\alpha_{LM} - (1/\ell_r)(M/P)$, shift the *LM* curve. An increase in the real money supply M/P reduces this intercept and thus shifts the *LM* curve down and to the right. An increase in the expected rate of inflation π^e reduces α_{LM} and shifts the *LM* curve down. An increase in real money demand arising from (for example) reduced liquidity of alternative assets raises ℓ_0, which raises α_{LM} and shifts the *LM* curve up.

General Equilibrium in the *IS–LM* Model

From the supply and demand relationships and equilibrium conditions in each market, we can calculate the general equilibrium values for the most important macroeconomic variables. We have already solved for the general equilibrium levels of the real wage, employment, and output in the labor market: The real wage is given by Eq. (10.A.5); employment equals its full-employment level $\bar{N}$, given by Eq. (10.A.6); and, in general equilibrium, output equals its full-employment level $\bar{Y}$, as given by Eq. (10.A.7).

Turning to the goods market, we obtain the general equilibrium real interest rate by substituting $\bar{Y}$ for Y in Eq. (10.A.14):

$$r = \alpha_{IS} - \beta_{IS}\bar{Y}. \qquad (10.A.22)$$

Having output $\bar{Y}$ and the real interest rate r (determined by Eq. 10.A.22), we use Eqs. (10.A.9), (10.A.8), and (10.A.10) to find the general equilibrium values of taxes T, consumption C, and investment I, respectively.

The final important macroeconomic variable whose equilibrium value needs to be determined is the price level P. To find the equilibrium price level, we work with the asset market equilibrium condition, Eq. (10.A.18). In Eq. (10.A.18), we substitute full-employment output $\bar{Y}$ for Y and use Eq. (10.A.22) to substitute the equilibrium value of the real interest rate for r. Solving Eq. (10.A.18) for the price level gives

$$P = \frac{M}{\ell_0 + \ell_Y \bar{Y} - \ell_r(\alpha_{IS} - \beta_{IS}\bar{Y} + \pi^e)}. \tag{10.A.23}$$

Equation (10.A.23) confirms that the equilibrium price level P is proportional to the nominal money supply M.

We can use these equations to analyze the effects of an adverse productivity shock on the general equilibrium, as in the text. We have already shown that an increase in the productivity parameter A increases the equilibrium real wage, the full-employment level of employment, and the full-employment level of output. Thus an adverse productivity shock (a reduction in A) reduces the general equilibrium levels of the real wage, employment, and output. Equation (10.A.22) indicates that an adverse productivity shock, because it reduces $\bar{Y}$, must increase the equilibrium real interest rate. Lower output and a higher real interest rate imply that both consumption and investment must decline (Eqs. 10.A.8 and 10.A.10). Finally, the decrease in $\bar{Y}$ resulting from an adverse productivity shock reduces the denominator of the right-hand side of Eq. (10.A.23), so the price level P must rise. All these results are the same as those found by graphical analysis.

CHAPTER 11

Classical Business Cycle Analysis: Market-Clearing Macroeconomics

Economists generally agree about the basic business cycle facts outlined in Chapter 9. They know that economic growth isn't necessarily smooth and that occasionally there are periods of recession in which output declines and unemployment rises. They know that recessions typically are followed by periods of recovery in which the economy grows more strongly than normal. And they also know a great deal about how other macroeconomic variables—such as productivity, interest rates, and inflation—behave during recessions.

Recall that recessions and booms in the economy raise two basic questions: (1) What are the underlying economic causes of these business cycles? and (2) What, if anything, should government policymakers do about them? Unfortunately, economists agree less about the answers to these two questions than about the basic business cycle facts.

The main disagreements about the causes and cures of recessions are between two broad groups of macroeconomists, the classicals and the Keynesians. As discussed first in Chapter 1 and again in Chapter 10, classicals and Keynesians—although agreeing on many points—differ primarily in their views on how rapidly prices and wages adjust to restore general equilibrium after an economic shock. Classical macroeconomists assume that prices and wages adjust quickly to equate quantities supplied and demanded in each market; as a result, they argue, a market economy is largely "self-correcting," with a strong tendency to return to general equilibrium on its own when it is disturbed by an economic shock or a change in public policy. Keynesians usually agree that prices and wages *eventually* change as needed to clear markets; however, they believe that *in the short run* price and wage adjustment is likely to be incomplete. That is, in the short run quantities supplied and demanded need not be equal and the economy may remain out of general equilibrium. Although this difference in views may seem purely theoretical, it has a practical implication: Because Keynesians are skeptical about the economy's ability to reach equilibrium rapidly on its own, they are much more inclined than are classicals to recommend that the government act to raise output and employment during recessions and to moderate economic growth during booms.

In this chapter and Chapter 12 we develop and compare the classical and Keynesian theories of the business cycle and the policy recommendations of the two groups, beginning with the classical perspective in this chapter. Conveniently, both the classical and Keynesian analyses can be expressed in terms of a common analytical framework, the *IS–LM* model. In this chapter we use the classical (or market-clearing) version of the *IS–LM* model, comprising the *IS–LM* model and the assumption that prices and wages adjust rapidly. The assumption that prices and wages adjust rapidly implies that the economy always is in or near general equilibrium and therefore that variables such as output and employment always are close to their general equilibrium levels.

In comparing the principal competing theories of the business cycle, we are particularly interested in how well the various theories explain the business cycle facts. The classical theory is consistent with many of the most important facts about the cycle. However, one business cycle fact that challenges the classical theory is the observation that changes in the money stock lead the cycle. Recall the implication of the classical assumption that wages and prices adjust quickly to clear markets: Money is neutral so that changes in the money supply do not affect output and other real variables. However, most economists interpret the fact that money leads the cycle as evidence that money is *not* neutral in all situations. If money is not neutral, we must either modify the basic classical model to account for monetary nonneutrality or abandon the classical model in favor of alternative theories (such as the Keynesian approach) that are consistent with nonneutrality. In Section 11.3 we extend the classical model to allow for nonneutrality of money. We then examine the implications of this extended classical approach for macroeconomic policy.

11.1 BUSINESS CYCLES IN THE CLASSICAL MODEL

We have identified two basic questions of business cycle analysis: What causes business cycles? and What can (or should) be done about them? Let's examine the classical answers to these questions, beginning with what causes business cycles.

The Real Business Cycle Theory

In general, a complete theory of the business cycle must have two components. The first component is a description of the types of shocks or disturbances believed to affect the economy the most. Examples of economic disturbances emphasized by various theories of the business cycle include supply shocks, changes in monetary or fiscal policy, and changes in consumer spending. The second component is a model that describes how key macroeconomic variables, such as output, employment, and prices, respond to economic shocks.

The model preferred by classical economists is the market-clearing version of the *IS–LM* model or some similar framework. However, the issue of which shocks are crucial in driving cyclical fluctuations remains.

An influential group of classical macroeconomists, led by Edward Prescott of the University of Minnesota and Finn Kydland of Carnegie Mellon University, developed a theory that takes a strong stand on the sources of shocks that cause cyclical fluctuations. This theory, the **real business cycle theory** (or RBC theory), argues that real shocks to the economy are the primary cause of business cycles.[1] **Real shocks** are disturbances to the "real side" of the economy, such as shocks that affect the production function, the size of the labor force, the real quantity of government purchases, and the spending and saving decisions of consumers. Economists contrast real shocks with **nominal shocks,** or shocks to money supply or money demand. In terms of the *IS–LM* model, real shocks directly affect only the *IS* curve or the *FE* line, whereas nominal shocks directly affect only the *LM* curve.

Although many types of real shocks could contribute to the business cycle, RBC theorists give the largest role to production function shocks—what we've called supply shocks and what the RBC theorists usually refer to as **productivity shocks.** Productivity shocks include the development of new products or production methods, the introduction of new management techniques, changes in the quality of capital or labor, changes in the availability of raw materials or energy, unusually good or unusually bad weather, changes in government regulations affecting production, and any other factor affecting productivity. According to RBC theorists, most economic booms result from beneficial productivity shocks, and most recessions are caused by adverse productivity shocks.

The Recessionary Impact of an Adverse Productivity Shock. Does the RBC theorists' idea that adverse productivity shocks lead to recessions (and, similarly, that beneficial productivity shocks lead to booms) make sense? We examined the theoretical effects on the economy of a temporary adverse productivity shock in Chapters 3 and 10.[2] In Chapter 3 we showed that an adverse productivity shock (or supply shock), such as an increase in the price of oil, reduces the marginal product of labor (*MPN*) and the demand for labor at any real wage. As a result, the equilibrium values of the real wage and employment both fall (see Fig 3.10). The equilibrium level of output (the full-employment level of output $\bar{Y}$) also falls, both because equilibrium employment declines and because the adverse productivity shock reduces the amount of output that can be produced by any amount of capital and labor.

We later used the complete *IS–LM* model (Fig. 10.8) to explore the general equilibrium effects of a temporary adverse productivity shock. We confirmed our earlier conclusion that an adverse productivity shock lowers the general equilibrium levels of the real wage, employment, and output. In addition, we showed that an adverse productivity shock raises the real interest rate, depresses consumption and investment, and raises the price level.

1. For a more detailed introduction to real business cycles, see Charles Plosser, "Understanding Real Business Cycles," *Journal of Economic Perspectives,* Summer 1989, pp. 51–78.

2. RBC theorists analyze permanent as well as temporary productivity shocks; we focus on temporary shocks because it is the slightly easier case.

Broadly, then, our earlier analyses of the effects of an adverse productivity shock support the RBC theorists' claim that such shocks are recessionary, in that they lead to declines in output. Similar analyses show that a beneficial productivity shock leads to a rise in output (a boom). Note that, in the RBC approach, output declines in recessions and rises in booms because the general equilibrium (or full-employment) level of output has changed and because rapid price adjustment ensures that actual output always equals full-employment output. As classical economists, RBC theorists would reject the Keynesian view (discussed in Chapter 12) that recessions and booms are periods of disequilibrium, during which actual output is below or above its general equilibrium level for a protracted period of time.

Real Business Cycle Theory and the Business Cycle Facts. Although the RBC theory—which combines the classical, or market-clearing, version of the *IS–LM* model with the assumption that productivity shocks are the dominant form of economic disturbance—is relatively simple, it is consistent with many of the basic business cycle facts. First, under the assumption that the economy is being continuously buffeted by productivity shocks, the RBC approach predicts recurrent fluctuations in aggregate output, which actually occur. Second, the RBC theory correctly predicts that employment will move procyclically—that is, in the same direction as output. Third, the RBC theory predicts that real wages will be higher during booms than during recessions (procyclical real wages), as also occurs.

A fourth business cycle fact explained by the RBC theory is that average labor productivity is procyclical; that is, output per worker is higher during booms than during recessions. This fact is consistent with the RBC theorists' assumption that booms are periods of beneficial productivity shocks, which tend to raise labor productivity, whereas recessions are the results of adverse productivity shocks, which tend to reduce labor productivity. The RBC theorists point out that without productivity shocks—allowing the production function to remain stable over time—average labor productivity wouldn't be procyclical. With no productivity shocks, the expansion of employment that occurs during booms would tend to reduce average labor productivity because of the principle of diminishing marginal productivity of labor. Similarly, without productivity shocks, recessions would be periods of relatively higher labor productivity, instead of lower productivity as observed. Thus RBC theorists regard the procyclical nature of average labor productivity as strong evidence supporting their approach.

A business cycle fact that does *not* seem to be consistent with the simple RBC theory is that inflation tends to slow during or immediately after a recession. The theory predicts that an adverse productivity shock will both cause a recession and increase the general price level. Thus, according to the RBC approach, periods of recession should also be periods of inflation, contrary to the business cycle fact.

Some RBC theorists have responded by taking issue with the conventional view that inflation is procyclical. For example, in a study of the period 1954–1989, real business cycle proponents Finn Kydland and Edward Prescott[3] showed that procyclical inflation is somewhat sensitive to the statistical methods

3. "Business Cycles: Real Facts and a Monetary Myth," *Quarterly Review*, Federal Reserve Bank of Minneapolis, Spring 1990, pp. 3–18.

used to calculate the trends in inflation and output. Using a different method of calculating these trends, Kydland and Prescott found evidence that, when aggregate output has been above its long-run trend, the price level has tended to be below its long-run trend, a result more nearly consistent with the RBC prediction about the cyclical behavior of prices. Kydland and Prescott suggested that standard views about the procyclicality of prices and inflation are based mostly on the experience of the economy between the two world wars (1918–1941), when the economy had a different structure and was subject to different types of shocks than the more recent economy. The fact that inflation surged following the oil price shocks of 1973–1974 and 1979–1980 is consistent with the prediction of the RBC theory. The issue of the cyclical behavior of prices remains controversial, however.[4]

APPLICATION

Calibrating the Business Cycle

Putting aside the debate about price level behavior, the RBC theory can account for some of the business cycle facts, including the procyclical behavior of employment, productivity, and real wages. However, real business cycle theorists argue that an adequate theory of the business cycle should be *quantitative* as well as *qualitative*. In other words, in addition to predicting generally how key macroeconomic variables move throughout the business cycle, the theory should predict numerically the size of economic fluctuations and the strength of relationships among the variables.

To examine the quantitative implications of their theories, RBC theorists developed a method called *calibration*. The idea is to work out a detailed numerical example of a more general theory. The results are then compared to observations to see whether model and reality broadly agree.

The first step in calibration is to write a simple classical model of the economy—such as the classical version of the *IS–LM* model—except that specific functions replace general functions. For example, instead of representing the production function in general terms as

$$Y = AF(K, N),$$

the person doing the calibration uses a specific algebraic form for the production function, such as[5]

$$Y = AK^{a}N^{1-a},$$

where a is a number between 0 and 1. Similarly, specific functions are used to describe the behavior of consumers and workers.

Next, the specific functions chosen are made even more specific by expressing them in numerical terms. For example, for $a = 0.3$, the production function becomes

$$Y = AK^{0.3}N^{0.7}.$$

In the same way, specific numbers are assigned to the functions describing the behavior of consumers and workers. Where do these numbers come from?

---

4. Another RBC response to this criticism is to note that in reality the money supply is not literally fixed, as we assumed in our analysis of the effects of a productivity shock in Chapter 10. To the extent that the money supply declines in recessions, the tendency for prices to rise will be less.

5. This production function is the Cobb–Douglas production function (Chapter 3). As we noted, although it is relatively simple, it fits U.S. data quite well.

Generally, they are *not* estimated from macroeconomic data but are based on other sources. For example, the numbers assigned to the functions in the model may come from previous studies of the production function or of the saving behavior of individuals and families.

The third step, which must be carried out on a computer, is to find out how the numerically specified model behaves when it is hit by random shocks, such as productivity shocks. The shocks are created on the computer with a random number generator, with the size and persistence of the shocks (unlike the numbers assigned to the specific functions) being chosen to fit the actual macroeconomic data. For these shocks, the computer tracks the behavior of the model over many periods and reports the implied behavior of key macroeconomic variables such as output, employment, consumption, and investment. The results are then compared to the behavior of the actual economy to determine how well the model fits reality.

One of the developers of RBC theory, Edward Prescott[6] of the University of Minnesota, performed an early and influential calibration exercise. Prescott used a model similar to the RBC model we present here, the main difference being that our version of the RBC model is essentially a two-period model (the present and the future), and Prescott's model allowed for many periods. The results of Prescott's computer simulations are shown in Figs. 11.1 and 11.2.

6. "Theory Ahead of Business Cycle Measurement," *Carnegie-Rochester Conference Series on Public Policy*, Volume 25, Autumn 1986, pp. 11–39. Reprinted in *Quarterly Review*, Federal Reserve Bank of Minneapolis, Fall 1986, pp. 9–22.

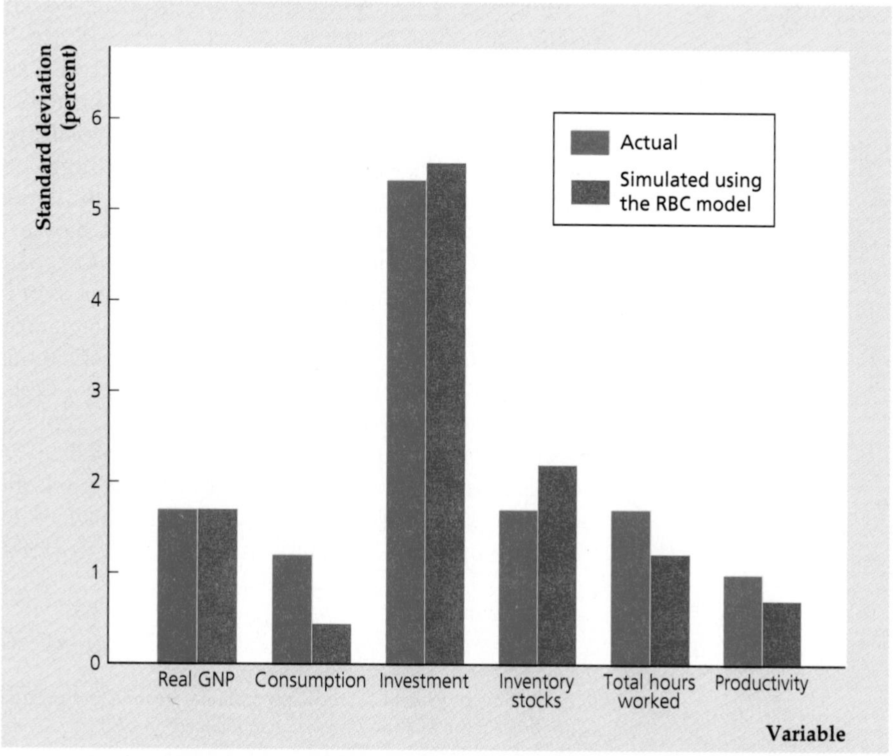

Figure 11.1
Actual versus simulated volatilities of key macroeconomic variables
The figure compares the actual volatilities of key macroeconomic variables observed in post–World War II U.S. data with the volatilities of the same variables predicted by computer simulations of Edward Prescott's calibrated RBC model. Prescott set the size of the random productivity shocks in his simulations so that the simulated volatility of GNP would match the actually observed volatility of GNP exactly. For these random productivity shocks, the simulated volatilities of the other five macroeconomic variables (with the possible exception of consumption) match the observed volatilities fairly well.

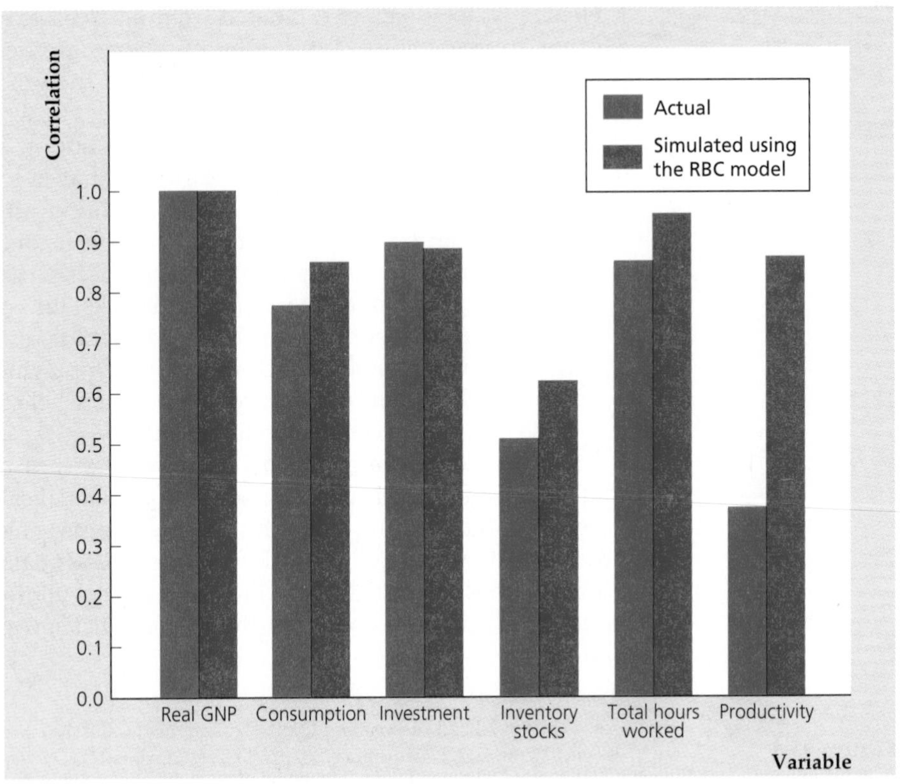

Figure 11.2
Actual versus simulated correlations of key macroeconomic variables with GNP
How closely a variable moves with GNP over the business cycle is measured by its correlation with GNP, with higher correlations implying a closer relationship. The figure compares the correlations of key variables with GNP that were actually observed in the post–World War II U.S. economy with the correlations predicted by computer simulations of Prescott's calibrated RBC model. Except for productivity, whose predicted correlation with GNP is too high, the simulations predicted correlations of macroeconomic variables with GNP that closely resemble the actual correlations of these variables with GNP.

Figure 11.1 compares the actually observed volatilities of six macroeconomic variables, as calculated from post–World War II U.S. data, with the volatilities predicted by Prescott's calibrated RBC model.[7] Prescott set the size of the random productivity shocks in his simulations so that the volatility of GNP in his model would match the actual volatility in U.S. GNP.[8] That choice explains why the actual and simulated volatilities of GNP are equal in Fig. 11.1. But he did nothing to guarantee that the simulation would match the actual volatilities of the other five variables. Note, however, that the simulated and actual volatilities for the other variables in most cases are quite close.

Figure 11.2 compares the actual economy with Prescott's calibrated model in another respect: how closely important macroeconomic variables move with GNP over the business cycle. The statistical measure of how closely variables move together is called *correlation.* If a variable's correlation with GNP is positive, the variable tends to move in the same direction as GNP over the business cycle (that is, the variable is procyclical). A correlation with GNP of 1.0 indicates that the variable's movements track the movements of GNP perfectly (thus the correlation of GNP with itself is 1.0), and a correlation with GNP of 0 indicates no relationship to GNP. Correlations with GNP between 0

7. The measure of volatility used is called the *standard deviation.* The higher the standard deviation, the more volatile is the variable being measured.

8. At the time of Prescott's study, the national income and product accounts of the U.S. focused on GNP rather than GDP, so Prescott also focused on GNP.

and 1.0 reflect relationships with GNP of intermediate strength. Figure 11.2 shows that Prescott's model generally accounts well for the strength of the relationships between some of the variables and GNP, although the correlation of productivity and GNP predicted by Prescott's model is noticeably larger than the actual correlation.

The degree to which relatively simple calibrated RBC models can match the actual data is impressive. In addition, the results of calibration exercises help guide further development of the model. For example, the version of the RBC model discussed here has been modified to improve the match between the actual and predicted correlations of productivity with GNP.

Are Productivity Shocks the Only Source of Recessions? Although RBC theorists agree in principle that many types of real shocks buffet the economy, in practice much of their work rests on the assumption that productivity shocks are the dominant, or even the only, source of recessions. Many economists, including both classicals and Keynesians, have criticized this assumption as being unrealistic. For example, some economists challenged the RBC theorists to identify the specific productivity shocks that they believe caused each of the recessions since World War II. The critics argue that, except for the oil price shocks of 1973, 1979, and 1990, historical examples of economywide productivity shocks are virtually nonexistent.

An interesting RBC response to that argument is that, in principle, economywide fluctuations could also be caused by the cumulative effects of a series of small productivity shocks. To illustrate the point that small shocks can cause large fluctuations, Fig. 11.3 shows the results of a computer simulation of

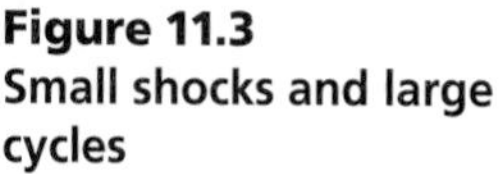

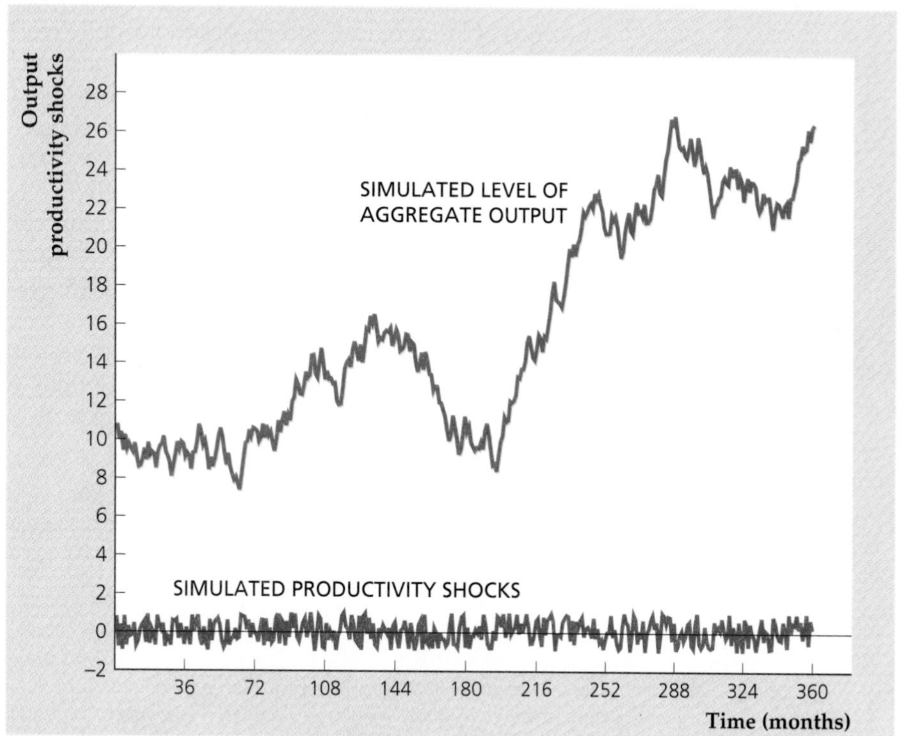

Figure 11.3
Small shocks and large cycles
A computer simulation of a simple RBC model is used to find the relationship between computer-generated random productivity shocks (shown at the bottom of the figure) and aggregate output (shown in the middle of the figure). Even though all the productivity shocks are small, the simulation produces large cyclical fluctuations in aggregate output. Thus large productivity shocks aren't necessary to generate large cyclical fluctuations.

productivity shocks and the associated behavior of output for a simplified RBC model. In this simple RBC model the change in output from one month to the next has two parts: (1) a fixed part that arises from normal technical progress or from a normal increase in population and employment; and (2) an unpredictable part that reflects a random shock to productivity during the current month.[9] The random, computer-generated productivity shocks are shown at the bottom of Fig. 11.3, and the implied behavior of output is displayed above them. Although none of the individual shocks is large, the cumulative effect of the shocks causes large fluctuations in output that look something like business cycles. Hence business cycles may be the result of productivity shocks, even though identifying specific, large shocks is difficult.

Theoretically, small productivity shocks could cause aggregate cyclical fluctuations, but history suggests that shocks other than productivity shocks also affect the economy; wars and military buildups are but one obvious example. Thus many classical economists favor a broader definition of classical business cycle theory that allows for both productivity and other types of shocks to have an impact on the economy.

The macroeconomic effects of shocks other than productivity shocks can be analyzed with the classical *IS–LM* model. Let's use it to examine the effects of a fiscal policy shock.

Fiscal Policy Shocks in the Classical Model

Another type of shock that can be a source of business cycles in the classical model is a change in fiscal policy, such as an increase or decrease in real government purchases of goods and services.[10] Examples of shocks to government purchases include military buildups (or more recently, build-downs) and the initiation of large road-building or other public works programs. Because government purchases are procyclical—and in particular, because national output tends to be above normal during wars and at other times when military spending is high—we need to explore how shocks to government purchases affect aggregate output and employment.

Let's consider what happens when the government purchases more goods, as it would, for example, when the country is at war. (Think of the increase in government purchases as temporary. Analytical Problem 2 at the end of the chapter asks you to work out what happens if the increase in government purchases is permanent.)

Figure 11.4 illustrates the effects of an increase in government purchases in the classical *IS–LM* model. Before the fiscal policy change the economy's general equilibrium is represented by point *E* in both (a) and (b). To follow what

---

9. Specifically, the model is $Y_t = Y_{t-1} + 0.01 + e_t$, where Y_t is output in month t, Y_{t-1} is output in the previous month, and e_t is the random productivity shock in month t. The productivity shocks are randomly chosen numbers between −1.0 and 1.0. A similar example is given in Numerical Problem 5 at the end of this chapter.

10. Another important example of a change in fiscal policy is a change in the structure of the tax code. Classical economists argue that the greatest effects of tax changes are those that affect people's incentives to work, save, and invest, and thus effect full-employment output. Because most classical economists accept the Ricardian equivalence proposition, they wouldn't expect lump-sum changes in taxes without accompanying changes in government purchases to have much effect on the economy, however.

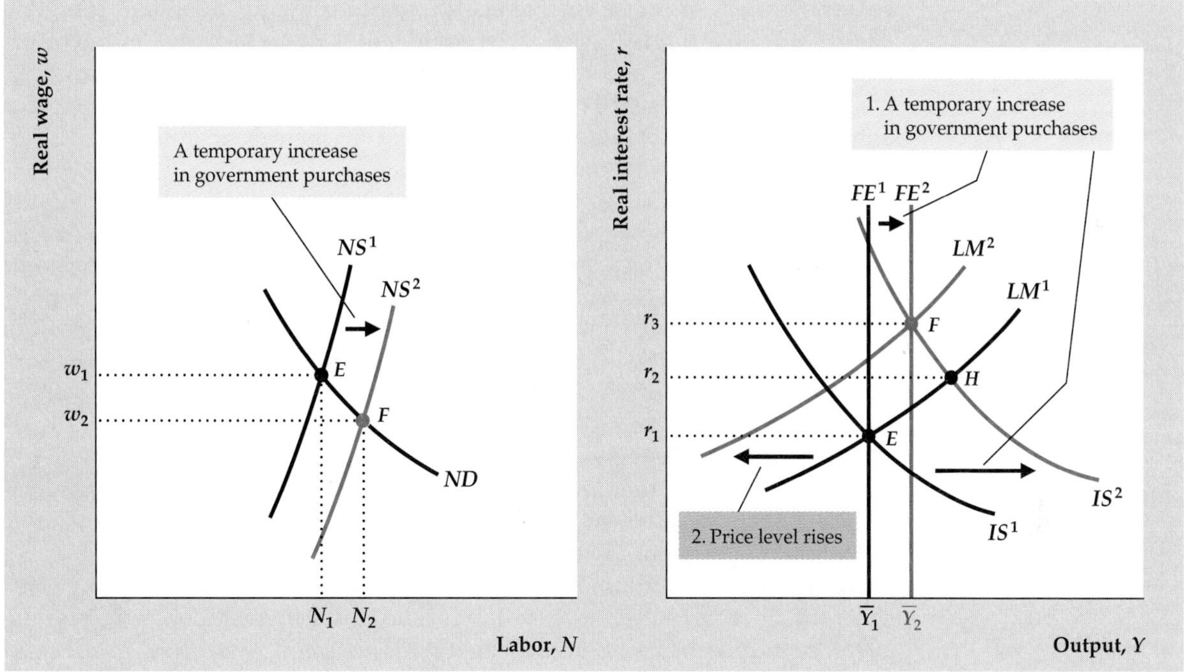

(a) Labor market

(b) General equilibrium

Figure 11.4
Effects of a temporary increase in government purchases
Initial equilibrium is at point E in both (a) and (b).
(a) A temporary increase in government purchases raises workers' current or future taxes. Because workers feel poorer, they supply more labor and the labor supply curve shifts to the right, from NS^1 to NS^2. The shift in the labor supply curve reduces the real wage and increases employment, as indicated by point F.
(b) The increase in employment raises full-employment output and shifts the FE line to the right, from FE^1 to FE^2. The increase in government purchases also reduces desired national saving and shifts the IS curve up, from IS^1 to IS^2. Because the intersection of IS^2 and LM^1 is to the right of FE^2, the aggregate quantity of output demanded is higher than the full-employment level of output $\bar{Y}_2$, so the price level rises. The rise in the price level reduces the real money supply and shifts the LM curve up, from LM^1 to LM^2, until the new general equilibrium is reached at point F. The effect of the increase in government purchases is to increase output, the real interest rate, and the price level.

happens after purchases rise, we start with the labor market in Fig. 11.4(a). The change in fiscal policy doesn't affect the production function or the marginal product of labor (the *MPN* curve), so the labor demand curve doesn't shift.

However, classical economists argue that an increase in government purchases will affect labor supply by reducing workers' wealth. People are made less wealthy because, if the government increases the share of the nation's output that it takes for military purposes, less output will be left for private consumption and investment. This negative impact of increased government purchases on private wealth is most obvious if the government pays for its increased military spending by raising current taxes.[11] However, even if the

11. For simplicity, assume that the tax increase is lump-sum. A tax increase that isn't lump-sum—for example, if it changes the effective tax rate on capital—has complicating effects.

government doesn't raise current taxes to pay for the extra military spending and borrows the funds it needs, taxes will still have to be raised in the future to pay the principal and interest on this extra government borrowing. So, whether taxes are currently raised or not, under the classical assumption that output is always at its full-employment level, an increase in government military spending effectively makes people poorer.

In Chapter 3 we showed that a decrease in wealth increases labor supply because someone who is poorer can afford less leisure. Thus, according to the classical analysis, an increase in government purchases—which makes people financially worse off—should lead to an increase in aggregate labor supply.[12] The increase in government purchases causes the labor supply curve to shift to the right, from NS^1 to NS^2 in Fig. 11.4(a). Following the shift of the labor supply curve, the equilibrium in the labor market shifts from point *E* to point *F*, with employment increasing and the real wage decreasing.[13]

The effects of the increase in government purchases in the classical *IS–LM* framework are shown in Fig. 11.4(b). First, note that, because equilibrium employment increases, full-employment output $\bar{Y}$ also increases. Thus the *FE* line shifts to the right, from FE^1 to FE^2.

In addition to shifting the *FE* line to the right, the fiscal policy change also shifts the *IS* curve. Recall that, at any level of output, a temporary increase in government purchases reduces desired national saving and raises the real interest rate that clears the goods market. Thus the *IS* curve shifts up, from IS^1 to IS^2. (See also Summary table 12, p. 322.) The *LM* curve isn't directly affected by the change in fiscal policy.

The new *IS* curve, IS^2, the initial *LM* curve, LM^1, and the new *FE* line, FE^2, have no common point of intersection. For general equilibrium to be restored, prices must adjust, shifting the *LM* curve until it passes through the intersection of IS^2 and FE^2 (point *F*). Will prices rise or fall? The answer to this question is ambiguous because the fiscal policy change has increased both the aggregate demand for goods (by reducing desired saving and shifting the *IS* curve up) and the full-employment level of output (by increasing labor supply and shifting the *FE* line to the right). If we assume that the effect on labor supply and full-employment output of the increase in government purchases isn't too large (probably a reasonable assumption), after the fiscal policy change the aggregate quantity of goods demanded is likely to exceed full-employment output. In Fig. 11.4(b) the aggregate quantity of goods demanded (point *H* at the intersection of IS^2 and LM^1) exceeds full-employment output $\bar{Y}_2$. Thus the price level must rise, shifting the *LM* curve to the left and causing the economy to return to general equilibrium at *F*. At *F* both output and the real interest rate are higher than at the initial equilibrium point, *E*.

Therefore the increase in government purchases increases output, employment, the real interest rate, and the price level. Because the increase in employment is

---

12. In theory the effect on labor supply of an increase in government purchases should be the strongest for spending, such as military spending, that extracts resources without providing any direct benefits to the private sector. Government purchases that effectively replace private consumption expenditures—for example, purchases of medical services, roads, or playgrounds—should in principle have a smaller negative impact on people's economic well-being and thus a smaller positive effect on labor supply.

13. Note that this labor supply effect was omitted from our discussion of the impact of increased government purchases in Chapter 4, as illustrated in Fig. 4.8.

the result of an increase in labor supply rather than an increase in labor demand, real wages fall when government purchases rise. Because of diminishing marginal productivity of labor, the increase in employment also implies a decline in average labor productivity when government purchases rise.

That fiscal shocks play some role in business cycles seems reasonable, which is itself justification for including them in the model. However, including fiscal shocks along with productivity shocks in the RBC model has the additional advantage of improving the match between model and data. We previously noted that government purchases are procyclical, which is consistent with the preceding analysis. Another advantage of adding fiscal shocks to a model that also contains productivity shocks is that it improves the model's ability to explain the behavior of labor productivity.

Refer back to Fig. 11.2 to recall a weakness of the RBC model with only productivity shocks: It predicts that average labor productivity and GNP are highly correlated. In fact, RBC theory predicts a correlation that is more than twice the actual correlation. However, as we have just shown, a classical business cycle model with shocks to government purchases predicts a negative correlation between labor productivity and GNP because a positive shock to government purchases raises output but lowers average productivity. A classical business cycle model that includes *both* shocks to productivity *and* shocks to government purchases can match the empirically observed correlation of productivity and GNP well, without reducing the fit of the model in other respects.[14] Thus adding fiscal shocks to the real business cycle model seems to improve its ability to explain the actual behavior of the economy.

Should Fiscal Policy Be Used to Dampen the Cycle? Our analysis shows that changes in government purchases can have real effects on the economy. Changes in the tax laws can also have real effects on the economy in the classical model, although these effects are more complicated and depend mainly on the nature of the tax, the type of income or revenue that is taxed, and so on. Potentially, then, changes in fiscal policy could be used to offset cyclical fluctuations and stabilize output and employment; for example, the government could increase its purchases during recessions. This observation leads to the second of the two questions posed in the introduction to the chapter: Should policymakers use fiscal policy to smooth business cycle fluctuations?

Recall that classical economists generally oppose active attempts to dampen cyclical fluctuations because of Adam Smith's invisible-hand argument that free markets produce efficient outcomes without government intervention. The classical view holds that prices and wages adjust fairly rapidly to bring the economy into general equilibrium, allowing little scope for the government to improve the macroeconomy's response to economic disturbances. Therefore, although in principle fiscal policy could be used to fight recessions and reduce output fluctuations, classical economists advise against using this approach. Instead, classicals argue that not interfering in the economy's adjustment to disturbances is better.

---

14. See Lawrence Christiano and Martin Eichenbaum, "Current Real-Business-Cycle Theories and Aggregate Labor-Market Fluctuations," *American Economic Review*, June 1992, pp. 430–450. The analysis of this paper is technically complex but it gives a flavor of much recent work in classical business cycle analysis.

This skepticism about the value of active antirecessionary policies does *not* mean that classical economists don't regard recessions as a serious problem. If an adverse productivity shock causes a recession, for example, real wages, employment, and output all fall, which means that many people experience economic hardship. But would offsetting the recession by, for example, increasing government purchases help? In the classical analysis, a rise in government purchases increases output by raising the amount of labor supplied, and the amount of labor supplied is increased by making workers poorer (as a result of higher current or future taxes). Thus, under the classical assumption that the economy is always in general equilibrium, increasing government purchases for the sole purpose of increasing output and employment makes people worse off rather than better off. Classical economists conclude that government purchases should be increased only if the benefits of the expanded government program—in terms of improved military security or public services, for example—exceed the costs to taxpayers. Classicals apply this criterion for useful government spending—that the benefits should exceed the costs—whether the economy is currently in recession or not.

So far we have assumed that, because fiscal policy affects the equilibrium levels of employment and output, the government is capable of using fiscal policy to achieve the levels of employment and output it chooses. In fact, the legislative process can lead to lengthy delays, or *lags,* between the time that a fiscal policy change is proposed and the time that it is enacted. Additional lags occur in implementing the new policies and in the response of the economy to the policy changes. Because of these lags, fiscal policy changes contemplated today should be based on where the economy will be several quarters in the future; but, unfortunately, forecasting the future of the economy is an inexact art at best. Beyond the problems of forecasting, policymakers also face uncertainties about how and by how much to modify their policies to get the desired output and employment effects. Classical economists cite these practical difficulties as another reason for not using fiscal policy to fight recessions.

Unemployment in the Classical Model

A major weakness of the classical model is that it doesn't explain why unemployment rises during business downturns. Indeed, in the simple classical, or supply-and-demand, model of the labor market, unemployment is literally zero: Anyone who wants to work can find a job at the market-clearing wage. Of course, in reality unemployment is never zero. Furthermore, the sharp increases in unemployment that occur during recessions are a principal reason that policymakers and the public are so concerned about economic downturns.

Classical economists are perfectly aware of this issue, and they have developed more sophisticated versions of the classical business cycle model to account for unemployment. The main modification they make to the simple supply-and-demand model of the labor market is to drop the model's implicit assumption that all workers and jobs are the same. Rather than all being the same, workers in the real world have different abilities, skills, and interests, among other things; jobs entail different skill requirements, work environments, locations, and other characteristics. Because workers and jobs both vary in so many ways, matching workers to jobs isn't instantaneous and free, but time-consuming and costly. The fact that someone who has lost a job or has just entered the labor force must spend time and effort to find a new job helps explain why there always are some unemployed people.

Some classical economists suggest that differences among workers and among jobs explain not only why the unemployment rate is always greater than zero, but also why unemployment rises so sharply in recessions. They argue that productivity shocks and other macroeconomic disturbances that cause recessions also often increase the degree of mismatch between workers and firms.[15] Thus a major adverse productivity shock might affect the various industries and regions within the country differently, with jobs being destroyed in some sectors but new opportunities emerging in others. An oil price shock, for example, would eliminate jobs in energy-intensive industries but create new opportunities in industries that supply energy or are light energy users.

Following such a shock, workers in industries and regions where labor demand has fallen will be induced to search elsewhere for jobs, which raises the frictional component of unemployment. Some of these workers will find that their skills don't match the requirements of industries with growing labor demand; these workers may become chronically unemployed, raising structural unemployment.[16] With many unemployed workers looking for jobs, and because creating new jobs takes a while, the time necessary to find a new job is likely to increase. For all these reasons, an adverse productivity shock may raise unemployment as well as reduce output and employment. Note that this predicted rise in frictional and structural unemployment during recessions is the same as an increase in the natural rate of unemployment (the sum of frictional and structural unemployment rates).

What is the evidence of worker–job mismatch and unemployment? The process of job creation and job destruction in American manufacturing has been studied in some detail by Steven Davis of the University of Chicago and John Haltiwanger[17] of the University of Maryland. Using data for 160,000 manufacturing plants, Davis and Haltiwanger showed that, during the 1973–1986 period, about 11% of all existing manufacturing jobs disappeared, on average, each year, reflecting plant closings and cutbacks. During a typical year, about 81% of these lost jobs were replaced by newly created jobs elsewhere in the manufacturing sector (so that, overall, employment in manufacturing shrank over the period). Thus Davis and Haltiwanger confirmed that a great deal of "churning" of jobs and workers occurs in the economy. They also showed that much of this churning reflected closing of old plants and opening of new ones *within the same industries,* rather than a general decline in some industries and growth in others. Thus reallocation of workers within industries seems to be as important as movement of workers between industries as a source of unemployment.

Table 11.1, on the next page, shows the rates of job creation and destruction in manufacturing for selected years, as found by Davis and Haltiwanger. Note

15. This idea was proposed in David Lilien, "Sectoral Shifts and Cyclical Unemployment," *Journal of Political Economy,* August 1982, pp. 777–793.

16. See Chapter 3 for definitions and discussion of frictional and structural unemployment.

17. "Gross Job Creation, Gross Job Destruction, and Employment Reallocation," *Quarterly Journal of Economics,* August 1992, pp. 819–864.

Table 11.1 Rates of Job Creation and Destruction in Manufacturing, 1973–1986

Year	Job Creation	Job Destruction
1973	13.2%	6.1%
1975	6.7%	16.6%
1976	11.3%	9.6%
1977	11.2%	9.6%
1978	11.6%	7.5%
1980	8.0%	9.3%
1981	7.0%	11.8%
1982	6.4%	15.2%
1983	8.6%	14.2%
1985	8.4%	11.7%
1986	8.8%	13.2%

Note: Job creation is the number of new manufacturing jobs created during the year, as a percentage of existing manufacturing jobs. Job destruction is the number of manufacturing jobs lost during the year as a result of closing or down-sizing plants, as a percentage of existing jobs.

Source: Table I in Steven Davis and John Haltiwanger, "Gross Job Creation, Gross Job Destruction, and Employment Reallocation," *Quarterly Journal of Economics*, August 1992, pp. 819–864. Data are not available for all years.

that in recession years, such as 1975 and 1981–1982, many more jobs were lost than created; but a significant number of new jobs were created even in recession years, reflecting shifts of workers in the labor market. Note also that the 1975 recession year was followed by three years in which job creation exceeded job destruction but that, after the 1981–1982 recession, manufacturing jobs showed continuing net declines.

It seems clear that increased mismatches between workers and jobs can't account for *all* the increase in unemployment that occurs during recessions. Much of that increase is in the form of temporary layoffs; rather than search for new jobs, many workers who are temporarily laid off simply wait until they are called back by their old firm. Moreover, if recessions were times of increased mismatch in the labor market, more postings of vacancies and help-wanted ads during recessions would be expected; but, in fact, both vacancies and new job openings fall in recessions.[18] Despite these objections, however, economists generally agree that the dynamic reallocation of workers from shrinking to growing sectors is an important source of unemployment.

Modifying the classical model to allow for unemployment doesn't change the classical view that fiscal policy should not be actively used to combat recessions. Classical economists point out that raising the aggregate demand for goods (by increasing government purchases, for example) doesn't directly address the problem of unemployment arising from the mismatch that exists at the microeconomic level between workers and jobs. A better approach, in the

18. See Katharine Abraham and Lawrence Katz in "Cyclical Unemployment: Sectoral Shifts or Aggregate Disturbances?" *Journal of Political Economy*, June 1986, pp. 507–522.

classical view, is to eliminate barriers to labor market adjustment, such as high legal minimum wages that price low-skilled workers out of the labor market or burdensome regulations that raise businesses' costs of employing additional workers.

11.2 MONEY IN THE CLASSICAL MODEL

So far we have focused on real shocks to the economy, such as productivity shocks and changes in government purchases. However, many macroeconomists believe that nominal shocks—shocks to money supply and money demand—also affect the business cycle. In the rest of the chapter we discuss the role of money and monetary policy in the classical approach to the business cycle.

Monetary Policy and the Economy

Monetary policy refers to the central bank's decisions about how much money to supply to the economy (Chapter 7). Recall that the central bank (the Federal Reserve in the United States) can control the money supply through open market operations, in which it sells government bonds to the public in exchange for money (to reduce the money supply) or uses newly created money to buy bonds from the public (to increase the money supply).

In Chapter 10 we used the *IS–LM* model to examine the effects of changes in the money supply (Fig. 10.9). We found that, after prices fully adjust, changes in the money supply are *neutral:* A change in the nominal money supply M causes the price level P to change proportionally, but a change in the money supply has no effect on real variables, such as output, employment, or the real interest rate. Our analysis left open the possibility that a change in the money supply would affect real variables, such as output, in the short run before prices had a chance to adjust. However, because classical economists believe that the price adjustment process is rapid, their theory predicts that money will be neutral even in the short run.

Monetary Nonneutrality and Reverse Causation

The prediction that money is neutral is a striking result of the classical model, but it seems inconsistent with the business cycle fact that money is a leading, procyclical variable. If an expansion of the money supply has no effect, why are expansions of the money supply typically followed by increased rates of economic activity? And, similarly, why are reductions in the money supply often followed by recessions?

Some classical economists have responded to these questions by pointing out that, although increases in the money supply tend to *precede* expansions in output, this fact doesn't necessarily prove that economic expansions are *caused* by those increases. After all, just because people put storm windows on their houses before winter begins doesn't mean that winter is caused by putting on storm windows. Rather, people put storm windows on their houses because they know that winter is coming.

Many classical economists, including RBC theorists in particular, argue that the link between money growth and economic expansion is like the link between putting on storm windows and the onset of winter, a relationship they call reverse causation. Specifically, **reverse causation** means that expected future increases in output cause increases in the current money supply and that expected future decreases in output cause decreases in the current money supply, rather than the other way around. Reverse causation explains how money could be a procyclical and leading variable even if the classical model is correct and changes in the money supply are neutral and have no real effects.[19]

Reverse causation might arise in one of several ways. One possibility (which you are asked to explore in more detail in Analytical Problem 4 at the end of the chapter) is based on the idea that money demand depends on expected future output as well as current output. Suppose that a firm's managers expect business to pick up considerably in the next few quarters. To prepare for this expected increase in output, the firm may need to increase its current transactions (for example, to purchase raw materials, hire workers, and so on) and thus it will demand more money now. If many firms do so, the aggregate demand for money may rise in advance of the actual increase in output.

Now suppose that the Fed observes this increase in the demand for money. If the Fed does nothing, leaving the money supply unchanged, the increase in money demand will cause the equilibrium value of the price level to fall. As one of the Fed's objectives is stable prices, it won't like this outcome; to keep prices stable, instead of doing nothing the Fed should provide enough extra money to the economy to meet the higher money demand. But if the Fed does so, the money supply will rise in advance of the increase in output, consistent with the business cycle fact—even though money is neutral.

Undoubtedly, reverse causation explains at least some of the tendency of money to lead output (see Box 11.1 for a seasonal example). However, this explanation doesn't rule out the possibility that changes in the money supply also sometimes cause changes in output so that money is nonneutral. That is, a combination of reverse causation and monetary nonneutrality could account for the procyclical behavior of money.

The Nonneutrality of Money: Additional Evidence

Because of reverse causation, the leading and procyclical behavior of money can't by itself establish that money is nonneutral. To settle the issue of whether money is neutral, we need additional evidence. One useful source is a historical analysis of monetary policy. The classic study is Milton Friedman and Anna J. Schwartz's, *A Monetary History of the United States, 1867–1960.*[20] Using a variety of sources, including Federal Reserve policy statements and the journals and correspondence of monetary policymakers, Friedman and Schwartz

19. Robert King and Charles Plosser, "Money, Credit, and Prices in a Real Business Cycle," *American Economic Review,* June 1984, pp. 363–380, explain reverse causation and present supporting evidence for the idea.
20. Princeton, N.J.: Princeton University Press for NBER, 1963.

BOX 11.1

Money and Economic Activity at Christmastime

According to the reverse causation argument, the association of higher-than-normal money growth with economic booms and lower-than-normal money growth with recessions occurs because money growth *responds* to changes in output, not because money growth *causes* changes in output. An example of reverse causation is provided by the behavior of money and economic activity at Christmastime: In the United States both the money supply and retail sales grow faster in the fourth quarter of the year than in any other quarter, as shown in the accompanying table. Clearly, the sharp increase in fourth-quarter retail sales (measured in real terms) results from Christmas gift buying and not from the fourth-quarter increase in the money supply. Thus at Christmastime higher economic activity must cause a higher money supply, rather than vice versa. Where does the extra money come from? The Federal Reserve regularly increases the money supply in the fourth quarter to meet the demands of merchants and shoppers for more money.

The existence of reverse causation from output to money in the fourth quarter doesn't rule out monetary nonneutrality, but it does mean that we have to be cautious in interpreting the positive association between money and output over the course of the business cycle. This association could arise because of monetary nonneutrality, reverse causation, or both. The relationship between money and economic activity at Christmastime shows that reverse causation does in fact occur and can be important.

Quarter	Growth of Money Supply	Growth of Real Retail Sales
Jan.–Mar.	−0.72%	−4.83%
Apr.–June	1.00	1.53
July–Sept.	0.52	−1.44
Oct.–Dec.	1.55	7.90

Note: Growth rates are measured quarter to quarter.

Sources: Money supply (M1, seasonally unadjusted), Board of Governors of the Federal Reserve System, *Banking and Monetary Statistics, 1941–1970,* and Board of Governors of the Federal Reserve System, *Annual Statistical Digest,* various issues; retail sales, total (seasonally unadjusted) and deflator (CPI-U), U.S. Department of Commerce, *Business Statistics, 1961–1988.*

carefully described and analyzed the causes of money supply fluctuations and the interrelation of money and other economic variables. They concluded:

> Throughout the near-century examined in detail we have found that:
>
> 1. Changes in the behavior of the money stock have been closely associated with changes in economic activity, [nominal] income, and prices.
> 2. The interrelation between monetary and economic change has been highly stable.
> 3. Monetary changes have often had an independent origin; they have not been simply a reflection of changes in economic activity. (p. 676)

The first two conclusions restate the basic business cycle fact that money is procyclical. The third conclusion states that reverse causation can't explain the entire relationship between money and real income or output. Friedman and Schwartz focused on historical episodes in which changes in the supply of money were not (they argued) responses to macroeconomic conditions but instead resulted from other factors such as gold discoveries (which affected money supplies under the gold standard), changes in monetary institutions, or changes in the leadership of the Federal Reserve. In the majority of these cases "independent" changes in money growth were followed by changes in the same direction in real output. This evidence suggests that money isn't neutral.

More recently, Christina Romer and David Romer,[21] of the University of California at Berkeley, reviewed and updated the Friedman–Schwartz analysis. Although they disputed some of Friedman and Schwartz's interpretations, they generally agreed with the conclusion that money isn't neutral. In particular, they argued that since 1960 half a dozen additional episodes of monetary nonneutrality have occurred. Probably the most famous one occurred in 1979, when Federal Reserve Chairman Paul Volcker announced that money supply procedures would change and that the money growth rate would be reduced to fight inflation. A minor recession in 1980 and a severe downturn in 1981–1982 followed Volcker's change in monetary policy. An economic boom followed relaxation of the Fed's anti-inflationary monetary policy in 1982.

Because of the Friedman–Schwartz evidence and episodes such as the 1979–1982 Volcker policy (and a similar experience in Britain at the same time), most economists now believe that money is *not* neutral. If we accept that evidence, contrary to the prediction of the classical model, we are left with two choices: Either we must adopt a different framework for macroeconomic analysis, or we must modify the classical model. In Section 11.3 we take the second approach and consider how monetary nonneutrality can be explained in a classical model.

11.3 AGGREGATE DEMAND, AGGREGATE SUPPLY, AND THE NONNEUTRALITY OF MONEY

To explore the issue of monetary neutrality more deeply, we introduce two new curves, the aggregate demand (*AD*) curve and the aggregate supply (*AS*) curve. These curves are consistent with the classical *IS–LM* model; they merely represent a different way of describing general equilibrium in the economy. Unlike the *IS* curve, the *LM* curve, and the *FE* line—which relate the real interest rate to real output—the *AD* and *AS* curves relate the price level to real output.

The Aggregate Demand Curve

The **aggregate demand curve** shows the relation between the aggregate quantity of goods demanded, $C^d + I^d + G$, and the price level, P. The aggregate demand curve slopes downward, just as the demand curve for a single product (apples, for example) does. Despite the superficial similarity between the *AD* curve and the demand curve for a specific good, however, there is an important difference between these two types of curves. The demand curve for apples relates the demand for apples to the price of apples *relative to the prices of other goods.* In contrast, the *AD* curve relates the aggregate quantity of output

21. "Does Monetary Policy Matter? A New Test in the Spirit of Friedman and Schwartz," in Olivier Blanchard and Stanley Fischer, eds., *Macroeconomics Annual,* Cambridge, Mass.: M.I.T. Press, 1989.

demanded to the *general price level.* If the prices of all goods increase by 10%, the price level P also increases by 10%, even though all relative prices of goods remain unchanged. Nevertheless, the increase in the price level reduces the aggregate quantity of goods demanded.

The reason that an increase in the price level P reduces the aggregate quantity of output demanded is illustrated in Fig. 11.5. Recall that, for a *given*

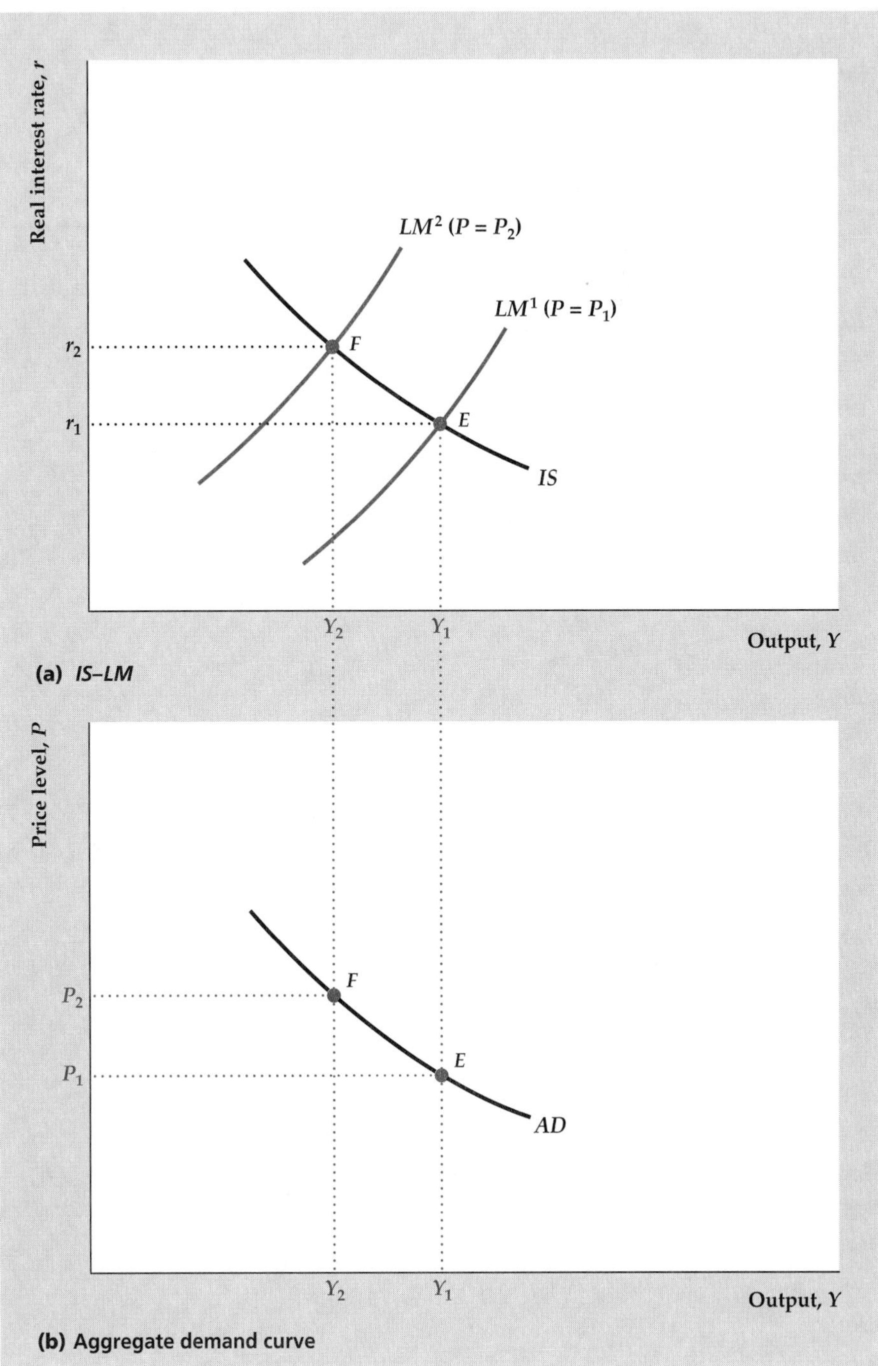

Figure 11.5 Derivation of the aggregate demand curve
For a given price level, the aggregate quantity of output demanded is determined where the *IS* and *LM* curves intersect. If the price level P is P_1 and the initial *LM* curve is LM^1, the initial aggregate quantity of output demanded is Y_1, corresponding to point *E* in both (a) and (b). To derive the aggregate demand curve, we examine what happens to the quantity of output demanded when the price level changes.
(a) An increase in the price level from P_1 to P_2 reduces the real money supply and shifts the *LM* curve up and to the left, from LM^1 to LM^2. Therefore the aggregate quantity of output demanded, represented by the intersection of the *IS* and *LM* curves, falls from Y_1 to Y_2.
(b) The increase in the price level from P_1 to P_2 reduces the aggregate quantity of output demanded from Y_1 to Y_2, so the aggregate demand curve slopes downward.

price level, the aggregate quantity of output that households, firms, and the government choose to demand is where the *IS* curve and the *LM* curve intersect. Suppose that the nominal money supply is M and that the initial price level is P_1. Then the real money supply is M/P_1, and the initial *LM* curve is LM^1 in Fig. 11.5(a). The *IS* and LM^1 curves intersect at point E, where the amount of output that households, firms, and the government want to buy is Y_1. Thus we conclude that when the price level is P_1, the aggregate amount of output demanded is Y_1.

Now suppose that the price level increases to P_2. With a nominal money supply of M, this increase in the price level reduces the real money supply from M/P_1 to M/P_2. Recall (Summary table 13, p. 328) that a decrease in the real money supply shifts the *LM* curve up and to the left, to LM^2. The *IS* and LM^2 curves intersect at point F, where the aggregate quantity of output demanded is Y_2. Thus the increase in the price level from P_1 to P_2 reduces the aggregate quantity of output demanded from Y_1 to Y_2.

This negative relation between the price level and the aggregate quantity of output demanded is shown as the downward-sloping *AD* curve in Fig. 11.5(b). Points E and F in Fig. 11.5(b) correspond to points E and F in Fig. 11.5(a). The *AD* curve slopes downward because an increase in the price level reduces the real money supply; the drop in the real money supply in turn shifts the *LM* curve up and to the left, reducing the aggregate quantity of output demanded.

Factors that Shift the *AD* Curve. The *AD* curve relates the aggregate quantity of output demanded to the price level. For a constant price level, any factor that changes the aggregate demand for output will cause the *AD* curve to shift, with increases in aggregate demand shifting the *AD* curve to the right and decreases in aggregate demand shifting it to the left. Aggregate demand is determined by the intersection of the *IS* and *LM* curves, so we can also say that, holding the price level constant, any factor that causes the intersection of the *IS* curve and the *LM* curve to shift to the right raises aggregate demand and shifts the *AD* curve to the right. Similarly, for a constant price level, any factor that causes the intersection of the *IS* and *LM* curves to shift to the left shifts the *AD* curve to the left.

An example of a factor that shifts the *AD* curve to the right, which we have considered before, is a temporary increase in government purchases. The effect of the increase in government purchases on the *AD* curve is illustrated in Fig. 11.6. The initial *IS* curve, IS^1, intersects the *LM* curve at point E in Fig. 11.6(a) so that the initial aggregate quantity of output demanded is Y_1. As we have shown, a temporary increase in government purchases shifts the *IS* curve, to the right to IS^2. With the price level held constant at its initial value of P_1, the intersection of the *IS* and *LM* curves moves to point F so that the aggregate quantity of output demanded increases from Y_1 to Y_2.

The shift of the *AD* curve resulting from the increase in government purchases is shown in Fig. 11.6(b). The increase in the aggregate quantity of output demanded at the price level P_1 is shown by the movement from point E to point F. Because the increase in government purchases raises the aggregate quantity of output demanded at any price level, the entire *AD* curve shifts to the right, from AD^1 to AD^2. Other factors that shift the *AD* curve are listed in Summary table 14 on page 376, and an algebraic derivation of the *AD* curve is presented in Appendix 11.A.

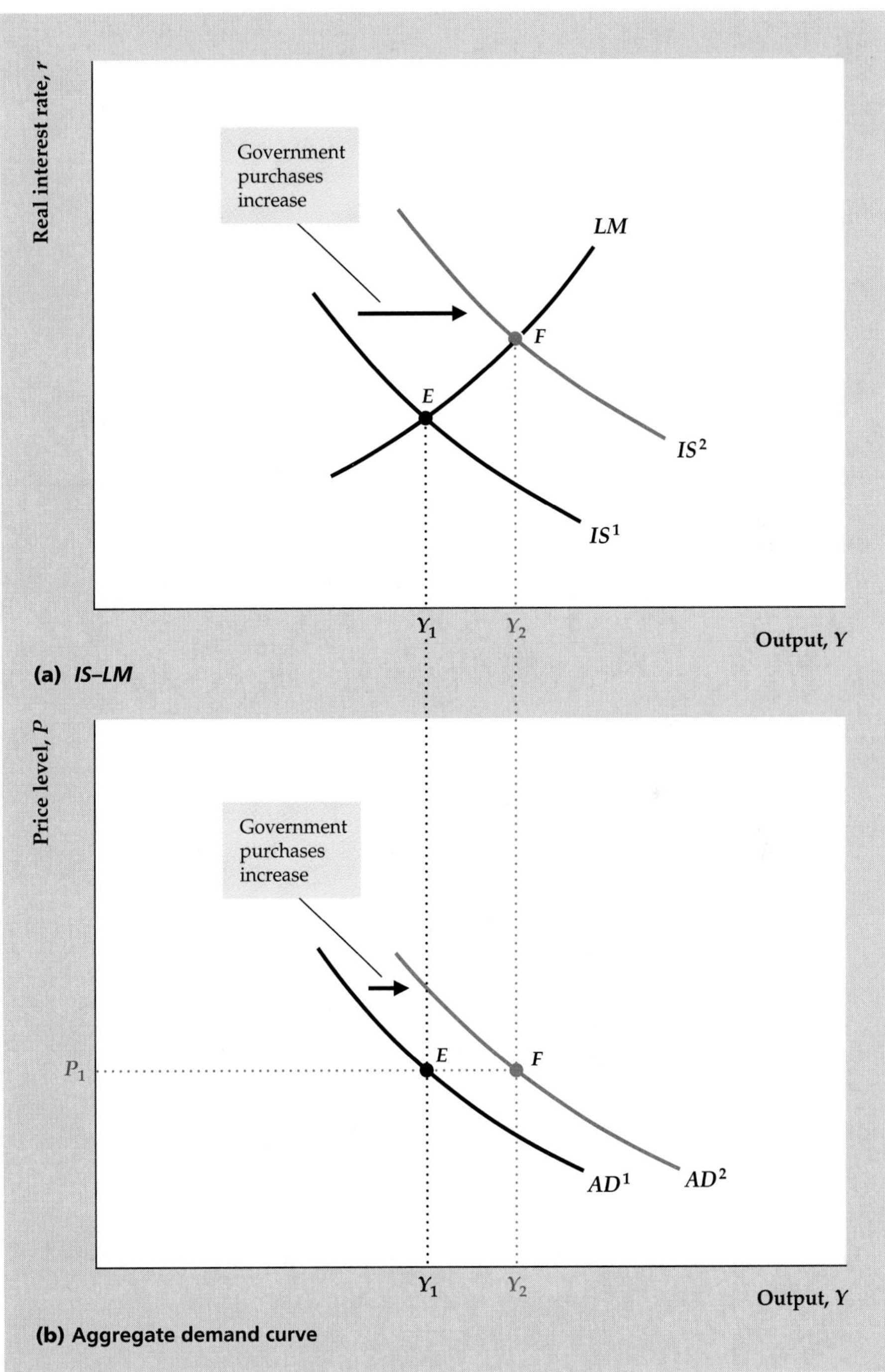

Figure 11.6
The effect of an increase in government purchases on the aggregate demand curve
(a) An increase in government purchases shifts the *IS* curve up and to the right, from IS^1 to IS^2. At the price level P_1, the aggregate quantity of output demanded increases from Y_1 to Y_2, as shown by the shift of the *IS*–*LM* intersection from point *E* to point *F*.
(b) Because the aggregate quantity of output demanded rises at any price level, the *AD* curve shifts to the right. Points *E* and *F* in (b) correspond to points *E* and *F* in part (a).

The Aggregate Supply Curve

The **aggregate supply curve** shows the relation between the price level and the aggregate amount of output that firms supply. In equilibrium in the classical model the labor market clears at the full-employment level of employment $\bar{N}$ and firms supply the full-employment level of output $\bar{Y}$ (their

SUMMARY 14

Factors that Shift the *AD* Curve

For a constant price level, any factor that shifts the intersection of the *IS* and *LM* curves to the right increases aggregate output demanded and shifts the *AD* curve to the right.

Factors that shift the *IS* curve up and to the right, and thus shift the *AD* curve to the right (see Summary table 12, p. 322) include:

- an increase in expected future output;
- an increase in wealth;
- an increase in government purchases, G;
- a reduction in taxes, T (assuming no Ricardian equivalence so that consumers respond by raising desired consumption);
- an increase in the expected future MPK; and
- a reduction in the effective tax rate on capital.

Factors that shift the *LM* curve down and to the right, and thus shift the *AD* curve to the right (see Summary table 13, p. 328) include:

- an increase in the nominal money supply, M;
- a rise in expected inflation, π^e;
- a decrease in the nominal interest rate on money, i^m; and
- any other change that reduces the real demand for money.

profit-maximizing level of output), regardless of the price level. Because in the classical model the amount of output that firms supply is fixed at $\bar{Y}$ and doesn't depend on the price level, the *AS* curve is a vertical line at $Y = \bar{Y}$, as shown in Fig. 11.7.

Factors that Shift the *AS* Curve. Any factor that increases the full-employment level of output $\bar{Y}$ shifts the aggregate supply curve to the right, and any factor that reduces $\bar{Y}$ shifts the aggregate supply curve to the left. Thus any change that shifts the *FE* line to the right in the *IS–LM* diagram also shifts the *AS* curve to the right. For instance, an increase in the labor force raises the full-employment levels of employment and output, shifting the *AS* curve to the right.

General Equilibrium in the *AD–AS* Model

General equilibrium in the economy is represented by the intersection of the *AD* and *AS* curves, as at point *E* in Fig. 11.8. At *E* output is at its full-employment level $\bar{Y}$, and the price level is P_1. In the classical model prices and wages adjust quickly so that the economy reaches its general equilibrium quickly. Let's examine how the price level adjusts by supposing that the price level happened to be P_2, which is lower than the equilibrium level P_1. In this case, the aggregate amount of output demanded is Y_2, which is greater than $\bar{Y}$. Because the aggregate quantity of output demanded exceeds full-employment output, wages and prices are bid up. The price level will continue to increase until it reaches P_1 and aggregate output demanded equals aggregate output

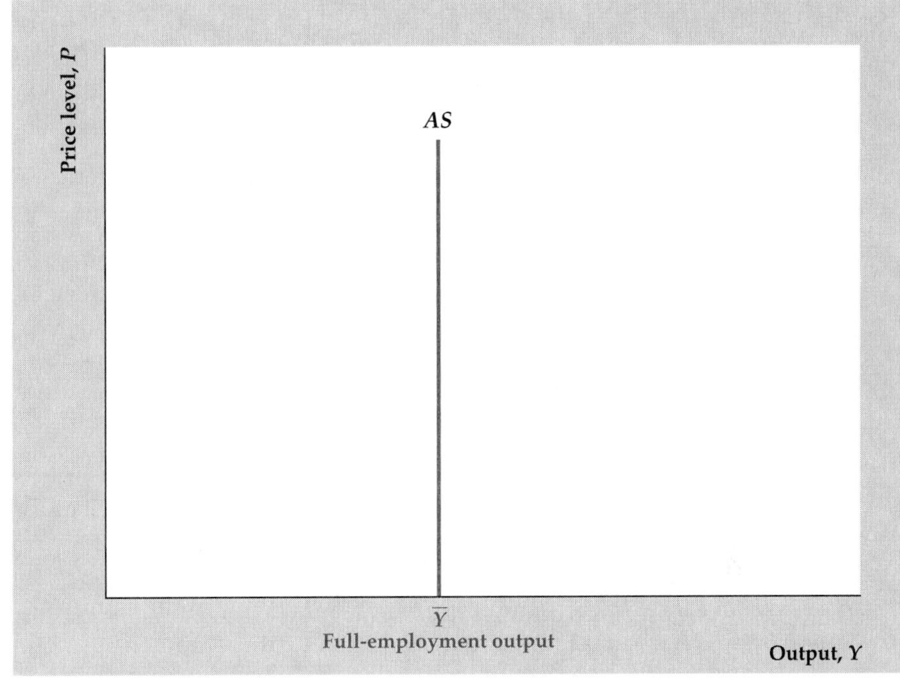

Figure 11.7
The classical aggregate supply curve
In the basic classical model, the labor market clears so that employment is always at its full-employment level. Therefore output is at its full-employment level $\bar{Y}$ regardless of the price level, and the aggregate supply curve is vertical.

supplied. Similarly, if the price level were higher than the equilibrium price level P_1, the aggregate quantity of goods demanded would be smaller than the aggregate quantity of goods supplied, and the price level would be bid down until it reached P_1.

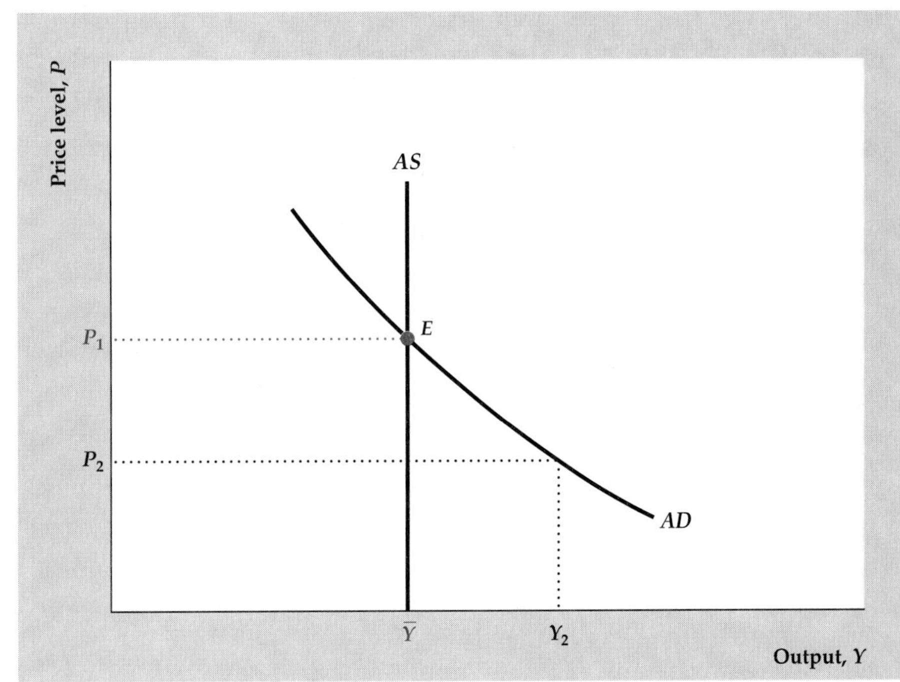

Figure 11.8
General equilibrium in the *AD–AS* model
The general equilibrium of the economy is located at the intersection of the *AD* and *AS* curves, point *E*, where output is $\bar{Y}$ and the price level is P_1. The general equilibrium is attained by price level adjustment. For example, if the price level is P_2, which is lower than P_1, the aggregate quantity of output demanded Y_2 exceeds full-employment output $\bar{Y}$. Hence the price level rises until it reaches P_1. Similarly, if the price level is above P_1, the aggregate quantity of output demanded will be less than $\bar{Y}$ and prices will fall to P_1.

The results obtained so far with the *AD–AS* model are identical to the results obtained with the classical *IS–LM* model. The only difference is that with the *AD–AS* model we focus on the relationship between output and the price level, rather than the relationship between output and the real interest rate, as we did in the *IS–LM* model.

Monetary Neutrality in the *AD–AS* Model

We can use the *AD* and *AS* curves to illustrate the neutrality of money in the classical model. Showing that money is neutral in terms of the *AD* and *AS* curves sets the stage for using the *AD–AS* diagram with an extension of the classical model that allows for monetary nonneutrality.

Suppose that the economy is initially in equilibrium at point *E* in Fig. 11.9 and that the money supply then increases by 10%. In the *IS–LM* model an increase in the money supply shifts the *LM* curve down and to the right, raising the aggregate quantity of output demanded at any particular price level. Thus an increase in the money supply also shifts the *AD* curve up and to the right, from AD^1 to AD^2.

Moreover, *when the money supply rises by 10%, the AD curve shifts vertically upward by 10% at each level of output demanded.* To see why, compare points *E* and *F*. Because *F* lies on AD^2 and *E* lies on AD^1, the nominal money supply *M* is 10% higher at *F* than at *E*. However, the aggregate quantity of output demanded is the same $(\bar{Y})$ at *F* and *E*. The aggregate quantity of output demanded can be the same at *F* and *E* only if the real money supply M/P, which determines the position of the *LM* curve and hence the aggregate quantity of output demanded, is the same at *F* and *E*. With the nominal money supply 10% higher at *F*, for the real money supply to be the same at the two points the

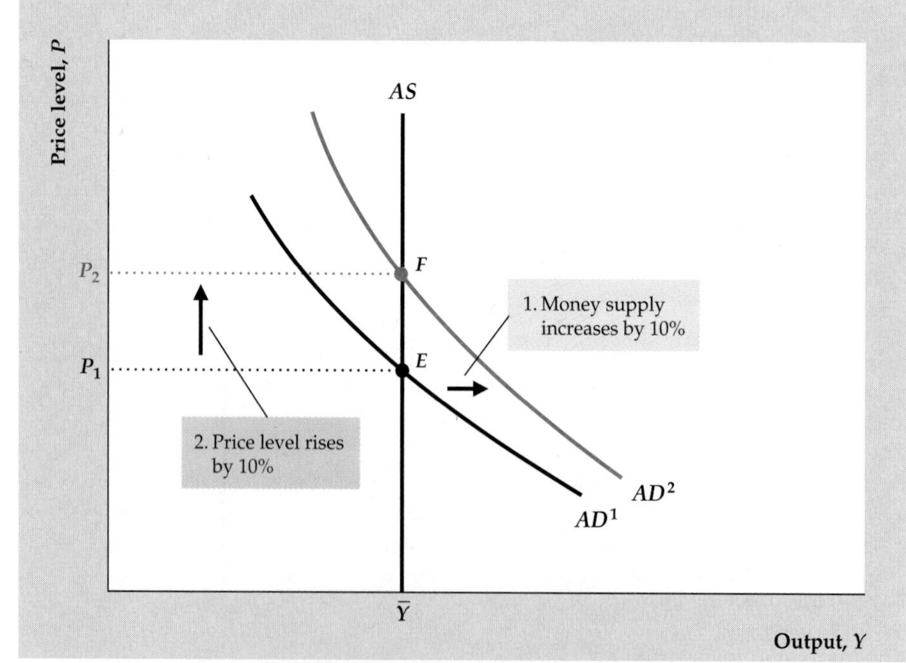

Figure 11.9
Monetary neutrality in the *AD–AS* framework
If we start from general equilibrium at point *E*, a 10% increase in the nominal money supply shifts the *AD* curve up by 10% at each level of output, from AD^1 to AD^2. The *AD* curve shifts up by 10% because at any given level of output, a 10% increase in the price level is needed to keep the real money supply, and thus the aggregate quantity of output demanded, unchanged. In the new equilibrium at point *F*, output is unchanged at $\bar{Y}$, and the price level P_2 is 10% higher than the initial price level P_1. Because the increase in the money supply raises prices but doesn't affect real variables such as output, money is neutral in this framework.

price level at F must be 10% higher than at E. Therefore P_2 is 10% higher than P_1. Indeed, for every level of output the price level is 10% higher on AD^2 than on AD^1.

The AS curve isn't affected by the increase in the nominal money supply because full-employment output doesn't depend on the money supply. Therefore, as a result of the increase in the money supply, the general equilibrium of the economy moves from E to F in Fig. 11.9, with the price level increasing by 10%. Because the price level rises by 10%, the real money supply M/P is unchanged between E and F, output is unchanged, and, again, money is neutral in the classical model.

Crucial to the neutrality of money, as illustrated in Fig. 11.9, is the fact that the AS curve is vertical. An increase in the money supply shifts the AD curve up, but because the AS curve in the classical model is vertical, the amount of output produced is unaffected. For an increase in the money supply to change the equilibrium amount of output produced, the aggregate supply curve must be nonvertical. We now turn to an extension of the classical model that features an upward-sloping aggregate supply curve, with the consequence that (at least sometimes) money isn't neutral.

The Misperceptions Theory

This extension to the classical model is based on a theory called the misperceptions theory. It was originally proposed by Nobel laureate Milton Friedman and then was rigorously formulated by Robert E. Lucas, Jr., of the University of Chicago.[22] According to the **misperceptions theory,** *the aggregate quantity of output supplied rises above the full-employment level* $\bar{Y}$ *when the aggregate price level* P *is higher than expected.* Thus for any expected price level, the aggregate supply curve relating the price level and the aggregate quantity of output supplied slopes upward.

If you took a course in the principles of economics, you learned that supply curves generally slope upward, with higher prices leading to increased production. However, just as the demand curves for individual goods differ from the aggregate demand curve, the supply curves for individual goods differ from the aggregate supply curve. An ordinary supply curve relates the supply of some good to the price of that good *relative to other prices.* In contrast, the aggregate supply curve relates the aggregate amount of output produced to the *general price level.* Changes in the general price level can occur while the relative prices of individual goods remain unchanged.

To understand the misperceptions theory and why it implies an upward-sloping aggregate supply curve, let's think about an individual producer of a particular good, say bread. For simplicity, consider a bakery owned and operated by one person, a baker. The baker devotes all his labor to making bread and earns all his income from selling bread. Thus the price of bread is effectively the baker's nominal wage, and the price of bread relative to the general price level is the baker's real wage. When the relative price of bread increases, the baker responds to this increase in his current real wage by working more and producing more bread. Similarly, when the price of bread falls

22. See Friedman, "The Role of Monetary Policy," *American Economic Review,* March 1968, pp. 1–17. Lucas's formalization of Friedman was first presented in Lucas's article, "Expectations and the Neutrality of Money," *Journal of Economic Theory,* April 1972, pp. 103–124.

relative to the other prices in the economy, the baker's current real wage falls and he decreases the amount of bread he produces.

But how does an individual baker know whether the relative price of bread has changed? To calculate the relative price of bread, the baker needs to know both the nominal price of bread and the general price level. The baker knows the nominal price of bread because he sells bread every day and observes the price directly. However, the baker probably is not as well informed about the general price level, because he observes the prices of the many goods and services he might want to buy less frequently than he observes the price of bread. Thus in calculating the relative price of bread, the baker can't use the actual current price level. The best he can do is to use his previously formed expectation of the current price level to estimate the actual price level.

Suppose that before he observes the current market price of bread, the baker expected an overall inflation rate of 5%. How will he react if he then observes that the price of bread increases by 5%? The baker reasons as follows: I expected the overall rate of inflation to be 5%, and now I know that the price of bread has increased by 5%. This 5% increase in the price of bread is consistent with what I had expected. My best estimate is that all prices increased by 5%, and thus I think that the relative price of bread is unchanged. There is no reason to change my output.

The baker's logic applies equally to suppliers of output in the aggregate. Suppose that all suppliers expected the nominal price level to increase by 5% and that in fact all prices do increase by 5%. Then each supplier will estimate that her relative price hasn't changed and won't change her output. Hence, if expected inflation is 5%, an actual increase in prices of 5% won't affect aggregate output.

For a change in the nominal price of bread to affect the quantity of bread produced, the increase in the nominal price of bread must differ from the *expected* increase in the general price level. For example, suppose that the baker expected the general price level to increase by 5% but then observes that the price of bread rises by 8%. The baker then estimates that the relative price of bread has increased so that the real wage he earns from baking is higher. In response to the perceived increase in the relative price, he increases the production of bread.

Again, the same logic applies to the economy in the aggregate. Suppose that everyone expects the general price level to increase by 5%, but instead it actually increases by 8%, with the prices of all goods increasing by 8%. Now all producers will estimate that the relative prices of the goods they make have increased, and hence the production of all goods will increase. Thus a greater-than-expected increase of the price level will tend to raise output. Similarly, if the price level actually increases by only 2% when all producers expected a 5% increase, producers will think that the relative prices of their own goods have declined; in response, all suppliers reduce their output.

Thus, according to the misperceptions theory, the amount of output that producers choose to supply depends on the actual general price level compared to the expected general price level. When the price level exceeds what was expected, producers are fooled into thinking that the relative prices of their own goods have risen, and they increase their output. Similarly, when the price level is lower than expected, producers believe that the relative prices of their goods have fallen, and they reduce their output. This relation between output and prices is captured by the equation:

$$Y = \bar{Y} + b(P - P^e), \tag{11.1}$$

where b is a positive number that describes how strongly output responds when the actual price level exceeds the expected price level. Equation (11.1) summarizes the misperceptions theory by showing that output Y exceeds full-employment output $\bar{Y}$ when the price level P exceeds the expected price level P^e.

To obtain an aggregate supply curve from the misperceptions theory, we graph Eq. (11.1) in Fig. 11.10. For given full-employment output $\bar{Y}$ and expected price level P^e, the aggregate supply curve slopes upward, illustrating the relation between the amount of output supplied Y and the actual price level P. Point E helps us locate the aggregate supply curve. At E the price level P equals the expected price level P^e so that (from Eq. 11.1) the amount of output supplied equals full-employment output $\bar{Y}$. When the actual price level is higher than expected ($P > P^e$), the aggregate supply curve shows that the amount of output supplied is greater than $\bar{Y}$; when the price level is lower than expected ($P < P^e$), output is less than $\bar{Y}$.

The aggregate supply curve in Fig. 11.10 is called the **short-run aggregate supply curve** (*SRAS*) because it applies only to the short period of time that P^e remains unchanged. In the long run people learn what is actually happening to prices, and the expected price level adjusts to the actual price level ($P = P^e$). When the actual price level equals the expected price level, no misperceptions remain and producers supply the full-employment level of output. In terms of Eq. (11.1), in the long run P equals P^e, and output Y equals full-employment output $\bar{Y}$. Hence in the long run the supply of output doesn't depend on the price level. Thus the **long-run aggregate supply curve** (*LRAS*) is vertical at the point where output equals $\bar{Y}$. The long-run aggregate supply curve is the same

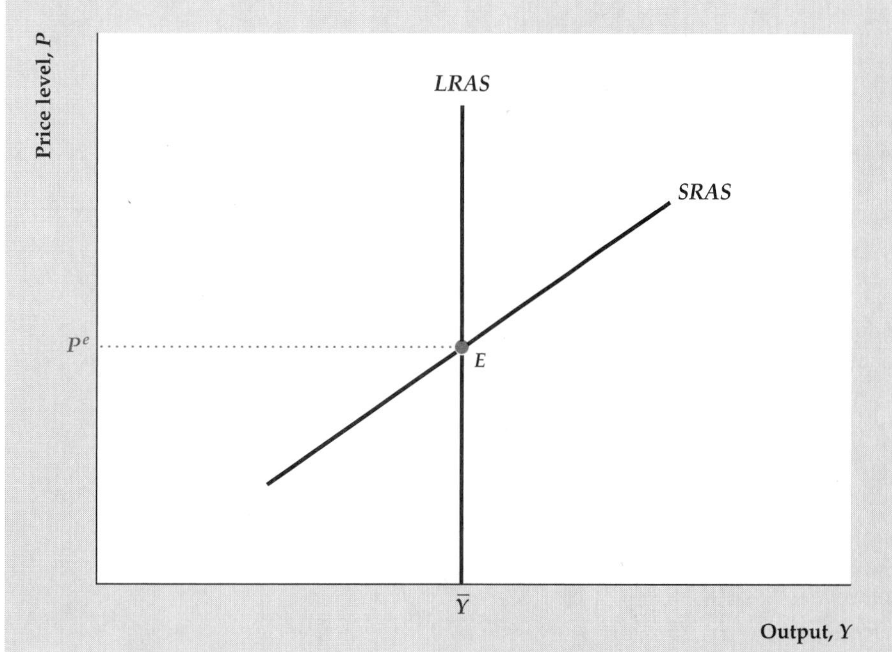

Figure 11.10
The aggregate supply curve in the misperceptions theory
The misperceptions theory holds that, for a given value of the expected price level P^e, an increase in the actual price level P fools producers into increasing output. This relationship between output and the price level is shown by the short-run aggregate supply curve *SRAS*. Along the *SRAS* curve, output equals $\bar{Y}$ when prices equal their expected level ($P = P^e$, at point E), output exceeds $\bar{Y}$ when the price level is higher than expected ($P > P^e$), and output is less than $\bar{Y}$ when the price level is lower than expected ($P < P^e$). In the long run, the expected price level equals the actual price level so that output equals $\bar{Y}$. Thus the long-run aggregate supply curve *LRAS* is vertical at $Y = \bar{Y}$.

as the vertical aggregate supply curve in the basic classical model without misperceptions.

Monetary Policy and the Misperceptions Theory

Let's now reexamine the neutrality of money in the extended version of the classical model. This framework highlights an important distinction between anticipated and unanticipated changes in the money supply: Unanticipated changes in the nominal money supply have real effects, but anticipated changes are neutral and have no real effects.

Unanticipated Changes in the Money Supply. Suppose that the economy is initially in general equilibrium at point *E* in Fig. 11.11, where AD^1 intersects $SRAS^1$. Here, output equals the full-employment level $\bar{Y}$, and the price level and the expected price level both equal P_1. Suppose that everyone expects the money supply and the price level to remain constant but that the Fed unexpectedly and without publicity increases the money supply by 10%. A 10% increase in the money supply shifts the *AD* curve up to AD^2, increasing the price level at each level of output by 10%. Given the expected price level P_1 the *SRAS* curve remains unchanged, still passing through point *E*.

The increase in aggregate demand bids up the price level to the new equilibrium level P_2, where AD^2 intersects $SRAS^1$ (point *F*). In the new short-run equilibrium at *F*, the actual price level exceeds the expected price level and output exceeds $\bar{Y}$. Because the increase in the money supply leads to a rise in output, money isn't neutral in this analysis.

The reason is that producers are fooled. Each producer misperceives the higher nominal price of her output as an increase in its relative price, rather

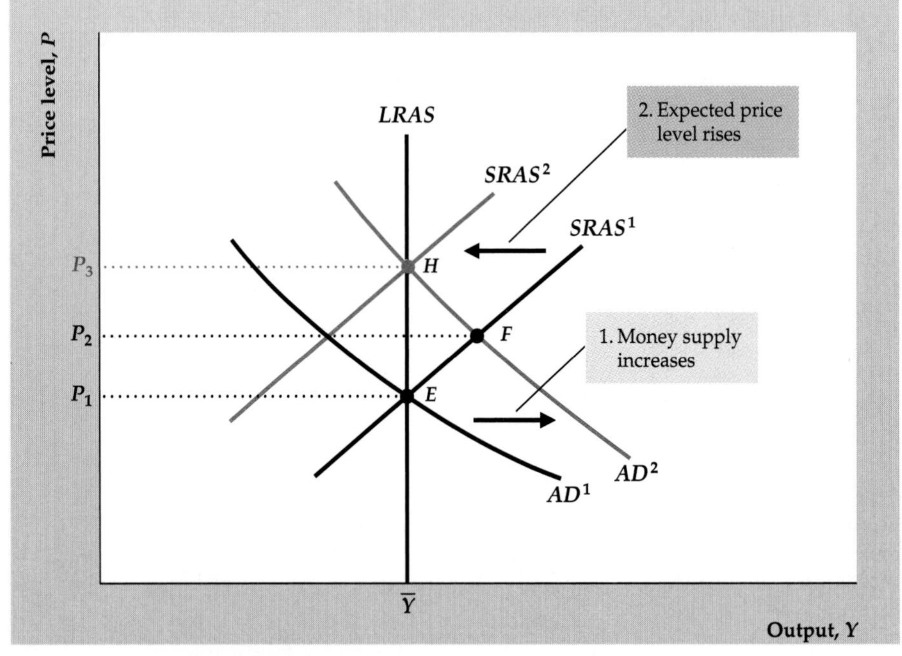

Figure 11.11
An unanticipated increase in the money supply
If we start from the initial equilibrium at point *E*, an unanticipated 10% increase in the money supply shifts the *AD* curve up by 10% at each level of output, from AD^1 to AD^2. The short-run equilibrium is located at point *F*, the intersection of AD^2 and the short-run aggregate supply curve $SRAS^1$, where prices and output are both higher than at point *E*. Thus an unanticipated change in the money supply isn't neutral in the short run. In the long run, people learn the true price level and the equilibrium shifts to point *H*, the intersection of AD^2 and the long-run aggregate supply curve *LRAS*. In the long-run equilibrium at *H*, the price level has risen by 10% but output returns to its full-employment level $\bar{Y}$ so that money is neutral in the long run. As expectations of the price level rise from P_1 to P_3, the *SRAS* curve also shifts up until it passes through *H*.

than as an increase in the general price level. Although output increases in the short run, producers aren't better off. They end up producing more than they would have if they had known the true relative prices.

The economy can't stay long at the equilibrium represented by point *F*, because at *F* the actual price level P_2 is higher than the expected price level P_1. Over time, people obtain information about the true level of prices and adjust their expectations accordingly. The only equilibrium that can be sustained in the long run is one in which people do not permanently underestimate or overestimate the price level so that the expected price level and the actual price level are equal. Graphically, when people learn the true price level, the relevant aggregate supply curve is the long-run aggregate supply curve *LRAS*, along which *P* always equals P^e. In Fig. 11.11 the long-run equilibrium is point *H*, the intersection of AD^2 and *LRAS*. At *H* output equals its full-employment level $\bar{Y}$, and the price level P_3 is 10% higher than the initial price level P_1. Because everyone now expects the price level to be P_3, a new *SRAS* curve, $SRAS^2$, passes through *H*.

Thus, according to the misperceptions theory, an unanticipated increase in the money supply raises output and isn't neutral *in the short run*. However, an unanticipated increase in the money supply *is* neutral in the long run, after people have learned the true price level.

Anticipated Changes in the Money Supply. In the extended classical model based on the misperceptions theory, the effects of an anticipated money supply increase are different from the effects of a surprise money supply increase. Figure 11.12 illustrates the effects of an anticipated money supply increase. Again, we suppose that the initial general equilibrium point is at *E*, where output equals its full-employment level and the actual and expected price

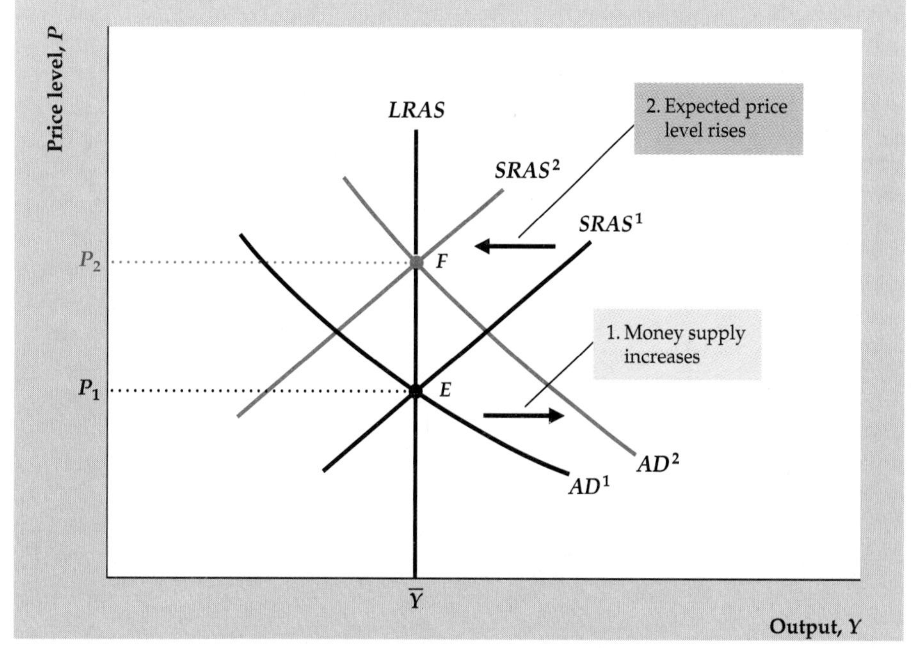

Figure 11.12
An anticipated increase in the money supply
The economy is in initial equilibrium at point *E* when the Fed publicly announces a 10% increase in the money supply. When the money supply increases, the *AD* curve shifts upward by 10%, from AD^1 to AD^2. But in addition, because the increase in the money supply is anticipated by the public, the expected price level increases by 10%, from P_1 to P_2. Thus the short-run aggregate supply curve shifts up from $SRAS^1$ to $SRAS^2$. The new short-run equilibrium, which is the same as the long-run equilibrium, is at point *F*. At *F* output is unchanged at $\bar{Y}$ and the price level is 10% higher than in the initial equilibrium at *E*. Thus an anticipated increase in the money supply is neutral in the short run as well as in the long run.

levels both equal P_1. We assume that the Federal Reserve announces that it is going to increase the money supply by 10% and that the public believes this announcement.

As we have shown, a 10% increase in the money supply shifts the AD curve up by 10% at each level of output, from AD^1 to AD^2. However, in this case the $SRAS$ curve also shifts up. The reason is that the public's expected price level rises as soon as people learn of the increase in the money supply. Suppose that people expect—correctly—that the price level will also rise by 10% so that P^e rises by 10%, from P_1 to P_2. Then the new $SRAS$ curve, $SRAS^2$, passes through point F in Fig. 11.12, where Y equals $\bar{Y}$ and both the actual and expected price levels equal P_2. The new equilibrium also is at F, where AD^2 and $SRAS^2$ intersect. At the new equilibrium, output equals its full-employment level, and prices are 10% higher than they were initially. The anticipated increase in the money supply hasn't affected output but has raised prices proportionally. Similarly, an anticipated drop in the money supply would lower prices but not affect output or other real variables. Thus *anticipated changes in the money supply are neutral in the short run as well as in the long run.* The reason is that, if producers know that increases in the nominal prices of their products are the result of an increase in the money supply and do not reflect a change in relative prices, they won't be fooled into increasing production when prices rise.

Rational Expectations and the Role of Monetary Policy

In the extended classical model based on the misperceptions theory, *unanticipated* changes in the money supply affect output, but *anticipated* changes in the money supply are neutral. Thus, if the Federal Reserve wanted to use monetary policy to affect output, it seemingly should use only unanticipated changes in the money supply. So, for example, when the economy is in recession, the Fed would try to use surprise increases in the money supply to raise output; when the economy is booming, the Fed would try to use surprise decreases in the money supply to slow the economy.

A serious problem for this strategy is the presence of private economic forecasters and "Fed watchers" in financial markets. These people spend a good deal of time and effort trying to forecast macroeconomic variables such as the money supply and the price level, and their forecasts are well publicized. If the Fed began a pattern of raising the money supply in recessions and reducing it in booms, forecasters and Fed watchers would quickly understand and report this fact. As a result, the Fed's manipulations of the money supply would no longer be unanticipated, and the changes in the money supply would have no effect other than possibly causing instability in the price level. More generally, according to the misperceptions theory, to achieve any systematic change in the behavior of output, the Fed must conduct monetary policy in a way that systematically fools the public. But there are strong incentives in the financial markets and elsewhere for people to try to figure out what the Fed is doing. Thus most economists believe that attempts by the Fed to surprise the public in a systematic way cannot be successful.

The idea that the Federal Reserve cannot systematically surprise the public is part of a larger hypothesis that the public has rational expectations. The hypothesis of **rational expectations** states that the public's forecasts of various economic variables, including the money supply, the price level, and GDP, are

BOX 11.2

Are Price Forecasts Rational?

Most classical economists assume that people have rational expectations about future economic variables; that is, people make intelligent use of available information in forecasting variables that affect their economic decisions. The rational expectations assumption has important implications. For example, as we have demonstrated, if monetary nonneutrality is the result of temporary misperceptions of the price level and people have rational expectations about future prices, monetary policy is not able to affect the real economy systematically.

The rational expectations assumption is attractive to economists—including many Keynesian as well as classical economists—because it fits well economists' presumption that people intelligently pursue their economic self-interests. If people's expectations aren't rational, the economic plans that individuals make won't generally be as good as they could be. But the theoretical attractiveness of rational expectations obviously isn't enough; economists would like to know whether people really do have rational expectations about important economic variables.

The rational expectations idea can be tested with data from surveys, in which people are asked their opinions about the future of the economy. To illustrate how such a test would be conducted, suppose that we have data from a survey in which people were asked to make a prediction of the price level one year in the future. Imagine that this survey is repeated each year for several years. Now suppose that, for each individual in the survey, we define

P^e_t = the individual's forecast, made in year $t - 1$, of the price level in year t.

Suppose also that we let P_t represent the price level that actually occurs in year t. Then the individual's *forecast error* for year t is the difference between the actual price level and the individual's forecast:

$P_t - P^e_t$ = the individual's forecast error in year t.

If people have rational expectations, these forecast errors should be unpredictable random numbers. However, if forecast errors are consistently positive or negative—meaning that people systematically tend to underpredict or overpredict the price level—expectations are not rational. If forecast errors have a systematic pattern—for example, if people tend to overpredict the price level when prices have been rising in the recent past—again, expectations are not rational.

Many statistical studies of price level forecasts made by consumers, journalists, academic economists, and others reject the rational expectations theory. A common finding is that people are too slow to incorporate new information into their forecasts. However, supporters of the rational expectations idea argue that the typical survey respondent isn't likely to think very hard about the forecast she gives to the survey-taker because she has little or no economic stake in the quality of her answer. They argue that a fairer test of rational expectations is to examine the expectations of people who do have a real stake in the quality of their forecasts—namely, professional economic forecasters. Michael Keane and David Runkle* of the Federal Reserve Bank of Minneapolis studied the price level forecasts of a panel of professional forecasters who have been surveyed by the American Statistical Association and the National Bureau of Economic Research since 1968. Perhaps not too surprisingly, Keane and Runkle found no evidence to refute the hypothesis that the professional forecasters had rational expectations. A plausible conclusion to draw from the research is that, the greater a person's economic incentives to make good forecasts about the future, the more likely that person is to have rational expectations.

* "Are Economic Forecasts Rational?" *Quarterly Review,* Federal Reserve Bank of Minneapolis, Spring 1989, pp. 26–33.

based on reasoned and intelligent examination of available economic data.[23] (The evidence for rational expectations is discussed in Box 11.2.) If the public has rational expectations, it will eventually understand the Federal Reserve's

23. The idea of rational expectations was first discussed by John F. Muth in his classic 1961 paper, "Rational Expectations and the Theory of Price Movements," *Econometrica,* July 1961, pp. 315–335. However, this idea wasn't widely used in macroeconomics until the new classical "revolution" of the early 1970s.

general pattern of behavior. If expectations are rational, purely random changes in the money supply may be unanticipated and thus nonneutral. However, because the Fed won't be able to surprise the public systematically, it can't use monetary policy to stabilize output. Thus, even if smoothing business cycles were desirable, according to the combination of the misperceptions theory and rational expectations, the Fed cannot systematically use monetary policy to do so.

Propagating the Effects of Unanticipated Changes in the Money Supply. The misperceptions theory implies that unanticipated changes in the money supply are nonneutral because individual producers are temporarily fooled about the price level. However, money supply data are available weekly and price level data are reported monthly, suggesting that any misperceptions about monetary policy or the price level—and thus any real effects of money supply changes—should be quickly eliminated.

To explain how changes in the money supply can have real effects that last more than a few weeks, classical economists stress the role of propagation mechanisms. A **propagation mechanism** is an aspect of the economy that allows short-lived shocks to have relatively long-term effects on the economy.

An important example of a propagation mechanism is the behavior of inventories. Consider a manufacturing firm that has both a normal level of monthly sales and a normal amount of finished goods in inventory that it tries to maintain. Suppose that an unanticipated rise in the money supply increases aggregate demand and raises prices above their expected level. Because increasing production sharply in a short period of time is costly, the firm will respond to the increase in demand partly by producing more goods and partly by selling some finished goods from inventory, thus depleting its inventory stocks below their normal level.

Next month suppose that everyone learns the true price level and that the firm's rate of sales returns to its normal level. Despite the fact that the monetary shock has passed, the firm may continue to produce for a while at a higher-than-normal rate. The reason for the continued high level of production is that besides meeting its normal demand, the firm wants to replenish its inventory stock. The need to rebuild inventories illustrates a propagation mechanism that allows a short-lived shock (a monetary shock, in this case) to have a longer-term effect on the economy.

CHAPTER SUMMARY

1. Classical business cycle analysis utilizes the classical *IS–LM* model along with the assumption that wages and prices adjust quickly to bring the economy into general equilibrium.
2. The real business cycle (RBC) theory is a version of the classical theory that emphasizes productivity shocks (shocks to the production function) as the source of business cycle fluctuations. In

the classical *IS–LM* model, a temporary decline in productivity reduces the real wage, employment, and output, while raising the real interest rate and the price level. The RBC theory can account for the observed procyclical behavior of employment, real wages, and labor productivity. However, the prediction of the RBC theory that prices are countercyclical is viewed by some as a failing.

3. Classical business cycle analysis allows for other shocks to the economy besides changes in productivity, including changes in fiscal policy. According to the classical *IS–LM* model, an increase in government purchases raises employment, output, the real interest rate, and the price level. Including both fiscal and productivity shocks in the classical model improves its ability to fit the data. Although fiscal policy can affect employment and output, classical economists argue that it should not be used to smooth the business cycle because the invisible hand leads the economy to an efficient outcome without government interference. Instead, decisions about government purchases should be based on comparisons of costs and benefits.

4. In the basic classical model (which includes RBC theory), money is neutral, which means that changes in the nominal money supply change the price level proportionally but do not affect real variables such as output, employment, and the real interest rate.

5. The basic classical model can account for the procyclical and leading behavior of money if there is reverse causation, that is, if anticipated changes in output lead to changes in the money supply in the same direction. For example, if firms increase their money demand in anticipation of future output increases, and if the Fed (to keep the price level stable) supplies enough extra money to meet the increase in money demand, increases in the money stock precede increases in output. This result holds even though changes in the money stock don't *cause* subsequent changes in output.

6. Examination of historical monetary policy actions suggests that money isn't neutral. Friedman and Schwartz identified occasions when the money supply changed for independent reasons, such as gold discoveries or changes in monetary institutions, and changes in output followed these changes in the money supply in the same direction. More recent experiences, such as the severe economic slowdown that followed Federal Reserve Chairman Volcker's decision to reduce money growth in 1979, also provide evidence for the view that money isn't neutral.

7. The effects of changes in the money supply on the economy can be studied using the aggregate demand–aggregate supply (*AD–AS*) model. It is consistent with the *IS–LM* model but, unlike the *IS–LM* model, focuses on the relationship between output and the price level.

8. The aggregate demand (*AD*) curve relates the aggregate quantity of output demanded—the level of output at the intersection of the *IS* and *LM* curves—to the price level. An increase in the price level reduces the real money supply and shifts the *LM* curve up and to the left, which reduces the aggregate quantity of output demanded. Because an increase in the price level reduces the aggregate quantity of goods demanded, the aggregate demand curve slopes downward. Factors that increase the aggregate quantity of output demanded at a given price level, such as increases in government purchases or the money supply, shift the *AD* curve to the right.

9. The aggregate supply curve relates the quantity of output supplied by firms to the price level. In the basic version of the classical model, output supplied always equals full-employment output $\bar{Y}$ regardless of the price level, so the aggregate supply curve is a vertical line that intersects the horizontal axis at $Y = \bar{Y}$. If the aggregate supply curve is vertical, money is neutral.

10. The misperceptions theory is based on the idea that producers have imprecise information about the current price level. According to the misperceptions theory, the amount of output supplied equals the full-employment level of output $\bar{Y}$ only if the actual price level equals the expected price level. When the price level is higher than expected, suppliers are fooled into thinking that the relative prices of the goods they supply have risen, so they supply a quantity of output that exceeds $\bar{Y}$. Similarly, when the

price level is lower than expected, the quantity of output supplied is less than $\bar{Y}$.

The short-run aggregate supply curve (*SRAS*), which is based on the misperceptions theory, slopes upward in describing the relation between output and the actual price level, with the expected price level held constant. In the long run the price level equals the expected price level so that the supply of output equals $\bar{Y}$; thus the long-run aggregate supply curve (*LRAS*) is a vertical line at the point where output equals $\bar{Y}$.

11. With the upward-sloping *SRAS* curve based on the misperceptions theory, an *unanticipated* increase in the money supply increases output (and is thus nonneutral) in the short run. However, because the long-run aggregate supply curve is vertical, an unanticipated increase in the money supply doesn't affect output (and so is neutral) in the long run. An *anticipated* increase in the money supply causes price expectations to adjust immediately and leads to no misperceptions about the price level; thus an anticipated increase in the money supply is neutral in both the short and long runs.

12. According to the extended classical model based on the misperceptions theory, only surprise changes in the money supply can affect output. If the public has rational expectations about macroeconomic variables, including the money supply, the Fed cannot systematically surprise the public because the public will understand and anticipate the Fed's pattern of behavior. Thus classical economists argue that the Fed cannot systematically use changes in the money supply to affect output.

KEY DIAGRAM 7

The Classical *AD–AS* Model

The classical *AD–AS* model shows how the aggregate demand for output and the aggregate supply of output interact to determine the price level and output in the classical model.

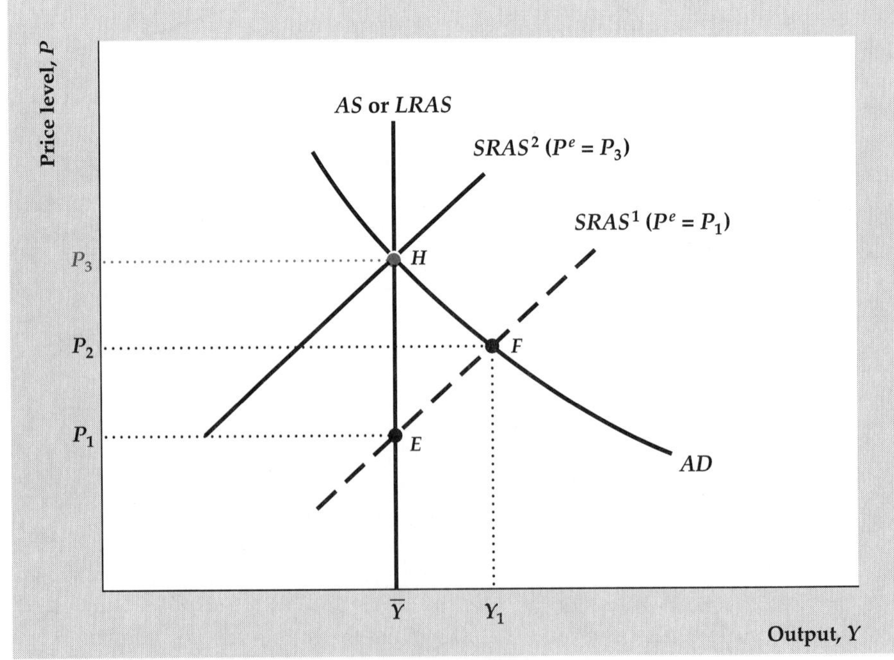

Diagram Elements

- The price level, P, is on the vertical axis, and the level of output, Y, is on the horizontal axis.

- The aggregate demand (AD) curve shows the aggregate quantity of output demanded at each price level. The aggregate amount of output demanded is determined by the intersection of the IS and LM curves (see Fig. 11.5). An increase in the price level P reduces the real money supply, shifting the LM curve up and to the left and reducing the aggregate quantity of output demanded. Thus the AD curve slopes downward.

- The aggregate supply (AS) curve shows the amount of output supplied at each price level. In the basic classical model, in which producers correctly perceive the relative prices of their products, producers supply the full-employment level of output—the level of output that maximizes their profits—regardless of the price level. Thus in the basic classical model the AS curve is a vertical line at $Y = \bar{Y}$.

- To allow for the possibility that money isn't neutral, the basic classical model is extended by adding to it the misperceptions theory. This theory is based on the assumption that producers have imperfect information about the general price level and hence don't know precisely the relative prices of their products. When producers misperceive the price level, an increase in the general price level above the expected price level fools suppliers into thinking that the relative prices of their goods have increased, so all suppliers increase output. The short-run aggregate supply curve ($SRAS$) shows the aggregate quantity of output supplied at each price level, with the expected price level held constant. Because an increase in the price level fools producers into supplying more output, in the extended classical model the short-run aggregate supply curve slopes upward, as shown by $SRAS^1$.

- The short-run aggregate supply curve $SRAS^1$ is drawn so that the expected price level P^e equals P_1. When the actual price level equals the expected price level, producers are not fooled and so supply the full-employment level of output $\bar{Y}$. Therefore at point E, where the actual price level equals the expected price level (both equal P_1), the short-run aggregate supply curve $SRAS^1$ shows that producers supply $\bar{Y}$.

- In the long run producers learn about the price level and adjust their expectations until the actual price level equals the expected price level. Producers then supply the full-employment level of output $\bar{Y}$, regardless of the price level. Thus, in the extended classical model with misperceptions, the long-run aggregate supply curve $LRAS$ is vertical at $Y = \bar{Y}$. The $LRAS$ curve is the same as the AS curve in the basic classical model.

Factors that Shift the Curves

- The aggregate quantity of output demanded is determined by the intersection of the IS curve and the LM curve. At a constant price level, any factor that shifts the IS–LM intersection to the right increases the aggregate quantity of goods demanded and thus also shifts the AD curve to the right. Factors that shift the AD curve are listed in Summary table 14.

- In the basic classical model any factor that increases full-employment output $\bar{Y}$ shifts the (vertical) AS curve to the right. Factors that increase full-employment output include beneficial supply shocks or an increase in labor supply. An increase in government purchases, because it induces workers to supply more labor, also shifts the AS curve to the right in the classical model.

- In the extended classical model with the misperceptions theory, any factor that increases full-employment output $\bar{Y}$ shifts both the short-run and the long-run aggregate supply curves to the right.

- In the extended classical model with the misperceptions theory, an increase in the expected price level shifts the short-run aggregate supply curve up.

Analysis

- In the basic classical model the economy's equilibrium is represented by the intersection of the AD curve and the (vertical) AS curve. There is no distinction between the short run and the long run, and output is always at its full-employment level $\bar{Y}$.

- In the extended classical model with the misperceptions theory, the short-run equilibrium is at the intersection of the AD curve and the $SRAS$ curve. For example, if the expected price level is P_1, the $SRAS$ curve is $SRAS^1$, and the short-run equilibrium is at point F. At F output Y_1 is higher than the full-employment level $\bar{Y}$, and the price level P_2 is higher than the expected price level P_1. As producers obtain information about the price level, the expected price level is revised upward, which shifts the $SRAS$ curve up. The long-run equilibrium is at point H, where the long-run aggregate supply curve $LRAS$ intersects the AD curve. In the long run (1) output equals $\bar{Y}$, and (2) the price level equals the expected price level (both equal P_3). In the long run, when the expected price level has risen to P_3, the short-run aggregate supply curve $SRAS^2$ passes through H.

Key Terms

aggregate demand curve, p. 372
aggregate supply curve, p. 375
long-run aggregate supply curve, p. 381
misperceptions theory, p. 379
nominal shocks, p. 356
productivity shocks, p. 356
propagation mechanism, p. 386
rational expectations, p. 384
real business cycle theory, p.356
real shocks, p. 356
reverse causation, p. 370
short-run aggregate supply curve, p. 381

Key Equation

$$Y = \bar{Y} + b(P - P^e) \quad (11.1)$$

The short-run aggregate supply curve, based on the misperceptions theory, indicates that the aggregate amount of output supplied, Y, equals full-employment output, $\bar{Y}$, when the price level, P, equals the expected price level, P^e. When the price level is higher than expected ($P > P^e$), output exceeds $\bar{Y}$; when the price level is lower than expected ($P < P^e$), output is less than $\bar{Y}$.

Review Questions

1. What main feature of the classical *IS–LM* model distinguishes it from the Keynesian *IS–LM* model? Why is the distinction of practical importance?
2. What are the two main components of any theory of the business cycle? Describe these two components for the real business cycle theory.
3. Define *real shock* and *nominal shock*. What type of real shock do real business cycle theorists consider the most important source of cyclical fluctuations?
4. What major business cycle facts does the RBC theory explain successfully? Does it explain any business cycle facts less well?
5. What effects does an increase in government purchases have on the labor market, according to the classical theory? What effects does it have on output, the real interest rate, and the price level? According to classical economists, should fiscal policy be used to smooth out the business cycle? Why or why not?
6. In the context of the relationship between the money supply and real economic activity, what is meant by *reverse causation*? Explain how reverse causation could occur. What business cycle fact is it intended to explain?
7. What two variables are related by the aggregate demand (*AD*) curve? Why does the *AD* curve slope downward? Give two examples of changes in the economy that shift the *AD* curve to the right, and explain why the shift occurs.
8. According to the misperceptions theory, what effect does an increase in the price level have on the amount of output supplied by producers? Explain. Does it matter whether the increase in the price level was expected?
9. What conclusion does the basic classical model (with no misperceptions of the price level) allow about the neutrality or nonneutrality of money? In what ways is this conclusion modified by the extended classical model based on the misperceptions theory?
10. Define *rational expectations*. According to the classical model, what implications do rational expectations have for the ability of the central bank to use monetary policy to smooth business cycles?

Numerical Problems

1. In a certain economy the production function is

$$Y = A(100N - 0.5N^2),$$

where Y is output, A is productivity, and N is total hours worked. The marginal product of labor associated with this production function is

$$MPN = A(100 - N).$$

Initially, $A = 1.0$, but a beneficial productivity shock raises A to 1.1.

a. The supply of labor is

$$NS = 45 + 0.1w,$$

where w is the real wage. Find the equilibrium levels of output, hours worked, and the real wage before and after the productivity shock. Recall (Chapter 3) that the *MPN* curve is the same as the labor demand curve, with the real wage replacing the *MPN*.

b. Repeat part (a) if the labor supply is

$$NS = 10 + 0.8w.$$

c. Some studies show that the real wage is only slightly procyclical. Assume for the sake of argument that this finding is correct. Would a calibrated RBC model fit the facts better if the labor supply is relatively insensitive to the real wage, or if it is relatively sensitive? Justify your answer diagrammatically and relate it to your answers to parts (a) and (b).

2. An economy is described as follows.

Desired consumption $C^d = 600 + 0.5(Y - T) - 50r$.
Desired investment $I^d = 450 - 50r$.
Real money demand $L = 0.5Y - 100i$.
Full-employment output $\bar{Y} = 2210$.
Expected inflation $\pi^e = 0.05$.

In this economy the government always has a balanced budget, so $T = G$, where T is total taxes collected.

a. Suppose that $M = 4320$ and $G = 150$. Use the classical *IS–LM* model to find the equilibrium values of output, the real interest rate, the price level, consumption, and investment. (*Hint:* In the classical model, output always equals its full-employment level.)

b. The money supply rises to 4752. Repeat part (a). Is money neutral?

c. With the money supply back at 4320, government purchases and taxes rise to 190. Repeat part (a). Assume for simplicity that $\bar{Y}$ is fixed (unaffected by G). Is fiscal policy neutral in this case? Explain.

3. Consider the following economy.

Desired consumption $C^d = 1275 + 0.5(Y - T) - 200r$.
Desired investment $I^d = 900 - 200r$.
Real money demand $L = 0.5Y - 200i$.
Full-employment output $\bar{Y} = 4600$.
Expected inflation $\pi^e = 0$.

a. Suppose that $T = G = 450$ and that $M = 9000$. Find an equation describing the *IS* curve. (*Hint:* Set desired national saving and desired investment equal, and solve for the relationship between r and Y.) Find an equation describing the *LM* curve. (*Hint:* Set real money supply and real money demand equal, and again solve for the relationship between r and Y, given P.) Finally, find an equation for the aggregate demand curve. (*Hint:* Use the *IS* and *LM* equations to find a relationship between Y and P.) What are the equilibrium values of output, consumption, investment, the real interest rate, and the price level? Assume that there are no misperceptions about the price level.

b. Suppose that $T = G = 450$ and that $M = 4500$. What is the equation for the aggregate demand curve now? What are the equilibrium values of output, consumption, investment, the real interest rate, and the price level? Assume that full-employment output $\bar{Y}$ is fixed.

c. Repeat part (b) for $T = G = 330$ and $M = 9000$.

4. An economy has the following *AD* and *AS* curves.

AD curve $Y = 300 + 30(M/P)$.
AS curve $Y = \bar{Y} + 10(P - P^e)$.

Here, $\bar{Y} = 500$ and $M = 400$.

a. Suppose that $P^e = 60$. What are the equilibrium values of the price level P and output Y? (*Hint:* The solutions for P in this part and in part (b) are multiples of 10.)

b. An unanticipated increase raises the money supply to $M = 700$. Because the increase is unanticipated, P^e remains at 60. What are the equilibrium values of the price level P and output Y?

c. The Fed announces that the money supply will be increased to $M = 700$, which the public believes. Now what are the equilibrium values of the price level P, the expected price level P^e, and output Y?

5. Try the following experiment: Flip a coin fifty times, keeping track of the results. Think of each "heads" as a small positive shock that increases output by one unit; similarly, think of each "tails" as a small negative shock that reduces output by one unit. Let the initial value of output Y be 50, and graph the level of output over time as it is hit by the "positive" and "negative" shocks (coin flips). For example, if your first four flips are three heads and a tail, output takes the values 51, 52, 53, 52. After fifty flips, have your small shocks produced any large cycles in output?

6. In a particular economy the labor force (the sum of employed and unemployed workers) is fixed at 100 million. In this economy, each month 1% of the workers who were employed at the beginning of the month lose their jobs, and 19% of the workers who were unemployed at the beginning of the month find new jobs.

a. The January unemployment rate is 5%. For the rates of job loss and job finding given, what will the unemployment rate be in February? In March?

b. In April an adverse productivity shock raises the job loss rate to 3% of those employed. The job loss rate returns to 1% in May, while the job finding rate remains unchanged at 19% throughout. Find the unemployment rate for April, May, June, and July.

7. (Appendix) Consider the following economy.

IS curve $r = 2.47 - 0.0004Y$.
Real money demand $L = 0.5Y - 500(r + \pi^e)$.
Short-run aggregate supply $Y = \bar{Y} + 100(P - P^e)$.

Here, r is the real interest rate, Y is output, and P is the price level. Assume that expected inflation $\pi^e = 0$, nominal money supply $M = 88{,}950$, and full-employment output $\bar{Y} = 6000$.

a. Use the notation of Appendixes 10.A and 11.A. What are the values of the parameters α_{IS}, β_{IS}, α_{LM}, β_{LM}, ℓ_r, and b? (*Hint:* Solve for asset market equilibrium to obtain the coefficients of the *LM* equation.)
b. What is the equation of the aggregate demand curve?
c. Suppose that the expected price level $P^e = 29.15$. What are the short-run equilibrium values of the price level P and output Y?
d. What are the long-run equilibrium values of the price level P and output Y?

Analytical Problems

1. The discovery of a new technology increases the expected future marginal product of capital.
   a. Use the classical *IS–LM* model to determine the effect of the increase in the expected future *MPK* on current output, the real interest rate, employment, real wages, consumption, investment, and the price level. Assume that expected future real wages and future incomes are unaffected by the new technology. Assume also that current productivity is unaffected.
   b. Find the effects of the increase in the expected future *MPK* on current output and prices from the *AD–AS* diagram based on the misperceptions theory. What accounts for the difference with part (a)?
2. Use the classical *IS–LM* model to analyze the effects of a permanent increase in government purchases of 100 per year (in real terms). The increase in purchases is financed by a permanent increase in lump-sum taxes of 100 per year.
   a. Begin by finding the effects of the fiscal change on the labor market. How does the effect of the permanent increase in government purchases of 100 compare with the effect of a temporary increase in purchases of 100?
   b. Because the tax increase is permanent, assume that at any constant levels of output and the real interest rate consumers respond by reducing their consumption each period by the full amount of the tax increase. Under this assumption, how does the permanent increase in government purchases affect desired national saving and the *IS* curve?
   c. Use the classical *IS–LM* model to find the effects of the permanent increase in government purchases and taxes on output, the real interest rate, and the price level in the current period. What happens if consumers reduce their current consumption by less than 100 at any level of output and the real interest rate?
3. Consider a business cycle theory that combines the classical *IS–LM* model with the assumption that temporary changes in government purchases are the main source of cyclical fluctuations. How well would this theory explain the observed cyclical behavior of each of the following variables? Give reasons for your answers.
   a. Employment
   b. The real wage
   c. Average labor productivity
   d. Investment
   e. The price level
4. This problem asks you to work out in more detail the example of reverse causation described in the text. Suppose that firms that expect to increase production in the future have to increase their current transactions (for example, they may need to purchase more raw materials). For this reason, current real money demand rises when expected future output rises.
   a. Under the assumption that real money demand depends on expected future output, use the classical *IS–LM* model to find the effects of an increase in expected future output on the current price level. For simplicity, assume that any effects of the increase in expected future output on the labor market or on desired saving and investment are small and can be ignored.
   b. Suppose that the Fed wants to stabilize the current price level. How will the Fed respond to the increase in expected future output? Explain why the Fed's response is an example of reverse causation.
5. Two countries called East and West agree to unify. The real value of full-employment output in East is 1 trillion widgets, and in West it is 2 trillion widgets. The combined full-employment output of the unified country is expected to be the sum of the two full-employment outputs, or 3 trillion widgets.

   Real money demand in the West is 10% of West's real output and will remain so after unification. In the East people don't have access to financial instruments, such as stocks and bonds, and so are forced to save in the form of money. As a result, real money demand in the East is 40% of East's real output. However, after unification easterners will have access to a full range of financial assets, and thus their real money demand will drop to 10% of output.

The unified country will use only the West's currency. As part of the unification plan, the West central bank has agreed to print new western currency and trade it for eastern currency, which will be destroyed. At the initial price levels the total real value of the western currency received by easterners equals the total real value of the eastern currency they give up.

Use the classical *IS–LM* model to find the effects on postunification output and prices of the currency swap. Give a quantitative estimate of the effect on the price level (measured in the western currency). Qualitatively, does your answer change if you use the *AD–AS* model based on the misperceptions theory? What can West's central bank do to offset the effects of the currency swap on the price level?

6. Starting from a situation with no government spending and no taxes, the government introduces a foreign aid program (in which domestically produced goods are shipped abroad) and pays for it with a temporary 10% tax on current wages. Future wages are untaxed.

What effects will the temporary wage tax have on labor supply? Use the classical *IS–LM* model to find the effects of the fiscal change on output, employment, the (before-tax) real wage, the real interest rate, and the price level.

APPENDIX 11.A AN ALGEBRAIC VERSION OF THE CLASSICAL *AD–AS* MODEL

Building on the algebraic version of the *IS–LM* model developed in Appendix 10.A, in this appendix we derive an algebraic version of the classical *AD–AS* model presented in this chapter. We present algebraic versions of the aggregate demand (*AD*) curve and the aggregate supply (*AS*) curve and then solve for the general equilibrium.

The Aggregate Demand Curve

Aggregate output demanded at any price level P is the amount of output corresponding to the intersection of the *IS* and *LM* curves. We begin with Eqs. 10.A.14 and 10.A.19, which describe the *IS* and *LM* curves as follows:

$$r = \alpha_{IS} - \beta_{IS}Y, \qquad IS \text{ curve}; \tag{11.A.1}$$

$$r = \alpha_{LM} - \left(\frac{1}{\ell_r}\right)\left(\frac{M}{P}\right) + \beta_{LM}Y, \qquad LM \text{ curve}. \tag{11.A.2}$$

Again, Y is output, r is the real interest rate, M/P is the real money supply, and α_{IS}, β_{IS}, α_{LM}, β_{LM}, and ℓ_r are positive numbers, as defined in Appendix 10.A. We find the value of Y at the intersection of the *IS* and *LM* curves by setting the right-hand sides of Eqs. (11.A.1) and (11.A.2) equal and solving for Y:

$$Y = \frac{\alpha_{IS} - \alpha_{LM} + (1/\ell_r)(M/P)}{\beta_{IS} + \beta_{LM}} \tag{11.A.3}$$

Equation (11.A.3) is the aggregate demand curve. For constant nominal money supply M, Eq. (11.A.3) shows that the aggregate quantity of goods demanded Y is a decreasing function of the price level P so that the *AD* curve slopes down. Note that the numerator of the right-hand side of Eq. (11.A.3) is the intercept of the *IS* curve minus the intercept of the *LM* curve. Thus, for a constant price level, any change that shifts the *IS* curve up (such as an increase in government purchases) or shifts the *LM* curve down (such as an increase in the nominal money supply) increases aggregate output demanded and shifts the *AD* curve to the right.

The Aggregate Supply Curve

The short-run aggregate supply curve based on the misperceptions theory is represented by Eq. (11.1), which, for convenience, we repeat here:

$$Y = \bar{Y} + b(P - P^e), \tag{11.A.4}$$

where b is a positive number. According to Eq. (11.A.4), producers supply the full-employment level of output $\bar{Y}$ when the price level P equals the expected price level P^e. When prices are greater than expected ($P > P^e$), producers are fooled into supplying more than the full-employment level of output; when prices are less than expected ($P < P^e$), producers supply less than the full-employment level of output. Equation (11.A.4) shows that the short-run aggregate supply curve shifts down and to the right when $\bar{Y}$ increases, and up and to the left when the expected price level P^e increases. In the long run, the expected price level equals the actual price level, so the long-run aggregate supply curve is vertical at $Y = \bar{Y}$.

General Equilibrium

For a given expected price level P^e, the short-run equilibrium value of the price level is determined by the intersection of the aggregate demand curve (Eq. 11.A.3) and the short-run aggregate supply curve (Eq. 11.A.4). Setting the right-hand sides of Eqs. (11.A.3) and (11.A.4) equal and multiplying both sides of the resulting equation by P yield a quadratic equation for the price level P:

$$a_2P^2 + a_1P - a_0 = 0, \tag{11.A.5}$$

where

$$a_2 = (\beta_{IS} + \beta_{LM})b;$$

$$a_1 = (\beta_{IS} + \beta_{LM})(\bar{Y} - bP^e) - \alpha_{IS} + \alpha_{LM};$$

$$a_0 = \frac{M}{\ell_r}.$$

The coefficients a_2 and a_0 are positive, and the coefficient a_1 could be positive, negative, or zero. Because both a_2 and a_0 are both positive, the solution of Eq. (11.A.5) yields one positive value of P and one negative value of P. The price level can't be negative, so the short-run equilibrium price level is the positive solution of this equation. Using the standard quadratic formula, we find the positive solution of equation (11.A.5) to be

$$P = \frac{-a_1 + \sqrt{a_1^2 + 4a_2a_0}}{2a_2}. \tag{11.A.6}$$

We obtain the short-run equilibrium level of output by substituting the value of the price level from Eq. (11.A.6) into either the aggregate demand curve Eq. (11.A.3) or the aggregate supply curve Eq. (11.A.4).

Note that an increase in the nominal money supply M increases the constant a_0 and thus, according to Eq. (11.A.6), it increases the equilibrium price level. Because an increase in M doesn't affect the aggregate supply curve but does increase the equilibrium price level, Eq. (11.A.4) shows that it increases output.

We focused on short-run equilibrium in this appendix. In the long run, the actual price level equals the expected price level so that, according to Eq. (11.A.4), output equals its full-employment level $\bar{Y}$. In the long run the economy reaches the general equilibrium described in Appendix 10.A.

CHAPTER 12

Keynesianism: The Macroeconomics of Wage and Price Rigidity

Chapter 11 presented the classical, or market-clearing, approach to business cycle analysis. In the classical approach wages and prices are assumed to adjust quickly so that markets are almost always in equilibrium. Classical economists argue that business cycles represent the economy's best response to disturbances, such as productivity shocks, so there is little justification for government attempts to smooth the cycle.

In contrast to the classicals, Keynesians are less optimistic about the ability of free-market economies to respond quickly and efficiently to shocks. One of the central ideas of Keynesianism is that wages and prices are "rigid" or "sticky" and do *not* adjust quickly to market-clearing levels. Wage and price rigidity implies that the economy can be away from its general equilibrium for significant periods of time. Thus a deep recession is not an optimal response of the free market to outside shocks; rather, it is a disequilibrium situation in which high unemployment reflects an excess of labor supplied over labor demanded. Keynesians believe that the government should act to eliminate—or at least minimize—these periods of low output and high unemployment.

As wage and price rigidity is the basis for Keynesian theory and policy recommendations, understanding the potential causes of rigidity is important. A telling criticism that the classicals aimed at the Keynesians in the early 1970s was that the Keynesians simply assumed that wages and prices are rigid, without giving a good economic explanation of why these rigidities occur. After all, argued the classicals, wages and prices are not simply "given" to the economy but are the results of decisions made by millions of individuals and firms. If excessively high wages are causing unemployment, why don't unemployed workers offer to work for lower wages until firms are willing to hire them? If prices aren't at the levels at which quantities supplied equal quantities demanded, why don't firms just change their prices? In effect, the classicals challenged the Keynesians to show how wage and price rigidity could be consistent with the idea—basic to almost all of economics—that individuals and firms are economically rational; that is, they do the best they can for themselves when making economic decisions.

Keynesian researchers accepted this challenge and have made progress in explaining wage and price rigidity in terms consistent with economic rationality. In the first part of this chapter we discuss some leading Keynesian explanations for wage and price rigidity. We then show how slow adjustment of wages and prices can be incorporated into the *IS–LM* model, converting it from a classical model to a Keynesian model. Using this model, we discuss the Keynesian answers to the two central questions about business cycles, namely, what causes business cycles and what should policymakers do about them?

12.1 REAL-WAGE RIGIDITY

Because Keynesian analysis and policy prescriptions depend so greatly on the assumption that wages and prices do not move rapidly to clear markets, we begin by discussing in some detail the possible economic reasons for slow or incomplete adjustment. In this section we focus on the rigidity of real wages, and in Section 12.2 we look at the slow adjustment of prices.

The main reason that Keynesians bring wage rigidity into their analysis is their dissatisfaction with the classical explanation of unemployment. Recall that classicals believe that most unemployment, including the increases in unemployment that occur during recessions, arises from mismatches between workers and jobs (frictional or structural unemployment). Keynesians don't dispute that mismatch is a major source of unemployment, but they are skeptical that it explains all unemployment.

Keynesians are particularly unwilling to accept the classical idea that recessions are periods of increased mismatch between workers and jobs. If higher unemployment during downturns reflected increased mismatch, Keynesians argue, recessions should be periods of particularly active search by workers for jobs and by firms for new employees. However, surveys suggest that unemployed workers spend relatively little time searching for work (many are simply waiting, hoping to be recalled to their old jobs), and help-wanted advertising and vacancy postings by firms fall rather than rise during recessions. Rather than times of increased worker–job mismatch, Keynesians believe that recessions are periods of generally low demand for both output and workers throughout the economy.

To explain the existence of unemployment without relying solely on worker–job mismatch, Keynesians argue for rejecting the classical assumption that real wages adjust relatively quickly to equate the quantities of labor supplied and demanded. In particular, if the real wage is above the level that clears the labor market, unemployment (an excess of labor supplied over labor demanded) will result. From the Keynesian perspective, the idea that the real wage moves "too little" to keep the quantity of labor demanded equal to the quantity of labor supplied is called **real-wage rigidity.**

Some Reasons for Real-Wage Rigidity

For a rigid real wage to be the source of unemployment, the real wage that firms are paying must be higher than the market-clearing real wage, at which quantities of labor supplied and demanded are equal. But if the real wage is higher than necessary to attract workers, why don't firms save labor costs by simply reducing the wage that they pay, as suggested by the classical analysis?

Various explanations have been offered for why real wages might be rigid, even in the face of an excess supply of labor. One possibility is that there are legal and institutional factors that keep wages high, such as the minimum-wage law and union contracts. However, most U.S. workers are neither union members nor minimum-wage earners, so these barriers to wage cutting can't be the main reason for real-wage rigidity. Furthermore, the minimum wage in the United States is specified in nominal terms so that workers who are paid the minimum wage would have rigid nominal wages rather than rigid real wages. (Union contracts may help explain real-wage rigidity in Western European and other countries in which a high proportion of workers are unionized, and in which nominal wages are typically adjusted for inflation in order to maintain the real wage at its negotiated level.)

Another explanation for why a firm might pay a higher real wage than it "has" to is that this policy might reduce the firm's **turnover costs,** or the costs associated with hiring and training new workers. By paying a high wage, the firm can keep more of its current workers, which saves the firm the cost of hiring and training replacements. Similarly, by developing a reputation for paying well, the firm can assure itself of more and better applicants for any position that it may have to fill.

A third reason that firms might pay real wages above market-clearing levels is that workers who are paid well may have greater incentives to work hard and effectively. If highly paid workers are more productive, the firm may profit from paying its employees well, even though it could attract all the workers it needs at a lower real wage. The idea that a worker's productivity depends on the real wage received, and that therefore firms may pay wages above the market-clearing level is the essence of the **efficiency wage model.** Because this model of wage determination has played a key role in recent Keynesian analyses and because it has several interesting aspects, we focus on it for the remainder of this section.

The Efficiency Wage Model

If better-paid workers are more productive, firms may gain by paying wages higher than the minimum necessary to attract workers. But why might a worker's productivity depend on the real wage received? The answer has both "carrot" and "stick" aspects.

The *carrot* or positive incentive is based on the idea that workers who feel well-treated will work harder and more efficiently. George Akerlof of the University of California at Berkeley argued that workers who believe that their employer is treating them fairly—say, by paying higher wages than required to retain them and by not cutting wages in slack times—will in turn want to treat the employer fairly by doing a good job. Akerlof called this motivation the *gift exchange motive*[1] because it's similar to the one that leads people to exchange gifts.

The *stick* or threat aspect of why a firm would pay a higher wage than necessary has been analyzed in an economic model called the "shirking" model of wage determination.[2] According to the *shirking model,* if a worker is paid only the minimum amount needed to attract her to a particular job, she won't be too concerned about the possibility of being fired if she doesn't perform well. After all, if the job pays the minimum amount necessary to induce her to take the job, she isn't much happier with the job than without the job. In this case the worker will be more inclined to take it easy at work and shirk her duties, and the employer will have to bear the cost either of the shirking or of paying supervisors to make sure that the work gets done. In contrast, a worker receiving a higher wage will place a greater value on keeping her job (it's not that easy to find another job as good) and will work hard to avoid being fired for shirking.

The gift exchange idea and the shirking model both imply that workers' efforts on the job depend on the real wages they receive. Graphically, the relation between the real wage and the level of effort is shown by the **effort curve** in Fig. 12.1 on the next page. The real wage w is measured along the horizontal axis, and the level of effort E is measured along the vertical axis. The effort curve passes through points O, A, and B. When real wages are higher, workers choose to work harder, for either "carrot" or "stick" reasons; therefore the effort curve slopes upward. We assume that the effort curve is S-shaped. At the lowest levels of the real wage workers make hardly any effort, and effort rises only slowly as the real wage increases. At higher levels of the real wage effort rises sharply, as shown by the steeply rising portion of the curve. The curve flattens at very high levels of the real wage because there is some maximum level of effort that workers really can't exceed no matter how motivated they are.

Wage Determination in the Efficiency Wage Model

The effort curve shows that effort depends on the real wage, but what determines the real wage? To make as much profit as possible, *firms will choose the level of the real wage that gets the most effort from workers for each dollar of real wages paid.* The amount of effort per dollar of real wages equals the amount of effort E divided by the real wage w. The ratio of E to w can be found graphically from Fig. 12.1. Consider, for example, point A on the effort curve, at which the real wage w_A induces workers to supply effort E_A. The slope of the line from the origin to A equals the height of the curve at point A, E_A, divided by the horizontal distance, w_A. Thus the slope of the line from the origin to A equals the amount of effort per dollar of real wages at A.

1. See George Akerlof, "Labor Contracts as Partial Gift Exchange," *Quarterly Journal of Economics,* November 1982, pp. 543–569.

2. See Carl Shapiro and Joseph E. Stiglitz, "Equilibrium Unemployment as a Worker Discipline Device," *American Economic Review,* June 1984, pp. 433–444.

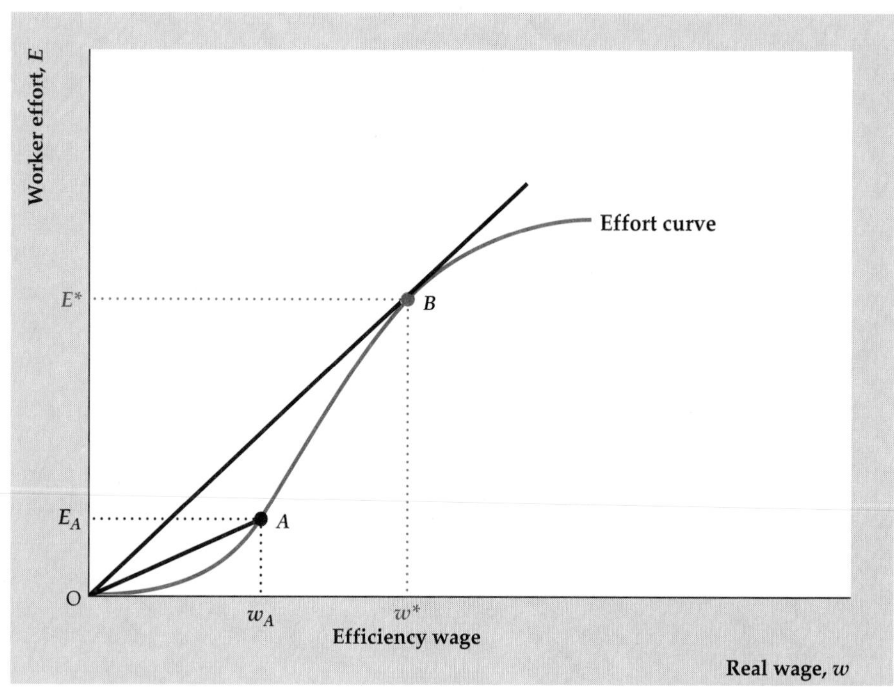

Figure 12.1
Determination of the efficiency wage
The effort curve shows the relation between worker effort, E, and the real wage workers receive, w. A higher real wage leads to more effort, but above a certain point higher wages are unable to spur effort much, so the effort curve is S-shaped. For any point on the curve, the amount of effort per dollar of real wage is the slope of the line from the origin to that point. At point A, effort per dollar of real wage is E_A/w_A. The highest level of effort per dollar of real wage is at point B, where the line from the origin is tangent to the curve. The real wage rate at B is the efficiency wage w^*, and the corresponding level of effort is E^*.

The real wage that achieves the highest effort per dollar of wages is at point B. The slope of the line from the origin to B, which is the amount of effort per dollar of real wage at B, is greater than the slope of the line from the origin to any other point on the curve. In general, to locate the real wage that maximizes effort per dollar of real wage, draw a line from the origin tangent to the effort curve; the real wage at the tangency point maximizes effort per dollar of real wage. We call the real wage that maximizes effort or efficiency per dollar of real wages the **efficiency wage.** In Fig. 12.1 the efficiency wage is w^*, and the corresponding level of effort is E^*.

The efficiency wage theory helps explain real-wage rigidity. Because the employer chooses the real wage that maximizes effort received per dollar paid, as long as the effort curve doesn't change, the employer won't change the real wage. Therefore the theory implies that the real wage is permanently rigid and equals the efficiency wage.

Employment and Unemployment in the Efficiency Wage Model

According to the efficiency wage theory, the real wage is rigid at the level that maximizes effort per dollar of wages paid. We now consider how the levels of employment and unemployment in the labor market are determined.

The workings of the labor market when there is an efficiency wage are shown in Fig. 12.2. The efficiency wage w^* is indicated by a horizontal line. Because the efficiency wage is determined solely by the effort curve, for the purpose of analyzing the labor market we can take w^* to be fixed. Similarly, we can take the level of effort E^* induced by the efficiency wage w^* as fixed at this stage of the analysis.

The upward-sloping curve is the standard labor supply curve, *NS*. As in the classical model, this curve shows the number of hours of work that people would like to supply at each level of the real wage.[3]

The downward-sloping curve is the demand curve for labor in the efficiency wage model. Recall from Chapter 3 that the amount of labor demanded by a firm depends on the marginal product of labor, or *MPN*. Specifically, the labor demand curve is identical to the *MPN* curve, which in turn relates the marginal product of labor *MPN* to the quantity of labor input *N* being used. The *MPN* curve—and hence the labor demand curve—slopes down because of the diminishing marginal productivity of labor.

In the classical model, the marginal product of labor depends only on the production function and the capital stock. A complication of the efficiency wage model is that the amount of output produced by an extra worker (or hour of work) also depends on the worker's effort. Fortunately, as we noted, the efficiency wage w^* and the effort level induced by that wage, E^*, are fixed at this stage of the analysis. Thus the labor demand curve in Fig. 12.2, ND^*, reflects the marginal product of labor *when worker effort is held fixed at* E^*. As in the classical case, an increase in productivity or in the capital stock shifts the labor demand curve ND^* to the right. In addition, any change in the effort curve that led to an increase in the optimal level of effort E^* would raise the *MPN* and the labor demand curve ND^* again would shift to the right.

3. For simplicity we assume that the number of hours of labor that people want to supply doesn't depend on the effort they must exert while on the job.

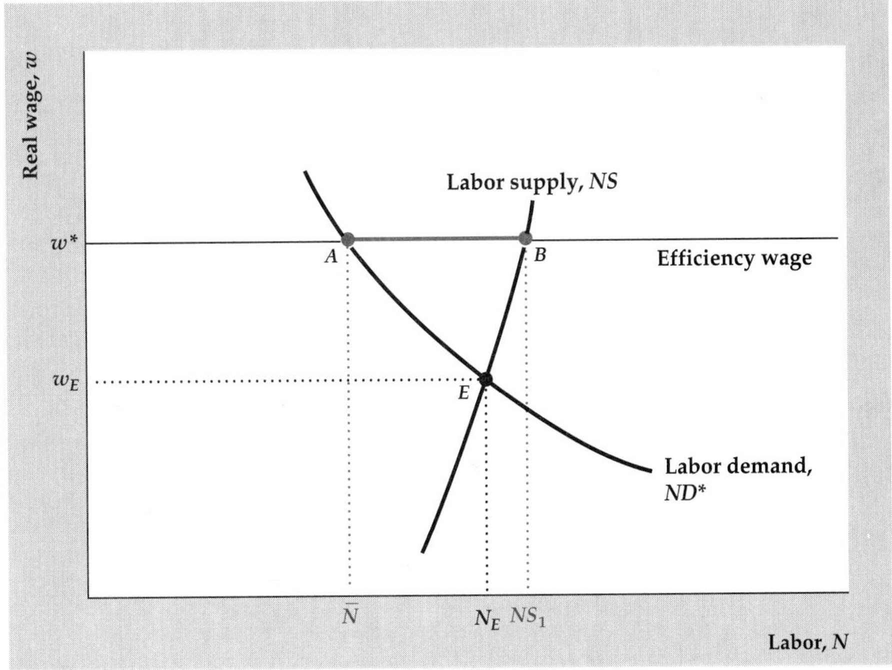

Figure 12.2
Excess supply of labor in the efficiency wage model
When the efficiency wage w^* is paid, the firm's demand for labor is $\bar{N}$, represented by point *A*. However, the amount of labor that workers want to supply at a real wage of w^* is NS_1. The excess supply of labor equals distance *AB*. We assume that the efficiency wage w^* is higher than the market-clearing wage w_E that would prevail if the supply of labor equaled the demand for labor at point *E*.

Now we can put the elements of Fig. 12.2 together to show how employment is determined. Point A on the labor demand curve ND^* indicates that, when the real wage is fixed at w^*, firms want to employ $\bar{N}$ hours of labor. Point B on the labor supply curve indicates that, when the real wage is fixed at w^*, workers want to supply NS_1 hours of labor, which is greater than the amount demanded by firms. At the efficiency wage the quantity of labor supplied is greater than the quantity demanded,[4] so the level of employment is determined by the labor demand of firms and hence equals $\bar{N}$. The demand-determined level of employment is labeled $\bar{N}$ because it represents the full-employment level of employment for this model; that is, $\bar{N}$ is the level of employment reached after full adjustment of wages and prices. (Note that the value of $\bar{N}$ in the efficiency wage model differs from the full-employment level of employment in the classical model of the labor market, which would correspond to N_E in Fig. 12.2.) Because the efficiency wage is rigid at w^*, in the absence of shocks the level of employment in this economy remains at $\bar{N}$ indefinitely.

Perhaps the most interesting aspect of Fig. 12.2 is that it provides a new explanation of unemployment. It shows that, even when wages have adjusted as much as they are going to and the economy is technically at "full employment," an excess supply of labor, $NS_1 - \bar{N}$ remains.[5]

Why don't the unemployed bid down the real wage and thus gain employment, as they would in the classical model of the labor market? Unlike the classical case, in a labor market with an efficiency wage the real wage can't be bid down by people offering to work at lower wages because employers won't hire them. Employers know that people working at lower wages will not put out as much effort per dollar of real wages as workers receiving the higher efficiency wage. Thus the excess supply of labor shown in Fig. 12.2 will persist indefinitely. The efficiency wage model thus implies that unemployment will exist even if there is no mismatch between jobs and workers.

The efficiency wage model is an interesting theory of real wages and unemployment, but does it explain actual behavior? Box 12.1 interprets a famous episode in labor history in terms of efficiency wage theory. In addition to this anecdotal evidence, studies of wages and employment in various firms and industries provide some support for the efficiency wage model. For example, Peter Cappelli of the University of Pennsylvania and Keith Chauvin of the University of Kansas[6] found that, consistent with one aspect of the theory, plants that paid higher wages to workers experienced less shirking, measured by the number of workers fired for disciplinary reasons.

A criticism of the efficiency wage model presented here is that it predicts that the real wage is literally fixed (for no change in the effort curve). Of course, this result is too extreme because the real wage does change over time (and over the business cycle, as demonstrated in Chapter 9). However, the

4. The result that there is an excess supply of labor requires the assumption that the efficiency wage w^* is higher than the real wage that would clear the labor market, shown as w_E in Fig. 12.2. We always assume that the efficiency wage is higher than the market-clearing wage; if it weren't, firms would have to pay the market-clearing wage to attract workers.

5. Because the unemployment represented by the excess supply of labor persists even when the economy is at full employment, it is considered part of structural unemployment.

6. "An Interplant Test of the Efficiency Wage Hypothesis," *Quarterly Journal of Economics,* August 1991, pp. 769–787.

BOX 12.1

Henry Ford's Efficiency Wage

During 1908–1914 Henry Ford instituted at Ford Motor Company a radically new way of producing automobiles.* Prior to Ford's innovations, automobile components weren't produced to uniform specifications. Instead, cars had to be assembled one by one by skilled craftsmen, who could make the parts fit even if sizes or shapes were off by fractions of an inch. Ford introduced a system of assembly-line production in which a standardized product, the Model T automobile, was produced from precisely made, interchangeable components. The production process also was broken into numerous small, simple steps, replacing the skilled craftsmen who had built cars from start to finish with unskilled workers who performed only a few operations over and over.

The high speed at which Ford ran the assembly line and the repetitiveness of the work were hard on the workers. As one laborer said, "If I keep putting on Nut No. 86 for about 86 more days, I will be Nut No. 86 in the Pontiac bughouse."† As a result, worker turnover was high, with the typical worker lasting only a few months on the job. Absenteeism also was high—about 10% on any given day—and morale was low. Worker slowdowns and even sabotage occurred.

In January 1914 Ford announced that the company would begin paying $5 a day to workers who met certain criteria, one being that the worker had been with the company at least six months. Five dollars a day was more than double the normal wage for production workers at the time. Although the motivation for Ford's announcement has been debated, its effect was stunning: Thousands of workers lined up outside the plant, hoping for jobs. Within the plant the number of people quitting dropped by 87%, absenteeism dropped by 75%, and productivity rose by 30% or more. The productivity increases helped increase Ford's profits, despite the higher wage bill and a cut in the price of a Model T.

Many results of Ford's $5 day can be predicted by the efficiency wage model, including improved efficiency and higher profits. As other automakers adopted Ford's technological innovations, they also adopted his wage policies. By 1928, before unions were important in the industry, auto industry wages were almost 40% higher than those in the rest of manufacturing.

---

* The source for this box is Daniel M. G. Raff and Lawrence H. Summers, "Did Henry Ford Pay Efficiency Wages?" *Journal of Labor Economics*, October 1987, pp. S57–S86.

† This quote is originally from Stephen Meyer, *The Five-Dollar Day: Labor Management and Social Control in the Ford Motor Company, 1908–1921*, Albany: State University of New York Press, 1981.

basic model can be extended to allow for changes in the effort curve that bring changes in the efficiency wage over time. For example, a reasonable assumption would be that workers are more concerned about losing their jobs during recessions, when finding a new job is more difficult, than during booms. Under this assumption, the real wage necessary to obtain any specific level of effort will be lower during recessions; hence the efficiency wage paid in recessions also may be lower. This extension may help the efficiency wage model match the business cycle fact that real wages are lower in recessions than in booms (procyclical real wages).

Efficiency Wages and the *FE* Line

In the Keynesian version of the *IS–LM* model, as in the classical version, the *FE* line is vertical, showing the full-employment level of output $\bar{Y}$. If we assume that employers pay efficiency wages, full-employment output $\bar{Y}$ in turn is the output produced when employment is at the full-employment level of employment $\bar{N}$, as shown in Fig. 12.2, and the level of worker effort is E^*.

As in the classical model, anything that changes full-employment output $\bar{Y}$ shifts the *FE* line. The classical model emphasizes two factors that shift the *FE* line: changes in the supply of labor and changes in productivity. In the efficiency wage model, however, labor supply doesn't affect employment, so *changes in labor supply don't affect the FE line in the Keynesian model* with efficiency wages. A change in productivity, however, *does* affect the *FE* line in the Keynesian model, as in the classical model. A drop in productivity reduces full-employment output $\bar{Y}$ and shifts the *FE* line to the left, for two reasons. First, by reducing the marginal product of labor at any given level of employment, a drop in productivity reduces the demand for labor at any fixed real wage. With the real wage fixed at w^*, the full-employment level of employment $\bar{N}$ falls. Second, a drop in productivity reduces the amount of output that can be produced with any particular amount of capital, labor, and effort.

12.2 PRICE STICKINESS

The rigidity created by efficiency wages is a *real* rigidity in that the real wage, rather than the nominal wage, remains fixed. Keynesian theories also emphasize *nominal* rigidities that occur when a price or wage is fixed in nominal, or dollar, terms and doesn't readily change in response to changes in supply or demand. Keynesians often refer to rigidity of nominal prices—a tendency of prices to adjust only slowly to changes in the economy—as **price stickiness.**

We explained in Section 12.1 that Keynesians introduced real-wage rigidity because of their dissatisfaction with the classical explanation of unemployment. Similarly, the assumption of price stickiness addresses what Keynesians believe is another significant weakness of the basic classical model: the classical prediction that monetary policy is neutral.

Recall that, in the basic classical model without misperceptions, the assumption that wages and prices adjust quickly implies that money is neutral. If money is neutral, an increase or decrease in the money supply changes the price level by the same proportion but has no effect on real variables, such as output, employment, or the real interest rate. However, recall also that empirical studies—including analyses of historical episodes—have led most economists to conclude that money probably is not neutral in the real world.

One approach to accounting for monetary nonneutrality (pursued in Chapter 11) is to extend the classical model by assuming that workers and firms have imperfect information about the current price level (the misperceptions theory). However, Keynesians favor an alternative way to explain monetary nonneutrality: Modify the classical assumption that prices adjust quickly. If prices are sticky, the price level can't adjust immediately to offset changes in the money supply, and money isn't neutral. Thus for Keynesians, the importance of price stickiness is that it helps explain monetary nonneutrality.

Although we focus on nominal-price rigidity in this section, a long Keynesian tradition emphasizes nominal-wage rigidity instead of nominal-price rigidity. An alternative version of the Keynesian model that rests on the assumption of nominal-wage rigidity is discussed in Appendix 12.A. This alternative model has similar implications to the Keynesian model with price rigidity, in particular, that money is not neutral.

Sources of Price Stickiness: Monopolistic Competition and Menu Costs

To say that price stickiness gives rise to monetary nonneutrality doesn't completely explain nonneutrality because it raises another question: Why are prices sticky? The Keynesian explanation for the existence of price rigidity relies on two main ideas: (1) most firms actively *set* the prices of their products rather than taking the prices of their output as given by the market; and (2) when firms change prices, they incur a cost, known as a menu cost.

Monopolistic Competition. Talking about price stickiness in a highly competitive, organized market—such as the market for corn or the stock exchange—wouldn't make much sense. In these markets prices adjust rapidly to reflect changes in supply or demand. Principal reasons for price flexibility in these competitive, highly organized markets include standardization of the product being traded (one bushel of corn, or one share of IBM stock, is much like any other) and the large number of actual or potential market participants. These two factors make it worthwhile to organize a centralized market (such as the New York Stock Exchange) in which prices can react swiftly to changes in supply and demand. These same two factors also promote keen competition among buyers and sellers, which greatly reduces the ability of any individual to affect prices.

Most participants in the corn market or stock market think of themselves as price takers. A *price taker* is a market participant who takes the market price as given. For example, a small farmer correctly perceives that the market price of corn is beyond his control. In contrast, a *price setter* has some power to set prices.

Markets having fewer participants and less standardized products than the corn or stock markets may exhibit price-setting rather than price-taking behavior. For example, consider the market for movies in a medium-sized city. This market may be fairly competitive, with many different movie theaters, each trying to attract customers from other theaters, home video stores, and so on. Although the market for movies is competitive, it isn't competitive to the same degree as the corn market. If a farmer tried to raise the price of a bushel of his corn by 5¢ above the market price, he would sell no corn; but a movie theater that raised its ticket prices by 5¢ above its competitors' prices wouldn't lose all its customers. Because the movie theater's product isn't completely standardized (it is showing a different movie than other theaters, its location is better for some people, it has different candy bars in the concession stand, a larger screen, or more comfortable seats, and so on), the theater has some price-setting discretion. It is a price setter, not a price taker.

Generally, a situation in which all buyers and sellers are price takers (such as the market for corn) is called **perfect competition.** In contrast, a situation in which there is some competition, but in which a smaller number of sellers and imperfect standardization of the product allow individual producers to act as price setters, is called **monopolistic competition.**

Perfect competition is the model underlying the classical view of price determination, and as we have said, price rigidity or stickiness is extremely unlikely in a perfectly competitive market. Keynesians agree that price rigidity wouldn't occur in a perfectly competitive market but point out that a relatively small part of the economy is perfectly competitive. Keynesians argue that price rigidity is possible, even likely, in a monopolistically competitive market.

To illustrate the issues, let's return to the example of the competing movie theaters. If the market for movie tickets were perfectly competitive, how would tickets be priced? Presumably, there would be some central meeting place where buyers and sellers of tickets would congregate. Market organizers would call out "bids" (prices at which they are willing to buy) and "asks" (prices at which they are willing to sell). Prices would fluctuate continuously as new information hit the market, causing supplies and demands to change. For example, a "two thumbs up" review by Siskel and Ebert would instantly drive up the price of tickets to that movie, but news of a prospective shortage of baby-sitters would cause all movie ticket prices to fall.

Obviously, though, this isn't how movie tickets are priced. Actual pricing by most theaters has the following three characteristics, which are also common to most price-setting markets:

1. Rather than accept the price of movies as completely determined by the market, a movie theater *sets* the price of tickets (or a schedule of prices), in *nominal* terms, and maintains the nominal price for some period of time.
2. At least within some range, the theater *meets the demand* that is forthcoming at the fixed nominal price. By "meets the demand" we mean that the theater will sell as many tickets as people want to buy at its fixed price, to the point that all its seats are filled.
3. The theater readjusts its price from time to time, generally when its costs or the level of demand changes significantly.

Can this type of pricing behavior maximize profits? Keynesian theory suggests that it can, if there are costs associated with changing nominal prices, and if the market is monopolistically competitive.

Menu Costs and Price Setting. The classic example of a cost of changing prices is the cost that a restaurant faces when it has to reprint its menu to show changes in the prices of its offerings. Hence the cost of changing prices is called a **menu cost.** More general examples of menu costs (which can apply to any kind of firm) include costs of remarking merchandise, reprinting price lists and catalogues, and informing potential customers. Clearly, if firms incur costs when changing prices, they will change prices less often than they would otherwise, which creates a certain amount of price rigidity.

A potential problem with the menu cost explanation for price rigidity is that these costs seem to be rather small. How, then, can they be responsible for an amount of nominal rigidity that could have macroeconomic significance?

Here is the first point at which the monopolistic competition assumption is important. For a firm in a perfectly competitive market, getting the price "a little bit wrong" has serious consequences: The farmer who prices his corn 5¢ a bushel above the market price sells no corn. Therefore the existence of a menu cost wouldn't prevent the farmer from pricing his product at precisely the correct level. However, the demand for the output of a monopolistically competitive firm responds much less sharply to changes in its price; the movie theater doesn't lose many of its customers if its ticket price is 5¢ higher than its competitors'. Thus as long as the monopolistic competitor's price is in the right general range, the loss of profits from not getting the price exactly right isn't too great. If the loss in profits is less than the cost of changing prices—the menu costs—the firm won't change its price.

Over time, the production function and the demand curve the firm faces will undergo a variety of shocks so that eventually the profit-maximizing price for a firm may be significantly different from the preset price. When the profits lost by having the "wrong" price clearly exceed the cost of changing the price, the firm will change its nominal price. Thus movie theaters periodically raise their ticket and popcorn prices to reflect general inflation and other changes in market conditions.

Empirical Evidence on Price Stickiness. Several studies have examined the degree of rigidity or stickiness in actual prices. Using data first collected by Nobel laureate George Stigler and James Kindahl for the low-inflation period 1957–1966, Dennis Carlton[7] of the University of Chicago documented that industrial prices can be very sticky. Table 12.1, taken from Carlton's study, shows the average number of months between price changes for various industrial product groups. Note that for three of eleven groups the average time between price changes is more than a year. Using a statistical analysis, Carlton also found that prices were less rigid in relatively more competitive industries, a finding that fits the theory.

There is also some evidence that prices of consumer goods can be sticky. Stephen Cecchetti,[8] now of Ohio State University, studied the price changes of

7. "The Rigidity of Prices," *American Economic Review,* September 1986, pp. 637–658.
8. "The Frequency of Price Adjustment: A Study of the Newsstand Prices of Magazines," *Journal of Econometrics,* April 1986, pp. 255–274.

Table 12.1 Average Times Between Price Changes for Various Industries

Product Group (Most to Least Rigid)	Average Time Between Price Changes (Months)
Cement	13.2
Steel	13.0
Chemicals	12.8
Glass	10.2
Paper	8.7
Rubber tires	8.1
Petroleum	5.9
Truck motors	5.4
Plywood	4.7
Nonferrous metals	4.3
Household appliances	3.6

Source: Dennis W. Carlton, "The Rigidity of Prices," *American Economic Review,* September 1986, pp. 637–658, Table 1.

thirty-eight newsstand magazines during the period 1953–1979. He found that magazine prices are remarkably sticky. During the low-inflation period 1953–1965 magazines changed their prices on average only once every seven and a half years. Even during the inflationary 1970s, price changes occurred on average less than once every three years. This degree of stickiness probably is greater than can be explained by simple menu costs. The direct cost of changing a magazine's price is virtually zero (a new cover that states the price must be printed for each issue anyway), and it isn't very expensive to inform newsstands and subscribers of a price change. However, most magazine revenue comes from advertisers and subscribers (who usually don't pay the newsstand price). Hence publishers may not have found it profitable to review their pricing policies frequently. Perhaps more likely, publishers may have feared that raising prices before their close competitors did would cause them to lose customers. Thus neither *Time* nor *Newsweek* may have been willing to move first to raise its price, until it was obvious to customers as well as newsstands that a price increase was appropriate.

In another study of price stickiness Anil Kashyap,[9] now of the University of Chicago, examined the prices of twelve individual items listed in the catalogues of L.L. Bean, Orvis, and Recreational Equipment, Inc., over a thirty-five-year period. Changing the prices listed in a new catalogue is virtually costless, yet Kashyap found that the nominal prices of many goods remained fixed in successive issues of the catalogue. When nominal prices were changed, Kashyap found both large and small changes. He interpreted the combination of small price changes and long periods of unchanged prices as evidence against menu costs. If menu costs are the reason that prices aren't changed frequently, prices should be changed only when they are relatively far out of line, and the price changes should be large; small changes seem to contradict this implication of menu costs. Even if menu costs aren't the underlying cause of pricing behavior, however, Kashyap's study confirms the findings by Carlton and Cecchetti of substantial nominal-price rigidity in the economy.

Meeting the Demand at the Fixed Nominal Price. When prices are sticky, firms react to changes in demand by changing the amount of production rather than by changing prices. According to Keynesians, why are firms willing to meet demand at a fixed nominal price? To answer this question, we again rely on the assumption of monopolistic competition. We've stated that a monopolistically competitive firm can raise its price some without risk of losing all its customers. The profit-maximizing strategy for a monopolistically competitive firm is to charge a price higher than its **marginal cost,** or the cost of producing an additional unit of output. The excess of the price over the marginal cost is the **markup.** For example, if a firm charges a price 15% above its marginal cost, the firm has a markup of 15%. More generally, if the firm charges a constant markup of η over marginal cost, the following markup rule describes its price:

$$P = (1 + \eta)MC, \tag{12.1}$$

9. "Sticky Prices: New Evidence from Retail Catalogs," Federal Reserve Board, FEDS Working Paper No. 112, February 1990, forthcoming in the *Quarterly Journal of Economics.*

where P is the nominal price charged by the firm and MC is the nominal marginal cost.[10]

When the firm sets its price according to Eq. (12.1), it has an idea of how many units will sell. Now suppose that, to the firm's surprise, customers demand several more units than the firm expected to sell at that price. Will it be profitable for the firm to meet the demand at this price?

The answer is "yes." Because the price the firm receives for each extra unit exceeds its cost of producing that extra unit (its marginal cost), the firm's profits increase when it sells additional units at the fixed price. Thus, as long as the marginal cost remains below the fixed price of its product, the firm gladly supplies more units at this fixed price. Furthermore, if the firm is paying an efficiency wage, it can easily hire more workers to produce the units needed to meet the demand, because there is an excess supply of labor.

The macroeconomic importance of firms' meeting demand at the fixed nominal price is that *the economy can produce an amount of output that is not on the full-employment line.* Recall that the *FE* line shows the amount of output that firms would produce after complete adjustment of all wages and prices. However, with nominal-price stickiness the prices of goods do not adjust rapidly to their general equilibrium values. During the period in which prices haven't yet completely adjusted, the amount of output produced need not be on the *FE* line. Instead, as long as marginal cost is below the fixed price, monopolistically competitive firms will produce the level of output demanded.

Effective Labor Demand. When a firm meets the demand for its output at a specific price, it may produce a different amount of output and employ a different amount of labor than it had planned. How much labor will a firm actually employ when it meets the demand? The answer is given by the effective labor demand curve, $ND^e(Y)$, shown in Fig. 12.3 on the next page. For any amount of output Y, the **effective labor demand curve** indicates how much labor is needed to produce that output, with productivity, the capital stock, and effort held constant.

We already have a concept that expresses the relationship between the amount of labor used and the amount of output produced: the production function. Indeed, the effective labor demand curve in Fig. 12.3 is simply a graph of the production function relating output and labor input, except that output Y is measured on the horizontal axis and labor N is measured on the vertical axis. (Reversing the units on the axes is convenient later.) The effective labor demand curve slopes upward from left to right because a firm needs more labor in order to produce more output.

We use the effective labor demand curve to determine the level of employment in the Keynesian model in Section 12.3. When the economy is not on the *FE* line and the price level is fixed, the effective labor demand curve gives the level of employment. Then, after complete adjustment of wages and prices, the economy returns to the *FE* line and the level of employment is given by the

---

10. Technical note: For a monopolistically competitive firm that faces a demand curve with a constant price elasticity and a fixed wage, the constant-markup rule in Eq. (12.1) will maximize profit. Also, in this case the labor demand curve is proportional to (rather than equal to) the marginal product of labor curve. Specifically, to maximize profits the firm equates the MPN to $(1 + \eta)w^*$, where w^* is the efficiency wage, rather than equating the MPN to w^* itself. This qualification doesn't affect any conclusions presented in this chapter.

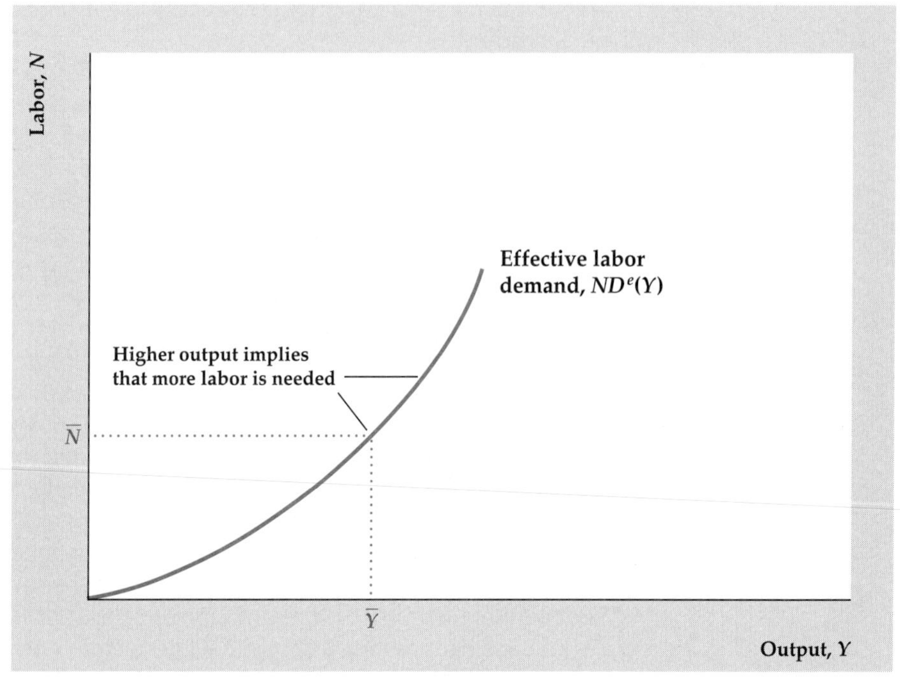

Figure 12.3
The effective labor demand curve
When a firm meets the demand for its output, it employs just the amount of labor needed to produce the quantity of output demanded. Because more labor is required to produce more output, firms must employ more labor when the demand for output is high. This relation between the amount of output demanded and the amount of labor employed is the effective labor demand curve. The effective labor demand curve is the same as the production function relating output and labor, except that labor is plotted on the vertical axis and output is plotted on the horizontal axis.

labor demand curve ND^* (Fig. 12.2). After wages and prices have completely adjusted, with output at its full-employment level $\bar{Y}$, the effective labor demand curve indicates that employment equals $\bar{N}$, as shown in Fig. 12.3.

12.3 MONETARY AND FISCAL POLICY IN THE KEYNESIAN MODEL

Let's now consider the complete Keynesian model. Like the classical model, the Keynesian model can be expressed in terms of the *IS–LM* diagram, or alternatively, in terms of the *AD–AS* diagram. Rather than describe the Keynesian model in the abstract, we put it to work analyzing the effects of monetary and fiscal policy. Appendix 12.B presents an algebraic analysis of the short-run behavior of the economy in the Keynesian model.

Monetary Policy

The main reason for introducing nominal-price stickiness into the Keynesian model was to explain monetary nonneutrality. We examine the link between price stickiness and monetary nonneutrality first in the Keynesian *IS–LM* framework and then in the *AD–AS* version of the Keynesian model.

Monetary Policy in the Keynesian *IS–LM* Model. The Keynesian version of the *IS–LM* model is quite similar to the *IS–LM* model discussed in Chapters 10 and 11. In particular, the *IS* curve and the *LM* curve are the same as in our earlier analyses. The *FE* line in the Keynesian model also is similar to the

FE line used earlier. The Keynesian *FE* line is vertical at the full-employment level of output $\bar{Y}$, which in turn depends on the full-employment level of employment determined in the labor market. However, the Keynesian and classical *FE* lines are different in two respects. First, in the Keynesian model the full-employment level of employment is determined at the intersection of the labor demand curve and the efficiency wage line, not at the point where the quantities of labor demanded and supplied are equal, as in the classical model. Second, because labor supply doesn't affect employment in the efficiency wage model, changes in labor supply don't affect the Keynesian *FE* line, although changes in labor supply do affect the classical *FE* line.

Because of price stickiness, in the Keynesian model the economy doesn't have to be in general equilibrium in the short run. However, in the long run when prices adjust, the economy reaches its general equilibrium at the intersection of the *IS* curve, the *LM* curve, and the *FE* line, as in the classical model.

According to Keynesians, what happens to the economy in the short run, if sticky prices prevent it from reaching general equilibrium? Keynesians assume that the asset market clears quickly and that the level of output is determined by aggregate demand. Thus, according to Keynesians, *the economy always lies at the intersection of the IS and LM curves.* However, because monopolistically competitive firms are willing to meet the demand for goods at fixed levels of prices, output can differ from full-employment output and the economy may not be on the *FE* line in the short run. When the economy is off the *FE* line, firms use just enough labor to produce the output needed to meet demand. Under the assumption that the efficiency wage is higher than the market-clearing real wage, there are always unemployed workers who want to work, and firms are able to change employment as needed to meet the demand for output without changing the wage.

Figure 12.4, on the next page, analyzes the effect of a decrease in the nominal money supply in the Keynesian *IS–LM* model. We assume that the economy starts at its general equilibrium point, *E*. Recall that a decrease in the money supply shifts the *LM* curve up and to the left, from LM^1 to LM^2 (Fig. 12.4a). Because a decrease in the money supply doesn't directly affect the goods or labor markets, the *IS* curve and the *FE* line are unaffected. So far this analysis is like that of the classical model.

Unlike the classical model, however, the Keynesian model assumes temporarily fixed prices (because of menu costs) so that the general equilibrium at *E* isn't restored immediately. Instead, the short-run equilibrium of the economy—that is, the resting point of the economy at the fixed price level—lies at the intersection of *IS* and LM^2 (point *F*), where output drops to Y_2 and the real interest rate rises to r_2.

Because the *IS–LM* intersection at point *F* is to the left of the *FE* line, aggregate output demanded Y_2 is less than the full-employment level of output $\bar{Y}$. Monopolistically competitive firms facing menu costs don't cut their prices in the short run, as competitive firms do. Instead they cut production to Y_2 to satisfy the lower level of demand. To reduce production, firms cut employment—for example, by laying off workers or putting some employees on part-time schedules. The level of employment is given by the effective labor demand curve in Fig. 12.4(b). Because the level of output falls from $\bar{Y}$ to Y_2 in the short run, the level of employment falls from $\bar{N}$ to N_2.

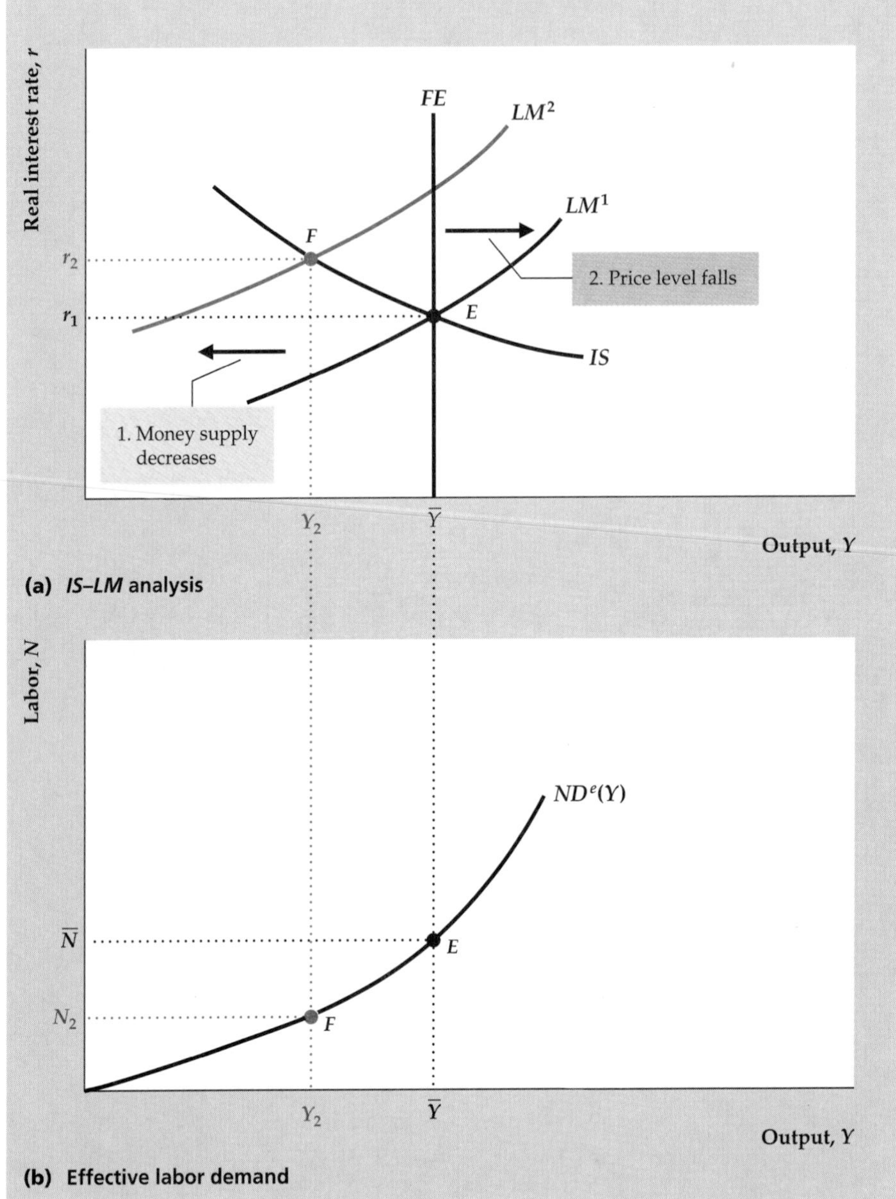

Figure 12.4
A decrease in the money supply
(a) If we start from an initial general equilibrium at point *E*, a decrease in the money supply shifts the *LM* curve up and to the left, from LM^1 to LM^2; the *IS* curve and the *FE* line remain unchanged. Because prices are fixed and firms meet the demand for output in the short run, the economy moves to point *F*, which is to the left of the *FE* line. Output falls to Y_2 and the real interest rate rises.
(b) Because firms produce less output, employment falls to N_2, as shown by the effective labor demand curve.

In the long run, the price level falls in the same proportion as the money supply, the real money supply returns to its initial level, and the *LM* curve returns to its initial position, LM^1, in (a). The economy returns to *E* in both (a) and (b), and money is neutral in the long run.

We refer to a monetary policy that shifts the *LM* curve up and to the left—and thus reduces output and employment—as a contractionary monetary policy, or "tight" money. Analogously, an expansionary monetary policy, or "easy" money, is an increase in the money supply that shifts the *LM* curve down and to the right, raising output and employment.

Why does tight money reduce output in the Keynesian model? In the Keynesian model prices are fixed in the short run, so a reduction in the nominal money supply M also is a reduction in the real money supply M/P. Recall that, for holders of wealth to be willing to hold more nonmonetary assets and less real money the real interest rate must rise.[11] Finally, the higher real interest rate reduces both consumption spending (because saving rises) and investment spending. With less demand for their output, firms cut production and lay off workers, taking the economy to point F in Fig. 12.4.

The rigidity of the price level isn't permanent. Eventually, firms will review and readjust their prices, allowing the economy to reach its long-run equilibrium. In the case of monetary contraction, firms find that demand for their products in the short run is less than they had planned (aggregate output demanded Y_2 is less than full-employment output $\bar{Y}$), so eventually they lower their prices. The decline in the price level returns the real money supply to its initial level, which shifts the LM curve back to LM^1 and restores the general equilibrium at point E in Fig. 12.4(a). This adjustment process is exactly the same as in the classical model, but it proceeds more slowly.

Thus, the Keynesian model predicts that *money is not neutral in the short run but is neutral in the long run.* In this respect the predictions of the Keynesian model are the same as those of the extended classical model with misperceptions. In the Keynesian model short-run price stickiness prevents the economy from reaching its general equilibrium, but in the long run prices are flexible, ensuring general equilibrium.

The Keynesian *AD–AS* Framework

Macroeconomic behavior in the Keynesian model can also be represented in terms of aggregate demand and aggregate supply. The aggregate demand (AD) curve in the Keynesian model (Fig. 12.5) is the same as that in the classical model (see Fig. 11.5). The AD curve relates the aggregate quantity of output demanded to the price level. Recall that an increase in the price level P reduces the real money supply M/P and shifts the LM curve up and to the left. Because the aggregate demand for goods corresponds to the intersection of the IS curve and the LM curve, a shift of the LM curve to the left reduces the aggregate quantity of output demanded. Because an increase in the price level reduces the aggregate quantity of output demanded, the AD curve slopes downward.

In the Keynesian model the short-run aggregate supply curve, $SRAS$, is a horizontal line, as shown in Fig. 12.5 on the next page. The reason is that, with monopolistic competition and menu costs, firms hold the price level P fixed in the short run and produce the level of output needed to satisfy demand. Thus the $SRAS$ curve is horizontal at the initial price level. However, in the long run, after complete price adjustment, firms produce the full-employment level of output $\bar{Y}$ regardless of the price level P. Because the amount of output supplied by firms doesn't depend on the price level in the long run, the long-run aggregate supply curve, $LRAS$, is a vertical line at $Y = \bar{Y}$, as in the classical version of the model. The economy's long-run equilibrium is at the intersection of the AD curve and the $LRAS$ curve, or point E in Fig. 12.5. At the long-run equilibrium point, output equals its full-employment level, and the price level equalizes the aggregate quantities of output demanded and supplied.

11. As we discussed in Chapter 10, the real interest rate is driven up by wealth-holders' attempts to exchange nonmonetary assets for money. The selling of nonmonetary assets drives down their prices, which is the same as increasing the real interest rate that they pay.

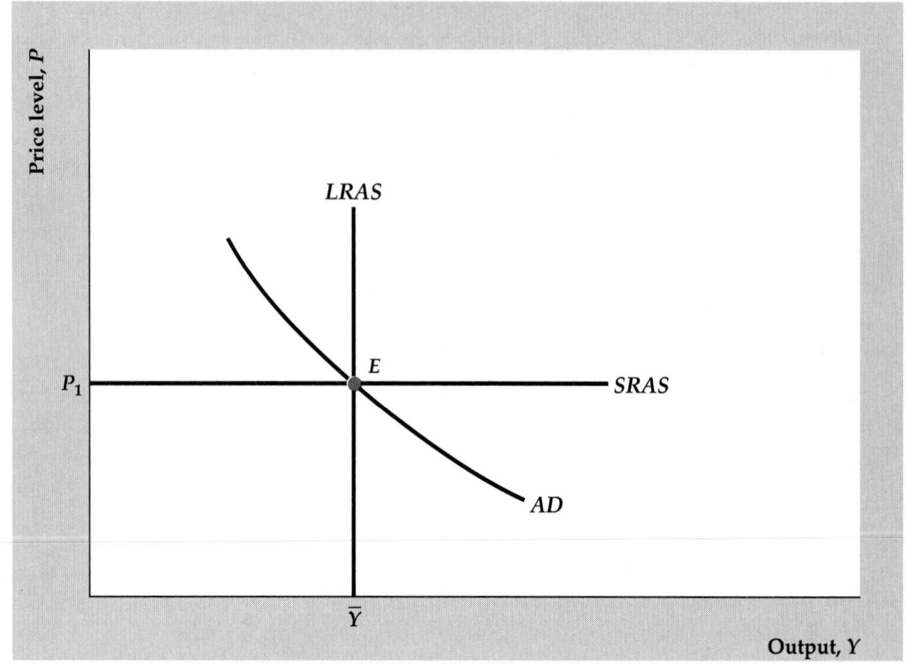

Figure 12.5
The Keynesian *AD–AS* framework
The aggregate demand (*AD*) curve slopes downward in the Keynesian model for the same reason it slopes downward in the classical model: An increase in the price level reduces the real money supply, which shifts the *LM* curve up and to the left and reduces the aggregate quantity of output demanded. The short-run aggregate supply (*SRAS*) curve is horizontal in the Keynesian model because firms meet the demand for their output at a fixed price. In the long run, prices adjust completely so that firms produce the full-employment level of output $\overline{Y}$ regardless of the price level. Thus the long-run aggregate supply (*LRAS*) curve is vertical at $Y = \overline{Y}$.

Let's examine monetary neutrality in the Keynesian *AD–AS* framework by supposing that the economy is initially in long-run equilibrium at point *E* in Fig. 12.6, that output equals $\overline{Y}$, that the price level equals P_1, and that the Fed then reduces the money supply by 10%. As in the classical model, the reduction in the money supply shifts the *AD* curve down by 10% at each level of output, from AD^1 to AD^2. The short-run equilibrium is at point *F*, where AD^2 intersects the short-run aggregate supply curve $SRAS^1$. At *F* the price level is unchanged from its initial value of P_1, and output equals the aggregate quantity of output demanded at that price level, Y_2. Point *F* is analogous to point *F* in the *IS–LM* diagram in Fig. 12.4, where the price level also equaled its initial value and output also equaled the quantity of output demanded at that price level.

The economy doesn't stay at point *F* forever. Because the quantity of output demanded Y_2 is smaller than the full-employment level of output $\overline{Y}$, firms eventually reduce their prices. The *SRAS* curve gives the price level at which firms are willing to meet the demand; thus as the prices set by firms fall, the *SRAS* curve moves down. In the long run the price level falls by 10%, and the economy reaches general equilibrium at point *H*, where the aggregate demand curve AD^2 intersects the long-run aggregate supply curve *LRAS*. The drop in the price level shifts the short-run aggregate supply curve down to $SRAS^2$, so that it too passes through *H* in the long run.

Because the *AD–AS* framework and the *IS–LM* model are equivalent, they lead to the same conclusions about monetary neutrality. In the short run the Keynesian *AD–AS* framework implies that money isn't neutral because the reduction in money supply causes output to fall (point *F* in Fig. 12.6). However, as in the *IS–LM* model, money is neutral in the long run in the

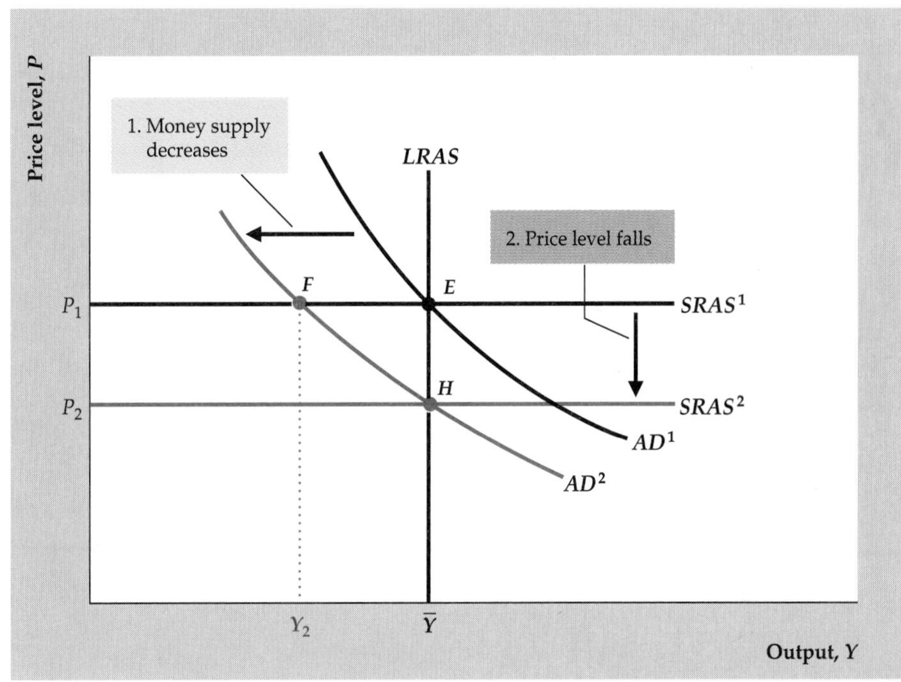

Figure 12.6
A decrease in the money supply in the Keynesian *AD–AS* framework
If we start from the full-employment general equilibrium at point *E*, a 10% reduction in the money supply shifts the *AD* curve down by 10% at each level of output, from AD^1 to AD^2. In the short run, the economy moves to point *F*, where the new aggregate demand curve AD^2 intersects the short-run aggregate supply curve $SRAS^1$. At *F* output has fallen to Y_2. Because aggregate output demanded is less than $\bar{Y}$, the price level falls. In the long run the economy returns to full-employment general equilibrium at point *H*, where AD^2 intersects the vertical long-run aggregate supply curve *LRAS*. Output returns to $\bar{Y}$, and the new price level P_2 is 10% lower than the initial price level P_1. Thus, again, money is neutral in the long run. As a result of the drop in the price level, the short-run aggregate supply curve shifts down, to $SRAS^2$.

AD–AS framework. Changes in the money supply leave output unchanged and affect only the price level (point *H* in Fig. 12.6).

Fiscal Policy

The Keynesian model was initially developed during the Great Depression as economists struggled to explain the worldwide economic collapse and find policies to help the economy return to normal. The early Keynesians stressed that fiscal policy, the government's decisions about government purchases and taxes, can significantly affect output and employment levels. Let's look at the Keynesians' conclusion that both increased government purchases and lower taxes can be used to raise output and employment.

The Effect of Increased Government Purchases. The Keynesian analysis of how increased government purchases affect the economy is shown in Fig. 12.7 on the next page. Again, we assume that the economy starts from full employment (later we discuss what happens if the economy starts from a recession). Point *E* represents the initial equilibrium in both (a) and (b). As before, a temporary increase in government purchases increases the demand for goods and reduces desired national saving at any level of the real interest rate, so that the *IS* curve shifts up and to the right, from IS^1 to IS^2 (see Summary table 12, p. 322). In the short run, before prices can adjust, the economy moves to point *F* in Fig. 12.7(a), where the new *IS* curve, IS^2, and LM^1 intersect. At *F* both output and the real interest rate have increased. Because firms meet the higher demand at the fixed price level, employment also rises, as shown by the movement from point *E* to point *F* along the effective labor demand curve in Fig. 12.7(b). A fiscal

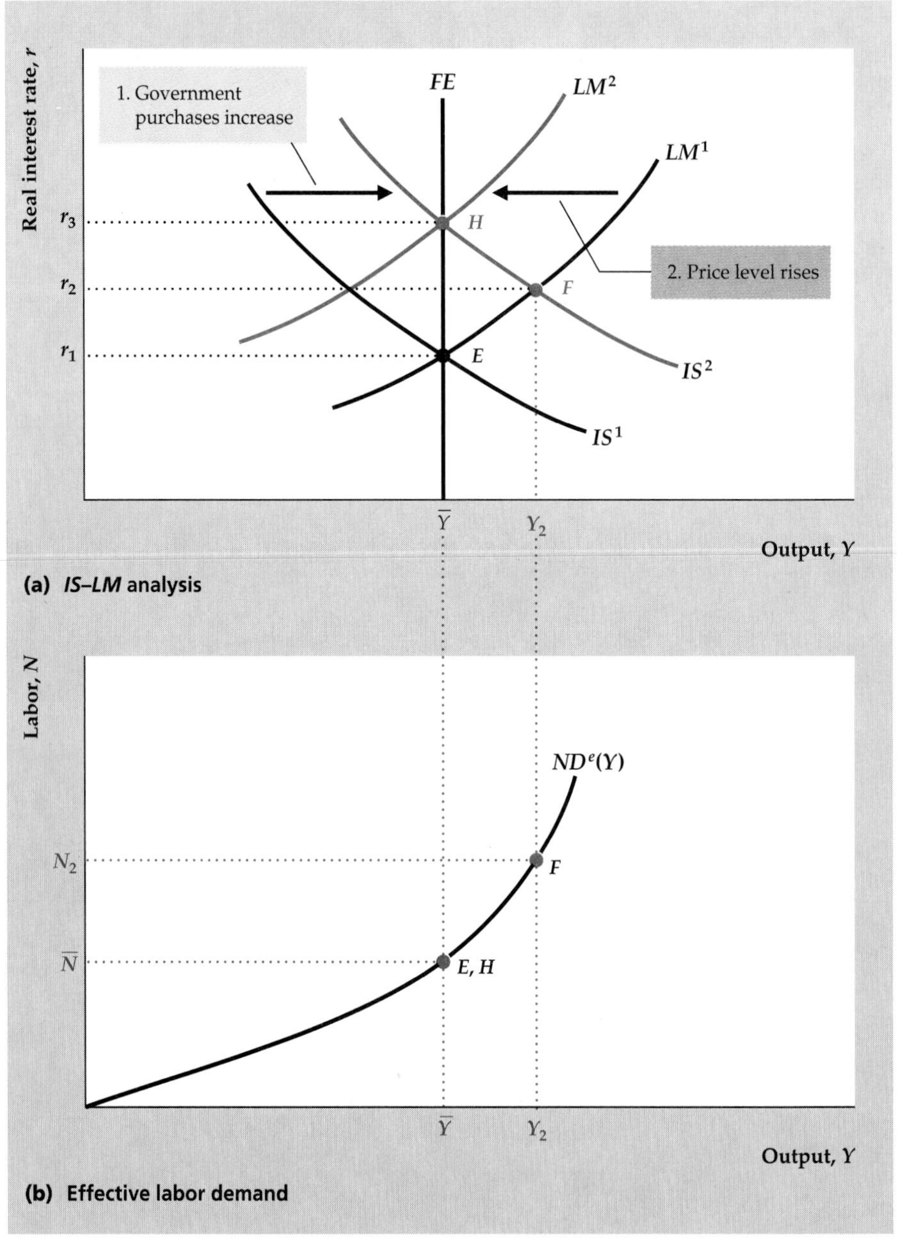

Figure 12.7
An increase in government purchases
(a) If we start from the general equilibrium at point *E*, an increase in government purchases reduces desired national saving and shifts the *IS* curve up and to the right, from IS^1 to IS^2. The short-run equilibrium is at point *F*, with output increasing to Y_2 and the real interest rate rising to r_2.
(b) As firms increase production to meet the demand, employment increases from $\bar{N}$ to N_2, as shown by the effective labor demand curve. However, the economy doesn't remain at point *F*. Because aggregate output demanded exceeds $\bar{Y}$ in the short run, the price level increases, reducing the real money supply and shifting the *LM* curve up and to the left, from LM^1 to LM^2. In the long run, with equilibrium at point *H*, output returns to $\bar{Y}$ and employment returns to $\bar{N}$, but the real interest rate rises further to r_3.

policy change, such as this one, that shifts the *IS* curve up and to the right and raises output and employment is an expansionary change. Similarly, a fiscal policy (such as a reduction in government purchases) that shifts the *IS* curve down and to the left and reduces output and employment is a contractionary change.

In discussing the effects of increased government purchases or other types of spending, Keynesians often use the multiplier concept. The **multiplier** associated with any particular type of spending is the short-run change in total output resulting from a one-unit change in that type of spending. So, for example, if the increase in government purchases analyzed in Fig. 12.7 is ΔG and the resulting short-run increase in output between points *E* and *F* in Fig. 12.7 is ΔY, the multiplier associated with government purchases is $\Delta Y/\Delta G$. Keynesians usually argue that the fiscal policy multiplier is greater than 1, so that if government purchases rise by \$1 billion, output will rise by more than \$1 billion. Unlike the classical analysis, which indicates that government spending diverts resources from the private sector, Keynesian analysis indicates that fiscal expansion can actually increase private sector resources in the short run, if the government purchases multiplier is greater than 1. We derive an algebraic expression for the government purchases multiplier in Appendix 12.B.

Recall that the classical version of the *IS–LM* model also predicts that a temporary increase in government purchases increases output, but in a different way. The classical analysis focuses on the fact that increased government purchases require higher current or future taxes to pay for the extra spending. Higher taxes make workers (who are taxpayers) effectively poorer, which induces them to supply more labor. This increase in labor supply shifts the *FE* line to the right and causes output to rise in the classical model. In contrast, the *FE* line in the Keynesian model doesn't depend on labor supply (because of efficiency wages) and thus is unaffected by the increase in government purchases. Instead, the increase in government purchases affects output by raising aggregate demand (that is, by shifting the *IS–LM* intersection to the right). Output increases above its full-employment level in the short run as firms satisfy extra demand at the initial price level.

The effect of increased government purchases on output in the Keynesian model lasts only as long as needed for the price level to adjust. (However, many Keynesians believe that price adjustment is sufficiently slow that this effect could be felt for several years.) In the long run, when firms adjust their prices, the *LM* curve moves up and to the left, from LM^1 to LM^2 in Fig. 12.7(a), and the economy reaches general equilibrium at point *H*, with output again at $\bar{Y}$. Thus an increase in government purchases doesn't raise output in the long run.

The effects of more government purchases also appear in the Keynesian *AD–AS* framework (Fig. 12.8 on the next page). Increased government purchases shift the *IS* curve up and to the right and raise the aggregate demand for output at any given price level. Thus as a result of expansionary fiscal policy, the aggregate demand curve shifts to the right, from AD^1 to AD^2. The increase in aggregate demand raises output above $\bar{Y}$, as shown by the shift from the initial equilibrium at point *E* to the short-run equilibrium at point *F*. At *F* the aggregate demand for output is greater than full-employment output, so firms eventually raise their prices. In the long run the economy reaches the full-employment general equilibrium at point *H*, with output again at $\bar{Y}$ and with a higher price level. These results are identical to those we obtained using the Keynesian *IS–LM* framework.

The Effect of Lower Taxes. Keynesians generally believe that, like an increase in government purchases, a lump-sum reduction in current taxes is expansionary. In other words, they expect that a tax cut will shift the *IS* curve up and to the right, raising output and employment in the short run. Similarly, they expect a tax increase to be contractionary, shifting the *IS* curve down and to the left.

Why does a tax cut affect the *IS* curve, according to Keynesians? The argument is that if consumers receive a tax cut, they will spend part of it on

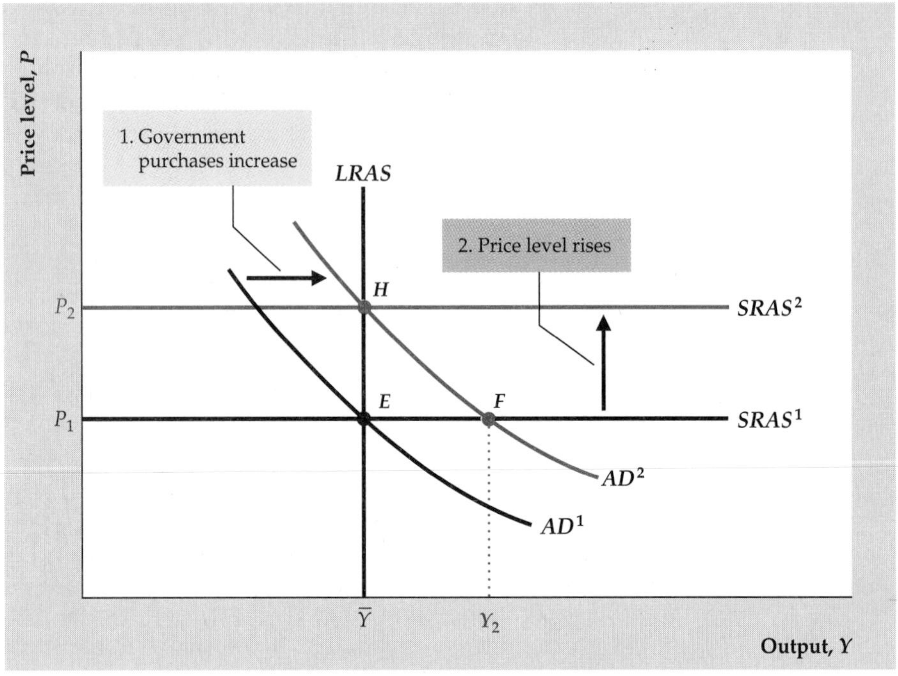

Figure 12.8
An increase in government purchases in the Keynesian *AD–AS* framework
An increase in government purchases raises the aggregate demand for output at any price level (see Fig. 12.7). Thus the aggregate demand curve shifts to the right, from AD^1 to AD^2. In the short run the increase in aggregate demand increases output to Y_2 (point *F*) but doesn't affect the price level, because prices are sticky in the short run. Because aggregate output demanded Y_2 exceeds $\bar{Y}$ at *F*, firms eventually raise their prices. The long-run equilibrium is at *H*, where AD^2 intersects the long-run aggregate supply curve *LRAS*. At *H*, output has returned to $\bar{Y}$ and the price level has risen from P_1 to P_2. The higher price level raises the short-run aggregate supply curve, from $SRAS^1$ to $SRAS^2$.

increased consumption. For any output *Y* and level of government purchases *G*, an increase in desired consumption arising from a tax cut will lower desired national saving, $Y - C^d - G$. A drop in desired saving raises the real interest rate that clears the goods market and shifts the *IS* curve up.[12]

If a tax cut raises desired consumption and shifts the *IS* curve upward, as Keynesians claim, the effects on the economy are similar to the effects of increased government purchases (Figs. 12.7 and 12.8). In the short run a tax cut raises aggregate demand and thus output and employment at the initial price level. In the long run, after complete price adjustment, the economy returns to full employment with a higher real interest rate than in the initial general equilibrium. The only difference between the tax cut and the increase in government purchases is that, instead of raising the portion of full-employment output devoted to government purchases, a tax cut raises the portion of full-employment output devoted to consumption.

APPLICATION

Macroeconomic Policy and the Real Interest Rate in the Early 1980s and the Early 1990s

In the early 1980s both U.S. monetary and fiscal policy changed significantly. The shift actually began in October 1979 with the announcement by Federal Reserve Chairman Paul Volcker that, to bring down inflation, which was running at a rate of about 11% per year, monetary policy would be tightened. Fiscal policy, in contrast, became more expansionary. In 1981 Congress passed the

12. In arguing that a tax cut raises desired consumption and lowers desired national saving, Keynesian economists reject the Ricardian equivalence proposition (Chapter 4), which states that a lump-sum tax cut should *not* affect consumption or national saving. Ricardian equivalence is discussed further in Chapter 16.

Economic Recovery Tax Act (ERTA), which reduced tax rates, at about the same time that government spending (notably military spending) began to rise.

The combined effects of tight money and easy fiscal policy are illustrated in Fig. 12.9. The economy was essentially at full employment in 1979 (unemployment was 5.8% of the labor force, close to its normal level, and the business cycle reached a peak in January 1980), so the initial situation in 1979 is represented by the full-employment general equilibrium at point *E*. Following Volcker's announcement, money growth fell below its previous trend, causing the *LM* curve to shift up and to the left, from LM^1 to LM^2. The easing of fiscal policy—from both the tax cut and the increase in military spending—shifted the *IS* curve up and to the right, from IS^1 to IS^2. As a result of the two policy changes, the economy shifted from point *E* to a short-run equilibrium at point *F*.

What effects did this policy mix have on the economy? According to the Keynesian analysis in Fig. 12.9, the effect on output is ambiguous, because tight monetary policy tends to lower output but expansionary fiscal policy tends to raise it. In other words, whether the short-run equilibrium at point *F* should be drawn to the right or to the left of the *FE* line is unclear. Actually, the economy suffered recessions in 1980 and 1981–1982, so we placed *F* to the left of the *FE* line.

Although the effect on output is unclear, the combination of tight monetary and easy fiscal policies has an unambiguous impact of raising the real interest rate. In fact, in the early 1980s the real interest rate in the United States soared to its highest level since the 1930s. (The real interest rate for the period 1960–1992 is shown in Fig. 2.4.)

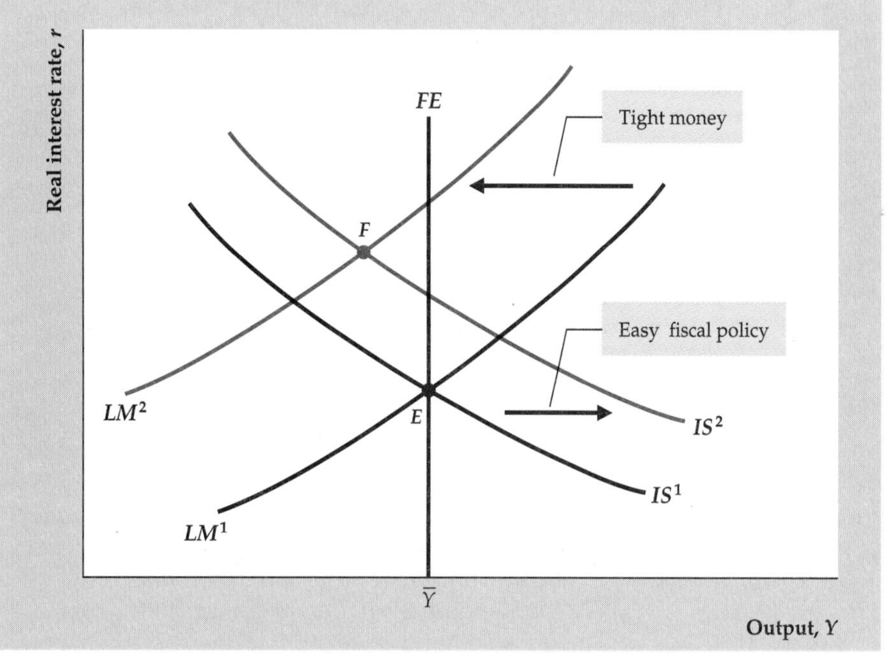

Figure 12.9
Tight money and easy fiscal policy
The U.S. economy was essentially at full employment in 1979 (point *E*), and late in the year the Fed tightened monetary growth in an attempt to reduce inflation. The reduction in monetary growth shifted the *LM* curve up and to the left, from LM^1 to LM^2. Then in 1981 the Economic Recovery Tax Act reduced taxes. This tax cut combined with an increase in government purchases shifted the *IS* curve up and to the right, from IS^1 to IS^2. With tight money and an easy fiscal policy, the economy moved to point *F* with a high real interest rate. Point *F* is drawn to the left of the *FE* line, indicating that the contractionary effects of tight money outweighed the expansionary effects of easy fiscal policy and caused a recession.

As the 1990s began, the economy again was at full employment (the business cycle reached a peak in July 1990) and again received doses of monetary and fiscal medicine. However, this time the policy changes were in the opposite direction from those at the beginning of the 1980s. On the fiscal side, a growing sense of urgency about the size of the Federal government's budget deficit led President Bush to agree to a deficit reduction bill in 1990; and in 1993 Congress approved a multiyear deficit reduction plan, proposed by President Clinton, involving both tax increases and spending cuts. Thus fiscal policy leaned toward contraction. On the monetary side, Fed Chairman Alan Greenspan began to ease policy in 1989 and 1990, and monetary policy remained relatively easy during the 1990–1991 recession and the subsequent slow recovery.

The Keynesian model predicts that this combination of tight fiscal policy and easy money should reduce the real interest rate (the reverse of what happened in the early 1980s, when the policy mix was tight money and easy fiscal policy)—and interest rates did fall. For example, between early 1989 and the spring of 1993, the three-month Treasury bill interest rate fell from almost 9% to less than 3%. Longer-term rates also fell, although less dramatically. Because inflation was stable, this drop in nominal interest rates largely reflected a drop in the real interest rate.

As often happens, reality was more complicated than suggested by these simple analyses. One important complication was that oil price shocks occurred both during 1979–1980 and in 1990 (see Fig. 3.11). Nevertheless, a Keynesian interpretation that focuses on the role of the policy mix seems to explain the behavior of at least one important macroeconomic variable, the real interest rate, fairly well.

12.4 THE KEYNESIAN THEORY OF BUSINESS CYCLES AND MACROECONOMIC STABILIZATION

Recall that there are two basic questions about business cycles that a macroeconomic theory should try to answer: (1) What causes recurrent fluctuations in the economy? and (2) What, if anything, should policymakers try to do about cycles? We are now ready to give the Keynesian answers to these two questions.

Keynesian Business Cycle Theory

An explanation of the business cycle requires not only a macroeconomic model but also some assumptions about the types of shocks hitting the economy. For example, RBC theorists believe that productivity shocks, which directly shift the *FE* line, are the most important type of macroeconomic shock.

In contrast to RBC theorists, most Keynesians believe that aggregate demand shocks are the primary source of business cycle fluctuations. **Aggregate demand shocks** are shocks to the economy that shift *either* the *IS* curve or the *LM* curve and thus affect the aggregate demand for output. Examples of aggregate demand shocks affecting the *IS* curve are changes in fiscal policy, changes in desired investment arising from changes in the expected future marginal product of capital,[13] and changes in consumer confidence about the future that affect desired saving. Examples of aggregate demand shocks affecting the *LM* curve are changes in the demand for money or changes in the money supply. The Keynesian version of the *IS–LM* model, combined with the view that most shocks are aggregate demand shocks, constitutes the Keynesian theory of business cycles.

Figure 12.10 uses the Keynesian model to illustrate a recession caused by an aggregate demand shock. Suppose that consumers become pessimistic about the long-term future of the economy and thus reduce their current desired consumption; equivalently, they raise their current desired saving. For any level of income, an increase in desired saving lowers the real interest rate that clears the goods market and thus shifts the *IS* curve down, from IS^1 to IS^2. The economy goes into recession at point *F*, and, as prices don't adjust immediately to restore full employment, it remains in recession for some period of time with output below its full-employment level. Because firms face below-normal levels of demand, they also cut employment.

Note that a decline in investment spending (reflecting, for example, pessimism of business investors) or reduced government purchases would have similar recessionary effects as the decline in consumer spending analyzed in Fig. 12.10. Alternatively, a shift to the left of the *LM* curve (because of either

13. A change in the expected future *MPK* might also be thought of as a technological shock because it involves a change in the future production function. However, because a change in the future *MPK* shifts the *IS* curve but doesn't affect the current *FE* line, Keynesians classify it as an aggregate demand shock.

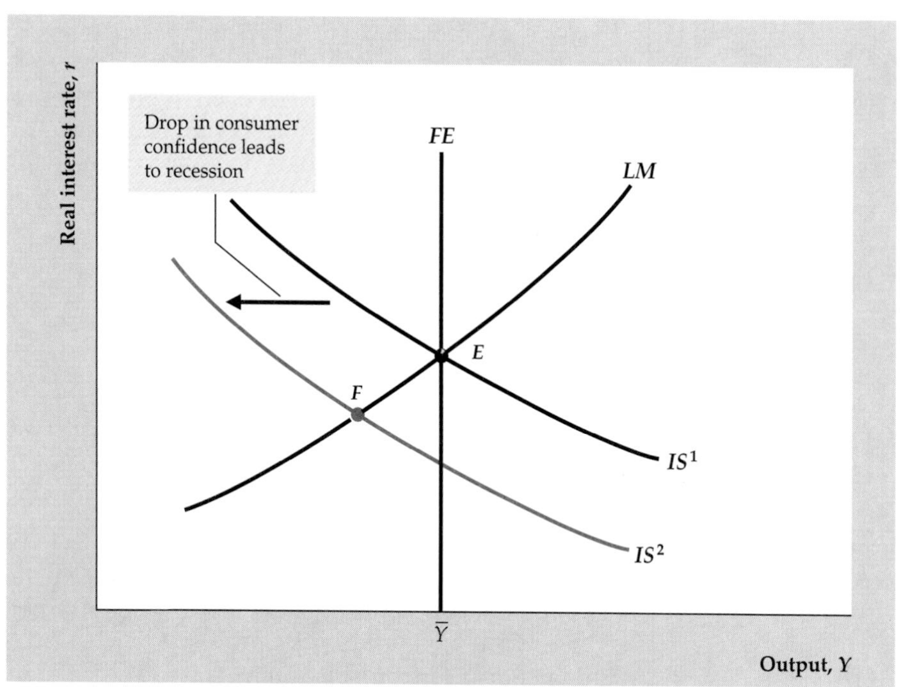

Figure 12.10
A recession arising from an aggregate demand shock
The figure illustrates how an adverse aggregate demand shock can cause a recession in the Keynesian model. The economy starts at general equilibrium at point *E*. A decline in consumer confidence about the future of the economy reduces desired consumption and raises desired saving so that the *IS* curve shifts down, from IS^1 to IS^2. The economy falls into recession at point *F*, with output below its full-employment level $\bar{Y}$.

increased money demand or reduced money supply) also could cause a recession in the Keynesian framework; in this case, high real interest rates caused by the "shortage" of money would cause the declines in consumer spending and investment. Thus Keynesians attribute recessions to "not enough demand" for goods, in contrast to classical economists who attribute recessions to "not enough supply."

Like the real business cycle theory, the Keynesian theory of cycles can account for several of the business cycle facts: (1) in response to occasional aggregate demand shocks, the theory predicts recurrent fluctuations in output; (2) the theory correctly implies that employment will fluctuate in the same direction as output; and (3) because it predicts that shocks to the money supply will be nonneutral, the theory is consistent with the business cycle fact that money is procyclical and leading.

A business cycle fact that we previously emphasized (Chapter 9) is that spending on investment goods and other durable goods is strongly procyclical and volatile. This cyclical behavior of durable goods spending can be explained by the Keynesian theory if shocks to durable goods demand are themselves a main source of cycles. The demand for durable goods would be a source of cyclical fluctuations if, for example, investors frequently reassessed their expectations of the future *MPK*. Keynes himself thought that waves of investor optimism and pessimism, which he called "animal spirits," were a significant source of cyclical fluctuations. A rise in the demand for investment goods or consumer durables (at fixed levels of output and the real interest rate) is expansionary because it shifts the *IS* curve to the right. Investment will also be procyclical in the Keynesian model whenever cycles are caused by fluctuations in the *LM* curve; for example, an increase in the money supply that shifts the *LM* curve down and to the right both increases output and (by reducing the real interest rate) increases investment.

Another important business cycle fact that is consistent with the Keynesian theory is the observation that inflation tends to slow during or just after recessions (inflation is procyclical and lagging). In the Keynesian view, as Fig. 12.10 illustrates, during a recession aggregate output demanded is less than the full-employment level of output. Thus when firms do adjust their prices, they will be likely to cut them in order to increase their sales. According to the Keynesian model, because demand pressure is low during recessions, inflation will tend to subside when the economy is weak.

Procyclical Labor Productivity and Labor Hoarding. Although the Keynesian model is consistent with many of the business cycle facts, one fact—that labor productivity is procyclical—presents problems for this approach. Recall that procyclical labor productivity is consistent with the real business cycle assumption that cycles are caused by productivity shocks—that recessions are times when productivity is unusually low and booms are times when productivity is unusually high. Unlike the RBC theorists, however, Keynesians assume that demand shocks rather than supply (productivity) shocks cause most cyclical fluctuations.

Because supply shocks are shifts of the production function, the Keynesian assumption that supply shocks usually are unimportant is the same as saying that the production function is fairly stable over the business cycle. But if the production function is stable, increases in employment during booms should *reduce* average labor productivity because of the diminishing marginal productivity of labor. Thus the Keynesian model predicts that average labor productivity is countercyclical, contrary to the business cycle fact.

To explain the procyclical behavior of average labor productivity, Keynesians modified their models to include labor hoarding. **Labor hoarding** occurs if, because of the costs of firing and hiring workers, firms retain some workers in a recession that they would otherwise lay off. These "redundant" workers represent "hoarded labor." They are being kept on the payroll so that the firm won't have to incur the costs of firing them and then hiring and training new workers when the economy revives. Hoarded labor either works less hard during the recession (there's less to do) or is put to work doing tasks, such as maintaining equipment, that aren't measured as part of the firm's output. When the economy revives, the hoarded labor goes back to working in the normal way. The presence of hoarded labor producing a reduced amount of measured output during recessions may explain why measured productivity is low during recessions and high during booms, even though the firm's production function is stable and exhibits diminishing marginal productivity.

There is evidence that labor hoarding does exist in at least some industries. In one well-known study, Jon Fay and James Medoff[14] of Harvard University sent questionnaires to large manufacturing enterprises, asking about employment and production during the most recent downturn experienced at each plant. Fay and Medoff found that during a downturn the average plant surveyed cut production by 31% and cut its total use of blue-collar hours to 23% below the normal level. Plant managers estimated that total hours could have been reduced by an additional 6% of the normal level without further reducing output. Of this 6% of normal hours, about half (3% of normal hours) were typically assigned to various types of useful work, including equipment maintenance and overhaul, painting, cleaning, reworking output, and training. The remaining 3% of normal hours were assigned to "make-work" and other unproductive activities. These numbers suggest that firms retain a fairly significant amount of redundant or hoarded labor during recessions.

Another interesting study, by John Shea[15] of the University of Wisconsin at Madison, examined the cyclical behavior of industrial injury rates. Shea reasoned that, if manufacturing workers work harder and more quickly during booms than during recessions, as suggested by the labor hoarding hypothesis, more workers should suffer injuries in booms. Shea found that, consistent with labor hoarding, industrial injury rates are procyclical.

Macroeconomic Stabilization

From the Keynesian explanation of why business cycles occur we turn to the Keynesian view on how policymakers should respond to recessions and booms. Briefly, Keynesians—unlike classical economists—generally favor policy actions to "stabilize" the economy by eliminating large fluctuations in

14. "Labor and Output Over the Business Cycle," *American Economic Review*, September 1985, pp. 638–655.

15. "Accident Rates, Labor Effort and the Business Cycle," SSRI working paper 9028, November 1990.

output and employment. Keynesian support of more active policy measures follows from the theory's characterization of business cycle expansions and contractions as periods in which the economy is temporarily away from its general equilibrium (or not at the *IS–LM–FE* intersection). According to Keynesians, recessions are particularly undesirable because in a recession employment may be far below the amount of labor that workers want to supply, which leads to hardships for the unemployed and to output that is "too low." Keynesians therefore argue that average economic well-being would be increased if governments tried to reduce cyclical fluctuations, especially recessions.

The Keynesian analysis of monetary and fiscal policies suggests that these policies could be used to smooth the business cycle. To understand how, consider Fig. 12.11. Suppose that the economy, initially in general equilibrium at point *E*, has been driven into recession at point *F*. Various types of shocks could have caused this recession. In Fig. 12.10, for example, we considered a drop in consumer confidence about the future of the economy. A drop in confidence would reduce current desired consumption and increase current desired saving, thereby shifting the *IS* curve down from IS^1 to IS^2.

How might policymakers respond to this recession? We consider three possibilities: (1) no change in monetary or fiscal policy; (2) an increase in the money supply; and (3) an increase in government purchases.

- *Scenario 1: No change in macroeconomic policy.* One policy option is to do nothing. With no government intervention, the economy eventually will correct itself. At point *F* in Fig. 12.11 aggregate output demanded is below the full-employment level of output $\bar{Y}$. Therefore, over time, prices will begin to fall, increasing the real money supply and shifting the *LM* curve down and to

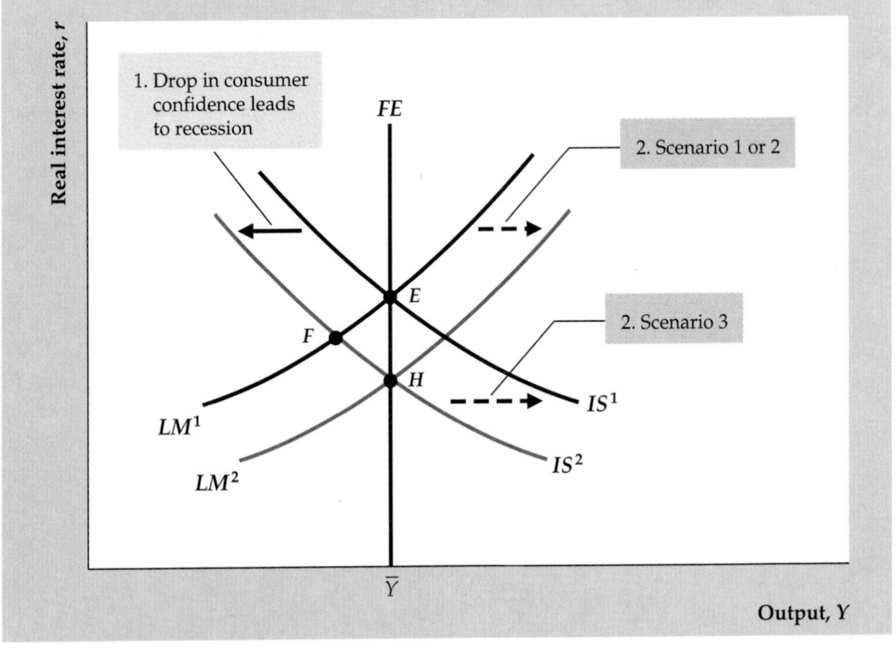

Figure 12.11
Stabilization policy in the Keynesian model
From point *E* the economy is driven into a recession at point *F* by a drop in consumer confidence and spending, which shifts the *IS* curve down, from IS^1 to IS^2. If the government took no action, in the long run price adjustment would shift the *LM* curve from LM^1 to LM^2 and restore general equilibrium at point *H* (scenario 1). Alternatively, the government could try to offset the recession through stabilization policy. For example, the Fed could increase the money supply, which would shift the *LM* curve directly from LM^1 to LM^2, speeding the recovery in output (scenario 2). Another possibility is a fiscal expansion, such as an increase in government purchases, which would shift the *IS* curve from IS^2 back to IS^1, again restoring full employment at *E* (scenario 3). Compared to a strategy of doing nothing, expansionary monetary or fiscal policy helps the economy recover more quickly but leads to a higher price level in the long run.

the right. In the long run price declines shift the LM curve from LM^1 to LM^2, restoring the economy to general equilibrium at point H. However, a disadvantage of this strategy is that, during the (possibly lengthy) price adjustment process, output and employment remain below their full-employment levels.

- *Scenario 2: An increase in the money supply.* Instead of waiting for the economy to reach general equilibrium through price adjustment, the Fed could increase the money supply, which also would shift the LM curve from LM^1 to LM^2 in Fig. 12.11. If prices adjust slowly, this expansionary policy would move the economy to general equilibrium at point H more quickly than would doing nothing.
- *Scenario 3: An increase in government purchases.* An alternative policy of raising government purchases will shift the IS curve up and to the right, from IS^2 to IS^1. This policy also takes the economy to full employment, although at point E in Fig. 12.11 rather than at point H.

In all three scenarios the economy eventually returns to full employment. However, the use of monetary or fiscal policy to achieve full employment leads to two important differences from the scenario in which no policy action is taken. First, if the government uses monetary or fiscal expansion to end the recession, the economy returns directly to full employment; if policy isn't changed, the economy remains in recession in the short run, returning to full employment only when prices have fully adjusted. Second, if there is no policy change (scenario 1), in the long run the price level falls relative to the nominal money supply. Indeed, the drop in the price level relative to the money supply increases the real money supply, shifts the LM curve down and to the right, and restores full employment at point H. In contrast, when monetary or fiscal policy is used to restore full employment (scenarios 2 and 3), the downward adjustment of the price level doesn't occur because expansionary policy directly returns aggregate demand to the full-employment level. Thus according to the Keynesian analysis, using expansionary monetary or fiscal policy has the advantage of bringing the economy back to full employment more quickly but the disadvantage of leading to a higher price level than if no policy action is undertaken.

Either monetary or fiscal policy can be used to bring the economy back to full employment. Does it matter which policy is used? Yes, there is at least one basic difference between the outcomes of the two policies: Monetary and fiscal policies affect the composition of spending (the amount of output that is devoted to consumption, the amount to investment, and so on) differently. In Fig. 12.11, although total output is the same at the alternative general equilibrium points E and H, at E (reached by an increase in government purchases) government purchases are higher than at H (reached by an increase in the money supply). Because government purchases are higher at E, the remaining components of spending—in a closed economy, consumption and investment—must be lower at E than at H. Relative to a monetary expansion, an increase in government purchases crowds out consumption and investment by raising the real interest rate, which is higher at E than at H. In addition, increased government purchases imply higher current or future tax burdens, which also reduces consumption relative to what it would be with monetary expansion.

Difficulties of Macroeconomic Stabilization. The use of monetary and fiscal policies to smooth or moderate the business cycle is called **macroeconomic stabilization.** Using macroeconomic policies to try to smooth the cycle is also sometimes called **aggregate demand management** because monetary and fiscal policies shift the aggregate demand curve. Macroeconomic stabilization was a popular concept in the heyday of Keynesian economics in the 1960s, and it still influences policy discussions. Unfortunately, even putting aside the debates between classicals and Keynesians about whether smoothing the business cycle is sensible, actual macroeconomic stabilization has been much less successful than the simple Keynesian theory suggests.

As discussed earlier in connection with fiscal policy, attempts to stabilize the economy run into some technical problems. First, because the ability to measure and analyze the economy is imperfect, gauging how far the economy is from full employment at any particular time is difficult. Second, the precise amount that output will increase in response to a monetary or fiscal expansion isn't known. These uncertainties make assessing how much of a monetary or fiscal change is needed to restore full employment difficult. Finally, even knowing the size of the policy change needed still wouldn't provide enough information. Because macroeconomic policies take time to implement and more time to affect the economy, their optimal use requires knowledge of where the economy will be six months or a year from now. But such knowledge is, at best, very imprecise.

Because of these problems, aggregate demand management has been likened to trying to hit a moving target in a heavy fog. These problems haven't persuaded most Keynesians to abandon stabilization policy; however, many Keynesians agree that policymakers should concentrate on fighting major recessions and not try to "fine-tune" the economy by smoothing every bump and wiggle in output and employment.

Beyond the technical problems associated with trying to find the right policies to stabilize the economy, economists also face the practical problem of convincing policymakers to take their advice. See the "Political Environment" box, p. 428, for a discussion of the role of the Council of Economic Advisers in formulating actual government policies.

Supply Shocks in the Keynesian Model

Until the 1970s the Keynesian business cycle theory focused almost exclusively on aggregate demand shocks as the source of business cycle fluctuations. Because aggregate demand shocks lead to procyclical movements in inflation, however, the Keynesian theory failed to account for the stagflation—high inflation together with a recession—that hit the U.S. economy following the 1973–1975 oil price shock. This experience led to much criticism of the traditional theory by both economists and policymakers, so Keynesians recast the theory to allow for both supply and demand shocks. Although Keynesians wouldn't go so far as to agree with RBC theorists that supply (productivity) shocks are a factor in most recessions, they now concede that there have been occasional episodes—the oil price shocks of the 1970s being the leading examples—in which supply shocks have played a primary role in an economic downturn.

Figure 12.12 shows a Keynesian analysis of the effects of a sharp temporary increase in the price of oil (a similar analysis would apply to other supply

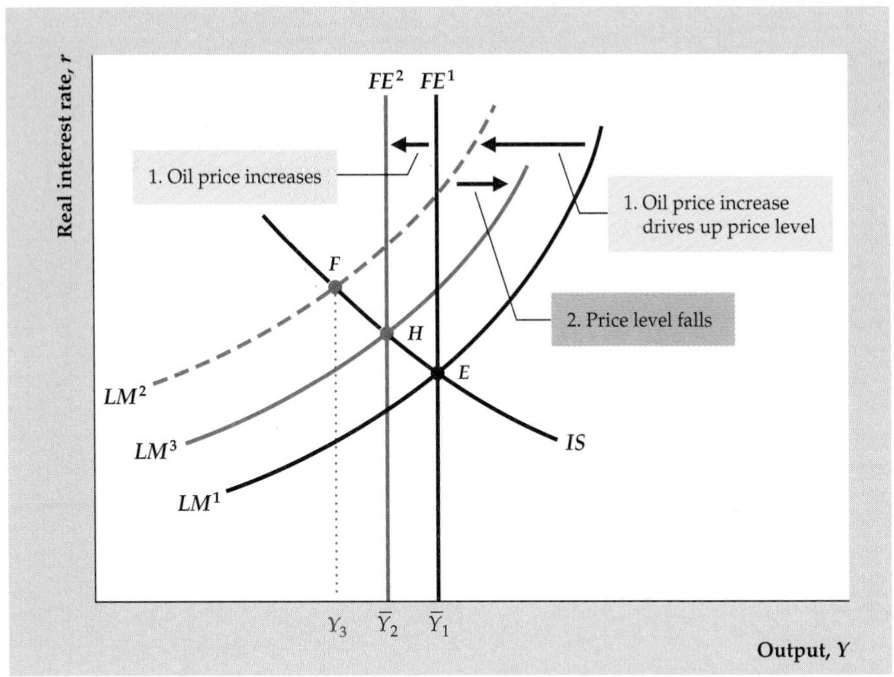

Figure 12.12
An oil price shock in the Keynesian model
An increase in the price of oil is an adverse supply shock that reduces full-employment output from $\bar{Y}_1$ to $\bar{Y}_2$ and thus shifts the *FE* line to the left. In addition, the increase in the price of oil increases prices in sectors that depend heavily on oil, whereas prices in other sectors remain fixed in the short run. Thus the average price level rises, which reduces the real money supply *M/P* and shifts the *LM* curve up and to the left, from LM^1 to LM^2. In the short run, the economy moves to point *F*, with output falling below the new, lower value of full-employment output and the real interest rate increasing. Because the aggregate quantity of goods demanded at *F* is less than the full-employment level of output $\bar{Y}_2$, in the long run the price level falls, partially offsetting the initial increase in prices. The drop in the price level causes the *LM* curve to shift down and to the right, from LM^2 to LM^3, moving the economy to full-employment equilibrium at point *H*.

shocks, such as a drought). As we showed in Chapter 3, if firms respond to an increase in the price of oil by using less energy, the amount of output that can be produced with the same amount of capital and labor falls. Thus the increase in the price of oil is an adverse supply shock, which reduces the full-employment level of output and shifts the *FE* line to the left, from FE^1 to FE^2. After complete wage and price adjustment, which occurs virtually immediately in the basic classical model but only in the long run in the Keynesian model, output falls to its new full-employment level $\bar{Y}_2$. Thus in the long run (after full wage and price adjustment), the Keynesian analysis and the classical analysis of a supply shock are the same.

However, the Keynesian analysis of the short-run effects of an oil price shock is slightly different from the classical analysis. To understand the short-term effects of the oil price shock in the Keynesian model, first think about the effects of the increase in the oil price on the general price level. Recall that firms facing menu costs will not change their prices if the "right" prices are only a little different from the preset prices. However, if the right prices are substantially different from the preset prices, so that firms would lose considerable profits by maintaining the preset prices, they will change their prices. In the case of a large increase in the price of oil, firms whose costs are strongly affected by the price of oil—including gas stations, suppliers of home heating oil, and airlines, for example—find that the right prices for their products are substantially higher than the preset prices. These oil-dependent firms increase their prices quickly, whereas firms in other sectors maintain their preset prices in the short run. Thus there is price stickiness in the sense that not all prices adjust to their equilibrium values, and yet the average price level rises in the short run.

Because a sharp increase in the price of oil raises the price level P in the short run, it also reduces the real money supply M/P. A decline in the real

THE POLITICAL ENVIRONMENT

THE ROLE OF THE COUNCIL OF ECONOMIC ADVISERS IN FORMULATING ECONOMIC POLICY

As World War II drew to an end in 1945, many people feared that the U.S. economy would revert to the Great Depression that prevailed in the 1930s. This concern prompted Congress to pass the Employment Act of 1946 "to promote maximum employment, production, and purchasing power." A more concrete provision of the Employment Act of 1946 was the establishment of the three-person Council of Economic Advisers (the CEA). In addition to advising the President on a variety of economic issues, the CEA prepares the annual *Economic Report of the President* and works with other agencies of the Federal government to forge economic policy.

Most CEA members have been professional economists who were drawn from leading research universities and nonprofit institutions (a recent example is Laura D. Tyson, a professor at the University of California at Berkeley when appointed CEA chair by President Clinton). Thus they often are newcomers to the political scene. Because they generally are at the frontier of economic research, CEA members bring fresh ideas and perspectives to policy discussions. However, being inexperienced in the political arena, most CEA members must also grasp the political dimensions of policymaking and develop a style for dealing with situations in which their views differ from those of others in the administration.

When President John F. Kennedy took office in 1961, he inherited a lackluster economy and promised to "start the country moving again." Kennedy's newly appointed CEA, chaired by Walter Heller, recommended tax cuts to stimulate the economy, but the President's belief in "fiscal responsibility" initially made him reluctant to propose any policies that would create government budget deficits.* The opposition to fiscal stimulus was shared by other administration officials, including Treasury Secretary Douglas Dillon and Commerce Secretary Luther Hodges. However, by working effectively within the administration, the CEA was able to convince the President and his aides to support expansionary fiscal policies. The result was a fiscal stimulus that was implemented in two stages: The Revenue Act of 1962 provided tax incentives for investment, and a more comprehensive tax reduction was instituted by the Revenue Act of 1964. This fiscal package was followed by a strong economic expansion and was widely regarded as a successful experiment in Keynesian demand management.

Twenty years later, the CEA was again at odds with the President and the administration about fundamental aspects of fiscal policy. In the early 1980s President Ronald Reagan advocated sharp cuts in income tax rates while the chairman of the CEA, Martin Feldstein, urged fiscal caution. Feldstein warned that tax cuts would lead to persistent government deficits, high real interest rates, and lower investment in the United States. When his warnings were repeatedly ignored by the Reagan administration, Feldstein made his views known to the public. Relations between the CEA and the administration then deteriorated to the point that the administration no longer relied on the CEA for economic advice, and the CEA temporarily lost its ability to influence economic policy. In testimony before Congress, Treasury Secretary Donald Regan recommended that the *Economic Report of the President* written by the CEA under Feldstein be thrown in the trash. In July 1984 Feldstein resigned from the CEA with his professional reputation intact and having earned a reputation for speaking his mind in the best interests of the country. However, the Reagan administration was so angered by the experience that it considered trying to abolish the CEA or to minimize its role in policymaking.

Did Feldstein do the right thing? In looking back at this incident, William Nordhaus, a member of the CEA under President Jimmy Carter, argued that "by taking the dispute public, Feldstein lost the trust of the President and of the President's confidants, thereby losing the Council's unique power to affect economic policy by persuading the President in close personal contacts."† However, we will never know whether President Reagan and his close advisors could have been persuaded to change their policies by behind-the-scenes discussion and negotiation. If not, the public interest may have been well served by Feldstein's public statements, which educated the Congress and the public about the potential risks of government budget deficits.

* The debate within the Kennedy administration about tax cuts is documented in Michael G. Rukstad, "The Zenith of Keynesian Economics", *Macroeconomic Decision Making in the World Economy,* Chicago: The Dryden Press, 1986, Chapter 6.

† William D. Nordhaus, "The Council of Economic Advisers: Conscience or Advocate?" in Karl Brunner and Allan Meltzer, eds., *Carnegie-Rochester Conference Series on Public Policy,* vol. 25, Amsterdam: North-Holland, 1986, p. 273.

money supply shifts the LM curve to left, from LM^1 to LM^2 in Fig. 12.12. As drawn, the LM curve shifts farther to the left than the FE line shifts, though this outcome isn't logically necessary. The short-run equilibrium is at point F, where LM^2 intersects the IS curve. Because F is to the left of the FE line, the economy is in a recession at F, with output (at Y_3) below the new value of full-employment output, $\bar{Y}_2$. In the short run the economy experiences stagflation, with both a drop in output *and* a burst of inflation. Note that, according to this analysis, the short-run decline in output has two components: (1) the drop in full-employment output from $\bar{Y}_1$ to $\bar{Y}_2$; and (2) the drop in output below the new full-employment level arising from the shift to the left of the LM curve (the difference between $\bar{Y}_2$ and Y_3).

Supply shocks of the type analyzed in Fig. 12.12 pose tremendous difficulties for Keynesian stabilization policies. First, monetary or fiscal policy can do little about the portion of the decline in output resulting from the shift of the FE line; attempts to expand the economy beyond the new full-employment output level $\bar{Y}_2$ will increase output only temporarily and worsen inflation. In contrast, the portion of the output decline arising from the shift to the left of the LM curve (the difference between $\bar{Y}_2$ and Y_3) represents an output level below the full-employment level and could, in principle, be eliminated by expansionary monetary or fiscal policies that raise output to $\bar{Y}_2$. However, by using expansionary policies at point F, rather than doing nothing, the government risks worsening the already-high rate of inflation. Hence in the face of a shock that induces stagflation like the one shown in Fig. 12.12, macroeconomic policy can neither avoid a sharp decline in output, nor can it restore output even to its new, lower full-employment level without potentially worsening inflation.

CHAPTER SUMMARY

1. Keynesians are skeptical that a mismatch between workers and jobs can explain all unemployment. They argue that some unemployment is caused by real wages that are rigid and above the level at which the quantities of labor demanded and supplied are equal.

2. One explanation for real-wage rigidity is based on the efficiency wage model, which assumes that workers work harder in response to an increase in the real wage. Firms can attain the highest level of profit by paying the real wage, known as the efficiency wage, that elicits the most worker effort per dollar of wages. If the effort curve relating effort provided by workers to the real wage doesn't change, the efficiency wage, and hence the real wage actually paid, is rigid.

3. At the efficiency wage, firms demand the level of employment $\bar{N}$ at which the marginal product of labor equals the efficiency wage. If the efficiency wage is above the market-clearing real wage, employment is determined by labor demand. The difference between the quantity of labor supplied and the quantity of labor demanded at the efficiency wage represents unemployment.

4. Full-employment output $\bar{Y}$ is the output that can be produced when employment is at its full-employment level $\bar{N}$ and worker effort is at the level induced by the efficiency wage. The FE line in the Keynesian IS–LM model is vertical where output equals its full-employment level. In the Keynesian model, full-employment output and

the *FE* line are affected by productivity shocks but not by changes in labor supply because changes in labor supply don't affect employment in the efficiency wage model.

5. Keynesians attribute the nonneutrality of money to price stickiness, which means that some firms may not change their prices in the short run even though the demand for or supply of their product has changed. Price stickiness is contrary to the assumption of the basic classical model that prices and wages are completely flexible.

6. Price stickiness can arise from the profit-maximizing behavior of monopolistically competitive firms that face menu costs, or costs of changing prices. Such firms are price setters rather than price takers, and once they set their prices they meet customer demand at that fixed price. These firms readjust prices only occasionally, generally when costs or demand have changed significantly.

7. In the Keynesian model with sticky prices, output is determined in the short run at the intersection of the *IS* and *LM* curves. The economy can be off the *FE* line in the short run because firms are willing to meet demand at predetermined prices. The level of employment in the short run is given by the effective labor demand curve, which shows the amount of labor needed to produce any given amount of output. In the long run, after prices and wages have completely adjusted, the *LM* curve moves to restore general equilibrium with full employment.

8. As in the classical model, the aggregate demand (*AD*) curve slopes downward in the Keynesian model. The reason is that an increase in the price level reduces the real money supply and shifts the *LM* curve up and to the left, which reduces aggregate demand. The Keynesian short-run aggregate supply (*SRAS*) curve is horizontal because in the short run the price level is fixed and firms supply the amount of output demanded. In the long run, after complete wage and price adjustment, firms supply the full-employment level of output $\bar{Y}$, regardless of the price level; so the long-run aggregate supply (*LRAS*) curve is vertical.

9. In the Keynesian model an increase in the money supply shifts the *LM* curve down and to the right, raising output and lowering the real interest rate in the short run. Thus money isn't neutral in the short run. In the long run, however, money is neutral; monetary expansion raises the price level proportionally but has no real effects.

10. In the Keynesian model an increase in government purchases or a cut in taxes shifts the *IS* curve up and to the right, raising output and the real interest rate in the short run. In the long run, output returns to the full-employment level but the real interest rate increases. Fiscal policy isn't neutral in the long run because it affects the composition of output among consumption, investment, and government purchases.

11. Keynesians attribute most business cycles to aggregate demand shocks. These shocks hit the *IS* curve (changes in government purchases, desired consumption, or desired investment) or the *LM* curve (changes in money supply or money demand). Keynesian business cycle theory, which has traditionally emphasized the importance of aggregate demand shocks, can account for the procyclical behavior of employment, money, inflation, and investment. To explain the procyclical behavior of average labor productivity, the Keynesian theory must include the additional assumption that firms hoard labor—that is, they employ more workers than necessary during recessions.

12. Macroeconomic stabilization, also called aggregate demand management, is the use of monetary or fiscal policy to try to eliminate recessions and keep the economy at full employment. The Keynesian theory suggests that macroeconomic stabilization is both desirable and possible. However, practical problems include the difficulty of measuring and forecasting the state of the economy and determining how much monetary and fiscal stimulus is needed at any particular time. Keynesian antirecessionary policies also lead to a higher price level than would occur in the absence of policy changes.

13. Following the oil price shocks of the 1970s, the Keynesian theory was modified to allow for supply shocks as well. Supply shocks lead to stagflation (a combination of inflation and recession) and pose great difficulties for stabilization policy.

KEY DIAGRAM 8

The Keynesian *AD–AS* Model

The Keynesian *AD–AS* framework shows how aggregate demand and aggregate supply interact to determine the price level and output in the Keynesian model.

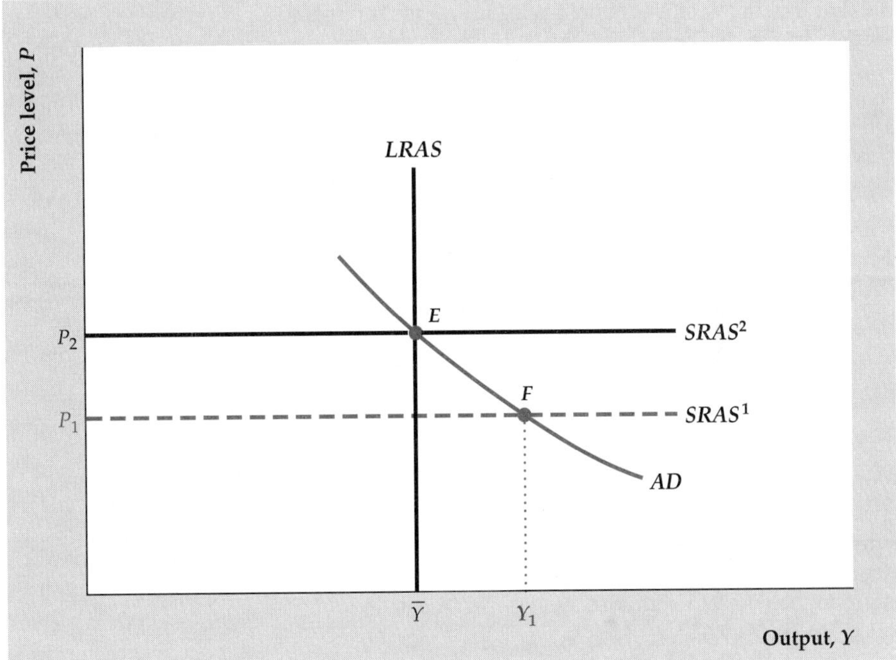

Diagram Elements

- The price level, P, is on the vertical axis, and output, Y, is on the horizontal axis.

- The aggregate demand (*AD*) curve, which shows the amount of output demanded at each price level, is identical to the *AD* curve in the classical model (Key Diagram 7, p. 388). An increase in the price level reduces the real money supply, shifts the *LM* curve up and to the left, and reduces the aggregate quantity of output demanded. Thus the *AD* curve slopes downward.

- The aggregate supply curve shows the amount of output supplied at each price level. In the short run monopolistically competitive firms that face menu costs meet demand for their output at fixed prices. Thus the short-run aggregate supply curve *SRAS* is horizontal at the initial price level.

- In the long run, after complete adjustment of prices, firms supply the full-employment level of output $\bar{Y}$ regardless of the price level. Thus the long-run aggregate supply curve *LRAS* is vertical at $Y = \bar{Y}$.

Factors that Shift the Curves

- The aggregate demand for output is determined by the intersection of the *IS* curve and the *LM* curve. For the given price level, any factor that shifts the *IS–LM* intersection to the right increases the aggregate demand for output and thus also shifts the *AD* curve to the right. Factors that shift the *AD* curve in the classical model, which also shift the Keynesian *AD* curve, are listed in Summary table 14 (p. 376). Note that Keynesians generally reject Ricardian equivalence, believing that a lump-sum tax cut increases aggregate demand and shifts the *AD* curve to the right.

- In the Keynesian model with monopolistic competition and menu costs, any factor that increases the price level in the short run, such as an increase in the price of oil, shifts the horizontal short-run aggregate supply (*SRAS*) curve up by the amount of the increase in the price level.

- Any factor that increases full-employment output $\bar{Y}$, such as a beneficial supply shock, shifts the long-run aggregate supply (*LRAS*) curve to the right. Changes in labor supply don't affect full-employment output in the Keynesian model with efficiency wages and thus don't affect the *LRAS* curve.

Analysis

■ In the short run the economy is located at the intersection of the *AD* curve and the initial *SRAS* curve, $SRAS^1$, at point *F*. At *F* the price remains at its initial level of P_1 and output is Y_1, which is greater than the full-employment level of output $\bar{Y}$. Output can exceed $\bar{Y}$ in the short run because monopolistically competitive firms facing menu costs are willing to meet the demand for their output at the initial price level.

■ If output exceeds $\bar{Y}$ in the short run, as at *F*, firms eventually raise their prices. In the long run, after complete adjustment of prices, the economy reaches general equilibrium at point *E*, where the *AD* curve intersects the long-run aggregate supply curve *LRAS*. At *E* the economy is at full employment, and the price level has risen from P_1 to P_2. Because the price level at which firms are willing to meet the demand has risen, the *SRAS* curve rises, from $SRAS^1$ to $SRAS^2$.

Key Terms

aggregate demand management, p. 426
aggregate demand shocks, p. 420
effective labor demand curve, p. 409
efficiency wage, p. 400
efficiency wage model, p. 398
effort curve, p. 399
labor hoarding, p. 423
macroeconomic stabilization, p. 426
marginal cost, p. 408
markup, p. 408
menu cost, p. 406
monopolistic competition, p. 405
multiplier, p. 416
perfect competition, p. 405
price stickiness, p. 404
real-wage rigidity, p. 398
turnover costs, p. 398

Review Questions

1. Define *efficiency wage*. What assumption about worker behavior underlies the efficiency wage theory? Why does it predict that the real wage will remain rigid even if there is an excess supply of labor?
2. How is full-employment output $\bar{Y}$ determined in the Keynesian model with efficiency wages? In this model, how is full-employment output affected by changes in productivity (supply shocks)? How is it affected by changes in labor supply?
3. What is price stickiness? Why do Keynesians believe that allowing for price stickiness in macroeconomic analysis is important?
4. Define *menu cost*. Why might small menu costs lead to price stickiness in monopolistically competitive markets but not in perfectly competitive markets? Why can a monopolistically competitive firm profitably meet demand at its fixed price when actual demand is greater than the firm anticipated?
5. What does the Keynesian model predict about monetary neutrality (both in the short run and in the long run)? Compare the Keynesian predictions about neutrality with those of the basic classical model and the extended classical model with misperceptions.
6. In the Keynesian model, how do increased government purchases affect output and the real interest rate in the short run? In the long run? How do increased government purchases affect the composition of output in the long run?
7. Describe three alternative responses available to policymakers when the economy is in recession. What are the advantages and disadvantages of each strategy? Be sure to discuss the effects on employment, the price level, and the composition of output. What are some of the practical difficulties in using macroeconomic stabilization policies to fight recessions?
8. Use the Keynesian model to explain the procyclical behavior of employment, money, inflation, and investment.

9. What does the Keynesian model predict about the cyclical behavior of average labor productivity? How does the idea of labor hoarding help bring the prediction of the model into conformity with the business cycle facts?
10. According to the Keynesian analysis, in what two ways does an adverse supply shock reduce output? What problems do supply shocks create for Keynesian stabilization policies?

Numerical Problems

1. A firm identifies the following relationship between the real wage it pays and the effort exerted by its workers.

Real Wage	Effort
8	7
10	10
12	15
14	17
16	19
18	20

The marginal product of labor for this firm is

$$MPN = \frac{E(100 - N)}{15},$$

where E is the effort level and N is the number of workers employed. If the firm can pay only one of the six wage levels shown, which should it choose? How many workers will it employ?

There are 200 workers in the town where the firm is located, all willing to work at a real wage of 8. Does this change your answer to the first part of this question? If so, how?

2. An economy is described by the following equations.

Desired consumption	$C^d = 130 + 0.5(Y - T) - 500r.$
Desired investment	$I^d = 100 - 500r.$
Government purchases	$G = 100.$
Taxes	$T = 100.$
Real money demand	$L = 0.5Y - 1000r.$
Money supply	$M = 1320.$
Full-employment output	$\bar{Y} = 500.$

Assume that expected inflation is zero so that money demand depends directly on the real interest rate.

a. Write the equations for the *IS* and *LM* curves. (These equations express the relationship between r and Y when the goods and asset markets are in equilibrium.)

b. Calculate the full-employment values of output, the real interest rate, the price level, consumption, and investment.

c. Now suppose that, because of investor optimism about the future marginal product of capital, the investment function becomes

$$I^d = 200 - 500r.$$

Assuming that the economy was initially at full employment, what are the new values of output, the real interest rate, the price level, consumption, and investment in the short run? In the long run? Show your results graphically.

3. Consider the following economy.

Desired consumption	$C^d = 325 + 0.5(Y - T) - 500r.$
Desired investment	$I^d = 200 - 500r.$
Government purchases	$G = 150.$
Taxes	$T = 150.$
Real money demand	$L = 0.5Y - 1000r.$
Money supply	$M = 6000.$
Full-employment output	$\bar{Y} = 1000.$

a. Calculate the full-employment values of the real interest rate, the price level, consumption, and investment.

b. Now suppose that government purchases are increased to 250, with no change in current taxes. Assuming that the economy was initially at full employment, what are the new values of output, the real interest rate, the price level, consumption, and investment in the short run? In the long run?

c. Repeat part (b) for an increase in the money supply to 7200. Assume that $G = 150$.

4. An economy is described by the following equations.

Desired consumption	$C^d = 300 + 0.5(Y - T) - 300r.$
Desired investment	$I^d = 100 - 100r.$
Government purchases	$G = 100.$
Taxes	$T = 100.$
Real money demand	$L = 0.5Y - 200r.$
Money supply	$M = 6300.$
Full-employment output	$\bar{Y} = 700.$

a. Write the equation for the aggregate demand curve. (*Hint:* Find the equations describing goods market equilibrium and asset market equilibrium. Use these two equations to eliminate the real interest rate. For any given price level the equation of the aggregate demand curve gives the level of output that satisfies both goods market equilibrium and asset market equilibrium.)

b. Suppose that $P = 15$. What are the short-run values of output, the real interest rate, consumption, and investment?
c. What are the long-run equilibrium values of output, the real interest rate, consumption, investment, and the price level?

5. (Appendix 12.A) Consider an economy in which all workers are covered by contracts that specify the nominal wage and give the employer the right to choose the amount of employment. The production function is

$$Y = 20\sqrt{N},$$

and the corresponding marginal product of labor is

$$MPN = \frac{10}{\sqrt{N}}.$$

Suppose that the nominal wage $W = 20$.
a. Derive an equation that relates the real wage to the amount of labor demanded by firms (the labor demand curve).
b. For the nominal wage of 20, what is the relation between the price level and the amount of labor demanded by firms?
c. What is the relation between the price level and the amount of output supplied by firms? Graph this relation.

Now suppose that the *IS* and *LM* curves of the economy (the goods market and asset market equilibrium conditions) are described by the following equations:

IS curve	$Y = 120 - 500r.$
LM curve	$M/P = 0.5Y - 500r.$

d. The money supply M is 300. Use the *IS* and *LM* equations to derive a relation between output Y and the price level P. This relation is the equation for the aggregate demand curve. Graph this relation on the same axis as the relation between the price level and the amount of output supplied by firms (the aggregate supply curve) from part (c).
e. What are the equilibrium values of the price level, output, employment, the real wage, and the real interest rate?
f. Now suppose that the money supply M is 135. What are the equilibrium values of the price level, output, employment, the real wage, and the real interest rate?

6. (Appendix 12.B) Consider the economy described in Numerical Problem 3.
a. What are the values of α_{IS}, β_{IS}, α_{LM}, β_{LM} and ℓ_r for this economy? (You'll have to refer back to Appendix 10.A for definitions of these coefficients.)
b. Suppose that the price level is fixed at $\bar{P} = 15$. What are the short-run equilibrium values of output and the real interest rate?
c. With the price level still fixed at $\bar{P} = 15$, suppose that government purchases increase from $G = 150$ to $G = 250$. What are the new values of α_{IS} and the short-run equilibrium level of output?
d. Use Eq. (12.B.10) to compute the government purchases multiplier. Use your answer to compute the short-run change in Y resulting from an increase in government purchases from $G = 150$ to $G = 250$. How does your answer here compare to your answer in part (c)?

Analytical Problems

1. According to the Keynesian *IS–LM* model, what is the effect of each of the following on output, the real interest rate, employment, and the price level? Distinguish between the short run and the long run.
a. Increased tax incentives for investment (the tax breaks for investment are offset by lump-sum tax increases that keep total current tax collections unchanged).
b. Increased tax incentives for saving [as in part (a), lump-sum tax increases offset the effect on total current tax collections].
c. A wave of investor pessimism about the future profitability of capital investments.
d. An increase in consumer confidence, as consumers expect that their incomes will be higher in the future.

2. According to the Keynesian *IS–LM* model, what is the effect of each of the following on output, the real interest rate, employment, and the price level? Distinguish between the short run and the long run.
a. Financial deregulation allows banks to pay a higher interest rate on checking accounts.
b. The introduction of sophisticated credit cards greatly reduces the amount of money that people need for transactions.
c. A severe water shortage causes sharp declines in agricultural output and increases in food prices.

d. A temporary beneficial supply shock affects most of the economy, but no individual firm is affected sufficiently to change its prices in the short run.

3. Suppose that the Fed has a policy of increasing the money supply when it observes that the economy is in recession. However, suppose that about six months are needed for an increase in the money supply to affect aggregate demand, which is about the same amount of time needed for firms to review and reset their prices. What effects will the Fed's policy have on output and price stability? Does your answer change if (a) the Fed has some ability to forecast recessions or (b) price adjustment takes longer than six months?

4. Classical economists argue that using fiscal policy to fight a recession doesn't make workers better off. Suppose, however, that the Keynesian model is correct. Relative to a policy of doing nothing, does an increase in government purchases that brings the economy to full employment make workers better off? In answering the question, discuss the effects of the fiscal expansion on the real wage, employment, consumption, and current and future taxes. How does your answer depend on (a) the direct benefits of the government spending program and (b) the speed with which prices adjust in the absence of fiscal stimulus?

5. Some labor economists argue that it is useful to think of the labor market as being divided into two sectors: a primary sector, where "good" (high-paying, long-term) jobs are located, and a secondary sector, which has "bad" (low-paying, short-term) jobs. Suppose that the primary sector has a high marginal product of labor and (because effort is costly for firms to monitor) firms pay an efficiency wage. The secondary sector has a low marginal product of labor and no efficiency wage; instead, the real wage in the secondary sector adjusts so that the quantities of labor demanded and supplied are equal in that sector. Workers are alike, and all would prefer to work in the primary sector. However, workers who can't find jobs in the primary sector work in the secondary sector.

What are the effects of each of the following on the real wage, employment, and output in both sectors?

a. Expansionary monetary policy increases the demand for primary sector output.

b. Immigration increases the labor force.

c. The effort curve changes so that a higher real wage is needed to elicit the greatest effort per dollar in the primary sector. Effort exerted at the higher real wage is the same as before the change in the effort curve.

d. There is a temporary productivity improvement in the primary sector.

e. There is a temporary productivity improvement in the secondary sector.

APPENDIX 12.A LABOR CONTRACTS AND NOMINAL-WAGE RIGIDITY

In the Keynesian theory the nonneutrality of money is a consequence of nominal rigidity. In this chapter we emphasized nominal-*price* rigidity. An alternative nominal rigidity that could account for the nonneutrality of money, which many Keynesians emphasize, is nominal-*wage* rigidity. Nominal-wage rigidity could reflect long-term labor contracts between firms and unions in which wages are set in nominal terms (the case we study here). In terms of the *AD–AS* framework the difference between nominal-price rigidity and nominal-wage rigidity is that nominal-price rigidity implies a horizontal short-run aggregate supply curve, whereas nominal-wage rigidity implies a short-run aggregate supply curve that slopes upward. However, this difference doesn't really affect the results obtained from the Keynesian model. In particular, in the Keynesian model with nominal-wage rigidity, money remains nonneutral in the short run and neutral in the long run.

The Short-Run Aggregate Supply Curve with Labor Contracts

In the United States most labor contracts specify employment conditions and nominal wages for a period of three years. Although labor contracts specify the nominal wage rate, they usually don't specify the total amount of employment. Instead, employers unilaterally decide how many hours will be worked and whether workers will be laid off. These factors imply that the short-run aggregate supply curve slopes upward.

We can see why the short-run aggregate supply curve slopes upward when labor contracts prespecify the nominal wage by considering what happens when the price level increases. With the nominal wage W already determined by the contract, an increase in the price level P reduces the real wage w, or W/P. In response to the drop in the real wage, firms demand more labor. Because firms unilaterally choose the level of employment, the increase in the amount of labor demanded leads to an increase in employment and therefore an increase in output. Thus an increase in the price level leads to an increase in the amount of output supplied, as shown by the *SRAS* curves in Fig. 12.A.1.

Nonneutrality of Money

Money is nonneutral in the short run in the model with long-term labor contracts, as illustrated in Fig. 12.A.1. The initial general equilibrium is at point *E*, where the initial aggregate demand curve AD^1 intersects the short-run aggregate supply curve $SRAS^1$. A 10% increase in the money supply shifts the *AD* curve up to AD^2. (For any level of output the price level is 10% higher on AD^2 than on AD^1.) In the short run the rise in the money supply increases the price level to P_2 and output to Y_2 at point *F*. Output is higher than its full-employment level at *F* because the rise in prices lowered the real wage, which leads firms to employ more labor and produce more output.

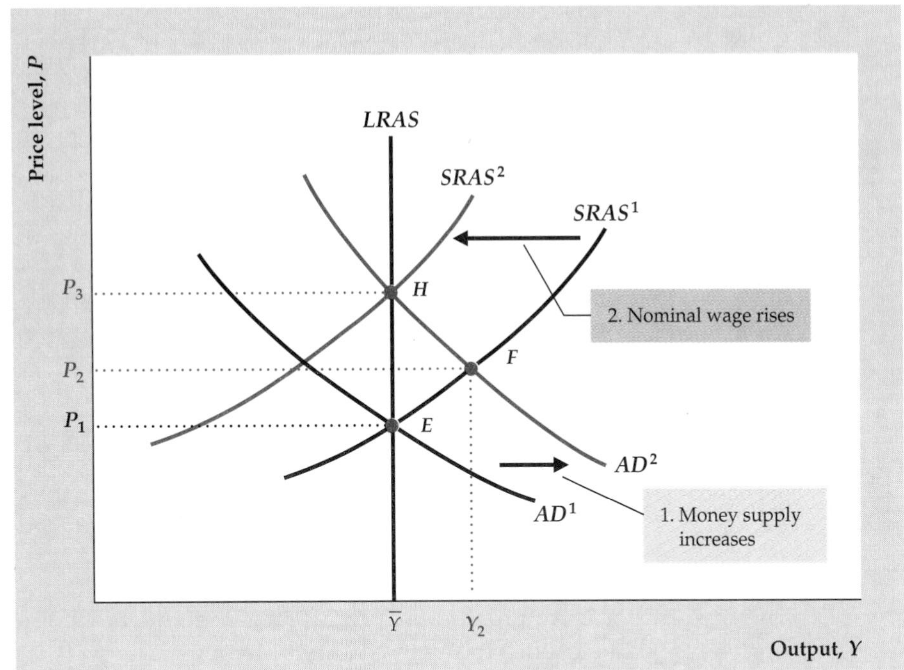

Figure 12.A.1 Monetary nonneutrality with long-term contracts
With long-term labor contracts that fix the nominal wage in the short run, an increase in the price level lowers the real wage and induces firms to employ more labor and produce more output. Thus the short-run aggregate supply curve $SRAS^1$ slopes upward. When nominal wages are rigid, money isn't neutral. From the initial equilibrium point *E* a 10% increase in the money supply shifts the *AD* curve up, from AD^1 to AD^2. In the short run both output and the price level increase, as shown by point *F*. Over time, contracts are renegotiated and nominal wages rise to match the increase in prices. As wages rise, the short-run aggregate supply curve shifts up, from $SRAS^1$ to $SRAS^2$, so that general equilibrium is restored at *H*. At *H* both the price level *P* and the nominal wage *W* have risen by 10%, so the real wage is the same as it was initially, and firms supply the full-employment level of output $\bar{Y}$.

At the short-run equilibrium point, *F*, however, workers will be dissatisfied because their real wages are lower than they had expected. Over time, as contracts are renewed or renegotiated, nominal wages will rise to offset the increase in prices. At any price level a rise in the nominal wage also raises the real wage, inducing firms to employ less labor and produce less output. Thus rising nominal wages cause the short-run aggregate supply curve to shift up, from $SRAS^1$ to $SRAS^2$. Eventually, general equilibrium is restored at point *H*.

In the long run at point *H*, the price level rises to P_3, which is 10% higher than its initial value P_1. At *H* the nominal wage *W* has also increased by 10% so that the real wage W/P has returned to its initial value. With the real wage back at its original value, firms employ the same amount of labor and produce the same amount of output ($\bar{Y}$) as they did at the initial equilibrium point, *E*. Thus, as in the Keynesian model based on efficiency wages and price stickiness, in the Keynesian model with nominal-wage rigidity, money is neutral in the long run but not in the short run.

Although nominal-wage rigidity arising from labor contracts can explain short-run monetary nonneutrality, some economists object to this explanation. One objection is that only about one-sixth of the labor force in the United States is unionized and covered by long-term labor contracts. However, many nonunion workers receive wages similar to those set in union contracts. For example, although most nonunion workers don't have formal wage contracts, they may have "implicit contracts" with their employers, or informal unwritten arrangements for comparable wages.

A second objection is that many labor contracts contain cost-of-living adjustments (COLAs), which tie the nominal wage to the overall price level, as measured, for example, by the consumer price index. Contracts with *complete* indexation increase the nominal wage by the same percentage as the increase in the price level. If wages are completely indexed to the price level, the short-run aggregate supply curve is vertical and money is neutral. To show why, let's suppose that the price level increases by 6%. If labor contracts are completely indexed, nominal wages also increase by 6% and the real wage W/P remains unchanged. Because the real wage doesn't change, firms choose the same levels of employment and output independent of the price level.

However, in most U.S. labor contracts wages aren't completely indexed to prices. In recent years, fewer than half the workers covered by major private industry bargaining agreements have had any COLA provisions at all.[16] Furthermore, most contracts with COLA provisions have partial rather than complete indexation. For example, under a contract that calls for 50% indexation, the nominal wage will increase by 50% of the overall rate of increase in prices. Thus, if the price level increases by 6%, the nominal wage increases by 3%. As a result, the real wage falls by 3% (a 3% increase in the nominal wage W minus a 6% increase in the price level P). The reduction in the real wage induces firms to increase employment and production. Thus with partial indexation the short-run aggregate supply curve again slopes upward, and money isn't neutral in the short run.

A third and final objection is that this theory predicts that real wages will be countercyclical, contrary to the business cycle fact that real wages are procyclical. For example, at point F in Fig. 12.A.1 output is higher than the full-employment level, but the real wage is lower than at full employment (indeed, the low real wage induces firms to produce the extra output). Thus the theory holds that real wages will fall in booms—that is, the real wage is countercyclical—which is inconsistent with the evidence.

However, perhaps both supply shocks and aggregate demand shocks affect real wages. For the real business cycle theory we showed that, if productivity shocks cause cyclical fluctuations, the real wage should be procyclical, perhaps strongly so. A combination of supply shocks (which cause the real wage to move procyclically) and aggregate demand shocks (which, as in Fig. 12.A.1, cause the real wage to move countercyclically) might average out to a real wage that is at least mildly procyclical. Some evidence for this view was provided in a recent study by Scott Sumner of Bentley College and Stephen Silver of Virginia Military Institute, which shows that the real wage has been procyclical during periods dominated by supply shocks but has been countercyclical during periods in which aggregate demand shocks were more important.[17]

---

16. The Bureau of Labor Statistics in the U.S. Department of Labor summarizes features of recent contracts in its monthly publication, *Compensation and Working Conditions* (prior to May 1991, this publication was called *Current Wage Developments*).

17. "Real Wages, Employment and the Phillips Curve," *Journal of Political Economy,* June 1989, pp. 706–720.

APPENDIX 12.B AN ALGEBRAIC VERSION OF THE SHORT-RUN KEYNESIAN MODEL

Further extending the algebraic analysis of Appendices 10.A and 11.A, this appendix examines short-run macroeconomic behavior in the Keynesian model. In the long run, the Keynesian model predicts that the economy reaches a general equilibrium much like that described in Appendix 10.A. Long-run equilibrium in the Keynesian model differs from the classical general equilibrium in only one respect: the full-employment level of employment $\bar{N}$ lies at the intersection of the labor demand curve and the efficiency wage line, rather than at the intersection of the labor demand and labor supply curves.

In the short run, the Keynesian model holds that prices are fixed and that output is determined by aggregate demand. Aggregate output demanded in turn is at the intersection of the *IS* and *LM* curves. Earlier we derived algebraic expressions for the *IS* and *LM* curves, Eqs. (10.A.14) and (10.A.19), as follows:

$$r = \alpha_{IS} - \beta_{IS}Y, \qquad IS \text{ curve;} \tag{12.B.1}$$

$$r = \alpha_{LM} - \left(\frac{1}{\ell_r}\right)\left(\frac{M}{P}\right) + \beta_{LM}Y, \qquad LM \text{ curve.} \tag{12.B.2}$$

In Eqs. (12.B.1) and (12.B.2), r is the real interest rate, Y is output, M/P is the real money supply, and α_{IS}, α_{LM}, β_{IS}, β_{LM} and ℓ_r are positive numbers defined in Appendix 10.A. The terms α_{IS} and α_{LM} capture factors that shift the *IS* curve (such as government purchases) and the *LM* curve (such as expected inflation), respectively.

As in Appendix 11.A, to find the aggregate quantity of output demanded, we set the right-hand sides of Eqs. (12.B.1) and (12.B.2) equal and solve for Y:

$$Y = \frac{\alpha_{IS} - \alpha_{LM} + (1/\ell_r)(M/P)}{\beta_{IS} + \beta_{LM}}. \tag{12.B.3}$$

In Eq. (12.B.3), which is the same as Eq. (11.A.3), Y is the aggregate quantity of output demanded at the intersection of the *IS* and *LM* curves. Equation (12.B.3) is also the equation for the aggregate demand curve; it states that, for constant money supply M, aggregate output demanded Y is a decreasing function of the price level P. Thus the aggregate demand curve slopes downward.

In the short-run Keynesian model, the price level is fixed at some initial level $\bar{P}$, so the Keynesian short-run aggregate supply curve is simply

$$P = \bar{P}. \tag{12.B.4}$$

We find the short-run equilibrium level of output by substituting the fixed price level $\bar{P}$ for the price level P in the aggregate demand curve, Eq. (12.B.3), to get

$$Y = \frac{\alpha_{IS} - \alpha_{LM} + (1/\ell_r)(M/\bar{P})}{\beta_{IS} + \beta_{LM}} \tag{12.B.5}$$

Equation (12.B.5) shows that the short-run equilibrium value of output in the Keynesian model increases in response to an increase in the nominal money supply *M*, or in response to any factor that shifts the *IS* curve up (an increase in α_{IS}) or the *LM* curve down (a decrease in α_{LM}).

To obtain the short-run equilibrium value of the real interest rate we substitute the short-run equilibrium level of output, from Eq. (12.B.5), into the *IS* curve, Eq. (12.B.1):

$$r = \frac{\alpha_{IS}\beta_{LM} + \beta_{IS}\alpha_{LM} - (\beta_{IS}/\ell_r)(M/\bar{P})}{\beta_{IS} + \beta_{LM}}. \qquad (12.B.6)$$

According to Eq. (12.B.6), the short-run equilibrium real interest rate in the Keynesian model increases in response to a decline in the nominal money supply *M*, or in response to any factor that shifts the *IS* curve up (an increase in α_{IS}) or the *LM* curve up (an increase in α_{LM}).

The Multiplier

In this chapter we defined the multiplier associated with any particular type of spending as the short-run change in total output resulting from a one-unit change in that type of spending. Here we derive the multiplier associated with government purchases *G*. We proceed in three steps: First, we calculate the effect on α_{IS} (the intercept of the *IS* curve in Eq. 12.B.1) of an increase in *G*. Then, we calculate the effect on the short-run equilibrium value of *Y*, shown by Eq. (12.B.5), of an increase in α_{IS}. Finally, we combine these two effects to calculate the effect on output *Y* of an increase in *G*.

To calculate the effect on α_{IS} of an increase in *G*, we repeat the definition of α_{IS}, Eq. (10.A.15):

$$\alpha_{IS} = \frac{c_0 + i_0 + G - c_Y t_0}{c_r + i_r}, \qquad (12.B.7)$$

where c_0, i_0, c_Y, c_r, i_r, and t_0 are parameters that determine desired consumption and desired investment (see Appendix 10.A). If *G* increases by ΔG, then α_{IS} increases by $\Delta G/(c_r + i_r)$, so

$$\Delta\alpha_{IS} = \frac{\Delta G}{c_r + i_r}. \qquad (12.B.8)$$

Next, observe from Eq. (12.B.5) that, if α_{IS} increases by $\Delta\alpha_{IS}$, output *Y* increases by $\Delta\alpha_{IS}/(\beta_{IS} + \beta_{LM})$, or

$$\Delta Y = \frac{\Delta\alpha_{IS}}{\beta_{IS} + \beta_{LM}}. \qquad (12.B.9)$$

Finally, if we substitute the right-hand side of Eq. (12.B.8) for $\Delta\alpha_{IS}$ on the right-hand side of Eq. (12.B.9) and then divide both sides of the resulting equation by ΔG, we obtain

$$\frac{\Delta Y}{\Delta G} = \frac{1}{(c_r + i_r)(\beta_{IS} + \beta_{LM})} \qquad (12.B.10)$$

The right-hand side of Eq. (12.B.10) is the increase in short-run equilibrium output Y that occurs for each one-unit increase in government purchases G. In other words, it is the government purchases multiplier. Similar calculations show that changes in desired consumption or desired investment (as reflected in the terms c_0 and i_0) have the same multiplier as government purchases.

Because c_r, i_r, β_{IS}, and β_{LM} all are positive, the multiplier is positive. However, depending on the specific values of those parameters, the multiplier may be greater or less than 1. A case in which the multiplier is likely to be large occurs when the LM curve is horizontal (that is, when the slope of the LM curve β_{LM} is 0). If the LM curve is horizontal, shifts in the IS curve induced by changes in spending have relatively large effects on output. Recall that Eq. (10.A.16) gives the slope of the IS curve β_{IS} as $[1 - (1 - t)c_Y]/(c_r + i_r)$. Making this substitution and setting the slope of the LM curve $\beta_{LM} = 0$ yield a simple form of the multiplier:

$$\frac{\Delta Y}{\Delta G} = \frac{1}{1-(1-t)c_Y}. \tag{12.B.11}$$

For example, suppose that the marginal propensity to consume $c_Y = 0.8$ and that the tax rate $t = 0.25$. Then the multiplier defined in Eq. (12.B.11) is $1/[(1 - (0.75)(0.8)] = 1/0.4$, or 2.5.

PART IV

Macroeconomic Policy: Its Environment and Institutions

CHAPTER 13

Unemployment and Inflation

The last several chapters focused on the concepts of the business cycle, macroeconomic stabilization, and classical and Keynesian approaches to business cycle analysis. Although these concepts are central to today's macroeconomics, actual policy discussions rarely involve such abstract terms. Policy debates tend to focus on highly publicized economic statistics such as inflation and unemployment. To make a stronger connection between business cycle theories and policy debates, we now take a closer look at unemployment and inflation, first together and then separately.

Unemployment and inflation—sometimes referred to as the "twin evils" of macroeconomics—are among the most difficult and politically sensitive economic issues that policymakers face. High rates of unemployment and inflation generate intense public concern because their effects are direct and visible: Almost everyone is affected by rising prices, and few workers can be confident that they will never lose their jobs.

Moreover, there is a long-standing idea in macroeconomics that unemployment and inflation are somehow related. In the first part of this chapter we discuss in some detail the concept of the Phillips curve—an empirical relationship between inflation and unemployment. According to the Phillips curve, inflation tends to be low when unemployment is high and high when unemployment is low. The Phillips curve relationship raises some important questions about how the economy works and how macroeconomic policies should be used.

We then look at unemployment and inflation separately. We examine the costs that each imposes on society and consider the options that policymakers have for dealing with these problems.

This chapter begins Part IV of the book, the purpose of which is to explore macroeconomic policymaking in greater detail. Following the discussion of inflation and unemployment in this chapter, Chapter 14 addresses the issue of how economic openness—as reflected in the trading and financial links among countries—affects macroeconomic policy. Chapter 15 takes a closer look at institutions and debates related to the making of monetary policy, and Chapter 16 provides a similar overview of fiscal policy.

13.1 UNEMPLOYMENT AND INFLATION: IS THERE A TRADE-OFF?

Newspaper editorials and public discussions about economic policy often refer to the "trade-off" between inflation and unemployment. The idea is that, to reduce inflation, the economy must tolerate high unemployment; or alternatively that, to reduce unemployment, more inflation must be accepted. This section examines the idea of an inflation–unemployment trade-off and its implications for macroeconomic policy.

The origin of the idea of a trade-off between inflation and unemployment was a 1958 article by economist A. W. Phillips.[1] Phillips examined ninety-seven years of British data on unemployment and nominal wage growth data; he found that, historically, unemployment tended to be low in years when nominal wages grew rapidly and high in years when nominal wages grew slowly. Economists who built on Phillips's work shifted its focus slightly by looking at the link between unemployment and inflation—that is, the growth rate of prices—rather than the link between unemployment and the growth rate of wages. During the late 1950s and the 1960s, many statistical studies examined inflation and unemployment data for numerous countries and time

1. "The Relation Between Unemployment and the Rate of Change of Money Wage Rates in the United Kingdom, 1861–1957," *Economica*, November 1958, pp. 283–299.

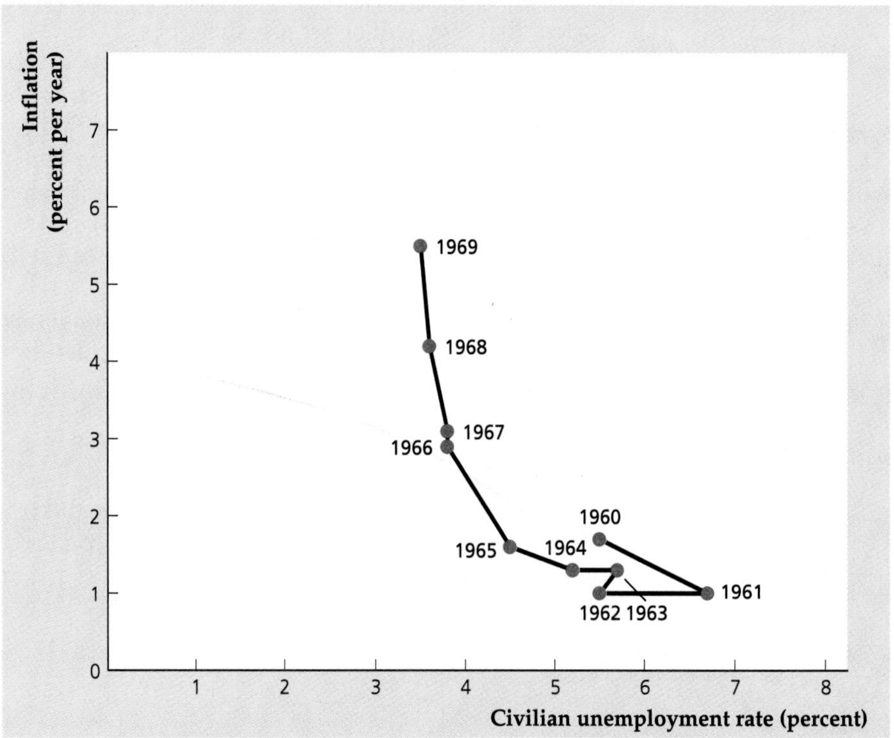

Figure 13.1
The Phillips curve and the U.S. economy during the 1960s
During the 1960s U.S. rates of inflation and unemployment seemed to lie along a Phillips curve. Inflation rose and unemployment fell fairly steadily during this decade, and policymakers apparently had decided to live with higher inflation in order to reduce unemployment.

Source: *Economic Report of the President,* February 1993; CPI inflation rate, year to year, Table B-59; Civilian unemployment rate, Table B-30.

periods, in many cases finding a negative relationship between the two variables. This negative empirical relationship between unemployment and inflation is known as the **Phillips curve.**

A striking example of a Phillips curve, shown in Fig. 13.1, occurred in the United States during the 1960s. The U.S. economy expanded throughout most of the 1960s, with unemployment falling and inflation rising steadily. In Fig. 13.1, the inflation rate is measured on the vertical axis, and the unemployment rate is measured on the horizontal axis. Note that years, such as 1961, that had high unemployment also had low inflation, and that years, such as 1969, that had high inflation also had low unemployment. The data produce an almost perfect downward-sloping relation between inflation and unemployment—that is, a Phillips curve. The experience of the United States in the 1960s, which came after Phillips's article had been published and widely disseminated, was viewed by many as a confirmation of his basic finding.

The policy implications of these findings were much debated. Initially, the Phillips curve seemed to offer policymakers a "menu" of combinations of inflation and unemployment from which they could choose. Indeed, during the 1960s some economists argued that, by accepting a modest amount of inflation, macroeconomic policymakers could keep the unemployment rate low indefinitely. This belief seemed to be borne out during the 1960s, when rising inflation was accompanied by falling unemployment.

In the following decades, however, this relationship between inflation and unemployment failed to hold: Figure 13.2 shows inflation and unemployment for the period 1970–1992. During those years, unlike the 1960s, there

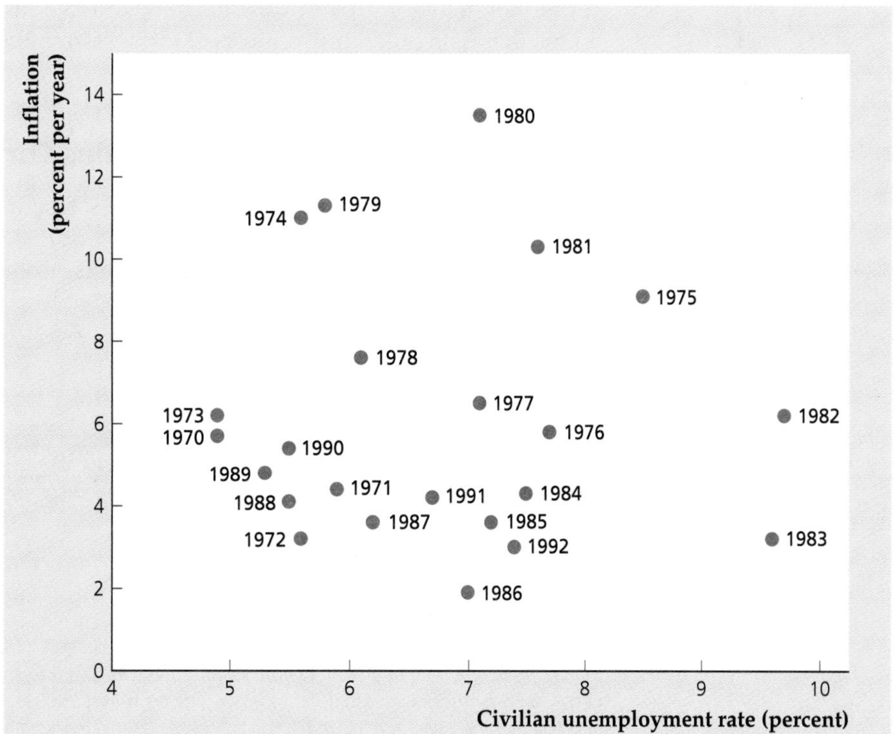

Figure 13.2
Inflation and unemployment in the United States, 1970–1992
The figure shows the combinations of inflation and unemployment experienced in the United States each year from 1970 to 1992. Unlike during the 1960s (see Fig. 13.1), after 1970 a clear negative relationship between inflation and unemployment in the United States didn't seem to exist.

Source: *Economic Report of the President*, February 1993; CPI inflation rate, year to year, Table B-59 (1992 rate from *Survey of Current Business*); Civilian unemployment rate, Table B-30.

seemed to be no reliable relationship between unemployment and inflation. From the perspective of the Phillips curve the most puzzling period was the mid 1970s, during which the country experienced high inflation and high unemployment simultaneously (stagflation). In 1975, for example, unemployment reached 8.5% of the labor force and the annual inflation rate was 9.1%. High unemployment, together with high inflation, is inconsistent with the Phillips curve.

The original empirical results of Phillips and others who extended his work, together with the unexpected experience of the U.S. economy after 1970, raises at least three important questions:

- Why was the original Phillips curve relationship between inflation and unemployment frequently observed historically, as in the cases of Great Britain in the century before 1958 and the United States in the 1960s?
- Why did the simple negative relationship between inflation and unemployment that seemed to exist during the 1960s in the United States vanish after 1970? In other words, was there in fact no systematic relationship between inflation and unemployment in the U.S. economy after 1970?
- Does the Phillips curve actually provide a menu of choices from which policymakers can choose? For example, by electing to maintain a high inflation rate can policymakers guarantee a *permanently* low rate of unemployment?

Economic theory provides reasonable answers to these questions; in particular, it explains the collapse of the Phillips curve after 1970. Interestingly, the key economic analysis of the Phillips curve—which predicted that this relationship would not be stable—was done during the 1960s, *before* the Phillips curve had actually broken down. Thus we have at least one example of economic theorists predicting an important development in the economy that policymakers and the public didn't anticipate.

The Expectations-Augmented Phillips Curve

Although the Phillips curve seemed to describe adequately the unemployment–inflation relationship in the United States in the 1960s, during the second half of the decade some economists, notably Milton Friedman[2] of the University of Chicago and Edmund Phelps[3] of Columbia University, questioned the logic of the Phillips curve. Friedman and Phelps argued—purely on the basis of economic theory—that there should not be a stable negative relationship between inflation and unemployment. Instead, a negative relationship should exist between *unanticipated* inflation (the difference between the actual and expected inflation rates) and *cyclical* unemployment (the difference between the actual and natural unemployment rates).[4]

2. "The Role of Monetary Policy," *American Economic Review*, March 1968, pp. 1–17.
3. "Money Wage Dynamics and Labor Market Equilibrium," in Edmund Phelps, ed., *Microeconomic Foundations of Employment and Inflation Theory*, New York: W.W. Norton, 1970, pp. 124–166.
4. In Chapter 3 we defined cyclical unemployment. Recall that the natural rate of unemployment is the unemployment rate that exists when output is at its full-employment level. The natural rate exceeds zero because of frictional and structural unemployment, also defined in Chapter 3.

Although these distinctions appear to be merely technical, they are crucial in understanding the relationship between the actual rates of inflation and unemployment.

Before discussing the significance of their analyses, we need to explain how Friedman and Phelps arrived at their conclusions. To do so we use the extended classical model, which includes the misperceptions theory. (Analytical Problem 3 at the end of the chapter asks you to perform a similar analysis using the Keynesian model.) We proceed in two steps, first considering an economy at full employment with steady, fully anticipated inflation. In this economy, both unanticipated inflation and cyclical unemployment are zero. Second, we consider what happens when aggregate demand growth increases unexpectedly. In this case both positive unanticipated inflation (inflation greater than expected) and negative cyclical unemployment (actual unemployment lower than the natural rate) occur. This outcome confirms the Friedman–Phelps point that a negative relationship exists between unanticipated inflation and cyclical unemployment.

We develop the first step of this analysis by using the extended classical model to analyze an economy with steady inflation (see Fig. 13.3). We assume that this economy is in full-employment equilibrium in which the money supply has been growing at 10% per year for many years and is expected to continue to grow at this rate indefinitely. With the money supply growing by 10% per year, the aggregate demand curve shifts up by 10% each year, from AD^1 in year 1 to AD^2 in year 2, and so on. For simplicity we assume that full-employment output $\bar{Y}$ is constant, but relaxing that assumption wouldn't affect our basic conclusions.

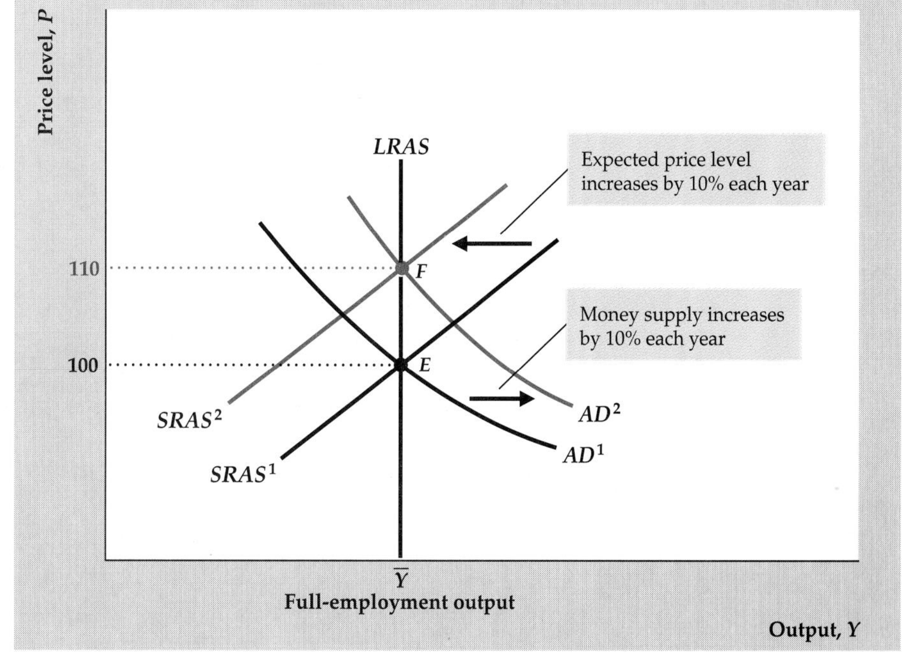

Figure 13.3
Ongoing inflation in the extended classical model

If the money supply grows by 10% every year, the *AD* curve shifts up by 10% every year, from AD^1 in year 1 to AD^2 in year 2, and so on. If the money supply has been growing by 10% per year for some time and the rate of inflation has been 10% for some time, the expected rate of inflation is also 10%. Thus the expected price level also grows by 10% each year, from 100 in year 1 to 110 in year 2, and so on. The 10% annual increase in the expected price level shifts the *SRAS* curve up by 10% each year, for example, from $SRAS^1$ in year 1 to $SRAS^2$ in year 2. The economy remains in full-employment equilibrium at the intersection of the *AD* curve and the *SRAS* curve in each year (point *E* in year 1 and point *F* in year 2), with output at $\bar{Y}$, unemployment at the natural rate of unemployment $\bar{u}$, and inflation and expected inflation both at 10% per year.

In Fig. 13.3 the short-run aggregate supply (*SRAS*) curve shifts up by 10% each year. Why? With the growth in money supply fully anticipated, there are no misperceptions. Instead, people expect the price level to rise by 10% per year (a 10% inflation rate), which in turn causes the *SRAS* curve to shift up by 10% per year. With no misperceptions, the economy remains at full employment with output at $\bar{Y}$. For example, when the expected price level is 100 in year 1, the *SRAS* curve is $SRAS^1$. At point *E* the price level is 100 (the same as the expected price level) and output is $\bar{Y}$. In year 2 the expected price level is 110, and the *SRAS* curve is $SRAS^2$. In year 2 equilibrium occurs at point *F*, again with output of $\bar{Y}$ and equal expected and actual price levels. Each year, both the *AD* curve and the *SRAS* curve shift up by 10%, increasing the actual price level and expected price level by 10% and maintaining output at its full-employment level.

What happens to unemployment in this economy? Because output is continuously at its full-employment level $\bar{Y}$, unemployment remains at the natural rate $\bar{u}$. With unemployment at its natural rate, cyclical unemployment is zero. Hence this economy has zero unanticipated inflation *and* zero cyclical unemployment.

Against this backdrop of 10% monetary growth and 10% inflation, suppose now that in year 2 the money supply grows by 15% rather than by the expected 10% (Fig. 13.4). In this case, instead of being 10% higher than AD^1 (as shown by $AD^{2,old}$), the aggregate demand curve in year 2 will be 15% higher than AD^1 (as shown by $AD^{2,new}$). If this increase in the rate of monetary growth is *unanticipated* at the beginning of year 2, the expected price level in year 2 remains at 110, and the short-run aggregate supply curve is

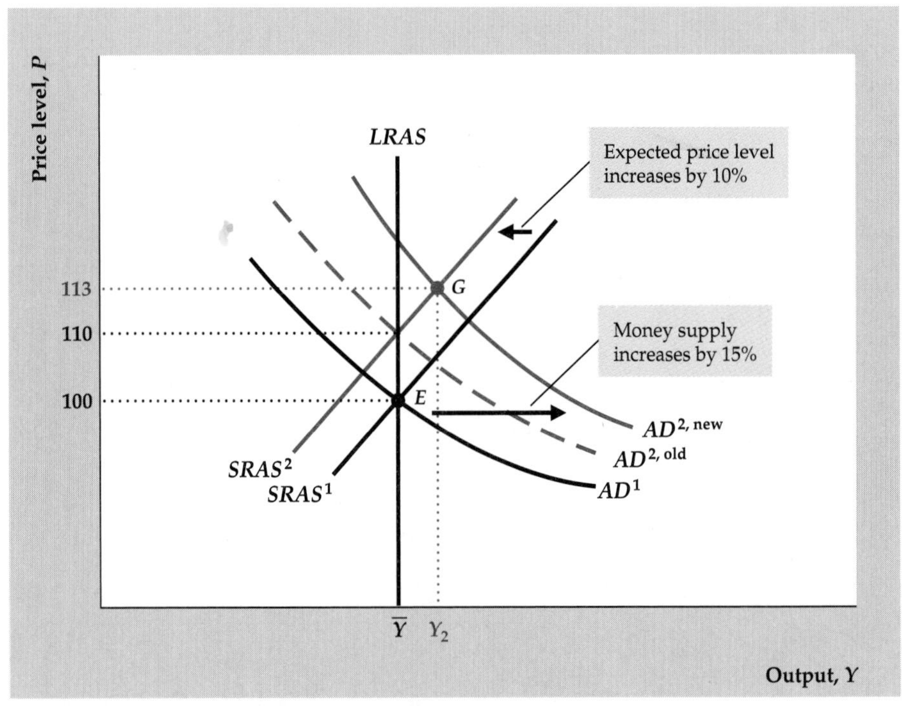

Figure 13.4
Unanticipated inflation in the extended classical model
If the money supply has been growing by 10% per year for a long time and is expected to continue growing by 10%, the expected price level increases by 10% each year. The 10% increase in the expected price level shifts the *SRAS* curve up from $SRAS^1$ in year 1 to $SRAS^2$ in year 2. Then, if the money supply actually increases by 15% in year 2 rather than by the expected 10%, the *AD* curve is $AD^{2,new}$ rather than $AD^{2,old}$. As a result of higher-than-expected money growth, output increases above $\bar{Y}$ in year 2 and the price level increases to 113, at point *G*. Because the price level rises by 13% rather than the expected 10%, unanticipated inflation is 3% in year 2. This unanticipated inflation is associated with output higher than $\bar{Y}$ and unemployment below the natural rate $\bar{u}$ (negative cyclical unemployment).

$SRAS^2$, as before. The short-run equilibrium in year 2 is at point G, the intersection of the $AD^{2,\text{new}}$ and $SRAS^2$ curves. At G the price level is 113, so the actual rate of inflation in year 2 is 13%. Because the expected rate of inflation was 10%, the 13% inflation rate implies unanticipated inflation of 3% in year 2. Further, because output is above its full-employment level $\bar{Y}$ at G, the actual unemployment rate is below the natural rate and cyclical unemployment is negative.

Why is output above its full-employment level in year 2? Note that, in year 2, the 13% rate of inflation is less than the 15% rate of money growth but greater than the 10% expected rate of inflation. Because the price level grows by less than does the nominal money supply in year 2, the real money supply M/P increases, lowering the real interest rate and raising the aggregate quantity of goods demanded above $\bar{Y}$. At the same time, because the price level grows by more than expected, the aggregate quantity of goods supplied also is greater than $\bar{Y}$ as producers are fooled into thinking that the relative prices of their products have increased.

Producers can't be fooled about price behavior indefinitely, however. In the long run producers learn the true price level, the economy returns to full employment, and the inflation rate again equals the expected inflation rate, as in Fig. 13.3. In the meantime, however, as long as actual output is higher than full-employment output $\bar{Y}$, and actual unemployment is below the natural rate $\bar{u}$, the actual price level must be higher than the expected price level. Indeed, according to the misperceptions theory, output can be higher than $\bar{Y}$ only when prices are higher than expected (and therefore when inflation is also higher than expected).

Thus in this economy, when the public correctly predicts aggregate demand growth and inflation, unanticipated inflation is zero, actual unemployment equals the natural rate, and cyclical unemployment is zero (Fig. 13.3). However, if aggregate demand growth unexpectedly speeds up, the economy faces a period of positive unanticipated inflation and negative cyclical unemployment (Fig. 13.4). Similarly, an unexpected slowdown in aggregate demand growth could occur, causing the AD curve to rise more slowly than expected; for a time unanticipated inflation would be negative (actual inflation less than expected) and cyclical unemployment would be positive (actual unemployment greater than the natural rate).

The relationship between unanticipated inflation and cyclical unemployment implied by this analysis is

$$\pi - \pi^e = -h(u - \bar{u}),$$

where

$\pi - \pi^e$ = unanticipated inflation (the difference between actual inflation π and expected inflation π^e);

$u - \bar{u}$ = cyclical unemployment (the difference between the actual unemployment rate u and the natural unemployment rate $\bar{u}$);

h = a positive number that measures the strength of the relationship between unanticipated inflation and cyclical unemployment.

The preceding equation expresses mathematically the idea that unanticipated inflation will be positive when cyclical unemployment is negative, negative when cyclical unemployment is positive, and zero when cyclical unemployment is zero.[5] If we add π^e to both sides of the equation, it becomes

$$\pi = \pi^e - h(u - \bar{u}). \tag{13.1}$$

Equation (13.1) describes the expectations-augmented Phillips curve. According to the **expectations-augmented Phillips curve,** actual inflation π exceeds expected inflation π^e if the actual unemployment rate u is less than the natural rate $\bar{u}$; and actual inflation is less than expected inflation if the unemployment rate exceeds the natural rate.

The Shifting Phillips Curve

Let's return to the original Phillips curve, which links the levels of inflation and unemployment in the economy. The insight gained from the Friedman–Phelps analysis is that the relationship illustrated by the Phillips curve depends on the expected rate of inflation and the natural rate of unemployment. If either factor changes, the Phillips curve will shift.

Changes in the Expected Rate of Inflation. Figure 13.5 shows how a change in the expected inflation rate affects the relationship between inflation

5. The equation also implies that the relationship between unanticipated inflation and cyclical unemployment is linear, but this is for convenience only. The relationship of the two variables might as easily be a curve as a line.

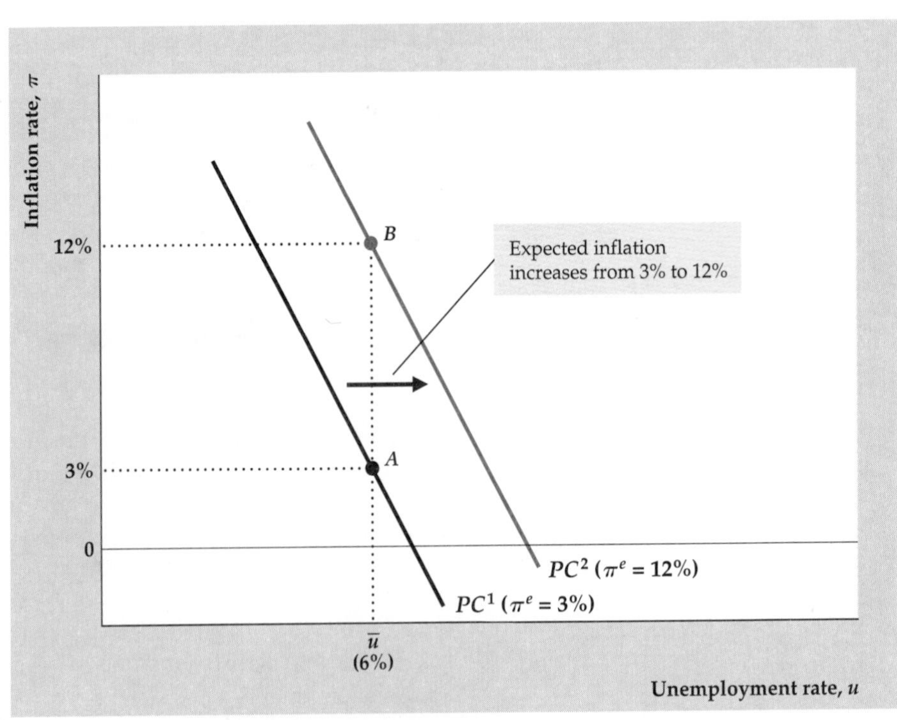

Figure 13.5
The shifting Phillips curve: An increase in expected inflation
The Friedman–Phelps theory implies that there is a different Phillips curve for every expected inflation rate. For example, PC^1 is the Phillips curve when the expected rate of inflation is 3%. To verify this claim, note from Eq. (13.1) that, when the actual unemployment rate equals the natural rate $\bar{u}$ (6% here), the actual inflation rate equals the expected inflation rate. At point *A*, the unemployment rate equals the natural rate and the inflation rate equals 3% on PC^1, so the expected inflation rate is 3% on PC^1. Similarly, at point *B* on PC^2, where the unemployment rate equals its natural rate, the inflation rate is 12%, so the expected inflation rate is 12% along PC^2. Thus an increase in the expected inflation rate from 3% to 12% shifts the Phillips curve up and to the right, from PC^1 to PC^2.

and unemployment, according to the Friedman–Phelps theory. The curve PC^1 is the Phillips curve for an expected rate of inflation of 3%. What identifies the expected rate of inflation as 3% along PC^1? Equation (13.1) indicates that, when the actual unemployment rate equals the natural rate (6% in this example), the actual inflation rate equals the expected inflation rate. Thus to determine the expected inflation rate on a Phillips curve, we find the inflation rate at the point where the actual unemployment rate equals the natural rate. For instance, at point *A* on curve PC^1 the unemployment rate equals the natural rate, and the actual and expected rates of inflation both equal 3%. As long as the expected inflation rate remains at 3% (and the natural unemployment rate remains at 6%), the Phillips curve PC^1 will describe the relationship between inflation and unemployment.

Now suppose that the expected rate of inflation increases from 3% to 12%. Figure 13.5 shows that this 9 percentage point increase in the expected rate of inflation shifts the Phillips curve up by 9 percentage points at each level of the unemployment rate, from PC^1 to PC^2. When the actual unemployment rate equals the natural rate on PC^2 (at point *B*), the inflation rate is 12%, confirming that the expected inflation rate is 12% along PC^2. Comparing PC^2 and PC^1 reveals that an increase in the expected inflation rate shifts the Phillips curve relationship between inflation and unemployment up and to the right.

Changes in the Natural Rate of Unemployment. The Phillips curve relationship between inflation and unemployment also is shifted by changes in the natural unemployment rate, as illustrated by Fig. 13.6. The Phillips curve PC^1 shows a natural unemployment rate at 6% and an expected inflation rate at

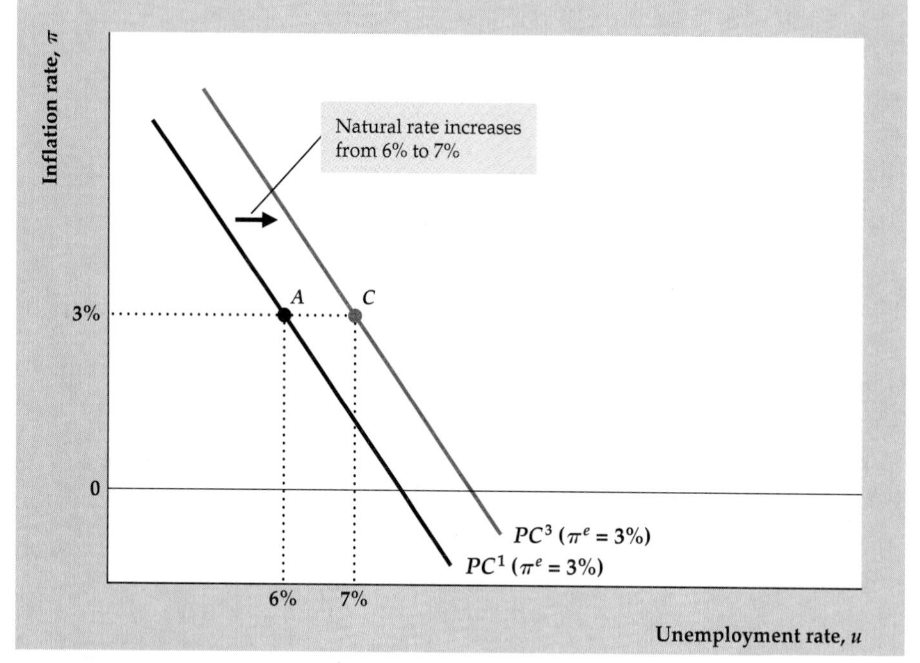

Figure 13.6
The shifting Phillips curve: An increase in the natural unemployment rate
According to the Friedman–Phelps theory, an increase in the natural unemployment rate shifts the Phillips curve up and to the right. At point *A* on PC^1, the actual inflation rate and the expected inflation rate are equal at 3%, so the natural unemployment rate equals the actual unemployment rate at *A*, or 6%. Thus PC^1 is the Phillips curve when the natural unemployment rate is 6% and the expected inflation rate is 3%, as in Fig. 13.5. If the natural unemployment rate increases to 7%, with expected inflation unchanged, the Phillips curve shifts to PC^3. At point *C* on PC^3, both expected and actual inflation equal 3%, so the natural unemployment rate equals the actual unemployment rate at *C*, or 7%.

3% (PC^1 in Fig. 13.6 is the same as PC^1 in Fig. 13.5). Now suppose that the natural unemployment rate increases to 7% but that the expected inflation rate remains unchanged at 3%. As Fig. 13.6 shows, the increase in the natural unemployment rate causes the Phillips curve to shift, from PC^1 to PC^3.

To confirm that the natural unemployment rate corresponding to Phillips curve PC^3 in Fig. 13.6 is 7%, look at point *C* on PC^3: At *C*, where the actual and expected inflation rates are equal, the unemployment rate is 7%. Thus the natural unemployment rate associated with Phillips curve PC^3 is 7%. This example illustrates that—like an increase in expected inflation—an increase in the natural unemployment rate causes the Phillips curve relationship between inflation and unemployment to shift up and to the right.

Supply Shocks and the Phillips Curve. The Friedman–Phelps theory holds that changes in either expected inflation or the natural unemployment rate will shift the Phillips curve. One type of economic disturbance that is likely to affect both factors is a supply shock. Recall that an adverse supply shock causes a burst of inflation, which may lead people to expect higher inflation.[6] An adverse supply shock also tends to increase the natural unemployment rate, although the reasons for this effect are different for the classical and Keynesian models.

Recall that, from the classical perspective, an adverse supply shock raises the natural rate of unemployment by increasing the degree of mismatch between workers and jobs. For example, an oil price shock eliminates jobs in heavy-energy-using industries but increases employment in energy-providing industries.

In the Keynesian model, recall that much of the unemployment that exists even when the economy is at the full-employment level is blamed on rigid real wages. In particular, if the efficiency wage is above the market-clearing real wage, the amount of labor supplied at the efficiency wage will exceed the amount of labor demanded at that wage (Fig. 12.2), leading to persistent structural unemployment. An adverse supply shock has no effect on the supply of labor,[7] but it does reduce the marginal product of labor and thus labor demand. With a rigid efficiency wage, the drop in labor demand increases the excess of labor supplied over labor demanded, raising the amount of unemployment that exists when the economy is at full employment. Thus, as in the classical model, the Keynesian model predicts that an adverse supply shock will raise the natural unemployment rate.

Because adverse supply shocks raise both expected inflation and the natural unemployment rate, according to the Friedman–Phelps analysis they should cause the Phillips curve to shift up and to the right. Similarly, beneficial supply shocks should shift the Phillips curve down and to the left. Overall, the Phillips curve should be particularly unstable during periods of supply shocks.

The Shifting Phillips Curve in Practice. Our analysis of the shifting Phillips curve (Figs. 13.5 and 13.6) helps answer the basic questions about the

---

6. The inflationary impact of a supply shock will be reinforced if, in an attempt to moderate the rise in unemployment caused by the shock, the central bank increases the money supply.

7. This statement is strictly true only for a temporary adverse supply shock. A permanent adverse supply shock, if it reduces expected future wages, would increase labor supply and thus cause an even larger rise in the natural rate of unemployment.

Phillips curve raised earlier in the chapter. The first question was: Why did the original Phillips curve relationship between inflation and unemployment apply to many historical cases, including the United States during the 1960s? The Friedman–Phelps analysis shows that a negative relationship between the levels of inflation and unemployment holds *as long as expected inflation and the natural unemployment rate are approximately constant.* As shown in Fig. 13.9 later in this chapter, the natural unemployment rate changes relatively slowly, and during the 1960s it was approximately constant. Expected inflation probably was also nearly constant in the United States in the 1960s, because at that time people were used to low and stable inflation and inflation remained low for most of the decade. Thus, not surprisingly, the U.S. inflation and unemployment data for the 1960s seem to lie along a single Phillips curve (Fig. 13.1).

The second question was: Why did the Phillips curve relationship, so apparent in the United States in the 1960s, seem to disappear after 1970 (Fig. 13.2)? The answer suggested by the Friedman–Phelps analysis is that, in the two decades after 1970, the expected inflation rate and the natural unemployment rate varied considerably more than they had in the 1960s, causing the Phillips curve relationship to shift erratically.

Contributing to the shifts of the Phillips curve after 1970 were the two large supply shocks associated with sharp increases in the price of oil that hit the U.S. economy in 1973–1974 and 1979–1980. Recall that adverse supply shocks are likely to increase both expected inflation and the natural rate of unemployment, shifting the Phillips curve up and to the right. Oil prices also varied considerably during the 1980s, declining precipitously in the middle of the decade and then temporarily rising again after the Iraqi invasion of Kuwait in August 1990.

Beyond the direct effects of supply shocks, other forces may have increased the variability of expected inflation and the natural unemployment rate after 1970. As we discuss later in the chapter, the natural unemployment rate rose during this period as a result of labor force composition changes and faster structural changes in the economy.

Expected inflation probably varied more after 1970 because actual inflation varied more (see Fig. 2.3 for the U.S. inflation rate for 1960–1992). After being relatively low for a long time, inflation, driven by monetary and fiscal policies that had probably been over-expansionary for several years, emerged as a problem at the end of the 1960s.[8] The 1970s were a period of high and erratic inflation, the result of the oil price shocks and macroeconomic policies that again were probably too expansionary, especially in the latter part of the decade. In contrast, following the tough anti-inflationary policies of the Federal Reserve during 1979–1982, inflation returned to a relatively low level during the 1980s. To the extent that expected inflation followed the path of actual inflation—high and erratic in the 1970s, low in the 1980s—our analysis suggests that the Phillips curve relationship between inflation and unemployment wouldn't have been stable over the period.

Does the unstable Phillips curve during 1970–1992 imply that there was no systematic relationship between inflation and unemployment during that period? The answer is no. According to the Friedman–Phelps analysis, a

8. Two sources of fiscal expansion during the 1960s were military expenditures associated with the Vietnam War and increased social spending for the Great Society programs.

negative relationship between *unanticipated* inflation and *cyclical* unemployment should appear in the data, even if expected inflation and the natural unemployment rate are changing. Measures of unanticipated inflation and cyclical unemployment for each year during the period 1970–1992 are shown in Fig. 13.7. These measures are approximate because we can't directly observe either expected inflation (needed to calculate unanticipated inflation) or the natural unemployment rate (needed to find cyclical unemployment). We assumed that expected inflation for each year was the average inflation rate of the previous two years, and we used estimates of the natural unemployment rate presented later in the chapter in Fig. 13.9.

Figure 13.7 suggests that, despite the instability of the traditional Phillips curve relationship between inflation and unemployment, a negative relationship between *unanticipated* inflation and *cyclical* unemployment did exist during the period 1970–1992, as predicted by the Friedman–Phelps analysis (compare Fig. 13.7 to Fig. 13.2).[9] In particular, note that inflation was much

9. In Fig. 13.7, the points corresponding to the years 1974, 1975, and 1980 lie somewhat above the curve defined by the rest of the points. Note that all three of those years follow oil price shocks, which were largely unexpected when they occurred. Our estimates of expected inflation for those years—based on inflation rates in the previous two years—may be too low, resulting in estimates of unanticipated inflation for those years that are too high. The years 1974 and 1975 also follow the 1971–1974 price control period, during which inflation was kept artificially low by government restrictions on price increases, so that again we may have underestimated the inflation rate actually expected in 1974 and 1975.

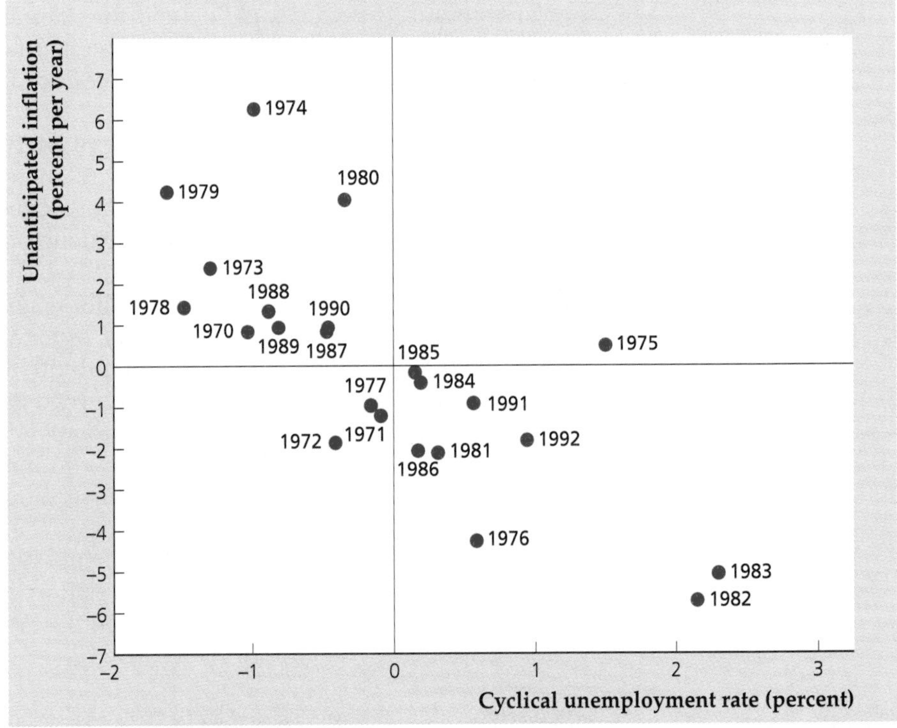

Figure 13.7
The expectations-augmented Phillips curve in the United States, 1970–1992
The expectations-augmented Phillips curve is a negative relationship between unanticipated inflation and cyclical unemployment. Shown is this relationship for the years 1970–1992 in the United States. Unanticipated inflation equals actual minus expected inflation, where expected inflation in any year is measured here as the average inflation rate for the preceding two years. Cyclical unemployment for each year is actual unemployment minus an estimate of the natural unemployment rate for that year (see Fig. 13.9). Note that years in which unanticipated inflation is high usually are years in which cyclical unemployment is low.

Source: Unemployment rate, all civilian workers, 1993 *Economic Report of the President,* Table B-37; natural rate of unemployment: see Figure 13.9; CPI inflation rate, year to year, all items (CPI-U): 1970–1991 from 1993 *Economic Report of the President,* Table B-59, 1992 value from *Survey of Current Business.*

lower than expected and that cyclical unemployment was high during 1982 and 1983, years that followed Fed Chairman Volcker's attempt to reduce inflation through tight monetary policy.

Macroeconomic Policy and the Phillips Curve

We have addressed two of the questions about the Phillips curve raised earlier in the chapter—the questions of why the Phillips curve was observed in historical data and why it seemed to shift after 1970. We still must answer the third question: Can the Phillips curve be thought of as a "menu" of inflation–unemployment combinations from which policymakers can choose? For example, can policymakers reduce the unemployment rate by increasing the rate of inflation (moving up and to the left along the Phillips curve)?

According to the expectations-augmented Phillips curve, unemployment will fall below the natural rate only when inflation is unanticipated. So the question becomes: Can macroeconomic policy be used systematically to create unanticipated inflation?

Classical and Keynesian economists disagree on the answer to this question. Classicals argue that wages and prices adjust quickly in response to new economic information, including information about changes in government policies. Furthermore, classicals believe that people have rational expectations, meaning that they make intelligent forecasts of future policy changes. Because prices and price-level expectations respond quickly to new information, the government can't keep actual inflation above expected inflation—as would be needed to drive unemployment below the natural rate—except perhaps for a very short time. According to classicals, policies (such as more rapid monetary expansion) that increase the growth rate of aggregate demand act primarily to raise actual *and* expected inflation and so do not lead to a sustained reduction in unemployment. Because any systematic attempt to affect the unemployment rate will be thwarted by the rapid adjustment of inflation expectations, classicals conclude that the Phillips curve does *not* represent a usable trade-off for policymakers. (Box 13.1, on the next page, explores a general lesson for policymakers of the shifting Phillips curve.)

In contrast, Keynesians contend that policymakers do have some ability—in the short run, at least—to create unanticipated inflation and thus to bring unemployment below the natural rate.[10] Although many Keynesians accept the notion that people have rational expectations, they argue that the expected rate of inflation that should be included in the expectations-augmented Phillips curve is the forecast of inflation made at the time that the oldest sticky prices in the economy were set. Because of price stickiness, when policymakers cause aggregate demand to rise above the expected level, time is needed for prices to fully reflect this new information. In the meantime some prices reflect older information, and the rate of inflation is higher than the expected inflation rate based on this older information. In response to increased inflation, therefore, unemployment may remain below the natural rate for a while.

---

10. As we discussed in Chapter 12, Keynesian economists also believe that macroeconomic policy can be used to return the unemployment rate to its natural level, if the economy starts out in a recession or a boom.

BOX 13.1

The Lucas Critique

Suppose that you observed, in a particular season, that the Houston Oilers of the National Football League punted 100% of the time when faced with fourth down in their own territory. Could you safely conclude, based on this empirical evidence, that the Oilers would punt on fourth down in their own territory next season? In most cases, you probably could safely make this prediction, even if you didn't know anything about football. But what if, during the off-season, the rules were changed to allow six attempts to make a first down? Would you still expect the Oilers to follow historical precedent and punt on fourth down? Certainly no one familiar with football would expect them to follow their old strategy, which would be foolish under the new rules. The simple lesson from this example is that, when the rules of the game change, people's behavior also changes.*

In an influential article,† Robert E. Lucas, Jr., of the University of Chicago, applied this lesson to macroeconomic policymaking. Frequently, in attempting to forecast the effects of a new set of policies, economists and policymakers assume that historical relationships between macroeconomic variables will continue to hold after the new policies are in place. Lucas objected to this assumption, asserting what has become known as the *Lucas critique.* According to the Lucas critique, because new policies change the economic "rules" and thus affect economic behavior, no one can safely assume that historical relationships between variables will hold when policies change.

A good example of the Lucas critique in action is the shifting Phillips curve. Historically, there seemed to be a stable relationship between inflation and unemployment, which led some policymakers to believe that they could permanently reduce unemployment by increasing inflation. However, as we have discussed, when policymakers allowed inflation to rise, the public's inflation expectations also rose. As a result, the Phillips curve shifted and the historical relationship between inflation and unemployment broke down.

The main message of the Lucas critique for economists is that, in order to predict the effects of policy changes on the economy, they must understand how economic behavior will change under the new policies. Understanding the impact of policy changes on behavior—particularly the introduction of policies that haven't been tried before—requires the use of economic theory as well as empirical analysis.

---

* The example is from Thomas Sargent, *Rational Expectations and Inflation,* New York: Harper & Row, 1986, pp. 1–2.

† "Econometric Policy Evaluation: A Critique," in K. Brunner and A. H. Meltzer, eds., *Carnegie-Rochester Conference Series on Public Policy,* vol. 1, 1976.

The Long-Run Phillips Curve

Although classicals and Keynesians disagree about whether the Phillips curve relationship can be exploited to reduce unemployment temporarily, they agree that policymakers can't keep the unemployment rate *permanently* below the natural rate by maintaining a high rate of inflation. Expectations about inflation eventually will adjust so that the expected and actual inflation rates are equal, or $\pi^e = \pi$. The expectations-augmented Phillips curve (Eq. 13.1) implies that, when $\pi^e = \pi$, the actual unemployment rate u equals the natural unemployment rate $\bar{u}$. Thus the actual unemployment rate equals the natural rate in the long run regardless of the inflation rate maintained.

The long-run relationship of unemployment and inflation is shown by the **long-run Phillips curve.** In the long run, because unemployment equals the natural rate regardless of the inflation rate, the long-run Phillips curve is a vertical line at $u = \bar{u}$, as shown in Fig. 13.8.

The vertical long-run Phillips curve is related to the long-run neutrality of money, discussed in Chapters 11 and 12. Classicals and Keynesians agree that changes in the money supply will have no long-run effects on real variables, including unemployment. The vertical long-run Phillips curve carries the

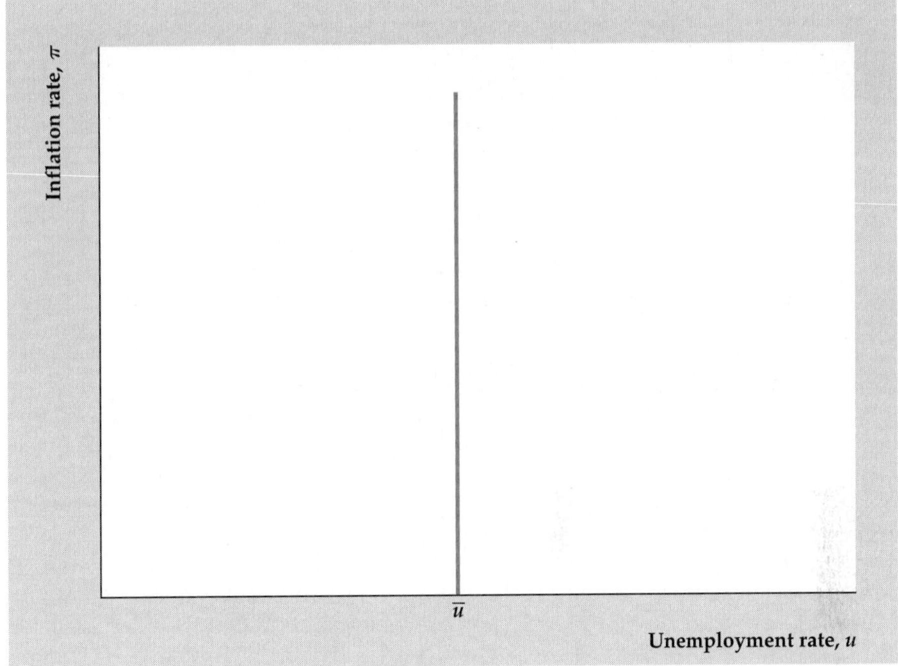

Figure 13.8
The long-run Phillips curve
Because people will not permanently overestimate or underestimate the rate of inflation, in the long run the expected and actual inflation rates are equal and the actual unemployment rate equals the natural unemployment rate. Because in the long run actual unemployment equals the natural rate regardless of the inflation rate, the long-run Phillips curve is vertical.

notion of monetary neutrality one step further by indicating that changes in the *growth rate* of money, which lead to changes in the inflation rate, also have no real effects in the long run.

At best, the Phillips curve can be exploited only temporarily, so why would policymakers attempt to reduce unemployment by creating surprise inflation? One possibility is that stimulating the economy may help the incumbent political party win elections; see the box "The Political Environment: Presidential Elections and Macroeconomic Policy," p. 460.

13.2 THE PROBLEM OF UNEMPLOYMENT

In the rest of the chapter we look more closely at unemployment and inflation, beginning with unemployment in this section. We start by discussing the costs of unemployment, then consider the factors that determine the long-run unemployment level, and conclude by exploring some ways in which macroeconomic policy can address unemployment.

The Costs of Unemployment

There are two principal costs of unemployment. The first is the loss of output that occurs because fewer people are productively employed. This cost is borne disproportionately by unemployed workers themselves, in terms of the income they lose because they are out of work. However, because the unemployed may stop paying taxes and instead receive unemployment insurance benefits or other government payments, society (in this case, taxpayers) also bears some of the output cost of unemployment.

THE POLITICAL ENVIRONMENT

PRESIDENTIAL ELECTIONS AND MACROECONOMIC POLICY

Among the many issues affecting presidential elections in the United States, macroeconomic policy and performance always are among the most important. The perception that the economy was performing poorly underlay both Bill Clinton's defeat of George Bush in 1992 and the surprisingly strong showing of third-party candidate Ross Perot. More generally, statistical studies of election results confirm that a growing economy and falling unemployment during an election year significantly improve the election prospects of the incumbent President (or a candidate of the incumbent President's party).*

Of course, Presidents are aware that an improving economy helps their reelection chances, and they undoubtedly consider these political benefits when planning macroeconomic policy. According to the theory of "political business cycles" introduced by William Nordhaus† of Yale University, we should expect incumbent Presidents to use expansionary aggregate demand policies to stimulate the economy during election years. Anecdotal evidence, at least, supports this theory: For example, many observers claimed that President Nixon used expansionary aggregate demand policies to improve his reelection chances in 1972.‡

Despite this anecdotal evidence, the data don't consistently support Nordhaus's political business cycle theory. One problem with the theory is the assumption that incumbents are motivated only by the prospects of reelection, which ignores the possibility that politicians have other goals, such as promoting policies that they favor. For example, an implication of the political business cycle theory is that the President's political party shouldn't matter in terms of the economy's performance, as the President will simply do what is needed to win reelection regardless of party affiliation. However, in general, economic performance under Republicans and Democrats isn't the same: Historically, Republicans have been more successful than Democrats at reducing inflation, but Democrats have done a better job at moderating unemployment.

To explain the difference in macroeconomic behavior during Democratic and Republican administrations, Douglas Hibbs§ of Harvard University proposed a "partisan theory" of macroeconomic policy in which Democrats, who typically have greater support among less affluent voters, are assumed to care relatively more about unemployment and relatively less about inflation than Republicans do. The partisan theory accounts for the fact that unemployment is more likely to fall and inflation is more likely to rise during Democratic administrations than during Republican administrations. A problem with the partisan theory is its assumption that a stable Phillips curve gives policymakers a choice among fixed combinations of unemployment and inflation. However, as we demonstrated, changes in the expected inflation rate shift the Phillips curve so that policymakers do *not* face a stable trade-off between inflation and unemployment.

Most recently, Alberto Alesina‖ of Harvard University has combined the partisan theory with rational expectations and an expectations-augmented Phillips curve to examine the effects of aggregate demand policy in Democratic and Republican administrations. The importance of rational expectations

How big is the output cost of unemployment? One estimate is provided by Okun's law (see Eq. 3.5), which states that each percentage point of *cyclical* unemployment is associated with a loss equal to 2.5% of full-employment output. Thus if full-employment output is \$6 trillion, Okun's law indicates that each percentage point of unemployment sustained for one year reduces output by \$150 billion.

The loss of output predicted by Okun's law reflects not only the direct impact of increased unemployment, but also other labor market changes that occur during recessions, such as shorter workweeks, reduced labor force participation, and lower productivity (Numerical Problem 10 in Chapter 3 illustrates these effects). Thus the output cost of unemployment estimated by Okun's law

THE POLITICAL ENVIRONMENT

(Continued)

and an expectations-augmented Phillips curve is that only surprises in policy can affect real variables such as output and unemployment. Alesina argues that surprises arising from electoral uncertainty occur only at the beginning of an administration because, when expectations of future inflation are formed before an election, the outcome of the election is unknown. Therefore the expected inflation rate is an average of the higher inflation that would prevail under a Democratic President and the lower inflation that would occur if a Republican is elected. If a Democrat wins the election, inflation is higher than expected and unemployment falls; if a Republican wins, inflation is lower than expected and unemployment rises. After expectations have completely adjusted to take into account the election outcome, however, aggregate demand policy doesn't yield systematically different results for Democrats and Republicans.

An important implication of Alesina's theory is that recessions are likely to occur early in Republican administrations, when inflation will be less than that expected before the election. However, there should be no difference between parties in the likelihood of recession later in administrations, when inflation expectations have had time to adjust. The accompanying table shows this implication to be generally true. In particular, with remarkable consistency, recessions have occurred in the second year of Republican administrations, whereas early in Democratic administrations growth has been strong. Economic growth in the second half of administrations, in contrast, hasn't varied much by party.

* An early study is Ray Fair,"The Effects of Economic Events on Votes for President," *The Review of Economics and Statistics*, May 1978, pp. 159–172.

† For a survey, see William Nordhaus, "Alternative Approaches to the Political Business Cycle," *Brookings Papers on Economic Activity*, 1989:2, pp. 1–49.

‡ Ibid., pp. 43–45.

§ "Political Parties and Macroeconomic Policy," *American Political Science Review*, December 1977, pp. 1467–1487.

‖ "Macroeconomics and Politics," in Stanley Fischer, ed., NBER *Macroeconomics Annual*, Cambridge, Mass.: M.I.T. Press, 1988.

Rate of growth of real output in Democratic and Republican administrations, by year of administration (percent)

Administration	Year of Administration: First	Second	Third	Fourth
Democrats				
Truman	0.0	8.5	10.3	3.9
Kennedy/Johnson	2.6	5.3	4.1	5.3
Johnson	5.8	5.8	2.9	4.1
Carter	4.7	5.3	2.5	−0.2[a]
Average	3.3	6.2	5.0	3.3
Republicans				
Eisenhower I	4.0	−1.3	5.6	2.1
Eisenhower II	1.7	−0.8	5.8	2.2
Nixon	2.4	−0.3	2.8	5.0
Nixon/Ford	5.2	−0.5	−1.3[a]	4.9
Reagan I	1.9	−2.5	3.6	6.4
Reagan II	3.4	2.8	3.4	4.6
Bush	1.5	−1.2	1.0	2.9
Average	2.9	−0.6	3.0	4.0

[a] Oil shock year.

Source: Alberto Alesina, "Comment on Nordhaus," *Brookings Papers on Economic Activity*, 1989:2, p. 54, Table 1. Alesina measures output by real GNP. Updated for Bush administration using GDP measure of output from *Survey of Current Business*, various issues.

probably is too high. Nevertheless, an output loss that was only one-quarter of that predicted by Okun's law would still be a significant cost, particularly if it were borne largely by the relatively poor and disadvantaged members of society.

The other substantial cost of unemployment is the personal or psychological cost faced by unemployed workers and their families. This cost is especially important for workers suffering long spells of unemployment and for the chronically unemployed. Workers without steady employment for long periods lose job skills and self-esteem, and suffer from stress. One study found that an increase in the unemployment rate of one percentage point maintained for six years is associated with 20,000 additional cardiovascular deaths, 4000 state mental hospital admissions, 3300 state prison admissions, 920 suicides, and 650 homicides.[11]

The costs of unemployment are real and serious, but two offsetting factors should be noted. First, to the extent that unemployed workers engage in economically productive activities such as searching for a job or acquiring new skills, the loss of output arising from current unemployment may be compensated for by increased output in the future. In particular, frictional unemployment—the result of workers and firms seeking appropriate matches—raises future productivity and output and thus may impose little net economic cost, or even lead to an economic gain.

A second offsetting factor is that unemployed people have more leisure time—to spend with family and friends, work around the house, and so on. However, the benefits of extra leisure time decrease as the amount of leisure increases, and most unemployed workers wouldn't feel that increased leisure was adequate compensation for their lost income.

The Long-Term Behavior of the Unemployment Rate

Classical and Keynesian economists agree that, although the actual unemployment rate may deviate from the natural unemployment rate in the short run, in the long run the actual rate equals the natural rate. Thus understanding the behavior of unemployment in all but the short run requires identifying the determinants of the natural rate of unemployment. In Chapter 3 we discussed the reasons for the natural unemployment rate always being greater than zero; here we focus more narrowly on the reasons for a rising natural rate in recent years in the United States and in Europe.

The Rising Natural Rate. The natural unemployment rate corresponds to full-employment output. Unfortunately, because we can't be sure when the economy is at full employment, we can't directly observe the natural rate and so must estimate it. Inevitably, therefore, there is some uncertainty about the value of the natural rate at any particular time. Figure 13.9 shows estimated values of the natural unemployment rate, along with the actual unemployment rate, for the period 1956–1992. Ellen Rissman of the Federal Reserve Bank of Chicago provided the estimated levels of the natural rate before 1987, based on her research; we estimated the levels of the natural rate since 1987.[12] Most current estimates, including those in Fig. 13.9, suggest a natural unemployment rate of about 6% of the labor force. In comparison, most estimates of the natural rate for the 1950s and 1960s were in the range of 4%–5%, though the estimates in Fig. 13.9 for that period are a bit higher. Hence the natural unemployment rate in the United States apparently has risen by one or two percentage points over the last thirty years.

Giving a fully satisfactory explanation of the rise in the natural rate of unemployment is difficult, but part of the increase seems to have been the result

---

11. The study, by Dr. Harvey Brenner of Johns Hopkins University, is cited in Barry Bluestone and Bennett Harrison, *The Deindustrialization of America,* New York: Basic Books, 1982, Chapter 3.

12. See Rissman, "Wage Growth and Sectoral Shifts: Phillips Curve Redux," *Journal of Monetary Economics,* June 1993, pp. 395–416 for a discussion of issues in estimating the natural unemployment rate. Unlike those in Rissman's article, estimates of the natural rate shown in Fig. 13.9 haven't been adjusted for changing demographics. We estimated the natural rate since 1987 as a weighted average of the actual unemployment rate and the year-earlier natural rate.

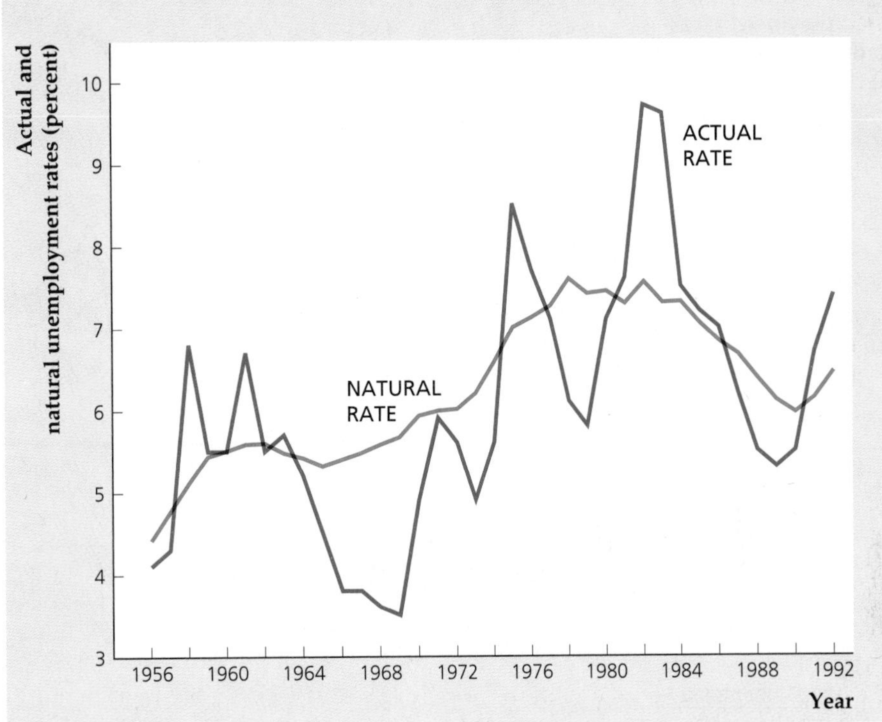

Figure 13.9
Actual and natural unemployment rates in the United States
The figure shows the actual unemployment rate and an estimate of the natural rate of unemployment in the United States for the period 1956–1992. The difference between the actual and natural unemployment rates is the cyclical unemployment rate. Note that the natural rate of unemployment has risen by one to two percentage points over this period.

Sources: Unemployment rate, all civilian workers, 1993 *Economic Report of the President,* Table B-37; natural rate of unemployment: 1970–1986 from Ellen Rissman, Federal Reserve Bank of Chicago, private communication; 1987–1992, estimated by the authors as a weighted average of the actual unemployment rate and the previous natural rate.

of demographic changes. Figures 13.10(a) and 13.10(b), on the next page, show unemployment levels for workers in different demographic groups (age, gender, and race) in the United States. Note that teenagers (aged sixteen through nineteen) have higher unemployment rates than adults, blacks have higher unemployment rates than whites, and for much of the post–World War II period (but not recently) women have had a higher unemployment rate than men.

A principal reason that teenagers, blacks, and other members of minority groups, and (until recently) women have higher unemployment rates is that these workers are less likely than white adult males to hold long-term, stable jobs. For example, because of discrimination, language problems, and lower educational attainment, blacks and other minority group members are more likely to hold temporary or "dead-end" jobs, with little prospect for advancement or long-term employment. Because these jobs don't last long, minority group members are frequently unemployed and must spend a relatively large amount of time looking for work. A cause of the historically higher unemployment rate for women is that, traditionally, women have spent more time than men in taking care of children and thus have had more interruptions in their careers. For women, moving in and out of the labor force often involves periods of unemployment. Teenagers have high unemployment rates both because they move in and out of the labor force frequently while they are in school and also because many teenagers work at low-skill jobs that don't provide long-term employment.

Since World War II, teenagers, members of minority groups, and women have emerged as a large portion of the U.S. labor force. This shift in the composition of the labor force toward groups that have higher unemployment rates may have raised the overall unemployment rate.

Figure 13.10 Unemployment rates by demographic group
(a) U.S. civilian unemployment rates are shown by race and gender for 1954 to 1992. Blacks have much higher unemployment rates than whites, and for much of the period (though not recently), women have had higher unemployment rates than men.

Source: *Economic Report of the President,* February 1993, Table B-38. Before 1972 black unemployment rates include unemployment of other nonwhite minorities.

(b) Teenage unemployment rates are shown by race and gender for 1954 to 1992. Black teenagers have higher unemployment rates than white teenagers. Teenagers in general also have considerably higher unemployment rates than adults (compare to Fig. 13.10a).

Source: Same as Fig. 13.10a.

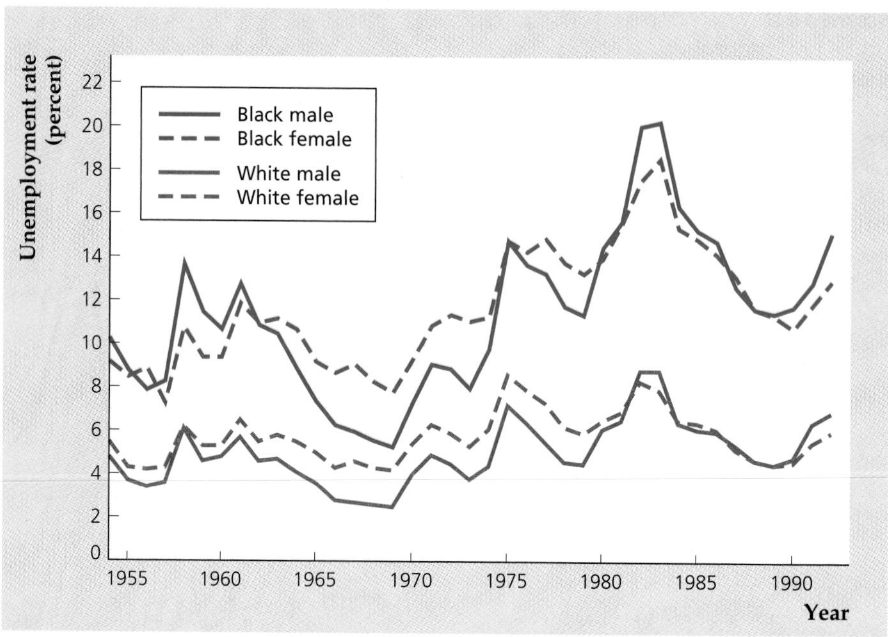

(a) Unemployment by race and gender

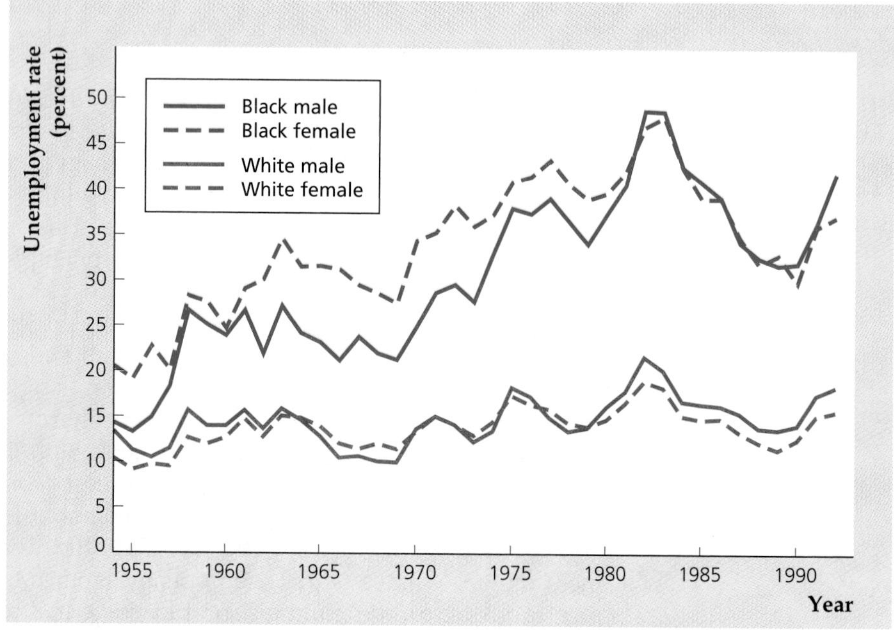

(b) Teenage unemployment

The demographic explanation of the increase in the natural unemployment rate has some merit but is incomplete for two reasons. First, the changes in labor force composition by age, gender, and race account only for a portion—probably less than one percentage point—of the increase in the natural rate.[13] Indeed, some demographic changes—such as the relative increase in college-educated workers, who typically have low unemployment rates—work in the direction of reducing the natural rate. Second, the unemployment rate has risen *within* each demographic category.[14] Thus even if there had been no change in labor force composition, the overall unemployment rate would have risen.

Another factor that may have contributed to the increase in the natural unemployment rate is a faster pace of structural change in the economy, which has taken several forms. Technological changes have increased the skill levels that firms demand from workers, reducing the employment opportunities for low-skilled or poorly educated workers (see the Application, "Technical Change and Wage Inequality," p. 88). Also, some industries and regions have grown significantly while others were suffering long-term declines; notably, the share of jobs in manufacturing has fallen while that in services has risen. Both changes worsen the problem of mismatch between jobs and workers, raising frictional and structural unemployment and hence the natural rate.

Hysteresis in Unemployment. Although economists would like to understand why the natural unemployment rate has risen, the one or two percentage point increase in the U.S. natural rate over the past several decades probably doesn't represent a large change in the operation of the labor market. A more serious and puzzling change in the natural unemployment rate occurred during the 1980s in several countries in Western Europe.

For thirty years after World War II many Western European countries maintained low unemployment rates. Then, after the oil price shocks and worldwide recessions of the 1970s, unemployment rates in those countries rose sharply. (Unemployment rates for Germany, France, and the United Kingdom are shown in Fig. 13.11 on the next page.) The unemployment rate in the United States also rose to high levels during the 1970s but fell quickly during the recovery that followed the 1981–1982 recession (see Fig. 13.9). In contrast, unemployment rates in Western Europe remained high throughout most of the decade, falling temporarily during the late 1980s but rising again in the early 1990s. This long-term increase in the Western European unemployment rate from only 1%–3% of the labor force in the early 1970s to much higher levels in the 1980s reflects an increase in the natural unemployment rate of five percentage points or more, according to some estimates. What accounts for this apparent large increase in the natural unemployment rate in Western Europe?

Some economists use a term taken from physics, hysteresis, to describe the behavior of European unemployment. Applied to unemployment, **hysteresis** means that the natural unemployment rate changes in response to the actual

---

13. See, for example, Ellen R. Rissman, "What Is the Natural Rate of Unemployment?" *Economic Perspectives*, Federal Reserve Bank of Chicago, September/October 1986, pp. 3–17, especially p. 6. See also Lawrence H. Summers, "Why Is the Unemployment Rate So Very High Near Full Employment?" *Brookings Papers on Economic Activity*, 1986:2, pp. 339–383.

14. See Kevin Murphy and Robert Topel, "The Evolution of Unemployment in the United States: 1968–1985," in Stanley Fischer, ed., NBER *Macroeconomics Annual*, Cambridge, Mass.: M.I.T. Press, 1987. Murphy and Topel examined eighteen years of individual data drawn from the Annual Demographic File of the Current Population Survey. They found that "unemployment has increased in all major industries, in all age and schooling groups, and in all major regions of the country. The timing and magnitudes of changes in unemployment are very similar across identifiable groups" (p. 12).

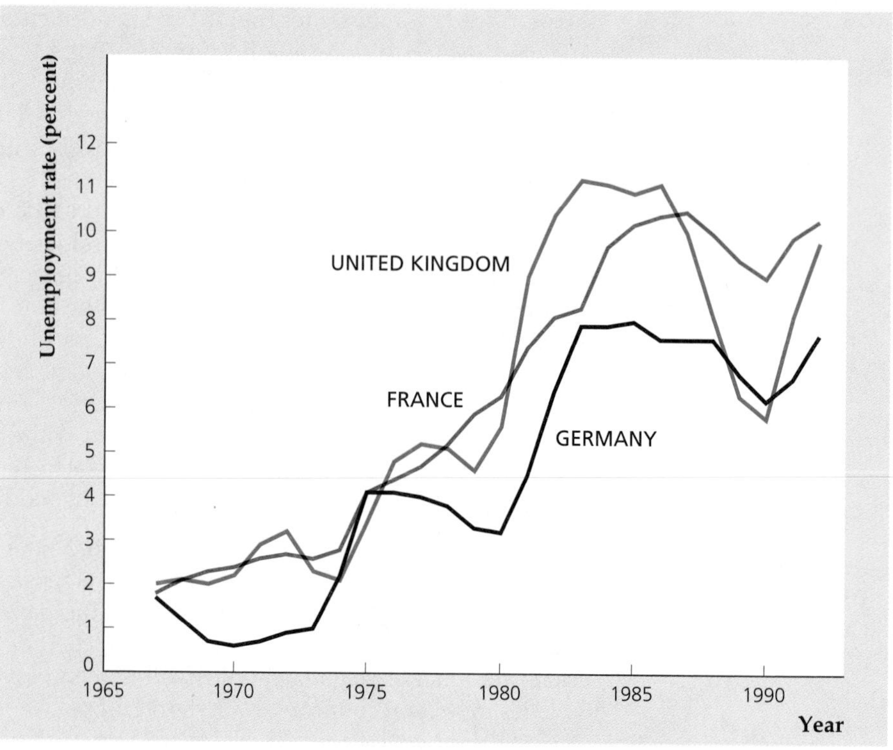

Figure 13.11
Unemployment rates in Western Europe
Unemployment rates in the United Kingdom, France, and Germany rose from less than 3% in the early 1970s to near double-digit range in the mid 1980s. The persistence of high unemployment suggests that the natural unemployment rate also increased. The increase in the natural rate, in response to an increase in actual unemployment, is an example of hysteresis.

Source: *OECD Historical Statistics*, various issues; updates from *IMF World Economic Outlook*. Data for Germany through 1990 refer to western Germany only.

unemployment rate, rising if the actual rate is above the natural rate and falling if the actual rate is below the natural rate. According to the proponents of hysteresis theory, the rise in Western European unemployment in the mid 1970s, originally because of factors such as rising oil prices and contractionary macroeconomic policies, also increased the natural unemployment rate. This increase in turn helps account for the continued high actual unemployment rate in these countries. When these countries return to long-run equilibrium with full employment, the actual rate equals the new higher natural rate.

There are several explanations of hysteresis in European unemployment. First, some economists suggest that, when a high unemployment rate idles workers for a long period of time, their skills deteriorate (or the workers fail to get training in the first place). Lower skill levels increase the mismatch between workers and firms and raise the natural unemployment rate.

Second, some economists argue that the bureaucratic aspects of firms and unions, as well as government regulation, interfere with the adjustment of the labor market in Western Europe. For example, in some European countries the government severely restricts the ability of firms to fire workers. Because firms know that firing workers is difficult, they are reluctant to hire additional workers unless they are confident that they won't have to reduce their work forces for a long time. Thus after many workers were laid off in the mid 1970s, firms were reluctant to rehire them or to hire new workers.

Third, the **insider–outsider theory** suggests that, when a union negotiates a labor contract with a firm, it seeks the highest real wage (including fringe benefits) possible without causing the firm to cut employment. This union behavior is in the best interests of currently employed workers, or insiders. But think about what happens if a contract is negotiated when unemployment is high. If the union succeeds in getting the highest wage consistent with continued employment of the insiders, the wage will be too high for the firm to increase employment and hire outsiders. Thus outsiders will remain unemployed.

The insider–outsider theory applies in a unionized setting. Because European labor markets are much more highly unionized than the U.S. labor market, the insider–outsider theory predicts that hysteresis is quantitatively more important in Europe than in the United States. This prediction is consistent with the fact that during the 1980s unemployment rates in Europe came down much more slowly than they did in the United States. Another difference is that unemployment insurance is more generous in Europe than in the United States. Box 13.2 discusses the implications of this difference for the behavior of the natural rate of unemployment.

BOX 13.2

The Effect of Unemployment Insurance on Unemployment

Most countries have unemployment insurance (UI) systems that provide income to unemployed workers. The purpose of UI systems is to soften the economic hardship associated with unemployment, but UI benefits have an additional effect: Because unemployed workers who receive UI benefits can afford to be more choosy when searching for a job, the availability of benefits may tend to increase the length of unemployment spells and the unemployment rate.

Some economists have suggested that the generous UI benefits in Europe are at least partly responsible for the persistent increase in unemployment that began there during the mid 1970s (see Fig. 13.11). Gary Burtless* of the Brookings Institution compared unemployment rates and the generosity of UI systems for the period 1966–1985 in Britain, France, Germany, Sweden, and the United States. To measure the generosity of UI systems, he focused on three factors:

1. the *replacement ratio,* which measures the size of unemployment benefits relative to lost wages (a replacement ratio of 2/3, as in the French, German, and Swedish systems, means that UI benefits are 2/3 of an unemployed worker's lost wages);
2. the *benefit duration,* which measures the amount of time that an unemployed worker may receive benefits; and
3. *eligibility requirements,* which specify who can collect UI benefits.

Burtless didn't find much evidence that more-generous UI systems lead directly to higher unemployment rates. For example, the UI system in the United States historically has been less generous than the four European systems, having a lower replacement ratio, a substantially shorter benefit duration, and more stringent eligibility requirements than its European counterparts. Nevertheless, before 1973 the U.S. unemployment rate was higher than the European unemployment rates, despite a relatively more restrictive UI system. Similarly, according to Burtless, changes in UI benefits can't explain increases in European unemployment rates after the mid 1970s, except possibly in the case of France where a sharp increase in unemployment followed a liberalization of the system.

Although the generosity of UI benefits doesn't seem closely related to unemployment rates, the *duration* of individual spells of unemployment—the length of time that an unemployed worker remains unemployed—apparently is affected by the generosity of UI benefits. Burtless found that unemployment spells were much longer in Europe (where UI systems were much more generous) than in the United States, even during the late 1960s and early 1970s when European unemployment rates overall were lower than in the United States. In particular, the longer benefit duration of European systems seems to account for the longer spells of unemployment in Europe.

---

* "Jobless Pay and High European Unemployment," in R. Lawrence and C. Schultze, eds., *Barriers to European Growth: A Transatlantic View,* Washington, D.C.: Brookings Institution, 1987.

Policies to Reduce the Natural Rate of Unemployment

Although we call the rate of unemployment toward which the economy gravitates in the long run the "natural" rate of unemployment, we don't mean to imply that it is necessarily desirable or optimal. Many people would argue that, for both economic and social reasons, economic policies should be used to try to lower the natural unemployment rate. Although no surefire method for reducing the natural rate exists, several strategies have been suggested:

1. *Government support for job training and worker relocation.* Firms have strong incentives to find and train capable workers, and unemployed workers have equally strong incentives to find productive jobs. However, some economists argue that the private incentives to match workers and jobs still are not as strong as they should be. For example, firms may be reluctant to train workers if they fear that, once trained, the workers will leave for other firms. Similarly, in deciding whether to retrain for a new job, an unemployed worker won't take into account the gain of his reemployment to taxpayers, who will no longer be responsible for financing his unemployment benefits. Thus a case can be made for policy measures such as tax breaks or subsidies for training or relocating unemployed workers. If these measures had their desired effect, the mismatch between workers and jobs would be eliminated more quickly and the natural unemployment rate would fall.

2. *Increased labor market flexibility.* Currently, government regulations mandate minimum wages, working conditions, workers' fringe benefits, conditions for firing a worker, and many other terms of employment. Such regulations may be well-intentioned but they also increase the cost of hiring additional workers, particularly workers with limited skills and experience. New and existing labor market regulations should be carefully reviewed to ensure that their benefits outweigh the costs they impose in higher unemployment.

3. *Unemployment insurance reform.* Although unemployment insurance (UI) provides essential support for the unemployed, it may also increase the natural unemployment rate by increasing the time that the unemployed spend looking for work (see Box 13.2) and by increasing the incentives for firms to lay off workers during slack times. Reforms to UI that preserve its function of supporting the unemployed but reduce incentives for increased unemployment are needed. For example, taxes on employers might be changed to force employers that use temporary layoffs extensively to bear a greater portion of the unemployment benefits that their workers receive.

4. *A high-pressure economy?* Classical and Keynesian economists generally agree that macroeconomic stabilization policies can't be used to affect the natural rate of unemployment; in other words, the long-run Phillips curve is vertical. However, some proponents of the hysteresis theory take issue with this view. They argue that if monetary and fiscal policy are used aggressively to keep unemployment as low as possible—a "high-pressure economy"—then, following the principle of hysteresis, the natural rate will eventually fall. So, for example, if current employment is stimulated by monetary expansion, workers may be able to acquire more on-the-job training, which reduces mismatch and lowers the natural unemployment rate in the long run. Opponents of this suggestion point out that there is much less evidence of hysteresis in the United States than in Europe. Opponents also express concern that a high-pressure strategy would reignite inflation.

13.3 THE PROBLEM OF INFLATION

In August 1971 President Nixon instituted a set of wage and price controls in an attempt to reduce U.S. inflation. These strong measures were taken even though the inflation rate was only 5% at the time. During the late 1970s, when the U.S. inflation rate approached "double-digits," surveys of voters found that they thought inflation was "public enemy number one"; one victim of the public's fear of inflation was President Jimmy Carter, who lost his reelection bid to Ronald Reagan in 1980 in part because of his perceived inability to control inflation. In this section we look at inflation, beginning with a discussion of inflation costs and then turning to the question of what can be done to control inflation.

The Costs of Inflation

The costs of inflation depend primarily on whether consumers, investors, workers, and firms are able to predict the inflation before it occurs. To illustrate this point, we discuss two extreme cases: an inflation that everyone is able to predict and an inflation that comes as a complete surprise.

Perfectly Anticipated Inflation. Let's first consider the case of an inflation that is perfectly anticipated by the public. Imagine, for example, that everyone knew that the inflation rate would be 4% per year. To keep things simple, assume also no change in relative prices so that the prices of all individual goods and services also are rising at the rate of 4% per year.

Why then does a fully anticipated inflation impose any costs? The prices you pay for groceries, movie tickets, and other goods would increase by 4% per year but so would your nominal wage or the nominal value of the goods or services you produce. Because your nominal income is rising along with prices, your purchasing power isn't hurt by the perfectly anticipated inflation.[15]

What about the money that you hold in your savings account? Although inflation reduces the purchasing power of money, perfectly anticipated inflation wouldn't hurt the value of your savings account. The reason is that the nominal interest rate would adjust to offset the drop in the purchasing power of money. For instance, with a zero inflation rate and a nominal interest rate on savings deposits of 3%, the real interest rate also is 3% per year. If inflation rises to a perfectly anticipated rate of 4% per year, an increase in the nominal interest rate to 7% per year will leave the real interest rate unchanged at 3%.

15. It may be true that, psychologically, people think of increases in their wages arising from ongoing inflation as being earned and thus "fair," but that increases in the prices they pay because of inflation are "unfair." This is a confusion, although one that may have real political consequences if it causes the public to demand strong action on inflation.

Because both savers and banks care only about the real interest rate, when inflation rises to 4% banks should be willing to offer 7% nominal interest, and savers should be willing to accept that nominal return. Thus neither banks nor savers are hurt by an anticipated increase in inflation.[16]

The suggestion that perfectly anticipated inflation imposes no economic costs isn't quite correct: Inflation erodes the value of currency, which leads people to keep less currency on hand—for example, by going to the bank or the automatic teller machine to make withdrawals every week instead of twice a month. Similarly, inflation may induce firms to reduce their cash holdings by introducing computerized cash management systems or adding staff to the accounting department. The costs in time and effort incurred by people and firms who are trying to minimize their holdings of cash are called **shoe leather costs.** For modest inflation rates, shoe leather costs are small but not completely trivial. For example, the shoe leather costs of a 10% perfectly anticipated inflation have been estimated to be about 0.3% of GNP, which is about $18 billion per year in the United States.[17]

A second cost of perfectly anticipated inflation arises from menu costs, or the costs of changing nominal prices. When there is inflation and prices are continually rising, sellers of goods and services must use resources to change nominal prices. For instance, mail-order firms have to print and mail catalogues frequently to report the increases in prices. Although some firms face substantial menu costs, for the economy as a whole these costs probably are small. Furthermore, technological progress, such as the introduction of electronic scanners in supermarkets, reduces the cost of changing prices.

Unanticipated Inflation. Much of the public's aversion to inflation is aversion to unanticipated inflation—inflation that is different from the rate expected. For example, if everyone expects the inflation rate to be 4% per year, but it actually is 6% per year, unanticipated inflation is 2% per year.

What is the effect of 6% inflation if (1) you expected 4% inflation and (2) your savings account pays 7% interest? When inflation is 6% per year instead of 4% per year, the actual real interest rate on your savings account is only 1% per year (the nominal interest rate of 7% minus the inflation rate of 6%) instead of the 3% per year that you expected. By earning a lower actual real interest rate, you lose as a result of the unanticipated inflation. However, your loss is the bank's gain because the bank pays a lower real interest rate than it expected. Note that the roles would have been reversed if the actual inflation rate had been lower than expected; in that case the real interest rate that you earn, and that the bank has to pay, would be higher than anticipated.

Similarly, suppose that your nominal salary is set in advance. If inflation is higher than expected, the real value of your salary is less than you expected, and your loss is your employer's gain. If inflation is lower than expected, however, you benefit and your employer loses.

These examples show that a primary effect of unanticipated inflation is to transfer wealth from one person or firm to another. People who lend or save at

16. This argument ignores the fact that interest is taxed on a nominal basis. If the after-tax real interest rate is to be kept constant, the nominal interest rate will have to rise by somewhat more than the increase in inflation.

17. See Stanley Fischer, "Towards an Understanding of the Costs of Inflation: II," in K. Brunner and A. Meltzer, eds., *Carnegie-Rochester Conference Series on Public Policy*, vol. 15, Autumn 1981.

fixed interest rates (creditors) and those with incomes set in nominal terms are hurt by unanticipated inflation, whereas people who borrow at fixed interest rates (debtors) or who must make fixed nominal payments are helped by unanticipated inflation.

For the economy as a whole, a transfer of wealth from one group to another isn't a net loss of resources and hence doesn't represent a true cost. However, from the viewpoints of individual people and firms in the economy, the *risk* of gaining or losing wealth as a result of unanticipated inflation is unwelcome. Because most people don't like risk, the possibility of significant gains or losses arising from unexpected inflation makes people feel worse off and hence is a cost of unanticipated inflation. Furthermore, any resources that people use in forecasting inflation and trying to protect themselves against the risks of unanticipated inflation represent an additional cost. However, some of these costs of unanticipated inflation can be eliminated by contracts that are indexed to the price level (see Box 13.3).

Another cost of unanticipated inflation relates to the fact that prices serve as signals in a market economy. For example, if wheat becomes more expensive

BOX 13.3

Indexed Contracts

In principle, much of the risk of gains and losses associated with unanticipated inflation can be eliminated by using contracts in which payments are indexed to inflation. If a bank wanted to offer a guaranteed 3% real interest rate on savings accounts, for instance, it could index the nominal interest rate to the rate of inflation by offering to pay a nominal interest rate equal to 3% plus whatever the rate of inflation turns out to be. Then if the actual inflation rate is 6%, the bank would end up paying a nominal interest rate of 9%—giving the depositor the promised 3% real interest rate. Similarly, other financial contracts, such as loans, mortgages, and bonds, can be indexed to protect the real rate of return against unanticipated inflation. Wage payments set by labor contracts can also be indexed to protect workers and employers against unanticipated inflation (we discussed the macroeconomic effects of wage indexation in Appendix 12.A).

How widespread is indexing? Most financial contracts in the United States are not indexed to the rate of inflation, although payments on some long-term financial contracts (adjustable-rate mortgages, for example) are indexed to nominal interest rates such as the prime rate charged by banks or the Treasury bill interest rate. Because nominal interest rates move roughly in step with inflation, these long-term financial contracts are to some extent indexed to inflation. Many labor contracts in the United States are indexed to the rate of inflation through provisions called cost-of-living adjustments, or COLAs. They provide for some increase in nominal wages if inflation is higher than expected, but usually a 1% increase in unanticipated inflation results in somewhat less than a 1% adjustment of wages. Because the public often expresses concern about inflation, economists are puzzled that indexed contracts are not more widely used in the United States.

In contrast, in countries that have experienced high and unpredictable inflation rates, indexed contracts are common. A case in point is Israel, which had a CPI inflation rate of 445% per year in 1984. At that time over 80% of liquid financial assets in Israel were indexed: For example, long-term government bonds were indexed to the CPI, and banks offered short-term deposits whose purchasing power was tied to that of the U.S. dollar. However, the fraction of financial assets that were indexed decreased after the Israeli hyperinflation ended in the second half of 1985.*

* See Stanley Fischer, "Israeli Inflation and Indexation," in J. Williamson, ed., *Inflation and Indexation: Argentina, Brazil, Israel,* Institute for International Economics, 1985, reprinted in Stanley Fischer, *Indexing, Inflation, and Economic Policy,* Cambridge, Mass.: M.I.T. Press, 1986; and Zalman F. Shiffer, "Adjusting to High Inflation: The Israeli Experience," Federal Reserve Bank of St. Louis *Review,* May 1986, pp. 18–29.

than corn, that is a signal to consumers to switch from wheat to corn and to farmers to produce more wheat and less corn. However, the prices that act as signals in the economy are *relative* prices, such as the price of wheat relative to the price of corn. Knowing that wheat is so many dollars per bushel doesn't help the consumer and farmer make good economic decisions unless they also know the price of corn. When inflation is unanticipated, particularly if it is erratic, people may confuse changes in prices arising from changes in the general price level with changes in prices arising from shifts in the supply or demand for individual goods. Because the signals provided by prices may be distorted by unanticipated inflation, the market economy works less efficiently. In addition, when there is a great deal of uncertainty about the true inflation rate, people must spend time and effort learning about different prices, by comparison shopping, for example.

The Costs of Hyperinflation. **Hyperinflation** occurs when the inflation rate is extremely high for a sustained period of time.[18] We mentioned the German hyperinflation of 1922–1923 in Chapter 1, and there are many other examples. During a twelve-month period beginning in August 1945, the average rate of inflation in Hungary was 19,800% *per month.*[19] In the more recent hyperinflation in Bolivia, the annual rate of inflation was 1281% in 1984, and soared to 11,750% in 1985, before dropping to 276% in 1986.[20] The costs of inflation during these hyperinflations were much greater than the costs associated with moderate inflation. For example, when prices are increasing at such mind-boggling rates, the incentives to minimize holdings of currency are powerful and the resulting shoe leather costs are enormous. In severe hyperinflations workers are paid much more frequently—perhaps even more than once a day—and they rush out to spend their money (or to convert their money into some other form, such as a foreign currency) before prices rise even further. The time and energy devoted to getting rid of currency as fast as possible wastes resources and disrupts production.

One early casualty of hyperinflations is the government's ability to collect taxes. In a hyperinflation taxpayers have an incentive to delay paying their taxes as long as possible. Because tax bills usually are set in nominal terms, the longer the taxpayer delays, the less the real value of that obligation is. The real value of taxes collected by the government falls sharply during hyperinflations, with destructive effects on the government's finances and its ability to provide public services.

Finally, the disruptive effect of inflation on market efficiency that we discussed earlier becomes most severe in the case of a hyperinflation. If prices change so often that they cease to be reliable indicators of the supply and demand for different goods and services, the invisible hand of the free market can't allocate resources efficiently.

---

18. Philip Cagan, in his classic study of hyperinflation ("The Monetary Dynamics of Hyperinflation," in Milton Friedman, ed., *Studies in the Quantity Theory of Money,* Chicago: University of Chicago Press, 1956), defined a hyperinflation as beginning in the month in which the rate of inflation first exceeds 50% *per month.*

19. *Ibid.,* Table 1.

20. See Table 7.3, Juan-Antonio Morales, "Inflation Stabilization in Bolivia," in Michael Bruno, Guido De Tella, Rudiger Dornbusch, and Stanley Fischer, eds., *Inflation Stabilization: The Experience of Israel, Argentina, Brazil, Bolivia, and Mexico,* Cambridge, Mass.: M.I.T. Press, 1988.

Fighting Inflation: The Role of Inflationary Expectations

Basically, inflation occurs when the aggregate quantity of goods demanded at any particular price level is rising more quickly than the aggregate quantity of goods supplied at that price level. (Fig. 13.3 illustrates such a situation.) Many factors can cause rapid increases in the aggregate quantity of goods demanded relative to the aggregate quantity supplied. Among these sources of inflation are increases in consumption or investment spending, expansionary fiscal policies, and adverse supply shocks. However, as discussed in Chapter 7, in general the only factor that can create *sustained* rises in aggregate demand, and thus ongoing inflation, is a high rate of money growth.

If rapid money growth is inflationary, why do central banks permit rapid monetary expansion? As mentioned in Chapter 7 (and discussed in more detail in Chapter 16), in developing or war-torn countries governments may not be able to raise enough revenue by taxing or borrowing, so they print money to finance their spending. However, in industrialized countries not engaged in or recovering from a war, governments usually are able either to tax or borrow enough to cover their expenditures. In these countries, rapid money growth usually is the result of past attempts to use expansionary monetary policy to fight recessions, not balanced by tighter monetary policies in periods when output is above the full-employment level.

Because ongoing inflation generally is the result of rapid money growth, the prescription for stopping inflation appears to be simple: Reduce the rate of money growth. Unfortunately, the process of **disinflation**—the reduction of the inflation rate—by slowing money growth may lead to a serious recession. In terms of the expectations-augmented Phillips curve, Eq. (13.1), if macroeconomic policy succeeds in reducing inflation below the expected rate, unemployment will rise above the natural rate. Unemployment will remain above the natural rate until expected inflation falls to the new, lower actual inflation rate.

Is there some way to reduce inflation without incurring serious unemployment costs? The expectations-augmented Phillips curve suggests one possibility: If the public's expected rate of inflation could be lowered as actual inflation was being brought down, unemployment wouldn't have to rise above the natural rate. (You should confirm that, in Eq. 13.1, if actual inflation π and expected inflation π^e fall by the same amount, cyclical unemployment $u - \bar{u}$ doesn't increase.) That is, if *expected* inflation can be reduced, the original Phillips curve relating inflation and unemployment can be shifted down and to the left, reducing the rate of inflation associated with any level of unemployment.

But how can policymakers reduce the public's inflationary expectations? In the rest of this section we discuss some suggested approaches for reducing both inflation and inflationary expectations.

Rapid Versus Gradual Disinflation. Some classical economists have proposed that disinflation should be implemented quickly by a rapid and decisive reduction in the growth rate of the money supply—a strategy sometimes referred to as **cold turkey.** Because a cold-turkey disinflation is dramatic and highly visible to the public, proponents of this policy argue that it will quickly and substantially reduce inflationary expectations, particularly if the policy is announced well in advance. If expected inflation falls sufficiently, the expectations-augmented Phillips curve implies that the unemployment costs of the disinflation will be minimal.

However, most Keynesian economists disagree with the idea that rapid disinflation can be achieved without significant costs in terms of increased cyclical unemployment. They argue that because of factors such as menu costs and nominal wage contracts several years may be required for prices and wages to adjust to a disinflationary policy; during the adjustment period cyclical unemployment could be high. Further, Keynesians point out that the cold-turkey strategy may not lower inflation expectations, because people may expect the government to abandon the policy if the resulting unemployment reaches politically intolerable levels.

Because they fear the possible unemployment consequences of the cold-turkey strategy, many Keynesians recommend a policy of **gradualism,** or reducing the rate of money growth and inflation gradually over a period of years. Keynesians argue that a gradual approach, which gives prices, wages, and expectations more time to adjust to the disinflation, will raise the unemployment rate by less than the cold-turkey strategy—although the period during which unemployment exceeds the natural rate may be longer. They further argue that, because the policy will be viewed as sustainable politically, gradualism may be as effective as the cold-turkey approach at reducing inflationary expectations.

Evidence on the relative advantages of the two approaches is limited. In one recent study Laurence Ball[21] of Johns Hopkins University examined 65 disinflation episodes in moderate-inflation, industrialized countries. Ball found that the unemployment costs incurred over an entire disinflationary episode were smaller for rapid disinflation than for gradual disinflation, supporting the cold-turkey approach. However, Ball also found that countries with slow wage adjustment (because of institutional factors such as unionization and government regulation of the labor market) suffered greater unemployment from disinflations of the same size, which is consistent with the results of the Keynesian approach.

Wage and Price Controls. Frustrated by the costs and difficulties of reducing inflation by reducing money growth, policymakers in some countries have taken a more direct approach and imposed wage and price controls—legal limits on the ability of firms to raise wages or prices. Supporters of wage–price controls (or of *incomes policies,* as wage–price controls are also called) argue that by using the force of law to stop price increases the government can "break the back" of inflationary expectations, allowing the disinflation to proceed without serious unemployment consequences.

Critics of price controls make two points. First, price controls are likely to cause shortages. In a free market the ever-changing forces of supply and demand lead to changes in relative prices, with the prices of some products rising more rapidly than the prices of others. If price controls prevent the price of a product from rising to the level at which quantity supplied equals quantity demanded, there will be excess demand for the product, that is, a shortage. These shortages and the disruptions they cause are a major cost of price controls.

Second, critics dispute that wage–price controls have a major effect on the public's inflation expectations. Although controls stop inflation for the

---

21. "What Determines the Sacrifice Ratio?" unpublished paper, March 1993.

moment, because they cause shortages and disrupt the economy they eventually have to be removed. Knowing that the controls are temporary, people may expect even greater inflation in the future.

One factor that may affect expectations of inflation during the period of controls is how the government handles monetary and fiscal policy. If macroeconomic policies allow aggregate demand to continue to grow rapidly, people may expect renewed inflation when the controls are lifted (see Analytical Problem 5 at the end of the chapter). This failure to reduce aggregate demand growth appears to have been the problem with the Nixon wage–price controls that began in 1971 (see the following Application). But if controls are accompanied by tight monetary and fiscal policy, the idea that inflation will not resume when controls are lifted is more plausible.

APPLICATION

The Nixon Wage–Price Controls

After increasing gradually during the 1960s, the inflation rate in 1970 and 1971 hovered at about 5% per year. Attempts to control this inflation by tighter monetary and fiscal policies weren't successful. Thus on August 15, 1971, in a surprise announcement, President Nixon instituted a program of price controls in the United States. The controls began with a ninety-day price freeze, known as Phase I, that prevented any prices from increasing. The program evolved haphazardly in response to economic events, reaching Phase IV before the program was finally terminated in April 1974.

As predicted by the basic economics of supply and demand, shortages developed during the period of price controls. To try to prevent shortages, the government exempted some prices, including the prices of raw agricultural products—feed grains, for example—from controls. But prices of final products, such as "broilers" (chickens sold to consumers in grocery stores), remained subject to controls. As feed grain prices increased, broiler producers could no longer make a profit by paying for feed grain at an uncontrolled price while selling broilers at a controlled price. When this profit squeeze caused broilers to disappear from grocery shelves, the government reclassified broilers as a raw agricultural product so that the price of broilers was no longer controlled. Broilers reappeared on the shelves but at 50% higher prices.[22] Shortages of other goods, including lumber and various steel products, also developed.

To study whether price controls succeeded in reducing inflation after the controls were lifted, Robert J. Gordon[23] conducted a statistical analysis of inflation in the United States during and after the period of price controls. He concluded that price controls reduced the rate of inflation during the period they were in effect (August 1971–April 1974). However, after the price controls were eliminated in April 1974, Gordon found that prices rose rapidly so that by the third quarter of 1975 the price level had reached the same level that it would have attained had there been no controls. In other words, the reduction in the rate of inflation during the period of controls was completely offset by an acceleration of inflation after price controls were removed. A probable

22. See George P. Shultz and Kenneth W. Dam, "The Life Cycle of Wage and Price Controls," in G. Shultz and K. Dam, eds., *Economic Policy Beyond the Headlines,* Stanford, Calif.: Stanford Alumni Association, 1977.

23. "The Impact of Aggregate Demand on Prices," *Brookings Papers on Economic Activity,* 1975:3, pp. 613–655.

reason that inflation accelerated after the removal of controls is that, as mentioned in the "Political Environment" box (p. 460), for political reasons the Nixon administration continued to use expansionary monetary and fiscal policy during the period of controls.

Credibility and Reputation. Classicals and Keynesians agree that, for disinflation to be achieved without high unemployment costs, reducing the public's expected inflation rate is important. Perhaps the most important factor determining how quickly expected inflation adjusts is the credibility, or believability, of the government's announced disinflationary policy. If the government (in the person of the President or the chairman of the Federal Reserve, for example) announces a policy to reduce the inflation rate—and if workers, consumers, and firms believe that the government means what it says—expected inflation should drop fairly rapidly.

How can a government improve its credibility with the public? One desirable way would be for the government to develop a reputation for carrying through on its promises; then when it announced a disinflation program, people would likely take this announcement seriously. Unfortunately, time is needed to develop such a reputation, and changes in administration may lead to relatively frequent changes in the people who make policy decisions.

Another strategy is to organize policymaking institutions in ways that create credibility with the public. For example, a strong and independent central bank, run by someone with well-known anti-inflation views, may have credibility with the public when it announces a disinflationary policy. However, if the central bank is controlled directly by the executive branch—and is therefore exposed to intense political pressure when unemployment rises—an announced disinflationary program is likely to be less credible. We explore the relationship among institutional structure, government credibility, and inflation expectations in greater detail in Chapter 15.

CHAPTER SUMMARY

1. Following the famous 1958 article by A. W. Phillips, empirical studies often showed that inflation is high when unemployment is low and low when unemployment is high. This negative empirical relationship between inflation and unemployment is called the Phillips curve. Inflation and unemployment in the United States conformed to the Phillips curve during the 1960s but not during the 1970s and 1980s.

2. Economic theory suggests that, in general, the negative relationship between inflation and unemployment should not be stable. Instead, in an economy in which there are unanticipated changes in the growth rate of aggregate demand, there should be a negative relationship between *unanticipated* inflation and *cyclical* unemployment. In particular, when actual and expected inflation are equal (so that unanticipated inflation is zero), the actual unemployment rate will equal the natural unemployment rate (so that cyclical unemployment is zero). This negative relationship between unanticipated inflation and cyclical unemployment is called the expectations-augmented Phillips curve.

3. According to the theory of the expectations-augmented Phillips curve, a stable negative

relationship between inflation and unemployment (a Phillips curve) will be observed only if expected inflation and the natural unemployment rate are constant. An increase in expected inflation or an increase in the natural unemployment rate shifts the Phillips curve up and to the right. Adverse supply shocks typically increase both expected inflation and the natural unemployment rate and also shift the Phillips curve up and to the right. Major supply shocks during the 1970s, a rising natural unemployment rate, and highly variable expected inflation rates explain why the Phillips curve shifted erratically in the United States after about 1970.

4. According to the expectations-augmented Phillips curve, macroeconomic policy can reduce unemployment below the natural rate only by surprising the public with higher-than-expected inflation. Classical economists argue that, because of rational expectations and rapid price adjustment, policy cannot be used systematically to create inflation higher than expected; thus policymakers cannot usefully exploit the Phillips curve relationship by trading higher inflation for lower unemployment. Keynesians believe that, because not all prices adjust rapidly to reflect new information, policymakers are able to create surprise inflation temporarily and thus trade off inflation and unemployment in the short run.

5. Classicals and Keynesians agree that, in the long run, expected and actual inflation rates are equal. Thus in the long run the actual unemployment rate equals the natural rate, regardless of the inflation rate. Reflecting the fact that there is no long-run trade-off between inflation and unemployment, the long-run Phillips curve is vertical at the natural unemployment rate.

6. The costs of unemployment include output lost when fewer people are working and the personal or psychological costs for unemployed workers and their families.

7. In the long run the unemployment rate is determined by the natural unemployment rate. According to some estimates, the natural unemployment rate in the United States has risen gradually over time. Explanations for this increase include demographic changes in the labor force and more rapid structural change in the economy.

8. The actual unemployment rate displays hysteresis if the natural rate increases whenever the actual rate is above the natural rate and decreases whenever the actual unemployment rate is below the natural rate. Hysteresis is thought to be a particularly serious problem in Western Europe. Explanations for hysteresis include loss of skills by the unemployed, bureaucratic and legal barriers to labor market adjustment, and wage-setting practices by unions that favor the currently employed (insiders) over those who are currently unemployed (outsiders).

9. Policies to reduce the natural unemployment rate include government support for job training and worker relocation, policies to increase labor market flexibility, and unemployment insurance reform. Some proponents of the hysteresis theory argue that pushing down the actual unemployment rate by means of expansionary policies (a "high-pressure" economy) will ultimately reduce the natural rate as well.

10. The costs of inflation depend on whether the inflation was anticipated or unanticipated. The costs of anticipated inflation, which (except in extreme inflations) are relatively minor, include shoe leather costs (resources used by individuals and firms to reduce their holdings of currency) and menu costs (costs of changing posted prices during an inflation). Unanticipated inflation causes unpredictable transfers of wealth among individuals and firms. The risk of unpredictable gains and losses, and the resources that people expend in trying to reduce this risk, are costs of unanticipated inflation. Unanticipated inflation may also reduce the efficiency of the market system by making it more difficult for people to observe relative prices.

11. Disinflation is a reduction in the rate of inflation. Attempts to disinflate by slowing money growth will cause cyclical unemployment to rise if actual inflation falls below expected inflation. To reduce the unemployment cost of disinflation, the public's expected inflation rate should be brought down along with the actual inflation rate. Strategies for reducing expected inflation include rapid and decisive reduction in the

growth rate of the money supply (the cold-turkey approach), wage and price controls, and taking measures to improve the credibility of government policy announcements.

Key Terms

cold turkey, p. 473
disinflation, p. 473
expectations-augmented Phillips curve, p. 452
gradualism, p. 474
hyperinflation, p. 472
hysteresis, p. 465
insider–outsider theory, p. 466
long-run Phillips curve, p. 458
Phillips curve, p. 447
shoe leather costs, p. 470

Key Equation

$$\pi = \pi^e - h(u - \bar{u}) \qquad (13.1)$$

The expectations-augmented Phillips curve states that unanticipated inflation, $\pi - \pi^e$, is negatively related to cyclical unemployment, $u - \bar{u}$. The expectations-augmented Phillips curve also implies that inflation, π, is negatively related to unemployment, u, only if the expected inflation rate π^e and the natural unemployment rate $\bar{u}$ are constant. Changes in the expected inflation rate or in the natural unemployment rate cause the relationship between inflation and unemployment—the traditional Phillips curve—to shift.

Review Questions

1. What is the Phillips curve? Does the Phillips curve relationship hold for U.S. data? Explain.
2. How does the expectations-augmented Phillips curve differ from the traditional Phillips curve? According to the theory of the expectations-augmented Phillips curve, under what conditions should the traditional Phillips curve relationship appear in the data?
3. How do changes in the expected inflation rate account for the behavior of the Phillips curve in the 1960s, 1970s, and 1980s in the United States? What role do supply shocks play in explaining the behavior of the Phillips curve in the United States?
4. Can policymakers exploit the Phillips curve relationship by trading more inflation for less unemployment in the short run? In the long run? Explain both the classical and Keynesian points of view.
5. Why is the natural unemployment rate an important economic variable? What factors explain the changes in the natural rate over time in the United States and in Europe? What government policies, if any, might be used to reduce the natural unemployment rate?
6. Give two costs of anticipated inflation and two costs of unanticipated inflation. How is the magnitude of each affected if, instead of a moderate inflation, hyperinflation occurs?
7. What is the greatest potential cost associated with disinflation? How does the responsiveness of the public's inflation expectations affect the size of this potential cost?
8. Discuss at least two strategies for reducing expected inflation rapidly. What are the pros and cons of these strategies?

Numerical Problems

1. Consider an economy in long-run equilibrium with an inflation rate π of 12% (0.12) per year and a natural unemployment rate $\bar{u}$ of 6% (0.06). The expectations-augmented Phillips curve is

$$\pi = \pi^e - 2(u - \bar{u}).$$

Assume that Okun's law holds so that a 1 percentage point increase in the unemployment rate maintained for one year reduces GDP by 2.5% of full-employment output.

a. Consider a two-year disinflation. In the first year $\pi = 0.04$ and $\pi^e = 0.08$. In the second year $\pi = 0.04$ and $\pi^e = 0.04$. In the first year, what is the unemployment rate? By what percentage does output fall short of full-employment output? In the second year, what is the unemployment rate? By what percentage does output fall short of full-employment output?

b. Now consider a four-year disinflation according to the following table.

Year	1	2	3	4
π	0.08	0.04	0.04	0.04
π^e	0.10	0.08	0.06	0.04

What is the unemployment rate in each of the four years? By what percentage does output fall short of full-employment output each year?

2. Consider the following extended classical economy.

AD	$Y = 300 + 10(M/P)$.
$SRAS$	$Y = \bar{Y} + P - P^e$.
Okun's law	$(Y - \bar{Y})/\bar{Y} = -2.5(u - \bar{u})$.
Full-employment output	$\bar{Y} = 500$.
Natural unemployment rate	$\bar{u} = 0.06$.

a. Suppose that the money supply $M = 1000$ and that the expected price level $P^e = 50$. What are the short-run equilibrium values of output Y, the price level P, and the unemployment rate u? What are the long-run equilibrium values of these three variables?

b. Now suppose that an unanticipated increase raises the nominal money supply to $M = 1260$. What are the new short-run equilibrium values of output Y, the price level P, and the unemployment rate u? What are the new long-run equilibrium values of these three variables? In general, are your results consistent with an expectations-augmented Phillips curve?

3. In a certain economy the expectations-augmented Phillips curve is

$$\pi = \pi^e - 2(u - \bar{u})$$

and

$$\bar{u} = 0.06.$$

a. Graph the Phillips curve of this economy for an expected inflation rate of 0.10. If the Fed chooses to keep the actual inflation rate at 0.10, what will be the unemployment rate?

b. An aggregate demand shock (resulting from increased military spending) raises expected inflation to 0.12 (the natural unemployment rate is unaffected). Graph the new Phillips curve and compare it with the curve you drew in part (a). What happens to the unemployment rate if the Fed holds actual inflation at 0.10? What happens to the Phillips curve and the unemployment rate if the Fed announces that it will hold inflation at 0.10 after the aggregate demand shock, and this announcement is fully believed by the public?

c. Suppose that a supply shock (a drought) raises expected inflation to 0.12 *and* raises the natural unemployment rate to 0.08. Repeat part (b).

4. Consider the following extended classical economy.

AD	$Y = 400 + 5\,(M/P)$.
$SRAS$	$Y = \bar{Y} + 40(P - P^e)$.
Okun's law	$(Y - \bar{Y})/\bar{Y} = -2.5(u - \bar{u})$.
Full-employment output	$\bar{Y} = 800$.
Natural unemployment rate	$\bar{u} = 0.08$.

a. Suppose that the nominal money supply has been constant for many years at $M = 2000$ and is expected to remain constant forever. What are the equilibrium values of the price level P, the expected price level P^e, output Y, and the unemployment rate u?

b. Suppose that as a complete surprise the nominal money supply increases to $M = 2912$. What are the short-run equilibrium values of the price level P (*Hint:* It's a whole number), the expected price level P^e, output Y, and the unemployment rate u? What are the values of cyclical unemployment and unanticipated inflation?

c. What is the slope of the expectations-augmented Phillips curve? (*Hint:* The slope of the expectations-augmented Phillips curve is $-h$ in Eq. 13.1.)

Analytical Problems

1. Suppose that the government institutes a program to help unemployed workers learn new skills, find new jobs, and relocate as necessary to take the new jobs.

a. If this program reduces structural unemployment, what is the effect on the expectations-augmented Phillips curve and the long-run Phillips curve?

b. The government program is expensive, and critics argue that a cheaper way to cut unemployment would be by monetary expansion. Comment.

2. Two extended classical economies (in which the misperceptions theory holds) differ only in one respect: In economy A money growth and inflation have been low and stable for many years, but in economy B money growth and inflation have fluctuated erratically between very low and very high levels. When producers in economy B observe changes in the prices of the goods they produce, from past experience they usually attribute these changes to fluctuations in the overall price level rather than to changes in the relative prices of their goods.

Will the slope of the short-run aggregate supply curve for economy B be flatter or steeper than the slope of the curve for economy A? What about the slope of the Phillips curve?

3. In this problem you are asked to show that the expectations-augmented Phillips curve (derived in the text using the extended classical model) can be derived using the Keynesian model.

Consider a Keynesian economy in which full-employment output is constant, and in which the nominal money supply has been growing at 10% per year for some time and is expected to keep growing at that rate in the future. To avoid some technical complications, suppose that, instead of growing continuously over time, the money supply is increased by 10% each December 31 and then held constant until the next December 31. Monopolistically competitive firms reset their prices on December 31 of each year at the level that they expect will allow them to sell the full-employment level of output during the coming year. Inflation is measured as the percentage change in prices between January 1 and December 31 of each year.

a. Show how the *AD* curve, *SRAS* curve, output, the price level, and the expected price level evolve over time in this economy. What are the values of unanticipated inflation and cyclical unemployment?

b. Now suppose that on June 30, 1995, the money supply is unexpectedly raised by an additional 5%. However, the central bank announces—and is believed by firms—that this extra increase in the money supply is a one-time-only increase and that next December 31 the central bank will return to its policy of increasing the money supply by 10%. (Thus the total increase in the money supply between January 1, 1995, and December 31, 1995, is 15%.) Firms don't change prices until December 31, as usual, but when they do they respond fully to the new information about money supply growth.

What are the actual and unanticipated inflation rates during 1995? Is cyclical unemployment positive, negative, or zero (on average) during 1995? Relate your results to the expectations-augmented Phillips curve.

4. Some economists have suggested that someday we will live in a "cashless society" in which all businesses (including stores) and banks will be linked to a centralized accounting system. In this system you will be able to pay for purchases directly from your bank account without using cash. What are the costs of anticipated inflation in a cashless society? What are the costs of unanticipated inflation?

5. To fight an ongoing 10% inflation, the government makes raising wages or prices illegal. However, the government continues to increase the money supply (and hence aggregate demand) by 10% per year. The economy starts at full-employment output, which remains constant.

a. Using the Keynesian *AD–AS* framework, show the effects of the government's policies on the economy. Assume that firms meet the demand at the fixed price level.

b. After several years in which the controls have kept prices from rising, the government declares victory over inflation and removes the controls. What happens?

CHAPTER 14

Exchange Rates, Business Cycles, and Macroeconomic Policy in the Open Economy

In Chapters 10–13 we focused on a closed economy, or one that doesn't interact with other economies. For some purposes ignoring the foreign sector simplifies the analysis. But the reality is that today, more than ever, we live in a highly interdependent world economic system.

There are two primary aspects of the interdependence of the world's economies. The first is international trade in goods and services, which has increased steadily in volume since World War II. Today firms produce goods and services with an eye on foreign *and* domestic markets, and they obtain many raw materials from distant sources. Expanded international trade has increased productivity by allowing economies to specialize in producing the goods and services best suited to their natural and human resources. However, expanded trade also implies that national economies are more dependent on what happens in other countries. For example, because Japan sells so much of its output to the United States, a U.S. recession or macroeconomic policy change may affect the Japanese economy as well.

The second is the worldwide integration of financial markets, which allows borrowers to obtain funds and savers to look for their best lending opportunities almost anywhere in the world, not just in their own countries. By allowing savings to flow to the highest-return uses regardless of where savers and investors happen to live, the integration of world financial markets increases worldwide productivity, as does the development of an integrated world trading system. But financial market linkages, like trade linkages, increase the sensitivity of individual economies to developments abroad. For example, because of closely connected financial markets, macroeconomic policies that change the real interest rate in one country may affect real interest rates and economic activity in other countries.

In this chapter we build on earlier analyses of the open economy (Chapter 5) and cyclical fluctuations (Chapters 9–12) to examine the macroeconomic implications of trading and financial links among countries. We are particularly concerned in this chapter with how economic openness affects fiscal and monetary policies and how macroeconomic policy changes affect the economies of a country's trading partners. We begin our discussion by introducing two new variables that play central roles in the international economy: the nominal exchange rate and the real exchange rate.

14.1 EXCHANGE RATES

In discussing exchange rates, we must distinguish between nominal and real exchange rates. Briefly stated, the nominal exchange rate is the answer to the question: How many units of a foreign *currency* can I get in exchange for one unit of my domestic *currency*? The real exchange rate is the answer to the question: How many units of the foreign *good* can I get in exchange for one unit of my domestic *good*?

Nominal Exchange Rates

Virtually all countries have their own national currencies:[1] The U.S. dollar, the Japanese yen, the British pound, the German mark, and the French franc are but a few well-known currencies. If someone in one country wants to buy goods, services, or assets from someone in another country, normally she will first have to exchange her country's currency for that of her trading partner's country.

The rate at which two currencies can be traded is the nominal exchange rate between the two currencies. For example, if the nominal exchange rate between the U.S. dollar and the Japanese yen is 110 yen per dollar, a dollar can buy 110 yen (ignoring transaction fees) in the **foreign exchange market,** which is the market for international currencies. Equivalently, 110 yen can buy 1 dollar in the foreign exchange market. More precisely, the **nominal exchange rate** between two currencies, e_{nom}, is the number of units of foreign currency that can be purchased with one unit of the domestic currency. For residents of the United States the domestic currency is the U.S. dollar, and the nominal exchange rate between the U.S. dollar and the Japanese yen is expressed as $e_{nom} = 110$ yen per dollar. The nominal exchange rate often is simply called the **exchange rate,** so whenever someone mentions the exchange rate without specifying real or nominal, the reference is taken to mean the *nominal* exchange rate.

The dollar–yen exchange rate isn't constant. The dollar might trade for 110 yen one day, but the next day it might rise in value to 112 yen or fall in value to 108 yen. Such changes in the exchange rate are normal under a flexible-exchange-rate system, the type of system in which many of the world's major currencies (including the dollar and the yen) are currently traded. In a **flexible-exchange-rate system,** or **floating-exchange-rate system,** exchange rates are not officially fixed but are determined by conditions of supply and

1. An exception is Panama, in which U.S. dollars are the official currency (some Panamanian coins are also used).

demand in the foreign exchange market. Under a flexible-exchange-rate system, exchange rates move continuously and respond quickly to any economic or political news that might influence the supplies and demands for various currencies. The box "In Touch with the Macroeconomy: Exchange Rates," p. 491, discusses exchange rate data.

The values of currencies haven't always been determined by a flexible-exchange-rate system. In the past, some type of **fixed-exchange-rate system** under which exchange rates were set at officially determined levels, often operated. Usually, these official rates were maintained by the commitment of nations' central banks to buy and sell their own currencies at the fixed exchange rate. For example, under the international gold standard system that operated in the late 1800s and early 1900s, the central bank of each country maintained the value of its currency in terms of gold by agreeing to buy or sell gold in exchange for currency at a fixed rate of exchange. The gold standard was suspended during World War I, was temporarily restored in the late 1920s, and then collapsed during the economic and financial crises of the 1930s.

A more recent example of a fixed-exchange-rate system was the Bretton Woods system, named after the town in New Hampshire where the 1944 conference establishing the system was held. Under the Bretton Woods system the values of various currencies were fixed in terms of the U.S. dollar, and the value of the dollar was set at $35 per ounce of gold. The Bretton Woods system functioned until the early 1970s, when inflation in the United States made keeping the price of gold from rising above $35 per ounce virtually impossible (see the Application, "Policy Coordination Failure...," p. 516, for a further discussion of the collapse of the Bretton Woods system). Since the breakdown of the Bretton Woods system, no fixed-exchange-rate system has encompassed all the world's major currencies. In particular, U.S. policymakers haven't attempted to maintain a fixed value for the dollar.

Although no worldwide system of fixed exchange rates currently exists, fixed exchange rates haven't disappeared entirely. Many individual countries, especially smaller ones, attempt to fix their exchange rates against a major currency. For example, several African countries tie their currencies to the French franc. By doing so, these countries hope to stabilize their own currencies and reduce the sharp swings in import and export prices that may result from exchange rate fluctuations. Also, some groups of countries, called **exchange rate unions,** have agreed to try to fix exchange rates among themselves, while allowing their currencies to fluctuate against those of countries outside the union. One example of an exchange rate union is the European Monetary System (EMS), founded in 1979, whose members include many of the Western European countries. The members of the EMS agreed to form an exchange rate union as part of a larger plan to increase economic integration among the countries of Western Europe (we discuss the EMS further in Section 14.5).

Real Exchange Rates

The nominal exchange rate doesn't tell you all you need to know about the purchasing power of a currency. If you were told, for example, that the nominal exchange rate between the U.S. dollar and the Japanese yen is 110 yen per dollar, but you didn't know anything else about the U.S. or Japanese economies, you might be tempted to conclude that someone from Kansas City could visit Tokyo very cheaply—after all, 110 yen for just 1 dollar seems like a good deal. But even at 110 yen per dollar, Japan is an expensive place to visit. The reason is that although 1 dollar can buy a lot of yen, it also takes a lot of yen (thousands or hundreds of thousands) to buy everyday goods in Japan.

Suppose, for example, that you want to compare the price of hamburgers in Tokyo and Kansas City. Knowing that the exchange rate is 110 yen per dollar doesn't help much. But if you also know that a hamburger costs 2 dollars in Kansas City and 1100 yen in Tokyo, you can compare the price of a hamburger in the two cities by asking how many dollars are needed to buy a hamburger in Japan. Because a hamburger costs 1100 yen in Tokyo, and 110 yen cost 1 dollar, the price of a hamburger in Tokyo is 10 dollars (calculated by dividing the price of a Japanese hamburger, ¥1100, by ¥110/$1, to obtain $10 per hamburger). The price of a U.S. hamburger relative to a Japanese hamburger is therefore ($2 per U.S. hamburger)/($10 per Japanese hamburger) = 0.20 Japanese hamburgers per U.S. hamburger. The Japanese hamburger is expensive in the sense that (in this example) one U.S. hamburger equals only one fifth of a Japanese hamburger.

The price of domestic goods relative to foreign goods—equivalently, the number of foreign goods someone gets in exchange for one domestic good—is called the **real exchange rate.** In the hamburger example the real exchange rate between the United States and Japan is 0.20 Japanese hamburgers per U.S. hamburger.

In general, the real exchange rate is related to the nominal exchange rate and to prices in both countries. To write this relation we use the following symbols:

e_{nom} = the nominal exchange rate (110 yen per dollar);
P_{For} = the price of foreign goods, measured in the foreign currency (1100 yen per Japanese hamburger);
P = the price of domestic goods, measured in the domestic currency (2 dollars per U.S. hamburger).

The real exchange rate e is the number of foreign goods (Japanese hamburgers) that can be obtained in exchange for one unit of the domestic good (U.S. hamburgers). The general formula for the real exchange rate is

$$
\begin{aligned}
e &= \frac{e_{\text{nom}}P}{P_{\text{For}}} \\
&= \frac{(¥110 / \$1)(\$2 / \text{U.S. hamburger})}{¥1100/\text{Japanese hamburger}} \qquad (14.1) \\
&= 0.20 \text{ Japanese hamburgers per U.S. hamburger.}
\end{aligned}
$$

In defining the real exchange rate as the number of foreign goods that can be obtained for each domestic good, we assume that each country produces a single, unique good. (Think of France producing only bottles of wine and Saudi Arabia producing only barrels of oil; then the French real exchange rate with respect to Saudi Arabia is the number of barrels of oil that can be purchased for one bottle of wine.) The assumption that each country produces a single good (which is different from the good produced by any other country) simplifies the theoretical analysis in this chapter.[2]

Of course, in reality countries produce thousands of different goods, so real exchange rates must be based on price indexes (such as the GDP deflator or the CPI) to measure P and P_{For}. Thus the real exchange rate isn't actually the rate of exchange between two specific goods but instead is the rate of exchange between a typical basket of goods in one country and a typical basket of goods in the other country. Changes in the real exchange rate over time indicate that, on average, the goods of the country whose real exchange rate is rising are becoming more expensive relative to the goods of the other country.

Appreciation and Depreciation

When the nominal exchange rate e_{nom} falls so that, say, a dollar buys fewer units of foreign currency, we say that the dollar has undergone a **nominal depreciation**. This is the same as saying that the dollar has become "weaker." If the dollar's nominal exchange rate e_{nom} rises, then the dollar has had a **nominal appreciation**. When the dollar appreciates, it can buy more units of foreign currency and thus has become "stronger."[3] The terms appreciation and depreciation are associated with flexible exchange rates. Under a fixed-exchange-rate system, in which exchange rates are changed only by official government action, different terms are used. Instead of a depreciation, a weakening of the currency is called a **devaluation.** A strengthening of the currency under fixed exchange rates is called a **revaluation,** rather than an appreciation. These terms are listed for convenience in Summary table 15.

An increase in the real exchange rate e is called a **real appreciation.** With a real appreciation, the same quantity of domestic goods can be traded for more

2. The assumption that different countries produce different goods is a change from Chapter 5, where we implicitly assumed that all countries produce an identical good that can be used for all purposes (consumption, investment, etc.). The assumption that all countries produce the same good implied that, in the analysis of that chapter, the real exchange rate was always equal to 1.

3. You will sometimes see the exchange rate defined as the number of units of domestic currency per unit of foreign currency, which is the reciprocal of how we have defined it. For example, the exchange rate between the British pound and the U.S. dollar is typically quoted in this form (for example, $1.90 per pound). Under this alternative definition an appreciation of the dollar corresponds to a fall in the nominal exchange rate. The two ways of defining the exchange rate are equally valid, as long as consistency is maintained. We have chosen to define the exchange rate as the number of units of foreign currency per unit of home currency because it is easier to remember that an appreciation (when the value of the dollar goes up) is associated with a rise in the exchange rate.

SUMMARY 15

Terminology for Changes in Exchange Rates

Type of Exchange Rate System	Exchange Rate Increases (Currency Strengthens)	Exchange Rate Decreases (Currency Weakens)
Flexible exchange rates	Appreciation	Depreciation
Fixed exchange rates	Revaluation	Devaluation

of the foreign good than before because e, the price of domestic goods relative to the price of foreign goods, has risen. A drop in the real exchange rate, which decreases the quantity of foreign goods that can be purchased with the same quantity of domestic goods, is called a **real depreciation.**

Real Versus Nominal Exchange Rate Movements

Let's now look at how movements in these two types of exchange rates are related. We can use the definition of the real exchange rate in Eq. (14.1), $e = e_{nom}P/P_{For}$, to calculate $\Delta e/e$, the percentage change in the real exchange rate. Because the real exchange rate is expressed as a ratio, its percentage change equals the percentage change in the numerator minus the percentage change in the denominator.[4] The percentage change in the numerator of the expression for the real exchange rate[5] is $\Delta e_{nom}/e_{nom} + \Delta P/P$, and the percentage change in the denominator is $\Delta P_{For}/P_{For}$. Thus the percentage change in the real exchange rate is

$$\frac{\Delta e}{e} = \frac{\Delta e_{nom}}{e_{nom}} + \frac{\Delta P}{P} - \frac{\Delta P_{For}}{P_{For}}. \tag{14.2}$$

In Eq. (14.2) the term $\Delta P/P$, the percentage change in the domestic price level, is the same as the domestic rate of inflation π, and the term $\Delta P_{For}/P_{For}$, the percentage change in the foreign price level, is the same as the foreign rate of inflation π_{For}. Making these substitutions and rearranging the equation, we rewrite Eq. (14.2) as

$$\frac{\Delta e_{nom}}{e_{nom}} = \frac{\Delta e}{e} + \pi_{For} - \pi. \tag{14.3}$$

Equation (14.3) is purely definitional and thus must always be satisfied. It states that the rate of nominal exchange rate appreciation $\Delta e_{nom}/e_{nom}$ equals the rate of real exchange rate appreciation $\Delta e/e$ plus the excess of foreign inflation over domestic inflation, $\pi_{For} - \pi$. Hence two factors contribute to strengthening a currency (a nominal appreciation): (1) an increase in the relative price of a country's exports (a real appreciation), which might occur if, for example, foreign demand for those exports rises; and (2) a rate of domestic inflation π lower than that of the country's trading partners π_{For}.

The Real Exchange Rate and Net Exports

We've defined the real exchange rate, but so far we haven't indicated why it is important in macroeconomic analysis. One reason that policymakers and the public should care about the real exchange rate is that it represents the rate at which domestic goods and services can be traded for those produced abroad. An increase in the real exchange rate—also sometimes referred to as the **terms of trade**—is good for a country in the sense that its citizens are able to obtain

---

4. Appendix A, Section A.7, describes how to calculate growth rates of products and ratios.
5. This result is obtained by using the rule that the percentage change in a product XY is the percentage change in X plus the percentage change in Y. See Appendix A, Section A.7.

more foreign goods and services in exchange for a given amount of domestic production.

A second reason is that the real exchange rate affects a country's net exports, or exports less imports. Changes in net exports in turn have a direct impact on the domestic industries that produce for export or that compete with imported goods in the domestic market. In addition, as we discuss later in the chapter, changes in net exports affect a country's overall level of economic activity and are a primary channel through which business cycle disturbances and macroeconomic policy changes are transmitted internationally.

What is the link between the real exchange rate and net exports? A basic determinant of the demand for any good or service—say, coffee or taxi rides—is the price of that good or service relative to alternatives. If the price of coffee is too high, some people will switch to tea; if taxi fares rise, more people will take the bus. Similarly, the real exchange rate—the price of domestic goods relative to foreign goods—helps determine the demand for domestic goods both in home and foreign markets.

Suppose that the real exchange rate is high so that a unit of the domestic good can buy relatively many units of the foreign good. For example, let's say that a domestically produced car costs twice as much as a comparable foreign car (both prices are measured in terms of the same currency). Domestic residents will then find that foreign cars are less expensive than domestic cars, so (all else being equal) their demand for imported autos will be high. Foreign residents, in contrast, will find that the domestic country's cars are more expensive than their own, so they will want to purchase relatively few of the domestic country's exports. With few cars being sold abroad and many cars being imported, the country's net exports of cars will be low, probably even negative.

Conversely, suppose that the real exchange rate is low; for example, imagine that a domestically produced automobile costs only half what a comparable foreign car costs. Then, all else being equal, the domestic country will be able to export relatively large quantities of cars and will import relatively few, so that its net exports of cars will be high.

The general conclusion, then, is that *the higher the real exchange rate is, the lower a country's net exports will be,* holding constant other factors affecting export and import demand. The reason for this result is the same reason that higher prices reduce the amount of coffee people drink or the number of taxi rides they take. Because the real exchange rate is the relative price of a country's goods and services, an increase in the real exchange rate induces both foreigners and domestic residents to consume less domestic production and more goods and services produced abroad, which lowers net exports.

The J Curve. Although the conclusion that (holding other factors constant) a higher real exchange rate depresses net exports is generally valid, there is one important qualification: Depending on how quickly importers and exporters respond to changes in relative prices, the effect of a change in the real exchange rate on net exports may be weak in the short run and may even go the "wrong" way.

To understand why, consider a country that imports most of its oil and suddenly faces a sharp increase in world oil prices. Because the country's domestic goods now can buy less of the foreign good (oil), the country's real exchange rate has fallen. In the long run, this decline in the real exchange rate may increase the country's net exports because high oil prices will lead domestic residents to reduce oil imports and the relative cheapness of domestic goods will stimulate exports (to oil-producing countries, for example). In the short run, however, switching to other fuels and increasing domestic oil production are difficult, so the number of barrels of oil imported may drop only slightly. For this reason, and because the real cost of each barrel of oil (in terms of the domestic good) has risen, for some period of time after the oil price increase the country's total real cost of imports (measured in terms of the domestic good) may rise. Thus in the short run a decline in the real exchange rate might be associated with a *drop* rather than a rise in net exports, contrary to our earlier conclusion. (Numerical Problem 2 at the end of the chapter provides an example of how a real depreciation can cause net exports to fall.)

Figure 14.1 shows the typical response pattern of a country's net exports to a drop in the real exchange rate (a real depreciation). The economy initially has negative net exports when the real exchange rate depreciates. In the short run the real depreciation reduces rather than increases net exports because the drop in the real exchange rate forces the country to pay more for its imports. Over time, however, as the lower real exchange rate leads to larger export quantities and smaller import quantities, net exports begin to rise (even taking into account the higher relative cost of imports). Eventually, the country's net exports rise relative to the initial situation. This typical response pattern of net exports to a real depreciation is called the **J curve** because the graph of net exports against time looks like the letter J lying on its back.

Figure 14.1
The J curve
The J curve shows the response pattern of net exports to a real depreciation. Here, net exports are negative at time zero, when the real exchange rate depreciates. In the short run net exports become more negative, as the decline in the real exchange rate raises the real cost of imports (measured in terms of the export good). Over time, however, increased exports and reduced quantities of imports more than compensate for the increased cost of imports, and net exports rise above their initial level.

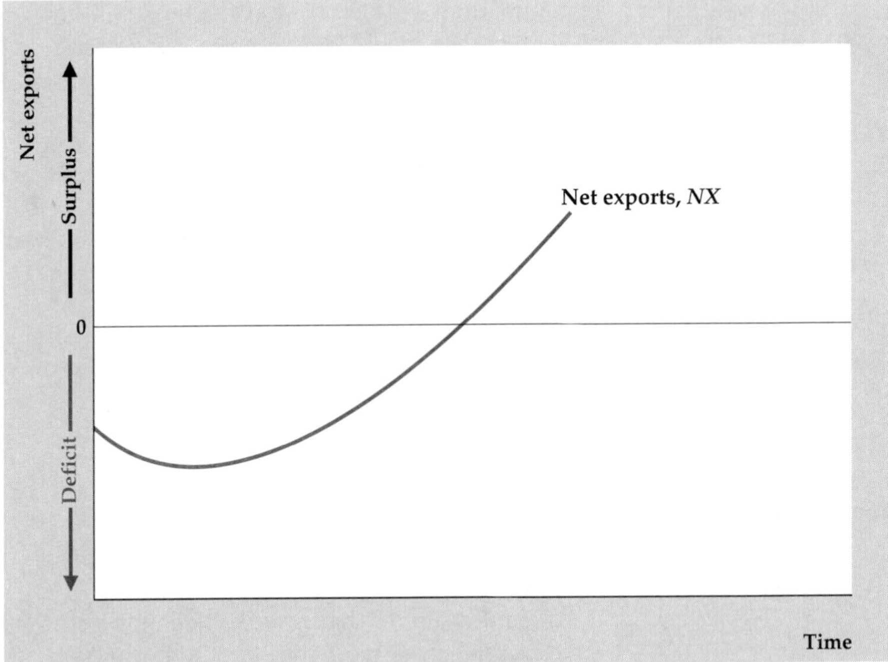

The macroeconomic analyses in this chapter are based on the assumption that the time period is long enough that (all else being equal) a real depreciation increases net exports and that a real appreciation reduces net exports. Keep in mind, though, that this assumption may not be valid for shorter periods—and in some cases, even for several years—as the following Application demonstrates.

APPLICATION

The Value of the Dollar and U.S. Net Exports in the 1970s and 1980s

In the early 1970s the major industrialized countries of the world switched from fixed to flexible exchange rates. Figure 14.2 shows the U.S. real exchange rate (the "real value of the dollar") and real U.S. net exports since the exchange rate began to float. Because the U.S. real exchange rate is the relative price of U.S. goods, the real value of the dollar and U.S. net exports should move in opposite directions (assuming that changes in the real exchange rate are the primary source of changes in net exports).

An apparent confirmation that the real exchange rate and net exports move in opposite directions occurred during the early 1980s. From 1980 to 1985 the real value of the dollar increased by about 50%. This sharp increase was followed, with a brief delay, by a large decline in U.S. net exports. At the time, many U.S. firms complained that the strong dollar was pricing their products out of foreign markets and, by making imported goods cheap for U.S. consumers, also reducing their sales at home.

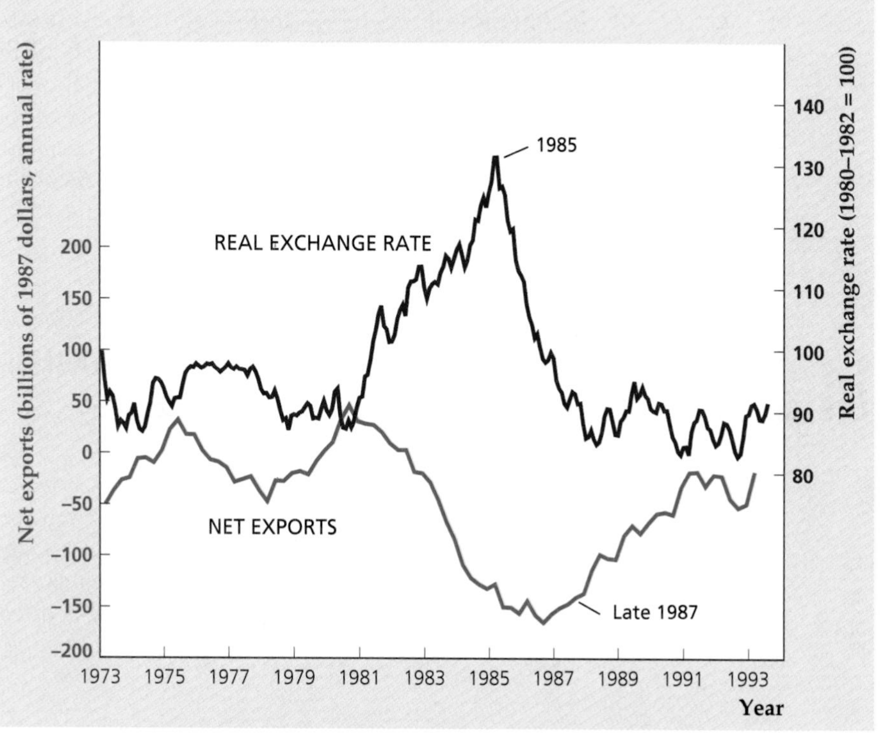

Figure 14.2
The U.S. real exchange rate and net exports, 1973–1993
U.S. real net exports are measured along the left vertical axis, and the U.S. real exchange rate (the real value of the dollar) is measured along the right vertical axis. The sharp increase in the real exchange rate in the first half of the 1980s was accompanied by a decline in U.S. net exports. The decline of the dollar after 1985 stimulated U.S. net exports, but with a delay that probably reflected the J-curve effect.

Source: Real exchange rate: U.S. real narrow effective exchange rate, 1980–1982 = 100, measured against 15 industrial-country currencies, courtesy of J. P. Morgan Economic Research; net exports (billions of 1987 dollars), *Survey of Current Business*, various issues.

After peaking in March 1985, the real value of the dollar fell sharply for almost three years. Despite this precipitous decline, U.S. net exports continued to fall until late in 1987, when they finally began to increase. During the two and a half years in which U.S. net exports continued to decline despite the rapid depreciation of the dollar, the public and policymakers expressed increasing skepticism about economists' predictions that the depreciation would lead to more net exports. Initially, economists reponded by saying that, because of the J curve, there would be some delay between the depreciation of the dollar and the improvement in net exports. By 1987, however, even the strongest believers in the J curve had begun to wonder whether net exports would ever begin to rise. Finally, U.S. real net exports did recover substantially, although they remained negative.

What took so long? One explanation suggests that, because the dollar was so strong in the first half of the 1980s (which made U.S. goods very expensive relative to foreign goods), U.S. firms lost many of their foreign customers. Once these foreign customers were lost, regaining them or adding new foreign customers was difficult, especially as many U.S. exporters reduced production capacity and cut back foreign sales operations when the value of the dollar was high. Similarly, the strong dollar gave foreign producers, including some who hadn't previously sold their output to the United States, a chance to make inroads into the U.S. domestic market. Having established sales networks and customer relationships in the United States, these foreign companies were better able than before to compete with U.S. firms when the dollar began its decline in 1985.

The idea that the strong dollar permanently increased the penetration of the U.S. market by foreign producers, while similarly reducing the capability of American firms to sell in foreign markets, has been called the "beachhead effect."[6] According to this view, if the effects of the strong-dollar period on U.S. net exports are to be undone, the real value of the dollar will have to fall back not just to its 1980 level, before the appreciation, but to a still lower level. Only with a very weak dollar will U.S. firms be able to regain the markets they lost when the dollar was unusually strong. As of the early 1990s the real value of the dollar had fallen to about its 1980 level.

14.2 HOW EXCHANGE RATES ARE DETERMINED: A SUPPLY-AND-DEMAND ANALYSIS

In flexible-exchange-rate systems, exchange rates change constantly. In fixed-exchange-rate systems, by definition, exchange rates are stable most of the time; but even under a fixed-rate system, large devaluations or revaluations are not uncommon. What economic forces cause a nation's exchange rate to rise or fall? In this section we address this question by using supply and

---

6. Empirical support for the beachhead effect is presented in Richard E. Baldwin, "Hysteresis in Import Prices: The Beachhead Effect," *American Economic Review*, September 1988, pp. 773–785.

IN TOUCH *WITH THE MACROECONOMY*

EXCHANGE RATES

Exchange rates are determined in foreign exchange markets, in which the currencies of different countries are traded. Principal foreign exchange markets are located in New York, London, Tokyo, and other financial centers. Because foreign exchange markets are in widely separated time zones, at least one of the markets is open at almost any time of the day, so trading in currencies essentially takes place around-the-clock.

Exchange rates among major currencies often are reported daily on radio and television, and daily quotations of exchange rates are printed in major newspapers and financial dailies. The exchange rates in the accompanying table were reported in the "Money and Investing" section of the *Wall Street Journal* on August 5, 1993, and apply to transactions of August 4, 1993.

Four exchange rates relative to the U.S. dollar are reported in the table for each country: a spot rate and three forward rates. All are expressed as units of foreign currency per U.S. dollar. The spot rate is the rate at which foreign currency can be traded immediately for U.S. dollars. For instance, the spot exchange rate for France, 5.9305, means that on August 4, 1993, one U.S. dollar could buy 5.9305 francs for immediate delivery.

Forward exchange rates are prices at which you can agree now to buy foreign currency at a specified date in the future. For example, on August 4, 1993, you could have arranged to buy or sell German marks 30 days later at an exchange rate of 1.7159 marks per dollar. Note that for each of the currencies listed, except for the Japanese yen, the 30-day forward exchange rate is higher than the spot exchange rate and that forward exchange rates increase for dates farther into the future (90 days and 180 days). This pattern of rising forward rates indicates that, as of August 4, 1993, participants in the foreign exchange market expected the value of the dollar relative to the other currencies (except the yen) to increase over the next six months. For the Japanese yen, the forward rates against the dollar are about the same as the spot rate, indicating that little change in the yen–dollar exchange rate was expected.

Exchange Rate Against U.S. Dollar

Country	Spot	30-Day Forward	90-Day Forward	180-Day Forward
Great Britain (pounds per U.S. dollar)	0.6669	0.6685	0.6714	0.6744
Canada (Canadian dollars per U.S. dollar)	1.2887	1.2897	1.2915	1.2946
France (francs per U.S. dollar)	5.9305	5.9695	6.0095	6.0380
Germany (marks per U.S. dollar)	1.7104	1.7159	1.7254	1.7367
Japan (yen per U.S. dollar)	104.84	104.85	104.83	104.63

demand to analyze the determination of exchange rates in a flexible-exchange-rate system (we return to fixed exchange rates in Section 14.5).

For clarity our supply-and-demand analysis focuses on the nominal exchange rate rather than the real exchange rate. However, recall from Eq. (14.1) that, for given levels of domestic and foreign prices, the real exchange rate and the nominal exchange rate are proportional. Because we hold price levels constant in this section, *all our conclusions about the nominal exchange rate apply equally to the real exchange rate.*

The nominal exchange rate e_{nom} is the value of a currency, say, the dollar. The value of the dollar, like that of any asset, is determined by supply and demand in the relevant market. For dollars the relevant market is the foreign exchange market, where banks and currency traders continuously trade dollars for other currencies.

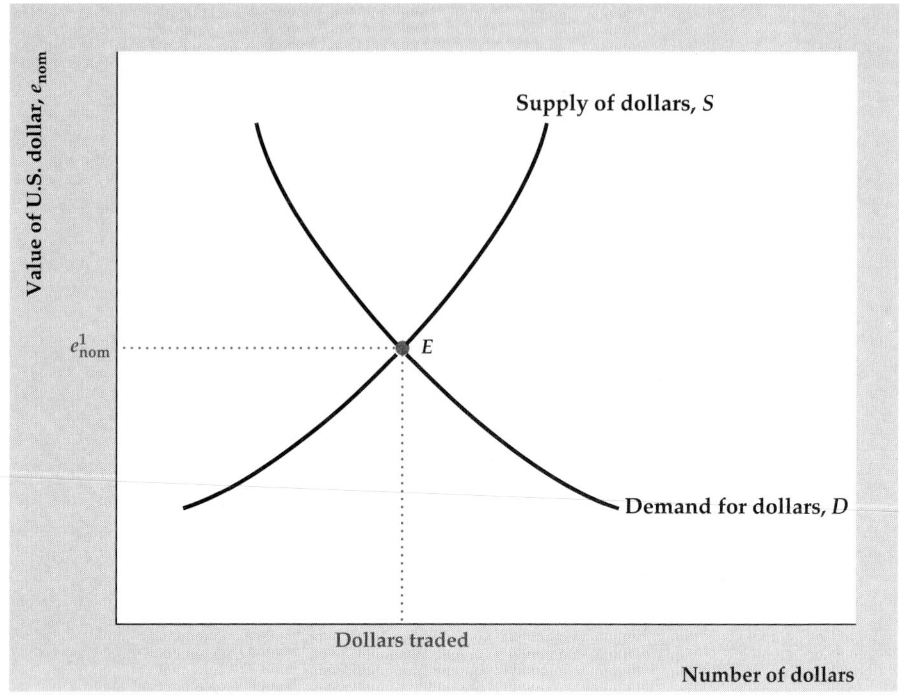

Figure 14.3
The supply of and demand for the dollar
The figure shows the determination of the value of the dollar in the foreign exchange market. The supply curve for dollars, *S*, indicates the number of dollars that people are willing to sell in the foreign exchange market at each value of the U.S. nominal exchange rate e_{nom}. The demand curve for dollars, *D*, shows the number of dollars that people want to buy at each nominal exchange rate. At equilibrium, point *E*, the value of the dollar, e^1_{nom}, is the nominal exchange rate at which the quantity of dollars supplied equals the quantity of dollars demanded.

Figure 14.3 shows the supply and demand for dollars. The horizontal axis of the diagram measures the quantity of dollars supplied or demanded, and the vertical axis measures the value of the dollar in terms of other currencies, or the nominal exchange rate e_{nom}. The supply curve for dollars, *S*, shows the number of dollars that people want to supply to the foreign exchange market at each "price" (nominal exchange rate). To supply dollars to the foreign exchange market means to offer to exchange dollars for some other currency. When the dollar's value in terms of other currencies is high, people are more willing to supply dollars to the market; thus the supply curve slopes upward. Similarly, the demand curve for dollars, *D*, shows the quantity of dollars that people want to buy in the foreign exchange market at each exchange rate. When the dollar is more expensive in terms of other currencies, people demand fewer dollars, so the demand curve slopes downward. The equilibrium value of the dollar at point *E* is e^1_{nom}, the exchange rate at which the quantity of dollars supplied and the quantity of dollars demanded are equal.

Figure 14.3 aids in understanding the forces that determine the value of the dollar, or any other currency. To go any further, though, we must ask why people decide to demand or supply dollars. Unlike apples or haircuts, dollars aren't demanded because people value them in themselves; rather, people value dollars because of what they can buy. Specifically, foreign individuals or firms demand dollars in the foreign exchange market for two reasons:

1. to be able to buy U.S. goods and services (U.S. exports), and
2. to be able to buy U.S. real and financial assets (U.S. capital inflows).

Note that the two types of transactions for which foreigners need dollars (to purchase U.S. exports and U.S. assets) correspond to the two components of the balance of payments accounts: the current account and the capital account.[7]

Similarly, Americans supply dollars to the foreign exchange market, thereby acquiring foreign currencies, for two reasons:

1. to be able to buy foreign goods and services (U.S. imports), and
2. to be able to buy real and financial assets in foreign countries (U.S. capital outflows).

Thus factors that increase foreigners' demand for U.S. exports and assets will also increase the foreign-exchange-market demand for dollars, raising the dollar exchange rate. Likewise, the value of the dollar will rise if Americans' demand for foreign goods and assets declines, so Americans supply fewer dollars to the foreign exchange market.

As an example, suppose that U.S. goods improve in quality, so that foreigners demand more of them. This increase in the demand for U.S. exports would translate into an increase in the demand for U.S. dollars. In Fig. 14.4 the demand for dollars shifts to the right, from D^1 to D^2, and the equilibrium value of the dollar rises from e^1_{nom} to e^2_{nom}. All else being equal, then, improvements in the quality of U.S. goods would lead to an appreciation of the dollar.

---

7. The current account and the capital account are defined and discussed in Chapter 5. The idea that foreigners must hold dollars to buy U.S. goods or assets isn't completely accurate, because many transactions between Americans and foreigners are done without anyone ever literally holding a supply of dollars or the foreign currency. Nevertheless, this way of thinking about the determination of exchange rates is fairly simple and gives the same answers as would a more complex analysis.

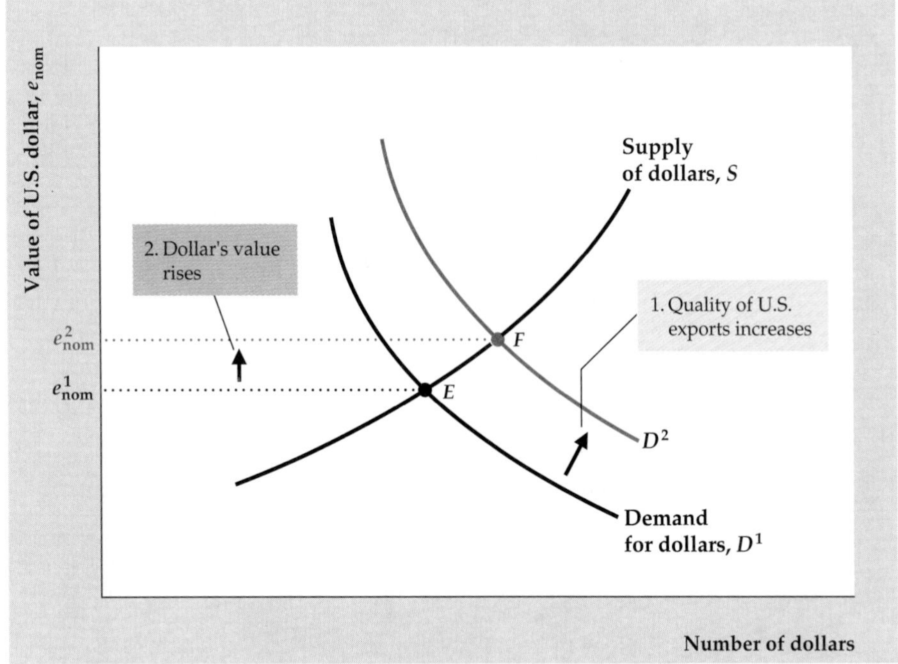

Figure 14.4
The effect of increased export quality on the value of the dollar
An increase in the quality of U.S. exports raises foreigners' demands for U.S. goods and hence their demand for U.S. dollars, which are needed to buy U.S. goods. The demand curve for dollars shifts, from D^1 to D^2, raising the value of the dollar (the nominal exchange rate) from e^1_{nom} to e^2_{nom}.

Macroeconomic Determinants of the Exchange Rate and Net Export Demand

In our previous *IS–LM* analyses we emphasized two key macroeconomic variables: real output (income) Y and the real interest rate r. In anticipation of the open-economy version of the *IS–LM* model presented in Section 14.3, we now consider how changes in real output or the real interest rate (either at home or abroad) are linked to the exchange rate and net exports. Again, because we are holding domestic and foreign price levels constant, the results we discuss here apply equally to the nominal exchange rate and the real exchange rate.

Effects of Changes in Output (Income). Imagine that domestic output (equivalently, domestic income) Y increases but that other factors (such as the real interest rate) remain unchanged. How would the increase in Y affect the exchange rate and net exports?

To consider the effect on net exports first is easier. We know that spending by consumers depends in part on their current incomes. When domestic income rises, consumers will spend more on all goods and services, *including imports.* Thus when domestic output (income) rises, net exports (exports minus imports) must fall, other factors held constant.[8]

To determine the effect of increased domestic output on the exchange rate, recall that, in order to increase their purchases of imports, domestic residents must obtain foreign currencies. Equivalently, domestic residents must supply more domestic currency to the foreign exchange market. An increased supply of domestic currency causes its value to fall, that is, the exchange rate depreciates.

We can also analyze the effects of an increase in the real output of the country's trading partners, Y_{For} (foreign output or income). An increase in Y_{For} leads foreign consumers to increase their spending on all goods and services, including the exports of the domestic country. Thus an increase in the income of Germany and Japan, for example, would increase those nations' demand for U.S. exports and raise U.S. net exports. The increase in foreign demand for U.S. goods also would increase foreigners' demand for U.S. dollars, raising the value of the dollar. Note that the effects of changes in foreign income are the opposite of the effects of changes in domestic income.

Effects of Changes in Real Interest Rates. A second key macroeconomic variable to be considered is the real interest rate. Imagine that the domestic country's real interest rate r rises, with other factors (including the foreign real interest rate) held constant.[9] In this case, the country's real and financial assets

8. The conclusion that an increase in output reduces net exports seems to contradict a result obtained in Chapter 5—that an increase in output owing to a beneficial supply shock raises net exports. There is no contradiction because a supply shock doesn't hold variables other than output constant as we are assuming here. See Analytical Problem 5 at the end of the chapter.

9. Note that, by holding the foreign real interest rate constant, we no longer assume (as we did in Chapter 5) that the domestic and foreign countries face the same world real interest rate. In general, real interest rates in different countries need not be the same when countries produce different goods, as we assume in this chapter. The reason is that real interest rates in different countries measure different things. For example, the Japanese real interest rate measures the growth of an asset's purchasing power in terms of Japanese goods, whereas the German real interest rate measures the growth of an asset's purchasing power in terms of German goods. If the Japanese–German real exchange rate is changing, the two need not be the same.

will become more attractive to foreign savers seeking the highest return on their funds. Because domestic currency can be used to buy domestic assets, a rise in the domestic real interest rate also increases the demand for domestic currency. An increased demand for domestic currency in turn leads to exchange rate appreciation.

A rise in the domestic real interest rate r has no *direct* effect on net exports, but it does have an *indirect* effect through the exchange rate. An increase in r raises the exchange rate so that domestic exports become more expensive and imports from abroad become cheaper. Thus, other factors being constant, an increase in r reduces the domestic country's net exports.

The effects of a change in the foreign real interest rate, r_{For}, are the opposite of the effects of a change in the domestic real interest rate. If the foreign real interest rate rises, for example, foreign assets will become more attractive to domestic savers. To get the foreign currency needed to buy foreign assets, domestic savers will supply domestic currency to the foreign exchange market. The increased supply of domestic currency will lead to a depreciation of the exchange rate. The depreciation of the exchange rate caused by the rise in r_{For} in turn raises the domestic country's net exports.

Summary tables 16 and 17, on the next page, list the effects of the various macroeconomic factors on the exchange rate and net exports.

14.3 THE *IS–LM* MODEL FOR AN OPEN ECONOMY

Now we're ready to explore how exchange rates and international trade interact with the behavior of the economy as a whole. To do so, we extend the *IS–LM* model to allow for trade and lending among nations. An algebraic version of this analysis is presented in Appendix 14.A.

Recall that the components of the *IS–LM* model are the *IS* curve, which describes goods market equilibrium; the *LM* curve, which describes asset market equilibrium; and the *FE* line, which describes labor market equilibrium. Nothing discussed in this chapter affects our analysis of the supply of or demand for money; so, in developing the open-economy *IS–LM* model, we use the same *LM* curve that we used for the closed economy model. Similarly, the labor market and the production function aren't directly affected by international factors, so the *FE* line also is unchanged.[10]

However, because net exports are part of the demand for goods, we have to modify the *IS* curve in order to describe the open economy. Three main points need to be made about the *IS* curve in the open economy:

1. Although the open-economy *IS* curve is derived somewhat differently than the closed-economy *IS* curve, it is a downward-sloping relationship between output and the real interest rate, as the closed-economy *IS* curve is.
2. All factors that shift the *IS* curve in the closed economy shift the *IS* curve in the open economy in the same way.

10. A case in which the *FE* line does depend on international considerations is when some raw materials (such as oil) are imported. In this book we have modeled oil price shocks as productivity shocks, which captures the main domestic macroeconomic effects. A full analysis that includes all the international aspects of an oil price shock is complex, so we do not present it here.

SUMMARY 16

Determinants of the Exchange Rate (Real or Nominal)

An Increase in	Causes the Exchange Rate to	Reason
Domestic output (income), Y	Fall	Higher domestic output raises demand for imports and increases supply of domestic currency.
Foreign output (income), Y_{For}	Rise	Higher foreign output raises demand for exports and increases demand for domestic currency.
Domestic real interest rate, r	Rise	Higher real interest rate makes domestic assets more attractive and increases demand for domestic currency.
Foreign real interest rate, r_{For}	Fall	Higher foreign real interest rate makes foreign assets more attractive and increases supply of domestic currency.
World demand for domestic goods	Rise	Higher demand for domestic goods increases demand for domestic currency.

SUMMARY 17

Determinants of Net Exports

An Increase in	Causes Net Exports to	Reason
Domestic output (income), Y	Fall	Higher domestic output raises demand for imports.
Foreign output (income), Y_{For}	Rise	Higher foreign output raises foreign demand for exports.
Domestic real interest rate, r	Fall	Higher real interest rate appreciates the real exchange rate and makes domestic goods more expensive relative to foreign goods.
Foreign real interest rate, r_{For}	Rise	Higher foreign real interest rate depreciates the real exchange rate and makes domestic goods cheaper relative to foreign goods.
World demand for domestic goods	Rise	Higher demand for domestic goods directly increases net exports.

3. In an open economy factors that change net exports also shift the *IS* curve. Specifically, for given values of domestic output and the domestic real interest rate, factors that raise a country's net exports shift the open-economy *IS* curve up; and factors that lower a country's net exports shift the *IS* curve down.

After discussing each point, we use the open-economy *IS–LM* model to analyze the international transmission of business cycles and the operation of macroeconomic policies in an open economy.

The Open-Economy *IS* Curve

For any level of output the *IS* curve gives the real interest rate that brings the goods market into equilibrium. In a closed economy the goods market equilibrium condition is that desired national saving S^d must equal desired investment I^d, or $S^d - I^d = 0$. In an open economy, as we showed in Chapter 5, the goods market equilibrium condition is that desired saving S^d must equal desired investment I^d plus net exports NX. Writing the goods market equilibrium condition for an open economy, we have

$$S^d - I^d = NX. \tag{14.4}$$

To interpret Eq. (14.4), recall that $S^d - I^d$, the excess of national saving over investment, is the amount that domestic residents desire to lend abroad. Recall also that net exports NX (which, if net factor payments are zero, is the same as the current account balance) equals the amount that foreigners want to borrow from domestic savers. Thus Eq. (14.4) indicates that, for the goods market to be in equilibrium, desired foreign lending must equal desired foreign borrowing.

An equivalent way to write the goods market equilibrium condition is as follows:

$$Y = C^d + I^d + G + NX. \tag{14.5}$$

We obtained Eq. (14.5) from Eq. (14.4) by replacing desired saving, S^d, with its definition, $Y - C^d - G$, and rearranging. Equation (14.5) states that the goods market is in equilibrium when the supply of goods, Y, equals the demand for goods, $C^d + I^d + G + NX$. Note that in an open economy the total demand for goods includes spending on net exports.

Figure 14.5, on the next page, illustrates goods market equilibrium in an open economy. The horizontal axis measures desired saving minus desired investment, $S^d - I^d$, and net exports NX. Note that the horizontal axis includes both positive and negative values. The vertical axis measures the domestic real interest rate, r.

The upward-sloping curve, $S - I$, shows the difference between desired national saving and desired investment for each value of the real interest rate r. This curve slopes upward because, with output held constant, an increase in the real interest rate raises desired national saving and reduces desired investment, raising the country's desired foreign lending.

The downward-sloping curve in Fig. 14.5, NX, shows the relationship between the country's net exports and the domestic real interest rate, other factors held constant. As discussed in Section 14.2, a rise in the real interest rate appreciates the exchange rate, which in turn reduces net exports (see Summary table 17). Hence the NX curve slopes downward.

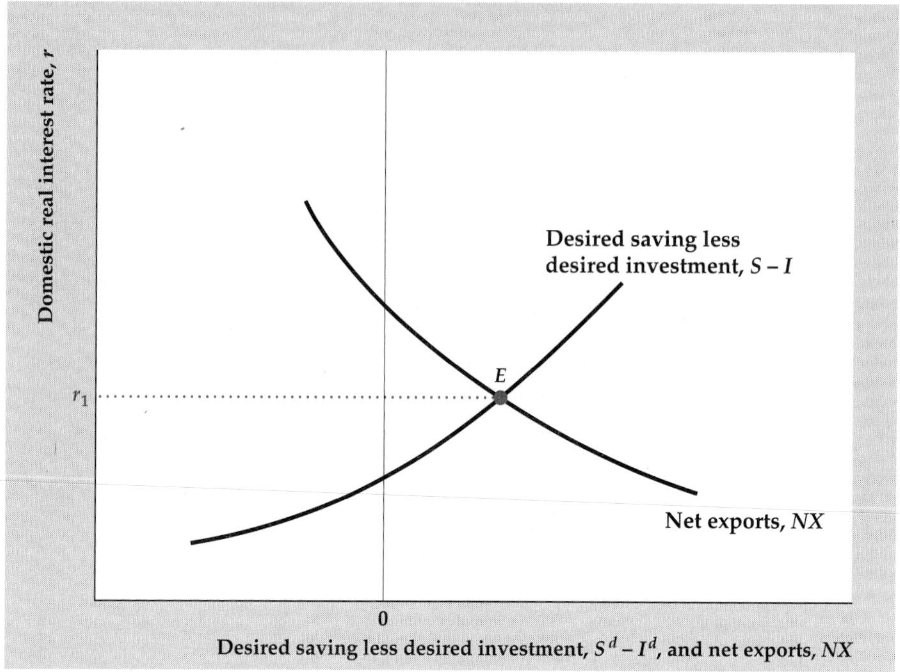

Figure 14.5
Goods market equilibrium in an open economy
The upward-sloping curve shows desired saving S^d less desired investment I^d. This curve slopes upward because a higher domestic real interest rate increases the excess of desired saving over desired investment. The *NX* curve relates net exports to the domestic real interest rate. This curve slopes downward because a higher domestic real interest rate causes the real exchange rate to appreciate, reducing net exports. Goods market equilibrium occurs at point *E*, where the excess of desired saving over desired investment equals net exports (equivalently, where desired lending abroad equals desired borrowing by foreigners). The real interest rate that clears the goods market is r_1.

Goods market equilibrium requires that the excess of desired saving over desired investment equal net exports (Eq. 14.4). This condition is satisfied at the intersection of the $S - I$ and *NX* curves at point *E*. Thus the domestic real interest rate that clears the goods market is the interest rate at *E*, or r_1.

To derive the open-economy *IS* curve, we need to know what happens to the real interest rate that clears the goods market when the current level of domestic output rises (see Fig. 14.6). Suppose that domestic output initially equals Y_1 and that goods market equilibrium is at point *E*, with a real interest rate of r_1. Now suppose that output rises to Y_2. An increase in current output raises desired national saving but doesn't affect desired investment, so the excess of desired saving over desired investment rises at any real interest rate. Thus the curve measuring the excess of desired saving over desired investment shifts to the right, from $(S - I)^1$ to $(S - I)^2$ in Fig. 14.6(a).

What about the *NX* curve? An increase in domestic income causes domestic consumers to spend more on imported goods, which (other factors held constant) reduces net exports (Summary table 17). Thus when output rises from Y_1 to Y_2, net exports fall, and the *NX* curve shifts to the left, from NX^1 to NX^2.

After the increase in output from Y_1 to Y_2, the new goods market equilibrium is at point *F* in Fig. 14.6(a), with the real interest rate at r_2. The *IS* curve in Fig. 14.6(b) shows that, when output equals Y_1, the real interest rate that clears the goods market is r_1; and that when output equals Y_2, the real interest rate that clears the goods market is r_2. Because higher current output lowers the real interest rate that clears the goods market, the open-economy *IS* curve slopes downward, as for a closed economy.

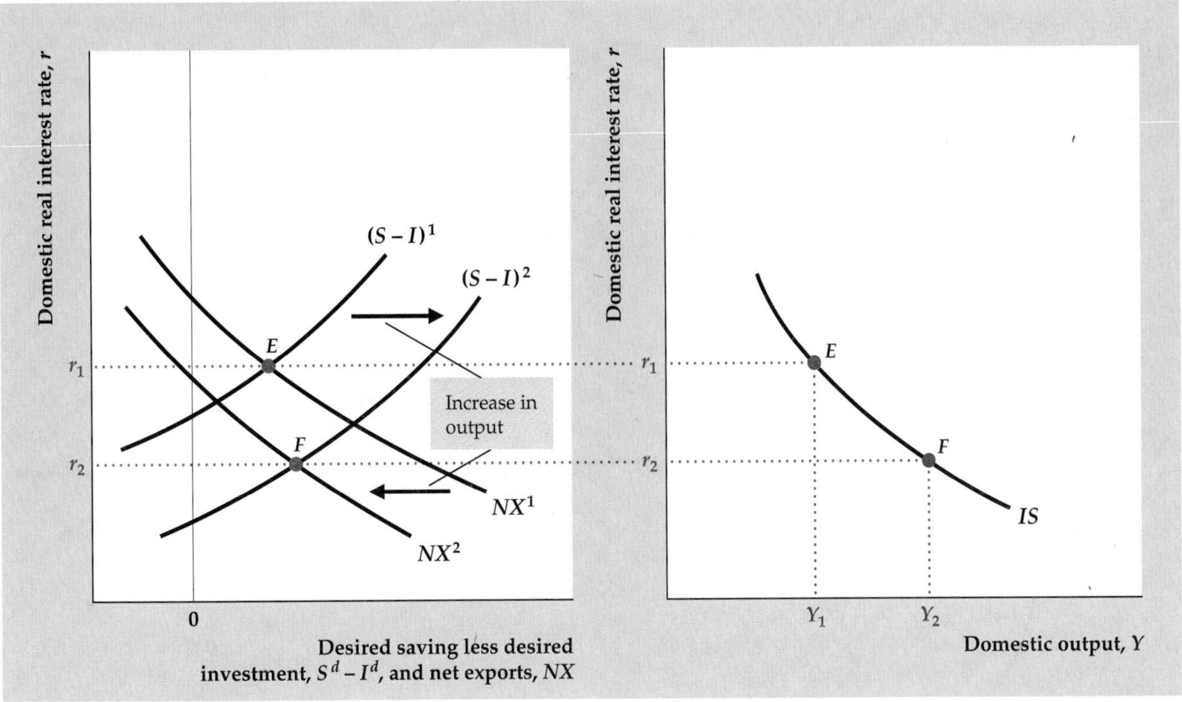

(a) Goods market equilibrium

(b) Open-economy *IS* curve

Figure 14.6
Derivation of the *IS* curve in an open economy
The initial equilibrium in the goods market is represented by point *E* in both (a) and (b).
(a) At point *E*, domestic output is Y_1 and the domestic real interest rate is r_1. An increase in domestic output from Y_1 to Y_2 raises desired national saving at each real interest rate and doesn't affect desired investment. Therefore the $S - I$ curve shifts to the right, from $(S - I)^1$ to $(S - I)^2$. The increase in output also raises domestic spending on imports, reducing net exports and causing the *NX* curve to shift to the left, from NX^1 to NX^2. At the new equilibrium point, *F*, the real interest rate is r_2.
(b) Because an increase in output from Y_1 to Y_2 lowers the real interest rate that clears the goods market from r_1 to r_2, the *IS* curve slopes downward.

Factors that Shift the Open-Economy *IS* Curve

As in a closed economy, in an open economy any factor that raises the real interest rate that clears the goods market at a constant level of output shifts the *IS* curve up. This point is illustrated in Fig. 14.7 on the next page, which shows the effects on the open-economy *IS* curve of a temporary increase in government purchases. With output held constant at Y_1, the initial equilibrium is at point *E*, where the real interest rate is r_1. A temporary increase in government purchases lowers desired national saving at every level of output and the real interest rate. Thus the $S - I$ curve shifts to the left, from $(S - I)^1$ to $(S - I)^2$, as shown in Fig. 14.7(a). The new goods market equilibrium is at point *F*, where the real interest rate is r_2.

Figure 14.7(b) shows the effect on the *IS* curve. For output Y_1, the increase in government purchases raises the real interest rate that clears the goods market from r_1 to r_2. Thus the *IS* curve shifts up and to the right, from IS^1 to IS^2.

In general, any factor that shifts the closed-economy *IS* curve up does so by reducing desired national saving relative to desired investment. Because a

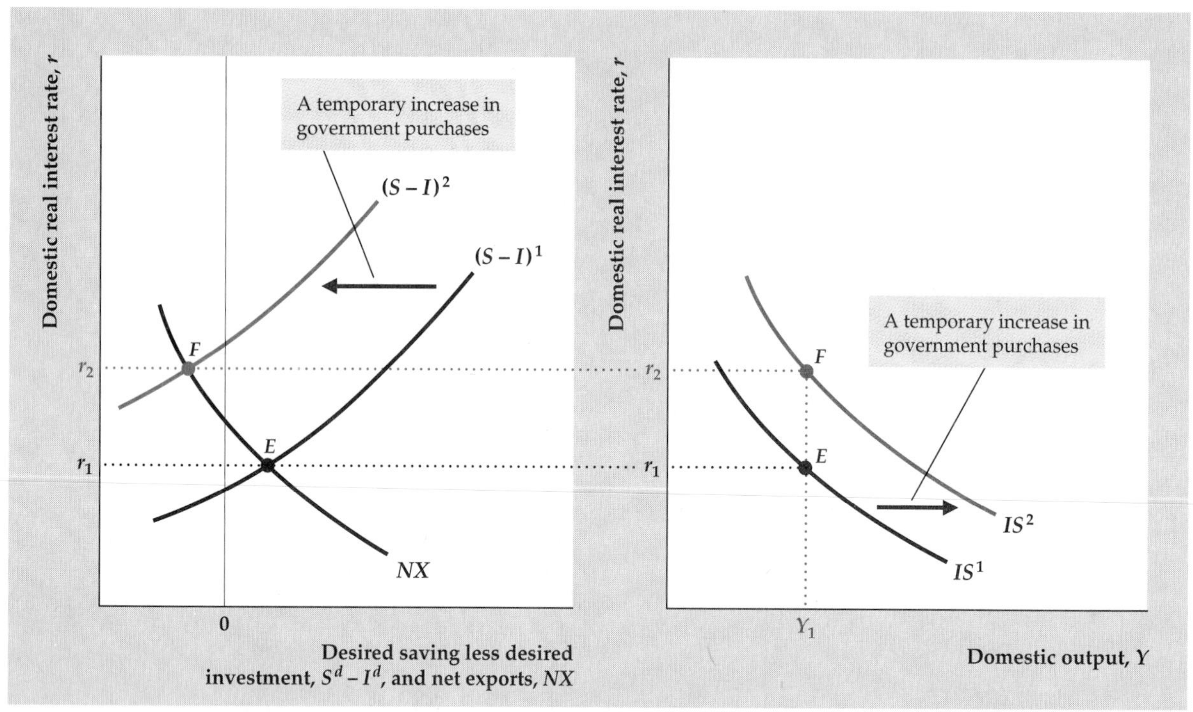

(a) Goods market equilibrium **(b) Open-economy *IS* curve**

Figure 14.7
Effect of an increase in government purchases on the open-economy *IS* curve
Initial equilibrium is at point *E*, where output is Y_1 and the real interest rate is r_1, in both (a) and (b).
(a) A temporary increase in government purchases lowers desired national saving at every level of output and the real interest rate. Thus the $S - I$ curve shifts to the left, from $(S - I)^1$ to $(S - I)^2$.
(b) For output Y_1, the real interest rate that clears the goods market is now r_2, at point *F* in both (a) and (b). Because the real interest rate that clears the goods market has risen, the *IS* curve shifts up and to the right, from IS^1 to IS^2.

change that reduces desired national saving relative to desired investment shifts the $S - I$ curve to the left (Fig. 14.7a), such a change also shifts the open-economy *IS* curve up.

In addition to the standard factors that shift the *IS* curve in a closed economy, some new factors affect the position of the *IS* curve in an open economy. In particular, anything that raises a country's net exports, given domestic output and the domestic real interest rate, will shift the open-economy *IS* curve up. This point is illustrated in Fig. 14.8.

At the initial equilibrium point, *E*, in both Fig. 14.8(a) and (b), domestic output is Y_1 and the domestic real interest rate is r_1. Now suppose that some change raises the country's net exports at any level of domestic output and the domestic real interest rate. This increase in net exports is shown as a shift to the right of the *NX* curve in Fig. 14.8(a), from NX^1 to NX^2. At the new goods market equilibrium point, *F*, the real interest rate has risen to r_2. Because the real interest rate that clears the goods market has risen for constant output, the *IS* curve shifts up and to the right, as shown in Fig. 14.8(b), from IS^1 to IS^2.

What might cause a country's net exports to rise, for any given domestic output and domestic real interest rate? We've discussed three possibilities at

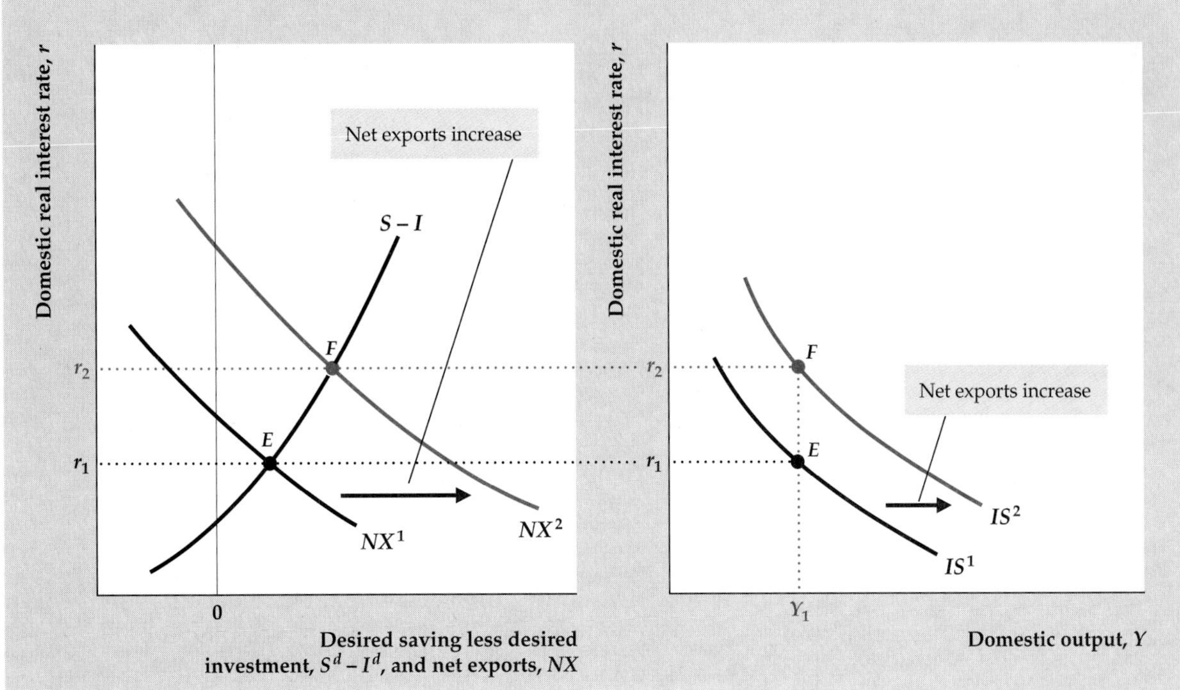

(a) Goods market equilibrium

(b) Open-economy *IS* curve

Figure 14.8
Effect of an increase in net exports on the open-economy *IS* curve
In both (a) and (b), at the initial equilibrium point, *E*, output is Y_1 and the real interest rate that clears the goods market is r_1.
(a) If some change raises the country's net exports at any given domestic output and domestic real interest rate, the *NX* curve shifts to the right, from NX^1 to NX^2.
(b) For output Y_1, the real interest rate that clears the goods market has risen from r_1 to r_2, at point *F* in both (a) and (b). Thus the *IS* curve shifts up and to the right, from IS^1 to IS^2.

various points in this chapter: an increase in foreign output, an increase in the foreign real interest rate, and a shift in world demand toward the domestic country's goods (see Summary table 17).

- *An increase in foreign output,* Y_{For}, increases purchases of the domestic country's goods by foreigners, directly raising the domestic country's net exports and shifting the *IS* curve up.
- *An increase in the foreign real interest rate,* r_{For}, makes foreign assets relatively more attractive to domestic savers, increasing the supply of domestic currency and causing the exchange rate to depreciate. A lower real exchange rate stimulates net exports, shifting the domestic country's *IS* curve up.
- *A shift in world demand toward the domestic country's goods,* as might occur if the quality of domestic goods improved, raises net exports and thus also shifts the *IS* curve up. A similar effect would occur if, for example, the domestic country imposed trade barriers that reduced imports (thereby increasing net exports); see Analytical Problem 1 at the end of the chapter. Summary table 18, on the next page, lists factors that shift the open-economy *IS* curve.

SUMMARY 18

International Factors that Shift the *IS* Curve

An Increase in	Shifts the *IS* Curve	Reason
Foreign output, Y_{For}	Up	Higher foreign output raises demand for home country exports.
Foreign real interest rate, r_{For}	Up	Higher foreign real interest rate depreciates the real exchange rate and raises net exports.
Demand for domestic goods relative to foreign goods	Up	Higher demand for domestic goods raises net exports.

The International Transmission of Business Cycles

In the introduction to this chapter we discussed briefly how trade and financial links among countries transmit cyclical fluctuations across borders. The analysis here shows that the impact of foreign economic conditions on the real exchange rate and net exports is one of the principal ways by which cycles are transmitted internationally.

For example, consider the impact of a recession in the United States on the economies for which the United States is a major export market, say, Japan. In terms of the *IS–LM* model a decline in U.S. output lowers the demand for Japanese net exports, which shifts the Japanese *IS* curve down. In the Keynesian version of the model this downward shift of the *IS* curve throws the Japanese economy into a recession, with output below its full-employment level, until price adjustment restores full employment (see, for example, Fig. 12.10). Japanese output also is predicted to fall in the classical model with misperceptions because the drop in net exports implies a decline in the Japanese aggregate demand (*AD*) curve and the short-run aggregate supply (*SRAS*) curve slopes upward. However, in the basic classical model without misperceptions, in which the aggregate supply curve is vertical at full-employment output, the decline in net exports wouldn't affect Japanese output.

Similarly, a country's domestic economy can be sensitive to shifts in international tastes for various goods. For example, a shift in demand away from Japanese goods—induced perhaps by trade restrictions against Japanese products—would shift the Japanese *IS* curve down, with the same contractionary effects as the decrease in foreign (U.S.) output had.

14.4 MACROECONOMIC POLICY IN AN OPEN ECONOMY WITH FLEXIBLE EXCHANGE RATES

A primary reason for developing the *IS–LM* model for the open economy is to determine how borrowing and trading links among countries affect fiscal and monetary policies. When exchange rates are flexible, the effects of macroeconomic policy on domestic variables such as output and the real interest rate are largely unchanged when foreign trade is added. However, adding foreign trade does raise two new questions: (1) How do fiscal and monetary policy affect a country's real exchange rate and net exports? and (2) How do the macroeconomic policies of one country affect the economies of other countries? With the open-economy *IS–LM* model, we can answer both of these questions.

To examine the international effects of various domestic macroeconomic policies, we proceed as follows:

1. We use the *IS–LM* diagram for the domestic economy to determine the effects of the policies on domestic output and the domestic real interest rate. This step is the same as in our analyses of closed economies in Chapters 10–12.
2. We apply the results of Section 14.2 (see in particular Summary tables 16 and 17) to determine how changes in domestic output and the domestic real interest rate affect the exchange rate and net exports.
3. We use the *IS–LM* diagram for the foreign economy to determine the effects of the domestic policies on foreign output and the foreign real interest rate. Domestic policies that change the demand for the foreign country's net exports will shift the foreign *IS* curve.

A Fiscal Expansion

To consider the effects of fiscal policy in an open economy, let's look again at a temporary increase in domestic government purchases. In analyzing this policy change we use the classical version of the *IS–LM* model (with no misperceptions) but also discuss the results that would be obtained in the Keynesian framework.

Figure 14.9, on the next page, shows two *IS–LM* diagrams, one for the domestic country (where the fiscal policy change is taking place) and one for the foreign country, representing the domestic country's major trading partners. Suppose that the original equilibrium is at point *E* in Fig. 14.9(a). As usual, the increase in government purchases shifts the domestic *IS* curve up and to the right, from IS^1 to IS^2. In addition, in the classical model the *FE* line shifts to the right, from FE^1 to FE^2. The reason for this shift is that the increase in government purchases raises present or future tax burdens; because higher taxes make workers poorer, they increase their labor supply, which raises full-employment output. The new equilibrium is represented by point *F*, the intersection of IS^2 and FE^2. The domestic price level rises, shifting the domestic *LM* curve to the left, from LM^1 to LM^2, until it passes through *F*. Comparing point *F* with point *E* reveals that the increase in government purchases increases both output Y *and* the real interest rate r in the domestic country. So far the analysis is identical to the classical analysis for a closed economy (Chapter 11). Note also that fiscal expansion raises output and the real interest rate—the same results that we would get from the Keynesian model.

To examine the role of international trade, we first consider the effects on the exchange rate of the increases in domestic output and the domestic real interest rate. Recall that an increase in output Y causes domestic residents to demand more imports and thus to supply more currency to the foreign exchange market. The increase in domestic output therefore depreciates the exchange rate. However, the rise in the domestic real interest rate makes

Figure 14.9
Effects of an increase in domestic government purchases
(a) In the classical *IS–LM* model, an increase in domestic government purchases shifts the domestic *IS* curve to the right, from IS^1 to IS^2. It also shifts the domestic *FE* line to the right, from FE^1 to FE^2. Therefore domestic output and the domestic real interest rate both increase. These increases reduce net exports but have an ambiguous effect on the real exchange rate. The results are similar in the Keynesian model.
(b) Because the domestic country's exports are the foreign country's imports and vice-versa, the decrease in the domestic country's net exports is equivalent to a rise in the foreign country's net exports. This increase shifts the foreign *IS* curve up, from IS^1_{For} to IS^2_{For}. In the classical model, prices adjust rapidly, shifting the *LM* curve from LM^1_{For} to LM^2_{For}. The new equilibrium is at point *F*, where the foreign real interest rate and price level are higher but foreign output is unchanged. In the Keynesian model, price stickiness would cause a temporary increase in foreign output at *H* before price adjustment restores general equilibrium at *F*.

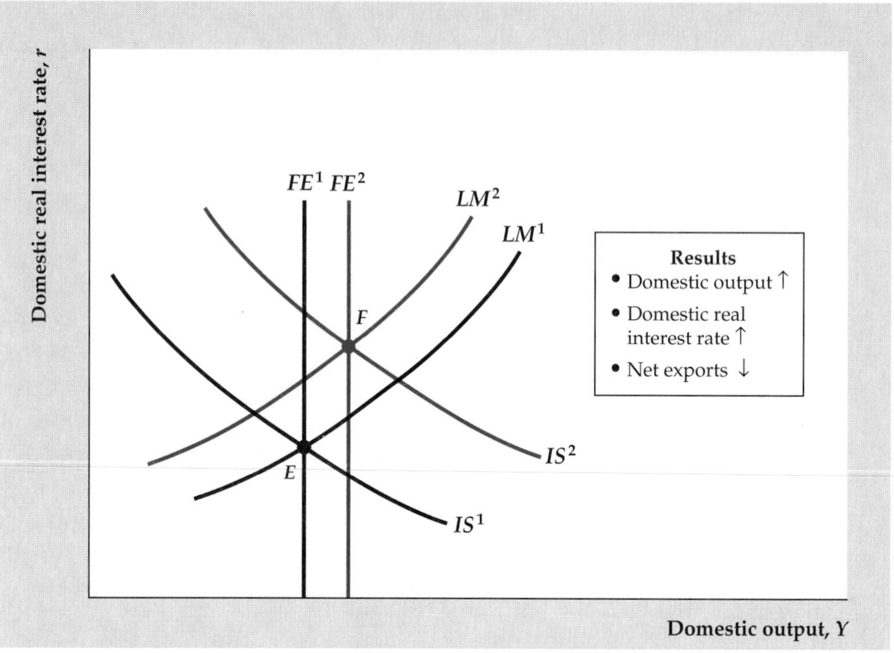

(a) Domestic country

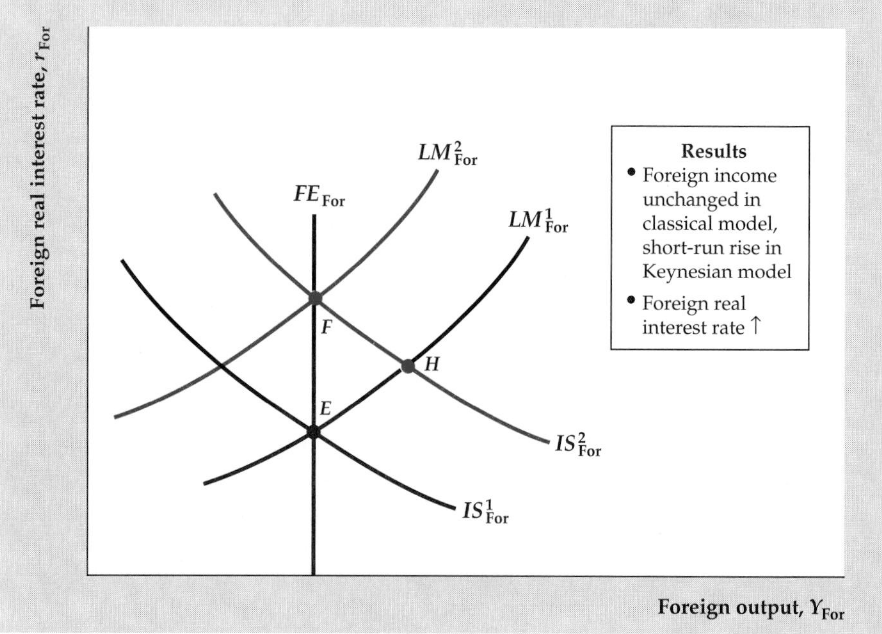

(b) Foreign country

domestic assets more attractive, causing foreign savers to demand the domestic currency and appreciating the exchange rate. The overall effect of the increase in government purchases on the exchange rate is ambiguous: We can't be sure whether the increase in government purchases will raise or lower the exchange rate.

The effect of the fiscal expansion on the country's net export demand isn't ambiguous. Recall that the increase in domestic output (which raises domestic consumers' demand for imports) and the increase in the real interest rate (which tends to appreciate the exchange rate) both cause net exports to fall. Thus the overall effect of the fiscal expansion clearly is to move the country's trade balance toward deficit. This result is consistent with the analysis of the "twin deficits" (the government budget deficit and the trade deficit) of Chapter 5.

In an interconnected world, the effects of macroeconomic policies in one country aren't limited to that country but also are felt abroad. Based on the analysis we've just finished, taking the extra step and finding out how the domestic fiscal expansion affects the economies of the domestic country's trading partners isn't difficult.

The effects of the domestic fiscal expansion on the rest of the world—represented by the foreign country *IS–LM* diagram in Fig. 14.9(b)—are transmitted through the change in net exports. Because the domestic country's imports are the foreign country's exports and vice-versa, the decline in net exports of the domestic country is equivalent to an increase in net exports for the foreign country. Thus the foreign country's *IS* curve shifts up, from IS^1_{For} to IS^2_{For}.

In the classical *IS–LM* model, the upward shift of the foreign *IS* curve doesn't affect foreign output; instead the price level rises immediately to restore general equilibrium (the *LM* curve shifts up from LM^1_{For} to LM^2_{For}). The foreign economy ends up at point *F*, with the real interest rate and the price level higher than they were initially.

If prices were sticky, as in the Keynesian model, the effects of the shift of the foreign country's *IS* curve would be slightly different. If prices don't adjust in the short run, the shift of the *IS* curve implies that the foreign economy would have *temporarily* higher output at the intersection of the *IS* and *LM* curves at point *H* in Fig. 14.9(b); only after firms adjust their prices would the economy arrive at point *F*. Otherwise, the implications of the classical and Keynesian analyses are the same.[11]

Therefore, in the open-economy versions of both the classical and Keynesian models, a temporary increase in government purchases raises domestic income and the domestic real interest rate, as in a closed economy. In addition, net exports fall; thus increased government purchases reduce, or crowd out, both investment and net exports. The effect on the real exchange rate is ambiguous: It can either rise or fall. In the foreign economy the real interest rate and the price level rise. In the Keynesian version of the model foreign output also rises, but only in the short run.

A Monetary Contraction

We can also use the open-economy *IS–LM* model to study the effects of monetary policy when exchange rates are flexible. For the Keynesian version of the *IS–LM* model we analyze the effects of a drop in the money supply in both the short and long run. Because the effects of monetary policy are the same in the basic classical model (without misperceptions) and the long-run Keynesian model, our analysis applies to the classical model as well.

---

11. In principle, we could continue the analysis by discussing how changes in foreign output and real interest rates in turn affect the domestic economy. However, these so-called *feedback effects* are generally small and thus don't reverse any of our conclusions, so we omit this discussion.

Short-Run Effects on the Domestic and Foreign Economies. The effects of a monetary contraction are shown in Fig. 14.10, which shows *IS–LM* diagrams corresponding to both the domestic and foreign countries. Suppose that the initial equilibrium is represented by point *E* and that a decrease in the money supply shifts the domestic *LM* curve up and to the left, from LM^1 to LM^2, in Fig. 14.10(a). In the Keynesian model, the price level is rigid in the short run, so the short-run equilibrium is at point *F*, the intersection of the *IS* and LM^2 curves. Comparing points *F* and *E* reveals that in the short run domestic output falls and the domestic real interest rate rises. This result is the same as for the closed economy (Chapter 12).

After the monetary contraction, the exchange rate appreciates in the short run, for two reasons. First, the drop in domestic income reduces the domestic demand for imports, leading domestic consumers to demand less foreign currency to buy imported goods. Second, the rise in the domestic real interest rate makes domestic assets relatively more attractive to foreign savers, increasing foreign savers' demand for the domestic currency.

What happens to the country's net exports? Here there are two competing effects: (1) The drop in domestic income created by the monetary contraction reduces the domestic demand for foreign goods and thus tends to increase the country's net exports; but (2) the rise in the real interest rate, which leads to exchange rate appreciation, tends to reduce net exports. The theory doesn't indicate for certain which way net exports will change. In our earlier discussion of the J curve, however, we noted that the effects of changes in the real exchange rate on net exports may be weak in the short run. Based on that analysis, we assume that in the short run exchange rate effects on net exports are weaker than the effects of changes in domestic income so that overall the country's net exports will increase.

The next question is: How does the domestic monetary contraction affect the economies of the country's trading partners? The effects on the typical foreign economy are illustrated by Fig. 14.10(b). If the domestic country's net exports are increased by the monetary contraction, the foreign country's net exports must decrease because the domestic country's exports are the foreign country's imports. Thus the *IS* curve of the foreign country shifts to the left, from IS^1_{For} to IS^2_{For}. The short-run equilibrium is at point *F*, where the IS^2_{For} and LM_{For} curves intersect. Output in the foreign country declines, and the foreign real interest rate falls.

These results show that a domestic monetary contraction also leads to a recession abroad. This transmission of recession occurs because the decline in domestic output also reduces domestic demand for foreign goods. The appreciation of the domestic real exchange rate works in the opposite direction by making foreign goods relatively cheaper, which tends to increase the net exports of the foreign country. However, we have assumed that the negative effect of declining domestic income on the foreign country's net exports is stronger than the positive effect of the appreciating domestic exchange rate. Thus a domestic monetary contraction leads to a recession in both the foreign country and the domestic country.

Long-Run Effects on the Domestic and Foreign Economies. In the long run after a monetary contraction, wages and prices decline in the domestic country, as firms find themselves selling less output than they desire. The

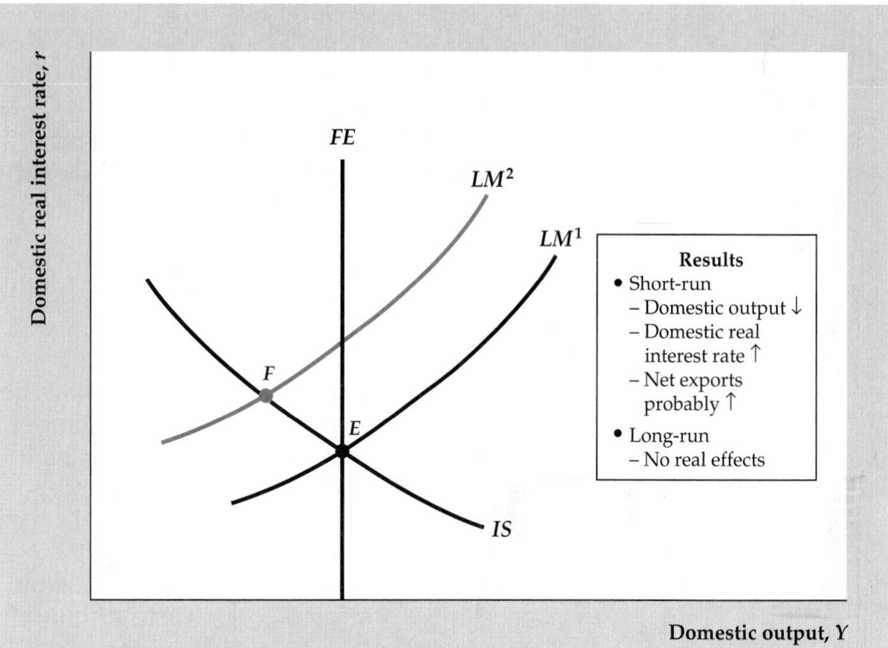

(a) Domestic country

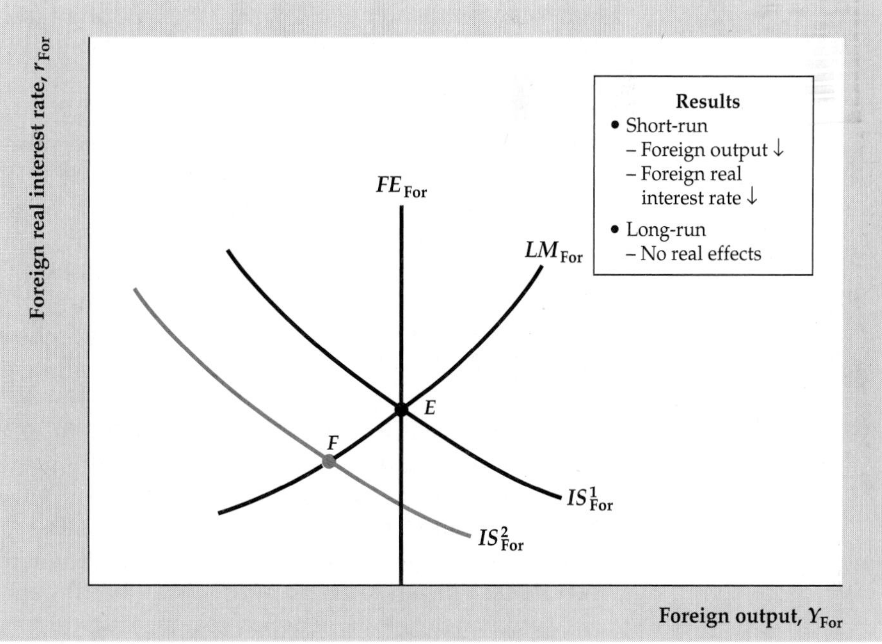

(b) Foreign country

Figure 14.10 Effects of a decrease in the domestic money supply

(a) A decrease in the domestic money supply shifts the domestic *LM* curve up, from LM^1 to LM^2. The short-run equilibrium in the Keynesian model is at point *F*, the intersection of the *IS* and LM^2 curves. The decline in the money supply reduces domestic output and increases the domestic real interest rate. The drop in domestic output and the rise in the real interest rate cause the real exchange rate to appreciate. The effect on net exports is potentially ambiguous; if we assume that the effect on net exports of the drop in domestic income is stronger than the effect of the appreciation of the exchange rate, net exports increase as domestic residents demand fewer goods from abroad.
(b) Because the domestic country's net exports increase, the foreign country's net exports fall and the foreign *IS* curve shifts down, from IS^1_{For} to IS^2_{For}. Thus output and the real interest rate fall in the foreign country in the short run.

In the long run, domestic prices fall and both economies return to equilibrium at point *E*. Thus in the long run money is neutral.

domestic country's *LM* curve returns to its initial position, LM^1 in Fig. 14.10(a), so that money is neutral in the long run. As all real variables in the domestic economy return to their original levels, the real exchange rate and the domestic demand for foreign goods also return to their original levels. As a result, the foreign country's *IS* curve shifts back to its initial position, IS^1_{For} in Fig. 14.10(b), and the foreign country's economy also returns to its initial equilibrium point, *E*. At *E*, all foreign macroeconomic variables (including the price level) are at their original levels. Hence, in the long run, the change in the domestic money supply doesn't affect any real variables, either domestically or abroad. In particular, the real exchange rate and net exports aren't affected by the monetary contraction in the long run.

Although monetary neutrality holds in the long run in the Keynesian model, it holds immediately in the basic classical model. So, in the basic classical model, monetary policy changes have no effect on real exchange rates or trade flows; they affect only the price level. In a monetary contraction, the domestic price level will fall (the foreign price level doesn't change).

Although money can't affect the *real* exchange rate in the long run, it does affect the *nominal* exchange rate by changing the domestic price level. (This is one case where the responses of the real and nominal exchange rates to a change in macroeconomic conditions differ.) As we have shown, the long-run neutrality of money implies that a 10% decrease in the nominal money supply will decrease the domestic price level by 10%. Recall (Eq. 14.1) that the nominal exchange rate e_{nom} equals eP_{For}/P, where e is the real exchange rate, P_{For} is the foreign price level, and P is the domestic price level. Because the real exchange rate e and the foreign price level P_{For} are unchanged in the long run by a domestic monetary contraction, the 10% drop in the domestic price level P raises the nominal exchange rate e_{nom} by (approximately) 10%. Thus a monetary contraction reduces the domestic price level and appreciates the nominal exchange rate by the same percentage as the drop in money supply.

APPLICATION

Why the Dollar Rose So High and Fell So Far in the 1980s

As Fig. 14.2 shows, the U.S. dollar appreciated strongly during the first half of the 1980s. Then after reaching its peak in March 1985, the dollar fell precipitously for nearly three years before stabilizing at a level close to where it had been in 1980. Associated with the rise in the dollar was a sharp decline in U.S. net exports, as Fig. 14.2 also shows. What were the ultimate causes of these fluctuations?

To explain these fluctuations Keynesians focus on the effects of macroeconomic policies during that decade—specifically, a combination of tight monetary policy and expansionary fiscal policy. The tight-money policy began in October 1979 when Federal Reserve Chairman Paul Volcker announced that money growth rates would be reduced to fight inflation, which at that time was worrisome. Contractionary monetary policy contributed to a short recession in 1980 and a deep recession in 1981–1982. Fiscal policy became expansionary in about 1981, when the tax cuts mandated by the Economic Recovery Tax Act (ERTA) began to be phased in. Military expenditures also increased, and the government's budget deficit rose significantly.

In the Keynesian analysis the effects on output of tight money and expansionary fiscal policy tend to cancel out, and, indeed, by 1983 the economy had begun a strong recovery from the 1981–1982 recession. However, the tight money and expansionary fiscal combination also led to a higher real interest rate, reaching record levels in the early 1980s (see Fig. 2.4). The high real interest rate in the United States attracted foreign investors; as foreigners demanded dollar-denominated assets, the real value of the dollar rose sharply. According to the Keynesians, because the dollar was so strong, U.S. net exports fell sharply in 1983 and 1984.

By the mid 1980s some of the factors keeping the dollar high had begun to reverse. Although budget deficits remained high, the ebbing of inflation reduced the need for tight money and the U.S. real interest rate declined (see Fig. 2.4). In 1985 and 1986 some major foreign countries, notably Japan and Germany, agreed to cooperate with the United States to help bring the value of the dollar down. At the same time, foreign savers, who had acquired large quantities of U.S. assets during the early 1980s, became reluctant to hold more dollar assets. Hence the dollar declined, ultimately bringing some improvement in the U.S. net export position.

An alternative (and to some degree complementary) explanation of the dollar's rise has been offered by some classical economists. Their explanation is based on the idea that during the early 1980s the United States became a relatively more attractive place to make real and financial investments. The argument is based on both a "push" and a "pull." The pull came from the liberalization of U.S. tax laws pertaining to investment and the generally probusiness attitude of the Reagan administration, both of which increased the profitability of investing in the United States. The push came from the failure of many developing countries to repay their international debts fully and on schedule. Savers both in the United States and abroad began to shy away from lending to these countries, preferring instead the safe haven of U.S. assets. According to the classical argument, the increased desirability of U.S. assets relative to foreign assets increased the demand for the dollar and raised the U.S. real exchange rate, which in turn reduced U.S. net exports.[12] Again, however, as the decade progressed foreign savers became "satiated" with U.S. assets, setting the stage for the ultimate decline in the value of the dollar.

14.5 FIXED EXCHANGE RATES

The United States has had a flexible exchange rate since abandonment of the Bretton Woods system of fixed exchange rates during the early 1970s. However, fixed-exchange-rate systems—in which exchange rates are officially set by international agreement—have been important historically and are still used by many countries. Let's now consider fixed-exchange-rate systems and address two questions: (1) How does the use of a fixed-exchange-rate system affect an economy and macroeconomic policy? and (2) Ultimately, which is the better system, flexible or fixed exchange rates?

Fixing the Exchange Rate

In contrast to flexible-exchange-rate systems—where exchange rates are determined by supply and demand in foreign exchange markets—in a fixed-exchange-rate system the value of the nominal exchange rate is officially set by

12. Analytical Problem 3 at the end of the chapter asks you to work out this argument in more detail.

the government, perhaps in consultation or agreement with other countries. For example, as members of the EMS, France and Germany have agreed on the exchange rate between French francs and German marks; similar agreements govern the rates at which francs and marks will trade for the currencies of other EMS members.[13]

A potential problem with fixed-exchange-rate systems is that the value of the exchange rate set by the government may not be the exchange rate determined by the supply and demand for currency. Figure 14.11 shows a situation in which the official exchange rate, $\bar{e}_{nom}$, is higher than the **fundamental value of the exchange rate,** e^1_{nom}, or the value that would be determined by free market forces without government intervention. When an exchange rate is higher than its fundamental value, it is an **overvalued exchange rate** (often referred to as an overvalued currency).

How can a country deal with a situation in which its official exchange rate is different from the fundamental value of its exchange rate? There are several possible strategies: First, the country can simply change the official value of its exchange rate so that it equals, or is close to, its fundamental value. For example, in the case of overvaluation shown in Fig. 14.11, the country could simply devalue (lower) its nominal fixed exchange rate from $\bar{e}_{nom}$ to e^1_{nom}. However,

13. Actually, members of the EMS agree to keep their exchange rates within a prespecified band above and below the official rate, rather than completely fixed. This band was widened significantly in August 1993 following a speculative crisis, discussed later in this section.

Figure 14.11
An overvalued exchange rate
The figure shows a situation in which the officially fixed nominal exchange rate, $\bar{e}_{nom}$, is higher than the fundamental value of the exchange rate, e^1_{nom} as determined by supply and demand in the foreign exchange market. In this situation the exchange rate is said to be overvalued. The country's central bank can maintain the exchange rate at the official rate by using its reserves to purchase its own currency in the foreign exchange market, in the amount of *AB* in each period. This loss of reserves also is referred to as the country's balance of payments deficit.

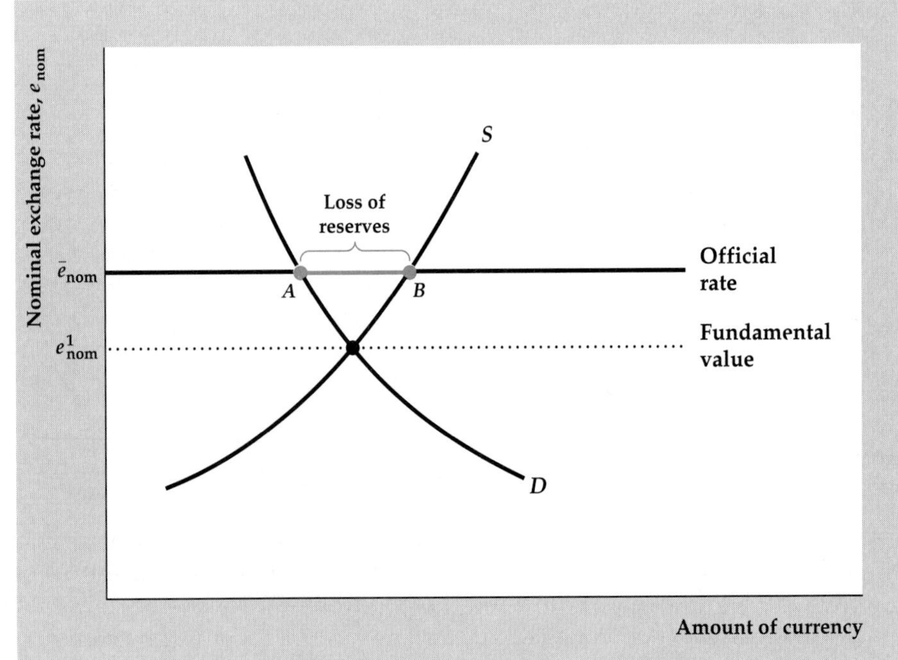

although occasional devaluations or revaluations can be expected under fixed-exchange-rate systems, if a country continuously adjusts its exchange rate it might as well switch to a flexible-rate system.

Second, the government could restrict international transactions—for example, by limiting or taxing imports or capital outflows. Such policies reduce the supply of the domestic currency to the foreign exchange market, thus raising the fundamental value of the exchange rate toward its fixed value. Some countries go even further and prohibit people from trading the domestic currency for foreign currencies without government approval; a currency that can't be freely traded for other currencies is said to be an **inconvertible currency.** However, direct government intervention in international transactions has many economic costs, including reduced access to foreign goods and credit.

Third, the government itself may become a demander or supplier of its currency in the foreign exchange market, an approach used by most of the industrialized countries having fixed exchange rates. For example, in the case of overvaluation shown in Fig. 14.11, the supply of the country's currency to the foreign exchange market (point *B*) exceeds private demand for the currency (point *A*) at the official exchange rate by the amount *AB*. To maintain the value of the currency at the official rate, the government could buy back its own currency in the amount *AB* in each period.

Usually, these currency purchases are made by the nation's central bank using official reserve assets. Recall that official reserve assets are assets other than domestic money or securities that can be used to make international payments (examples are gold, foreign bank deposits, or special assets created by international agencies such as the International Monetary Fund). During the gold standard period, for example, gold was the basic form of official reserve asset, and central banks offered to exchange gold for their own currencies at a fixed price. If Fig. 14.11 represented a gold standard country, *AB* would represent the amount of gold the central bank would have to use to buy back its currency in each period to equalize the quantities of its currency supplied and demanded at the official exchange rate. Recall also that the decline in a country's official reserve assets during a year equals its *balance of payments deficit.* Thus amount *AB* measures the reserves the central bank must use to support the currency and corresponds to the country's balance of payments deficit.

Although a central bank can maintain an overvalued exchange rate for a time by offering to buy back its own currency at a fixed price, it can't do so forever because it has only a limited supply of official reserve assets. During the gold standard period, for example, central banks did not own unlimited amounts of gold. Attempting to support an overvalued currency for a long period of time would have exhausted a central bank's limited gold reserves, leaving the country no choice but to devalue its currency.

A central bank's attempts to support an overvalued currency can be ended quickly and dramatically by a speculative run. A **speculative run** occurs when financial investors begin to fear that an overvalued currency may soon be devalued, reducing the value of assets denominated in that currency relative to assets denominated in other currencies. To avoid losses, financial investors frantically sell assets denominated in the overvalued currency. The panicky sales of domestic assets associated with a speculative run on a currency shift

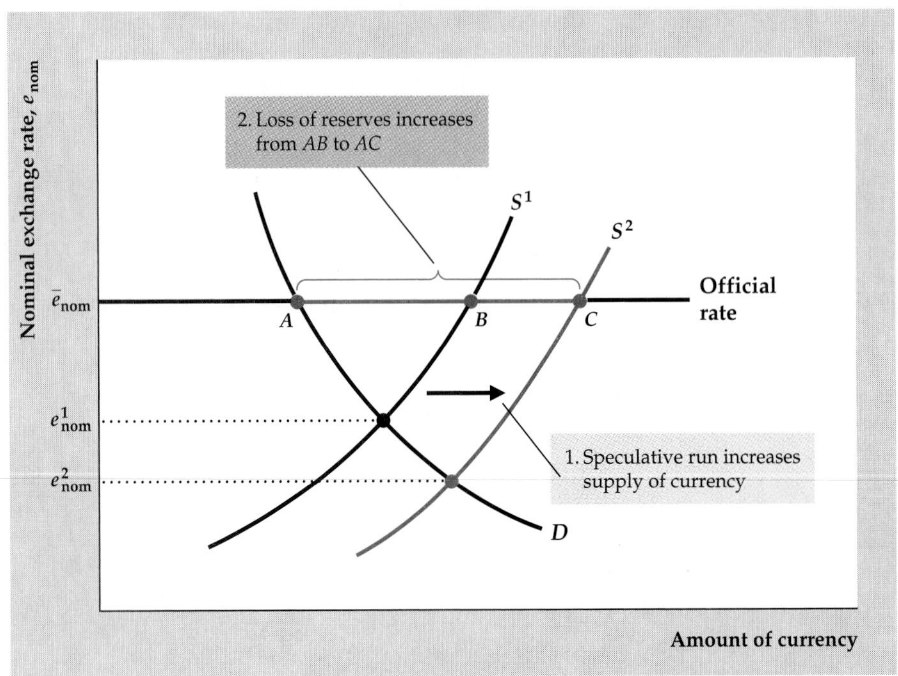

Figure 14.12
A speculative run on an overvalued currency
Initially, the supply curve of the domestic currency is S^1 and, to maintain the fixed exchange rate, the central bank must use amount *AB* of its reserves each period to purchase its own currency in the foreign exchange market. A speculative run occurs when holders of domestic assets begin to fear a devaluation, which would reduce the values of their assets (measured in terms of foreign currency). Panicky sales of domestic-currency assets lead to more domestic currency being supplied to the foreign exchange market, which shifts the supply curve of the domestic currency to the right, from S^1 to S^2. The central bank must now purchase its currency and lose reserves in the amount *AC*. This more rapid loss of reserves may force the central bank to stop supporting the overvalued currency and to devalue it, confirming the market's expectations.

the supply curve for that currency sharply to the right (see Fig. 14.12), increasing the gap between the quantities supplied and demanded of the currency from amount *AB* to amount *AC*. This widening gap increases the rate at which the central bank has to spend its official reserve assets to maintain the overvalued exchange rate, speeding devaluation and confirming the financial investors' expectations.

Without strong restrictions on international trade and finance (themselves economically costly), we conclude that an overvalued exchange rate isn't sustainable for long. If the exchange rate is overvalued, the country must either devalue its currency or make some policy change to raise the fundamental value of the exchange rate. We show in the next section that the basic tool for changing the fundamental value of the exchange rate is monetary policy.

We've focused on overvaluation, but an exchange rate also could be undervalued. As illustrated in Fig. 14.13, an **undervalued exchange rate** (or undervalued currency) exists if the officially fixed value is less than the value determined by supply and demand in the foreign exchange market. In this case, instead of buying its own currency, the central bank sells its currency to the foreign exchange market and accumulates reserves in the amount *AB* each period. With no limit to the quantity of reserve assets (gold, for example) a central bank could accumulate, an undervalued exchange rate could apparently be maintained indefinitely. However, a country with an undervalued exchange rate can accumulate reserves only at the expense of trading partners who have overvalued exchange rates and are therefore losing reserves. Because the country's trading partners cannot continue to lose reserves indefinitely, eventually they will put political pressure on the country to bring the fundamental value of its exchange rate back in line with the official rate.

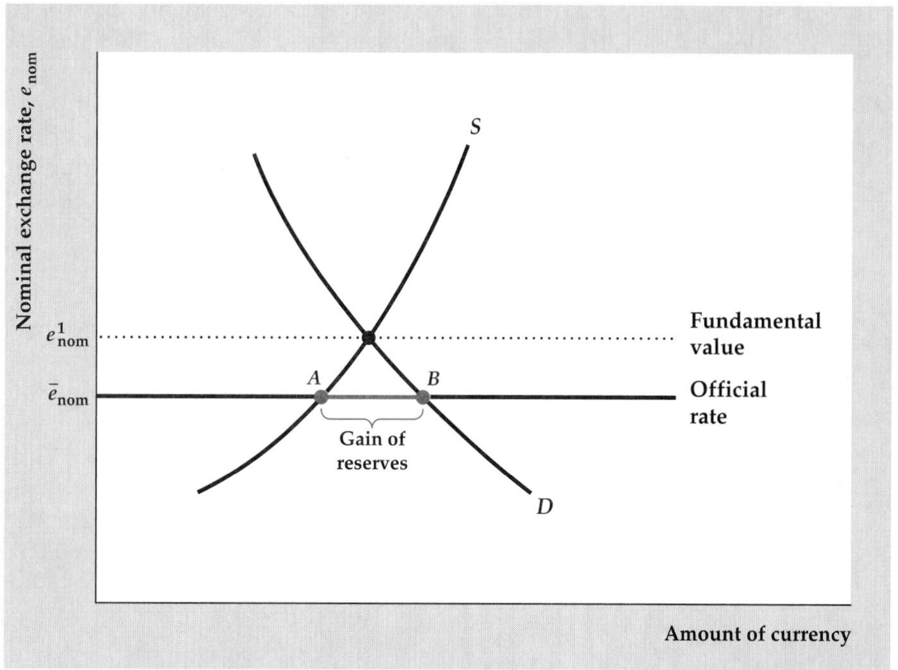

Figure 14.13
An undervalued exchange rate
The exchange rate is undervalued when the officially determined nominal exchange rate, $\bar{e}_{nom}$, is less than the fundamental value of the exchange rate as determined by supply and demand in the foreign exchange market, e^1_{nom}. To maintain the exchange rate at its official level, the central bank must supply its own currency to the foreign exchange market in the amount *AB* each period, thereby accumulating foreign reserves.

Monetary Policy and the Fixed Exchange Rate

Suppose that a country wants to eliminate currency overvaluation by raising the fundamental value of its nominal exchange rate until it equals the fixed value of the exchange rate. How can it achieve this goal? Economists have long recognized that the best way for a country to do so is through contraction of its money supply.

To demonstrate why a monetary contraction raises the fundamental value of the nominal exchange rate, we first rewrite Eq. (14.1), which defined the relationship of the real and nominal exchange rates:

$$e_{nom} = \frac{eP_{For}}{P}. \tag{14.6}$$

Equation (14.6) states that, for any foreign price level P_{For}, the nominal exchange rate e_{nom} is proportional to the real exchange rate e and inversely proportional to the domestic price level P.

In our earlier discussion of monetary policy in the Keynesian model with flexible exchange rates, we showed that a monetary contraction causes the real exchange rate to appreciate in the short run by reducing domestic output and increasing the real interest rate. Because short-run domestic and foreign price levels are fixed in the Keynesian model, Eq. (14.6) indicates that the short-run appreciation of the real exchange rate also implies a short-run appreciation of the nominal exchange rate. In the long run money is neutral; hence a monetary contraction has no effect on the real exchange rate, but it does cause the domestic price level to fall. In the long run the domestic price level P falls but the real exchange rate e is unaffected, so Eq. (14.6) implies that the nominal exchange rate rises (appreciates) both in the long run and the short run. Thus in both the short and long run a monetary contraction increases the fundamental value of the nominal exchange rate, or the value of the nominal exchange rate determined by supply and demand in the foreign exchange market.[14] Conversely, a monetary easing reduces the fundamental value of the nominal exchange rate in both the short and long run.

Figure 14.14 illustrates the relationship between the nominal exchange rate and the money supply in a country with a fixed exchange rate.[15] The downward-sloping curve shows the relationship of the money supply to the fundamental value of the nominal exchange rate. This curve slopes downward because, other factors being equal, an increase in the money supply reduces the fundamental value of the nominal exchange rate. The horizontal line in Fig. 14.14 is the officially determined exchange rate. The value of M_1 on the horizontal axis is the money supply that equalizes the fundamental value of the exchange rate and its officially fixed value. If the money supply is more than M_1, the country has an overvaluation problem (the fundamental value of the exchange rate is below the official value), and if the money supply is less than M_1 the country has an undervaluation problem.

Figure 14.14 suggests that, in a fixed-exchange-rate system, individual countries typically are *not* free to expand their money supplies in order to try

14. Because money is neutral in both the short and long run in the basic classical model, a monetary contraction increases the fundamental value of the nominal exchange rate in both the short and long run in the basic classical model also.

15. The country's money supply is the amount of money in circulation domestically, as in previous chapters. It is *not* the supply of currency to foreign exchange markets, which depends only on domestic residents' demands for foreign goods and assets.

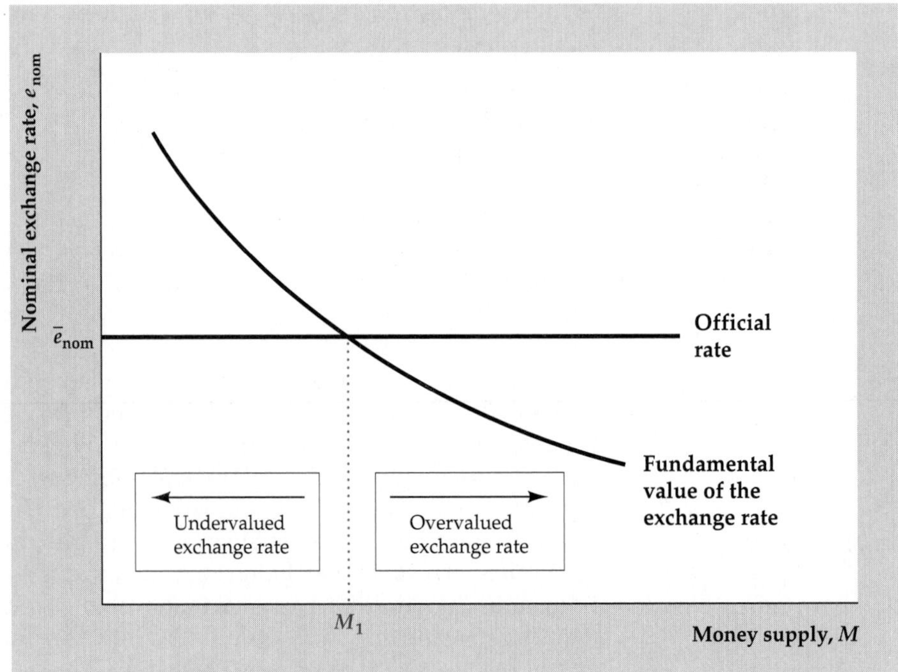

Figure 14.14 Determination of the money supply under fixed exchange rates
The downward-sloping fundamental value curve shows that a higher domestic money supply causes a lower fundamental value of the exchange rate. The horizontal line shows the officially fixed nominal exchange rate. Only when the country's money supply equals M_1 does the fundamental value of the exchange rate equal the official rate. If the central bank increased the money supply above M_1, the exchange rate would become overvalued. A money supply below M_1 would result in an undervalued currency.

to raise output and employment. Instead, the money supply is governed by the condition that the official and fundamental values of the exchange rate be the same. If the country represented in Fig. 14.14 wanted to expand its money supply to fight a recession, for example, it could do so only by creating an overvaluation problem (most likely leading to a future devaluation) or by devaluing its currency immediately. Under fixed exchange rates, then, a central bank cannot use monetary policy to pursue macroeconomic stabilization goals.

Although one member of a group of countries in a fixed-exchange-rate system generally isn't free to use monetary policy by itself, the group *as a whole* may be able to do so, *if* they coordinate their policies. For example, suppose that Spain and Portugal have a fixed exchange rate between their two currencies and that, because of a recession in both countries, both want to expand their money supplies. If Portugal attempts a monetary expansion on its own, from M_1 to M_2 in Fig. 14.15, its exchange rate will become overvalued (its fundamental value, at the intersection of M_2 and FV^1, would be lower than the official exchange rate). As a result, the Bank of Portugal would lose reserves, ultimately forcing Portugal to undo its attempted expansion.

Suppose, however, that Spain goes ahead with its own money supply expansion. If Portugal's money supply remains constant, an increase in Spain's money supply reduces Spain's (nominal) exchange rate, which is equivalent to raising Portugal's exchange rate. In terms of Fig. 14.15, the increase in Spain's money supply increases the fundamental value of Portugal's exchange rate at any level of its money supply. The fundamental value curve in Fig. 14.15 shifts up from FV^1 to FV^2. Now Portugal can expand its money supply, from M_1 to M_2, without creating an overvaluation problem (the fundamental value of the Portuguese exchange rate, at the intersection of M_2 and FV^2, is the same as the

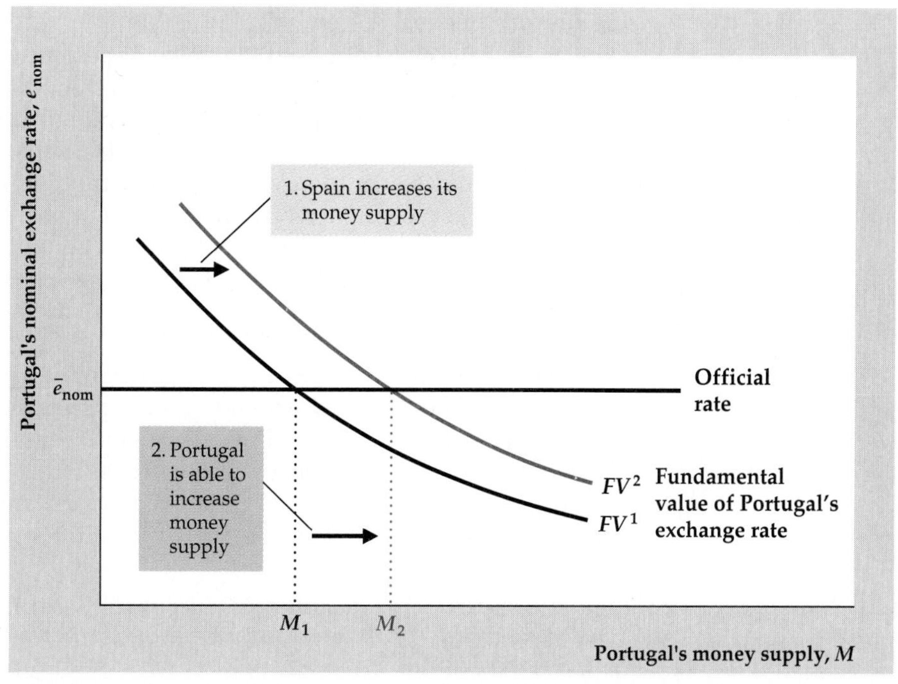

Figure 14.15
Coordinated monetary expansion
Suppose that Spain and Portugal are members of a fixed-exchange-rate system and that both are suffering from recessions. Initially, the fundamental value of Portugal's exchange rate as a function of the country's money supply is FV^1, and its money supply level consistent with maintenance of the official exchange rate is M_1. If Portugal raises its money supply to M_2 in an attempt to stimulate its economy, the fundamental value of its exchange rate will fall below the official fixed rate, and Portugal's currency would be overvalued.

Now suppose that Spain also expands its money supply in a coordinated effort to stimulate both economies. For any level of Portugal's money supply, the increase in Spain's money supply will depreciate the fundamental value of Spain's exchange rate and appreciate the fundamental value of Portugal's exchange rate. The fundamental value curve of Portugal's exchange rate shifts up from FV^1 to FV^2. Portugal can now increase its money supply to M_2 without creating an overvaluation problem. Thus Spain and Portugal have achieved a coordinated monetary expansion.

official exchange rate). Thus if Spain and Portugal cooperate by changing their money supplies in the same direction, both countries can achieve their stabilization goals without either country experiencing overvaluation.

As this example shows, fixed exchange rates are most likely to work well when the countries in the system have similar macroeconomic goals and can cooperate on monetary policies. As the following application illustrates, the failure of nations to cooperate within a fixed-exchange-rate system can lead to severe problems, including the potential breakdown of the system.

APPLICATION

Policy Coordination Failure and the Collapse of Fixed Exchange Rates: The Cases of Bretton Woods and the EMS

After World War II, the world's industrialized nations established the Bretton Woods system, under which exchange rates were fixed (with occasional adjustments).[16] The United States, by far the world's largest economy at the time, played a central role in the system and U.S. dollars were widely used by other countries as official reserve assets. Other countries were willing to do so because the United States pledged to maintain the exchange rate between dollars and gold at $35 per ounce. In other words, the U.S. dollar was "as good as gold." All in all, the Bretton Woods system seemed to perform well. While the system was fully operational (1959–1971)[17] most countries recorded solid macroeconomic growth and stability. However, the inability of the principal member countries to coordinate their monetary policies created severe strains in the system and eventually led to its collapse.

Several international disputes erupted over monetary policy during the Bretton Woods era, but the one that ultimately proved fatal was triggered by American monetary policy during the 1960s. The U.S. money supply grew more and more rapidly, reflecting the Federal Reserve's aggressive attempts to promote growth in output and employment and its desire to keep interest rates low despite expansionary fiscal policies. (U.S. government spending increased significantly during the 1960s both because of the Vietnam War and expansion of Great Society social programs.) Increasing money growth and the inflation that followed caused the dollar to become increasingly overvalued.

Normally, in a fixed-exchange-rate system, a country's loss of international reserves makes sustaining an overvalued currency impossible. However, the United States avoided the loss of its reserves for a time by persuading foreign central banks to buy the excess supply of dollars in the foreign exchange market. Foreign central banks at first were willing to use their own currencies to buy U.S. dollars because they could use the dollars as international reserves. Ultimately, however, the foreign central banks grew tired of accumulating dollars and complained about what they considered to be overexpansionary U.S. monetary policy.

The solution suggested by U.S. policymakers was for the other Bretton Woods members to increase their money supplies, thereby eliminating the dollar overvaluation problem. However, several countries, notably Germany, refused to accept the inflationary consequences of this proposal and began to demand instead that the United States redeem its dollars with gold. Fearing a huge drain on its gold reserves, the United States was reluctant to redeem its

16. For a detailed recent study of the Bretton Woods system, see Michael D. Bordo and Barry Eichengreen, eds., *A Retrospective on the Bretton Woods System*, Chicago: University of Chicago Press for NBER, 1993.

17. Before 1959 not all currencies in the system were convertible.

dollars. A series of crises in the foreign exchange markets followed, and in August 1971 President Nixon announced that the United States would no longer exchange gold for dollars. This announcement effectively ended the Bretton Woods system and left the world's major currencies to float freely against each other.

Two decades later a different kind of dispute over monetary policy threatened the European Monetary System (EMS), a system of fixed exchange rates among Western European nations. Because of its large economy, Germany was the most influential country in the EMS. In 1992, concerned about increased inflation after German reunification, the Bundesbank tightened Germany's monetary policy, raising interest rates significantly. This action undervalued the mark and overvalued other EMS currencies, putting considerable pressure on other members of the EMS to tighten monetary policies as well. However, Great Britain and other countries at the time were mired in serious recessions and didn't want to go along with German contractionary policies.

In September 1992, participants in the foreign exchange market became convinced that Great Britain would not tighten monetary policy and that, as a result, the Bank of England would eventually have to devalue the pound. This fear led to a speculative run on the pound. After losing large quantities of reserves in attempts to maintain the value of the pound relative to other currencies in the EMS, Great Britain decided to leave the fixed-exchange-rate system and allowed the value of the pound to fall. Several other countries refused to match Germany's tight monetary policies and were forced to devalue or leave the system. The 1992 EMS crisis substantially delayed progress toward the ultimate goal of a single European currency. Indeed, new speculative crises in the summer of 1993 led many observers to question whether this system will survive much longer.

In the Bretton Woods case, the dominant country in the system followed a monetary policy that was more expansionary than the other members wanted; in the EMS case, the dominant country followed a monetary policy that was tighter than the other members preferred. In both instances, however, international disagreements about the appropriate rate of monetary growth posed a severe threat to the very existence of the fixed-exchange-rate system.

Fixed Versus Flexible Exchange Rates

We have discussed some of the problems that arose in the Bretton Woods and EMS fixed-exchange-rate systems. However, flexible-exchange-rate systems have problems of their own, primarily the volatility of exchange rates, which introduces uncertainty for people and businesses in their transactions with other countries. Each type of system has its problems, so which is preferable?

Proponents of fixed-exchange-rate systems stress two major benefits. First, relative to a situation in which exchange rates fluctuate continuously, stable exchange rates make trading goods and assets among countries easier and less costly. Thus a system of fixed rates may promote economic and financial integration and improve economic efficiency. Second, fixed exchange rates may improve monetary policy "discipline," in the sense that countries with fixed exchange rates typically are less able to carry out highly expansionary monetary policies; the result may be lower inflation in the long run.

The other side of the monetary discipline argument is that fixed exchange rates take away a country's ability to use monetary policy flexibly to deal with recessions.[18] This inability is particularly serious if the different countries in the fixed-exchange-rate system have different policy goals and face different types of economic shocks. As the preceding Application illustrated, disagreements among countries in a fixed-exchange-rate system about the conduct of monetary policy may even lead to the breakdown of the system.

Which system is better depends on the circumstances. Fixed exchange rates (or even a common currency) among a group of countries are useful when large benefits can be gained from increased trade and integration and when the countries in the system coordinate their monetary policies closely. Countries that value the ability to use monetary policy independently—perhaps because they face different macroeconomic shocks than other countries or hold different views about the relative costs of unemployment and inflation —should retain a floating exchange rate.

18. Keynesians consider this a cost, but classicals don't.

CHAPTER SUMMARY

1. The nominal exchange rate is the number of units of foreign currency that can be obtained for one unit of domestic currency. The real exchange rate is the number of units of foreign goods that can be obtained for one unit of the domestic good. There are two major types of exchange rate systems: flexible- or floating-exchange-rate systems, in which the value of the nominal exchange rate is determined by market forces; and fixed-exchange-rate systems, in which the value of the exchange rate is officially set by a government or group of governments. In a flexible-exchange-rate system, an exchange rate increase is called an appreciation, and an exchange rate decrease is called a depreciation.

2. The real exchange rate is important because it affects net exports, or exports minus imports. Other factors held constant, a decline in the real exchange rate makes domestic goods cheaper relative to foreign goods and thus tends to increase net exports in the long run. Because a drop in the real exchange rate raises the cost of imports, however, it may cause net exports to fall in the short run before physical flows of exports and imports have had time to adjust. The characteristic pattern of the response of net exports to a drop in the real exchange rate—falling net exports in the short run but rising net exports in the long run—is called the J curve.

3. In a flexible-exchange-rate system, the value of the (nominal) exchange rate is determined by supply and demand in the foreign exchange market. Foreigners demand the domestic currency to buy domestic goods and assets. Domestic residents supply the domestic currency to obtain the foreign currency needed to buy foreign goods and assets.

4. Other factors held constant, an increase in domestic output leads domestic residents to demand more imports, reducing the country's net exports and depreciating its exchange rate. An increase in the domestic real interest rate makes domestic assets more attractive, increasing the demand for the domestic currency and appreciating the exchange rate; the higher exchange rate in turn reduces net exports. The effects of changes in foreign output and the foreign real interest rate on the domestic country's net exports and exchange rate are the opposite of the effects of changes in domestic output and the domestic real interest rate.

5. The *IS–LM* model for an open economy is similar to that for the closed economy. The principal difference is that, in the open-economy *IS–LM* model, factors (other than output or the real interest rate) that increase a country's net exports cause the *IS* curve to shift up. Among the factors that increase net exports are a rise in foreign output, an increase in the foreign real interest rate, or a shift in world demand toward the domestic country's goods. Economic shocks or policy changes are transmitted from one country to another by changes in net exports that lead to *IS* curve shifts.

6. In an open economy with flexible exchange rates, a fiscal expansion increases domestic output, domestic prices, and the domestic real interest rate, as in a closed economy. The effect on the exchange rate is ambiguous. The increase in output raises the demand for imported goods, which weakens the exchange rate, but the higher real interest rate makes domestic assets more attractive, which strengthens the exchange rate. Because increased output raises the demand for imports, net exports fall. The fiscal expansion is transmitted to the foreign country by the increase in demand for the foreign country's exports.

7. In an open economy with flexible exchange rates, changes in the money supply are neutral in the basic classical model. Changes in the money supply also are neutral in the long run in the Keynesian model. In the short run in the Keynesian model, however, a decrease in the domestic money supply reduces domestic output and raises the domestic real interest rate, causing the current real exchange rate to appreciate. Net exports by the domestic country increase, if the effect of lower output (which increases net exports) is stronger than the effect of the rise in the real exchange rate (which tends to reduce net exports). The monetary contraction is transmitted to the foreign country by the effect on the foreign country's net exports, which decline.

8. In a fixed-exchange-rate system, nominal exchange rates are officially determined. If the officially determined exchange rate is greater than the fundamental value of the exchange rate as determined by supply and demand in the foreign exchange market, the exchange rate is said to be overvalued. The central bank can maintain the exchange rate at an overvalued level for a time by using official reserves (such as gold or foreign-currency bank deposits) to buy its own currency in the foreign exchange market. A country that tries to maintain an overvalued exchange rate for too long will run out of reserves and be forced to devalue its currency. If financial investors expect a devaluation, they may sell large quantities of domestic assets (a speculative run). A speculative run increases the supply of the domestic currency in the foreign exchange market and increases the rate at which the central bank must pay out its reserves.

9. To raise the fundamental value of its exchange rate, the central bank can tighten monetary policy. There is only one value of the domestic money supply at which the fundamental value of the exchange rate equals its officially fixed rate. With fixed exchange rates, individual countries aren't free to use expansionary monetary policies to fight recessions because such policies result in an overvalued exchange rate. However, a group of countries in a fixed-exchange-rate system can use expansionary monetary policies effectively if they coordinate their policies.

10. The advantages of a fixed-exchange-rate system are that it may promote economic and financial integration among countries and that it imposes discipline on the monetary policies of individual countries. A fixed-exchange-rate system won't work well if member countries have different macroeconomic policy goals or face different macroeconomic disturbances and thus are unable or unwilling to coordinate their monetary policies.

Key Terms

devaluation, p. 485
exchange rate, p. 482
exchange rate unions, p. 483
fixed-exchange-rate system, p. 483
flexible-exchange-rate system, p. 482
floating-exchange-rate system, p. 482
foreign exchange market, p. 482
fundamental value of the exchange rate, p. 510
inconvertible currency, p. 511

J curve, p. 488
nominal appreciation, p. 485
nominal depreciation, p. 485
nominal exchange rate, p. 482
overvalued exchange rate, p. 510
real appreciation, p. 485
real depreciation, p. 486
real exchange rate, p. 484
revaluation, p. 485
speculative run, p. 511
terms of trade, p. 486
undervalued exchange rate, p. 512

Key Equations

$$e = \frac{e_{nom}P}{P_{For}} \tag{14.1}$$

The real exchange rate, e, or the number of foreign goods that can be obtained for one domestic good, is defined in terms of the nominal exchange rate e_{nom} (the amount of foreign currency that can be obtained for one unit of domestic currency), the domestic price level P, and the foreign price level P_{For}.

$$\frac{\Delta e_{nom}}{e_{nom}} = \frac{\Delta e}{e} + \pi_{For} - \pi \tag{14.3}$$

The percentage change in the nominal exchange rate, $\Delta e_{nom}/e_{nom}$, equals the percentage change in the real exchange rate, $\Delta e/e$, plus the excess of the foreign rate of inflation over the domestic rate of inflation, $\pi_{For} - \pi$.

$$S^d - I^d = NX \tag{14.4}$$

In an open economy, goods market equilibrium (the *IS* curve) requires that the excess of desired national saving over desired investment equal net exports. Equation (14.4) is equivalent to the condition that output, Y, must equal the aggregate demand for goods, $C^d + I^d + G + NX$, Eq. (14.5).

Review Questions

1. Define *nominal exchange rate* and *real exchange rate.* How are changes in the real exchange rate and the nominal exchange rate related?
2. What are the two main types of exchange rate systems? Currently, which type of system determines the values of the major currencies, such as the dollar, yen, and mark?
3. What is the J curve? What explains the behavior of net exports represented by the J curve?
4. For a given real exchange rate, how are a country's net exports affected by an increase in domestic income? An increase in foreign income? How does an increase in the domestic real interest rate affect the real exchange rate and net exports? Explain.
5. Why do foreigners demand dollars in the foreign exchange market? Why do Americans supply dollars to the foreign exchange market? Give two examples of changes that would lead to an increased demand for dollars and two examples of changes that would lead to an increased supply of dollars in the foreign exchange market.
6. How does the *IS–LM* model for an open economy differ from the *IS–LM* model for a closed economy? Illustrate the use of the open-economy *IS–LM* model in describing how a recession in one country may be transmitted to other countries.
7. How are net exports affected by expansionary fiscal policy? By expansionary monetary policy? What is the potential ambiguity in determining these effects?
8. What effects does expansionary monetary policy have on the nominal exchange rate in both the short and long run? Explain.
9. What is the *fundamental value* of a currency? What does saying that a currency is *overvalued* mean? Why is an overvalued currency a problem? What can a country do about an overvalued currency?
10. Why is a country limited in changing its money supply under a fixed-exchange-rate system? Explain how policy coordination among countries on a fixed-exchange-rate system can increase the degree to which monetary policy may be used to pursue macroeconomic goals.

Numerical Problems

1. West Bubble makes ordinary soap bars that are sold for 5 guilders each. East Bubble makes deluxe soap bars that are sold for 100 florins each. The real exchange rate between West and East Bubble is two ordinary soap bars per deluxe soap bar.
   a. What is the nominal exchange rate between the two countries?
   b. During the following year West Bubble has 10% domestic inflation and East Bubble has 20% domestic

inflation. Two ordinary soap bars are still traded for a deluxe soap bar. At the end of the year what has happened to the nominal exchange rate? Which country has had a nominal appreciation? Which has had a nominal depreciation?

2. Japan produces and exports only cameras, and Saudi Arabia produces and exports only barrels of oil. Initially, Japan exports 40 cameras to Saudi Arabia and imports 64 barrels of oil. The real exchange rate is 4 barrels of oil per camera. Neither country has any other trading partners.

a. Initially, what is the real value of Japan's net exports, measured in terms of its domestic good? (*Hint:* You have to use the real exchange rate to express Japan's oil imports in terms of an equivalent number of cameras. Then calculate Japan's net exports as the number of cameras exported minus the real value of its imports in terms of cameras.)

b. The real exchange rate falls to 3 barrels of oil per camera. Although the decline in the real exchange rate makes oil more expensive in terms of cameras, in the short run there is relatively little change in the quantities of exports and imports, as Japan's exports rise to 42 cameras and its imports fall to 60 barrels of oil. What has happened to the real value of Japan's net exports?

c. In the longer run, quantities of exports and imports adjust more to the drop in the real exchange rate from 4 to 3, and Japan's exports rise to 45 cameras and its imports of oil fall to 54 barrels. What are Japan's real net exports now?

d. Relate your answers to parts (b) and (c) to the J-curve concept.

3. Consider the following classical economy.

Desired consumption	$C^d = 300 + 0.5Y - 200r$.
Desired investment	$I^d = 200 - 300r$.
Government purchases	$G = 100$.
Net exports	$NX = 150 - 0.1Y - 0.5e$.
Real exchange rate	$e = 20 + 600r$.
Full-employment output	$\bar{Y} = 900$.

a. What are the equilibrium values of the real interest rate, the real exchange rate, consumption, investment, and net exports?

b. Now suppose that full-employment output increases to 940. What are the equilibrium values of the real interest rate, the real exchange rate, consumption, investment, and net exports?

c. Suppose that full-employment output remains at 940 and that government purchases increase to 132. What are the equilibrium values of the real interest rate, the real exchange rate, consumption, investment, and net exports?

4. Consider the following Keynesian economy.

Desired consumption	$C^d = 200 + 0.6(Y - T) - 200r$.
Desired investment	$I^d = 300 - 300r$.
Taxes	$T = 20 + 0.2Y$.
Government purchases	$G = 152$.
Net exports	$NX = 150 - 0.08Y - 500r$.
Money demand	$L = 0.5Y - 200r$.
Money supply	$M = 924$.
Full-employment output	$\bar{Y} = 1000$.

a. What are the general equilibrium (that is, long-run) values of output, the real interest rate, consumption, investment, net exports, and the price level?

b. Starting from full employment, government purchases are increased by 62, to 214. What are the effects of this change on output, the real interest rate, consumption, investment, net exports, and the price level in the short run? In the long run?

c. With government purchases at their initial value of 152, net exports increase by 62 at any income and real interest rate so that $NX = 212 - 0.08Y - 500r$. What are the effects of this change on output, the real interest rate, consumption, investment, net exports, and the price level in the short run? In the long run? Compare your answer to that for part (b).

5. Consider the following classical economy.

AD	$Y = 400 + 50\,M/P$.
AS	$Y = \bar{Y} = 1000$.

This economy produces only wine, its output is measured in terms of wine, and its currency is francs. It trades with a country that produces only cheese, and the currency of that country is crowns. The real exchange rate e equals 5 wedges of cheese per bottle of wine. The foreign price level is 20 crowns per wedge of cheese, and the domestic money supply is 48 francs.

a. What is the domestic price level? What is the fundamental value of the (nominal) exchange rate?

b. Suppose that the domestic country fixes its exchange rate at 50 crowns per franc. Is its currency overvalued, undervalued, or neither? What will happen to the domestic central bank's stock of official reserve assets if it maintains the exchange rate at 50 crowns per franc?

c. Suppose that the domestic country wants a money supply level that equalizes the fundamental value of the exchange rate and the fixed rate of 50 crowns per franc. What level of the domestic money supply achieves this goal? (*Hint:* For the given real exchange rate and foreign price level, what domestic price level is consistent with the official rate? What domestic money supply level will yield this price level?)

Analytical Problems

1. Recessions often lead to calls for protectionist measures to preserve domestic jobs. Suppose that a country that is in a recession imposes restrictions that sharply reduce the amount of goods imported by the country.
a. Using the Keynesian *IS–LM* model, analyze the effects of import restrictions on the domestic country's employment, output, real interest rate, and real exchange rate, keeping in mind that the country is initially in a recession.
b. What are the effects of the country's action on foreign employment, output, real interest rates, and real exchange rates? What happens if the foreign country retaliates by imposing restrictions on goods exported by the domestic country?
c. Suppose that the domestic economy is at full employment when it imposes restrictions on imports. Using the basic classical model without misperceptions, find the effects on the country's employment, output, real interest rate, and real exchange rate.

2. "U.S. government budget deficits not only crowd out investment in the United States but also reduce capital formation in other countries."

Is this statement true? To analyze it, use the Keynesian model to work out the effects on investment, both at home and abroad, of a government budget deficit. Assume that the deficit was the result of a large tax cut and assume also that households respond to the tax cut by increasing desired consumption (Ricardian equivalence doesn't hold). Consider both the short and long run. Does your answer change if Ricardian equivalence holds so that desired consumption is unaffected by the tax cut?

3. The Application at the end of Section 14.4 discussed the idea that the United States became a relatively more attractive place to invest in the early 1980s. Analyze this argument by using the classical *IS–LM* model for two countries. Assume that because of more favorable tax laws, the user cost of capital falls in the domestic country and that, because of the LDC debt crisis, the expected future marginal product of capital falls in the foreign country. Show that these changes lead to an appreciation of the home country's real exchange rate and a drop in the domestic country's net exports. Assume no change in current productivity or current labor supply in either country. What is happening to capital flows? Why?

4. East Bubble's main trading partner is West Bubble. To fight inflation, West Bubble undertakes a contractionary monetary policy.
a. What is the effect of West Bubble's contractionary monetary policy on East Bubble's real exchange rate in the short run, assuming no change in East Bubble's policies? In the long run? Use the Keynesian model with flexible exchange rates.
b. What is the effect of West Bubble's monetary contraction on East Bubble's *nominal* exchange rate in the short run and in the long run?
c. Suppose now that East Bubble has fixed its exchange rate with West Bubble. If East Bubble wants to keep the exchange rate equal to its fundamental value, how will East Bubble have to respond to West Bubble's monetary tightening? What will happen to East Bubble's output, real exchange rate, and net exports in the short run if it maintains the fixed exchange rate at its fundamental value? Compare your answer to that for part (a).
d. Suppose that, after West Bubble's monetary tightening, East Bubble decides not to change any of its own macroeconomic policies (the exchange rate is still fixed). What will happen? Describe some alternative scenarios.

5. Use a diagram like Fig. 14.6 to analyze the effect on a country's net exports of a beneficial supply shock that temporarily raises full-employment output by 100 per person. Assume that the basic classical model applies so that income is always at its full-employment level.
a. Suppose that, in response to the temporary increase in income, the residents of the country do not change the amount they desire to spend at any real interest rate (on either domestic or foreign goods). What is the effect of the supply shock on the country's net exports? (*Hint:* What is the effect of the increase in income on the curve representing desired

saving minus desired investment? What is the effect on the curve representing net exports?)

b. Now suppose that, in response to a temporary increase in income, the residents of the country increase their desired spending at any real interest rate by 100 per person. A portion of this increased spending is for foreign-produced goods. What is the effect on the country's net exports?

c. More difficult: If the increase in income is temporary, would the spending behavior assumed in part (a) or the spending behavior assumed in part (b) be more likely to occur? Based on your answer, do the results of this problem confirm or contradict the prediction of the model in Chapter 5 of the response of net exports to a supply shock? Explain.

APPENDIX 14.A AN ALGEBRAIC VERSION OF THE OPEN-ECONOMY *IS–LM* MODEL

The *IS–LM* model for the open economy is basically the same as the closed-economy *IS–LM* model derived in Appendix 10.A, with the exception that the goods market equilibrium condition (the *IS* curve) is expanded to include net exports. The *LM* curve and the *FE* line are unchanged from previous analyses.

To derive the *IS* curve for the open economy, we begin with the equations describing desired consumption and desired investment, Eqs. (10.A.8) and (10.A.10):

$$C^d = c_0 + c_Y[Y - (t_0 + tY)] - c_r r, \qquad (14.A.1)$$

$$I^d = i_0 - i_r r. \qquad (14.A.2)$$

Equation (14.A.1) shows that desired consumption depends positively on disposable income, $Y - T$, and negatively on the real interest rate, r. (In Eq. 14.A.1 we used Eq. 10.A.9 to substitute for taxes, T.) Equation (14.A.2) states that desired investment depends negatively on the real interest rate r. Other factors influencing desired consumption and desired investment are included in the constant terms c_0 and i_0, respectively.

In an open economy net exports also are a source of demand for domestic output. We assume that net exports are

$$NX = x_0 - x_Y Y + x_{YF} Y_{For} - x_r r + x_{rF} r_{For}, \qquad (14.A.3)$$

where x_0, x_Y, x_{YF}, x_r, and x_{rF} are positive numbers. According to Eq. (14.A.3), a country's net exports depend negatively on domestic income Y (increased domestic income raises spending on imports) and positively on foreign income Y_{For} (increased foreign income raises spending on exports). Net exports also depend negatively on the domestic real interest rate r (a higher real interest rate appreciates the real exchange rate, making domestic goods relatively more expensive) and positively on the foreign real interest rate r_{For} (a higher foreign real interest rate depreciates the domestic country's real exchange rate). Other factors influencing net exports, such as the qualities of domestic and foreign goods, are reflected in the constant term x_0 in Eq. (14.A.3).

The goods market equilibrium condition for an open economy, Eq. (5.5), is

$$Y = C^d + I^d + G + NX. \qquad (14.A.4)$$

The alternative version of the open-economy goods market equilibrium condition, $S^d = I^d + NX$, which is emphasized in the text, could be used equally well.

If we substitute the equations for desired consumption, Eq. (14.A.1), desired investment, Eq. (14.A.2), and net exports, Eq. (14.A.3), into the goods market equilibrium condition, Eq. (14.A.4), we get

$$Y = c_0 + c_Y(Y - t_0 - tY) - c_r r + i_0 - i_r r + G + x_0 - x_Y Y + x_{YF} Y_{For} - x_r r + x_{rF} r_{For}. \qquad (14.A.5)$$

Collecting the terms that multiply Y on the left-hand side yields

$$[1-(1-t)c_Y+x_Y]Y=c_0+i_0+G-c_Yt_0+x_0+x_{YF}Y_{\text{For}}+x_{rF}r_{\text{For}}-(c_r+i_r+x_r)r, \quad (14.A.6)$$

Equation (14.A.6) relates output Y to the real interest rate r that clears the goods market and thus defines the open-economy *IS* curve. To put Eq. (14.A.6) in a form that is easier to interpret graphically, we rewrite it with r on the left-hand side and Y on the right side to obtain

$$r=\alpha'_{IS}-\beta'_{IS}Y, \qquad \text{open-economy } IS \text{ curve}. \quad (14.A.7)$$

Here, α'_{IS} and β'_{IS} are positive numbers defined as

$$\alpha'_{IS}=\frac{c_0+i_0+G-c_Yt_0+x_0+x_{YF}Y_{\text{For}}+x_{rF}r_{\text{For}}}{c_r+i_r+x_r}; \quad (14.A.8)$$

and

$$\beta'_{IS}=\frac{1-(1-t)c_Y+x_Y}{c_r+i_r+x_r}. \quad (14.A.9)$$

If there are no net exports, so that $x_0=x_Y=x_{YF}=x_r=x_{rF}=0$, the coefficients α'_{IS} and β'_{IS} reduce to the coefficients of the closed-economy *IS* curve, α_{IS} and β_{IS} (compare Eqs. 14.A.8 and 14.A.9 to Eqs. 10.A.15 and 10.A.16).

We use the open-economy *IS* curve equation, Eq. (14.A.7), to confirm the three points made about the curve in the text. First, it slopes downward (the slope of the *IS* curve is $-\beta'_{IS}$ which is negative). Second, any factor that shifts the closed-economy *IS* curve also shifts the open-economy *IS* curve (any factor that changes the intercept α_{IS} also changes the intercept α'_{IS} in the same direction). Finally, for a given output and real interest rate, any factor that increases net exports shifts the open-economy *IS* curve up. That is, an increase in Y_{For} or r_{For}, or some other change that increases the demand for net exports as reflected in an increase in x_0, raises the intercept term α'_{IS} and thus shifts the *IS* curve up.

General equilibrium in the open-economy *IS–LM* model is determined as in the closed-economy model, except that the open-economy *IS* curve (Eq. 14.A.7) replaces the closed-economy *IS* curve (Eq. 10.A.14). Similarly, classical and Keynesian *AD–AS* analysis in the open economy is the same as in the closed economy (Appendixes 11.A and 12.B), except that the coefficients α_{IS} and β_{IS} in the equation for the aggregate demand curve, Eq. (11.A.3), are replaced by their open-economy analogues, α'_{IS} and β'_{IS}.

For values of output Y, the real interest rate r, and the price level P determined by the open-economy *IS–LM* or *AD–AS* model, exchange rates can be determined from:

$$e=e_0-e_YY+e_{YF}Y_{\text{For}}+e_rr-e_{rF}r_{\text{For}}, \quad (14.A.10)$$

where e_0, e_Y, e_{YF}, e_r, and e_{rF} are positive numbers; and

$$e_{\text{nom}}=\frac{eP_{\text{For}}}{P}. \quad (14.A.11)$$

According to Eq. (14.A.10), an increase in foreign income Y_{For} or the domestic interest rate r, either of which raises the demand for the domestic currency, appreciates the real exchange rate e. Also, an increase in domestic income Y or the foreign real interest rate r_{For}, either of which increases the supply of domestic currency, depreciates the real exchange rate. Eq. (14.A.11), which is the same as Eqs. (14.1) and (14.6), states that the nominal exchange rate e_{nom} depends on the real exchange rate e and the foreign and domestic price levels, P_{For} and P.

To illustrate the use of Eqs. (14.A.10) and (14.A.11), let's consider the effects of a monetary expansion in the Keynesian model. In the short run, an increase in the money supply raises domestic output Y, lowers the domestic real interest rate r, and leaves the domestic price level P unchanged. For these changes Eqs. (14.A.10) and (14.A.11)—holding constant foreign output Y_{For} and the foreign real interest rate r_{For}—imply a lower real exchange rate e and a lower nominal exchange rate e_{nom} (both a real and a nominal depreciation). In the long run, money is neutral, so Y and r return to their original levels. Equation (14.A.10) indicates, therefore, that the real exchange rate e also returns to its original value in the long run. However, a monetary expansion leads to a long-run increase in the domestic price level P. Hence from Eq. (14.A.11) we see that the nominal exchange rate e_{nom} also depreciates in the long run.

CHAPTER 15

MONETARY POLICY AND THE FEDERAL RESERVE SYSTEM

Monetary policy—the government's decisions about how much money to supply to the economy—is one of the two principal tools available for affecting macroeconomic behavior. (The other, fiscal policy, is discussed in Chapter 16.) Monetary policy decisions have widespread implications for the economy. The macroeconomic models that we have presented predict that changes in the money supply will affect nominal variables such as the price level and the nominal exchange rate. In addition, theories that allow for nonneutrality (including the extended classical theory with misperceptions and the Keynesian theory) imply that, in the short run, monetary policy also affects real variables such as real GDP, the real interest rate, and the unemployment rate. Because monetary policy has such pervasive economic effects, the central bank's announcements and actions are closely monitored by the media, financial market participants, and the general public.

In this chapter we look more closely at monetary policy, concentrating first on the basic question of how the nation's money supply is determined. We demonstrate that, although a nation's central bank (the Federal Reserve System in the United States) can exert strong influence over the level of the money supply, the money supply also is affected by the banking system's behavior and the public's decisions.

In the second part of the chapter, we explore the question: How should the central bank conduct monetary policy? Not surprisingly, because of classical and Keynesian differences over the effects of monetary policy and the desirability of trying to smooth the business cycle (Chapters 11 and 12), the question is controversial. Keynesians usually argue that monetary authorities should have considerable latitude to try to offset cyclical fluctuations. Opposing the Keynesian view, both classical economists and a group of economists called *monetarists* believe that monetary policy shouldn't be left to the discretion of the central bank but instead should be governed by simple rules. Although establishing rules for monetary policy might seem to tie policymakers' hands unnecessarily, monetarists and classicals argue that the use of rules would lead to a more stable and less inflationary economy in the long run. After examining the arguments for and against the use of rules, we compare the performances of rules-based monetary policies in the United States, Germany, and Japan. We also discuss how the debate about rules is related to questions of how monetary policymaking institutions should be designed. For example, should the central bank be largely independent from the rest of the government, as in Germany and the United States, or should it be more directly controlled by the executive and legislative branches?

15.1 PRINCIPLES OF MONEY SUPPLY DETERMINATION

How is the nation's money supply determined? So far we have assumed that the money supply, M, is controlled directly by the central bank. Although this assumption is a useful simplification, it isn't literally true. The central bank's control of the money supply is only indirect and depends to some extent on the structure of the economy.

Most generally, three groups affect the money supply: the central bank, depository institutions, and the public.

1. In nearly all countries the **central bank** is the governmental institution responsible for monetary policy.[1] Examples of central banks are the Federal Reserve System in the United States, the Bundesbank in Germany, and the Bank of Japan.
2. **Depository institutions** are privately owned banks and thrift institutions (such as savings and loan associations) that accept deposits from and make loans directly to the public. We refer to depository institutions as banks, for short.
3. The public includes every person or firm (except banks) that holds money, either as currency and coin or as deposits in banks—in other words, virtually the whole private economy outside of the banking system.

Before investigating how these groups interact to set the money supply in a financially complex country like the United States, we begin with an example of a primitive agricultural economy, which we call Agricola. Examining the introduction of money and the development of banking in Agricola identifies clearly the factors involved in the determination of the money supply. Additionally, the development of the monetary and banking systems in fictitious Agricola loosely parallels the actual evolution of such systems over the centuries in many countries.

The Money Supply in an All-Currency Economy

The imaginary country of Agricola is an agricultural nation that produces a variety of fruits, nuts, vegetables, and grains. Initially, Agricola has no money supply, so all trading is done by barter, or the direct trading of goods for

1. Most industrialized countries established central banks in the nineteenth century or early twentieth century. Prior to the establishment of central banks, national Treasury Departments often were responsible for currency issue and other matters pertaining to the money supply.

goods. Recall, however, that a trading system based on barter is extremely inconvenient (Chapter 7). Under a barter system a farmer who wants to trade barley for pomegranates must find someone willing to exchange pomegranates for barley, which involves a costly and time-consuming search.

The benevolent leader of Agricola recognizes this inconvenience and decides to create a national money to ease trade among the people. The first step in establishing a national money is to create a government agency called the Agricolan Central Bank. The Central Bank then prints paper certificates[2] and decrees the value of each certificate to be one florin (abbreviated fl), which becomes the national currency of Agricola. The government of Agricola prohibits anyone other than the Agricolan Central Bank from printing these certificates.

To get the florins into general circulation, the Central Bank uses them to buy some real assets from the public. In the agricultural economy of Agricola real assets are storable agricultural products such as coconuts, so the Central Bank uses newly printed florins to buy coconuts from the public. Why do people in Agricola willingly surrender valuable coconuts in exchange for paper certificates? In general, people accept paper money in payment for goods, services, or assets because they expect to be able to use it to buy other goods, services, or assets in the future. In other words, people accept paper money because they believe that other people also will accept it. The belief that money has value becomes self-justifying: If most people believe that money has value, then it has value.[3] The government helps convince the public that paper money has value, usually by decreeing that the money is *legal tender*—that is, creditors are required to accept the money in settlement of debts—and by stating its own willingness to accept money from the public in payment of taxes.

Suppose that the people of Agricola accept the new currency and that the Central Bank trades 1 million florins to the public for 1 million coconuts. The balance sheet of the Agricolan Central Bank is

Agricolan Central Bank			
ASSETS		LIABILITIES	
Coconuts	1,000,000 fl	Currency	1,000,000 fl

On the left-hand side of the balance sheet are the Central Bank's assets—what it owns or is owed, in this case, the coconuts. On the right-hand side are the bank's liabilities—what it owes to others. Because the florins are technically debt obligations of the Central Bank, they are entered as liabilities in the balance sheet. The liabilities of the Central Bank that are usable as money are called the **monetary base,** or, equivalently, **high-powered money.** The monetary base of Agricola is thus 1 million florins.

Assume that Agricola initially has no banking system. With no banks and hence no bank deposits, the total money supply is the currency held by the public. That is, the paper certificates distributed by the Agricolan Central Bank are used directly as money. Thus the money supply in Agricola equals 1 million

2. In most countries the actual printing of paper money is done by a separate agency, not by the central bank itself.

3. Also possible is that no one believes that money has value, which would again be a self-justifying belief because no one would then accept money in payment.

florins, which in turn equals the monetary base (the liabilities of the Agricolan Central Bank). Hence *in an all-currency economy (one with no bank deposits) the money supply equals the monetary base.*

The Money Supply Under Fractional Reserve Banking

As the people of Agricola become financially more sophisticated, a system of private banks emerges. The banks announce their willingness to accept deposits from the public.

For the time being, let's assume that, because currency is easily lost or stolen, Agricolans want to hold *all* their money in bank deposits rather than in currency. After the Agricolans deposit all their currency (1 million florins) in banks, the combined, or consolidated, balance sheet of all the banks is

Consolidated Balance Sheet of Banks

ASSETS		LIABILITIES	
Currency	1,000,000 fl	Deposits	1,000,000 fl

The banking system's assets are the 1,000,000 paper florins in bank vaults. The banking system's liabilities are the deposits, which are the banks' debts or obligations to the public. The balance sheet of the Central Bank remains the same.

Liquid assets held by banks to meet the demands for withdrawals by depositors or to pay the checks drawn on depositors' accounts are called **bank reserves.** In general, bank reserves comprise currency held by private banks in their vaults and deposits held by private banks at the Central Bank. Here, all bank reserves are held as currency in the banks' vaults. Note that the bank reserves equal total deposits of 1,000,000 fl. This type of banking system is called **100% reserve banking** because bank reserves equal 100% of deposits. Under 100% reserve banking, banks are nothing more than a safekeeping service for the public's currency. Indeed, the only way that banks could cover their expenses and make a profit under 100% reserve banking would be to charge depositors a fee for holding their money for them (that is, to pay negative interest on deposits).

However, one day an enterprising Agricolan banker notices that the paper florins the bank has accepted from depositors are just sitting idly in neat stacks in the bank's vault. True, a few florins flow out when a depositor writes a check to someone who banks elsewhere, or when a depositor switches an account to another bank. However, this outflow is balanced by a roughly equivalent inflow, when the bank's depositors receive checks drawn on other banks or the bank attracts a depositor away from another bank. The banker calculates that keeping florins in the vault equal to, say, 20% of outstanding deposits would more than cover this random ebb and flow. The remaining 80% of the florins on deposit could be lent to earn interest for the bank!

Under the Agricolan banker's scheme the reserves held by the bank will equal only a fraction of the bank's outstanding deposits. In this case, the **reserve–deposit ratio,** or reserves divided by deposits, equals 20%. A banking system in which banks hold only a fraction of their deposits in reserve, so that the reserve–deposit ratio is less than 1, is called **fractional reserve banking.**

Fractional reserve banking is profitable for banks because, instead of sitting in the vault earning no interest for the bank, a portion of the funds received from depositors can be used to make interest-earning loans.

All the bankers of Agricola quickly grasp the idea of fractional reserve banking, and decide to hold reserves of 20% of deposits and lend the other 80% (800,000 fl) to farmers. The farmers use the loans to buy fertilizer for their farms. The sellers of the fertilizer receive 800,000 fl in payment, and, because everyone prefers having bank deposits to holding currency, they deposit the 800,000 fl in the banking system. After these deposits are made all of the florins are back in the banks, and the consolidated balance sheet of the banking system is

Consolidated Balance Sheet of Banks

ASSETS		LIABILITIES	
Currency (reserves)	1,000,000 fl	Deposits	1,800,000 fl
Loans to farmers	800,000 fl		
Total	1,800,000 fl	Total	1,800,000 fl

The banks' assets now include the 800,000 fl in loans to farmers (the loans are owed to the banks, so they are assets of the banks). The banks' assets also include 1,000,000 paper florins: 200,000 fl originally kept in reserve plus the 800,000 fl deposited by the sellers of the fertilizer.

The banks' consolidated liabilities equal 1,800,000 fl in deposits: the 1,000,000 fl in original deposits and the 800,000 fl in new deposits from the fertilizer sellers.

At this point, as the bankers examine their balance sheets, they note that their reserves (holdings of paper florins) are back up to 1,000,000 fl. Their deposits equal 1,800,000 fl. Based on the principle that reserves need be only 20% of deposits, their reserves of 1,000,000 fl are too high. The bankers need to hold only 360,000 fl, or 0.20(1,800,000 fl). The other 640,000 fl, or 1,000,000 fl − 360,000 fl, can be lent again to earn more interest.

So the banks make additional interest-bearing loans in the amount of 640,000 fl. The banks' borrowers use the funds to make purchases. As before, these florins eventually are redeposited in the banking system. At this point the consolidated balance sheet of all the banks is

Consolidated Balance Sheet of Banks

ASSETS		LIABILITIES	
Currency (reserves)	1,000,000 fl	Deposits	2,440,000 fl
Loans to farmers	1,440,000 fl		
Total	2,440,000 fl	Total	2,440,000 fl

The assets of the banks now include 1,000,000 paper florins (the 360,000 fl kept as reserves and the 640,000 fl redeposited by the public) and 1,440,000 fl in loans (the 800,000 fl of first-round loans and the 640,000 fl of second-round loans). The liabilities are 2,440,000 fl in deposits (the 1,800,000 fl from earlier deposits and the 640,000 fl in new deposits).

The process doesn't stop here. Checking their balance sheets after this latest round of loans and redeposits, the bankers find that their reserves

(1,000,000 fl) still exceed 20% of their deposits, or 0.20(2,440,000 fl) = 488,000 fl. So yet another round of loans and redeposits of loaned funds will occur.

This process of **multiple expansion of loans and deposits,** in which fractional reserve banking increases an economy's loans and deposits, will stop only when the reserves of the banking system equal 20% of its deposits. The reserves of the banks always equal 1,000,000 fl (the entire supply of paper florins) at the end of each round, so the process will stop when total bank deposits equal 1,000,000 fl/0.20, or 5,000,000 fl. At this final point the consolidated balance sheet of the banks is

Consolidated Balance Sheet of Banks			
ASSETS		LIABILITIES	
Currency (reserves)	1,000,000 fl	Deposits	5,000,000 fl
Loans to farmers	4,000,000 fl		
Total	5,000,000 fl	Total	5,000,000 fl

At this final stage the ratio of reserves to deposits equals the ratio desired by banks (20%). No further expansion of loans and deposits can occur after this point because the ratio of reserves to deposits is at its minimum acceptable level.

What is the money supply in Agricola at the end of this process? Recall that the public doesn't hold any currency but, instead, deposits any currency received in the banking system, where it is held in the form of bank reserves. The reserves in the banks' vaults aren't available for transactions and thus aren't counted as money. However, the public *is* holding deposits. Because they are liquid and can be used for transactions, bank deposits are counted as part of the money supply.[4] Indeed, as there is no public holding of currency in Agricola, bank deposits *are* the money supply. Therefore the money supply equals 5,000,000 fl, or the total quantity of deposits.

What is the relationship between the money supply and the monetary base with fractional reserve banking and no holding of currency by the public? We use the following variables to answer this question algebraically:

M = the money supply;
$BASE$ = the monetary base;
DEP = total bank deposits;
RES = total bank reserves;
res = the banks' desired reserve–deposit ratio = RES/DEP.

With no currency being held by the public, the money supply equals the quantity of bank deposits:

$$M = DEP. \tag{15.1}$$

For any level of deposits DEP, the amount of reserves that banks want to hold is $(res)(DEP)$. At the end of the multiple-expansion process, bank reserves

4. Recall from Chapter 7 that the most narrowly defined monetary aggregate M1 includes demand deposits and other checkable deposits. Slightly less liquid deposits, such as savings deposits and time deposits, are included in broader monetary aggregates.

must equal the amount of currency distributed by the Central Bank (the monetary base). Therefore

$$(res)(DEP) = BASE. \tag{15.2}$$

Solving Eq. (15.2) for deposits yields $DEP = BASE/res$. Because the money supply equals deposits in this example,

$$M = DEP = \frac{BASE}{res}. \tag{15.3}$$

Hence *in an economy with fractional reserve banking and no currency held by the public, the money supply equals the monetary base divided by the reserve–deposit ratio.* In Agricola the monetary base is 1,000,000 fl, and the reserve–deposit ratio chosen by the banks is 0.20. The money supply is therefore 1,000,000 fl/0.20, or 5,000,000 fl, as we have already shown.

The multiple expansion of loans and deposits allows the economy to create a money supply that is much larger than the monetary base. Each unit of monetary base allows $1/res$ units of money to be created, leading to a money supply that is a multiple of the monetary base. Because each unit of monetary base permits creation of several units of money supply, the base is also called *high-powered money*.

Bank Runs

Fractional reserve banking works on the assumption that outflows and inflows of reserves will roughly balance, and in particular that a large fraction of a bank's depositors will never want to withdraw their funds at the same time. If a large number of depositors attempt to withdraw currency simultaneously (more than 20% of the bank's deposits in Agricola), the bank will run out of reserves and be unable to meet all its depositors' demands for cash.

Historically in the United States, there were episodes in which rumors circulated that a particular bank had made some bad loans and was at risk of becoming bankrupt. On the principle of "better safe than sorry," the bank's depositors lined up to withdraw their money. From the depositors' perspective withdrawal avoided the risk that the bank would fail and not be able to pay off depositors in full. A large-scale, panicky withdrawal of deposits from a bank is called a **bank run.** Even if the rumors about the bank's loans proved untrue, a large enough run could exhaust the bank's reserves and force it to close.[5] We discuss the link between bank runs and the money supply in the Application "The Money Multiplier During the Great Depression," p. 537.

The Money Supply with both Public Holdings of Currency and Fractional Reserve Banking

In most economies the public holds some currency (as at first in Agricola) and there is also a fractional reserve banking system (as later in Agricola). Currency in the public's hands and bank deposits both may be used for transactions, so

5. To stop a run, a bank had to convince customers that it was "sound"—financially solvent—and had plenty of funds available. This was Jimmy Stewart's strategy in the movie *It's A Wonderful Life.*

both are forms of money. When the public holds both currency, CU, and bank deposits, DEP, the money supply M is

$$M = CU + DEP. \tag{15.4}$$

In this situation the monetary base has two uses: Some of the monetary base is held as currency by the public, and the rest is held as reserves by banks. Therefore the monetary base equals the sum of the two, or

$$BASE = CU + RES. \tag{15.5}$$

The central bank controls the amount of monetary base but doesn't directly control the money supply. To relate the money supply to the monetary base, we first divide the money supply, Eq. (15.4), by the monetary base, Eq. (15.5), to get

$$\frac{M}{BASE} = \frac{CU + DEP}{CU + RES}. \tag{15.6}$$

Next, we divide both the numerator and the denominator on the right-hand side of Eq. (15.6) by DEP to obtain

$$\frac{M}{BASE} = \frac{(CU/DEP) + 1}{(CU/DEP) + (RES/DEP)}. \tag{15.7}$$

The right-hand side of Eq. (15.7) contains two important ratios. The first is the **currency–deposit ratio** (CU/DEP, or cu), which is the ratio of the currency held by the public to the public's deposits in banks. The currency–deposit ratio is determined by the public and depends on the amount of money the public wants to hold as currency versus the amount it wants to hold as deposits. The public can raise the currency–deposit ratio to any level that it wants by withdrawing currency from banks (which increases currency held and reduces deposits); similarly, by depositing currency in banks, the public can lower the currency–deposit ratio.

The second important ratio on the right-hand side of Eq. (15.7) is the reserve–deposit ratio (RES/DEP, or res), which we've already discussed. The reserve–deposit ratio is determined by banks' decisions about how much of their deposits to lend.[6]

When the process of multiple expansion of loans and deposits is complete, the currency–deposit ratio equals the ratio desired by the public, cu, and the reserve–deposit ratio equals the ratio desired by the banks, res. Substituting cu for CU/DEP and res for RES/DEP in Eq. (15.7) and multiplying both sides of Eq. (15.7) by $BASE$, we obtain

$$M = \left(\frac{cu + 1}{cu + res}\right) BASE. \tag{15.8}$$

Equation (15.8) states that the money supply is a multiple of the monetary base. The relation of the money supply to the monetary base depends on the currency–deposit ratio chosen by the public and the reserve–deposit ratio chosen

6. As we discuss later in this chapter, government regulations may set minimum levels for banks' reserve–deposit ratios.

by banks. The factor $(cu + 1)/(cu + res)$, which is the number of dollars of money supply that can be created from each dollar of monetary base, is called the **money multiplier.** The money multiplier will be greater than 1 as long as *res* is less than 1 (that is, with fractional reserve banking). Note that if the public holds no currency ($cu = 0$), the money multiplier equals $1/res$, or the same value as that in Agricola when all money was held as bank deposits (Eq. 15.3).

Table 15.1 uses U.S. data to illustrate the money multiplier and the relation among currency, reserves, monetary base, and the money supply. With these data, you can verify that the currency–deposit ratio is 0.3980 and that the reserve–deposit ratio is 0.0748. Thus the money multiplier, $(cu + 1)/(cu + res)$, equals 2.96. You may verify this formula by dividing the money supply ($1058.4 billion) by the monetary base ($357.9 billion) to obtain 2.96.

It can be shown algebraically that the money multiplier decreases when either the currency–deposit ratio *cu* or the reserve–deposit ratio *res* increases.[7] Recall that the reason that the monetary base gets "multiplied" is that, under fractional reserve banking, banks use some of the currency received as deposits to make loans to the public. The public can either hold the money it borrows from banks as currency or redeposit its borrowings in the banking system, but in either case the result is a higher total money supply than existed before the loans were made. When the reserve–deposit ratio rises, banks lend a smaller fraction of each dollar of deposits, creating less money for the same amount of monetary base; thus an increase in the reserve–deposit ratio lowers the money multiplier. When the currency–deposit ratio rises, the public puts a smaller fraction of its money in banks, which means that banks have less money to loan. With banks lending less, less money is created from the same amount of monetary base, again reducing the money multiplier.

7. That the money multiplier decreases when *cu* increases is not obvious, as *cu* appears in both the numerator and the denominator of the money multiplier. However, as you can confirm by trying numerical examples or by taking a derivative, an increase in *cu* reduces the money multiplier as long as *res* is less than 1, which must always be the case under fractional reserve banking.

Table 15.1 The Monetary Base, the Money Multiplier, and the Money Supply in the United States

Currency in circulation, *CU*	$301.3 billion
Bank reserves, *RES*	$56.6 billion
Monetary base, *BASE* (=*CU* + *RES*)	$357.9 billion
Deposits, *DEP*	$757.1 billion
Money supply, *M* (=*CU* + *DEP*)	$1058.4 billion
Reserve–deposit ratio, *res* (=*RES*/*DEP*)	0.0748
Currency–deposit ratio, *cu* (=*CU*/*DEP*)	0.3980
Money multiplier, $(cu + 1)/(cu + res)$	2.96
Ratio of money supply to base, *M*/*BASE*	2.96

Source: *Federal Reserve Bulletin,* July 1993, Tables 1.12 and 1.21. Deposits are transactions, deposits plus travelers' checks, and the money supply is M1. Data are for April 1993.

Open-Market Operations

We have shown how the monetary base and the money multiplier determine the money supply. To change the level of the money supply, a central bank must change the amount of monetary base or change the money multiplier. In Section 15.2 we discuss how the central bank can affect the money multiplier. For now we focus on the most direct and frequently used way of changing the money supply: raising or lowering the monetary base. For any value of the money multiplier Eq. (15.8) indicates that a change in the monetary base will cause a proportional change in the money supply.

Suppose that the Agricolan Central Bank decides to increase the monetary base by 10%, from 1,000,000 to 1,100,000 fl. How would it actually do so? First, the Central Bank has to print the extra 100,000 fl. Then it can use the 100,000 new florins to buy assets (coconuts) from the public. After purchasing the additional coconuts, the Agricolan Central Bank's balance sheet is

Agricolan Central Bank			
ASSETS		LIABILITIES	
Coconuts	1,100,000 fl	Currency	1,100,000 fl

By purchasing 100,000 fl of coconuts, the Central Bank puts 100,000 more paper certificates (florins) into circulation. The monetary base, which is the same as the total liabilities of the Central Bank, rises to 1,100,000 fl. If the money multiplier remains unchanged, the money supply also increases by 10%.

Suppose, instead, that the Agricolan Central Bank wanted to reduce the monetary base by 10%. To do so it would sell 100,000 fl of coconuts to the public for 100,000 fl in currency. The 100,000 florins collected by the Central Bank are retired from circulation. (The retired florins aren't treated as assets of the Central Bank; if you paid off a debt and retrieved your IOU, you wouldn't consider the IOU to be an asset.) The Agricolan Central Bank's balance sheet now is

Agricolan Central Bank			
ASSETS		LIABILITIES	
Coconuts	900,000 fl	Currency	900,000 fl

The Agricolan Central Bank's liabilities outstanding (the monetary base) have been reduced to 900,000. With a constant money multiplier the money supply will fall proportionately.

Recall (Chapter 7) that a purchase of assets by the central bank is called an **open-market purchase.**[8] It increases the monetary base and thus the money supply. A sale of assets to the public by the central bank is called an **open-market sale.** It reduces the monetary base and the money supply. Open-market purchases and sales are collectively called open-market operations. Open-market operations are the most direct way for central banks to change their national money supplies.

8. The term *open market* refers to the fact that the central bank's transactions with the public take place in regular asset markets that are open to and used by the public.

APPLICATION

The Money Multiplier During the Great Depression

The money multiplier usually is relatively stable, but not always. During 1930–1933, in the early part of the Great Depression, the money multiplier fell sharply, creating serious problems for monetary policy.

The source of the instability in the money multiplier, as discussed in detail by Milton Friedman and Anna Schwartz in their *Monetary History of the United States, 1867–1960*,[9] was a series of severe banking panics. A banking panic is an episode in which many banks suffer runs by depositors, with some banks being forced to close. The U.S. panics resulted from both financial weakness in the banking system and the arrival of bad economic and financial news. Among the causes of banking panics emphasized by Friedman and Schwartz were: (1) the effects of falling agricultural prices on the economies of farm states in the autumn of 1930; (2) the failure of a large New York bank called the Bank of the United States, in December 1930 (a private bank, despite its name); (3) the failure in May 1931 of Austria's largest bank, which led to a European financial crisis; and (4) Great Britain's abandonment of the gold standard in September 1931. The most severe banking panic began in January 1933 and was halted only when the newly inaugurated President Roosevelt proclaimed a "bank holiday" that closed all the banks in March 1933. By that time more than a third of the banks in the United States had failed or been taken over by other banks. Banking reforms that were passed as part of Roosevelt's New Deal legislation restored confidence in the banking system and halted bank runs after March 1933.

The banking panics affected the money multiplier in two ways. First, people became very distrustful of banks, fearing that their banks might suddenly fail and not be able to pay them the full amounts of their deposits. (These events occurred before deposits were insured by the Federal government, as they are today.) Instead of holding bank deposits, people felt safer holding currency, perhaps under the mattress or in coffee cans buried in the backyard. Conversion of deposits into currency caused the currency–deposit ratio to rise, as shown in Fig. 15.1 on the next page, with a spectacular rise in the first quarter of 1933.

Second, in anticipation of possible runs, banks began to hold more reserves (including vault cash) to back their deposits, as shown by the behavior of the reserve–deposit ratio. Banks hoped to convince depositors that there was enough cash in the banks' vaults to satisfy withdrawals so that the depositors would not be tempted to start a run.

As discussed earlier, increases in either the currency–deposit ratio or the reserve–deposit ratio cause the money multiplier to fall. As shown in Fig. 15.2(a) on page 539, as a result of the banking panics, the money multiplier fell precipitously, from 6.6 in March 1930 to 3.6 by the bank holiday in March 1933. Thus, even though the monetary base grew by 20% during that three-year period, the money multiplier fell by so much that the money supply fell by 35%, as shown in Fig. 15.2(b) on page 539. There is some controversy about whether the drop in the money supply was a primary cause of the decline in output during 1930–1933 (Friedman and Schwartz argue that it was), but there is general agreement that the drastic decline in the price level (by about a third) in this period was the result of the plunge in the money supply.

9. Princeton, N.J.: Princeton University Press for NBER, 1963.

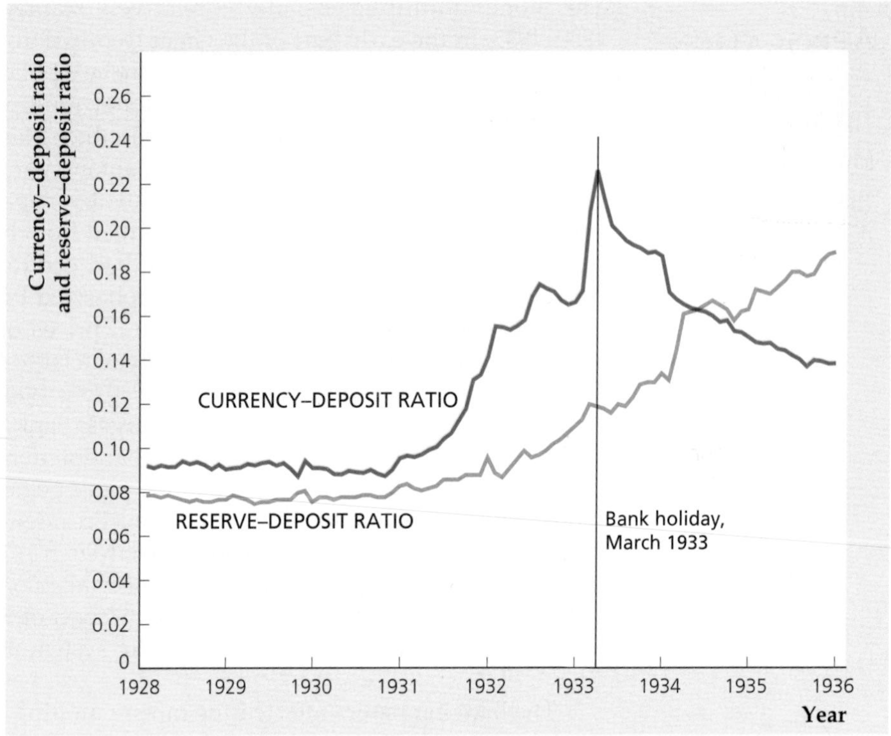

Figure 15.1
The currency–deposit ratio and the reserve–deposit ratio in the Great Depression
During the Great Depression people worried about the safety of their money in banks and increased the ratio of currency in circulation to deposits. In anticipation of possible bank runs banks increased the ratio of reserves to deposits.

Source: Milton Friedman and Anna Schwartz, *A Monetary History of the United States, 1867–1960:* Currency—Table A-1, column (1); deposits, total commercial banks (demand and time)—Table A-1, column (4); bank reserves—Table A-2, column (3).

15.2 MONETARY CONTROL IN THE UNITED STATES

The principles of money supply determination developed in the Agricola example can be applied directly to actual economies by adding a few institutional details. In this section we link these general principles to monetary institutions in the United States.

The Federal Reserve System

The central bank of the United States is called the Federal Reserve System, or the Fed for short. It was created by the Federal Reserve Act in 1913 and began operation in 1914. One of Congress's primary motives in establishing the Fed was the hope that a central bank would help eliminate the severe financial crises (combinations of stock market crashes, business failures, and banking panics) that had periodically afflicted the United States before World War I. Ironically, the most severe financial crisis in U.S. history occurred in 1930–1933, barely a decade and a half after the creation of the Fed.

The Federal Reserve Act established a system of twelve regional Federal Reserve Banks, each associated with a geographical area called a Federal Reserve district. The locations of the twelve Federal Reserve Banks are shown in Fig. 15.3 on page 540. Technically, the regional Federal Reserve Banks are

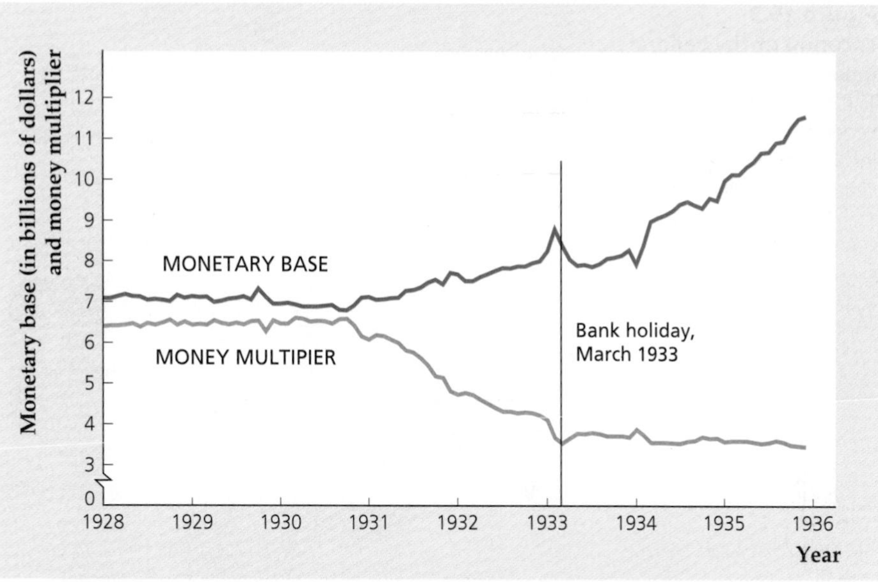

(a) The monetary base and the money multiplier in the Great Depression

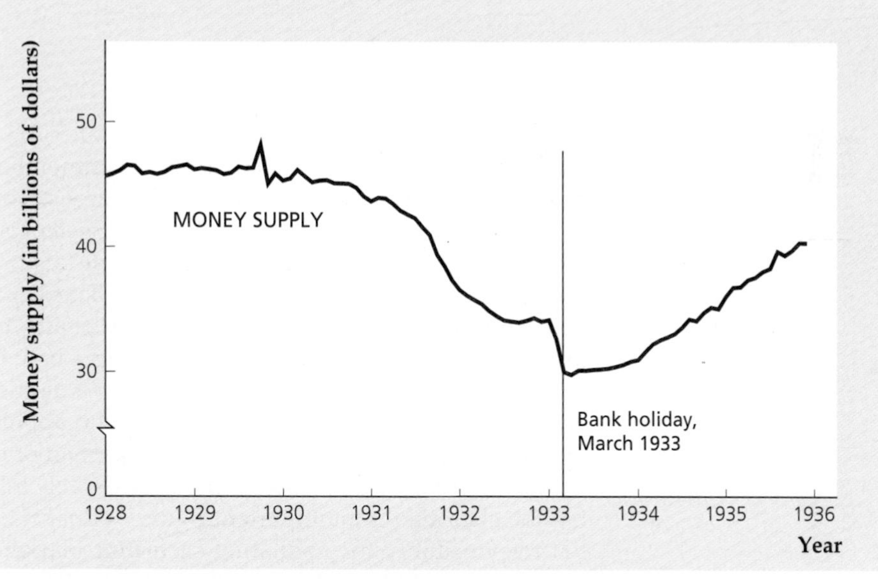

(b) The money supply in the Great Depression

Figure 15.2 Monetary variables in the Great Depression
(a) As a result of the increases in the currency–deposit ratio and the reserve–deposit ratio, the money multiplier fell sharply during the Great Depression. The monetary base rose during the Great Depression.
(b) Although the monetary base rose during the Great Depression, the money multiplier fell so much that the money supply—the product of the money multiplier and the monetary base—declined sharply.

Source: Milton Friedman and Anna Schwartz, *A Monetary History of the United States, 1867–1960:* Currency—Table A-1, column (1); deposits, total commercial banks (demand and time)—Table A-1, column (4); bank reserves—Table A-2, column (3); base = currency + reserves; money multiplier = (currency + deposits)/base; money = currency + deposits.

owned by the private banks within the district who are members of the Federal Reserve System. All federally-chartered private banks are members of the Federal Reserve System, and state-chartered banks may join. Whether an individual bank is a member of the system has ceased to mean much, however, because Congress passed legislation in 1980 extending the responsibilities and privileges of member banks to all banks. Before 1980 member banks faced

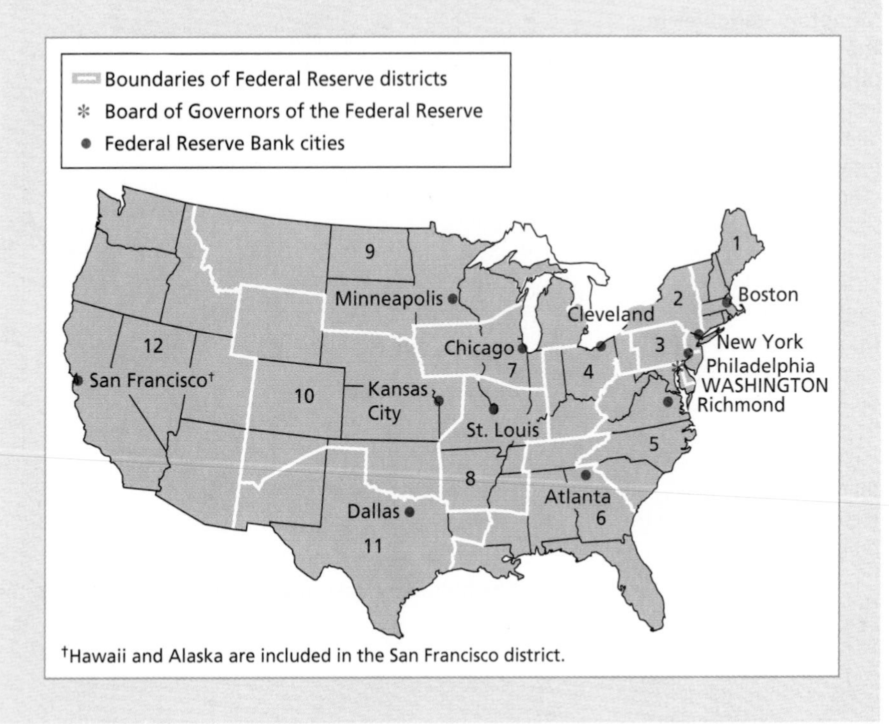

Figure 15.3
Location of the Federal Reserve Banks
The twelve regional Federal Reserve Banks are located in twelve major cities in the United States. The Board of Governors of the Federal Reserve System is located in Washington, D.C.

stricter regulatory requirements than nonmembers but also had access to some useful services (such as check-clearing services).[10]

The leadership of the Federal Reserve System is provided by the **Board of Governors of the Federal Reserve System** (also called the Federal Reserve Board), located in Washington, D.C. The Board consists of seven governors, appointed by the President of the United States to staggered fourteen-year terms, with one of the governors beginning a new term every other year. (See "The Political Environment" box, p. 548, for a discussion of how closely governors follow the wishes of the President who appointed them.) The President appoints one Board member to be the chairman of the Board of Governors for a term of four years. Besides having considerable influence over monetary policy, the chairman is an important figure in financial markets (the Fed has partial responsibility for regulating securities markets and the banking sector) and often is consulted by Congress and the President on matters of national economic policy.

Decisions about monetary policy are the responsibility of the **Federal Open Market Committee** (FOMC). The FOMC consists of the seven governors, the president of the Federal Reserve Bank of New York, and four of the presidents of the other regional Federal Reserve Banks, who serve on the FOMC on a rotating basis. The FOMC meets about eight times a year to review

10. Thrift institutions, such as savings and loans, are not allowed to be members of the Federal Reserve System, but they can hold deposits at the Fed and can use the check-clearing facilities of the Fed.

the state of the economy and to plan the conduct of monetary policy. The FOMC can meet more frequently (in person or by conference call) if developments in the economy seem to warrant discussion.

The Federal Reserve's Balance Sheet and Open-Market Operations

The balance sheet of the Federal Reserve System (all Federal Reserve Banks taken together) as of April 1993 is shown in Table 15.2. The Fed's largest asset by far is its holdings of U.S. Treasury securities, or government bonds. Indeed, the Fed owns about 10% of outstanding U.S. government bonds. It also owns gold and makes loans to banks (depository institutions), which count as assets for the Fed. The category "Other assets" includes foreign exchange, bonds issued by Federal agencies, and other relatively small items.

The largest liability of the Fed is currency outstanding. Some of this currency ($29.6 billion) is held in the vaults of private banks and is known as **vault cash.** The remainder of currency outstanding, $301.3 billion, is in circulation (that is, held by the public) and corresponds to what we label *CU*.

The other principal liability of the Fed is deposits made by depository institutions, such as banks, savings and loan associations, and mutual savings banks. In accepting deposits from depository institutions, the Fed acts as the

Table 15.2 The Balance Sheet of the Federal Reserve System (Billions of Dollars)

Assets		**Liabilities**		
Gold	$11.1	Currency		$330.9
		Vault cash[a]	$29.6	
Loans to depository institutions	$0.1	In circulation[b]	$301.3	
U.S. Treasury securities	$305.4	Deposits of depository institutions[c]		$27.0
Other assets	$51.5			
		Other liabilities and net worth[d]		$10.2
Total	$368.1	Total		$368.1

Addenda

Reserves = deposits of depository institutions + vault cash = $56.6 billion.
Monetary base = currency in circulation + reserves = $357.9 billion.

[a]Table 1.12, line 3.

[b]Table 1.21, line 27.

[c]Table 1.12, line 1.

[d]Calculated as total minus the sum of the other figures in the column.

Source: *Federal Reserve Bulletin,* July 1993, Table 1.18. Data are for April 1993.

"banks' bank." Depository institutions make deposits at the Fed because it is a convenient way of holding reserves. These accounts at the Fed ($27.0 billion), together with vault cash ($29.6 billion), equal the total reserves of the banking system ($56.6 billion), what we call *RES*.

Recall from Eq. (15.5) that the monetary base equals bank reserves ($56.6 billion) plus currency in circulation ($301.3 billion), or $357.9 billion. As shown in Fig. 15.4, the monetary base can be calculated equivalently as the sum of total currency outstanding ($330.9 billion) plus deposits of depository institutions at the Fed ($27.0 billion), which again is $357.9 billion.[11]

Like the Agricolan Central Bank, if the Fed wants to change the money supply, its primary tool is open-market operations. To increase the money supply, for example, the Fed could conduct an open-market purchase, in which it would buy U.S. Treasury securities (instead of coconuts, as in Agricola) from the public. A purchase of $1 billion in securities would increase the Fed's assets by $1 billion. To pay for these securities, the Fed would write a check on itself, redeemable by a bank either as a deposit at the Fed or as currency. In either case the monetary base would rise by $1 billion. Because of the money multiplier, an increase in the monetary base translates into a proportional increase in the money supply.

To reduce the money supply, the Fed could use an open-market sale. The Fed could sell $1 billion of Treasury securities to the public, receiving checks

11. The Fed also has other liabilities, including accounts held by the U.S. Treasury and by foreign central banks. Because these accounts are not owned by the public or the U.S. banking sector, they aren't counted as part of the monetary base.

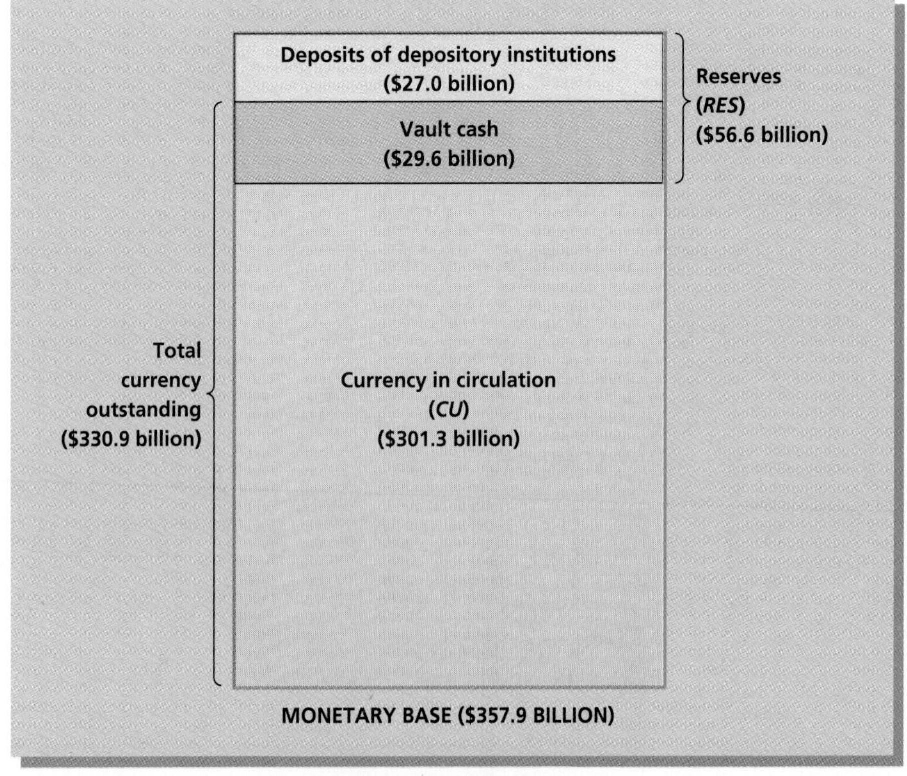

Figure 15.4
Components of the monetary base
The monetary base equals currency in circulation *CU* plus bank reserves *RES*. The monetary base also may be expressed as the sum of deposits at the Fed by depository institutions and total currency outstanding (currency in circulation and vault cash).

drawn on banks in exchange. The Fed's assets would fall by $1 billion (it owns $1 billion less in securities). The Fed would use the $1 billion in checks it receives to eliminate $1 billion in deposits of depository institutions, so that the monetary base would fall by $1 billion.

Other Means of Controlling the Money Supply

Although open-market operations are the main way that the Fed affects the money supply, it has two other methods available: changes in reserve requirements and discount window lending. The effects of these and other factors on the money supply are listed in Summary table 19.

Reserve Requirements. The Fed sets the minimum fraction of each type of deposit that banks must hold as reserves. An increase in reserve requirements forces banks to hold more reserves and increases the reserve–deposit ratio. A higher reserve–deposit ratio reduces the money multiplier, so an increase in reserve requirements reduces the money supply for any level of the monetary base.

Over the past several years the Fed has phased out reserve requirements on many types of deposits so that, currently, reserve requirements apply only to transactions deposits (primarily checking accounts and NOW accounts). As of December 1992, banks were required to hold reserves equal to 3% of the first $46.8 million of transactions deposits and 10% of the transactions deposits over $46.8 million.[12]

12. For the most recent reserve requirements, see Table 1.15 of the *Federal Reserve Bulletin*.

SUMMARY 19

Factors Affecting the Monetary Base, the Money Multiplier, and the Money Supply

Factor	Effect on Monetary Base, *BASE*	Effect on Money Multiplier, $(cu + 1)/(cu + res)$	Effect on Money Supply, *M*
An increase in the reserve–deposit ratio, *res*	Unchanged	Decrease	Decrease
An increase in the currency–deposit ratio, *cu*	Unchanged	Decrease	Decrease
An open-market purchase	Increase	Unchanged	Increase
An open-market sale	Decrease	Unchanged	Decrease
An increase in reserve requirements	Unchanged	Decrease	Decrease
An increase in discount window borrowing	Increase	Unchanged	Increase
An increase in the discount rate	Decrease	Unchanged	Decrease

Note: The relationship among the money supply, the money multiplier, and the monetary base is $M = [(cu + 1)/(cu + res)]BASE$.

Discount Window Lending. A principal reason that the Fed was created was to try to reduce severe financial crises. The Fed was supposed to accomplish this goal mainly by acting as a "lender of last resort," that is, by standing ready to lend reserves to banks that need cash to meet depositors' demands or reserve requirements. The Fed's lending of reserves to banks is called **discount window lending,** and the interest rate it charges for lending reserves is called the **discount rate.**

Although financial panics and bank runs are no longer common, the Fed still lends reserves to banks through the discount window, which affects the monetary base. For example, if banks borrow $1 billion from the Fed and deposit these borrowings in their reserve accounts at the Fed, the Fed's balance sheet is affected in two ways: (1) on the asset side, loans to depository institutions rise by $1 billion; and (2) on the liability side, deposits held by depository institutions also rise by $1 billion, increasing the monetary base by $1 billion. Thus an increase in borrowing from the discount window raises the monetary base, and a decrease in discount window borrowing lowers the monetary base.

From time to time the Fed changes the discount rate it charges. An increase in the discount rate makes borrowing at the discount window more costly. If banks reduce their borrowing in response to the higher discount rate, the monetary base falls. For a constant money multiplier, a drop in the monetary base implies a decline in the money supply as well.

Although banks may borrow reserves through the discount window, the Fed discourages banks from using the discount window frequently. Instead of borrowing from the Fed, a bank can borrow reserves from other banks that have extra reserves. These borrowed funds are called Federal funds, or Fed funds, and the interest rate charged on these loans is the **Fed funds rate.** Despite its name, the Fed funds rate is not an interest rate charged by the Fed; it is the interest rate charged on loans from one bank to another. Figure 15.5 shows the behavior of the Fed funds rate and the discount rate. The Fed funds rate is a market interest rate determined by the forces of supply and demand and changes much more frequently than the discount rate, which the Fed sets. The Fed funds rate usually exceeds the discount rate, because banks are willing to pay a premium to avoid borrowing from the Fed.

The existence of the discount window doesn't affect the Fed's ultimate control over the monetary base. If the Fed thinks that banks are borrowing too much, it can discourage borrowing by raising the discount rate or simply refuse to lend. Moreover, the Fed can offset any effects of bank borrowing on the monetary base through open-market operations.

Intermediate Targets

In conducting monetary policy, the Fed has certain goals, or ultimate targets, such as price stability and stable economic growth. In trying to reach these goals, the Fed can use the monetary policy tools, or **instruments,** that we've discussed: reserve requirements, the discount rate, and especially open-market operations. The problem the Fed faces is how to use the instruments that it controls directly, particularly open-market operations, to achieve its goals. Because there are several steps between open-market operations and the ultimate behavior of prices and economic activity—and because these steps often

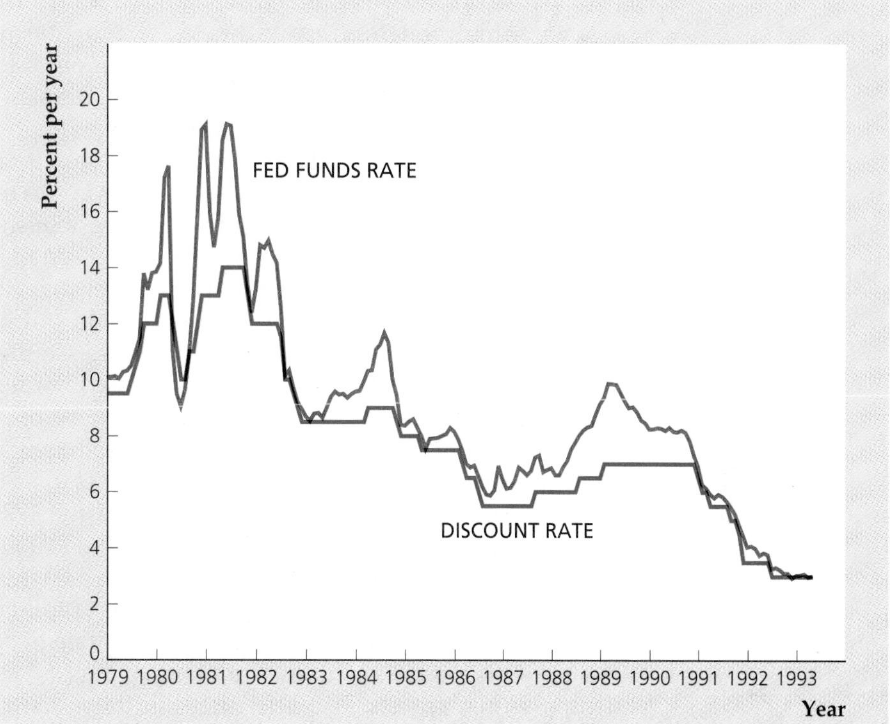

Figure 15.5
The discount rate and the Fed funds rate
Banks can borrow reserves from the Fed at the discount window and pay the discount rate, or they can borrow reserves from other banks and pay the Fed funds rate. Because the Fed discourages borrowing at the discount window, banks are willing to pay a premium to borrow in the Fed funds market rather than to borrow from the Fed. As a result, the Fed funds rate is usually higher than the discount rate.

Source: *Federal Reserve Bulletin*, various issues, Table 1.35.

can't be predicted accurately—the Fed uses intermediate targets to guide monetary policy. **Intermediate targets,** also sometimes called indicators, are macroeconomic variables that the Fed cannot control directly but can influence fairly predictably, and that in turn are related to the goals the Fed is trying to achieve.[13]

The most important and frequently used intermediate targets are monetary aggregates, such as M1 and M2, and short-term interest rates, such as the Fed funds rate.[14] By using open-market operations, the Fed can directly control the level of the monetary base, which influences the monetary aggregates. Fluctuations in the money supply in turn affect interest rates, at least temporarily, by causing the *LM* curve to shift. Neither monetary aggregates nor short-term interest rates are important determinants of economic welfare in and of themselves, but both influence the state of the macroeconomy. Because monetary aggregates and short-term interest rates are affected in a predictable way by the Fed's policies and both in turn affect the economy, these variables qualify as intermediate targets.

13. For a discussion of the use of intermediate targets and further references, see Richard Davis, "Intermediate Targets and Indicators for Monetary Policy: An Introduction to the Issues," in Federal Reserve Bank of New York, *Quarterly Review*, Summer 1990, 71–82.

14. Other intermediate targets that have been suggested include the exchange rate, the price level, and nominal GDP. The latter two pose problems because the control of the Fed over prices and nominal GDP is indirect and operates only with a lag.

At various times the Fed has guided monetary policy by attempting to keep either monetary growth rates or short-term interest rates at or near preestablished target ranges (the Application "Monetary Targeting in Germany, Japan, and the United States," p. 559, discusses the historical experience with money-growth targets). Note that, although the Fed may be able to stabilize one or the other of these variables, it cannot target both simultaneously. For example, suppose that the Fed were trying to target both the money supply and the Fed funds rate and that the preestablished target ranges called for an increase in both variables. How could the Fed meet these targets simultaneously? If it raised the monetary base in order to raise the money supply, in the short run the increase in money supply would shift the *LM* curve down and to the right, which would lower rather than raise the Fed funds rate. Alternatively, if the Fed lowered the monetary base in order to try to increase the Fed funds rate, the money supply would fall instead of rising, as required. Thus, in general, the Fed cannot simultaneously meet targets for *both* interest rates and the money supply, unless those targets are set to be consistent with each other.

In recent years—and during much of the 1970s—the Fed's short-term monetary policies often involved attempts to stabilize the Fed funds rate at a target level. Figure 15.6 shows a situation in which this strategy is useful. When the *LM* curve is LM^1, the economy is at full-employment equilibrium at point *E*, with output at $\bar{Y}$ and a real interest rate of r_1. Suppose that most of the shocks hitting the economy are nominal shocks, including shocks to money supply (perhaps because of changes in the money multiplier) and to money demand. Without intervention by the Fed, these nominal shocks cause the *LM*

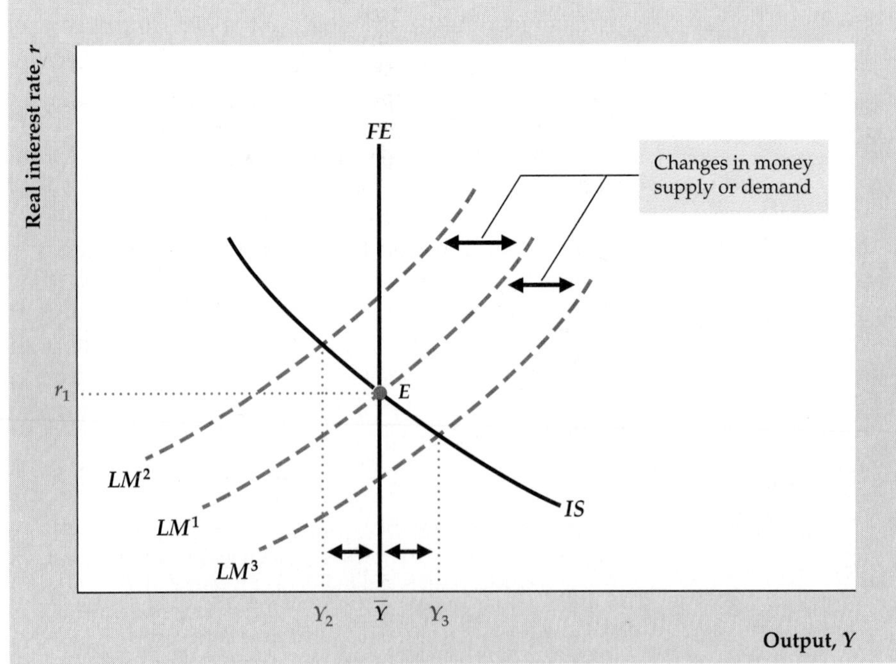

Figure 15.6
Interest rate targeting
The figure shows an economy that is buffeted by nominal shocks. Changes in money supply or money demand cause the *LM* curve to shift between LM^2 and LM^3 and aggregate demand to move erratically between Y_2 and Y_3. A Fed policy of keeping the real interest rate at r_1, by raising the monetary base whenever the interest rate exceeds r_1 and lowering the base whenever the interest rate falls below r_1, will keep the economy at full employment at *E*.

curve to shift between LM^2 and LM^3, leading aggregate demand to shift erratically between Y_2 and Y_3. In either the extended classical model or the Keynesian model, random shifts in aggregate demand cause undesirable cyclical fluctuations in the economy.

The Fed could reduce the instability caused by nominal shocks by using monetary policy to hold the real interest rate at r_1.[15] In other words, whenever the LM curve shifted up to LM^2, the Fed could increase the money supply to restore the LM curve to LM^1; similarly, shifts of the LM curve to LM^3 could be offset by reductions in the money supply to return the LM curve to LM^1. In this case stabilizing the intermediate target, the interest rate, also would stabilize output at its full-employment level. For interest rate targeting to be a good strategy, however, nominal shocks must be the main source of instability. As discussed in Analytical Problem 2 at the end of the chapter, if other types of shocks to the economy are more important than nominal shocks, the use of monetary policy to stabilize the interest rate could instead destabilize output.

15.3 THE CONDUCT OF MONETARY POLICY: RULES VERSUS DISCRETION

How should monetary policy be used? On some aspects of this question, there is broad agreement. Most classicals and Keynesians agree that money is neutral in the long run so that changes in money growth affect inflation but not real variables in the long run. Therefore most would accept that the main long-run goal of monetary policy should be to maintain a low and stable inflation rate. However, there is much less agreement about the effects of monetary policy and its appropriate use in the short run (Chapters 11 and 12). Most Keynesians believe that monetary policy can and should be used to smooth the business cycle, but most classicals don't. In this section we revisit the debate about the appropriate use of monetary policy by addressing a long-standing question in macroeconomics: Should monetary policy be conducted according to fixed rules or at the discretion of the central bank?

The use of rules in monetary policy has been advocated primarily by a group of economists called monetarists and by classical macroeconomists. Supporters of **rules** believe that monetary policy should be essentially automatic. In particular, in its control of the money supply, the central bank should be required to follow a set of simple, prespecified, and publicly announced rules. Many such rules can be imagined. For example, the Fed might be instructed to increase the monetary base by 1% each quarter. An alternative rule, which has been used historically, is to require the central bank to conduct monetary policy to keep the price of gold at a predetermined level (this rule was the essence of the gold standard).

Although the exact form of the rule chosen isn't crucial, supporters of the rules-based approach emphasize that the monetary rule should be simple;

---

15. The Fed actually targets nominal interest rates. Over a short period of time, in which expected inflation is constant, targeting nominal interest rates and targeting real interest rates are the same.

THE POLITICAL ENVIRONMENT

RELIABILITY OF FED GOVERNORS

Although the Federal Reserve System was created by an act of Congress and is ultimately responsible to Congress and the President, under normal circumstances the Fed has the authority to conduct monetary policy as it chooses without having to get their approval. The most direct control that the President has over the policies of the Fed is through the appointment of Federal Reserve governors. But because governors have fourteen-year terms, they don't have to worry about pleasing the President who appointed them in order to be reappointed. Thus if the President wants the Fed to conduct monetary policy in accordance with the administration's general economic philosophy, the President will have to select appointees who are "reliable"—that is, people who are loyal and persuasive and who share the President's views on economic policy.

Is there some systematic characteristic that a President can look for in trying to appoint a reliable Fed governor? To answer this question, Thomas Havrilesky of Duke University and John Gildea of Wheaton College* studied individual governors' voting records at FOMC meetings during the period 1959–1987. Although governors may hold different views on any given issue, the desire to present a unified stance on monetary policy leads most governors to vote with the majority most of the time. As the accompanying table shows, governors who were professional economists dissented only 7.6% of the time, and noneconomists dissented only 8.9% of the time. More interesting is the timing of the dissenting votes. The first row shows that economists were more likely to dissent during a presidential term of the opposing party than during a presidential term of the governor's own party (a governor's own party was taken to be the party of the President that appointed that governor). For noneconomists the pattern of dissent was just the opposite. Noneconomists dissented 13.3% of the time during their own party's presidential tenure and only 5.4% of the time during the opposing party's presidential tenure.

Fraction of Votes in Which a Governor Dissents from the Majority

Profession	Dissents During Own Party's Tenure	Dissents During Opposing Party's Tenure	Total
Economist	5.1%	9.5%	7.6%
Noneconomist	13.3%	5.4%	8.9%

Source: Based on Havrilesky and Gildea (1990), Table 1.

Havrilesky and Gildea found that among ten characteristics of the governors only a Ph.D. in economics, an academic background, and experience as an economist seemed to be systematically associated with reliability. There are two explanations for the reliability of economists: A charitable explanation is that economists are professionals with coherent and consistent viewpoints that they maintain over a long period of time; an uncharitable explanation is that they are stubborn ideologues.

If economists are systematically more reliable, why would a President appoint noneconomists? Havrilesky and Gildea argue that noneconomists chosen as governors generally are better connected politically than are economists, and their connections may help in presidential campaigns. Thus economists bring reliability to the job of Fed governor, and noneconomists bring political clout to the job. Thus it would make sense to appoint economists near the beginning of a presidential term to take advantage of a long period of reliability and to appoint noneconomists near the end of a presidential term for their value in the campaign. Havrilesky and Gildea point out that this pattern holds in most administrations. An exception was President Carter, who failed to appoint a persuasive economist early in his term and, according to Havrilesky and Gildea, suffered the consequences in terms of low Fed reliability.

* "Packing the Board of Governors," *Challenge*, March/April 1990, pp. 52–55.

IN TOUCH *WITH THE MACROECONOMY*

DECODING THE POLICY DIRECTIVES OF THE FOMC

One of the most important decisions reached at Federal Open Market Committee (FOMC) meetings is whether to ease or tighten monetary policy. The FOMC transmits its decision to the Federal Reserve Bank of New York (where open-market operations are actually executed) in a domestic policy directive that guides monetary policy in the subsequent weeks. The directive and the discussion at FOMC meetings remain confidential for several weeks, being made public three days after the following meeting. Then this information is published in the *Federal Reserve Bulletin* in a section called "Record of Policy Actions of the Federal Open Market Committee."

Policy directives typically contain cryptic sentences such as: "In the implementation of policy for the immediate future, the Committee seeks to decrease slightly the existing degree of pressure on reserve positions. Taking account of progress toward price stability, the strength of the business expansion, the behavior of the monetary aggregates, and developments in foreign exchange and domestic financial markets, slightly greater reserve restraint might or somewhat lesser reserve restraint would be acceptable in the intermeeting period." This carefully worded statement, which is taken from the domestic policy directive of the November 13, 1990, FOMC meeting,* means that the Fed plans to ease monetary policy and probably will continue to do so until the next FOMC meeting. (At the time of the meeting the economy was in the midst of the 1990–1991 recession.)

The following guidelines (suggested to us by experienced Fed watchers) are helpful in decoding policy directives.

1. Increased "pressure" or "restraint" on reserves means a reduction in the growth of monetary base and thus a monetary tightening. Similarly, decreased "pressure" or "restraint" on reserves means that an easier monetary policy is planned.
2. The Fed is more likely to change reserve restraint in a direction that "would be acceptable" than in a direction that "might be acceptable."
3. The word "somewhat" refers to a larger change in reserve restraint and interest rates than the term "slightly."

Thus in the excerpted statement, "*slightly* greater reserve restraint *might* or *somewhat* lesser reserve restraint *would* be acceptable in the intermeeting period" [italics added] means that money could become either tighter or easier but that the tendency is toward easier money.

---

* *Federal Reserve Bulletin*, February 1991, p. 103.

there can't be dozens of exceptions and conditions. Furthermore, the rule should be stated in terms of variables that the Fed can control directly or nearly directly. Because the Fed can control the monetary base precisely, a prespecified growth rate for the monetary base is acceptable as a rule. But as the Fed's control over, say, the national unemployment rate is indirect and imperfect, an instruction to the Fed to "keep the unemployment rate at 4%" isn't acceptable to advocates of a rules-guided monetary policy.

The opposite of the rules approach, which has been supported by most (though not all) Keynesian economists, is called **discretion.** The idea behind discretion is that the central bank should be free to conduct monetary policy in any way that it believes will advance the ultimate objectives of low and stable inflation, high economic growth, and low unemployment. In particular, the central bank should continuously monitor the economy and, using the advice of economic experts, should change the money supply as needed to best achieve its goals. For example, if inflation is currently low and economic indicators suggest that the economy is slipping into recession, under a strategy of discretion the central bank would be free to increase the money supply to try to stimulate the economy. In contrast, under an approach based on rules the central bank would have to follow its preannounced policy and wouldn't be free to apply such a stimulus. Because a strategy of discretion involves active responses by the central bank to changes in economic circumstances, such a strategy sometimes is called *activist*.

From this description of rules and discretion, you may have trouble understanding why many economists advocate the use of rules. After all, why should anyone arbitrarily and unnecessarily tie the hands of the central bank? The idea that giving the central bank the option of responding to changing economic conditions is always better than putting monetary policy in a straitjacket dictated by rules is the essence of the Keynesian case for discretion.

This basic argument for discretion is sound, but a strong case also may be made for rules. Next we discuss the traditional monetarist argument for rules. We then consider a relatively new argument for rules: that the use of rules increases the credibility of the central bank.

The Monetarist Case for Rules

Monetarism emphasizes the importance of monetary factors in the macroeconomy. Although monetarists have included numerous outstanding economists, the dominant figure and leader of the group is Milton Friedman. For many years Friedman has argued that monetary policy should be conducted by rules, and this idea has become an important part of monetarist doctrine.[16]

Friedman's argument for rules may be broken down into a series of propositions.

Proposition 1. *Monetary policy has powerful short-run effects on the real economy. In the longer run, however, changes in the money supply have their primary effect on the price level.*

Friedman's research on U.S. monetary history (with Anna Schwartz) provided some of the earliest and best evidence that changes in the money supply can be nonneutral in the short run (Chapter 11). Friedman and other monetarists believe that fluctuations in the money supply historically have been one of the most significant—if not the most significant—sources of business cycle fluctuations. On long-run neutrality Friedman (along with Edmund Phelps) was one of the first to argue that, because prices eventually adjust to changes in the money supply, the effect of money on real variables can only be temporary (Chapter 13).

Proposition 2. *Despite the powerful short-run effect of money on the economy, there is little scope for using monetary policy actively to try to smooth business cycles.*

Friedman backs this proposition with several points (several of which we discussed in connection with macroeconomic policy more generally in earlier chapters). First, time is needed for the central bank and other agencies to

16. Friedman's 1959 book, *A Program for Monetary Stability* (New York: Fordham University Press) presents a clear early statement of his views.

gather and process information about the current state of the economy. These information lags may make it difficult for the central bank to determine whether the economy actually is in a recession and whether a change in policy is appropriate.

Second, there is considerable uncertainty about how much effect a given change in the money supply will have on the economy and how long the effect will take to occur. Friedman has emphasized that there are *long and variable lags* between monetary policy actions and their economic results. From his empirical research Friedman claims that, on average, monetary changes take about a year to have a significant impact on the economy (that is, the lag is long). Furthermore, the time required for policy to have an effect is unpredictable and may vary from as little as six months to as much as eighteen months (the lag is variable).

Third, wage and price adjustment, although not instantaneous, is fast enough that, by the time the Fed recognizes that the economy is in a recession and increases the money supply, the economy may already be heading out of the recession. If the expansion in the money supply stimulates the economy with a lag of about a year, the stimulus may take effect when output has already recovered and the economy is in a boom. In this case the monetary expansion will cause the economy to overshoot full employment and cause prices to rise. Thus the monetary increase, intended to fight the recession, may actually be destabilizing (causing more variability of output than there would have been otherwise), as well as inflationary.

Proposition 3. *Even if there is some scope for using monetary policy to smooth business cycles, the Fed cannot be relied on to do so effectively.*

One reason that Friedman doesn't trust the Fed to manage an activist monetary policy effectively is political. He believes that despite its supposed independence, the Fed is susceptible to short-run political pressures from the President and others in the administration. For example, the Fed might be pressured to stimulate the economy during an election year. If timed reasonably well, an election-year monetary expansion could expand output and employment just before voters go to the polls, with the inflationary effects of the policy not being felt until after the incumbents were safely reelected (see "The Political Environment: Presidential Elections and Macroeconomic Policy" box, p. 460).

More fundamentally, though, Friedman's distrust of the Fed arises from his interpretation of macroeconomic history. From his work with Anna Schwartz, Friedman concludes that for whatever reason—incompetence, shortsightedness, or bad luck—monetary policy historically has been a greater source of economic instability than stability. The primary example cited by Friedman is the 1929–1933 period, when the Fed was unable or unwilling to stop the money supply from falling by one third in the wake of widespread runs on banks. Friedman and Schwartz argued that this monetary contraction was one of the main causes of the Great Depression. Thus Friedman concludes that eliminating monetary policy as a source of instability would substantially improve macroeconomic performance.

How could the Fed be removed as a source of instability? This question leads to Friedman's policy recommendation, the last proposition:

> Proposition 4. *The Fed should choose a specific monetary aggregate (such as M1 or M2) and commit itself to making that aggregate grow at a fixed percentage rate, year in and year out.*

For Friedman the crucial step in eliminating the Fed as a source of instability is to get it to give up activist, or discretionary, monetary policy and to commit itself—publicly and in advance—to following some rule. Although the exact choice of a rule isn't critical, Friedman believes that a constant-money-growth rule would be a good choice for two reasons. First, the Fed has considerable influence, though not complete control, over the rate of money growth. Thus if money growth deviated significantly from its target, the Fed couldn't easily blame the deviation on forces beyond its control. Second, Friedman argues that steady money growth would lead to smaller cyclical fluctuations than the supposedly "countercyclical" monetary policies utilized historically. He concludes that a constant money growth rate would provide a "stable monetary background" that would allow economic growth to proceed without concern about monetary instability.

Friedman doesn't advocate a sudden shift from discretionary monetary policy to a low, constant rate of money growth. Instead, he envisions a transition period in which the Fed, by gradual preannounced steps, would steadily reduce the growth rate of money. Ultimately, the growth rate of the monetary aggregate selected would be consistent with an inflation rate near zero. Importantly, after the constant growth rate has been attained, the Fed wouldn't respond to modest economic downturns by changing money growth but would continue to follow the policy of maintaining a fixed rate of money growth. However, in some of his writings Friedman appears to leave open the possibility that the monetary rule could be temporarily suspended in the face of major economic crises, such as a depression.

Rules and Central Bank Credibility

Much of the monetarist argument for rules rests on pessimism about the competence or political reliability of the Federal Reserve. Economists who are more optimistic about the ability of the government to intervene effectively in the economy (which includes many Keynesians) question the monetarist case for rules. A "policy optimist" could argue as follows:

> Monetary policy may have performed badly in the past. However, as time passes, we learn more about the economy and the use of policy gets better. For example, U.S. monetary policy clearly was handled better after World War II than during the Great Depression. Imposing rigid rules just as we are beginning to learn how to use activist policy properly would be foolish. As to the issue of political reliability, that problem affects fiscal policymakers and indeed all our branches of government. We just have to trust in the democratic process to ensure that policymakers will take actions that for the most part are in the best interests of the country.

For policy optimists this reply to the monetarist case for rules seems perfectly satisfactory. During the past decade and a half, however, a new argument for rules has been developed that applies even if the central bank knows exactly how monetary changes affect the economy and is completely public-spirited. Thus the new argument for rules is a challenge even to policy optimists. It holds that the use of monetary rules can improve the **credibility** of the central bank, or the degree to which the public believes central bank announcements about future policy, and that the credibility of the central bank influences how well monetary policy works.

Dad, the Kids, and the Game: Credible Threats and Commitment. To help explain what credibility is, why it may be enhanced by rules, and why it may be important to monetary policy, let's look at a simple example drawn from family life. Knowing that Mom will be going to a business meeting, Dad has bought tickets to a baseball game for himself and the two kids, Junior and Sis. Dad likes baseball, as do the kids. Unfortunately, the kids also like to fight with each other. Dad has warned the kids: "Don't fight. If you do, we just won't go to the baseball game." Dad can't go to the baseball game without both kids because Mom won't be home to baby-sit and on such short notice he won't be able to find a sitter. We are interested in the following questions about the behavior of Dad and the kids: (1) Will the kids fight? and (2) Will Dad take the kids to the baseball game?

Before we analyze this situation, let's discuss it informally. The kids know that, because Dad wants to go to the game himself, he will be reluctant to impose the punishment he has threatened. That is, Dad's threat isn't credible (believable) to the kids. Therefore the kids will fight anyway, assuming that when push comes to shove, Dad won't be able to bring himself to waste the tickets and they'll go to the game.

Figure 15.7 illustrates this situation. The two columns of the diagram correspond to the two possible actions that the kids can take: *fight* and *don't fight*.

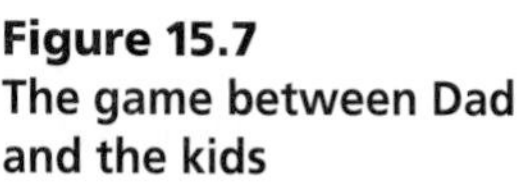

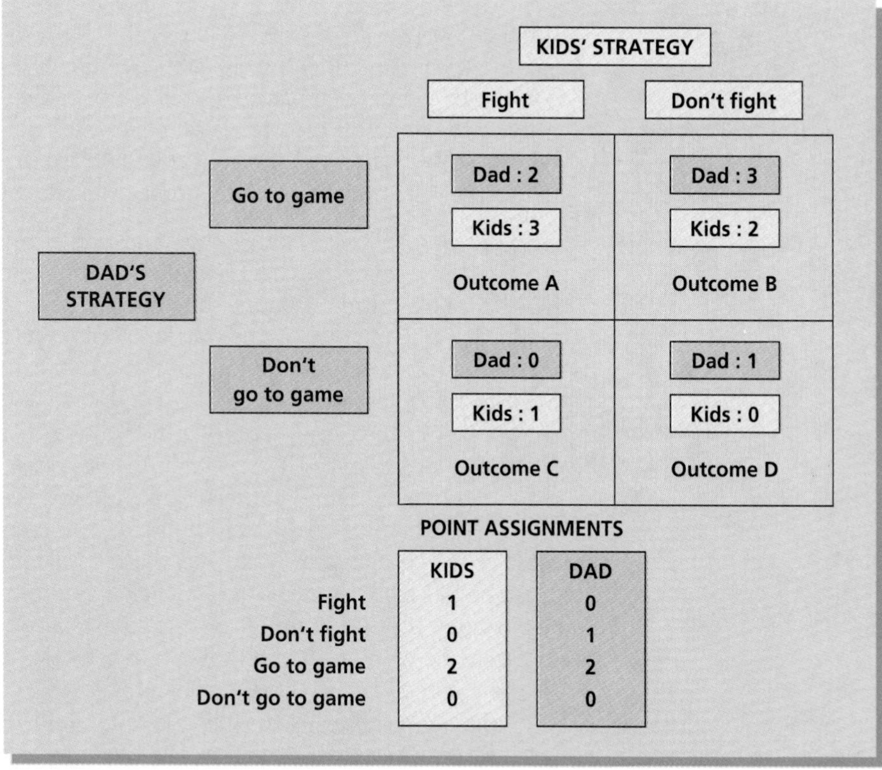

Figure 15.7
The game between Dad and the kids
Each square represents a combination of an action by the kids and an action by Dad. The points assigned to each combination of actions (shown in each square) measure how much each set of players likes each outcome. The kids "move" first by picking a column; then Dad "moves" by picking a row. The equilibrium is outcome A, in which the kids fight and still get to go to the game.

The two rows correspond to the two actions that Dad can take: *go to game* and *don't go to game.* Each of the four squares in the diagram thus refers to a possible outcome: Square A corresponds to the outcome *kids fight and Dad takes kids to game;* square B refers to *kids don't fight and Dad takes kids to game;* and so on.

Dad and the kids each have preferences about the four possible outcomes. Let's measure preferences in terms of points: The more points someone assigns to an outcome, the more he or she likes it. Dad likes baseball, so let's assume that he assigns 2 points to going to the game. Also, he assigns 1 point to having the kids not fight. The total number of points Dad assigns to each outcome is shown in each square. Dad's preferred outcome (worth 3 points) is B, in which the kids don't fight and they all go to the game. Dad's worst outcome is C, in which the kids fight and no one goes to the game, an outcome that gets 0 points from Dad.

The kids also like baseball, and they also assign 2 points to going to the game. However, they also like to fight, and they assign 1 point to fighting. The kids' point totals for each outcome are also shown in each box. The kids' favorite outcome, worth 3 points, is A (they fight and still get to go to the game). Their least favorite outcome, worth 0 points, is D (no fight and no game).

The sequence of actions is as follows. First, the kids decide whether to fight (after hearing the warning), and then Dad decides whether to take the kids to the game. In terms of Fig. 15.7 the kids get to pick the column (*fight* or *don't fight*). After the kids pick the column, Dad gets to pick whether they will be in the top square (*go to game*) or the bottom square (*don't go to game*). We assume that at each stage both the kids and Dad make the choices that attain their preferred outcome.

The kids reason as follows:

> Suppose we pick *fight* (the left column). That leaves Dad with the choice of A (*go to game*) or C (*don't go to game*). Outcome A is worth 2 points to Dad; C is worth 0 points. So Dad will pick A over C and, if we fight, we still get to go to the game. If we pick *don't fight* (the right column), Dad will pick B over D, so we also go to the game in that case. But because we like to fight, and we get to go to the game in either case, we might as well fight.

In terms of Fig. 15.7, the kids know that once they factor in their Dad's response, they effectively have a choice between A and B. They prefer A to B, so they pick the left column (that is, they fight).

This type of diagram is a standard tool from a branch of mathematics, much used in economics, called game theory. **Game theory** explores situations (games) in which strategy is used by individuals (players) to achieve their goals, possibly at the expense of the other players. An equilibrium of a game is an outcome that occurs if all players do the best they can for themselves.

In the game here, the "players" are Dad and the kids. The equilibrium of the game is outcome A, in which the kids fight and still go to the game. Outcome A is the equilibrium because the kids recognize that Dad's threat isn't credible; he has a strong incentive to back away from his threat when the time comes to carry it out. Indeed, if Dad is smart enough to realize that his threat has no force, he won't bother to make it in the first place.

Is there some way for Dad to make his threat credible and thereby get the kids to behave? Yes; the key to credibility for Dad is to find some way by which he can commit himself to carrying out the threat. In other words, Dad must convince the kids that, should they fight, he will have *no choice* but to keep everybody home from the game. Suppose, for example, that Dad gives the game tickets to Mom, with instructions to hide them and not to reveal their whereabouts if the kids fight. Suppose that Mom is indifferent about whether Dad and the kids go to the game and can be counted on to carry out these instructions.

How does Mom's hiding the tickets affect the equilibrium of the game? Formally, the effect is to cross out square A (kids fight, go to game) as a possible outcome. If the kids fight, going to the game will not be a possible choice for Dad. Thus the kids know that if they choose the left column (*fight*), Dad will be forced to choose square C (*don't go to game*), an outcome that yields 1 point for the kids. On the other hand, if the kids choose the right column (*don't fight*), Dad's preferred choice between his options B and D will be B (*go to game*). Because the kids prefer B (2 points) to C (1 point), they will pick the right column and not fight. The key conclusion of this analysis is that by committing in advance to carry out his threat, Dad has made his threat credible. If the kids act in their own best interests, Dad achieves the outcome (B) that he likes the best.

A Game Between the Central Bank and Firms. We can use game theory to think about the credibility of the central bank. Consider a situation in which the macroeconomy is in general equilibrium so that the *IS* and *LM* curves cross at the *FE* line (point *E* in Fig. 15.8a). Initially, suppose that both the money supply and the price level are growing steadily at 10% per year. As *M* and *P* are growing at the same rate, the real money supply M/P is constant, and the *LM* curve, LM^1, remains fixed and passes through *E*. Thus the economy is initially at full employment with the unemployment rate at the natural rate, say, 6%, and the inflation equal to 10% per year.

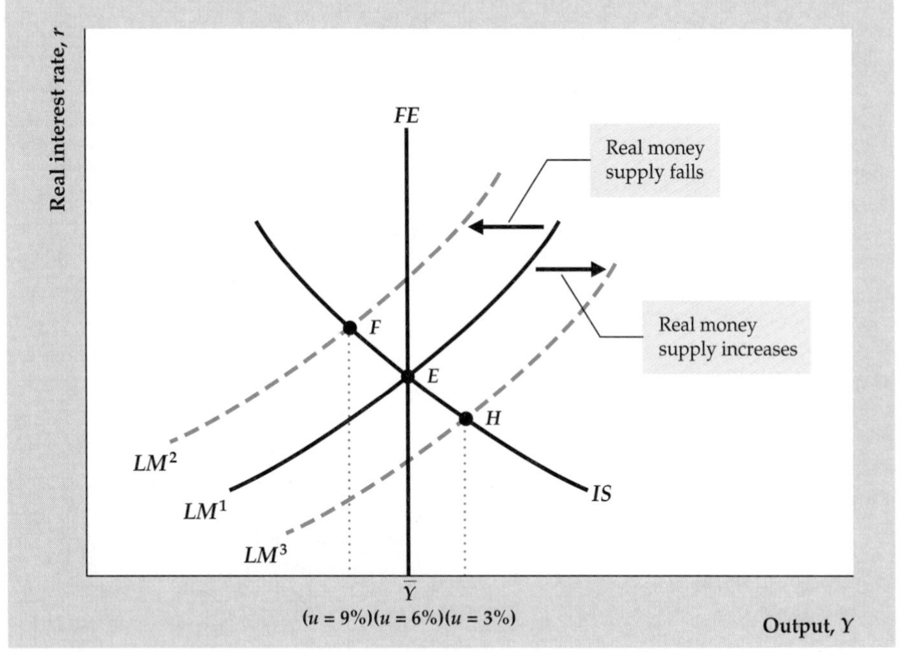

Figure 15.8
The game between the Fed and the firms
(a) This part of the figure shows the possible outcomes of the game between the Fed and the firms. Initially, the economy is at point *E* (full employment) with 10% inflation. The real money supply *M/P* depends both on the price level *P* chosen by firms and the money supply *M* chosen by the Fed. If the real money supply doesn't change, the economy remains at full employment at *E*. If the real money supply falls, the *LM* curve shifts from LM^1 to LM^2, and the economy goes into a recession with 9% unemployment at point *F*. If the real money supply increases, the *LM* curve shifts from LM^1 to LM^3, and the economy goes into a boom with 3% unemployment at point *H*.

The central bank (the Fed, let's say) wants to reduce the inflation rate to zero without increasing the unemployment rate. Suppose that the Fed makes the following announcement to all the firms in the economy:

> There's no reason why we should be suffering from this 10% inflation. Let's make a deal. If you businesses hold prices P constant this period, rather than raising them by 10%, we will hold the money supply M constant. With M and P both constant, the real money supply M/P won't change and the LM curve won't shift. Thus the economy will remain at full employment, with an unemployment rate of 6%, but we'll all be better off with no inflation. However, if you insist on raising prices, we'll still keep the money supply constant. In this case the real money supply M/P will fall by 10%, the LM curve will shift up and to the left to LM^2, and we'll all suffer from both high unemployment and continued inflation (point F).

How will the firms respond to this statement by the Fed? As we show, the Fed's threat to reduce the real money supply if firms raise prices isn't credible because the Fed doesn't want a recession. As a result, the firms will go ahead and raise prices.

The game between the Fed and the firms is analyzed formally in Fig. 15.8(b). The firms' choices, *raise P* (by 10%) and *don't raise P*, correspond to the two columns of the diagram. The Fed's two choices, *raise M* (by 10%) and *don't raise M* correspond to the two rows. Square A represents the outcome *firms raise P and Fed raises M;* square B represents the outcome *firms don't raise P and Fed raises M;* and so on.

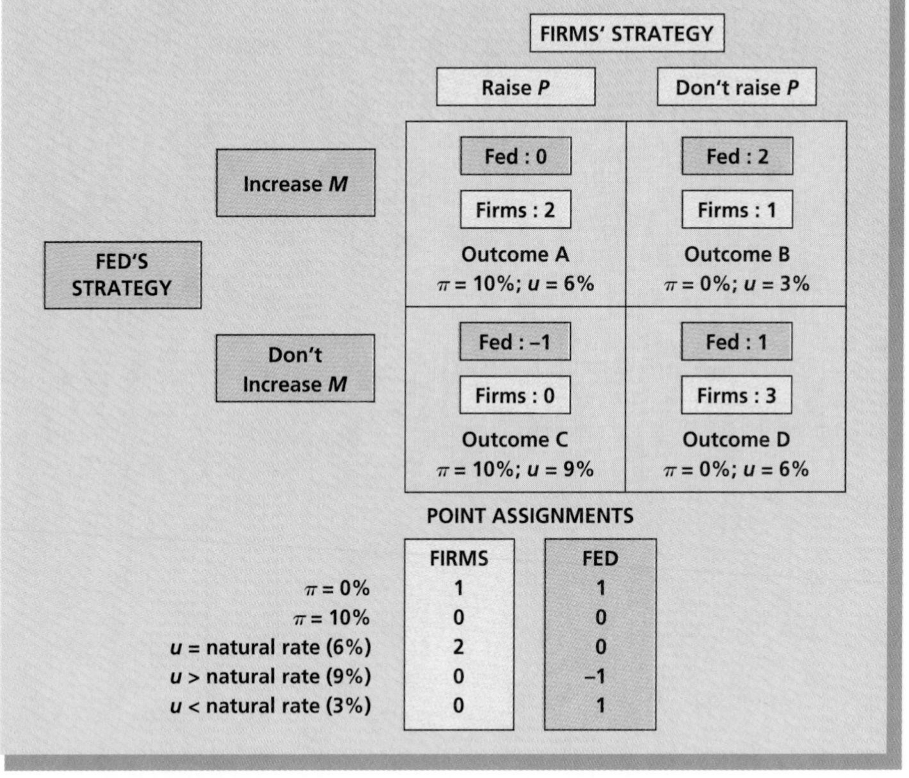

Figure 15.8
(b) This part of the figure shows the possible moves in the game between the Fed and the firms. The firms move first by deciding whether to raise the price level P, choosing the column. Then the Fed moves by deciding whether to increase the money supply M, choosing the row. If M and P both rise (outcome A) or both stay the same (outcome D), the real money supply is unchanged, and the economy remains at full employment at point E in (a). In outcome B, M increases and P remains the same; thus the real money supply rises and unemployment falls as at point H in (a). In outcome C, M remains the same and P increases, so the real money supply falls and unemployment increases as at point F in (a). Point assignments show the preferences of the Fed and firms for each outcome. The equilibrium of the game is outcome A, in which the firms raise prices and the Fed increases the money supply.

What happens to the economy in each case? Determining what happens to inflation is easy: In squares A and C, firms raise prices by 10%, so inflation π is 10%; in squares B and D firms don't raise prices, so $\pi = 0$.

What about unemployment? In square A both money and prices rise by 10%, so M/P is unchanged and the economy remains at full employment (point E in Fig. 15.8a). Similarly, in square D neither M nor P changes, so M/P is unchanged and the economy remains at full employment. Thus in squares A and D the unemployment rate u remains at the natural rate of 6%. In square C, P rises but M doesn't. Thus M/P falls, the LM curve shifts up and to the left to LM^2, and the economy goes into recession at point F in Fig. 15.8(a), with the unemployment rate increasing to 9%. Finally, in square B, M rises but P doesn't, so M/P rises and the LM curve shifts down and to the right to LM^3. In this case the economy goes into a boom (point H in Fig. 15.8a), and the unemployment rate falls to 3%.

The next step is to determine the points that each player assigns to each outcome. Let's start with the Fed, which doesn't like inflation. It assigns 1 point to zero inflation (B and D) and no points to a positive rate of inflation (A and C). However, the Fed also doesn't like unemployment. It assigns 0 points to the natural unemployment rate (A and D), 1 point to unemployment below the natural rate (B), and –1 point to unemployment above the natural rate (C). The total point scores for the Fed are shown in each square. The Fed's preferred outcome is B, with no inflation and 3% unemployment; its least favorite outcome is C, with 10% inflation and 9% unemployment.

The firms' profits are maximized on the *FE* line, that is, when the economy is at full employment. Therefore the firms assign 2 points to the natural unemployment rate (A and D). Firms prefer zero inflation to positive inflation, so they assign 1 point to zero inflation (B and D). Total scores for firms are also shown in each box.

Now let's find the equilibrium, assuming that firms first decide whether to raise prices and then the Fed decides whether to increase the money supply. The firms reason as follows:

> Suppose that we raise prices. This action leaves the Fed the choice between outcomes A and C. The Fed doesn't want a recession, so it will choose A; that is, it will increase the money supply. If we don't raise prices, the Fed has a choice of B or D. The Fed prefers B to D because, with no inflation, it prefers unemployment below the natural rate to unemployment at the natural rate. In this case the Fed also will increase the money supply. Therefore, no matter what we do, the Fed will increase the money supply. The Fed's claim that it will maintain a constant money supply if we raise prices just isn't credible. If we raise prices we get outcome A, and if we don't raise prices we get outcome B. We prefer A to B (we'd rather be at full employment than off the *FE* line and above full employment), so we will raise prices.

The equilibrium of the game is therefore outcome A, in which the firms raise prices and the Fed (failing to carry through on its threat) raises the money supply. Because the Fed's threat isn't credible, the firms ignore it. Note that *both the Fed and the firms prefer outcome D (full employment and no inflation) to the equilibrium outcome A.* Yet because the Fed's promise to hold the money supply constant isn't credible, the economy doesn't attain outcome D.

In contrast, suppose that the Fed could credibly promise not to increase the money supply under any circumstances and that the firms believed this promise. The firms would reason: "If we raise prices, the Fed will pick outcome C (inflation and a recession). If we don't raise prices, the Fed will pick D (no inflation and no recession). We prefer D to C, so we won't raise prices."

The equilibrium in this case would be outcome D, which is preferred by everyone to the no-credibility outcome A. In outcome D disinflation is achieved without increasing unemployment because the central bank is credible.

Rules, Commitment, and Credibility. The formal analysis shows why central bank credibility is important. If a central bank is credible, it can reduce money growth and inflation without incurring high unemployment. But how can a central bank achieve credibility?

One possibility is for the central bank to develop a reputation for carrying out its promises. Suppose that in the preceding example firms raise their prices, fully expecting the Fed to increase the money supply. However, the Fed holds the money supply constant, causing a recession. The next time, the firms may take the Fed's promises more seriously, and the economy may attain outcome D. Similarly, if Dad crosses up the kids and refuses to take them to the game after they fight, he will improve his reputation for carrying out his threats; the next time, the kids may take him seriously.

The problem with this strategy is that it may involve serious costs while the reputation is being established: The economy suffers a recession while the central bank establishes its reputation; Dad and the kids miss the game while Dad establishes his. Is there some less costly way to achieve credibility?

Advocates of rules suggest that, by forcing the central bank to keep its promises, rules may substitute for reputation in establishing credibility. Suppose that there is an ironclad rule—ideally, enforced by some outside agency—that the Fed must gradually reduce the growth of the money supply. Observing the existence of this rule, the firms might well believe that money supply growth is going to decline no matter what, and painless disinflation (outcome D) can be achieved. Similarly, in the case with Dad and the kids, if there is an unbreakable family rule that fighting suspends all privilegess—and Mom is there to help enforce it—Dad's threat not to go to the game might be more credible. Note that if it increases credibility, a rule improves central bank performance even if the central bank is competent and public-spirited. Hence this reason for monetary policy rules is different from the monetarists' argument presented earlier.

How do advocates of discretion respond to the credibility argument for rules? Keynesians argue that there may be a trade-off between credibility and flexibility. For a rule to establish credibility, it must be virtually impossible to change—otherwise, no one will believe that the Fed will stick to it. In the extreme, the monetary growth rule would be added as an amendment to the Constitution, which could then be changed only at great cost and with long delays. But if a rule is completely unbreakable, what happens (ask the Keynesians) if some unexpected crisis arises—for example, a new depression? In that case the inability of the Fed to take corrective action—that is, its lack of flexibility—could prove disastrous. Therefore, Keynesians argue, establishing a rule ironclad enough to create credibility for the central bank would, by eliminating policy flexibility, also create unacceptable risks.

APPLICATION

Monetary Targeting in Germany, Japan, and the United States

During the mid and late 1970s, in response to rising inflation, central banks in various industrialized countries established targets for the growth rates of one or more monetary aggregates.[17] The strategy of trying to hit predetermined monetary targets seems quite similar to Friedman's recommended strategy of a constant growth rate for money. Indeed, many observers and sometimes the central banks themselves used monetarist arguments to justify this strategy. Did monetary targeting actually conform to what Friedman recommended? Did monetary targeting improve central bank credibility? And did the use of monetary targets improve macroeconomic performance? To try to answer these questions, we briefly consider the experiences of three countries that experimented with monetary targeting: Germany,[18] Japan, and the United States.

Germany. The Bundesbank introduced targets for money growth in 1975 in response to a flare-up of inflation. The Bundesbank targeted only one monetary aggregate, a broad monetary measure called central bank money (CBM), a weighted sum of currency, checking accounts, savings accounts, and time deposits. In choosing only one aggregate to target, the Germans conformed to Friedman's conclusion that central banks can effectively control only one monetary aggregate at a time.[19] From 1975 to 1978, the Bundesbank set a single target for money growth for the coming year; beginning in 1979 the Bundesbank began to announce target ranges, specifying minimum and maximum acceptable money growth rates. Over time, the Bundesbank lowered its money-growth targets in an attempt to squeeze inflation out of the system.

The targets and actual values for German money growth are shown in Fig. 15.9(a) on the next page. From 1975 to 1985 the Bundesbank did a reasonably good job of achieving its targets, except in 1978. However, in the 1986–1988 period officials at the Bundesbank worried that the strength of the German mark relative to the dollar might depress German exports. To weaken the mark, the Bundesbank allowed the money growth rate to exceed its target. This deviation from the money target in order to affect short-run economic conditions is not in the spirit of the monetarist constant-growth-rate rule.

German money-growth targeting ran into additional problems in the latter part of the 1980s. First, the relationship between the targeted money aggregate (central bank money) and the economy seemed to become increasingly unreliable, primarily because of unpredictable shifts in the demand for currency (a major component of central bank money). Fearing that continued targeting of central bank money would destabilize the economy, in 1988 the Bundesbank began to target a different monetary aggregate, M3.[20] Second, the reunification of East and West Germany in 1989 posed new economic problems for the central bank, including a resurgence of inflation. Under political pressure to deal

---

17. For more on recent monetary policy in the major industrialized countries, see Ben Bernanke and Frederic Mishkin, "Central Bank Behavior and the Strategy of Monetary Policy: Observations from Six Industrialized Countries," in Olivier Blanchard and Stanley Fischer, eds., NBER *Macroeconomics Annual*, 1992.

18. Prior to 1990, "Germany" refers to West Germany.

19. Only one monetary aggregate can be targeted at a time for much the same reason that the central bank cannot simultaneously target a monetary aggregate and an interest rate. If the central bank uses open-market operations to cause one monetary aggregate to hit its target, it cannot simultaneously use open-market operations to force a different aggregate to hit a different target.

20. This switch is reflected in the target and money growth data in Fig. 15.9.

Figure 15.9
Money targeting in Germany
(a) Upper and lower target ranges and actual money growth rates are shown for Germany. From 1975 to 1985 the Bundesbank came close to its targets for monetary growth, except in 1978. From 1986 to 1988 concern that the mark was too strong relative to the dollar prompted the Bundesbank to allow money supply growth to exceed the target.

Source: George A. Kahn and Kristina Jacobson, "Lessons from West German Monetary Policy," in Federal Reserve Bank of Kansas City, *Economic Review*, April 1989, pp. 18–35. Update from International Monetary Fund (IMF), *World Economic Outlook*, May 1993, Table 23. Data refer to West Germany prior to 1990 and to unified Germany thereafter.

(b) During the money-targeting period inflation in Germany was brought down, but unemployment rose and remained stubbornly high.

Source: Unemployment: see Fig. 13.11. Inflation: *OECD Main Economic Indicators, 1969–88*, p. 385, and IMF, *World Economic Outlook*, May 1993, Table 23.

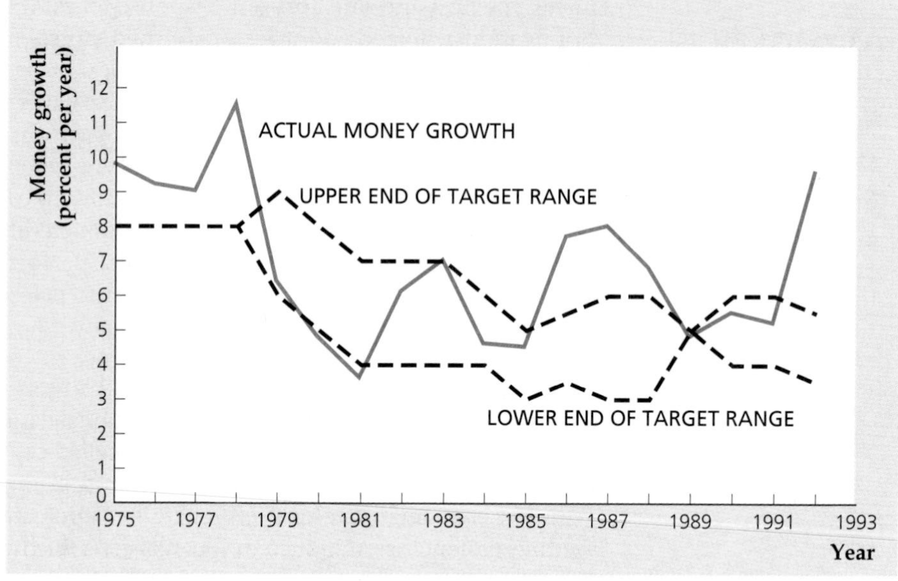

(a) Money growth and targets in Germany

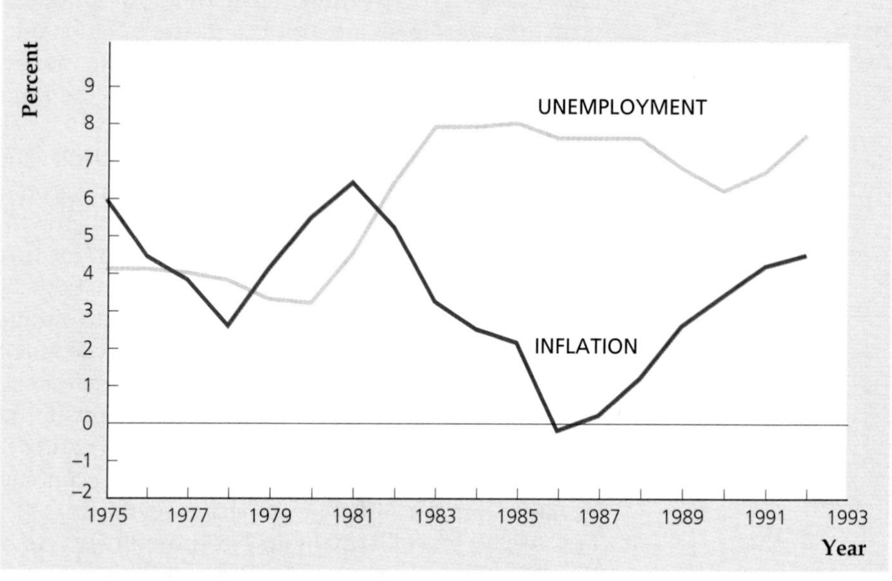

(b) Inflation and unemployment in Germany

more actively with these problems, after reunification the Bundesbank reduced somewhat the role of monetary targets in its policymaking.

How did the German economy perform during the Bundesbank's experiment with money targeting? As shown in Fig. 15.9(b), the inflation rate fell after the introduction of money targeting, rose temporarily at about the time of the 1979 oil price shock, and then remained low for most of the 1980s. As mentioned in the discussion of hysteresis in unemployment (Chapter 13), the German unemployment rate increased significantly in the early 1980s and has remained relatively high since then. Thus, although monetary targeting seems to have helped reduce inflation in Germany, evidently it didn't help prevent higher unemployment.

Japan. Like Germany, Japan adopted monetary targeting in response to inflation. In July 1978 the Bank of Japan began announcing a quarterly target for M2 growth. The targeted money aggregate was expanded to include certificates of deposit (CDs) when they began to be issued in May 1979.

Figure 15.10(a), on the next page, shows the target ranges and actual growth rates of money in Japan since 1979. The Japanese apparently were remarkably successful in hitting their money-growth targets. However, the Bank of Japan revises its targets quarterly to reflect its expectation of money growth. In other words, Japanese money-growth targets serve more as short-term forecasts of money growth than as actual targets for monetary policy. When the Bank of Japan decided to contract money growth sharply in 1991 (to slow what it feared was an overheating economy), it lowered the money-growth targets at the same time. This loose commitment to money-growth targets would not be supported by monetarists; on the other hand, monetarists would like the fact that, before 1991, Japanese money growth was in fact fairly stable.

Judging by the performance of the Japanese economy (Fig. 15.10b) on the next page, Japanese monetary policy has been quite successful. Unlike the German case, the subduing of inflation in the early 1980s in Japan was not accompanied by a large increase in unemployment.

United States. Unlike Germany and Japan, and counter to Friedman's advice, in 1975 the United States announced target growth rates for three different monetary aggregates: M1, M2, and M3. The target and actual growth rates for M2 are shown in Fig. 15.11(a) on page 563. Throughout most of the period M2 growth was within or slightly above its target range, although most recently M2 growth has been low and below its target range. As Friedman would have predicted, however, the Fed wasn't able to achieve all three monetary aggregate targets simultaneously: M1 growth in particular was consistently above its target, and the Fed abandoned attempts to target M1 in 1987.

As in Germany and Japan, inflation in the United States dropped and then stabilized in the 1980s (see Fig. 15.11b on page 563). Unemployment rose during the 1981–1982 recession but then declined steadily until a new recession hit in 1990. Overall, then, U.S. monetary policy during the period of money-growth targeting was reasonably successful.

Despite this relative success, however, the Fed became increasingly dissatisfied with the strategy of targeting money growth. The main problem was that, because of rapid changes in the U.S. financial system, at times the demand for money was quite unstable and unpredictable (see the Application, "Financial Innovation and the 'Case of the Missing Money,'" p. 234). Recall that, if money demand is unstable so that the *LM* curve moves randomly back and forth, varying the money supply to keep interest rates constant leads to more stable aggregate demand than does holding the money stock constant (see Fig. 15.6). Accordingly, after 1982 the Fed relied more and more on interest-rate targets (particularly the Fed funds rate) and less on money-growth targets in making policy. In 1993, following a period in which the demand for M2 appeared to be particularly volatile, the Fed announced it was dropping money-growth targets entirely.

Figure 15.10
Money targeting in Japan

(a) The figure suggests that the Japanese were very successful in hitting money growth targets. However, because the Bank of Japan revised its targets quarterly to reflect its expectations of future money growth, that impression is overstated.

Source: Takatoshi Ito, "Is the Bank of Japan a Closet Monetarist? Monetary Targeting in Japan, 1978–88," NBER Working Paper no. 2879, March 1989. Update from IMF, *World Economic Outlook,* May 1993, Table 23.

(b) Following the oil price shocks of the 1970s, inflation in Japan was brought down without any substantial increase in unemployment.

Source: *OECD Main Economic Indicators, 1969–88:* Unemployment, p. 120; inflation, p. 126. Updates from IMF, *World Economic Outlook,* May 1993: Unemployment, Table A-4; inflation, Table 23.

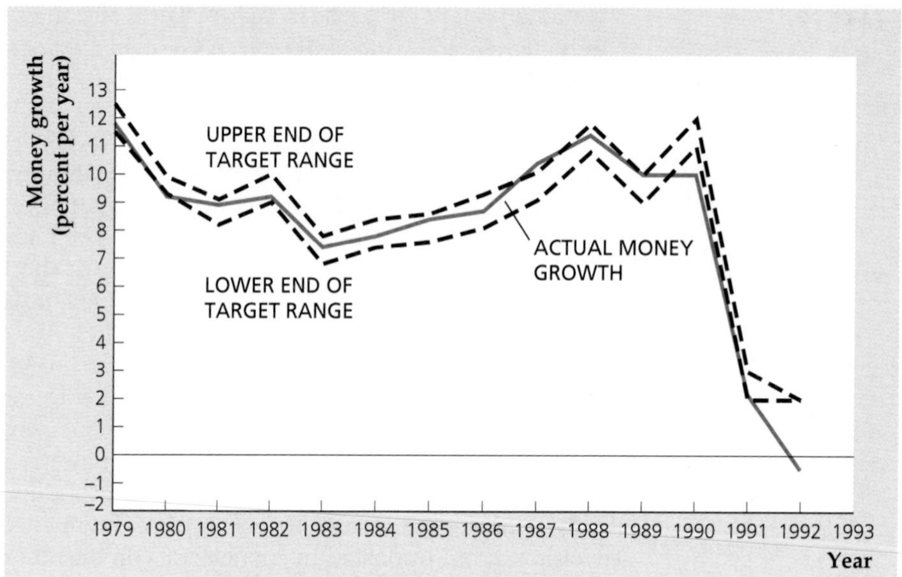

(a) Money growth and targets in Japan

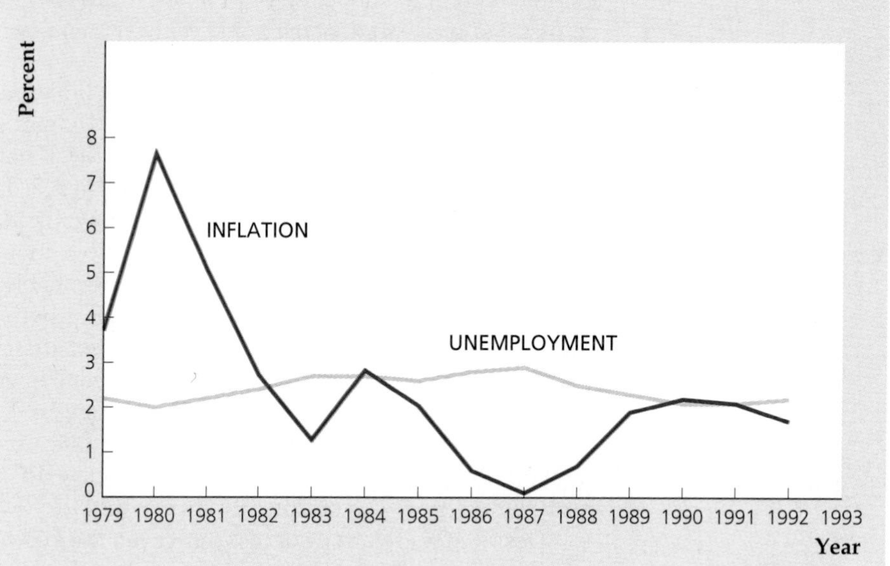

(b) Inflation and unemployment in Japan

Lessons. What do the experiences of Germany, Japan, and the United States tell us about the use of money-growth targets as a monetary policy rule? One important lesson is that, although governments have been willing to try money targeting, they don't seem willing to tie the hands of the central bank to the degree recommended by the monetarists. For example, Germany ignored its money-growth targets to meet exchange-rate goals and to deal with problems of reunification, the United States ultimately dropped money targets

Figure 15.11
Money targeting in the United States

(a) In 1975 the United States began targeting three money aggregates: M1, M2, and M3. The figure shows targeted and actual growth of M2. Although the Fed was reasonably successful in meeting its targets for M2 growth, instability in the demand for M2 led the Fed to drop M2 targets in 1993.

Source: Stanley Fischer, "Monetary Policy and Performance in US, Japan and Europe, 1973–86," NBER working paper no. 2475, December 1987. Update from IMF, *World Economic Outlook,* May 1993, Table 23.

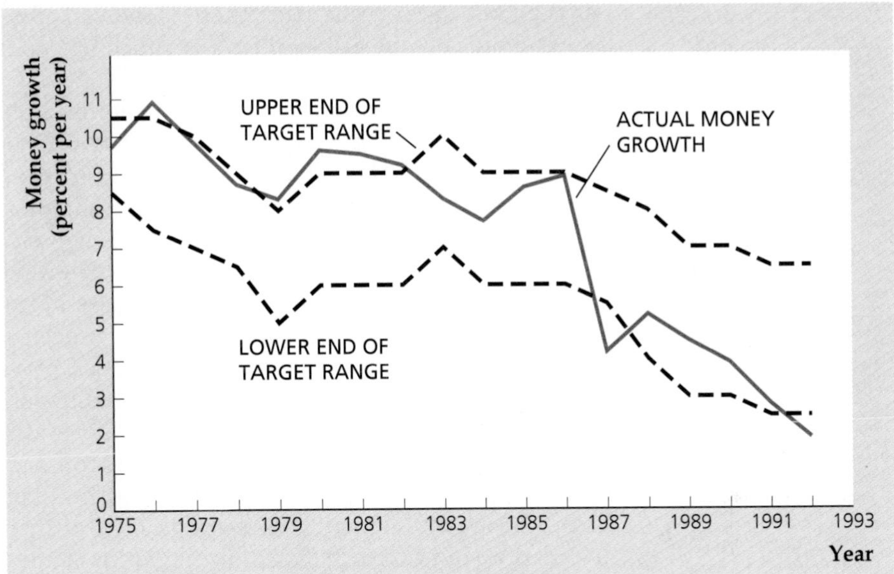

(a) Money growth and targets in the United States

(b) The rate of inflation in the United States fell sharply during the early 1980s and stabilized. The unemployment rate increased significantly during the early part of this disinflation but fell during the long expansion from 1983 to 1990.

Source: Inflation, see Fig. 2.3; unemployment, see Fig. 13.9.

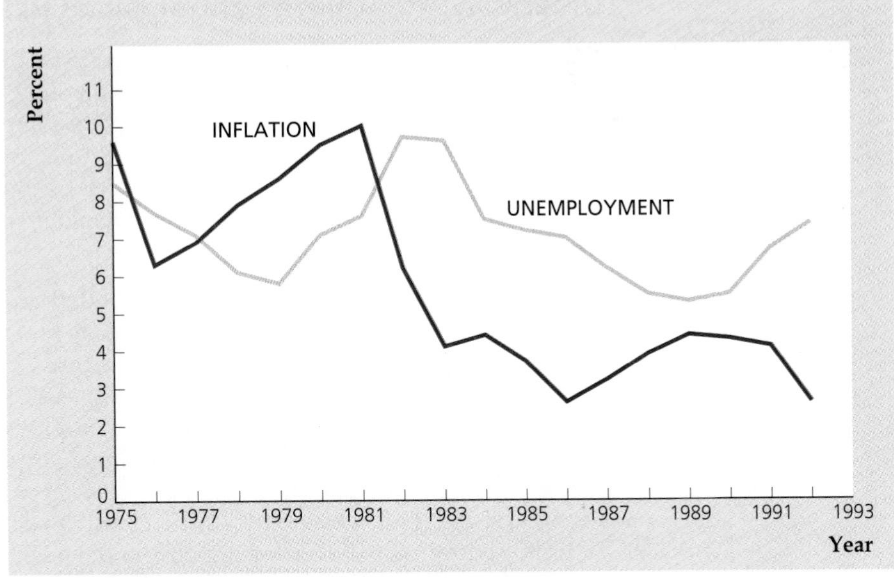

(b) Inflation and unemployment in the United States

in favor of interest-rate targets, and Japan treated its targets more as forecasts of money growth then as actual targets. An important reason for the unwillingness of central banks to commit more strongly to money-growth targets is that the demand for money, and therefore the link between specific money aggregates and the economy, often has proved to be unstable.

Because central banks have never made irrevocable commitments to meeting specific money-growth targets, monetarists can claim that their strict targeting strategy has never really been tried. However, critics can reply that if a strategy is politically infeasible, it isn't of much use no matter how appealing it is in theory.

Even if the preannounced targets weren't as ironclad as monetarists would have liked, did they yield any benefits? One clear result of the experience with targeting is that a concerted effort by the central bank can bring inflation under control; in all three countries inflation was sharply reduced by attempts to moderate money growth. However, advocates of rules have claimed that not only can adherence to money-growth targets reduce inflation, but it can do so without significant increases in unemployment. The experiences of these three countries don't provide much support for the idea that the use of money-growth targets reduces the unemployment costs of disinflation. In particular, the Bundesbank was very credible and had a reasonably good track record at hitting its targets, yet the German disinflation coincided with a sharp and persistent increase in unemployment. The United States also experienced significant unemployment costs during disinflation, although its increase in unemployment was more transitory than Germany's. Only Japan avoided a significant increase in unemployment, even though the Bank of Japan may have been the least committed of the three to hitting monetary targets.

Other Ways to Achieve Central Bank Credibility

The preceding application suggests that adopting money-growth targets doesn't generally give the central bank credibility, possibly because central banks are unwilling or unable to commit to meeting those targets. Are there other ways to increase the central bank's credibility and thus improve the performance of monetary policy? Three possibilities have been suggested: to appoint a "tough" central banker; to change central bankers' incentives; and to increase the central bank's independence.

1. *Appointing a "tough" central banker.* By definition, a credible central bank is one that will be believed by the public when it states its intention to reduce money growth and inflation. One way to increase credibility is for the President to appoint a Fed chairman who strongly dislikes inflation and who people believe is willing to accept increased unemployment if necessary to bring inflation down. Thus, when President Jimmy Carter faced a serious inflation problem in 1979, he appointed Paul Volcker—an imposing individual with a strong anti-inflation reputation—to be chairman of the Fed. In appointing a "tough" central banker, Carter hoped to convince the financial markets and the public that he was serious about reducing inflation. Volcker succeeded in getting rid of inflation, but, because unemployment rose significantly in the process, his appointment didn't completely solve the credibility problem.[21]

2. *Changing central bankers' incentives.* A second way to enhance the central bank's credibility is to give its leadership strong incentives to be "tough" on

21. The point that appointing a tough central banker may improve central bank credibility was made by Kenneth Rogoff, "The Optimal Degree of Commitment to an Intermediate Monetary Target," *Quarterly Journal of Economics,* November 1985, 1169–1189. Keynesians might argue that Volcker was credible but that long-lived stickiness in wages and prices led unemployment to increase in 1981–1982 anyway.

inflation (and to ignore any unemployment costs associated with disinflation).[22] If the incentives are strong enough and are publicly known, people may find the central bank's anti-inflation pronouncements to be credible. An interesting recent example of this approach is a law passed in New Zealand that sets explicit inflation targets for the central bank and provides for the replacement of the head of the central bank if those targets aren't met. Inflation has come down significantly in New Zealand, but unemployment has risen. Again, credibility problems haven't been completely solved.

3. *Increasing central bank independence.* A third strategy is to increase the independence of the central bank from the other parts of the government—for example, by limiting the legal ability of the executive and legislative branches to interfere in monetary policy decisions. The rationale is that a more independent central bank will be less subject to short-term political pressures to try to expand output and employment (say, before an election) and will be more strongly committed to maintaining a low long-run inflation rate. Because the public will recognize that an independent central bank is less subject to political pressures, announcements made by the central bank should be more credible.

Considerable evidence supports the idea that independent central banks are more credible. Figure 15.12, taken from a study by Alberto Alesina and

22. An analysis of central bankers' incentives is Carl Walsh, "Optimal Contracts for Central Bankers," unpublished paper, University of California-Santa Cruz and Federal Reserve Bank of San Francisco, 1992.

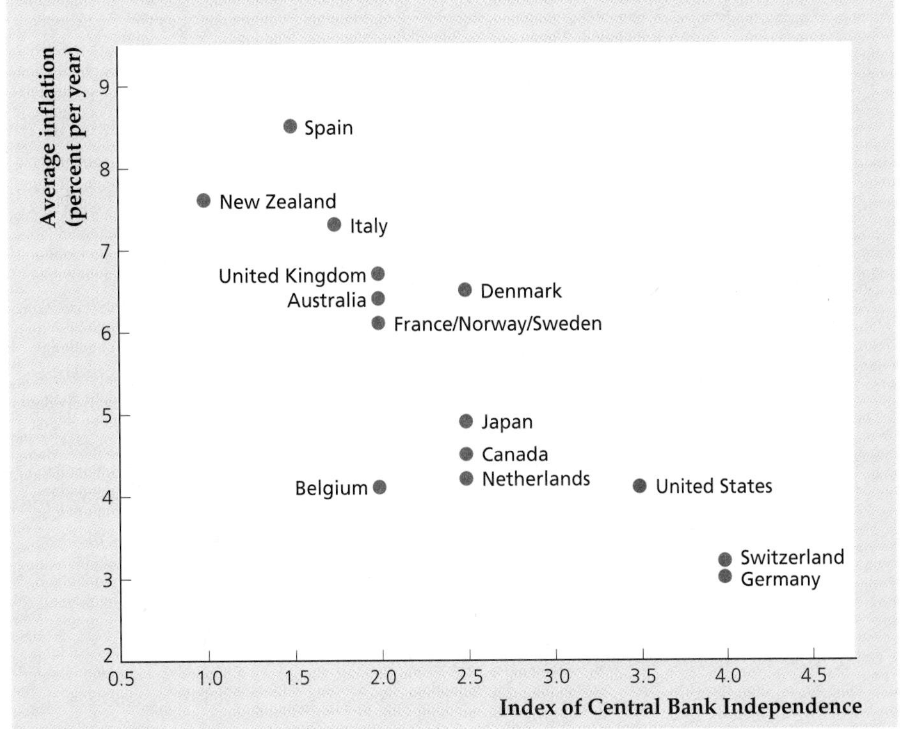

Figure 15.12
Central bank independence and inflation
The figure compares average inflation to an index of central bank independence from the rest of the government (higher values of the index imply that the central bank is more independent) for each of sixteen countries for the period 1955–1988. It shows that countries with more independent central banks have lower average inflation rates.

Source: Alberto Alesina and Lawrence Summers, "Central Bank Independence and Macroeconomic Performance," *Journal of Money, Credit and Banking,* May 1993, 151–162, Table A1 and Fig. 1a.

Lawrence Summers[23] of Harvard University, shows the relationship between central bank independence and inflation in sixteen industrialized countries. The vertical axis measures average inflation for each country for the period 1955–1988. The horizontal axis shows an index of central bank independence (based on factors such as the ease with which the government can dismiss the head of the central bank or reverse central bank decisions). Countries with relatively independent central banks, such as Germany, Switzerland, and the United States, clearly have lower long-run inflation rates than countries without independent central banks, such as the United Kingdom, New Zealand,[24] Italy, and Spain. A similar figure in the Alesina–Summers study shows that countries with independent central banks don't have higher long-run rates of unemployment. This evidence supports the idea that increased central bank independence raises credibility and thus lowers the unemployment cost of keeping inflation low. Reflecting growing acceptance of the idea that increased central bank independence improves macroeconomic performance, in 1993 France took several steps expressly designed to increase the independence of its central bank, the Bank of France.

23. "Central Bank Independence and Macroeconomic Performance," *Journal of Money, Credit and Banking,* May 1993, 151–162.

24. The evaluation of the independence of New Zealand's central bank preceded the recent reforms in New Zealand's central banking laws mentioned earlier.

CHAPTER SUMMARY

1. Three groups help determine the money supply: the central bank, private banks, and the general public. The central bank sets the monetary base, which is the quantity of central bank liabilities that can be used as money. The monetary base equals the sum of bank reserves (deposits by banks at the central bank plus currency in the vaults of banks) and currency in circulation. Private banks and the general public interact to determine the money multiplier, which is the ratio of the money supply to the monetary base.

2. In an all-currency economy the monetary base consists entirely of currency in circulation. Therefore the money supply equals the monetary base, and the money multiplier equals 1.

3. In an economy with fractional reserve banking and no currency held by the public, the money supply is $1/res$ times the monetary base, where res is the ratio of reserves to deposits desired by banks. The money supply is greater than the monetary base in this case because banks lend part of the deposits they receive. When those funds are redeposited in the banking system, bank deposits and thus the money supply increase.

4. In an economy with both fractional reserve banking and currency in circulation, the money multiplier equals $(cu + 1)/(cu + res)$, where cu is the public's desired ratio of currency to deposits. The money supply equals deposits plus currency in circulation and also equals the money multiplier times the monetary base. An increase in the desired currency–deposit ratio cu or in the desired reserve–deposit ratio res reduces the money multiplier. During the Great Depression in the United States, banking panics caused both cu and res to increase, and the money multiplier and the money supply both fell sharply.

5. The central bank can affect the size of the monetary base and thus the money supply through open-market operations. An open-market sale (in which central bank assets are sold for currency or bank reserves) reduces the monetary base. An open-market purchase (in which the central bank uses money to buy assets, such as government securities, from the public) increases the monetary base.

6. The central bank of the United States is called the Federal Reserve System, or the Fed. The leadership of the Fed is the Board of Governors, which in turn is headed by the chairman of the Federal Reserve. The Federal Open Market Committee (FOMC) meets several times each year to set monetary policy.

7. The Fed affects the U.S. money supply primarily through open-market operations. Discount window lending and changes in reserve requirements can also be used to affect the money supply. An increase in discount window lending raises the monetary base and thus the money supply. An increase in reserve requirements raises the reserve–deposit ratio, lowering the money multiplier and the money supply.

8. The Fed often focuses on intermediate targets such as the money supply or short-term interest rates (primarily the Fed funds rate) to guide monetary policy. Stabilizing interest rates is a useful strategy when fluctuations in money supply or demand would otherwise cause the *LM* curve to shift randomly back and forth.

9. Monetary policy may be conducted either by rules or by discretion. Under rules the central bank is required to follow a simple predetermined rule for monetary policy, such as a requirement for constant money growth, and isn't allowed to respond to current economic conditions. Under discretion the central bank is expected to monitor the economy and use monetary policy actively to maintain full employment and to keep inflation low. Discretion for monetary policy is favored by Keynesians, who argue that it gives the Fed maximum flexibility to stabilize the economy.

10. Monetarists, led by Milton Friedman, argue that, because of information problems and lags between the implementation of policy changes and their effects, the scope for using monetary policy to stabilize the economy is small. Furthermore, they argue, the Fed cannot be relied on to use active monetary policy wisely and in the public interest. Monetarists advocate a constant-growth-rate rule for the money supply in order to discipline the Fed and keep monetary fluctuations from destabilizing the economy.

11. An additional argument for rules is that they increase central bank credibility. Supporters of rules claim that the use of ironclad rules will cause the public to believe the central bank if it says (for example) that money supply growth will be reduced, with the implication that inflation can be reduced without a large increase in unemployment.

12. Although some countries have experimented with money-growth targets—similar in spirit to the monetarists' constant-growth-rate rule—central banks haven't been willing or able to make strong commitments to meet their targets. One reason for their reluctance is that fluctuations in the demand for money have led the relationship between specific monetary aggregates and the macroeconomy to be unstable or unpredictable at times. The use of money-growth targets seems to have helped central banks bring inflation under control, but there isn't much evidence that money targeting has reduced the unemployment cost of disinflation.

13. Possible alternatives for increasing a central bank's credibility are to appoint a central banker who is "tough" on inflation; to increase central bankers' incentives to reduce inflation; and to increase the central bank's independence from other parts of the government.

Key Terms

bank reserves, p. 530
bank run, p. 533
Board of Governors of the Federal Reserve System, p. 540
central bank, p. 528
credibility, p. 553
currency–deposit ratio, p. 534

depository institutions, p. 528
discount rate, p. 544
discount window lending, p. 544
discretion, p. 549
Federal Open Market Committee (FOMC), p. 540
Fed funds rate, p. 544
fractional reserve banking, p. 530
game theory, p. 554
high-powered money, p. 529
instruments, p. 544
intermediate targets, p. 545
monetarism, p. 550
monetary base, p. 529
money multiplier, p. 535
multiple expansion of loans and deposits, p. 532
100% reserve banking, p. 530
open-market purchase, p. 536
open-market sale, p. 536
reserve–deposit ratio, p. 530
rules, p. 547
vault cash, p. 541

Key Equations

$$M = CU + DEP \qquad (15.4)$$

The money supply, M, is the sum of currency in circulation, CU, and deposits held by the public at banks, DEP.

$$BASE = CU + RES \qquad (15.5)$$

The monetary base, or the liabilities of the central bank that are usable as money, equals the sum of currency in circulation, CU, and bank reserves, RES.

$$M = \left(\frac{cu + 1}{cu + res}\right) BASE \qquad (15.8)$$

The money supply, M, equals the monetary base times the money multiplier, $(cu + 1)/(cu + res)$, where cu is the currency–deposit ratio chosen by the public and res is the reserve–deposit ratio chosen by banks.

Review Questions

1. Define *monetary base.* What is the relationship between the monetary base and the money supply in an all-currency economy?
2. Define *money multiplier.* What is the value of the money multiplier in a system of 100% reserve banking? What is the value of the money multiplier in a system of fractional reserve banking, if all money is held in the form of deposits? Why is the money multiplier higher under fractional reserve banking than under 100% reserve banking?
3. Discuss how actions of the public and banks can cause the money multiplier to rise or fall. Does the fact that the public and banks can affect the money multiplier imply that the central bank cannot control the money supply? Why or why not?
4. What is the effect on the monetary base of an open-market purchase of U.S. Treasury securities? What is the effect on the money supply?
5. Who determines monetary policy in the United States? What role does the President play?
6. Besides open-market operations, what other means does the Federal Reserve have for controlling the money supply? Explain how these alternative methods work.
7. What are intermediate targets? How do they differ from monetary policy goals? List the two principal types of intermediate targets that the Fed has used.
8. "It is plain to see that discretion is a better way to run monetary policy than following a rule because a policy of discretion gives the central bank the ability to react to news about the economy." What is the monetarist response to the statement? What is the more recent argument for using rules rather than discretion?
9. Has the use of money-growth targets significantly improved central bank credibility? Besides adopting money-growth targets, what other actions can a country take to increase the credibility of its central bank?

Numerical Problems

1. The Agricolan monetary base is 1,000,000 florins. The public always holds half its money supply as currency and half as deposits. Banks hold 20% of deposits in the form of reserves. Starting with the initial creation of a monetary base that accompanies the purchase by the central bank of 1,000,000 fl worth of coconuts from the public, show the consolidated balance sheet of the banks after they first receive deposits, after a first round of loans and redeposits, and after a second round of loans and redeposits. (*Hint:* Don't forget that the public keeps only half its money in the form of bank deposits.)

Show the balance sheets of the central bank, the banking system, and the public at the end of the process of multiple expansion of loans and deposits. What is the final value of the money supply?

2. **a.** The money supply is \$6,000,000, currency held by the public is \$2,000,000, and the reserve–deposit ratio is 0.25. Find deposits, bank reserves, the monetary base, and the money multiplier.
b. In a different economy vault cash is \$1,000,000, deposits by depository institutions at the central bank are \$4,000,000, the monetary base is \$10,000,000, and bank deposits are \$20,000,000. Find bank reserves, the money supply, and the money multiplier.

3. When the real interest rate increases, banks have an incentive to lend a greater portion of their deposits, which reduces the reserve–deposit ratio. In particular, suppose that

$$res = 0.4 - 2r,$$

where *res* is the reserve–deposit ratio and r is the real interest rate. The currency–deposit ratio is 0.4, the price level is fixed at 1.0, and the monetary base is 60. The real quantity of money demanded is

$$L(Y, i) = 0.5Y - 10i,$$

where Y is real output and i is the nominal interest rate. Assume that expected inflation is zero so that the nominal interest rate and the real interest rate are equal.
a. If $r = i = 0.10$, what are the reserve–deposit ratio, the money multiplier, and the money supply? For what real output Y does a real interest rate of 0.10 clear the asset market?
b. Repeat part (a) for $r = i = 0.05$.
c. Suppose that the reserve–deposit ratio is fixed at the value you found in part (a) and isn't affected by interest rates. If $r = i = 0.05$, for what output Y does the asset market clear in this case?
d. Is the *LM* curve flatter or steeper when the reserve–deposit ratio depends on the real interest rate than when the reserve–deposit ratio is fixed? Explain your answer in economic terms.

4. This question asks you to analyze a game played by two players, player I and player II. Player I can choose one of two actions, A and B. Player II also has two actions to choose from, a and b. Both players are affected by their own action and by the action of the other player. The points that each player assigns to each possible outcome (combination of actions) are shown in the following table.

Outcome	Points for Player I	Points for Player II
(A, a)	2	2
(A, b)	5	0
(B, a)	0	5
(B, b)	3	3

The first row indicates that, if player I chooses action A and player II chooses action a, player I gets 2 points and player II gets 2 points. The more points a player gets, the happier she is with the outcome. Players don't care about how many points the other player gets.
a. If player I moves (chooses an action) first and then player II moves, what action will each player take? (Set up a game theory diagram like Fig. 15.7.) What is the outcome of the game? Does your answer change if player II moves first?
b. Suppose that player I moves first, but before player I moves, player II announces which action (a or b) she will take when it is her turn. Player II's announcement is legally binding. What is the outcome of the game now?
c. Before player I makes the first move, player II is allowed to make a threat, telling player I what action she will take on her turn if player I chooses A and what action she will take if player I chooses B. Player II's threats are legally binding. What is the outcome of the game now? Is player I made worse off or better off by player II's ability to threaten her?

Analytical Problems

1. How would each of the following affect the U.S. money supply? Explain.
a. Banks decide to hold more excess reserves. (Excess reserves are reserves over and above what banks are legally required to hold against deposits.)
b. People withdraw cash from their bank accounts for Christmas shopping.
c. The Federal Reserve sells gold to the public.
d. The Federal Reserve begins to pay interest on deposits of depository institutions held at the Fed (it currently doesn't pay interest).
e. The introduction of automatic teller machines, which allow people to withdraw cash from the

bank as needed, makes deposits relatively more convenient.

f. The Federal government covers \$20 billion of its fiscal deficit by selling bonds to the Federal Reserve. The proceeds of the sale are used to pay government employees.

g. The Federal Reserve sells some of its government securities in Tokyo for yen.

2. Suppose that the central bank strictly followed a rule of keeping the real interest rate at 3% per year. That rate happens to be the real interest rate consistent with the economy's initial general equilibrium.

a. Assume that the economy is hit only by money demand shocks. Under the central bank's rule, how will the money supply respond to money demand shocks? Will the rule make aggregate demand more stable or less stable than it would be if the money supply were constant?

b. Assume that the economy is hit only by *IS* shocks. Under the central bank's interest-rate rule, how will the money supply behave? Will the interest-rate rule make aggregate demand more stable or less stable than it would be if the money supply were constant? Will the central bank be able to follow its rule in the long run?

c. Assume that the economy is hit only by supply shocks (shocks to the *FE* line). Repeat part (b).

3. In the game between the Fed and the firms shown diagrammatically in Fig. 15.8(b), what happens if the Fed doesn't value having the unemployment rate below the natural rate $\bar{u}$? Specifically, assume that the Fed assigns 0 points to a situation in which u equals $\bar{u}$ and assigns -1 points to a situation in which u is either above or below $\bar{u}$. How does this modification affect the outcome of the game? (Assume that if the Fed is indifferent between two actions, it chooses the one that makes the firms better off.)

4. Why do many governments have policies against negotiating with hostage-taking terrorists? Under what conditions, if any, are such policies likely to reduce hostage taking? Discuss the analogy to monetary rules.

CHAPTER 16

GOVERNMENT SPENDING AND ITS FINANCING

At every level of government, from the town hall to the White House, fiscal policy—government decisions about how much to spend, what to spend for, and how to finance its spending—is of central importance. Politicians and the public understand that the government's fiscal choices have a direct impact on the "bread and butter" issues of how much they pay in taxes and what government benefits and services they receive. Equally important are the effects of fiscal policy on the economy. In recent years people have become more aware of the macroeconomic effects of fiscal policy as the economic implications of government budget deficits, tax reform, and other aspects of fiscal policy have been extensively debated.

This chapter takes a closer look at fiscal policy and its macroeconomic effects. To provide some background, we begin with definitions and facts about the government's budget. We then discuss some basic fiscal policy issues, including the effects of government spending and taxes on economic activity, the burden of government debt, and the link between budget deficits and inflation.

16.1 THE GOVERNMENT BUDGET: SOME FACTS AND FIGURES

Before getting into the analytical issues of fiscal policy, we set the stage by looking at the components of the government budget and their recent trends. We discuss three main aspects of the budget: (1) spending, or outlays; (2) tax revenues, or receipts; and (3) the budget deficit. Our discussion reviews and builds on Chapter 2, which introduced basic budget concepts.

Government Outlays

Government outlays, the total spending by the government during a period of time, are divided into three primary categories: government purchases, transfer payments, and net interest payments.

1. *Government purchases* (*G*) are government spending on currently produced goods and services. Examples are spending on military hardware or highway repairs and government workers' salaries.
2. *Transfer payments* (*TR*) are payments made to individuals for which the government does not receive *current* goods or services in exchange. Examples of transfers are Social Security benefit payments, military and civil service pensions, unemployment insurance, welfare payments (Aid to Families with Dependent Children), and Medicare.[1]
3. *Net interest payments* (*INT*) are the interest paid to the holders of government bonds less the interest received by the government—for example, on outstanding government loans to students or farmers.

In addition there is a minor category called *subsidies less surpluses of government enterprises.* Subsidies are government payments that are intended to affect the production or prices of various goods. Examples are price support payments to farmers and fare subsidies for mass transit systems. The surpluses of government enterprises represent the profits of government-run enterprises such as the Tennessee Valley Authority (an electricity producer). This category of outlays is relatively small, so for simplicity we ignore it in the equations later in this chapter.

In the United States total government outlays (Federal, state, and local) are about a third of GDP. Figure 16.1 shows the trends since 1939 in the three main

1. Although government outlays for Medicare and Medicaid are used to pay for current medical services, they are treated as transfer payments to individuals who then purchase these services.

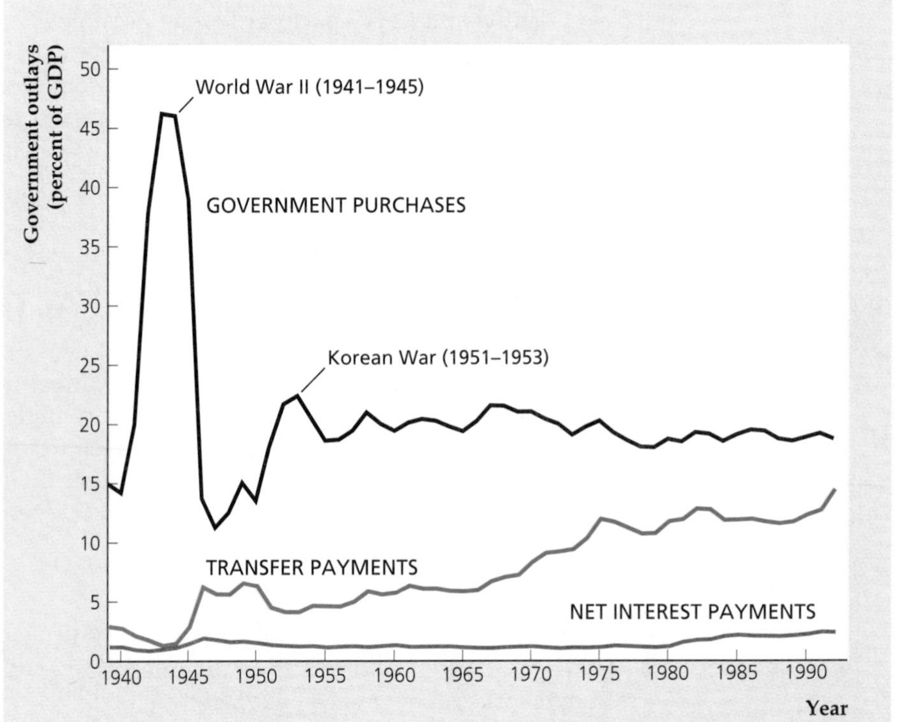

Figure 16.1
Government outlays: Federal, state, and local, 1939–1992
The figure shows the behavior since 1939 of the three major components of government outlays, for all levels of government combined and measured as a percentage of GDP. Government purchases rose most sharply during World War II (1941–1945) and the Korean War (1951–1953). Transfer payments have risen steadily as a share of GDP. Interest payments rose most sharply during World War II and in the 1980s.

Source: GDP from *Survey of Current Business,* December 1992 (1939–1991) and May 1993 (1992 value); Government purchases, transfer payments, and net interest: *Economic Report of the President,* 1991, Table B-80 (1939–1958); *Economic Report of the President,* 1993, Table B-78 (1959–1991); *Survey of Current Business,* May 1993 (1992 value).

categories of government outlays, expressed as a percentage of GDP. The most obvious feature of Fig. 16.1 is the enormous increase in government purchases during World War II: In 1943 and 1944, when the war effort was at its peak, government purchases exceeded 45% of GDP. The impact of the Korean War (1951–1953) also is evident, though less dramatic: Government purchases of goods and services increased from 13.5% of GDP in 1950 to 22.4% of GDP in 1953. Since the mid 1950s, the share of GDP devoted to government purchases has remained fairly steady at about 20%.

Figure 16.1 also shows that transfer payments rose steadily as a share of GDP from the early 1950s until the early 1980s, doubling their share of GDP during that thirty-year period. Transfers are currently about 13%–14% of GDP. The long-term increase in transfer payments is the result of the creation of new social programs (such as Medicare and Medicaid in 1965), the expansion of benefits under existing programs (such as Social Security), and the increased number of people covered by the various programs. Reforms to the health care system proposed by President Clinton in 1993, if passed by Congress, may ultimately have significant effects on the level of transfer payments; however, it is too early to predict what those effects will be.

Finally, Fig. 16.1 shows how net interest payments—interest payments, for short—have evolved. Because interest payments are much smaller than the other two categories of government outlays, they appear to fluctuate less. However, interest payments rose sharply as a percentage of GDP in two periods. First, interest payments doubled from 0.96% of GDP in 1941 to 1.93% of GDP in 1946, reflecting the large amount of government borrowing done to finance the war effort during World War II. Second, interest payments as a share of GDP almost doubled during the 1980s, rising from 1.15% in 1979 to 2.14% in 1989. This increase reflected both higher rates of borrowing by the government and the generally high level of interest rates during the 1980s.

How does the rate of government expenditure in the United States compare with rates in other countries with similar living standards? Because official accounting rules for measuring the government budget vary widely among countries, the answer isn't as straightforward as you might think. Nevertheless, Table 16.1, on the next page, compares the ratios of government spending to GDP for seven industrialized countries. Shown are ratios for both central government spending (Federal, in the United States) and total government spending (including state and local, in the United States). The United States has a lower rate of government spending than the Western European countries and Canada, but a higher rate than Japan. The lower rate of government spending in the United States relative to the Western European countries and Canada largely reflects the more extensive government-financed social welfare programs (such as national health insurance) in those countries.

Taxes

On the revenue side of the government's budget are tax receipts. There are four principal categories of tax receipts: personal taxes, contributions for social insurance, indirect business taxes, and corporate taxes. Figure 16.2, on page 575, shows the history of revenues from these four major categories of taxes in the United States, all expressed as a percentage of GDP. Note that the share of taxes in GDP has risen steadily, nearly doubling from 17.0% of GDP in 1939 to 30.7% of GDP in 1992.

Table 16.1 Government Spending in Seven Industrialized Countries, Percentage of GDP, 1990

Country	Central Government	All Government
Italy	37.6%	48.1%
France	20.5%	46.3%
Canada	22.2%	44.0%
Germany	14.7%	42.6%
United Kingdom	29.9%	38.1%
United States	17.4%	34.6%
Japan	13.9%	26.2%

Source: OECD, *National Accounts, 1978–1990*. All data are from 1990, except those for the United States, which are from 1989. Data for the "Central government" in the United States, Japan, Germany, France, and the United Kingdom exclude social security payments, but these payments are included in the "All Government" category. Data for "Central Government" in Canada and Italy include some social security benefits.

The largest category of tax receipts is *personal taxes,* which are primarily personal income taxes and property taxes. Income taxes were first introduced at the Federal level in the United States (at very low rates and for only the richest people) during the Civil War. However, this tax faced a series of legal challenges, and eventually the Supreme Court declared the income tax unconstitutional. In 1913 the Sixteenth Amendment to the Constitution gave Congress the right to impose an income tax. Used lightly at first, this tax is now a major source of revenue for government.

Personal taxes took their biggest jump during World War II, rising from 2.6% of GDP in 1940 to 9.8% of GDP in 1945. The general upward drift in personal tax receipts since 1945 has been interrupted by several tax cut bills, notably the Kennedy–Johnson tax cut of 1964 and the Reagan tax cut of 1981.

Figure 16.2 shows that a large share of the increase in tax receipts since World War II reflects the increase in the second category of taxes, *contributions for social insurance* (primarily Social Security taxes). Social insurance contributions usually are levied as a fixed percentage of a worker's salary, up to a ceiling; income above that ceiling isn't taxed. In most cases the worker's contributions are matched by the employer so that the deduction appearing on the worker's paycheck reflects only about half the total tax levied. Increases in social insurance contributions are the result of increases both in the contribution rate and higher ceilings on the amount of income subject to the tax.

The third category of tax receipts is *indirect business taxes,* mainly sales taxes. These taxes declined as a share of GDP during World War II and haven't shown any significant long-term increase or decrease since.

The final category of tax receipts is *corporate taxes,* particularly corporate profit taxes. Figure 16.2 shows that corporate taxes rose sharply during World War II and the Korean War, then drifted gradually downward as a share of GDP from the mid 1950s until the mid 1980s. Changes in the tax code in 1986 were intended to increase corporate tax receipts (while reducing personal income taxes collected by the Federal government), and between 1985 and 1988

Figure 16.2
Taxes: Federal, state, and local, 1939–1992
Shown is the history of revenues collected from various types of taxes, for all levels of government combined and measured as a percentage of GDP. Total taxes have drifted upward during the past five decades. Most of this increase in taxes is accounted for by increases in contributions for social insurance and in personal taxes.

Source: GDP as in Fig. 16.1; total tax receipts, personal taxes, corporate profit taxes, indirect business taxes, and contributions for social insurance: same sources as expenditure components, Fig. 16.1.

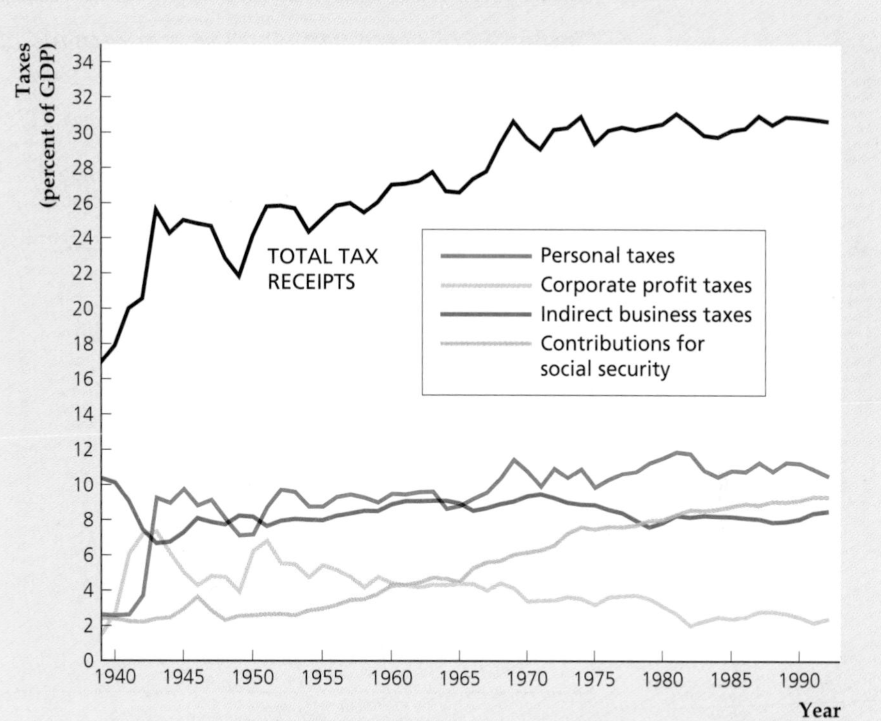

corporate tax receipts as a share of GDP rose from 2.39% to 2.80% of GDP. However, by 1992 corporate taxes as a share of GDP had fallen back to 2.36%. Corporate tax rates, along with income tax rates for high-income individuals, were raised in 1993.

The Composition of Outlays and Taxes: The Federal Government Versus State and Local Governments. The components of government spending shown in Fig. 16.1 and the components of taxes shown in Fig. 16.2 lump together Federal, state, and local governments. For most purposes of macroeconomic analysis, combining Federal, state, and local fiscal policy is the most sensible course. The macroeconomic effect of a new highway-building program, for example, shouldn't depend on whether the new highways are financed from the Federal, state, or local budgets—or from a combination of those budgets. In this respect the tendency of many news stories about fiscal policy to focus exclusively on the Federal government's budget can be misleading.

Nevertheless, it is useful to know that in the United States Federal government budgets have a much different composition, on both the expenditure and the revenue sides, from those of state and local governments. A summary of the major components of both the Federal and the combined state and local government budgets for 1992 is given in Table 16.2 on the next page. Note in particular the following points:

1. *Goods and services.* By far the largest part of state and local outlays (more than four fifths) is for goods and services. In contrast, less than a third of Federal outlays is for goods and services, and 70% of this amount is for national

Table 16.2 Government Outlays and Receipts, 1992

	Federal		State and Local	
	Billions of Dollars	**Percentage of Outlays**	**Billions of Dollars**	**Percentage of Outlays**
Outlays				
Goods and services	449.1	30.8	665.8	81.0
National defense	*315.8*		*0*	
Nondefense	*133.4*		*665.8*	
Transfer payments	623.3	42.7	233.6	28.4
Grants in aid	173.0	11.9	0	0
Net interest paid	186.7	12.8	–43.8	–5.3
Subsidies less surpluses of government enterprises and less dividends received	26.2	1.8	–33.3	–4.0
Total outlays	1458.3	100.0	822.3	100.0

	Federal		State and Local	
	Billions of Dollars	**Percentage of Receipts**	**Billions of Dollars**	**Percentage of Receipts**
Receipts				
Personal taxes	474.1	40.9	153.2	18.3
Contributions for social insurance	489.7	42.2	63.7	7.6
Indirect business taxes	81.5	7.0	422.7	50.5
Corporate taxes	115.0	9.9	25.2	3.0
Grants in aid	0	0	173.0	20.6
Total receipts	1160.4	100.0	837.8	100.0
Deficit (outlays less receipts; surplus, if negative)	298.0		–15.5	
Primary deficit	111.3		28.3	

Note: Figures may not add due to rounding.

Source: *Survey of Current Business*, June 1993, p. 9, Tables 3.2 and 3.3.

defense. *About five sixths of government spending on nondefense goods and services in the United States is done by state and local governments.*

2. *Transfer payments.* The Federal budget is more heavily weighted toward transfer payments (particularly, benefits from Social Security and related programs) than state and local budgets are.

3. *Grants in aid.* Grants in aid are payments made by the Federal government to state and local governments to help support various education, transportation, and welfare programs. Grants in aid appear as an outlay for the Federal government and as a receipt for state and local governments. In 1992 these grants made up more than 20% of state and local government receipts.

4. *Net interest paid.* Because of the large quantity of Federal government bonds outstanding, net interest payments are an important component of Federal spending. In contrast, net interest payments for state and local governments are actually *negative,* meaning that state and local governments (who hold substantial amounts of Federal government bonds) receive more interest than they pay out.

5. *Composition of taxes.* About 83% of Federal government receipts come from personal taxes (primarily the Federal income tax) and contributions for social insurance. Only about 10% of Federal revenues are from corporate taxes and only about 7% are from indirect business taxes such as sales taxes. In contrast, indirect business taxes account for half of state and local revenues. About a quarter of state and local revenues come from personal taxes (both income taxes and property taxes) and contributions for social insurance. As already mentioned, state and local governments also count as revenue the grants in aid they receive from the Federal government.

Deficits

Government outlays need not equal tax revenues in each period. In Chapter 2 we showed that, when government outlays exceed revenues, there is a government budget deficit (or simply a deficit); and when revenues exceed outlays, there is a government budget surplus. For ease of reference we write the definition of the deficit as

$$\begin{aligned}\text{deficit} &= \text{outlays} - \text{tax revenues}\\ &= \text{government purchases} + \text{transfers} + \text{net interest} - \text{tax revenues}\\ &= G + TR + INT - T. \qquad (16.1)\end{aligned}$$

A second deficit concept, called the **primary government budget deficit,** excludes net interest from government outlays:

$$\begin{aligned}\text{primary deficit} &= \text{outlays} - \text{net interest} - \text{tax revenues}\\ &= \text{government purchases} + \text{transfers} - \text{tax revenues}\\ &= G + TR - T. \qquad (16.2)\end{aligned}$$

The primary deficit is the amount by which government purchases and transfers exceed tax revenues; the primary deficit plus net interest payments equals the deficit. Figure 16.3, on the next page, illustrates the relationship between the two concepts.

Why have two deficit concepts? The reason is that each answers a different question. The standard or total budget deficit answers the question: How much does the government currently have to borrow to pay for its total outlays? When measured in nominal terms, the deficit during any year is the number of additional dollars that the government must borrow during that year.

The primary deficit answers the question: Can the government afford its *current* programs? If the primary deficit is zero, the government is collecting just enough tax revenue to pay for its current purchases of goods and services and its current social programs (as reflected by transfer payments). If the

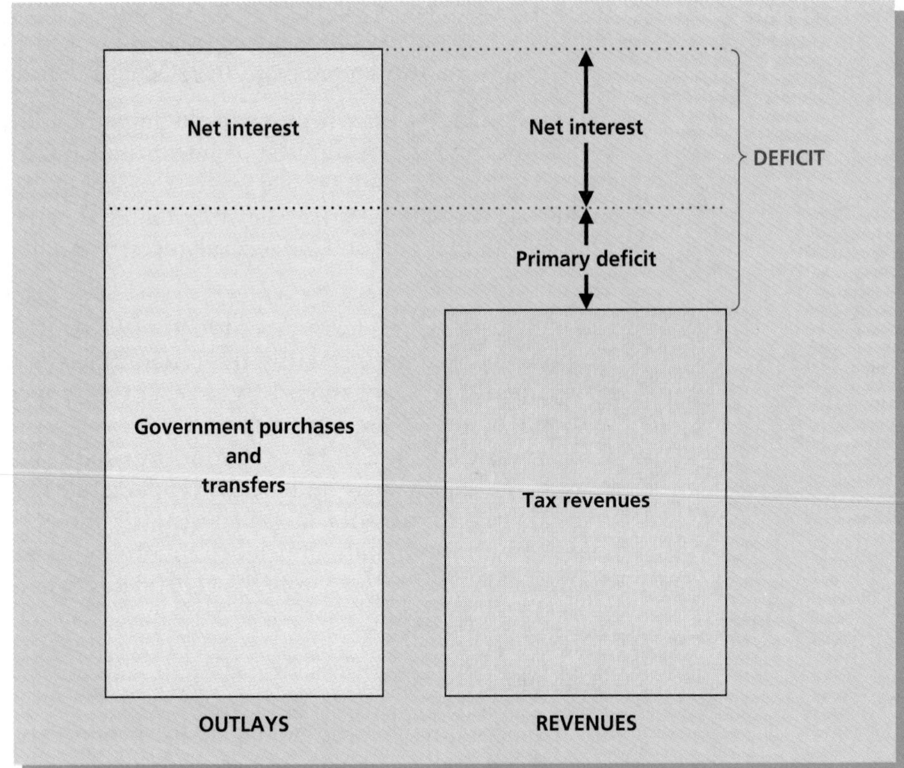

Figure 16.3
The relationship between the total budget deficit and the primary deficit
The standard measure of the total government budget deficit is the amount by which government outlays exceed tax revenues. The primary deficit is the amount by which government purchases plus transfers exceed tax revenues. The total budget deficit equals the primary deficit plus net interest payments.

primary deficit is greater than zero, current government purchases and social programs cost more than current tax revenue can pay for. Net interest payments are ignored in the primary deficit because they represent not current program costs but costs of past expenditures financed by government borrowing.

Figure 16.4 shows the deficit and primary deficit for all levels of government combined as a percentage of GDP since 1940. Again, the World War II period stands out; the government financed only part of the war effort with taxes and thus ran large primary and overall deficits. Large deficits (using both concepts) also occurred in the mid 1970s and through much of the 1980s, although the primary deficit for all levels of government combined was eliminated and turned into a primary surplus in 1988 and 1989. By the early 1990s, a substantial primary deficit had reemerged.

16.2 GOVERNMENT SPENDING, TAXES, AND THE MACROECONOMY

How does fiscal policy affect the performance of the macroeconomy? Economists emphasize three main ways by which government spending and taxing decisions influence macroeconomic variables such as output, employment, and prices: (1) aggregate demand, (2) government capital formation, and (3) incentives.

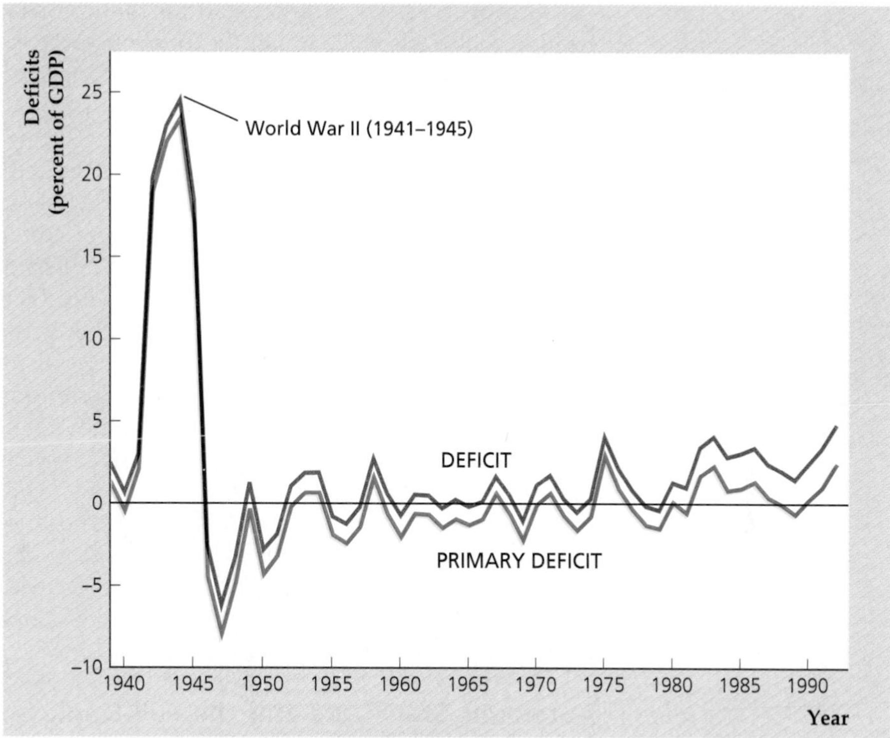

Figure 16.4
Deficits and primary deficits: Federal, state, and local, 1940–1992
Shown are the total government budget deficit and the primary deficit, both measured as a percentage of GDP, since 1940. The government ran large deficits during World War II. Deficits and primary deficits also occurred during the 1980s. The widening gap between the deficit and the primary deficit in recent years reflects increasing interest payments on the government's accumulated debt.

Source: Same as Figs. 16.1 and 16.2.

Fiscal Policy and Aggregate Demand

Fiscal policy can affect economic activity by influencing the total amount of spending in the economy, or aggregate demand. Recall that aggregate demand is represented by the intersection of the *IS* and *LM* curves. In either the classical or the Keynesian *IS–LM* model, an increase in government purchases reduces desired national saving and shifts the *IS* curve up and to the right, thereby raising aggregate demand.

Classical and Keynesian economists have different beliefs about the effect of tax changes on aggregate demand. Classicals usually accept the Ricardian equivalence proposition, which says that lump-sum tax changes do not affect desired national saving and thus have no impact on the *IS* curve or aggregate demand.[2] Keynesians generally disagree with this conclusion; in the Keynesian view, a cut (for example) in taxes is likely to stimulate desired consumption and reduce desired national saving, thereby shifting the *IS* curve up and to the right and raising aggregate demand.

Classicals and Keynesians also disagree over the question of whether fiscal policy should be used to fight the business cycle. Classicals generally reject attempts to smooth business cycles, by fiscal policy or by other means. In contrast, Keynesians argue that using fiscal policy to stabilize the economy and maintain full employment—for example, by cutting taxes and raising spending when the economy is in a recession—is desirable.

2. We introduced Ricardian equivalence in Chapter 4. We discuss this idea further in Section 16.3.

However, even Keynesians admit that the use of fiscal policy as a stabilization tool is difficult. A significant problem is *lack of flexibility.* The government's budget has many purposes besides macroeconomic stabilization, such as maintaining national security, providing income support for eligible groups, developing the nation's infrastructure (roads, bridges, and public buildings), and supplying government services (education and public health). Much of government spending is committed years in advance (as in weapons development programs) or even decades in advance (as for Social Security benefits). Expanding or contracting total government spending rapidly for macroeconomic stabilization purposes thus is difficult without either spending wastefully or compromising other fiscal policy goals. Taxes are somewhat easier to change than spending, but the tax laws also have many different goals and may be the result of a fragile political compromise that isn't easily altered.

Compounding the problem of inflexibility is the problem of *long time lags* that result from the slow-moving political process by which fiscal policy is made (see the Political Environment box, "The Federal Budget Process," p. 587). From the time a spending or tax proposal is made until it goes into effect is rarely less than eighteen months to two years. This lag makes effective countercyclical use of fiscal policy difficult because (for example), by the time an antirecession fiscal measure actually had an impact on the economy, the recession might already be over.

Automatic Stabilizers and the Full-Employment Deficit. One way to get around the problems of fiscal policy inflexibility and long lags that impede the use of countercyclical fiscal policies is to build automatic stabilizers into the budget. **Automatic stabilizers** are provisions in the budget that cause government spending to rise or taxes to fall automatically—without legislative action—when GDP falls. Similarly, when GDP rises, automatic stabilizers cause spending to fall or taxes to rise without any need for direct legislative action.

A good example of an automatic stabilizer is unemployment insurance. When the economy goes into a recession and unemployment rises, more people receive unemployment benefits, which are paid automatically without further action by Congress. Thus the unemployment insurance component of transfers rises during recessions, making fiscal policy automatically more expansionary.[3]

Quantitatively, the most important automatic stabilizer is the income tax system. When the economy goes into a recession, people's incomes fall, and they pay less income tax. This "automatic tax cut" helps cushion the drop in disposable income and (according to Keynesians) prevents aggregate demand from falling as far as it might otherwise. Likewise, when people's incomes rise during a boom, the government collects more income tax revenue, which helps restrain the increase in aggregate demand. Keynesians argue that this automatic fiscal policy is a major reason for the increased stability of the economy since World War II.

A side effect of automatic stabilizers is that government budget deficits tend to increase in recessions because government spending automatically

3. This statement assumes that the Keynesian view is right, so that an increase in transfers—which is equivalent to a reduction in taxes—raises aggregate demand.

rises and taxes automatically fall when GDP declines. Similarly, the deficit tends to fall in booms. In order to distinguish changes in the deficit caused by recessions or booms from changes caused by other factors, some economists advocate the use of a deficit measure called the full-employment deficit. The **full-employment deficit** indicates what the government budget deficit *would be*—given the tax and spending policies currently in force—if the economy were operating at its full-employment level.[4] Because it eliminates the effects of automatic stabilizers, the full-employment deficit measure is affected primarily by changes in fiscal policy reflected in new legislation. In particular, expansionary fiscal changes—such as increases in government spending programs or (in the Keynesian model) reduced tax rates—raise the full-employment budget deficit, whereas contractionary fiscal changes reduce the full-employment deficit.

Figure 16.5 shows the actual and full-employment budget deficits (as percentages of GDP) of the Federal government since 1962. Note that the actual budget deficit substantially exceeded the full-employment budget deficit during the recessions of 1973–1975, 1981–1982, and 1990–1991 when output was below its full-employment level. The difference between the two deficit measures reflects the importance of automatic stabilizers in the budget.

4. In practice, the calculation of full-employment deficits uses the Keynesian assumption that recessions reflect deviations from full employment rather than the classical assumption that (in the absence of misperceptions) recessions reflect changes in full-employment output.

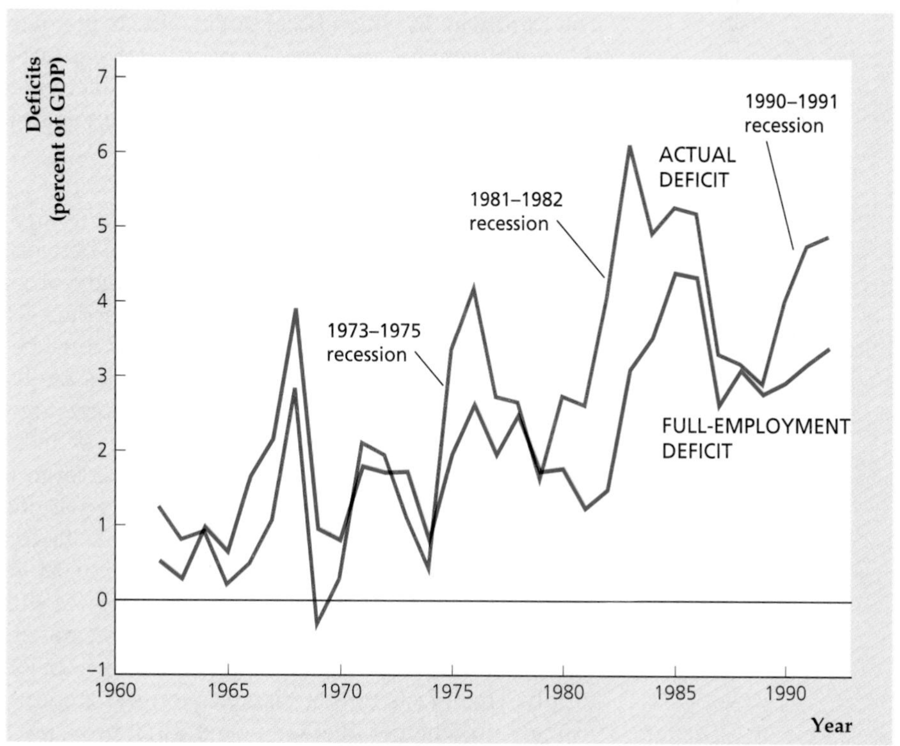

Figure 16.5
Full-employment and actual budget deficits, 1962–1992
The actual and full-employment Federal budget deficits are shown as a percentage of GDP. The actual budget deficit exceeded the full-employment deficit by substantial amounts during the 1973–1975, 1981–1982, and 1990–1991 recessions, reflecting the importance of automatic stabilizers.

Source: GDP as in Fig. 16.1; deficits: *The Economic and Budget Outlook: Fiscal Years 1994–1998,* Congressional Budget Office, Tables E-1 and E-2.

Government Capital Formation

The health of the economy depends not only on *how much* the government spends but also on *how* it spends its resources. For example, as we discussed in Chapter 6, the quantity and quality of public infrastructure—roads, schools, public hospitals, and so on—are potentially important for the rate of economic growth. Thus the formation of **government capital**—long-lived physical assets owned by the government—is one way that fiscal policy affects the macroeconomy. The government budget affects not only physical capital formation but also human capital formation. At least part of government expenditures on health, nutrition, and education are an investment, in the sense that they will lead to a more productive work force in the future.

An ideal government budget accounting system would distinguish between expenditures on current items, such as the salaries of police officers or agricultural subsidies, and expenditures on capital items, such as the construction of mass transit systems or flood-control dams. Corporate financial accounts distinguish current from capital expenditures, as do the accounts of governments in some other countries, but the U.S. government's budget doesn't make this distinction. Some people have advocated the introduction of separate current and capital accounts in the Federal budget to allow better evaluation of the amount of government capital formation. One practical problem would be the difficulty of allocating expenditures having a partial investment component—such as those on health and nutrition—between the two accounts.

Incentive Effects of Fiscal Policy

The third way in which fiscal policy affects the macroeconomy is by its effects on incentives. Tax policies in particular can affect economic behavior by changing the financial rewards to various activities. For example, Chapter 4 showed how tax rates influence the incentives of households to save and of firms to make capital investments.

Average Versus Marginal Tax Rates. To analyze the effects of taxes on economic incentives, we need to distinguish between average and marginal tax rates. The **average tax rate** is the total amount of taxes paid by a person (or a firm), divided by the person's before-tax income. The **marginal tax rate** is the fraction of an *additional* dollar of income that must be paid in taxes. For example, suppose that in a particular country no taxes are levied on the first $10,000 of income, and a 25% tax is levied on all income above $10,000 (see Table 16.3). Under this income tax system a person with an income of $18,000 pays a tax of $2000. Thus her average tax rate is 11.1% ($2000 in taxes divided by $18,000 in before-tax income). However, this taxpayer's marginal tax rate is 25%, because a $1.00 increase in her income will increase her taxes by $0.25. Table 16.3 shows that everyone with an income higher than $10,000 faces the same marginal tax rate of 25% but that the average tax rate increases with income.

We can show why the distinction between average and marginal tax rates is important by considering the individual's decision about how much labor to supply. The effects of a tax increase on the amount of labor supplied depend strongly on whether average or marginal taxes are being increased. Economic

Table 16.3 Marginal and Average Tax Rates: An Example (Total Tax = 25% of Income over $10,000)

Income	Income – $10,000	Tax	Average Tax Rate	Marginal Tax Rate
$ 18,000	$ 8,000	$ 2,000	11.1%	25%
50,000	40,000	10,000	20.0%	25%
100,000	90,000	22,500	22.5%	25%

theory predicts that an increase in the average tax rate, with the marginal tax rate held constant, will *increase* the amount of labor supplied at any (before-tax) real wage. In contrast, theory predicts that an increase in the marginal tax rate, with the average tax rate held constant will *decrease* the amount of labor supplied at any real wage.

To explain these conclusions, let's first consider the effects of a change in the average tax rate. Returning to our example from Table 16.3, imagine that the marginal tax rate stays at 25% but that now all income over $8000 (rather than all income over $10,000) is subject to a 25% tax. The taxpayer with an income of $18,000 finds that her tax bill has risen from $2000 to $2500, or 0.25($18,000 – $8000), so her average tax rate has risen from 11.1% to 13.9%, or $2500/$18,000. As a result, the taxpayer is $500 poorer. Because she is effectively less wealthy, she will increase the amount of labor she supplies at any real wage (see Summary table 4, p. 84). Hence an increase in the average tax rate, holding the marginal tax rate fixed, shifts the labor supply curve (in a diagram with the before-tax real wage on the vertical axis) to the right.[5]

Now consider the effects of an increase in the marginal tax rate, with the average tax rate constant. Suppose that the marginal tax rate on income is raised from 25% to 40% and is accompanied by other changes in the tax law that keep the average tax rate—and thus the total amount of taxes paid by the typical taxpayer—the same. To be specific, suppose that the portion of income not subject to tax is increased from $10,000 to $13,000. Then for the taxpayer earning $18,000, total taxes are $2000, or 0.40($18,000 – $13,000), and the average tax rate of 11.1%, or $2000/$18,000, is the same as it was under the original tax law.

With the average tax rate unchanged, the taxpayer's wealth is unaffected, and so there is no change in labor supply stemming from a change in wealth. However, the increase in the marginal tax rate implies that the taxpayer's after-tax reward for each extra hour worked declines. For example, if her wage is $20 per hour before taxes, at the original marginal tax rate of 25%, her actual take-home pay for each extra hour of work is $15 ($20 minus 25% of $20, or $5, in taxes). At the new marginal tax rate of 40% the taxpayer's take-home pay for each extra hour of work is only $12 ($20 in before-tax wages minus $8 in

5. In terms of the analysis of Chapter 8, the increase in the average tax rate has a pure income effect on labor supply.

taxes). Because extra hours of work no longer carry as much reward in terms of real income earned, at any specific before-tax real wage the taxpayer is likely to work fewer hours and enjoy more leisure instead. Thus, if the average tax rate is held fixed, an increase in the marginal tax rate causes the labor supply curve to shift to the left.[6]

APPLICATION

Labor Supply and Tax Reform in the 1980s

Twice during the 1980s Congress passed tax reform legislation that dramatically reduced marginal tax rates. At the beginning of the decade the highest marginal tax rate on labor income was 50%. The Economic Recovery Tax Act of 1981 (known as ERTA) reduced personal income tax rates in three stages, with a complete phase-in by 1984.[7] The Tax Reform Act of 1986 further reduced personal tax rates. By the end of the 1980s the marginal tax rate on the highest levels of personal income had fallen to 28%.[8]

The 1981 tax act was championed by a group of economists, politicians, and journalists who favored an approach to economic policy called **supply-side economics.** The basic belief of supply-side economics is that all aspects of economic behavior—such as labor supply, saving, and investment—respond to economic incentives and, in particular, to incentives provided by the tax code. Although most economists agree with this idea in general, "supply-siders" went further, claiming that the incentive effects of tax policy are much larger than most economists have traditionally believed. In particular, supply-siders argued that the amount of labor supplied would increase substantially as a result of the tax reductions in ERTA.

What does the theory discussed in this section predict about the likely response of labor supply to ERTA? Along with the sharp reduction in marginal tax rates, the average tax rate also fell after 1981 (see the accompanying table). Between 1981 and 1984 Federal taxes fell from 21.1% of GDP to 19.2% of GDP, and the combined taxes collected by Federal, state, and local governments fell from 31.1% of GDP to 29.7% of GDP. The theory suggests that the reduction in marginal tax rates should have increased labor supply and that the decline in average tax rates should have reduced labor supply, leading to an ambiguous and probably small effect overall. Actually, the labor force participation rate (the proportion of adults who are working or actively searching for jobs) didn't change noticeably after 1981, so apparently any effect that ERTA had on labor supply was indeed small.

The 1986 Tax Reform Act also reduced the marginal tax rate on labor income but, unlike ERTA, it caused a small increase in the average tax rate. Between the passage of tax reform in 1986 and its full phase-in in 1988, the average Federal tax rate rose from 19.4% of GDP to 19.8% of GDP. The average combined tax rate of Federal, state, and local governments also rose, increasing from 30.2% to 30.5% of GDP. Because the 1986 Tax Reform Act reduced the marginal tax rate and raised the average tax rate slightly, the overall result should have been an increase in labor supply. There is some evidence that this

6. In terms of the discussion in Chapter 8, a change in the marginal tax rate with no change in the average tax rate has a pure substitution effect on labor supply.

7. For a description of ERTA, see the *Economic Report of the President,* February 1982.

8. However, because of a quirk in the tax law, some people with relatively high income, but not those with the highest incomes, faced a 33% marginal tax rate.

Average Tax Rates in the United States, 1981–1988

	Federal Taxes		Federal, State, and Local Taxes	
Year	Real Tax Revenue (Billions of 1987 Dollars)	Average Tax Rate (% of GDP)	Real Tax Revenue (Billions of 1987 Dollars)	Average Tax Rate (% of GDP)
1981	809.9	21.1	1193.8	31.1
1982	758.2	20.2	1146.2	30.5
1983	756.9	19.4	1165.6	29.9
1984	797.6	19.2	1234.7	29.7
1985	835.4	19.5	1289.2	30.1
1986	853.7	19.4	1332.1	30.2
1987	913.8	20.1	1405.2	31.0
1988	935.8	19.8	1436.4	30.5

Source: *Economic Report of the President,* 1993. Tax revenues from Table B-77, GDP from Table B-1 and GDP deflator from Table B-3.

increase in labor supply occurred. For example, after gradually declining since at least 1950, the labor force participation rate for men leveled off in 1988 and actually increased in 1989 for the first time in more than a decade.

Overall, the responses of labor supply to the revisions to the tax law in the 1980s are consistent with our analysis of the effects of average and marginal tax changes. However, contrary to the predictions of the supply-siders, the actual changes in labor supply were quite small. One study estimated that the Tax Reform Act of 1986 increased the labor supply of men by 0.9%, and the 1981 ERTA increased the labor supply of men by only 0.4%.[9]

Tax-Induced Distortions and Tax Rate Smoothing. Because taxes affect economic incentives, they change the pattern of economic behavior. If the invisible hand of free markets is working properly, the pattern of economic activity in the absence of taxes is the most efficient, so changes in behavior caused by taxes reduce economic welfare. Tax-induced deviations from efficient, free-market outcome are called **distortions.**

To illustrate the idea of a distortion, let's go back to the example of the worker whose before-tax real wage is $20. Because profit-maximizing employers demand labor up to the point that the marginal product of labor equals the real wage, the real output produced by an extra hour of the worker's labor (her marginal product) also is $20. Now suppose that the worker is willing to sacrifice leisure to work an extra hour if she receives at least $14 in additional real earnings. Because the value of what the worker can produce in an extra hour of labor exceeds the value that she places on an extra hour of leisure, her working the extra hour is economically efficient.

9. Jerry A. Hausman and James M. Poterba, "Household Behavior and the Tax Reform Act of 1986," *Journal of Economic Perspectives,* Summer 1987, pp. 101–119. Cited results are from p. 106.

In an economy without taxes this efficient outcome occurs, because the worker is willing to work the extra hour for the extra $20 in real wages. She would also be willing to work the extra hour if the marginal tax rate on earnings was 25%, because at a marginal tax rate of 25% her after-tax real wage is $15, which exceeds the $14 real wage minimum that she is willing to accept. However, if the marginal tax rate rises to 40%, so that the worker's after-tax wage falls to only $12, she would decide that it isn't worth her while to work the extra hour, even though for her to do so would have been economically efficient. The difference between the number of hours the worker would have worked had there been no tax on wages and the number of hours she actually works when there is a tax reflects the distorting effect of the tax. The higher the tax rate is, the greater the distortion is likely to be.

Because doing without taxes entirely isn't possible, the problem for fiscal policymakers is how to raise needed government revenues while keeping distortions relatively small. Because high tax rates are particularly costly in terms of economic efficiency, economists argue that keeping tax rates roughly constant at a moderate level is preferable to alternate periods of very low and very high tax rates. For example, if the government's spending plans require it to levy a tax rate that over a number of years averages 20%, most economists would advise the government *not* to set the tax rate at 30% half the time and 10% the other half. The reason is the large distortions that the 30% tax rate would cause in the years that it was effective. A better strategy is to hold the tax rate constant at 20%. A policy of maintaining stable tax rates so as to minimize distortions is called **tax rate smoothing.**

Has the Federal government had a policy of tax rate smoothing? Statistical studies typically have found that Federal tax rates are affected by political and other factors and hence aren't as smooth as is necessary to minimize distortions.[10] Nevertheless, the idea of tax smoothing is still useful. For example, what explains the U.S. government's huge deficit during World War II (Fig. 16.4)? The alternative to deficit financing of the war would have been a large wartime increase in tax rates, coupled with a drop in tax rates when the war was over. But high tax rates during the war would have distorted the economy when productive efficiency was especially important. By financing the war through borrowing, the government effectively spread the needed tax increase over a long period of time (as the debt was repaid) rather than raising current taxes by a large amount. This action is consistent with the idea of tax smoothing.

16.3 GOVERNMENT DEFICITS AND DEBT

The single number in the Federal government's budget that is the focus of most public debate is the size of the budget deficit. During the 1980s and early 1990s a series of unprecedentedly large (for peacetime) deficits led to a barrage of claims and counterclaims about the potential impact of big deficits on the economy. In the rest of this chapter we discuss the government budget deficit, the government debt, and their effects on the economy.

---

10. David Bizer and Steven Durlauf, "Testing the Positive Theory of Government Finance," *Journal of Monetary Economics*, August 1990, pp. 123–141.

The Political Environment

THE FEDERAL BUDGET PROCESS

Enacting the Federal government's budget is a long and complex process, involving both the executive and legislative branches. The budget process has three main phases: (1) development of a proposed budget and its presentation to Congress by the President; (2) congressional action on the budget; and (3) implementation of the budget, primarily by the executive branch.

The President usually submits the proposed budget to Congress eight or nine months before October 1, the beginning of the fiscal year. About nine months are required to formulate the budget, so this submission deadline implies that budget planning must begin a full year and a half before the beginning of the fiscal year to which the budget applies. The President is assisted in developing his budget by his staff, the Office of Management and Budget (OMB), the Treasury, the Council of Economic Advisers, and other members of the executive branch, all of whom gather information and requests for funds from the various government agencies.

After receiving the President's budget proposal, Congress usually modifies it extensively. Congressional consideration of the budget begins in the House of Representatives, where spending plans are first considered by the Appropriations Committee and proposals for raising revenue are considered by the Ways and Means Committee. After the various appropriations and tax bills are approved by the House, they are sent to the Senate, which conducts its own review. Differences between the House and Senate versions of the various bills are reconciled by a conference committee, consisting of members from both the House and Senate, and the reconciled legislation is returned to the full memberships of the House and Senate for approval. Finally, the appropriations and revenue bills are sent to the President for signature or veto.

When some of the appropriations bills are not completed by the beginning of the fiscal year—which has happened frequently in recent years—Congress passes a *continuing resolution* to allow the government to keep operating until the new budget is finalized.

Upon approval of the budget the process enters the third phase—the actual spending and collection of taxes. Overseeing this process is the responsibility of the President and the executive branch. The actual allocation of funds to the various government agencies is done by the director of the OMB. If more money is needed during the year, the President may request a supplementary appropriation from Congress.

Over the past two decades Congress has reformed the budget process several times, primarily to reduce the size of the budget deficit. In 1985 Congress adopted the Balanced Budget and Emergency Deficit Control Act (better known as the Gramm–Rudman–Hollings bill), which required a steadily decreasing deficit leading to a balanced budget in fiscal year 1991. The original legislation failed to achieve significant deficit reduction and has been revised several times. In the 1990 revision, limits were placed on various categories of government spending. According to the law, if spending in any category exceeds its limit, all spending items in that category will be automatically cut.

Sources: Office of Management and Budget, *The United States Budget in Brief,* and *Economic Report of the President,* February 1991, pp. 65–69.

The Growth of the Government Debt

There is an important distinction between the government budget deficit and the government debt (also called the national debt). The government budget *deficit* (a flow variable) is the difference between expenditures and tax revenues in any fiscal year. The **government debt** (a stock variable) is the total value of government bonds outstanding at any particular time. Because the excess of government expenditures over revenues equals the amount of new borrowing that the government must do—that is, the amount of new government debt that it must issue—any year's deficit (measured in dollar, or nominal, terms) equals the change in the debt in that year. We can express the relationship between government debt and the budget deficit by

$$\Delta B = \text{nominal government budget deficit,} \qquad (16.3)$$

where ΔB is the change in the nominal value (or face value) of government bonds outstanding.

In a period of persistently large budget deficits, such as that experienced recently by the United States, the nominal value of the government's debt will grow quickly. For example, between 1980 and 1992, Federal government debt outstanding more than quadrupled in nominal terms, from $906 billion in 1980 to $4062 billion in 1992.[11] Measured in terms of 1987 dollars, the (real) value of government debt outstanding in 1992 ($3360 billion) was two and two thirds times as large as in 1980 ($1264 billion).

Because countries with a high GDP have relatively more resources available to pay the principal and interest on the government's bonds, a useful measure of government indebtedness is the quantity of government debt outstanding divided by the GDP, or the *debt–GDP ratio.* Figure 16.6 shows the history of the debt–GDP ratio in the United States. The upper curve shows the debt–GDP ratio when the measure of total government debt outstanding includes both government bonds held by the public and government bonds held by government agencies and the Federal Reserve. The lower curve includes in the measure of debt outstanding only the government debt held by the public.

11. *Economic Report of the President,* January 1993, Table B–82.

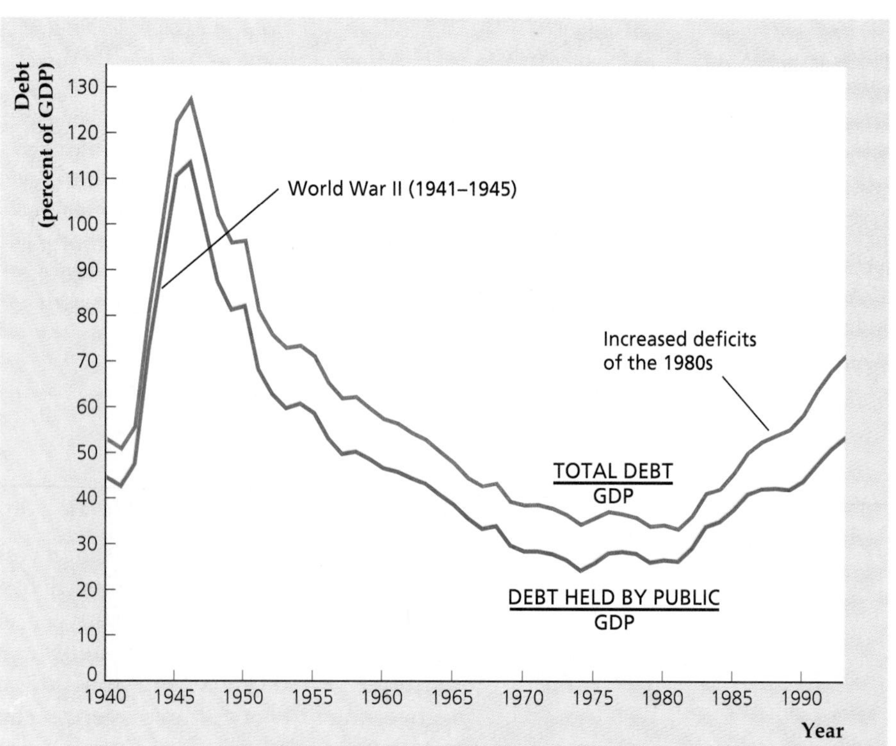

Figure 16.6
Ratio of Federal debt to GDP, 1939–1993
The upper curve shows the ratio of total government debt—including government bonds held by government agencies and the Federal Reserve—to GDP. The lower curve shows the ratio of government bonds held by the public to GDP. The debt–GDP ratio rose dramatically during World War II, fell steadily for the next thirty-five years, and then rose again from 1980 until the present.

Source: *Economic Report of the President,* 1993, Table B-76.

The most striking feature of Fig. 16.6 is the large increase in the debt–GDP ratio that occurred during World War II when the government sold bonds to finance the war effort. By the end of the war the debt–GDP ratio exceeded 1.0, implying that the value of government debt outstanding was greater than a year's GDP. Over the following thirty-five years the government steadily reduced its indebtedness relative to GDP. Beginning in about 1980, though, greater budget deficits caused the debt–GDP ratio to rise, which it did throughout the decade. Despite this increase, by 1990 the ratio of Federal debt to GDP was still less than half its size at the end of World War II.

We can describe changes in the debt–GDP ratio over time by the following formula (derived in Appendix 16.A at the end of the chapter):

$$\text{growth rate of debt–GDP ratio} = \frac{\text{primary deficit}}{B} + i - \text{growth rate of nominal GDP}, \qquad (16.4)$$

where B is the nominal quantity of government bonds outstanding and i is the nominal interest rate. Recall that the primary deficit is the total budget deficit less interest payments, measured here in nominal terms. Equation (16.4) emphasizes three factors that cause the debt–GDP ratio to rise quickly:

- a high primary deficit;
- a high interest rate, which increases the interest payments the government must make on its outstanding debt and thus increases the total budget deficit; and
- a slow rate of GDP growth.

Equation (16.4) helps account for the pattern of the debt–GDP ratio shown in Fig. 16.6. The sharp increase during World War II was the result of large primary deficits. In contrast, for the three and a half decades after World War II, the Federal government's primary deficit was small or even negative and interest rates were generally lower than GDP growth, so the debt–GDP ratio declined. The debt–GDP ratio increased during the 1980s and 1990s because the Federal primary deficit was relatively high and because interest rates exceeded GDP growth rates for much of the period. A factor that may reduce the U.S. debt–GDP ratio in the not-too-distant future is discussed in Box 16.1 on the next page.

The Burden of the Government Debt on Future Generations

People often express concern that the trillions of dollars of Federal government debt accumulated in recent years will impose a crushing financial burden on their children and grandchildren, who will someday be taxed to pay off these debts. (Box 16.2, on page 593, discusses the relative tax burdens borne by different generations.) In this view, high rates of government borrowing amount to "robbing the future" to pay for government spending that is too high or taxes that are too low in the present.

This conventional argument ignores the fact that most U.S. government bonds are owned by U.S. citizens. Therefore, although our descendants someday may face heavy taxes to pay the interest and principal of the government debt, these future taxpayers also will inherit the outstanding government bonds and thus will be the *recipients* of most of those interest and principal payments. To a substantial degree, we owe the government debt to ourselves,

BOX 16.1

The Social Security Surplus and the Federal Deficit

As the generation born in the years after World War II —the "baby boomers"—ages, the average age in the general U.S. population will also rise. In 1990 there were about twenty Americans over the age of 65 for every hundred people of working age (20–64 years). From 2010 to 2030, as the baby boomers retire, this ratio will double to about forty people over age 65 for every hundred people of working age. The prospect of so many retirees raises the question: How will the Social Security system be able to pay promised retirement benefits?

Traditionally, the Social Security system was *pay as you go;* that is, Social Security taxes collected from workers approximately equaled current benefits paid out to retirees *in each year.* However, under a pay-as-you-go system, the prospective bulge in the number of retirees in the twenty-first century would require very high taxes on future workers. To avoid this problem, in 1983 Congress changed the method of financing Social Security. Under the system now in effect, funds intended to pay retirement benefits in the twenty-first century are being accumulated in advance. Primarily by raising current Social Security taxes, the Social Security Amendment of 1983 provided for surpluses in the Social Security Trust Fund (the government account that keeps track of Social Security taxes and benefits) until several years after the turn of the twenty-first century. The planned surpluses are large: According to the Congressional Budget Office, Social Security taxes will exceed benefits paid out by $88 billion in fiscal year 1998.*

Social Security taxes collected and benefits paid in each year are both counted as part of the current Federal government budget. Hence the prospective Social Security surpluses will have a large impact on the overall Federal deficit. Because of the growing Social Security surpluses, over the next two decades the Federal budget deficit will be significantly lower than it otherwise would have been and (according to some projections) may even become a budget surplus.

Do the large projected Social Security surpluses solve the problem of high Federal budget deficits? No, not really. A problem with the standard calculation of the deficit (which counts Social Security taxes and benefits as part of the current budget) is that it ignores the Federal government's obligation to pay Social Security benefits to the retiring baby boomers in the future. When the baby boomers retire, the Social Security system will pay benefits to retirees that far exceed the taxes collected from workers at that time. Thus the Social Security system itself will run large deficits during the middle third of the next century. If the Social Security surpluses over the next several decades are used simply to offset deficits in the rest of the Federal budget, when the time comes to pay the baby boomers' benefits, no resources will have been accumulated and a new fiscal crisis will occur.

---

* *The Economic and Budget Outlook: Fiscal Years 1992–98,* Congressional Budget Office, January 1991, Table 2-1, p. 28.

so the debt isn't a burden in the same sense that it would be if it were owed entirely to outsiders.

Although the popular view of the burden of the government debt is faulty, economists have pointed out several ways in which the government debt can become a burden on future generations. First, if tax rates have to be raised substantially in the future to pay off the debt, the resulting distortions could cause the economy to function less efficiently and impose costs on future generations.

Second, most people hold small amounts of government bonds or no government bonds at all (except perhaps indirectly, as through pension funds). In the future people who hold few or no bonds may have to pay higher taxes to pay off the government debt than they receive in interest and principal payments; people holding large quantities of bonds may receive more in interest and principal than they pay in increased taxes. Bondholders are richer on average than nonbondholders, so the need to service the government debt might lead to a transfer of resources from the relatively poor to the relatively rich. However, this transfer could be offset by other tax and transfer policies—for example, by raising taxes on high-income people.

The third argument is probably the most significant: Many economists claim that government deficits reduce national saving; that is, when the government runs a deficit, the economy accumulates less domestic capital and fewer foreign assets than it would have if the deficit had been lower. If this argument is correct, deficits will lower the standard of living for our children and grandchildren, both because they will inherit a smaller capital stock and because they will have to pay more interest to (or receive less interest from) foreigners than they otherwise would have. This reduction in the future standard of living would constitute a true burden of the government debt.

Crucial to this argument, however, is the idea that government budget deficits reduce national saving. As we have mentioned at several points in this book (notably in Chapter 4), the question of whether budget deficits affect national saving is highly controversial. We devote most of the rest of this section to further discussion of this issue.

Budget Deficits and National Saving: Ricardian Equivalence Revisited

Under what circumstances will an increased government budget deficit cause national saving to fall? Virtually all economists agree that an increase in the deficit caused by a rise in government purchases—say, to fight a war—reduces national saving and imposes a real burden on the economy. However, whether a deficit caused by a cut in current taxes or an increase in current transfers reduces national saving is much less clear. Recall that advocates of Ricardian equivalence argue that tax cuts or increases in transfers will not affect national saving, whereas its opponents disagree.

Ricardian Equivalence: An Example. To illustrate Ricardian equivalence let's suppose that, holding its current and planned future purchases constant, the government cuts this year's taxes by \$100 per person. (Assuming that the tax cut is a lump sum allows us to ignore incentive effects.) What impact will this reduction in taxes have on national saving? In answering this question, we first recall the definition of national saving (Eq. 2.8):

$$S = Y - C - G. \tag{16.5}$$

Equation (16.5) states that national saving S equals output Y less consumption C and government purchases G.[12] If we assume that government purchases G are constant and that output Y is fixed at its full-employment level, we know from Eq. (16.5) that the tax cut will reduce national saving S only if it causes consumption C to rise. Advocates of Ricardian equivalence assert that, if current and planned future government purchases are unchanged, a tax cut will *not* affect consumption and thus won't affect national saving.

Why wouldn't a tax cut that raises after-tax incomes cause people to consume more? The answer is that—if current and planned future government purchases don't change—a tax cut today must be accompanied by an offsetting

12. We assume that net factor payments from abroad, NFP, are zero.

increase in expected future taxes. To see why, note that if current taxes are reduced by \$100 per person without any change in government purchases, the government must borrow an additional \$100 per person by selling bonds. Suppose that the bonds are one-year bonds that pay a real interest rate r. In the following year, when the government repays the principal (\$100 per person) and interest (\$100 $\times$ r per person) on the bonds, it will have to collect an additional \$100(1 + r) per person in taxes. Thus when the public learns of the current tax cut of \$100 per person, they should also expect their taxes to increase by \$100(1 + r) per person next year.[13]

Because the current tax cut is balanced by an increase in expected future taxes, it doesn't make taxpayers any better off in the long run despite raising their current after-tax incomes. Indeed, after the tax cut, *taxpayers' abilities to consume today and in the future are the same as they were originally.*[14] That is, if no one consumes more in response to the tax cut—so that each person saves the entire \$100 increase in after-tax income—in the following year the \$100 per person of additional saving will grow to \$100(1 + r) per person. This additional \$100(1 + r) per person is precisely the amount needed to pay the extra taxes that will be levied in the future, leaving people able to consume as much in the future as they had originally planned. Because people aren't made better off by the tax cut (which must be coupled with a future tax increase), they have no reason to consume more today. Thus national saving should be unaffected by the tax cut, as supporters of Ricardian equivalence claim.

Ricardian Equivalence Across Generations. The argument for Ricardian equivalence rests on the assumption that current government borrowing will be repaid within the lifetimes of people who are alive today. In other words, any tax cuts received today are offset by the higher taxes that people must pay later. But what if some of the debt the government is accumulating will be repaid not by the people who receive the tax cut but by their children or grandchildren? In that case, wouldn't people react to a tax cut by consuming more?

Harvard economist Robert Barro[15] has shown that, in theory, Ricardian equivalence may still apply even if the current generation receives the tax cut and future generations bear the burden of repaying the government's debt. To state Barro's argument in its simplest form, let's imagine an economy in which every generation has the same number of people and suppose that the current generation receives a tax cut of \$100 per person. With government purchases held constant, this tax cut increases the government's borrowing and outstanding debt by \$100 per person. However, people currently alive are not taxed to repay this debt; instead, this obligation is deferred until the next generation. To repay the government's increased debt, the next generation's taxes (in real terms) will be raised by \$100(1 + R) per person, where 1 + R is the real value of a dollar borrowed today at the time the debt is repaid.[16]

---

13. The government might put the tax increase off for two, three, or more years. Nevertheless, the general conclusion that the current tax cut must be offset by future tax increases would be unchanged.

14. Section 8.2 discusses this point in more detail.

15. "Are Government Bonds Net Wealth?" *Journal of Political Economy*, November/December 1974, pp. 1095–1117.

16. For example, if the debt is to be repaid in thirty years and r is the one-year real interest rate, then $(1 + R) = (1 + r)^{30}$.

BOX 16.2

Generational Accounts

How are the costs and benefits of a government program, such as Social Security, distributed among the population? We could try to answer this question by noting that in a particular year (say, 1994) Social Security benefits were received primarily by older people while younger people paid most of the taxes used to fund those benefits. However, to conclude that Social Security helps old people at the expense of young people fails to recognize that the currently retired paid Social Security taxes when they were young, and that the people who are paying Social Security taxes today will someday receive benefits. A better way to measure how the costs and benefits of Social Security are distributed would be to compare taxes paid and benefits received by various individuals over their *entire lifetimes.* For example, by projecting the lifetime pattern of Social Security taxes and benefits of a worker who is currently thirty years old, we could determine whether, overall, Social Security is a "good deal" for that worker, whereas looking at only one year wouldn't allow us to conclude anything about whether the worker should be satisfied to be part of the Social Security system.

The same lifetime perspective can be applied to all government taxes and transfers combined to see how any group of people—members of a particular generation, for example—fares in terms of benefits and burdens. Alan Auerbach of the University of Pennsylvania, Jagadeesh Gokhale of the Federal Reserve Bank of Cleveland, and Laurence Kotlikoff* of Boston University have calculated the taxes paid and transfers received as a fraction of lifetime income for each generation of Americans, starting with people born in 1900 and including projections of taxes and transfers for people who will be born in the future.

Some of their results are summarized in the accompanying table, which shows lifetime gross tax rates, transfer rates, and net tax rates for various generations. For each generation, the gross tax rate is lifetime taxes paid (Federal, state, and local) as a percentage of lifetime income, and the transfer rate is lifetime transfers received (such as Social Security and Medicare) as a percentage of lifetime income. The net tax rate, or the gross tax rate minus the transfer rate, is a measure of the net burden of government borne by each generation. The net tax rate grew with each generation until the generation born in 1980, implying that, among those alive today, older people have borne a smaller overall burden than younger people have borne or can expect to bear.

The most striking number in the table is the projected 71.1% lifetime net tax rate of U.S. citizens who are yet unborn. This figure is based on numerous projections about the future of the economy and is necessarily speculative. What you should conclude from this calculation is that *without substantial changes in current fiscal policies* future generations will pay significantly higher taxes and receive fewer transfers than generations alive today. However, shifts in fiscal policy could avoid this outcome. For example, Auerbach, Gokhale, and Kotlikoff calculate that if real, per-person expenditures on Medicare, Medicaid, and several other programs could be held at current levels, the net tax rate faced by future generations would fall to 41.3%.

* "Generational Accounts and Lifetime Tax Rates, 1900–1991," in Federal Reserve Bank of Cleveland, *Economic Review,* First Quarter 1993, pp. 2–13.

Lifetime Tax and Transfer Rates by Generation (percent)

Generation's Year of Birth	Gross Tax Rate	Transfer Rate	Net Tax Rate
1900	24.8	3.3	21.5
1910	29.8	5.2	24.7
1920	32.5	6.2	26.3
1930	35.3	7.2	28.1
1940	37.3	8.0	29.3
1950	39.9	9.3	30.6
1960	42.3	10.2	32.1
1970	44.5	11.3	33.2
1980	45.5	11.7	33.8
1990	45.7	12.2	33.6
1991	45.8	12.2	33.5
Future generations	Not available		71.1

Source: Alan Auerbach, Jagadeesh Gokhale, and Laurence Kotlikoff, "Generational Accounts and Lifetime Tax Rates, 1900–1991," in Federal Reserve Bank of Cleveland, *Economic Review,* First Quarter 1993, 2–13, Table 5.

Seemingly, the current generation of people, who receive the tax cut, should increase their consumption because the reduction in their taxes isn't expected to be balanced by an increase in taxes during their lifetimes. However, Barro argued that people in the current generation shouldn't increase their consumption in response to a tax cut if they care about the well-being of the next generation. Of course, people do care about the well-being of their children, as is reflected in part in the economic resources devoted to children, including funds spent on children's health and education, gifts, and inheritances.

How does the concern of this generation for the next affect the response of people to a tax cut? A member of the current generation who receives a tax cut—call him Joe—might be inclined to increase his own consumption, all else being equal. But, Barro argues, Joe should realize that, for each dollar of tax cut he receives today, his son Joe Junior will have to pay $1 + R$ dollars of extra taxes in the future. Can Joe do anything on his own to help out Joe Junior? The answer is yes. Suppose that, instead of consuming his \$100 tax cut, Joe saves the \$100 and uses the extra savings to increase Joe Junior's inheritance. By the time the next generation is required to pay the government debt, Joe Junior's extra inheritance plus accumulated interest will be $\$100(1 + R)$, or just enough to cover the increase in Joe Junior's taxes. Thus, by saving his tax cut and adding these savings to his planned bequest, Joe can keep both his own consumption and Joe Junior's consumption the same as they would have been if the tax cut had never occurred.

Furthermore, Barro points out, Joe *should* save all his tax cut for Joe Junior's benefit. Why? If Joe consumes even part of his tax cut, he won't leave enough extra inheritance to allow Joe Junior to pay the expected increase in his taxes, and so Joe Junior will have to consume less than he could have if there had been no tax cut for Joe. But if Joe wanted to increase his own consumption at Joe Junior's expense, he could have done so without changes in the tax laws—for example, by contributing less to Joe Junior's college tuition payments or by planning to leave a smaller inheritance. That Joe didn't take these actions shows that he was satisfied with the division of consumption between himself and Joe Junior that he had planned before the tax cut was enacted; there is no reason that the tax cut should cause this original consumption plan to change. Therefore if Joe and other members of the current generation don't consume more in response to a tax cut, Ricardian equivalence should hold even when debt repayment is deferred to the next generation.

This analysis can be extended to allow for multiple generations and in other ways. These extensions don't change the main point, which is that, if taxpayers understand that they are ultimately responsible for the government's debt, they shouldn't change their consumption in response to changes in taxes or transfers that are unaccompanied by changes in planned government purchases. As a result, deficits created by tax cuts shouldn't reduce national saving and therefore shouldn't burden future generations.

Departures from Ricardian Equivalence

The arguments for Ricardian equivalence are logically sound, and this idea has greatly influenced economists' thinking about deficits. Although twenty-five years ago most economists would have taken for granted that a tax cut would substantially increase consumption, today there is much less agreement a this claim. Although Ricardian equivalence seemed to fail spectacularly in 1980s in the United States—when high government budget deficits were accompanied by extremely low rates of national saving—data covering longer periods of time suggest little relation between budget deficits and national saving rates in the United States. In some other countries, such as Canada and Israel, Ricardian equivalence seems to have worked quite well at times.[17]

Our judgment is that tax cuts that lead to increased government borrowing probably affect consumption and national saving, although the effect may be small. We base this conclusion both on the experience of the United States during the 1980s and on the fact that there are some theoretical reasons to expect Ricardian equivalence not to hold exactly. The main arguments against Ricardian equivalence are the possible existence of borrowing constraints, consumers' shortsightedness, the failure of some people to leave bequests, and the non-lump-sum nature of most tax changes.

1. *Borrowing constraints.* Many people would be willing to consume more if they could find lenders who would extend them credit. However, consumers often face limits, known as *borrowing constraints,*[18] on the amounts that they can borrow. A person who wants to consume more, but who is unable to borrow to do so, will be eager to take advantage of a tax cut to increase consumption. Thus the existence of borrowing constraints may cause Ricardian equivalence to fail.

2. *Shortsightedness.* In the view of some economists, many people are shortsighted and don't understand that as taxpayers they are ultimately responsible for the government's debt. For example, some people may determine their consumption by simple "rules of thumb," such as the rule that a family should spend fixed percentages of its current after-tax income on food, clothing, housing, and so on, without regard for how its income is likely to change in the future. If people are shortsighted, they may respond to a tax cut by consuming more, contrary to the prediction of Ricardian equivalence. However, Ricardians could reply that ultra-sophisticated analyses of fiscal policy by consumers aren't necessary for Ricardian equivalence to be approximately correct. For example, if people know generally that big government deficits mean future problems for the economy (without knowing exactly why), they may be reluctant to spend from a tax cut that causes the deficit to balloon, consistent with the Ricardian prediction.

3. *Failure to leave bequests.* If people don't leave bequests, perhaps because they don't care or think about the long-run economic welfare of their children, they will increase their consumption if their taxes are cut, and Ricardian equivalence won't hold. Some people may not leave bequests because they

17. For surveys of the evidence by a supporter and an opponent of Ricardian equivalence, respectively, see Robert Barro, "The Ricardian Approach to Budget Deficits," *Journal of Economic Perspectives,* Spring 1989, pp. 37–54; and B. Douglas Bernheim, "Ricardian Equivalence: An Evaluation of Theory and Evidence," in Stanley Fischer, ed., NBER *Macroeconomics Annual,* Cambridge, Mass.: M.I.T. Press, 1987.

18. Section 8.2 discussed the effect of borrowing constraints on consumption and their implications for Ricardian equivalence.

expect their children to be richer than they are and thus not need any bequest. If people continue to hold this belief after they receive a tax cut, they will increase their consumption and again Ricardian equivalence will fail.

4. *Non-lump-sum taxes.* In theory, Ricardian equivalence holds only for lump-sum tax changes, with each person's change in taxes being a fixed amount that doesn't depend on the person's economic decisions, such as how much to work or save. As we discussed in Section 16.2, when taxes are not lump-sum, the level and timing of taxes will affect incentives and thus economic behavior. Thus non-lump-sum tax cuts will have real effects on the economy, in contrast to the simple Ricardian view.

We emphasize, though, that with non-lump-sum taxes, the incentive effects of a tax cut on consumption and saving behavior will depend heavily on the tax structure and on which taxes are cut. For example, a temporary cut in sales taxes would likely stimulate consumption, but a reduction in the tax rate on interest earned on savings accounts might increase saving. Thus we cannot always conclude that, just because taxes aren't lump-sum, a tax cut will increase consumption. That conclusion has to rest primarily on the other three arguments against Ricardian equivalence that we presented.

A Balanced-Budget Amendment? The Policy Debate

The large and persistent Federal budget deficits of recent years have convinced many observers that the President and Congress will not willingly make the tough political decisions—the spending cuts and tax increases—needed to reduce the deficit. To force action on the deficit, numerous politicians and others advocate an amendment to the U.S. Constitution that would require a balanced Federal budget, except perhaps in extreme circumstances, as when the country is at war. Several such amendments have been proposed in Congress, and legislatures in more than thirty states have passed resolutions calling for a Constitutional Convention for the purpose of discussing a balanced-budget amendment.

As demonstrated by the debate over Ricardian equivalence, economists don't agree on whether government budget deficits represent a serious threat to the economy. However, even accepting the premise that large deficits are harmful and should be reduced, two questions remain: (1) Is it desirable to have a balanced budget in *every year*? and (2) will a balanced-budget amendment actually succeed in eliminating the budget deficit?

In answering the first question, Keynesians and classicals both point out problems with having a balanced budget every year. Keynesians argue that a balanced budget every year would undo the beneficial effects of automatic stabilizers, which increase government expenditures and reduce taxes during a recession. Because they tend to create deficits during recessions, automatic stabilizers would have to be eliminated. Otherwise, new fiscal measures to offset their effects on the budget would have to be introduced in order to balance the budget every year. Keynesians also worry that requiring a balanced budget every year would eliminate any flexibility that the President and Congress have to use fiscal policy actively to fight recessions.

Classical economists also object to a balanced-budget amendment, but on different grounds. Many classicals believe that a balanced-budget amendment would divert attention from a more valid issue: the share of the economy's total resources used by the government. Because they believe that the true burden of the government on the economy is reflected in the government's total use of resources and not in the deficit itself, these economists prefer an amendment limiting the ratio of government spending to GDP.

Opponents of the balanced-budget amendment also point out that tax rates should be smooth over time to minimize distortions in the economy. Under a balanced-budget amendment tax rates would have to rise and fall to offset temporary increases and declines in government spending. Year-to-year fluctuations in tax rates would increase the average amount of tax-induced distortion in the economy.

In responding to the second question, economists of all persuasions express doubts that such an amendment could be enforced. One problem is that, because tax collections and spending under some programs can't be perfectly predicted in advance, the government would have to balance its budget only on an expected or projected basis. To avoid tax increases or cuts in spending while satisfying the requirement of a *projected* balanced budget, policymakers might use optimistic economic forecasts (implying, for example, that tax collections will be high) to make the projected deficit look smaller than it might reasonably be expected to be.

Experience with similar types of budgetary restrictions isn't encouraging for advocates of a balanced-budget amendment. For example, the 1985 Balanced Budget and Emergency Deficit Control Act (also known as the Gramm–Rudman–Hollings bill) set legal limits on the Federal budget deficit beginning in fiscal year 1986 (October 1, 1985–September 30, 1986) and required a balanced budget in fiscal year 1991. The actual Federal budget deficit in fiscal year 1991 was $321.7 billion. At a different level of government, many individual states have constitutional restrictions requiring balanced budgets, but some have run large deficits nevertheless. For example, when Michigan rewrote its state constitution in 1963, it included a requirement that the state budget be balanced. However, between 1975 and 1982 Michigan ran budget deficits that increased its debt by $850 million.[19]

Because of these problems with the balanced-budget amendment, both in principle and in practice, most economists do not consider a balanced-budget amendment to be the answer to large budget deficits. However, in the absence of any good alternative, some economists might consider this measure preferable to taking no action at all to arrest the growth of government debt.

16.4 DEFICITS AND INFLATION

In this final section of the chapter we discuss one more concern that has been expressed about government budget deficits: that deficits are inflationary. We show that the principal link between deficits and inflation is that in some

19. Daniel B. Suits and Ronald C. Fisher, "A Balanced Budget Constitutional Amendment: Economic Complexities and Uncertainties," *National Tax Journal*, December 1985, pp. 467–477.

circumstances deficits lead to higher rates of growth in the money supply and that high rates of money growth in turn cause inflation.

The Deficit and the Money Supply

Inflation—a rising price level—results when aggregate demand increases more quickly than aggregate supply. In terms of the *AD–AS* framework, suppose that the long-run aggregate supply curve (which reflects the productive capacity of the economy) is fixed. Then for the price level to rise, the aggregate demand curve must rise over time.

Both the classical and Keynesian models of the economy imply that deficits can cause aggregate demand to rise more quickly than aggregate supply, leading to an increase in the price level. In both models a deficit owing to increased government purchases reduces desired national saving, shifting the *IS* curve upward and causing aggregate demand to rise. This increase in aggregate demand causes the price level to rise.[20] If we assume (as Keynesians usually do) that Ricardian equivalence doesn't hold, a budget deficit resulting from a cut in taxes or an increase in transfers also reduces desired national saving, increases aggregate demand, and raises the price level. Thus deficits resulting from expansionary fiscal policies (increased spending or reduced taxes) will be associated with inflation.

However, an increase in government purchases or a cut in taxes causes only a one-time increase in aggregate demand. Therefore, although we expect expansionary fiscal policies to lead to a one-time increase in the price level (that is, a temporary burst in inflation), we don't expect an increase in government purchases or a cut in taxes to cause a *sustained* increase in inflation. In general, the only factor that can sustain an increase in aggregate demand, leading to continuing inflation, is sustained growth in the money supply. Indeed, high rates of inflation are almost invariably linked to high rates of national money growth (Chapter 7). The key question therefore is: Can government budget deficits lead to ongoing increases in the money supply?

The answer is yes. The link is the printing of money to finance government spending when the government cannot (or does not want to) finance all of its spending by taxes or borrowing from the public. In the extreme case, imagine a government that wants to spend \$10 billion (say, on submarines) but has no ability to tax or borrow from the public. One option is for this government to print \$10 billion worth of currency and use this currency to pay for the submarines. The revenue that a government raises by printing money is called **seignorage.** Any government with the authority to issue money can use seignorage; governments that do not have the authority to issue money, such as state governments in the United States, can't use seignorage.

Actually, governments that want to finance their deficits through seignorage don't simply print new currency but use an indirect procedure. First, the Treasury authorizes government borrowing equal to the amount of the budget deficit (\$10 billion in our example), and a corresponding quantity of new government bonds are printed and sold. Thus the deficit still equals the change in

20. The classical analysis predicts that an increase in government purchases causes aggregate supply to rise also, but we have assumed that the supply effect is smaller than the demand effect.

the outstanding government debt (Eq. 16.3). However, the new government bonds aren't sold to the public. Instead, the Treasury asks (or requires) the central bank to purchase the \$10 billion in new bonds. The central bank pays for its purchases of new bonds by printing \$10 billion in new currency,[21] which it gives to the Treasury in exchange for the bonds. This newly issued currency enters general circulation when the government spends it on its various outlays (the submarines). Note that the purchase of bonds by the central bank increases the monetary base by the amount of the purchase (see Chapter 15), as when the central bank purchases government bonds on the open market.

The precise relationship between the size of the deficit and the increase in the monetary base is

$$\text{deficit} = \Delta B = \Delta B^p + \Delta B^{cb} = \Delta B^p + \Delta BASE. \tag{16.6}$$

Equation (16.6) states that the (nominal) government budget deficit equals the total increase in (nominal) government debt outstanding, ΔB, which can be broken into additional government debt held by the public, ΔB^p, and by the central bank, ΔB^{cb}. The increase in government debt held by the central bank in turn equals the increase in the monetary base, $\Delta BASE$. The increase in the monetary base equals the amount of seignorage collected by the government.

The final link between the budget deficit and the money supply has to do with the relationship between the money supply and the monetary base. In general, the increase in the money supply M equals the money multiplier times the increase in the monetary base (Eq. 15.8). In an all-currency economy the money supply and the monetary base are the same and the money multiplier is 1. Nothing significant in this discussion depends on the value of the money multiplier, so for simplicity we focus on an all-currency economy, in which the change in the money supply equals the change in the monetary base. Based on this assumption, Eq. (16.6) implies that

$$\text{deficit} = \Delta B = \Delta B^p + \Delta B^{cb} = \Delta B^p + \Delta M, \tag{16.7}$$

where $\Delta BASE = \Delta M$.

Why would governments use seignorage to finance their deficits, knowing that continued money creation ultimately leads to higher inflation? Under normal conditions developed countries rarely use seignorage. For example, in recent years the monetary base in the United States has typically increased about \$20 billion per year, which is less than 10% of the Federal budget deficit and about 1.5% of Federal government outlays. Heavy reliance on seignorage usually occurs in war-torn or developing countries, in which military or social conditions dictate levels of government spending well above what the country can raise in taxes or borrow from the public.

Real Seignorage Collection and Inflation

The amount of real revenue that the government collects from seignorage is closely related to the inflation rate. To examine this link let's consider an all-currency economy in which real output and the real interest rate are fixed and the rates of money growth and inflation are constant. In such an economy the

21. The new money created by the central bank could also be in the form of deposits at the central bank; the ultimate effect is the same.

real quantity of money demanded is constant[22] and hence, in equilibrium, the real money supply must also be constant. Because the real money supply M/P doesn't change, the growth rate of the nominal money supply $\Delta M/M$ must equal the growth rate of the price level, or the rate of inflation π:

$$\pi = \frac{\Delta M}{M}. \tag{16.8}$$

Equation (16.8) expresses the close link between an economy's inflation rate and money growth rate.

How much seignorage is the government collecting in this economy? The *nominal* value of seignorage in any period is the increase in the amount of money in circulation ΔM. Multiplying both sides of Eq. (16.8) by M and rearranging gives an equation for the nominal value of seignorage:

$$\Delta M = \pi M. \tag{16.9}$$

Real seignorage revenue, R, is the real value of the newly created money, which equals nominal seignorage revenue ΔM divided by the price level P. Dividing both sides of Eq. (16.9) by the price level P gives

$$R = \frac{\Delta M}{P} = \pi \frac{M}{P}. \tag{16.10}$$

Equation (16.10) states that the government's real seignorage revenue R equals the inflation rate π times the real money supply M/P.

Equation (16.10) illustrates why economists sometimes call seignorage the **inflation tax.** In general, for any type of tax, tax revenue equals the tax rate multiplied by the tax base (whatever is being taxed). In the case of the inflation tax the tax base is the real money supply and the tax rate is the rate of inflation. Multiplying the tax base (the real money supply) by the tax rate (the rate of inflation) gives the total inflation tax revenue.

How does the government collect the inflation tax and who pays this tax? The government collects the inflation tax by printing money (or by having the central bank issue new money) and using the newly created money to purchase goods and services. The inflation tax is paid by any member of the public who holds money, because inflation erodes the purchasing power of money. For example, when the inflation rate is 10% per year, a person who holds currency for a year loses 10% of the purchasing power of that money and thus effectively pays a 10% tax on the real money holdings.

Suppose that a government finds that the seignorage being collected doesn't cover its spending and begins to increase the money supply faster. Will this increase in the money growth rate cause the real seignorage collected by the government to rise? Somewhat surprisingly, it may not. As Eq. (16.10) shows, the real seignorage collected by the government is the product of two terms—the rate of inflation (the tax rate) and the real money supply (the tax base). By raising the money growth rate, the government can increase the inflation rate. However, at a constant real interest rate, a higher rate of inflation will raise the

22. Real money demand depends on real output and the nominal interest rate (we assume that the interest rate paid on money is fixed). Output is constant, and because the real interest rate and the inflation rate are constant, the nominal interest rate also is constant. Thus the real quantity of money demanded is constant.

nominal interest rate, causing people to reduce the real quantity of money held. Thus whether real seignorage revenue increases when the money growth rate increases depends on whether the rise in inflation π outweighs the decline in real money holdings M/P.

This point is illustrated by Fig. 16.7, which shows the determination of real seignorage revenue at an assumed constant real interest rate of 3%. The real

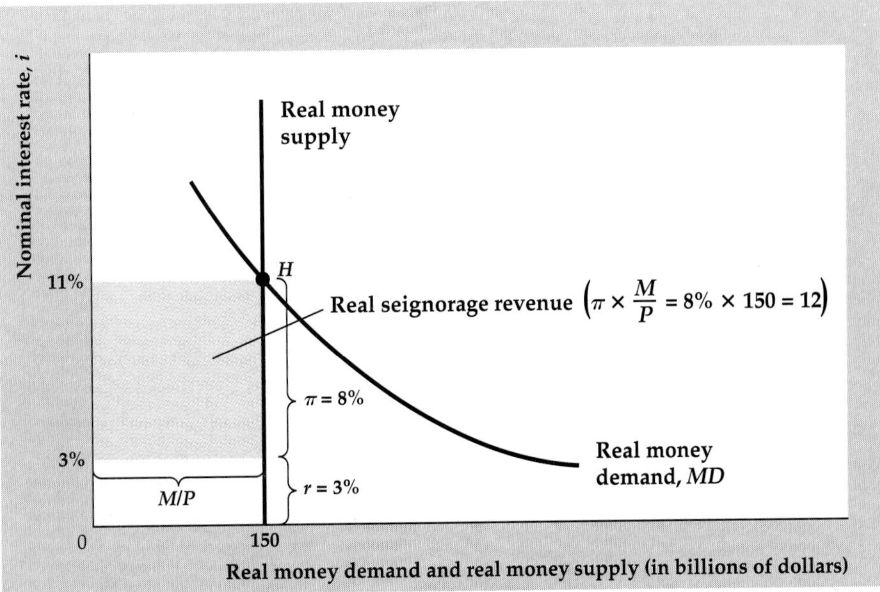

(a) Determination of real seignorage revenue for $\pi = 8\%$

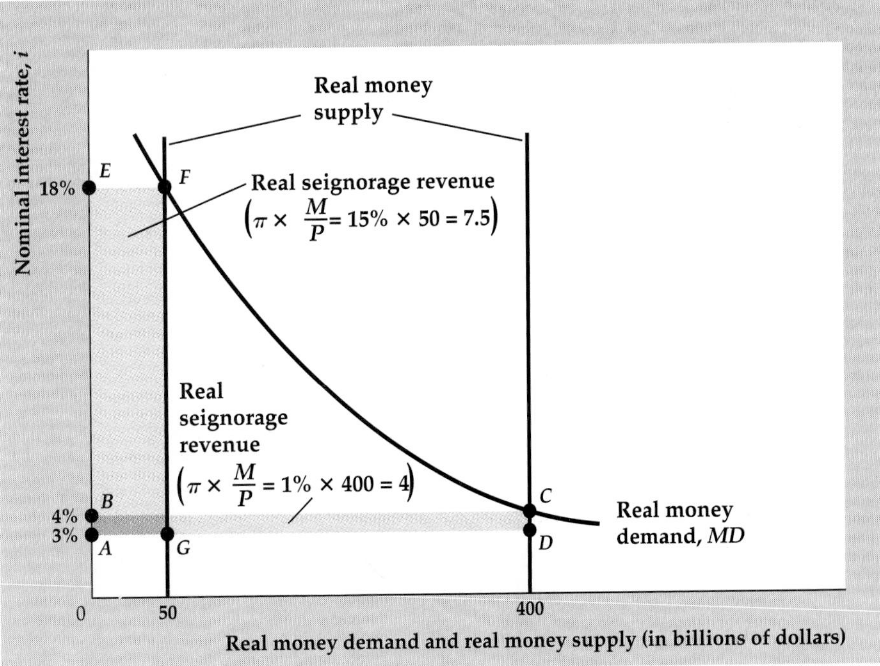

(b) Determination of real seignorage revenue for $\pi = 1\%$ and $\pi = 15\%$

Figure 16.7
The determination of real seignorage revenue
(a) The downward-sloping curve *MD* is the money demand function for any level of real income. The real interest rate is assumed to be 3%. When the rate of inflation is 8%, the nominal interest rate is 11%, and the real quantity of money held by the public is $150 billion (point *H*). Real seignorage revenue collected by the government, represented by the area of the shaded rectangle, equals the rate of inflation (8%) times the real money stock ($150 billion), or $12 billion.
(b) The money demand function *MD* is the same as in (a), and the real interest rate remains at 3%. When the inflation rate is 1%, the nominal interest rate is 4%, and the real quantity of money held by the public is $400 billion. In this case real seignorage revenue equals the area of the rectangle, *ABCD*, or $4 billion. When the rate of inflation is 15%, the nominal interest rate is 18%, and the real money stock held by the public is $50 billion. Real seignorage revenue in this case equals the area of the rectangle *AEFG*, or $7.5 billion.

quantity of money is measured along the horizontal axes, and the nominal interest rate is measured along the vertical axes. The downward-sloping *MD* curves show the real demand for money; they slope downward because an increase in the nominal interest rate reduces the real quantity of money demanded.

In Fig. 16.7(a) the actual and expected rate of inflation is 8%, so that (for a real interest rate of 3%) the nominal interest rate is 11%. When the nominal interest rate is 11%, the real quantity of money that people are willing to hold is $150 billion (point *H*). Using Eq. (16.10), we find that the real value of seignorage revenue is 0.08($150 billion), or $12 billion. Real seignorage revenue is represented graphically by the area of the shaded rectangle. The rectangle's height equals the inflation rate (8%) and the rectangle's width equals the real quantity of money held by the public ($150 billion).

Figure 16.7(b) shows the real amount of seignorage revenue at two different inflation rates. The real interest rate (3%) and the money demand curve in Fig. 16.7(b) are identical to those in Fig. 16.7(a). When the rate of inflation is 1% per year, the nominal interest rate is 4%, and the real quantity of money that the public holds is $400 billion. Real seignorage revenue is 0.01($400 billion) = $4 billion, or the area of rectangle *ABCD*. Alternatively, when the rate of inflation is 15% per year, the nominal interest rate is 18%, and the real value of the public's money holdings is $50 billion. Real seignorage revenue in this case is $7.5 billion, or the area of rectangle *AEFG*.

Comparing Fig. 16.7(a) and Fig. 16.7(b) reveals that real seignorage revenue is higher when inflation is 8% per year than when inflation is either 1% per year or 15% per year. Figure 16.8 shows the relationship between the inflation rate and seignorage revenue. At low inflation rates an increase in the inflation rate increases real seignorage revenue. However, at high inflation rates an increase in inflation reduces real seignorage revenue. In Fig. 16.8 the

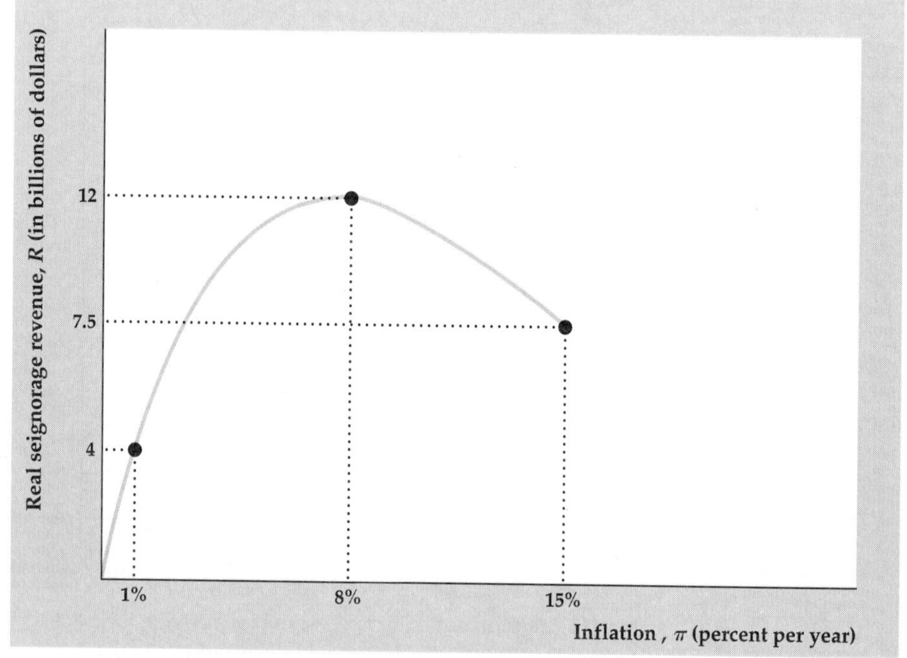

Figure 16.8
The relation of real seignorage revenue to the rate of inflation
Continuing the example of Fig. 16.7, this figure shows the relation of real seignorage revenue R, measured on the vertical axis, to the rate of inflation π, measured on the horizontal axis. From Fig. 16.7(a), when inflation is 8% per year, real seignorage revenue is $12 billion. From Fig. 16.7(b), real seignorage is $4 billion when inflation is 1% and $7.5 billion when inflation is 15%. At low rates of inflation, an increase in inflation increases seignorage revenue. At high rates of inflation, increased inflation can cause seignorage revenue to fall. In this example the maximum amount of seignorage revenue the government can obtain is $12 billion, which occurs when the inflation rate is 8%.

maximum possible real seignorage revenue is \$12 billion, which is achieved at the intermediate level of inflation of 8% per year.

What happens if the government tries to raise more seignorage revenue than the maximum possible amount? If it does so, inflation will rise but the real value of the government's seignorage will fall as real money holdings fall. If the government continues to increase the rate of money creation, the economy will experience a high rate of inflation or even hyperinflation. Inflation will continue until the government reduces the rate of money creation either by balancing its budget or by finding some other way to finance its spending.

In some hyperinflations, governments desperate for revenue raise the rate of money creation well above the level that maximizes real seignorage. For example, in the extreme hyperinflation that hit Germany after World War I, rapid money creation drove the rate of inflation to 322% *per month*. In contrast, in his classic study of the German hyperinflation, Philip Cagan[23] of Columbia University calculated that the constant rate of inflation that would have maximized the German government's real seignorage revenue was "only" 20% per month.

23. "The Monetary Dynamics of Hyperinflation," in Milton Friedman, ed., *Studies in the Quantity Theory of Money*, Chicago: University of Chicago Press, 1956.

CHAPTER SUMMARY

1. Government outlays are government purchases of goods and services, transfers, and net interest. To pay for them, the government collects revenue by four main types of taxes: personal taxes, contributions for social insurance, indirect business taxes, and corporate taxes.

2. The government budget deficit equals government outlays minus tax revenues and indicates how much the government must borrow during the year. The primary government budget deficit is the total deficit less net interest payments. The primary deficit indicates by how much the cost of current programs (measured by current government purchases and transfers) exceeds tax revenues during the year.

3. Fiscal policy affects the economy through its effects on aggregate demand, government capital formation, and incentives.

4. Increases or decreases in government purchases affect aggregate demand by changing desired national saving and shifting the *IS* curve. If Ricardian equivalence doesn't hold, as Keynesians usually argue, changes in taxes also affect desired national saving, the *IS* curve, and aggregate demand. Automatic stabilizers in the government's budget allow spending to rise or taxes to fall automatically in a recession, which helps cushion the drop in aggregate demand during a recession. The full-employment deficit is what the deficit would be—given current government spending programs and tax laws—if the economy were at full employment. Because of automatic stabilizers that increase spending and reduce taxes in recessions, the actual deficit rises above the full-employment deficit in recessions.

5. Government capital formation contributes to the productive capacity of the economy. Government capital formation includes both investment in physical capital (roads, schools) and investment in human capital (education, child nutrition).

6. The average tax rate is the fraction of total income paid in taxes, and the marginal tax rate is the fraction of an additional dollar of income that must be paid in taxes. Changes in average tax rates and changes in marginal tax rates have different effects on economic behavior. For example, an increase in the average tax rate (with no change in the marginal tax rate) increases labor supply, but an increase in the marginal tax rate (with no change in the average tax rate) decreases labor supply.

7. Policymakers must be concerned about the fact that taxes induce distortions, or deviations in economic behavior from that which would have occurred in the absence of taxes. One strategy for minimizing distortions is to hold tax rates approximately constant over time (tax rate smoothing), rather than alternating between high and low tax rates.

8. The national debt equals the value of government bonds outstanding. The government budget deficit, expressed in nominal terms, equals the change in the government debt. The behavior of the debt–GDP ratio over time depends on the ratio of the primary deficit to outstanding government debt and on whether the interest rate is greater or less than the GDP growth rate.

9. Deficits are a burden on future generations if they cause national saving to fall because lower national saving means that the country will have less capital and fewer foreign assets than it would have had otherwise. Ricardian equivalence indicates that a deficit caused by a tax cut won't affect consumption and therefore won't affect national saving. In the Ricardian view, a tax cut doesn't affect consumption because the increase in consumers' current income arising from the tax cut is offset by the prospect of increased taxes in the future, leaving consumers no better off. In theory, Ricardian equivalence still holds if the government debt isn't repaid by the current generation, provided that people care about the well-being of their descendants and thus choose not to consume more at their descendants' expense.

10. Ricardian equivalence may not hold—and thus tax cuts may affect national saving—if (1) borrowing constraints prevent some people from consuming as much as they want to; (2) people are short-sighted and don't take expected future changes in taxes into account in their planning; (3) people fail to leave bequests; or (4) tax cuts aren't lump-sum. The empirical evidence on Ricardian equivalence is mixed.

11. Deficits are linked to inflation when a government finances its deficits by printing money. The amount of revenue that the government raises by printing money is called seignorage. The real value of seignorage equals the inflation rate times the real money supply. Increasing the inflation rate doesn't always increase the government's real seignorage because higher inflation causes the public to hold a smaller real quantity of money. Attempts to push the collection of seignorage above its maximum can lead to hyperinflation.

Key Terms

automatic stabilizers, p. 580
average tax rate, p. 582
distortions, p. 585
full-employment deficit, p. 581
government capital, p. 582
government debt, p. 587
inflation tax, p. 600
marginal tax rate, p. 582
primary government budget deficit, p. 577
seignorage, p. 598
supply-side economics, p. 584
tax rate smoothing, p. 586

Key Equations

$$\Delta B = \text{nominal deficit} \quad (16.3)$$

The change in the nominal value of the government debt equals the nominal government deficit.

$$\text{growth rate of debt–GDP ratio} = \frac{\text{primary deficit}}{B} + i - \text{growth rate of nominal GDP} \quad (16.4)$$

The growth rate of the ratio of government debt outstanding to GDP depends on the ratio of the primary deficit to outstanding government debt, B, and on the difference between the nominal interest rate, i, and the growth rate of nominal GDP.

$$\text{deficit} = \Delta B = \Delta B^p + \Delta B^{cb} = \Delta B^p + \Delta M \quad (16.7)$$

The government budget deficit equals the increase in the stock of government debt outstanding, B, which in turn equals the sum of additional holdings of government debt by the public, B^p, and by the central bank, B^{cb}. The increase in debt held by the central bank equals the increase in the monetary base, which in an all-currency economy is the same as the increase in the money supply, M.

$$R = \frac{\Delta M}{P} = \pi \frac{M}{P} \quad (16.10)$$

In an all-currency economy, real seignorage revenue, R, equals the increase in the money supply, M, divided by the price level, P. This ratio in turn equals the inflation rate (the tax rate on money) multiplied by the real money supply (the tax base).

Review Questions

1. What are the major components of government outlays? What are the major sources of government revenues? How does the composition of the Federal government's outlays and revenues differ from that of state and local governments?
2. Explain the difference between the overall government budget deficit and the primary deficit. Why are two deficit concepts needed?
3. How is government debt related to the government deficit? What factors contribute to a high growth rate of the debt–GDP ratio?
4. What are the three main ways that fiscal policy affects the macroeconomy? Explain briefly how each channel of policy works.
5. Define *automatic stabilizer* and give an example. For proponents of anti-recessionary fiscal policies, what advantage do automatic stabilizers have over other types of taxing and spending policies?
6. Give a numerical example that shows the difference between the average tax rate and the marginal tax rate on a person's income. For a constant before-tax real wage, which type of tax rate most directly affects how wealthy a person feels? Which type of tax rate affects the reward for working an extra hour?
7. Why do economists suggest that tax rates be kept roughly constant over time, rather than alternating between high and low levels?
8. In what ways is the government debt a potential burden on future generations? What is the relationship between Ricardian equivalence and the idea that government debt is a burden?
9. Discuss four reasons why the Ricardian equivalence proposition isn't likely to hold exactly.
10. Define *inflation tax* (also called *seignorage*). How does the government collect this tax, and who pays it? Can the government always increase its real revenues from the inflation tax by increasing money growth and inflation?

Numerical Problems

1. The following budget data are for a country having both a central government and provincial governments:

Central purchases of goods and services	200
Provincial purchases of goods and services	150
Central transfer payments	100
Provincial transfer payments	50
Grants in aid (central to provincial)	100
Central tax receipts	450
Provincial tax receipts	100
Interest received from private sector by central government	10
Interest received from private sector by provincial governments	10
Total central government debt	1000
Total provincial government debt	0
Central government debt held by provincial governments	200
Nominal interest rate	10%

   Calculate the overall and primary deficits for the central government, the provincial governments, and the combined governments.
2. Congress votes a special one-time \$1 billion transfer to bail out the buggy whip industry. Tax collections don't change, and no change is planned for at least several years. By how much will this action increase the overall budget deficit and the primary deficit in the year that the transfer is made? In the next year? In the year after that? Assume that the nominal interest rate is constant at 10%.
3. Because of automatic stabilizers, various components of the government's budget depend on the level of output Y. The following are the main components of that budget:

Tax revenues	$1000 + 0.1Y$
Transfers	$800 - 0.05Y$
Government purchases	1800
Interest payments	100

Full-employment output is 10,000. Find the actual budget deficit and the full-employment budget deficit for

a. $Y = 12{,}000$. **b.** $Y = 10{,}000$. **c.** $Y = 8000$.

In general, how does the relationship between the actual deficit and the full-employment deficit depend on the state of the economy?

4. Suppose that the income tax law exempts income under \$8000 from the tax, taxes income between \$8000 and \$20,000 at a 25% rate, and taxes income greater than \$20,000 at a 30% rate.

a. Find the average tax rate and the marginal tax rate for someone earning \$16,000 and for someone earning \$30,000.

b. The tax law is changed so that income of less than \$6000 is untaxed, income from \$6000 to \$20,000 is taxed at 20%, and income of more than \$20,000 continues to be taxed at 30%. Repeat part (a).

c. How will the tax law change in part (b) affect the labor supply of the person initially making \$16,000? How will it affect the labor supply of the person making \$30,000?

5. Suppose that all workers value their leisure at 90 goods per day. The production function relating output per day Y to the number of people working per day N is

$$Y = 250N - 0.5N^2.$$

Corresponding to this production function, the marginal product of labor is

$$MPN = 250 - N.$$

a. Assume that there are no taxes. What are the equilibrium values of the real wage, employment N, and output Y? (*Hint:* In equilibrium the real wage will equal both the marginal product of labor and the value of a day's leisure to workers.)

b. A 25% tax is levied on wages. What are the equilibrium values of the real wage, employment, and output? In terms of lost output, what is the distortion cost of this tax?

c. Suppose that the tax on wages rises to 50%. What are the equilibrium values of the real wage, employment, and output? In terms of lost output, what is the distortion cost of this higher tax rate? Compare the distortion caused by a 50% tax rate with that caused by a 25% tax rate. Is the distortion caused by a 50% tax rate twice as large, more than twice as large, or less than twice as large as that caused by a 25% tax rate? How does your answer relate to the idea of tax smoothing?

6. Find the largest nominal primary deficit that the government can run without raising the debt–GDP ratio, under each of the following sets of assumptions:

a. Nominal GDP growth is 10%, the nominal interest rate is 12%, and outstanding nominal debt is 1000.

b. Nominal interest payments are 800, outstanding nominal debt is 10,000, inflation is 6%, and the economy has zero real growth.

7. In this problem you are asked to analyze the question: By issuing new bonds and using the proceeds to pay the interest on its old bonds, can government avoid ever repaying its debts?

a. Suppose that nominal GDP is \$1 billion and the government has \$100 million of bonds outstanding. The bonds are one-year bonds that pay a 7% nominal interest rate. The growth rate of nominal GDP is 5% per year. Beginning now the government runs a zero primary deficit forever and pays interest on its existing debt by issuing new bonds. What is the current debt–GDP ratio? What will this ratio be after 1, 2, 5, and 10 years? Suppose that, if the debt–GDP ratio exceeds 10, the public refuses to buy additional government bonds. Will the debt–GDP ratio ever reach that level? Will the government someday have to run a primary surplus in order to repay its debts, or can it avoid repayment forever? Why?

b. Repeat part (a) for nominal GDP growth of 8% per year and a nominal interest rate on government bonds of 7% per year.

8. Real money demand in an economy is

$$L = 0.2Y - 500i,$$

where Y is real income and i is the nominal interest rate. In equilibrium real money demand L equals real money supply M/P. Suppose that Y is 1000 and the real interest rate r is 0.04.

a. Draw a graph with real seignorage revenue on the vertical axis and inflation on the horizontal axis. Show the values of seignorage for inflation of 0, 0.02, 0.04, 0.06,..., 0.30.

b. What inflation rate maximizes seignorage?

c. What is the maximum amount of seignorage revenue?

d. Repeat parts (a)–(c) for $Y = 1000$ and $r = 0.08$.

9. Consider an economy in which the money supply consists of both currency and deposits. The growth rate of the monetary base, the growth rate of the money supply, inflation, and expected inflation all are constant at 10% per year. Output and the real interest rate are constant. Monetary data for this economy as of January 1, 1994, are as follows.

Currency in circulation	\$200
Bank reserves	\$50
Monetary base	\$250
Deposits	\$600
Money supply	\$800

a. What is the nominal value of seignorage over the year? (*Hint:* How much monetary base is created during the year?)
b. Suppose that deposits and bank reserves pay no interest, and that banks lend deposits not held as reserves at the market rate of interest. Who pays the inflation tax (measured in nominal terms), and how much do they pay? (*Hint:* The inflation tax paid by banks in this example is negative.)
c. Suppose that deposits pay a market rate of interest. Who pays the inflation tax, and how much do they pay?

Analytical Problems

1. Why is some state and local spending paid for by grants in aid from the Federal government, instead of having every state and locality pay for its own spending by levying taxes on its residents? What are the advantages and disadvantages of a system of grants in aid?
2. Using the *Economic Report of the President,* compare the Federal government's budget in 1979, 1986, and 1992. Express the main components of Federal spending and receipts in each year as fractions of GDP. Have increased deficits since 1979 been more the result of increased spending or reductions in revenues?
3. Both transfer programs and taxes affect incentives. Consider a program designed to help the poor that promises each aid recipient a minimum income of \$10,000. That is, if the recipient earns less than \$10,000, the program supplements his income by enough to bring him up to \$10,000.
   Explain why this program would adversely affect incentives for low-wage recipients. (*Hint:* Show that this program is equivalent to giving the recipient \$10,000, then taxing his labor income at a high marginal rate.) Describe a transfer program that contains better incentives. Would that program have any disadvantages? If so, what would they be?
4. **a.** Show that Eq. (16.4), which describes how the debt–GDP ratio evolves, still holds if the primary budget deficit, the outstanding stock of government bonds, the interest rate, and the growth rate of GDP all are expressed in real rather than nominal terms. (*Hint:* Use the growth-rate formulas in Appendix A, Section A.7, to show that the growth rate of nominal GDP equals the growth rate of real GDP plus the inflation rate.)
   b. Show that, if the primary deficit is zero, the real stock of outstanding government debt grows at a rate equal to the real interest rate. (*Hint:* In this case, the government budget deficit is iB, its nominal interest payments.)

APPENDIX 16.A THE DEBT–GDP RATIO

In this appendix we derive Eq. (16.4), which shows how the debt–GDP ratio evolves. If we let Q represent the ratio of government debt to GDP, by definition

$$Q = \frac{B}{PY}, \tag{16.A.1}$$

where B is the nominal value of government bonds outstanding (government debt), P is the price level, and Y is real GDP (so that PY is nominal GDP). A useful rule is that the percentage change in any ratio equals the percentage change in the numerator minus the percentage change in the denominator (Appendix A, Section A.7). Applying this rule to Eq. (16.A.1) gives

$$\frac{\Delta Q}{Q} = \frac{\Delta B}{B} - \frac{\Delta(PY)}{PY}. \tag{16.A.2}$$

The increase in the nominal value of government bonds ΔB equals the nominal value of the government budget deficit (Eq. 16.3). The budget deficit equals the nominal value of the primary deficit plus interest payments on the government debt so that

$$\Delta B = PD^P + iB, \tag{16.A.3}$$

where D^P is the real value of the primary deficit, PD^P is the nominal value of the primary deficit, i is the nominal interest rate, and iB is the nominal value of interest payments on the government debt. Using Eq. (16.A.3) to substitute for ΔB on the right-hand side of Eq. (16.A.2), we obtain

$$\frac{\Delta Q}{Q} = \frac{PD^P}{B} + i - \frac{\Delta(PY)}{PY}. \tag{16.A.4}$$

As PD^P/B is the ratio of the primary deficit to the government debt and $\Delta(PY)/PY$ is the growth rate of nominal GDP, Eq. (16.A.4) is equivalent to Eq. (16.4).

Some Useful Analytical Tools

This appendix reviews some basic algebraic and graphical tools that are used in this book.

A.1 FUNCTIONS AND GRAPHS

A function is a relationship among two or more variables. For an economic illustration of a function, suppose that in a certain firm each worker employed can produce five units of output per day. Let

N = the number of workers employed by the firm;
Y = total daily output of the firm.

In this example, the relationship of output Y to the number of workers N is:

$$Y = 5N. \qquad (A.1)$$

Equation (A.1) is an example of a function relating the variable Y to the variable N. Using this function, for any number of workers N we can calculate the total amount of output Y that the firm can produce each day. For example, if $N = 3$, then $Y = 15$.

Functions can be described graphically as well as algebraically. The graph of the function $Y = 5N$, for values of N between 0 and 16, is shown in Fig. A.1. Output Y is shown on the vertical axis, and the number of workers N is shown on the horizontal axis. Points on the line $0AB$ satisfy Eq. (A.1). For example, at point A, $N = 4$ and $Y = 20$, a combination of N and Y that satisfies Eq. (A.1). Similarly, at point B, $N = 12.5$ and $Y = 62.5$, which also satisfies the relationship $Y = 5N$. Note that (at B, for example) the relationship between Y and N allows the variables to have values that are not whole numbers. Allowing fractional values of N and Y is reasonable because workers can work part-time or overtime, and a unit of output may be only partially completed during a day.

Functions such as $Y = 5N$ whose graph is a straight line are called *linear functions*. Functions whose graph is not a line are called *nonlinear*. An example of a nonlinear function is

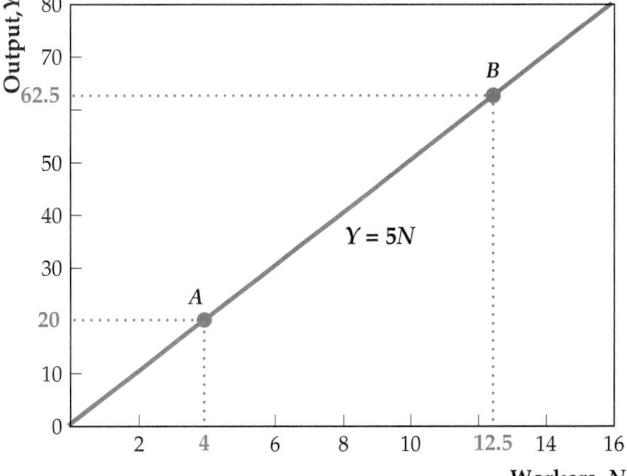

Figure A.1
Points on the line $0AB$ satisfy the relationship $Y = 5N$. Because the graph of the function $Y = 5N$ is a straight line, this function is called a linear function.

$$Y = 20\sqrt{N}. \qquad (A.2)$$

The graph of the nonlinear function $Y = 20\sqrt{N}$ is shown in Fig. A.2 on the next page. All points on the curve satisfy Eq. (A.2). For example, at point C, $N = 4$ and $Y = 20\sqrt{4} = 40$. At point D, $N = 9$ and $Y = 20\sqrt{9} = 60$.

Both examples of functions given so far are exact numerical relationships. We can also write functions in more general terms, using letters or symbols. For example, we might write:

$$Y = G(N). \qquad (A.3)$$

Equation (A.3) states that there is some general relationship between the number of workers N and the amount of output Y, which is represented by a function G. The numerical functions given in Eqs. (A.1) and (A.2) are specific examples of such a general relationship.

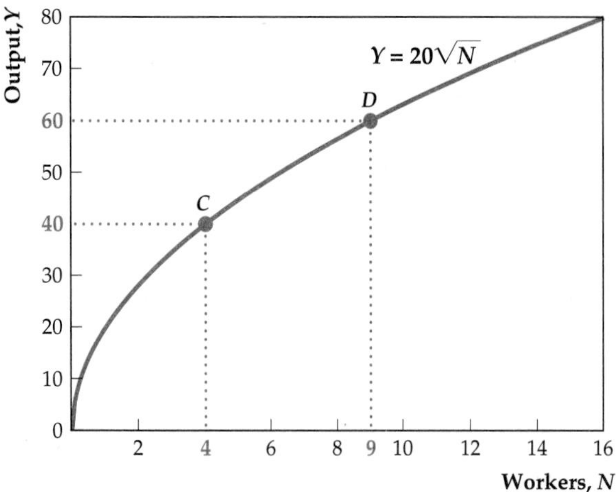

Figure A.2
The function $Y = 20\sqrt{N}$, whose graph is shown in this figure, is an example of a nonlinear function.

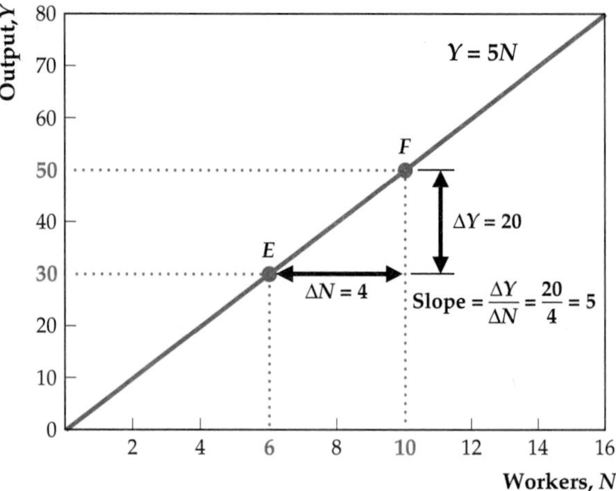

Figure A.3
The slope of a function equals the change in the variable on the vertical axis (Y) divided by the change in the variable on the horizontal axis (N). For example, between points E and F the increase in N, ΔN, equals 4 and the increase in Y, ΔY, equals 20. Therefore the slope of the function between E and F, $\Delta Y/\Delta N$, equals 5. In general, the slope of a linear function is constant, so the slope of this function between any two points is 5.

A.2 SLOPES OF FUNCTIONS

Suppose that two variables N and Y are related by a function $Y = G(N)$. Generally speaking, if we start from some given combination of N and Y that satisfies the function G, the *slope* of the function G at that point indicates by how much Y changes when N changes by one unit.

To define the slope more precisely, we suppose that the current value of N is a specific number N_1 so that the current value of Y equals $G(N_1)$. Now consider what happens if N is increased by an amount ΔN (ΔN is read "the change in N"). Output Y depends on N; therefore if N changes, Y must also change. The value of N is now $N_1 + \Delta N$, so the value of Y after N increases is $G(N_1 + \Delta N)$. The *change* in Y is

$$\Delta Y = G(N_1 + \Delta N) - G(N_1).$$

The slope of the function G, for an increase in N from N_1 to $N_1 + \Delta N$, is

$$\text{slope} = \frac{\Delta Y}{\Delta N} = \frac{G(N_1 + \Delta N) - G(N_1)}{(N_1 + \Delta N) - N_1}. \quad \text{(A.4)}$$

Note that if $\Delta N = 1$, the slope equals ΔY, the change in Y.

Figures A.3 and A.4 show graphically how to determine slopes for the two functions discussed in the preceding section. Figure A.3 shows the graph of the function $Y = 5N$ (as in Fig. A.1). Suppose that we start from point E in Figure A.3, where $N = 6$ and $Y = 30$. If N is increased by 4 (for example), we move to point F on the graph, where $N = 10$ and $Y = 50$. Between E and F, $\Delta N = 10 - 6 = 4$ and $\Delta Y = 50 - 30 = 20$, so the slope $\Delta Y/\Delta N = 20/4 = 5$.

In general, the slope of a linear function is the same at all points. You can prove this result for the linear function $Y = 5N$ by showing that for any change ΔN, $\Delta Y = 5\,\Delta N$. So for this particular linear function, the slope $\Delta Y/\Delta N$ always equals 5, a constant number.

For a nonlinear function, such as $Y = 20\sqrt{N}$, the slope isn't constant but depends on both the initial value of N and the size of the change in N. These results are illustrated in Fig. A.4 on the next page, which displays the graph of the function $Y = 20\sqrt{N}$ (as in Fig. A.2). Suppose that we are initially at point G, where $N = 1$ and $Y = 20$, and we increase N by 8 units. After the increase in N we are at point D, where $N = 9$ and $Y = 20\sqrt{9} = 60$. Between G and D, $\Delta N = 9 - 1 = 8$ and $\Delta Y = 60 - 20 = 40$. Thus the slope of the function between G and D is $40/8 = 5$. Geometrically, the slope of the function between G and D equals the slope of the straight line between G and D.

Starting once again from point G in Fig. A.4, if we instead increase N by 3 units, we come to point C, where $N = 4$ and $Y = 20\sqrt{4} = 40$. In this case $\Delta N = 3$ and $\Delta Y = 40 - 20 = 20$, so the slope between G and C is $20/3 = 6.67$, which isn't the same as the slope of 5 that we calculated when earlier we increased N by 8 units. Geometrically, the slope of the line between G and C is greater than the slope of the line between G and D; that is, line GC is steeper than line GD.

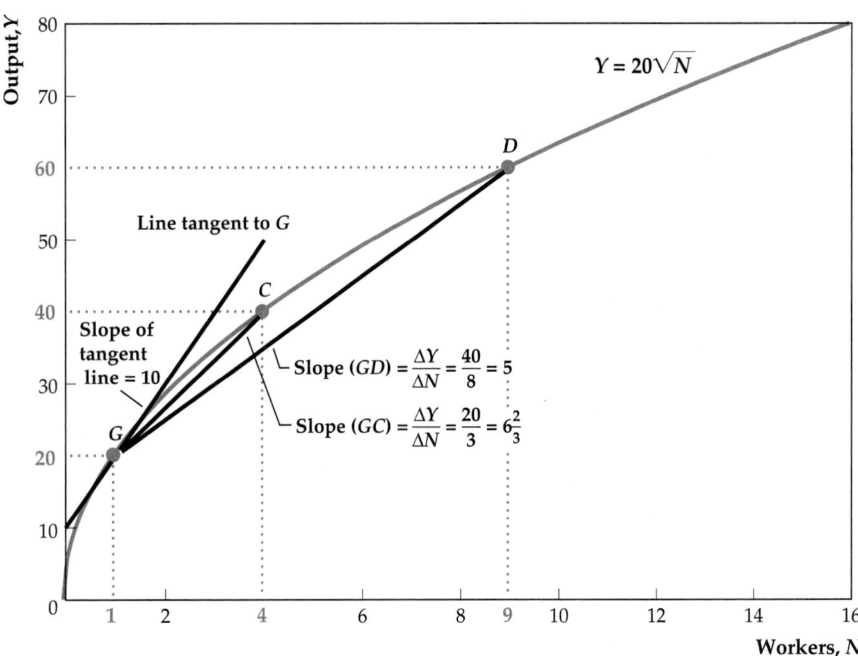

Figure A.4
Between points *G* and *D* the change in *N* (ΔN) is 8 and the change in *Y* (ΔY) is 40, so the slope of the function between points *G* and *D* is $\Delta Y/\Delta N = 40/8 = 5$. This slope is the same as the slope of the line *GD*. Similarly, the slope of the function between points *G* and *C* is $\Delta Y/\Delta N = 20/3 = 6.67$. The slope of the line tangent to point *G*, which equals 10, approximates the slope of the function for very small changes in *N*. Generally, when we refer to the slope of a nonlinear function at a specific point, we mean the slope of the line tangent to the function at that point.

In Fig. A.4 we have also drawn a line that touches but does not cross the graph of the function at point *G*; this line is *tangent* to the graph of the function at point *G*. If you start from point *G* and find the slope of the function for different values of ΔN, you will discover that the smaller the value of ΔN is, the closer the slope will be to the slope of the tangent line. For example, if you compare the slope of line *GD* (for which $\Delta N = 8$) with the slope of line *GC* (for which $\Delta N = 3$), you will see that of the two the slope of line *GC* is closer to the slope of the line tangent to point *G*. For values of ΔN even smaller than 3, the slope would be still closer to the slope of the tangent line.

These observations lead to an important result: *For small values of ΔN the slope of a function at any point is closely approximated by the slope of the line tangent to the function at that point.* Unless specified otherwise, in this book when we refer to the slope of a nonlinear function, we mean the slope of the line tangent to the function at the specified point. Thus in Fig. A.4, the slope of the function at point *G* means the slope of the line tangent to the function at point *G*, which happens to be 10.[1]

The numerical example illustrated in Fig. A.4 shows that the slope of a nonlinear function depends on the size of the increase in *N* being considered. The slope of a nonlinear function also depends on the point at which the slope is being measured. In Fig. A.4 note that the slope of a line drawn tangent to point *D*, for example, would be less than the slope of a line drawn tangent to point *G*. Thus the slope of this particular function (measured with respect to small changes in *N*) is greater at *G* than at *D*.

A.3 ELASTICITIES

Like slopes, elasticities indicate how much one variable responds when a second variable changes. Suppose again that there is a function relating *Y* to *N*, so that when *N* changes, *Y* changes as well. The *elasticity* of *Y* with respect to *N* is defined to be the percentage change in *Y*, $\Delta Y/Y$, divided by the percentage change in *N*, $\Delta N/N$. Writing the formula, we have

$$\text{elasticity of } Y \text{ with respect to } N = \frac{\Delta Y/Y}{\Delta N/N}.$$

Because the slope of a function is $\Delta Y/\Delta N$, we can also write the elasticity of *Y* with respect to *N* as the slope times (N/Y).

If the elasticity of *Y* with respect to *N* is large, a 1% change in *N* causes a large percentage change in *Y*. Thus a large elasticity of *Y* with respect to *N* means that *Y* is very sensitive to changes in *N*.

1. Showing that the slope of the line tangent to point *G* equals 10 requires basic calculus. The derivative of the function $Y = 20\sqrt{N}$, which is the same as the slope, is $dY/dN = 10/\sqrt{N}$. Evaluating this derivative at $N = 1$ yields a slope of 10.

A.4 FUNCTIONS OF SEVERAL VARIABLES

A function can relate more than two variables. To continue the example of Section A.1, suppose that the firm's daily output Y depends on both the number of workers N the firm employs and the number of machines (equivalently, the amount of capital) K the firm owns. Specifically, the function relating Y to K and N might be

$$Y = 2\sqrt{K}\,\sqrt{N}. \qquad \text{(A.5)}$$

So, if there are 100 machines and 9 workers, by substituting $K = 100$ and $N = 9$ into Eq. (A.5), we get the output $Y = 2\sqrt{100}\,\sqrt{9} = 2 \times 10 \times 3 = 60$.

We can also write a function of several variables in general terms using symbols or letters. A general way to write the relationship between output Y and the two inputs, capital K and labor N, is

$$Y = F(K, N).$$

This equation is a slight simplification of a relationship called the production function, which we introduce in Chapter 3.

The graph of a function relating three variables requires three dimensions. As a convenient way to graph such a function on a two-dimensional page, we hold one of the right-hand-side variables constant. To graph the function in Eq. (A.5), for example, we might hold the number of machines K constant at a value of 100. If we substitute 100 for K, Eq. (A.5) becomes

$$Y = 2\sqrt{100}\,\sqrt{N} = 20\sqrt{N}. \qquad \text{(A.6)}$$

With K held constant at 100, Eq. (A.6) is identical to Eq. (A.2). Like Eq. (A.2), Eq. (A.6) is a relationship between Y and N only and thus can be graphed in two dimensions. The graph of Eq. (A.6), shown as the solid curve in Fig. A.5, is identical to the graph of Eq. (A.2) in Fig. A.2.

A.5 SHIFTS OF A CURVE

Suppose that the relationship of output Y to machines K and workers N is given by Eq. (A.5) and we hold K constant at 100. As in Section A.4, with K held constant at 100, Eq. (A.5) reduces to Eq. (A.6) and the solid curve in Fig. A.5 shows the relationship between workers N and output Y. At point C in Fig. A.5, for example, $N = 4$ and $Y = 20\sqrt{4} = 40$. At point D, where $N = 9$, $Y = 20\sqrt{9} = 60$.

Now suppose that the firm purchases additional machines, raising the number of machines K from 100 to 225. If we substitute this new value for K, Eq. (A.5) becomes

$$Y = 2\sqrt{225}\,\sqrt{N} = 30\sqrt{N}. \qquad \text{(A.7)}$$

Equation (A.7) is shown graphically as the dashed curve in Fig. A.5. Note that the increase in K has shifted the curve up. Because of the increase in the number of machines, the amount of daily output Y that can be produced for any given number of workers N has risen. For example, initially when N equaled 9, output Y equaled 60 (point D in Fig. A.5). After the increase in K, if $N = 9$, then $Y = 30\sqrt{9} = 90$ (point J in Fig. A.5).

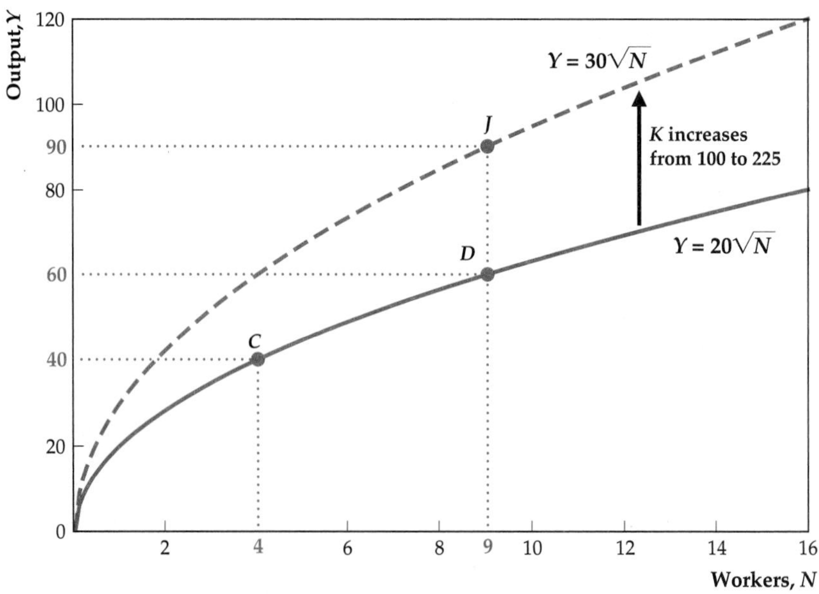

Figure A.5
Suppose that output Y depends on capital K and workers N, according to the function in Eq. (A.5). If we hold K fixed at 100, the relationship between Y and N is shown by the solid curve. If K rises to 225, so that more output can be produced with a given number of workers, the curve showing the relationship between Y and N shifts upward, from the solid curve to the dashed curve. In general, a change in any right-hand-side variable that doesn't appear on an axis of the graph causes the curve to shift.

This example illustrates some important general points about the graphs of functions of several variables.

1. To graph a function of several variables in two dimensions, we hold all but one of the right-hand-side variables constant.
2. The one right-hand-side variable that isn't held constant (N in this example) appears on the horizontal axis. Changes in this variable don't shift the graph of the function. Instead, changes in the variable on the horizontal axis represent movements *along* the curve that represents the function.
3. The right-hand-side variables held constant for the purpose of drawing the graph (K in this example) don't appear on either axis of the graph. If the value of one of these variables is changed, the entire curve shifts. In this example, for any number of workers N the increase in machines K means that more output Y can be produced. Thus the curve shifts up, from the solid curve to the dashed curve in Fig. A.5.

A.6 EXPONENTS

Powers of numbers or variables can be expressed by using superscripts called *exponents.* In the following examples, 2 and 4 are the exponents:

$$5^2 = 5 \times 5, \quad \text{and} \quad Z^4 = Z \times Z \times Z \times Z.$$

For any numbers Z, a, and b, exponents obey the following rules:

$$Z^a \times Z^b = Z^{a+b}, \quad \text{and} \quad (Z^a)^b = Z^{ab}.$$

An illustration of the first rule is $5^2 \times 5^3 = (5 \times 5) \times (5 \times 5 \times 5) = 5^5$. An illustration of the second rule is $(5^3)^2 = (5^3) \times (5^3) = (5 \times 5 \times 5) \times (5 \times 5 \times 5) = 5^6$.

Exponents do not have to be whole numbers. For example, $5^{0.5}$ represents the square root of 5. To understand why, note that by the second of the two rules for exponents, $(5^{0.5})^2 = 5^{(0.5)2} = 5^1 = 5$. That is, the square of $5^{0.5}$ is 5. Similarly, for any number Z and any whole number q, $Z^{1/q}$ is the qth root of Z. Thus $5^{0.25}$ means the fourth root of 5, for example. Using exponents, we can rewrite Eq. (A.5) as

$$Y = 2K^{0.5}N^{0.5},$$

where $K^{0.5} = \sqrt{K}$ and $N^{0.5} = \sqrt{N}$.

In general, consider any number that can be expressed as a ratio of two whole numbers p and q. Using the rules of exponents, we have

$$Z^{p/q} = (Z^p)^{1/q} = q\text{th root of } Z^p.$$

Thus, for example, as 0.7 equals 7/10, $N^{0.7}$ equals the tenth root of N^7. For values of N greater than 1, $N^{0.7}$ is a number larger than the square root of N, $N^{0.5}$, but smaller than N itself.

Exponents also may be zero or negative. In general, the following two relationships hold:

$$Z^0 = 1, \quad \text{and} \quad Z^{-a} = \frac{1}{Z^a}.$$

Here is a useful way to relate exponents and elasticities: Suppose that two variables Y and N are related by a function of the form

$$Y = kN^a, \tag{A.8}$$

where a is a number and k can be either a number or a function of variables other than N. Then the elasticity of Y with respect to N (see Section A.3) equals a.

A.7 GROWTH RATE FORMULAS

Let X and Z be any two variables, not necessarily related by a function, that are changing over time. Let $\Delta X/X$ and $\Delta Z/Z$ represent the growth rates (percentage changes) of X and Z, respectively. Then the following rules provide useful approximations (proofs of the various rules are included for reference).

Rule 1. The growth rate of the product of X and Z equals the growth rate of X plus the growth rate of Z.

Proof. Suppose that X increases by ΔX and Z increases by ΔZ. Then the absolute increase in the product of X and Z is $(X + \Delta X)(Z + \Delta Z) - XZ$, and the growth rate of the product of X and Z is

$$\begin{aligned} \text{growth rate of } (XZ) & \qquad\qquad\qquad \text{(A.9)} \\ &= \frac{(X + \Delta X)(Z + \Delta Z) - XZ}{XZ} \\ &= \frac{(\Delta X)Z + (\Delta Z)X + \Delta X \Delta Z}{XZ} \\ &= \frac{\Delta X}{X} + \frac{\Delta Z}{Z} + \frac{\Delta X \Delta Z}{XZ}. \end{aligned}$$

The last term on the right-hand side of Eq. (A.9), $(\Delta X\, \Delta Z)/XZ$, equals the growth rate of X, $\Delta X/X$, times the growth rate of Z, $\Delta Z/Z$. This term is generally small; for example, if the growth rates of X and Z are both 5% (0.05), the product of the two growth rates is only 0.25% (0.0025). If we assume that this last term is small enough to ignore, Eq. (A.9) indicates that the growth rate of the product XZ equals the growth rate of X, $\Delta X/X$, plus the growth rate of Z, $\Delta Z/Z$.

Rule 2. The growth rate of the ratio of X to Z is the growth rate of X minus the growth rate of Z.

Proof. Let W be the ratio of X to Z, so $W = X/Z$. Then $X = ZW$. By Rule 1, as X equals the product of Z and W, the growth rate of X equals the growth rate of Z plus the growth rate of W:

$$\frac{\Delta X}{X} = \frac{\Delta Z}{Z} + \frac{\Delta W}{W}.$$

Rearranging this equation to put $\Delta W/W$ on the left-hand side and recalling that $\Delta W/W$ equals the growth rate of (X/Z), we have

$$\text{growth rate of } (X/Z) = \frac{\Delta X}{X} - \frac{\Delta Z}{Z}. \quad \text{(A.10)}$$

Rule 3. Suppose that Y is a variable that is a function of two other variables X and Z. Then

$$\frac{\Delta Y}{Y} = \eta_{Y,X}\frac{\Delta X}{X} + \eta_{Y,Z}\frac{\Delta Z}{Z}, \quad \text{(A.11)}$$

where $\eta_{Y,X}$ is the elasticity of Y with respect to X and $\eta_{Y,Z}$ is the elasticity of Y with respect to Z.

Proof (informal). Suppose that only X changes so that $\Delta Z/Z = 0$. Then Eq. (A.11) boils down to the definition of an elasticity, $\eta_{Y,X} = (\Delta Y/Y)/(\Delta X/X)$, as in Section A.3. Similarly, if only Z changes, Eq. (A.11) becomes $\eta_{Y,Z} = (\Delta Y/Y)/(\Delta Z/Z)$, which is the definition of the elasticity of Y with respect to Z. If both X and Z change, Eq. (A.11) indicates that the overall effect on Y is approximately equal to the sum of the individual effects on Y of the change in X and the change in Z.

Rule 4. The growth rate of X raised to the power a, or X^a, is a times the growth rate of X,

$$\text{growth rate of } (X^a) = a\frac{\Delta X}{X}. \quad \text{(A.12)}$$

Proof. Let $Y = X^a$. Applying the rule from Eq. (A.8) and setting $k = 1$, we find that the elasticity of Y with respect to X equals a. Therefore, by Eq. (A.11) the growth rate of Y equals a times the growth rate of X. Because $Y = X^a$, the growth rate of Y is the same as the growth rate of X^a, which proves the relationship in Eq. (A.12).

Example: The real interest rate. To apply the growth rate formulas, we derive the equation that relates the real interest rate to the nominal interest rate and the inflation rate, Eq. (2.12).

The real value of any asset, say, a savings account, equals the nominal or dollar value of the asset divided by the price level:

$$\text{real asset value} = \frac{\text{nominal asset value}}{\text{price level}}. \quad \text{(A.13)}$$

The real value of an asset is the ratio of the nominal asset value to the price level, so, according to Rule 2, the *growth rate* of the real asset value is approximately equal to the *growth rate* of the nominal asset value minus the *growth rate* of the price level. The growth rate of the real value of an interest-bearing asset equals the real interest rate earned by that asset; the growth rate of the nominal value of an interest-bearing asset is the nominal interest rate for that asset; and the growth rate of the price level is the inflation rate. Therefore, Rule 2 implies the relationship

Real interest rate = nominal interest rate – inflation rate,

which is the relationship given in Eq. (2.12).

PROBLEMS

1. Graph the function $Y = 3X + 5$ for $0 \le X \le 5$. What is the slope of this function?

2. Graph the function $Y = X^2 + 2$ for $0 \le X \le 5$. Starting from the point at which $X = 1$, find the slope of the function for $\Delta X = 1$ and $\Delta X = -1$. What is the slope of the line tangent to the function at $X = 1$? (See Problem 3.)

3. For the function $Y = X^2 + 2$, use Eq. (A.4) to write a general expression for the slope. This expression for the slope will depend on the initial value of X, X_1, and on the change in X, ΔX. For values of ΔX sufficiently small that the term $(\Delta X)^2$ can be ignored, show that the slope depends only on the initial value of X, X_1. What is the slope of the function (which is the same as the slope of the tangent line) when $X_1 = 1$?

4. Suppose that the amount of output Y that a firm can produce depends on its amount of capital K and the number of workers employed N, according to the function

$$Y = K^{0.3}N^{0.7}.$$

a. Suppose that $N = 100$. Give the function that relates Y to K and graph this relationship for $0 \le K \le 50$. (You need calculate only enough values of Y to get a rough idea of the shape of the function.)

b. What happens to the function relating Y and K and to the graph of the relationship if N rises to 200? If N falls to 50? Give an economic interpretation.

c. For the function relating Y to K and N, find the elasticity of Y with respect to K and the elasticity of Y with respect to N.

5. Use a calculator to find each of the following.

a. $5^{0.3}$

b. $5^{0.3}5^{0.2}$

c. $(5^{0.25})^2$

d. $(5^{0.5}5^{0.3})^2\ 5^{0.4}$

e. $5^{0.2}/5^{0.5}$

f. $5^{-0.5}$

6. a. Nominal GDP equals real GDP times the GDP deflator (see Section 2.4). Suppose that nominal GDP growth is 12% and real GDP growth is 4%. What is inflation (the rate of growth of the GDP deflator)?

b. The "velocity of money," V, is defined by the equation

$$V = \frac{PY}{M},$$

where P is the price level, Y is real output, and M is the money supply (see Eq. 7.4). In a particular year velocity is constant, money growth is 10%, and inflation (the rate of growth of the price level) is 7%. What is real output growth?

c. Output Y is related to capital K and the number of workers N by the function

$$Y = 10K^{0.3}N^{0.7}.$$

In a particular year the capital stock grows by 2% and the number of workers grows by 1%. By how much does output grow?

GLOSSARY

(The number in parentheses after the glossary term is the chapter in which that term first appears or is most extensively discussed.)

absorption: (5) total spending by domestic residents, firms, and governments, equal to $C + I + G$. (p. 157)

activist: (15) describes a policy strategy that involves active responses by the central bank to changes in economic circumstances. See *discretion*.

acyclical: (9) not displaying a regular pattern of behavior over the business cycle. See *procyclical, countercyclical*. (p. 300)

aggregate demand: (10, 11) the economywide demand for output when the goods market and the asset market are in equilibrium; the level of output corresponding to the intersection of the *IS* and *LM* curves.

aggregate demand (*AD*) curve: (11) in a diagram with output on the horizontal axis and the price level on the vertical axis, the downward-sloping relation between the price level and the economywide demand for output. (p. 372)

aggregate demand for labor: (3) the sum of the labor demands of all employers in an economy. (p. 80)

aggregate demand management: (12) the use of monetary and fiscal policies, which shifts the aggregate demand curve, to try to smooth out the business cycle; also known as macroeconomic stabilization or stabilization policy. (p. 426)

aggregate demand shocks: (12) shocks to the economy that shift the *IS* curve or the *LM* curve and thus affect the aggregate demand for output. (p. 420)

aggregate supply: (11) the amount of output supplied by firms in the economy at any given price level; in the long run, when prices and price expectations have adjusted to their equilibrium levels, aggregate supply equals full-employment output.

aggregate supply (*AS*) curve: (11) in a diagram with output on the horizontal axis and the price level on the vertical axis, the relation between the price level and the total amount of output that firms supply. (p. 375)

aggregate supply of labor: (3) the sum of the labor supplied by everyone in the economy. (p. 80)

aggregation: (1) the process of adding individual economic variables to obtain economywide totals. (p. 13)

appreciation: (14) see *nominal appreciation, real appreciation*.

automatic stabilizers: (16) provisions in the government's budget that automatically cause government spending to rise or taxes to fall when GDP falls. (p. 580)

average labor productivity: (1) the amount of output produced per unit of labor input (per worker or per hour of work). (p. 5)

average tax rate: (16) the total amount of taxes paid divided by the taxpayer's income. (p. 582)

balance of payments: (5) the net increase (domestic less foreign) in a country's official reserve assets; also known as the official settlements balance. (p. 151)

balance of payments accounts: (5) the record of a country's international transactions, consisting of the current account and the capital account. (p. 146)

bank reserves: (15) liquid assets held by banks to meet the demands for withdrawals by depositors or to pay the checks drawn on depositors' accounts. (p. 530)

bank run: (15) a large-scale withdrawal of deposits from a bank, caused by depositors' fear that the bank may go bankrupt and not pay depositors in full. (p. 533)

bequest motive: (8) the desire to leave inheritances. (p. 268)

Board of Governors of the Federal Reserve System: (15) a group of seven governors, appointed by the President of the United States to staggered fourteen-year terms, that provides the leadership of the Federal Reserve System. (p. 540)

boom: (9) in a business cycle, the period of time during which aggregate economic activity grows; also known as an expansion. (p. 291)

borrowing constraint: (8) a restriction imposed by lenders on the amount that someone can borrow. If a borrowing constraint causes an individual to borrow less than he or she would choose to borrow in the absence of the constraint, the borrowing constraint is *binding*; otherwise it is *nonbinding*. (p. 265)

budget constraint: (8) a relation that shows how much current and future consumption a consumer can afford given the consumer's initial wealth, current and future income, and the interest rate. (p. 251)

budget deficit: (2) government outlays minus government receipts. See *government outlays, government receipts*. (p. 41)

budget line: (8) the graph of the consumer's budget constraint; the budget line shows graphically the combinations of current and future consumption a consumer can afford given the consumer's initial wealth, current and future income, and the interest rate. (p. 252)

budget surplus: (2) government receipts minus government outlays. See *government outlays, government receipts, government saving*. (p. 41)

business cycle: (9) a decline in aggregate economic activity (a contraction or recession) to a low point (a trough), followed by a recovery of activity (an expansion or boom) to a high point (a peak). A complete business cycle can be measured from peak to peak or from trough to trough. (p. 291)

business cycle chronology: (9) a history of the dates of business cycle peaks and troughs. (p. 290)

capital account: (5) the record of a country's international trade in existing assets, either real or financial. (p. 150)

capital account balance: (5) the value of capital inflows (credit items) minus the value of capital outflows (debit items) in a country's capital account. (p. 150)

capital good: (2) a good that is produced, is used to produce other goods, and—unlike an intermediate good—is not used up in the same period that it is produced. (p. 31)

capital inflow: (5) a credit (plus) item in a country's capital account that arises when a resident of the country sells an asset to someone in another country. (p. 150)

capital–labor ratio: (6) the amount of capital per worker, equal to the capital stock divided by the number of workers. (p. 195)

capital outflow: (5) a debit (minus) item in a country's capital account that arises when a resident of the country buys an asset from abroad. (p. 150)

central bank: (15) the governmental institution responsible for monetary policy, such as the Federal Reserve System in the United States, the Bundesbank in Germany, and the Bank of Japan in Japan. (p. 528)

chronically unemployed: (3) workers who are unemployed a large fraction of the time. (p. 96)

classical approach: (1) an approach to macroeconomics based on the assumption that wages and prices adjust quickly to equate quantities supplied and demanded in each market. Classical economists generally argue that free markets are a good way to organize the economy and that the scope for government intervention in the economy—for example, to smooth out the business cycle—should be limited.

closed economy: (1) a national economy that does not have trading or financial relationships with the rest of the world. (p. 9)

coincident variable: (9) a variable with peaks and troughs that occur at about the same time as the corresponding business cycle peaks and troughs. See *lagging variable, leading variable*. (p. 300)

cold turkey: (13) a rapid and decisive reduction in the growth rate of the money supply aimed at reducing the rate of inflation; in contrast with *gradualism*. (p. 473)

comovement: (9) the tendency of many economic variables to move together in a predictable way over the business cycle. (p. 293)

conditional convergence: (6) the tendency of living standards within groups of countries with similar characteristics to become more equal over time. See *unconditional convergence*. (p. 207)

consumer price index: (2) a price index calculated as the current cost of a fixed basket of consumer goods divided by the cost of the basket in the base period. (p. 51)

consumption: (2) spending by domestic households on final goods and services. (p. 34)

consumption-smoothing motive: (8) the preference of most people for a relatively constant or stable pattern of consumption over time, as opposed to having high consumption at some times and low consumption at others. (p. 256)

contraction: (9) in a business cycle, the period of time during which aggregate economic activity is falling; also known as a recession. (p. 291)

contractionary policy: (12) a monetary or fiscal policy that reduces aggregate demand.

convergence: (6) a tendency of living standards in different countries to become equal over time. See *conditional convergence, unconditional convergence*.

countercyclical: (9) tending to move in the opposite direction of aggregate economic activity over the business cycle (up in contractions, down in expansions). See *procyclical, acyclical.* (p. 300)

credibility: (15) the degree to which the public believes the central bank's announcements about future policy. (p. 553)

currency: (7) paper money and coin issued by the government; cash.

currency–deposit ratio: (15) the ratio of the currency held by the public to the public's deposits in banks. (p. 534)

current account: (5) the record of a country's international trade in currently produced goods and services. (p. 147)

current account balance: (2, 5) payments received from abroad in exchange for currently produced goods and services (including factor services), minus the analogous payments made to foreigners by the domestic economy. (pp. 42, 149)

cyclical unemployment: (3) the excess of the actual unemployment rate over the natural rate of unemployment; equivalently, unemployment that occurs when output is below its full-employment level. (p. 97)

debt–GDP ratio: (16) the quantity of government debt outstanding divided by GDP.

deflation: (1) a situation in which the prices of most goods and services are falling over time. (p. 8)

demand for money: (7) the quantity of monetary assets, such as cash and checking accounts, that people choose to hold in their portfolios. (p. 245)

depository institutions: (15) privately owned banks and thrift institutions (such as savings and loans) that accept deposits from and make loans directly to the public. (p. 528)

depreciation: 1. (2) the amount of capital that wears out during a given period of time. (p. 38) 2. (14) a decline in the exchange rate; see *nominal depreciation, real depreciation.* (p. 485)

depression: (9) a particularly severe and prolonged downturn in economic activity. (p. 291)

desired capital stock: (4) the amount of capital that allows a firm to earn the highest possible expected profit. (p. 121)

devaluation: (14) a reduction in the value of a currency by official government action under a fixed exchange rate system. (p. 485)

diminishing marginal productivity: (3) a feature of production functions that implies that, the more a particular factor of production is used, the less extra output can be gained by increasing the use of that factor still further (with the usage of other factors of production held constant). For example, for a given capital stock, adding an extra worker increases output more when employment is initially low than when it is initially high. (p. 70)

discount rate: (15) the interest rate charged by the Fed when it lends reserves to banks. (p. 544)

discount window lending: (15) the lending of reserves to banks by the Fed. (p. 544)

discouraged workers: (3) people who stop searching for jobs because they have become discouraged by lack of success at finding a job; discouraged workers are not included in the official unemployment rate. (p. 94)

discretion: (15) the freedom of the central bank to conduct monetary policy in any way that it believes will advance the ultimate objectives of low and stable inflation, high economic growth, and low unemployment; in contrast to *rules*. (p. 549)

disinflation: (13) a fall in the rate of inflation. (p. 473)

distortions: (16) tax-induced deviations in economic behavior from the efficient, free-market outcome. (p. 585)

duration: (3) the length of time that an unemployment spell lasts. (p. 95)

economic model: (1) a simplified description of some aspect of the economy, usually expressed in mathematical form. (p. 15)

economic theory: (1) a set of ideas about the economy that have been organized in a logical framework. (p. 15)

effective labor demand curve: (12) in a diagram with output on the horizontal axis and the quantity of labor on the vertical axis, an upward-sloping curve that shows how much labor is needed to produce a given amount of output, with productivity, the capital stock, and effort held constant. (p. 409)

effective tax rate: (4) a single measure of the tax burden on capital that summarizes the many provisions of the tax code that affect investment. (p. 126)

efficiency wage: (12) the real wage that maximizes worker effort or efficiency per dollar of real wages received. (p. 400)

efficiency wage model: (12) a model of the labor market in which, because workers exert more effort when they receive a higher real wage, profit-maximizing employers choose to pay a real wage that is higher than the real wage that clears the labor market; the efficiency wage model can be used to help explain real-wage rigidity and the existence of unemployment. (p. 398)

effort curve: (12) the relation between the level of effort put forth by workers and the real wage; its positive slope indicates that a higher real wage induces workers to exert greater effort. (p. 399)

empirical analysis: (1) a comparison of the implications of an economic theory or model with real-world data. (p. 16)

employment ratio: (3) the fraction of the adult population that is employed. (p. 93)

equilibrium: (1) a situation in which the quantities demanded and supplied in a market or set of markets are equal. (p. 19)

exchange rate: (14) the number of units of foreign currency that can be purchased with one unit of the home currency; also known as the nominal exchange rate. (p. 482)

exchange rate union: (14) a group of countries that agree to fix exchange rates among themselves while allowing their currencies to fluctuate against those of countries outside the union. (p. 483)

expansion: (9) in a business cycle, the period of time during which aggregate economic activity is rising; also known as a boom. (p. 291)

expansionary policy: (12) a monetary or fiscal policy that increases aggregate demand.

expectations-augmented Phillips curve: (13) an inverse relation between unanticipated inflation and cyclical unemployment. (p. 452)

expected after-tax real interest rate: (4) the nominal after-tax rate of return (equal to the nominal interest rate times 1 minus the tax rate) minus the expected rate of inflation; equals the expected increase in the real value of an asset after payment of taxes on interest income. (p. 115)

expected real interest rate: (2) the nominal interest rate minus the expected rate of inflation; equals the expected increase in the real value of an asset. (p. 54)

expected returns: (7) the rates of return on real or financial assets that financial investors expect to earn. (p. 226)

expenditure approach: (2) a procedure for measuring economic activity by adding the amount spent by all purchasers of final goods and services. (p. 28)

factors of production: (3) inputs to the production process, such as capital goods, labor, raw materials, and energy. (p. 64)

FE line: (10) see *full-employment line*.

Federal Open Market Committee (FOMC): (15) a twelve-member committee (consisting of the seven governors of the Federal Reserve Board, the president of the Federal Reserve Bank of New York, and four of the presidents of the other regional Federal Reserve Banks) that decides the course of monetary policy. (p. 540)

Fed funds rate: (15) the interest rate charged on reserves that one bank loans to another. (p. 544)

final goods and services: (2) goods and services that are the end products of the productive process, in contrast to intermediate goods and services. (p. 31)

fiscal policy: (1) policy concerning the level and composition of government spending and taxation. (p. 11)

fixed-exchange-rate system: (14) a system in which exchange rates are set at officially determined levels and are changed only by direct governmental action. (p. 483)

fixed-weight price index: (2) a price index that measures how much a fixed "basket" of goods costs in each year, relative to its cost in a base period. (p. 51)

flexible-exchange-rate system: (14) a system in which exchange rates are not officially fixed but are determined by conditions of supply and demand in the foreign exchange market; also known as a floating-exchange-rate system. (p. 482)

floating-exchange-rate system: (14) see *flexible-exchange-rate system*. (p. 482)

flow variable: (2) a variable that is measured per unit of time; an example is GDP, which is measured as output per year or quarter. See *stock variable*. (p. 44)

foreign exchange market: (14) the market in which the currencies of different nations are traded. (p. 482)

fractional reserve banking: (15) a banking system in which banks hold reserves equal to a fraction of their deposits so that the reserve–deposit ratio is less than 1. (p. 530)

frictional unemployment: (3) the unemployment that arises as the result of the matching process in which workers search for suitable jobs and firms search for suitable workers. (p. 96)

full-employment deficit: (16) what the government budget deficit *would be*, given the tax and spending policies currently in force, if the economy were operating at its full-employment level. (p. 581)

full-employment (*FE*) line: (10) a vertical line representing full-employment output in a diagram with output on the horizontal axis and the real interest rate on the vertical axis. (p. 317)

full-employment level of employment: (3) the equilibrium level of employment, achieved after wages and prices fully adjust. (p. 84)

full-employment output: (3) the level of output that firms supply when wages and prices in the economy have fully adjusted to their equilibrium levels. (p. 85)

fundamental identity of national income accounting: (2) the accounting identity that states that total production, total income, and total expenditure during a given period are equal. (p. 29)

fundamental value of the exchange rate: (14) the value of the exchange rate that would be determined by the forces of supply and demand in the foreign exchange market, in the absence of government intervention. (p. 510)

game theory: (15) the study of situations (games) in which individuals (players) use strategy in attempting to achieve their goals, possibly at the expense of the other players. (p. 554)

GDP: (2) see *gross domestic product*.

GDP deflator: (2) a variable-weight measure of the price level, calculated as the ratio of current nominal GDP to current real GDP. (p. 50)

general equilibrium: (10) a situation in which all markets in an economy are simultaneously in equilibrium. (p. 331)

GNP: (2) see *gross national product*.

government capital: (16) long-lived physical assets owned by the government, such as roads and public schools. (p. 582)

government debt: (16) the total value of government bonds outstanding at any given time. (p. 587)

government outlays: (2) the government's purchases of goods and services plus transfers and interest payments; also known as government expenditures. (p. 41)

government purchases: (2) spending by the government on currently produced goods and services. (p. 35)

government receipts: (2) taxes and other revenues collected by the government. (p. 41)

government saving: (2) the government's tax receipts minus its outlays; equal to the government budget surplus. (p. 41)

gradualism: (13) a prescription for disinflation that involves reducing the rate of monetary growth and the rate of inflation gradually over a period of several years; in contrast to *cold turkey*. (p. 474)

gross domestic product (GDP): (2) the market value of final goods and services newly produced within a nation's borders during a fixed period of time. (p. 29)

gross investment: (4) the total purchase or construction of new capital goods. (p. 128)

gross national product (GNP): (2) the market value of final goods and services newly produced by domestically owned factors of production during a fixed period of time. (p. 33)

growth accounting: (6) a method for breaking down total output growth into parts attributable to growth of capital, labor, and productivity. (p. 187)

growth accounting equation: (6) the production function written in growth rate form; it states that the growth rate of output is the sum of (1) the growth rate of productivity, (2) the elasticity of output with respect to capital times the growth rate of capital, and (3) the elasticity of output with respect to labor times the growth rate of labor. (p. 186)

high-powered money: (15) the liabilities of the central bank, consisting of bank reserves and currency in circulation, that are usable as money; also known as the monetary base. (p. 529)

human capital: (6) the productive knowledge, skills, and training of individuals. (p. 209)

hyperinflation: (13) a situation in which the rate of inflation is extremely high for a sustained period of time; one suggested definition is a 50% monthly rate of inflation. (p. 472)

hysteresis: (13) the tendency of the natural rate of unemployment to change in response to the actual unemployment rate, rising if the actual unemployment rate is above the natural rate and falling if the actual unemployment rate is below the natural rate. (p. 465)

income approach: (2) a procedure for measuring economic activity by adding all income received, including taxes and after-tax profits. (p. 28)

income effect: (8) a change in economic behavior (such as the amount a person saves or works) in response to a change in income or wealth; graphically, a change in behavior induced by a parallel shift in the budget line. (p. 261)

income effect (of real interest rate on saving): (8) the tendency of savers to consume more and save less in response to an increase in the real interest rate because they are made wealthier; the tendency of borrowers to consume less and save more in response to an increase in the real interest rate because they are made less wealthy. (p. 273)

income effect (of real wage on labor supply): (8) the tendency of workers to supply less labor in response to an increase in the real wage; arises because an increase in the real wage makes workers wealthier and leads them to want to consume more leisure. (p. 277)

income elasticity of money demand: (7) the percentage change in money demand resulting from a 1% increase in real income. (p. 233)

income-expenditure identity: (2) the accounting identity that states that total income (product) equals the sum of the four types of expenditure: consumption, investment, government purchases, and net exports. (p. 34)

inconvertible currency: (14) a currency that cannot be traded freely for other currencies, usually because of government-imposed restrictions. (p. 511)

index of leading indicators: (9) a weighted average of eleven economic variables that lead the business cycle, used for forecasting future business activity. (p. 300)

indicators: (15) see *intermediate targets*.

indifference curve: (8) shows graphically the combinations of current and future consumption that yield any given level of utility. (p. 255)

industrial policy: (6) a strategy for economic growth by which the government, using taxes, subsidies, or regulation, attempts to influence the nation's pattern of industrial development. (p. 213)

inflation: (1) a situation in which the prices of most goods and services are rising over time. (p. 8)

inflation tax: (16) the resources raised by the government by issuing money and creating inflation; also known as seignorage. (p. 600)

insider–outsider theory: (13) attributes hysteresis of the natural unemployment rate to the supposed tendency of unions to try to obtain the highest real wage consistent with continued employment of employed members (insiders), without taking account of the interests of unemployed workers (outsiders). See *hysteresis*. (p. 466)

instruments: (15) the policy tools that the Fed can use to influence the economy; these include reserve requirements, the discount rate, and, especially, open-market operations. (p. 544)

interest elasticity of money demand: (7) the percentage change in money demand resulting from a 1% increase (different from a 1 percentage point increase) in the interest rate. (p. 245)

interest rate: (2) the rate of return promised by a borrower to a lender. (p. 52)

intermediate goods and services: (2) goods and services that are used up in the production of other goods and services in the same period that they themselves were produced; an example is wheat used up in making bread. (p. 31)

intermediate targets: (15) macroeconomic variables that the Fed cannot control directly but can influence fairly predictably and that, in turn, are related to the ultimate goals the Fed is trying to achieve; also known as indicators. Examples of intermediate targets are the growth rates of monetary aggregates and short-term interest rates. (p. 545)

inventories: (2) stocks of unsold finished goods, goods in process, and production materials held by firms. (p. 31)

investment: (2) spending for new capital goods, called fixed investment, and increases in firms' inventory holdings, called inventory investment. See *gross investment, net investment*. (p. 34)

invisible hand: (1) the idea (proposed by Adam Smith) that, if there are free markets and individuals conduct their economic affairs in their own best interests, the economy as a whole will work well. (p. 18)

***IS* curve**: (10) in a diagram with output on the horizontal axis and the real interest rate on the vertical axis, a downward-sloping curve that shows the value of the real interest rate that clears the goods market for any given value of output. At any point on the *IS* curve, desired national saving equals desired investment (in a closed economy); equivalently, the aggregate quantity of goods demanded equals the aggregate quantity of goods supplied. (p. 318)

***J* curve**: (14) the typical time pattern of the response of net exports to a depreciation of the real exchange rate, in which net exports initially decline but then increase. (p. 488)

Keynesian approach: (1) an approach to macroeconomics based on the assumption that wages and prices may not adjust quickly to equate quantities supplied and demanded in each market. Keynesian economists are more likely than classical economists to argue that government intervention in the economy—for example, to smooth out the business cycle—may be desirable.

Keynesian consumption function: (4) a relationship that states that desired consumption depends on current aggregate output. (p. 110)

labor force: (3) the number of people willing to work, including unemployed people actively searching for work, as well as employed workers. (p. 92)

labor hoarding: (12) a situation that occurs if, because of the costs of firing and hiring workers, firms continue to employ some workers in a recession that they otherwise would have laid off. (p. 423)

lagging variable: (9) a variable with peaks and troughs that tend to occur later than the corresponding peaks and troughs in the business cycle. See *coincident variable, leading variable*. (p. 300)

large open economy: (5) an economy that trades with other economies and is large enough to affect the world real interest rate. (p. 168)

leading variable: (9) a variable with peaks and troughs that tend to occur earlier than the corresponding peaks and troughs in the business cycle. See *coincident variable, lagging variable*. (p. 300)

leisure: (3) all off-the-job activities, including eating, sleeping, recreation, and working in the yard and on the house. (p. 81)

life-cycle model: (8) a multiperiod version of the basic two-period model of consumer behavior that focuses on the patterns of income, consumption, and saving over the various stages of an individual's life. (p. 266)

liquidity: (7) the ease and quickness with which an asset can be exchanged for goods, services, or other assets. (p. 245)

***LM* curve**: (10) in a diagram with output on the horizontal axis and the real interest rate on the vertical axis, an upward-sloping curve that shows the value of the real interest rate that clears the asset market for any given value of output. At any point on the *LM* curve, the quantities of money supplied and demanded are equal. (p. 327)

long-run aggregate supply (*LRAS*) curve: (11) in a diagram with output on the horizontal axis and the price level on the vertical axis, a vertical line at full-employment output; indicates that in the long run the supply of output does not depend on the price level. (p. 381)

long-run Phillips curve: (13) in a diagram with unemployment on the horizontal axis and inflation on the vertical axis, a vertical line at the natural rate of unemployment; indicates that in the long run the unemployment rate equals the natural rate, independent of the rate of inflation. (p. 458)

M1: (7) the most narrowly defined monetary aggregate, made up of currency and travelers' checks held by the public, demand deposits (non-interest-bearing checking accounts) at commercial banks, and other checkable deposits. (p. 223)

M2: (7) a monetary aggregate that includes everything in M1 and a number of other assets that are somewhat less moneylike, such as savings deposits, small-denomination (under $100,000) time deposits, noninstitutional holdings of money market mutual funds (MMMFs), and money market deposit accounts (MMDAs). (p. 223)

macroeconomics: (1) the study of the structure and performance of national economies and of the policies that governments use to try to affect economic performance. (p. 3)

macroeconomic stabilization: (12) the use of monetary and fiscal policies to moderate cyclical fluctuations and maintain low inflation; also known as aggregate demand management or stabilization policy. (p. 426)

marginal cost: (12) the cost of producing an additional unit of output. (p. 408)

marginal product of capital (MPK): (3) the amount of output produced per unit of additional capital. (p. 68)

marginal product of labor (MPN): (3) the amount of output produced per unit of additional labor. (p. 70)

marginal propensity to consume (MPC): (4) the amount by which desired consumption rises when current output rises by one unit. (p. 110)

marginal revenue product of labor (MRPN): (3) the extra revenue obtained by a firm when it employs an additional unit of labor and sells the resulting increase in output; for competitive firms, equal to the price of output times the marginal product of labor. (p. 74)

marginal tax rate: (16) the fraction of an additional dollar of income that must be paid in taxes. (p. 582)

markup: (12) the difference between the price charged for a good and its marginal cost of production, expressed as a percentage of marginal cost. (p. 408)

medium of exchange: (7) an asset used in making transactions. (p. 220)

menu cost: (12) the cost of changing prices, for example, the cost of printing a new menu or remarking merchandise. (p. 406)

merchandise trade balance: (5) a country's merchandise exports (exports of goods) minus its merchandise imports. (p. 147)

misperceptions theory: (11) predicts that, because of producers' inability to observe directly the general price level, the aggregate quantity of output supplied rises above the full-employment level when the aggregate price level is higher than expected; hence the short-run aggregate supply curve is upward-sloping. (p. 379)

monetarism: (15) a school of macroeconomic thought that emphasizes the importance of monetary factors in the macroeconomy, but which opposes the active use of monetary policy to stabilize the economy. (p. 550)

monetary aggregates: (7) the official measures of the money supply, such as M1 and M2. See *M1, M2*. (p. 222)

monetary base: (15) the liabilities of the central bank, consisting of bank reserves and currency in circulation, that are usable as money; also known as high-powered money. (p. 529)

monetary neutrality: (10) characterizes an economy in which changes in the nominal money supply change the price level proportionally but have no effect on real variables. The basic classical model predicts neutrality; the classical model with misperceptions and the Keynesian model predict that neutrality holds in the long run but not in the short run. (p. 341)

monetary policy: (1) policies determining the level and rate of growth of the nation's money supply, which are under the control of a government institution known as the central bank (the Federal Reserve System in the United States). (p. 11)

money: (7) assets that are widely used and accepted as payment. (p. 220)

money demand function: (7) the function that relates the real demand for money to output and the interest rate paid by nonmonetary assets. (p. 231)

money multiplier: (15) the number of dollars of money supply that can be created from each dollar of monetary base, calculated as the ratio of the money supply to the monetary base. (p. 535)

money supply: (7) the total amount of money available in an economy, consisting of currency in circulation and deposits; also known as the money stock. (p. 224)

monopolistic competition: (12) a market situation in which some competition exists but in which a relatively small number of sellers and imperfect standardization of the product allow individual producers to act as price setters rather than as price takers. (p. 405)

multiple expansion of loans and deposits: (15) in a fractional reserve banking system, the process in which banks lend out some of their deposits, the loaned funds are ultimately redeposited in the banking system, and the new deposits are lent out again; as a result of the multiple-expansion process, the money supply can greatly exceed the monetary base. (p. 532)

multiplier: (12) for any particular type of spending, the short-run change in output resulting from a one-unit change in that type of spending. (p. 416)

national income: (2) the amount of income available to distribute among producers, equal to the sum of employee compensation, proprietors' income, rental income of persons, corporate profits, and net interest. Also measured as gross domestic product plus net factor payments less depreciation and indirect business taxes. (p. 36)

national income accounts: (2) an accounting framework used in measuring current economic activity. (p. 26)

national saving: (2) the saving of the economy as a whole, including both private saving (business and household) and government saving. (p. 41)

national wealth: (2) the total wealth of the residents of a country, consisting of the country's domestic physical assets (such as its stock of capital goods and land) and its net foreign assets. (p. 39)

natural rate of unemployment: (3) the rate of unemployment that exists when the economy's output is at its full-employment level; consists of frictional unemployment and structural unemployment. (p. 97)

net exports: (2) exports of goods and services minus imports of goods and services. (p. 36)

net factor payments from abroad (NFP): (2) income paid to domestic factors of production by the rest of the world, minus income paid to foreign factors of production by the domestic economy. (p. 33)

net foreign assets: (2) a country's foreign assets (for example, foreign stocks, bonds, and factories owned by domestic residents) minus its foreign liabilities (domestic physical and financial assets owned by foreigners). (p. 44)

net investment: (4) the change in the capital stock over the year, equal to gross investment minus depreciation of existing capital. (p. 129)

net national product (NNP): (2) GNP minus depreciation. (p. 38)

new growth theory: (6) research that extends the Solow growth model to include theoretical explanations of why productivity changes over time. (p. 215)

no-borrowing, no-lending point: (8) on the budget line, the point at which current consumption equals current income plus initial wealth; if the consumer chooses the consumption combination corresponding to this point, he or she neither borrows nor carries over resources into the future. (p. 270)

nominal appreciation: (14) an increase in the nominal exchange rate in a flexible-exchange-rate system. (p. 485)

nominal depreciation: (14) a decrease in the nominal exchange rate in a flexible-exchange-rate system. (p. 485)

nominal exchange rate: (14) the number of units of foreign currency that can be purchased with one unit of the home currency; also known as the exchange rate. (p. 482)

nominal GDP: (2) the value of an economy's final output measured using current market prices; also known as current-dollar GDP. (p. 48)

nominal interest rate: (2) the rate at which the nominal value of an interest-bearing asset increases over time; equivalent to the market interest rate. (p. 53)

nominal shocks: (11) shocks to money supply or money demand, which cause the *LM* curve to shift. (p. 356)

nominal variables: (2) variables measured in terms of current market prices. (p. 47)

normative analysis: (1) an analysis of policy that tries to determine whether a certain policy should be used; involves both analysis of the consequences of the policy and value judgments about the desirability of those consequences. See *positive analysis*. (p. 18)

official reserve assets: (5) assets held by central banks, other than domestic money or securities, that can be used in making international payments; examples are gold, foreign bank deposits, and special assets created by the International Monetary Fund. (p. 150)

official settlements balance: (5) the net increase (domestic less foreign) in a country's official reserve assets; also known as the balance of payments. (p. 151)

Okun's law: (3) a rule of thumb that says that output falls by 2.5% for each percentage point increase in the cyclical unemployment rate. (p. 97)

100% reserve banking: (15) a banking system in which banks hold reserves equal to 100% of their deposits. (p. 530)

open economy: (1) a national economy that has significant trading and financial relationships with other national economies. (p. 9)

open-market operation: (7) an open-market purchase or sale of assets by the central bank, used to affect the money supply. See *open-market purchase, open-market sale.* (p. 225)

open-market purchase: (15) a purchase of assets (such as Treasury securities) from the public by the central bank, used to increase the money supply. (p. 536)

open-market sale: (15) a sale of assets (such as Treasury securities) to the public by the central bank, used to reduce the money supply. (p. 536)

overvalued exchange rate: (14) in a fixed-exchange-rate system, an exchange rate that is higher than its fundamental value. See *fundamental value of the exchange rate.* (p. 510)

participation rate: (3) the fraction of adults who are in the labor force. (p. 93)

peak: (9) in a business cycle, the point in time when economic activity stops increasing and begins to decline. (p. 291)

perfect competition: (12) a market situation in which there is a standardized good and many buyers and sellers so that all buyers and sellers are price takers. (p. 405)

permanent income theory: (8) a theory that states that consumption depends on the present value of lifetime resources, with the implication that consumption responds much less to temporary than to permanent changes in income. (p. 261)

persistence: (9) the tendency for declines in economic activity to be followed by further declines and for growth in economic activity to be followed by more growth. (p. 293)

Phillips curve: (13) a downward-sloping relationship between the inflation rate and the unemployment rate; theory suggests that a Phillips curve will be observed in the data only in periods in which expected inflation and the natural rate of unemployment are relatively stable. See *expectations-augmented Phillips curve, long-run Phillips curve.* (p. 447)

portfolio allocation decision: (7) a wealth holder's decision about which assets and how much of each asset to hold. (p. 226)

positive analysis: (1) an analysis of the economic consequences of a policy that doesn't address the question of whether those consequences are desirable. See *normative analysis.* (p. 18)

present value: (8) the value of a future payment in terms of today's dollars; equal to the amount of money that must be invested today at a given interest rate to be worth the specified payment at the specified date in the future. (p. 253)

present value of lifetime consumption (PVLC): (8) the present value of current and future consumption, which equals PVLR according to the budget constraint. (p. 254)

present value of lifetime resources (PVLR): (8) the present value of current and expected future income plus initial wealth; corresponds to the horizontal intercept of the budget line. (p. 254)

price index: (2) a measure of the average level of prices for some specified set of goods and services, relative to the prices of a specified base period. (p. 50)

price setter: (12) a market participant with some power to set prices; see *monopolistic competition.*

price stickiness: (12) in Keynesian theory, the tendency of prices to adjust only slowly to changes in the economy; also known as price rigidity. (p. 404)

price taker: (12) a market participant who takes the market price as given; see *perfect competition.*

primary government budget deficit: (16) a measure of the deficit that excludes government interest payments from total outlays; equal to government purchases of goods and services plus transfers minus tax revenues. (p. 577)

private disposable income: (2) the income of the private sector (households and businesses taken together) after payment of taxes and receipt of transfer payments and interest from the government. (p. 38)

private saving: (2) the saving of the private sector (households and businesses), equal to private disposable income minus consumption. (p. 40)

private sector (2) the household sector and the business sector taken together.

procyclical: (9) tending to move in the same direction as aggregate economic activity over the business cycle (up in expansions, down in contractions). See *acyclical, countercyclical.* (p. 300)

product approach: (2) a procedure for measuring economic activity by adding the market values of goods and services produced, excluding any goods and services used up in intermediate stages of production; equivalently, by summing the values added of all producers. (p. 27)

production function: (3) a function that shows the amount of output that can be produced (by a firm or by an entire economy) by using any given quantities of capital and labor. (p. 64)

productivity: (3) a measure of the overall effectiveness with which the economy uses capital and labor to produce output; also known as total factor productivity. (p. 63)

productivity shock: (11) a change in an economy's production function; equivalently, a change in the amount of output that can be produced using given quantities of capital and labor; also known as a supply shock. (p. 356)

propagation mechanism: (11) an aspect of the economy, such as the behavior of inventories, that allows short-lived shocks to have longer term effects on the economy. (p. 386)

quantity theory of money: (7) a theory that asserts that nominal money demand is proportional to nominal GDP so that velocity is constant. (p. 235)

rational expectations: (11) expectations about the future values of economic variables that are based on reasoned and intelligent examination of available economic data; although they may make forecast errors, people with rational expectations cannot be *systematically* surprised by changes in macroeconomic policy or in the economy. (p. 384)

real appreciation: (14) an increase in the real exchange rate, which increases the quantity of foreign goods that can be purchased with a given quantity of domestic goods. (p. 485)

real business cycle (RBC) theory: (11) a version of the classical theory that assumes that productivity shocks (supply shocks) are the primary source of cyclical fluctuations. (p. 356)

real depreciation: (14) a fall in the real exchange rate, which decreases the quantity of foreign goods that can be purchased with a given quantity of domestic goods. (p. 486)

real exchange rate: (14) the quantity of foreign goods that can be obtained in exchange for one domestic good; also known as the terms of trade. (p. 484)

real GDP: (2) the market value of an economy's final output measured in terms of the prices that prevailed during some fixed base period; also known as constant-dollar GDP. (p. 48)

real interest rate: (2) the rate at which the real value or purchasing power of an interest-bearing asset increases over time; equal to the nominal interest rate minus the rate of inflation. (p. 53)

real shocks: (11) disturbances to the "real side" of the economy, such as shocks that affect the production function, the size of the labor force, the real quantity of government purchases, or the spending and saving decisions of consumers; real shocks affect the *IS* curve or the *FE* line. (p. 356)

real variable: (2) a variable measured in terms of the prices of a fixed base year; a measure intended to represent physical quantities produced or used. (p. 47)

real wage: (3) the real value (measured in terms of goods) of what firms must pay per unit of labor input that they employ; equal to the nominal (dollar) wage divided by the price level. (p. 75)

real-wage rigidity: (12) from the Keynesian perspective, the apparent tendency of real wages to move too little over the business cycle to keep the quantity of labor supplied equal to the quantity of labor demanded. (p. 398)

recession: (9) in a business cycle, the period of time during which aggregate economic activity is falling; also known as a contraction. (p. 291)

reserve–deposit ratio: (15) the ratio of reserves held by banks to the public's deposits in banks. (p. 530)

reserves: 1. (15) see *bank reserves*. 2. (5) see *official reserve assets*.

revaluation: (14) an increase in the value of a currency by official government action under a fixed-exchange-rate system. (p. 485)

reverse causation: (11) the tendency of expected future changes in output to cause changes in the current money supply in the same direction; used by real business cycle theorists to explain why the money supply leads the cycle. (p. 370)

Ricardian equivalence proposition: (4) the proposition that changes in the government budget deficit caused entirely by changes in (lump-sum) tax collections have no effect on the economy. (p. 119)

risk: (7) the possibility that the actual return received on an asset will be substantially different from the expected return. (p. 226)

rules: (15) a set of simple, prespecified, and publicly announced guidelines for conducting monetary policy; in contrast to discretion. (p. 547)

saving: (2) current income minus spending on current needs. (p. 40)

seignorage: (16) government revenue raised by printing money; also known as the inflation tax. (p. 598)

shoe leather costs: (13) the costs incurred in the process of economizing on holdings of cash, for example, in more frequent trips to the bank. (p. 470)

short-run aggregate supply (*SRAS*) curve: (11, 12) in a diagram with output on the horizontal axis and the price level on the vertical axis, the relationship between the price level and the amount of output supplied by firms that applies in the short run. In the extended classical model, the *SRAS* curve slopes upward, as producers are fooled into supplying more output when the price level is higher than expected; the short run in this model is the period of time during which the expected price level remains unchanged. In the Keynesian model the *SRAS* curve is horizontal, as firms meet demand at their initially set prices; the short run corresponds to the period during which prices remain unchanged. (p. 381)

small open economy: (5) an economy that trades with other economies but is too small to affect the world real interest rate. (p. 158)

speculative run: (14) a situation in which financial investors, fearing the imminent devaluation of a currency in a fixed-exchange-rate system, rush to sell assets denominated in that currency. (p. 511)

spell of unemployment: (3) see *unemployment spell*.

statistical discrepancy: (5) the amount that would have to be added to the sum of the current and capital account balances for this sum to reach its theoretical value of zero; arises because of errors of measurement and incomplete reporting. (p. 153)

steady state: (6) a situation in which the economy's output per worker, consumption per worker, and capital stock per worker are constant over time. (p. 215)

stock variable: (2) an economic quantity that is defined at a specific time; examples are wealth or the money supply. See *flow variable*. (p. 44)

store of value: (7) a means of holding wealth over time. (p. 221)

structural unemployment: (3) long-term and chronic unemployment arising from imbalances between the skills and other characteristics of workers in the market and the needs of employers. (p. 96)

substitution effect (of real interest rate on saving): (8) the tendency of consumers to save more, and thereby substitute future consumption for current consumption, in response to a higher reward for saving. (p. 271)

substitution effect (of real wage on labor supply): (8) the tendency of workers to substitute work for leisure in response to a higher real wage. (p. 277)

supply shock: (3) a change in an economy's production function, that is, in the amount of output that can be produced by using given quantities of capital and labor; also known as a productivity shock. (p. 71)

supply-side economics: (16) a school of economic thought based on the premise that all aspects of economic behavior—such as labor supply, saving, and investment—respond strongly to economic incentives, and, in particular, to incentives provided by the tax code. (p. 584)

tax-adjusted user cost of capital: (4) indicates how large the before-tax expected future marginal product of capital must be in order to make a proposed investment profitable; equivalently, the (unadjusted) user cost of capital divided by 1 minus the effective tax rate. (p. 126)

tax rate smoothing: (16) a policy of maintaining stable tax rates over time in order to minimize the distortions created by the tax code. See *distortions*. (p. 586)

terms of trade: (14) the quantity of foreign goods that can be obtained in exchange for one domestic good; also known as the real exchange rate. (p. 486)

trade deficit: (1) a nation's excess of imports over exports. (p. 10).

trade surplus: (1) a nation's excess of exports over imports. (p. 10).

transfers: (2) payments by the government, excluding payments made in exchange for current goods or services; examples of transfers are Social Security and Medicare benefits, unemployment insurance, and welfare payments. (p. 36)

trough: (9) in a business cycle, the time when economic activity stops falling and begins rising. (p. 291)

turning points: (9) peak or troughs in the business cycle. (p. 291)

turnover costs: (12) the costs associated with hiring and training new workers. (p. 398)

unanticipated inflation: (13) the actual rate of inflation minus the rate of inflation that was expected to occur.

unconditional convergence: (6) a tendency for the living standards of different countries to become more equal over time, independently of the particular characteristics of individual countries. See *conditional convergence*. (p. 207).

underground economy: (2) the portion of the economy that includes both legal activities hidden from government record-keepers and illegal activities. (p. 130)

undervalued exchange rate: (14) in a fixed-exchange-rate system, an exchange rate that is lower than its fundamental value. See *fundamental value of the exchange rate*. (p. 512)

unemployment: (1) the number of people who are available for work and actively seeking work but cannot find jobs. (p. 7)

unemployment rate: (3) the fraction of the labor force that is unemployed. (p. 93)

unemployment spell: (3) the period of time that an individual is continuously unemployed. (p. 95)

unilateral transfers: (5) payments made from one country to another that do not correspond to the purchase of any good, service, or asset; examples are foreign aid and gifts by domestic residents to foreigners. (p. 149)

unit of account: (7) the basic unit for measuring economic value (dollars, for example). (p. 220)

user cost of capital: (4) the expected real cost of using a unit of capital for a specified period of time; equal to the depreciation cost plus the interest cost. (p. 122)

uses-of-saving identity: (2) the accounting identity that states that private saving equals the sum of investment, the government deficit, and the current account balance. (p. 42)

utility: (8) an individual's economic satisfaction or well-being. (p. 255)

value added: (2) for any producer, the value of output minus the value of purchased inputs.

variable-weight price index: (2) a price index that starts with the set of goods and services produced in the current period, then compares the cost of those goods and services today with what they would have cost in the base period. (p. 50)

vault cash: (15) currency held in the vaults of banks; vault cash forms a portion of banks' reserves. (p. 541)

velocity: (7) the number of times the money stock "turns over" each period; calculated as nominal GDP divided by the nominal money supply. (p. 235)

wealth: (2) the assets minus the liabilities of an individual, firm, or country; also known as net worth. (p. 39)

world real interest rate: (5) the real interest rate that prevails in the international capital market in which individuals, businesses, and governments borrow and lend across national borders. (p. 158)

Name Index

(Note: When page numbers are followed by *n* the reference appears in a footnote.)

INDEX

Note: Page numbers in boldface type indicate pages where terms are defined; when page numbers are followed by *n* the reference appears in a footnote.

Year	Nominal GDP[a] (*PY*)	Real GDP[b] (*Y*)	Consumption[b] (*C*)	Investment[b] (*I*)	Government Purchases[b] (*G*)	Net Exports[b] (*NX*)
1929	103.1	821.8	554.5	152.8	112.6	1.9
1933	55.6	587.1	447.4	26.6	116.1	–3.0
1941	125.0	1070.6	629.3	149.4	289.1	2.8
1945	213.1	1602.6	714.6	82.6	829.4	–23.9
1950	287.0	1418.5	874.3	256.4	284.5	3.2
1955	404.3	1768.3	1047.0	284.8	441.7	–5.2
1960	513.4	1970.8	1210.8	290.8	476.9	–7.6
1961	531.8	2023.8	1238.4	289.4	501.5	–5.5
1962	571.6	2128.1	1293.3	321.2	524.2	–10.5
1963	603.1	2215.6	1341.9	343.3	536.3	–5.8
1964	648.0	2340.6	1417.2	371.8	549.1	2.5
1965	702.7	2470.5	1497.0	413.0	566.9	–6.4
1966	769.8	2616.2	1573.8	438.0	622.4	–18.0
1967	814.3	2685.2	1622.4	418.6	667.9	–23.7
1968	889.3	2796.9	1707.5	440.1	686.8	–37.5
1969	959.5	2873.0	1771.2	461.3	682.0	–41.5
1970	1010.7	2873.9	1813.5	429.7	665.8	–35.2
1971	1097.2	2955.9	1873.7	475.7	652.4	–45.9
1972	1207.0	3107.1	1978.4	532.2	653.0	–56.5
1973	1349.6	3268.6	2066.7	591.7	644.2	–34.1
1974	1458.6	3248.1	2053.8	543.0	655.4	–4.1
1975	1585.9	3221.7	2097.5	437.6	663.5	23.1
1976	1768.4	3380.8	2207.3	520.6	659.2	–6.4
1977	1974.1	3533.3	2296.6	600.4	664.1	–27.8
1978	2232.7	3703.5	2391.8	664.6	677.0	–29.9
1979	2488.6	3796.8	2448.4	669.7	689.3	–10.6
1980	2708.0	3776.3	2447.1	594.4	704.2	30.7
1981	3030.6	3843.1	2476.9	631.1	713.2	22.0
1982	3149.6	3760.3	2503.7	540.5	723.6	–7.4
1983	3405.0	3906.6	2619.4	599.5	743.8	–56.1
1984	3777.2	4148.5	2746.1	757.5	766.9	–122.0
1985	4038.7	4279.8	2865.8	745.9	813.4	–145.3
1986	4268.6	4404.5	2969.1	735.1	855.4	–155.1
1987	4539.9	4539.9	3052.2	749.3	881.5	–143.1
1988	4900.4	4718.6	3162.4	773.4	886.8	–104.0
1989	5250.8	4838.0	3223.3	784.0	904.4	–73.7
1990	5522.2	4877.5	3260.4	739.1	929.9	–51.8
1991	5722.9	4861.4	3258.6	675.7	946.3	–19.1
1992	6038.5	4986.3	3341.8	732.9	945.2	–33.6
1993	6374.0	5132.7	3452.5	820.9	938.6	–79.3

a in billions of dollars
b in billions of 1987 dollars
c base year 1987 = 100